1995

California Tax Handbook

by

Robert A. Petersen, CPA

Petersen/Ginner, Inc., CPAs
Menlo Park, California

Edited by
Jose A. Curammeng, Jr., LL.B.

RESEARCH INSTITUTE OF AMERICA

HOW TO USE THIS HANDBOOK

This *1995 California Tax Handbook* gives immediate help on California tax laws and regulations. You can get quick and in-depth answers to practically any California tax question by following the simple steps explained below.

Charts and calendar.   In the front section of this handbook you'll find these major features. The Chart of State Tax System at ¶11 shows at a glance the general set-up of California taxes. For important tax dates consult the tax calendar at ¶13.

Federal and state forms.   A list of both federal and state forms and the paragraphs of the handbook explanation where they appear is in the index at page 3051.

How to get answers to tax problems.   First, to locate the explanation of a specific tax, consult the general table of contents at page 4. It leads you to the place where the tax is explained in depth. At the explanation section for each tax there is also a detailed table of contents listing the topics covered in the explanation. If you have a specific subject in mind, go to the index at page 3051 to find where it is covered. Refer to the case table at page 3001 of the handbook to find where leading California tax cases are explained. List of legal rulings of the California Franchise Tax Board and the handbook paragraphs where they appear is at page 3003. Federal revenue rulings and procedures are listed in the same manner at page 3004.

Federal-California and California-Federal law tables.   If you want to know how the Internal Revenue Code is tied into the California law for income taxes on individuals, corporations, and banks, go to the tables that appear in the explanation sections on these taxes. The tables take you from the federal code to the California law and from the California law to the federal code. Tables will tell you where California conforms to the federal provisions.

Citations to official materials.   Throughout this book, references are made to sections of the California Revenue and Taxation Code, other relevant statutes of the regulations and rulings of the Franchise Tax Board, rulings of the State Board of Equalization, and to federal Internal Revenue Code sections and federal regulations. Cases decided by the state and federal courts carry citations to the official reporters, where available. Some recently decided cases, not yet published in any reporter, are cited to the court, the docket number, and the date of the decision.

PREFACE

California taxes are enacted by the California Legislature; they are created and shaped, and perhaps reshaped, by politicians. Simply stated, the political choices and compromise create complexity. When the state tax law differs from its federal counterpart, as is sure to happen with different legislative bodies enacting our laws, confusion reins. Taxes then are not easily understood by the general public and are on occasion confusing even to the seasoned tax practitioner. Conformity of state tax law with the Internal Revenue Code should be the goal; California's conformity is a myth. And yet, our clients expect us to be prompt and efficient in preparing tax returns, resolving their tax compliance questions, and effectively identifying those planning opportunities which might be available for them.

This year added complexity will be found in the California Revenue & Taxation Code, even though the number of new tax laws which have been adopted are not great. Rather, for the first time in many years the California individual income tax law is far out of sync with the Internal Revenue Code because California has conformed with little, if any, of the federal *Revenue Reconciliation Act of 1993*. Conformity with the Internal Revenue Code has not been achieved for 1994, even for those California sections which are usually conformed. California law which provides for automatic conformity refers only to the Internal Revenue Code as of January 1, 1993 - only a limited number of the federal changes thereafter have been specifically adopted by California. I am fearful that the Legislature's failure to adopt a conformity date of January 1, 1994, is a forbearer of the future. The conformity which the California tax practitioner has sought for many years has now been seriously eroded, and may be lost in the future. After all, there has been little conformity in those sections of the California tax code applicable to corporations. Let us be thankful that we now use computers to help us monitor the federal - California differences in return preparation; and let us not hesitate to tell our client that we must at least refer to the *California Tax Handbook* before giving any response to a question which is even a little unique, or involves significant dollars.

Candidly, many tax questions do not require in-depth research. The *California Tax Handbook* is meant to be a quick reference guide which should be kept at the practitioner's desk so that timely and reliable responses may be given to everyday technical questions. The use of the *California Tax Handbook* will result in a higher confidence level that the correct answers are being given. With an expectation that tax practitioners are more familiar with the Internal Revenue Code because that is where they have received most of their training, the *California Tax Handbook* is designed to highlight the differences between federal and California law and to minimize research time with those repetitive questions where the practitioner wants confidence without the costly time that in-depth research requires. The user should recognize that not all questions are going to be resolved with the use of this handbook - it is not meant to be an exhaustive treatise; the *RIA California State and Local Taxes Service* fulfills this expanded need. However, even when further research is required before a conclusion is reached, or action taken, a quick reference to the *California Tax Handbook* may guide the user to the expected answer.

I have been asked to identify the most useful part of the *California Tax Handbook*. I believe it is the federal - California code comparison tables found in Section II, commencing at ¶85, for personal income tax matters, and in Section VII, Chapter 11, commencing at ¶991, for bank and corporation tax matters. The first question one should ask is: "Are California and federal law the same?" If so, then the question being researched is generally solved by research in the federal code. This handbook may still be consulted for forms information, etc., but the basic question has been answered. Read carefully however, because even those sections which appear to confirm may have hidden traps.

The preparation of the *California Tax Handbook* is not an individual task. Numerous individuals are involved. Thanks goes to my partner Wanda Ginner who makes sure the practice runs even when I choose to write. RIA personnel contribute many valuable hours to the preparation of this handbook - particularly Doreen O'Hare, Esquire, who makes sure that nothing is lost in the flow of paper between my fax machine in Menlo Park, and RIA's fax in New York; and José A. Curammeng, Jr., Esquire who is a very talented editor at RIA and one in whom I have the greatest of confidence. If I have not said "Thank You" sufficiently loud to be heard in New York, let me again shout my thanks now. And for my wife Carol, thanks again for your continuing support for this, and all those other projects for which I have not yet learned to say 'no'.

Robert A. Petersen, CPA

Menlo Park, California

December, 1994

Robert A. Petersen, CPA has been an active participant in the California tax arena for over 20 years. In his professional practice he has ably represented many individual and business taxpayers in resolving disputes with the Franchise Tax Board and State Board of Equalization. He has testified on tax changes before committees of both the California and Florida legislatures. In his professional activities he has been President of the 28,000-member California Society of CPAs, President of the California CPA Foundation for Education and Research, and was a member of governing Council of the American Institute of CPAs for seven years. He has also served as a member of the Internal Revenue Service Commissioner's Advisory Group. He has written and taught the *California Combined Reporting* and *California Sales Tax: Procedures and Compliance* courses of the California CPA Foundation for Education and Research. Mr. Petersen is currently a member of the Responsibilities in Tax Practice of the American Institute of CPAs and is also currently the Chair of the RIA Advisory Board for loose-leaf tax publications. Mr. Petersen practices in the firm of Petersen/Ginner, Inc., CPAs, which is located in Menlo Park, California.

Table of Contents

¶

ROUNDUP OF MAJOR 1994 LEGISLATIVE CHANGES

¶6   1994 California Legislation

Individuals—income taxes.

Indexed personal exemption credits for 1994. The credit is $65 for single, dependent, blind or elderly persons. For married persons and heads of household, the credit is $130 (¶141). Joint custody head of household credit is 30% of the taxpayer's net tax up to $259 (¶155).

Credit for maintaining a dependent parent in the household. The maximum amount of the credit is $259 (¶155).

Senior head of household credit. The credit is 2% of taxable income up to a maximum of $792. Taxpayers whose adjusted gross income (AGI) exceeds $42,031 cannot claim the credit. (¶155).

Personal income tax brackets. For single persons, married persons filing separately, and fiduciaries, the 1994 rates range from 1% of the first $4,722 of taxable income to 11% of taxable income over $214,929. For spouses filing jointly, and surviving spouses with dependents, the rates range from 1% of the first $9,444 of taxable income to 11% of taxable income over $429,858. For unmarried heads of household, the rates range from 1% of the first $9,445 of taxable income to 11% of taxable income over $292,550. (¶87).

Standard deduction. For heads of household, surviving spouses, and married persons filing jointly, the 1994 standard deduction is $4,862. For all other taxpayers, the deduction is $2,431. (¶322).

Itemized deduction threshold. The limits are: $107,464 for single taxpayers and spouses filing separately; $161,196 for heads of household; and $214,929 for married persons filing jointly and surviving spouses (¶322).

Return filing requirement for certain dependent. An individual who can be claimed as a dependent as set in IRC § 63(c)(5) must file a California return when the individual's gross income from all sources exceeds the standard deduction allowed under the IRC. (¶110).

Child adoption costs credit. For tax years beginning on or after 1-1-94, a credit against tax in an amount equal to 50% of the costs for adopting a minor child who is a U.S. citizen or legal resident and who is in the custody of a California public agency is allowed, up to a maximum of $2,500 per child. The credit shall only be allowed for the taxable year in which the order or decree of adoption is entered. However, the allowable credit claimed may include adoption costs incurred in any prior tax year. If the credit exceeds the net tax, the excess may be carried over until exhausted. Any deduction allowed under the Personal Income Tax Law for any amount incurred by the taxpayer on which the credit is based is reduced by the amount of the credit. (¶143).

Salmon and trout habitat restoration credit: For taxable years beginning on or after 1-1-95 and before 1-1-2000, a credit against tax is allowed for 10% of the qualified costs paid or incurred by a taxpayer for salmon and steelhead trout habitat restoration and improvement projects. The credit shall be claimed in the return for the income year in which the expense was paid or incurred. Excess credits may be carried over until exhausted. The aggregate amount of the credit granted under both the Bank & Corporation Tax Law and the Personal Income Tax Law can't exceed $500,000 per year. (¶154).

Manufacturer's investment credit. Effective for taxable years beginning on or after 1-1-94, costs paid on or after 1-1-94, under a binding contract existing on or before that date, should be allocated based on a ratio of costs paid before 1-1-94 to total costs. Binding contract includes successor or replacement contracts and option contracts (but not option contracts where the option holder is liable for an amount less than 10% of the price if option is not exercised). Qualified costs include only costs on which sales-use tax has been paid and which are properly chargeable to a capital account. Exception is made to include as qualified costs capitalized labor costs for special purpose buildings and other qualified equipment. The credit is extended to equipment acquired under an operating lease if the lessor has fully paid sales-use taxes. Only tangible property that is IRC § 1245 property and which is used in manufacturing qualify for the credit. (¶142).

Low-income housing credit. For taxable years beginning on or after 1-1-94, various conforming changes were made to the low-income housing credit, including: (1) clarifying the credit limit for buildings located in designated difficult development areas or qualified census tracts by providing the maximum state credit on condition that the amount of the allocated federal credit is computed on 100% of the qualified adjusted basis of the building; (2) changing the requirement that buildings which are "at risk of conversion" be eligible for prepayment from three to two years after the credit application; (3) clarifying which federal provisions don't apply for purposes of the limitations on the aggregate credit dollar amount available for allocation. (¶156).

Child care credits. The credit for startup expenses for child care programs or constructing a child care facility and costs for child care information and referral services is extended to taxable years beginning before 1-1-98.

The employer's credit for contributions to a qualified care plan on behalf of an employee's qualified dependent is also extended to tax years beginning before 1-1-98. However, for taxable years beginning on or after 1-1-95 and before 1-1-98, the credit is reduced to 30% from 50% of the amount of the contribution, up to $360 from $600. The age requirement for qualified dependents is reduced to 12 from 15 years. (¶144; 145).

Enterprise zones. A specific program area or part of a program area may be redesignated as an enterprise zone if the city council enacts a resolution or ordinance effecting such redesignation. Taxpayers conducting business within the redesignated area will be eligible for enterprise zone tax incentives, rather than program area incentives. (The language of the statute identifying the program area qualifying for redesignation describes only the portion of the Sacramento program area within the closed Army Depot). (¶159).

The Trade and Commerce Agency is authorized to designate 2 new enterprise zones each of which must meet at least 2 of the following criteria: (1) the unemployment rate in the area has been double the state average for each of the preceding 5 years; (2) the median household income for the area is less than 90% of the median household income for the county in which it is located; (3) the designated area has grown at least 8% in population per year for each of the preceding 2 years but has not had a corresponding percentage growth in area employment. The existing enterprise zone credits will be extended to the new enterprise zones. (¶159).

For taxable years beginning on or after 1-1-95, the definition of "qualified disadvantaged individual" is expanded for purposes of the enterprise zone employer credit. Qualified disadvantaged individuals are no longer required to be in a state or federal jobs program; it is sufficient that they are eligible for such programs. But priority is given to those who are enrolled in a qualified program under the federal Job Training Partnership Act or the Greater Avenues of Independence Act or those who are eligible under the federal Targeted Jobs Tax Credit Program. (¶159).

Los Angeles Revitalization Zone (LARZ) incentives. For taxable years beginning on or after 1-1-94, the LARZ hiring credit for nonconstruction workers can be used to reduce the regular tax below the tentative minimum tax.

The formula for determining income attributable to business activities within the LARZ is revised to apply taxpayer specific and California only factors rather than the factors of the unitary group. The business income attributable to California is first determined by considering the unitary group and using the standard apportionment formula. The result is then apportioned to the LARZ by using a 2-factor formula based on taxpayer's California property and payroll in the LARZ and in California. (¶161).

The Trade and Commerce Agency must determine whether an approved LARZ map complies with the statutory criteria and void any approved map that is determined to be not in compliance with such criteria. Beginning in the next taxable year after the LARZ map is changed, taxpayers engaged in a trade or business in an area deleted from the map won't be allowed the LARZ incentives. However, any unused credit may be carried forward until exhausted. (¶161).

Disaster relief. Effective for taxable years beginning on or after 1-1-94, taxpayers may claim a disaster loss deduction for losses suffered as a result of: (1) the November 1993 fires in the counties of Los Angeles, Orange, Riverside, Ventura, San Bernardino, and San Diego; (2) the earthquake that occurred in the counties of Los Angeles, Orange, and Ventura in January 1994; and (3) the August 1994 fire in San Luis Obispo county. Taxpayers may carry a qualifying casualty loss back to the taxable year immediately preceding the year of loss and excess loss may be carried forward for the next five taxable years; 50% of such loss may be carried over for the next 10 taxable years. (¶327).

The 2.5% penalty for premature or early distributions from an IRA, or from a plan qualified under IRC § 401(a) or 403(a) to a self-employed individual is eliminated if the distributee or a member of his/her household suffered a personal injury or property damage as a result of the Northridge earthquake of 1994. This treatment applies to distributions made on or after 1-17-94 and before 1-18-95 and is operative only for tax years in which a substantially similar treatment is allowed under federal law. (¶298).

Taxpayers who sustained a significant property loss, or who lost employment due to property damage to their employer, or who realized a significant loss of business income from a business located within the Northridge area, as a result of the 1994 earthquake are allowed an extension of 6 months from the original due date of their return within which to pay their tax (as shown on the original returns to be filed during calendar year 1994) provided they timely filed their returns (not later than the extended due date granted by FTB). If the tax isn't paid within the extended period, the penalty for failure to pay is assessed from the original due date of the return. (¶338).

Renter's credit suspended. For taxable years beginning on or after 1-1-93, and before 1-1-96, the renter's credit is suspended. The credit will be available again for the 1996 tax year. (¶150).

Crime hotline rewards. For taxable years beginning on or after 1-1-94, gross income does not include any income received as a reward from a crime hotline authorized by any government entity. The exclusion does not apply to an employee of the agency or organization establishing or operating the hotline or to an employee of an organization that has contributed to the reward offered by the hotline. (¶290).

Exclusion for ridesharing benefits. Effective for tax years beginning on or after 1-1-95, the exclusion from gross income for compensation or benefits (other than salary and wages) received by an employee for participating in a ridesharing arrangement is expanded to include compensation or benefits for: (1) bicycling to or from an employee's workplace; (2) commuting by ferry; (3) using an alternative transportation method that reduces the use of a motor vehicle by a single occupant to travel to and from the place of employment; and (4) traveling to and from a telecommuting facility. (¶283).

Cost-share payments to forest landowners. For taxable years beginning on or after 1-1-94, gross income does not include cost-share payments received by forest landowners from the Department of Forestry and Fire Protection pursuant the California Forest Improvement Act of 1987 or from the U.S. Department of Agriculture, Forest Service under the Forest Stewardship Program and the Stewardship Incentives Program, pursuant to the Cooperative Forestry Assistance Act, as amended. Any cost-share payments so excluded won't be considered in determining the basis of property acquired or improved by the taxpayer or in computing any allowable deduction to which taxpayer may otherwise be entitled. (¶289).

Sales of unprocessed timber. For income years beginning on or after 1-1-94, and before 1-1-2000, California conforms to the recently enacted federal law which provides that income from the sale of unprocessed timber that is softwood and was cut from an area located in the U.S. is treated as a U.S. source income. (¶201).

Net operating losses. The net operating loss deduction is extended indefinitely. Effective for taxable years beginning on or after 1-1-94, new businesses and qualifying small businesses are subject to revised rules for carrying forward their losses. In addition, new rules are established for determining whether a trade or business activity qualifies as a new business. (¶295A).

Amortization of goodwill and other intangibles. For taxable years beginning on or after 1-1-94, California has adopted with modifications IRC § 197, as added by the federal Revenue Reconciliation Act of 1993, which requires goodwill and other intangibles acquired after 8-10-93 (7-25-91, if elected) in connection with the purchase of the assets of a business or a substantial portion of one to be amortized over 15 years. It also adopted IRC § 167(f), which provides for amortizing of intangibles that are excluded from the application of IRC § 197. (¶371).

Employment tax amnesty. The Employment Development Department is required to develop an employment tax amnesty program to be conducted for three months beginning 4-1-95. Under the program, the department must waive: (1) all outstanding penalties and interest owed on unpaid penalties imposed on or before 12-31-93 as a result of the nonpayment or underpayment of withholding tax on personal income or the failure to file reports for the tax reporting periods for which amnesty is requested; (2) penalties and interest imposed or imposable for the tax reporting periods for which amnesty is sought that are owed as a result of nonreporting or underreporting of tax liabilities or for failing to file reports for tax reporting periods ended on or before 12-31-93; and (3) all penalties that may be imposed and taxes that may be due for wages paid before 3-17-92 that the employer certifies on the amnesty application as owed due to the misclassification of workers as independent contractors and their reclassification as employees. Waiver under (3) above applies only to workers who are reclassified as employees as a result of the clarification of the common law rules for determining employer-employee relationship. (¶5021A).

Report on wage withholding. Beginning in 1995, the requirement to file a quarterly payroll tax return is eliminated. Instead, employers will be required to file a quarterly wage report showing the: (1) employee's name; (2) social security number; (3) total wages paid; and (4) total personal income tax withheld. Personal income tax withholding deposits will be reconciled once a year using an annual reconciliation return. In addition, employers will no longer be required to file copies of the employee wage statements (W-2) with the Employment Development Department.

The threshold for deposits of withholding taxes will increase to over $500 of accumulated state tax from over $75 for employers that are required to make withholding tax deposits for federal income tax purposes. Beginning in 1996, the $500 amount will be adjusted annually based on annual average rate of interest. (¶5008).

Corporate, business and investment tax changes.

Limited liability companies. Limited liability companies may now organize and engage in any lawful activity in California. Foreign LLCs must register with the Secretary of State. LLCs may elect to be treated as corporations or partnerships for California tax purposes. LLCs treated as partnerships are subject to the $800 minimum tax. Effective for tax years beginning on or after 1-1-94 and before 1-1-99, LLCs treated as partnerships must also pay a fee ranging from $500 for LLCs with total income of $250,000, to $4,000 ($4,500 after 1995) for LLCs with total income of at least $5 million. The fees for tax years beginning on or after 1-1-99 will be set by the FTB depending on a study. Members of an LLC that is treated as a partnership will be taxed on their distributive share of the LLC's income under the Personal Income Tax Law. (¶1040).

Combined reporting—new bright-line unity-of-ownership test. For income years beginning on or after January 1, 1995, the income and apportionment factors of two or more corporations must be included in a combined report if they are members of a commonly controlled group. A "commonly controlled group" means: (1) a parent corporation and any one or more corporations or chains of corporations, connected through stock ownership (or constructive ownership) with the parent and the parent owns stock possessing more than 50% of the voting power of at least one corporation, and, if applicable, stock cumulatively representing more than 50% of the voting power of each of the corporations, except the parent, is owned by the parent or one or more of the other corporations; (2) any two or more corporations, if stock representing more than 50% of the voting power of the corporations is owned (including constructive ownership) by the same person; (3) any two or more corporations constituting stapled entities; and (4) any two or more corporations all of whose stock representing more than 50% of the voting power of the corporations is cumulatively (without regard to constructive ownership) by, or for the benefit of, members of the same family. (¶1166A).

Allocation and apportionment—savings and loan. Effective for income years beginning on or after 1-1-94, the apportionment formula for businesses deriving 50% of their gross business receipts from a savings and loan activity is revised to allow the use of a single-weighted sales factor, rather than the double-weighted factor applicable to most businesses.

¶6

Operative on the adoption by the FTB of the Proposed Multistate Tax Commission Formula for the Uniform Apportionment of Net Income from Financial Institutions (or its equivalent), businesses deriving 50% of their gross business receipts from a banking or financial business activity may also use a single-weighted sales factor in apportioning their business income. (¶1180).

If the income and apportionment factors of two or more affiliated banks, savings associations, or corporations are required to be included in a combined report, the application of the "50% of gross business receipts" test is made with respect to the gross business receipts of the entire group, excluding gross receipts from sales or transactions between members of the group. The entire business income of the group must be apportioned using a single-or double-weighted sales factor, as applicable. (¶1180).

Net operating losses. Effective for income years beginning on or after 1-1-94, new businesses and qualifying small businesses are subject to revised rules for carrying forward their losses. In addition, new rules are established for determining whether a trade or business activity qualifies as a new business. (¶1145).

Alternative minimum tax. Effective for income years beginning on or after 1-1-94, California modifies IRC § 56(g), relating to adjustments based on current earnings, to provide that for corporations whose income is subject to allocation and apportionment, the determination of adjusted current earnings is made at the individual entity level, rather than on the combined report of the unitary group. (¶2004).

Credit for increasing research activities. California does not conform to the IRC 41(h) termination date of 6-30-95. For income years beginning on or after 1-1-94, California adopts the IRC § 41(g) rule for the passthrough of the credit, with modifications. For those receiving the benefit from pass-thru entities, the amount of credit allowed in any income year can't exceed the portion of the tax attributable to the income from the trade or business from which the credit was generated. If the credit amount exceeds the limit, the excess may be carried over to other income years, subject to the same limitation. (¶1237).

Low-income housing credit. Effective retroactive to income years beginning on or after 1-1-93, the definition of a bank or corporation is modified by substituting "voting common stock" for "voting stock." Various conforming and technical changes are made to the credit. (¶1239).

Salmon and trout habitat restoration credit: For income years beginning on or after 1-1-95 and before 1-1-2000, a credit against tax is allowed for 10% of the qualified costs paid or incurred by a taxpayer for salmon and steelhead trout habitat restoration and improvement projects. The credit shall be claimed in the return for the income year in which the expense was paid or incurred. Excess credits may be carried over until exhausted. The aggregate amount of the credit granted under both the Bank & Corporation Tax Law and the Personal Income Tax Law can't exceed $500,000 per year. (¶1252A).

¶6

Manufacturer's investment credit. Effective for income years beginning on or after 1-1-94, costs paid on or after 1-1-94, under a binding contract existing on or before that date, should be allocated based on a ratio of costs paid before 1-1-94 to total costs. Binding contract includes successor or replacement contracts and option contracts (but not option contracts where the option holder is liable for an amount less than 10% of the price if option is not exercised). Qualified costs include only costs on which sales-use tax has been paid and which are properly chargeable to a capital account. Exception is made to include as qualified costs capitalized labor costs for special purpose buildings and other qualified equipment. The credit is extended to equipment acquired under an operating lease if the lessor has fully paid sales-use taxes. Only tangible property that is IRC § 1245 property and which is used in manufacturing qualify for the credit. (¶1252).

Child care credits. The credit for startup expenses for child care programs or constructing a child care facility and costs for child care information and referral services is extended to income years beginning before 1-1-98.

The employer's credit for contributions to a qualified care plan on behalf of an employee's qualified dependent is also extended to income years beginning before 1-1-98. However, for income years beginning on or after 1-1-95 and before 1-1-98, the credit is reduced to 30% from 50% of the amount of the contribution, up to $360. The age requirement for qualified dependents is reduced to 12 from 15 years. (¶1245; 1246).

Enterprise zones. A specific program area or part of a program area may be redesignated as an enterprise zone if the city council enacts a resolution or ordinance effecting such redesignation. Taxpayers conducting business within the redesignated area will be eligible for enterprise zone tax incentives, rather than program area incentives. (The language of the statute identifying the program area qualifying for redesignation describes only the portion of the Sacramento program area within the closed Army Depot). (¶1236B).

The Trade and Commerce Agency is authorized to designate 2 new enterprise zones each of which must meet at least 2 of the following criteria: (1) the unemployment rate in the area has been double the state average for each of the preceding 5 years; (2) the median household income for the area is less than 90% of the median household income for the county in which it is located; (3) the designated area has grown at least 8% in population per year for each of the preceding 2 years but has not had a corresponding percentage growth in area employment. The existing enterprise zone credits will be extended to the new enterprise zones. (¶1236B).

For income years beginning on or after 1-1-95, the definition of "qualified disadvantaged individual" is expanded for purposes of the enterprise zone employer credit. Qualified disadvantaged individuals are no longer required to be in a state or federal jobs program, it is sufficient that they are eligible for such programs. But priority is given to those who are enrolled in a qualified program under the federal Job Training Partnership Act or the Greater Avenues of Independence Act or those who are eligible under the federal Targeted Jobs Tax Credit Program. (¶1236B).

¶6

Los Angeles Revitalization Zone (LARZ) incentives. For income years beginning on or after 1-1-94, the LARZ hiring credit for nonconstruction workers can be used to reduce the regular tax below the tentative minimum tax.

The formula for determining income attributable to business activities within the LARZ is revised to apply taxpayer specific and California only factors rather than the factors of the unitary group. The business income attributable to California is first determined by considering the unitary group and using the standard apportionment formula. The result is then apportioned to the LARZ by using a 2-factor formula based on taxpayer's California property and payroll in the LARZ and in California. (¶1236C).

The Trade and Commerce Agency must determine whether an approved LARZ map complies with the statutory criteria and void any approved map that is determined to be not in compliance with such criteria. Beginning in the next income year after the LARZ map is changed, taxpayers engaged in a trade or business in an area deleted from the map won't be allowed the LARZ incentives. However, any unused credit may be carried forward until exhausted. (¶1236C).

Cost-share payments to forest landowners. For income years beginning on or after 1-1-94, gross income does not include cost-share payments received by forest landowners from the Department of Forestry and Fire Protection pursuant the California Forest Improvement Act of 1987 or from the U.S. Department of Agriculture, Forest Service under the Forest Stewardship Program and the Stewardship Incentives Program, pursuant to the Cooperative Forestry Assistance Act, as amended. Any cost-share payments so excluded won't be considered in determining the basis of property acquired or improved by the taxpayer or in computing any allowable deduction to which taxpayer may otherwise be entitled. (¶1102).

Sales of unprocessed timber. For income years beginning on or after 1-1-94, and before 1-1-2000, California conforms to the recently enacted federal law which provides that income from the sale of unprocessed timber that is softwood and was cut from an area located in the U.S. is treated as a U.S. source income.

For purposes of apportioning income to California, income from the sales of unprocessed timber which is cut in California and delivered to a buyer outside the U.S. must be included in the numerator of the sales factor of the apportionment formula. (¶1184).

Amortization of goodwill and other intangibles. For income years beginning on or after 1-1-94, California has adopted with modifications IRC § 197, as added by the federal Revenue Reconciliation Act of 1993, which requires goodwill and other intangibles acquired after 8-10-93 (7-25-91, if elected) in connection with the purchase of the assets of a business or a substantial portion of one to be amortized over 15 years. California also adopted IRC § 167(f), which provides for amortizing of intangibles that are excluded from the application of IRC § 197. (¶371).

Nonprofit farm cooperatives. Effective for income years beginning on or after 1-1-94, nonprofit farm cooperative associations organized under the Food and Agricultural Code are exempt from paying the annual $800 minimum franchise tax if they get a certificate from the county where they have their principal place of business that they meet certain requirements. A cooperative will be issued the required certificate if it shows that: (1) it is located in an economically distressed area; (2) at least 90% of its members are, or have been, within the previous 12 months unemployed or dependent on public services for their income; and (3) the request for the certificate is made during the cooperative's first income year.

The exemption applies only to cooperatives organized on or after 1-1-94 and for five consecutive income years, beginning with the income year for which the certificate is issued. (¶1211).

Transitory rule for dissolved partnerships. For taxable years beginning on or after 1-1-93, limited partnerships that have dissolved but failed to inform the Secretary of State of their dissolution are exempt from paying the $800 minimum tax if: (1) they ceased doing business before January 1, 1993; (2) they filed a final return with the Franchise Tax Board for a taxable year ending before January 1, 1993; and (3) they file a certificate of cancellation with the Secretary of State no later than 12- 31-94.

Short period returns. For income years beginning on or after 1-1- 95, a California short period return must be filed at the same time that a federal short period return is filed if one is required. If no federal short-period return is required to be filed, the return must be filed within two months and 15 days after the close of the taxpayer's income year.

A taxpayer that exists during only part of what would otherwise be its income year need not file a short period return if the termination of its corporate life is due to an IRC § 368(a)(1)(F) reorganization.

Retroactive to income years beginning on or after 1-1-91, taxpayers required to file a California short period return must compute their alternative minimum tax as provided under IRC § 443(d). (¶1274).

Water's-edge election. Taxpayers making a water's-edge election are no longer required to list in the information return each state and county where it has payroll, property, or sales. A clarification is made that existing water's-edge contracts are rescinded for income years beginning on or after 1-1-94 and that the requirement to pay water's-edge election fees applied to income years beginning before 1-1-94. (¶1184A).

Disaster relief. Effective for income years beginning on or after 1-1-94, taxpayers may claim a disaster loss deduction for losses suffered as a result of: (1) the November 1993 fires in the counties of Los Angeles, Orange, Riverside, Ventura, San Bernardino, and San Diego; (2) the earthquake that occurred in the counties of Los Angeles, Orange, and Ventura in January 1994; and (3) the August 1994 fire in San Luis Obispo county. Taxpayers may carry a qualifying casualty loss back to the taxable year immediately preceding the year of loss and excess loss may be carried forward for the next five taxable years; 50% of such loss may be carried over for the next 10 income years. (¶1157).

Effective 9-21-94, taxpayers who sustained a significant property loss or who realized a significant loss of business income from a business located within the Northridge area as a result of the 1994 earthquake are allowed an extension of 7 months from the original due date of their return within which to pay their tax (as shown on the original returns to be filed during calendar year 1994) provided they timely filed their returns (not later than the extended due date granted by FTB). If the tax isn't paid within the extended period, the penalty for failure to pay is assessed from the original due date of the return. (¶1321).

Sales-use taxes.

Manufacturing equipment exemption. On or after 1-1-95, the exemption for manufacturing equipment of a new trade or business from the state sales-use tax is reduced to 5% from 6%. Such equipment will continue to be subject to local sales-use taxes. New rules are established for purposes of determining when a new trade or business activity qualify for the exemption. (¶4008A).

Meals served to elderly. Effective 1-1-95, meals served to the elderly by a duly-licensed residential care facility (license not required if exempt from licensing requirement), or a facility operated by the U.S., or any state or federal program-financed housing serving the elderly are exempt. (¶4008).

Nonprofit organization's fundraising auctions. Effective 1-1-95, items sold at fund raising auctions conducted by, or affiliated with, a religious, charitable, scientific, literary, educational, or other nonprofit organization exempt from tax under Rev & TC § 23701d are not subject to tax if the purpose of the auction is to get revenue for the funding of a shelter for the homeless and the funds are actually spent for such purpose. The exemption does not apply to any auction sale conducted more than once during any 12-month period. (¶4008).

Prescription drug samples. Effective 1-1-95, free samples of prescription drugs furnished by a drug manufacturer or distributor to a licensed physician, surgeon, dentist, podiatrist, or health facility for the treatment of persons or to an institution of higher education for instruction or research are exempt. The exemption also covers the materials used to package and the constituent elements and ingredients used to produce the drugs. (¶4008).

Endangered or threatened animals or plants. Effective 1-1-95, the exemption for endangered animal or plant species is expanded to include any transfer of an endangered or threatened animal or plant species acquired or disposed of through a trade or exchange between members of the American Zoo and Aquarium Association and a nonprofit zoological society. But any retailer (other than a nonprofit zoological society) storing, using, or otherwise consuming in-state endangered or threatened animal or plant species acquired through a trade or exchange with a nonprofit zoological society is subject to use tax. (¶4008).

Carbon dioxide. Effective 1-1-95, carbon dioxide (dry ice) used in packing and shipping or transporting fruits and vegetables for human consumption and nonreturnable materials containing the carbon dioxide atmosphere are exempt if the fruits or vegetables are not sold to the ultimate consumer in a package that contains the carbon dioxide. (¶4008).

Nexus—use of on-line computer services. Effective 1-1-95, out-of- state retailers won't acquire nexus in California if they take orders from California customers through an in-state computer telecommunications network which is not directly or indirectly owned by them and the order results from the electronic display of products on such network. This exclusion applies only to a computer telecommunications network consisting substantially of on-line communications services other than the displaying and taking of orders for products. (¶4004A).

Deficiency determination—out-of-state retailers—time limit. Effective 1-1-95, the limitation period for issuing a deficiency determination against out-of-state retailers is reduced to 3 years from 8 years if the retailer: (1) is located out-of-state and has not previously registered with the SBE; (2) is engaged in business in-state; (3) voluntarily registers with the SBE; (4) has not been previously contacted by the SBE regarding its doing business in-state; and (5) failed to report or pay tax due to reasonable cause and not due to negligence or intentional disregard of the law, or due to fraud or an intent to evade the provisions of the Sales-Use Tax Law. If the SBE finds that such failure to file or pay is due to reasonable cause and circumstances beyond the retailer's control, it shall relieve the retailers of all penalties. (¶4004A).

Recovery of erroneous refunds. Effective 1-1-95, as an alternative to filing suit for the recovery of refunds erroneously made or credits mistakenly allowed, the SBE may issue a deficiency or jeopardy determination. Except in the case of fraud, the determination must be made within 3 years from the last day of the month following the quarterly period in which the SBE certified to the Controller that the amount refunded or allowed was in excess of the sum legally due.

Aiding in preparation of false claims. Effective 1-1-95, it is a misdemeanor for any person to willfully aid, assist in, or procure, counsel, or advise in, the preparation or presentation of a return, affidavit, claim, or other document that is fraudulent or false as to any material matter, whether or not such falsity or fraud is known or consented to by the person authorized or required to file the return, affidavit, claim, or other document. Each offense is punishable by a fine of not less than $1,000 but not more than $5,000 and/or imprisonment of not over 1 year.

EFT payments—penalty. Effective 1-1-95, failure to timely remit tax by electronic transfer is subject to additional penalty of 10% of the tax due if such failure results in the SBE's issuance of a deficiency determination.

Trade shows. Operators of a swap meet, flea market, or special event are exempt from the requirement to get written evidence that a seller who rents or leases space holds a valid seller's permit if: (1) the event or show is one for which all exhibitors' contract prohibit any sale of tangible personalty and in fact no such sales occur; (2) the event or show is conducted for informational or educational purposes only and at which no sale of tangible personalty occurs; and (3) it's a trade show. A "trade show" for this purpose is one that: (a) is not open to the general public; (b) only orders for tangible personalty are solicited or taken from sellers for purposes of resale; and (c) the event or show is operated by an IRC § 501(c) organization. (¶4004).

Refund in-lieu of investment tax credit. A taxpayer who has paid sales or use tax on purchases of property for which a manufacturing and research equipment credit may be claimed under the Bank & Corporation Tax law or the Personal Income Tax Law has the option of claiming a sales tax refund in lieu of claiming the manufacturing and research equipment credit. The claim must be filed no earlier than the date a claim for credit or carryover of credit may be made and must be for an amount not in excess of the amount of credit that could have been used to offset personal income or corporate tax liability. (¶4008A).

SBE's settlement authority made permanent. The SBE's authority to settle civil tax matter disputes has been extended on a permanent basis effective 7-7-94. (¶4016-A).

Additional sales-use tax. The County Stanislaus, on voter approval, to impose an additional transactions (sales) and use tax of ¹/₈ of 1% for a period not to exceed five years and in any succeeding period not to exceed five years. The revenues from the additional tax must be used to fund countywide library programs and operations.

On voter approval Lakeport City may collect a transaction and use tax of up to 1% (in multiples of .25%) to fund road projects. Clearlake City may collect .25% or .5% for public safety services. (¶4012).

Exemption for hand tools. Effective 9-11-94, the first $20,000 of personal property consisting of hand tools that are owned and supplied by an employee and are required as a condition for employment are exempt from tax. (¶3005).

Vessels. Effective 7-1-95, a vessel engaged in carrying 7 or more persons for hire for commercial passenger fishing purposes will continue to be assessed at 4% of full cash value even if it is occasionally used—no more than 15% of operating time—for dive, tour, or whale watching purposes. (¶3007).

Transfer of base-year value. Effective 1-1-94, counties may adopt an ordinance allowing the transfer of the Proposition 13 base year value of property substantially damaged or destroyed in a disaster to comparable replacement property of equal or lesser value in another county if the receiving county has adopted an ordinance accepting such transfer. The replacement property must be acquired or newly constructed within three years of the damage to or destruction of, the original property. (¶3018).

¶6

Limitation periods for escape assessments. Effective 1-1-95, the 8-year limitation period applicable to escape assessments resulting from unrecorded changes in ownership or control of property is eliminated. If property escapes taxation or is underassessed following a change in ownership, the applicable limitations periods (4 or 6 years) won't start until the beginning of the assessment year in which a change of ownership statement was filed. The 4-and 6-year limitation periods applicable to supplemental assessments will start in the assessment year in which a statement reporting a change of ownership or completion of a new construction is filed. (¶3018).

Penalties—willful evasion or fraud. Effective 1-1-95, the penalty for fraudulently preventing assessment or fraudulently causing an underassessment is increased to 75% from 25% of the amount of the additional assessed value. (¶3011).

Penalty relief—limitation. On adoption by the county of a resolution or ordinance to this effect, penalty relief for a taxpayer who failed to pay tax on an assessment that is the subject of a pending assessment appeal is limited to the difference between the final determination of value by the county board of equalization or an assessment appeals board and the value on the assessment roll for the fiscal year covered by the application for reduction of assessment. (¶3008).

Insurance taxes.

Surplus line brokers. Effective 1-1-95, payment due date for the surplus line brokers' gross premiums tax is changed to March 1 from April 1. Also, surplus line brokers whose annual tax for the preceding calendar year was at least $5,000 must now make monthly, rather than quarterly, installment payments. The monthly payments must be remitted by the 1st day of the 3rd calendar month following the end of the accounting month in which the business was done. The annual report of surplus line brokers must contain an account of the business done for the previous year. (¶6008).

Other taxes.

Diesel fuel tax. Effective 7-1-95, California imposes a diesel fuel tax on the removal, entry, sale, and delivery of diesel fuel in-state at the rate of 18¢ per gallon. The tax also applies to interstate truckers. Licenses are required for suppliers, exempt bus operators, vendors, highway vehicle operators, and end sellers. (¶6505).

Propane safety inspection surcharge. Effective 7-1-95, a surcharge is imposed on the owner of mobilehome parks or of propane distribution systems at a rate to be determined by the State Board of Equalization. The surcharge for mobilehome park owners can't be more than 25¢ per month. (¶6521).

Petroleum underground storage tank fee. Effective 1-1-95, an additional fee of .001¢ per gallon of petroleum placed in underground storage will be imposed on the owners of underground storage tanks. The additional fee will increase to .002¢ effective 1-1-96 and to .003¢ effective 1-1-96. (¶6522).

General Administrative Provisions

FTB's settlement authority permanently extended. The FTB's authority to settle civil tax matter disputes has been extended on a permanent basis effective 7-7-94. Settlements involving reductions in tax or penalties not exceeding $5,000 are now settled with the joint approval of the executive officer and chief counsel, without need of FTB approval or review by the Attorney General. (¶340; 1308-A).

Out-of-state businesses—voluntary disclosure program. Effective 8-26-94, a voluntary disclosure program is adopted which allows business entities, other than those organized under California law or those that have qualified to do business in California, to enter into negotiations with the FTB for the waiver of taxes, additions to tax, fees, or penalties with respect to each taxable or income year ending before six years from the signing date of the voluntary disclosure agreement. For the first six years before such signing date, the FTB may waive certain specified penalties. (¶338A; 1326).

Unintentional noncompliance with new statutory provisions. Beginning 9-30-94 and before 1-1-95, the Franchise Tax Board may adopt resolutions waiving penalties or allowing taxpayers to perfect deficient elections with respect to new provisions in the Bank & Corporation Tax Law, Personal Income Tax Law, Administrative Tax Law, and Nonadmitted Insurance Tax Law. Such relief may only be granted for the first taxable or income year for which the new statutory provision is operative and only when substantial unintentional noncompliance with the new provisions was made by a class of affected taxpayers. In addition, relief will only be granted to taxpayers who timely paid taxes and other required amounts shown on their return consistent with the election and who timely filed their returns (with regard for extension). (¶350).

Tax payments. Effective 1-1-95, check payments of tax, interest, or penalties to the Franchise Tax Board must be payable in U.S. funds. The Franchise Tax Board may offer a voluntary electronic funds transfer payment program to personal income taxpayers. (¶1293).

Dynamic revenue estimating. The Legislative Analyst and the Department of Finance, to the extent that any fiscal estimate of the annual state budget involves changes in state tax law having a designated impact, must prepare the estimate on the basis of assumptions that estimate the behavioral responses of taxpayers, businesses, and other citizens to the proposed changes. A statement identifying those assumptions must be included in the estimate. This requirement applies to a proposed change in tax law determined by the Legislative Analyst and Department of Finance, using a static fiscal estimate, to have a fiscal impact of over $10 million.

¶6

State Board of Control approvals. Effective 9-21-94, the State Board of Control's approval is no longer required for refunds of over $50,000 ($15,000 for certain taxes such as the gross premiums tax and private railroad car tax) or for cancellations of any amount in excess of $50,000 (or $15,000) illegally determined by the taxpayer or the SBE. Also repealed is the requirement that the SBC approve SBE recommendations for the reimbursement to taxpayers of reasonable fees and expenses in relation to SBE hearings. Instead, refund or cancellation determinations by the SBE of over $50,000 (or $15,000) or any proposed award for fees and expenses will be made available as a public record for at least 10 days before the effective date of the determination or award.

Nontax debt collection by FTB. Effective 1-1-95, the FTB's child support collection program is made permanent and available to all counties within two years.

Effective 1-1-95, the FTB is authorized to collect fines, state or local penalties, forfeitures, restitution fines, or restitution orders imposed by a California superior, municipal, of justice court if the amount due in the aggregate is at least $250.

Effective 7-1-95, the FTB is authorized to collect delinquent fees, wages, penalties, costs, and interest for the Department of Industrial Relations when such amounts due have been assessed under specified provisions of the Labor Code. (¶349).

Section I/*Charts, Calendars*

¶10 **Administrative Departments**

Franchise Tax Board. The FTB administers the franchise (income) tax of corporations and the corporation income tax. The FTB also administers the personal income tax and the tax on nonadmitted insurers.

State Controller. Motor fuel license tax and use fuel tax are paid to the controller. He also enforces the state tax, the generation-skipping transfer tax, the collection of oil and gas production charge, and reviews assessments.

State Treasurer. Payment of oil and gas production charge is made to treasurer.

State Board of Equalization. The SBE is the largest tax administering agency of the state. The SBE hears appeals from decisions of the Franchise Tax Board on additional assessments and refunds of corporation franchise (income) tax and corporation income tax; also assessments and refunds of personal income tax. The SBE exercises general administration of the state sales and use tax, and of state-administered local sales-use taxes; equalizes county assessment levels, and notifies county auditors of changes made in county assessment books; administers the motor vehicle fuel and use fuel taxes; assesses property of public utilities for taxation by counties, administers motor vehicle license fee, and assesses private car tax.

County Assessors. Assessors assess property for county and school districts, and sometimes for city taxes; they also receive returns for county and school district taxes, and assess omitted property.

County Boards of Equalization. The County Boards of Equalization review assessments of property and hear complaints.

County Auditor. The Auditor makes changes in the county assessment book on notice from state board of equalization and completes tax roll.

County Recorders. The county recorders receive payments of recordation taxes on sales or transfers of realty.

County Supervisors. The county supervisors receive and act on claims for refund of local property taxes because of specified grounds, such as illegal or erroneous collection.

County Tax Collectors. The county tax collectors collect county and school district taxes, and in some cases, city taxes.

City Assessors. The assessor assesses real and personal property for city tax, where separately assessed, and receives returns in such cases.

City Tax Collectors. The city tax collectors collect property taxes in certain cities.

Department of Conservation. The Department of Conservation receives report for oil and gas production charge, determines the rate and gives notice of completion of assessment and of time for correction of assessment, and levies the charge.

Department of Employment Development. The Department of Employment Development administers the withholding of personal income tax from employees' pay, and employment taxes for unemployment insurance and disability benefits.

Public Utilities Commission. The Public Utilities Commission administers the Highway Carriers' Act and City Carriers' Act, and receives reports and fees from transportation companies.

Insurance Commissioner. The Insurance Commissioner administers the taxes on general insurers, surplus line brokers, ocean marine insurers, and the retaliatory tax on foreign insurers.

¶11   Chart Of California Tax System

Italics indicate taxes applicable to business corporations.

Kind of tax	Measure and Rate of Tax	Reports—Payments Due
* *Initial taxes—domestic corporations including state banks*	Filing fee: Stock corporations, $100 nonstock, $30 plus minimum franchise tax (below). Annual statement and designation, stock corporation, $5; mutual and public nonprofit benefit corps., $5; nonstock corps., no fee.	To Secretary of State by end of calendar year in which original articles filed. Pay fees to Secretary of State when filing papers.
* *Entrance fees—foreign corporations*	Flat fee of $350 for stock corporations; nonstock, $30 plus minimum franchise tax (below); includes deisgnation of agent; filing any document, $6; affixing certificate and seal of State, $5.	Before doing business in state, file papers with Secretary of State, pay fees and get certificate.
* *Initial fees—limited liability companies*	Filing articles of organization or applying for registration, $80.	Pay fees to Secretary of State when filing papers.
Franchise (income) tax—Business corporations, public utility companies and banks	General corporations, 9.3% of net income attributable to California; for banks and financial corporations, general corporation rate, plus personal property tax and business license tax equivalent. Minimum tax is $800 ($25 for certain gold mines). Credit unions pay no tax. Minimum tax payable at time of incorporation or qualification.	To Franchise Tax Board 2 months and 15 days after end of income year. Payment of estimated tax required if tax estimated to be over minimum tax by 4-1, pay 25% by 4-15, 6-15, 9-15 and 12-15; by 6-1, pay 33$1/3$% by 6-15, 9-15 and 12-15; by 9-1, pay 50% by 9-15 and 12-15; by 12-1, pay 100% by 12-15. Payment by electronic transfer starts January 1, 1993.
	S corporation rate is 1.5% for income years beginning on or after 1-1-94 (formerly, 2.5%). Financial corporation qualified as S corporation pays regular rate plus personal property tax and business license tax equivalent.	Same as above.
	For tax years beginning on or after 1-1-94, limited liability companies treated as partnerships pay the minimum franchise tax if they are doing business in-state or their articles of organization have been accepted by, or their certificates of registeration issued by, the Secretary of State. Also, they must pay an annual fee ranging from $500 to $4,000 ($4,500 after 1995), depending on their total income.	Minimum franchise tax must be paid to Franchise Tax Board by the 15th day of the 4th month of the taxable year. Annual fees must be paid by the due date of the annual return, which is due within 3 months and 15 days after the close of the LLCs tax or income year.
Corporation income tax—All corporations except banking corporations	Tax is 9.3% of net income attributable to California exclusive of income included in measure of franchise tax.	Same as for franchise tax above.

* Not a periodic tax. All other taxes are imposed periodically (usually every year).

Kind of tax	Measure and Rate of Tax	Reports—Payments Due
Retail sales and use tax	Basis is nonexempt tangible personalty. State sales tax rate is 6%; combined state, city and county rate is 7.25%; combined state, city and county and district rates range from 7.50% to 8.25%. Interest on refunds or judgments from 1-1-95 to 6-30-95, based on rate of 13-week treasury bills is 3%; underpayment rate is 11% from 1-1-95 to 6-30-95. Smog impact fee, $300; not applicable to commercial vehicles with unladen weight of over 6,000 lbs.	Report to State Board of Equalization in month after end of quarter. Pay with report. For tax base over $17,000 ($50,000 if certified by Attorney-General) in first, third and fourth calendar quarters, prepay not less than 90% of state tax by 24th day next following end of each of first two monthly periods; in second calendar quarter, prepay 95% for first monthly period by 24th day following end of period; for second monthly period, prepay either (1) 95% of liability for that period, plus 95% of liability for first 15 days of third monthly period; or (2) 95% of liability for second monthly period, plus 50% of 95% of such liability by 23rd day of third monthly period. Fuel distributors and brokers with more than 75% of gross receipts from retail sale of motor fuel prepay at rate set by Board each 4-1 by 25th of following month. Payable on registration of motor vehicle.
Property tax	Full cash value of realty and tangible personalty. Rates vary locally; assessment ratios are at full value. No state tax since 1910. Notes, debentures, stocks, bonds, etc., exempt from property tax.	Report to County Assessor—not later than last Friday in May unless he sets earlier date, not before April 1. Realty: pay to County or City Tax Collector, half by Dec. 10, balance by April 10. Personalty taxes; on secured roll Dec. 10; unsecured roll, Aug. 31.
Timber yield tax	6% of immediate harvest value.	Report and pay taxes to State Board of Equalization by last day of month following quarter of scaling date.
* Recordation tax	Every document conveying interest in realty. Rates: *County:* 55¢ for each $500 of consideration of value over $100. *City:* ¹/₂ county rate in taxing county. Credit allowed for city tax. Otherwise same as county.	Pay County Recorder when filing document.
Gasoline or motor fuels tax	Rate for 1994 and later is 18¢ per gallon; 1992, 16¢; 1993, 17¢ per gallon.	Report, pay to State Board of Equalization on or before 25th of each month. Make remittance payable to State Controller. Prepay 25% of tax by 15th of each month.
Use fuel tax	Rate for 1994 and later is 18¢ per gallon; 1992, 16¢; 1993, 17¢ per gallon. Liquefied petroleum gas, 6¢ a gallon. Natural gas liquid, 6¢ per gallon; nonliquid compressed, 7¢ per 100 cu. ft. For ethanol or methanol, rate is 9¢ per gallon for 1994; 8¢ for 1992; 8.5¢ for 1993. Annual flat rate for liquefied petroleum or natural gas for vehicles 4,000 lbs. or less, $36; 4,001 lbs. to 8,000, $72; 8,001 lbs. to 12,000, $120; 12,001 lbs. or more, $168.	Report, pay to State Board of Equalization on or before 25th of each month. Flat rate tax starting 1-1-88 is annual tax. Annual per period is from end of month in which tax paid to end of month prior to following year.
Diesel fuel tax	18c per galon beginning 7-1-95.	Report, pay to State Board of Equalization by the last day of each calendar month. Interstate truckers report, pay quarterly.

Kind of tax	Measure and Rate of Tax	Reports—Payments Due
Oil and gas production charge	Amount of oil produced and gas produced (unless used in oil production or withdrawn from underground storage) in calendar year preceeding filing of report at rate fixed by Department of Conservation.	Report to Department of Conservation by March 15 of each year. Pay State Treasurer first half Aug. 15, second half February 1. Charges due and payable July 1 on assessments of $10, but less than $500. For assessments of $500 or more, half of charges will be delinquent, if not paid by August 15th; balance is delinquent, if not paid by following February 1.
Public utilities— property tax	Subject to same property tax as ordinary business corporations except that all property other than franchise is assessed by State Board of Equalization.	Report to State Board of Equalization by April 1. Payment dates are same as for other property taxes; see "Property Tax" above.
Private railroad car tax	Assessed value of private railroad cars, at rate equal to preceding year's average rate of taxation in state.	Report to State Board Equalization by April 30. Pay State Board of Equalization by Dec. 10.
Express corporations, freight forwarders, motor transportation brokers, motor carriers of property	1/3 of 1% (unless administratively reduced) of gross operating revenue, plus $10 (quarterly) filing fee.	Report, pay Public Utilities Commn. by 15th of Jan., April, July, and Oct.
Railroads, vessel operators	$10 (quarterly) filing fee.	Same as for express corporations above.
Personal income tax on resident and nonresident individuals and estates and trusts.	Resident's entire net income and nonresident's net income from instate sources. Rates range from 1% to 11%, and are indexed annually. All taxpayers with taxable income, except those who income average, compute tax from Tax Table. Alternative minimum tax at 8.5% flat rate.	Report and pay to Franchise Tax Board at time of filing return. Reports are due on or before April 15, or 15th day of fourth month after close of fiscal year. Payment of estimated tax is required if tax for preceding taxable year less credits, or tax computed on estimated income for taxable year is $100 in case of single person, or married persons filing jointly, or $50 or more for married persons filing separately, or less than 80% of tax will be paid by withholding. If requirements are first met by 4-1, file and pay in 4 installments on 4-15, 6-15, 9-15, and 1-15 of following year; if met by 6-1, file and pay in 3 installments, by 6-15, 9-15, and 1-15 of following year; if met by 9-1, file and pay in 2 installments by 9-15 and 1-15 of following year; if met after 9-1, pay in full with declaration by 1-15 of following year. California adopts IRC § 6654(d) limits on use of prior year's tax.
Withholding personal income tax	Every employer paying wages to residents for both in-state and out-of-state services, and nonresidents for in-state services must withhold tax. Tables can be used to determine amount to be withheld.	Report and pay to Employment Development Dept. in Sacramento. *Electronic funds transfer:* For calendar years beginning before 1-1-95, if, in the 12-month period ending June 30 of the prior year, the cumulative average payment for any deposit period is $50,000 or more ($20,000

Kind of tax	Measure and Rate of Tax	Reports—Payments Due
		or more, eff. January 1, 1995), employers must remit within the time prescribed by IRC § 6302. Payments must be made starting January 1 for one year. *Quarterly—monthly:* Employers required to deposit federal taxes must deposit state taxes within the same number of banking days that deposits of federal taxes are due if the accumulated amount of state tax withheld is more than $500 (over $75 before 1-1-95) (this includes the federal one-banking day rule). *Monthly:* Employers that are not required to deposit state taxes according to the federal schedule must remit the total amount withheld during each month of a calendar quarter by the 15th day of the next month, if the amount withheld for one or cumulatively for two or more months of a calendar quarter is $350 or more. Remittances are made with Form DE 88. *Quarterly:* By 4-30, 7-31, 10-31 and 1-31.
Gross premiums tax	Insurers pay a 2.35% tax on gross premiums, less return premiums, received on business done in-state.	Return and payment due by April 1 to Insurance Commr., covering premiums received during the preceding calendar year. Prepay 25% of preceding year's tax every quarter if preceding year's tax is at least $5,000.
Surplus line brokers tax	Surplus line brokers pay 2.35% on gross premiums, less return premiums.	Return and payment due to Insurance Commr. by March 1 for premiums received during preceding calendar year. Prepay in monthly installment of 25% based on gross premiums for business done in preceding quarter if preceding calendar year's tax was at least $5,000.
Title insurers	Title insurers pay a 2.35% tax on gross income from business done in-state except interest, dividends, rents from realty, profits from disposition of investments, and income from investments.	Return and payment due to Insurance Commr. by April 1 for premiums received during preceding calendar year. Prepay 25% of tax reported for preceding year quarterly if preceding calendar year's tax is at least $5,000.
Ocean marine insurance	Ocean marine insurers pay a 5% tax on proportion of their total underwriting profits allocable to California, less deductible losses and expenses.	Return and pay to Insurance Commr. by June 15.
Retaliatory tax	Variable.	Return and pay to Insurance Commr. by April 1. Prepay in quarterly installment of 25% of preceding year's tax if such preceding year's tax is at least $5,000.
Nonadmitted insurance tax	Insurers not admitted to do business in-state pay gross premiums tax of 3%, less 3% returned premiums, of business done in-state.	Return and pay to the Franchise Tax Board by 1st day of 3rd month following close of calendar quarter during which a taxable insurance took effect or was renewed.
Unemployment insurance	New employers pay 3.4% of total taxable wages; all others have their rates determined by the Employment Development Dept. from one of seven schedules, depending on various factors. There is also a 0.1% employment and training tax imposed on certain employers.	Quarterly returns and payments are made to Employment Development Dept. by last day of month following the end of a calendar quarter.

¶12 **Estate Tax and Generation-Skipping Transfer Tax—Chart of Rates**

CALIFORNIA ESTATE TAX—CHART OF RATES
→ **APPLICABLE TO ESTATES OF DECEDENTS DYING ON OR AFTER 6-9-82** →

Adjusted Taxable Estate (Federal taxable estate reduced by $60,000)	Rate of Tax	Adjusted Taxable Estate (Federal taxable estate reduced by $60,000)	Rate of Tax
$40,000 to $90,000	.8%	$2,540,000 to $3,040,000	8.8%
$90,000 to $140,000	1.6%	$3,040,000 to $3,540,000	9.6%
$140,000 to $240,000	2.4%	$3,540,000 to $4,040,000	10.4%
$240,000 to $440,000	3.2%	$4,040,000 to $5,040,000	11.2%
$440,000 to $640,000	4.0%	$5,040,000 to $6,040,000	12.0%
$640,000 to $840,000	4.8%	$6,040,000 to $7,040,000	12.8%
$840,000 to $1,040,000	5.6%	$7,040,000 to $8,040,000	13.6%
$1,040,000 to $1,540,000	6.4%	$8,040,000 to $9,040,000	14.4%
$1,540,000 to $2,040,000	7.2%	$9,040,000 to $10,040,000	15.2%
$2,040,000 to $2,540,000	8.0%	exceeding $10,040,000	16.0%

ESTATE TAX—RESIDENTS AND NONRESIDENTS

The estate tax is equal to the portion, if any, of the maximum allowable federal credit for state death taxes, which is attributable to property located in California. The estate tax cannot result in a total tax liability to California and the U.S. in excess of the death tax liability to the U.S. which would result if the California estate tax were not in effect.

GENERATION-SKIPPING TRANSFER TAX—RESIDENTS AND NONRESIDENTS—A generation-skipping transfer tax is also imposed to absorb the federal credit when the original transferor is a resident of California at the date of original transfer, or the property transferred is in California.

California Estate Tax—Rapid Tax Calculator

Showing Rates and Amounts of Tax on Adjusted Taxable Estate

In California the tax is assessed against the entire estate and not against such individual beneficiary.[1]

To find the tax on the entire adjusted taxable estate (for example, an adjusted taxable estate of $900,000):

(1) Find in column A, the figure nearest to, but less than the entire adjusted taxable estate; thus the figure nearest to but less than $900,000 is $840,000.

(2) Find in column B, the tax on that figure; thus, the tax on $840,000 is $27,600. This roughly is the tax. To find the tax exactly, proceed as follows:

(3) Compute the tax on the excess, which is at the rate indicated in column D; thus the excess of $900,000 over $840,000 is $60,000; the rate of tax on the excess is 5.6% (found in column D) because $900,000 falls in the bracket which includes adjusted taxable estates of $840,000 (column A) to $1,040,000 (column C). This percentage of $60,000 is $3,360. Add that to the tax on $840,000 ($27,600), which results in a tax of $30,960 on the entire adjusted taxable estate of $900,000.

Amount of adjusted taxable estate[1]	Tax on adjusted taxable estate shown in (A)	Amount of adjusted taxable estate in excess of (A) but not more than	Tax rate on amount in excess of (A) but not in excess of (C)
(A)	(B)	(C)	(D)
$ 40,000	$ 0	$ 90,000	.8%
$ 90,000	$ 400	$ 140,000	1.6%
$ 140,000	$ 1,200	$ 240,000	2.4%
$ 240,000	$ 3,600	$ 440,000	3.2%
$ 440,000	$ 10,000	$ 640,000	4.0%
$ 640,000	$ 18,000	$ 840,000	4.8%
$ 840,000	$ 27,600	$ 1,040,000	5.6%
$ 1,040,000	$ 38,800	$ 1,540,000	6.4%
$ 1,540,000	$ 70,800	$ 2,040,000	7.2%
$ 2,040,000	$ 106,800	$ 2,540,000	8.0%
$ 2,540,000	$ 146,800	$ 3,040,000	8.8%
$ 3,040,000	$ 190,800	$ 3,540,000	9.6%
$ 3,540,000	$ 238,800	$ 4,040,000	10.4%
$ 4,040,000	$ 290,800	$ 5,040,000	11.2%
$ 5,040,000	$ 402,800	$ 6,040,000	12.0%
$ 6,040,000	$ 522,800	$ 7,040,000	12.8%
$ 7,040,000	$ 650,800	$ 8,040,000	13.6%
$ 8,040,000	$ 786,800	$ 9,040,000	14.4%
$ 9,040,000	$ 930,800	$10,040,000	15.2%
$10,040,000	$ 1,082,800	. . . .	16.0%

(1) The tax is based on the maximum credit allowable under § 2011 of the 1954 Internal Revenue Code. The adjusted taxable estate means the federal taxable estate reduced by $60,000.

The tax cannot result in a total tax liability to California and the U.S. in excess of the death tax liability to the U.S. which would result if the California tax was not in effect.

¶12

¶13   **California Tax Calendar—Annual Dates**

The following calendar lists dates for returns, payments, and other duties of taxpayers. Last day for performance without penalty is shown, unless otherwise noted. No cognizance is taken of Sundays and holidays, it being generally true that, in such cases, taxpayers' time is extended to the next business day.

Date		Item
JAN.	1	Property taxes—State-assessed property; first day for State Board of Equalization to mail notice of assessed value, date for declaration of intent to file and reassessment petition
	15	Carriers—Quarterly report, fee; also, (for all but railroads and vessel operators) gross operating revenue fee to Public Utilities Commission.)
		Personal income tax—Declaration and payment of estimated income tax to Franchise Tax Board
	22	Property taxes—State assessed property, earliest date for filing declaration of intent to petition for reassessment
	31	Taxes on corporate income—Withholding return to Franchise Tax Board
		Personal income tax—Quarterly payroll report, pay taxes withheld to Employment Development Department
		Disability insurance contributions—Quarterly return and payment due with personal income taxes income taxes withheld
		Personal income tax—Return and payment of tax withheld at source from nonresident not subject to withholding
		Sales-use taxes—Quarterly return and balance of tax to State Board of Equalization
		Timber yield tax—Timber owners report-pay timber yield tax to State Board of Equalization
		Unemployment compensation tax—Quarterly return and payment due
		Personal income tax—Information statement must be given to recipients of $600 or more
		Withholding—Personal income tax—Annual reconciliation return is delinquent if not filed by this date
FEB.	1	Oil and gas producer's tax—2nd $1/2$ delinquent; additional penalty for failure to pay 1st $1/2$; not applicable to assessments of less than $500
3rd Mon.		Oil and gas producer's tax—Action against State Treasurer to recover taxes paid under protest
	21	Property taxes—State assessed property, earliest date for filing petition for reassessment
	24	Sales-use taxes—Prepay to State Board of Equalization if so ordered
	28	Personal income tax—Information to Franchise Tax Board
MAR.	1	Property taxes—Assessment date
		Property taxes—Taxes become lien on realty
		Property taxes—File statement of separate ownership of land and improvements with assessor before this date
		Property taxes—File property statement pertaining to state assessed property with State Board of Equalization
		Insurance companies—Surplus line brokers report and pay gross premiums tax
	15	Oil and gas producer's tax—Report to Department of Conservation
		Taxes on corporate income—Report (except by farmers' cooperative) and tax to Franchise Tax Board (15th day 3rd month after fiscal year)
		Property taxes—Exemption affidavits (except church, religious, veterans, homeowners and vessels) to county assessor

¶13

Date		Item
		Disability insurance contributions—Payment due with personal income tax withheld.
MAR.	16	Property taxes—Airport owner or operator lists aircraft owners with county assessor
	24	Sales-use taxes—Prepay to State Board of Equalization if so ordered
	31	Property taxes—Affidavit to assessor, church and religious exemption
APR.	1	Property taxes—Affidavit to assessor, documented vessel
		Insurance companies—General insurers report and pay gross premiums tax
		Insurance companies—Prepayments of gross premiums tax due if annual tax for preceding year was $5,000 or more.
		Insurance companies—Retaliatory tax report and payment due; information return due.
	10	Property taxes—Last day to pay county tax collector 2nd $1/2$ realty tax
	15	Carriers—Quarterly report, fee; also (for all but railroads and vessel operators) gross operating revenue fee to Public Utilities Commission
		Property taxes—Veteran's affidavit and homeowner's affidavit to county assessor
		Personal income tax—Return and tax to Franchise Tax Board (15th day 4th month after fiscal year)
		Personal income tax—Declaration and payment of estimated tax to Franchise Tax Board
		Taxes on corporate income—Declaration and payment of estimated tax
		Franchise tax—Limited liability companies pay minimum franchise tax to Franchise Tax Board
	30	Personal income tax—Quarterly payroll report, pay taxes withheld to Employment Development Department
		Disability insurance contributions—Quarterly payment due with personal income tax withheld
		Sales-use taxes—Quarterly return and balance of tax to State Board of Equalization
		Private car companies—Annual report to State Board of Equalization
		Timber yield tax—Timber owners report-pay timber yield tax to State Board of Equalization
		Unemployment compensation tax—Quarterly payment due
MAY	15	Taxes on corporate income—Exempt corporations, information returns to Franchise Tax Board (15th day 5th month after fiscal year)
	24	Sales-use taxes—Prepay State Board of Equalization if so ordered
Last Fri.		Property taxes—File property statement with assessor unless he sets earlier date, not before Apr. 1
	31	Property taxes—State-assessed property; last day for notice of assessed value of unitary property
JUNE	8	Property taxes—Collector publishes notice of power and intent to sell tax-defaulted property
	15	Personal income tax—Declaration and payment of estimated income tax to Franchise Tax Board
		Taxes on corporate income—Declaration and payment of estimated tax
		Insurance companies—Ocean marine insurers report and pay gross premiums tax
		Insurance companies—Prepayments of gross premiums tax due if annual tax for preceding year was $5,000 or more.
		Ocean marine insurance—Additional retaliatory tax and payment due.
	20	Property taxes—State-assessed property; assessee has to at least this date to file declaration of intent to petition for reassessment of unitary property
	23	Sales-use taxes—Prepay State Board of Equalization if so ordered
	30	Property taxes—Senior citizens; last day FTB may accept assistance claims for preceding fiscal year

¶13

Date	Item
JULY 1	Oil and gas producer's tax—Charges due and payable if over $10
Before **1st Mon.**	Oil and gas producer's tax—Apply to correction to State Controller
2	Property taxes—First day to file assessment complaints with County Board of Equalization
15	Carriers—Quarterly report, fee; also (for all but railroads and vessel operators) gross operating revenue fee to Public Utilities Commission
	Property taxes—State-assessed property, State Board of Equalization must transmit estimate of total assessed value to county auditor
20	Property taxes—State-assessed property; assessee has to at least this date to file petition for reassessment of unitary property
30	Property taxes—State-assessed property; last day for notice of assessment of nonunitary property
31	Personal income tax—Quarterly payroll report, pay taxes withheld to Employment Development Department
	Disability insurance contributions—Payment due with personal income tax withheld
	Sales-use taxes—Return and tax (or balance after prepayment) to State Board of Equalization
	Property taxes—State assessed property, last day for State Board of Equalization to transmit roll to county auditor
	Property taxes—State assessed property, last day for State Board of Equalization to transmit changes in estimate of total assessed value to county auditor
	Timber yield taxes—Timber owners report-pay timber yield tax to State Board of Equalization
	Unemployment compensation tax—Quarterly return and payment due.
AUG. 15	Oil and gas producer's tax—Full payment due on charges of $10 to less than $500; first half tax due on charges of $500 or more.
20	Property taxes—State-assessed property; assessee has to at least this date to file declaration of intent to petition for reassessment of nonunitary property
	Insurance companies—Prepayments of gross premiums tax due if annual tax for preceding year was $5,000 or more
24	Sales-use taxes—Prepay to State Board of Equalization if so ordered
31	Property taxes—Pay collector taxes on unsecured roll
SEPT. 15	Property taxes—Last day to file assessment complaints
	Personal income tax—Declaration and payment of income tax to Franchise Tax Board
	Taxes on corporate income—Declaration and payment of estimated tax
	Taxes on corporate income—Farmers' cooperative reports to Franchise Tax Board (15th day of 9th month after fiscal year)
24	Sales-use taxes—Prepay to State Board of Equalization if so ordered
OCT. 15	Carriers—Quarterly report, fee; also (for all but railroads and vessel operators) gross operating revenue fee to Public Utilities Commission
31	Sales-use taxes—Quarterly return and balance of tax to SBE
	Personal income tax—Quarterly return of taxes withheld to Employment Development Department
	Disability insurance contributions—Quarterly return and payment due with personal income tax withheld
	Timber yield tax—Timber owners report-pay timber yield tax to State Board of Equalization
	Withholding—Personal income tax—Quarterly payroll report, pay taxes withheld to Employment Development Department
	Unemployment compensation tax—Quarterly return and payment due
NOV. 15	Insurance companies—Prepayments of gross premiums tax due if annual tax for preceding year was $5,000 or more
24	Sales-use taxes—Prepay to State Board of Equalization if so ordered
DEC. 10	Private car operators' tax—Pay State Board of Equalization
	Property taxes—Last day to pay county tax collector personalty taxes secured by realty and 1/2 realty taxes

¶13

Date	Item
15	Taxes on corporate income—Declaration and payment of estimated income tax
24	Sales-use taxes—Prepay to State Board of Equalization if so ordered
31	Property taxes—State-assessed property; last day for SBE decision on petitions for reassessment of unitary and nonunitary property

¶14   California Tax Calendar—Monthly Dates

The following calendar, which is supplementary to the annual calendar, lists those items which recur on the same date each month during the year. The headnote for the annual calendar applies to this calendar.

Every Month on the	Item
1st	Alcoholic beverages—Carriers report and pay tax to State Board of Equalization
	Gross premiums tax—Surplus line brokers whose annual tax for preceding calendar year was at least $5,000 pay monthly installments
15th	Alcoholic beverages—Distillers report and pay tax to State Board of Equalization
	Alcoholic beverages—Beer and wine manufacturers, wine growers, and importers, report and pay tax to State Board of Equalization
	Gasoline tax—Distributors prepay 95% of tax if estimated monthly liability $900,000 or more
20th	Taxes on corporate income—Withholding agent's return and payment of nonresident's tax withheld at source to Franchise Tax Board if over $2,500 was withheld or accumulated in last calendar month
	Personal income tax—Withholding agent's return and payment of nonresident's tax withheld at source to Franchise Tax Board if over $2,500 was withheld or accumulated in last calendar month
25th	Cigarettes—Report, and pay tax not covered by stamps, to State Board of Equalization
	Gasoline tax—Distributors, aircraft jet fuel dealers, producers and importers report; pay tax
	Gasoline tax—Users and vendors of fuel report; pay tax
	Sales tax—Distributors and brokers of motor vehicle fuel prepay taxes collected.
Last day	Motor fuel—Give State Board of Equalization export certificates for third previous month
	Diesel fuel tax—Beginning 7-1-95, report, pay to State Board of Equalization (except interstate truckers who report, pay quarterly)
Payroll	Withholding—Personal income tax—Employers required to deposit federal taxes must deposit state taxes within the same number of banking days that deposits of federal taxes are due (this includes the federal one-day banking rule), if the accumulated amount of state tax withheld is more than $500 ($75 before 1-1-95 in any deposit period. For calendar years beginning on or after 1-1-95, electronic funds transfer is required, if, in the 12-month period ending 6-30 of the prior year, the cumulative average payment of withholding for any deposit period was $20,000 or more. Payment is due as specified for federal taxes under IRC § 6302.

¶15   Personal Income Tax—1994 Tax Table

1994 California Tax Table

Use the Tax Table below if your taxable income on Form 540EZ, line 16; Form 540A, line 16; or Form 540, line 19 is $50,000 or less.
Use the Tax Rate Schedules on page 46 if your taxable income on Form 540A, line 16 or Form 540, line 19 is more than $50,000.
Find Your Tax:
• Read down the column labeled "If Your Taxable Income Is . . ." to find the range that includes your taxable income.
• Read across the columns labeled "The Tax For Filing Status" until you find the tax that applies for your taxable income and filing status.
Filing status: 1 or 3 (Single; Married filing Separately)   2 or 5 (Married filing Joint; Qualifying Widow(er))   4 (Head of Household)

At Least	But Not Over	1 Or 3 Is	2 Or 5 Is	4 Is	At Least	But Not Over	1 Or 3 Is	2 Or 5 Is	4 Is	At Least	But Not Over	1 Or 3 Is	2 Or 5 Is	4 Is
1	50	0	0	0	6,451	6,550	83	65	65	12,951	13,050	249	166	166
51	150	1	1	1	6,551	6,650	85	66	66	13,051	13,150	253	168	168
151	250	2	2	2	6,651	6,750	87	67	67	13,151	13,250	257	170	170
251	350	3	3	3	6,751	6,850	89	68	68	13,251	13,350	261	172	172
351	450	4	4	4	6,851	6,950	91	69	69	13,351	13,450	265	174	174
451	550	5	5	5	6,951	7,050	93	70	70	13,451	13,550	269	176	176
551	650	6	6	6	7,051	7,150	95	71	71	13,551	13,650	273	178	178
651	750	7	7	7	7,151	7,250	97	72	72	13,651	13,750	277	180	180
751	850	8	8	8	7,251	7,350	99	73	73	13,751	13,850	281	182	182
851	950	9	9	9	7,351	7,450	101	74	74	13,851	13,950	285	184	184
951	1,050	10	10	10	7,451	7,550	103	75	75	13,951	14,050	289	186	186
1,051	1,150	11	11	11	7,551	7,650	105	76	76	14,051	14,150	293	188	188
1,151	1,250	12	12	12	7,651	7,750	107	77	77	14,151	14,250	297	190	190
1,251	1,350	13	13	13	7,751	7,850	109	78	78	14,251	14,350	301	192	192
1,351	1,450	14	14	14	7,851	7,950	111	79	79	14,351	14,450	305	194	194
1,451	1,550	15	15	15	7,951	8,050	113	80	80	14,451	14,550	309	196	196
1,551	1,650	16	16	16	8,051	8,150	115	81	81	14,551	14,650	313	198	198
1,651	1,750	17	17	17	8,151	8,250	117	82	82	14,651	14,750	317	200	200
1,751	1,850	18	18	18	8,251	8,350	119	83	83	14,751	14,850	321	202	202
1,851	1,950	19	19	19	8,351	8,450	121	84	84	14,851	14,950	325	204	204
1,951	2,050	20	20	20	8,451	8,550	123	85	85	14,951	15,050	329	206	206
2,051	2,150	21	21	21	8,551	8,650	125	86	86	15,051	15,150	333	208	208
2,151	2,250	22	22	22	8,651	8,750	127	87	87	15,151	15,250	337	210	210
2,251	2,350	23	23	23	8,751	8,850	129	88	88	15,251	15,350	341	212	212
2,351	2,450	24	24	24	8,851	8,950	131	89	89	15,351	15,450	345	214	214
2,451	2,550	25	25	25	8,951	9,050	133	90	90	15,451	15,550	349	216	216
2,551	2,650	26	26	26	9,051	9,150	135	91	91	15,551	15,650	353	218	218
2,651	2,750	27	27	27	9,151	9,250	137	92	92	15,651	15,750	357	220	220
2,751	2,850	28	28	28	9,251	9,350	139	93	93	15,751	15,850	361	222	222
2,851	2,950	29	29	29	9,351	9,450	141	94	94	15,851	15,950	365	224	224
2,951	3,050	30	30	30	9,451	9,550	143	96	96	15,951	16,050	369	226	226
3,051	3,150	31	31	31	9,551	9,650	145	98	98	16,051	16,150	373	228	228
3,151	3,250	32	32	32	9,651	9,750	147	100	100	16,151	16,250	377	230	230
3,251	3,350	33	33	33	9,751	9,850	149	102	102	16,251	16,350	381	232	232
3,351	3,450	34	34	34	9,851	9,950	151	104	104	16,351	16,450	385	234	234
3,451	3,550	35	35	35	9,951	10,050	153	106	106	16,451	16,550	389	236	236
3,551	3,650	36	36	36	10,051	10,150	155	108	108	16,551	16,650	393	238	238
3,651	3,750	37	37	37	10,151	10,250	157	110	110	16,651	16,750	397	240	240
3,751	3,850	38	38	38	10,251	10,350	159	112	112	16,751	16,850	401	242	242
3,851	3,950	39	39	39	10,351	10,450	161	114	114	16,851	16,950	405	244	244
3,951	4,050	40	40	40	10,451	10,550	163	116	116	16,951	17,050	409	246	246
4,051	4,150	41	41	41	10,551	10,650	165	118	118	17,051	17,150	413	248	248
4,151	4,250	42	42	42	10,651	10,750	167	120	120	17,151	17,250	417	250	250
4,251	4,350	43	43	43	10,751	10,850	169	122	122	17,251	17,350	421	252	252
4,351	4,450	44	44	44	10,851	10,950	171	124	124	17,351	17,450	425	254	254
4,451	4,550	45	45	45	10,951	11,050	173	126	126	17,451	17,550	429	256	256
4,551	4,650	46	46	46	11,051	11,150	175	128	128	17,551	17,650	433	258	258
4,651	4,750	47	47	47	11,151	11,250	177	130	130	17,651	17,750	438	260	260
4,751	4,850	49	48	48	11,251	11,350	181	132	132	17,751	17,850	444	262	262
4,851	4,950	51	49	49	11,351	11,450	185	134	134	17,851	17,950	450	264	264
4,951	5,050	53	50	50	11,451	11,550	189	136	136	17,951	18,050	456	266	266
5,051	5,150	55	51	51	11,551	11,650	193	138	138	18,051	18,150	462	268	268
5,151	5,250	57	52	52	11,651	11,750	197	140	140	18,151	18,250	468	270	270
5,251	5,350	59	53	53	11,751	11,850	201	142	142	18,251	18,350	474	272	272
5,351	5,450	61	54	54	11,851	11,950	205	144	144	18,351	18,450	480	274	274
5,451	5,550	63	55	55	11,951	12,050	209	146	146	18,451	18,550	486	276	276
5,551	5,650	65	56	56	12,051	12,150	213	148	148	18,551	18,650	492	278	278
5,651	5,750	67	57	57	12,151	12,250	217	150	150	18,651	18,750	498	280	280
5,751	5,850	69	58	58	12,251	12,350	221	152	152	18,751	18,850	504	282	282
5,851	5,950	71	59	59	12,351	12,450	225	154	154	18,851	18,950	510	284	284
5,951	6,050	73	60	60	12,451	12,550	229	156	156	18,951	19,050	516	286	286
6,051	6,150	75	61	61	12,551	12,650	233	158	158	19,051	19,150	522	288	288
6,151	6,250	77	62	62	12,651	12,750	237	160	160	19,151	19,250	528	290	290
6,251	6,350	79	63	63	12,751	12,850	241	162	162	19,251	19,350	534	292	292
6,351	6,450	81	64	64	12,851	12,950	245	164	164	19,351	19,450	540	294	294

1994 California Tax Table — Continued

Section 1

If Your Taxable Income is...		The Tax For Filing Status		
At Least	But Not Over	1 Or 3 Is	2 Or 5 Is	4 Is
19,451	19,550	546	296	296
19,551	19,650	552	298	298
19,651	19,750	558	300	300
19,751	19,850	564	302	302
19,851	19,950	570	304	304
19,951	20,050	576	306	306
20,051	20,150	582	308	308
20,151	20,250	588	310	310
20,251	20,350	594	312	312
20,351	20,450	600	314	314
20,451	20,550	606	316	316
20,551	20,650	612	318	318
20,651	20,750	618	320	320
20,751	20,850	624	322	322
20,851	20,950	630	324	324
20,951	21,050	636	326	326
21,051	21,150	642	328	328
21,151	21,250	648	330	330
21,251	21,350	654	332	332
21,351	21,450	660	334	334
21,451	21,550	666	336	336
21,551	21,650	672	338	338
21,651	21,750	678	340	340
21,751	21,850	684	342	342
21,851	21,950	690	344	344
21,951	22,050	696	346	346
22,051	22,150	702	348	348
22,151	22,250	708	350	350
22,251	22,350	714	352	352
22,351	22,450	720	354	354
22,451	22,550	726	358	358
22,551	22,650	732	362	362
22,651	22,750	738	366	366
22,751	22,850	744	370	370
22,851	22,950	750	374	374
22,951	23,050	756	378	378
23,051	23,150	762	382	382
23,151	23,250	768	386	386
23,251	23,350	774	390	390
23,351	23,450	780	394	394
23,451	23,550	786	398	398
23,551	23,650	792	402	402
23,651	23,750	798	406	406
23,751	23,850	804	410	410
23,851	23,950	810	414	414
23,951	24,050	816	418	418
24,051	24,150	822	422	422
24,151	24,250	828	426	426
24,251	24,350	834	430	430
24,351	24,450	840	434	434
24,451	24,550	846	438	438
24,551	24,650	853	442	442
24,651	24,750	861	446	446
24,751	24,850	869	450	450
24,851	24,950	877	454	454
24,951	25,050	885	458	458
25,051	25,150	893	462	462
25,151	25,250	901	466	466
25,251	25,350	909	470	470
25,351	25,450	917	474	474
25,451	25,550	925	478	478
25,551	25,650	933	482	482
25,651	25,750	941	486	486
25,751	25,850	949	490	490
25,851	25,950	957	494	494
25,951	26,050	965	498	498
26,051	26,150	973	502	502
26,151	26,250	981	506	506
26,251	26,350	989	510	510
26,351	26,450	997	514	514

Section 2

If Your Taxable Income is...		The Tax For Filing Status		
At Least	But Not Over	1 Or 3 Is	2 Or 5 Is	4 Is
26,451	26,550	1,005	518	518
26,551	26,650	1,013	522	522
26,651	26,750	1,021	526	526
26,751	26,850	1,029	530	530
26,851	26,950	1,037	534	534
26,951	27,050	1,045	538	538
27,051	27,150	1,053	542	542
27,151	27,250	1,061	546	546
27,251	27,350	1,069	550	550
27,351	27,450	1,077	554	554
27,451	27,550	1,085	558	558
27,551	27,650	1,093	562	562
27,651	27,750	1,101	566	566
27,751	27,850	1,109	570	570
27,851	27,950	1,117	574	574
27,951	28,050	1,125	578	578
28,051	28,150	1,133	582	582
28,151	28,250	1,141	586	586
28,251	28,350	1,149	590	590
28,351	28,450	1,157	594	594
28,451	28,550	1,165	598	598
28,551	28,650	1,170	602	602
28,651	28,750	1,181	606	606
28,751	28,850	1,189	610	610
28,851	28,950	1,197	614	615
28,951	29,050	1,205	618	621
29,051	29,150	1,213	622	627
29,151	29,250	1,221	626	633
29,251	29,350	1,229	630	639
29,351	29,450	1,237	634	645
29,451	29,550	1,245	638	651
29,551	29,650	1,253	642	657
29,651	29,750	1,261	646	663
29,751	29,850	1,269	650	669
29,851	29,950	1,277	654	675
29,951	30,050	1,285	658	681
30,051	30,150	1,293	662	687
30,151	30,250	1,301	666	693
30,251	30,350	1,309	670	699
30,351	30,450	1,317	674	705
30,451	30,550	1,325	678	711
30,551	30,650	1,333	682	717
30,651	30,750	1,341	686	723
30,751	30,850	1,349	690	729
30,851	30,950	1,357	694	735
30,951	31,050	1,365	698	741
31,051	31,150	1,375	702	747
31,151	31,250	1,384	706	753
31,251	31,350	1,393	710	759
31,351	31,450	1,403	714	765
31,451	31,550	1,412	718	771
31,551	31,650	1,421	722	777
31,651	31,750	1,431	726	783
31,751	31,850	1,440	730	789
31,851	31,950	1,449	734	795
31,951	32,050	1,458	738	801
32,051	32,150	1,468	742	807
32,151	32,250	1,477	746	813
32,251	32,350	1,486	750	819
32,351	32,450	1,496	754	825
32,451	32,550	1,505	758	831
32,551	32,650	1,514	762	837
32,651	32,750	1,524	766	843
32,751	32,850	1,533	770	849
32,851	32,950	1,542	774	855
32,951	33,050	1,551	778	861
33,051	33,150	1,561	782	867
33,151	33,250	1,570	786	873
33,251	33,350	1,579	790	879
33,351	33,450	1,589	794	885

Section 3

If Your Taxable Income is...		The Tax For Filing Status		
At Least	But Not Over	1 Or 3 Is	2 Or 5 Is	4 Is
33,451	33,550	1,598	798	891
33,551	33,650	1,607	802	897
33,651	33,750	1,617	806	903
33,751	33,850	1,626	810	909
33,851	33,950	1,635	814	915
33,951	34,050	1,644	818	921
34,051	34,150	1,654	822	927
34,151	34,250	1,663	826	933
34,251	34,350	1,672	830	939
34,351	34,450	1,682	834	945
34,451	34,550	1,691	838	951
34,551	34,650	1,700	842	957
34,651	34,750	1,710	846	963
34,751	34,850	1,719	850	969
34,851	34,950	1,728	854	975
34,951	35,050	1,737	858	981
35,051	35,150	1,747	862	987
35,151	35,250	1,756	866	993
35,251	35,350	1,765	870	999
35,351	35,450	1,775	875	1,005
35,451	35,550	1,784	881	1,011
35,551	35,650	1,793	887	1,017
35,651	35,750	1,803	893	1,023
35,751	35,850	1,812	899	1,031
35,851	35,950	1,821	905	1,039
35,951	36,050	1,830	911	1,047
36,051	36,150	1,840	917	1,055
36,151	36,250	1,849	923	1,063
36,251	36,350	1,858	929	1,071
36,351	36,450	1,868	935	1,079
36,451	36,550	1,877	941	1,087
36,551	36,650	1,886	947	1,095
36,651	36,750	1,896	953	1,103
36,751	36,850	1,905	959	1,111
36,851	36,950	1,914	965	1,119
36,951	37,050	1,923	971	1,127
37,051	37,150	1,933	977	1,135
37,151	37,250	1,942	983	1,143
37,251	37,350	1,951	989	1,151
37,351	37,450	1,961	995	1,159
37,451	37,550	1,970	1,001	1,167
37,551	37,650	1,979	1,007	1,175
37,651	37,750	1,989	1,013	1,183
37,751	37,850	1,998	1,019	1,191
37,851	37,950	2,007	1,025	1,199
37,951	38,050	2,016	1,031	1,207
38,051	38,150	2,026	1,037	1,215
38,151	38,250	2,035	1,043	1,223
38,251	38,350	2,044	1,049	1,231
38,351	38,450	2,054	1,055	1,239
38,451	38,550	2,063	1,061	1,247
38,551	38,650	2,072	1,067	1,255
38,651	38,750	2,082	1,073	1,263
38,751	38,850	2,091	1,079	1,271
38,851	38,950	2,100	1,085	1,279
38,951	39,050	2,109	1,091	1,287
39,051	39,150	2,119	1,097	1,295
39,151	39,250	2,128	1,103	1,303
39,251	39,350	2,137	1,109	1,311
39,351	39,450	2,147	1,115	1,319
39,451	39,550	2,156	1,121	1,327
39,551	39,650	2,165	1,127	1,335
39,651	39,750	2,175	1,133	1,343
39,751	39,850	2,184	1,139	1,351
39,851	39,950	2,193	1,145	1,359
39,951	40,050	2,202	1,151	1,367
40,051	40,150	2,212	1,157	1,375
40,151	40,250	2,221	1,163	1,383
40,251	40,350	2,230	1,169	1,391
40,351	40,450	2,240	1,175	1,399

1994 California Tax Table — Continued

If Your Taxable Income Is...		The Tax For Filing Status			If Your Taxable Income Is...		The Tax For Filing Status			If Your Taxable Income Is...		The Tax For Filing Status		
At Least	But Not Over	1 Or 3 Is	2 Or 5 Is	4 Is	At Least	But Not Over	1 Or 3 Is	2 Or 5 Is	4 Is	At Least	But Not Over	1 Or 3 Is	2 Or 5 Is	4 Is
40,451	40,550	2,249	1,181	1,407	43,951	44,050	2,574	1,391	1,710	47,451	47,550	2,900	1,601	2,036
40,551	40,650	2,258	1,187	1,415	44,051	44,150	2,584	1,397	1,720	47,551	47,650	2,909	1,607	2,045
40,651	40,750	2,268	1,193	1,423	44,151	44,250	2,593	1,403	1,729	47,651	47,750	2,919	1,613	2,054
40,751	40,850	2,277	1,199	1,431	44,251	44,350	2,602	1,409	1,738	47,751	47,850	2,928	1,619	2,064
40,851	40,950	2,286	1,205	1,439	44,351	44,450	2,612	1,415	1,748	47,851	47,950	2,937	1,625	2,073
40,951	41,050	2,295	1,211	1,447	44,451	44,550	2,621	1,421	1,757	47,951	48,050	2,946	1,631	2,082
41,051	41,150	2,305	1,217	1,455	44,551	44,650	2,630	1,427	1,766	48,051	48,150	2,956	1,637	2,092
41,151	41,250	2,314	1,223	1,463	44,651	44,750	2,640	1,433	1,775	48,151	48,250	2,965	1,643	2,101
41,251	41,350	2,323	1,229	1,471	44,751	44,850	2,649	1,439	1,785	48,251	48,350	2,974	1,649	2,110
41,351	41,450	2,333	1,235	1,479	44,851	44,950	2,658	1,445	1,794	48,351	48,450	2,984	1,655	2,120
41,451	41,550	2,342	1,241	1,487	44,951	45,050	2,667	1,451	1,803	48,451	48,550	2,993	1,661	2,129
41,551	41,650	2,351	1,247	1,495	45,051	45,150	2,677	1,457	1,813	48,551	48,650	3,002	1,667	2,138
41,651	41,750	2,361	1,253	1,503	45,151	45,250	2,686	1,463	1,822	48,651	48,750	3,012	1,673	2,147
41,751	41,850	2,370	1,259	1,511	45,251	45,350	2,695	1,469	1,831	48,751	48,850	3,021	1,679	2,157
41,851	41,950	2,379	1,265	1,519	45,351	45,450	2,705	1,475	1,841	48,851	48,950	3,030	1,685	2,166
41,951	42,050	2,388	1,271	1,527	45,451	45,550	2,714	1,481	1,850	48,951	49,050	3,039	1,691	2,175
42,051	42,150	2,398	1,277	1,535	45,551	45,650	2,723	1,487	1,859	49,051	49,150	3,049	1,699	2,185
42,151	42,250	2,407	1,283	1,543	45,651	45,750	2,733	1,493	1,868	49,151	49,250	3,058	1,707	2,194
42,251	42,350	2,416	1,289	1,552	45,751	45,850	2,742	1,499	1,878	49,251	49,350	3,067	1,715	2,203
42,351	42,450	2,426	1,295	1,562	45,851	45,950	2,751	1,505	1,887	49,351	49,450	3,077	1,723	2,213
42,451	42,550	2,435	1,301	1,571	45,951	46,050	2,760	1,511	1,896	49,451	49,550	3,086	1,731	2,222
42,551	42,650	2,444	1,307	1,580	46,051	46,150	2,770	1,517	1,906	49,551	49,650	3,095	1,739	2,231
42,651	42,750	2,454	1,313	1,589	46,151	46,250	2,779	1,523	1,915	49,651	49,750	3,105	1,747	2,240
42,751	42,850	2,463	1,319	1,599	46,251	46,350	2,788	1,529	1,924	49,751	49,850	3,114	1,755	2,250
42,851	42,950	2,472	1,325	1,608	46,351	46,450	2,798	1,535	1,934	49,851	49,950	3,123	1,763	2,259
42,951	43,050	2,481	1,331	1,617	46,451	46,550	2,807	1,541	1,943	49,951	50,000	3,130	1,769	2,266
43,051	43,150	2,491	1,337	1,627	46,551	46,650	2,816	1,547	1,952					
43,151	43,250	2,500	1,343	1,636	46,651	46,750	2,826	1,553	1,961	OVER $50,000 YOU MUST COMPUTE				
43,251	43,350	2,509	1,349	1,645	46,751	46,850	2,835	1,559	1,971	YOUR TAX USING THE TAX RATE				
43,351	43,450	2,519	1,355	1,655	46,851	46,950	2,844	1,565	1,980	SCHEDULES BELOW.				
43,451	43,550	2,528	1,361	1,664	46,951	47,050	2,853	1,571	1,989					
43,551	43,650	2,537	1,367	1,673	47,051	47,150	2,863	1,577	1,999					
43,651	43,750	2,547	1,373	1,682	47,151	47,250	2,872	1,583	2,008					
43,751	43,850	2,556	1,379	1,692	47,251	47,350	2,881	1,589	2,017					
43,851	43,950	2,565	1,385	1,701	47,351	47,450	2,891	1,595	2,027					

1994 Tax Rate Schedules

Caution: Use only if your taxable income (Form 540A, line 16 or Form 540, line 19) is more than **$50,000.** If $50,000 or less, use the Tax Table.

	If the amount on Form 540A, line 16 or Form 540, line 19, is: over—	But not over—	Enter on Form 540A, line 17 or Form 540, line 20		of the amount over—
Schedule X – Use if your filing status is **Single or Married Filing Separate**	$ 0	$ 4,722	$ 0.00	+ 1.0%	$ 0
	4,722	11,192	47.22	+ 2.0%	4,722
	11,192	17,662	176.62	+ 4.0%	11,192
	17,662	24,519	435.42	+ 6.0%	17,662
	24,519	30,987	846.84	+ 8.0%	24,519
	30,987	107,464	1,364.28	+ 9.3%	30,987
	107,464	214,929	8,476.64	+ 10.0%	107,464
	214,929	AND OVER	19,223.14	+ 11.0%	214,929
Schedule Y – Use if your filing status is **Married Filing Joint or Qualifying Widow(er) with Dependent Child**	$ 0	$ 9,444	$ 0.00	+ 1.0%	$ 0
	9,444	22,384	94.44	+ 2.0%	9,444
	22,384	35,324	353.24	+ 4.0%	22,384
	35,324	49,038	870.84	+ 6.0%	35,324
	49,038	61,974	1,693.68	+ 8.0%	49,038
	61,974	214,928	2,728.56	+ 9.3%	61,974
	214,928	429,858	16,953.28	+ 10.0%	214,928
	429,858	AND OVER	38,446.28	+ 11.0%	429,858
Schedule Z – Use if your filing status is **Head of Household**	$ 0	$ 9,445	$ 0	+ 1.0%	$ 0
	9,445	22,383	94.45	+ 2.0%	9,445
	22,383	28,852	353.21	+ 4.0%	22,383
	28,852	35,709	611.97	+ 6.0%	28,852
	35,709	42,179	1,023.39	+ 8.0%	35,709
	42,179	146,274	1,540.99	+ 9.3%	42,179
	146,274	292,550	11,221.83	+ 10.0%	146,274
	292,550	AND OVER	25,849.43	+ 11.0%	292,550

¶16   Franchise and Income Taxes—1994 Rates

A.   General corporations.   For income years ending in 1994, the franchise and income tax rate for general corporations is 9.3%.

B.   S corporations.   The rate for S corporations is 1.5% for income years beginning on or after 1-1-94. Previously, it was 2.5%.

C.   Banks and financial corporations.   Calendar year taxpayers.   For banks and financial corporations that are not S corporations, the rate is 11.470% for 1994. For S financial corporations, the rate is 3.670%. The rate for S financial corporations reflects the reduction of the regular franchise tax rate from 2.5% to 1.5%.

Fiscal year taxpayers.   For fiscal year taxpayers, the rate is prorated as follows:

Month ending	Banks and financial corporations that are not S corporations	S financial corporations
January 1994	11.137%	4.337%
February	11.168%	4.367%
March	11.198%	4.398%
April	11.228%	4.428%
May	11.258%	4.458%
June	11.288%	4.488%
July	11.319%	4.519%
August	11.349%	4.549%
September	11.379%	4.579%
October	11.409%	4.609%
November	11.440%	4.640%

The rates for S financial corporations reflect the 2.5% rate. The reduction in the S corporation tax rate is effective for income years beginning on or after 1-1-94. The above rates must be used in computing estimated tax payments for income years ending in 1994, not the rates shown in Form 100-ES.

Section II/*Personal Income Tax*

CODE TABLES, TAX RATES AND TAX TABLES

CODE TABLES

¶85   **Federal—California Code Table**

Listed in the table below are the federal Internal Revenue Code section numbers, the comparable California Personal Income Tax Law and Administrative Tax Law section numbers, and the paragraph numbers in this handbook where they are explained or to which they relate.

Federal IRC § No.	Subject	Calif. Law No.	Handbook ¶ No.
1	Tax imposed	17041	121; 137
2	Definitions and special rules	17042; 17046	121; 123; 141
3	Tax tables for individuals	17048	131
21	Expenses for household and dependent care services necessary gainful employment	N	143; 158
26	Limitation based on tax liability; definition of tax liability	17039	106
28	Clinical testing expenses for certain drugs for rare diseases or conditions	17057	154
30	Credit for electric vehicles	17052.11	153
41	Credit for increasing research activities	17052.12	148
42	Low income housing credit	17058	156
48	Energy credit	17052.5	151
51-52	Amount of targeted jobs credit	17053.7	149; 158
53	Credit for prior year minimum tax liability	17063	135
55—59	Alternative minimum tax	17062	135
61	Gross income	17071; 17131.5; 17132; 17133; 17133.5; 17135; 17136; 17140.5; 17141; 17153.5; 17156; 17160	115; 251; 252
62	Adjusted gross income	17072	115; 182; 291—295; 297; 298; 302
63	Taxable income defined; standard deduction	17073; 17073.5; 17301	115; 321—322
64	Ordinary income	17074	115
65	Ordinary loss	17075	115
66	Treatment of community income	18402.8	201
67	2-percent floor on miscellaneous itemized deductions	17076	292; 293
68	Overall limitation on itemized deductions	17077	322
71	Alimony and separate maintenance payments	17081	218; 301
72	Annuities; life insurance contracts	17085	214; 215
73	Services of child	17081	208
74	Prizes and awards	17081	204
75	Dealers in tax-exempt securities	17081	216
77	Commodity credit loans	17081	219

Federal IRC § No.	Subject	Calif. Law No.	Handbook ¶ No.
78	Dividends received from foreign corporations by domestic corporations choosing tax credit	17081	217
79	Group-term life insurance purchased for employees	17095	203
80	Restoration of value of certain securities	17081	251
82	Reimbursement for expenses of moving	17081	203
83	Property transferred in performance of services	17081	212; 221; 309
84	Transfer of appreciated property to political organization	17081	361
85	Unemployment compensation	17083	203
86	Social security and railroad retirement benefits	17087	209
88	Certain amounts with respect to nuclear decommissioning costs	17081	354
90	Illegal federal irrigation subsidies	17081	224
101	Certain death benefits	17131	209, 251, 253
102	Gifts and inheritances	17131	251; 254
103	Interest on state and local bonds	17143	216
104	Compensation for injuries or sickness	17131	251, 255
105	Amounts received under accident and health plans	17095	220; 251; 256
106	Contributions by employer to accident and health plans	17131	251
107	Rental value of parsonages	17131	251; 257
108	Income from discharge of indebtedness	17144	220; 251; 258
109	Improvements by lessee on lessor's property	17131	251; 259
111	Recovery of tax benefit items	17142	251; 260
112	Combat pay of members of the Armed Forces	17131	206; 251
115	Income of states; municipalities	17131	251
117	Qualified scholarships	17131	205; 251
119	Meals or lodging for convenience of employer	17131	251; 263

Federal IRC § No.	Subject	Calif. Law No.	Handbook ¶ No.
121	One-time exclusion of gain from sale of principal residence by age 55	17152	251; 261
122	Certain reduced uniformed services retirement pay	17131; 17153	251; 264
123	Amounts received under insurance contracts for certain living expenses	17131	251; 262
125	Cafeteria plans	17158	251; 264; 272
126	Governmental payments for environmental conservation	17131	271
127	Educational assistance programs	17151	251; 269; 272
129	Dependent care assistance	17131; 17095	275
130	Assignments of personal injury liability	17131	255
131	Foster care	17131	272
132	Certain fringe benefits	17090; 17095; 17134; 17149	282
133	Interest on loans to acquire employer securities	17131	216; 1094
134	Certain military benefits	17131	206
135	U.S. Savings bonds used to pay higher education tuition and fees	17131	251
136	Cross references to other acts; ship contractors	17138; 17139	251
151	Allowance of deductions for personal exemptions	17054	122; 141
152	Dependent defined	17056	123; 141
161	Itemized deductions	17201; 17274; 17275; 17278; 17299.8; 17299.9	291; 321
162	Trade or business expenses	17201; 17202; 17269; 17270; 17270(a); 17286; 17289	291; 292; 293; 294; 302; 324; 328; 1236
163	Interest	17201; 17224; 17230; 17231; 17232; 17233	182; 291; 325
164	Taxes	17220	291; 324
165	Losses	17201; 17207; 17208-17208.3	182; 291; 295; 298; 327; 328
166	Bad debts	17201	291; 295; 403; 404
167	Depreciation	17201; 17250; 17250(d); 17250(e); 17250(f)	291; 370; 387; 388; 391
168	Accelerated cost recovery system	17201; 17858	81
169	Amortization of pollution control facilities	17201; 17250(c)	291; 306
170	Charitable, etc., contributions and gifts	17201; 17241	291; 265; 326

¶85

Federal IRC § No.	Subject	Calif. Law No.	Handbook ¶ No.
171	Amortizable bond premium	17201	291
172	Net operating losses	17276; 17276.1; 17276.2; 17276.3; 17310	295
173	Circulation expenditures	17201	303
174	Research and experimental expenditures	17201	291; 304
175	Soil and water conservation expenditures	17201	291; 305
176	Payments to employees of certain foreign corporations	17201	203; 1145
178	Amortization of cost of acquiring a lease	17201	291
179	Expensing certain depreciable assets	17201; 17252.5; 17255; 17265; 17266	385; 461
180	Expenditures by farmers for fertilizer, etc.	17201	291; 305
183	Activities not engaged in for profit	17201	291; 308
186	Recoveries of damages for antitrust violations, etc.	17201	291
190	Expenditures to remove architectural and transportation barriers to the handicapped and elderly	17201	291
192	Black lung benefit trust	17201	326
193	Tertiary injectants	17260(a)	291
194	Reforestation expenditures	17201	115; 305
194A	Contributions to employer liability trusts	17201	326
195	Business start-up expenses	17201	392
197	Amortization of goodwill and other intangibles	17249; 17279	371
211	Allowance of deductions	17201	291; 321
212	Expenses for production of income	17201	291; 328
213	Medical, dental, etc., expenses	17024.5(b-10)	291; 323
215	Alimony, etc., payments	17302	291; 301
216	Deduction of taxes, interest, and business depreciation by cooperative housing corporation tenant-stockholder	17201	291
217	Moving expenses	17201	291; 297
219	Retirement savings	17272	213; 291; 299
261	General rule for disallowance of deductions	17201	321

Federal IRC § No.	Subject	Calif. Law No.	Handbook ¶ No.
262	Personal, living, and family expenses	17201	321
263	Capital expenditures	17201; 17260(b)	354; 366; 394-5; 402
263A	Capitalization and inclusion in inventory costs; certain expenses	17261	411
264	Certain amounts paid in connection with insurance contracts	17201	321
265	Expenses and interest relating to tax-exempt income	17201; 17280	291; 325
266	Carrying charges	17201	363
267	Losses, expenses, and interest between related tax-payers	17201	365
268	Sale of land with unharvested crop	17201	401; 402
269	Acquisitions made to evade or avoid income tax	17201	224; 292; 1145
269A	Personal service corporation used to avoid or evade income tax	17201; 17287	354
271	Debts owed by political parties, etc.	17201	325
272	Disposal of coal or domestic iron ore	17201	295
273	Holders of life or terminable interest	17201	321
274	Disallowance of certain entertainment, etc., expenses	17201; 17271	292; 293
275	Certain taxes	17222	291; 324
276	Certain indirect contributions to political parties	17283	328
277	Certain membership organizations	17201	328
279	Interest on indebtedness incurred by corporation to acquire another corporation's stock	17201	1082
280A	Disallowance of certain expenses in connection with business use of home, rental of vacation homes, etc.	17201	302
280B	Demolition of structures	17201	291
280C	Expenses for which credits are allowable	17201; 17270(c); 17270(d)	291—293
280E	Expenditures in connection with illegal sale of drugs	17281-82	292

Federal IRC § No.	Subject	Calif. Law No.	Handbook ¶ No.
280F	Limitation on investment tax credit and depreciation for luxury automobiles; limitation where certain property used for personal purposes	17201	396
280G	Golden parachute payments	17201	328
280H	Limitations on amounts paid to owner-employees by personal service corporations	17201	213
301	Distributions of property	17321	1116
302	Distributions in redemption of stock	17321; 17322	334; 335; 1117
303	Distributions in redemption of stock to pay death taxes	17321	1124
304	Redemption through use of related corporations	17321	1119
305	Distributions of stock and stock rights	17321	1120
306	Dispositions of certain stock	17321	362; 1123
307	Basis of stock and stock rights acquired in distributions	17321	362
311	Taxability of corporations on distributions	17321	201
312	Effect on earnings and profits	17321	1115
316	Dividend defined	17321	1115
317	Other definitions	17321	1115
318	Constructive ownership of stock	17321	1118
331	Gain or loss to shareholders in corporate liquidations	17321	1125
332	Liquidation of subsidiaries	17321	1131
334	Basis of property received in liquidations	17321	1126
336	Gain or loss recognized on property distributed in complete liquidation	17321	1130
337	Nonrecognition for property distributed to parent in liquidation of subsidiary	17321	1130
338	Stock purchases treated as asset acquisitions	17321	1130
341	Collapsible corporations	17321	1029
346	Definition and special rule	17321	1117; 1126

Federal IRC § No.	Subject	Calif. Law No.	Handbook ¶ No.
351	Transfer to corporation controlled by transferor	17321	1103
354	Exchanges of stock and securities in certain reorganizations	17321	1104
355	Distribution of stock and securities of a controlled corporation	17321	1104
356	Receipt of additional consideration	17321	1104
357	Assumption of liability	17321	362
358	Basis to distributees	17321	1104
361	Nonrecognition of gain or loss to corporations	17321	1103; 1104
362	Basis to corporations	17321	1103; 1104
367	Foreign corporations	17321	362
368	Definitions relating to corporate reorganizations	17321	1104
381-384	Carryovers	17321	1017; 1104; 1134
385	Treatment of certain interests in corporations as stock or indebtedness	17321	104; 331
401	Qualified pension, profit-sharing, and stock bonus plans	17501; 17502	210; 300
402	Taxability of beneficiary of employees' trust	17501; 17504	210; 212
403	Taxation of employee annuities	17501; 17506	209; 210
404	Deduction for contributions of an employer to an employees' trust or annuity plan and compensation under a deferred-payment plan	17501	300
404A	Foreign deferred compensation plan	17501	292
406	Certain employees of foreign affiliates	17501	209—211
407	Certain employees of domestic subsidiaries engaged in business outside the United States	17501	209—211
408	Individual retirement accounts	17501; 17507; 17508	136; 211; 299
409	Retirement bonds. (Repealed.)	17501	211
409	Qualifications for tax credit ESOPs	17501	309
410	Minimum participation standards	17501	209—211

Federal IRC § No.	Subject	Calif. Law No.	Handbook ¶ No.
411	Minimum vesting standards	17501; 17555	209—211
412	Minimum funding standards	17501	209—211
413	Collectively bargained plans	17501; 17509	209—211
414	Definitions and special rules	17501	209—210
415	Limitations on benefits and contributions under qualified plans	17501; 17512	209—211; 292; 300
416	Special rules for top-heavy plans	17501	209—213; 299-300
417	Minimum survivor annuity requirements	17501	209—213; 299-300
418— 418E	Multiemployer plans	17501	209—213; 299-300
419	Treatment of funded welfare benefit plans	17501	292
419A	Qualified asset account; limitation of additions to account	17501	292
420	Transfers of excess pension assets to retiree health accounts	17501	209—211
421	General rules	17501	309
422	Incentive stock options	17501	309
423	Employee stock purchase plans	17501	309
424	Definitions and special rules	17501	309
441	Period for computation of taxable income	17551; 17551.5; 17554; 17565	351
442	Change of annual accounting period	17551; 17556	351
443	Returns for a period of less than 12 months	17551; 17552	351
444	Election of taxable year other than required taxable year	17551	351
446	General rule for methods of accounting	17551	183; 352
447	Method of accounting for corporation or partners engaged in farming	17551	183; 352
448	Limitation on use of cash method of accounting	17551; 17562	352
451	General rule for taxable year of inclusion	17081; 17551; 17559	353
453— 453-B	Installment sales	17551; 17560	364; 394; 395; 407; 453
454	Obligations issued at discount	17551; 17553	353
455	Prepaid subscription income	17551	353

Federal IRC § No.	Subject	Calif. Law No.	Handbook ¶ No.
456	Prepaid dues income of certain membership organizations	17551	353
457	Deferred compensation plans for state and local governments	17551; 17566	353
458	Magazines, paperbacks, and records returned after close of tax year	17551	353
460	Special rules for long-term contracts	17551; 17564	353
461	General rule for taxable year of deduction	17551	292; 324; 325; 354; 454
464	Limitations on deductions in case of farming syndicates	17551	354
465	Deductions limited to amount at risk	17551	354; 428
467	Certain payments for the use of property or services	17551; 17558	353
468	Special rules for mining and solid waste reclamation and closing costs	17551	354
468A	Special rules for nuclear decommissioning costs	17551	354
468B	Special rules for designated settlement funds	17551	354
469	Passive activity losses and credits; limits	17551; 17561	354
471	General rule for inventories	17551	411
472	Last-in, first-out inventories	17551	411
473	LIFO inventories; liquidation	17551	411
474	Simplified dollar-value LIFO method; certain small businesses	17551	411
481	Adjustments required by changes in method of accounting	17551	352
482	Allocation of income and deductions among taxpayers	17551	354
483	Interest on certain deferred payments	17551	216; 325
501	Exemption from tax on corporations, certain trusts, etc.	17631-32	954
503	Requirements for exemption	17635—17640	951—963
505	Additional requirements for organizations described in paragraph (9) or (20) of section 501(c) (added)	17631-32	954

Federal IRC § No.	Subject	Calif. Law No.	Handbook ¶ No.
511	Imposition of tax on unrelated business income of charitable, etc., organizations	17651	954
512	Unrelated business taxable income	17651	954
513	Unrelated trade or business	17651	954
541-547	Personal holding companies	17024.5	106; 1028
584	Common trust funds	17671	475
611	Allowance of deduction for depletion	17681	402
612	Basis for cost depletion	17681	402
613	Percentage depletion	17681; 17682; 17683	402
613A	Limitations on percentage depletion in case of oil and gas wells	17682	402
614	Property defined	17681	402
616	Development expenditures	17681	402
617	Deduction and recapture of certain mining exploration expenditures	17681	401—402
631	Gain or loss in the case of timber, coal, or domestic iron ore	17681	402
636	Income tax treatment of mineral production payments	17681	402
641	Imposition of tax	17731; 17734; 17742; 17743; 17744; 17745; 17745.1	455; 456
642	Special rules for credits and deductions	17731-17733; 17736	455; 461; 462; 472
643	Definitions applicable to subparts A, B, C, and D	17731; 17750	459; 462
644	Special rule for gain on property transferred to trust at less than fair market value	17731	455
645	Taxable year of trusts	17731	455
651	Deduction for trusts distributing current income only	17731	455; 462
652	Inclusion of amounts in gross income of beneficiaries of trusts distributing current income only	17731	455; 462
661	Deduction for estates and trusts accumulating income or distributing corpus	17731; 17735	455; 462

Federal IRC § No.	Subject	Calif. Law No.	Handbook ¶ No.
662	Inclusion of amounts in gross income of beneficiaries of estates and trusts accumulating income or distributing corpus	17731	474
663	Special rules applicable to sections 661 and 662	17731	462
664	Charitable remainder trusts	17731	474
665	Definitions applicable to subpart D	17731; 17779	462
666	Accumulation distribution allocated to preceding years	17731; 17779	462
667	Treatment of amounts deemed distributed in preceding years	17731; 17779	462; 463
668	Interest charge on accumulation distributions from foreign trusts	17731; 17779	462
671	Trust income deductions, and credits attributable to grantors and others as substantial owner	17731	473
672	Definitions and rules	17731	473
673	Reversionary interest	17731	473
674	Power to control beneficial enjoyment	17731	473
675	Administrative powers	17731	473
676	Power to revoke	17731	473
677	Income for benefit of grantor	17731	473
678	Person other than grantor treated as substantial owner	17731	473
679	Foreign trusts with U.S. beneficiaries	17024.5	471
681	Limitation on charitable deduction	17731	462
682	Income of an estate or trust in case of divorce, etc.	17731; 17737	218; 455
683	Use of trust as an exchange fund	17731	1103
691	Recipients of income in respect of decedents	17731	453
692	Income taxes of members of Armed Forces on death	17731; 17800	206; 453
701	Partners, not partnership, subject to tax	17851	422
702	Income and credits of partner	17851-17852	423
703	Partnership computations	17851; 17853	426

Federal IRC § No.	Subject	Calif. Law No.	Handbook ¶ No.
704	Partner's distributive share	17851; 17858	421—423; 428
705	Determination of basis of partner's interest	17851	425
706	Taxable years of partner and partnership	17851	422
707	Transactions between partner and partnership	17851; 17854	426; 429
708	Continuation of partnership	17851	426; 429
709	Treatment of organization and syndication fees	17851	426
721	Nonrecognition of gain or loss on contribution	17851	424
722	Basis of contributing partner's interest	17851	424
723	Basis of property contributed to partnership	17851	425
724	Character of gain or loss on contributed unrealized receivables, inventory items, and capital loss property	17851	424
731	Extent of recognition of gain or loss on distribution	17851	432
732	Basis of distributed property other than money	17851	433
733	Basis of distributee partner's interest	17851	433
734	Optional adjustment to basis of undistributed partnership property	17851	434
735	Character of gain or loss on disposition of distributed property	17851	433
736	Payments to a retiring partner or a deceased partner's successor in interest	17851	431
737	Recognition of precontribution gain	17851	424
741	Recognition and character of gain or loss on sale or exchange	17851	430
742	Basis of transferee partner's interest	17851	361
743	Optional adjustment to basis of partnership property	17851	434
751	Unrealized receivables and inventory items	17851; 17855; 17856; 17857	430; 433
752	Treatment of certain liabilities	17851	423
753	Partner receiving income in respect of decedent	17851	453

Federal IRC § No.	Subject	Calif. Law No.	Handbook ¶ No.
754	Manner of electing optional adjustment to basis of partnership property	17851	434
755	Rules for allocation of basis	17851	434
761	Terms defined	17851	421
851	Definition of regulated investment company	17088	216
852	Taxation of regulated investment companies and their shareholders	17088; 17145	216
853	Foreign tax credit allowed to shareholders	17088; 17024.5(b-07)	216
856	Definition of real estate investment trust	17740	1004
857	Taxation of real estate investment trusts and their beneficiaries	17740	1004
858	Dividends paid by real estate investment trust after close of taxable year	17740	1004
860A— 860G	Real estate mortgage investment conduits (REMICs)	17940	216; 1038
893	Employees of foreign country	17146	251
911	Citizens or residents of the U.S. living abroad	17024.5(b-08)	203
988	Treatment of certain foreign currency transactions	17078	115
991—999	Domestic International Sales Corporations (DISCs)	17024.5(b-02)	1026
1001	Determination of amount of and recognition of gain or loss	18031; 18041.5	361
1011	Adjusted basis for determining gain or loss	18031	361
1012	Basis of property—cost	18031	361
1013	Basis of property included in inventory	18031	362
1014	Basis of property acquired from a decedent	18031	459
1015	Basis of property acquired by gifts and transfers in trust	18031	362; 459
1016	Adjustments to basis	18031; 18036	361
1017	Discharge of indebtedness	18031	220; 251; 258
1019	Property on which lessee has made improvements	18031	362
1021	Sale of annuities	18031	361

Federal IRC § No.	Subject	Calif. Law No.	Handbook ¶ No.
1031	Exchange of property held for productive use or investment	18031; 18043	362
1033	Involuntary conversions	18031; 18037; 18586.5	334; 335; 361
1034	Rollover of gain on sale of principal residence	18031; 18044; 18586.4	361
1035	Certain exchanges of insurance policies	18031	362
1036	Stock for stock of same corporation	18031	362
1037	Certain exchanges of U.S. obligations	18031	361
1038	Certain reacquisitions of real property	18031	362
1040	Transfer of certain farm, etc., real property	18031; 18038	362
1041	Transfers of property between spouses or incident to divorce	18031	361
1042	Sales of stock to stock ownership plans or certain cooperatives	18031; 18042	309
1051	Property acquired during affiliation	18031	362
1052	Basis established by the Revenue Act of 1932 or 1934 or by the Internal Revenue Code of 1939	18031; 18039	362
1053	Property acquired before March 1, 1913	18031	362
1055	Redeemable ground rents	18031	362
1056	Basis limitation for player contracts transferred in connection with the sale of a franchise	18031	362
1058	Transfers of securities under certain agreements	18031	362
1059	Corporate shareholder's basis in stock reduced by nontaxed portion of extraordinary dividends	18031	362
1059A	Limitation on taxpayer's basis or inventory cost in property imported from related persons	18031	362
1060	Special allocation rules for certain asset acquisition	18031	362
1061	Nonrecognition of gain; certain vessels	18031; 18040	362
1071	Gain from sale or exchange to effectuate policies of F.C.C.	18031	362

Federal IRC § No.	Subject	Calif. Law No.	Handbook ¶ No.
1081	Nonrecognition of gain or loss on exchanges or distributions in obedience to orders of S.E.C.	18031	362; 1104
1082	Basis for determining gain or loss	18031	362
1091	Loss from wash sales of stock or securities	18031	362
1092	Straddles	18031	366
1211	Limitation on capital losses	18151	361
1212	Capital loss carrybacks and carryovers	18151; 18155	361
1221	Capital asset defined	18151	361
1222	Other items related to capital gains or losses	18151	361
1223	Holding period of property	18151	361
1231	Property used in the trade or business and involuntary conversions	18151	401
1233	Gains and losses from short sales	18151	361
1234	Options to buy or sell	18151	361
1234A	Certain terminations; gain or loss	18151	361
1235	Sale or exchange of patents	18151	361
1236	Dealers in securities	18151	361
1237	Real property subdivided for sale	18151	361
1239	Gain from sale of depreciable property between certain related taxpayers	18151	361; 1103
1241	Cancellation of lease or distributor's agreement	18151	361
1242	Losses on small business investment company stock	18151	361
1243	Loss of small business investment company	18151	361
1244	Losses on small business stock	18151	296
1245	Gain from dispositions of certain depreciable property	18151	401
1250	Gain from dispositions of certain depreciable realty	18151; 18171; 18171.5	401
1252	Gain from disposition of farm land	18151	401
1253	Transfers of franchises, trademarks, and trade names	18151	361; 401

Federal IRC § No.	Subject	Calif. Law No.	Handbook ¶ No.
1254	Gain from disposition of interest in oil, gas, geothermal, or other mineral property	18151	401
1255	Gain from disposition of § 126 property	18151	401
1256	Section 1256 contracts marked to market	18151	366
1257	Disposition of wetlands or highly erodible croplands	18151	401
1271	Treatment of amounts received on retirement or sale or exchange of debt instruments	18151	106; 353
1272	Current inclusion in income of original issue discount (added)	18151; 18178	106; 353
1273	Determination of amount of original issue discount	18151	106; 353
1274	Determination of issue price in the case of certain debt instruments issued for property	18151	106; 353
1274A	Certain transactions; stated principal amount does not exceed $2,800,000	18151	401
1275	Other definitions and special rules	18151; 18177; 18803.2	106; 353
1276	Disposition gain representing accrued market discount treated as ordinary income	18151	106; 353
1277	Deferral of interest deduction allocable to accrued market discount	18151	106; 353
1278	Definitions and special rules	18151	106; 353
1281	Current inclusion in income of discount on certain short-term obligations	18151	106; 353
1282	Deferral of interest deduction allocable to accrued discount	18151	106; 353
1283	Definitions and special rules	18151	106; 353
1286	Tax treatment of stripped bonds	18151	106; 353
1287	Denial of capital gain treatment for gains on certain obligations not in registered form	18151	106; 353
1288	Treatment of original issue discount on tax-exempt obligations	18151	106; 353

¶85

Federal IRC § No.	Subject	Calif. Law No.	Handbook ¶ No.
1385	Amounts includable in patron's gross income	17086	217; 334; 335
1445	Withholding of tax on dispositions of U.S. real property interests	18662	341
1446	Withholding tax on amounts paid by partnerships to foreign partners	18666	341
3401	Definitions	UIC	5021-5024
3402	Income tax collected at source	18551; 18661; 18663; 18667	5021—5024
3403	Liability for tax	18668	5021—5024
3505	Liability of third parties	18677	5021—5024
6011	General requirement of return	18552; 19524	165
6012	Persons required to make returns	18501; 18503—18510	110; 121; 165
6013	Joint returns	18521—18533; 18635	110; 121; 165
6031	Partnership returns	18535; 18633	110; 422
6032	Common trust funds	17677	110
6039	Information; options	18636	341
6039C	Returns with respect to foreign persons holding direct investments in U.S. real property interests	18645	346
6041	Information at source	18637	341
6041A	Payments of remuneration for services and direct sales	18638	346
6042	Returns regarding payments of dividends and corporate earnings and profits	18639	346
6044	Patronage dividends reporting	18640	344
6045	Returns of brokers	18643	346
6049	Returns on payment of interest	18639	341
6050A	Fishing boat operators	18644	338
6050H	Returns relating to mortgage interest received in trade or business from individuals	18645	346
6050I	Returns relating to cash received in trade or business	18645	346
6050J	Returns relating to foreclosures and abandonments of security	18645	346

¶85

Federal IRC § No.	Subject	Calif. Law No.	Handbook ¶ No.
6050K	Returns relating to exchanges of certain partnership interests	18645	346
6050L	Returns relating to certain dispositions of donated property	18645	346
6050N	Returns regarding payments of royalties	18645	346
6052	Group-life insurance reporting	18647	346
6065	Verification of returns	18621	165
6072	Time for filing returns	18566	165; 172; 422
6081	Extension of time for filing	18567	171; 172; 422
6091	Place for filing returns	18621	111; 166
6102	Computations on returns	18623	110
6103	Disclosure; confidentiality	19544—19547; 19549; 19551; 19553—19555; 19562	344
6109	Identifying numbers	18624	338
6111	Registration of tax shelters	18547	346
6112	Organizers and sellers of potentially abusive tax shelters must keep lists of investors	18648	346
6151	Time for paying tax on return	19001; 19004—19006	172
6201	Assessment authority	19054	208; 321
6211	Definition of deficiency	17013; 19043	335; 6602
6212	Notice of deficiency	19031—19036; 19049—19050	331; 6602
6315	Payment of estimated tax—on account	19007	171
6402	Authority to make refunds and credits	19301; 19314; 19354; 19362	336
6404	Abatements	19104; 19431	336
6501	Limitations on assessment and collection	19057—19058; 19063; 19065—19067; 19087	334; 335
6511	Limitations on credits and refunds	19306; 19308—19309; 19311—19313	173; 334; 335
6532	Limitation; refund suits	19384—19385; 19388—19389	336
6601	Interest on underpayment, etc.	19101—19103; 19105—19106; 19108; 19110; 19115	172; 335
6611	Interest on overpayments	19340—19341; 19349; 19351	172; 338

Federal IRC § No.	Subject	Calif. Law No.	Handbook ¶ No.
6621	Determination of rate of interest	19521(a)	172; 337
6651	Additions - failure to file return and pay tax	19131—19132	338
6654	Failure to pay estimated tax	18682.5; 18682.6; 18682.7	171; 338
6657	Bad checks	19134	338
6662	Imposition of accuracy-related penalty	19164	338
6663	Imposition of fraud penalty	19164	338
6664	Definitions and rules	19164	338
6665	Applicable rules	19164	338
6693	Failure to provide reports on IRAs; annuities	19184	338
6694	Understatement; preparer	19166	338
6695-6	Negotiation by preparer	19167—19169; 19712	338
6698	Failure to file partnership return	19172	338
6700	Abusive tax shelters	19174; 19177	338
6701	Understatement	19178	338; 344
6702	Frivolous return	19179	338
6703	Applicable rules	19180	338
6706	Original issue discount information requirements	19181	106; 338
6707	Failure to furnish information regarding tax shelters	19182	338
6708	Failure to maintain lists of investors in potentially abusive tax shelters	19173	338
6721	Failure to file information returns	19183	338
6861	Jeopardy assessments	19081; 19086; 19092	333
6863	Stay of collection jeopardy assessments	19083—19085	333; 6602
6867	Cash; gross income presumption	19093	333; 6602
6871	Claims in receivership proceedings	19088—19090	332
6872	Suspension of period of assessment	19089	332; 334; 335
6873	Unpaid claims	19091	332
6901	Transferred assets	19071—19072	339
7121	Closing agreements	19441	340
7202	Willful failure to collect or pay tax	19707—19709	338
7203	Willful failure to file return	19701; 19705	338
7206	Fraud and false statements	19706	338
7213	Unathorized disclosure of information	19542; 19552	1321

Federal IRC § No.	Subject	Calif. Law No.	Handbook ¶ No.
7215	Offenses with respect to collected taxes	19713	338
7408	Abusive tax shelters; injunction	19715	338
7508	Time for performing certain acts	18570—18571	165; 172
7512	Separate accounting for collected taxes	19009	341
7609	Third-party summons	19064	331; 6602
7623	Expenses of detection and punishment of frauds	19525	344
7701	Definitions	017003-17035; 17510	101; 104-105; 110; 112; 116; 118; 121; 291-294; 326; 331; 333-335; 351-352; 421; 451; 455; 457-458
7702	Life insurance contract	17020.6	253
7702A	Modified endowment contract defined	17020.6	253
7703	Determination of marital status	17021.5	122
7704	Publicly traded partnerships	17008.5	421
7872	Treatment of loans with below-market interest rates	18180	353

¶86 **California-Federal Code Table**

Listed in the table below are the California Personal Income Tax Law and Administrative Tax Law section numbers, the comparable Federal Internal Revenue Code (IRC) section number and the paragraph number in this handbook where they are explained or to which they relate. N means none.

Calif. Law No.	Federal IRC § No.	Handbook ¶ No.
17003	7701(a)(11)	104; 331
17004	7701(a)(14)	105
17005	N	105
17006	7701(a)(6)	451, 457—458
17007	7701(a)(1)	110
17008	7701(a)(2)	421
17008.5	7704	421
17009	7701(a)(3)	110
17010	7701(a)(23)	351
17011	7701(a)(24)	351
17012	7701(a)(25)	352
17013	6211	333—335
17014	N	112; 181
17015	N	112; 181
17016	N	112; 181
17017	7701(a)(9)	112; 181
17018	7701(a)(10)	112; 181
17019	N	112; 181
17020	7701(a)(26)	115; 291—294
17020.1	7701(a)(42)	361
17020.2	7701(a)(43)	361
17020.3	7701(a)(44)	361
17020.4	7701(a)(45)	361
17020.5	7701(g)	361
17020.6(a)	7702	203; 253
17020.6(b)	7702A	253
17020.7	7701(a)(46)	209—211
17020.8	7701(e)	222
17020.9	7701(a)(19)	216
17020.11	7701(h)	353
17020.12	7701(a)(20)	203
17020.13	7701(k)	326
17021	7701(a)(17)	110
17021.5	7703	122
17022	7701(a)(15)	110
17024.5	7806; 991-999; 541-547; 1246; 679; 853; 911; 213	103
17026	7851	102
17029.5	N	140
17034	N	105
17035	7701(a)(16)	5021—5025
17037	7806	105
17038	N	115; 122; 123

Calif. Law No.	Federal IRC § No.	Handbook ¶ No.
17039	26	140
17041	11(g)	115; 131; 322
17042	2(b)	121
17045	N	137
17046	2(a)	121
17048	3	131
17052.11	30	153
17052.12	41	148
17052.13	N	159; 160
17052.15	N	161
17052.17	N	145
17052.18	N	146
17052.25	N	143
17053	161	163
17053.1	N	163
17053.10	N	161
17053.11	N	160
17053.17	N	161
17053.45	N	164 A
17054	151(c)	123; 141
17054.1	151(d)	141
17054.5	N	155
17054.7	N	123
17055	N	322
17056	152	123
17057	28	154
17057.5	N	156
17058	42	156
17061	N	152
17062	55—59	135
17063	53	135
17071	61	115; 222; 251; 402
17072	62	115; 182; 291; 292; 293; 294; 295; 297; 298; 302
17073	63	115; 321
17073.5	63	115; 322
17074	64	115
17075	65	115
17076	67	216; 328; 952
17077	68	322
17078	988	115

Calif. Law No.	Federal IRC § No.	Handbook ¶ No.
17081	71-90	115; 145; 201(b); 203; 204; 208; 210; 215-218; 219; 222; 251; 291; 334; 335; 354; 402
17083	85	203
17085	72	215
17085.5	72	136
17086	1385	217; 334; 335
17087	86	209
17087.5	1361-1379	145; 266
17088	851-860G	216
17090	61	115; 250; 252
17091	865(b)	1184
17131	101-136	201; 205; 206; 209; 216; 251; 253-264; 269; 270; 272; 275
17131.5	61	263
17132	61	251
17133	61	251
17133.5	61	216
17135	61	282; 292
17136	61	281
17137	137	251
17138	61	286
17140.5	61	181
17141	61	272
17142	111	251; 260
17143	103	251
17144	108	258
17145	852	216
17146	893	251
17149	61	283
17151	127	269
17152	121	261
17153.5	61	284
17201	161-280H	156; 182; 213; 265; 291-308; 321-328; 363; 364; 370; 381; 382; 383; 387; 388; 390; 391; 401-404; 461

Calif. Law No.	Federal IRC § No.	Handbook ¶ No.
17202	162(2)	291; 292
17207	165	327
17208.1	165	327
17208.2	165	327
17208.3	165	327
17208.4	165	327
17220	164	324
17222	275	291
17224	163	325
17230	163	182; 291; 325
17231	163	325
17233	163	325
17249	167(c); (f)	371
17250	168—169	156; 291; 370; 381; 382; 387; 388; 391
17252.5	179	394
17256	179A	385A
17260(a)	193	370; 394; 395
17260(b)	263	354; 366; 394-5; 402
17265	179	394; 395
17266	179	395
17269	162	292
17270(a)	162(a)	149; 292
17270(b)	280C(a)	292
17270(c)	280C(c)	292
17271	274	292; 293
17273	162(l)	323
17274	161	292; 328
17275	161	291
17276	172	295
17276.1	172	295
17276.2	172	295
17276.3	172	295
17278	161	291—293
17279	197	371
17280	265	291; 325
17281	280E	292
17282	280E	292
17283	276	328
17286	162(c)	291
17287	269A	354
17299.8	161	292
17299.9	161	324; 325; 370
17301	63	182
17302	215	182; 301
17303	61	182
17310	172	182

Calif. Law No.	Federal IRC § No.	Handbook ¶ No.	Calif. Law No.	Federal IRC § No.	Handbook ¶ No.
17321	301—385	334; 335; 362; 1029; 1103; 1104; 1115-1120; 1123-1126; 1128; 1130; 1132			462-463; 472-474; 1103
			17732	642	455
			17733	642	455
			17734	641	455
17322	302	334; 335	17735	661	455
17501	401-424	136; 209; 210; 211; 212; 213; 292; 293; 300; 309	17736	642	461
			17737	682	218; 455
			17742	641	455
			17743	641	455
			17744	641	455
17504	402	210; 212	17745	641	455
17506	403	209; 210	17745.1	641	455
17507	408	210; 211; 299	17748	642	371
			17750	643	459
17508	408	299	17779	665-668	462-463
17509	413	209-210	17851	701-761	110; 361; 421-426; 428-434
17510	7701(j)	209; 285			
17551	441-483	183; 216; 292; 324; 325; 331; 351-354; 364; 407; 411; 428; 453-454; 482	17852	702	328; 423
			17853	703	426
			17854	707	426
			17855	751	430
			17856	751	430
			17857	751	430
			17858	704	426; 428
17551.5	441	351	17951	N.	182
17552	443	351	17952	N.	182
17553	454	353	17953	N.	182
17554	441	183	17954	N.	182
17555	61	331	17955	N.	182
17556	442	351	18001	N.	145
17560	453; 453A	364	18002	N.	145
17561	469	354	18003	N.	145
17563	463	364	18004	N.	145
17564	460	353	18005	N.	145
17565	441	351	18006	N.	145
17631	501(a)	951-963	18007	N.	145
17632	501(b)	951-963	18008	N.	145
17635	503(a)	951-963	18009	N.	145
17636	503(a)	951-963	18011	N.	145
17637	503(b)	951-963	18031	1001—1092	220; 251; 258; 334; 335; 361; 362; 366; 367; 459; 1104
17638	503(c)	951-963			
17639	503(e)	951-963			
17640	503(f)	951-963			
17651	511—512	954			
17671	584	110			
17677	6032	110	18035	1016	371
17681	611; 612; 613; 613A; 614—617; 631; 636; 638	402	18036	1016	361; 362
			18037	1033(g)	361
			18038	1040	362
17731	641—692	206; 218; 353; 455; 461;	18039	1052	362
			18040	1061	362
			18041.5	1001	361

Calif. Law No.	Federal IRC § No.	Handbook ¶ No.
18042	1042	362
18043	1031	362
18060	1060	371
18151	1201—1297	296; 353; 361; 365; 366; 401; 459; 1103
18155	1212	296; 361
18165—18166	1245	371
18171	1250	401
18171.5	1250	401(c)
18173	1253	371
18177	1275	353
18178	1272	353
18180	7872	353
18401	N	110; 451
18405	N	350
18412—18414	7807	110; 326
18501	6012(a)	326
18503	6012(b)	326
18504	6012	326
18505—18506	6012(b)	326
18507—18509	6012	326
18510	6012(c)	326
18521	6013	326
18522	6013(b)	326
18523—18524	6013(b)(1)	326
18525—18526	6013(b)(2)	326
18527—18528	6013(b)(3)	326
18529	6013(b)(4)	326
18530—18531	6013(b)(5)	326
18532	6013(d)	326
18533	6013(e)	326
18534	66	326
18535	6031	326
18542	N	326
18547	6111	326
18551	3402	172
18552	6011	
18566	6072	
18567	6081	
18570	7508	
18571	7508	
18602	N	331
18604	6081	
18605	N	
18606	6012(b); 6065	
18621	6065; 6091	339
18621.5	N	
18622	N	339
18623	6102	110
18624	6109	338
18625	6107	338

Calif. Law No.	Federal IRC § No.	Handbook ¶ No.
18631	N	346
18632	N	346
18633—18633.5	6031	110; 422
18635	6013(a)	346
18636	6039	341
18637	6041	341
18638	6041A	346
18639	6042; 6049	341; 346
18640	6044	346
18641	6045	333
18642	6045	333
18643	6045	333
18644	6050A	338
18645	6039C; 6050H—6050L; 6050N; 6050P	333
18646	6050M	333; 6602
18648	6112	334
18649	1275	332
18661	3402	5021-5024
18662	1445; 3402	341
18663	3402	5021-5024
18664	N	5021-5024
18665	N	5021-5024
18666	1446	341
18667	3402	5021-5024
18668	3403	5021-5024
18669	N	5021-5024
18670	N	5021-5024
18671	N	5021-5024
18672	N	5021-5024
18674	N	5021-5024
18675	6414	5021-5024
18676	N	5021-5024
18677	3505	5021-5024
18701—18796	N	328
18801—18804	N	326
18821—18824	N	326
18831—18834	N	326
19001	6151	172
19002	6513	172
19004	6151; 6655	172
19005	6151	172
19006	6151	172
19007	6315	171
19008	N	172
19009	7512	341
19010	6655	171
19021	N	1254
19022	N	1254
19023	6655(g)	1254
19024	6655(g)	1254
19025	6655(c); (d)	1254

Calif. Law No.	Federal IRC § No.	Handbook ¶ No.
19026	6655	1254
19027	6655	1255
19031	6212	331; 6602
19032	6212	331; 6602
19033	6212	331; 6602
19034—19036	6212	331; 6602
19041	6213	6602
19042	6213	6602
19043	6211	335; 6602
19044	6213	6602
19045	N	6602
19046—19048	6213	6602
19049	6212	331; 6602
19050	6212	331; 6602
19051	6213	336
19052	N	336
19053	N	173; 334; 335
19054	6201	336
19057	6501	336; 6602
19058	6501(e)	336; 6602
19059	N	6602
19060	N	6602
19061	1032; 1033(a)(2)(A)—(D)	6602
19062	1034	337
19063	6501(a)	334; 335
19064	7609	331; 6602
19065	6501(c)	331; 6602
19066	6501(b)	331; 6602
19067	6501(c)	331; 6602
19071—19074	6901	339
19081	6861	336
19082	6862	336
19083	6863	336
19084	6863	336
19085	6863	336
19086	6861	6602
19087	6501(c)	6602
19088	6871	6602
19089	6036; 6872	6602
19090	6871	331
19091	6873	332
19092	6861	333
19093	6867	333; 6602
19101	6601(a)	172; 335
19102	6601(b)	172; 335
19103	6601(b)	172; 335
19104	6404	336
19105	6601	172; 335
19106	6601(e)	172; 335
19107	6401	333; 6602
19108	6601	172; 335
19110	6601	172; 335
19111	6601(e)	172; 335
19112	6601	172; 335

Calif. Law No.	Federal IRC § No.	Handbook ¶ No.
19113	6601(f)	172; 335
19114	6601(g)	172; 335
19115	6601(h)	172; 335
19131	6651	336
19132	6651	340
19132.5	6651	338
19134	6657	338
19135	N	338
19136	6654	171; 338
19141	N	338
19141.5	6038A; 6038B 6038C	338; 346
19142	6655(a)	331; 338
19144	6655(b)	331; 338
19145	6655	331; 338
19147	6655(d)	331; 338
19148	6655	331; 338
19149	6655	331; 338
19150	6655	331; 338
19151	6655	331; 338
19161	6658	338
19164	6662; 6663; 6664; 6665	338
19166	6694	338
19167	6695(a); 6695(c); 6695(d)	338
19168	6696	338
19169	6695(f)	338
19172	6698	338
19173	6708	338
19174	6700	338
19175	N	338
19176	6682	338
19177	6700	338
19178	6701	338; 344
19179	6702	338
19180	6703	338
19181	6706	106; 338
19182	6707	338
19183	6721; 6722; 6723; 6724	338
19184	6693	338
19201	N	348
19202	N	348
19203	N	348
19204	N	348
19205	N	348
19206—19209	6325	348
19221	6321	348
19222	6311	348
19223	N	348
19224	N	348
19231	6331	348
19232	N	348

¶86

Calif. Law No.	Federal IRC § No.	Handbook ¶ No.
19233	N	348
19234	N	348
19235	N	348
19251—53	N	104; 345
19254	N	6601
19256	7504	6601
19262	6331	342
19263	N	342
19271	N	347
19272	N	344
19273	N	344
19280—19283	N	349
19301	6402	336
19302	N	336
19306	6511(a)	336
19307	N	335
19308	6511(c)	335
19309	6511(c)	335
19311	6511	335
19312	6511(d)	338
19313	6511(g)	335
19314	6402	336
19321	N	336
19322	N	336
19323	N	336
19324	N	336
19325	N	336
19331	N	336
19332—19334	6213	336
19335	N	336
19340	6611(b)	337
19341	6611(e)	337
19342	N	337
19343	N	336; 337
19344	N	336; 337
19345—19348	N	336; 337
19349	6611	337
19350	N	337
19351	6611(b)	335
19354	6402	336
19355	N	336
19361	6414	336
19362	6402	336
19363	6402	336
19364	6402	336
19371	6502	335; 348
19372—19376	N	348
19377	6301	348
19378	6301	348
19381	7421	336
19382	7422	336
19383	7422	336
19384	6532	336
19385	6532	336
19387	7422	336

Calif. Law No.	Federal IRC § No.	Handbook ¶ No.
19388	6532	336
19389	6532	336
19390	N	336
19391	6612	337
19392	N	336
19411	6602; 7405	337
19412	N	337
19413	N	337
19431	6404	336
19441	7121	340
19442	N	340
19501	7621(a)	6601
19502	7621(b)	6601
19503	7805	6601
19504	7602	6601
19505	7803	6601
19506—19509	N	6601
19511	7622	6601
19512	6903	6601
19513—19515	N	457
19516	6905	451
19517	N	451; 455
19518	N	455
19521(a)	6621	172; 337
19521(b)	6622	172; 337
19522—19523	N	6601
19524	6011	346
19525	7623	344
19526—19531	N	344
19542	7213	344
19543—19544	6103(b)	344
19545	6103(h)	344
19546	6103(f)	344
19547	6103(h)	344
19548	N	344
19549	6103(b)	344
19551	6103(d)	344
19552	7213	344
19553—19555	6103	344
19556—19561	N	344
19562	6103	344
19563	6108	344
19564	6108	344
19565	6104	344
19581—19583	N	1269
19701	7203	338
19701.5—19704	N	338
19705	7203	338
19706	7206	338
19707—19709	7202	338
19710	N	338
19711	7205	338
19712	6695	338
19713	7215	338
19714	6673	338

Calif. Law No.	Federal IRC § No.	Handbook ¶ No.
19715	7408	338
19717—19719....	N....................	338
19801—19802....	N....................	338

Calif. Law No.	Federal IRC § No.	Handbook ¶ No.
21001—21022....	7811	347; 1324
U.I.C.d §		
13021	6302	5009

TAX RATES FOR PERSONAL INCOME TAX

¶87   1994 Tax Rate Schedules

The tax rate schedules for (1) single taxpayers, married persons filing separate returns, and fiduciary tax returns; (2) joint taxpayers and surviving spouses with dependents; and (3) unmarried heads of household are shown below. These schedules must be used by taxpayers (1) to whom §1750(b) relating to the tax on lump-sum distributions applies for the taxable year; (2) who make short period returns under IRC §443(a)(1); and (3) who file returns for estates or trusts.

The tax tables must be used by all other taxpayers to compute their taxes. The tax rate schedules have been indexed for inflation.

TAX SCHEDULES

SCHEDULE 1. (A) Single Taxpayers
(B) Married Filing Separate Returns
(C) Fiduciary Tax Returns

If the Taxable Income Is: Over	But not Over:	Computed Tax Is:			Of Amount Over:
$ 0.........	$ 4,722	$ 0.00	Plus	1.0%........................	$ 0
$ 4,722.........	$ 11,192............	$ 47.22	Plus	2.0%........................	$ 4,722
$ 11,192.........	$ 17,662............	$ 176.62	Plus	4.0%........................	$ 11,192
$ 17,662.........	$ 24,519............	$ 435.42	Plus	6.0%........................	$ 17,662
$ 24,519.........	$ 30,987............	$ 846.84	Plus	8.0%........................	$ 24,519
$ 30,987.........	$107,464............	$ 1,364.28	Plus	9.3%........................	$ 30,987
$107,464.........	$214,929............	$ 8,476.64	Plus	10.0%........................	$107,464
$214,929.........	AND OVER.......	$ 19,223.14	Plus	11.0%........................	$214,929

¶87

SCHEDULE 2. (A) Joint Taxpayers
(B) Surviving Spouses With Dependents

If The Taxable Income Is: Over	But Not Over:	Computed Tax Is:		Of Amount Over:
$ 0.........	$ 9,444	$ 0.00	Plus 1.0%........................	$ 0
$ 9,444.........	$ 22,384............	$ 94.44	Plus 2.0%........................	$ 9,444
$ 22,384.........	$ 35,324............	$ 353.24	Plus 4.0%........................	$ 22,384
$ 35,324.........	$ 49,038............	$ 870.84	Plus 6.0%........................	$ 35,324
$ 49,038.........	$ 61,974............	$ 1,693.68	Plus 8.0%........................	$ 49,038
$ 61,974.........	$214,928............	$ 2,728.56	Plus 9.3%........................	$ 61,974
$214,928.........	$429,858............	$16,953.28	Plus 10.0%........................	$214,928
$429,858.........	AND OVER.......	$38,446.28	Plus 11.0%........................	$429,858

SCHEDULE 3. (A) Unmarried Head of Household

If Taxable Income Is: Over	But Not Over:	Computed Tax Is:		Of Amount Over:
$ 0.........	$ 9,445	$ 0.00	Plus 1.0%........................	$ 0
$ 9,445.........	$ 22,383............	$ 94.45	Plus 2.0%........................	$ 9,445
$ 22,383.........	$ 28,852............	$ 353.21	Plus 4.0%........................	$ 22,383
$ 28,852.........	$ 35,709............	$ 611.97	Plus 6.0%........................	$ 28,852
$ 35,709.........	$ 42,179............	$ 1,023.39	Plus 8.0%........................	$ 35,709
$ 42,179.........	$146,274............	$ 1,540.99	Plus 9.3%........................	$ 42,179
$146,274.........	$292,550............	$11,221.83	Plus 10.0%........................	$146,274
$292,550.........	AND OVER.......	$25,849.43	Plus 11.0%........................	$292,550

¶87

CHAPTER **1**

INDIVIDUALS—RETURNS, RATES, PERSONAL EXEMPTIONS, CREDITS

INTRODUCTION

¶ 101   **Scope of Chapter**

This chapter explains the history and gives an overview of the tax on personal income, including the state's adoption of the federal IRC starting in 1983.

¶ 102   **History of Tax**

The Personal Income Tax Act was enacted in 1935. The Act is codified in Sections 17001–19452 of the California Revenue and Taxation Code.

¶ 103   **The California Tax System**

Residents of California are taxed on their entire taxable income wherever derived. Nonresidents are taxed only on income derived from California sources. Net income taxes paid to other states may be allowed as credits against California tax. Local income taxes are not imposed by counties, cities or local governments in California.[1]

¶ 104   **Administration of Tax**

The Personal Income Tax Law is administered by the California Franchise Tax Board. This Board includes the State Controller, the Director of the Department of Finance and the Chairman of the State Board of Equalization. Historically, the Board has been concerned only with major overall policy decisions with the actual operations of the Income and Franchise Tax Departments delegated to the Executive Officer.[2]

¶ 105   **Imposition of Tax**

The tax is imposed on every resident taxpayer's income from all sources wherever derived, and on every nonresident's income derived from sources in California. "Taxpayer" is any individual, fiduciary, estate or trust subject to the tax. "Individual" means a natural person.[3] Law changes during the taxable year with respect to the imposition and computation of taxes, that affect additions to tax, penalties, or the allowance of credits against the tax apply to taxable years starting on or after January 1 of the year the act takes effect. Other provisions apply on and after the date the act becomes law.[4]

¶ 106   **Federal Conformity**

WARNING   FEDERAL CONFORMITY REMAINS AS OF JANUARY 1, 1993

Generally California has confirmed significant parts of its Personal Income Tax Law (commencing with Rev & TC § 17001) with the Internal Revenue Code by adopting, by reference, selected IRC provisions as of January 1 of each year. This simplified the filing of California returns for

---

(1) § 17041.5.
(2) § 19251–19260; Govt C § 15700–15702.

(3) § 17001–17009; 17041.
(4) § 17034.

the vast majority of individuals, partnerships, and fiduciaries, because California law generally mirrored the federal code so that differences were minimized. The California individual income tax return reflected this conformity by having the taxpayer first report items as shown on the federal return, and then the taxpayer only had to make limited adjustments to arrive at California taxable income.

As in the past, the Legislature passed legislation for 1994 to conform to selected provisions of the IRC as of 1–1–94, only to have that legislation (AB 2370) vetoed by the Governor. Accordingly when California law makes reference to specific provisions of the Internal Revenue Code, it is to those provisions as reflected in the IRC at 1–1–93, unless specific provisions of the Internal Revenue Code were adopted through the passage of other tax legislation. Provisions conforming at 1–1–94 are limited in number.

One of the reasons for not conforming California law at 1–1–94 was that California could not determine if the provisions of the IRC added or modified by the passage of the *Revenue Reconciliation Act of 1993,* would result in increased or decreased California taxes. Specifically the Governor in his veto message said "It would be irresponsible to enact a selected group of conformity items for a single year without a debate on the entirety of the conformity issues raised by the federal tax changes."

Care should therefore be exercised in treating California law as conforming to federal law. Some provisions will conform at 1–1–94 because individual tax bills may have resulted in limited conformity. In general however, those provisions enacted for federal purposes through the *Revenue Reconciliation Act of 1993,* and other federal tax legislation for 1993 as well, have not been adopted for California purposes.

The California Legislature first amended the Personal Income Tax Law in 1983 (c. 488 and c. 498) to adopt by reference the provisions of the federal Internal Revenue Code (IRC) on gross income, adjusted gross income and taxable income with specified modifications (Rev & TC § 17024.5). Conformity is not automatic; in addition, the IRC is constantly changing. It is therefore necessary to specify a date each year which freezes state law to the IRC already then in effect and the Legislature generally sets the specified date as of the beginning of the calendar year for which the conformity legislation is intended. If the Legislature chooses to conform to any retroactive changes in federal law, the state language must specifically provide for retroactive application. The specified dates for conformity for each year starting in 1983 are contained in Rev & TC § 17024.5(a)(1). For 1993 the conformed sections relate to the IRC as enacted on 1–1–93.[5]

---

(5) § 17024.5.

Approximately one-half of the Personal Income Tax Law was repealed in 1983 and replaced with references to federal law. The remaining portion is primarily provisions dealing with the administration of the tax.

The incorporation process requires specific language in state law. In some instances an entire subchapter is incorporated by reference. In other cases conformity is limited to a particular section or subsection.

IRC operative and inoperative dates—application. Unless otherwise specifically provided by California law, any IRC provision which is operative on or after the specified date for that taxable year also is operative on the same date for purposes of the Personal Income Tax Law. The same applies to an IRC provision that becomes inoperative on or after the specified date for that taxable year. Unless otherwise specifically provided, uncodified provisions in federal laws enacted on or after 1–1–87, that relate to provisions of the IRC that are incorporated into the Personal Income Tax Law by a change in the specified date of the conformity statute in Rev & TC § 17024.5(a)(1), apply to the same taxable years as specified in that paragraph.[6]

Exceptions to IRC adoption. Unless California law otherwise specifically provides, provisions of the federal Internal Revenue Code relating to the following are not applicable under the California Personal Income Tax Law:

(1) Except as provided in Chapter 4.5 (commencing with Rev & TC § 23800) of the Bank and Corporation Tax Law, relating to the tax treatment of S corporations and their shareholders, an electing small business corporation, as defined in IRC § 1361(b).

(2) Domestic International Sales Corporations (DISCs) as defined in IRC § 992(a).

(3) Personal holding company, as defined in IRC § 542.

(4) Foreign personal holding company, as defined in IRC § 552.

(5) Foreign investment company, as defined in IRC § 1246(b).

(6) Foreign trust, as defined in IRC § 679.

(7) Foreign income taxes and foreign tax credits.

(8) IRC § 911 relating to U.S. citizens living abroad.

(9) Foreign corporation, except that IRC § 367 applies.

(10) The federal tax credits and carryovers of federal tax credits, except as provided in IRC § 162(l)(3) (coordination with medical deductions) and IRC § 213(f) (coordination with the health insurance credit of IRC § 32).

(11) Nonresident aliens.

(12) Deduction for personal exemptions, as provided in IRC § 151.

(13) Tax on generation-skipping transfers imposed by IRC § 2601.

(14) Tax, relating to estates, imposed by IRC § 2001 or 2101.[7]

California and federal regulations. When applying the IRC, regulations issued by "the secretary" in effect as of the applicable effective date of the Internal Revenue Code sections referred to in Rev & TC § 17024.5(a)

---

(6) § 17024.5.   (7) § 17024.5(b).

shall be applicable to the extent they do not conflict with the Personal Income Tax Law or with Franchise Tax Board regulations.[8]

Elections. Whenever the Personal Income Tax Law allows taxpayer to make an election, the following rules apply:

(1) A proper election filed in accordance with IRC or regulations issued by "the secretary" shall be deemed a proper election, unless Personal Income Tax Law or FTB regulations otherwise provide.

(2) Copy of election must be furnished to Franchise Tax Board on request.

(3) To obtain treatment other than that elected for federal purposes, a separate election shall be filed with the Franchise Tax Board.[9]

Application or consent. Whenever the Personal Income Tax Law allows or requires a taxpayer to file an application or seek consent, the rules set forth with respect to elections shall apply to such application or consent.[10]

Statute of limitations. When applying the IRC in determining the statute of limitations under the Personal Income Tax Law, any reference to a period of three years must be modified to read four years for purposes of the Personal Income Tax Law.[11]

"Secretary"—"Franchise Tax Board." Unless the Personal Income Tax Law otherwise provides, when applying the IRC, any reference to the "secretary" means "Franchise Tax Board."[12]

Adjusted gross income. Unless the Personal Income Tax Law provides, when applying any IRC section, any reference to "adjusted gross income" (AGI) means the amount computed as adjusted gross income in accordance with Rev & TC § 17072, on the California income tax return for the same taxable year. For purposes of computing limitations based on a percentage of adjusted gross income, "adjusted gross income" means the amount required to be shown as adjusted gross income on the federal tax return of the same taxable year.[13]

Application of IRC. Unless otherwise specifically provided, when applying the Internal Revenue Code for purposes of the California Personal Income Tax Law, any reference to a specific provision of the Internal Revenue Code includes modifications of that provision by the California Personal Income Tax Law.[14]

WHO MUST FILE RETURNS

¶ 110 Who Must File Returns

Residents of California are required to file a return if they meet one of the following requirements:

---

(8) § 17024.5(c).
(9) § 17024.5(d).
(10) § 17024.5(e).
(11) § 17024.5(f).

(12) § 17024.5(g).
(13) § 17024.5(h).
(14) § 17024.5(i).

(1) Single, married filing a separate return, head of household, qualified widow or widower—adjusted gross income in excess of $6,000 or gross income of $8,000 (regardless of the amount of adjusted gross income).

(2) Married filing joint return—combined adjusted gross income of $12,000 or gross income of $16,000.[15]

If a married couple has a combined adjusted gross income of $12,000, or gross income of $16,000, and they choose not to file a joint return, then each must file a return (married filing separately).[16]

If an individual can be claimed as a dependent of another as set forth in IRC § 63(c)(5), than that individual must file a California return reporting their income if that income is in excess of the standard deduction amount allowed under federal law.[16a]

Estates and trusts.   Estates with net income over $1,000, trusts with net income over $100 or estates and trusts with gross income over $8,000 regardless of the amount of net income must file a return.[17]

Common trust funds.   Common trust funds maintained by banks, etc., must file information returns irrespective of the amount of gross or taxable income of the trust fund taxable to the beneficiaries.[18]

Partnerships.   Every partnership doing business in California or in receipt of income from California sources, regardless of the amount, is required to file a tax return. Even if a partnership is not required to file a California partnership return within the requirements of the preceding sentence, if it has one or more California resident partners and an election is required to be made by the partnership affecting the computation of income (e.g., installment method, accounting method, etc.), a return must be filed. The resident partner of a nonresident partnership may be required to furnish a copy of the partnership return to determine whether or not there is any California tax liability on his share of the partnership income.[19] Group returns can be required of partnerships and S corps. on behalf of electing nonresident partners and shareholders.[20]

Nonresident and part-year resident.   Any individual who is a resident for any portion of the year and any nonresident deriving income from California sources.[21]

Military personnel.   A California resident is not subject to tax on military pay when serving at an out-of-state post of duty under permanent orders. A return may be required if the spouse remains a resident of California or either has income from within California.[22]

Refund claimant.   Any person who is not required to file an income tax return should file a return to get a refund if California income tax was

---

(15) § 18401(a)–(c).
(16) § 18401.
(16a) § 18501, as amended by Stats. 1994, c. 948, § 1.
(17) § 18405.

(18) § 17677.
(19) § 18633.
(20) § 18408.
(21) § 18405.5
(22) LR 300, 4–23–65.

withheld, or to get a Renter's Credit or excess state disability insurance refund.

¶ 111   Return Forms

The basic form for use by resident individuals is Form 540. Residents can choose to use Short Form 540A. Nonresidents and part-year residents use Form 540NR; they cannot use Short Form 540A.[23] Qualifying widows and widowers must use Form 540.

The required returns must be in the form established by the Franchise Tax Board including, but not limited to, paper, magnetic media under Rev & TC § 19272, or by electronic imaging technology under Rev & TC § 17431.2. Failure to receive or secure a form does not relieve a taxpayer from making any return, declaration or statement, or other document. Any return, declaration, statement or other document must contain or be verified by a written declaration that it is made under penalties of perjury.[24]

Electronic filing. Returns which are filed electronically are not considered complete until the electronic filing declaration is signed by the taxpayer, or the authorized signer in the case of an estate, trust, or partnership. California accepted only a limited number of returns electronically for the 1993 tax year to test its electronic filing procedures. Testing will continue for the 1994 tax year.[25]

RESIDENT INDIVIDUALS

¶ 112   Who Is a Resident

Taxation of residents.   Residents of California are taxed on their entire income wherever derived. Nonresidents are taxed only on income derived from sources in California and are generally not taxed on income from intangible assets like interest and dividends.

Definition of "resident."   The term "resident" includes:

(1) Every individual who is in this state for other than a temporary or transitory purpose; and
(2) Every individual who has his permanent home (domicile) in California but who is outside this state for a temporary or transitory purpose.

Nonresidents.   Nonresidents are individuals who are not residents.[26]

"Resident" and "domicile."   "Resident" and "domicile" are two different concepts (see "domicile" below). An individual may be a "resident" although not domiciled in California. This happens when the individual is present in the state for an indefinite period (i.e., for other than a temporary or transitory purpose). Conversely, an individual domiciled in California may be

---

(23) Form 540A, Instructions.
(24) § 18431; 18431.2.

(25) § 17932.
(26) § 17014.

treated as a nonresident when he is out of the state for other than a temporary or transitory purpose.

An individual who becomes a resident by being physically present in California for other than a temporary or transitory purpose remains a resident even though temporarily absent from the state.

Employment-related absence.   For tax years beginning on or after January 1, 1994, an individual who is domiciled in California who is absent from the state for an uninterrupted period of at least 546 consecutive days under an employment-related contract shall be considered outside the state for other than a temporary or transitory purpose. If the spouse accompanies the taxpayer during the 18 month period, then the spouse too will be considered outside the state for other than a temporary of transitory purpose. The taxpayer's return to California for up to 45 days during the tax year will be disregarded in determining the 546 consecutive days period. This exception to the general rule will not apply if: (1) the individual has income from stocks, bonds, notes, or other intangible personal property in excess of $200,000 in any taxable year in which the employment-related contract is in effect, or (2) if the principal purpose of the individual's absence is to avoid tax.[27]

Factors used administratively.   A review of court cases and rulings as well as the information requested by the Franchise Tax Board auditors indicates that the following factors are considered important in determining whether or not an individual is a California resident after he leaves California to accept employment outside the state on a temporary or indefinite basis:

(1) Retention of home in California;
(2) Whether or not wife and children remained in California or accompanied the taxpayer out of the state;
(3) Whether or not such children were placed in school at the new location;
(4) Location of insurance agent;
(5) Location of stock broker;
(6) Location of registration for voting;
(7) Location of car registration;
(8) Location of bank accounts;
(9) Location of financial institutions issuing credit cards and charge accounts;
(10) Location of attorneys and accountants; doctors and dentists;
(11) Membership in church or temple; business, social and country clubs.

---

(27) § 17014, as amended by Stats. 1994, c. 1243,
§ 4.

ILLUSTRATIVE COURT DECISIONS

In the *Appeal of Nathan H. & Julia M. Juran, SBE 1–8–58,* a motion picture director who had been a California resident for many years went to Europe under an employment contract for 16 weeks. After that he accepted an offer for three additional films which engaged him in Europe for another lengthy period. Although the taxpayer returned only once to California during the period, he maintained his California home throughout the period, continued to receive mail at the home in California and kept financial accounts with California institutions throughout the period. The Board of Equalization decided that he was out of California for a temporary or transitory purpose and was, therefore, taxable on the foreign income earned in 1962 through 1964 because he maintained a California home and kept his financial accounts in California even though he was physically absent from the State for most of the period.

In a later Board of Equalization decision, the *Appeal of Brent Berry, SBE 3–22–71,* a professional football player who resided in California for eight months of the year, spending the balance of time during the football season in Canada while maintaining a bank account, driver's license and car in California, did not establish a Canadian domicile and was liable for California income tax as a resident under Rev & TC § 17014. He rented an apartment in Canada on a month-to-month basis, leased a car and opened a bank account in Canada which he closed when he returned to California.

In the *Appeal of John B. and Beverly Simpson, SBE 8–19–75,* a taxpayer was absent from California for over a year while working overseas on a joint assignment with a foreign government, the U.S. government and Philco Ford. The Board decided that he was a California resident throughout his absence since his family, personal belongings and bank accounts remained there. He claimed he intended to leave California permanently, and, therefore, he was absent from the State for other than a temporary or transitory purpose.

In another instance, in the *Appeal of John Haring, SBE 8–19–75,* a merchant seaman spent approximately 9–10 months at sea each year with one-third to one-half of the remainder of the time in California. The Board decided that because he had retained bank accounts in California and used professional services there, had the car registered there and obtained a California driver's license as he was employed primarily by California employers, he was considered to be a resident.

In the *Appeal of Pierre E. and Nicole Salinger, SBE 6–30–80,* the taxpayer argued that his employment in Europe was of indefinite duration and, therefore, was for other than a temporary or transitory purpose out of California. The taxpayers maintained California bank accounts, charge accounts, business interests, investments, rental property, had California driver's licenses, car registration and were registered to vote in California for the years in question. The taxpayers stated that they intended to establish a new domicile outside of California. However, they returned to California after only one year's employment abroad and had significant personal, financial and business contacts in the State. The Board ruled that taxpayers did not give up California residence status.

Conversely, in the *Appeal of Richards L. and Kathleen Hardman, SBE 8–19–75,* a professional writer who accepted employment in England on a project which was supposed to take 3–4 years but which was cancelled in less than a year, was not considered a resident even though he had been a resident of California for a number of years prior to accepting the foreign employment. The taxpayer's actions, such as the purchase of a one-way ticket, enrollment of his daughter in English schools, the retention of a lawyer and a literary agent in England, were considered to be consistent with his intention to remain in England indefinitely.

Persons moving in-state. If an individual from another location is in California for business purposes which will require a long or indefinite period to accomplish or is employed in a position that may last permanently or indefinitely in California or has retired from business and moved to California with no definite intention of leaving shortly thereafter, he or she is in the state for other than a temporary or transitory purpose and, accordingly, is a resident taxable upon the entire net income even though he or she may retain his or her permanent home in some other state or country. In such cases, the criteria used by the Franchise Tax Board to determine the State in which the taxpayer has the closest ties, are the following:

> (1) The time spent in each state for each year,
> (2) The taxpayer's principal residence and whether or not it is owned or leased. If he has one in each state, respective sizes and investment in each are considered,
> (3) Location of taxpayer's business connections,
> (4) Location of taxpayer's social and family ties,
> (5) Other factors such as vehicle or voter's registration and driver's licenses.

Presumption of residence—nine-month rule. If an individual spends, in the aggregate, more than nine months of any taxable year in California, it will be presumed that he is a resident of the state. The presumption is not conclusive and may be overcome by satisfactory evidence that the individual is in the state for temporary or transitory purposes. It does not follow, however, that a person is not a resident simply because nine months of a particular taxable year are not spent in the state. On the contrary, a person may be a resident even though not in the state during any portion of the year.[28]

One of the oldest landmark cases was the 1951 Board of Equalization *Appeal of Edgar M. Wooley, SBE 7–15–51,* involving a famous stage and movie actor. Although he was in California for more than nine months he

---

(28) § 17016.

overcame the presumption that he was a California resident. He retained a permanent home in New York while he lived in a hotel in California.

The decision in *Appeal of Ada Wrigley, SBE 11–17–55 & 7–17–57,* is significant because the taxpayer, during the last several years involved in the Appeal, was in a coma and unable to be moved from California. Coming to California for many years during the winter months, she maintained two large homes here. She had extensive business and property holdings in Chicago. Her banking interests and voting registration were there. The Board of Equalization decided that she was in California for other than a temporary or transitory purpose and determined that she was a resident. The importance of the decision was that she had a large income from dividends and interest which were taxable by the state of residence.

The Board of Equalization decision in the *Appeal of Ruby Loyal, SBE 8–1–66,* was similar to the Wrigley Case in that the taxpayer went to California for a short visit to her daughter. While there, she became ill and remained there from 1943 until her death in 1951. She was determined to be a "resident" of California even though she held a life estate in the family home in Massachusetts, kept her securities, jewelry and checking accounts in Massachusetts and voted and filed Federal income tax returns there. The principal determining factor in the case was her uninterrupted presence in California for eight years.

Presumption of nonresidence—six-month rule.   An individual whose presence in California does not exceed a total of six months within the taxable year and who maintains a permanent home outside of the state will be considered as being in California for temporary or transitory purposes provided he or she does not engage in any activity or conduct within this state other than that of a seasonal visitor, tourist or guest. Incidentally, an individual may be considered to be a seasonal visitor, tourist or guest even though he or she owns and maintains a home in California or has a bank account in this state for purposes of paying personal expenses, or joins local social clubs.

The Court of Appeals in the First District, reversing the Superior Court in the case of *Whittell v. Franchise Tax Board (1964) 231 Cal App 2d 278,* determined a California residency in a situation where a taxpayer lived in an elaborate home in California for eight or nine months out of the year, spending only the summer months in his home in Nevada, had substantial business and family connections in California, maintained bank accounts here and professional connections as well. The taxpayer insisted that his residence was in Nevada rather than California. The Court said that voluntary or physical presence in the state is a factor of greater significance than the mental intent or outward formalities of ties to another state.

Meaning of domicile.   Domicile has been defined as a place where an individual has his true, fixed, permanent home and principal establishment and to which place he has, whenever he is absent, the intention of returning.

An individual can, at any one time, have but one domicile which is retained until another is acquired elsewhere. For example, an individual domiciled in Illinois, who comes to California for a rest, vacation or business or for some other purpose, but intends to either return to Illinois or to go elsewhere as soon as his or her stay in California is complete, retains his or her domicile in Illinois and does not acquire a domicile in California; even though he or she maintains a home here, has his or her family with him or her and remains here a considerable period of time. Likewise, an individual who is domiciled in California and who leaves the State, retains California domicile as long as he or she has a definite intention of returning regardless of the length of time or the reasons he or she is absent from the state.

Domicile of wife and minors. Generally, a married woman has the same domicile as her husband. The domicile of a minor ordinarily is that of the minor's father, or of the mother if the father is deceased. Accordingly, if a man is domiciled in California, his wife and minor children generally are likewise domiciled there and, depending on the facts of the case, may be taxable on their entire net income as residents of the State.

Domicile of certain public officials. Another significant California resident's problem arose during the presidential term of Richard M. Nixon. As a result of a public disclosure that he had filed income tax returns as a nonresident of California (which were accepted by the Franchise Tax Board after a review of the facts), Rev & TC § 17014 was amended by the legislature. The law now provides that certain persons and their wives, who are domiciled in California but are outside the state are to be considered residents whether or not they are outside the state, for temporary or transitory purposes. These enumerated individuals are: the President of the United States, the Vice-President of the United States, Congressmen, staff employees of a California Congressman and certain persons holding presidential pleasure appointments (not including military officers and career diplomat appointees).

Residence of military personnel. A resident of California in the military service who leaves California under permanent military orders will be considered to be a nonresident for tax purposes. If his wife remains in California, she will be taxable on one half of the military pay for the duration of her stay in California. The Soldiers' and Sailors' Civil Relief Act provides that nonresident military persons serving in California bases cannot be taxed unless they transfer their domicile to this state. This exclusion applies to the spouse of the military person even though she may live in a community property state.

COMPUTATION OF TAX

¶ 115   What's Involved in the Computation

In accumulating the information for the preparation of the individual income tax return, a taxpayer or return preparer must know (1) gross income, (2) deductions in arriving at adjusted gross income, (3) adjusted gross income, (4) itemized deductions, (5) standard deduction and (6) taxable income.[29]

Gross income. Gross income includes all income from whatever source derived including (but not limited to) compensation, business income, gains from property, dividends, rents, interest, royalties and similar items. The sum total of all of these items is considered to be the gross income to be reflected on the return. Gross income for California purposes is defined by IRC § 61.[30]

Adjusted gross income. For California purposes adjusted gross income is defined by IRC § 62.[31] In arriving at adjusted gross income, the taxpayer deducts from gross income:

(1) Expenses directly incurred in carrying on a trade or business (not as an employee).
(2) Reimbursed expenses in connection with one's employment.
(3) Expenses paid or incurred by qualified performing artist in connection with performance by the artist of services in the performing arts as an employee.
(4) Deduction for losses from sales or exchange of property.
(5) Deductions for property held for the production of rents and royalties.
(6) Deductions for contributions to self-employment retirement plans.
(7) Deductions for contributions to individual retirement plans.
(8) Deductions for penalties forfeited because of premature withdrawal from savings accounts.
(9) Deductions for alimony.
(10) Reforestation expenditures (IRC § 62(14)).
(11) Deduction of life tenant, income beneficiary of property, or heir, legatee, or devisee of estate for depreciation allowed by IRC § 67, and depletion deduction allowed by IRC § 611.
(12) Deduction for repayment to supplemental unemployment trust of supplemental unemployment compensation benefits received, if required because of receipt of trade readjustment allowances.
(13) Jury duty pay remitted to employer.[32]

The allowable amount of the deductions considered in arriving at adjusted gross income may be limited under various code sections.

Arrangements not treated as reimbursement arrangements. California adopts IRC § 62(c). Under this federal rule, an arrangement will in no event be treated as a reimbursement arrangement, or other expense allowance arrangement, if (1) such arrangement does not require the employee to substantiate the expenses covered by the arrangement to the person providing the reimbursement, or (2) the arrangement provides the employee the right to retain any amount in excess of the substantiated expenses covered. This rule does not apply to any expense to the extent substantiation is not required under IRC § 274(d) for the expense by reason of federal regs. under that IRC section.

---

(29) § 17071–17073.
(30) § 17071.

(31) § 17072.
(32) IRC § 62(a)(1)–(13); § 17072.5.

IMPORTANT   *Moving expenses.* Unlike federal law, California does not recognize moving expense as a deduction in arriving at adjusted gross income.

Taxable income. California tax is figured on "taxable income." Taxable income is defined by IRC § 63. In arriving at taxable income, the taxpayer may deduct itemized deductions from adjusted gross income including medical expenses, property taxes, interest on credit cards, purchases of personal property and mortgage interest, charitable contributions and miscellaneous expenses including tax preparation fees, union dues and similar items. The overall deduction limit in IRC § 68 applies in California, as modified by the state. The miscellaneous deduction 2% floor, required by IRC § 67, applies in California. California also adopts IRC § 67(c)(1) that disallows indirect deduction through pass-thru entities of amounts not allowable as a deduction if paid or incurred directly by an individual. It also adopts the IRC § 67(c)(2) treatment of publicly offered regulated investment companies, cooperatives, real estate investment trusts, and, unless otherwise provided by regulations, estates and trusts, that makes the IRC § 67(c)(1) rule inapplicable. Instead of itemizing deductions, a taxpayer may elect to take the California standard deduction. The indexed California standard deduction for 1994 for single persons and married persons filing separately is $2,431. For married persons filing jointly, heads of household and surviving spouses, the deduction is $4,862.[33]

IMPORTANT   California tax tables are indexed for inflation. California has replaced deductions for personal exemptions with exemption tax credits. These, and other tax credits, are subtracted from the tax as determined under the tax tables.

Ordinary income and loss.   California adopts the federal IRC definition of ordinary income. Ordinary income is defined in IRC § 64 to include any gain from the sale or exchange of property that is neither a capital asset nor property described in IRC § 1231(b) (property used in trade or business). Any gain treated under other IRC provisions on income tax as ordinary income will be treated as gain from sale or exchange of property that is neither capital asset or property described in IRC § 1231(b).[34] California adopts the federal IRC definition of ordinary loss. Ordinary loss is defined by IRC § 65 to include any loss from the sale or exchange of property that is not a capital asset. Any loss from such sales or exchanges considered under other provisions as ordinary loss will be treated as loss from a sale or exchange of property that is not a capital asset.[35]

Foreign currency transactions. California will treat these transactions as ordinary gain or loss, capital gain or loss, or interest as specified in IRC § 988. However, IRC § 988(a)(3) doesn't apply for California.[36]

---

(33) § 17073.5; 17076; 17077.
(34) § 17074.

(35) § 17075.
(36) § 17078.

Kiddie tax—unearned income of child under 14.   For purposes of Rev & TC § 17041 that imposes the California income tax rates for individuals, the taxation of the unearned income of a minor child who has not attained the age of 14 before the close of the taxable year and who has a parent living at the close of the taxable year will be determined in accordance with IRC § 1(g).

California modifications to IRC § 1(g).   IRC § 1(g)(B)(ii)(II), relating to income included on a parent's return is modified by substituting $5 for $75, and 1% for 15%.

The child's net unearned income is taxed to the child at the parent's top marginal rate—that is, the peak tax bracket of the parent. Thus, income received from bank accounts, CDs, money market funds, stocks, and the like regardless of who set up or bought the property that belonged to one or both parents is taxed to the child at the parent's top rate. This provision applies if (1) the child has not attained age 14 before the close of the tax year, and (2) either parent of the child is alive at the close of the tax year.

How to calculate tax.   The tax is imposed on a child's net unearned income and equals the greater of: (1) the tax that would be imposed on the child's income without the special rules on the child's unearned income; or (2) the sum of the tax that would be payable had the child not received unearned income, and the child's share of the parental-source tax. The child will pay tax at the parent's rates on his or her *net unearned income*. The child's net unearned income, is the child's unearned income less the sum of $500 and the greater of: (1) $500 of the standard deduction or $500 of itemized deductions, or (2) the deductions allowed the child that are directly connected with the production of the child's unearned income. The net unearned income cannot exceed the child's total taxable income for the year in question.

Exemption from the under-14 rules.   Certain kinds of income are exempt from the under-14 rules and continue to be taxed at the child's rate. The exemption is for all wages earned by the child, whether the wages come from babysitting, delivering newspapers, or even from a job with a business owned by a parent.[37]

Reporting on parents' return.   California allows a parent to report unearned income of a minor child up to $5,000 on the parent's return.[37]

FILING STATUS

¶ 121   Determining Your Filing Status

Use same filing status as federal.   When filing returns, an individual is required to use the same filing status as that used on the federal income tax

---

(37) § 17041(g).

return for the same taxable year. In case of a husband and wife filing jointly, if one spouse was a resident for all of the taxable year, and the other was a nonresident for all or any portion of the taxable year, a joint nonresident income tax return must be filed. Rev & TC § 18402 rules on use of federal filing status, and filing joint nonresident return do not apply to either (1) a married couple, when either spouse was an active member of the armed forces or any auxiliary branch during the taxable year, (2) a married couple when either spouse was a nonresident of the state for the taxable year and had no California source income during the taxable year, or (3) a married couple when either spouse is a nonresident alien as determined under federal law. The married couple may file either separate returns or a single joint return on such forms or in such manner as the Franchise Tax Board prescribes.[38]

Married persons filing joint returns. If a joint federal income tax return for the same taxable year is filed, the income of a husband and wife may be included in a single joint return. Tax will be computed on the aggregate income, using the income-splitting provisions of Rev & TC § 17045. A nonresident joint return must be made if: (1) one spouse was resident for the entire year, and (2) the other spouse was a nonresident for all or any portion of the taxable year. This rule on filing a nonresident joint return does not apply if either (a) a nonresident or his or her spouse was an active member of the U.S. Armed Forces or any auxiliary branch during the taxable year; or (b) the nonresident spouse has no income from California sources for the taxable year. This exception applies only to a husband and wife who file a joint federal return. Married couples who file separately for federal purposes must file separate California returns. A joint return cannot be filed if the husband and wife have different taxable years. An exception to this rule is the situation where the taxable years start on the same day, and end on different days because of the death of either or both spouses. In that case, a joint return may be made with respect to the taxable year of each spouse. California conforms to IRC § 6013(a)(2)–(3). This exception will not apply if the surviving spouse remarries before the close of his or her taxable year. It also does not apply if the taxable year of either spouse is a fractional part of a year under IRC § 443(a).[39]

Married filing separate returns. The California requirements for filing status as married filing separate returns, are the same as federal. The filing of separate returns is optional. However, since California is a community property state, community income and deductions must be divided equally between spouses. Separate returns must be filed if a husband and wife have different taxable years, unless the taxable years start on the same day and end on different days because of the death of either or both spouses. In such a case, a joint return will be allowed. This exception does not apply if the surviving spouse remarries before the close of his or her taxable year. The

---

(38) § 17043(a)–(d); ¶ 18, 402(b); (d).   **(39)** § 17045; 18521.

¶ 121

exception also does not apply if the taxable year of either spouse is a fractional part of the year under IRC § 443(a).[39] State taxing agencies must honor the decisions of California courts on the marital status of parties regardless of conflicting decisions of foreign courts. If a California court declares a foreign divorce invalid, a joint return will not be allowed with later spouse.[40]

If two individuals are married at the end of the taxable year, live separate and apart from each other with no present intent to resume marital relationship for all or part of the year, and do not file a joint return, the earnings and accumulations of each during the separation must be reported on each spouse's return as separate income.[1]

Qualifying widow(er) with dependent child.   The filing status requirements for California are the same as federal. The requirements for filing a joint return with the deceased spouse are the same as federal.[2]

Abandoned spouse.   If a taxpayer lives apart from his or her spouse for the entire taxable year and pays more than one-half the cost of maintaining a home which is the principal residence, for over one-half of that year, of a dependent child, such taxpayer may file a separate return as though unmarried. Because of the lower federal tax rates, for a single person, there is a federal tax advantage. California has adopted the same tax treatment for the so-called "abandoned spouse." But in order to make it worthwhile for California tax purposes, it would be necessary to look at the community property status of the joint income and the use of itemized vs. the standard deduction. The principal advantage from a California standpoint would be if the qualifying dependent lives in the house maintained by the taxpayer for the entire taxable year, the taxpayer may qualify as "head of household" and can use the lower rates and higher personal exemption credit on his California return.[3]

Head of household.   California adopts federal IRC § 2(b) and (c) rules. An individual is considered a head of household if he or she qualifies under IRC § 2(b) or 2(c). A taxpayer qualifies as a head of household if all of the following conditions are met for the year.[4]

(1) Taxpayer must be an unmarried person. "Unmarried person" is one who has never been married; or who is a widow(er) whose spouse died in a prior year; or one who has obtained a final decree of divorce or separate maintenance. Interlocutory decree of divorce does not result in "unmarried" status. *Appeal of Mohammed M. Siddiqui, SBE 9–14–72.*

(2) Taxpayer must maintain as his or her home for more than one-half of the taxable year a household in which lives a person who qualifies under the following classes of relationship:

(a) Sons and daughters (including adopted children) and their descendants, or step-children—but not descendants of step-children. (If any of these

---

(40) LR 319, 1–10–67.
(1) Civ Cd § 5118.
(2) § 17045; 18521.

(3) § 17042; IRC § 2(c); 7703(b); Fed Reg No. 1.143.1.
(4) § 17042.

persons are unmarried, he or she has income of $1,000 or more or if the taxpayer contributed less than half to his support, he would still qualify the taxpayer as head of household if other conditions are met.)

(b) Any other relative (except a cousin) who qualifies the taxpayer for a dependency exemption. If the dependent is the taxpayer's mother or father, it is not necessary that they live in the taxpayer's home. Maintaining a parent in a rest home or a home for the aged qualifies for head of household rules. Taxpayer would get household head status when he stays with a dependent for a substantial portion of the year (8 to 10 months) and periods of separation are temporary. *Appeal of J.M. Troxler, SBE 12–13–60.* However, the status would be denied when taxpayer maintained separate residences for himself and his dependent. *Appeal of John V. Durand, SBE 11–5–63.*

(3) Taxpayer must contribute over half of the cost of maintaining the home. Such cost includes property taxes, mortgage interest, rent, utilities, insurance and food; but does not include clothing, education, medical expenses, life insurance, transportation and other services rendered the taxpayer.[3]

Note: Federal law treats U.S. taxpayers as unmarried individuals as qualifying for head of household status if the U.S. taxpayer is married to a nonresident alien at any time during the tax year (IRC § 2(b)(2)(B)). This rule does not apply for California purposes (see Rev & TC § 17024.5(b)(11) which provides that all federal provisions referring to nonresident aliens will be ignored in determining California tax).[5]

TAX RATES AND ALTERNATIVE MINIMUM TAX

¶ 131 Tax Rates

Generally. California rates range from 1% to 11%. Tax brackets are indexed to account for the effects of inflation. To put this indexation into operation, the California Department of Industrial Relations submits to the Franchise Tax Board each year, the percentage change in the California Consumer Price Index for the fiscal year then ended on that June 30. For each tax year starting in 1988 the Franchise Tax Board will recompute the income brackets by multiplying the prior year's taxable income bracket figure by the appropriate Inflation Adjustment Factor rounded to the nearest $1. The Franchise Tax Board must use the California Consumer Price Index for All Urban Consumers as modified for rental equivalent of homeownership.[6]

Tax tables. At the present time there are tax tables issued by the Franchise Tax Board, for use by single persons, and married persons filing separate returns and married spouses filing jointly and qualifying widow(er)s. The tables can also be used by head of household taxpayers.

The tax tables cannot be used by (1) individuals to whom tax on lump-sum distributions under § 17504(b) applies; (2) individuals making returns under IRC § 443(a)(1) for period of less than 12 months on account of change in annual accounting; and (3) estates or trusts.[7]

---

(5) § 17024.5
(6) § 17038(b).

(7) § 17048(b).

¶ 135   Alternative Minimum Tax

California adopts the IRC § 55–59 alternative minimum tax provisions, but imposes its own rate of tax. For taxable years starting on or after 1–1–91 and before 1–1–96, the California rate is 8.5%. Starting 1–1–96, the 7% rate will again apply. Alternative minimum taxable income means taxable income for the taxable year, determined with the adjustments provided in IRC § 56 and § 58, and increased by the amount of items of tax preference described in IRC § 57. California modifies IRC § 56(b)(1)(E), disallowing the standard deduction and personal exemptions to deny its own standard deduction under Rev & TC § 17073.5. Regular tax means regular California tax liability before reduction for any credits against the tax, less any amount imposed under Rev & TC § 17560(d)(1) and (e)(1), relating to increase of tax by interest in the case of dealer dispositions and special rules for nondealers.[8] Tax, as reduced, by credit for taxes paid other states, is used as "regular tax liability" for purposes of computing the minimum tax credit under IRC § 53.[9] IRC § 57(a)(5), relating to tax-exempt interest and IRC § 57(a)(6)(B), relating to tangible personal property do not apply in California. IRC § 59(a), relating to the alternative minimum tax foreign tax credit also does not apply.

Nonresidents and part-year residents. The tentative minimum tax must be computed as if a nonresident or part-year resident were a resident for the entire taxable year, multiplied by the ratio of adjusted gross income from California sources, as modified for purposes of the alternative minimum tax, to total adjusted gross income from all sources, as modified for the purposes of the alternative minimum tax. California adjusted gross income includes each of (1) for any period taxpayer was a resident of the state, all items of gross income, as modified for purposes of the alternative minimum tax, regardless of source; and (2) for periods during which taxpayer was not a resident of this state, only those items of adjusted gross income, as modified, which were derived from sources within California.

Exemptions. In case of joint return, or surviving spouse, $40,000. In case of unmarried individual who is not surviving spouse, $30,000. In case of married individual who files separately, or an estate or trust, $20,000. Surviving spouse is defined in IRC § 2(a). Marital status is determined by IRC § 7703. Exemption phaseout (25%) applies to amounts of alternative minimum taxable income in excess of $150,000 for married filing jointly and surviving spouse; $112,500 for individuals not surviving spouse; and $75,000 in case of married persons filing separately, and estates or trusts.[9]

Adjustments in computing alternative minimum taxable income. California conforms to IRC § 56(a)–(b), (d) and (e) rules that apply to individuals. These rules cover: (1) depreciation; (2) mining exploration and development costs; (3) certain long-term contracts; (4) alternative tax net operating loss deduction; (5) pollution control facilities; (6) installment sales of certain

---

(8) § 17062.   (9) § 17063.

property; (7) adjusted basis; (8) itemized deduction limits; (9) circulation and research and experimental expenditures; and (10) incentive stock options.[10]

Items of tax preference. California conforms to IRC § 57 which specifies items of tax preference including: (1) depletion allowable under IRC § 611 in excess of adjusted basis of property at the end of the taxable year, determined without regard to depletion deduction for the year; (2) for oil, gas or geothermal property, the amount by which the amount of excess intangible drilling costs arising in the taxable year exceeds 65% of net income from such properties; (3) amount by which the deduction for appreciated property would be reduced if all capital gain property were taken into account in adjusted basis; (4) accelerated depreciation on property placed in service before 1–1–87—applies to accelerated depreciation on real property and leased personal property, amortization of certified pollution control facilities, and accelerated cost recovery deduction not subject to current IRC § 56(1); or (5) 50% of gain on the sale or exchange of qualified small business stock excluded from income under § 18152.5 (because of the five year holding period set forth in § 18152.5(a), the 50% exclusion for such gains will not be available until at least 1998 for qualifying sales or exchanges after 8–10–93).[10]

CAUTION	California continues to treat as an item of tax preference, appreciation on contributions of tangible personal property gifted after 6–31–92, and before 1–1–93. It has not adopted § 13171 of the Revenue Reconciliation Act of 1993.

Losses denied. California conforms to the provisions of IRC § 58 that deny farm loss and losses from passive activity, and provide special rules for insolvent taxpayers, and loss on disposition of farm shelter activity.[10]

Minimum tax credit. A minimum tax credit, determined in accordance with IRC § 53, is allowed. References to "regular tax liability" determined under IRC § 53(c)(1) mean the regular tax, as defined by Rev & TC § 17062(b)(2), reduced by the sum of the credits allowed by the Personal Income Tax Law, other than the credits containing refundable provisions, but not carryover provisions under Rev & TC § 17039(a)(7), and the portion of any credit that reduces tax below the tentative minimum tax, as provided in Rev & TC § 17039(c)(1). Under IRC § 53, taxpayers can use the amount of the minimum tax they pay as a credit that reduces the following year's regular tax, net of other nonrefundable credits (or the excess of this regular tax over the tentative minimum tax, if that's less). Unused credits can be carried over indefinitely, but can't be carried back. They can be carried over as tax attributes in corporate acquisitions covered by IRC § 381(a). The year's minimum tax credit is in general composed of the aggregate post-1986 liability for alternative minimum tax reduced by regular tax, to the extent it wasn't previously used as a credit. However, taxpayers take into account in

---

(10) § 17062.

the alternative minimum tax computation only those liabilities that result from deferral preferences—but not from preferences that result from permanent exclusions for regular tax purposes. California includes the 50% excluded gain on the sale of qualifying small business stock as an exclusion preference as defined in IRC § 53(d)(1)(B)(ii)(II).[11] So the minimum tax for this credit is reduced by the amount of minimum tax liability that would have been incurred if the only preferences were the exclusion preferences, which are percentage depletion and regular tax itemized deductions that are denied for minimum tax purposes. The minimum tax credit can't be used to reduce the alternative minimum tax under Rev & TC § 17062.[11]

¶ 136 Tax on Premature Distributions

An individual who receives a premature distribution or enters into certain prohibited transactions in connection with his Individual Retirement Account or Keogh Plan is required to pay a tax at the rate of 10% of the amount for federal purposes.[12] The rate is 2.5% for California.[13]

Prohibited transaction. Prohibited transaction includes:

(a) Borrowing from the Individual Retirement Account;
(b) Using the assets or the income of the Individual Retirement Account as a basis for obtaining a benefit; or
(c) Pledging the account as security for a loan, etc.

Engaging in prohibited transactions causes the Individual Retirement Account to be considered to be terminated so that the entire value in the account at the beginning of the year is deemed to be distributed.

Premature distribution. Premature distribution includes:

(a) Any actual distribution to a person not yet 59½ years of age; and
(b) Income earned in the year on excess contributions when returned before the due date of the return.

Excluded from the premature distributions is a distribution in the form of a "rollover" of contributions to another plan, amounts distributed due to disability and amounts transferred to a spouse under a divorce decree.

Exclusion from penalty-Northridge earthquake victims. The 2½% penalty tax on premature or early distributions from a qualified pension plan, employee annuity, or an IRA, does not apply where the distribution is made to any individual who suffered a hardship as a result of the Northridge earthquake during January, 1994, or any related aftershock or related casualty. The exception applies to any distribution between January 17, 1994, and before January 18, 1995. The exclusion is limited to those individuals who have suffered a hardship which includes, but is not limited to personal injury or property damage of the distributee or any member of the distribu-

---

(11) § 17063.   **(13)** § 17085(c).
(12) IRC § 72(m), 408(e); § 408(f)(1).

tee's household. The exclusion applies only if the federal government grants a similar waiver.[13a]

¶ 137 Income-splitting

The tax on a California return is twice the tax imposed on a single person or married person filing a separate return with one-half of the income. Income-splitting applies to normal taxes.[14] By way of comparison, on the federal return a husband or wife filing jointly pays more than twice the tax which would be imposed on a single person with one-half of the income.[15]

CREDITS AGAINST TAX

¶ 140 Tax Credits—Generally

California law defines "net tax" (i.e., the basic figure against which credits are applied) as the personal income tax imposed under Rev & TC §§ 17041 and 17048 (tax schedules and tables), plus the tax imposed under Rev & TC § 17504, relating to lump-sum distributions, less the credits allowed by Rev & TC § 17054, relating to the personal exemption credits, and any amount imposed under Rev & TC § 17560(d)(1) and § 17560(e)(1), relating to dealer dispositions and nondealer special rules, for addition of interest under Rev & TC §§ 453(l)(3)(B) and 453A(c)(2). The "net tax" can not be less than the tax imposed under § 17054, relating to the separate tax on lump-sum distributions.

Credits are allowed against the net tax in the following order:

(1) Credits which do not contain carryover or refundable provisions, except for taxes paid to other states, and the minimum tax credit allowed by Rev & TC § 17063.

(2) Credits which contain carryover provisions but do not contain refundable provisions.

(3) Credits which contain both carryover and refundable provisions.

(4) The minimum tax credit allowed by Rev & TC § 17063.

(5) Credits for taxes paid to other states.

(6) Credits which contain refundable provisions but do not contain carryover provisions.

The order within each category is determined by the Franchise Tax Board. These credits are by law put in category (6): renters' credit (Rev & TC § 17053.5); excess California State Disability Insurance contributions (Rev & TC § 17061); California income tax withheld (Rev & TC § 19002).[16]

Nonresidents and part-year residents are allowed all credits, except the renter's credit, and a nonresident's credit for taxes paid in the state of residence, in the same proportion as the ratio used to determine the basis for tax under Rev & TC § 17041. The rule doesn't apply to credits allowed that

---

(13a) § 17085.5, as added by Stats. 1994, c. 735, § 1.
(14) § 17045.

(15) IRC § 2.
(16) § 17039.

are conditional on the transaction occurring wholly within the state. These credits are allowed in their entirety.[17]

Tax credits that reduce tax imposed below tentative minimum tax. No tax credit can reduce the tax imposed under Rev & TC §§ 17041 and 17048 plus the tax imposed under Rev & TC § 17504 on lump-sum distributions below the tentative minimum tax, except the following credits, but only after the allowance for the minimum tax credit allowed by Rev & TC § 17063: (1) the credit allowed by former Rev & TC § 17052.4, relating to solar energy; (2) the credit allowed by former Rev & TC § 17052.5, relating to solar energy; (3) the credit allowed by Rev & TC § 17052.5, relating to solar energy; (4) the credit allowed by Rev & TC § 17052.12, relating to research expenses; (5) the credit allowed by Rev & TC § 17052.13 relating to the sales and use tax credit; (6) the credit allowed by Rev & TC § 17052.15 relating to the Los Angeles Revitalization Zone sales tax credit; (7) the credit allowed by Rev & TC § 17053.8 relating to the enterprise zone hiring credit; (8) the credit allowed by Rev & TC § 17053.10 relating to the Los Angeles Revitalization Zone hiring credit for construction work; (9) the credit allowed by Rev & TC § 17053.11 relating to the program area hiring credit; (10) the credit allowed by Rev & TC § 17053.17 relating to the LA Revitalization Zone hiring credit; (11) the credit allowed by Rev & TC § 17053.49 relating to qualified property; (12) the credit allowed by Rev & TC § 17057, relating to clinical testing expenses; (13) the credit allowed by Rev & TC § 17058, relating to low-income housing; (14) the credit allowed by Rev & TC § 17061, relating to refunds under the Unemployment Insurance Code; (15) the credits for taxes paid to other states allowed by Ch. 12, starting with Rev & TC § 18001; (16) the credit allowed by Rev & TC § 19002, relating to tax withholding. Any of these credits partially or totally denied can be carried over to later tax years, if that credit's provisions allow a carryover, when it exceeds net tax. Any remaining carryover of a credit allowed by a section that has been repealed or made inoperative by law shall continue to be carried over and applied against the net tax, until exhausted, unless California law provides otherwise.[18]

Two or more taxpayers—division of credits. Unless otherwise provided, if two or more taxpayers, other than a husband and wife, share in the costs that would be eligible for a credit against tax under the Personal Income Tax Law, they can take the tax credit in proportion to his or her respective share of the costs paid or incurred. In the case of a partnership, the credit may be divided among partners according to a written partnership agreement in accordance with IRC § 704, relating to partner's distributive share. In the case of a husband and wife who file separate returns, the credit can be taken by either, or equally divided between them.[19]

---

(17) § 17055.
(18) § 17039(c)(1).

(19) § 17039(e).

¶ 141 **Personal and Dependency Credits**

In California, personal and dependency exemptions are credits against tax. Credits against tax apply to tax as computed by the tax schedules or tax tables, but not against the tax imposed on lump-sum distributions under Rev & TC § 17504, or the increases to tax for interest imposed by Rev & TC § 17560(d)(1) and 17560(e)(1). They are not subtractions or deductions from adjusted gross income as under federal rules. Personal and dependency credits are indexed annually based on percentage change in the California Consumer Price Index. This index will be modified for rental equivalent homeownership.[20]

Indexed tax credit amounts for 1994:

Single individual	$65
Married filing separate return	$65
Married filing joint return	$138
Qualifying widow(er) with dependent child	$138
Head of household	$138
Persons 65 or older	$65
Blind—one spouse	$65
Blind—both spouses	$65
Dependent	$65

IRC § 151(c) determines dependents for whom an exemption is allowable.

Credit reduction provisions. For taxable years starting on or after 1–1–91, a reduction will be made to the credits allowed by Rev & TC § 17054 (personal exemptions, dependents, blind persons, surviving spouses, individuals over 65), and § 17054.6 (individuals not eligible for dependent credit). The threshold amount is indexed annually. For 1994, the amount that triggers a reduction is $214,929 in case of a joint return, or surviving spouse; $161,196 in case of a head of household, $107,464 in case of an individual who is not married, and is not a surviving spouse or head of household, and $107,464 in case of a married individual filing separately. Each credit will be reduced by $6 for each $2,500 by which the taxpayer's adjusted gross income (AGI) exceeds the threshold amount. For joint returns or surviving spouses, the reduction will be $12 instead of $6; for married individuals filing separately, the reduction will be $6 for each $1,250 in excess of the threshold amount. The credit cannot be reduced below zero. In the case of nonresidents and part-year residents, the reductions apply to the tax as computed under Rev & TC § 17041(b) and (d) before proration of the tax. Marital status is determined under Rev & TC § 17021.5. Indexing started in 1992.[21]

---

(20) § 17054–17055.

(21) § 17054.1.

¶ 142 **Investment Tax Credit For Manufacturing Equipment**

For acquisitions of qualified property on or after January 1, 1994, qualified taxpayers will be entitled to a 6% credit against the "net tax" as defined in Rev & TC Section 17039, of the amount paid or incurred on or after January 1, 1994, for qualified property that is placed in service in California.

Time for taking credit for the 1994 year. For qualified cost paid or incurred on or after January 1, 1994, and prior to the first taxable year of a qualified taxpayer beginning on or after January 1, 1995, the credit shall be claimed for the first taxable year beginning on or after January 1, 1995.

Special transition rules apply for those contracts in existence on or before January 1, 1994, but for which costs are incurred after December 31, 1993. Contract costs for qualified property which qualify for the credit shall be the amount determined by the ratio of cost actually paid before January 1, 1994, and total contract cost actually paid. For this purpose, a cost paid shall include contractual deposits and option payments. For any contract that is entered into on or after January 1, 1994, that is a replacement contract to a contract that was binding prior to January 1, 1994, shall be treated as a binding contract in existence prior to January 1, 1994. An option contract in existence prior to January 1, 1994, shall be treated as a binding contract for purposes of determining the credit. Special rules apply when the option holder will forfeit an amount less than 10% of the fixed option price in the event that option is not exercised. Contracts shall be considered binding even if they are subject to conditions.

Qualifying persons. Qualifying persons entitled to the credit for acquisitions of qualifying property are those who are engaged in those lines of business described in Codes 2,000 to 3,999, inclusive of the Standard Industrial Classification Manual published by the U.S. Office of Management and Budget, 1987 edition (these are generally referred to as SIC Codes). Generally, Codes 2,000 to 3,999 include all manufacturing businesses but exclude agriculture, communication, construction, forestry, fishing, mining, real estate, retail trade, services, transportation, utilities and wholesale trade.

Manufacturing is defined in the Code and generally means converting or conditioning property by changing the form, composition, quality, or character of the property for ultimate sale at retail or use in the manufacturing of a product to be ultimately sold at retail. It includes any improvements to tangible personal property that result in a greater service life or greater functionality than that of the original property. Fabricating means to make, build, create, produce, or assemble components or property to work in a new or different manner.

Qualified property. Qualified property means all of the following:

(1) Tangible personal property purchase for use primarily (defined as 50% or more) in any stage of the manufacturing, processing, refining, fabricating, or recycling of property, beginning at the point any raw materials are received by the qualified person and are introduced into the process and ending at the point at

which the manufacturing, processing, refining, fabricating, or recycling has altered the property to its completed form.

(2) Tangible personal property purchased for use primarily (defined as 50% or more) in research and development.

(3) Tangible personal property purchased to be used primarily (defined as 50% or more) to maintain, repair, measure, or test any property which is otherwise qualified property.

(4) For pollution control that meets or exceeds standard established by any local or regional governmental agency within the state.

(5) Recycling equipment.

The value of any capitalized labor cost that is directly allocable to the construction or modification of property which is otherwise qualifying property, is included in the cost subject credit.

In the case of any qualified taxpayer engaged in manufacturing activities described in SIC Codes 357 or 367, or for those activities related to biotech processes described in SIC Code 8731, or those activities related to biopharmaceutical establishments only that are described in SIC Codes 2830 to 2836 inclusive, "qualified property" also include special purpose buildings that are constructed or modified for use by a qualified taxpayer primarily in a manufacturing, processing, refining, or fabricating process, or as research of storage facility primarily used in connection with a manufacturing process. Such costs for special purpose buildings include capitalized labor costs. Special rules are included limiting the definition of "special purpose building and foundation". If the entire building does not qualify as a "special purpose building" a taxpayer may establish that a portion of the building, and foundation, qualify. Biopharmaceutical activities are specifically defined.

Qualified properties specifically excludes furniture, facilities used for warehousing purposes after completion of the manufacturing process, inventory, equipment used in the extraction process, equipment used to store finished products that have completed the manufacturing process, tangible personal property that is used in administration, general management, or marketing, and any vehicle for which credit is claimed as a low-emission vehicle under Section 17052.11. Qualifying property includes property that is acquired by or subject to a lease by a qualified taxpayer subject to special rules set forth in Rev & TC Section 17053.49(f).

Recapture. If the qualified property is removed from the state of California in the same taxable year as the property is first placed in service, no credit shall be allowed. If qualified property for which a credit was allowed is thereafter removed from the state of California, or disposed of to an unrelated party, or used for any purpose not qualifying for the credit within one year from the date the qualified property is first placed in service in California, the amount of the credit allowed will be recaptured by adding that credit to the net tax of the qualified taxpayer for the taxable year in which the qualified property is disposed of, removed, or put to ineligible use.

¶ 142

Carryover of unused credit. THe credit in excess of the amount allowed in any one year can be carried over for seven years. A "small business" can carry the credit over for an additional two years for a total of nine years. A "small business" is one which either has less than $50 million in gross receipts, less than $50 million in net assets, or a total credit of less than $1 million in the year for which the credit is allowed.

Coordination with sales tax exemption. No credit shall be allowed for any qualified property for which an exemption from sales and use taxes was allowed and claimed as provided in Rev & TC § 6377.[22]

¶ 143 Credit for Adoption Costs

For taxable years beginning on or after January 1, 1994, a credit shall be allowed for adoption costs equal to 50% of those costs incurred or paid by the taxpayer for the adoption of a minor child who is a citizen or legal resident of the United States and was in custody of a public agency of California or political subdivision of California. The credit shall not exceed $2,500 per minor child.

The costs eligible for credit include fees for required services of either the Department of Social Services or a licensed adoption agency, and travel and related expenses for the adoptive family that are directly related to the adoption process. In addition, medical fees that are not reimbursed by insurance and are directly related to the adoption are qualified expenses. This credit may be claimed for the taxable year in which the decree or order of adoption is entered as provided in Family Code § 8612. The credit may include costs paid or incurred in any prior taxable year. There is a carryover provision where the credit allowed exceeds the "net tax" in the year of adoption. The excess may be carried over to the following year, and succeeding years, if necessary until the total credit is exhausted.

If any of the expenses for which a credit is claimed or otherwise deductible, that deduction will be reduced by the amount of the credit allowed.[23]

¶ 144 Expanded California Child Care Credit

For taxable years starting on or after 1–1–91 and before 1–1–94, a credit of $1,000 will be allowed for a qualified parent. "Qualified parent" must qualify as a head of household under IRC § 2(b) and § 2(c), or as a surviving spouse under IRC § 2(a), or be considered married for tax purposes at the end of the taxable year, and file a joint return with his or her spouse for the taxable year. The qualified parent must attach a copy of the birth certificate of the child who meets the following requirements: (1) the child must not have reached the age of 13 months, and (2) must be a dependent, within the meaning of IRC § 152, of the qualified parent.[24]

---

(22) § 17053.49, as added by Stats. 1994, c. 751, § 2.

(23) Former § 17052.6, as added by Stats. 1994, c. 827.

(24) § 17052.20.

The credit allowed must be reduced by two hundred dollars ($200) for each $1,000, or fraction by which the qualified parent's adjusted gross income for the taxable year exceeds an amount which is indexed annually. For 1993, the amounts are: (1) $42,476, if the qualified parent is a married person filing jointly, or a surviving spouse under IRC § 2(a); (2) $30,264, if the qualified parent is a head of household, as defined under IRC § 2(b). The 1992 indexed amounts were $41,440 and $29,526.

"Qualified parent" is defined as an individual who meets all the following requirements, determined on a month-by-month basis: (1) maintains as his or her home, or if married, the qualified parent and his or her spouse maintain as their home a household that includes at least one member who is a child who has not reached the age of 13 months, and a dependent within meaning of IRC § 152; (2) qualified parent has no income; (3) qualified parent is resident of California; (4) qualified parent or qualified parent's spouse does not have expenses for which credit under Rev & TC § 17052.6 (child care credit) is claimed.

¶ 145   Employers' Child Care Credit

Start-up expenses—child care program—construction of facility. For taxable years starting on or after 1–1–88 and before 1–1–98, a credit is allowed for 30% of either or both of (1) start-up expenses of establishing a child care program, or constructing a child care facility in California for the benefit of the employees of the taxpayer; and (2) cost paid by taxpayer for contributions to California child care information and referral services for the employees of the taxpayer. This credit is extended for years beginning on or after 1–1–93 for expenses incurred by the taxpayer for the start-up expenses of establishing a child care program or constructing a child care facility in California, to be used primarily by the children of employees of tenants leasing commercial or office space in a building owned by the taxpayer. The amount of credits allowed cannot exceed $50,000 for any taxable year. In the case of a child care facility established by two or more taxpayers, credit is allowed if the facility is to be used primarily by children of employees of each of taxpayers. If two or more taxpayers, other than a husband or wife, share in the costs eligible for the credit allowed, each taxpayer may receive a tax credit in proportion to their respective share of the cost. If the husband and wife file separately, either may take the credit, or they may divide it equally. Carry-overs are allowed. A $50,000 limit applies in any year. No deduction will be allowed, as otherwise provided by the Personal Income Tax Law, for expenses paid or incurred that are equal to amount of credit allowed attributable to those expenses. Instead of taking the credit, a taxpayer can elect to take a depreciation under Rev & TC § 17250. Also, a taxpayer can take a depreciation for the cost of a facility in excess of amount of tax credit claimed. The basis of a child care facility must be reduced by the amount of the credit attributable to the facility, in the year the credit is taken. The costs of a program or facility must be certified to the FTB. If a child care center is disposed of or ceases operation within 60 months after completion, the portion of the credit that represents the rest of the 60-month period must be added to the taxpayer's tax liability in the taxable year of that disposition or nonuse.[25] The credit to employers incurring start-up expenses of establishing a child care program, or constructing a child care facility, is claimed on FTB form 3501.

¶ 146   Employers' Qualified Dependent Care Plan Credit

Contributions to qualified plan on behalf of dependent of employee. For taxable years beginning on or after 1–1–88 and before 1–1–95, a credit is allowed for 50% of the cost paid or incurred by a taxpayer for contributions to a qualified care plan made on behalf of any dependent of the taxpayer's California employee who is under the age of 15. The amount of the credit allowed in any taxable year cannot exceed $600 per qualified dependent. For taxable years beginning on or after 1–1–95 and before 1–1–98, the credit is reduced to 30% of the amount of the cost paid or incurred, up to $360. Also, the age requirement for qualified dependents goes down to 11 years or under.

"Qualified care plan" includes, but is not limited to, onsite service, center-based service, dependent care center, in-home care or home-provider care, if the facility is located in California, and operated under the authority of a license when required by state law. "Contributions" include employer reimbursements to an employee's qualified care plan expenses, or direct payment to child care programs or providers, or both. IRC § 401(c)(1), relating to self-employed individuals, is embraced in the definition of "employee."

If an employer makes contributions to a qualified care plan and also collects fees from parents to support a child care facility owned and operated by the employer, no credit will be allowed for contributions, in the amount, if any, by which the sum of contributions and fees exceeds the cost of providing child care. In cases where child care received is of less than 42-week duration, employers may claim a prorated portion of the credit, using a ratio of the number of weeks of care received, divided by 42 weeks. Carryovers of credit are allowed. The credit is not available to an employer if the care provided on behalf of an employee is provided by an individual who qualifies as a dependent of that employee or the employee's spouse, or son, stepson, daughter or stepdaughter. Contributions to the plan can't discriminate. No deduction is allowed where expenses equal the credits. The basis must be reduced by the amount of the credit. Two or more taxpayers, other than a husband or wife, sharing in the costs get a proportionate credit. A husband and wife filing separately may equally divide the credit, or either may take the entire credit. The credit expires for tax years beginning on or after January 1, 1995.[26]

---

(25) § 17052.17.   **(26)** § 17052.18.

¶ 147 "Other State" Net Income Tax Credit

Generally. The California Personal Income Tax Law allows a credit against the California tax for taxes paid by residents, part-year residents and certain nonresidents to another state, the District of Columbia or a territory or possession of the United States. Credit is made on a reciprocal basis. Qualifying out-of-state taxes are those based on net income or taxable income, (i.e., gross income less direct expenses applicable thereto). Also, the other state's taxes must have been imposed on income derived from sources within the other state. This requirement rules out a tax paid on the income from intangible property (dividends, interest, and the like) because California considers intangible property to have a situs in the state of residence of the owner (i.e., the "income-source state"). The requirement also eliminates a tax paid to another state measured by gross income. The California law and its associated case decisions are the authority for the determination of the source of income, or any matter affecting the computation regardless of any provision or interpretation of the law of the other state. California considers the source of compensation for services is in California or in the other state only to the extent the services are actually rendered in each location. No credit is allowed for income taxes paid to any city, county, the federal government or a foreign country. Special taxes which may have been added to the other state's income tax are not allowable in the tax credit computation.[27] The District of Columbia unincorporated business franchise tax isn't a net income tax for purposes of the California credit.[28] The credit for qualifying income taxes paid to other states is claimed on Schedule S of the individual income tax return, FTB Form 540.

Administrative practice. The Franchise Tax Board and the State Board of Equalization have uniformly followed the California Supreme Court decision in *Miller v. McColgan (1941) 17 Cal 2d 432.* In *Miller,* the tax credit was denied a resident who paid Philippine income tax on dividends received on stock in a Philippine corporation based on the ground that the dividend's source was the stock itself and the stock's situs was California. So the dividend was not properly taxable by the Philippine government. The same rule was applied to gains from the sale of such stocks even though the certificates were in the Philippines and the sale was made there. A contrary ruling in *Henley v. Franchise Tax Board (1953) 122 Cal App 2d 1* is not being followed by tax officials. In *Henley,* the credit was allowed for Canadian taxes paid on dividends distributed by Canadian corporations that had no operations in California. The court ruled that the dividends were from Canadian sources.

In the *Appeal of Stanley K. and Beatrice L. Wong, SBE 5-4-78,* the credit was denied for other state taxes paid on interest income from promissory notes held in connection with the sale of real estate in the other state. The Board of Equalization ruled that the source of the interest was the debt

---

(27) Reg 18001-1–18001-2.   (28) LR 240, 10-28-59.

which had situs at the creditor's residence (California). The same result was reached in the *Appeal of Hallie L. Bills, SBE 4–5–65.* See also the *Appeal of Hugh S. and Nina J. Livie, SBE 10–28–64,* and the *Appeal of John K. and Patricia J. Withers, SBE 9–1–66.*

Residents. Residents of California are allowed a tax credit on income derived from sources within the following states or territories on which a net income tax to such state or territory was paid and which was also taxed by California:

Alabama, American Samoa, Arkansas, Colorado, Connecticut, Delaware, Georgia, Hawaii, Idaho, Illinois, Iowa, Kansas, Kentucky, Louisiana, Maine, Maryland, Massachusetts, Michigan, Minnesota, Mississippi, Missouri, Montana, Nebraska, New Hampshire (business profits tax), New Jersey, New Mexico, New York (allowable for both the personal income tax, including the unincorporated business tax, where both are paid on the same income), North Carolina, North Dakota, Ohio, Oklahoma, Pennsylvania, Puerto Rico, Rhode Island, South Carolina, Utah, Vermont, Virginia (dual residents—U.S. officials only), Virgin Islands, West Virginia, Wisconsin, and the District of Columbia dual residents—U.S. officials only.[29]

WARNING	Local income taxes should be excluded from the computation of the credit for taxes paid to another state. A local income tax is not an "Income tax to the state" and, therefore, does not qualify for the California credit for taxes paid to another state.

The credit is the lesser of: (a) the actual tax paid to the other state or proportionate tax paid on income from sources within that state and also taxable by California; or (b) that proportion of the California tax which the income taxable by both states bears to the entire income taxable by California.[30] The formula is as follows:

$$\frac{(A)}{(B)} \times (C) = (D)$$

Meaning of symbols:

(A) Income derived from sources within other state and also taxable by California
(B) California adjusted gross income
(C) California tax liability before credit for tax paid to other state
(D) Credit limitation (cannot exceed tax paid to other state on income from sources within other state).

Taxes paid to the other state do not include any preference, alternative, or minimum tax comparable to the tax imposed by Rev & TC § 17062, relating to the alternative minimum tax.

---

(29) Form 540, Sch S.   **(30)** § 18001.

Net income tax paid to another state by a resident of California includes the taxpayer's pro rata share of any taxes, on, or according to, or measured by income or profits, paid or accrued, that were paid by a partnership or S corporation, as provided in Rev & TC § 18006. The rule on S corporations will apply only if (1) the state imposing the tax does not allow corporations to elect to be treated as an S corporation; or (2) the state imposes a tax on S corporations and the corporation has elected to be treated as an S corporation in the other state.[31]

Rev & TC § 17014(b) provides that certain individuals are taxed as residents. These individuals, who are domiciled in California, are classified as residents for income tax purposes even though they are out of California for an extended period of time. This applies to elected United States officials, congressional staff members and presidential appointees subject to senate confirmation, other than military and foreign service career appointees. For purposes of the tax credit limitation above, they are entitled to compute their credit on income taxed by other states regardless of its source.

Part-year residents. If a taxpayer is a resident of California for part of a year and then moves to another state or is a nonresident of California and moves into California during the year so that he is a resident in the latter part of the year, his allowable credit is computed on Form 540, Schedule S.

Nonresidents of California. If a taxpayer is a resident of another state or territory and pays an income tax (not including any preference, alternative, or minimum tax comparable to the tax imposed under alternative minimum tax provisions of Rev & TC § 17062) to such state or territory on income which is also taxed by California, the taxpayer may claim a credit against his California net tax on Form 540NR. The states or territories are: Arizona, Guam, Indiana, Maryland, and Virginia.

A state tax credit to reduce California tax has been allowed to a Connecticut resident for Connecticut taxes paid on capital gains from the sale of California real estate partnerships which were sourced in California. The fact that Connecticut taxed its residents only on net capital gains and divided income did not preclude the tax being classified as an income tax for which a credit could be claimed against the income tax assessed by California on nonresidents. *Harry J. Gray, et. al. v. Franchise Tax Board,* CA2 (1991) 286 Cal Rptr 453. The State Board of Equalization has denied a subsequent appeal of a Connecticut taxpayer with similar facts indicating that the State Board of Equalization is unwilling to follow the Appellate Court's decision in *Gray Appeal of Megan Thomas* (1992). *(Note:* This action of the Board was taken by summary decision which cannot be cited as a precedent.)

The credit is limited to: (a) the portion of the resident state's tax (not including any preference, alternative, or minimum tax comparable to the tax

---

(31) § 18001(c); 18006.

imposed under alternative minimum tax provisions of Rev & TC § 17062) which the income taxable by both states bears to the entire income taxable by the state of residence not to exceed (b) that proportion of the California net tax which the income taxable by both states bears to the entire income taxable by California.[32] The formula is as follows:

$$\frac{(E)}{(F)} \times (G) = (H)$$

Meaning of symbols:

(E) Income derived from sources within California and also taxable by state of residence.
(F) Total income reported to state of residence.
(G) Tax paid to state of residence.
(H) Credit limitation (cannot exceed tax paid to other state).

Net income taxes paid to another state by a nonresident includes the taxpayer's pro rata share of any taxes on, or according to, or measured by, income or profits paid or accrued, which were paid by partnership or S corporation, as provided by Rev & TC § 18006.

Reciprocity.   A California resident is allowed a credit for taxes paid to another state if the other state does not a credit. See *Appeal of Frank E. Tompkins, SBE 2–8–78,* where a Californian was denied credit for Arizona taxes since Arizona allowed a credit for California taxes paid on the same income. A nonresident is allowed the credit provided the other state either allows a California resident a credit against California net tax or does not tax the California resident on income from sources within that state.

TAX TIP   It is necessary for the taxpayer to pay the tax to the other state by the time he claims the credit against the California tax. He may claim it at the time of filing the California return if he has paid the foreign state's tax by then or he may file an amended return as a claim for refund if he pays the tax later. Schedule S (Form 540) must accompany the amended return with a copy of the other state's income tax return. The credit is applied only against California tax paid for the year in which the income is taxed. If, for example, a tax to another state is paid as a deficiency tax in a later year, the taxpayer does not use that tax in a computation for credit against the California tax in the year of payment but he must file a claim for credit for the prior year in which the income was taxed by California.

IMPORTANT   If a taxpayer has received a refund or a reduction of the tax paid to the other state or any portion of it on which he has received a California credit, he is required to notify the Franchise Tax Board of the refund or

---

(32) § 18002; 18006.

¶ 147

credit and pay the California tax and interest resulting from the change.[33]

Married couples. When a husband and wife file separate California returns and a joint return in another state, each taxpayer is allowed a credit based upon the portion of the other state tax allocable to the husband or wife on his or her own income. The total tax paid to the other state is prorated to each spouse on the basis of the income that is included in the joint return and also taxed on the separate California returns. If a joint return is filed in California, the entire amount of taxes paid by either or both spouses to the other state may be claimed as a credit regardless of whether a joint return or separate returns are filed in the other state.

The California credit for taxes paid to another state is somewhat similar to the foreign tax credit allowed by the Internal Revenue Code.[34] However, the federal foreign income tax credit, if not used in a given year because of the formula limitation, is allowed as a carryover to subsequent years.[35] In California the credit has to be used in the year in which the income is also taxed by California or it is lost because there is no carryover provision.

Estates and trusts. The credit for taxes paid to other states is allowed to an estate or trust where it is treated as a "resident" of California and also of another state. For this purpose it is considered to be a resident of any state which taxes its income irrespective of whether the income is derived from sources within that state.[36] The credit is subject to the following limitations:

(1) Amount of credit may not exceed the same proportion of the total tax paid to the other state as the income taxed in both states bears to the total income taxed in the other state; and

(2) The amount of the credit is limited to the same proportion of the total California tax as the income taxed in both states bears to the total income taxed by California.

Beneficiaries. The credit is also allowed to the beneficiary of an estate or trust where a beneficiary who is a California resident pays California tax on income which has been taxed to the estate or trust in another state.[37] The credit is limited to the following extent:

(1) The amount of the credit may not exceed the same proportion of the total tax paid to the other state by the estate or trust as the income taxed to the beneficiary in California and also to the estate or trust in the other state bears to the total income taxed by the other state; and

(2) The amount of the credit is limited to the same proportion of the total California tax paid by the beneficiary as the income taxed to the beneficiary in California and also to the estate or trust in the other state bears to the beneficiary's total income taxed by California.

---

(33) § 18007–18009; 19269.
(34) IRC § 901, 903.
(35) IRC § 904.

(36) § 18003; 18004.
(37) § 18005.

With respect to income from intangibles, a California resident who was an income beneficiary of an active Hawaiian trust composed of intangible personal property was entitled to a credit for Hawaii income taxes paid on his income from the trust because the source of that income was in Hawaii where the trustees, who had possession, management and control of the trust corpus, lived. *Appeal of Estate of Douglas C. Alexander, Deceased, et al., SBE 1–4–66.* Resident beneficiaries receiving accumulation distribution from a Minnesota trust were allowed a credit for taxes paid to Minnesota by the trust to the extent it would have been allowed if the trust income had been distributed to the taxpayers ratably in the year of distribution and five preceding years.[38]

Partnerships. For the purpose of determining the credit under Rev & TC § 18001, relating to residents, or § 18002, relating to nonresidents, a member of a partnership shall be allowed to treat their pro rata share of net income taxes paid to another state by the partnership as if those taxes had been paid directly by the partner.[39] This credit is subject to the following conditions:

(1) Credit may not exceed the same proportion of the total tax paid to the other state by the partnership as the income taxed to the partner in California and also to the partnership in the other state bears to the total income taxed by the other state; and

(2) Credit is limited to the same proportion of the total California tax as the income taxed to the partner in California and also to the partnership in the other state bears to the partner's total income taxed by California.

EXAMPLE   A California resident whose distributive share of income from a New York partnership was taxed twice by New York, once on the partnership and once on the partner as an individual, was not allowed a combined tax credit in excess of the amount of California tax on that income derived from the New York partnership. *Appeal of William A. and Dorothy Salant, SBE 5–10–67.*

S corporations. A shareholder of a corporation electing to be treated as an S corporation under Ch. 4.5 of Part 11 shall be allowed to treat their pro rata share of net income taxes to another state as if those taxes had been paid by the shareholder. This rule applies only when (1) the state imposing the tax does not allow a corporation to elect to be treated as an S corporation, or (2) the state imposes a tax on S corporations, and the S corporation has elected to be treated as an S corporation in the other state.[40]

¶ 148   Research Expenditures Credit

A credit against tax is allowed for amounts paid or incurred for research in accordance with IRC § 41, as modified by California. The research credit is claimed on FTB Form 3523. The research credit for start-up companies is claimed on FTB Form 3505.

---

(38) LR 375, 11–19–74.
(39) § 18006.

(40) IRC § 1371, 1372; 17087.5; 18006. 23800–23810.

California modifications.   The applicable percentage is 8% (20% federal) of qualified research expenses for 1993 determined in accordance with IRC § 41. IRC § 41(a)(2), relating to basic research payments, does not apply in California. The term "qualified research" includes only research conducted in California.

Rules applicable in California for computation of base amount.   When computing gross receipts under IRC § 41(c)(5), the California computation is modified to take into account only those gross receipts from the sale of property held primarily for sale to customers in the ordinary course of the taxpayer's trade or business that is delivered or shipped to a purchaser in California, regardless of F.O.B. point or other conditions of sale.[1]

CAUTION	The amendments made by § 13112 of the Revenue Reconciliation Act of 1993 to IRC § 41 relating to the credit for increased research activities, shall apply for California purposes only to taxable years beginning on or after January 1, 1994.

Carryovers.   In the case where the credit allowed under this section exceeds the net tax, the excess may be carried over to reduce the net tax in the following year, and succeeding years, until exhausted.

Pass-thru of Credits.   Credits may be passed through from partnerships, Estates or trusts, or S corporations. For individual sole proprietors, and for those receiving the benefit from pass-thru entitles, the amount of credit allowed in any taxable year can not exceed the portion of tax attributable to the income from the trade or business from which the credit was generated. The carryover credit is also limited in the year for which the carryover is used, to that portion of the tax attributable to the income from the trade or business.[1a]

Federal termination date not applicable.   IRC § 41(h), relating to termination, does not apply in California.

¶ 149   **Jobs Tax Credit**

For federal purposes, employers are allowed a credit against taxes for wages paid to certain classes of disadvantaged or "targeted" employees. The employer's deduction for wages is reduced by the amount of the credit. California has a plan which is similar in purpose but essentially different in many of the details of application.[2]

The California credit is 10% of the amount of wages paid to each employee who is certified by the Employment Development Department to meet the requirements of Sec. 328 of the Unemployment Insurance Code. The credit is against "net tax" and cannot exceed $600 per qualified employee. The term "wages" does not include any amount paid or incurred to

---

(1) § 17052.12.

(1a) § 17052.12, as amended by Stats. 1994, c. 1243, § 5.

(2) § 17053.7.

an individual who begins work for the employer after 12–31–93. The credit does not apply to wages paid in excess of $3,000 to the same individual. The jobs tax credit is claimed on FTB Form 3524.

Unlike the federal Targeted Jobs Credit plan, the credit is applied to wages paid to each qualified employee during the 24-month period starting on date employee begins working for employer.

The credit doesn't apply to an individual, unless, on or before the day of the start of work for the employer, the employer has received a certification from the Employment Development Department, or requested the certification in writing. If, by the day of the start of work, the individual has received from the Department a written preliminary determination that he or she is member of targeted group, the certification requirements will apply on the fifth day on which the individual starts work.

The credit also doesn't apply to wages paid to an individual who is a dependent of the taxpayer, as described in IRC § 152(a)(1)–(8), or if the taxpayer is an estate or trust, is a grantor, beneficiary, or fiduciary, or a person related to such grantor, etc., or who is a dependent as described in IRC § 152(a)(9), or, if taxpayer is an estate or trust, a dependent of a grantor, beneficiary, or fiduciary of estate or trust.

The credit doesn't apply to wages paid to an individual, if before hiring date, that individual was employed at any time during which there was no certification for the employee.[3]

A taxpayer can elect to have the jobs tax credit provisions not apply for any taxable year. The election may be made or revoked at any time before the end of the four-year period starting on the last date for filing the return for the taxable year, determined without regard to extensions. It must be made in the manner set by the Franchise Tax Board.[4]

In case of a successor employer referred to in IRC § 3306(b)(1), the determination of the amount of the credit with respect to wages paid by that employer will be made in the same manner as if the wages were paid by the predecessor employer.[5]

The credit will not be determined with respect to remuneration paid by an employer to an employee for services performed by that employee for another person, unless the amount reasonably expected to be received by the employer for those services from that other person exceeds the remuneration paid.[4]

---

(3) § 17053.7(a); (b); (d).
(4) § 17053.7(h).

(5) Unemployment Ins Cd § 328.

OBSERVATION Unlike the federal provisions, however, the employer may deduct the salaries on which the credit is computed, in addition to taking the credit against the net tax.

TAX TIP California does not provide for a carryback or carryover of the excess credits not usable in the taxable year.

Payments for services during wage disputes. "Wages" do not include these payments.

The Employment Development Department, on any applicant's request, that, at time of hiring, applicant was a registrant under the Greater Avenues of Independence Act of 1985.[5]

OBSERVATION A partner of an employer partnership will receive the credit from the partnership and use it as an offset against the tax on his own Individual Income Tax Return.

Duration of credit. The credit expires 12–31–93.[6]

¶ 150 Renter's Credit

The renter's credit has been suspended for tax years beginning on or after January 1, 1993 through tax year 1995. For tax years beginning on or after January 1, 1996, the credits will be allowed without reference to the taxpayers' adjusted gross income. The credit is $120 for married spouses filing jointly, heads of households, and surviving spouses, and $60 for all other qualified renters.[7]

A married couple filing separate returns may divide the credit equally or either spouse may take the entire amount. Any individual who is a non-resident for any part of taxable year can claim credits at the rate of 1/12 for each full month of residence. If both of the spouses are residents for only part of the year, the credit shall be divided equally between them and each will be allowed 1/12 of the credit for each full month of residence in California. If one is a resident for the entire taxable year and the other is a nonresident for all or part of the year, the resident person will be allowed one-half of the credit and the nonresident person will be allowed one half of the credit apportioned according to the number of months he or she is a resident of the state. If the husband and wife lived apart and resided in California for the entire taxable year, each may claim one half of the credit if they qualify, but there is no option to allow one or the other to take the full credit. The credit is applied against the tax computed on the return after deducting all other credits. Any refund of credit is excluded from gross income. A claim for refund will be denied, even though the return is timely filed, if the claim is filed more than four years after the due date. If the filing of the return is more than four years delinquent, the credit will be allowed to the extent it offsets tax liabil-

---

(6) § 17053.7(g).

(7) § 17053.5, as amended by Stats. 1994, c. 144.

ity. The renter's credit is claimed by attaching Schedule H to the individual income tax return, FTB Form 540, or by completing part II of Form 540A.

Qualified renter. "Qualified renter" means an individual who (1) was a resident of the state and (2) rented and occupied premises in California that constituted his or her principal place of residence during at least 50% of the taxable year. *The term does not include:* (1) an individual who, for more than 50% of the taxable year, rented and occupied premises exempt from property taxes, except that an individual, otherwise qualified, will be deemed qualified renter if the individual or landlord pays possessory interest taxes, or the owner of premises makes a payment in lieu of property taxes substantially equivalent to the property taxes paid on properties of comparable market value; (2) an individual whose principal place of residence for more than 50% of the taxable year is with any other person who claimed such individual as a dependent for income tax purposes; (3) an individual, or spouse of that individual, granted a homeowners' property tax exemption for the taxable year. This rule does not apply to an individual whose spouse was granted such exemption, but who maintained a separate residence for the entire taxable year.

Military personnel who are not residents of California do not qualify for the renter's credit. However, if the military person's spouse enters California to stay during the tour of duty of the military person, the non-military spouse is considered to be a resident and may claim the renter's credit during the months spent in California if otherwise qualified.

If credits exceed tax liability, qualified renters may credit excess against other amounts due. The balance, if any, will be refunded.

¶ 151 **Commercial Solar Energy System Credit**

For taxable years beginning on or after 1–1–90 and before 1–1–94, there is allowed as a credit against the amount of net tax (as defined in Rev & TC § 17039) an amount equal to 10% of the cost of a solar energy system installed on premises, used for commercial purposes, which are located in California and which are owned by the taxpayer during the taxable year. For purposes of taxpayers who lease a solar energy system, the tax credit shall apply only to the principal recovery portion of lease payments for the term of the lease not to exceed 10 years, which are made during the taxable year, and to the amounts which are expended on the purchased portion of the solar energy system, including installation charges, during the taxable year.[8] The commercial solar electric system credit is claimed on FTB Form 3556.

When claimed. The solar energy tax credit shall be claimed on the state income tax return for the taxable year in which the solar energy system was installed. The solar energy tax credit may not be claimed for any solar energy system with a generating capacity in excess of 30 megawatts for any taxable year for which the Internal Revenue Code does not allow at least a

---

(8) 17052.5.

10% tax credit for solar energy systems with a generating capacity in excess of 30 megawatts that is equivalent in scope to the credit available under the IRC for the 1989 taxable year. A taxpayer who claimed the solar energy tax credit in the state income tax return for the taxable year in which the solar energy system was installed may claim the credit in subsequent years for additions to the system or additional systems by the amount prescribed in subdivision (a).

Cost reduced by grant of public entity. For purposes of computing the credit, the cost of any solar energy system eligible for the credit shall be reduced by any grant provided by a public entity for that system.

Basis reduced by credit and grant of utility or public agency. The basis of any system for which a credit is allowed shall be reduced by the amount of the credit and the amount of any grant provided by a utility or public agency for the solar energy system. The basis adjustment shall be made for the taxable year for which the credit is allowed.

More than one owner. With the exception of a husband and wife, if there is more than one owner of a premises on which a solar energy system is installed, each owner is eligible to receive the solar energy tax credit in proportion to his or her ownership interests in the premises. In the case of a husband or wife who files a separate return, the credit may be taken by either or equally divided between them. In the case of a partnership, the solar energy tax credit may be divided between the partners pursuant to a written partnership agreement.

Carryovers. When the credit allowed under this section exceeds the "net tax" for the taxable year, that portion of the credit which exceeds the "net tax" may be carried over to the "net tax" in succeeding taxable years, until the credit is used. The credit is applied first to the earliest years possible.

No credit-expenditures claimed as tax credit for energy conservation measures. No tax credit may be claimed under this section for any expenditures which have been otherwise claimed as a tax credit for the current or any prior taxable year as energy conservation measures under this part.

Lessees of solar energy system. Taxpayers who lease a solar energy system installed on premises in California receive a credit, if the lessee can confirm, if necessary, by a written document signed by the lessor that (1) the lessor irrevocably elects not to claim a state tax credit for the solar energy system, and (2) if the system is installed in a locality served by a municipal solar utility, that the lessor holds a valid permit from the municipal solar utility. Leasing requirements may be established by the State Energy Resources Conservation and Development Commission as part of the solar energy system eligibility criteria.

Guidelines and criteria. The State Energy Resources Conservation and Development Commission is required to establish limits on eligible costs

¶ 151

of solar energy systems in terms of dollars per kilowatt and guidelines and criteria for solar energy systems which shall be eligible for the credit provided by this section. These guidelines and criteria may include, but are not limited to, minimum requirements for safety, cost-effectiveness in terms of dollars per kilowatt, market readiness, reliability and durability. Any solar energy system with a generating capacity in excess of 100 kilowatts is eligible for the credit only if the owner of that system first obtains a finding from the Commission that the system is eligible for the credit under the guidelines and criteria established. Any solar energy system certified by the Commission under Public Resources Code, Division 15, Chapter 6 (starting with § 25500) is deemed eligible for the credit. The Franchise Tax Board shall prescribe such regulations as may be necessary to carry out the purposes of this section. The State Energy Resources Conservation and Development Commission may obtain a claimant's social security or taxpayer identification number through its tax credit application and certification process in order to identify a qualifying taxpayer to the Franchise Tax Board. This information may be used solely for state tax administrative purposes.

Start of construction or making of expenditures within tax year. Any taxpayer that, during or by the end of the tax year, has started construction or made expenditures in connection with the installation of a solar energy system, is eligible for a tax credit to the extent of the cost paid or incurred in that tax year for construction and expenditures. The installation must be completed by the end of the sixth month of the taxpayer's next tax year.

¶ 152   Excess State Disability Insurance

Employees who work for more than one employer during the year may have paid more than the maximum state disability insurance, through overwithholding. The maximum state disability payment for 1993 and 1994 is 1.3% of $31,767. Any amounts withheld in excess of such totals are returned to the employee through the medium of his receiving a credit against his California Personal Income Tax.[9]

If more than the maximum was withheld by one employer, the employee cannot claim the excess as a credit against his income tax return but must contact that employer to receive a refund.

The State Disability Insurance deducted by the employer must be shown on the W–2 Forms attached to the employee's return in order for such employee to get the credit for the excess.

For married couples filing joint returns, the excess credit must be computed separately for each spouse.

---

(9) § 17061.

¶ 153   **Low-emission Motor Vehicle Credit**

For taxable years beginning on or after 1–1–91 and before 1–1–96 a credit is allowed against the net tax equal to 55% of the costs, including installation, but excluding interest charges, of a device designed to and installed to convert a motor vehicle, that is intended to be used on the public roads and highways of the state, to a low-emission motor vehicle. The credit also applies to 15% of the purchase price of a nonrecreational motor vehicle that is low-emission and is intended to be used on private roads, private school campuses, or commercial or industrial worksites in California.[10] The credit can be claimed in the taxable year the device is installed. The credit cannot exceed $1,000 per automobile, motorcycle, or two person passenger vehicle, or $3,500 for a vehicle whose weight is in excess of 5,750 lbs. Credit will also be allowed for the differential cost of a new motor vehicle which is equipped from the factory to operate as a low-emission vehicle and is certified by the state board (the Air Resources Board) to be a low-emission motor vehicle. Differential cost is determined by the California Energy Commission. To qualify for the credit, all vehicles must be registered in the state. The taxpayer or partnership must make application to the California Energy Commission which must certify that (1) the device or vehicle qualifies for the credit under Rev & TC § 17052.11; and (2) credit allocation is available. The application for credit allocation and certification must contain all the information required by the Energy Commission. Taxpayers must notify the Commission that the device or vehicle has actually been purchased. Copy of the Commission certificate must be retained. The Franchise Tax Board can require taxpayers to make the certification available. A partnership must disclose on its return the partner's social security number or identification number, and the name of each partner receiving a credit allocation, and the amount of the allocation. S corporations must disclose similar information. Guidelines and criteria are to be established by the California Energy Commission. The credit can be carried over to subsequent years if it exceeds the net tax in the year the credit is earned.

The differential costs for which the credit may be claimed must be reduced by those costs for which a federal credit is allowed under IRC § 30 for qualified electric vehicles. The low-emission vehicles credit is claimed on FTB Form 3554.

¶ 154   **Salmon And Steelhead Trout Habitat Credit**

Beginning January 1, 1995, taxpayers will be entitled to a credit of 10% of the qualified costs paid or incurred by the taxpayer or partnership for salmon and steelhead trout habitat restoration and improvement projects. The credit is allowed for the taxable year in which the expense for the habitat restoration or improvement project is paid or incurred. The California Department of Fish and Game must certify that the requirements as set forth in the Code have been met. These conditions include: (1) that the

---

(10) § 17052.11.

project meets the objective of the Salmon, Steelhead Trout, and Anadromous Fisheries Program Act of California, (2) the project provides employment to persons previously employed in the commercial fishing or forest products industry within a county with a rate of unemployment that is higher than the mean annual unemployment rate as specified in the Code, (3) the work to be undertaken in not otherwise required to be carried out purusant to the Public Resources Code of the state of California, and (4) the project does not involve certain activities as listed in Rev & TC § 17053.66(b)(4). Carryover provisions are provided. The credit will remain in effect until December 1, 2000.[11]

¶ 155 **Head of Household and Dependent Parent Credits**

A credit against net tax is allowed to a qualified joint custody head of household for 30% of the net tax. The credit is also available to a qualified taxpayer with a dependent parent. The Franchise Tax Board must index this credit for each taxable year.[12] For 1994, the amount is the lesser of $259 or 30% of the net tax.

Qualified joint custody head of household and qualified taxpayer. "Qualified individual" means each of the following: (1) a qualified joint custody head of household; (2) a qualified taxpayer.

"Qualified taxpayer" means an individual who meets all of following requirements: (1) is married and files a separate return; (2) during the last six months of the taxable year, taxpayer's spouse was not a member of taxpayer's household; (3) maintains a household, whether or not the taxpayer's home, that constitutes the principle place of abode of dependent mother or father of taxpayer for the taxable year; (4) furnishes over half the cost of maintaining the household during that year.

"Qualified joint custody head of household" is an individual who meets all of the following requirements: (1) is not married at the close of the taxable year, or files a separate return and does not have his or her spouse as a member of his or her household during the entire taxable year; (2) maintains as his or her home a household which constitutes for the taxable year the principal place of abode for a qualifying child, for no less than 146 days of the taxable year but no more than 219 days of the taxable year, under a decree of dissolution or separate maintenance, or under a written agreement between the parents prior to the issuance of a decree of dissolution or separate maintenance where the proceedings have been initiated; (3) furnishes over one-half the cost of maintaining the household during the taxable year; (4) does not qualify as a head of household under Rev & TC § 17042 or as a surviving spouse under Rev & TC § 17046.

"Qualifying child" means a son, stepson, daughter, or stepdaughter of the taxpayer or a descendant of a son or daughter of the taxpayer, but if that

---

(11) § 17053.66, as added by Stats. 1994, c. 1296, § 1.

(12) § 17054.5.

son, stepson, daughter, stepdaughter, or descendant is married at the close of the taxpayer's taxable year, only if the taxpayer is entitled to a credit for the taxable year for that person under Rev & TC § 17054.

Qualified senior head of household. For taxable years starting on or after 1–1–90, a credit for a qualified senior head of household will be allowed in an amount equal to 2% of taxable income. For 1994 the credit cannot exceed $792. "Qualified senior head of household" means an individual who meets all of the following: (1) attained the age of 65 before the close of the taxable year; (2) qualified as head of household under Rev & TC § 17042 for either of the two taxable years immediately preceding the taxable year by providing a household for a qualifying individual who died during either of the two taxable years immediately preceding the taxable year; and (3) whose adjusted gross income for the 1994 tax year does not exceed $42,031.[13]

¶ 156 Low-income Housing Credit

A California low-income housing credit is allowed in an amount determined by IRC § 42, subject to certain California modifications outlined below. Originally the federal and California credits were to expire on June 30, 1992. The federal *Revenue Reconciliation Act of 1993* however reinstated the federal credit retroactively to July 1, 1992. As Rev & TC § 17058(q) provides that the California credit will remain in effect during the same periods that the federal credit is operative, California automatically reinstated the low-income housing credit retroactively to July 1, 1992. The low-income housing credit is one of those credits that may reduce tax below the tentative minimum tax.

The California credit is claimed on Form 3521, which must be attached to the return together with a Certificate of Final Award of California Low-Income Housing Tax Credits (Form 3521A) issued by the Mortgage Bond and Tax Credit Allocation Committee.

Note: Due to the retroactive reinstatement of the California low-income housing credit, refund claims may be appropriate for the 1992 tax year.

California Tax Credit Allocation Committee authorizations. California requires that credit allocated to a housing sponsor be authorized by this committee based on the project's need for credit for economic feasibility. It is the intent of the Legislature that the amount of the state low-income housing tax credit allocated to a project shall not exceed an amount in addition to the federal credit that is necessary for the financial feasibility of the project and its viability throughout the extended use period.

The low-income housing project must be located in California, and must satisfy either of the following requirements: (1) the housing sponsor of the project must have been allocated a credit for federal income tax purposes by the Committee under IRC § 42; or (2) the project must qualify for credit under IRC § 42(h)(4)(B), providing for special rule where 70% or more of the

---

(13) § 17054.7.

building is financed with exempt bonds subject to a volume cap. The committee can't require fees for credit under California law in addition to the fees required for credit application under IRC § 42. The committee must certify to the housing sponsor the amount of state tax credit to which a taxpayer is entitled for each credit period. In the case of a partnership or S corporation, the housing sponsor must provide a copy of the California Tax Credit Allocation Committee certification to the taxpayer who must attach it to the return. Special rule applies to any government assisted building, and any building purchased by a qualified nonprofit organization that agrees to satisfy the requirements of IRC § 42(g) for the useful life of the building. All elections made by the taxpayer pursuant to IRC § 42 apply to California. No credit shall be allocated to buildings located in a difficult development area or a qualified census tract, as defined in IRC § 42, for which the eligible basis of a new building or the rehabilitation expenditure of an existing building is 130% of that amount pursuant to IRC § 42(d)(5)(C), unless the committee reduces the amount of federal credit, with approval of the applicant, so that the combined federal and state amount does not exceed total credits allowed by § 17058 and IRC § 42(b), computed without regard to IRC § 42(d)(5)(C).

Applicable percentage. California modifies IRC § 42(b) to provide (1) in case of qualified income housing placed in service by the housing sponsor during 1987, applicable percentage means 9% for the first three years, and 3% for the fourth year for new buildings, whether or not the building is federally subsidized, and for existing buildings (federal is 9% for new buildings not federally subsidized, or 4% for new building federally subsidized, and existing buildings); (2) in case of any qualified low-income building placed in service after 1989 that is a new building not federally subsidized, the applicable percentage means either (a) for each of the first three years, the percentage prescribed by the Secretary of the Treasury for new buildings which are not federally subsidized for the taxable year, determined in accordance with IRC § 42(b)(2) instead of the percentage prescribed in IRC § 42(b)(1)(A), or (b) for the fourth year the difference between 30% and the sum of the applicable percentages for the first three years. In the case of a qualified low-income building that receives an allocation after 1989, and that is a new building that is federally subsidized, or an existing building that is at risk of conversion, applicable percentage means: (1) for the first three years, the percentage set by the Secretary of the Treasury for new buildings federally subsidized for the taxable year; (2) for the fourth year, the difference between 13% and the sum of the applicable percentages for the first three years. "At risk of conversion" is defined by § 17058(c)(4).

Qualified low-income housing project. California modifies IRC § 42(c)(2) by adding the following requirements: (1) the taxpayer must be entitled to receive a cash distribution from the operations of the project, after funding required reserves, which, at the election of the taxpayer, is equal to (a) an amount not to exceed 8% of the lessor of the owner equity which shall include the amount of capital contributions actually paid to the housing sponsor, and shall not include any amounts until they are paid on an investor note, or 20% of the adjusted basis of the building as of the close of the first taxable year of the credit period; or (b) the amount of the cash flow from those units in the building that are not low-income units. For purposes of computing cash flow, operating costs are allocated using "floor space fraction." Any amount allowed to be distributed under (a) that is not available for distribution during the first five years of the compliance period may be accumulated and distributed at any time during the first 15 years of the compliance period, but not thereafter. The limitation on return shall apply to the partners if the housing sponsor is a partnership and in the aggregate to shareholders if the housing sponsor is an S corporation. (2) The housing sponsor must apply any cash available for distribution in excess of the above amount to reduce rent on rent-restricted units, or increase number of rent-restricted units subject to IRC § 42(g)(1) tests.

Credit period. California uses a 4-year period instead of the federal 10-year period. California does not apply the special federal rule under IRC § 42(f)(2) for the first taxable year of the period. California modified the IRC § 42(f)(3) rule on the increase in qualified basis after the first year of the credit period. If, as of the close of any taxable year after the first year of the credit period, the qualified basis of any building exceeds the qualified basis as of the close of the first year of the credit period of the credits, the housing sponsor to the extent of its tax credit allocation shall be eligible for a credit on the excess in an amount equal to the applicable percentage determined for state purposes of the four-year period starting with the later of the taxable year in which the increase occurs.

Qualified low-income housing project. California adopts the definition in IRC § 42(g)(1) providing that taxpayer can elect either 20–50 or 40–60 test for rent restriction and income. The state also adopts the definition of rent-restricted units in IRC § 42(g)(2); rules on date for meeting requirements on restriction and income in IRC § 42(g)(3); rules on determination of low-income qualification in IRC § 42(g)(4); and election after compliance period in IRC § 42(g)(5).

Limitation on aggregate credit allowable on projects located in—state. California adopts IRC § 42(h)(1) limiting the credit to that allocated to the building. California does not adopt IRC § 42(h)(2); instead, the total amount for the four-year period of the housing credit dollars allocated in a calendar year to any building reduces the aggregate housing credit dollar amount of the California Tax Credit Allocation Committee for the calendar year in which the allocation is made. California does not adopt IRC § 42(h)(3)–(5), (6)(E)(i)(II), (6)(F), (6)(G), (6)(I), (7) and (8). Notwithstanding Rev & TC § 17058(m), aggregate housing credit dollar amount allocable annually by Committee is an amount equal to the sum of the following: (1) $35 million; (2) the unused housing credit ceiling, if any, for the preceding calendar years; (3) the amount of the housing credit ceiling returned in the calendar year. The amount in (3) equals the housing credit dollar amount previously allo-

¶ **156**

cated to a project that does not become a qualified low-income project within the period required by § 17058, or to any project with respect to which an allocation is canceled by mutual consent to the Committee and the allocation recipient.

Definitions and special rules of IRC § 42(i).   The definitions and special rules under IRC § 42(i) are adopted, but the state uses a 30-yr. compliance period instead of the federal 18-yr. period.

Recapture of credit.   California does not follow IRC § 42(j). It provides that a regulatory agreement be entered into between the Committee and the housing sponsor as to enforcement of state provisions on low income housing credit. The agreement may be subordinated, when necessary, to any lien or encumbrance of banks or financial institutions. The regulatory agreement entered into pursuant to Health & Safety Cd § 50199.14(f) shall apply, subject to specified conditions.

Carryovers.   Carryovers of excess credits are provided, and may extend beyond the expiration date.

Aggregate amount of tax credits.   The aggregate granted by Rev & TC § 17058 and 23610.5 cannot exceed $35 million per year. The committee cannot authorize any credit if the total authorized in any year under both Bank and Corporation and Personal Income Tax laws exceeds $35 million. The aggregate granted under Rev & TC § 23610.5 in 1989 could exceed $35 million by an amount equal to the unallocated credit from 1987 and 1988.

Acceleration of credit—election not applicable.   California has not adopted the provisions of federal P.L. 101–508, § 11407(c), relating to the election to accelerate the low-income housing credit.

Sunset date of credit.   Rev & TC § 17058 will remain in effect for as long as IRC § 42 remains in effect.[13a]

¶ 157   Other Tax Credits

Estimated taxes.   Estimated taxes paid are treated as advance payment on account of income taxes imposed.[14]

Withholding taxes.   Personal income taxes withheld under Rev & TC §§ 18662 (withholding at source) 18666 (amounts paid by partnership to foreign partners) and § 13020 of the Unemployment Insurance Code (salaries and other compensation) are allowed as credits against tax to the recipients of the income. In case of a partnership filing a group return as the agent for electing nonresident partners under Rev & TC § 18535, the amount withheld under Rev & TC §§ 18662 or 18666 must be allowed as a credit attributable to the partnership on the group return for the taxable year the tax was withheld.[15]

(13a) § 17058.
(14) § 19007.

(15) § 19002, 18662, 18666; Unemployment Ins Cd § 13020.

¶ 158   **Table of Tax Credits**

This table has been prepared principally for comparison with the federal credits available. The information is necessarily brief and therefore should not be considered to include all of the data and limitations related to each of the credits. The notations in brackets below the name of the credit show whether the credit applies to individuals (IND.), estates and trusts (E&T), and corporations (CORP.).

Credit	California	Federal
Alcohol Fuels	None	60¢ a gallon credit for alcohol of at least 190 proof (45¢ for alcohol between 150 and 190 proof) to persons producing alcohol or using in a trade or business. [IRC § 40.]
Qualified parent (IND)	For taxable years starting on or after 1–1–91 and before 1–1–94, credit is $1,000. For 1993, credit must be reduced by $200 for each $1,000 or fraction by which qualified parent's adjusted gross income (AGI) for taxable year exceeds $42,476, if qualified parent is married filing jointly, or surviving spouse; if qualified parent is head of household, credit is reduced by $200 for each $1,000 or fraction that AGI exceeds $30,264. [§ 17052.20.]	None
Employer's child care (IND.) (CORP.)	30% of either or both of (1) cost of start-up expenses of establishing program or constructing facility to be used by employees' children; (2) cost paid or incurred for contributions to information and referral services. Limit is $30,000 for any taxable year. [§ 17052.17; 23617.] Repealed 12–31–98.	None

Credit	California	Federal
Dependent care (IND.) (CORP.)	50% (30% for taxable years beginning on or after 1–1–95) of cost paid or incurred for contributions to qualified care plan for dependent under 15 (for taxable years beginning 1–1–95, under 12 years old) of taxpayer's employee. Limit: $600 ($360 for taxable years beginning on or after 1–1–95) for contribution to full-time qualified care plan; $300 for contribution to part-time plan. [§ 17052.18; 23617.5.] Repealed 12–31–98.	None
Adoption costs (IND.)	For taxable years beginning on or after 1–1–94, a credit is allowed for 50% of adoption costs of a minor child who is a citizen or legal resident of the U.S. and is in custody of a California public agency, up to $2,500 per child. [§ 17052.25, as added by Stats. 1994, c. 827, § 1.]	None
Credit for the Elderly (IND.)	None	15% of eligible amount reduced by Soc. Sec., Railroad Retirement, V.A. administered benefits; or otherwise excluded income. Also reduced by half of AGI in excess of $7,500 for singles; $10,000 for married filing joint; $5,000 for married filing separately. Different rules for over and under 65. [IRC § 22.]
Personal—Exemption and Dependents (IND.)	Single Married—joint Married—separate Head of Household Blind Dependent Over 65	None
Joint Custody Head of Household; Dependent Parent Credit (IND.)	Credit is 30% of net tax. It is allowed, to qualified joint custody head of household and qualified taxpayer. For 1994, $259 or 30%. [§ 17054.5.]	None

Credit	California	Federal
Qualified senior head of household (IND.)	For taxable years starting on or after 1–1–90, a credit is allowed in an amount equal to 2% of taxable income. Indexed credit for 1994 is $792. Qualifications: (1) 65 or over by end of taxable year; (2) qualified as head of household under § 17042 for either of two taxable years immediately preceding; (3) adjusted gross income for 1994 tax year cannot exceed $42,032. [§ 17054.7.]	None
Earned Income Credit (IND.)	None	Applies to low-income worker, married, surviving spouse or head of household, who maintains a home in the U.S. for at least one child. Credit is 14% of earned income up to $5,714. Credit can't exceed excess of above amount, over 10% of AGI, or earned income, if greater, that exceeds $9,000 AGI. [IRC § 32.] Indexed.
Excess Employee's Payroll Tax. (IND.)	Employees who work for more than one employer and have paid more than the maximum SDI. [§ 17061.]	Same for excess withholding FICA taxes. [IRC § 31(b).]
Fuel Production from Unconventional Sources	None	Credit of $3 for each quantity of fuel that yields energy equal to 5.8 million BTU is allowed the producer. Sources include shale, tar sands, coal seams, processed wood fuels, etc. [IRC § 29.]
Gasoline and Special Fuels	None	Credit for excise taxes paid on gasoline or oil and special fuels when used for farming off-the-highway uses, and for buses and public transportation. [IRC § 34.]
Investment Tax Credit	Eff. 1–1–94, 6% of qualified purchases for use in manufacturing [§ 17053.49, added by Stats. 1993, c.881.]	Credit of 10% for qualified investment in Sec. 38 property as well as 10% or 20% for qualified rehabilitation expenditures. [IRC § 46.]

Credit	California	Federal
Jobs Tax Credit (IND.) (CORP.)	Employer gets credit for 10% of wages paid to employee certified by the Employment Development Department to meet the requirements of Sec. 328 of California Unemployment Insurance Code. [§ 17053.7; 23621.]	Targeted Jobs Tax Credit—40% of the first $6,000 of the qualified first-year wages; also 40% of $3,000 wages paid to certain summer jobs. [IRC § 51.]
Enterprise zones—jobs tax credit (IND.) (CORP)	Employer doing business in zone can take credit for 50% of qualified wages in year 1, 40% in year 2, 30% in year 3, 20% in year 4, and 10% in year 5. [§ 17053.8; 23612.]	None
Enterprise zones—employee wage credit (IND.)	Qualified employee is allowed credit against tax for 5% of qualified wages [§ 17053.9.]	None
Program areas—jobs tax credit (IND.) (CORP)	Qualified businesses in program areas, credit against tax for hiring qualified employee, if unemployed at least 6 months before hiring: 50% of qualified wages in first yr. of employment; 40% of qualified wages in second yr.; 30% of qualified wages in third yr.; 20% of qualified wages in fourth yr.; 10% of qualified wages in fifth yr.; if employee is unemployed at least three months, but less than 6 months before hiring, credit is 25% of qualified wages for first yr.; 40% of qualified wages for second yr.; 30% of qualified wages for third yr.; 20% of qualified wages for fourth yr.; and 10% of qualified wages for fifth yr. [§ 17053.11; 23623.]	None
Low income housing (IND.) (CORP.)	Similar to IRC § 42 but modified by Calif. Conforms to IRC § 42 as set forth in Revenue Reconciliation Act of 1993.	9% of qualified basis of qualified low-income bldg., if not federally subsidized; 4% for building subsidized, and existing buildings. [IRC § 42.] Federal credit period is ten years starting with year placed in service.

Credit	California	Federal
Regulated Investment Company Capital Gains Tax Credit to Shareholder	None	Shareholder can take credit for tax on long-term capital gains retained by the investment company, provided the taxpayer includes the gain in taxable income. [IRC § 852(b)(3)(d).]
Renter's Credit (IND.)	Suspended for tax years 1993 through 1995. For taxable years beginning on or after 1–1–96, a credit of $120 is allowed to married spouses filing jointly, heads of households, and surviving spouses, and $60 for all others. [§ 17053.5, as amended by Stats. 1994, c. 144.]	None
Research Expenditures (IND.) (CORP.)	Similar to federal, but applicable percentage is 8% of excess qualified research expenses over base amount. Includes only research conducted in California. [§ 17052.12.; 23609]	Expenditures in a trade or business for qualified research expenses provide a credit of 20% of the excess of such expenditures for the year over the average base period research expense for the three prior years, and 20% of specified basic research payments. [IRC § 41.]
Salmon and Steelhead Trout (IND.)(CORP.)	Credit is allowed for 10% of qualified costs of habitat restoration and improvement, effective for costs paid or incurred on or after 1–1–95 and before 12–1–2000. [§ 17053.66; 23666.]	None
Ride-Sharing Credit (IND.) (E&T) (CORP.)	Employer's sponsoring ride-sharing incentive programs get 20% credit of cost of purchase, lease or contracting for, company buses, vans, or motor pool vehicles. 20% of cost of subsidized transit passes. Nonemployer sponsored van pool programs equal to 40% of subscriptions, not in excess of $480. Husband and wife can each take $480 credit. [§ 17053; 17053.1; 23605]. On or after 1–1–89, and before 1–1–96.	None

Credit	California	Federal
Commercial solar energy credit (IND.) (CORP.)	Credit of 10% of cost of solar energy system installed on premises used for commercial purposes in California. Expired 12–31–93. [§ 17052.5; 23601.5]	None
Taxes Paid Other States (IND.)	Credit is allowed against California tax for taxes paid to other states on "double-taxed" income to a maximum based on computation relating the income taxed to the total income taxed by California. [§ 18001–18002.]	Federal Foreign Tax Credit is similar on taxes paid to foreign countries on income which is also taxed by the United States. [IRC § 33; 901.]
Vehicle conversion to low-emission vehicle (IND.)	For taxable years starting on or after 1–1–91 and before 1–1–95, credit is allowed in amount of 55% of the costs, including installation, but excluding interest charges, of a device to convert a motor vehicle intended for use on public roads and highways, to a low-emission vehicle. Credit also applies to 15% of purchase price of low-emission nonrecreational motor vehicle intended to be used on private roads, private school campuses, or commercial or industrial worksites. Credit can be claimed in year device is installed. Credit cannot exceed $1,000 per automobile, or $3,500 for vehicle whose weight is in excess of 5,750 lbs. [§ 17052.11, as amended by Stats. 1993, c. 873, § 2.5.]	None
Program areas and enterprise zones—credit against tax for sales or use tax paid on purchase of machinery and machinery parts (IND.) (CORP.)	Qualified businesses in program area can take credit for amount of sales or use tax paid or incurred in purchase of machinery and machinery parts used for fabricating, processing, assembling and manufacturing up to value of $1 million [§ 17052.13; 23612.]	None

¶ **158**

Credit	California	Federal
Recycling equipment (IND.) (CORP.)	40% of cost of qualified property, up to $625,000, purchased and placed in service, on or after 1–1–89 and before 1–1–94 [§ 17052.14; 23612.5]	None
Prison inmate labor (IND.) (CORP.)	Credit is allowed for 10% of the amount of wages paid to each prisoner employed in a joint venture program established under California Penal Code. [§ 17053.6; 23624.]	None

¶ 159   Enterprise Zones—Credits

Employers' credit. For taxable years starting on or after designation of an enterprise zone, taxpayers doing business in that zone can take a credit against tax for: (1) 50% of qualified wages in the first year of employment; (2) 40% of such wages in the second year of employment; (3) 30% in the third year of employment; (4) 20% in the fourth year of employment; and (5) 10% in the fifth year of employment. "Qualified wages" means wages paid or incurred by employer during taxable year to qualified disadvantaged individuals. Term means that portion of hourly wages that does not exceed 150% of minimum wage. Qualified wages does not include amounts paid or incurred after the enterprise zone designation is terminated.

"Qualified disadvantaged individual" means an individual who is: (1) a qualified employee; (2) hired by the employer after the designation of the area as an enterprise zone; and (3) is any of the following: (a) an individual who is eligible for services under the federal Job Training Partnership Act (29 USC 1501 et seq.); (b) an individual eligible for voluntary or mandatory registration under Greater Avenues for Independence Act of 1985 (Welfare & Institutions Cd., Div. 9, Pt. 3, Ch. 2, Art. 3.2); (c) any individual who is eligible under the federal Targeted Jobs Tax Credit program as long as that program is in effect. The employer must obtain, and have available for the FTB, certification that the employee qualifies as set forth in (3) above.

"Qualified employee" is an individual at least 90% of whose services for the taxpayer during the taxable year are directly related to the trade or business of the taxpayer located in an enterprise zone, and who performs at least 50% of those services during the taxable year in the enterprise zone.

Enterprise employers credit must be reduced by jobs tax credit allowed under Rev & TC § 17053.7. It must also be reduced by IRC § 51 targeted jobs credit.

In addition, any deduction otherwise allowed by the Personal Income Tax Law for wages or salaries paid or incurred by the taxpayer upon which the credit is based must be reduced by the amount of the credit.

The credit may be carried over, when it exceeds net tax, to succeeding taxable years for number of taxable years in which enterprise zone designation is operative, or 15 years, if longer, until it is used.

The credit in any taxable year can't exceed the amount of tax that would be imposed on income attributed to the business activities of the taxpayer within the enterprise zone. The amount of attributed income will be determined under a factor apportionment formula method provided under the allocation and apportionment provisions of UDITPA (Rev & TC §§ 25120–25141). A two-factor formula of property and payroll will apply for taxable years starting on or after 1–1–91, and ending on or before 1–1–96.[16]

The taxpayer claiming this credit must also maintain and have available for the FTB, the average number of full-time (defined as 35 or more hours per week), part-time or seasonal employees working within the enterprise zone for the year the credit is claimed, and for the "base year" means the first taxable year beginning on or after January 1, 1995, or the first year the credit is claimed.

The enterprise zone employee credit is claimed on FTB Form 3553. The credit for sales/use tax paid on equipment purchases used in an enterprise zone is claimed on FTB Form 3805Z. The Franchise Tax Board also publishes a separate booklet detailing the deductions and credits that businesses may earn if they are operating in an enterprise zone or program area.

Qualified employees. Qualified employees are allowed credit against tax for 5% of their qualified wages. "Qualified employee" is an individual: (1) defined as such under the provisions of Rev & TC § 17053.8 governing employer's credit; and (2) who is not an employee of the federal government, California, or any of its political subdivisions. "Qualified wages" don't include any compensation received from the federal government, California or its political subdivisions. The term has the meaning given to "wages" by IRC § 3306(b) attributable to services performed for an employer with respect to which an employee is a qualified employee in an amount not in excess of the 150% of IRC § 3306(b) dollar limit.

For each dollar of income received over qualified wages, the credit will be reduced by 9¢.

The amount of credit in any taxable year can't exceed the amount of tax that would be imposed on income attributed to employment within the enterprise zone, as if such income was all of taxpayer's net taxable income.[17] The credit sunsets 1–1–96.

---

(16) § 17053.8.   **(17)** § 17053.9.

Sales or use tax credit. A person or entity engaged in a trade or business within a designated enterprise zone can take credit for amount of sales or use tax paid or incurred in the purchase of qualified property. "Qualified property" means machinery and machinery parts used for fabricating, processing, assembling and manufacturing, and machinery and machinery parts used to produce renewable energy resources, or air or water pollution control mechanisms, up to a value of $1 million. The property must be used exclusively in the enterprise zone. A use tax credit will only be allowed if qualified property of a comparable quality or price is not timely available for purchase in-state. Excess credit can be carried over to succeeding years until used. A basis increase for property, otherwise required by IRC § 164(a), can't be made by a taxpayer who takes this credit. The credit can't exceed the amount of tax that would be imposed on income attributed to the business activities of taxpayer within the enterprise zone, as if that attributed income represented the taxable income of taxpayer. The amount of attributed income will be determined under UDITPA. A two factor formula of property and payroll applies from 1–1–91 through 12–31–96.[18]

¶ 160 **Program Areas—Credits**

Qualified employees. Qualified businesses engaged in the active conduct of trade or business in a program area during the period of its designation as a neighborhood economic or targeted economic development area will be allowed a credit against tax for hiring a qualified employee. The credit for each qualified employee who has been unemployed for at least six months before being employed is an amount equal to the sum of each of the following: (1) 50% for qualified wages in the first year of employment; (2) 40% for qualified wages in the second year of employment; (3) 30% for qualified wages in the third year of employment; (4) 20% for qualified wages in the fourth year of employment; and (5) 10% for qualified wages in the fifth year of employment. If a qualified employee has been unemployed for at least three and less than six months, the credit is 25% of qualified wages for the first year of employment; 40% of qualified wages for the second year of employment; 30% of qualified wages for the third year of employment; 20% of qualified wages in the fourth year of employment; and 10% of qualified wages in the fifth year of employment.

The credits which are earned by a taxpayer operating in a program zone are claimed on the FTB Form 3805Z.

The credit can be carried over to succeeding taxable years until used, but must be applied to the earliest years possible. It can't exceed the amount of tax on income that would be imposed on income attributed to the business activities within the program area as if it represented all of taxpayer's income. Attribution will be made under UDITPA rules. A two factor formula of property and payroll will apply from 1–1–91 through 12–31–96.

---

(18) § 17052.13.

The credit must be reduced by the credit allowed under Rev & TC § 17053.7, and the credit allowed under IRC § 51. In addition, any deduction otherwise allowed by the Personal Income Tax for wages and salaries incurred by the taxpayer upon which the credit is based shall be reduced by the amount of the credit.

"Qualified wages" means that portion of wages not in excess of 150% of the minimum wage paid or incurred by a qualified business during the taxable year to a qualified employee.

If the employment of any employee for whom qualified wages are taken into account in computing the credit is terminated by the taxpayer at any time during the first 270 days of employment, whether or not consecutive, or before the close of the 270th calendar day after the day in which the employee completes 90 days of employment with the taxpayer, the tax imposed for the income year of termination must be increased by the amount of the credit allowed for that taxable year, and all prior taxable years attributable to qualified wages. This increase will not be treated as a tax for the purpose of determining the amount of any allowable credit. Exceptions to the termination rule apply to employees who leave voluntarily, become disabled, are terminated for misconduct, replaced by other qualified employees, or discharged because a of substantial reduction in the taxpayer's trade or business operations.

"Qualified business" means a person, corporation or other entity certified by the city, county and town applying for a program area designation and the Trade and Commerce Agency that, during the period of the program area designation, is engaged in the active conduct of business in the program area, and has either: (1) an annual average of at least 50% of employees who are residents of a high density unemployment area; (2) has at least 30% of employees in such category, and has set up approved community service programs; or (3) is a joint venture between an existing business and a business set up by residents of a program area. Financial institutions may qualify. Percentage requirements on employment of residents of a high-density unemployment area are applicable only to employees that were hired within the 12 months immediately preceding the date the business seeks certification from the Trade and Commerce Agency and not to the entire workforce of the business. For purposes of Rev & TC § 17053.11 only, a business will be qualified if the Trade and Commerce Agency certifies that it meets the requirements of Govt. Cd § 7082.

"Qualified employee" means an employee who has been an unemployed resident of a high density unemployment area before being hired by a qualified business. Participation by a prospective employee in a state or federally funded job training or work demonstration program does not constitute employment, or effect the eligibility of an otherwise qualified employee. Qualified employee includes an otherwise qualified employee who is employed by a qualified business in the 90 days before its certification by the

Trade and Commerce Agency as a qualified business for purposes of becoming eligible for that certification.[19]

Sales or use tax credit. Qualified businesses in a program area can take a credit for the amount of sales or use tax paid or incurred in the purchase of qualified property. If the taxpayer has purchased property on which use tax is paid or incurred, the credit will be allowed only if qualified property of comparable quality and price is not timely available for purchase in-state. "Qualified property" means machinery and machinery parts used for fabricating, processing, assembling and manufacturing, and machinery and machinery parts used to produce renewable energy resources or air and water pollution control mechanisms, up to a value of $1 million. Excess credit can be carried over to later years until used. A basis increase required by IRC § 164(a) can't be made if the credit is taken. The credit can't exceed the amount of tax that would be due on income attributed to business activities in the program area, using allocation rules. For taxable years starting 1–1–91 and ending on or before 12–31–96, a two-factor formula of property and payroll will apply.[20]

¶ 161   Los Angeles Revitalization Zone–Hiring and Sales Tax Credits

A "Los Angeles Revitalization Zone" has been established in Los Angeles County and within cities that suffered from civil disturbances in April and May, 1992. Local jurisdictions are responsible for identifying and mapping business areas damaged during the civil disturbances. These designated zones must be approved by the Department of Commerce by January 1, 1993. In the event that the designated zones are later amended, the incentive programs identified below (e.g., hiring credits for construction workers and others, and the sales tax credit) become inoperative for the next following tax year. Prior credits are not lost retroactively, and any unused credits for periods prior to the amendment of the designated zone may continue to be carried forward.[21]

Hiring credits—construction workers. For each tax year beginning on or after 1–1–92 and before 1–1–98, a hiring credit is allowed to employers who hire construction workers who are residents of a "supportive residential area" equal to the sum of:

(1) for the period between May 1, 1992, and June 30, 1993, 100% of the wages not exceeding $6.38 per hour earned during that period by employees who were hired during that period, and

(2) for the next six month period, 75% of the wages not exceeding $6.38 per hour earned during that period by employees hired during that period, and

(3) for the next four years, 50% of the wages not exceeding $6.38 per hour earned during that period by employees hired during that period.

The credit is recaptured in the event of early termination in the same manner as credit is recaptured for Program Area Credits (see ¶ 160) except

---

(19) § 17053.11.
(20) § 17052.13.

(21) §§ 17052.15, 17053.10 & 17053.17, as amended by Stats. 1994, c. 756, § 2, 3, & 5.

that termination as a result of a contractual agreement won't result in recapture. No deduction is allowed for wages for which a credit is claimed. The amount of the credit in any taxable year can not exceed the amount of tax that would be imposed on income attributed to the business conducted in the "Los Angeles Revitalization Zone." Special rules are included for the determination of income earned in the Revitalization Zone. Carryovers are allowed for excess credits.

A "business zone" is a defined area within which businesses can take advantage of the tax benefits granted for the Los Angeles Revitalization Zone. A "supportive residential area" is an area where employees must reside in order for employees to receive job-related tax incentives.

The hiring credit must be reduced by other credits available including the Jobs Tax Credit (Rev & TC § 17053.7), the Enterprise Zone Employer's Credit (Rev & TC § 17053.8), the Program Zone Employer's Credit (Rev & TC § 17053.11), and the Enterprise Zone Employer's Credit (Rev & TC § 17053.17).

Hiring credits—employees other than construction workers. For each tax year beginning on or after 1–1–92, and before 1–1–98, a hiring credit will be allowed to employers who hire qualified disadvantaged individuals on or after 5–1–92. The credit against the "net tax" (as defined by Rev & TC § 17039) is equal to the sum of the following: (1) 50% of qualified wages in the first year of employment; (2) 40% of qualified wages in the second year of employment; (3) 30% of qualified wages in the third year of employment; (4) 20% of qualified wages in the fourth year of employment; and (5) 10% of qualified wages in the fifth year of employment. The period for measuring the credit commences with the first day the individual commences employment within the Los Angeles Revitalization Zone.

Qualified wages means the wages, not in excess of 150% of the hourly minimum wage, paid or incurred by the employer during the taxable year to qualified disadvantaged individuals.

A qualified disadvantaged individual is one who is a resident in the Los Angeles Revitalization Zone who performs services for the taxable year which are at least 90% directly related to the conduct of the taxpayer's trade or business located in the Zone, and who performs at least 50% of the services in the Zone. Special rules apply to multiple businesses under common control which have not been incorporated.

The credit is recaptured if an employee's employment is terminated by the taxpayer at any time during the first 270 days of that employment, or before the close of the 270th calendar day after the day in which the employee completes 90 days of employment with the taxpayer. Recapture does not apply if the termination of employment is voluntarily, the employee becomes disabled, the termination is due to misconduct, there is a substantial reduction in the trade or business of the employer, the employee is replaced by other qualified employees so as to create a net increase in both

¶ 161

the number of employees and the hours of employment, there is a mere change in the form of conduction the trade or business and the employee continues to be employed, or if an employer acquired the major portion of a trade of business of another employer, or the major portion of a separate unit of a trade or business of a predecessor, and the employee continues to be employed in that trade or business.

The credit allowed as a hiring credit shall be reduced by the credit allowed under Rev & TC §§ 17053.7 (jobs tax credit), 17053.8 (enterprise zone employers' credit), 17053.10 (credit for wages paid to a construction employee in the Los Angeles Revitalization Zone - discussed above), 17053.11 (employers' credit for employees within a program area), and by the credit allowed under IRC § 51. The deduction for wages paid such qualified employees will be reduced by the amount of the credit.

The credit may be carried over to subsequent years for a maximum of 15 years.

The credit can only offset the amount of tax that would be imposed on income attributed to business activities within the Zone as if it represented all of the taxpayer's income. Special rules are included for the determination of the income earned in the revitalization zone.[21]

Sales tax credit.   A sales tax credit may be claimed by a person or entity engaged in a trade or business within the Los Angeles Revitalization Zone for (1) construction materials to repair or replace the taxpayer's building and fixtures, and (2) machinery and equipment used exclusively in the zone. The credit is equal to the sales or use tax paid or incurred for the purchase of qualified property. No depreciation shall be allowed on the amount claimed as a credit. Recapture of the credit is required if the property is no longer used by the taxpayer in the Los Angeles Revitalization Zone at the end of the second taxable year after the property is placed in service.

The amount of sales tax credit which can be claimed in any one year is limited to the tax on the income earned in the Los Angeles Revitalization Zone. Special rules are provided for determining the amount of tax which can be reduced by the credit. Carryovers are available for excess credits.[21]

¶ 162   Recycling Equipment

A credit against net tax is allowed in an amount equal to 40% of the cost of qualified property purchased and placed in service on or after January 1, 1989 and before January 1, 1994.[22]

Qualified property.   Qualified property means machinery or equipment located in California that has not been previously certified and is used by the taxpayer exclusively to manufacture finished products composed of at least 50% secondary waste material with at least 10% composed of post-consumer waste generated from within California. Qualified property may

---

(22) § 17052.14.

include manufacturing equipment that utilizes 100% secondary waste including at least 80% post-consumer waste where all of that material is contained within a finished product regardless of the finished product's percent post-consumer content. It can include deinking equipment use to produce fine quality paper and equipment used to reclaim plastic used as raw material or in the fabrication or manufacture of finished products, equipment utilized in the production of compost, equipment that processes used plastic milk bottles into flakes, equipment that processes resin pellets from the flakes, and equipment that manufactures toys from the pellets.

How claimed? 20% of the cost as limited shall be allowed for the taxable year the qualified property is placed in service; 15% in the taxable year immediately succeeding the taxable year the qualified property is placed in service; 5% of the cost in the following taxable year. The amount of credit cannot exceed $625,000 per facility over the 5-year tax credit period.

The credit for qualified purchases of recycling equipment is claimed on FTB Form 3527.

Basis reduced by credit. The basis of any qualified property, for which the credit is allowed must be reduced by the amount of the credit; adjustment is made in the year the credit is allowed.

Conditions of credit. The credit shall only be allowed if: (1) the total adjusted basis of all qualified property owned on the last day of the taxable year exceeds the largest total adjusted basis of all qualified property owned at any time during the base year; (2) the total capacity to used recycled materials, of items of qualified property on the last day of the taxable year exceeds the largest total capacity of qualified property at any time during the base year. In case of replacement, eligible costs shall be proportional to the increase in capacity.

California Integrated Waste Management Board. The California Integrated Waste Management Board must certify the purchase and use by the taxpayer, and provide an annual listing to the Franchise Tax Board of qualified taxpayers who were issued certification. It must also provide the taxpayer with a copy of the certification for the taxpayer's records.

Taxpayer's duties. A taxpayer must provide the California Integrated Waste Management Board with documents to verify his or her purchase of qualified property, and that the machinery or equipment meets recycling requirements. The taxpayer must also retain the board certificate in its records.

Carryover of credit. Excess credit may be carried over to succeeding years until exhausted. Carryover also applies beyond the law's 12–1–94 repeal date.

Disposal of qualified property. Any amount otherwise allowable as a credit for the year of disposition or nonuse will not be allowed.

Two or more taxpayers. Each taxpayer sharing in expenses is eligible to receive the credit in proportion to his or her respective share of the expenses paid or incurred. In case of a partnership, the credit may be divided between the partners pursuant to the written partnership agreement. A husband and wife may divide the credit equally, or either one may take the entire credit.

¶ 163   **Ridesharing**

Purchase of company shuttle and commuter buses or vans, or motorpool vehicles. An employer with 200 or more employees is allowed a credit for 20% of the cost paid or incurred for the purchase of company shuttle buses, commuter buses or vans, motor pool vehicles provided as part of an employer-sponsored ridesharing incentive program for employees conducted principally in California. An employer with less than 200 employees will be allowed a credit of 30% of the cost.

The credit must be claimed in the state income tax return for the taxable year the vehicles are purchased and placed in service. Credit is claimed on FTB Form 3518.

The basis of any ridesharing vehicle purchased must be reduced by the amount of credit. Adjustment is made in the year for which the credit is allowed.

In the event of disposal of the vehicle, or nonuse within three years of acquisition, the portion of the credit that represents the pro rata share of that remaining three-year period is added to the employer's tax liability in the year of disposition or nonuse. The basis of the vehicle must be increased by the amount added to the employer's tax liability.[23]

Cost of leasing or contracting for vehicles. An employer with 200 or more employees, will be allowed a credit of 20% of the cost paid or incurred. The credit is based on the total payments to the lessor or vehicle provider during the life of the lease or contract. The lessor or vehicle provider is not eligible for the credit. An employer with less than 200 employees will be allowed a credit of 30% of the cost.

The credit claimed in the state income tax return for the taxable year in which the vehicles are first placed in service under the lease or contract. If first leased or contracted prior to the 1989 taxable year, the credit may be claimed on the 1989 return based on the total payments to the lessor or vehicle provider in that year, and the total payments to be made during the remaining life of the contract.

In case of disposal or nonuse, the portion of credit representing a pro rata share of the remaining life of the lease or contract will be added to the employer's tax liability in the year of disposition or nonuse.[23]

---

(23) § 17053.

Subsidized transit passes. The credit will be allowed for cost paid or incurred by employers for providing subsidized public transit passes to employees: (1) 40% of cost if employers provide no free or subsidized parking; (2) 20% of cost if the employers provide subsidized parking; (3) 10% of cost if employers provide free parking.

Carryovers. Excess credits may be carried over until exhausted, even beyond the 12–1–96 repeal date of the credit.

Credit in lieu of deduction. The credit is in lieu of any other deduction to which the employer might be entitled under the Personal Income Tax Law.

When vehicle credits do not apply. The credit will not be allowed for the cost of the purchase, lease or contract of vehicles that would otherwise be required as part of an employer's business activities in the absence of the ridesharing program.[23]

Non-employer sponsored vanpool programs. A credit will be allowed employees in non-employer sponsored programs in an amount equal to 40% of all vanpool subscription costs, for which receipts are available. In the case of a husband and wife, each shall be allowed a credit equal to 40% of their individual vanpool subscription costs. The credit shall not exceed $480 applied separately to a husband or wife. If a husband and wife file separately, and each qualify for the credit, each shall claim his or her allowable credit, or, if only one is qualified, the credit may be taken by either, or equally divided between them.

Employee. Employee means an individual who performs services for an employer for at least 10 hours per week for remuneration, and who vanpools to and from work at least three days a week or 15 days a month for at least six months of the year. An employee, within the meaning of the definition of "employee," whose employer is not subject to the personal income tax or corporate income taxes, will be deemed to be an employee in a non-employer-sponsored vanpool program.

Carryover. Excess credits can be carried over until exhausted.[24]

¶ 164   **Prison inmate labor**

A credit is allowed for 10% of the amount of wages paid to each prisoner employed in a joint venture program established under the Penal Code, Part 3, Title 1, Ch 5, Art 1.5 through agreement with the Director of Corrections. The Department of Corrections must forward to the Franchise Tax Board annually a list of all employers it certified as active participants in a joint venture program. The list must include the certified participant's federal employer identification number.[25] The credit for prison inmate labor is claimed on FTB Form 3507.

---

(24) § 17053.1.   (25) § 17053.6.

¶ 164a   **Local Agency Military Base Recovery Area—Incentives**

The California Trade and Commerce Agency is authorized to specify certain geographical areas as Local Agency Military Base Recovery Areas [LAMBRA]. For taxable years beginning on or after January 1, 1995, and before January 1, 2003, a taxpayer engaged in a trade or business within a LAMBRA is entitled to certain incentives including a sales tax credit, a hiring credit, an accelerated deduction for the cost of specified property acquired by purchase for exclusive use in the LAMBRA, and special treatment of net operating loss carryovers.[26]

To be eligible for the incentives the taxpayer must be doing business in the LAMBRA, and generate at least one additional new full time job in the state, and in the LAMBRA, within the first two taxable years of doing business in the LAMBRA. Specific methods for calculating if a new job has been created are provided.

If there are similar incentives available to the taxpayer under more than one part of the Revenue and Taxation Code, then the taxpayer may elect the section under which the incentive will be claimed.

The amount of credits which may be used in any one year, including carryovers, is limited to the amount of tax that would be imposed on the income attributable to business activities within the LAMBRA. The income of a taxpayer operating within and outside a LAMBRA is apportioned based on the property and payroll factors, divided by 2. Credits may be carried forward if not fully utilized in the year the credit is earned by the taxpayer.

Sales tax credits. A credit against the taxpayer's income tax equal to the amount of sales or use tax paid in connection with the purchase of qualified property is allowed. Qualified property may not exceed $1 million cumulative cost of qualifying property. Qualified property must be used exclusively in a LAMBRA, and is defined as: (1) high technology equipment; (2) aircraft maintenance equipment; (3) aircraft components; and (4) any property that is IRC § 1245 property as defined in IRC § 1245(a)(3). To be eligible for credit the property must be manufactured in California unless qualified property of a comparable quality and price is not available for timely purchase and delivery from a California manufacturer.

The sales tax credit is recaptured if the property is disposed of, or moved outside the LAMBRA, before the close of the second tax year following the date the property is placed in service. The credit previously claimed will be recaptured on the return for the second taxable year after the property was placed in service.[26]

Hiring credits. A credit will be allowed for hiring a disadvantaged individual, or a qualified displaced employee, during a taxable year equal to the sum of the following:

---

(26) § 17053.46.

(1) 50% of qualified wages in the first year of employment,
(2) 40% of qualified wages in the second year of employment,
(3) 30% of qualified wages in the third year of employment,
(4) 20% of qualified wages in the fourth year of employment,
(5) 10% of qualified wages in the fifth year of employment.

Qualified wages means the amount paid to qualified disadvantaged individuals, or qualified displaced individuals. These are individuals who work at least 90% of the time in activities directly related to the taxpayer's business in a LAMBRA, and who spend at least 50% of their time actually in the LAMBRA. The wages for which a credit is claimed can not exceed that portion of a wage paid to an individual which exceeds 150% of the minimum wage, and cannot exceed $2 million during years one through five. The credit is also limited to those wages paid to employees hired after the designation of the area as a LAMBRA. A qualified disadvantaged employee is one who has been determined eligible for service under the federal Job Training Partnership Act; any voluntary or mandatory registrant under the California Greater Avenues for Independence Act of 1985; or any individual who has been certified eligible by the Employment Development Department under the federal Targeted Jobs Tax Credit Program. A qualified displaced employee means an individual who was a civilian or military employee of a base or former base that has been displaced as a result of a federal base closure act. Provisions are made for recapture of the credit if an employee is terminated within 270 days of employment, whether or not consecutive, or within 270 calendar days after the day in which that employee completes 90 days of employment. Special rules are provided for termination because of disability, mergers and divestitures, misconduct, or substantial reduction in operations of the taxpayer. The tax upon recapture will be added to the tax otherwise due by the taxpayer for the year in which the termination occurred. All employees of trades or business that are under common control shall be treated as employed by a single employer, and each business shall be entitled to the credit based on their proportionate share of qualifying wages.

The amount of credit will be reduced by credits claimed under Rev & TC § 17053.7 [Calif. Jobs Tax Credit], and by the credit allowed under IRC § 51 [federal Targeted Jobs Tax Credit].

Deduction for qualifying property acquisitions. Taxpayers may elect to deduct the cost of qualifying property purchased for exclusive use in a trade or business conducted within a LAMBRA in the year of acquisition. The election will be made on the taxpayer's return and may not be revoked except with the consent of the Franchise Tax Board. No form is specified for the election, and as with property claimed as a deduction under IRC § 179, the election is made by the decision, as reflected in the computation of tax, to deduct the qualifying property. Qualifying property means property as defined in IRC § 1245(a)(3) used exclusively in a trade or business conducted with in a LAMBRA. A purchase does not include: property acquired from a person whose relationship to the person acquiring the property would result in the disallowance of losses under IRC §§ 267 or 707(b), but with modifica-

¶ **164a**

tion of the federal attribution rules under IRC § 267(c)(4); where the basis of the property in the hands of the acquiring person is determined by reference to the adjusted basis of the property in the hands of the person from whom it was acquired; or, where the basis is determined under IRC § 1014 relating to property acquired from a decedent.

Eligible property excludes that property for which no election can be made under IRC § 179 because of the rules set forth in IRC § 179(d).

The deduction shall not exceed the following amounts for the taxable year of the designation of a LAMBRA and each taxable year thereafter:

Taxable year of designation, and

the first year thereafter.. $5,000 per year

Second and third taxable year following

designation of a LAMBRA.. 7,500 per year

Each taxable year thereafter.. 10,000 per year

Recapture of the deduction is provided if the property ceases to be used in the trade or business within a LAMBRA at any time before the close of the second taxable year after it has been placed in service.

Any taxpayer who elects to deduct property under this provision will not be entitled to claim a deduction for the same property under IRC § 179.[26]

Special treatment of net operating losses. Rather than the normal 5 year period for carryover of net operating losses, the net operating loss incurred in a LAMBRA may be carried over for 15 years. The net operating loss carryover shall be a deduction only with respect to income attributed to the business activities of the taxpayer in the LAMBRA by applying the two factor formula based on payroll and property as described above.[26]

RETURNS AND PAYMENT OF TAX

¶ 165   Time for Filing Returns

Generally. California individual income tax returns (Form 540, 540A, or 540NR) must be filed by residents, part-year residents and nonresidents by April 15 after the end of the taxable year. Partnership returns of information (Form 565), and the fiduciary income tax returns of estates and trusts (Form 541) when filed on a calendar-year basis are due April 15 following the close of the taxable year. Fiscal year returns are to be filed by the fifteenth day of the fourth month following the close of the fiscal period.[27] IRC § 7503 provides that when a due date falls on Saturday, Sunday, or a legal holiday, the filing date is postponed to the first day following that which is not a Saturday, Sunday or holiday. Although a similar provision has not been included in the California Personal Income Tax Law, the wording of Reg 18433.1 and

---

(27) § 18566.

Govt. Cd. § 6702[28] give the same result. Returns, when filed by U.S. mail, are considered to be filed on time if the envelope or wrapper bears a U.S. postmark on or before the due date of the return. A postmark from a postage meter is acceptable if it is dated on or before the due date. However, the taxpayer may be asked to prove that it was timely filed if it was received later than other returns filed at the same time.

Short period returns.   Tax returns filed for a short period must be filed within the same time after the end of the period as if the short year were a fiscal year. The final return of a decedent is due on the same date as the return would have been due had the decedent lived the entire tax year.

IRC § 6072 requires that the final return of an estate or a trust must be filed by the 15th day of the fourth month after closing the estate or ending the trust. Federal regulations state that: "In general, the requirements with respect to the filing of returns and the payment of tax for a short period where the taxpayer has not been in existence for the entire taxable year are the same as for the filing of a return and the payment of the tax for a taxable year of 12 months ending on the last day of the short period".[29]

¶ 166   Extension of Time To File

Automatic extension.   A person shall automatically be granted an extension of time for six months for filing an individual California return if the taxpayer qualified for a federal extension and paid the tax due with the federal extension.[30] There is no requirement to apply for this extension; rather a copy of the federal application should be attached to the California return when it is filed. If California tax is due, it should be mailed with the Payment Voucher for Automatic Extension for Individuals (FTB form 3519) by the original due date for the return. Late payment penalties may be assessed if 100% of the California tax due is not paid at the original due date for the return, although as a practical matter the FTB waives any penalties if 90% of the tax shown on the return when filed is paid on or before the original due date.

Persons outside the United States.   Persons who are residing or traveling outside the United States on the ordinary due date of their return are granted an automatic extension of time for filing to the fifteenth day of the sixth month following the close of the taxable years.[31] There is no requirement to file an extension application. An additional six month automatic extension of the filing date can be obtained to December 15. The Rev & TC provides that the automatic extension for those traveling outside the United States does not automatically extend the time for payment of the tax. However, the instructions accompanying the 1992 Form 3519, Payment Voucher for Automatic Extension, stated that the tax did not have to be paid until the fifteenth day of the sixth month. For those obtaining the additional exten-

---

(28) Reg 18433.1; Govt. Cd. § 6707.   **(30)** § 21022.
(29) Fed Reg 1.443.1(a)(2).   **(31)** § 18567

sion to December 15, 100% of the tax due must be paid on or before the fifteenth day of the sixth month after the close of the tax year to avoid late filing penalties.

It should be noted that the federal rule for an automatic extension for persons outside the United States is more restrictive and applies only to those whose abode or tax home is outside the United States, or Puerto Rico, on the ordinary due date for the return.

TAX TIP	While not required by the Rev & TC or regulations, it is good practice to attach the California Special Handling Required form (FTB 3595) to the face of the return when it is filed and note that the due date for the return had been extended since the taxpayer was traveling or residing outside the United States on the original due date. A copy of the federal extension application should be attached to the return when it is filed.

Members of the Armed Forces. California law provides that an individual serving in the armed forces of the United States or an auxiliary branch of the services, or the merchant marine, outside of the United States is granted an automatic extension without applying for it for filing the return and payment of the tax (except withheld income tax) until 180 days after his or her return to the United States. In addition, the period for performing the following acts is automatically extended for a period ending 180 days after the return to the United States: (1) filing a protest to a notice of proposed assessment issued by the Franchise Tax Board, (2) appealing the FTB's action on a protest to the State Board of Equalization, (3) filing a claim for credit or refund, (4) appeal the FTB's denial of a claim for credit or refund, and (5) filing an appeal of the FTB fails to act within six months of filing a claim for credit or refund.[32]

Commencing with those returns or other actions required to be taken on or after 8–2–90, California includes those identified in IRC § 7508, military personnel serving in combat zones, including those hospitalized and in a missing status and their spouses as qualifying for the automatic extension of time for filing, etc. set forth in Rev & TC § 18570. For purposes of determining interest on overpayments and refunds to which the benefits of Rev & TC § 18570 apply, IRC § 7508(b) as amended by P.L. 102–2 shall apply.

The California automatic six-month extension may be terminated at any time by the Franchise Tax Board by mailing a notice of termination to the taxpayer(s) or the person who requested the extension for the taxpayer(s). The notice will be mailed at least 10 days prior to the termination date designated in the notice.

Where to file. All Form 540 returns, payments or extension requests, other than original returns on which refund is claimed, should be mailed to the Franchise Tax Board, Sacramento, California 95867. This requirement also applies to amended returns on Form 540X, including those on which

---

(32) § 18570.

refund claim is made. Form 540 returns on which refund is claimed should be mailed to the Franchise Tax Board, Sacramento, California 95840.[33]

¶ 171   **Payment of Estimated Tax**

California has enacted Rev & TC § 19136 that covers underpayments of estimated tax. This section provides that an amount shall be added to the tax imposed by the tax schedules (Rev & TC § 17041) or tax tables (Rev & TC § 17048) for any underpayment of tax. The amount shall be determined in accordance with IRC § 6654 except as modified (see below).[34]

IRC § 6654(a) provides for the addition to the tax for underpayment of estimated tax at the applicable annual rate established under IRC § 6621 governing the determination of the rate of interest. For California purposes, the determination will be governed by Rev & TC § 19521. The interest applies to the amount of the underpayment for the period of the underpayment.[35]

California follows IRC § 6654(b), which states that the amount of the underpayment is the excess of the required installment over the amount of the installment paid on or before the due date for the installment. The period of the underpayment runs from the due date of the installment to the earlier of the 15th day of the fourth month following the close of the taxable year, or with respect to any part of the underpayment, to the date on which that part is paid. Individuals outside the U.S. on the ordinary due date for the first installment of estimated tax receive an automatic two-month extension in which to pay the first installment. If payment is not made by June 16, then, for purposes of computing the underpayment penalty, the period and amount of underpayment will be calculated without regard to the extension.[34]

IRC § 6654(c) requires installments to be paid by April 15, June 15, September 15, and January 15 of the following taxable year. Under IRC § 6654(d) except in the case of annualized installments, the amount of any required installment is 25% of required annual payment. The required annual payment means the lesser of 90% of the tax shown on the return, or if no return is filed 90% of the tax for the taxable year, or 100% of the tax shown on the return of the individual for the previous year (not applicable to short years, or where no return is filed). California modifies this rule by requiring an annual payment of 80% of the tax shown on the return for the taxable year, or, if no return is filed, 80% of the tax for that year, or 100% of the tax shown on the return of the individual for the preceding taxable year. The annualized income installment for California purposes does not include alternative minimum taxable income, or adjusted self-employment income.[36]

California has not adopted IRC § 6654(e)(1) that provides that no addition to tax will be imposed if the tax shown on the return, or the tax, if no

---

(33) § 18621.
(34) § 19136(a).

(35) § 19136(b).
(36) § 19136(c)(i);(3).

return is filed, reduced by withheld tax credit under IRC § 31, is less than $500.[37]

California has not adopted IRC § 6654(e)(2), but provides that no addition to the tax shall be imposed if the tax (1) for the preceding taxable year, minus the sum of any credits allowed, or (2) computed on estimated income for the taxable year less credits is less than $100 ($50 in case of married persons filing separately). No addition to tax will be made if 80% or more of the tax for the preceding year less the credit for withheld taxes was paid, or 80% or more of the estimated tax will be paid by withholding, or 80% or more of adjusted gross income consists of wages subject to withholding, provided the employee does not file false or fraudulent withholding certificate.[38]

California has adopted IRC § 6654(e)(3) that allows a waiver of underpayment penalty in case of casualty, disaster, or other unusual circumstances, or in case of retired or disabled taxpayers for good cause shown.[34]

Because California requires that only 80% of the annualized tax be paid at each installment date as compared with the federal requirement of 90%, California modified the percentages found in IRC § 6654(d)(2)(C)(ii) to provide that the respective percentages are:[39]

Required Installment	Applicable Percentage
1st	20%
2nd	40
3rd	60
4th	80

California does not follow IRC § 6654(f) defining tax computed after application of credits. For California purposes, tax means the tax computed under the tax tables or schedules less allowable credits and withholding. The definition of tax withheld on wages under Rev & TC § 19002 will apply.[40]

Nonresidents are subject to above estimated tax underpayment rules.[1]

An estimated tax payment need not be made if withholding is enough to cover your estimated tax. If a taxpayer does not have enough tax withheld during the year, he may file a new federal Form W–4, Employee's Withholding Allowance Certificate, with his employer to have an adjustment made in the amount of withholding. The amount paid through withholding should equal 80% of the tax liability or be sufficient to leave a balance due exclusive of taxes on items of tax preference of less than $100 or $50 for married persons filing separate returns. Married couples who file joint returns and who are both employed may have a problem of underwithholding of state income taxes.

(**37**) § 19136(d)(1).
(**38**) § 19136(c).
(**39**) § 19136(c)(2).

(**40**) § 19136(e)—(f).
(**1**) § 19136(g).

For federal purposes as well as California, the amount of withholding tax paid is equally divided between the installment periods for purposes of determining the estimated tax unless the taxpayer proves a different allocation. This gives the taxpayer an opportunity to compute his current year's total tax liability on the best information available late in the taxable year and if it appears that he will be underpaid, ask his employer to withhold a larger amount before the end of the year to avoid penalties for underpayment of estimated taxes.

WARNING   Although the addition to tax for an underpayment is computed in the same manner as the interest, both the IRS and the California Franchise Tax Board have announced that they will not allow a deduction for the addition to tax (the penalty).[2]

High income taxpayers. California adopted IRC § 6654(d)(1)(C)–(F) effective 1–1–93 which requires estimated tax payments for certain high income taxpayers to be based solely on annualized income. The federal change, first effective 1–1–92, was substantially modified by the Revenue Reconciliation Act of 1993. California has not incorporated amendments made to IRC § 6654 by the Revenue Reconciliation Act of 1993 that allow high income taxpayers for federal purposes to base estimated tax payments on 110% of the preceding year's tax. A high income taxpayer is one who has an increase in modified adjusted gross income of more than $40,000 as compared with the prior year ($20,000 in the case of a separate return for the current year by a married individual), adjusted gross income on the current year's return in excess of $75,000 ($37,500 in the case of a separate return for the current year by a married individual), and has made estimated tax payments during the preceding three years or was assessed a penalty for failing to make such payments.

WARNING   California has not adopted federal law which provides that the penalty for underpayment of estimated tax by high income taxpayers can be avoided by paying 110% of the prior year's tax.

In addition, none of the safe harbor exemptions from the under payment penalty set forth in Rev & TC § 19136 will apply if a false or fraudulent withholding certificate has been filed for the year.

TAX TIP   For purposes of determining the amount of tax paid by withholding during the year so as to avoid an addition to tax for underpayment of estimated tax, the instructions for the completion of form 5805, which is used for calculating the amount of underpayment penalty, allows amounts withheld pursuant to Rev & TC § 18662 (relating to tax withheld on income sourced in California, including the sale of real property), and Rev & TC § 18666 (relating to tax withheld on certain distributions

(2) LR 358.

¶ 171

to partners not resident in the United States), to be treated the same as amounts withheld from wages during the year.

¶ 172 Payment of Taxes

The balance of tax shown on the tax return after taking the credit for the income tax withheld during the year and estimated tax payments is required to be paid in full by the time and place fixed for filing the tax return.[3] Payments must be made in U.S. funds.[4] (Note: A grant of an extension of time for filing the return, does not extend the time to pay.) If the last date for payment falls on a Saturday, Sunday or legal holiday, payment is due on the first business day following without a penalty. The Franchise Tax Board may accept payments in the form of a credit account number and an authorization to draw upon a specified credit account. Remittances must include an amount, not to exceed 2% of the balance due, to pay the discount rates associated with the account draw. Remittances may also be drawn upon on an account with a financial institution.

Extension of time to pay. A reasonable extension for payment of tax may be granted by the Franchise Tax Board when in its judgment good cause exists. Except for a taxpayer residing or traveling abroad, no extension shall be for more than six months. In the case of taxpayers residing or traveling abroad, returns shall be filed no later than the 15th day of the sixth month following the close of the taxable year, unless the requirements for extension have been fulfilled on or before that date. An extension of time under Rev & TC § 18567 and § 21022 is not an extension of time for payment. Underpayment penalties will be imposed as provided by law without regard to any extension granted under Rev & TC § 18567 and 21022.[5] There is no application form available to request extensions of time to pay the taxes due. It should be done by contacting an office of the Board.

Late payment penalty. A late payment penalty may be imposed when a taxpayer applies for an automatic extension of time for filing the return and paying the tax "due." If the amount paid is less than the tax per the return filed, the penalty for late payment is 5% of the unpaid tax plus 0.5% per month for each month the tax is unpaid. In addition, interest is assessed from the original due date of the return to the date of payment at the rate determined in accordance with the provisions of IRC § 6621, except that the overpayment rate specified in IRC § 6621(a)(1) must be modified to be equal to the underpayment rate determined under IRC § 6621(a)(2).[6]

When automatic extension applies. A member of the Armed Forces of the United States or any auxiliary branch or the merchant marine serving beyond the boundaries of the United States will receive an automatic extension, without application being made for payment of the tax the same as he

---

(3) § 18551–18554.
(4) § 19005.

(5) § 18567.
(6) § 19132; 19102; 19521.

would for filing the tax return until 180 days after returning to the United States.[7]

Installment payments—financial hardship. The Franchise Tax Board, may, in cases of financial hardship, as determined by the Board, allow a taxpayer to enter into installment payment agreements with the Board to pay the taxes due, and applicable interest and penalties, over the life of the installment period. Failure to comply with terms of the agreement renders it null and void, unless the Board determines that the failure was due to reasonable cause. In the event the agreement is void, the total amount of the tax, interest and all penalties, shall be immediately due and payable.[8]

¶ 173   Amended Returns

The Franchise Tax Board has issued Form 540X (substantially similar to the Federal 1040X) to be used in amending the income reported for a prior year on annual return Form 540, 540A or 540NR. Form 540X is to be used to claim a refund of individual income taxes previously paid. A refund must be filed within four years after the original due date of the return without regard to any extension of time for filing the return, or within one year from the date of overpayment whichever expires the later.[9] Amended returns must be filed to report federal adjustments (¶ 174). The requirements for filing an amended declaration of estimated tax are at ¶ 171.

¶ 174   Reporting Federal Adjustments

If the amount of gross income or deductions reported to the Internal Revenue Service for any year is changed, either by the taxpayer of the Internal Revenue Service, the taxpayer must notify the Franchise Tax Board of the change within 6 months of the "final determination" of such change. However, such change or correction need not be reported to the FTB if it does not affect the California income tax payable.[10]

Changes that must be reported to California include:

(1) Amendments made on a return filed by the taxpayer with the IRS,
(2) Results of revenue agent's examination, or other changes or corrections by the IRS,
(3) Change or correction by any other officer of the U.S. or other competent authority, or
(4) Renegotiation of a contract or subcontract with the U.S.

If the change is timely reported, then the Franchise Tax Board has two years to assess the tax as a result of such change, or the taxpayer has 2 years for filing a claim for refund as a result of the change.

What happens if you do not report the change. If a taxpayer does not report a change or correction as required, or fails to file an amended return with the state, the statute of limitations upon the assessment by the

---

(7) § 18570.   (9) § 19306.
(8) § 19008.   (10) § 18622.

Franchise Tax Board is suspended and the Board may issue the assessment at any time.

If the taxpayer advises the Board of such change, but does so only after the expiration of the 6 month period for reporting, then the Franchise Tax Board has 4 years from the date the change is reported to issue an assessment with respect to the change.[11]

IMPORTANT	It should be noted that the extension of the statute of limitations applies only to the changes made by the US government, and does not allow the Franchise Tax Board to propose other adjustments to taxable income, if the ordinary statute of limitations has expired.

Note: It should be noted that the "final determination" may be the date on which the revenue agent's report was issued, but if the assessment is protested, and an appeal is taken to the Tax Court or higher, the final determination does not occur until the final court has issued its determination even if the tax has been assessed previously.[12]

TAX TIP	In instances when the federal audit adjusts a year which is closed for federal assessment except for loss carryover purposes, the taxpayer is not required to report the results to the Franchise Tax Board.[12]

State exchanges info with IRS. Through the reciprocity arrangement with the IRS, the Franchise Tax Board receives copies of the examination reports directly from the IRS, and does not wait until it receives a notice from the taxpayer to issue its own assessment. The authority is in IRC § 6103(d).

The Franchise Tax Board audit staff handles the information it receives from the IRS by means of a revenue agent's report or the results of a protested action in a confidential manner. When the federal findings are requested by or are to be discussed with a person other than the taxpayer, a written authorization or power-of-attorney is required unless the representative has a copy of the IRS information.

Furthermore, disclosure of the IRS information to other than the Board's staff or the taxpayer or his authorized representative is prohibited unless it is required by the Legal Division in connection with administrative or judicial proceedings.

What are effects of federal changes. Once there is a federal adjustment or change, the affected taxpayer is required to concede the accuracy of the federal determination, or state "wherein it is erroneous." The burden of proof is on the taxpayer to prove that the federal adjustments are not applicable to the California income. *(Appeal of Bernard J. and Elia C. Smith, SBE 1–9–79.* The converse, however, is not true. For example, a federal tax refund would not automatically result in a state tax refund. A case in point is the *Appeal of Herman D. and Russell Mae Jones, SBE 4–10–79,* where the IRS had offset overpayments from two years against 1973 tax deficiency, resulting in federal refunds of tax. This federal treatment did not, said the Board of

---

(11) § 19060.   (12) LR 098.

¶ 174

Equalization, substantiate the right of the taxpayers to deduct the amounts disallowed by the IRS and administrative authorities.

In using the federal reports to make similar California changes for the purpose of issuing deficiency notices, the state adjustments will generally follow the federal changes, when federal and California laws are substantially similar. Even adjustments resulting from negotiations between the taxpayer and the revenue agent in effecting an agreed or even a compromise settlement will routinely be followed by the California audit staff if there is an apparent basis for the treatment followed. Otherwise, the staff will request further information from the taxpayer before assessing the additional tax.

Even when the federal adjustment pertains to a factual situation which involves an exercise of judgment, the state will follow the federal action unless it can be clearly shown that the federal action was in error. The same is true when it becomes clear that the federal auditor has reviewed the factual situation and proposed no adjustment. Typical of this type of adjustment would be the determination of business vs. nonbusiness entertainment expenses, personal vs. business use of automobiles or facilities, reasonableness of salaries, etc.

Because the existence of operating loss carryovers or carrybacks—California law modifies federal rules—may affect the federal treatment, the Board's auditors will make a separate determination for state purposes as to whether or not to follow the revenue agent's recommendations.

Note: If a taxpayer reports the results of a federal audit to the Franchise Tax Board and the federal audit adjustments affect a number of related taxpayers, the state adjustments will be made for all taxpayers.

In appeals to the Board of Equalization, the Franchise Tax Board will be sustained in a state adjustment which follows the federal adjustment when the laws are shown to be the same. However, the Franchise Tax Board has the burden of proving the correctness of any adjustment inconsistent with the federal report. For this reason, it makes adjustments contrary to those in a federal examination only to the extent these adjustments are substantial or have importance, either as precedents or having a continuing revenue effect.

If a fraud penalty has been assessed in a federal audit, it will usually be assessed by the state. In the *Appeal of M. Hunter and Martha J. Brown, SBE 10-7-74,* the Board of Equalization sustained the Franchise Tax Board's position with respect to asserting deficiencies in income tax based on the federal findings, but not including the fraud penalty as assessed by the federal government. The appellate body stated that the burden of proof was on the Franchise Tax Board to establish that fraud was present and that such proof must be presented by "clear and convincing evidence." However, the California Supreme Court in the case of *Calhoun v. Franchise Tax Board*

(1978) 20 Cal 3d 851, 153 Cal Rptr 692, 574 P2d 763 reversed the trial court which had denied the Franchise Tax Board claim for income tax deficiencies and the fraud penalty based on the federal audit. Although the Supreme Court did not discuss any specifics with respect to the fraud penalty, the Franchise Tax Board presumably will follow the case and assert fraud penalties when it considers they are warranted.

¶ 175　**Privacy Act Information**

The Franchise Tax Board is required by the provisions of the Information Practices Act of 1977 and the federal Privacy Act to comply with provisions of those federal laws to protect individual taxpayers. In that regard, the Board is authorized by law to furnish information shown on the return to the IRS, the proper official of any state imposing an income tax or a tax measured by income, to the Multistate Tax Commission, and the California Attorney General, Auditor General, Board of Control, Board of Equalization, California Parent Locator Service, county welfare departments and probation officers, Department of Finance, Department of Social Services, District Attorneys, Employment Development Department, Legislative Analyst, Legislative Committees, local tax administrators, Office of the State Controller, the Public Employees Retirement System, and the Registry of Charitable Trusts.[13]

California will also share tax information with tax officials of Mexico if a reciprocal agreement exists. The information to be shared with Mexico by California is limited to those pertaining to Mexican nationals. Conversely, California would be entitled to receive information only on California residents.[14]

An individual has the right of access to records containing his/her personal information that are maintained by the Franchise Tax Board.

Note: In order to gain access to such information, the request should be directed to: Director, Taxpayer Services, Franchise Tax Board, Sacramento, California 95867.

NONRESIDENTS AND PART-YEAR RESIDENTS

¶ 181　**Who Are Nonresidents and Part-Year Residents**

Persons who are permanently living in California are residents and are still considered to be residents even though they are temporarily out of the state. Persons who spend more than nine months of the year in California are presumed to be residents for the period while in California.

Persons who are California residents for part of the year and nonresidents for the remainder of the year are part-year residents. Persons who are in California temporarily, or who are not in California at all, are considered to be nonresidents.[15]

---

(13) § 19542—19565.
(14) § 19551.

(15) § 17014; 17016; Reg 17014–17016.

A person who was a California resident for part of the year and a nonresident for the remainder of the year (part-year resident), is required to file Form 540NR, rather than Form 540. All part-year residents and nonresidents are required to file Form 540NR if the return as prepared shows a tax liability, whether or not credits for withholding and other credits would eliminate any additional payment. A nonresident joint return must be made if one spouse was a resident for entire year and the other spouse was a nonresident for all or any portion of the taxable year. This provision does not apply if the nonresident or his or her spouse was an active member of the armed forces of the United States or any auxiliary branch thereof during the taxable year, or the nonresident spouse had no income from California sources during the taxable year.[16]

> *Note:* In case of a part-year resident, income from sources in-state includes income from whatever source derived during period of residence in California.[17]

Employment-related absence.   For tax years beginning on or after 1–1–94, an individual who is domiciled in California who is absent from the state for an uninterrupted period of at least 546 consecutive days under an employment-related contract shall be considered outside the state for other than a temporary or transitory purpose. If the spouse accompanies the taxpayer during the 18 month period, then the spouse too will be considered outside the state for other than a temporary of transitory purpose. The taxpayer's return to California for up to 45 days during the tax year will be disregarded in determining the 18 consecutive month period. This exception to the general rule will not apply if: the individual has income from stocks, bonds, notes, or other intangible personal property in excess of $200,000 in any taxable year in which the employment-related contract is in effect, or (2) if the principal purpose of the individual's absence is to avoid tax.[18]

How tax is imposed.   Tax is imposed on a taxable income of the nonresident or part-year resident equal to tax computed as if they were a resident multiplied by the ratio of California source adjusted gross income to total adjusted gross income from all sources. For this purpose, the term "California adjusted gross income" includes (1) for any period during which taxpayer was resident of California, all items of adjusted gross income, regardless of source; (2) for any period during which taxpayer was not a resident of California, only those items of adjusted gross income which were derived from sources within California, determined in accordance with Ch 11, Gross Income of Nonresidents, Rev & TC §§ 17951–17954.[19]

Military personnel.   Nonresident military personnel serving at post of duty at California are not subject to tax on their military pay. A return may be required if California is made the permanent residence of the military person or the military person or his spouse has income from California

---

(16) § 18521.

(17) § 17303.

(18) § 17014, as amended by Stats. 1994, c. 1243, § 4.

(19) § 17041(b); (d); 17951–17954.

sources. As with Form 540, a nonresident should file a tax return (Form 540NR) to get a refund of any California tax withheld or to obtain the renter's credit. After a 1986 announcement by the Franchise Tax Board that it intended to change its policy and tax a resident spouse's community share of the earnings of a nonresident member of the armed forces, the California Legislature enacted a law excluding from gross income the earnings of such nonresident not domiciled in-state and attributable to a resident spouse solely because of the application of any community property law or rule. This 1986 change is applicable to all taxable years in which the limitation for mailing of the notice of deficiency assessment has not expired.[20]

Net operating loss. For purposes of computing tax, and gross income from all sources, the net operating loss deduction provided in IRC § 172, as modified by Rev & TC § 17276, must be computed as if the taxpayer was a resident for all prior years.[19]

¶ 182   **How to Prepare Nonresident Return**

It is usually an advantage to prepare your federal income tax return and then prepare the California nonresident tax return. The reason is that the California nonresident return requires that all income be reported, not just the items which may be subject to California tax liability.

Form 540NR which is filed by nonresidents or part-year residents of California reflects both federal income as reported by the individual on their federal individual income tax returns with the modifications as provided in the California Revenue & Taxation Code, and also their California source income which is detailed on Schedule SI to the nonresident or part-year resident return. The tax computed on federal income as adjusted for California purposes is then apportioned based on the ratio of California source income to total taxable income [ie., the federal income with California modifications as appropriate]. The California tax before personal exemptions is the tax which bears the same amount to total tax, as California source income bears to total income. This effectively results in the nonresident or part-year resident computing their tax at the same graduated rate brackets as used for computing the tax of a resident.

GROSS INCOME FROM CALIFORNIA SOURCES

Income from tangibles located in-state. California gross income is income from real or tangible personal property located in California, such as rental property. Any gain resulting from the sale or exchange of real or tangible personal property located in California is to be included regardless of where the sale was consummated.

Any other type of income from the ownership, control or management of real or personal property located in California, whether or not in connection

---

(20) § 17140.5; LR 300, 4–23–65.

with a trade, business or profession in California, is to be included as California source income reflected on Schedule SI.[21]

Trade, business or professional income.   If a nonresident's business, trade or profession is carried on entirely without the state, no portion of the gross income is to be reported as California source income. On the other hand, if the business is conducted wholly within the state, the entire gross income must be reported.[22]

Separate accounting.   If the nonresident's business is conducted partly within and partly without California and the part within the state is so separate and distinct from the part without the state that the taxable income can be determined by separate accounting, only that amount should be reported for California purposes. As an example, if a nonresident operates a hotel in California and a manufacturing business in another state, the nonresident would report only the gross income from the hotel as California source income.[23]

Unitary business income.   Most of the problems in connection with reporting a nonresident's income arise from a business, trade or profession which is carried on within the state as an integral part of a "unitary business" carried on both within and without the state. In such a case, the entire gross income from the unitary business must be reported and then adjusted to arrive at the California portion of the income.[24]

The first step is the determination of which portion of the nonresident's income consists of business income and nonbusiness income in accordance with Rev & TC § 25120 and the regulations pertaining to it. The items of business income are allocated specifically to the states depending on the nature of the income and the type and location of the property earning the income.

In determining the portion of a nonresident's unitary business income from California sources, the Franchise Tax Board generally follows the Uniform Division of Income for Tax Purposes Act (Rev & TC § 25120—25139).[25]

Long-term contracts.   A nonresident reporting income from long-term contracts may use either the percentage of completion method or the completed contract method as discussed in the chapter dealing with accounting methods. However, if the long-term contract is a part of the operations within and without California, it would be necessary to go to the regulations implementing Rev & TC § 25137(f)(1) applicable to corporations reporting income from long-term contracts with allocation involved.[26] California has modified selected provisions of the UDITPA, including double weighing the sales factor of the apportionment formula.

---

(21) Reg 17951–3.

(22) Reg 17951–4(a).

(23) Reg 17951–4(b).

(24) Reg 17951–4(c).

(25) § 25120–25129.

(26) Reg 17951–4(d); Reg 25137(f).

Partnership income. California source income is not produced by a partnership for its partners who are resident outside California if the investment by the partners in the capital of the partnership is for long-term appreciation, even though the partnership has offices and employees in California to trade in securities and profit from short-term price changes (*Appeal of Robert M. and Ann T. Bass, SBE 1–25–89*).

Income of nonresidents through California investment partnerships. A nonresident of the State of California who's only contact with the state is through a broker, dealer, investment adviser, investment partnership, corporate fiduciary managing an investment account for a beneficiary of a qualifying estate or trust, or who is a unit holder in a regulated investment company, located in California does not realize California source income from interest, dividends, or gains and losses from qualifying investment securities. An investment partnership is one which has at least 90% of the partnership's cost of its total assets in qualifying investment securities, deposits at banks or other financial institutions, and office space and equipment reasonably necessary to carry on its activities, and no less than 90% of its gross income from interest, dividends, and gains from the sale or exchange of qualifying investment securities.[27]

Qualifying investment securities include: common stock, including preferred shares or debt securities convertible into common stock, and preferred stock; bonds, debentures, and other debt securities; foreign and domestic currency deposits or equivalents and securities convertible into foreign securities; mortgage- or asset-backed securities secured by federal, state, or local government agencies; repurchase agreements and loan participations; foreign currency exchange contracts and forward and futures contracts on foreign currencies; stock and bond index securities and futures contracts, options on any of the fore-mentioned investments, and regulated futures contracts. Qualifying investment securities does not include an interest in a partnership unless that partnership is itself an investment partnership.

Partnerships' professional income. If the business, trade or profession carried on within or without the state is a partnership and if the income is from professional services, then the formula for apportioning the income from California sources for nonresident partners is set forth and illustrated in the Section IV of this book dealing with partnerships.[28]

Personal service income. The regulations cover rules for calculating the California gross income from the performance of personal services.[29]

(1) *Sales persons' commissions.* The gross income from commissions earned by a nonresident taxpayer within California such as a traveling salesman, an agent or other employee whose compensation depends directly on the volume of business transacted includes in California gross income the ratio of the California total applied to the total gross income received.

---

(27) § 17955.
(28) Reg 17951–4(e).

(29) Reg 17951–4(f)–(h); Reg 17951–5.

(2) *Entertainers and athletes.* Actors, singers, performers, entertainers and professional athletes include in California gross income the gross amount received for performances in the state;

(3) *Professionals.* Attorneys, physicians, accountants and other professional people—even though they do not regularly engage in carrying on their profession in California, must include in California gross income the entire amount of fees or compensation paid them for services performed in California on behalf of their clients;

(4) *Employees.* Nonresident employees including officers of the corporations, when they are employed continuously in the state for a definite portion of any year, will include in California gross income the entire compensation for the period employed in the state;

(5) *Nonresident career employees.* Nonresident career employees who are in California at intervals throughout the year as they would be if employed in operating trains, boats, planes, buses, trucks and who are paid on a daily, weekly or monthly basis, would report their gross income for California purposes based on the portion of their total compensation, which the total number of working days, within the state bears to the total number of working days everywhere. If the employees are paid on a mileage basis, the gross income from California would be that portion of the total compensation which the number of miles traveled in California bears to the total number of miles traveled within and without the State.

If they are paid on some other basis, the total compensation must be apportioned between the states in a manner to allocate to California that portion of the total compensation which is "reasonably attributable to personal services performed in this state."

Income from intangibles. Income from intangible personal property such as stocks, bonds, notes generally is assigned to the state of residence of the owner unless the property has attained a business situs elsewhere (*Miller v McColgan (1941) 17 Cal 2d 432, 110 P2d 419; Appeals of Amyas and Evelyn P. Ames, et al, SBE, 6/17/87*). Intangible property has a business situs in California when the asset becomes identified with the economic activity in California (*Holly Sugar Corp v Johnson, (1941) 18 Cal 2d 218; 115 P2d 8*). This occurs when either (1) the intangible property is employed as capital in California; or (2) the possession and control of the property have been localized in connection with a business, trade, or profession in California so that its substantial use and value attach to and become an asset of the business in California.[30] For example, if a nonresident pledges stocks, bonds, or other intangible personal property as security for the payment of indebtedness, taxes, etc., incurred in connection with a business in the state, the property has a business situs in California. Again, if a nonresident maintains a branch office in the state and a bank account in which the agent in charge of the branch office may draw for the payment of expenses in connection with the activities locally, the bank account has a California business situs.[31]

---

(30) Reg. 17952(c).   (31) Reg. 17952.

Another example would be in the case of royalties, patents, copyrights, trademarks, and so on, which are used by a business operating in California. A letter ruling provides that patent percentage payments to nonresidents are from the sale of intangible personalty not having an in-state situs.[32] Payments couldn't be determined with reasonable accuracy at the time taxpayers changed their residence to another state; they didn't accrue before the change of residence. Royalty income of nonresident from sale of books written in-state while he was a resident is taxable. Royalty income from revision done in-state is also taxable, but not taxable if done out-of-state while a nonresident.[33]

Buying-selling stocks in-state. If a nonresident buys or sells intangible property in the state, or places orders with brokers in the state to buy or sell such property so regularly, systematically, and continuously as to constitute doing business in California, the profit or gain from this type of activity is income from sources within the state, irrespective of the situs of the property.[31]

Alimony received by a nonresident is not taxable by California even though it is paid by a California resident who gets a deduction for the payment (*Francis v. McColgan, Calif Ct Appl (1951) 107 Cal App 2d 823, 238 P2d 72; Silberberg v. FTB, Calif Ct Appl (1951) 107 Cal App 2d 826, 238 P2d 72*).

Income from estates or trusts. Nonresident beneficiaries of estates and trusts are taxable by California on income distributed or distributable out of income of the estate or trust derived from sources in California. However, the nonresident beneficiary would be considered to be the owner of intangible personal property held by the estate or trust, so that the income from such property would be excluded from California income.[34]

Gains or profits. No capital loss carry-over is allowable if the loss arose from a capital transaction which occurred while the taxpayer was a nonresident.[31]

Installment sale gains. Installment sale gains which arose from a sale when the taxpayer was a nonresident are not taxable to a California resident.[31]

Gain from the sale or exchange of the principal residence. A nonresident who sells his out-of-state residence and becomes a resident of California by purchasing a home in the state within an 18-month period is entitled to take as his basis the cost of the property to him without reducing it by the gain on the sale of his own residence. On the other hand, if a California resident sells his home in the state at a gain and moves out of California, he is still entitled to postpone the gain on his California residence if he buys a home in another state.[35]

---

(32) LR 340, 10–5–70.
(33) LR 345, 10–5–70;.

(34) § 17953; Reg 17953.
(35) LR 329.

A nonresident receiving both principal and interest payments on an installment note arising from the sale of a personal residence in California is taxable on the gain arising from the sale of the California real property. Gain continues to be reported to California on the installment method following the taxpayers move out-of-state. Interest income, however, as income earned on an intangible asset, is subject to tax only by the new state in which the taxpayer resides (*Appeal of Christian M. and Lucille V. McCririe, SBE 12–6–77*).

ADJUSTMENTS TO GROSS INCOME

California adjustments to gross income.   The following items of possible adjustments to the taxpayer's 540NR are mentioned only briefly here. If they are pertinent, you should look at Chapter 4 covering adjustments to gross income for more details.

(1) *Employee business expenses*. Generally the same as federal provisions. Federal Form 2106 or FTB 3805N may be submitted;

(2) *Payments to IRA*. California follows federal.

(3) *Payments to a Keogh Retirement Plan*. The California law is the same as the federal law.

(4) *Payments to a self-employed "defined benefit plan."* California law is same as federal.

(5) *Interest penalty on early withdrawal of savings*. Rev & TC § 17072(i) follows IRC 62(12) in allowing a deduction for the "penalty" on the premature withdrawal from long-term savings accounts.

(6) *Disability income exclusion*. California law is the same as federal.

(7) *Alimony*. California has adopted IRC § 215.

(8) *Net operating loss*. The amount of net operating loss sustained in any taxable year during any part of which taxpayer was not a California resident is limited to sum of: (1) portion of net operating loss attributable to part of year in which taxpayer is a resident; and (2) portion of net operating loss which, during part of year taxpayer is not a resident, is attributable to California source income and deductions.[36]

DEDUCTIONS

Statutory deductions.   The following items should be noted in connection with determining the allowable itemized deductions on the nonresident California return:

(1) *Interest*. Interest paid on the purchase price of California property and interest on mortgages on such property are deductible, and

(2) *Casualty losses*. Losses of property located in California even though not connected with a trade or business are deductible if the losses arise from fires, storms, shipwreck, or other casualty or from theft.

---

(36) § 17041(i); 17310.

Note: Deductions of nonresidents relating to income from sources within and without the state must be apportioned and allocated according to rules prescribed by the Franchise Tax Board.[37]

CREDITS AGAINST TAX

California tax credits are explained starting at ¶ 140. Nonresidents and part-year residents are not eligible for the tax credit for elderly; they can qualify for the other state tax credits if they meet the requirements. The tax credit for income tax paid by nonresidents to their home state is explained at ¶ 147.

Proration of nonresident and part-year resident credits. Nonresidents and part-year residents will be allowed all credits in the same proportion as the ratio used to determine tax under Rev & TC § 17041—adjusted gross income from California sources to adjusted gross income from all sources.

Exceptions: (1) Credits allowed that are conditional upon a transaction occurring within California will be allowed in their entirety; (2) no credit for the elderly will be allowed to a nonresident; (3) no proportionate credit under Rev & TC § 17055 will be allowed under Rev & TC § 17053.5, relating to renter's credit, and § 18002, relating to taxes paid to another state.[38]

¶ 183 **Change of Status—Resident or Nonresident**

When the status of a taxpayer changes from resident to nonresident or from nonresident to resident, the accrual method is used to determine the status of income and deductions before and after the date of the change. In other words, income which had accrued to a nonresident prior to the time he moved to California and took up residence in the state is not includable in taxable income, even though received after the date of the change. In the same fashion, deductions which had accrued prior to the change are not deductible against California income after the date of the change.[39]

The income and deductions for the year of the change and for subsequent years are reported under the taxpayer's regular method of accounting—cash or accrual.[40]

EXAMPLE If a California resident (reporting on a cash basis) earned $8,000 in California prior to becoming a resident of New York on July 1 and received half of this amount in December and the balance in January, after he has acquired a New York residence, he must report in his California return $4,000 in one year, and $4,000 in the second year. Under the same facts, except that the taxpayer is a New York resident who

---

(37) § 17301.
(38) § 17055.

(39) § 17554.
(40) LR 58, 12–5–58.

became a California resident on July 1, all such income earned in New York would not be subject to the California income tax.

Problems when residence is changed. The decisions and rulings on change of residence are excerpted below to better illustrate areas where problems exist:

ILLUSTRATIVE DECISIONS

Pensions—employer contributions while nonresident, excludable. The general rule that nonresidents are taxed only on income from California sources applies to payments received from an employee's pension trust. Even if the taxpayer is on the cash basis and is now a California resident, amounts received during the year are excludable from gross income because they represent employer contributions and interest nonforfeitably credited to the employee's pension fund account while he was a nonresident of California. The tax does apply to amounts received during the year based on employer contributions and interest credited after the employee became a California resident (Appeal of E.W.L. Tydeman, (SBE 1–5–90). A letter ruling states that pensions aren't excludable merely because they are attributable to services performed outside California before the taxpayer became a resident (see *Flaherty* case below). It also states that amounts such as those in *Tydeman* case are excludable as accrued to the nonresident before he became a resident to the extent payable to the employee if he were to terminate employment before becoming a resident. If the taxpayer retired before becoming a resident, all pension payments from outside sources payable to him, or to which he became entitled before he became a resident, are excludable.[40]

IMPORTANT

Noncontributory pensions. *Payments received while resident—taxable.* Pension payments received by the taxpayer, a California resident, under two noncontributory pension plans were subject to tax in California even though the services entitling the taxpayer to the pensions had been rendered outside of California while he was a nonresident. The taxpayer's right to the pension income did not "accrue" prior to its actual receipt, since each monthly payment was contingent upon his continued life and no definite lump sum was payable to him, to his estate, or to any named beneficiary (Appeal of Edward B. and Marion R. Flaherty, SBE 1–6–96). The taxpayer received pensions from a municipality and from the United States Navy, under an arrangement whereby the payments were to terminate when the taxpayer died. In other words, his beneficiary would not receive a lump-sum settlement nor monthly payments. Taxpayer had to be alive in order for the payment to be received.

Pensions connected with California employment—taxable. In a similar, but opposite situation, California residents moved to the state of

Idaho while receiving monthly pension payments from a municipal pension plan. Under the plan the taxpayer's right to receive the pension income was contingent upon his continued life. The Board of Equalization decided that the payments were taxable income from sources within California. The basis for the decision is that the payments were directly attributable to the taxpayer's former employment within California, citing that retirement annuity is a form of deferred compensation for personal services. The Board of Equalization stated that the source of the income from personal services is a place of actual performance, not the residence of the taxpayer or the place of payment *(Appeal of John J. and Virginia Baustian, (SBE 3-7-79).*

Income in respect of decedent. Annuity payments received by a California resident, as the beneficiary of a retirement pension earned by a nonresident father for services performed in Pennsylvania, were not taxable to the recipient because of the provisions regarding income in respect to a decedent. The purpose of these provisions is to place the beneficiary in the shoes of the decedent who would not have been taxable had he been alive and receiving the annuity payments. However, the Board of Equalization in its decision then went on to say that for an annuity contract, if purchased by an employer for an employee under a qualified noncontributory plan, the amounts received as annuity payments by a beneficiary after the death of an employee or retired employee are included in the gross income of that beneficiary. Therefore, the amounts received by the taxpayer as the current beneficiary should be included in her gross income because she is a resident of California. Her tax liability is not altered by the circumstance that the income was derived from sources outside of California *(Appeal of Preston T. and Virginia R. Kelsey, SBE 3-8-76).*

Gain realized from the sale of stock did not accrue prior to the taxpayers' becoming California residents. Furthermore, the taxpayers' distributive share of income from an Illinois partnership was not ascertainable until the close of the partnership's taxable year, which occurred after the taxpayers became California residents. *(Appeal of Jerald L. and Joan Katleman SBE 12-15-76).* When liquidation gain accrued at the time taxpayers had not yet become residents of California, it wasn't taxable. Assets and liabilities of liquidating out-of-state company had become known with enough certainty to ascertain the amount of final dividend.[1]

Royalties. Royalty income of a recording artist does not accrue until the records on which the royalty is based are sold. Consequently, a recording artist is taxable only on those royalties accruing while he is a resident of California or resulting from personal services performed within California.[2]

Moving expense reimbursements. The reimbursement of nonresident taxpayers' pre-move travel expenses and expenses incurred in connection

---

(1) LR 248, 10-30-59.   (2) LR 132, 12-5-58.

with the sale of their Illinois home constituted California source income because the payments were directly related to the taxpayers' California employment and represented compensation for services to be performed in California. *(Appeal of William H. Harmount and Estate of Dorothy E. Harmount, SBE 8–28–77; (Appeal of James H. and Heloise A. Frame, SBE 11–14–79).*

Professional athletes. A nonresident professional football player must compute his California income for the working days spent in California from the first practice day; for the first regular season game through the team's post-season game. *(Appeal of Michael D. and L. Joy Eischeid, SBE 10–6–76).*

The Franchise Tax Board used a "working day" formula to apportion the salary of a nonresident football player in and out of California, rather than a "games played" formula used by other states, or California for other sports. The Board of Equalization said that it was not discriminatory to use the working days formula when the games played formula would fail to give a reasonable allocation required by the statute. *(Appeal of Dennis F. and Nancy Partee, SBE 10–6–76).*

CHAPTER **2**

GROSS INCOME—INCLUSIONS

¶ 201   **Gross Income**

Gross income means all income from whatever source derived unless excluded by law. Gross income means income realized in any form whether in money or services. Income may be realized, therefore, in the form of services, meals, accommodations, stock or other property, or cash. California has adopted the IRC § 61 definition of gross income.[1]

To whom income is taxable.   Salaries and other forms of pay for services rendered generally are income to the person who performs the services. Income from property and gain from the sale of property generally are income to the property's owner. However, income received by an agent is not taxable to the agent—the income is taxable to the principal. Income received by reservation Indians from reservation sources is exempt. But income earned outside the reservation is not. The basis of the exemption is federal preemption of state laws.[2]

Community property income.   California is a community property state so that a husband and wife domiciled in California may each report one-half of the community income in separate returns. Generally, income earned by the spouses through their efforts or investments after their marriage is community income. Income from property acquired after the marriage by either the husband or wife or both (except property acquired by gift, bequest, devise or inheritance) generally is community income.

In the Appeal of Annette Bailey, SBE 3–8–76, it was determined that one-half of the husband's earnings from an out-of-state business was taxable to the wife in California even though the taxpayers were not living together and the wife didn't receive any part of the earnings. The husband was a nonresident of California but was a California domiciliary so that the wife was taxable on her one-half of community income.

When a husband lived and worked in another community property state, his wife as a resident of California was taxable by California on one-half of his salary (see *the Appeal of George F. and Magdalena Hermann, SBE 8–6–62.)* The California District Court of Appeals in *Todd v. McColgan (1949) 89 Cal App 2d 509* stated that in determining the community and separate portions of income derived by a husband from his separate property (a partnership interest in a business he owned prior to marriage), the separate portion of the partnership income, representing a fair return on his investment, could be based on an 8% return on invested capital.

Note: Starting in 1981, a spouse is taxed only on her separate income—without including community income of the other spouse—when a separate return is filed. It must be shown, however, that the spouses are separated and have no intent to resume marital relationship [Civ Cd § 5118].

Allocation of income between spouses.   In any case where a husband and wife file separate returns, the Franchise Tax Board has the authority to

---

(1) § 17071.   (2) LR 399, 1–19–77.

distribute, apportion, or allocate gross income between the spouses if necessary to properly reflect income.[3] There is no similar provision in the Internal Revenue Code.

IRC adopted. California has adopted the following provisions of the Internal Revenue Code (IRC), enacted as of 1–1–93, relative to items of income that must be included in gross income:

- IRC § 71, Alimony and separate maintenance payments (¶ 218);
- IRC § 72, Annuities (¶ 214);
- IRC § 73, Services of a child (¶ 208);
- IRC § 74, Prizes and awards (¶ 203);
- IRC § 75, Dealers in tax-exempt securities (¶ 216);
- IRC § 77, Commodity credit loans (¶ 219);
- IRC § 79, Group-term life-insurance purchased for employee (¶ 202);
- IRC § 82, Reimbursement for moving expenses (¶ 202);
- IRC § 83, Property transferred in connection with performance of services (¶ 221); and
- IRC § 84, Transfer of appreciated property to political organization (¶ 361).

Exceptions. California has not adopted the following:

- Penalties for premature plan distributions under IRC § 72(m)(5) and § 72(o)(2) are 2½% in California;
- 10% under federal;
- IRC § 85, tax on unemployment compensation does not apply in California;
- IRC § 72(f)(2) on special rules for computing employee's contributions applies without respect to exceptions for income of US citizens living abroad;
- non-cash patronage allocations (¶ 217).

¶ 202   Compensation for Personal Services

An employee must include the entire compensation in gross income before payroll deductions are taken out. The employment may be temporary, part-time, seasonal or casual. Compensation for personal services received from persons other than an employer, such as tips, is still taxable. The Franchise Tax Board requires withholding for tips in the same manner as for federal purposes. See ¶ 275 for dependent care assistance.

Employee's moving expenses and losses. Reimbursement and other payments to employees for moving expenses from one residence to another in connection with their employment are included in gross income. They may be received directly or indirectly and in the form of money, property or services. An employer's payment to an employee for loss on sale of his residence caused by the relocation must be included in the employee's income.

Parking cash-out programs. Amounts which an employee receives from an employer under an employer-sponsored parking subsidy program ("parking cash-out program") will be included in the employees gross income. A

---

(3) § 17555.

"parking cash-out program" is one which gives the employee the option of receiving subsidized parking or an equivalent cash allowance.

Fees.   Offerings, marriage fees, and similar items received for services rendered by a clergyman are includable in gross income as are jury fees exclusive of mileage reimbursement.[4] Fees to executives for serving on the boards of directors of corporations are taxable income.

TAX TIP	Even in situations where the taxpayer is a participant in a profit-sharing retirement plan, or pension plan of his employer, the director's fees from independent corporations may be the basis for his establishing his own self-employed retirement plan (Keogh).

Group-term life insurance.   California has adopted the federal IRC § 79 provision that group term life insurance purchased for employees by the employer is included in gross income of the employee to the extent that the cost exceeds the sum of the cost of $50,000 of such insurance. Employee contributions reduce the taxable amount. Employer-paid premiums for coverage over $50,000 are not income to the employee if the employer is directly or indirectly the beneficiary.[5]

Group health or hospitalization insurance.   California has adopted the federal IRC § 106 provision that premiums paid by employers are not taxable to employees. Premiums, including reimbursements to employees, paid by employers under sick pay plans are not taxable.[6] The gross income of an employee does not include employer-provided coverage under an accident or health plan.

Employees of a foreign country.   The taxability of compensation of employees of a foreign country is determined under IRC § 893 that excludes such compensation from taxation if: (1) the employee is not a U.S. citizen, or is a citizen of the Philippine Republic, whether or not a U.S. citizen; and (2) in the case of an employee of a foreign government, the services are of a character similar to those performed by US government employees in foreign countries, and (3) the foreign government employer grants an equivalent exemption to U.S. government employees performing similar service in the foreign country.[7]

OBSERVATION	*Compensation earned outside the U.S.* California has not adopted IRC § 911 which provides an exclusion for certain income earned outside the U.S. by U.S. citizens or resident aliens living abroad. Income earned in a foreign country is taxed by California if earned by a resident or domiciliary of California.[8]

Unemployment compensation.   California has not adopted IRC § 85 that taxes all of unemployment compensation paid under federal govern-

---

(4) Fed Reg No. 1.61–2(a).

(5) § 17081.

(6) § 17131.

(7) § 17146.

(8) IRC § 911; § 17024.5.

ment programs. Under IRC § 85, gross income includes unemployment compensation.[9]

¶ 203   **Compensation Distinguished From Gift**

Outright gifts are not included in gross income. But gifts received from one who is also paying for services, or from one who is receiving services without paying an adequate amount for them, the "gifts" may be deemed to be includable in gross income. Of principal importance in deciding whether or not an item received is a gift or compensation is payor's intent to make a gift. If he does not deduct it in his own return, it is evidence that he considered it to be a gift and vice versa. *In the Appeal of Ida Rogers, SBE 11–27–56* and the *Appeal of Irma Livingston, SBE 11–27–56* the Board of Equalization decided that a corporation's payments to a widow and dependent were gifts on the basis that there was no obligation to pay, and the payor derived no benefit from the payment and the payee provided no services.

Awards and prizes.   California has adopted IRC § 74.[10] Under federal IRC § 74(a)–(b), awards and prizes are part of a taxpayer's gross income unless they are paid principally to recognize religious, charitable, scientific, educational, literary or civic achievement. In the latter case it must be shown that the recipient was selected without any action on his part to enter the contest or the proceedings, that, he is not required to render present or substantial future services for the award, and the prize or award is transferred by the payor to the governmental unit or organization described in IRC § 170(c)(1)–(2) (US, state, political subdivision, possession, or DC, or religious, charitable, etc. organization), pursuant to a designation made by the recipient.

California also adopts IRC § 74(c) that excludes from gross income the value of an employment achievement award, as defined in IRC § 274(j), received by a taxpayer if the cost to the employer of the award does not exceed the amount allowable as a deduction to the employer for the cost of the award. If the cost of the award exceeds the amount allowable as a deduction to the employer, gross income includes the greater of: (1) the portion of the cost not allowable as a deduction, not in excess of the award's value, or (2) the amount by which the award's value exceeds the amount allowable as a deduction. The value of a trip to Rome, awarded by an airline as a prize for an editorial on aviation was includable in the recipient's income. *Appeal of Joseph A. and Elizabeth Kugelmass, SBE 10–10–64.* California State Lottery prizes are exempt from state and local taxes under Govt Cd § 8880.68.

Under IRC § 274(j), adopted by California, the deduction for the cost of an employee achievement award made by an employer to an employee that is: (1) not a qualified plan award, when added to the cost for all other such employee achievement awards made to an employee during a taxable year,

---

(9) IRC § 85; § 17083.   (10) § 17081.

cannot exceed $400; (2) a qualified plan award, when added to the cost of all other such employee achievement awards, during the taxable year, including those that are not qualified plan awards, cannot exceed $1,600.

¶ 204   **Qualified Scholarships**

California has adopted by reference in Rev & TC § 17131, all of the provisions of IRC § 117 which provides an exclusion from gross income for qualified scholarships.

> *Note:* Under the law, unreimbursed work-related educational expenses are deductible as miscellaneous itemized expenses subject to a 2% floor (see ¶ 328).

Medical residency.   In the *Appeal of Charles B. and Irene L. Larkin, Board of Equalization, SBE 6–22–76,* it was determined that payments to a doctor while in resident training in psychiatry at a state hospital and in a clinical fellowship at a county medical center were not scholarship or fellowship grants and therefore not excludable (see also Fed Reg 1.117–3). A similar result was reached by the Board in the *Appeal of William W. and Barbara R. Clover, SBE 5–10–77.*

Christa McAuliffe Fellows-interim treatment.   California has adopted TAMRA § 6005, an uncodified section of the 1988 Act, for taxable years starting on or after 1–1–88. The amount of such a fellowship, received by a teacher before 7–1–90, and expended in accordance with the terms of the award on an approved school project for the benefit and use of a school or school system will be treated as an award to the school and will not be included in the gross income of the teacher. The award must be used only for an education project approved by the federal Department of Education.[11]

¶ 205   **Employer Educational Assistance Programs**

California has adopted IRC § 127 which provides a limited exclusion from gross income for a maximum amount of $5,250 per year for employer provided educational assistance. Educational assistance generally means the provision of, or payment of, an employee's educational expenses for tuition, fees, books, supplies, equipment and similar expenses. The California exclusion will remain in effect for only those tax years, or portions thereof, to which the federal exclusion applies.

Meals, lodging, or transportation, and tools or supplies which may be retained by the employee after the completion of the educational program cannot be excluded under these provisons. The exclusion does not apply to any education or benefits involving sports, games, or hobbies.[12]

¶ 206   **Military Pay**

Payment for services in the armed forces of the United States is fully taxable for federal income tax purposes for officers, enlisted personnel and the students at the Service Academies. Monthly allotments chargeable to the

---

(11) § 17160.   (12) § 17024.5.

serviceman's pay must be included in gross income but the monthly basic allowance for quarters for dependents is not to be considered in determining gross income.

Combat pay. California has adopted federal IRC § 112(a)–(c) to the effect that compensation received for active service by an enlisted man in the U.S. Armed Forces for any month in which he served in a combat zone or was hospitalized as a result of wounds, disease or injury incurred while serving in the combat zone, is not to be included in income. Compensation which does not exceed $500 received for active service by a commissioned officer in the Armed Forces is similarly excluded.[13] Service is performed in a "combat zone" only if performed on or after the date designated by the President by executive order as the date of the commencing of combatant activities in such zone.

MIAs. California has adopted IRC § 112(d) which provides that gross income also does not include compensation received for active service as a member of the U.S. Armed Forces or a civilian employee for any month during any part of which such member or employee is in a missing status during the Vietnam conflict as a result of such conflict.[13] A presidential order designated end of the Vietnam conflict.

Military or civilian employees of U.S. dying as result of injuries sustained overseas. California adopts the provisions of IRC § 692(c), that exempt from taxation military or civilian employees of the U.S. who die as result of wounds or injury incurred outside the U.S. in terroristic or military action. Tax does not apply with respect to the taxable year in which the date of death falls, and any prior taxable year in the period starting with the last taxable year ending before the taxable year in which the wounds or injury were incurred.[14]

¶ 207 Bargain Purchases by Employees or Independent Contractors

When an employee or an independent contractor buys property at less than market value from a person for whom services are performed, the difference between the amount paid and the property's fair market value is taxable to the buyer as compensation. The basis of the property for gain or loss on a later sale is increased by the amount of the income taxed. Fed Reg § 1.61–2(d)(2) interpreting IRC § 61 applies in California. The FTB has issued no regulations.[15]

¶ 208 Services of a Child

California has adopted IRC § 73 and § 6203.[16] Under IRC § 73, any amounts received for the services of a child are to be included in the gross income of the child and not in the gross income of the parent even though such amounts are not received by the child. Any expenditures by the parent or the

---

(13) § 17131.
(14) § 17731.

(15) § 17024.5; 17071.
(16) IRC § 73; § 17081.

child attributable to the amounts which are includable in the child's gross income are treated as though paid or incurred by the child. Under IRC § 6203, any income tax assessed on the amounts includable in the gross income of the child and not of the parent by reason of this provision will—if not paid by the child—be considered as having also been properly assessed against the parent.

¶ 209   **Pensions and Other Payments to Retired Employees**

Pensions and retirement allowances are taxable when distributed. California conforms to federal law. If the employee did not contribute to the cost of the pension and was not taxed on his employer's contributions, the full amount of the pension must be included in his gross income. Payments to a deceased employee's widow by the employer may be exempt as a gift or may be taxable compensation for the deceased employee's past services. The taxability of pensions where the employee has contributed to the cost depends on the annuity rules.[17]

Death benefit exclusion.   California has adopted the federal IRC § 101(b) under which payments up to $5000 made by the employer to the deceased employee's beneficiary by reason of the death of the employee are not taxable, although any amount over $5000 is taxable. If the payments exceed $5000 and are made to more than one beneficiary of the employee, the non-taxable amount is allocated among the beneficiaries.[18] There is no exclusion for amounts to which the employee had a vested right except when a lump-sum distribution is paid to the beneficiary by an exempt employee's trust or under a qualified annuity plan.

Employees of exempt organizations.   California has adopted IRC § 403(b) that applies the death benefit exclusion to total distributions under an annuity contract purchased for an employee by a tax-exempt organization or for an employee who performs services for an educational institution by an employer which is a state or a political subdivision of a state. When the employee's rights under the contract are nonforfeitable, the amounts contributed by such employer are excluded from the gross income of the employee for the taxable year to the extent that the aggregate of such contributions does not exceed the exclusion allowance.

The exclusion allowance is an amount equal to the excess of the amount determined by multiplying 20% of his annual includable compensation by the number of years of service, over the aggregate of the amounts contributed by the employer for annuity contracts, and excludable from the gross income of the employee for any prior taxable year.[17]

Tax sheltered annuities-contributions-limit reduction.   California has adopted IRC § 402(g) which provides that the amount an employee of a public school or tax-exempt organization can elect to defer in any one year under all elective deferral plans in which the employee participates is lim-

---

(17) § 17501.   (18) § 17131.

ited to the greater of $9,500, or the cash or deferred arrangement cap, as indexed. The cash or deferred arrangment cap for 1994 is $9,240. For 1993 the cap was $8,994, and for 1992, $8,728.

> *Note:* Since the maximum limitation for contributions to all elective deferral plans is $9,500, or the indexed cap, the limitation for contributions to a tax-sheltered annuity for a teacher would have to be reduced by, for instance, contributions to the State Teachers Retirement System.

Social security and tier 1 railroad retirement benefits. California has not adopted the provisions of IRC § 86 that, includes social security and tier 1 railroad retirement benefits in gross income.[19]

Tier 2 railroad retirement benefits. California has not adopted the provisions of IRC § 72(r) that treat these benefits as if they were distributed from qualified retirement plans.[20]

Sick pay under Railroad Unemployment Insurance Act. California has not adopted the provisions of IRC § 105(h) that include these benefits in gross income.[21]

California Legislature's pension plans for legislative employees. IRC § 414(h)(2) permits employers' contributions to pension plans established by state or local governments even though they may be designated under a plan as employee contributions. California has adopted this federal rule.[17] These contributions can be excluded from the federal and California gross income of the employee until distributed or made available by the employer. The employee, to get the benefit of this tax treatment, can't have the option of choosing to receive the contributed amounts directly. IRC § 415(b)(10), relating to special contribution and benefit limits for government plans applies in California as are the IRC § 415(b)(2) rules.[22]

¶ 210 **Lump-Sum Distributions**

A lump-sum distribution is the payment of the total amount due to an employee under a qualified plan, within one taxable year. Such distributions must be attributable to the employee's death or a separation from employment or made after the employee has attained the age of 59½ or is disabled. California law follows federal treatment under IRC § 402 using the tax rates, set forth in Rev & TC § 17041, without regard to Rev & TC § 17045.

Subtractions for contributions. In determining the taxable portion of a lump-sum distribution, it is necessary to subtract from the total amount the amounts contributed to the plan by the employee and the unrealized appreciation of any securities of the employer included in the distribution. California has adopted IRC § 402(a)(1).[23] If there are appreciated securities, the gain on unrealized appreciation at the time of distribution is a long-term

---

(19) IRC § 86; § 17087(a).
(20) IRC § 72(r); § 17087(b).
(21) IRC § 105(i); § 17087(c).

(22) § 17512(b)–(c).
(23) § 17501.

capital gain. The balance at the time of sale is subject to California capital gain rules.[24]

Capital gains.   California imposes a tax on lump-sum distributions computed in accordance with IRC § 402(e) using the rates and brackets prescribed in Rev & TC § 17041(a) for individuals other than heads of household, without regard to the husband and wife income-splitting provisions of Rev & TC § 17045. IRC § 402(e) applies only to distributions prior to 12–31–92. California does not use the rates and brackets set by IRC § 1(c). California has adopted the age 59½ requirement of IRC § 402(e)(4)(B)(i) in the case of lump-sum distributions received by an individual who attained age 50 before 1–1–86.

"Roll-over" of lump-sum distributions.   Taxes on lump-sum distributions which are "rolled over" into an Individual Retirement Account or into another qualified plan provide a deferral of taxes for both federal IRC § 402(a)(5)–(7) and California purposes.[23]The assets distributed under the plan must not be retained by the taxpayer for a period of longer than 60 days before the reinvestment into the new IRA or another qualified plan is made. The rollover feature is available only once during any one-year period. Partial rollover is permitted.

Key employees in top-heavy plans.   California has adopted federal IRC provisions that permit a rollover of a Keogh plan distribution to a qualified plan, including another Keogh plan, or an annuity plan if the distribution is not attributable to contributions made while an individual was a key employee in a top-heavy plan.[25]

¶ 211   **Self-Employed and Individual Retirement Plans**

Lump-sum distribution rules for employee plans (¶ 210) also apply to distributions from self-employed plans. California uses its own rates and tax brackets, and does not follow federal transitional rules. It is necessary to compute separately the amounts which are not taxable on a distribution under the two laws because of the differences in deductibility of the contributions in prior years.[26]

Note: In distributions from Individual Retirement Accounts or self-employment plans generally, if the funds are invested in "retirement bonds," California and federal law (as enacted 1–1–84) provided a different treatment when the bonds are redeemed. Both laws provided that the full proceeds of redemption of such bonds were fully taxable but the interest portion of the redemption was not subject to California tax, if the redeemed bonds were obligations of the United States.[27] The 1984 federal Tax Reform Act (TRA) repealed IRC §§ 405 and 409 relating to qualified bond purchase plans and retirement bonds for obligations issued after 1983. Previously issued obligations remain subject to their original terms. IRC § 402(e) allows individuals to redeem these bonds before age 59½ and roll them over into an IRA or qualified plan within 60 days.

---

(24) IRC § 402(b); § 17085(d); 17505.
(25) IRC § 402(a)(5)(A); 403(a)(4)(A); 403(b)(8)(A); § 17506(a).

(26) § 17085(a)–(c).
(27) § 17133; 17145.

Because California did not adopt the individual retirement account provisions in 1975, any contribution in that particular year to an individual retirement account is not part of an exempt plan. Interest earned on the 1975 contribution in 1976 was subject to California tax when earned and therefore would not be taxable when distributed. Interest earned in 1977 and later years on the 1975 contribution was not includible in gross income and will be taxable on distribution.[28]

IRC § 408(d)(1)–(2) provide that any amount paid or distributed out of an individual retirement plan shall be included in gross income by the payee or distributee as provided in IRC § 72. For purposes of applying IRC § 72 to such amount, all individual retirement plans shall be treated as one contract, all distributions shall be treated as one distribution, and the value of the contract, income on the contract, and investment in the contract must be computed as of close of calendar year with or within which the taxable year ends. The value of the contract must be increased by the amount of any distributions during the calendar year. For taxable years starting on or after 1–1–83, and before 1–1–87, the basis of any person in such account or annuity is amount of contributions not allowed as deductions under former Rev & TC § 17272(a), (e), or (g), as amended by Stats 1985, c 1461 on account of purchase of account or annuity. The rules for the recovery of basis are governed by Rev & TC § 17085.[29]

¶ 212 Non-Exempt Trust or Plan

For purposes of both federal IRC § 402(b) and California law, employer contributions to a trust or plan which is not exempt are taxable to the employee when they are made except where his right to the contributions are subject to a substantial risk of forfeiture as defined in federal IRC § 83. The value of the employee's interest in the trust is substituted for the fair market value of the property. The contributions are not taxable to the employee when made because of the substantial risk of forfeiture provision. The distributions are taxable to the employee when made to him under the annuity rules.[30]

¶ 213 Simplified Pension Plans

California adopts IRC § 219; 402; 404(h); and 408(k) that permit employees who participate in a simplified employee pension plan to have contributions made to the simplified employee pension plan or paid to them in cash. Contributions to the simplified employee pension plan (SEP) pursuant to that election are not taxable to the employee, and are not treated as employee contributions. Elective deferrals under a SEP are treated like elective deferrals under a qualified cash or deferred arrangement, and are subject for 1993, to a $8,994 cap which is indexed annually. These elective deferrals under a SEP are exclusions from income. There is a $200,000 limit on compensation taken into account in determining SEP contributions, and

---

(28) § 17507(a)(1).
(29) § 17085(b); 17504(a)(3); 17506(c); 17507(b).
(30) § 17501.

a $300 threshold for participation. Employer's SEP contributions are excluded from employees' income.[31]

¶ 214   Annuities

California has adopted IRC § 72.[32] Under IRC § 72, gross income includes any amount received as an annuity (whether for a period certain or during one or more lives) under an annuity endowment or life insurance contract. However, gross income does not include that part of any amount received as an annuity under an annuity endowment or life insurance contract which bears the same ratio to such amount as the investment in the contract as of the annuity starting date bears to the expected return under the contract. Any excess of the total amount received as an annuity during the taxable year over the amount determined by the formula is included in gross income of the recipient for the taxable year of receipt. For individuals retiring after 1986, the total amount of annuity income that is excluded over the years as a return on investment may not exceed their total investment reduced by the value of any refund feature. Any unrecovered investment at a retiree's or last annuitants death is allowed as a deduction in the last tax year.

EXAMPLE   A taxpayer purchased an annuity contract providing for payments of $100 per month for a consideration of $12,650. Assuming that the expected return under the contract is $16,000, the exclusion ratio used is $12,650/$16,000 or 79.1%. That percentage of the total received during the year is excluded from gross income, and the balance is taxable.

The expected return, if it depends in whole or in part on the life expectancy of one or more individuals, will be determined by actuarial tables. Otherwise, the expected return is the amount received under the contract as an annuity. Whether or not the recipient outlives his actuarial life, the exclusion is unchanged.

Note: California does not adopt exceptions to special rules for computing employees contributions under IRC § 72(f)(2) for income of U.S. citizens living abroad.[33]

Deferred annuity contracts—restrictions. California has adopted IRC § 72u providing that income from annuity contracts held by a person that is not a natural person (partnerships, corporations and trusts) will not be treated as an annuity contract for income tax purposes. All income on contract is treated as ordinary income received or accrued by the owner during the taxable year. [30]

¶ 215   Employee Annuities

The federal rule in IRC § 72(d) was repealed for retirees whose annuity starting dates were after 7–1–86. An annuity starting date is the later of the first day of the first period for which the retiree receives an annuity payment under the contract, or the date the obligation under the contract becomes fixed. Under California law, retirees whose annuity starting dates are on or

---

(31) IRC § 219; 402; 404(h); 405(k); § 17024.5; 17201; 17501.

(32) § 17081.
(33) § 17084.

after 1–1–87 must report their annuity payments under the general rule. Under this rule, a retiree's contributions are recovered tax-free on a prorated basis, and not in full at the beginning. Part of each payment will be nontaxable and part taxable. Generally, the nontaxable part is the prorated return of the retiree's contributions. The annuity is fully taxable once the retiree's investment, minus the value of any refund feature, has been recovered tax-free. If the retiree dies before full recovery, a special deduction is allowed for the unrecovered amount. Election can be made by a taxpayer whose annuity starting date is after 7–1–86 but before 1–1–87 to be subject to the rules that apply to annuity starting dates on or after 1–1–87. The amount of distribution includible in gross income for federal purposes must be reduced, for California purposes, by the lesser of: (1) the amount includable in federal gross income, or (2) the amount equal to the basis in the annuity allowed by Rev & TC § 17507 remaining after adjustments for prior years. IRC § 72(f)(2) applies without exceptions immediately following that paragraph.[34]

California adopts the IRC § 72(e) rule that if any amount is received under an annuity, endowment, or life insurance contract but not as an annuity, then such amount if received on or after the annuity starting date, will be included in gross income if when added to amounts already received under the contract, it exceeds the aggregate premiums or other consideration paid. Amounts not received as an annuity include any amount received in a single sum or otherwise under a contract in full discharge of the obligation under the contract and any amount received under a contract on its surrender, redemption or maturity. California also adopts the IRC § 72(h) provision that, if, under the terms of the contract, the employee is entitled to receive a lump sum subject to an option to receive an annuity in lieu of the lump sum and such option is exercised within 60 days, the lump sum will not be included in taxable income.[34]

Supplemental railroad retirement annuities are exempt from state tax; federal law (45 USC § 228c(j)(4)) authorizes only federal tax.[35]

State Teacher's Retirement System (STRS) annuities are subject to special rules. (See LR 425, 12–5–84).

> *Note:* The California penalty for premature plan distributions to beneficiaries of qualified employer plan or government plan is 2½% of the amount includible in gross income. Tax on premature distributions is discussed at ¶ 136.

¶ 216   Interest

All interest received or credited to a taxpayer's account is taxable unless it is specifically exempt from tax. Interest on obligations of the United States, its agencies or its instrumentalities is fully taxable for federal purposes, including interest on tax refunds.[36] Interest on bonds that California is prohibited from taxing includes interest on bonds issued by California and local governments in the state. The determination as to whether a bond is issued by the

---

(34) § 17081; LR 425, 12–5–84.   (36) § 17133.
(35) LR 338, 3–5–70.

state or local government must be made without regard to: (1) source of payment or security for bond; or (2) whether or not public improvements are financed by the bond. IRC § 1286(d) applies to treatment of stripped bonds and coupons.[36] Interest on bonds issued by the territories of Alaska and Hawaii before they became states is exempt, but interest on bonds issued thereafter is not exempt from tax.[37] Although interest on such bonds and other obligations of the United States is exempt from taxation, gains and profits from the sale or other disposition of such bonds and obligations are taxable in California to the same extent as other property.[38] California has not adopted the provisions of IRC § 103, § 141 to § 150 that exclude interest on state and local and private activity bonds.

California's treatment of interest on various types of popular federal securities is as follows (LR 255):

> Federal Land Banks—Exempt
> Federal National Mortgage Associations—Taxable
> Housing Authority Bonds—Exempt for California projects only
> Federal Home Loan Bank Bonds—Exempt
> Banks for Cooperatives—Exempt
> Federal Intermediate Credit Banks—Exempt Government National Mortgage Association "Pass-through" securities—Taxable.[39]
> Puerto Rico Bonds and other obligations—Exempt.

Regulated investment companies. California has adopted IRC §§ 851–855 by reference with the exceptional noted below. IRC § 852(b)(5) allows a regulated investment company which invests in tax-exempt state and local bonds to pass through the interest on such bonds to be tax exempt in the hands of the shareholders if at least 50% of its assets is invested in tax-exempt bonds at the close of each quarter, and if at least 90% of its net tax exempt interest is paid during the taxable year of the fund or within 45 days thereafter. These dividends must be identified by written notice to the shareholders within the same period.

Rev & TC § 17145 applies instead of IRC § 852(b)(5). IRC § 852(b)(3)(D), relating to treatment by shareholders of undistributed capital gains does not apply in California. California adopts IRC § 852(f), relating to treatment of certain load charges. California allows a "management company" or series thereof a similar pass-through of "exempt interest dividends." A company is qualified to pay exempt-interest dividends to its shareholders, if, at the close of each quarter of its taxable year, at least 50% of the value of its total assets consists of obligations which, when held by an individual, the interest therefrom is exempt from taxation by California. An "exempt interest dividend" means any dividend or part paid by a management company, or series thereof, in an amount not exceeding the interest

---

(37) LR 266.
(38) § 17133.5.

(39) LR 255, 8–21–64.

received by it during its taxable year on obligations which, when held by an individual, the interest therefrom is exempt from taxation. If the aggregate amount so designated, including exempt-interest dividends paid after the close of the calendar year as described in IRC § 855, is greater than the excess of: (1) the amount of interest received by the company on exempt-interest obligations, as defined; over (2) the amounts that, if the company were treated as an individual, would be disallowed as deductions under Rev & TC § 17280, relating to expenses and interest that relate to tax-exempt income, or IRC § 171(a)(2), relating to amortizable bond premium on tax-exempt bonds, the portion of the distribution that constitutes an exempt-interest dividend shall be only that proportion of the amount so designated as the amount of the excess for that taxable year bears to the amount so designated. A company must designate the dividend as an exempt-interest dividend in a written notice mailed to shareholders not later than 60 days after the close of its taxable year.

¶ 217 Dividends

Dividends received in cash are taxable. California does not adopt IRC § 852(b)(3)(D), relating to treatment by shareholders of a regulated investment company of undistributed capital gains. Also, Rev & TC § 17145, relating to exempt-interest dividends applies instead of IRC § 852(b)(5). (See ¶ 216 above).[40] See Chapter 17 for explanation of non-cash dividends. (¶ 1115–1122)

Patronage dividends. Under California law, a taxpayer can elect to be taxed on non-cash patronage dividends from farmers' cooperatives paid in capital stock, revolving fund certificates, retained certificates or certificates of indebtedness, and letters of advice. The taxpayer reports the dividends as gross income for the taxable year in which received at the face amount of such dividends.

If a taxpayer elects to exclude such dividend in the taxable year in which received, the income will be included in gross income in the year that the certificates are redeemed or realized. If the taxpayer elects this second method, the face amount of such patronage allocations must be disclosed in the return for the taxable year in which they were received. The same method of computing income shall be used with respect to all subsequent taxable years unless a change to a different method is authorized with the approval of the Franchise Tax Board.[1] In the *Appeal of Vito J. LaTorre, SBE 3-25-68,* the taxpayer's election to include the face amount of one type of non-cash patronage allocation in gross income when received constituted an election to report a second type of non-cash allocation in the same way.

The federal law requires that all of the above allocations be included in income in the year of receipt.

---

(40) § 17088; 17145.   (1) § 17086.

¶ 218 **Alimony**

California has adopted IRC § 71, relating to alimony and separate maintenance payments.[2]

Alimony and separate maintenance—general rule. Gross income includes amounts received as alimony or separate maintenance payments.

Alimony and separate maintenance payments defined. The term "alimony or separate maintenance payment" means any payment in cash, if: (1) the payment is received by, or on behalf of a spouse under a divorce or separation instrument; (2) the divorce or separation instrument does not designate the payment as a payment that is not includible in gross income under IRC § 71, and not allowable as a deduction for alimony or separate maintenance payments under IRC § 215; (3) in the case of an individual legally separated from his or her spouse under a decree of divorce or separate maintenance, the payee spouse and the payor spouse are not members of the same household at the time the payment is made; and (4) there is no liability to make the payment for any period after the death of the payee spouse, and there is no liability to make any payment, in cash or property as a substitute for such payments after the death of the payee spouse.

Divorce or separation instrument. Divorce or separation instrument means (1) a decree of divorce or separate maintenance or written instrument incident to such decree; (2) a written separation agreement; or (3) a decree, not described in (1) above, requiring a spouse to make payments for the support or maintenance of the other spouse.

Support payments for children. IRC § 71(a), which includes amounts received as alimony and separate maintenance in gross income, does not apply to any part of the payments that by terms of the divorce or separation instrument fix, in terms of an amount of money, or part of a payment, as a sum that is payable for support of the children of the payor spouse. If any amount specified in the instrument will be reduced: (1) on the happening of a contingency specified in the instrument relating to a child, such as attaining specified age, marriage, death, leaving school, etc., or (2) at a time that can clearly be associated with the above contingencies, an amount equal to the reduction amount will be treated as payable for support of the children of the payor spouse. Where the payment is less than the amount specified in the instrument, so much of that payment that does not exceed the sum payable for support, will be considered a payment for support.

Spouse. Spouse includes a former spouse.

Joint returns. IRC § 71 (gross income treatment) and § 215 (deductions for payment) do not apply to spouses that make a joint return.

Excess front-loading of alimony payments—recomputation. If there are excess alimony payments, the payor spouse must include the amount of

---

(2) IRC § 71; § 17024.5.

those payments in gross income for the payor spouse's taxable year, starting in the third post-separation year, and the payee spouse will be allowed a deduction in computing adjusted gross income for the amount of those excess payments for the payee's taxable year beginning in the third post-separation year.

Excess alimony payments are the sum of (1) the excess payments for the first post-separation year, and (2) the excess payments for the second post-separation year.

Excess alimony payments for the first post-separation year. These excess payments are the excess of (1) the amount of alimony or separate maintenance payments made by the payor spouse during the first post-separation years, over (2) the sum of (a) the average of (i) the alimony or separate maintenance payments paid by the payor spouse during the second post-separation year, reduced by the excess payments for that year, and (ii) the alimony and separate maintenance payments paid during the third post-separation year, plus (b) $15,000.

Excess payments for the second post-separation year. Excess payment for the second post-separation year are the excess of (1) the amount of alimony or separate maintenance payments paid during the second post-separation year, over (2) the sum of those payments made during the third post-separation year plus $15,000.

Post-separation years. The first post-separation year is the first calendar year the payor spouse made payments to the payee spouse of the payments to which the IRC § 71 applies. The second and third years are the first and second succeeding calendar years respectively.

Exceptions to above rules. The rule on excess front-loading of alimony payments in IRC § 71(f)(1) does not apply if either spouse dies or the payee spouse remarries before the close of the third post-separation year, and the alimony or separate maintenance payments cease by reason of such death or remarriage.

Fluctuating payments. Any payment to the extent made pursuant to a continuing liability, over a period of not less than three years to pay a fixed portion or portions of the income from a business or property or from compensation for employment or self-employment is not included within the definition of "alimony or separate maintenance payment."

¶ 219   **Commodity Credit Loans**

California has adopted IRC § 77 which provides that amounts received as loans from the Commodity Credit Corporation may be considered as income for the taxable year in which received by an election on the part of the taxpayer. The election must be followed for all subsequent taxable years unless a change to a different method is approved by the Franchise Tax Board.[3]

¶ 220   Cancellation of Indebtedness

Both California and federal IRC § 108 and § 1017 provide that if a debt of a solvent taxpayer is cancelled or forgiven for consideration, he realizes income in the amount of the debt cancelled. However, gross income does not include any amount otherwise includable in gross income by reason of the discharge of debt if: (1) the discharge occurs in a Title 11 case, or (2) the discharge occurs when the individual is insolvent. If (1) applies, the rule on discharge when insolvent does not apply. If (2) applies, the amount can't exceed the amount by which the taxpayer is insolvent. Debt charges must be recognized in income immediately. [4] The taxpayer must file a consent to the adjustment with his return on Form 982 for both California and federal purposes. The adjustment is made against particular properties in the order prescribed by regulations.

¶ 221   Restricted Property

If a taxpayer, after June 30, 1969, receives restricted stock or property for services performed, the value of the property received over the amount paid for it is included in gross income in the first taxable year in which the taxpayer's interest is transferrable or is not subject to a substantial risk of forfeiture. A substantial risk of forfeiture means that the taxpayer's rights to full enjoyment of the property depend directly or indirectly upon the future performance (or refraining from performing) of substantial services by the taxpayer or any person. The appreciation in value of the property between the time it is received and when it is included in income is ordinary income. Any appreciation after it is included in income is treated as capital gain. As an exception the employee can elect, by filing a written statement, to have the fair market value of the restricted property in excess of cost taxed in the year received even though the restrictions are in effect. Any later appreciation of the property would be subject to capital gain rates.[5] California adopted these provisions of the Tax Reform Act of 1969 with the same effective dates and transitional rules.[6]

¶ 222   Rents

Rental payments must be included in gross income and offset by deductions for depreciation, mortgage interest, taxes and all other ordinary and necessary expenses of operating the property. Improvements made by the lessee on the lessor's real property reverting to the lessor on the termination of a lease in the form of buildings or other improvements are not includable in taxable income of the lessor.[7]

---

(3) § 17081.
(4) § 17131.
(5) IRC § 83; Fed Reg 1.83–1—1.83–8.

(6) § 17081.
(7) § 17071; 17132.

¶ 223   **State Officials' Expense Allowances**

California Government Code § 11034 provides that certain officials of the state of California can exclude from gross income up to $10,000 per year of amounts they receive from the state for an expense allowance for all ordinary and necessary expenses incurred in carrying out the functions and duties of their office, including entertainment expenses.[8] Under IRC § 162(h), state legislators are treated as having spent the higher of the federal per diem or state per diem (but it cannot exceed the federal's by 10%) in the state capitol as travel expenses away from home. It is necessary, however, that the state legislator elect to use his legislative district as his tax home. A legislator is deemed away from home on each legislative day and each day he attends committee hearings.

¶ 224   **Illegal Payments, Bribes, Kickbacks**

Income from illegal activities is taxable. Examples of such activities are gambling, betting, winnings, extortion, embezzlement and fraud. [9]

California adopts IRC § 90, relating to illegal federal irrigation subsidiaries. Under IRC § 90, gross income includes an amount equal to any illegal federal irrigation subsidy received by a taxpayer during the taxable year. "Illegal federal irrigation subsidy" is the excess, if any, of the amount required to be paid for any federal irrigation water delivered to the taxpayer during the taxable year, over the amount paid for such water. No deduction is allowed by reason of any inclusion in gross income.[10]

¶ 225   **Credits and Treatment of Credit Carryovers**

California has adopted IRC § 111(b)(1)–(2), relating to credits and IRC § 111(c), relating to treatment of carryovers. California conformity statute bars adoption of IRC § 111(b)(3), relating to the investment tax credit under IRC § 46 and the foreign tax credit.

Under IRC § 111(b)(1), if a credit was allowable with respect to any amount for any prior taxable year, and during the taxable year there is a downward price adjustment, or similar adjustment, the tax imposed for the taxable year must be increased by the amount of the credit attributable to the adjustment. This rule does not apply to the extent that the credit allowable to the recovered amount did not reduce the amount of tax imposed.

Under IRC § 111(c), an increase in a carryover that has not expired before the beginning of the taxable year in which the recovery or adjustment takes place must be treated as reducing the tax.[11]

¶ 226   **Other Items of Gross Income**

Items of income that are related to exclusions from gross income are covered in Chapter 3. They include: interest earned after insured's death (¶ 253);

---

(8) § 17071; 17132.

(9) § 17071.

(10) § 17024.5.

(11) § 17142.

amounts not considered as gifts (¶ 254); settlement received for loss of profits (¶ 255); certain amounts received under accident and health plans (¶ 256); bad debts later recovered (¶ 260). Items of income related to adjustments to income in Chapter 4 are taxable portion of capital gains (¶ 296); unreimbursed moving expenses (¶ 297); premature distributions from retirement plans (¶ 299; 300); certain amounts realized under stock option plans either on exercise of option or sale of stock received (¶ 309). Under Section III, Tax Concepts for Individuals and Corporations, items of income explained are: Gain or loss from sale or exchange of property (¶ 361–362); income from installment sales (¶ 364); depreciation recapture (¶ 401); and income produced by inventories (¶ 411).

CHAPTER **3**

GROSS INCOME—EXCLUSIONS

¶ 251   What Are Exclusions From Gross Income

Gross income is income less the income exempt from tax. Exempt items are commonly called exclusions. They should not be confused with exemptions allowed by law. An item may be excluded from gross income because:

(1) Under the U.S. Constitution it is not taxable by the federal or the state government;

(2) Under the Constitution of California it is not taxable by the state;

(3) It does not come within the definition of the term "income" such as a return of capital;[1] or

(4) It is expressly excluded by the statutes of the United States or California.[2]

IRC adoption.   California has adopted the following provisions of the Internal Revenue Code (IRC), enacted as of 1–1–93, which provides for certain exclusions from gross income:

- IRC § 101, Certain death payments (¶ 253);
- IRC § 102, Gifts and inheritances (¶ 254);
- IRC § 104, Compensation for injuries and sickness (¶ 255);
- IRC § 105, Amounts received under accident and health plans (¶ 256);
- IRC § 106, Contributions by employer to accident and health plans (¶ 256);
- IRC § 107, Rental value of parsonages (¶ 257);
- IRC § 108, Income from discharge of indebtedness (¶ 258);
- IRC § 109, Lessee's improvements on lessor's property (¶ 259);
- IRC § 111, Recovery of tax benefit items (¶ 260);
- IRC § 112, Certain combat pay of members of armed forces (¶ 206);
- IRC § 117, Scholarship and fellowship grants (¶ 204);
- IRC § 119, Meals or lodging furnished for convenience of employers (¶ 263);
- IRC § 121, Sale or exchange of residence—one-time exclusion (¶ 261);
- IRC § 122, Certain reduced uniformed services retirement pay (¶ 206);
- IRC § 123, Living expense insurance payments (¶ 262);
- IRC § 125, Cafeteria plans (¶ 264);
- IRC § 126, Governmental payments for environmental conservation (¶ 271);
- IRC § 127, Educational assistance programs (¶ 269);
- IRC § 129, Dependent care assistance programs (¶ 275);
- IRC § 130, Personal injury liability assignments (¶ 255);
- IRC § 131, Foster care payments (¶ 287);
- IRC § 893, Exclusion of compensation of employees of foreign governments (¶ 203);
- IRC § 115, Exclusion of income of states and political divisions derived from any public utility, or exercise of governmental functions (¶ 271).

Additional exclusions.   California provided additional exclusions for (1) expenses of government officials (¶ 223), and (2) stipends, meals, transportation received under foster grandparent and senior companion programs (¶ 272).

---

(1) § 17071.   (2) § 17131—17150.

Modifications or exceptions. California does not follow the federal rule for management company exempt-interest dividends but has adopted a modification of this rule (¶ 216). California does not allow the exclusion found in IRC § 136(a)(4) for ship contractor's payments deposited in special funds under § 607(d) of the Merchant Marine Act of 1936.

¶ 253 Life Insurance

Under federal IRC § 101(a), adopted by California, gross income does not include amounts received (whether in a single sum or otherwise) under a life insurance contract if such amounts are paid by reason of the death of the insured person. Proceeds of group life insurance contracts paid for by a taxpayer's employer are within this exclusion. If a life insurance contract or an interest in one is transferred for a valuable consideration by assignment or otherwise, the exclusion of the death proceeds is limited to the consideration paid plus the premiums or other sums subsequently paid by the buyer. However, all of the proceeds are excludable if the buyer's basis is determined by reference to the seller's basis in the contract or the transfer of the contract was to the insured or a corporation in which the insured is a shareholder or officer.

Interest earned after insured's death. California has adopted federal IRC § 101(d)(1) which provides that when the beneficiary receives the proceeds in installments that include interest earned after the insured's death, the interest element of the payment is taxable to the beneficiary.[3]

"Amounts held by an insurer". Amounts held by an insured under an insurance contract with respect to any beneficiary must be prorated over the period that payments are to be made. The prorated amounts are excluded from income. Amounts in excess of the exclusion are taxable as interest. California has adopted this federal IRC § 101(d)(2)(A) rule.[3]

Option to receive lump sum. California has adopted IRC § 101(d)(2)(B). Under this federal provision if one of the options in the insurance contract is to take a specific amount in a lump sum, that is the amount that is prorated. But when the contract does not have an option providing for a payment of a lump-sum amount upon the death of the insured, the amount that can be excluded is determined by finding the value (with respect to each beneficiary on a particular contract) of the agreement as of the date of death of the insured, discounted on the basis of the interest rate and mortality tables used in determining payment.[3]

Public Employees Retirement System. Exempt status is generally given to group insurance proceeds and other benefits received by survivors of state employees; annuity rules also apply to these persons.[4] Annuity rules are explained at ¶ 214.

---

(3) § 17131.   (4) LR 412, 1–16–79.

Life insurance contract. The definition of a life insurance contract in IRC § 7702 has been adopted by California. A life insurance contract, for both California and federal purposes, means any contract that, under applicable law, is a life insurance contract, but only if the contract meets the cash value accumulation test of IRC § 7702(b), guideline premium requirements of IRC § 7702(c), and falls within the cash value corridor of § 7702(d). If a contract does not meet these requirements, the income on the contract for any taxable year of the policyholder will be treated as ordinary income received or accrued by the policyholder during that year. These rules also apply to endowment contracts.[5]

¶ 254   Gifts and Inheritance

California follows IRC § 102 that provides that gross income does not include the value of property acquired by gift, bequest, devise or inheritance. However, the income from any property received as a gift or bequest is not excluded. Also, when the gift, bequest, devise or inheritance is of income from property, the amount of such income is taxable.[6] California also follows IRS Rev Rulings 74–22 and 74–23. Under IRS Rev Rul 74–23, political campaign contributions are not taxable to a candidate. However, interest and cash dividends and gains on sales of contributed securities are includable in gross income. Amounts diverted from political campaign contributions to the personal use of the candidate are taxable and must be reported by him in year diverted (IRS Rev Rul 74–22).

> *Note:* When under the terms of the gift, bequest, devise or inheritance, the payment is to be made at intervals, then to the extent that it is paid out of income from property, it is taxable to the recipient.

Gifts of specific sums or property.   A gift or bequest of a specific sum of money or specific property is exempt even though paid out of income, if it is required under the terms of the governing instrument to be paid or credited all at once or in not more than three installments. If the terms of the instrument require it to be paid or credited in more than three installments or if it can be paid or credited only out of income, the gift or bequest is taxable.[7]

In order to qualify as a gift or bequest of a specific sum of money or of specific property, the amount of money or the identity of the specific property must be ascertainable under the terms of a will as of the date of death, or under the terms of an inter vivos trust instrument as of the date of the inception of the trust. For example, bequests to a decedent's son of the decedent's interest in the partnership and to his daughter of a sum of money equal to the value of the partnership interest are bequests of specific property and of a specific sum of money, respectively. On the other hand, a bequest to the decedent's spouse of money or property to be selected by the decedent's executor equal in value to a fraction of the decedent's "adjusted

---

(5) § 17020.6.
(6) § 17131.

(7) Federal Reg 1.663(a)–1(a).

gross estate" is neither a bequest of a specific sum of money nor of specific property.[8]

Amounts not considered as gifts or bequests of a sum of money or property:

(1) An amount that can be paid or credited only from the income of an estate or trust whether from the income for the year of payment or crediting or from the income accumulated from a prior year;

(2) An annuity or periodic gift of specific property in lieu of, or having the effect of, an annuity;

(3) A residuary estate or the corpus of a trust; or

(4) A gift or bequest paid in a lump sum or in not more than three installments if the gift or bequest is required to be paid in more than three installments under the terms of the governing instrument.[9]

Courts have defined a gift as a gratuitous transfer of property. The central elements of a gift are:

(a) A donor competent to make the gift;

(b) A clear and unmistakable intention on his part to make it;

(c) A donee able to take the gift; and

(d) A conveyance, assignment or transfer vesting legal title in the donee without power of revocation at the will of the donor and a relinquishment of dominion in control of the subject matter of the gift by delivery to the donee.

¶ 255   Compensation for Injury or Sickness

California has adopted the IRC § 104 rules on excluded compensation for injury or sickness. The exclusion is limited to physical injuries and sickness. It does not include awards for discrimination or unfair labor practices. The following are excluded from gross income of the taxpayer under federal IRC § 104:

(1) Amounts received under Workmen's Compensation Acts as compensation for personal injuries or sickness,

(2) Amounts received as damages (whether by suit or agreement) on account of personal injuries or sickness,

(3) Amounts received through accident or health insurance for personal injuries or sickness attributable to the taxpayer's own contributions,

(4) Amounts received as a pension, annuity, or similar allowance for personal injuries or sickness resulting from acts of service while in the armed forces or certain other public service categories on or before September 24, 1975 or taxpayer was entitled to receive amounts for personal injuries or sickness on that date or received reimbursements for combat-related injury or illness expenses,[10]

(5) Amounts received by an individual as disability income attributable to injuries incurred as a direct result of violent attack that Secretary of State determines to be a terrorist attack that occurred while that individual was an employee of the U.S. engaged in the performance of his official duties outside the U.S.

Public employees. Disability retirement pensions and death benefits of San Francisco police and fire personnel are nontaxable so long as they are

---

(8) Federal Reg 1.663(a)–1(b)(1).

(9) Federal Reg. 1.663(a)–1(b)(2).

(10) § 17131.

not measured, under the city retirement plan, by service retirement allowance.[10] A similar rule applies to salaries paid to Oakland firemen and policemen during disability or when under disability pensions,[10], and Los Angeles firemen and policemen.[11]

Payments by employer to disability fund. California follows IRS Rev Rul 72–191. Voluntary payments made by an employer to a state sponsored fund to provide nonoccupational disability benefits are not taxable to employees.

Structured settlements. California has conformed to IRC § 130. Favored treatment of structured settlement agreements is limited to assignments requiring payment of damages on account of a claim for personal injuries involving the claimant's physical injury or sickness, including damages for wrongful death arising from physical injury or sickness. A settlement company that pays damages in a series of periodic payments can the exclude income received for the contract if it is used to buy qualified funding assets. The basis of the assets is reduced by exclusion; on disposal of funding assets, gains are ordinary income. A taxpayer liable for damages to an injured party can deduct the amount of damages as if they were paid in lump sum.[12]

¶ 256   Amounts Received Under Accident and Health Plans

Generally. Under IRC § 105(a), adopted by California, amounts received by an employee through an accident or health insurance for personal injuries or sickness are taxable and to be included in gross income to the extent the payments are (1) the result of contributions by the employer that were not includable in the employee's gross income; or (2) they are paid by the employer. However, any payment received under an accident or health insurance policy which has been paid for by the taxpayer generally is not taxable. Similarly, accident and health benefits employees receive from company plans attributable to their own contributions are not taxable.[13]

Three types of benefits resulting from an employer's contributions to the plan may be excluded from the employee's income entirely or in part. These are:

● Payments to reimburse a taxpayer for expenses incurred by him for medical care for himself, his spouse and his dependents provided they are not deducted as medical expenses.[14]

● Amounts which are in payment for the permanent loss or loss of use of a member or function of the body or the permanent disfigurement of the taxpayer and/or his dependents, if payments are based on the nature of the injury and not on the time the employee is absent from work (the employee can also take the medical expense deductions).[15]

● Under IRC § 106, gross income of an employee does not include employer-provided coverage under an accident or health plan. P.L. 101–40, § 203, relating to

---

(11) LR 365, 12–14–73; LR 178, 12–5–58; LR 097, 12–5–58.
(12) IRC § 104; 130; 468B; § 17024.5; 17131.
(13) § 17131.
(14) IRC § 105(b); § 17131.
(15) IRC § 105(c); § 17131.

the reinstatement of pre-1986 act nondiscrimination rules applies in California to the same taxable years as provided by federal law.[16]

Accident and health plan limits. California follows IRC § 105(e)–(h), including restrictions on the excess reimbursements paid to a highly compensated individual for the years commencing January 1, 1980. A highly compensated individual is defined as one of the five highest paid officers who is among the highest paid 25% of all employees or who is a shareholder owning more than 10% of the company stock. In order for the provision not to apply, the plan must provide for certain nondiscrimination requirements. To meet the non-discrimination requirements a plan must benefit at least 70% of all of the employees or 80% of all eligible employees (if at least 70% of all employees are eligible) or a class of employees found not to discriminate in favor of highly compensated individuals, by the IRS or the Franchise Tax Board. Part-time workers, employees under age 25 or with less than three years of service, and certain employees excluded as a result of a collective bargaining agreement may be excluded from the coverage. "Excess reimbursements" are amounts reimbursed as plan benefits which are available to highly compensated employees but not to other participants.[17]

Allocating benefits based on an employer and employee contribution. When contributions are made jointly by the employee and the employer, the benefits received must be allocated between them. For an individual policy under a contributory insured plan, the amount resulting from the employer's contributions is proportionate to the premiums he paid for the policy year.[18]

For a group policy, the amount resulting from the employer's contributions is proportionate to the net premiums contributed by the employer for the last three policy years before the calendar year of receipt that the policy was in force and for which the amount of net premiums is known on the first day of such calendar year. If the policy has not been in force for three years, then the period that it had been in force is used.[19]

If an employee receives an amount under a contributory noninsured plan, the portion resulting from the employer's contribution is proportionate to the employer's contributions for the three calendar years (or a lesser period during which the plan was in effect) before the year of receipt.[20]

¶ 257 **Rental Value of Parsonages**

California adopts IRC § 107 which provides that, for a minister or clergyman, gross income does not include the rental value of the home furnished to him as part of his compensation, or the rental allowance paid to him as part of his compensation to the extent that he uses it to rent or provide a home.[21]

---

(16) § IRC § 106; § 17024.5.

(17) § IRC § 105(h); § 17024.5.

(18) Fed Reg. 1.105–(1)(d)(1).

(19) Fed. Reg. 1.105–1(d)(2).

(20) Fed. Reg. No. 1.105–1(e).

(21) § 17131.

¶ 258 **Income From Discharge of Indebtedness**

Both California and federal IRC § 108, give a specific exclusion from gross income of the amount of income otherwise includable in gross income by reason of the disc'.arge, in whole or in part, of an individual's indebtedness if: (1) the discharge occurs in a Title 11 (bankruptcy) case; (2) when taxpayer is insolvent; or (3) the indebtedness discharged is a qualified farm indebtedness. The exclusion for insolvency does not apply in a Title 11 case. The insolvency exclusion is limited to the amount of the insolvency. It takes precedence over the qualified farm exclusion. The amount excluded from gross income must be applied to reduce the tax attributes of the taxpayer in the following order: (a) any net operating loss for tax year of discharge, and any net operating loss carryover to such tax year; (b) any carryover to or from the tax year of discharge of an amount for purposes of determining the amount allowable as a general business credit; (c) any net capital loss for taxable year of discharge, and any capital loss carryover to such taxable year under IRC § 1212; (d) basis of property. Foreign tax credit carryovers do not apply in California. Excluded indebtedness must be used to reduce any carryover to or from the discharge year of general business credits allowed under California law. Rev & TC specifies a reduction in the credit carryover of 11.1¢ of each dollar excluded; the federal reduction is 33⅓¢ for each dollar.

Indebtedness of an individual means any indebtedness for which an individual is liable, or subject to which an individual holds property. Insolvent means excess of liabilities over fair market value of assets. In case of any discharge, questions of whether or not the taxpayer is insolvent, and the amount thereof, will be determined on the basis of assets and liabilities immediately before the discharge. Title 11 case means a case under USC Title 11 (bankruptcy), but only if the taxpayer is under the jurisdiction of the court in such case, and the discharge of indebtedness is granted by the court, or pursuant to a plan approved by the court. The taxpayer may elect to apply any part of the reduction to the reduction under IRC § 1017 (adopted by California) of the basis of the depreciable property of the taxpayer. The amount to which the election will apply cannot exceed the aggregate adjusted bases of depreciable property held by the taxpayer at the beginning of the taxable year following the taxable year of discharge. This election may be made on the taxpayer's return for the taxable year of discharge, or such other time as the administrative authorities prescribe. It may be revoked only with their consent.[22]

Note: Although California does not have an election form, federal Form 982 should be attached to the California return for the year in which the debt reduction occurs. Based on Rev & TC § 17024.5(d) and § 23051.5(g), a federal election to adjust basis would be equally applicable for California purposes, unless a separate statement of nonelection were filed with the California return. As with federal law, if a taxpayer establishes to the satisfaction of the Franchise Tax Board that the failure to file the Form 968 with the

---

(22) § 17131; 18031; Fed. Reg. No. 1.108 (a)–1—1.108(a)–2.

original return was due to reasonable cause, the form may be filed with an amended return or claim for credit or refund. See ¶ 265 for rules on cancellation of student loan.

Special rules for qualified farm indebtedness. Under IRC § 108(g), the exclusion provisions apply only if the discharge is by a qualified person. The meaning of a qualified person is that given by IRC § 46(c)(8)(D)(iv), except that the term includes any state, federal or local government agency, or instrumentality. Indebtedness is treated as a qualified farm indebtedness if (1) incurred directly in connection with the operation by the taxpayer of the trade or business of farming, and (2) 50% or more of the aggregate gross receipts of the taxpayer for the 3 taxable years preceding the taxable year of occurrence of the discharge is attributable to the trade or business of farming. The amount excluded cannot exceed the sum of the adjusted tax attributes and business and investment assets. For California purposes, the general business credit carryover attribute is multiplied by nine; under IRC § 108(g)(3), it is multiplied by three.[23]

Debt for debt and stock for debt exchanges. Under IRC § 108(e)(10)–(11), adopted by California, in determining a debtor's income from discharge of indebtedness, a debtor that issues a debt instrument in satisfaction of indebtedness is treated as having satisfied it with an amount of money equal to the issue price of the debt instrument. The rule that allows insolvent debtors and taxpayers in Title 11 cases to issue stock in satisfaction of debt without creating cancellation of debt income does not apply to stock that has a stated redemption price and a fixed redemption date, if the issuer has the right to redeem it one or more times, and the stockholder has the right to require redemption at one or more times. California's adoption applies to tax years starting on or after 1–1–91; the applicable federal date is 10–10–90.[24]

¶ 259   Lessee's Improvements on Lessor's Property

California follows IRC § 109 that provides that when at the termination of a lease of real property (due to forfeiture or otherwise) the lessor obtains title to buildings erected or other improvements made by the lessee upon the leased property, the value of the improvements is excluded from gross income. However, if the facts disclose that such buildings or improvements represent, in whole or in part, a liquidation in kind of rental, the exclusion from gross income does not apply to that portion.[25]

¶ 260   Recovery of Tax Benefit Items

Under IRC § 111(a), adopted by California, gross income does not include income attributable to the recovery during the tax year of any amount deducted in any prior taxable year to the extent that amount *did not* reduce the tax imposed.

---

(23) § 17144.
(24) § 17131.

(25) § 17131; Fed. Reg. No. 1.109–1.

EXAMPLE   A taxpayer in 1984 with an adjusted gross income of $20,000 has a casualty loss deduction of $30,000 and thus has a taxable income of minus $10,000 and pays no tax. In 1985 the taxpayer receives a settlement of an additional $2,000. All of the $2,000 recovered in 1985 will be included in the taxpayer's income since $20,000 of the total $30,000 casualty loss *did* reduce taxable income.

California adopts IRC § 111(b)(1)–(2). These rules provide that if a credit was allowable with respect to any amount for any prior taxable year, and during that year there was a downward price or similar adjustment, the tax will be increased by the amount of the credit attributable to the adjustment, unless the credit allowable did not reduce the amount of the tax imposed. California does not adopt the IRC § 111(b)(3) exception for investment credits and foreign tax credits. California also adopts the IRC § 111(c) rule on treatment of carryovers. It does not adopt the IRC § 111(d) special rules for accumulated earnings tax and personal holding company tax.[26]

> *Note:* It should be noted that the tax benefit rule for California and federal purposes may not be the same because for federal purposes consideration must be given to the net operating loss carrybacks and carryovers or capital loss carryovers resulting from the bad debt deduction.

¶ 261   Sale or Exchange of Residence

Special one-time exclusion.   California adopts IRC § 121 which provides that gain from the sale or exchange of a taxpayer's principal residence may be excluded up to $125,000 of the gain realized on the sale. For federal and California purposes, this one-time exclusion applies to taxpayers who have attained age 55 years prior to the date of sale. For both the California and federal exclusion provisions, the taxpayer must have owned and used the residence as his or her principal residence for a total of at least three years during the five-year period ending on the date of the sale. The election is not available to any sale or exchange by the taxpayer if a similar election by the taxpayer or taxpayer's spouse is in effect involving another sale or exchange. However, the election may be made or revoked at any time during a four-year period from the date on which the tax return was originally due to be filed. In the case of a taxpayer who is married, an election or a revocation of an election may be made only if the taxpayer's spouse joins. If the taxpayer is a tenant stockholder in cooperative housing or owns a condominium as his principal residence, the exclusion also applies. The destruction, theft, seizure, requisition or condemnation of property is treated as the sale of the property. The dollar amount is the same as allowed by federal rules even though the taxpayer is barred from filing a joint return under Rev & TC § 18402.[27]

Special rules for those incapable of self-care.   California has adopted IRC § 121(d)(9). This federal IRC rule provides that a taxpayer who; (1) becomes physically or mentally incapable of self-care, and (2) owns property and uses such property as his or her principal residence for periods aggregat-

---

(26) § 17131; Fed. Reg. 1.111–1.   **(27)** § 17131; 17152.

ing at least one year during the 5-year period ending on the date of the sale or exchange will be treated as using the property as the taxpayer's principal residence at any time during the 5-year period in which the taxpayer owns the property, and resides in any facility, including a nursing home, licensed by a state or political subdivision to care for individuals in taxpayer's condition.[27]

Special rules for Peace Corp volunteers. For tax years beginning on or after 1–1–92, California has modified the federal rule which requires that the taxpayer use the property as a principal residence for three of the prior five years if rollover of the gain is to be permitted. The three-year period of required use is reduced by the period, not in excess of 18 months, during which the taxpayer is serving in the Peace Corp during the five year test period. There is no comparable provision in federal law.

Rollover of gains. Under federal IRC § 1034(a), adopted by California, a taxpayer who sells his home will not be taxed on the gain from the sale if he rolls over his gain by buying or building a more expensive home within 24 months before or after the sale of his old home. Put another way, taxpayer's gain will be taxed only to extent that the selling price of the old home (minus fixing expenses) exceeds the cost of buying or building the new home. California has adopted federal rule in IRC § 1034(k) relating to the suspension of the rollover time period when the taxpayer has a tax home abroad or overseas.[28] California has adopted provisions that extend the rollover period up to eight years for military personnel stationed outside the U.S. or required to reside in on-base quarters. California has also adopted IRC § 1034(g) that allows a surviving spouse to defer reporting gain from the sale of the old residence when the other spouse has died after the sale of the old residence and before the purchase of the new residence.[29]

OBSERVATION Federal rules adopted by California also govern replacement period [IRC § 1034(a)]; start of construction and purchase of more than one residence [IRC § 1034(c)]; sale of residence following prior rollover [IRC § 1034(d)]; and suspension for military duty [IRC § 1034(h)].

¶ 262 Living Expense Insurance Payments

California follows the IRC § 123 provisions that gross income does not include amounts received by an individual under insurance contracts for living expenses for himself and members of his household resulting from the loss of use or occupancy of a residence because of damage by fire, storm or other calamity or denial by government authorities of access to a residence because of the occurrence (or threat of occurrence) of any of the above events.[29]

Living benefits contracts. For taxable years starting on or after 1–1–91, gross income does not include any amounts received by a person

---

(28) § 18031; 18044.   (29) § 17131; Fed. Reg. No. 1.123–1.

owning a life insurance policy, whether in a single sum or otherwise, under any policy of life or endowment insurance or contracts supplemental thereto, if paid pursuant to a living benefits contract under Insurance Code § 10113.1–10,113.2.[30]

¶ 263   **Meals and Lodging Furnished by Employer**

Under IRC § 119(a)–(d) and California law, an employee is not required to include in gross income the value of meals and lodging furnished to him or her on the employer's premises when they are for the convenience of the employer and the employee is required to accept such meals and lodging as a condition of employment.[31] The exclusion applies to (1) meals and lodging for employee's spouse and dependents; and (2) meals for a fixed charge. The provisions relating to employees living in camps in foreign countries considered to be part of the employer's business premises also apply. Gross income does not include the value of qualified campus lodging furnished to employees of an educational institution described in IRC § 170(b)(1)(A)(ii).

¶ 264   **Cafeteria Plans**

California adopts the IRC § 125 exclusion for cafeteria plan benefits.[32] "Cafeteria plans" or flexible benefit plans permit covered employees to select the fringe benefits they want from a package of employer-provided fringe benefits. Under IRC § 125, except as provided in § 125(b) for highly compensated participants and key employees, no amount shall be included in the gross income of a participant in a cafeteria plan solely because, under the plan, the participant may choose among the benefits of the plan. In the case of highly compensated participants, the rule excluding cafeteria plan benefits does not apply to any benefit attributable to a plan year for which the plan discriminates in favor of highly compensated individuals as to eligibility to participate, or highly compensated participants as to contributions and benefits. In the case of a key employee (see IRC § 416(i)(1)), the rule on exclusion of cafeteria benefits does not apply to a plan benefit attributable to a plan for which the statutory nontaxable benefits provided key employees exceed 25% of the aggregate of all benefits provided for all employees. In determining the taxable year of inclusion, any benefit that is considered discriminatory in favor of highly compensated participants and key employees will be treated as received or accrued in the taxable year of the key employee or highly compensated participant in which the plan year ends. A cafeteria plan does not discriminate where qualified benefits and total benefits (or employer contributions thereto) do not discriminate in favor of highly compensated participants.

With certain exceptions, a cafeteria plan does not include any plan that provides for deferred compensation. The exceptions are: (1) a profit-sharing, stock bonus, or rural cooperative plan within the meaning of IRC § 401(k)(7);

---

(30) § 17131.5.
(31) IRC § 125 17131.

(32) § 17095; 17131.

(2) a plan maintained by an educational organization to extent of amounts covered employee may elect to have employer pay as contributions for post-retirement group insurance. All contributions for this insurance must be made before retirement, and there can be no cash surrender value.

Qualified benefits for a cafeteria plan are any benefits that are not includible in the income of the employee under IRC Subtitle A, Ch. 1B, Part III, §§ 101–136, other than § 117 (qualified scholarships), § 124 (qualified transportation), § 127 (educational assistance programs), or 132 (certain fringe benefits). The term can include group term life insurance benefits exceeding IRC § 79 limitation. Special rules apply to health benefits, collectively bargained plans, participation eligibility rules, and certain controlled groups.

California adopts federal IRC § 122, that lets members or former members of the uniformed services of the United States to make an election under the Retired Serviceman's Family Protection Plan to receive a reduced amount of retirement pay (or detainer pay) to provide annuities for their survivors.[32]

¶ 265 Cancellation of Student Loan

California has adopted federal IRC § 108(f) that provides a permanent exclusion for income from income for cancellation of certain student loans where a student works for a certain period of time in certain professions for any of a broad class of employers. "Student loan" means any loan to an individual to assist that individual in attending an organization that normally maintains a regular faculty and curriculum and normally has a regularly enrolled body of pupils or students in attendance at place where its educational activities are regularly carried on. The loan can be made by the U.S., a state, territory or possession of the U.S., D.C., an instrumentality and agency of the U.S., an exempt public benefit corporation, or any educational organization.[33]

¶ 266 S Corporation Shareholders

California tax treatment of S corporations and their shareholders will be determined under IRC Subtitle A, Chapter 1, Subchapter S, §§ 1361–1379. The corporation must have in effect a valid election for federal purposes under IRC § 1362(a) for the same income year, or it cannot elect to be treated as S corporation for California purposes. Election provisions cover 1987, 1988, 1989 and 1990 and later taxable years. Each nonresident shareholder or fiduciary must file with the S corporation return a statement of consent to California's jurisdiction to tax the shareholder's pro rata share of income attributable to California sources. The S corporation must include in its return for each income year a list of shareholders in the form and manner set by the Franchise Tax Board. IRC §§ 1366–1368 relating to tax treatment of shareholders of an S corporation dealing with pass-thru of items to shareholders, adjustments to shareholder's basis of stock, and distributions will

---

(**33**) IRC § 108(f); § 17024.5.

apply. California modifies IRC § 1366(a) to provide that a shareholder's pro rata share of the corporation's credits includes the credit for political contributions. The termination of the federal election terminates the California S corporation election.[34] Before 1987, California Bank and Corporation Franchise Tax Law did not include the federal provisions recognizing S corporations. The California Personal Income Tax Law, therefore, had no provisions that required a shareholder of an S corporation to include in his California income his share of the corporation's profit.

¶ 268   Payments to Vacate Real Property

Federal law specifically excludes from gross income the payments for reasonable relocation expenses for persons required to vacate real property at the request of public utility. California enacted similar legislation under California Government Code § 7269.[35] This section states that no payment received by any person under this chapter will be considered as income for the purposes of the Personal Income Tax Law. Also, neither will such payments be considered as income or resources to any recipient of public assistance and such payments will not be deducted from the amount of aid to which the recipient would otherwise be entitled.

¶ 269   Educational Assistance Programs

California has adopted the federal exclusion for employer-provided educational assistance as set forth in IRC § 127. California has also adopted the federal exclusion provided in IRC § 117 for qualified scholarships received by candidates for a degree at a qualified educational institution.[36]

¶ 271   Conservation Cost-Sharing Program Payments

California has adopted IRC § 126 which provides that a taxpayer can exclude from gross income those payments received under a federal, or state, or local government cost-sharing conservation programs such as the rural clean water program, the rural abandoned mine program, water bank program and others. The exclusion is allowed if the payments would ordinarily be considered to be capital items.[37]

¶ 272   Grants Under Assistance Programs

California has provided assistance programs to benefit various categories of less advantaged groups of persons under its Welfare and Institutions Programs. Under federal law, 42 USC § 5058, the state programs set forth below are exempt from all taxes, state and federal.

Senior Companion Program expenses. Meals, stipends, transportation and other items pursuant to Chapter 7 of Division 8.5 of the Welfare and Institutions Code.

---

(34) IRC § 1361–1369; § 23800–23810.
(35) LR368.

(36) § 17131; 17151.
(37) § 17131.

Foster Grandparent Program expenses. Stipends, meals, transportation and other expenses pursuant to Chapter 8 of Division 8.5 of the Welfare and Institutions Code.

¶ 275 **Dependent Care Assistance Programs**

Under IRC § 129, adopted by California, employees can exclude from gross income amounts paid or incurred by their employers for furnishing dependent care assistance under a written dependent care assistance program. The exclusion is also available to self-employed individuals and partners of a partnership. The exclusion applies to payments and provided services that would qualify for the dependent care credit (¶ 143). No other deduction or credit will be allowed for any excluded amount. Also, the amount excluded cannot exceed the individual's earned income for the year. If the person is married, the exclusion cannot exceed the lesser of his earnings for the year or the earnings of his spouse. Aggregate amount excluded can't exceed $5,000 ($2,500 in case of separate return by married individual). If one spouse is a student or is incapable of self-care, he or she is treated as having earnings of $200 a month if there is one dependent or $400 if there are two or more dependents.[38]

¶ 276 **Cash or Deferred Profit-Sharing Arrangement—401(k) Plans**

California conforms to federal provisions for 401k plans. The maximum 1993 deferral under state and federal laws is $8,994 which is indexed annually (1992 amount was $8,728; 1991 was $8,475).[39] Under IRC § 401(k), employees who participate in a qualified cash or deferred profit-sharing or stock option plan, may elect to receive cash payments from their employer, or defer them by having the employer contribute them on their behalf to a trust. The deferral is considered a deductible employer contribution and is not includible in the employee's gross income. The arrangement may be in the form of a salary reduction agreement whereby the employee reduces his or her current pay in favor of a contribution to a plan. Amounts held by the trust that are attributable to employer contributions can't be distributed to participants or other beneficiaries before retirement, death, disability, or separation from service, hardship, or attainment of age 59½. They are not distributable merely by reason of a stated period of participation or lapse of a fixed number of years. The plan must provide that the employee's right to accrued benefit derived from employer contributions to the trust pursuant to the employee's election is nonforfeitable. The plan can't discriminate in favor of highly compensated employees.

¶ 280 **Individual 65 Years of Age or Over**

California grants a personal exemption credit to individuals age 65 or over. The credit is indexed, annually. The 1999 amount is $65. The credit was $64 in 1993.[40]

---

(38) § 17131.
(39) § 17501.

(40) § 17054(c).

¶ 281   Boundary Waters Canoe Act Payments

Effective for payments made in taxable years starting on or after 1–1–85, qualified resort operators and commercial outfitters can exclude from gross income equity grants paid by the U.S. Forest Service as a result of restricting motorized traffic in the Boundary Waters Canoe Area.[1]

¶ 282   Fringe Benefits

California has adopted IRC § 132, that lists the following fringe benefits excluded from employee's gross income:

- no additional cost services;
- qualified employee discounts;
- working condition fringes; and
- de minimis fringes.[2]

Federal regulation § 1.61–21 that covers taxation of fringe benefits and valuation of automobiles, aircraft and meals provided by an employer also applies in California. Federal or state special agents are not subject to income and wage inclusion rules.[3]

¶ 283   Ridesharing

For taxable years starting on or after 1–1–90, gross income does not include compensation or the fair market value of any other benefit, except salary or wages, received by an employee from an employer for participation in any ridesharing arrangement in California. There is no comparable federal provision. "Ridesharing arrangement" means the transportation of persons in a motor vehicle when that transportation is incidental to another purpose of the driver. The exclusion covers the value of free or subsidized parking received by employees participating in ridesharing arrangements. The exclusion also exempts any compensation or the fair market value of any other benefit received for:

For periods after July 31, 1990

(1) Commuting in a vanpool.
(2) Commuting in a private commuter bus or buspool.
(3) A transit pass for use by the employee or his or her dependents, other than transit passes for use by elementary and secondary school students who are dependents of the employee.
(4) Commuting in a subscription taxipool.
(5) Commuting in a carpool.
(6) Free or subsidized parking.

In addition, beginning January 1, 1995, the following are added:

(7) An employee's bicycling to or from his or her place of employment.
(8) Commuting by ferry.
(9) The use of an alternative transportation method that reduces the use of a motor vehicle by a single occupant to travel to or from that individual's place of employment.

---

(1) § 17136.   (3) § 17135.
(2) § 17024.5.

(10) Travel to or from a telecommuting facility.[4]

¶ 284 Empty Beverage Containers

Gross income does not include any amount received for empty beverage containers by a consumer from a recycling center or location as the recycling value.[5]

¶ 285 Reparation Payments to Persons of Japanese Ancestry

Gross income does not include any amount received pursuant to any federal law enacted in 1988 to provide reparation payments to redress the injustice done to United States citizens and resident aliens of Japanese ancestry who were interned during World War II.[6]

¶ 286 Water Conservation Water Closet Expenses

Any amount received as a rebate from a local water agency or supplier for any expenses a taxpayer has paid or incurred for the purchase or installation of each water conservation water closet will be treated as a refund or price adjustment of the amounts payable to that water agency or supplier. The water closet must meet the performance standards of the American National Standards Institute Standard A112.19.2, and use no more than one gallon per flush.[7]

¶ 287 Foster Care Payments

California has adopted IRC § 131 which provides a limited exclusion for payments received for providing foster care and difficult care payments. California and federal law both establish limits based on the ages of individuals in the foster care home, and only apply to qualified payments from the state or political subdivisions, or qualified placement agencies as described in IRC § 501(c)(3).[8]

¶ 288 Energy Subsidies Paid By Public Utilities

California has adopted IRC § 136 which provides an exclusion from taxable income for energy subsidies paid by a public utility to its customers for the purchase or installation of any energy conservation devise. The California exclusion is available only for amounts received on or after 1–1–93, and before 1–1–95. The exclusion applies only to amounts received with respect to a dwelling unit.[9]

¶ 289 Cost-share Payments Received by Forest Landowners

Gross income does not include cost-share payments received by forest landowners from the Department of Forestry and Fire Protection pursuant to the California Forest Improvement Act of 1978, or from the United States Forest Stewardship Program and the Stewardship Incentives Program, pursuant to

---

(4) § 17149, as amended by Stats. 1994, c. 622, § 3.
(5) § 17153.5.
(6) § 17156.

(7) § 17138.
(8) § 17024.5; IRC § 131.
(9) § 17139.

the Cooperative Forestry Assistance Act. Such receipts also do not effect the determination of basis of property, or any other allowable deduction to which the taxpayer may otherwise be entitled. This exclusion is effective January 1, 1994.[10]

¶ 290   Crime Hotline Awards

For taxable years beginning on or after January 1, 1994, California gross income does not include any amount which is received as a reward from a crime hotline that is authorized by any governmental unit. "Crime hotline" means any method of direct communication established by a government agency or a private, non-profit organization exempt from tax under Rev & TC § 23701d for the purpose of permitting individuals to report criminal activity to the agency or organization, or any other designated agency. This exclusion does not apply to employees of the organization establishing or operating the crime hotline.[11]

---

(10) § 17135.5, as added by Stats. 1994, c. 22, § 1.

(11) § 17147.7, as added by Stats. 1994, c. 481.

CHAPTER **4**

ADJUSTMENTS TO INCOME

¶ 291   **Deductions for Adjusted Gross Income**

Deductions are classified as (1) those expenses which are subtracted from gross income to arrive at adjusted gross income[1] and (2) those expenses which are subtracted from adjusted gross income in arriving at taxable income.[2] The latter group of expenses are known as itemized deductions and, under both IRC § 63(e) and California law, may not be used unless taxpayer elects to itemize.[3] For taxpayers who do not elect to itemize, the standard deduction is allowed in computing taxable income.[4]

This chapter explains the deductions from gross income to arrive at adjusted gross income. Itemized deductions are covered in Chapter 5.

IRC conformity.   California uses Internal Revenue Code (IRC) § 62 to define adjusted gross income.

California adjustments to federal adjusted gross income.   California adjustments to federal adjusted gross income listed on Schedule CA to Form 540 are:

- *Subtractions—*
    - (1) state income tax refund;
    - (2) unemployment compensation;
    - (3) social security benefits;
    - (4) California nontaxable income;
    - (5) railroad retirement benefits and sick pay;
    - (6) California lottery winnings;
    - (7) IRA distributions;
    - (8) pensions and annuities;
    - (9) passive activity loss;
    - (10) depreciation and amortization;
    - (11) capital gains and losses and other gains and losses; and
    - (12) any other subtractions.
- *Additions—*
    - (1) interest on state and municipal bonds from a state other than California;
    - (2) passive activity loss;
    - (3) depreciation and amortization;
    - (4) capital gains and losses and other gains and losses; and
    - (5) any other additions.

Performing artists.   California has adopted IRC § 62(a)(2)(B) that allows performing artists to deduct from gross income the IRC § 162 deductions consisting of expenses paid or incurred by qualified performing artists in connection with their performance of services in the performing arts as employees. California has also adopted the IRC § 62(b) provisions defining a qualified performing artist, disregarding a nominal employer if service receipts in a taxable year are less than $200, and the special rule for married couples that require the filing of a joint return.

---

(1) § 17072.
(2) § 17201–17299.9.

(3) § 17073.
(4) § 17073; 17073.5.

Certain arrangements not treated as reimbursement arrangements. California has also adopted IRC § 62(c). This IRC rule provides that, for purposes of reimbursed expenses of employees, an arrangement shall in no event be treated as a reimbursement, or other expense allowance arrangement if: (1) such arrangement does not require the employee to substantiate expenses covered to the person providing the reimbursement, or (2) the arrangement gives the employee the right to retain any amount in excess of the substantiated expenses covered. These requirements do not apply to any expense to the extent substantiation is not required under IRC § 274(d) for that expense by reason of regulations of the Secretary of the Treasury.

¶ 292   Business Expenses

Under IRC § 62(1)—(2) and § 162(a), an expense, to be deductible from gross income must be ordinary and necessary and must have been paid or incurred in the year as an expense of a trade or business regularly carried on. Deductible trade or business expenses include the following:

(a) A reasonable allowance for salaries or other compensation for personal services actually rendered;

(b) Amounts expended for meals and lodging and travel expenses other than amounts which are lavish or extravagant under the circumstances while away from home in pursuit of the trade or business;

(c) Rentals or other payments required to be made in the trade or business for property in which the taxpayer has no equity. California adopts federal provisions.[5]

Overview of business travel and entertainment expenses. California has conformed to federal law[6] so that:

● A business meal is deductible only if it is "directly related" or "associated with" the active conduct of a taxpayer's trade or business. In other words, you must talk business at the table or have the meal before or after a substantial and bona fide business discussion. Under prior law, a "quiet business meal"—one held in an atmosphere conducive to business—was deductible even though business was not actually discussed.

● As a general rule, the deduction for business meals and business entertainment is limited to 50% of cost. (The deduction was 80% for tax years beginning prior to 1–1–94.) This rule also applies to meals consumed while away from home overnight on business.

● There are limits on business-entertainment deductions for "skyboxes" at sports events.

● For years after 1993, deductions for tickets to entertainment events are generally limited to 50% of face value; for tax years beginning prior to 1–1–94, entertainment expenses deduction is limited to 80% of cost.

● Deductions for each day of business travel by luxury water transport are limited to twice the highest domestic federal per diem reimbursement rate.

● Unreimbursed employee expenses for business travel, transportation, and entertainment become miscellaneous itemized deductions subject to a 2%-of-AGI "floor."

---

(5) § 17072; 17201; 17286.   (6) § 17024.5.

Other restrictions on deductions for travel expenses. Expenses for travel as a form of education and certain types of charitable travel are nondeductible. Finally, the 1986 TRA eliminated deductions for attending investment-related seminars and conventions.

Business meals. A business meal, like business entertainment, is deductible subject to the 50% rule for 1994 only if it is "directly related to" or "associated with" the active conduct of a taxpayer's trade or business.

Directly related. In general, a business meal or business entertainment is "directly related" if four conditions are met:

- The taxpayer has more than a general expectation of deriving income, or a specific business benefit, from the meal or entertainment. However, the taxpayer is not required to show that income or a specific business benefit actually resulted.
- The taxpayer did in fact engage in business discussions during the meal or entertainment (or if he didn't, it was for reasons beyond his control).
- The principal nature of the expense was the active conduct of the taxpayer's trade or business.
- The meal or entertainment expense was for the taxpayer, his business guest or guests, and their spouses.

Associated with. A meal or entertainment is deductible if it directly precedes or follows a substantial and bona fide business (or practice) related discussion. The business discussion (or negotiation, transaction, conference, etc.) must be substantial in relation to the meal or entertainment. If the taxpayer's business guest is from out of town, the meal or entertainment can take place the day before or after the business discussion.

Additional requirements. The cost of a business meal, like the cost of business entertainment, is not deductible to the extent it is "lavish and extravagant" under the circumstances. And the cost of beverages and food is deductible as a business meal only if the taxpayer (or his representative) is present at the meal. The representative can be the taxpayer's employee, or an independent contractor acting on his behalf.[7]

50% rule. For years beginning after 12–31–93, the deduction for otherwise allowable business meals and business entertainment is limited to 50% of cost. The limited deduction also applies to (1) meals while away from home overnight on business, and (2) meals provided by employers to employees (but see exceptions, below). Meals consumed during a job-related move are affected as well. For years prior to 1–1–94, the deduction was limited to 80% of cost.[8]

Besides meals and entertainment, expenses subject to the 50% rule include taxes and tips related to the meal or entertainment and other related expenses (e.g., nightclub cover charges, room rental for cocktail party, and parking at the theater or sports arena). Transportation to and from the business meal or entertainment is not subject to the 50% rule.

---

(7) IRC § 274(e); 274(k); § 17024.5.   (8) IRC § 274(n); § 17024.5.

Meals while on travel status.   A taxpayer may deduct 50% of the cost of meals consumed while he is away from home overnight on business. Being on travel status automatically qualifies meals as being directly related to the taxpayer's trade or business, *but only if the taxpayer eats alone,* or eats with non-business-connected persons and claims a deduction for his meal only. Apparently, if a taxpayer on travel status has a meal with a business client or associate, he can deduct 50% of the cost only if the meal is directly related to or associated with his trade or business.

Reimbursed expenses.   If a taxpayer is reimbursed for the cost of business meals or entertainment (and makes an adequate accounting), the rule limiting the deduction applies to the one who makes the reimbursement, not the taxpayer.

Per-diem arrangements.   An employer may reimburse employees for away-from-home travel at a fixed per-diem rate. If the reimbursement does not exceed the government-approved maximum, the expenses are deemed accounted for if the employee: (1) keeps a record of the time, place, and business purpose of his expenses, and (2) gives the same information to the employer. The employee is not required to keep track of actual expenses for travel, lodging, or meals.

Note: More than 10% owners must keep complete records, including the amount of each expense.

In general, an employer may deduct only 50% of its reimbursement for away-from-home meals. But if the employee isn't required to keep track of meal expenses, how will the employer know what part of the per diem is subject to the 50% rule?

Probable result.   As long as the per diem doesn't exceed the government maximum, the employer will continue to deduct 100% of its reimbursement. An analogy can be made to the rules for business travel by luxury water transport. The 50% rule is not applied if the cost of onboard meals is not separately stated or clearly identifiable. The same rule should hold true for per-diem reimbursement arrangements.

Interplay of 50% rule and other limitations.   In general, the rule limiting the deduction is imposed *after* the application of the limits imposed by IRC § 162 and 274 (for example, disallowance of lavish and extravagant expenses), but *before* the application of the 2% floor for "second tier" miscellaneous itemized deductions.

EXAMPLE
During the 1994 tax year, Bob Smith, an employee, incurs $1,000 of business entertainment expenses for which he is not reimbursed. Of the total $1,000 expenses, $200 is deemed lavish and extravagant. Smith's AGI is $50,000 and he has $500 of other "second tier" miscellaneous itemized deductions. Here's how he figures his deduction:

Total business entertainment expense $1,000
Less amount deemed lavish and extravagant .... (200)
800

Less 50% reduction .... (400)
400

Plus other "second tier" miscellaneous
itemized deductions 800
1,200

Less 2% of adjusted gross income .... (1,000)

Deductible amount .... $ 200

A special rule applies for business travel by luxury water transport. If the cost of meals and entertainment is separately stated, then the 50% rule is applied *before* computation of the new deduction limit on luxury water transport expenses.

Exceptions to 50% rule. Expenses that fall in the following categories are not subject to the rule limiting the deduction and are deductible in full:

● *Amounts treated as compensation:* The full value of the benefit must be treated as compensation to the recipients, whether or not they are employees.

● *De minimis fringe benefits:* These include items excludable under IRC § 132 as a subsidized eating facility or a de minimis fringe (e.g., holiday gifts of turkeys, hams, etc.).

● *Employer-provided recreation:* This consists of amounts paid for recreational, social, or similar activities or employee events (e.g., holiday parties or summer outings).

● *Samples or promotions:* Items made available to the public as samples or promotional material.

● *Meals and entertainment sold to customers:* The taxpayer must sell the item in a bona fide transaction for adequate and full consideration. For example, a restaurant can deduct the full cost of the meals it supplies to patrons.

● *Sports tickets:* Expenses to a sports event, to the extent otherwise allowable as a business deduction, are deductible in full if three conditions are met: (1) the event's primary purpose is to benefit an IRC § 501(c)(3) charity, (2) the entire net proceeds must go to the charity, and (3) the event uses volunteers to perform substantially all the event's work.

Qualified banquet meeting meals are subject to the 50% disallowance rule in the same way as other meals.

Oil and gas platforms and drilling rigs. California has adopted IRC § 274(n)(2)(F)(iii)–(iv) which provides that the limitation on meal deduction will not apply to food and beverages provided on an oil and gas platform or drilling rig, if the platform or rig is located offshore, or provided on an oil and gas platform or drilling rig, or at a support camp that is integral and in proximity to the platform or rig, if the platform or rig is located in the U.S. north of 54 degrees north latitude. California has adopted the provisions of IRC § 274(n)(2)(F)(i)–(ii) relating to commercial vessels and crew members.[9]

Skybox rentals. A business may entertain its clients and customers by letting them use its leased skybox at a sports arena. The taxpayer must use the skybox for "directly related" or "associated with" entertainment. If this

---

(9) § 17271.

condition is satisfied, the taxpayer's deduction is limited to the sum of the face value of the nonluxury box seat tickets for the seats in the leased skybox. All the seats in the skybox are counted, even though the box is not fully occupied during the event. However, the taxpayer may not deduct the excess cost of the skybox.[10]

The taxpayer may also deduct stated charges for food and beverages under the general rules for business entertainment.

Reminder: The deduction for skybox seats, food, and beverages is limited to 50% of cost beginning in 1994.

Ticket deductions—face value limit. Federal law limits deductions for tickets to entertainment events to 50% beginning in 1994 of their face value, which includes tax. The face-value limitation bars payment to (1) a scalper for a ticket, even if not otherwise disallowed under IRC § 162(a)(2) as an illegal payment; and (2) a legitimate ticket agency for the part of the cost in excess of the ticket's face value.[11]

Charitable fund raisers' exception. The full deduction remains available for tickets for sporting events that are considered charitable fund raisers. A qualifying event must turn over the entire net proceeds to a charity and use volunteers for substantially all the work performed in carrying out the event.

Luxury water travel. Federal and California law generally limits deductions for business travelers who use ocean liners, cruise ships, or other forms of "luxury water transportation." There is no exemption for someone who uses luxury water transportation because of an illness or disability that rules out travel on an airplane. The deduction per day on the boat cannot exceed twice the highest per-diem amount paid by the U.S. government to traveling employees in the coterminous U.S., disregarding any limited special exception, such as a higher limit authorized only for high-ranking executive personnel.[12]

The cost of on-board meals and entertainment is subject to the deduction limit if these charges are separately stated. However, if the cost of on-board meals and entertainment is not separately stated and is not clearly identifiable, then the rule limiting the deduction does not apply. The taxpayer may claim a deduction equal to twice the applicable federal per-diem limit.

Exceptions. Federal and California expressly bars application of the per diem rules to expenses that are allocable to business-related conventions, seminars, or other meetings on cruise ships. IRC § 274(h)(2) allows a deduction of up to $2,000 for certain cruise-ship conventions, provided the ship is a U.S. flagship and all ports of call are in the U.S. or its possessions.

---

(10) IRC § 274(l)(2); § 17024.5.
(11) IRC § 274(l)(1); § 17024.5.

(12) IRC § 274(m)(1); § 17024.5.

¶ 292

Travel as a form of education. No deduction is allowed for travel expenses by teachers and others when their travel is a form of education. But both federal and California law allow deductions for travel that is necessary to engage in activities that give rise to deductible education. Even if taxpayer steers clear of the educational-travel prohibition, his travel deduction is trimmed by following limitations: (1) meals must be reduced by 20% (50% beginning 1994); and (2) the remaining unreimbursed away-from-home travel expenses are allowable only to the extent they exceed 2% of his adjusted gross income.[13]

Charitable deduction denied for certain travel. No deduction is allowed for "charitable" trips that are disguised vacations. Charitable deductions are limited for travel expenses, including meals and lodging, incurred by volunteer workers who perform services away from their homes on behalf of charities. The deductions are allowable only if there is "no significant element of personal pleasure, recreation, or vacation" in the away-from-home travel. The travel-expense disallowance rules apply to payments made directly by the taxpayer of his or her own expenses or of an associated person, such as a member of the taxpayer's family, as well as indirectly through reimbursement by the charity. A reimbursement includes any arrangement for the taxpayer to make a payment to the charity and its payment of the taxpayer's travel outlays. To stop an end run around the disallowance rules, reciprocal arrangements, where two unrelated taxpayers pay each other's expenses or members of a group contribute to a fund that pays for all of their expenses, are barred.

Exception. The deduction remains available for payment by the taxpayer of expenses for third parties who are participants in the charitable activity.

EXAMPLE   Virginia Hickey, a Girl Scout leader, takes her scouts on a camping trip. She gets a deduction for her payment of expenses for girls who belong to the group and are unrelated to her, but not for expenses for her own children.

You don't lose a deduction for your own expenses merely because you enjoy taking care of chores for a charity. For example, what about Hickey's own expenses? They are deductible, provided she is on duty in a genuine and substantial sense throughout the trip, even if she enjoys the trip or supervising children. But her expenses are nondeductible if she (1) only has nominal duties relating to the performance of services for the group, or (2) for significant portions of the trip is not required to perform services.

No effect on other deductions. The disallowance rules do not apply to deductions for travel (other than for charitable travel) on behalf of a charitable organization. These rules, for example, don't affect the deductibility of an IRC § 162 business expense incurred by an employee of a charity.[14]

---

(13) IRC § 274(m)(2); § 17024.5.   (14) IRC § 170(k); § 17024.5.

Investment seminars. No deduction is allowed for costs of attending conventions, seminars, or similar meetings for investment purposes unrelated to carrying on a trade or business. The disallowance is aimed solely at expenses that serve an IRC § 212 purpose, such as production of income, not those that serve an IRC § 162 trade-or-business purpose.[15]

Illegal activities, bribes or kickbacks. No deductions shall be allowed on gross income, including cost of goods sold, from illegal activities set in specified California criminal statutes. The same rule applies to income from other acts promoting or connected with illegal activities. Under IRC § 62(1)–(2) and § 162(c), adopted by California, no deduction is allowed for any payment made directly or indirectly to an official or employee of any government if the payment constitutes an illegal bribe or kickback. Any payment to an official or employee of a foreign government which would be unlawful under the laws of the United States would also not be a deduction.[16]

Clubs that discriminate. Beginning 1–1–94, no deduction is allowed for any club dues.[17]

Other business deductions. Depreciation and amortization, depletion and bad debts are explained in Section III of this handbook. Child care subsidies, lobbying expenses, contributions to foreign deferred compensation plan, and donations of food are treated as business expenses (¶ 1145).

Compensation for services. Under IRC § 62 and § 162(a)(1), adopted by California, a taxpayer-employer must be able to prove that the payments were made for services actually rendered. It's not necessary that the services be performed during the year, but the compensation for past services must be actually paid or incurred during the year in which the deduction is taken. If a taxpayer uses the accrual method, the deduction for salary and wages is allowable when the obligation to pay the amount is established.[18]

TAX TIP

As a sole proprietor, you cannot deduct your own salary or any type of withdrawal for your personal use. You can, however, take a deduction for salaries or wages or expenses paid to relatives, even including a minor child, if the payments are for services actually rendered and meet the tests as to reasonableness, etc.

The compensation paid to the employee must be reasonable in amount; an amount that would ordinarily be paid for like services by like enterprises under like circumstances. Whether the payments are called wages, salaries, commissions, bonuses, fees or vacation or retirement pay, or they are paid at a flat rate or on a contingent basis, paid in cash or other property, such payments are deductible as long as they meet the tests of reasonableness and are paid for services rendered in connection with the trade or business.[19]

---

(15) IRC § 274(h)(7); § 17024.5.
(16) § 17281; 17282.
(17) § 17269.

(18) § 17072; 17201; 17551.
(19) Fed. Reg. No. 1.162–7.

Factors used in determining reasonableness of payments include:

(1) Duties performed by the person.
(2) Volume of business handled.
(3) Character and amount of responsibility.
(4) Ease or difficulty of the work.
(5) Amount of time required.
(6) Working conditions.
(7) Cost of living in the vicinity.
(8) Particular ability of the individual.
(9) Technical and professional training of the person.
(10) Comparison with others performing the same or similar duties.
(11) Length of service or seniority of the person.
(12) Taxpayer's overall policy on payroll.
(13) Number of persons available with the same skills for the job.[19]

WARNING   The Franchise Tax Board may disallow the deduction if the person or entity making payments of compensation for personal service fails to report the payments on information returns to the Franchise Tax Board by 2–28, and make written statements to the payees by 1–31 of the succeeding year as required by Rev & TC § 18637, furnish a written statement with respect to services required by Rev & TC § 18638, and make annual statements to employees by 1–31 of the succeeding year as required by § 13050 of the Unemployment Insurance Code.[20]

California adopts the provisions of IRC § 280C that bar deductions of certain expenses for which credits are allowable. The California rule applies to the credit for qualified clinical testing expenses (IRC § 280C(b)), and the credit for increasing research activities (IRC § 280C(c)). It does not apply to the rule for targeted jobs credit (IRC § 280C(a)).[21] California modifies IRC § 280C(c)(3)(B), relating to the amount of reduced credit election, to refer to Rev & TC § 17041 instead of IRC § 11(b)(1).[22]

Expenses "away from home." For travel expenses to be deductible, they must be incurred "away from home." Federal Rev. Rul. 73–529 points out that a taxpayer's "home" is considered to be located at (1) his regular or principal place of business (if he has more than one) or, (2) if he has no regular or principal place of business because of the nature of his work, then at his regular place of abode in a real and substantial sense. If the taxpayer does not fall within either category, he is considered to be an itinerant who has his home wherever he happens to be working and thus is never away from home for the purpose of a traveling expense deduction. Travel expenses are deductible only if the taxpayer is away from home overnight.[23]

Substandard housing. No deduction is allowed for interest, taxes, depreciation, or amortization paid or incurred in a tax year with respect to substandard housing, with the exception of property rendered substandard solely by reason of a change in the applicable state or local housing stan-

---

(20) § 17299.8.
(21) § 17270.

(22) § 17270(d).
(23) Rev. Rul. 73–259.

dards. This exception will not apply if the violations cause substantial danger to the occupants of the property.[24]

Substantiation requirements. The substantiation requirements of IRC § 274(d) with respect to the amount of the expense, time and place of the travel, entertainment, recreation, use of property, etc., business purpose, and business relationship apply in California.[25] The requirements don't apply to federal and state special agents.[26]

Board of Equalization decisions. The following decisions of the Board of Equalization illustrate the business and travel expense deduction:

Automobile expenses incurred by an employee in his work for which he could have been reimbursed had he filed the proper request with his employer are not "necessary" expenses and are therefore not deductible. The taxpayer made trips to various Lockheed Aircraft facilities throughout southern California. *(Appeal of Ario and Florence Pagliasotti, SBE 4–22–75).*

Away from home living expenses were disallowed since the taxpayer worked for three years in another city and should have moved his permanent residence. His permanent home was in Fullerton where his wife and children lived. He was employed as a doctor for about three years in King City, in northern California *(Appeal of Stuart D. and Kathleen Whetstone, SBE 1–7–75).* See also the *Appeal of Francis L. and Mary J. Stein, SBE 8–16–77* and the *Appeal of Carroll P. Page, SBE 5–9–79* for the same holding on similar facts.

Travel expenses incurred by an executive whose job was located in California where he lived while his wife and children remained in New York to sell their house, as well as airfare for visits to New York, were disallowed because there was no direct connection with his employment *(Appeal of James E. and E. Elizabeth Friden, SBE 6–13–74).*

¶ 293 **Employee Business Expenses**

Travel and transportation expenses up to the amount of the reimbursement are to be claimed above the line. Reimbursement agreement must require substantiation by the employee. However, expenses in excess of any reimbursement become below-the-line miscellaneous deductions and are subject to the 2% floor. The same holds true for an employee's business-entertainment expenses. Expenses up to the amount of any reimbursement are claimed above the line; excess expenses are claimed below the line and are subject to the 2% floor.[27]

The following chart shows how an employee handles his business-connected travel, transportation, and entertainment expenses:

---

(24) § 17274.
(25) § 17270.5.
(26) § 17135.

(27) IRC § 62(2); 67(a)–(b); § 17024.5; 17072; 17201.

¶ **293**

EMPLOYEE BUSINESS EXPENSES

TYPE OF EXPENSE	TAX TREATMENT
Travel & Transportation * (1) Employee is fully reimbursed and makes an adequate accounting.	Neither expenses nor reimbursements are reported on the return.
* (2) Employee is fully reimbursed but does not make an adequate accounting.	Reimbursement reported as income. Expenses reported above the line. Meal expenses while on travel status are subject to the 50% rule beginning 1994.
(3) Expenses exceed reimbursements.	Reimbursement reported as income. Expenses up to reimbursement claimed above the line; excess expenses claimed below the line, subject to 2% floor. 50% rule beginning 1994 applies to unreimbursed meals.
(4) No employer reimbursement.	Expenses claimed below the line, subject to 2% floor. Meal expense subject to 50% rule beginning 1994.
Business entertainment. (5) Reimbursement equals expenses and employee accounts for expenses.	Same as Item (1), above.
(6) Reimbursement equals expenses, but no accounting by employee.	Same as Item (2), above. 50% rule beginning 1994 applies to expenses.**
(7) Expenses exceed reimbursement.	Reimbursement reported as income. Reimbursed expenses reported above the line. Expenses in excess of reimbursement reported below the line. Deduction for unreimbursed expenses limited to 50% of cost; and expenses reported below the line are subject to the 2% floor.
(8) No employer reimbursement.	Expenses claimed below the line, but subject to 50% rule beginning 1994 and 2% floor.

* An adequate accounting to the employer generally consists of the time, date, place, business purpose and amount of expense (or mileage, in the case of car travel). For travel and transportation expenses, accounting is simplified if reimbursement does not exceed Government-approved per-diem or per-mile rate. Expenses for business travel, transportation, and entertainment are deductible by the employee only if he or she has kept the proper records.
** If the employee does not account for expenses, employer deducts 100% of reimbursement as compensation, and employee is subject to the 50% rule beginning 1994.

Outside salespersons' expenses. Consistent with federal law, California treats outside salespersons the same as other employees for purposes of deduction of business expenses. The 2% floor comes into play after all other deduction limitations are taken into account.

Estates and trusts. In general, estates or trusts compute their AGI in the same way as individuals. However, expenses paid or incurred in connection with trust or estate administration that would not have been incurred had the property not been held in a trust or estate, are deductible in arriving at adjusted gross income.[28]

Special break for performers. Qualifying performing artists can report their income and expenses as if they were independent contractors. Such artists will be entitled to a new above-the-line deduction for business expenses if they meet all of these conditions:

- They are employed as performing artists by two or more employers during the tax year;
- Expenses relating to the profession of being a performing artist exceed 10% of gross income attributable to services as a performing artist; and
- Adjusted gross income (before expenses relating to performing) does not exceed $16,000.[29]

Reporting—substantiation. California has adopted IRC § 274 and the regulations under that section that provide reporting requirements for employers and for employees to substantiate entertainment, amusement or recreation expenses as well as limitations on gifts and foreign travel.[30]

An employee who does account to his employer for his travel and entertainment expenses does not have to disclose these on his tax return if they are paid for by the employer either directly or through reimbursement. However, reimbursements in excess of expenses must be reported.

Records. The employee must keep adequate records to maintain an adequate accounting to his employer. Records must include the amount, the time and the place, the business purpose and the business relationship of the entertained person. To substantiate travel expenses a detailed record must be kept such as a diary account book or other statement of expense. The taxpayer must have documentary evidence for any lodging expense while traveling away from home and for any other expenditures of $25 or more.[30] Employee's travel and transportation expenses, meals and lodging cost for outside salesperson expenses which exceed the amount paid to him by his employer are deductible in arriving at adjusted gross income. The taxpayer must file a Form 2106 or a statement showing the total of all amounts received from or charged to his employer, the amount of business expenses broken down into broad subject classifications and the number of days away from home on business. California will accept a properly completed Form 2106 or California Form FTB 3805N.

---

(28) IRC § 67(e); § 17024.5.
(29) IRC § 62(2); 67(b); § 17024.5.

(30) § 17270.5; Fed. Reg. 1.162–17(d).

Mileage allowances. California follows the federal 1994 mileage rate for business transportation paid by employers to employees of 29¢ (1992 and 1993, 28¢) per mile. When used by an employer to reimburse an employee's automobile expenses, it is considered to meet substantiation and adequate accounting requirements. The 1994 business use rate is 29¢ per mile. For the use of an automobile for charitable activities, the rate stays at 12¢ a mile. For medical and moving expense purposes, the rate stays at 9¢ a mile. Taxpayers may deduct either the business standard mileage rate or actual expenses for business use of an automobile. In addition to the standard mileage rate, taxpayers may deduct the business portion of parking fees or tolls. (Rev. Proc. 91–67.)

Rural mail carriers—mileage rates. An employee of the U.S. postal service who furnishes his or her own automobile for the collection and delivery of mail on a rural route may compute the deduction for business use of that automobile in performing these services by using 150% of the standard mileage rate. California is the same. The 1994 rate is 43.5¢ (1993 rate is 42¢, 1992 rate was 42¢) per mile. (Rev. Proc. 90–59.) This federal rule does not apply if the automobile is fully depreciated, or the employee claimed a depreciation for any taxable year starting after 1987.[31]

¶ 294   Rent or Royalty Expenses

Federal and California law provides that expenses such as interest, taxes, depreciation, etc., are deductible in determining adjusted gross income. The property does not have to be income producing as long as it is held for the production of rents or royalties.[32]

¶ 295   Losses on Business Property

Federal and California law provides that losses from sales or exchanges of business capital assets and losses that are treated as losses from sales or exchange of capital assets (such as losses on worthless stocks and bonds and on nonbusiness bad debts) are allowable deductions from gross income.[33]

¶ 295–A   Net Operating Losses

For tax years beginning on or after 1–1–93, California has adopted the provisions of IRC § 172 relating to net operating loss carryovers, except as provided in Rev & TC §§ 17276.1 and 17276.2 (see below). IRC § 172(b)(2) is generally modified for California purposes to provide that only 50% of the entire amount of the net operating loss for any taxable year is eligible for carryover to any later taxable year. In addition, the carryover must be adjusted to eliminate the exclusion for gains provided in Rev & TC § 18152.5 for sales of qualifying small business stock; because of a five year holding

---

(31) § 17289.
(32) IRC § 62; 165(a)–(h); 166(a)–(e); § 17072; 17201; Fed. Reg. No. 1.62–1(c)(8); Fed. Reg. No. 1.162–11.

(33) IRC § 62; 165(a)–(h); 166(a)–(e); 17072; 17201; Fed. Reg. No. 1.62–1(c)(7); Fed. Reg. No. 1.165–1(c)(3); 1.165–4; 1.165–5; 1.166–1(g).

period requirement for the gain to be eligible for exclusion, this adjustment is not required until 1998. No carrybacks are allowed.[34]

For the 1991 and 1992 tax years the deduction for net operating loss carryovers was suspended. For tax years beginning in 1993 the deduction for NOLs has been reinstated. With exceptions discussed below, the carryover period is generally 5 tax years.

Extended NOL period Because of the prior suspension of the NOL deduction, the carryover period for NOL's arising in tax years beginning in 1991 is seven years, and for those arising in tax years beginning in 1992, the carryover period is six years.

Year NOL Generated	Last Year Allowed
1986 or prior	Expired
1987	1994
1988	1995
1989	1996
1990	1997
1991	1997
1992	1997
1993	1998

New and small-businesses allowed 100% deduction of their NOLs, and new businesses have an extended carryover period. For tax years beginning on or after 1-1-94, new businesses, or qualifying small-businesses, are allowed to deduct 100% of their NOL carryovers. A new business is one organized and first commending business in California on or after 1-1-94. For new businesses, the extended carryover provision are limited to losses incurred in the first three years of operations. A new business may carryover its loss for its first tax year for 8 years; its second tax year for 7 years; and its third tax year for 6 years.[34]

A small-business is one which has total receipts of less than $1 million.

Special rules are provided for those situations where the taxpayer conducts more than one business so that only the new business, or qualifying small business, losses are treated in a preferential manner. In addition Rev & TC § 17276(f) addresses those situations where a taxpayer acquires a portion of the assets of an existing trade or business.

The net operating loss rules of Rev & TC § 17276 also apply to individuals, S corporations, and partnerships.[35]

Taxpayers in bankruptcy. Taxpayers who are under the jurisdiction of a federal court under USC Title 11, any time prior to 1-1-94, or who are in receipt of assets acquired in a tax-free reorganization under IRC § 368(a)(1)(G) may carry over their net operating loss for years beginning on

---

(34) § 17276.

(35) § 17276, as amended by Stats. 1994, c. 949, § 1.

or after 1–1–87, and before 1–1–94, for 10 years. The extended carryover period does not apply to any loss incurred in an income year after the income year in which the business is no longer subject to jurisdiction of the court in a Title 11 proceeding.

Program areas—NOL deduction. Qualified taxpayers, as defined in Rev & TC § 17276.2, may elect to take the deduction provided by IRC § 172, relating to the net operating loss deduction with the following exceptions: (1) Rev & TC § 17276(a), relating to the years in which allowable losses are sustained shall not be applicable; and (2) Rev & TC § 17276(b), relating to the 50% reduction of losses shall not be applicable. A statement of election must be attached to the original return, timely filed for the year of the claim; the election is irrevocable. "Qualified taxpayers" are those: (1) engaged in the conduct of a qualified business within a program area; and (2) engaged in the conduct of a trade or business within the enterprise zone. In the case of a program area, the net operating loss for any taxable year starting on or after the date the taxpayer becomes a qualified business can be carried over to each of the 15 taxable years following the taxable years of the loss. In the case of a trade or business within an enterprise zone, carryover is to any taxable year starting on or after the date the area in which the business is conducted is designated an enterprise zone that ends before the expiration or revocation of the zone designation, or to each of 15 years following taxable years of loss, whichever is longer. Notwithstanding the provisions of Rev & TC § 17276, the amount of loss determined under Rev & TC § 17276.2 shall be the only net operating loss allowed to be carried over from that taxable year, and the designation under Rev & TC § 17276.2(c) shall be included in the election under Rev & TC § 17276.1. For taxable years starting 1–1–91 and ending on or before 12–31–96, taxpayers engaged in business in enterprise zones or program areas will determine attributed loss using a two-factor formula of property and payroll instead of the regular three-factor formula of property, payroll and sales.[36]

TAX TIP	It is only the loss which arises from business done in the program areas (Govt. Code § 7082) or in an enterprise zone (Govt. Code § 7073) which qualifies for the loss carryforward.

Los Angeles Revitalization Zone and Local Agency Military Base Recovery Area—net operating loss deductions. Special net operating loss carryover provisions are available for businesses operating in a designated Los Angeles Revitalization Zone or a local agency Military Base Recovery Area. 100% of the losses incurred by a business located in the zone or area and attributable to the business activity in the zone or area may be carried forward for up to 15 years to offset taxable income earned in the zone or area. Rules are provided for determining both the loss incurred from conducting business in a qualified zone or area, and for determining the income against which the loss carryover may be applied.[37]

---

(36) § 17276.1; 17276.2.   (37) § 17276.2.

¶ 296 **Capital Gain Deduction**

Generally. For 1987 and later, California, like federal, does not allow a capital gain deduction. Unlike federal, however, California does not set a maximum rate for taxing long-term capital gains.[38]

Small business corporations. Effective 10–1–87, California repealed a § 18162.5 former Rev & TC which provided for the total or partial exclusions from gross income of gain recognized upon the sale or other taxable disposition of stock of a small business corporation (not to be confused with 'Small Business Stock' under IRC § 1244 which has been adopted by reference in California Rev & TC § 18151 which is discussed below).

However, there continues to be litigation as to the definition of qualifying stock of small business corporations and whether the special exclusion from tax carries over through a nontaxable exchange. The FTB in Legal Ruling 428 (August 19, 1987) held that the small business stock benefits did not carry over in a nontaxable corporate reorganization. One California Appellate court has agreed and ruled that the small business tax attributes do not carry over in a tax-free, reorganization, but that for preference tax purposes the gain on the disposition of the small-business stock was not a preference item irrespective of the date acquired. *(Mervin G. Morris et al. v. Franchise Tax Board, California Ct. Appl., 2nd Dist., Dkt. No. B065778, 8–19–93).* Another has ruled that the gain on the sale of small-business stock was subject to preference tax even though an acquisition date for such shares was not specified in the statute *(James P. Lennane et al. v. FTB, California Ct. Appl., 1st Dist., Dkt. No. A057655, 6–29–93).* The California Supreme Court has accepted the *Morris* decision, but a ruling has not yet been issued.

Loss on "Small Business Stock" (or Rev & TC § 1244 stock). California adopts IRC § 1244 which provides that a taxpayer may take an ordinary deduction for the loss sustained on "small business stock" issued to an individual or a partnership. For any year, the ordinary loss shall not exceed $50,000 or, $100,000 on a joint return. The federal law provides that the excess may be carried back or forward similar to a net operating loss.[38]

¶ 297 **Moving Expenses**

Moving expenses are deducted *from* adjusted gross income to arrive at taxable income. They are not subject to the 2% of AGI floor. A taxpayer who claims the standard deduction and does not itemize forfeits the deduction. California follows the federal rule. Under IRC § 217(b)(1), the term "moving expenses" means reasonable expenses of moving household goods and personal effects and of traveling (including meals and lodging) from the former residence to the new place of residence. In addition, traveling expenses (including meals and lodging) from the former residence to the general location of the principal place of work and return for the principal purpose of looking for a new home after obtaining employment are deductible. Meals

---

(38) § 17024.5

and lodging while occupying temporary quarters in the general location of the new principal place of work for a period of 30 consecutive days after obtaining employment are deductible. For both federal (IRC § 217(b)(2)) and California purposes, qualified selling, purchase or lease expenses of the old and new residences may be included in the definition but they must be incident to the sale or exchange. This includes such items as real estate commissions, title fees, loan charges and the like. The 80% deduction limit generally applies to meal expenses that qualify for the moving expense deduction under IRC § 217. The limit applies to reimbursed moving expenses as well as unreimbursed moving expenses.[39]

Limits on deductible amounts. California also adopts federal IRC § 217(b)(3)(A)–(C). Under these provisions, the aggregate amount allowable as a deduction which is attributable to the expenses of looking for a new residence or the temporary quarters during the 30-day period cannot exceed $1,500. The total amount allowable as a deduction which is attributable to qualified residence sale, purchase or lease expenses shall not exceed $3,000 reduced by the amount attributable to the temporary living expenses or house-hunting trips included in the $1,500. If a husband and wife both commence work at a new principal place of work within the same general location, the rules are to be applied as if there was only one commencement of work. In the case of a husband and wife filing separate returns, the limits are $750 and $1,500.[39]

Distance and work requirements. California has adopted the IRC § 217(c)(1) rules on distance and work requirements.[39]

Moving expenses claimed for the storage of household furniture that was not needed in the new location were not considered to be within the definition of "expenses of moving household goods and personal effects from the former residence to the new residence." *Appeal of Harold J. and Jo Ann Gibson, SBE 10–6–76.*

Military personnel. California has adopted the federal IRC § 217(g) rules for military personnel. The distance and work requirements of IRC § 217(c) do not apply to members of the Armed Forces transferring as an incident to a permanent change of station while on active duty. Moving and storage expenses furnished in kind by military means or by cash reimbursements and allowances to the extent of expenses actually paid are not includable in the income of the serviceman.[39]

¶ 298   **Interest Penalty Due to Early Withdrawal of Savings**

California has adopted IRC § 62(a)(9). Under these federal provisions, a taxpayer is required to report the gross amount of interest paid or credited during the year on a time savings account without reduction for the amount of any early withdrawal penalty. In arriving at adjusted gross income, however, a taxpayer may deduct the amount charged by a bank, mutual savings

---

(39) § 17201.

bank, savings and loan association, building and loan association, etc., as a penalty for the early withdrawal of funds from a time savings deposit, certificate of deposit or similar types of deposits.[40]

¶ 299   Individual Retirement Arrangements

California conforms to federal rules relating to deductions for contributions and acquisition basis for nondeductible contributions. Federal law reduces the deduction proportionately for adjusted gross income (AGI) between $40,000 and $50,000 for married taxpayers filing jointly, and for adjusted gross income between $25,000 and $35,000 for individual taxpayers, if taxpayer or husband or wife filing jointly are active participants in an employer-maintained retirement plan for any part of plan year ending with or within taxpayer year. For married taxpayers filing separately, deductible contributions are phased out between zero and $10,000 if a spouse participates in an employer-sponsored plan. A minimum contribution of $200 is allowed a taxpayer whose AGI is not above the phase-out range. The phase-out is based on AGI determined before reduction for deductible contributions. Nondeductible contributions are allowed up to $2,000 ($2,250 for spousal IRA).[1]

Federal law allows an individual who is covered by an employer plan, self-employed retirement plan or charitable annuity to set up his own plan to which he can contribute and deduct 100% of his compensation up to $2,000 from gross income each year. The maximum deduction is figured separately for each individual. A husband and wife must keep his or her own compensation separate whether or not they file a joint return or live in a community property state and one or both may have an IRA subject to the 100% and $2,000 limitations. A contribution may be made to an Individual Retirement Account or an Individual Retirement Annuity or Bond. The deduction limit for a spousal IRA is $2,250. There is no compensation requirement for spousal IRAs. They are available if a spouse either has no compensation for the tax year, or elects to be treated as having no compensation. If a claim is made on a joint return for the tax year, the spouse is deemed to have made the election.[2] Contributions to an Individual Retirement Account or annuity which are above the permissible limits plus any income earned on the excess can be withdrawn by the due date for the tax return, including extensions; otherwise the excess is subject to a 6% excise tax. California does not impose this penalty. This excise tax is nondeductible.

Excess contributions made in one year may be applied against contribution limits in a later year if contributions in that year are less than limit. Overstatement of nondeductible contributions in any year incurs $100 penalty.[3] Distributions from a retirement account or annuity plans which occur before an individual reaches age 59½ are subject to a 10% nondeductible excise tax (2½% in California) unless the individual is disabled. Distributions from Individual Retirement Plans must begin April 1 following the

---

(40) § 17201; Fed. Reg. 1.165–1(e)(2).
(1) § 17085; 17508; 18681.9.

(2) IRC § 219(b); (c)(1)(B); § 17024.5.
(3) IRC § 408(o); 6693(b); § 17024.5.

year in which the participant reaches age 70½. If not, a nondeductible 50% excise tax is imposed on the difference between what was paid out and what should have been paid out. An individual can withdraw his or her entire interest in the retirement plan without penalty or tax if that interest is recontributed to an individual retirement arrangement within 60 days of receipt. A "rollover" contribution to an individual retirement arrangement is an allowable contribution not deductible on the taxpayer's return. A taxpayer can make a partial rollover of lump-sum distributions. If part of the distribution consists of property, the property rolled over must be identical to the property distributed. The part not rolled over is subject to current income tax and is not eligible for the five-year averaging provision.[4]

Note: The provisions on partial rollovers for IRA's [IRC § 408(d)(3)(C)] and retirement bond redemptions [IRC § 409(b)(3)(D), effective for obligations issued before 1–1–84] are followed by California.[5]

IRA distributions. The California treatment of the periodic distributions from IRA's is necessarily different from the federal provision that all income is taxable when distributed. Rev & TC § 17507(b) provides for a modification of IRC § 408(d) so that an individual has a basis for annuity computation purposes in any contributions to an IRA not allowed as a deduction for California purposes by reason of Rev & TC 17272 (a), (e), or (g) (in effect before 1987). In other words, for an IRA, the excess contributions over the lesser allowable California contributions ($2,000 vs $1,500, for example) becomes the basis which when distributed is not taxed.[6]

The following table sets forth the maximum allowable IRA contributions for all years and the California basis to be excluded from the first distributions until the basis is recovered.

Year	Maximum amount of IRA contribution which was deductible:		California basis if maximum federal contributions were made:
	Federal	California	
1975	$ 1,500	–0–	$1,500
1976	1,500	$ 1,500	———
1977	1,500	1,500	———
1978	1,500	1,500	———
1979	1,500	1,500	———
1980	1,500	1,500	———
1981	1,500	1,500	———
1982	2,000	1,500	500
1983	2,000	1,500	500
1984	2,000	1,500	500
1985	2,000	1,500	500
1986	2,000	1,500	500
	$20,500	$16,500	$4,000

(4) IRC § 219; 408; § 17024.5.
(5) § 17501.

(6) § 17507.

Simplified employee plans. For taxable years starting on or after 1–1–87, California adopts the provisions of IRC § 219, 402, 404 and 408 with respect to simplified employee pensions (SEPS). Amounts contributed to a SEP by an employer on behalf of an employee and the elective deferrals under SEP are to be excluded from gross income. The amount excludable is the lesser of 15% of compensation or $30,000 reduced in the case of a highly compensated employee by the amounts taken into account for contributions and benefits under Chapter 2 of the Internal Revenue Code (relating to tax on self-employment income, Chapter 21 (relating to Federal Insurance Contribution Act), Title II of the Social Security Act, or any other federal or state law (Social Security Taxes). Any excess of the amount excludable is treated as distributed or made available to the employee. In addition, the act provides that the elective deferrals are to be included as wages for the purpose of the employment tax.

The SEP participation requirements require that an employer make contributions for a year on behalf of each employee (100% participation) who (1) has attained the age of 21, (2) has performed service for the employer during at least three of the immediately preceding five years, and (3) received for 1994, $396 in compensation from the employer for the year. The compensation amount is indexed annually ($385 for 1993, $374 for 1992; $363 for 1991).

The 100% participation requirement applies separately to elective arrangements and, for purposes of such elective arrangements, an individual who is eligible is deemed to receive an employer contribution.

For purposes of the SEP participation requirements, employees covered by a collective bargaining agreement and nonresident aliens who receive no earned income are excluded from consideration.

In addition, employees who are eligible to have contributions made on their behalf under a salary reduction SEP are treated, for purposes of the SEP participation requirements, as receiving an employer contribution.[7]

IRA and SEP rules in California. Where there are both an employer contribution to a SEP and a contribution to an IRA, the deduction is limited to the greater of the amounts allowed for contributions to the SEP or IRA.[8]

IRA, SEP and endowment contract reports. These reports must be filed with the federal Secretary of Treasury. Copies must be filed with the Franchise Tax Board.[9]

Funded tax-exempt trusts. California has adopted IRC §§ 219 and 501 provisions allowing employees who participate in a tax-exempt trust pension plan to elect to make deductible contributions up to the lesser of $9,240 for 1994 ($8,994 for 1993; $8,728 for 1992) or 25% of compensation. These amounts are indexed annually. The amounts contributed to the plan reduce

---

(7) § 17024.5.

(8) FTB 4–9–86.

(9) § 17507(d).

the 1993 $8,994 annual cap on elective deferrals under 401(k) plans and simplified employee pensions but do not reduce deferrals under tax sheltered annuities for employees of schools or tax-exempt charitable organizations. In addition, the election to make deductible contributions to tax-exempt trust pension plans is subject to a nondiscrimination test similar to the test applicable to qualified cash or deferral arrangements. If the test is not satisfied, rules similar to the rules applicable to excess contributions under a qualified cash or deferred arrangement are to apply.[10]

¶ 300 Keogh Plans

California adopts federal IRC § 401 and § 404. Self-employed individuals can take tax deductions for contributions they make to formal pension or profit-sharing plans for themselves and their employees (HR 10 plan). Income earned on their contributions is not taxed until it is withdrawn from the retirement fund. A self-employed individual who owns an unincorporated business or is a partner owning a more than 10% capital or profits interest (an owner-employee) cannot get full coverage for himself unless he provides coverage for all full-time employees (including those whose services and wage costs are shared by others) with more than two years service. Any owner-employee controlling more than one business must cover all the qualifying employees in all of his controlled businesses.[11]

Defined benefit plans. Starting in 1987, the normal retirement age under a defined benefit plan is raised from 62, to the social security retirement age (SSRA) which is currently age 65; however, it will be incrementally raised to age 67 over a twenty-year period. The law limits the annual benefits to the lesser of $118,800 for 1994 ($115,641 for 1993; $112,221 for 1992; $108,963 for 1991) or 100% of compensation for the year. These amounts are indexed annually. If, however, a participant retires before attaining the SSRA, the annual limit must be actuarially reduced so that it is equivalent to $90,000 at SSRA.

The annual limit is also reduced by the shortness of the duration of service, rather than the duration of plan participation. For participants with 10 years of service or less, the limit on annual benefits is reduced by 10% for each year of service less than 10. It will never be less than 10% of the annual limit.

The reduction of the benefit limitation for retirement prior to reaching the SSRA, does not apply to airline pilots, police and firefighters, or participants in government and tax-exempt plans who retire early.

The maximum benefit limitation, phased in over 10 years, is also to be applied to any benefit increases of a qualified defined benefit plan as if such increase were a new plan. It is anticipated that regulations will be drafted to provide for the application of a concentration test under which this phase-in would not apply to a benefit increase, if the increase in benefits is not

---

(10) § 17024.5; 17201; 17501.

(11) § 17024.5; 17501.

primarily for highly compensated employees, (i.e., update of compensation scales, cost of living increases for retirees, etc.)

California adopts the special rule for state and local government plans under IRC § 415(g)(10). Under this rule, the limit for a qualified participant cannot be less than the accrued benefit under the plan determined without regard to any benefit increases adopted after 10–14–87.[11]

Combined plans. California adopts IRC § 415(f) relating to the application of the limitations of IRC § 415(b)(c) and (e) on all defined benefit plans and all defined contribution plans. All defined benefit plans of an employer are treated as one defined benefit plan; the same applies to defined contribution plans. IRC § 415(f)(2) sets the rules for the annual compensation to be taken into account for defined benefit plans. The Secretary of the Treasury has power to disqualify one or more trusts, accounts or plans, or any combination until such plans do not exceed the prescribed limitations in IRC § 415.[12]

Includible compensation. Under prior federal law, the amount of compensation that could be taken into account for SEPs and top-heavy plans was limited to $200,000. This $200,000 limit is now extended to all qualified plans.

IRC § 415 limits on benefits and contributions under qualified plans. All members of a county retirement system who joined the system before 1–1–90 would be exempted from the IRC § 415 limits under the grandfather option of IRC § 415(b)(10). This rule does not apply in Los Angeles County. Each 1937 Act county would be deemed to have elected to contract with the Public Employees Retirement System for the administration of replacement benefits for those IRC § 415 affected members whose retirement benefits cannot be fully maximized under the 1937 Act.[13]

Keogh distributions. Because of the difference between the maximum allowable federal and California contributions annually, Keogh plan holders have the same situation at the time periodic distributions begin as the taxpayers who have IRAs as explained in ¶ 299.

However, there is no statutory authority in California law such as Rev & TC § 17507(b) to cover Keogh plans. California Publication 1005 provides guidance for treating recovery of amounts not previously deducted. The legal staff of the Franchise Tax Board has indicated in a letter ruling that the excess contributions are properly considered as investments in the "annuity contract" and become a return of capital. The following table discloses the amounts involved for all years in which defined contribution Keogh plans have been in effect.

---

(12) 17024.5; 17501.   (13) Govd. Cd. § 31538; 31899.1–31899.10.

	Maximum amount of Keogh contribution which was deductible		California basis if maximum federal contributions were made
Year	Federal	California	
1963	$ 2,500	–0–	$ 2,500
1964	2,500	–0–	2,500
1965	2,500	–0–	2,500
1966	2,500	–0–	2,500
1967	2,500	–0–	2,500
1968	2,500	–0–	2,500
1969	2,500	–0–	2,500
1970	2,500	–0–	2,500
1971	2,500	2,500	—
1972	2,500	2,500	—
1973	2,500	2,500	—
1974	7,500	2,500	5,000
1975	7,500	2,500	5,000
1976	7,500	2,500	5,000
1977	7,500	2,500	5,000
1978	7,500	2,500	5,000
1979	7,500	2,500	5,000
1980	7,500	2,500	5,000
1981	7,500	2,500	5,000
1982	15,000	2,500	12,500
1983	15,000	2,500	12,500
1984	30,000	2,500	27,500
1985	30,000	2,500	27,500
1986	30,000	2,500	27,500
TOTALS	$207,500	$40,000	$167,500

It should be noted that there are similar differences in the maximum allowable amounts of contributions to defined benefit plans with the differences excludable from income when distributed.

Annual reports. An annual report must be filed with the Internal Revenue Service by the end of the seventh month following the end of the plan year—ordinarily the calendar year. Form 5500 is used for plans with more than 100 participants. Failure to file on time calls for a penalty of $25 per day up to a maximum of $15,000. The annual report Form 5500–C is not required to be filed for a plan in which the only participant is the owner-employee. If there are fewer than 100 plan participants and no owner-employee, Form 5500–C may be filed every third year with Form 5500–R filed for the intervening two years. The Franchise Tax Board will accept copies of these federal forms when filed with them as part of general information pertaining to the tax returns. Plans with only one participant, and

¶ 300

less than $100,000 in total assets, may meet the filing requirements by filing Form 5500–EZ annually.

TAX TIP   An individual who is self-employed may set up a Keogh plan and take the deduction even though he is an employee of another business and a participant in that business's pension or profit-sharing plan. For example, an executive of a corporation who receives director's fees from unrelated corporations may set up a Keogh plan with respect to that self-employed income.

The nondiscrimination provisions for a qualified plan must provide for immediate vested benefits for all "covered" employees. If it is a profit-sharing plan, it must have a definite formula for determining contributions to be made on behalf of employees (other than owner-employees). Benefits to an employee start at age 70½ or the year he retires, whichever is later, or to an owner-employee not later than age 70½. Benefits cannot be paid to an owner-employee before he reaches age 59½ unless he becomes disabled, even if the plan is terminated. A premature distribution to an owner-employee is taxed as ordinary income and is subject to a 10% penalty tax.

The owner-employee plan can be funded by: (1) direct cash contributions to a trust created for that purpose if the trustee is a bank, building and loan association or federal credit union, unless all the trust funds are invested in an annuity endowment or life insurance contracts; (2) direct cash contributions to a custodial account held by a bank, building and loan association or Federal credit union; (3) purchase of nontransferrable annuity contracts from a life insurance company; (4) direct investment in a special series of United States retirement plan bonds; or (5) direct purchase from an investment company of so-called face amount certificates as defined in the Investment Company Act of 1940.[14]

¶ 301   **Alimony Payments**

Alimony payments are deductible in arriving at adjusted gross income as long as the amounts are includable in the gross income of the spouse receiving the payment. California's definition of alimony and separate maintenance payments is the same as federal. IRC § 215(b) refers to IRC § 71(b) for the definition of those payments.[15] Generally, the payments are not deductible unless they are includable in the income of the recipient. Nonperiodic payments are examples. Nonresident and part-year residents can't subtract alimony payments for any part of year they are not residents of California.[16]

OBSERVATION   In the case of *Francis vs. McColgan (1951) 107 Cal App 2d 823,* a resident of this state was allowed to deduct periodic alimony payments made to his nonresident former wife under a written property settlement agreement incident to a decree of divorce. In other words, the husband

---

(14) § 17501.   **(16)** § 17302.
(15) § 17201.

¶ 301

was allowed to deduct the periodic alimony payments even though the spouse did not include the alimony payments in California income.

Note: It should be noted that the husband cannot deduct support payments made pursuant to an informal oral agreement and prior to a formal court order or written agreement. *Appeal of Paul A. Pflueger, Jr., SBE 3–26–74;* LR 319, 1–16–67.

¶ 302 Business Use of Home

California has adopted federal IRC § 280A. A taxpayer cannot deduct any expenses for the use of his home for business purposes unless he can prove that a specific part of the residence or a separate structure is set aside and used *exclusively* on a regular basis as (1) a principal place of business, or (2) a place where the taxpayer meets with patients, clients or customers. An employee is allowed a home/office deduction if it is used for the convenience of the employer. The deduction for the business use of the home is limited to the amount of gross income from that use reduced by the sum of otherwise allowable expenses such as taxes, interest and casualty losses and the deductions allocable to the trade or business or rental activity of the taxpayer in which the use occurs, but are not allocable to such use as business, storage of inventory, rental, or day care services, specified in IRC § 280A(c)(1)–(4). Excess home office deductions can be carried forward to later years, but will be subject to income limitations in effect in those years, whether or not the dwelling is used as a residence. Home office deduction is denied if the employee rents home space to the employer.[17] See *Appeal of John H. Roy, SBE 3–8–76; Appeal of Frederick A. Sebring, SBE 12–9–80.*

California has also adopted the provisions of IRC § 280A that allow a deduction for items allocable to the use of any portion of a dwelling unit on a regular basis in the taxpayer's trade or business of providing day care for children, individuals 65 or over, or individuals mentally or physically incapable of caring for themselves.[18]

¶ 303 Circulation Expenditures

Under IRC § 173, adopted by California, all expenditures to establish, maintain or increase the circulation of a newspaper, magazine or other periodical are deductible. This does not include expenditures for the purchase of land or depreciable property or for the acquisition of circulation through the purchase of any part of the business of another publisher of a newspaper, magazine or other periodical. The taxpayer may elect, in accordance with the Franchise Tax Board's regulation, to capitalize the total amount of the expenditures which are chargeable to the capital account. The election is binding for all subsequent taxable years.[19]

For many years, the IRS has allowed write-offs of pre-publication costs paid or incurred for the writing, editing, compiling, designing and illustrating and similar costs of a book, teaching aid or similar product. Such costs

---

(17) § 17201.
(18) § 17201.

(19) § 17201.

are allowed to be deducted currently rather than capitalized. The write-off is allowed if the publisher's past practice has been to expense the items on a consistent basis. The special provision is applicable until the final regulations are issued by the Service. California will follow the lead of the Service and allow similar treatment.[20]

¶ 304   Research and Experimental Expenditures

Under IRC § 174, adopted by California, a taxpayer may deduct research or experimental expenditures which are paid or incurred by him during the taxable year in his trade or business as expenses. Only reasonable research expenditures are deductible. The method adopted shall apply to all expenditures and must be used for all subsequent taxable years unless permission is received to change to a different method. The taxpayer may elect to treat as deferred expenses those research or experimental expenditures which are paid or incurred in his trade or business and which are not treated as expenses and are not of a character which is subject to the allowance for depreciation. In computing taxable income, deferred expenses will be allowed as a deduction ratably over a period of not less than 60 months as may be selected by the taxpayer.[21] For adjustments to basis of property, see IRC § 1016(a)(14).[22]

> *Note:* California allows a credit against taxes, based on the IRC § 41 credit for increasing research activities, as modified by California (¶ 146.)[23]

OBSERVATION   The optional 10-year write-off of research and experimental expenditures allowed by IRC § 59(e) has been adopted by California. Write-off takes the place of preference item treatment.

¶ 305   Farmers' Expenses

Soil and water conservation expenditures. California has adopted federal IRC § 175. Under this section, a farmer can deduct expenditures made for the purpose of soil and water conservation and the prevention of erosion of land used in farming. *Deductible* are expenditures for the cultivation of earth including, but not limited to, leveling, grading and terracing, contour-furrowing, the construction of diversion channels and drainage ditches, the control and protection of diversion channels, drainage ditches, earthen dams, water courses, outlets and ponds, the planting and cultivation of cover and protective crops, the eradication of brush, and the planting of windbreaks. *Nondeductible* are expenses incurred in the purchase, construction, installation or improvement of structures, appliances and facilities such as tanks, reservoirs, pipes, conduits, canals, dams, wells and pumps which are subject to the allowance for depreciation.[24]

---

(20) Fed. Reg. No. 1.173–1.
(21) § 17201; Fed. Regs. No. 1.174–1–1.174.4.
(22) § 18031; 18036.

(23) § 17052.12.
(24) § 17024.5; 17201.

How much can be deducted. For both California and federal purposes the amount deductible in any year is limited to 25% of the gross income from farming for that year. Any excess expenses over the limitation may be carried over and deducted in the subsequent year subject to the same 25% limitation for that year.[25]

Land used for farming. The term land used for farming means land used by the taxpayer or his tenant for the production of crops, fruits, or other agricultural products, or for the sustenance of livestock.[26]

Election to deduct fertilizer and lime expenses. IRC § 180 allows a farmer to deduct rather than capitalize the amount paid or incurred for the purchase of fertilizer, lime, ground limestone, marl, or other materials to enrich, neutralize, or condition the land used in farming. California has the same provision.[27]

Reforestation expenditures. California has adopted IRC § 194.[28] Under IRC § 194, a taxpayer may elect to amortize the amortizable basis of qualified timber property over a period of 84 months. The aggregate amount of the amortizable basis acquired during the taxable year that may be taken into account is $10,000 ($5,000 in case of separate return by married individual). "Amortizable basis" means portion of basis of qualified timber property attributable to reforestation expenditures. "Reforestation expenditures" means direct costs incurred in forestation or reforestation by planting or artificial or natural seeding.

¶ 306   Amortization of Pollution Control Facility

California determines the deduction for amortization of pollution control facilities in accordance with IRC § 169.[29] Under this provision, instead of depreciation a taxpayer may elect to take a deduction for the amortization of the amortizable basis of any "certified pollution control facility" based on the period of 60 months. The election of the taxpayer to take the amortization deduction on a 60-month period is to begin with the month following the month in which the facility is completed or acquired or with the taxable year succeeding the taxable year in which such facility is completed or acquired.[30]

The term "certified pollution control facility" means a new identifiable treatment facility which is used in connection with a plant or other property in operation before 1976 to abate or control water, air or atmospheric pollution or contamination by removing, altering, disposing, storing, or preventing the emission or creation of pollutants, contaminants, waste or heat which the State Air Resources Board in the case of air pollution or the State Water Resources Control Board in the case of water pollution and the federal authorities have certified.[31]

---

(25) IRC § 175; Fed. Reg. 1.175–1.175–4.
(26) IRC § 175(c)(2).
(27) IRC § 180; Fed. Reg. 1.180–1–1.180–2; § 17201.

(28) § 17024.5; 17072.
(29) IRC § 169; § 17250(f).
(30) IRC § 169(a)–(b); § 17250(c).
(31) IRC § 169(f); § 17250(c).

Note: California allows deduction only with respect to facilities located instate. California law also specifies that "State certifying authority" referred to in IRC § 169(d)(2) is State Air Resources Board in the case of air pollution or the State Water Resources Control Board in the case of water pollution.[32]

Cogeneration or alternative energy equipment. For tax years beginning before 1–1–91, California allowed a 12-month or 60-month write-off of "cogeneration" equipment or alternative energy equipment. These are types of equipment used to generate energy by secondary recovery sources from waste steam or from thermal energy sources.

¶ 308 Activities Not Engaged in for Profit

California has adopted IRC § 183.[33] Under federal IRC § 183, a taxpayer engaged in a business which is not considered to be engaged in for profit is not allowed deductions for expenses except the deductions which would be allowable without regard to whether or not such activity is engaged in for profit, such as taxes, interest and carrying charges.

Presumption activity is for profit. If the gross income derived from an activity exceeds deductions for three or more of the taxable years in the period of five consecutive taxable years which ends with a taxable year, then such activity will be presumed for such taxable year to be actively engaged in for profit. In the case of an activity which consists in major part of the breeding, training, showing or racing of horses, the period is two out of seven years.[33]

The three-out-of-five year rule is only a presumption on the part of the tax authorities, however. It may be overcome by taxpayer's showing that he is in the business to ultimately arrive at a taxable profit. Among things considered would be the capital investment, the background and history of the taxpayer related to the particular type of business involved, a projection of future outlook for customers and income, etc.

TAX TIP	A taxpayer may file federal Form 5213 to postpone until the end of the fifth year (or seventh) a determination by the Internal Revenue Service as to whether the rule applies.

The Board of Equalization had ruled that taxpayers were not engaged in a rental business for profit when they (1) conducted no preliminary investigation of profitability of rental property in the vicinity (2) didn't use expert advice and services in acquiring and operating the property (3) made minimal efforts in advertising and promoting the rental and (4) failed to take action to convert the losses to profits. *Appeal of Walter E. and Gladys M. Sherbondy, SBE 4–10–79.*

¶ 309 Employee Stock Options

California has adopted IRC §§ 421—424 governing stock options.[34]

---

(32) § 17250(f).
(33) § 17201; Fed. Reg. No. 1.183–1–1.183–2.

(34) § 17501.

An employee stock option is essentially an offer by a corporation to sell stock to its employees at a bargain price. Usually, employees have taxable income if they receive *nonstatutory* options to buy stock (or other property), unless the options are subject to a substantial risk of forfeiture or have no readily ascertainable value. However, if they receive *statutory* options, special rules generally postpone the tax until the employees sell their stock. There are four kinds of statutory stock options: qualified stock options, employee stock purchase plans, incentive stock options and restricted stock options.

Generally, if all requirements are met, employees realize no income when they receive an option or when exercising it.

Under IRC § 421, if stock acquired under an option is not held for the required length of time, the employee realizes ordinary income. Generally, the income is reported when the stock is disposed of, and the corporation can then deduct the same amount as compensation paid to the employee. No deduction is allowed to the corporation when it transfers the stock on exercise of an option. Payments received for cancellation of an option are taxed as ordinary income.

Employee stock purchase plan.   Under this arrangement the employee has no income when he receives the option or when he exercises the option if he has been employed from the time of the grant to a point three months before the exercise. The option price can be as low as 85% of the fair market value at the date of grant or exercise. If the stock is sold after being held for a period of more than one year after acquisition and at least two years after the date of the grant, the employee has ordinary income to the extent of the excess of the fair market value at the date of the grant over the option price. The basis of the stock is increased by the amount of the ordinary income. The difference between the increased basis and the selling price is capital gain or loss. If the option price is expressed as a percent of the value at the date of exercise, the option price is determined as if the option were exercised at the date of the grant.[35]

Nonstatutory stock option.   If a stock option plan does not meet the requirement of a qualified stock option or a restricted stock plan or under an employee stock purchase plan or any option granted after 5–20–76, the employee realizes income at the date of the exercise. The taxable portion is considered to be ordinary income as additional compensation. To the extent of such compensation, the employer, of course, would get a deduction. If the option itself is considered to be compensation and the fair market value is measurable, then the amount is considered to be ordinary income to the employee. If the non-statutory option has no ascertainable market value when granted, the difference between the option price and the market value is ordinary taxable compensation.

---

(35) IRC § 423.

Restricted stock plan. Under IRC § 83, adopted by California, stock received by an employee for services after 6–30–69 under restrictions is taxable when the restrictions lapse or the stock is no longer subject to a substantial risk of forfeiture. The amount taxable is the excess of the fair market value over the cost. The employer gets a deduction when the employee reports income from the restricted stock plan. A "substantial risk of forfeiture" means that the person's right to the property is conditioned on future performance of substantial services by the individual.

The appreciation in the value of the stock from the time it was received until the restrictions lapse would be deemed to be ordinary income, and later appreciation would be taxed as a capital gain on disposition of the stock.

Election to treat restricted property as pay. If an employee chooses, he may treat restricted property as compensation at the time he receives it and ignore the postponement due to the substantial risk of forfeiture provision. His or her income would be the excess of the fair market value over any consideration he pays for it. The later appreciation would be capital gain. The election has to be made within 30 days of the transfer of the property by filing a statement with the Internal Revenue Service Center used by the employee to file his return and the Franchise Tax Board, as the case may be. If the property is issued subject to restrictions which never lapse, such as a requirement that the employer will be offered the stock by the employee on termination of employment, some special rules apply. If the stock under such a restriction can be sold at a formula price, such as book value, then the formula price would be the fair market value unless the Internal Revenue Service Commissioner or the Franchise Tax Board determine a different amount. If the restriction is later cancelled, the employee has compensation income on the excess of the full value over the sum of the restricted value, plus any consideration paid for the cancellation. The above rule doesn't apply if the employee is able to show that the cancellation was not compensatory. California follows the federal rule that an individual's rights in property are subject to substantial risk of forfeiture, and not transferable so long as the sale of the property at a profit could subject the individual to suit under the insider trading rules of the Securities and Exchange Act of 1934, § 16(b).[36]

Employee stock ownership plan (ESOP). This is a tax-qualified retirement plan (defined benefit plan) which invests primarily in the securities of the employer. The plan cannot be used to replace other employee benefits, but an existing plan can be amended to provide these additional benefits for the employees.

The shares of stock are allocated to the employee as of the end of each plan year. The apportionment is made on the basis of the compensation paid to each to the total compensation paid to all of those eligible. Salary paid to any one employee over $100,000 will be disregarded for this computation.

---

(36) § 17081.

The receipt of the stock and the dividends the stock earns are not taxable to the employee even though there is immediate vesting of the stock to the employee. It must be retained in the plan for at least seven years except in cases where the employee is terminated, disabled or dies.

California has adopted the provisions of IRC § 1042 for taxable years starting on or after 1–1–90 and before 1–1–95. These provisions do not apply in California for taxable years beginning on or after 1–1–88 and before 1–1–90, and for taxable years beginning on or after 1–1–95.[37]

Incentive stock options. California has adopted the provisions of IRC § 422. The incentive stock option (ISO) gets much the same favorable tax treatment that previously applied to restricted and qualified options.

What options qualify. To qualify, the terms of the incentive stock option itself must satisfy these conditions:[38]

●Option must be granted under a plan that specifies the number of shares of stock to be issued and the employees or class of employees eligible to receive options. Also, the plan must be approved by stockholders within 12 months before or after the plan is adopted.

●Option must be granted within 10 years of the date the plan is adopted or is approved by the shareholders, whichever is earlier.

●Option must be exercisable only within 10 years of the date it is granted.

●Option price must equal or exceed the stock's fair market value when the option is granted. Fair market value must be determined without regard to any restriction other than a restriction that by its terms will never lapse.

●Option must not be transferable other than on death.

● Employee must not, immediately before the option is granted, own over 10% of the voting power of the employer corporation or its parent or subsidiary. However, this limitation is waived if the option price is at least 110% of the stock's fair market value when the option is granted and the option must be exercised within five years of the date it is granted.

TAX TIP   Keep the periods during which an option can be exercised reasonably short. Remember that an employee won't be able to exercise a second option until the first option is either fully exercised or lapses. And if the terms of the first option are excessively long, such as 10 years or more, it will be a long time before the second option will be of any practical use to the employee.

Tax treatment. The employee realizes no taxable income when the incentive option is granted or when it's exercised. If the employee doesn't dispose of his option stock within two years after the option is granted, and has held the stock itself for at least one year, any gain he realizes on the sale of the option stock will be long-term capital gain and his employer won't get any deduction. If the two-year holding period requirement is not met, gain will be treated as ordinary income instead of capital gain and his employer gets a deduction. The amount of ordinary income, and the amount of the

---

(37) § 18042.   (38) IRC § 422A(b); (c)(10).

employer's deduction, is limited to the difference between the amount realized on the sale and the option price.

> *Note:* IRC § 6039(a) requiring written statements to be given to any employee exercising a stock option.[39]

¶ 311 Welfare Benefit Plans

California has adopted IRC § 419 relating to the treatment of funded welfare benefit plans, and IRC § 419A relating to the limits on additions to a qualified asset account. Under IRC § 419, if employer contributions to a welfare fund, even though they are not deductible under Subchapter D, Deferred Compensation, are otherwise deductible, they can be deducted, up to the amount of the fund's qualified cost, in the tax year when made. "Welfare benefit fund" means any fund that is (1) part of the employer's plan through which it provides benefits to employee's or their beneficiaries. "Welfare benefit" is any benefit other than a benefit to which IRC § 83(h) relating to property transferred in performance of service, IRC § 404 relating to contributions to qualified plan, or IRC § 404A relating to contributions to foreign deferred compensation plan applies. "Fund" is any organization described in IRC § 501(c)(7), (9), (17), or (20), any trust, corporation, or other organization not exempt from tax, and, to the extent provided in regulations, any account held for an employer by any person. "Fund" does not include amounts held by an insurance company under a qualified nonguaranteed contract that is a life insurance contract described in IRC § 264(a)(1) (policy on life of office, employee, or financially interested person), or such contract is a qualified non-guaranteed contract. A method or arrangement of employer contributions having the effect of a plan will be treated as a plan. Plans are extended to include independent contractors.

Contributions allowable are limited to the fund's qualified cost for the tax year. This cost is computed by adding the fund's direct qualified cost, which are benefits provided by the plan that would have been deductible if provided by the employer, and any addition by the fund to the qualified asset account, subject to limitations in IRC § 419A(b), and reducing this figure by the fund's after-tax income. Excess contributions can be carried over to the succeeding taxable year. The employer is taxed on the fund's deemed unrelated income.[40]

---

(39) § 17501; 17514; 18802.7; 24622.   **(40)** § 17501.

CHAPTER **5**

ITEMIZED DEDUCTIONS

501

¶ 321   **General**

An individual taxpayer must make an election to deduct from adjusted gross income certain "itemized" deductions—principally medical expenses, taxes, interest, charitable contributions, casualty losses and miscellaneous expenses. Itemized deductions are also known as "statutory" deductions because they are not related to one's trade or business and can offset items of gross income because the taxing authorities have provided for their deduction through legislation.[1]

IRC conformity.   For tax year 1993, California has adopted the Internal Revenue Code as enacted on 1–1–93. Under IRC § 63(d), "itemized deductions" means deductions allowable other than:

(1) those allowed in arriving at adjusted gross income; and

(2) the deduction for personal exemptions provided by IRC § 151.

For adjustments in arriving at California itemized deductions, see Form 540, Schedule CA instructions, and FTB 1001, Supplemental Guidelines. California does not allow deduction for personal exemptions. Instead the state allows credits for personal exemptions.

Overall limit on itemized deductions.   California adopts IRC § 68, but substitutes 6% for 3% of the excess adjusted gross income over the applicable amount in IRC § 68(a)(1). For the purposes of Rev & TC § 17077, the applicable amount for the 1994 tax year means $107,464 for a single individual, or a married individual making a separate return; $161,196, in case of a head of household; and $214,929, in case of a surviving spouse or husband or wife making a joint return. The amounts are indexed annually.

> *Note:* IRC § 68(c), adopted by California, makes the limitation inapplicable to the deduction for medical expenses (IRC § 213), the deduction for investment interest (IRC § 163(d)), and the deduction for casualty and theft losses (IRC § 165(c)(3) and (d)). IRC § 68 does not apply to any estate or trust.

Time and manner of election to itemize.   Election must be made on taxpayer's return as prescribed by the Franchise Tax Board.[2]

Change of treatment.   Under Franchise Tax Board regulations, a change of election with respect to itemized deductions for any taxable year may be made after filing a return for such year. A change will not be allowed if the taxpayer's spouse filed a separate return for the year corresponding to the taxpayer's unless certain conditions are met.[3]

¶ 322   **Standard Deduction**

The California standard deduction is indexed annually. The deduction for taxable year 1994 is $2,431 for taxpayers other than married persons filing jointly, heads of household and surviving spouses; and $4,862 for married persons filing jointly, heads of household or surviving spouses.[4]

---

(1) § 17073; 17201.
(2) IRC § 63(e)(1)–(2); § 17024.5(d).

(3) IRC § 63(e)(3); § 17073.
(4) IRC § 63(c); (f); (h); § 17073.5.

For 1994, additional standard deductions of $750 for aged and blind persons, and $950 if such individuals are not married or are not surviving spouses are allowed by the federal IRC. California does not allow these deductions, but gives personal exemption credits for single and married individuals, heads of household and surviving spouses, and aged and blind persons.[4]

California standard deductions, when elected by a taxpayer, is in place of all other deductions other than those that are subtracted from gross income in computing adjusted gross income. California provisions on standard deduction are applied instead of federal provisions for standard deduction (IRC § 63(c)); and additional amounts for aged and blind (IRC § 63(f)). However, California adopts the IRC § 63(c)(5) limits on deduction for certain dependents, and IRC § 63(c)(6), relating to certain individuals not eligible for the standard deduction. The IRC § 63(c)(4) provisions on indexing apply to the limited deduction under IRC § 63(c)(5).

Indexing of standard deduction is provided by both state and federal laws.[4]

¶ 323   **Medical Expenses**

Generally.   An individual taxpayer who itemizes personal deductions may deduct medical expenses he pays for himself, his spouse and his dependents. Any medical expense that is reimbursed during the year is reduced by the amount of the reimbursement before the percentage limitations are applied. Only amounts actually paid during the tax year for medical expenses incurred in the tax year or prior tax years may be included in computing the medical expense deduction.

Deduction amount.   California follows federal treatment of medical expenses (IRC § 213) which allows taxpayers to deduct medical expenses only to the extent they exceed 7.5% of adjusted gross income. California does not separately compute the 7.5% reduction amount. Rather, the 7.5% reduction amount computed for state purposes is based on federal adjusted gross income so that the medical expense deduction is the same amount for federal and California purposes. Medical insurance premiums are combined with other medical expenses subject to the 7.5% floor.[5] Amounts paid for medicine or drugs can be taken into account only if medicine is a prescribed drug or insulin.[5] California also follows federal rules which disallow a deduction for medical insurance premiums claimed as a credit under IRC § 32 (Earned Income Credit).

Medical expenses of a decedent paid out of his estate within one year after his death are considered paid by a decedent at the time incurred. If the expenses are also deductible for estate tax purposes, the taxpayer can deduct them only if he files a statement that deduction has not been claimed for estate tax purposes and files a waiver of the right to claim a deduction for

---

(5) § 17201.

estate tax purposes. These federal IRC § 213(c) provisions have also been adopted by California.[5]

Taxpayer—spouse—dependent. Expenses paid must be for medical care of the taxpayer, the spouse, or a dependent. In community property states, medical expenses paid out of community funds are deductible in equal amounts on separate returns. However, those paid out of the separate funds of either are deductible only by the spouse paying them. California follows this federal IRC § 213(a) rule.[5]

What are medical expenses. California has adopted federal rules relative to what constitutes deductible and undeductible medical expenses. The state follows IRC § 213(d) that denies a medical deduction for unnecessary cosmetic surgery and similar procedures. "Medical expenses" under federal IRC § 213(d) include any payment for diagnosis, cure, treatment, mitigation or prevention of disease or for the purpose of affecting any bodily function or structure, cost of insurance to cover medical care and also transportation expenses primarily for and essential to medical care. This definition of medical expenses is fairly broad and includes payments to physicians, surgeons, dentists, ophthalmologists, optometrists, chiropractors, osteopaths, podiatrists, psychiatrists, psychologists, Christian Science practitioners and others for medical services. Also included are payments for hospital services, therapy and similar services, nursing services (including nurses' meals provided by the taxpayer), ambulance hire and laboratory, surgical, obstetrical, diagnostic, dental and X-ray fees. Among the expenses which are also considered medical expenses are payments for a legal abortion, payments for an operation legally performed to make a person unable to have children, payments for a face-lifting operation, payments for acupuncture and payments to a treatment center for drug addicts or alcoholics, including meals and lodging provided by the center during the treatment.[5]

Home improvements. The full cost of installing an elevator or making similar permanent improvements to property is deductible if the improvement does not increase the value of the property and otherwise qualifies as a medical expense. If the improvement increases the property's value, only the part of the cost that exceeds the increase in value is deductible.[6]

Medical reimbursement plans. Under federal regulations also applicable in California, if medical expenses deducted in one year are reimbursed in a later year, the amount is income to the extent attributable to, but not in excess of the deduction. The amount taxable in this case is the lesser of the amount received as reimbursement or the deduction allowed.[7] However, if no tax benefit was obtained from the deduction for medical expense, than the reimbursement in the later year would be excluded from income under Rev & TC § 24310 which is substantially similar to IRC § 111 (Recovery of Tax Benefit Items).

---

(6) Fed. Reg. § 1.213–1(g).   (7) Fed. Reg. 1.213–(g).

Amounts paid for lodging away from home. California has adopted IRC § 213(d)(2) that treats amounts paid for lodging away from home as deductible. These amounts must be primarily for and essential to medical care which must be provided by a physician in a licensed hospital or equivalent medical care facility. No significant pleasure, recreation or vacation can be involved in travel away from home. Deduction will be denied if amounts paid are lavish or extravagant. It is limited to $50 a night for each individual.[5]

Child of divorced parents. California has adopted the IRC § 213(d)(5) rule that regards any child to whom IRC § 152(e) governing support test in case of divorced parents applies as dependent of both parents. This means that noncustodial parent can deduct medical expenses paid for children, even though it can't claim dependency exemption, as long as one of the parents can claim child as dependent.[5]

Child care credit taken. Any expense allowed as credit under the IRC § 21 provisions for child care credit will not be treated as deductible expense for medical care.[5]

Dogs purchased and maintained for use by blind and deaf individuals. California has adopted IRC § 213 governing the deduction of medical expenses. Federal regulation 1.213–1(e)(iii) and Rev Rulings 57–461 and 68–295, that apply in California in the absence of state regulations, provide that the purchase and maintenance of dogs for use by blind and deaf individuals qualify for medical expense deductions.[5]

Transportation expenses. Under federal IRC § 213(d)(1)(B), the cost of transportation required for medical assistance is deductible including family visits if required as a medical necessity.[8] California rules are the same as federal. Actual automobile expenses, excluding depreciation, relating to medical travel are deductible. California also follows federal Rev. Proc. 91–67 that allows the use of an optional mileage rate deduction of 9¢ a mile for computing the medical expense deduction for the use of a personal automobile which is in lieu of the actual costs, and avoids detail substantiation requirements to document actual cost.

Health insurance costs of self-employed individuals. California adopts IRC § 162(1) which allows a self-employed individual a deduction of 25% of health insurance costs. Special rules limit the deductions which can be claimed by partnerships and S Corporations with respect to certain partners or employee-shareholders. The cost of the health insurance in excess of the 25% credit amount is added to other medical expenses subject to the 7.5% floor. These provisions remain in effect only as long as IRC § 162(1), relating to health insurance costs of self-employed individuals remains in effect.

Originally, the deduction of health insurance costs for self-employed individuals expired on June 30, 1992. Consistent with federal law, the Cali-

---

(8) Lichterman v. Commissioner, 37 TC 586.

fornia deduction has been retroactively extended to provide deductions for insurance payments for the period July 1, 1992 to December 31, 1994.

REFUND OPPORTUNITY

Self-employed individuals who did not claim deductions for the medical insurance payments for the last six months of 1992, may file a claim for refund to recover excess tax payments as a result of this deduction being allowed retroactively.

CAUTION

The deduction for health insurance costs of self-employed persons was not extended by the federal Congress before it recessed in October, 1994. Accordingly the deduction expires both for federal and California purposes on December 31, 1994. Watch for federal legislation in 1995 to see if the deduction is extended for federal purposes, but exercise caution because California may not conform automatically.

Adoption expenses. California no longer allows a deduction for adoption expenses.

¶ 324 Taxes

These taxes are deductible for both the federal and California individual income tax returns:

- Real property tax (state, local or foreign).
- Personal property tax (state or local).

State, local and foreign taxes not included above are also deductible if incurred in carrying on a trade or a business or an activity for the production of income.[9]

State or local taxes are those imposed by the 50 states or any of their political subdivisions (such as a city or county) and the District of Columbia.[10]

Income taxes paid states and foreign countries. Federal IRC § 164(a)(3) allows a deduction for state, local and foreign income taxes. California *does not* allow a deduction for state, local and foreign income, war profits, and excess profits taxes.[11]

Limited partnerships and S corporations. California does not allow a deduction for taxes paid under corporate tax provisions, Rev & TC, Part 11, starting with Rev & TC § 23001, which includes the tax on limited partnerships, and tax on S corporations.[11]

Japanese tax withheld from receipts paid to nonresident from domestic source income such as royalties, dividends, and motion picture rentals is not deductible.[12] California beneficiaries of Hawaiian trust that paid Hawaiian gross income tax liability, but failed to pay California tax, must report

---

(**9**) IRC 164(a); (d); § 17201.
(**10**) IRC § 164(b)(2); § 17201.

(**11**) § 17220.
(**12**) LR 336, 3–5–70.

shares of entire gross income to California, when distributed, or distributable, and can't deduct Hawaiian tax.[13]

Real property taxes are deductible.   Under federal IRC § 164(a)(1) and California law, deductible taxes are those paid to any state, local or foreign government on real property levied for the general public welfare. Not deductible under federal IRC § 164(c) and California law are those taxes charged for local benefits and improvements that increase the value of the property.[14]

Under IRC § 461(c), an accrual basis taxpayer may elect to accrue real property taxes ratably over the taxable year of the tax assessing authority. The election may be made without the consent of the taxing authority for the first taxable year in which the taxpayer incurs real property taxes. An election may be made at a later time with the consent of the commissioner. California has adopted this federal provision.[15] If the taxpayer does not elect to accrue the real property tax ratably, the general rule is that the state property tax accrues on the assessment date.

IMPORTANT   For California the assessment date is March 1 of each year and the tax year for that accrual date is from July 1 following to June 30 of the next year.[16]

Tenant stockholders of co-op apartment or housing corporation.   Tenant stockholders of co-op apartments or housing corporations can deduct amounts paid that represent taxes.[17]

California has adopted IRC § 164(d) that provides that if real estate is sold during the year, the real estate taxes are divided between the buyer and the seller. The taxes are prorated according to the number of days in the tax year (the period through which the tax imposed relates) that each owned the property. The seller pays the taxes up to the date of the sale and the buyer pays the taxes from that date to the end of the tax year, irrespective of the lien date or the assessment date.[9]

Sales taxes.   Sales taxes are not deductible.

Capitalization of sales tax paid, if not otherwise deductible.   California adopts IRC § 164(a) that requires taxes incurred in the acquisition of property used in trade or business to be considered part of the cost of acquisition, and taxes incurred in the disposition of property used in trade or business to be used to reduce amount realized on the disposition. This rule does not apply to taxpayers electing a credit under Rev & TC § 17052.13 for sales or use tax paid or incurred in connection with the purchase of qualified property used in an enterprise zone, a Los Angeles Revitalization Zone, a Local Agency Military Base Recovery Zone, or program area.[18]

---

(13) LR 371, 1–22–74.
(14) § 17201.
(15) § 17551.

(16) § 2192; 17551.
(17) § 17052.13; ¶ 58,118.
(18) IRC § 164(a); 17024.5; 17052.13.

Motor vehicle license and registration fees.   IRC § 164(b), adopted by California, allows deduction for personal property taxes defined as annual ad valorem tax imposed on personal property. You can deduct California motor vehicle license fees, less the annual registration fee. Vehicles with commercial license plates must also subtract weight fees from the total license fee in accordance with a table contained in the instructions for the return.

Withholding taxes.   No deduction is allowed for tax deducted and withheld under Rev & TC § 18805 and Unemployment Insurance Code § 13020 either to the employer or to the recipient of the income.[19]

State disability insurance contributions.   California law requires that employers withhold a percentage of wages for State Disability Insurance. For 1994 and 1995 the taxable wage base is $31,767. The employee's rate for disability tax purposes is 1.3% for 1994 and 1995. The IRS, in a news release in 1978 (IR–1967, March 10, 1978), announced that it would allow a deduction for the employee's contribution to the disability insurance fund, as a state income tax paid, based on the Tax Court Decision in A. Trujillo (68 TC 670).

OBSERVATION   As indicated above, California does not allow a deduction for income taxes and, therefore, does not allow an employee a deduction for the disability insurance withheld by employers. For federal purposes the disability insurance is treated as an income tax but only if the employer participates in the state-sponsored plan. Employee contributions to an employer's self-insured plan are not treated as an income tax and are not deductible by the employee for federal or state purposes.

WARNING   Deduction for taxes can be lost by owners and transferors of an interest in real property or mobile homes that fail to provide information as to social security numbers, identification numbers (if not individuals), and identification of property interests to the FTB as required by Rev & TC § 18802.3, or who provide false, misleading or inaccurate information in return. Deduction will be denied from 60 days after due date of Rev & TC § 18802.3 return until the FTB determines there is compliance. If noncompliance does not cover the entire calendar year, the denial of deductions is at the rate of one-twelfth for each full month of noncompliance.[20] Taxpayers deriving income from substandard housing can lose the deduction.[21]

¶ 325   **Interest**

California has adopted IRC § 163 that provides that all interest, other than personal interest, paid or accrued within the taxable year on indebtedness is deductible if it results from a debtor-creditor relationship and is based on a

---

(19) § 17222.
(20) § 17299.9.

(21) § 17274.

valid obligation to pay a fixed or determinable sum of money. The obligation must be one for which the taxpayer is legally liable.

For an accrual basis taxpayer the interest is deductible ratably over the period for which it accrues without consideration of the date paid, while a cash basis taxpayer deducts interest in the year paid.[22]

Prepaid interest. IRC § 461(g)(1), adopted by California, states that a cash basis taxpayer who prepays interest is not allowed to deduct the interest in the year of prepayment. The prepaid interest must be capitalized and deducted on the accrual basis. In effect, the prepaid interest is allocated to the tax year or years as a cost of using the borrowed money. This prepayment rule covers interest paid for personal, business or investment purposes.[23]

First-time home buyers—"buy-down mortgage plan." Payments made by these buyers to the California Housing Agency under such plans are considered deductible interest payments. Under the plan, the Agency purchases from the mortgage lender a buy-down of the effective interest to the borrower on the mortgage loan. It also obtains a note and deed of trust from the borrower which is subordinate to the mortgage loan. This subordinate mortgage or deed of trust may provide that all amounts due and payable be paid at the end of the sixth year, or be repaid on an amortized basis starting at the seventh year and extending through the thirtieth year, or a term selected by the agency between the end of the sixth year and the end of the thirtieth year. The amount of the subordinate note and mortgage must be equal to the contract amount advanced by the agency to the mortgage lender, plus interest on such amounts that will cover the costs of funds to the agency, and administrative costs less any funds returned to the agency by the lender that were not earned by the lender because of prepayment of the mortgage for any reason before the end of the buy-down period. The federal IRC has no comparable provision.[24]

Tenant-stockholders in cooperative housing corporation. Cooperative housing corporations that charge tenant-stockholders with a portion of the cooperative's interest or taxes in a manner that reasonably reflects the cost to the cooperative of the interest or taxes allocable to each tenant-stockholder's dwelling unit, may elect to have the tenant-stockholders deduct for income tax purposes the separately allocated amounts (rather than amounts based on proportionate ownership of shares of the cooperative). In addition, the tax treatment accorded individuals who are tenant-stockholders is extended to corporations, trusts, and other entities that are stockholders. Also, maintenance and lease expenses are disallowed where payments by tenant-stockholders are allocable to amounts properly chargeable to the capital account of the cooperative.[25]

---

(22) IRC § 163; § 17201; Fed Reg No. 1.446–1(c) (11).
(23) IRC § 461(g)(1) § 17551.

(24) Health & Safety Cd § 52500–52519; § 17230.
(25) § 17201.

Redeemable ground rents. Annual or periodic rentals under a redeemable ground rent arrangement (other than payments in redemption thereof) are deductible as interest under IRC § 163(c) as adopted by California.[26]

Personal interest. No deduction is allowed for personal interest regardless of when the loan was obtained. Personal interest means any interest allowable as a deduction, except:

(1) interest paid or accrued on debt incurred or continued in connection with a trade or business, other than employee's services;

(2) any investment interest;

(3) any interest taken into account under IRC § 469 in computing income or loss from passive activity;

(4) any qualified residence interest; and

(5) any interest payable on unpaid portion of estate tax for period in which extension of time to pay is in effect.[27]

TAX TIP   Interest paid on deferred federal or California income, estate, or gift taxes may be claimed as cost of administration for estate tax purposes under IRC § 2053(a)(2), even though the interest is not deductible as interest for income tax purposes under IRC § 163 (*Estate of Charles A. Bahr, Sr., Deceased,* 68 TC 74 (1977); *Estate of Webster,* 65 TC 968 (1976)). Interest paid to banks for loans to finance the payment of income, estate, or gift taxes may also be a cost of administration for estate tax purposes (*Estate of Todd,* 57 TC 288 (1971)).

Qualified residence interest. California adopts the 1987 OBRA amendments to IRC § 163(h)(3)–(4). For both California and federal purposes, interest on a home mortgage is generally deductible as home mortgage interest to the extent the amount borrowed on the mortgage does not exceed the cost of the home, that is, the qualified principal or second residence, plus the cost of improvements. "Qualified residence interest" means any interest paid or accrued during the taxable year on acquisition indebtedness with respect to any qualified residence, or home equity indebtedness with respect to any qualified residence. "Acquisition indebtedness" means any indebtedness that is incurred in constructing, acquiring or substantially improving any qualified residence, and is secured by that qualified residence. The aggregate amount of acquisition indebtedness cannot exceed $1,000,000, or $500,000 in the case of a married individual filing separately. "Home equity indebtedness" means any indebtedness, other than acquisition indebtedness, secured by a qualified residence to the extent that the aggregate amount does not exceed the fair market value of such qualified residence, reduced by the amount of acquisition indebtedness. The aggregate cannot be more than $100,000, or $50,000 in case of a married individual filing separately.

---

(26) IRC § 163(c); § 17201.   (27) IRC § 163(h)(1)–(2). § 17024.5.

CAUTION	Interest on home equity indebtedness is fully deductible for determination of one's regular California income tax liability as set forth above. However, if the proceeds of the home equity indebtedness was used for any purpose other than the acquisition of the home, or improvements with respect thereto, then the interest on that home equity indebtedness is not deductible for alternative minimum tax purposes.

Indebtedness incurred on or before 10–13–87 is treated as acquisition indebtedness, and the one million dollar limitation does not apply. The limitation must be reduced, but not below zero, by the aggregate amount of pre-10–13–87 indebtedness. The term includes indebtedness incurred after 10–13–87 to refinance pre-10–13–87 debt secured by a qualified residence on 10–13–87 to the extent that, immediately after the refinancing the principal amount of debt resulting from refinancing does not exceed the principal amount of debt before the refinancing. The refinancing rule does not apply to any debt after the expiration of the term of the debt incurred on or before 10–13–87 that was secured by a qualified residence on 10–13–87, or, if the principal of the debt is not amortized over its term, the expiration of the term of the first refinancing of such indebtedness, or, if earlier, the date that is 30 years after the date of the first refinancing.

Special rules apply to:

(1) cooperative housing corporations;

(2) unenforceable security interests; and

(3) estates or trusts.[28]

Points. Loan processing fees and loan origination fees are both referred to as "points." Loan processing fees a mortgagor-borrower pays as a bonus or premium to get a conventional mortgage loan are treated as interest. Loan origination fees paid in lieu of specific service charges in connection with a loan are service charges and are not deductible as interest. Nor is a loan placement fee that a seller pays to secure a loan for a buyer.

Deductible "points" as described above, paid in connection with buying or improving a taxpayer's qualified residence, are deductible in full in the year paid. If paid to refinance an existing mortgage, they may be deducted ratably over the loan period. (IRC § 461(g)). One circuit court has allowed a prepaid interest deduction for points paid in obtaining a long-term permanent mortgage used to replace a three-year mortgage on the taxpayers' residence and a home improvement loan secured by a second mortgage on the home.

The IRS will not follow this circuit court case (Huntsman, CA–8) outside the Eighth Circuit. (AOD 1991–02, 2/25/91.) The IRS has notified mortgage lenders to report points charged in connection with the acquisition

---

(28) IRC § 163(h)(1), (3)–(4); § 17024.5.

of a principal residence as paid directly by the borrower in virtually all cases. IRC § 6050H.

Investment interest.   Taxpayers other than corporations are limited by IRC § 163(d) in the amount they can deduct for interest on debt incurred to buy or carry property held for investment. Investment interest is deductible only to the extent of net investment income each year, with an indefinite carryforward of disallowed investment interest. Interest subject to the limitation includes all interest (except consumer interest, qualified residence interest, and certain interest to borrow money for a passive activity) on debt not incurred in a person's active trade or business.

Interest on loans borrowed to purchase or carry investment property is investment interest. Also, if you have a trade or business in which you do not materially participate, any interest expense allocable to the business activity is investment interest provided the activity in not a "passive activity" under the passive loss rule. If you borrow money to purchase or carry an interest in a passive activity, your interest expense will be investment interest to the extent the interest is attributable to the activity's portfolio income.[29]

The language of the definition of investment interest is conformed to the language of a related provision that allocates interest expense to portfolio income under the passive loss rule. So investment interest is that which is properly allocable to property held for investment. The result is consistency in the language of the provisions allocating interest expense to the category of investment interest, and permits consistent application of a standard for allocation of interest. According to the Treasury Committee Reports, this change is not intended to suggest the adoption of any particular method of allocation, but rather to give the IRS the ability to devise allocation rules as simple as possible, consistent with the objectives of the provision.[29]

Investment income.   Federal law and California law conforms the definition of investment income to the definition of investment interest. It does this by deleting the provision that amounts are treated as investment income only to the extent they are not derived from the conduct of a trade or business.[29]

Deduction for net interest received on debt payments.   A taxpayer can deduct the amount of net interest received in payment on indebtedness of either:

(1) a qualified business, as defined in Govt. Cd. § 7082 (economic development program area);

(2) a person or entity engaged in conduct of a trade or business located in an enterprise zone, as defined in Govt. Cd. § 7073; or

---

(29) IRC § 461(a); § 17024.5.

(3) a person or entity engaged in a trade or business located in a Los Angeles Revitalization Zone, as defined in Govt. Cd. § 7102.

No deduction will be allowed unless at the time the indebtedness is incurred, each of the following requirements is met:

(1) qualified business must be located solely within a program area, the Los Angeles Revitalization Zone or an enterprise zone;

(2) indebtedness is incurred solely in connection with a trade or business within the targeted or neighborhood economic development area, an enterprise zone or the Los Angeles Revitalization Zone. The taxpayer, to claim the deduction, cannot have an equity or other ownership interest in the debtor.[30]

In the event that the designated zones are later amended, the deduction for the net interest received will become inoperative for the next following tax year. Prior deductions are not lost retroactively.

Nondeductible interest expenses. California law does not allow a deduction for interest expenses connected with income exempt from tax in California.[31] Both federal IRC § 265(2) and California law include a similar provision prohibiting a deduction for interest incurred or continued to carry obligations whose income is exempt from the law. No deduction is allowed for interest on debt incurred or continued to purchase or carry shares, or a series thereof, of a management company that, during taxable year of holder, distributes exempt-interest dividends. Interest includes amounts paid or incurred in connection with personal property used in short sale by person making sale, or person using property as collateral. This rule does not apply to sellers providing cash as collateral and receiving no material earnings on that cash during sale period. This often leads to a different interest expense deduction for California because of the difference in the treatment of interest income by California and federal laws. No deduction must be denied under Rev & TC § 17280 for interest on a mortgage on, or real property taxes on, the home of a taxpayer by reason of receipt of an amount as either: (1) a military housing allowance; or (2) a parsonage allowance excludible from income under IRC § 107. Rev & TC § 17280 specifies that state rules govern instead of IRC § 265.[32]

Registration required obligation. California adopts IRC § 163(f) that disallows interest deduction for any registration required obligation unless it is in fact registered. Rules similar to IRC § 149(a)(3) on book entries apply.[33]

Original issue discount. The California deduction is based on the amount deductible on the federal return. California adopts IRC § 463(e) concerning high-yield original issue discount obligations. This yield is split to create an interest element that is deductible when paid and a dividend or

---

(30) § 17231; 17233.
(31) § 17280(b)(2); LR323, 5–3–67.

(32) § 17280.
(33) § 17201.

return of capital element that is not deductible. The dividend element can be deducted as a dividends-received deduction (¶ 1081;1153).

WARNING	The deduction for interest can be lost by owners and transferors of an interest in real property or mobilehomes that fail to provide information as to social security numbers, identification numbers (if not individuals), and identification of property interests to the FTB as required by Rev & TC § 18802.3, or who provide false, misleading or inaccurate information in return. Deduction will be denied from 60 days after due date of Rev & TC § 18802.3 return until the FTB determines there is compliance. If noncompliance does not cover the entire calendar year, the denial of deductions is at the rate of one-twelfth for each full month of noncompliance.[34] Renters of substandard housing can lose the deduction.[35]

¶ 326   Charitable Contributions

California has adopted the IRC § 170(b)(1) 50% of adjusted gross income limitation on charitable contributions.[36] The state also conforms to the IRC § 170(g) deduction of $50 a month for the maintenance of individual students as members of the taxpayer's household. The individual maintained can't be a dependent, as defined in IRC § 152, or a relative of the taxpayer. The student must be a full-time pupil or student in the twelfth or any lower grade at an educational organization that maintains a regular faculty and curriculum and normally has a regularly enrolled student body in attendance at the place where the educational activities are regularly carried on. The rule doesn't apply to any compensation or reimbursement received by the taxpayer.

A taxpayer can deduct contributions to or for the use of qualified organizations, that may be public or private or a governmental unit. Contributions to public charities that cannot be deducted in the year they are paid may be carried over and deducted in the following year.

Deductible contributions.   A deduction is allowed under both federal IRC § 170(c) and California law for contributions to:

(1) *Organizations created and operated exclusively for religious, charitable, scientific, literary or educational purposes* or to foster national or international amateur sports competition or for the prevention of cruelty to children or animals if the organizations are organized under state or federal laws or the laws of United States possessions and are nonprofitable. For years commencing prior to 1-1-93, educational expenses included in IRC § 170(c)(2), the term "educational purposes" includes the providing of care of children away from home if (1) substantially all the care provided by the organization is to enable individuals to be gainfully employed; and (2) the services provided by the organization are available to the general public.[37]

(2) *Domestic fraternal societies* operating under the lodge system if contributions are to be used exclusively for the purposes listed in (1) above.

---

(34) § 17299.9.   (36) IRC § 170; § 17024.5; 17201.
(35) § 17274.   (37) § 17240.

(3) *United States, any state or U.S. possession* or any political subdivision thereof or the District of Columbia if contributions are for exclusively public purposes.

(4) *Nonprofit veterans' groups* or trusts or foundations for such groups organized in the United States or any of its possessions.

(5) *Nonprofit cemetery companies* owned and operated exclusively for the benefit of their members, the funds of which must be irrevocably dedicated to the cemetery as whole and not for a particular lot or crypt.[38]

Limitations on deductible contributions. Under federal law, the charitable contribution deduction is limited to 50% of adjusted gross income but only if the contribution is in cash or similar property and is made to certain designated "50%" organizations. The deduction for appreciated capital gain property donated is limited to 30% and the deduction for contributions to "private foundations" is limited to 20%. Contributions over the 30% and 50% limitations may be carried over five years. There is no carryover allowed for contributions in excess of 20% made to nonoperating private foundations.[39] California rules and deduction limits are generally the same.

Appreciated property. The amount deductible for a contribution of property which has appreciated in value depends on whether it is ordinary income property or capital gain property.

Ordinary income property is defined as inventory, stock and trade, works of art and short-term capital assets. The deduction for such property is the fair market value at the time of the contribution reduced by any amount which would be treated as ordinary income if the property had been sold. Therefore, the contribution deduction is, in effect, limited to the basis of the property in the hands of the taxpayer. If a taxpayer donates tangible personal property and it is not used by the charity directly in its exempt functions, the deduction is the fair market value of the property reduced by the federal long-term capital gain that would have resulted if it had been sold at the fair market value.[40]

If the receiving charity uses the personal property in its exempt functions, the deduction is computed on the basis of the fair market value. Gifts of intangible capital gain properties such as capital stock and made to a charity qualifying for the 50% limitation are subject to a ceiling of 30% of adjusted gross income. A taxpayer may elect to deduct these gifts under the 50% limitation if he elects to reduce his contributions deduction by the potential long-term capital gain which would result if the property were sold.[1]

In instances where contributions of appreciated capital gain property are in excess of the 30% limit and carried over, the excess is added to actual contributions of capital gain property in the carryover year to figure the 30%

---

(38) § 17201.
(39) IRC § 170(b)–(d).

(40) IRC § 170(e)(1).
(1) IRC § 170(b)(1)(C); (c)(1)(B).

limit for that year. In addition, the contribution of the capital gain property is also subject to the 50% of adjusted gross income limitation.[2]

CAUTION   California has not conformed to federal law that excludes the unrecognized gain on charitable contributions of appreciated property from the calculation of the alternative minimum tax. Federal and California law are not the same.

Gift of rent-free use of property.   No charitable deduction is allowed for gift to charity of the rent-free use of property.[3]

Gifts of less than total interest in property.   When less than the total interest of a taxpayer in a property is contributed he is not allowed a charitable deduction except when the contribution consists of a remainder interest in personal residences and farms, or a qualified conservation contribution. It is, of course, possible to transfer an undivided interest in a portion of a piece of property.[4]

If the contribution is less than entire interest in the property, a deduction would be allowable to the same extent as if the property had been transferred to a trust. A transfer of the right to use the property would be considered the same as the transfer of a partial interest for this purpose.[5]

In determining the value of the real property remainder interest straight line depreciation and depletion have to be taken into account and the value further reduced by an annual discount rate of 6%, unless the Secretary of the Treasury prescribes a different rate.[6]

A charitable contribution deduction is not allowed where a taxpayer transfers to a charitable organization the future interest in tangible personal property such as a painting or other art object.[7]

California has adopted IRC § 170(h) that allows a deduction for contribution of a partial interest in real property even if there is a retention of a qualified mineral interest subject to conditions on the separation of ownership of the surface and mineral interest and negligible probability of surface mining.[8]

Gifts to lobby groups.   Both the federal IRC § 170(f)(6) and California laws disallow a deduction for payments made to an organization for the purpose of influencing legislation—except that this exclusion does not apply to payments made to churches.[38]

Educational purposes—providing care of children away from home. For purposes of IRC § 170(c)(2), the term "educational purposes" includes the providing of care of children away from home if both of the following are satisfied: (1) substantially all the care provided by the organization is for the

---

(2) IRC § 170(b)(1)(C); (d).
(3) IRC § 170(f)(3).
(4) IRC § 170(f)(3)(B).
(5) IRC § 170(f)(3)(A).

(6) IRC § 170(f)(4).
(7) IRC § 170(a)(3).
(8) IRC § 170(h).

purpose of enabling individuals to be gainfully employed; and (2) the services provided by the organization are available to the general public.[9]

Treatment of certain amounts paid to institutions of higher education. California has adopted IRC § 170(m). This section allows 80% of any amount paid by a taxpayer to or for the benefit of an educational organization, described in IRC § 170(b)(1)(A)(ii), that is an institution of higher education, as defined in IRC § 3304(f) will be treated as a charitable deduction, if such amount would be allowable as a deduction under IRC § 170, but for the fact that the taxpayer receives, directly or indirectly, as a result of paying such an amount, the right to purchase tickets for seating at an athletic event in an athletic stadium of such institution. If any portion of a payment is for the purchase of such tickets, that portion, and the remaining portion, if any will be treated as separate amounts.

Traveling expenses. California and federal laws allow a deduction for your reasonable out-of-pocket expenses for travel in rendering services to charitable organizations or to the extent of 12¢ a mile.[10]

Voluntary contributions. Contributions may be designated on tax returns as additions to tax liability. Such contributions either increase tax due, or reduce refund. With the exception of contributions to the California Election Campaign Fund, the contributions listed below are deductible. Contributions may be made to:

(1) California Election Campaign Fund;[11]

(2) California Fund for Senior Citizens;[12]

(3) Endangered Rare Fish, Wildlife and Plant Species Conservation and Enhancement Account;[13]

(4) State Children's Trust Fund for the prevention of child abuse;[14]

(5) Alzheimer's Disease and Related Disorders Research Fund;[15]

(6) Seniors' Special Fund;[16]

(7) Veterans Memorial Account;[17]

(8) California Breast Cancer Research Fund;[18]

(9) Mexican American Veterans Memorial Beautification and Enhancement Fund;[19]

(10) California Firefighters' Memorial Fund;[20]

(11) California Public School Library Protection Fund;[21] and

---

(9) § 17240.
(10) Rev Proc. 91–67.
(11) § 18703.
(12) § 18721.
(13) § 18741.
(14) § 18711.
(15) §§ 18763.

(16) § 18771.
(17) § 18731.
(18) § 18793.
(19) § 18821.
(20) § 18801.
(21) § 18812.

(12) Olympic Training Fund (for 1995).[22]

California State Lottery. Purchaser of lottery ticket receives full consideration with each ticket. None of the payment made is a gift deductible as a charitable contribution. Motivation of purchase is not unselfish generosity, but hope of winning substantial prize.[23]

Ethics in government—payments to charity. California has adopted IRC § 7701(k). Under this federal rule, in case of any payment which, except for the Ethics in Government Act of 1978, § 501(b), might be made to any officer or employee of the federal government, but which is made instead on behalf the officer or employee to an IRC § 170(c) (charitable contribution defined) organization, the payment shall not be treated as received by such officer or employee for all purposes of the IRC title, and any state or local tax law, and no deduction shall be allowed under state or federal tax laws to the officer or employee because he or she had such payment made to an IRC § 170(c) organization. For purposes of this rule, representatives, delegates or resident commissioners are treated as federal officers or employees; senators or officers, other than the Vice-President, or employees of the Senate are not so treated.[23]

¶ 327 Casualty Losses

Losses of property not connected with a trade or business and which are not covered by insurance are deductible if caused by fire, storm, earthquake or other casualty. A "casualty" is an event due to some sudden, unexpected or unusual cause. Generally, this means an accident or some sudden invasion by a hostile agency. It need not be due to natural causes. However, the progressive deterioration of property through a steadily operating cause is not a casualty.[24]

The amount deductible as casualty loss is the lesser of the actual value of the property just before the casualty, less its value immediately after the casualty, or the adjusted basis of the property for determining the loss on a sale. The actual loss or the adjusted basis for determining loss must be reduced by $100, and the insurance proceeds or the amounts received from an employer or disaster relief agency. California has adopted the IRC § 165(h)(4)(E) provision that, to the extent a personal casualty loss of an individual is covered by insurance, it will be taken into account in computing the deduction only if the individual files a timely insurance claim for it.[24]

California has adopted the federal 10%-of-adjusted-gross-income floor on the deduction of total personal casualty and theft losses for the year. This, in addition to keeping the $100-per-occurrence limit, effectively eliminated any casualty deduction at all for the average taxpayer.[25]

---

(22) § 18831, as added by Stats. 1994, c. 997, § 1.
(23) § 17020.13.

(24) IRC § 165(c)(3); (h); § 17201; Fed Reg No. 1.165–1; 1.165–7.
(25) IRC § 165(c)(3); (h).

When deductible. California has adopted IRC § 165(c)(3).[24] Under this federal rule, the loss is deductible in the year incurred, regardless of the year in which payments for repairs or replacement are made. Proceeds received after the year when the casualty loss was deducted are income in the year received.

Loss from theft or embezzlement. Loss from theft or embezzlement is deductible in the year in which the taxpayer discovers the loss. California follows IRC § 165(c); (e).[26]

Disaster losses. California has adopted IRC § 165(i). Under this federal rule, any loss from a disaster in an area subsequently determined by the President of the United States to warrant federal assistance under an applicable federal disaster act may be taken on the return for the year in which the loss occurred, or the taxpayer may elect to deduct the loss on his return for the preceding taxable year. The election to take the disaster loss in the prior year must be made on or before the due date of the taxpayer's return for the year in which the loss occurred. The loss may be claimed by filing an amended return for the prior year.[27] California has also adopted IRC § 165(k) providing a deduction for forced demolition or relocation.

Special rules apply to disaster losses, to the extent that those losses, as computed under IRC § 165(a), exceed taxable income of the year of loss, or, if an IRC § 165(i) election is made, the taxable income of year preceding loss. Losses covered by IRC § 165(c)(1)—(2), relating to trade or business losses or losses from a transaction entered into for profit, and losses covered by IRC § 165(c)(3), relating to personal casualty losses may, at the election of the taxpayer, be carried forward to each of five taxable years following year loss is claimed.

DISASTER AREAS

Those California disasters which result in losses qualifying for the special carryback and carryover rules include:

(1) forest fire or other related casualty occurring in California during 1985;

(2) storm, flooding or any other related casualty occurring in California during February, 1986;

(3) forest fires or any other related casualty occurring during 1987;

(4) earthquake, aftershock, or any other related casualty occurring in California during October, 1987;

(5) earthquake, aftershock, or any other related casualty occurring in California during October, 1989;

(6) fire or any other related casualty occurring in the County of Santa Barbara, California during 1990;

---

(26) § 17201; Fed Reg No. 1.165–1; 1.165–8.   (27) § 17201; Fed Reg No. 1.165–11.

(7) Oakland/Berkeley fire losses of 1991 or any other related casualty;

(8) storm, flooding or any other related casualty occurring in California during February, 1992;

(9) earthquake, aftershock, or any other related casualty during April, 1992 in the County of Humboldt;

(10) losses as a result of riots, arson, or any other related casualty occurring in April or May, 1992;

(11) the Fountain Fire occurring in the County of Shasta in August, 1992, or any other related casualty;

(12) earthquakes occurring in the County of San Bernardino in June, and July of 1992 and any other related casualty;

(13) fires in the Counties of Calaveras and Trinity that occurred in August, 1992, or other related casualty;

(14) any loss sustained as a result of a fire that occurred in the County of Los Angeles, Orange, Riverside, San Bernardino, San Diego, or Ventura, during October or November, 1993, or any other related casualty;

(15) losses in the County of Los Angeles, Orange, or Ventura on or after January 17, 1994, as a result of earthquake, aftershocks, or any other related casualty; and

(16) losses sustained as a result of a fire that occurred in the County of San Luis Obispo during August, 1994.[28]

The entire amount of any excess loss must be carried to the earliest of the taxable years to which it may be carried. The part of loss carried to each of the other taxable years is the excess of the amount of "excess loss" over the sum of the taxable income for each of the prior taxable years to which the "excess loss" may be carried. If there is any "excess loss" remaining after the five-year period, then 50% of that excess loss may be carried forward to each of the next 10 taxable years. The rule applies to any county or city in California proclaimed by the Governor to be in a state of disaster. Losses taken into account under Rev & TC § 17207 may not be taken into account in computing a net operating loss deduction under Rev & TC § 17201, as modified by Rev & TC § 17276, 17276.1 and 17276.2.[29] For the purposes of Rev & TC § 17207, the IRC § 1212(b) definition of adjusted gross income applies in California.[30]

IRC § 1231 gains and losses. Personal casualty and theft losses must exceed 10% of federal adjusted gross income (AGI) to be deductible.

Personal casualty and theft losses are not subject to IRC § 1231. IRC § 1231 will be applied regardless of these gains and losses. Gains and losses from personal casualties (regardless of the period the property was held) are

---

(28) § 17207, as amended by Stats. 1994, c. 1245, § 4.

(29) § 17207.

(30) § 17207(f).

netted. If the recognized gains exceed the losses from these transactions, then all gains and losses are treated as capital gain and losses, and the losses won't be subject to the 10% floor. The amount of any loss is subject to the $100 floor before netting. If losses exceed gains, all losses to the extent of gains are allowed in full. Losses exceeding gains are subject to the 10% of AGI floor. The rules for computing adjusted gross income also apply to estates and trusts.

California follows federal rules on the recapture of ordinary losses under IRC § 1231(c).[31]

Losses on deposits in insolvent financial institutions. California has adopted IRC § 165(l). The law allows qualified individuals to elect to deduct losses on deposits arising from the insolvency or bankruptcy of a qualified financial institution as a casualty loss in the year in which the amount of the loss is reasonably estimated. The election must be made on the tax return for the taxable year and once made, cannot be changed without the IRS's consent. The provisions of IRC § 166 on bad debts do not apply to any loss taken under IRC § 165(e). Unless the deposit was created or acquired in connection with the taxpayer's trade or business, the loss was treated as a short-term capital loss.

Interest treatment on frozen deposits. Frozen deposits are deposits which, as of the close of the calendar year, may not be withdrawn because the qualified financial institution is threatened with bankruptcy or insolvency or is actually bankrupt or insolvent. Accrued, but unpaid interest on a deposit in a qualified financial institution isn't includible in the depositor's taxable income for the taxable year when such interest isn't subject to withdrawal at the end of the taxable year. The interest income is includible in gross income in the taxable year in which the interest is withdrawable. Interest not included in gross income is treated as credited in the next calendar year. Qualified financial institutions can't take deductions for interest not includible in gross income until the interest is includible in gross income.[32]

¶ 328   Miscellaneous Deductions

Pass-through entities—estates, trusts and mutual funds. An individual's miscellaneous itemized deductions are deductible for federal and California purposes only to the extent they exceed 2% of AGI. Federal regulations prevent an individual's use of pass-through entities to deduct expenses that wouldn't have been deductible had the individual incurred them directly. For example, under these regulations, partnerships wouldn't deduct their miscellaneous expenses from partnership income, but would report each partner's share of miscellaneous deductions separately from his share of income. The 2% floor would be applied at the individual partner level.

---

(31) § 18151.   (32) IRC § 451(g); § 17024.5.

"First tier" miscellaneous itemized deductions. The following expenses are not subject to the 2% floor:

- Interest [IRC § 163].
- Taxes [IRC § 164].
- Charitable contributions [IRC § 170].
- Amounts paid and permanently set aside for a charitable purpose [IRC § 642(c)].
- Medical and dental expenses [IRC § 213].
- Pre-1994 moving expenses [IRC § 217].
- In connection with property used in a short sale [IRC § 263; 265].
- Impairment-related work expenses of handicapped individuals [IRC § 67(d)].
- Certain adjustments when a taxpayer restores amounts held under a claim of right [IRC § 1341].
- Amortizable bond premium [IRC § 171].
- Gambling losses to the extent of gambling winnings [IRC § 165(d)].
- Deductions allowable in connection with personal property used in a short sale.

Impairment-related work expenses are expenses of a handicapped individual [IRC § 190(b)(3)] for attendant care services at the individual's place of employment, or other expenses necessary for the individual to work, which are deductible under IRC § 162.

Other expenses that are deductible without regard to a percent-of-AGI floor include certain terminated annuity payments [IRC § 72(b)(3)] and certain costs of cooperative housing corporations [IRC § 216]. California conformity statute bars deduction of the federal estate tax on income in respect of a decedent [IRC § 691(c)].

"Second tier" miscellaneous itemized deductions. Expenses in this category are deductible only to the extent they cumulatively exceed 2% of adjusted gross income. There are two groups of expenses subject to the 2% floor:[33]

(1) Miscellaneous expenses. This group consists of miscellaneous expenses *other than* those expenses placed in the first-tier class of miscellaneous itemized deductions.

Employee expenses

- Dues to professional societies
- Employment-related education
- Malpractice insurance premiums
- Expenses of looking for a job, including employment agency fee
- Cost of having resume prepared
- Office-at-home expenses
- Subscriptions to professional journals and magazines
- Work clothes and uniforms
- Union dues and fees

---

(33) IRC § 67; 165; 212; § 17042.5; 17201.

● 80% of unreimbursed business-entertainment expenses (50% for tax years starting on or after 12–31–93)

Expenses for production of income

● Legal and accounting fees
● Custodial fees related to income-producing property
● Fees paid to an IRA custodian
● Fees paid to collect interest or dividends
● Hobby expenses up to hobby income
● Investment counsel fees
● Rental cost of safe deposit box used to store non-tax-exempt securities

Other expenses

● Fees paid for investment counsel
● Tax counsel and assistance
● Cost of tax services, periodicals, return preparation manuals, and similar expenses related to the determination, collection, or refund of a tax
● Appraisal fees establishing a casualty loss or charitable contribution

(2) Employee business expenses. Employee travel and transportation expenses up to the amount of the reimbursement continue to be claimed above the line. However, expenses in excess of any reimbursement become below-the-line miscellaneous deductions and are subject to the 2% floor. The same holds true for an employee's business-entertainment expenses. Expenses up to the amount of any reimbursement are claimed above the line; excess expenses are claimed below the line and are subject to the 2% floor.[33]

Note: For a more complete coverage of employee business expenses, see ¶ 293.

Application of 2% floor. The 2% floor comes into play after all other deduction limitations are taken into account.

EXAMPLE   During the tax year 1993, Ted Smith, an employee of XYZ Corp., incurs $2,000 of unreimbursed business-entertainment expenses. Smith's adjusted gross income for 1993 is $60,000. For simplicity, we'll assume Smith does not have other second-tier miscellaneous itemized deductions. *Result:* Smith's deduction for business entertainment is computed as follows:

Total entertainment expenses	$2,000
Less statutory 20% reduction	(400)
	$1,600
Less 2% of AGI	(1,200)
Net second-tier miscellaneous itemized deduction	$ 400

Personal living and family expenses. These expenses are not deductible. California follows IRC § 262.

Gambling losses. California adopts federal IRC § 165(d) that allows a taxpayer to deduct gambling losses on Schedule A but not more than the gambling winnings reported in gross income.[34] California state lottery losses are not deductible because winnings are exempt from tax.[35]

Capital expenditures. California adopts IRC § 263(a), as modified. Under IRC § 263(a), no deduction is allowed for any amount paid out for new buildings or permanent improvements or betterments made to increase the value of any property or estate. This rule does not apply to:

(1) expenditures for the development of mines or deposits deductible under IRC § 616;

(2) research and experimental expenditures deductible under IRC § 174;

(3) soil and water conservation expenditures deductible under IRC § 175;

(4) expenditures by farmers for fertilizer deductible under IRC § 180;

(5) expenditures for removal of architectural barriers and transportation barriers to the handicapped and elderly elected for deduction under IRC § 190;

(6) expenditures for tertiary injectants deductible under IRC § 193 (California limits deduction to depreciation); and

(7) expenditures for certain depreciable business assets under IRC § 179.[36]

No deduction is allowed for any amount expended in restoring property or in making good the exhaustion thereof for which an allowance has been made.

The IRC § 263(a) rule does not apply to expenditures under a Rev & TC § 17265 election to treat 40% of Rev & TC § 17265 property cost as an expense not chargeable to a capital account. Rev & TC § 17265 expenditures are those incurred under the California Employment and Economic Employment Act as set forth in Government Code § 7082.

Repairing and remodeling costs on behalf of handicapped or elderly. California adopted IRC § 190 which provides that a taxpayer may elect to treat qualified architectural and transportation barrier removal expenses paid or incurred during the taxable year as expenses not chargeable to a capital account. Expenditures so treated are allowed as a deduction. The maximum amount of the deduction for any taxable year is $15,000. IRC § 190 defines the deductible expenses for architectural and transportation barrier removal as those made to any facility or vehicle owned or leased by the taxpayer for use in connection with his trade or business to make the facility, etc. more accessible to handicapped or elderly.

---

(34) § 17201; Fed Reg 1.165–10.
(35) Franchise Tax Board 2–26–86.

(36) § 17024.5; 17201; 17260; 17265.

Political contributions.   California does not allow a deduction for political contributions.

Designation on return.   Every individual, lawfully able to make contributions to qualified political parties in California, may designate payment of $1, $5, $10 or $25 on his return. This voluntary contribution is in addition to his or her income tax liability and will be paid over to the California Election Campaign Fund. In case of a joint return, each spouse may separately designate the above amounts. The taxpayer must designate on the tax return which of the qualified political parties of state, contribution shall benefit.[37]

Indirect contributions.   California has not adopted IRC § 276 that denies a deduction for certain indirect contributions to political parties.[38]

Golden parachute payments.   California adopts IRC § 280G. Under that federal section, payments in money or property in excess of the "base amount" under a "golden parachute" agreement entered into or amended after 6–14–84 are nondeductible. Also, the recipient is subject to a nondeductible 20% excise tax on such excess and also subject to Social Security (FICA) taxes.

A "golden parachute agreement" is an agreement: (1) that calls for payments or property transfers that are contingent on a change in the ownership or control of the corporation or a significant portion of its assets; (2) under which payments are to be made to a disqualified individual i.e., officer, shareholder or highly compensated employee, independent contractor or other person including personal service corporation that performs services for the corporation; (3) where the present value of the contingent payments (determined under IRC § 1274) equal or exceed 300% of the individual's annualized includible compensation from the corporation for any tax year during the 5-year period preceding the change in ownership—the so-called base amount; (4) where at least some part of the payments isn't reasonable compensation for services actually rendered. Excess payments under an agreement which meets conditions (1)–(3), are rebuttably unreasonable compensation. The base amount is allocated to any parachute payment in the same ratio that the present value of such payment bears to the aggregate value of all such payments. Under IRS Regulations, the "golden parachute" rules can also cover agreements that the SEC classifies as unreasonable in threatened corporate takeover situations.[39]

Transfers of franchises, trademarks and trade names.   Under IRC § 1253, transferees of franchises, trademarks and trade names can treat any amounts paid or incurred during the taxable year as a deduction for a trade or business expense under IRC § 162(a), in computing taxable income, if the amounts are contingent on the productivity, use or disposition of the franchise, trademark or trade name, and paid as part of a series of payments

---

(**37**) § 18720.
(**38**) § 17283.

(**39**) IRC § 280G; 4999; § 17024.5.

that are: (1) payable not less frequently than annually throughout the term of the transfer agreement, and (2) are substantially equal in amount, or are payable under a fixed formula.

Payments in discharge of principal sums can also be deducted, if a transfer of a franchise, trademark or trade name is not treated as the sale or exchange of a capital asset. This rule applies only if the payment does not qualify as a contingent serial payment under IRC § 1253(d)(1). In the case of a single payment made in discharge of a principal sum, the deduction may be taken ratably over the taxable years starting with the taxable year the payment is made, and ending with the ninth succeeding taxable year, or the last taxable year starting in the period of the transfer, whichever is shorter. If the payment is one of a series of approximately equal payments, the deduction may be taken over the period of the transfer agreement, or a period of more than ten taxable years, whether ending before or after the end of the transfer agreement period. In the case of any other kind of payment, the deduction may be taken in the years specified by regulations issued by the tax administrative authorities. The deduction is limited to $100,000. Amounts to which the rules on contingent serial payments, or principal sum payments do not apply can, at the election of the taxpayer, be charged to a capital account and amortized over a 25-year period starting with the taxable year of the transfer.[40]

These rules apply, for both federal and California purposes, to taxable years starting after 10–2–89, unless the transfer is made under a binding written contract then in effect and before the transfer.

Substandard housing.   No deduction is allowed for interest, taxes, depreciation, or amortization paid or incurred in a tax year with respect to substandard housing, with the exception of property rendered substandard solely by reason of a change in the applicable state or local housing standards. This exception will not apply if the violations cause substantial danger to the occupants of the property.[1]

---

(40) IRC § 1253; 17024.5; 23051.5.   (1) § 17274.

CHAPTER **6**

ADMINISTRATION AND ENFORCEMENT OF PERSONAL INCOME TAX

OVERVIEW OF 1993 LEGISLATIVE CHANGES IN CODE NUMBERING

The California Legislative reformatted the administrative provisions of the Revenue & Taxation Code effective 1–1–94. For years prior to 1994 the Personal Income Tax (Part 10, Rev & TC §§ 17801–19452) contained the administrative provisions applicable to individuals, and the Bank And Corporation Tax (Part 11, Rev & TC §§ 23001–26491) contained substantially similar administrative provisions applicable to corporate income and franchise taxpayers. Effective 1–1–94 the administrative provisions, and those relating to enforcement, interest, and penalties in each of these laws were repealed and consolidated into a new substantially similar Administration Law (Part 10.2, Rev & TC §§ 18401 to 19802) was added. The references to Revenue & Taxation Code sections in this chapter are to the new section numbers effective 1–1–94.

¶ 331   **Processing of Returns**

The principal office of the Franchise Tax Board is in Sacramento. All of the returns filed by California taxpayers are processed through the Sacramento office and the instructions on the tax forms state that they should be sent there. The FTB maintains field offices within the State of California, and in Chicago and New York to provide assistance to the taxpayer and to carry out their audit and collection program. Returns filed in these offices would be forwarded to Sacramento for processing.

ASTRA system used.   Once the returns are in Sacramento, they are reviewed for completeness, mathematical errors, proper credits, etc. Whereas the Internal Revenue Service Center uses a computer generated DIF selection system, the California system is called ASTRA (automated selection of tax returns for audit).

OBSERVATION   Those returns which are selected for further action and possible examination are then handled by Sacramento correspondence or by transferring the files to one of the field offices for personal contact with the taxpayer or his representative and a review of requested information or books and records.

Mathematical errors.   If the preliminary review by the Headquarters office of the Franchise Tax Board shows that the return contained a mathematical error, the FTB will issue a notice to the taxpayer to that effect with a demand for payment. Any amount of tax in this notice in excess of that on the tax return as filed, due to the mathematical error, is not a deficiency assessment. This means simply that the taxpayer does not have the right to protest or appeal based on that notice. The tax erroneously omitted in the return can be assessed and collected by the Franchise Tax Board the same as a deficiency resulting from an examination of the return.[1]

(1) § 19051.

The denial of a credit or refund based on the renter's credit provisions is considered in the same manner as a mathematical error for processing, except in such cases the taxpayer does have the right of protest and appeal if he does not agree.[2]

The tax understatement resulting from the overstatement of estimated tax paid or of withholding tax paid may be assessed in same manner as provided in case of mathematical error. No unpaid amount of estimated tax under Rev & TC §§ 19025 or 19136 shall be assessed.[3]

If the Franchise Tax Board makes or allows a refund or credit that it determines to be erroneous, in whole or in part, the amount erroneously made or allowed may be assessed and collected after notice and demand pursuant to Rev & TC § 19051, pertaining to mathematical errors. Rights of protest and appeal apply with respect to amounts assessable as deficiencies without regard to the running of any period of limitations provided elsewhere in Article 5, Interest and Penalties, Rev & TC §§ 19131—19184. A notice and demand for repayment must be made within two years after the refund or credit was made or allowed, or during the period in which the Franchise Tax Board may mail a notice of proposed additional assessment, whichever ends later. Interest on amounts erroneously made or allowed will not accrue until 30 days from the date the Franchise Tax Board mails the notice and demand for repayment.[4]

In case of an assessment of interest, the Franchise Tax Board may abate the assessment of all or any part of that interest for any period if either (1) any deficiency is attributable in whole or in part to any error or delay by an officer or employee of the FTB, acting in an official capacity, in performing a ministerial act; or (2) to the extent that any payment of tax described in Rev & TC § 19033 (tax disclosed on return less than tax disclosed by examination) is delayed because an officer or employee was dilatory in performing a ministerial act. The error or delay must be taken into account only if no significant aspect of that error or delay can be attributed to the taxpayer, and after the Board has contacted the taxpayer in writing with respect to the deficiency or payment.[4]

The franchise Tax Board must abate an assessment of interest on any erroneous refund for which an action for recovery is provided under Rev & TC § 19411 until the date of demand for repayment, unless either (1) the taxpayer, or a related party, has in any way caused the erroneous refund; or (2) the refund involved exceeds $50,000.[4]

Bad checks are perfected and enforceable state tax lien to the extent of their amount on the assets of the drawee bank. The same applies to the issuer of money orders.

---

(2) § 19052.
(3) § 19054.

(4) § 19104.

¶ 332 **Bankruptcy**

If a receiver for any taxpayer is appointed in any receivership proceeding, the Franchise Tax Board under Rev & TC § 19088 has the right to immediately assess any deficiency together with interest or additions to the tax provided by law. The assessment can also be made against a debtor's estate in a USC Title 11 case, or debtor, but only if the liability for tax has become res judicata pursuant to a determination in the case under Title 11.[5]

Fiduciary to give notice. Every trustee in a case under USC Title 11 or receiver or assignee for the benefit of creditors, or similar fiduciary is required to give notice to the Franchise Tax Board of his appointment in any case under Title 11 USC or receivership.[6]

In case the fiduciary is required to give notice to the Franchise Tax Board in writing of his appointment, the statute of limitations is suspended for a period beginning with the date when the case under Title 11 USC or receivership proceedings commenced until a date 30 days after the required notice is received by the Franchise Tax Board, but in no event will the suspension period be longer than two years.[7]

FTB claims. If the Franchise Tax Board has filed a claim in a case under Title 11 USC, or a receivership proceeding for the tax deficiency and interest, then additional amounts and additions to the tax may be presented for adjudication by the court. If the claims are allowed by the court and not recovered in the distribution of the assets, the liability of the taxpayer is not extinguished by the discharge of the proceedings. An unpaid amount of the claim may be collected, the same as any other delinquent tax, at any time within six years after the termination of the receivership proceedings.[8]

¶ 333 **Jeopardy Assessments**

If the Franchise Tax Board determines that the assessment or collection of a tax or a deficiency for any year will be jeopardized by a delay, it is entitled to mail or issue a notice of its finding to the taxpayer with a demand for immediate payment of the tax or the deficiency declared to be in jeopardy, plus interest and penalties. Any assessment issued is also an assessment for a deficiency issued under Rev & TC § 18583, if such an assessment under that section has not already been issued.

Termination of tax year. If the Franchise Tax Board for the current period finds that an assessment or collection of tax will be jeopardized in whole or in part by delay, it may declare that the taxpayer's current taxable year is immediately terminated. When it mails or issues its notice of finding and declaration together with a demand for a return and payment of the tax, the tax is immediately due and payable and collection procedures can be commenced at the same time.[9]

---

(5) § 19088.
(6) § 19089.
(7) § 19089.

(8) § 19090—19091.
(9) § 19081—19082.

TAX TIP	The taxpayer may stay the collection by filing a bond with the Franchise Tax Board in an amount equal to the amount plus interest determined to be in jeopardy, or other security in an amount which the Franchise Tax Board deems necessary, but not in excess of double the amount of the tax and interest in jeopardy.[10]

Written statement of information. A written statement of information upon which the Franchise Tax Board relied in issuing a notice and demand for payment under Rev & TC § 19081, or a notice and demand for a return and payment under Rev & TC § 19082, must be mailed or issued to taxpayer within five days after the date of issuance or mailing of notice and demand under either Rev & TC §§ 19081 or 19082.[11]

Petition for review. Within 30 days after the date on which the taxpayer is furnished with a written statement of information, or within 30 days after the last day of the 5-day period for furnishing the statement, the taxpayer may petition the Franchise Tax Board to review whether its finding under Rev & TC §§ 19081—19082 is reasonable. The petition must specify the grounds. The filing of the petition does not stay collection. It can only be stayed by the procedure specified in Rev & TC § 19083 (see "Tax Tip" above). The petition will also be considered a protest against an additional tax under Rev & TC § 19041. If the petition is not made within the 30-day period, the finding of the Franchise Tax Board will be final.[12]

Hearing. After a petition for review is filed, the Franchise Tax Board must determine whether or not its issuance of notice and demand is reasonable. In making this determination, it must grant taxpayer, or representative an oral hearing, if so requested. The burden of proof on the issue of the existence of jeopardy as to collection or assessment rests on the Franchise Tax Board. A determination by the FTB must be made within 90 days of filing of the petition for review, unless the taxpayer requests additional time in writing. The determination must consider all relevant factors, including the likelihood of jeopardy of collection, assets of the taxpayer, and the amount of assessment as it relates to the existence of a jeopardy status. The burden of proof is on the taxpayer as to the amount of assessment for purpose of determining jeopardy status.[13]

Appeals to State Board of Equalization. Taxpayers can appeal to the State Board of Equalization within 60 days after earlier of (1) the day the FTB notifies the taxpayer of its determination on the reasonableness of the issuance of the notice and demand; or (2) one day after the 90-day time period. If appeal is not made within these periods, the FTB determination is final.[14] The filing of the appeal does not stay the collection of the jeopardy assessment.[15]

---

(10) § 19083.

(11) § 19084(a)(1).

(12) § 19084(a)(2)–(3).

(13) § 19084(a)(4)–(6).

(14) § 19084(b)(1)–(2).

(15) § 19084(b)(3)–(6); § 19085.

¶ 333

Superior court action. The State Board of Equalization decision on the reasonableness of the notice and demand may be subject to an action brought by either party.[16]

Individual in physical possession of cash in excess of $10,000. If an individual who is in physical possession of cash in excess of $10,000 does not claim the cash as belonging to (1) that individual; or (2) another person whose identity the Franchise Tax Board can readily ascertain, and who acknowledges ownership of that cash, for purposes of Rev & TC §§ 19081—19082, it will be presumed that such cash represents gross income of a single individual for the taxable year in which the possession occurs, and the collection will be jeopardized by delay. The income will be treated as taxable at the maximum rate set by Rev & TC § 17041. The possessor of the cash will be treated as the taxpayer, solely with respect to that cash, for purposes of the Rev & TC §§ 19001—19180 rules on payment and assessment of tax, and Rev & TC §§ 18631—19256 rules on collection of tax. California adopts IRC § 6050I(d) that provides that cash includes foreign currency, and any monetary instrument to the extent set by the Secretary of the Treasury, with a face amount of, not more than $10,000. Checks drawn on account of the writer in specified financial institutions are excepted. If after the assessment, the assessment against the possessor is abated and replaced by an assessment against the owner, the later assessment relates back to the date of the original assessment for purposes of all laws relating to lien, levy and collection.[17]

¶ 334   **Collection of Tax When No Return or False Return Filed**

If a taxpayer fails to file a return, or files a false or fraudulent return with intent to evade the tax for any year, the Franchise Tax Board, at any time, may demand that a return or an amended return under penalties of perjury be filed.

As an alternative, the Franchise Tax Board may make an estimate of the taxpayer's net income from any available information and may propose to assess the amount of tax, interest, and penalties due under the law.[18]

Remedies for taxpayer. In such circumstances the taxpayer will have the right to protest any deficiency issued under this section and to have an oral hearing, if requested, and take an appeal to the State Board of Equalization from the Franchise Tax Board's action on the protest, if necessary.

¶ 335   **Time Limits for Assessments and Refunds**

The California statute of limitations operates like the federal statutes in that the expiration date is based on the last date open on any of the expiration dates in effect for a given year or assessment. It provides a list of

---

(16) § 19084.   (18) § 19087.
(17) § 19093.

expiration dates for tax deficiency assessments and for filing claims for refunds.

STATUTES OF LIMITATIONS
(INDIVIDUALS, PARTNERSHIPS, ESTATES AND TRUSTS)

Situation	Tax Deficiency	Claim For Refund
Normal	4 years from the date return was filed or 4 years after the due date, (including extensions), whichever is later. May be extended 60 days on receipt of document showing taxpayer owes additional amount [§ 19057].	4 years from the due date (including extensions) or 1 year from date of payment, whichever is later. [§ 19306]. 4 years for return filed showing credit for tax withheld under §§ 18662 or 18664, or estimated tax overpaid under § 19136 [§ 19307.1].
California waiver of the statute	The period of the waiver [§ 19067].	The period of the waiver or 1 year from date of overpayment, whichever is later [§ 19308].
Federal waiver	6 months from expiration of federal waiver [§ 19065].	6 months from expiration of federal waiver [§ 19308].
Omission of 25% of gross income	6 years from due date or the date return was filed, whichever is later [§ 19058].	Not applicable.
Federal change reported by taxpayer (or amended return filed), within 6 months.	2 years after notification by the taxpayer or amended return filed with California (applies for federal adjustments but no other changes), or within § 19057 and 19058 periods, whichever is later [§ 19053].	2 years after notification by the taxpayer or amended return filed with California [§ 19038].

Situation	Tax Deficiency	Claim For Refund
Federal change *not* reported by taxpayer within 6 months, or amended California return not filed.	At any time; statute of limitations suspended [§ 19060].	Not applicable.
Federal change reported by taxpayer, or amended California return filed, but after 6-month period for timely reporting had expired	4 years from the final determination by the Internal Revenue Service, or from date amended return filed (applies only to federal changes [¶ 19060(b)].	Not applicable.
Bad debt, worthless security, or erroneous inclusion of recoveries	Not applicable.	7 years after the due date of the return [§ 19312].
Election regarding gain on involuntary conversions	3 years after notification by taxpayer of replacement or intention not to replace [§ 19061].	Not applicable.
Patronage dividends (noncash dividends elected to be excluded)	4 years after the date taxpayer notifies the FTB of gain realized from noncash dividends [§ 17086].	Not applicable.
Title 11 cases; receivership	Running of period of limitations suspended up to 60 days after end of time FTB is prohibited from mailing notice [§ 19057]. Appointment of receiver; debtor's estate, or debtor under title 11; immediate assessment [§ 19088]. Trustee, Title 11 case; period suspended to 30 days after notice of qualification, but not for more than 2 years [§ 19089].	Not applicable.

Situation	Tax Deficiency	Claim For Refund
Gain on sale of principal residence	3 years after notification by taxpayer of cost of new residence, intention not to purchase, or failure to purchase within the period specified [§ 19062].	Not applicable.
Joint return after filing separate returns	1 year after the joint return is filed [§ 18529].	4 years after due date (without regard to any extension of time for filing return) [§ 18527].
Request by fiduciary for clearance certificate	18 months after written request [§ 19517].	Not applicable.
Fraud or no return filed	No limitation.	Not applicable.
Reacquisition after disproportionate redemption	1 year after notice by taxpayer of reacquisition of stock [§ 17322].	Not applicable.
Motion to quash subpoena under Govt. Cd. § 7465–7476	Period of limitations suspended under § 19057 (deficiency assessments), § 19087 (false or fraudulent returns), or § 19704 (criminal prosecutions) for period in which proceeding and appeals as to enforcement of subpoena is pending [§ 19064].	Not applicable.
Absence of resolution of response to subpoena served on third-party recordkeeper, as defined in IRC § 7609	Period of limitations suspended under § 19057 (deficiency assessments), § 19087 (false or fraudulent returns), or § 19704 (criminal prosecutions), if person subpoenaed makes no motion to quash starting on date 6 mos. after service of subpoena, and ending with resolution of response [§ 19064.]	Not applicable.

Situation	Tax Deficiency	Claim For Refund
Prosecutions for (1) fraud; (2) willful attempt to evade or defeat tax; (3) willful aiding, procuring, etc. of false or fraudulent return; (4) willful failure to file return or supply information; (5) false return or statement; (6) willful failure to pay estimated tax; (7) supplying false information; (8) counseling evasion	Six years from date of offense [§ 19701; 19704; 19705; 19706].	Not applicable.
Prosecutions for all other offenses	6 years after commission [§ 19704].	Not applicable.

Extensions of the statute. FTB 3570 is the form used by the Franchise Tax Board to get extensions of the statute of limitations. The form is prepared by the FTB's auditors and given to the taxpayer in instances where the auditor has insufficient time between the date he completes his audit and the expiration of the statute of limitations, or in cases where it is necessary to delay the audit pending receipt of additional information, or completion of a federal examination of the same year(s), etc.

IMPORTANT   It has been the usual policy of the FTB to ask that an extension of time for one year be given to keep the statute open until the expiration of the statute for the following year. In other words, a one-year extension in ordinary circumstances. If the taxpayer does not wish to keep the statute open for that length of time, he may sign for a lesser period. It should be kept in mind, however, that if one refuses to sign a waiver, or will not extend the statute for a sufficient period of time, the FTB can issue a jeopardy assessment or proposed assessment based on the information it has, and put the burden on the taxpayer to have the assessment withdrawn or revised by cooperating to supply the appropriate information.

The same Form FTB 3570 is used for personal income tax and corporation franchise and income tax. If it is for a joint return, the waiver should be signed by both husband and wife, or "their authorized representative."[19]

---

(19) § 19067.

¶ 335

¶ 336 **Refund Claims**

Generally, if the Franchise Tax Board or the State Board of Equalization finds that there has been an overpayment of tax, or penalty or interest by a taxpayer for any year for any reason, the amount of the overpayment is credited against any amount then due from the taxpayer and the balance refunded to him.[20] "Valid claim" is asserted when the entire amount of tax and penalties assessed have been paid.[21] Every claim for refund must be in writing and signed by the taxpayer or authorized representative. Specific grounds must be stated. A claim filed on behalf of a class must (1) be accompanied by a written authorization of each taxpayer sought to be included in the class; (2) be signed by the taxpayer or representative; (3) state specific grounds upon which it is founded. It's not necessary to use a particular form, if necessary information is provided (see "How to Claim" below). An IRS agent's report, filed by the taxpayer or representative, accompanied by a refund request will be considered a valid claim if sufficient explanation is provided. If the IRS report is submitted within the statutory periods and establishes overpayment by the taxpayer, FTB may initiate a credit or refund.[21]

How to claim. On the other hand, the taxpayer can initiate a claim for refund by filing with the Franchise Tax Board one of the following:

●*Form 540X*. This form, the amended individual California income tax form, is to be used to file a claim for refund in most cases.

●*Form 540A*. This is the short form of the personal income tax return and if you are filing only for the purpose of receiving the Renter's Credit you are to use Form 540A.

●*Federal Form 1310—deceased taxpayer*. The surviving spouse, executor or administrator who files a return for a decedent on which a refund is due may use federal Form 1310.

● *Ordinary letter*. The Franchise Tax Board will accept a letter from the taxpayer as a claim for refund if it states the reason for the claim with enough information so that the Franchise Tax Board may process the letter as a claim for refund.

● *Protest or appeal*. If a taxpayer pays the tax which he has protested before the Franchise Tax Board has acted upon his protest, or if the taxpayer has filed an appeal with the State Board of Equalization before it has handled the appeal, the Franchise Tax Board treats the protest or the appeal as a claim for a refund.

How refunds are processed. Generally, claims for refund are handled by the Claims and Protest Unit for the Franchise Tax Board. They are processed as expeditiously as is possible, because of the interest element involved. In some cases, it is necessary to defer action on a claim for a refund for a period of time. This would be true when a similar claim has been filed with the IRS and the Franchise Tax Board is awaiting a final federal determination on the claim. Form 540X specifically asks if the taxpayer has filed an amended return with the IRS on the similar basis (refund claim) and

---

(20) § 19301.   (21) LR 402, 1–27–77; LR 386, 8–25–75.

requires explanation of changes to income, deductions and credits. It also requires taxpayer to indicate whether or not the original federal return was or is being audited. Also, claims for refund cases which are in the Appeals and Review Office (Protest Section) may not be satisfied until the matters at protest are handled.[22]

Denial of claim—remedies. If the Franchise Tax Board disallows the claim for refund and notifies the taxpayer to that effect, he has 90 days from the mailing of the notice to appeal in writing to the Board of Equalization.[23] If the Franchise Tax Board does not mail a notice of action on any refund claim within six months from the date the claim is filed, the taxpayer may consider the claim disallowed and appeal to the State Board of Equalization or file a suit in the California civil courts. Title 11, § 505(a)(2), USC permits a substitution of the 120 day period in Title 11 cases.[24] A refund of excess tax withheld under Rev & TC §§ 18662 or 18664, or estimated tax overpaid under Rev & TC § 19136, or any refunds made under § 13020 of the Unemployment Insurance Code is not a determination of the correctness of the return.[25]

Appeal to State Board of Equalization. Two copies of the appeal from the denial of the claim for refund and two copies of the supporting documents should be addressed and mailed to the State Board of Equalization in Sacramento. Upon receipt of the appeal, the State Board of Equalization shall provide one copy of the appeal and one copy of the supporting documents to the Franchise Tax Board. After the SBE issues its decision, the determination is final after 30 days from the date it was issued, unless the taxpayer or the Franchise Tax Board files a petition for a rehearing with the SBE. The determination then becomes final on the expiration of 30 days from the date the SBE issued its opinion on the petition for rehearing.[26]

Suit for refund. After payment of the tax and denial of the Franchise Tax Board of a claim for refund, or the denial of an appeal by the State Board of Equalization on a claim for refund, the taxpayer may initiate a suit to be heard by the Superior Court of California.[27] The suit must be filed within four years from the last date for filing the return or within one year from the date the tax was paid or within 90 days after: (a) notice of action by the Franchise Tax Board on any claim for refund or (b) final notice of action by the State Board of Equalization on an appeal from the action of the Franchise Tax Board on a claim for refund, whichever period expires the later.[28] If the Franchise Tax Board fails to mail a notice of action on any refund claim within six months after the claim was filed, the taxpayer may, before the mailing of the notice of action on the refund claim, consider the claim disallowed, and bring an action for refund. Title 11, § 505(a)(2), USC permits substitution of the 120-day period for the six-month period.[29]

---

(22) § 19302.
(23) § 19324.
(24) § 19331.
(25) § 19355.

(26) § 19301—19334.
(27) § 19382.
(28) § 19384.
(29) § 19385.

Service of papers on FTB. It is required that a copy of the complaint and summons filed with the courts shall also be served on the Franchise Tax Board or its Executive Officer.

Where suit is filed. Any action against the Franchise Tax Board must be commenced and tried in any city or city and county in which the Attorney General maintains an office. Inasmuch as these are suits against the State of California, the Attorney General and the Attorneys for the Franchise Tax Board will work together to defend the action.[30]

Note: Any individual, after protesting a notice or notices of deficiency assessment issued because of an alleged residence in California and after appealing to the Board of Equalization, may file an action in the Superior Court of the counties of Sacramento, Los Angeles, Fresno or city and county of San Francisco within 60 days after the action of the Board of Equalization becomes final to determine the facts of his residence in California during the years in question.[31]

¶ 337   Interest on Overpayments

Interest on a refund will be allowed at an adjusted rate established in accordance with the provisions of IRC § 6621, except that the overpayment rate specified in IRC § 6621(a)(1) must be modified to equal the underpayment rate determined under IRC § 6621(a)(2). The federal rate provisions are modified by California so that the state rate is determined semi-annually. The rate for January applies during the following July through December; the rate for July shall apply during the following January through June.

Interest rates on deficiencies and refunds are:

---

(30) § 19388—19389.   (31) § 19381.

From		To	Rate
January 1, 1987	—	September 30, 1987	8%
October 1, 1987	—	December 31, 1987	10%
January 1, 1988	—	March 31, 1988	11%
April 1, 1988	—	September 30, 1988	10%
October 1, 1988	—	June 30, 1989	11%
July 1, 1989	—	December 31, 1989	12%
January 1, 1990	—	June 30, 1991	11%
July 1, 1991	—	June 30, 1992	10%
July 1, 1992	—	December 31, 1992	9%
January 1, 1993	—	June 30, 1993	8%
July 1, 1993	—	December 31, 1993	7%
January 1, 1994	—	June 30, 1994	7%
July 1, 1994	—	December 31, 1994	7%
January 1, 1995	—	June 30, 1995	8%

Interest is figured from the date of the overpayment to a date preceding the date of the refund warrant by not more than 30 days. In the case of a credit, it starts from the date of the overpayment to the due date of the amount for which the credit is allowed.[32]

If any overpayment of tax is refunded or credited within 90 days after the return is filed, or within 90 days after the last date for filing the return (determined without regard to any extension of time), whichever is later, no interest will be allowed on such overpayment. Overpayment of tax for years prior to 1993 includes a refund in excess of tax liability under Rev & TC § 17053.5 (renter's credit). When a return is filed after the due date (including extensions), no interest will be allowed on the refund claim for any day before the return is filed.[33]

If an overpayment of tax is credited as a payment of estimated tax for a succeeding year, the credit will be treated as a payment of tax for the succeeding year, and no claim for credit or refund of that overpayment shall be allowed for the income or taxable year in which the overpayment of tax arises.[34]

WARNING   Rev & TC § 19349 states that if a payment is not made for a bona fide and orderly discharge of an actual liability or one reasonably assumed to be

---

(32) § 19340; 19521.
(33) § 19341.

(34) § 19364, as added by Stats. 1994, c. 1243, § 56.

imposed by law, it would not be considered to be an overpayment and, therefore, interest would not be paid on it. *Interest will not be allowed* in the following situations: (1) taxpayer pays a larger estimate than he had filed; (2) taxpayer fails to take a credit for estimated tax payments on the return; (3) taxpayer voluntarily makes duplicate estimated tax payments.[35]

The franchise Tax Board may recover any refund or credit erroneously allowed plus interest at the adjusted annual rate determined under Rev & TC § 19521. Interest applies from the date the demand for recovery was made, in an action brought in a court of competent jurisdiction in Sacramento County within two years after the refund or credit was made, or during the period within which the FTB may mail the notice of proposed additional assessment, whichever expires later.[36]

¶ 338   **Penalties**

The following penalties may be assessed:

Penalty for failure to file return on time. The penalty for failure to file a return by the original or the extended due date is 5% of the unpaid tax shown on the return for each month or fraction of a month from the due date (without regard to any extension of time for filing) to the date on which the return was filed, but not in excess of 25% of the tax. In case of failure to file a return within 60 days of the due date, determined with regard to extensions, the penalty is not less than the lesser of $100 or 100% of the tax required to be shown on the return, unless it's shown the failure was due to a reasonable cause, and not willful neglect. The amount of tax required to be shown on the return must be reduced for any payment before the due date or any credit that can be claimed. These rules do not apply to any failure to pay any estimated tax required by Rev & TC § 19136. If any failure to file a return is fraudulent, the above rules must be applied by substituting 15% for 5% of the unpaid tax, and 75% for 25% of the tax. In most cases the Franchise Tax Board will waive the penalties for the same reasons that the Internal Revenue Service will accept.[37] A partnership's failure to file on time, or to file a return showing information on gross income, deductions and the persons entitled to distributive shares is subject to a monthly penalty, not to exceed five months, of $10 multiplied by the number of persons who were partners during the taxable year, unless it is shown that the failure was due to reasonable cause.[38]

WARNING   *Filing enforcement fee.* The Franchise Tax Board may impose a filing enforcement fee if a taxpayer required to file a return under Part 10 of the Revenue & TC (relating to individuals) fails or refuses to make and file a tax return within 25 days after a formal legal demand to file the return is mailed by the Franchise Tax Board. The fee for the 1994–95

(35) § 19349.

(36) § 19411; 19521.

(37) § 19131.

(38) § 19172.

¶ **338**

fiscal year of the state is $114 for an individual, partnership, or fiduciary return. The filing enforcement fee is in addition to the failure to file penalty. The amount assessed as a filing enforcement fee will not bear interest.[39]

Accuracy-related penalty—general—negligence. California adopts IRC § 6662, relating to an accuracy-related penalty. Under this federal section, a penalty of 20% of the amount of the underpayment of tax is imposed if the portion of the underpayment is due to one or more of the following:

(1) negligence or disregard of rules or regulations;
(2) any substantial understatement of income tax;
(3) any substantial valuation misstatement;
(4) any substantial overstatement of pension liabilities;
(5) any substantial estate or gift valuation understatement. This rule does not apply to IRC § 6663, relating to the fraud penalty. The term "negligence" is defined in IRC § 6662(c).[1]

When the amount shown by the husband and wife on a joint return as tax exceeds the aggregate of the amounts shown as tax upon a separate return of each spouse, and any part of the excess is attributable to negligence or intentional disregard of the rules and regulations, but without intent to defraud, at the time of making a separate return, then 20% of the amount of the excess will be assessed, collected and paid instead of the 20% addition to tax provided in Rev & TC § 19164 (accuracy-related penalty).[1]

Accuracy-related penalty—substantial understatement of income tax. Under IRC § 6662(d), there is a substantial understatement of income tax for any taxable year if the amount of the understatement for the taxable year exceeds the greater of 10% of the tax required to be shown on the return, or $5,000. In the case of corporations, other than S corporations, or personal holding company, as defined in IRC § 542, substitute $10,000 for $5,000. "Understatement" means the excess of the amount of the tax required to be shown for the taxable year on the return, over the amount of the tax imposed that is shown on the return, reduced by any IRC § 6211(b)(2) rebate. A reduction of an understatement can be made due to the position of taxpayer on a disputed item. Special rules apply to tax shelters. Administrative authorities can prescribe, and revise, not less frequently than annually, a list of positions for which they believe there is no substantial authority, and affect a significant number of taxpayers.[1]

Accuracy-related penalty—substantial valuation misstatement under Chapter 1. Under IRC § 6662(e), there is a substantial valuation overstatement under Ch. 1 of the IRC if (1) the value of any property, or the adjusted basis of any property, claimed on any return of tax imposed by that chapter is 200% or more of the amount determined to be the correct amount of such valuation or adjusted basis, or (2) the price for any property or services, or for the use of any property claimed on any return in connection with any trans-

---

(39) § 19254.   (1) IRC § 6013(b)(5); § 6662; 6663; § 18530; 19164.

action between persons described in IRC § 482 is 200% or more, or 50% or less of the amount determined under IRC § 482 to be the correct amount of the price, or the net IRC § 482 transfer price adjustment for the tax year exceeds $10 million. For purpose of the 40% gross misstatement penalty, substitute 400% for 200%, 25% for 50%, and $20 million for $10 million. No penalty applies unless the portion of the underpayment for the taxable year attributable to the substantial valuation overstatement exceeds $5,000 or $10,000 in case of a corporation other than an S corporation or personal holding company.[1]

Net IRC § 482 transfer price adjustment. California has adopted the provisions of IRC § 6662(e)(3), relating to net IRC § 482 transfer price adjustment. The term "net IRC § 482 transfer price adjustment" means the net increase in taxable income for the tax year, determined without regard to any amount carried to such tax year from another tax year, resulting from adjustments under IRC § 482 in the price for any property or services, or for the use of property. Certain adjustments must be made in determining the $10 million threshold requirement for net IRC § 482 transfer price adjustment.[1]

Accuracy-related penalty—substantial overstatement of pension liabilities. California adopts IRC § 6662(f). The penalty will apply if the actuarial determination of liabilities taken into account in computing the deduction under IRC § 404(a)(1) or § 404(a)(2) is 200% or more of the amount determined to be correct. For purposes of the 400% gross misstatement penalty, substitute 400% for 200%. No penalty applies unless the underpayment for the taxable year attributable to the substantial overstatement of these liabilities exceeds $1,000.[1]

Accuracy-related penalty—substantial estate or gift tax valuation understatement. Under IRC § 6662(g), adopted by California, there is a substantial estate tax valuation understatement if the value of any property included on any return of tax imposed by Subtitle B, Estate and Gift Tax is 50% or less of the amount determined to be the correct amount. For purposes of the gross valuation misstatement penalty, substitute 25% for 50%. No penalty applies unless the portion of the underpayment attributable to the understatements exceeds $5,000.[1]

Accuracy-related penalty—definitions and special rules. California adopts IRC § 6664, relating to the definition of underpayment, charitable deduction property, qualified appraiser, qualified appraisal, and special rules on reasonable cause exception and valuation overstatements.[1]

Fraud penalty. California adopts IRC § 6664 which provides that if any part of any underpayment of tax required to be shown on the return is due to fraud, an addition to tax will be made in an amount equal to the sum of 75% of the portion of the underpayment attributable to fraud. If the FTB establishes that any part of the underpayment is attributable to fraud, the entire underpayment will be treated as so attributable, except for any portion that the taxpayer establishes not to be attributable. In case of a joint return, this rule on fraud will not apply to a spouse, unless some part of the underpayment is due to that spouse's fraud.[2] If any part of the excess shown as tax on a joint return under Rev & TC § 18522 by the husband and wife over the amount shown on a separate return of each spouse is attributable to fraud with intent to evade tax at the time of making a separate return, then 75% of the total amount of the excess must be assessed, collected and paid instead of the 75% addition to tax provided by Rev & TC § 19164 (accuracy-related penalty).[3]

Failure to pay tax by due date. In case of failure to pay either (1) the amount of tax shown on the return by the due date, without regard to any extension; or (2) any amount in respect of any tax required to be shown on return that is not so shown, including excess tax assessed due to a mathematical error, within 10 days of the date of notice and demand, unless it is shown that the failure is due to reasonable cause and not willful neglect, a penalty is imposed of (a) 5% of the total tax unpaid; and (b) an amount computed at the rate of ½% per month of the remaining tax for each additional month or fraction during which that tax is greater than zero. The aggregate amount of penalty that can be imposed cannot exceed 25% of the total unpaid tax. The penalty is due and payable upon notice and demand by Franchise Tax Board. No interest shall accrue on the "remaining tax" part of the penalty. "Total tax unpaid" means the amount of tax shown on the return, reduced by the amount of tax paid by the due date, and any credit that may be claimed on the return. "Remaining tax" means the total tax unpaid reduced by the amount of payment. If the amount of tax required to be shown on return is less than the amount shown, the penalty provisions will be applied by substituting the lower amount. Penalty is not assessed if, for the same taxable year, the penalties for failure to file, or failure to file after demand are equal to or greater than this penalty for failure to pay the tax. If the penalty for unpaid tax is greater than the sum of the penalties for failure to file, or failure to file after notice and demand, the penalty imposed for the unpaid tax is an amount that exceeds the sum of those penalties.[4] Interest applies to extended payment, and extended installment payment.[5]

WAIVER OF LATE PAYMENT PENALTIES.

Late payment and late filing penalties will be waived for qualified taxpayers who as a result of the Northridge earthquake in January 1994, suffered a (1) significant property loss, (2) a loss of employment due to property damage suffered by his or her employer, or (3) a significant loss of business income from a business located in the Northridge earthquake area. The late payment will be waived only if the tax is paid by an individual, partnership, or fiduciary within 6 months of the original due date of the return, or by a corporation within 7 months from the original

---

(2) IRC § 6613; 19164.   (4) § 19132.
(3) 18530.   (5) § 19102.

due date of the return. The return must be filed timely, including extensions, for the waiver of the late payment penalty to apply.[6]

WARNING	*Collection costs.* The Franchise Tax Board is empowered to add a fee when any person taxable under Part 10 of the Rev & Tax C (relating to individual taxes) fails to respond to a notice to the person for payment of tax, penalty, addition to tax, interest, or other liability imposed and delinquent. This fee can be imposed only after a notice has been mailed to the person for payment that advises the taxpayer that continued failure to pay the amount due may result in collection action, including the imposition of a collection cost recovery fee. The fee for the 1994–95 fiscal year of the state is $103. The assessment of collection costs is in addition to failure to pay penalty. The amount assessed as a collection fee will not bear interest.[7]

Failure to disclose gains on straddles. An accuracy-related penalty for negligence applies for failure to disclose gains on straddles. California has adopted IRC § 6662.

Failure to file information returns and interest statements. California adopts the IRC § 6050I intentional disregard penalty for returns relating to cash received in a trade or business. The penalty is the greater of $25,000 or the amount of cash received, not over $100,000; the $250,000 limit does not apply. The penalty for failure to file an information return will be determined by IRC § 6721. Under that federal section, the general penalty imposed is $50 for each failure; the maximum penalty for all such failures during any calendar year is $250,000. In case of intentional disregard in connection with one or more failures, the penalty is $100 for each failure, with the same maximum limit of $250,000. But, if a greater penalty would result from applying 10% of the aggregate amount of items required to be reported, that penalty will apply, and the maximum limit of $250,000 will be disregarded. California modifies IRC § 6721 by providing that Rev & TC § 18641 (brokers) applies instead of the federal rule under IRC § 6045(a), and the reference to IRC § 6041A(b) (service remuneration and direct sales) does not apply in California. IRC § 6721(e) and California except from the 10% rule returns covering mortgage interest, foreclosures and abandonment of security, exchanges of partnership interests, and dispositions of certain donated property. The 5% rule under IRC § 6721(e) applies to exchanges of partnership interests and dispositions of certain donated property in California. The $250,000 limit does not apply.[8]

California has adopted IRC § 6722 which provides the penalty for failure to furnish certain payee statements. This federal rule imposes a penalty of $50 for each failure to furnish the statement and required information. The $100,000 limit applies. California modifies IRC § 6722(c), relating to the penalty in case of intentional disregard to substitute Rev & TC § 18641 rule

---

(6) § 19132.5, as added by Stats. 1994, c. 735, § 2.　　　　(8) § 19183.
(7) § 19254.

on brokers for IRC § 6045(b), and provides that IRC §§ 6041A(b) and 6041A(e), relating to service remuneration and direct sales, do not apply. The penalty for intentional disregard with respect to furnishing correct payee statements, subject to the above modification, is $100, or if greater, 10% of the aggregate amount of items required to be reported correctly, or in the case of exchanges of partnership interests and dispositions of certain donated property, 5%. The $100,000 limit does not apply.[8]

California also adopts IRC § 6723 which provides for a penalty for failure to comply with other information reporting requirements. Under IRC § 6723 the penalty is $50 for each failure with a $100,000 maximum.[8]

Subject to certain state modifications listed below, California adopts IRC § 6724, relating to waiver, definitions and special rules. California has adopted its own code sections modifying IRC § 6724(d)(1) with respect to the following:

Subject	IRC §	California Rev & TC §
Information return	6041(a)	18637
Service renumeration	6041A(a)	18638
Patronage dividends, rebates or refunds	6044(a)(1)	18640
Brokers	6045(a)	18641
Boat operators	6050A(a)	18644
Group-term life insurance	6052(a)	18647

The payee statement rules found in IRC § 6074(d)(2) are modified to refer to the following California code sections:

Subject	IRC §	California Rev & TC §
Statement to beneficiary of trust or estate	6034A	18505
Transfer of shares on exercise of stock options	6039(a)	18636
Patronage dividends, etc.	6044(e)	18640
Brokers' reports to customers	6045(b)	18641
Boat operators	6050A(b)	18644
Group-term life insurance	6052(b)	18647

Other references to diesel fuel reports, pass-through entities, direct sales and services, brokers, receipts from employees, reports of tips under the IRC do not apply to California.

A $10 penalty is imposed for each failure to provide a written explanation to recipients of distributions eligible for rollover treatment as required by IRC § 402(f). The total penalty can't exceed $5,000 in any calendar year.[8]

Individual retirement accounts—annuities—reports.   Any person required to file a report on individual retirement accounts or annuities pursuant to Rev & TC § 17507 must pay a penalty of $50 for each failure, unless it is shown that such failure is due to a reasonable cause. Any individual required to furnish information under Rev & TC § 17508 as to the amount designated as nondeductible contributions made for any taxable year, must pay a penalty of $100 for each overstatement of those contributions unless it is shown that the overstatement is due to a reasonable cause. The failure to file the form under Rev & TC § 17508 incurs a $50 penalty. Article 2, relating to deficiency procedures does not apply to the assessment or collection of this penalty.[9]

Original issue discount reporting requirements.   A penalty is imposed for failing to meet the requirements of Rev & TC § 18649 that a copy of the information furnished to the IRS under IRC § 1275(c)(2) on offering to the public of debt instruments having original issue discount be furnished to the Franchise Tax Board. The penalty is determined under IRC § 6706. The penalty is equal to 1% of the aggregate price of such issue, not in excess of $50,000 for that issue.[10]

Failure to furnish information on tax shelters.   The failure to furnish information on tax shelters with respect to registration, registration numbers, and include tax shelter identification numbers on the return as required by Rev & TC § 18547 incurs a penalty determined under IRC § 6707—the greater of $500 or 1% of the aggregate amount invested in the shelter.[11]

Failure to pay estimated income tax.   An addition to tax is made at the adjusted rate of interest determined under Rev & TC § 19521 based on the amount of underpayment and period of underpayment (see ¶ 171) for failure to pay estimated tax. Estates and trusts are subject to the estimated tax rules of IRC § 6654(l).[12]

No addition to tax will be made for any installment of tax due after 1–1–93, to the extent the underpayment of estimated tax of a California resident is attributable to a change in the laws of another state which makes Rev & TC § 18001 inapplicable which causes a loss of the California credit for taxes paid to the other state.[13]

Tax preparers—failure to furnish copy of return.   The failure of a tax preparer to furnish a copy of return to the taxpayer will incur a $50 penalty for each failure as set by IRC § 6695(a). The failure to furnish an identifying

---

(9) § 19184.
(10) § 19181.
(11) § 19182.

(12) § 19136.
(13) § 19136.5.

number on the return or refund claim incurs a similar $50 penalty. A $50 penalty applies for failure to retain the copy of the return, claim for refund, or list of name and identifying number of taxpayer. These penalties are additional to others set by law. Penalty includes the failure to retain an electronic filing declaration as required by Rev & TC § 18621.5.[14]

Identifying number—failure to include in return or furnish to another. California adopts IRC § 6723 that imposes a $50 penalty for each failure to comply with a specified information reporting requirement on or before the date set for that compliance. The total amount of such penalty cannot exceed $100,000.[15] Identifying numbers are those required under IRC § 6109 except IRC § 6109(e) relating to the furnishing of numbers for certain dependents, and IRC § 6109(h) relating to the furnishing of numbers for certain seller-provided financing do not apply.

Promoting abusive tax shelters. The penalty for promoting abusive tax shelters is $1000 or 20% of the gross income derived or to be derived, whichever is greater—same as IRC § 6700.[16]

Aiding and abetting understatement. The penalty for aiding and abetting understatement is $1,000 per person per period—same as IRC § 6701.[17]

Filing frivolous return. The penalty for filing a frivolous return is $500—same as IRC § 6702. The provisions for partial payment of penalty and judicial review under IRC § 6703 do not apply. Authorities can counterclaim for the balance of the penalty.[18]

Tax shelter promoter. A tax shelter promoter required to file an information return under Rev & TC § 18648 who (1) fails to file such return for any calendar year within 60 days of an FTB request; or (2) fails to show the required information on such return; or (3) fails to furnish the required statement to each investor is subject to a penalty that is the product of the number of investors required to be shown on the return times $1,000. If number of investors can't be determined, the amount of the penalty is $100,000.[19] A tax shelter promoter who fails to keep the records required by Rev & TC § 18648(d) is subject to a penalty of $1,000 multiplied by the number of investors with respect to whom the failure occurs. If the number can't be determined, the penalty is $100,000. It applies to each calendar year for which the failure occurs.[20]

Failure to report amounts paid as personal service remuneration. Any person or entity that fails to report amounts paid as remuneration for personal services under the information return requirements of Rev & TC § 18802, the payee statement requirements of the same section, the statement on services required by Rev & TC § 18637, and the employee statement

---

(14) § 17024.5; 18624; 18625; 19167; 19168.
(15) § 19183.
(16) § 19177.
(17) § 19178.

(18) § 17024.5; 19179.
(19) § 19173.
(20) § 19174.

requirements of Rev & TC § 13050 may be subject to a penalty of the maximum tax rate under Rev & TC § 17041 multiplied by the unreported amounts. The penalty is in addition to that for failure to file information returns and interest statements. Reasonable cause is no excuse. The deficiency assessment provisions do not apply. If the penalty is imposed by both Rev & TC § 19175 and Unemployment Insurance Cd § 13052.5, only the latter penalty will apply. The penalty imposed by Unemployment Insurance Cd § 13052.5 can be assessed in lieu of or in addition to the penalty imposed by Unemployment Insurance Cd § 13052 with respect to the failure to furnish a withholding statement.[21]

Interest on assessable penalties. Except as provided in Rev & TC § 19111, relating to the payment of the amount within 10 days of notice, interest is imposed under Rev & TC § 19101 with respect to any penalty assessed under the Personal Income Tax Law or the Bank and Corporation Tax Law. In case of penalty, additional amount, or addition to tax that, when assessed, is due and payable on notice and demand, (other than a penalty for failure to file a return by the due date under Rev & TC § 19131, or a penalty under Rev & TC § 19132, relating to underpayment of tax) or Rev & TC § 19164, relating to accuracy-related penalty, interest is imposed from the date of the notice and demand to the date of payment. If the penalty, additional amount, or addition to tax is initially assessed as a deficiency or addition to tax, other than Rev & TC § 19131 penalty for failure to file a return by the due date, Rev & TC § 19172 relating to underpayment of tax, or Rev & TC § 19164, relating to accuracy-related penalty, interest is imposed from the date of notice of the proposed assessment to the date of payment. In case of Rev & TC § 19131, 19132, and 19164 penalties, interest is assessed for the period that starts on the date on which the tax return subject to the penalty is required to be filed, including extensions, and ends on the date of payment of the addition to tax.[22]

Bad checks. The provisions of IRC § 6657, relating to bad checks, apply in California. Under IRC § 6657, if a check or money order is not duly paid, in addition to any other penalties, the person who tendered such check, upon notice and demand from the taxing authorities, must pay as penalty an amount equal to 2% of the amount of the check. If the amount of the check is less than $750, the penalty is $15 or the amount of the check, whichever is less. The penalty does not apply, if that person tendered the check in good faith and with reasonable cause to believe that it would duly be paid. For checks received on or after January 1, 1993, the penalty will be applied to all payments regardless of the tax year for which the payment is made.[23]

Case pending under title 11, USC. No addition to tax shall be made under Rev & TC § 19132 or § 19136 for failure to make a timely payment of tax during any period in which a case is pending under Title 11(1), if such tax

---

(21) § 19175; UI Cd § 13052.5.   (23) § 19134.
(22) § 19106.

was incurred by the estate and the failure occurred pursuant to an order of the court finding a probable insufficiency of funds of the estate to pay administrative expenses; or (2) if such tax was incurred by the debtor by the earlier of the order of relief, or the appointment of the trustee in an involuntary proceeding, and the petition was filed before the due date, including extensions, for filing the return, or the date for making the addition to tax occurs on or after the day the petition was filed. The rule doesn't apply to liability for tax arising from the failure to pay or deposit withholding taxes.[24]

Failure to provide information for foreign-owned corporations, transfers to foreign-owned corporations, and foreign-owned corporations doing business in the U.S. California has adopted IRC §§ 6038A, 6038B, and 6038C which imposes penalties for failure to provide information with respect to, or for transfers to, certain foreign-owned corporations. Basically a copy of the information required to be filed with the U.S. tax return is to be filed with the California return. The California penalties are the same as provided in federal law.[25]

Failure to provide information on qualifying small business stock. Issuers of qualified small business stock under Rev & TC § 18152.5(d)(1)(D), are required to submit those reports to the Franchise Tax Board and to shareholders as the Franchise Tax Board may required to carry out the purposes of the qualifying small business stock incentive. Failure to provide that information will result in a penalty of $50 for each report with respect to which there is a failure. In the case of a required report which covers two or more years, the penalty of $50 will be multiplied by the number of years for which there was a failure to provide the report. If the failure to file the report is due to negligence or intentional disregards of the regulations, the penalty will increase to $100 per failure to file a required report. As of 12–1–93, the Franchise Tax Board had not yet proscribed regulations setting forth a reporting requirement.[26]

Criminal penalties. In addition to the above, Rev & TC § 19705–19715 provide severe fines and in some cases jail sentences for criminal and willful violations of the laws with respect to filing false returns, failing to file returns, failure to collect and pay withheld taxes, furnishing information, etc.[27] The identification of those subject to criminal penalty is broad so as to include the taxpayer, any member of the taxpayer's family, or any agent, fiduciary, or representative of, or any other individual acting on behalf of the taxpayer who willfully makes, aids or assists in, counsels, or advises, as to the filing for a false statement or return; simulates or falsely or fraudulently executes documents; removes, deposits, or conceals records; etc.

---

(24) § 19161.

(25) § 19141.5, as amended by Stats. 1994, c. 948, § 2.

(26) § 19133.5.

(27) § 19176; 19583; 19705–19715.

Spouses filing joint return. Generally, each spouse is liable for the entire tax and any penalties imposed. However, under certain conditions, an innocent spouse may be relieved of liability for tax on unreported income.[28]

Forging spouse's signature. Any person who signs his or her spouse's name on any income tax return, or any schedules or attachments thereto, or electronically, without the consent of the spouse is guilty of misdemeanor. Upon conviction, that person can be fined up to $5,000, or imprisoned for a term not to exceed one year, or both, together with costs of investigation and prosecution.[29] Exceptions are provided in the case of incapacity if the spouse's name is followed by the words "By ———, Husband (or Wife)," and by the signature of the signing spouse. A statement required by Rev & TC § 19701.5 must be attached.

Abusive tax shelters—aiding and abetting understatement of tax. A civil action to enjoin the promotion may be brought in the county of residence or principal place of business of defendants, or in the County of Sacramento if the defendant has no such residence or place of business.[30]

Litigation costs. In case of any civil proceeding brought by or against the State of California in connection with the determination, collection, or refund of any tax, interest, or penalty under the Personal Income Tax Law brought in a court of record, the prevailing party may be awarded a judgment for reasonable litigation costs. Exhaustion of administrative remedies is required.[31]

Waiver—reliance on board opinion. The franchise Tax Board is required to waive interest, additions to tax, and penalties if it determines that the following conditions are satisfied:

(1) taxpayer or its representative requested in writing an opinion as to tax consequences of particular acts or activities contemplated, setting forth all pertinent facts;

(2) based on facts presented and applicable law, board issued written opinion as to tax consequences that was reasonably relied on when activities were started and action taken;

(3) tax consequences were not later changed by change in statutory law, case law, federal interpretation on which board's opinion was based, or material facts or circumstances relating to taxpayer.

A taxpayer seeking relief must file the required documents, including the request and opinion. A misrepresentation or omission of one or more material facts makes this rule inapplicable. Waiver extends only to penalties and interest attributable to actions taken after receipt of the opinion.[32] The ruling can be obtained by writing the Legal Counsel, Franchise Tax Board, P.O. Box 942867, Sacramento, CA 94267–0040.

---

(28) § 18533; 18534; 19006.
(29) § 19701.5.
(30) § 19177; § 19707; 19715.

(31) § 19717.
(32) § 21012.

Waiver of interest—extreme financial hardship. The Franchise Tax Board may waive interest for any period for which it determines that taxpayer demonstrates inability to pay that interest solely because of extreme financial hardship caused by significant disability or other catastrophic circumstances. Fraud, malfeasance, misrepresentation, or omission of any material fact will cause withdrawal of waiver. The rule applies only to interest accruing on and after 1–1–87.[33]

¶ 338–A   Voluntary Disclosure Program for Business Entities

Effective August 26, 1994, the State of California has adopted a voluntary disclosure program which allows business entities, other than those organized under the laws of the state of California, or those which have qualified to do business in California, to enter into negotiations with the Franchise Tax Board for the waiver of taxes, additions to tax, fees, or penalties with respect to each taxable or income year ending prior to six years from the signing date of the voluntary disclosure agreement. For the first six years prior to the signing of the voluntary disclosure agreement, the Franchise Tax Board could waive certain specified penalties. The voluntary disclosure program is more fully described in Chapter 22, and paragraph 1326.[34]

¶ 339   Secondary or Transferee Liability

The taxes assessed against any taxpayer for which any other person is liable may be assessed against such other person in the manner provided for the assessments of deficiencies. For example, an assessment can be made against a distributee of an estate where the decree of distribution did not give the Franchise Tax Board adequate notice of the probate proceedings. These taxes may be assessed against the secondary liability at any time within which deficiency assessments can be made against the taxpayers. There is also a provision, however, that the running of the statute of limitations on the assessment of any liability is suspended during the period in which the taxpayer is carrying on a protest procedure.[35]

¶ 340   Closing Agreements

The Franchise Tax Board itself or any other person it authorizes in writing may enter into an agreement with a taxpayer to settle any matter pertaining to the taxes under the Personal Income Tax Law. The agreement must be approved by the Franchise Tax Board, and the matter cannot be reopened, except upon showing of fraud, malfeasance, or misrepresentation of material fact, by any officer, employee, or agent of the Franchise Tax Board and in any suit, action or proceeding, any agreement made in accordance with the section shall not be annulled, modified, or disregarded.[36]

---

(33) § 19112.

(34) § 19191, as added by Stats. 1994, c. 367, § 2.

(35) § 19071.

(36) § 19441.

Settlement authority. The Franchise Tax Board may settle civil tax disputes.[37] The executive officer of chief counsel of the Franchise Tax Board must first submit the proposed recommendations to the Attorney General who, within 30 days of receiving the recommendation, must advise the executive officer or chief counsel of the Franchise Tax Board of the Attorney General's conclusions as to whether the recommendation is reasonable from an overall perspective. Once submitted to the Franchise Tax Board, following the receipt of the Attorney General's findings, the Franchise Tax Board will have 45 days to accept or disapprove the recommendation for settlement. If there has been no action within 45 days of submission, the recommendation shall be deemed approved. All settlements pursuant to Rev & TC § 19442 will be final and nonappealable.

Whenever a reduction of tax in excess of $500 is approved pursuant to the settlement authority granted to the Franchise Tax Board, a public record will be created to show the name of the taxpayer, the amount originally involved, the amount of the settlement, a summary of the reasons why the settlement is in the best interests of the State of California, and the Attorney General's conclusions that the recommendation of settlement was reasonable from an overall perspective.

A settlement of any civil tax matter in dispute involving a reduction of tax or penalties which does not exceed $5,000, may be approved by the executive officer and chief counsel of the Franchise Tax Board without referral to the Attorney General's office.[37]

¶ 341   **Withholding of Tax From Nonresidents**

Every individual who is a resident or has a place of business in California, and every bank, corporation, or partnership and in fact, any business entity subject to the laws of the state is required to withhold from any payment of income derived from sources within this state by individuals who are nonresidents and transmit the withheld amount to the Franchise Tax Board.[38]

Items of income subject to withholding. Items of income subject to withholding are interest, dividends, rent, prizes and winnings, premiums, annuities, emoluments, compensation for personal services, partnership income or gains, and other fixed amounts of determinable annual or periodical gains, profits and income.[39]

Withholding of tax at source. Withholding of tax at source is required in the case of payments to nonresidents of compensation for personal services rendered in California, except for wages subject to withholding under Unemployment Insurance Code § 13020, or exempt from withholding under § 13009 of the Unemployment Insurance Code, or exempt from withholding under federal law. Withholding at source is also required in the case of rentals or royalties for the use of, or for the privilege of using in California,

---

(37) § 19442, as amended by Stats. 1994, c. 138, § 3.

(38) § 18662; Reg 18805–1–18805–3.
(39) Reg 18805–2.

patents, copyrights, secret processes and formulas, goodwill, trademarks, brands, franchises and other like property of such intangible property having a business or taxable situs as defined in the regulations[40] in California. Withholding at source is also required from payments of prizes, premiums, rewards, winnings, etc. to nonresidents participating, or entering cars, horses, etc. in races or other contests in California.[39] For supplemental wages paid on or after 1–1–92, the rate of withholding that may be applied instead of wage withholding is 6%. Supplemental wages include, but are not limited to bonus payments, overtime payments, commissions, sales awards, back pay including retroactive wage increases, and reimbursements for nondeductible moving expenses that are paid for the same or a different period, or without regard to a particular period.[1]

Notice to withhold from Franchise Tax Board.   In the case of payments to nonresidents of items of income not specified in the paragraph entitled "Withholding of tax at source" above, and in the case of persons not making payments to nonresidents of items of income subject to withholding listed in the paragraph preceding "Withholding of tax at source," but having control, receipt, custody or disposal of such income, withholding at source is required when the person subject to withholding, as specified in California Reg 18805–1, is notified by the Franchise Tax Board or its representative to withhold tax.[39]

Compensation for personal services.   Compensation for personal services besides wages and salaries includes:

(1) payment of expenses of nonresident employees for services rendered in California;

(2) commissions paid nonresident salesmen for instate services;

(3) fees for nonresidents professional services rendered instate;

(4) payments to nonresident actors, performers, etc. for performances instate; and

(5) payments to independent contractors, such as leaders, managers, or owners of bands, orchestras, dance teams, circuses, and similar groups pursuant to contracts where these contractors agreed to furnish in-state services.[39]

PL 86–272 (see ¶ 1163) doesn't exempt nonresident salesmen who solicit orders from California residents. The law refers to income of person engaged in interstate commerce, not income of a salesman.[2] (Note: Withholding on residents' pay is explained at Section XI of this book.)

Withholding threshold.   Withholding under California Reg 18805–2 is not required unless and until income payments with respect to each payee by the same payor either exceed $1,500 during the calendar year, or the payor is directed to withhold by the Franchise Tax Board.[39]

Amount of tax to be withheld.   This is computed by applying the 7% rate, or the lesser rate authorized by the FTB in writing. The FTB will

---

(40) Reg 17951–17951–5; 17952; 17953.   (2) LR 372, 1–22–74.
(1) § 18663.

consider documentation to the effect the 7% rate will result in overwithholding. The FTB may, after consideration of the documents submitted, waive withholding, or set a lower rate. The payee will be required to submit a security to the FTB by bond, deposit, or otherwise. Notices of the waiver must be given in writing the by FTB. The payor can repay the overwithholding to the payee.[3] A California resident payee should submit the executed Certificate of Residence (Form 590) if withholding is to be waived. However, in order to avoid incurring liabilities for failure to withhold, the payor should file on behalf of the payee the executed Form 590 with the Franchise Tax Board prior to making the payment to the payee.

When withholding return due. *Annual.* On or before January 31st of each year each person, firm or corporation subject to withholding requirements is required to make a return of tax withheld at source on Form 592 for the preceding calendar year and submit it to the Franchise Tax Board. Form 591, Report of Tax Withheld at Source, that replaces Certificate of Nonresidence and Claim for Personal Exemption Credit must be filed with Form 592.

Monthly. If the total amount withheld by a withholding agent exceeds $2,500, a return of tax withheld at source on Form 592 together with the amount of tax withheld, must be filed within 20 days following the month in which the accumulated total of $2,500 was reached.[4] The payor is relieved of liability only where the FTB lowers or waives withholding.

Foreign persons disposing of real property interest in United States. In case of any disposition of a California real property interest by a person subject to IRC § 1445, relating to withholding of tax on dispositions of US real property interests, the transferee must deduct and withhold a tax equal to one-third of the amount required to be withheld by the transferee under IRC § 1445. California real property interest means an interest in real property described in IRC § 897(c)(1)(A)(i) that is located in California.[5]

A transferee must withhold a tax equal to 3⅓% of the sales price of the California real property conveyed in the case of any disposition by a person, but not a partnership, when the return required to be filed by the US Treasury under IRC § 6045(e) indicates, or authorization for disbursement of transaction's funds instructs that the funds be disbursed either to the transferor with a last-known street address outside the boundaries of California at the time of transfer of title. The withholding requirement does not apply to the transferee in any taxable year in which transfer of title occurs, if the transferee has received a homeowners' property tax exemption for the property conveyed. Also, transferee need not withhold if the sales price does not exceed $100,000. The transferee does not need to withhold if a written notice of the withholding requirements has not been provided by the real estate escrow person. No transferee is required to withhold any amount

---

(3) Reg 18805–3.
(4) Reg 18805–8.

(5) IRC § 1445; § 18662.

under Rev & TC § 18662, if the transferee, in good faith, and based on all the information of which he or she has knowledge, relies on a written certificate executed by the transferor, certifying under penalty of perjury that the transferor is a resident of California, or that the California real property being conveyed is the principal residence of the transferor, within the meaning of IRC § 1034.[6] For liability of transferor, transferee and real estate escrow person, and a form for escrow person's notice to transferee see Rev & TC § 18668.[7]

Amounts paid by partnerships to foreign partners.   IRC § 1446 applies in California to the extent that the amounts paid by partnerships to foreign partners represent income from California sources, unless California law otherwise provides. Under IRC § 1446, if a partnership has effectively connected taxable income for any taxable year, and any portion of that income is allocable under IRC § 704 to a foreign partner, the partnership must pay withholding tax. This withholding tax payable, as a general rule, must be equal to the applicable percentage of effectively connected taxable income of the partnership. The applicable percentage, for California purposes, is the maximum tax rate specified in Rev & TC § 17041 rather than the rate specified in IRC § 1. For banks and corporations who are foreign partners the applicable tax rate is the rate specified in Rev & TC §§ 23151, 23181, or 23183, as applicable, rather than the rate specified in IRC § 11.[8]

Notice to withhold taxes.   Notice to withhold taxes from property belonging to the taxpayer and the transmit amounts of tax due to the Franchise Tax Board may be given by the FTB to persons in possession of this property of taxpayer or an employer or person who has failed to withhold taxes. The notice may also be given to state officers, agencies and subdivisions.

¶ 342   Franchise Tax Board Certificate

If the assets of an estate are distributable to one or more nonresident beneficiaries, the probate court is not allowed to certify the final account of the executor or other fiduciary until he obtains from the Franchise Tax Board and files with the court a certificate that all taxes imposed on the estate or the decedent which have become payable have either been paid or secured by bond or deposit.[9]

The above rule applies only if the total value of the assets of the estate exceeds $400,000 and assets having a total value of $100,000 or more are distributable to one or more of the beneficiaries living outside of California.

The Franchise Tax Board is required to issue the certificate within 30 days after receiving the request or notify the fiduciary of the amount of bond,

---

(6) § 18662.
(7) § 18668.

(8) IRC § 1446; § 18666.
(9) § 19513.

deposit, or other security that should be furnished in order to have the certificate issued.[10]

The fiduciary or any other person liable for the tax may request that the Franchise Tax Board issue any notices proposing to assess the tax or commence any proceeding in court without assessment within 18 months after the request.[11]

¶ 343 **Notice of Fiduciary**

For federal purposes a fiduciary is required to give notice to the Internal Revenue Service when he assumes the duties of the fiduciary. Form 56 "Notice Concerning Fiduciary Relationship" is provided for this service.

Rev & TC § 19512 provides that the same Notice be given to the Franchise Tax Board. No form has been prepared by the Franchise Tax Board, but it will accept federal Form 56 for this purpose.[12]

¶ 344 **Disclosure of Information**

It is a misdemeanor for a member of the Franchise Tax Board or any employee of the state, or former officer or employee or other individual, to disclose any information as to the amount of income or other information included in the tax returns filed with the state.

Information may be disclosed, however, to:

● *Courts.* Courts may inspect returns provided a proper judicial order is in effect, but only for purposes of enforcement of the tax laws or prosecutions for the violations of the tax laws;

● *Legislative committees.* Legislative committees may inspect returns on request, but again it is a misdemeanor for any member of the committee or clerk to disclose any of the particulars of the information furnished except to a law enforcement officer for the purposes of aiding the detection or prosecution of crimes committed in violation of the tax laws;

● *Attorney General.* The Attorney General or his representatives may inspect the returns in connection with action to recover any tax or any penalty or to enforce any of the provisions of the tax law;

●*Commissioner of Internal Revenue or California tax officials.* The Commissioner of Internal Revenue or California tax officials or the Multistate Tax Commission or the proper officer of any state imposing an income tax or a tax measured by income may inspect the tax returns when allowed by the Franchise Tax Board. But this information must be furnished only for tax purposes;

● *Director of Social Services or deputy directors.* The Director of Social Services may inspect income tax records but only for applicants or recipients of assistance under the Welfare and Institutions Code and responsible relatives. The Department of Social Services must annually inform the Franchise Tax Board of names and Social Security numbers of all applicants for or recipients of public social services programs. On receipt of such information, the FTB will inform the department of any such applicant who received dividends or interest within prior calendar year. The FTB must provide information to the department with infor-

---

(10) § 19514.
(11) § 19517.

(12) § 19512.

mation identifying amount of dividends and interest paid, and address and name of payor;

● *State Controller.* The Franchise Tax Board may provide the State Controller with the address or other identification or location information from income tax returns which may be necessary for the State Controller to locate owners of unclaimed property, pursuant to Title 10 of the Code of Civil Procedure.

● *Franchise Board and Public Employees' Retirement System (PERS).* Subject to the limitations of Rev & TC § 19558, and federal law, the Franchise Tax Board may provide the Public Employees' Retirement System with names and addresses and other location or identification information from income tax returns and other records required under the Personal Income Tax Law, solely for the purposes of disbursing unclaimed benefits. Neither PERS, nor its agents, nor any of its current or former officers or employees shall disclose or use any information obtained, except as provided in Rev & TC § 19558.

● *National taxing officials of Mexico.* Mexico national taxing officials may inspect returns if a reciprocal agreement exists and if the reciprocal agreement is limited to the exchange of information which is essential for tax administration purposes only. Taxing officials of Mexico shall be granted tax information only on Mexican nationals. California will receive information only on California residents.[13]

● *Franchise Tax Board.* Cities with access to computerized recordkeeping or information system that assess business tax must annually furnish the Franchise Tax Board, for all businesses subject to tax in the preceding business year: (1) name and address of business; (2) federal employer identification number or owner's name and Social Security number; (3) type of business activity; (4) amount of annual business tax; and (5) any other information prescribed by regulation.[14]

● *Franchise Tax Board.* A reward program for information resulting in identification of unreported or underreported income may be developed by the Franchise Tax Board.[15]

● *Franchise Tax Board.* A cross-reference file to be used as part of non-wage earner filing enforcement program may be developed and maintained by FTB.[16]

● *Debt collection agencies.* Debt collection agencies may be used by the FTB to assist in collection of taxes out-of-state. The agency may refer the debt to legal representatives for collection in the name of the board.[17]

Note: High income data. The Franchise Tax Board can publish as of each December 31 information on the amount of tax paid by individual taxpayers with high total incomes. The total income for this purpose is to be calculated and set forth in two ways: by adding to adjusted gross income any items of tax preference excluded from or deducted in arriving at adjusted gross income, and by subtracting any investment expenses incurred in the production of such income to the extent of the investment income. The data is to include the number of such individuals with total income over $200,000, who owe no state income tax after credits and the deductions, exclusions or credits used by them to avoid tax.[18]

Standards and data used for audit selection. If the disclosure of a requested audit criteria would seriously impair tax assessment, collection or enforcement, the law can't be construed to require the disclosure of stan-

---

(13) § 19551.	**(16)** § 19526.
(14) § 19542—19565.	**(17)** § 19376; 19377.
(15) § 19525.	**(18)** § 19564.

dards used or to be used for audit selection, or data used or to be used in setting standards.[19]

California Parent Locator Service.   The Franchise Tax Board may, upon request of the California Parent Locator Service, disclose to that service pursuant to Welfare & Institutions Cd §§ 11478 and 11478.5, any taxpayer return information that may be of assistance in locating alleged abducting or absent parents, spouses or former spouses in enforcing their liability for child or spousal support, establishing a parent and child relationship, and locating and returning abducted children. Information can only be used for purposes specified in above sections of Welfare and Institutions Code.[20]

California Student Aid Commission.   The California Student Aid Commission may annually inform the Franchise Tax Board of the names and Social Security numbers of (1) all applicants for or recipients of student financial aid; (2) parents of dependent applicants for, or recipients of student financial aid; and (3) spouses of applicants for, and recipients of student aid. Applicants have to authorize this disclosure as part of their student aid application. Upon receipt of the names and social security numbers, the Franchise Tax Board may provide the Student Aid Commission, from state tax returns of the above individuals, their California adjusted gross income, and the California income adjustments necessary to calculate their federal adjusted gross income, or any other information from the state tax return needed to administer the student aid program. Board may audit authorization and report all audit findings to the Commission.[21]

Welfare recipients—names and Social Security numbers.   The State Department of Social Services and the State Department of Health Services must inform the Franchise Tax Board of the names and Social Security numbers of applicants for or recipients of public social service programs. The FTB on receipt of such information may inform those departments of any applicant or recipient who received unearned income within the most recent available tax year as reflected on magnetic tape information returns supplied to the FTB by payers, or on the magnetic tape prepared by the FTB which reflects paper information returns supplied to the FTB by payers. Also, the FTB may provide the departments, from those sources, with the payee's name, Social Security number, and address, and the payer's name or federal employer identification number, and address, and the dollar amount of unearned income and any identifying account numbers. The FTB must return all information received from the departments after completing the information exchange.[22]

---

(19) § 19544.
(20) § 19548.

(21) § 19557.
(22) § 19555.

¶ 345   **Regulations**

Office of Administrative Law. No state agency can issue, use, enforce or attempt to enforce any guideline, order, standard of general application, or any other rule to implement or make specific the law it is required to enforce unless such rules, guidelines or orders have been adopted as regulations and filed with the Secretary of State. If the Office of Administrative Law is notified or learns of any action by a state agency not in compliance with these requirements it may issue a determination that the action taken by the agency is a regulation. It must notify the agency involved, the Governor and the Legislature, and publish its determination in the California Administrative Notice Register. A court or administrative agency need not consider the determination of the Office if the court or administrative agency proceeding:

(1) involves the party that sought the determination;
(2) began before the Office's determination; and
(3) is considering the question of whether the agency action is a regulation.[23]

Franchise Tax Board. The Franchise Tax Board has the power to issue regulations. Absent California regulations on a specific subject, federal regulations are considered persuasive in the interpretation of a California law provision when the California law is substantially identical with the federal code section being interpreted by the federal regulation. In the case of *Rihn v. Franchise Tax Board,* 131 Cal App 2d 356, 280 P2d 593, the California Court of Appeal, 2nd Dist., stated that where federal and state statutes and regulations are substantially identical, the interpretations and effect given them by the federal courts are highly persuasive. When applying the Internal Revenue Code, any reference to regulations prescribed by Secretary of Revenue will not apply if the FTB has adopted and issued regulations. IRC regulations will apply in the absence of state regulations if not in conflict with state law.[24]

¶ 346   **Information Returns**

Every individual, partnership, corporation, joint stock company or association, insurance company, business trust or Massachusetts trust engaged in trade or business in-state, and making payment in the course of such trade or business to another person, including lessees and mortgagors of real or personal property, fiduciaries, employers, and all officers and employees of the state of California, or its political subdivision, or any city organized under a freehold charter, or any political body, not a subdivision or agency of the state, having control, receipt, custody, disposal, or payment of interest, other than bearer coupons, dividends, rents, salaries, wages, premiums, annuities, compensation, remuneration, emoluments, or other fixed or determinable annual or periodical gains, profits and income amounting to $600 or more, paid or payable to any taxpayer must make a verified return to the Franchise Tax Board. Instead of an information return, the Franchise

---

(23) Govt Cd § 11347.5.   **(24)** § 17024.5.

Tax Board may require a copy of the federal information return to be filed. Nonprofit organizations must also make a return.[25] A written statement must be given to each person listed on the return indicating the name, address, and identification number of the person making the return and the aggregate amount of payments by Jan. 31 of the year following the calendar year for which the return was made.

Returns and statements are also required of:

(1) corporations and cooperatives allocating amounts as patronage dividends, rebates or refunds;

(2) brokers;

(3) employers providing group-term life insurance;

(4) corporations transferring shares pursuant to exercise of stock option; starting 1–1–91, California adopts IRC § 6039, and has repealed former Rev & TC § 18802.7;

(5) boat operators with respect to shares of catch by each person performing services; and

(6) heads of state agencies entering into any contract.[26]

Any person required to file an information return with the IRS under IRC § 6042 (payment of dividends), or IRC § 6049 (payment of interest) must report that information to the Franchise Tax Board, and furnish a statement to each person named in the return. A similar requirement applies to issuers of original issue discount bonds.[27] The name and address of the recipient must be furnished.[28]

Copies of federal information returns. The Franchise Tax Board may require that a copy of a federal information return to be filed with it, if a federal information return was required under:

● IRC § 6050H, relating to mortgage interest received in trade or business from individuals, including points paid by borrower or withheld from loan;

● IRC § 6050J, relating to foreclosure and abandonments of security;

● IRC § 6050K, relating to exchanges of certain partnership interests;

● IRC § 6050L, relating to certain dispositions of donated property;

● IRC § 6050N, relating to returns regarding payments of royalties; and

● IRC § 6039C, relating to returns with respect to foreign persons holding direct investments in United States real property interests, if those persons hold direct investment in California real property interest, as defined in Rev & TC § 18662 (interest in real property described in IRC § 897(c)(1)(A)(i) that is located in California).

Every person required to make such returns must furnish a statement to each person required to be named in the return, as required by the IRC. A transferor of partnership interest must notify the partnership of the transfer in accordance with IRC § 6050K(c). The Franchise Tax Board must require a copy of the federal information required to be filed, if a federal information return was required under IRC § 6050I, relating to cash received in trade or

---

(25) § 18637.

(26) § 18640—18646.

(27) § 18639; 18649.

(28) § 18661.

business. The California Attorney-General, on court order following an ex parte showing to a magistrate of articulable suspicion of a felony offense, must be provided a copy of the federal information return filed with the Franchise Tax Board. This return can be made available to a District Attorney. Regulations must require the District Attorney to specify the reasons for its suspicion that a felony offense has been committed. The information received is confidential.[29]

A charitable trust must file information return showing income, deductions, payments to beneficiaries, assets, liabilities and net worth.[30]

Return due date. Information returns must be filed by February 28 with the Franchise Tax Board, P.O. Box 942840, Sacramento, Ca. 94240–2000. Extensions may be granted.[31]

> *Note:* Interest on tax-exempt bonds and other exempt obligations is not subject to information return provisions.

Magnetic tapes—discs. California follows federal Rev Proc 75–20 that spells out the requirements for filing magnetic tapes or discs for payments to nonemployees.

Tax shelter registrants. Tax shelter registrants under IRC § 6111 with the Secretary of Treasury must, if the tax shelter is organized in California, send a duplicate of its registration information to the Franchise Tax Board not later than the day on which the first offering for sale of interests in that shelter occurs. A registrant who receives a tax registration number from the Secretary of Treasury must, within 30 days after the FTB request, file a statement with the FTB of that number. IRC § 6111(b) relating to inclusion of tax shelter identification number on taxpayer's return applies in California.[32]

Tax shelter promoters. Tax shelter promoters must, within 60 days of request, make a complete return to the Franchise Tax Board containing a full identification of each investment sold during the reporting period (each calendar year specified on request of the FTB). The return must provide, for each investment:

> (1) name of investment;
> (2) description of business activities of investment;
> (3) form of investment, such as limited partnership plan, investment plan, or arrangement;
> (4) list of investors showing the full name, address, social security number, and amount invested by each investor during the reporting period;
> (5) total amount invested by all investors during the reporting period; and
> (6) any other related information the FTB may request.

Promoters who make returns must also furnish, within 60 days of the request, to each investor whose name is set forth in the return a written statement showing: (1) the name and address of the person making the

---

(**29**) § 18802.6; 18805; 18645; 18662.
(**30**) § 18635.

(**31**) Regs 18801–18804(a)–18802.1.
(**32**) § 18547.

return; and (2) the aggregate amount of investments of each investor as shown on the return for the reporting period.[33]

Owners and transferors of interest in realty. Owners and transferors of an interest in real property or a mobile home must file a return on written request of the Franchise Tax Board that includes their social security number, or federal identification number, or other identification number prescribed by the FTB, if not an individual, identification of property interest, and any other pertinent information about interest prescribed by regulation. The FTB must give notice of this requirement at least 60 days before the due date of the return. The return requirement doesn't apply to property not assessed by the county assessor, or subject to homeowner's property tax exemption. Failure to file subjects owners and transferors to Rev & TC § 19183 penalty of $50 per failure, up to $10,000 in any calendar year, 10% of aggregate amount without limit in case of intentional disregard, and disallowance of interest, taxes, depreciation and amortization under Rev & TC § 17299.9.[34]

If a transaction involves real property in California, any person required to file a return with the Secretary of the Treasury under IRC § 6045(e), relating to real estate brokers, must send a copy of that return to the Franchise Tax Board at the time set for filing the return with the Secretary. Failure to comply is subject to penalties set out in Rev & TC § 19183.[35]

Brokers and barterers. Brokers and barterers must, when required by the FTB, make a return showing the name and address of each customer, with details as to gross proceeds, and any other information the FTB requires. A person, including a governmental agency, managing a farm for another is not treated as a broker. A written statement must be furnished each customer showing the name and address of the person required to make the return, and the information on the return with respect to the customer. A copy of the return filed with the IRS under IRC § 6045 may be filed instead.[36]

Service recipients. Taxpayers subject to both Bank and Corporation Tax and Personal Income Tax who are engaged in a trade or business, and in the course of such trade or business, pay remuneration to any person for services performed in any calendar year of $600 or more must file a return, and furnish a written statement to the person whose name is required to be set forth on the return, as prescribed by the Franchise Tax Board, setting forth the aggregate amount of such payments, and the names and addresses of the recipients, as required by IRC § 6041A. No return is required if (1) a statement with respect to the services must be furnished under Unemployment Insurance Cd., Div. 6, relating to withholding tax on wages, or Rev &

(**33**) § 18648.
(**34**) § 17299.9; 19183; 18642.

(**35**) § 19183; 18643.
(**36**) § 18641.

TC § 18647, relating to a return by an employer providing a group term life insurance; or (2) with respect to direct sales under IRC § 6041A(b).[37]

Cafeteria plans. Information return requirements apply to these plans. IRC § 6039D sets forth reporting requirements.[38]

Information on licensees. The Franchise Tax Board may require any Board (as defined in Bus. & Prof. Cd. § 22), State Bar, the Department of Real Estate, and Insurance Commissioner to provide the following information with respect to every licensee:

(1) name;
(2) address or addresses of record;
(3) federal employer identification number, if entity is partnership, or owner's name and social security number, for all others;
(4) type of license;
(5) effective date of license or renewal;
(6) expiration date of license;
(7) whether license is active or inactive, if known;
(8) whether license is new or renewal.

A notice may be sent to a licensee failing to provide the identification number. Failure to provide the information within 30 days of notice incurs a $100 penalty payable on notice and demand. Information furnished under Bus. & Prof. Cd. § 30 or Ins. Cd. § 1666.5 is not public or open to public for inspection.[39]

¶ 347   **Taxpayers' Bill of Rights**

Rev & TC §§ 21001–21022 govern the audit, assessment, and collection of personal income taxes by the Franchise Tax Board. The purpose of these provisions is to protect the privacy of taxpayers and their property rights. The Franchise Tax Board is required to establish the position of Taxpayers' Rights Advocate to coordinate the resolution of taxpayers' complaints and problems. The FTB must also establish a taxpayer education and information program. Annually, it must systematically identify areas of taxpayer noncompliance. The performance of FTB officers and employees in contact with taxpayers must be evaluated. Also, a plan must be developed to reduce the time required to resolve refund claims, protests, and appeals. Other important provisions deal with protest hearing procedures, surveillance restriction, and penalties imposed on employees for reckless disregard of FTB procedures.

¶ 348   **Collection Remedies**

The Franchise Tax Board may bring an action to collect tax, use collection agents[40] and file certificate of amount of taxes, interest, penalties, etc. due,

---

(**37**) IRC § 6041A; § 18638.
(**38**) IRC § 125(h); 6652(f).

(**39**) § 19528.
(**40**) § 19371—19377.

and obtain and record judgment on certificate. [1] Other provisions on collection cover lien of tax [2] and warrant for collection.[3]

¶ 349   Collection of Nontax Amounts by the Franchise Tax Board

Child Support.   The Controller of the State of California, is required upon request of a city or county, to withhold from income tax refunds due individual taxpayers, amounts which are owed by the taxpayers for child support, and to cities and counties of the State of California. In addition, the Franchise Tax Board will collect delinquent child support from the obligated parent in the same manner as the collection of a delinquent tax amount due. The collection of child support is not related to a tax return, or refund; rather the collection procedures and apparatus of the Franchise Tax Board will be used to collect amounts referred to it by the State Department of Social Services. For purposes of collecting any child support delinquency from an obligated parent who is out-of-state, the Franchise Tax Board may utilize the procedures and mechanisms which it currently has available for the collection of taxes owed from out-of-state taxpayers.[4]

Department of Industrial Relations.   Effective 7–1–95, the Franchise Tax Board is authorized to collect delinquent fees, wages, penalties, and costs, and any interest thereon, for the Department of Industrial Relations when such amounts due have been assessed pursuant to specific sections of the Labor Code.[5]

Court fines, penalties, forfeitures, restitution fines, and restitution orders.   Commencing 1–1–95, the Franchise Tax Board is authorized to collect fines, state or local penalties, forfeitures, restitution fines, or restitution orders imposed by a superior, municipal, or justice court of the state of California if the amount due, in the aggregate is at least $250 or more. Such collections may be affected in the same manner as the Franchise Tax Board is authorized to collect delinquent personal income tax liabilities, including levy, and withholding orders for taxes. Interest on obligations referred to the Franchise Tax Board accrue interest at the greater amount of (1) interest as provided on the obligation referred to the Board, or (2) the interest which accrues on delinquent tax obligations. If the amount owed is paid to the Franchise Tax Board within 10 days after the date of the notice, interest shall not be added for the period after the date of notice.[6]

Application of amounts collected.   In the event a debtor has more than one debt being collected by the Franchise Tax Board and the amount collected is insufficient to satisfy the total amount owing, the amount collected shall be first applied to the payment of any taxes, additions to tax, penalties, interest, fees, or other amounts due and payable under the personal income tax law commencing with Rev & TC § 17001, or the bank and corporation tax

---

(1) § 19201—19209.

(2) § 19221—19224.

(3) § 19231—19235.

(4) § 19271.

(5) § 19290, as added by Stats. 1994, c. 1117, § 2.

(6) § 19280, as added by Stats. 1994, c. 1242, § 8.

law commencing with Rev & TC § 23001. Any additional collections are to be applied as specified in the Code.[7]

¶ 350   **Relief for Unintentional Nonconformity with New Law**

The Franchise Tax Board, by resolution of the Board, is authorized to waive penalties, or allow the perfection of elections, when there has been unintentional noncompliance with a new statutory provision. Relief can only be made available for the first taxable or income year of the new statutory provision. Such relief can be granted only to those who timely paid taxes and other required amounts shown on the return consistent with the election and who timely filed their return. An election can be perfected where there is substantial evidence with the filed return that the taxpayer intended to make the election and does not include making an election where one was not previously attempted to be made. A new statutory provision includes only a complete newly established tax program, credit, exemption, deduction, exclusion, penalty, or reporting or payment requirement and does not mean amendments made to existing tax provisions that make minor modifications or technical changes.

This provision applies only to resolutions adopted by the FTB between the date of enactment on 9–19–94, and 12–31–94. The resolution granting relief can apply to any year still open for adjustment under the statute of limitations. On or before March 1, 1995, the Franchise Tax Board is to report to the Legislature on the use of this authority.[8]

---

(7) § 19532, as added by Stats. 1994, c. 1243, § 59.

(8) § 18405, as added by Stats. 1994, c. 1243, § 34.

Section III/*Tax Concepts For Individuals and Corporations*

CHAPTER 7

ACCOUNTING, SALES—EXCHANGES, DEDUCTIONS, INVENTORIES

TAX ACCOUNTING

¶ 351 Accounting Period

California conforms to the IRC § 441 rules on the period for computing taxable income.[1] Under IRC § 441, income is computed on the basis of a taxpayer's annual accounting period, which may be either a calendar year or a fiscal year. A fiscal year means an accounting period of 12 months ending on the last day of any month other than December or, if the taxpayer so elects, an annual accounting period varying from 52–53 weeks as explained below. If a taxpayer does not keep books, the taxable income must be computed on the basis of the calendar year. In no event can a tax year cover more than a 12-month period. If an individual operates a business as a sole proprietor, he must report that income and his income from all other sources on the basis of the same tax year.

Taxable year of taxpayer same as federal. A taxpayer's taxable year may not be different from federal, unless initiated or approved by the Franchise Tax Board. Whenever a taxpayer must file a federal return for a period of less than 12 months, that period will be deemed to be a taxable year, and Rev & TC § 17552, relating to termination will apply.[2]

Partnership. A partnership is required to use the same income year as all of its principal partners. If its principal partners are on different reporting years, it is not necessary for a new partnership to obtain approval from the IRS or the Franchise Tax Board regarding the adoption of a calendar or a fiscal year unless the partnership intends to adopt a reporting year which is different from that of the principal partners. California follows Rev Proc 72–51 that shows the partnership how to apply for permission to adopt a different reporting year from that of its principal partners.

First return of a newly organized corporation. The first return of a newly organized corporation may generally be filed on a fiscal year basis without the prior approval of the Internal Revenue Service or the Franchise Tax Board provided the books are kept in accordance with that year-end.

Election of tax year other than required tax year. California has adopted IRC § 444. IRC § 444(c)(1), relating to the effect of the election (required payments) does not apply in California. IRC § 441(c)(2), relating to personal service corporation and IRC § 280H deduction limits applies in California. Generally, a partnership, S corporation, or personal service corporation may elect to have a taxable year other than the required taxable year. Under IRC § 444(b)(1), an election may be made only if the deferral period of the taxable year elected is not longer than three months. In the case of an entity changing a taxable year, an election may be made only if the deferral period of the taxable year is no longer than three months, or the deferral period of the taxable year being changed. The "deferral period" with

---

(1) § 17551; 24631.   (2) § 17565.

respect to any taxable year of the entity means the months between the beginning of such year, and the close of the first required taxable year ending in such year. Any election made under IRC § 444(a) remains in effect until the partnership, S corporation, or personal service corporation changes its taxable year. Any change to a required taxable year may be made without consent of the taxing authorities. If the election is terminated, the partnership, S corporation, or personal service corporation may not make another election. No election may be made with respect to an entity that is part of a tiered structure other than a tiered structure comprising one or more partnerships or corporations all of which have the same taxable year.[3]

52–53-Week year.   California conforms to federal IRC provisions. Under IRC § 441(f), a taxpayer who wants to end his fiscal accounting period on the same day of the week each year may elect to use for reporting purposes a "52–53 Week Year." That day of the week would be: (1) a day that occurs for the last time in a calendar month, or (2) the day which falls nearest to the end of the calendar month. It should be noted that the year may end as many as six days before the end of the month in the first instance or three days before or as many as three days after the end of the month in the second instance. It is important to realize that the due dates of returns are the effective dates of provisions effective for tax years beginning or ending with reference to the first or last day of a specified calendar month. 52–53 week year begins on the first day of the calendar month nearest to the first day of the 52–53 week year and ends on the last day of the calendar month ending nearest to the last day of the 52–53 week year.[4]

Change of accounting period.   California conforms to federal IRC § 442 on change of accounting periods. IRC § 442 requires prior permission of the Commissioner of Internal Revenue and the filing of a return for the short period for a taxpayer to change from one accounting period to another. Such a change will be generally approved if it can be established that there exists a substantial business purpose for making the change. However, approval will not be given where the sole purpose of changing the accounting period is to maintain or obtain a preferential tax treatment. The California Personal Income Tax Law and the Bank and Corporation Tax Law each provide that it is necessary that a taxpayer obtain prior approval to change its accounting period, but the Franchise Tax Board has not issued any form for the application and no time limit within which to file for permission has been established. For federal purposes, the taxpayer files Form 1128, Application to Adopt, Change, or Retain a Tax Year, with the Commissioner of Internal Revenue in Washington, D.C. on or before the 15th day of the second calendar month following the close of the short period required to effect the change. The application requests that the taxpayer state the reasons why the change in period is requested.[5]

---

(3) IRC § 444(a); (b); (d); § 17551; 17551.5; 24637.   **(5)** § 17551; 24633.
(4) § 17551; 24631(f).

IMPORTANT   The Franchise Tax Board will accept Form 1128. When you apply to the Commissioner of Internal Revenue you should send a copy of the same Form 1128 to the Franchise Tax Board. In practice, it is usual that even though no request for approval has been sent to the Franchise Tax Board it will go along with the federal approval or disapproval because California insists that it's the same as that for federal purposes.

When IRS consent isn't needed. A corporation may change its accounting period without obtaining the Internal Revenue Service's prior consent if it meets all of the following tests:

(1) The corporation has not changed its accounting period at any time within ten years ending with the calendar year which includes the short period;

(2) The corporation would not have a net operating loss for the short period;

(3) The taxable income for the short period is annualized and is at least 80% of the taxable income of the preceding taxable year, and

(4) The corporation has the same special status (if any) for the short period and for the tax year immediately preceding the short period. Special status in this instance means a personal holding company (foreign or domestic), an exempt organization or a foreign corporation not engaged in trade or business within the United States.

Note: The California regulations do not include regulations to federal Regulation 1.442–1(c), which provides for the automatic change of period. The Franchise Tax Board would recognize the automatic change since they adopt the federal regulations by reference in California Rev & TC § 17024.5(c) for personal income tax purposes, and Rev & TC § 23051.5(f) for corporate tax purposes, if there are no California regulations. If however, there was a valid reason to retain a different year for California purposes, an application to retain the existing year would have to be separately filed with the Franchise Tax Board.

Partnership. A partnership may change its accounting period without obtaining permission only if all of the partners having an interest of 5% or more in the partnership profits or capital have the same taxable year to which the partnership changes or if all those who do not have such a taxable year change to that year at the same time. This federal regulation applies in California. California law conforms to federal, and the FTB has issued no regulations.[6]

Debtor's estate. A debtor's estate subject to tax under USC, Title 11, § 346(b)(2) may change its annual accounting period once without approval. California allows an estate to change its accounting period once without FTB approval.[7]

Taxpayer using the 52–53 week year. California conforms to IRC § 441(f)(2) that allows taxpayer to switch to or from this special accounting period with the following results: (1) if a change results in the short period of more than 359 days, the short tax period is considered a full tax year; (2) if a change results in the short period of less than seven days, the short tax

---

(6) Fed Reg § 1.442–1; § 17024.5(c).   (7) IRC § 1398(j)(1); § 17556.

period is added to and becomes a part of the following tax year; (3) if a change results in the short period of more than seven days and less than 359 days, the short tax period is considered a short tax year and must be annualized. To do this, it is necessary to multiply the income by 365 days and divide the result by the number of days in the short period. The tax for the short period is the same part of the tax computed on such income placed on an annual basis as the number of days in the short period is of 365 days. Federal Reg 1.441–2 applies.[8]

The general method of computing the tax for a short period because of a change in period is to put the taxable income on an annual basis by multiplying such income by 12 and dividing the result by the number of months in the short period. An individual making a change in period and thus having a short period is not allowed to use the standard deduction for California purposes.

The rule for annualizing income in the short period return applies only to a change in accounting period. It does not apply to the short period return of a new corporation, the final return of a dissolving corporation, the return of a decedent, the first or final return of a decedent's estate, or to a new member of an affiliated group filing a consolidated return for federal purposes. A taxpayer who must annualize income computes tax based on actual income for a 12-month period starting with the first day of the short period and multiplying the tax on that income by a fraction, the numerator of which is the actual taxable income for the short period and the denominator of which is the taxable income for the 12-month period. The tax would be the lesser of the short period tax or this alternative tax. This alternative tax may be based on a period of 12 months ending at the close of the last day of the short period if, at the end of the 12 months referred to above, beginning with the first day of the short period, the taxpayer is not in existence.[9]

TAX TIP   California conforms to IRC § 443.[10] Exceptions to IRC conformity are: (1) Notwithstanding Rev & TC § 17265, a return for period of less than 12 months, required by IRC § 443, must also be made when the Franchise Tax Board terminates taxpayer's taxable year under Rev & TC § 18642, relating to tax in jeopardy; (2) IRC § 443(c) provisions, relating to adjustment in deduction for personal exemption apply to the credit allowed under Rev & TC § 17054 for personal exemptions, dependents and blind persons, instead of the deductions allowed under IRC § 151.[11]

CAUTION   Except for cooperative associations, for income years beginning on or after January 1, 1995, if a short period return is required by Rev & TC § 24634, then the return is due when the federal return is due which includes the net income of the taxpayer for the short period. If no federal return is required to be filed for the period that includes the short period

---

(8) § 17551; 24631(f)(2).
(9) IRC § 443; Fed Reg 1.443–1.
(10) § 17551; 24636.

(11) § 17024.5(a); (b)(18); 17551; 17552; 23051.5; 24634; 24636.

California return, then the California return is due on the fifteenth day of the third month following the close of the short period.[12]

Use of calendar year as taxable year. All partnerships, S corporations, personal service corporations, and trusts (other than tax-exempt and wholly charitable trusts) must change their accounting periods to conform to the taxable years of their owners or beneficiaries. This rule applies for both California and federal purposes. The change of period will be treated as initiated by taxpayers with the consent of the Franchise Tax Board. Any income in excess of expenses for the short period resulting from the change may be taken into account ratably in each of the first four taxable years, including the short year, that starts after 12–31–86, unless the beneficiary, partner or shareholder elects to include all that income in the short year. The spreading of income over four years will not apply unless the taxpayer receives a similar treatment for federal income tax purposes.[13]

For taxable years starting on or after 1–1–87, the adjusted basis of any partner's interest on a partnership or shareholder's stock in an S corporation must be determined as if all of the income to be taken into account ratably in the four taxable years referred to in Rev & TC § 17551.5(b) or 24633.5(b) were included in gross income for the first of those taxable or income years. If any interest in a partnership or stock in an S corporation is disposed of before the last taxable or income year of the spread period, all amounts which would be included in the gross income of the partner or shareholder for later taxable or income years in the spread period under Rev & TC § 17551.5(b) or 24633.5(b) and attributable to the stock or interest disposed of must be included in gross income for the taxable or income year in which the disposition occurs.[13]

¶ 352   **Accounting Methods**

The two principal methods of accounting for tax purposes are the cash receipts and disbursements method (which is commonly called the "cash" basis) and the accrual basis. If income is solely from wages, it is not necessary to keep a set of accounting books. The information and the method may be established from the tax returns filed, your deposit slips and similar financial records. If a taxpayer is engaged in two or more separate and distinct businesses, it is possible to use a different method of accounting for each of them; that is, you may use a cash basis for one and the accrual method for the other.[14]

TAX TIP   Ordinarily, a combination of accounting methods is permitted by the tax authorities if it clearly reflects income and is used on a consistent basis. For example, the accrual basis may be used for purchases and sales while the cash basis may be used for all other income and expense items.

---

(12) § 18601, as amended by Stats. 1994, c. 35, § 1.   **(14)** IRC § 446.
(13) IRC § 267; 269; 441; 645; 706; 1378;
§ 17024.5; 17551.5; 24633.5.

However, if the cash basis is used in figuring business gross income, it must also be used in figuring business expenses. Or, if the accrual basis is used for business expenses, it must also be used for items involving business gross income.[15]

Note: California has adopted IRC § 446–447 rules on accounting methods. If a taxpayer does not file with the authorities a request to change method of accounting, the absence of the authorities' consent to the change will not be taken into account to prevent the imposition of any penalty, or the addition of any amount to tax, or to diminish the amount of the penalty or addition to tax.[16] California has adopted the 1987 changes to IRC § 447, relating to family farm corporations required to use the accrual method of accounting. These changes allow a family farm corporation that has gross receipts of $25 million or less to use the cash, instead of the accrual method of accounting. A family corporation is defined as any corporation if at least 50% of the total combined voting power of all classes of stock entitled to vote, and at least 50% of all other classes of stock of the corporation, are owned by members of the same family. The gross receipts test involves taking into account the applicable percentage of gross receipts of any other member of a controlled group of corporations. Special rule applies to family farm corporation's holdings in pass-thru entities such as partnerships, estates and trusts, etc. The suspense account rules of IRC § 447 also apply to these corporations.[17]

Cash method. Under the cash method of accounting, income is reported for the year when it is actually or constructively received either in the form of cash or other property. Deductions are taken for the year in which they are actually paid in the usual sense. However, certain items such as depreciation and prepaid expenses for a tax basis taxpayer may be deducted in the year other than that in which the actual cash is paid. This is not true for income, however. Income must be reported in the year in which it is received.[18]

Constructive receipt. A cash basis taxpayer may be required to include in income in any year the amount of income "constructively" received. This is income which the taxpayer does not actually possess but which is within his control and disposition as to the time of actual receipt. Money which is subject to the taxpayer's command is constructively received whether he actually accepts it or not. Income cannot be shifted to another year by refusing to accept payment which has been properly offered under the arrangements in effect. For example, an employee would be considered to have constructively received his salary if the money is credited to him and he can draw upon it at any time even though he has not in fact reduced it to his possession. Similarly, interest on bank savings accounts is to be included in income in the year in which the bank credits it to the depositor's account even though the depositor may not receive the entry for the interest until the following quarter.[19]

---

(15) Fed Reg No. 1.446–1(c)(iv).
(16) § 17024.5; 17551; 23051.5; 24651.1.
(17) § 24652(b).

(18) Fed Reg No. 1.446–1(c)(i).
(19) Fed Reg No. 1.451–2.

¶ 352

Limitations on the cash method.   California has adopted IRC § 448 which provides that the cash method of accounting cannot be used by a tax shelter, a C corporation, a partnership with a C corporation as a partner, or certain trusts. Exceptions are provided for corporations in the farming business, qualified personal service corporations, and certain types of businesses with average annual gross receipts that do not exceed $5 million for the taxable three-year period ending with the prior taxable year. These exceptions to the general rule do not apply to tax shelters. Any adjustments due to the change from the cash method are to be taken into account over a period generally not to exceed four years.[20]

Accrual basis.   Accrual basis taxpayers include in gross income all income which accrues during the year. In other words, all income which is earned as compared to income which has been earned but not payable to the recipient. Such income accrues when all events have occurred that fix the right to receive it and the amount can be reasonably estimated. When a reasonable estimate is made, any difference in the estimated and the actual amount is to be taken into income in the year of the exact determination.[21]

TAX TIP   The accrual method must be used for purchases and sales in a trade or business in which inventories are acquired to be maintained, except in instances when the taxpayer is authorized by the Internal Revenue Service and/or the Franchise Tax Board to use another method to clearly reflect the proper amount of income.

Method must reflect income.   Whichever accounting method is used, that is, the cash or accrual method or a hybrid method, it must clearly reflect income in the particular taxpayer's situation.[22]

Change of accounting method.   Once a particular method of accounting is clearly established for tax purposes, it cannot be changed to another method, without the prior consent of the Commissioner of Internal Revenue and the Franchise Tax Board. It is true even when the new method is appropriate and would in fact clearly reflect the proper amount of income under methods permitted by the Code and the Regulations. Form 3115 is provided by the Treasury Department and it must be filed with the Commissioner of Internal Revenue, Washington, D.C. within 180 days after the start of the year in which the change is effected.[23] When the application has been filed for federal purposes, it is deemed to have been filed for California purposes as well. However, the FTB has issued instructions that it will accept a copy of Form 3115. You may file a copy of Form 3115 with the Franchise Tax Board at the same time you file one with the Commissioner of Internal Revenue.[24]

---

(20) IRC § 448; § 17024.5; 17551; 23051.5; 24651; 24654.
(21) Fed Reg No. 1.446–1(c)(ii).
(22) IRC § 446(b).
(23) Fed Reg No. 1.446–1(e)(3).
(24) § 17551; 24651.

¶ 352

TAX TIP	It might be more practical to file the Form 3115 with the Commissioner of Internal Revenue. And when you obtain approval from the Commissioner for the change in method, send a request to the Franchise Tax Board for a similar change and cite the fact that you have obtained permission from the Internal Revenue Service. The approval of the Franchise Tax Board then would be automatic because the FTB insists that you be on the same basic method for state and federal purposes.
TAX TIP	The Franchise Tax Board requires a taxpayer to initially adopt the same accounting methods for California purposes as are adopted for federal tax reporting purposes. If a request for change is filed with the Internal Revenue Service, California Rev & TC § 17024.5(d)(1) deems that the federal application shall be a proper election for California purposes, unless otherwise provided in the California Code or regulation issued by the Franchise Tax Board. California has not issued regulations with respect to a change in accounting method so that the federal regulations apply for California purposes. If the taxpayer desires to change an accounting method only for federal purposes, an application must be filed with the Franchise Tax Board to retain the existing method for California purposes.

What are accounting method changes. A change in the method of accounting includes a change in the overall method of accounting for items of gross income or deductions, but it also includes a change in the treatment of any material item. This would be any item which involves the proper time for the inclusion of an item in income or the taking of a deduction. It is necessary to obtain consent even in instances when the change is made from an unacceptable method of accounting to an acceptable method. Some of the changes in accounting methods which are specified include the following:

- Change from the cash to an accrual method or vice versa;
- Change from the cash or accrual method to a method for long-term contracts or vice versa;
- Change in the method or the basis used in valuing inventories;
- Change in any specialized method of figuring taxable income such as the crop method; and
- Change in the treatment of any other material item of income or expense.

Not accounting method changes. A change in the method of accounting does not include the correction of mathematical or posting errors or errors in the computation of tax liabilities. Also, a change in the method of accounting does not include adjustment of any item of income or deduction which does not involve the proper time or the inclusion of the item of income or the taking of a deduction. For example, corrections of items that are deducted as interest or salary or which are in fact payments of dividends and of items that are deducted as business expenses but which are in fact personal expenses are not changes in the method of accounting. In addition, a change in the method of accounting does not include an adjustment with respect to the addition to a reserve for bad debts or any adjustment in the useful life of a depreciable asset. Even though this type of adjustment involves the question of the proper time for the taking of a deduction, such items are traditionally corrected by adjustments in the current year but a taxpayer's request for a change in his accounting *practice* with respect to a material item or to change any other accounting method will receive favorable consideration if the taxpayer agrees to take the resulting adjustment into account ratably over a ten-year period.[25]

Adjustments required by change. A change in the method of reporting requires an adjustment to avoid duplication or omission of items of income or deductions. The income of the year of change would consist of income computed under the new method and also adjustments to pick up the variations between the new and the old methods. Ordinarily, unless there is a specific requirement otherwise, the entire adjustment is made in the year of change, if the total is not more than $3,000. If the adjustments increase taxable income in the changeover year by more than $3,000, you may reduce your tax through one of two methods, whichever gives the lower tax.[26]

TAX TIP

These methods are: (1) *Three-year spread.* The increase in tax in the changeover year is limited to the sum of the tax increases that would occur if the increased income from the change were prorated over the tax year and the two preceding years. (2) *Spread under new accounting method.* If the taxpayer establishes his taxable income under the new method for one or more tax years consecutively preceding the changeover year, the tax is reduced by the amount of tax that would have been paid if the tax for those preceding years were figured under the new method and the then remaining adjustments were allocated to the changeover year.

If the accounting method change is initiated by the taxpayer, all adjustments must be taken into account. If, however, the change in the method of accounting is involuntary (that is, required by the Internal Revenue Service), the adjustments apply after 1953.

Note: Consent of the IRS and the Franchise Tax Board is not required under the following circumstances: (1) when the installment method is adopted, changed to or discontinued but consent is required if a new election is made within five years of discontinuance; (2) when a subsidiary corporation must change its method to conform to that of the consolidated group of which it is a member; (3) when changing from the declining balance to the straight line depreciation method; and (4) when changing to accrual method to avoid the recapture of deducted farm losses as ordinary income.

If your change in accounting method involves the depreciation method, a simplified procedure has been adopted by the Internal Revenue Service. Form 3115 should be filed within the first 180 days of the tax year which is the normal requirement but it should be filed with the Service Center where you file your tax return rather than with the Commissioner's office in Wash-

---

(25) Fed Reg No. 1.446–1(e)(2).   (26) Fed Reg No. 1.481–1–1.481–2.

ington, D.C. If Form 3115 is timely filed, the consent of the Commissioner is automatic.

Through an administrative procedure the Commissioner has established a method to be followed when adjustments to be made are only those which are based on 1954 Internal Revenue Code years.

TAX TIP

The Franchise Tax Board has adopted all of the above provisions with respect to changes in method of accounting, except that in the instance of involuntary changes, the adjustments are to be made only to the extent that they are based on income years beginning in 1955 rather than 1954. By adopting the procedures set forth in Rev Proc 64–16 and 70–27 the FTB has also set a time limit of 180 days for a corporate application for change of method.

California follows federal Rev Proc 67–10 on change from cash to accrual method. It also follows Rev Proc 80–51 specifying the general procedure for obtaining consent to a change of accounting method, Rev Proc 82–19, and Rev Proc 82–32 on change of method of deducting vested vacation pay to the year of accrual.

Change of status—resident or nonresident. California requires that in determining income from sources within or without the state, income and deductions accrued before the change in status must be reported to California if California is the state of residence prior to the change in status. If the taxpayer is not a California resident prior to the change then income which is not California source income accrued prior to California residence is not reported to California, and the deductions are not allowable for determining California income if accrued prior to the change in status. The time for reporting the income or deductions does not chage and is based on the taxpayer's previously adopted accounting method.[27]

EXAMPLE

Cash basis taxpayer is a resident of Nevada prior to December 1, 1991, and a California resident thereafter. Salary income earned from Nevada sources during November, 1991, but received in January, 1992 is not California income since it was accrued prior to the change in status. However, it continues to be a 1992 item included for federal purposes and reflected as an exclusion adjustment in determining 1992 California income.

If the taxpayer were a California resident prior to the change in status, and became a Nevada resident on December 1, 1992, income earned in November, 1991, but received in January, 1992 would be California source income. A 1992 California return would be required from the taxpayer to report the income even though the taxpayer was no longer a resident of California in 1992. The income had accrued while the taxpayer was a California resident.

¶ 353   Taxable Year of Inclusion of Items of Gross Income

Generally speaking, the amount of any item of gross income is to be included in the taxable year in which received by the taxpayer unless under the

---

(27) § 17554.

method of accounting used such amount is to be properly accounted for in a different period. California laws conform to this federal rule.[28]

TAX TIP

Advance payments. Generally, amounts which are paid for future services without restriction as to the use of the funds by the recipient are income when received *whether the taxpayer is on the cash or the accrual basis.* An accrual basis taxpayer, however, may defer reporting such advance payments until the year following the year of payment *if under the agreement the services is to be performed by that time.* If any part of the services is not performed by that time, the entire amount must nevertheless be included in gross income in that succeeding year regardless of when the services are performed. California follows federal Rev Proc 71–21.

"Claim of right" theory. A for-profit trade association received fees from its members in one year but did not include them in income for that year. On the "accrual" basis, the association included the amounts in income in the following year when it began rendering services to its members. The Board of Equalization upheld the Franchise Tax Board in stating that the income had been received in the first year and was reportable then under the "claim of right" theory. *Appeal of Western Outdoor Markets, SBE 1–4–72; Affd. 10–7–74.*

Fees under terminable contracts. An accrual basis taxpayer earns its income from selling fast food franchises and providing services and supplies to franchisees. The franchise fees were received and deposited in the taxpayer's checking account without any restriction as to their use. The Board of Equalization said that the fees were income when received even though if no suitable location for a fast food outlet was found in 24 months, either party could terminate the contract and the fee would be returned. *Appeal of Der Wienerschnitzel International, Inc., SBE 4–10–79; Affd. 6–28–79.*

Interest. Interest is taxable when actually or constructively received for a cash basis taxpayer as indicated above. Accrual basis taxpayers report interest for the year in which it accrues unless it is received in an earlier period.

Original issue discount. California conforms to IRC § 454(a) which provides that when a noninterest-bearing obligation is issued at a discount, a cash basis taxpayer may elect to report annually the increment in the redemption price rather than reporting the entire amount in the year of sale or redemption. An accrual basis taxpayer would be required to pick up the annual increase—the election is not available to him. The obligation can be issued by a corporation or government agency, but it principally applies to Series E bonds of the U.S. Treasury.[29]

---

(28) IRC § 451(a); § 17551; 24661.   **(29)** § 17551; 24674(a).

California adopts the IRC § 454(b) rule that for government issues maturing in one year or less, the option is not available for either cash or accrual taxpayers.[30]

California has not adopted IRC § 454(c) that permits holders of matured U.S. Savings bonds who hold such bonds to maturity, and under Treasury regulations retain investment in such bonds in U.S. obligation other than current income obligation, or exchange such bond for another nontransferable obligation of the U.S. in exchange upon which gain or loss is not recognized to include the increase in redemption value in gross income for the taxable year of redemption or final maturity.[31]

California has adopted the provisions of Subchapter P, Part V of the Internal Revenue Code, §§ 1271–1288 that contain special rules for bonds and other debt instruments. California Personal Income Tax Law makes the following modifications:

(1) IRC § 1275(a)(3) defining tax-exempt obligations does not apply in California; the term "tax-exempt obligations" means obligations the interest of which is exempt from tax under the California Personal Income Tax Law;

(2) IRC § 1272 is modified by providing that, for California purposes, for taxable years starting on or after 1–1–87, and before the tax year in which the debt obligation matures or is sold, exchanged, or otherwise disposed, the amount included in gross income shall be the same as that included in gross income on the federal return, and the difference between the federal and California gross income inclusions, with respect to obligations issued after 12–31–84, for taxable years starting before 1–1–87, must be included in gross income in the taxable year in which the debt obligation matures, or is sold, exchanged or otherwise disposed;

(3) starting in 1989, IRC § 7872, relating to treatment of loans with below market interest rates will apply, with the exception of the 1989 Support for East European Democracy (SEED) Act, § 307;

(4) starting 6–11–87, IRC § 1286(d), relating to special rules for tax-exempt obligations, will apply in California. The California Bank and Corporation Tax Law makes similar conforming provisions and modifications, and also applies IRC § 1272 to obligations issued on or after the first day of the taxpayer's income year starting on or after 1–1–87.[32] Federal regulations provide that the term "other evidence of indebtedness" includes certificates of deposit, time deposits, bonus plans and other deposit arrangements of banks, savings and loan institutions and similar financial institutions etc.

Money market certificates. The Internal Revenue Service has reversed its original and secondary positions on so-called "money-market certificates," which are time deposit certificates similar to, and with interest rates based on, six-month Treasury bills. The present rule for obligations issued after 1978 indicates that no interest would be constructively received prior to the date of the certificate's maturity. The California Franchise Tax Board has announced that it would follow the same policy.

Dividends. Dividends are subject to tax for a cash basis taxpayer when they are actually or constructively received. If a dividend is payable on

---

(30) IRC § 454(b); § 17551; 24674(b).
(31) § 17553.

(32) § 18151; 18177; 18178; 18180; 23051.5; 24990–24994.

December 31st, but the payor corporation puts the dividend in the mail and the taxpayer does not receive it until January, the dividend is January income because there would be no "constructive receipt" in December.

Rents. Rent is taxable when received by a cash basis taxpayer. However, rent accrues ratably over the period of the lease as income for an accrual basis taxpayer unless it is paid in advance. See also discussion of "deferred payments for use of property or services" below.

Income from prepaid subscriptions. California conforms to IRC § 455, with one exception (see "Note" below). Under IRC § 455, income from subscriptions for a cash basis taxpayer is income in the year in which it is received. An accrual basis publisher may elect to report prepaid subscriptions over the subscription period instead of reporting it all in the year in which it is received. The election applies to all prepaid subscriptions of the trade or business for which it is made. However, a special provision indicates that income which will be earned within 12 months of receipt may be either included in the election or reported in the year received. The election can be made for federal and also California purposes without obtaining prior consent for the first tax year subscription income is received if a statement is attached to the return with the details relating to the prepaid income. Otherwise, it is necessary to file an application to the Commissioner of Internal Revenue in Washington within 90 days after the beginning of the first year to which the election is to apply.[33]

> *Note:* An application for permission to use the elective method is also required by the California Franchise Tax Board, but no provision is made in the laws for a limitation on the period within which to make the application.

Repayment of income previously reported. For federal purposes, if a cash basis taxpayer receives income without restriction as to its disposition under a claim of right, it is income in the year received. This is proper even though the taxpayer's right to retain the income may be disputed and all or part of it may have to be repaid in a later year. If, in fact, the taxpayer is required to repay the income previously reported, he is entitled to a deduction for the amount of the payment for the year paid. If the amount of repayment exceeds $3,000, the taxpayer may recompute his tax for the earlier year after eliminating the amount of the income reported. In that case, the tax of the repayment year is figured without the deduction minus the decrease in tax for the prior year due to the exclusion of the repaid item. If the decrease in tax for the prior year is greater than the tax due for the repayment year, the excess is refunded or credited as an overpayment for the repayment year.[34]

(**33**) § 17551; 24676.   (**34**) IRC § 1341.

TAX TIP	California has not adopted IRC § 1341, so the year of payment is when the deduction would be taken for California.

Blocked foreign income. Taxpayers having income from foreign countries which have monetary or exchange restrictions which prevent the conversion of foreign currency into U.S. dollars can elect to defer the tax until the conversion can be made or the conversion is actually made. The tax could also be deferred until the income is used for non-deductible personal expenses or disposed of by way of gift, bequest, device or inheritance or by dividend or other distribution. In order to make the election the taxpayer files with his federal income tax return a separate return using the same type of form reporting the deferrable income and declaring that it will be included in income when it is no longer deferrable. The election must be made no later than the due date for filing the return (including any extension) for the first year for which the election will apply.[35]

IMPORTANT	The Franchise Tax Board will accept the same federal information and election to permit the postponement of the time to report the income. However, in the case of a combined group of corporations reporting on a unitary return, the blocked funds should be included in income used in the computation of the tax. In addition, the property, payroll, and sales factors of the foreign affiliate having the blocked income should be included in the allocation formula in the normal manner. This treatment follows the Franchise Tax Board's traditional concept that the only income taxed in a combined report is that portion of the total income which is derived from California sources.

Membership organizations—prepaid dues income. California Personal Income Tax Law has adopted IRC § 456 that allows membership organizations on an accrual basis that have liability to render services or make available membership privileges over a period of time not exceeding 36 months to include prepaid dues income in gross income ratably over that period of time. When the taxpayer's liability ceases, so much of the prepaid dues income that was not includible in gross income for the preceding taxable years must be included in gross income for the taxable year the liability ends. A similar rule applies to the year of taxpayer's cessation.[36]

Deferred compensation salary reduction plans of state and local government employees. California Personal Income Tax Law has adopted IRC § 457 that allows state and local government or tax-exempt rural electric cooperative to establish a deferred compensation plan under which part of an employee's compensation is not taxed until distributed or made available on separation from service, or in the event of an unforeseeable emergency. The maximum that can be deferred each year is the lesser of $7,500 or one-third of the employee's compensation. This amount may be increased in one

(35) IRC § 964(b)–(c); Reg 1.964–3. (36) § 17551.

or more of the last three years of the participant's employment to the lesser of $15,000, or the sum of the plan ceiling amount plus the unused ceiling amounts for previous years.[36]

Magazines, paperbacks and records returned. California conforms to IRC § 458 treatment. Accrual basis taxpayer may elect not to include in gross income for the taxable year the income attributable to the qualified sale of any magazine, paperback or record returned before the close of the merchandise return period. This return period is the two months and 15 days first occurring after close of taxable year in case of magazines. For paperbacks and records, the period is the four months and 15 days first occurring after the close of the taxable year. The election applies to the taxable year made and all later taxable years until the taxpayer gets a consent to revocation. Taxpayers must establish a suspense account in case of paperbacks and records instead of applying change of accounting rules.[37]

Deferred payments for use of property or services. California has adopted IRC § 467.[38]

Rental and interest income attributable to a deferred rental agreement (or IRC § 467 rental agreement) must be reported and deducted as if both parties were on the accrual method of accounting. Generally, a deferred rental payment agreement is any agreement for the use of tangible property involving more than $250,000 in rental payments under which either: (1) at least one amount is allocable to the use of property during a calendar year which is to be paid after the close of the next calendar year, or (2) there are increases in the amount of rent to be paid under the agreement. The rules will apply if payment of rent is in a lump sum at the end of the lease term unless the term is no more than two years or if the rents are stepped (small in the early years, large in the later years), unless the parties can show the absence of a tax-avoidance motive.

Tax-avoidance test. IRC § 467 uses a presumptive tax-avoidance test under which rents payable under the lease are leveled. That is, the parties must take into account annually the "constant rental amount" and interest on unpaid rentals from prior years. The test applies to "disqualified leasebacks or long-term agreements"—IRC's § 467 rental agreements under which the leaseback or rental term exceeds 75% of the recovery period for such property and such increasing (or stepped) rentals are principally tax-avoidance motivated. IRC § 467 provides safe harbors for rental increases based on CPI formulas, reasonable rent holidays, percentage-of-receipts formulas and changes in additional rent amounts paid to unrelated third parties (under net leases). Lessors who pass the tax-avoidance test are subject to a special recapture provision on disposition of the leased property. Any gain realized will be ordinary income to the extent rent accruals, that would have been taken into account had the rent leveling provision applied, exceed actual accruals to the date of transfer.

---

(37) IRC § 458; § 17551; 24676.5.   (38) § 24688.

Constant rental amount. Generally, the amount includible in any taxable year is that portion of the constant rental amount and that portion of the annual interest amount allocable to that taxable year. The term "constant rental amount" is the amount which, if paid as of the close of each lease period (the 12-month period beginning on the first day the agreement applies) would have a present value (using a discount rate of 110% of the applicable federal rate), equal to the present value of the aggregate payments required. The lessor must report and the lessee must deduct an annual interest amount, at a rate equal to 110% of the applicable federal rate compounded semi-annually, equal to the sum of the constant rental amount over payments made during the lease period plus any unpaid annual interest amount as of the close of the lease period for any preceding year. So payments will occur either at the end of the lease (lump-sum payments) or on an incremental basis in period when rent exceeds the constant rental amount (step-rental agreement).

Long-term contracts. California has adopted the IRC § 460 special rules for long-term contracts. California taxpayers must, as a general rule, account for long-term contracts under the percentage-of-completion method of accounting. The completed contract method may not be used. Under the percentage of completion method, instead of recognizing income and costs from the long-term contract as the contract is being completed, taxpayers can elect to postpone recognition until the first income year in which at least 10% of the contract costs have been incurred by the end of the year. Before 1990, California required either a percentage-of-completion method or the percentage-of-completion capitalized cost method. Under the current rules, adjustments to income must be made on completion of the contracts to correct any overreporting or underreporting.[39]

For purposes of applying IRC § 460(b)(2)(3)(4) and (5), relating to the lookback method, any adjustment in income computed shall be deemed to have been reported in the taxable year from which the adjustment arose, not the taxable year of completion. Long-term contract cost allocation rules also apply to past-service pension costs under California law for taxable or income years starting on or after 1–1–90.[40]

In general, California also requires that all costs that directly benefit or are incurred because of a long-term contract are to be allocated to the contract in accordance with the regulations that currently apply to extended period long-term contracts. Moreover, additional general and administrative costs attributable to cost-plus contracts and to federal government contracts requiring certification of costs are treated as contract costs. Some types of costs which include "independent research and development costs," expenses incurred in making unsuccessful bids and proposals, and marketing, selling, and advertising expenses are considered current deductions rather than capitalized expenditures.

---

(39) IRC § 460; § 17024.5; 24673.2.   **(40)** § 17564.

In addition, any incorrect total cost or income estimates using the above long-term contract methods will generally give rise to interest liabilities or income (look-back rule) upon completion of the contract. The completion percentage cannot be determined on the basis of the estimated percentage of work completed.

An exception from the long-term contract rules and the cost allocation rules (except for the production interest rules) provides that these rules are not to apply to contracts for the construction or improvement of real property if the contract (1) is expected to be completed within the two-year period beginning on the commencement date, and (2) is performed by a taxpayer with average annual gross receipts of $10 million or less for the three tax years preceding the tax year in which the contract is entered into. Gross receipts of all commonly controlled trades or businesses (including partnerships and proprietorships) and members of a controlled group of corporations during the three years are taken into account.

Utility services. California has adopted the provisions of IRC § 451(f), that requires utilities to include sales in gross income in year services were provided to customers.[1]

¶ 354 Taxable Year for Taking Deductions

Generally. Generally, deductions may be taken by a taxpayer on the cash basis in the year in which payment is made in cash or the equivalent of cash.

An accrual basis taxpayer takes a deduction at the time the expense accrues.

California has adopted the IRC § 461(h) rules on satisfaction of "all-events" test when economic performance occurs.[2]

Except as provided in the IRS Regulations, economic performance is determined as follows:

● If payment is made to another person for services or property provided economic performance occurs when the items are provided;
● If payment must be made for the use of property, economic performance occurs as it's used;
● If the taxpayer must provide property or services, economic performance occurs when the taxpayer so provides;
● If payments arise under any workers' compensation act, tort, and contract to provide benefits to employees, economic performance occurs as the payments are made.

Exceptions are made for certain recurring items (generally paid within 8½ months of year end that are either immaterial or better match expense to income), as well as items for which the tax law provides specific timing rules. They include: accrual of vacation pay; qualified discount coupons; and any other provision of the tax law which provides a reserve for estimated

---

(1) IRC § 451(f).   (2) IRC § 461(a); (c); (h); § 17551; 24681; 24686.2.

expenses. Presumably, payments to qualified retirement plans are generally recurring items.

Disputed liabilities.   California conforms to federal rules.[3] Under IRC § 461(f), if an accrual basis taxpayer disputes his liability to pay a certain amount, the deduction is generally postponed until the dispute is settled between the parties or by the courts. If, however, the taxpayer pays the disputed amount, he is entitled to take a deduction in the year of the payment even though the liability is still being contested. When the dispute is settled an adjustment is made as an increase or decrease in income in the year of settlement. Cash basis taxpayers may deduct a disputed liability in the year of payment. For either the accrual taxpayer or a cash basis taxpayer "payment" includes depositing the disputed amount in an escrow account. IRC § 461(h) economic performance test for accruals also applies to disputed liabilities.

Vacation pay.   For income and taxable years starting on or after 1–1–90, California picks up the 1987 OBRA § 10201 repeal of IRC § 81 and IRC § 463.[4] Before 1990, California followed IRC § 463, as amended by the 1986 TRA that provided that accrual basis employers could elect to accrue and deduct vacation pay when earned by their employees even though the employees did not take the vacation or receive vacation pay until a subsequent year. (Vacation pay did not include holiday or sick pay.)

Current federal law provides that the vacation pay deduction for any taxable or income year is generally limited to the amount of vacation pay earned during the year to the extent that the amount is paid to employees during the year, or the amount is vested as of the last day of the tax year, and is paid to the employees within two and one-half months after the end of the taxable or income year. Vacation pay earned during any taxable or income year, but not paid to employees within two and one-half months after the end of the taxable or income year, is deductible in the year in which it is paid to the employees.

In the case of taxpayers who elected the deduction for their last taxable year before 1990, and must change their method of accounting, the change is treated as initiated by the taxpayer with the consent of the Franchise Tax Board. The adjustments that must be taken into account because of the change of method must be taken into account over a two-year period, unless the provisions governing the change of method call for a shorter period. The adjustments are reduced by the balance in the taxpayer's suspense account.[4]

Taxes.   A cash basis taxpayer can deduct taxes. However, the deduction is limited to the amount of tax actually paid during the year. Accrual basis taxpayers deduct taxes as they accrue. The discussion above with respect to contested items, specifically applies to tax liabilities.[5]

---

(3) § 17551; 24684; 24686.2.
(4) § 17094; 17551; 17563; 24685.

(5) IRC § 461(c).

Property taxes. Generally, property taxes accrue on the date liability for the tax becomes fixed. This is usually called the assessment date or the lien date set up by the appropriate tax law and is generally the date on which the owner becomes personally liable for the taxes. As indicated above, a cash basis taxpayer deducts property taxes, including real property taxes, in the year in which they are paid. An accrual basis taxpayer will deduct the taxes during the year in which the lien date or the assessment date falls. However, both the IRC § 461(c) and the California tax laws[6] provide that an accrual basis taxpayer may elect to accrue and deduct real property taxes over the period for which the tax is imposed. It is not required that consent be obtained from the tax authorities for the first tax year in which the taxpayer incurs real property taxes if the election is made by the time for filing returns for the tax year (including extensions). For adoption at any other time, it is necessary that a written request be filed with the Internal Revenue Service not later than 90 days after the start of the tax year to which the election applies. This should be accompanied by a computation of the deduction for the first year of the election and any other information necessary to explain the deduction. Both the California Personal Income Tax Law and the Bank and Corporation Tax Law provide that an accrual basis taxpayer may, with the consent of the Franchise Tax Board, make an election under this section at any time. The laws do not specify how the request is to be submitted or the time limit or whether any other information is required.

TAX TIP   For California purposes, the tax authorities' fiscal year runs from July 1 to June 30 each year and the lien date or the assessment date is March 1 of each year. The accrual basis taxpayer, therefore, by making the election may defer the deduction for real property taxes accrued on March 1 of a given year to the period commencing the following July 1 and ending the subsequent June 30. The taxpayer is allowed to pay real property taxes in two installments without penalty. The first installment would be due not later than December 10 of the year following the March 1 lien date and the second installment would be due April 10 in the subsequent year.[7]

Interest. California conforms to IRC § 461(g). Under IRC § 461(g), as with other expenses, the taxpayer on the cash basis deducts interest when it is actually paid and an accrual basis taxpayer deducts interest as it accrues ratably over the period. However, if the interest is paid in advance, and chargeable to a period after the close of the taxable year in which it is paid, a cash basis taxpayer must capitalize the interest and deduct it in the proper period of the loan. Bank and Corporation law also conforms to federal.[8] California also follows the IRC § 461(g)(2) rule which indicates that "points" paid on a mortgage incurred in connection with the purchase or improvement of a taxpayer's *principal residence* can be fully deducted in the year of

---

(6) § 17551; 24681(b).   (8) § 17551; 23051.5.
(7) § 17551; 23051.5.

¶ 354

payment provided that this payment of points is an established business practice in the area in which such indebtedness is incurred and the amount of such payment does not exceed the amounts generally charged for home loans in that area. (see ¶ 325).

Bad debts. Bad debts are deductible in the year in which they become worthless.

Losses. Losses are deductible in the year sustained. They must be evidenced by closed and completed transactions fixed by identifiable events.

Loss deductions limited to amounts at risk. California has adopted the IRC § 465 at risk rules as applied to the activity of holding real property. An exception is made for real estate losses to the effect that certain qualified nonrecourse financing is treated as an amount at risk. In case of nonrecourse financing from related persons, terms of loan must be commercially reasonable and on substantially the same terms as loans involving unrelated persons. IRC § 465 limits a taxpayer's loss to the amount that the taxpayer has at risk in a venture. The provisions apply to individuals, tax option corporations and personal holding companies. For California purposes, it would apply only to individuals inasmuch as California does not follow federal with respect to tax option corporations or personal holding companies. The amount which a taxpayer has at risk in a venture consists of the money and the adjusted basis of any other property contributed to the activity as well as loans to the extent to which the investor is personally liable or for which property has been pledged (other than property used in the activity). Any arrangement by which the taxpayer is protected against loss by insurance, non-recourse financing, guarantees, stop loss agreements or similar arrangements, are not considered to be at risk. Any loss which exceeds the risk investment is treated as a deduction allocable to the activity in the first succeeding taxable year and in that year it is also subject to the risk limits. California has adopted the federal rule excluding from the at-risk rules active closely held businesses.[9]

When at risk rules apply. At risk rules apply to all activities engaged in as a trade or business or for the production of income except the leasing of equipment by a closely held corporations (one with five or fewer stockholders owning more than 50% of the stock) if 50% or more of its gross receipts are attributable to equipment leasing.

Passive activity losses and credits—limits. California has adopted IRC § 469, that sets limits on losses and credits from passive activity. California has also adopted federal rules repealing the phase-out of deduction equivalent (credit limitation) for persons with AGI over $200,000. California has also adopted the following federal provisions:

(1) definition of portfolio income (IRC § 469(e)(1)(A));

---

(9) IRC 465; § 17024.5(b)(1); (3); 17551.

(2) deduction of suspended passive activity losses upon disposition of entire interest in passive activity (IRC § 469(g)(1));

(3) rental real estate activities; active participation requirement; application of phase-in rule (IRC § 469(m));

(4) disposition of interest in publicly traded partnership (IRC § 469(k)(3));

(5) rental use of dwelling; overlap of limits under IRC § 280A(c)(5) and § 469 (IRC § 469(j)(10));

(6)affiliated groups (IRC § 469(j)(11));

(7) distribution of passive activity interests by trusts or estates (IRC § 469(j)(12)); and

(8) pre-1987 installment sales (1986 TRA § 501(c)(4)).

"Passive activity" means any activity that involves the conduct of any trade or business in which the taxpayer does not materially participate. It includes any rental activity. Working interests in oil and gas property are not included within meaning of term. Passive activity losses mean the amounts by which aggregate losses from all passive activities for the taxable year, exceed aggregate income from all passive activities for such year. Passive activity credit means the amount by which the sum of credits for all passive activities allowable for taxable year under provisions for business-related credits, or foreign tax credit, exceeds regular tax liability for taxable year allocable to all passive activities. California does not adopt federal foreign credit provisions. (See California modifications to IRC § 469 below.)

Federal passive loss restrictions, adopted by California, apply only to individuals, trusts, estates, closely held corporations and personal service corporations. Rental losses can be offset against other income up to the amount of $25,000 only if taxpayer has at least 10% interest in rental activity and actively participates in its management. Passive losses cannot be offset against wage, salary or portfolio income.[10]

California modifications to IRC § 469. The state modifies IRC § 469(d)(2) to refer to following California credits against tax:

(1) Rev & TC § 17052.12 credit for research expenses;

(2) Rev & TC § 17053.7 credit for certain wages paid;

(3) Rev & TC § 17057 credit for clinical testing expenses;

(4) Rev & TC § 17058 credit for low-income housing.

For purposes of applying IRC § 469(i), relating to the $25,000 offset for rental real estate activities, the dollar limit for the Rev & TC § 17058 credit for low income housing is $75,000. The 1986 transitional rules for low-income housing applies in California. The provisions on publicly traded partnerships under IRC § 469 also apply.[11]

WARNING The *Revenue Reconciliation Act of 1993* provides an exemption [IRC § 469(c)(7)] from the federal limit on passive losses arising from rental activities for real estate professionals. This federal change applies for

---

(10) IRC § 469.   (11) § 17561.

tax years beginning after 12–31–93. California has not adopted this exemption.

Special rules for tax shelters. Under IRC § 461(i)(3), adopted by California, a tax shelter is: (1) any enterprise, other than a C corporation, if at any time interests in such enterprise have been offered for sale in any offering required to be registered with any federal or state agency having authority to regulate the offering of securities for sale; (2) any syndicate within the meaning of IRC § 1256(e)(3)(B); and (3) any tax shelter within the meaning of IRC § 6661(b)(2)(C)(ii). In the case of a tax shelter, economic performance must be determined without regard to the IRC § 461(h)(3) exceptions for certain recurring items.

Economic performance, as defined by IRC § 461(h), with respect to amounts paid during the taxable or income year for drilling an oil or gas well shall be treated as having occurred within that year if drilling of the well starts before the close of the 90th day after the close of the taxable year. The taxpayer must have paid for the drilling activity by the end of the taxable year. The deduction is limited to cash basis of partner.

In the case of the trade or business of farming, as defined in IRC § 464(e), any tax shelter will be treated as a farming syndicate for purposes of the IRC § 464 deduction limits on farming, but this rule does not apply for determining the income of an individual meeting the requirements of IRC § 464(c)(2) on holdings attributable to active management. IRC § 464 on deduction limits for certain farming will be applied before IRC § 461(i)(4) special rules on farming. In determining whether an entity is a tax shelter, the IRC § 464(c) definition of a farming syndicate will be substituted for the tax shelter definitions of IRC § 461(i)(3).[12]

Limitations on deductions for certain farming. Under IRC § 464, farming syndicates must deduct expenses for feed, seed, fertilizer and similar supplies only when used or consumed rather than when paid, capitalize the cost of poultry purchased for use in the trade or business, and deduct cost of poultry purchased for sale in taxable year of sale or other disposition. The rule applies to excess prepaid farm supplies of a taxpayer not using the accrual method and not a qualified farm related taxpayer.[13]

"Farming syndicate." Farming syndicate means a partnership or any other enterprise other than a corporation not an S corporation engaged in the trade or business of farming if, at any time, interests in such partnership or enterprise have been offered for sale in an offering required to be registered with any federal or state agency having authority to regulate the offering of securities for sale. Also included is a partnership or any other enterprise other than a corporation engaged in the trade or business of farming if more than 35% of the losses during any period are allocable to limited partners or limited entrepreneurs.

---

(12) IRC § 461(i); § 17024.5; 23051.5.   **(13)** IRC § 464; § 17024.5; 23051.5.

Limited partner or entrepreneur. An individual will *not* be considered a limited partner or a limited entrepreneur if: (1) he has actively participated (for a period of not less than five years) in the management of any trade or business of farming; or (2) whose principal residence is on a farm at which the business enterprise is conducting farming operations; or (3) an individual who is actively participating in the management of the farming enterprise (regardless of whether he actively participates in the management of the activity); or (4) who is actively participating in the management of any trade or business of farming involving the raising of livestock or any participation in the further processing of livestock which were raised in such enterprise. Any member of the family of an individual who meets any of the above conditions, who owns an interest in a farming enterprise which is attributable to such individual's participation, will not be treated as a limited partner or a limited entrepreneur.

Accounting for trading stamps and coupons. California has adopted Section 821 of the federal Tax Reform Act of 1986 that repealed IRC § 466 allowing a current year deduction for the cost of redeeming qualified discount coupons received after the close of the taxable year. Only redemption costs actually incurred before the end of the taxable year can be deducted currently. Any adjustment required to be made as result of a change in the method of accounting will be reduced by the amount of any suspense account and reflected in income over a period not longer than four years.[14]

Allocation of income and deductions among taxpayers. California has adopted IRC § 482 that requires that in any case of two or more businesses (whether or not incorporated, and whether or not affiliated, owned or controlled directly or indirectly by the same interests), the Secretary may distribute, apportion, or allocate gross income, deductions, credits or allowances between or among them if it is determined that such allocation is necessary in order to: (1) prevent evasion of taxes, or (2) clearly reflect the income of any of them.[15] In addition, California has an additional section with essentially the same wording applicable to the filing of separate returns for husbands and wives.[15]

The Franchise Tax Board's authority to allocate income and deductions under IRC § 482 is modified in the case of a corporation electing "water's edge" treatment under Article 1.5 (commencing with Rev & TC § 25110) of Chapter 17. Special allocation rules are included in the "water's edge" contract which is signed by those making that election.[16]

---

(14) § 17024.5; 17551; 23051.5.   (16) § 24725.
(15) § 17555; 24725.

IMPORTANT   IRC § 482 is actively used, particularly in connection with the allocation of income between U.S. corporations with operations and/or affiliated companies in foreign countries.

If an allocation under IRC § 482 is made, then Rev Proc 65–31, 1965–2 CB 1024, requires for federal purposes that if the parent corporation does not elect to have its subsidiary pay back the amount of income allocated to the parent corporation under IRC § 482, than that amount will be added to the basis of the parent corporation's stock in the subsidiary. If California chooses to allocate income under IRC § 482, then Rev Proc 65–31 must be applied and California can not use IRC § 481 for the allocation of income and then ignore the logical consequences of its action (*Appeal of Signal Companies, Inc., SBE 11–19–86*).

Personal service corporations.   Personal service corporations are corporations whose principal activity is the performance of personal services substantially by their employee-owners (employees owning more than 10% of the corporation's stock). The IRS may allocate tax benefits between a personal service corporation and its employee-owners if substantially all of the services are performed for one other entity and its principal purpose is tax avoidance or evasion.[17]

> *Note:* California has adopted the provisions of IRC § 269A with one modification. "California Personal Income Tax" is substituted for "Federal income tax."[18]

Mine and solid waste reclamation costs.   California has adopted the IRC § 468 treatment of mine and solid waste reclamation costs.[19] IRC § 468 provides that such costs can be accrued only as economic performance occurs, i.e., as the reclamation or closing activities occur. However, an exception is provided. A taxpayer can elect to adopt the uniform method for deducting site reclamation and closing costs of deep and surface mines and disposal sites for solid, liquid, or hazardous waste (except superfund sites) associated with meeting the requirements of federal or state law. To get the deduction for any taxable year, the taxpayer must so elect and establish separate accounts for qualified reclamation and qualified closing costs. Any reserve established for qualified reclamation or closing expenses is treated as a book sinking fund. The fund will be increased by the amount of current reclamation or closing costs, credited with phased-in increases in interest based on applicable IRC § 1274 rates using the Federal short-term rate and reduced by the amount paid from the fund for qualified reclamation and closing expenses. Any "excess" deduction, or reserve amount returned to the taxpayer, is taken into income on revocation of the election or the closing or disposition of the reserve property. In addition to the reserve deduction provided under the election, a deduction will be allowed for qualified reclamation and closing costs in excess of reserve limits in the taxable year in which economic performance occurs.[20]

---

(17) IRC § 269A; Fed. Reg 1.269A–1.
(18) § 17287.

(19) § 17551; 24689.
(20) IRC § 468.

Nuclear power plant decommissioning.   California has adopted the provisions of IRC § 88 and § 468A. The state has not adopted the special carryback period for losses incurred in decommissioning a nuclear power plant provided in IRC § 172(k)(2). It does not allow loss carrybacks.[21]

Under IRC § 88, any taxpayer required to include the amount of any nuclear decommissioning costs in cost of service for ratemaking purposes must include that amount in gross income for any taxable year.[22]

The law generally allows reduction only as the decommissioning is performed. However, the company can make an election to deduct contributions, within annual limitations, to a qualified nuclear decommissioning reserve fund set up to pay future costs of decommissioning a nuclear power plant.

To get a deduction, the utility company must request and receive a schedule of "ruling amounts" from the IRS. The ruling must establish the maximum annual deduction that can be claimed for contributions to the fund. The term "ruling amount" for any year is the amount IRS says is necessary: (1) to fund the future decommissioning costs; and (2) to prevent excess funding or funding at a rate more rapid than level funding. The actual deduction is limited to the lesser of the amount of nuclear decommissioning costs included in the costs of service, charged to customers, and included in the taxpayer's income, or the amount contained in the IRS ruling. The amounts are only deductible to the extent the contributions are deposited in a separate qualified reserve fund. Contributions may be made up to 2½ months after the end of the taxable or income year. The owner of the nuclear power plant must include in income: amounts distributed from the fund, other than the fund's administrative costs (unless distributed to the owner), amounts deemed distributed on disqualification; and the balance left in the fund on termination. In addition to qualifying contributions to the fund, amounts paid for reasonable decommissioning costs are deductible from the plant owner's income in the year of payment (as economic performance occurs). Tax on fund income is instead of any other income tax state or federal. Fund is treated as a corporation. Contributions and administrative costs are not income. California modifies its adoption of IRC § 468A to tax fund income at state corporate rate.[23]

Designated settlement funds.   The special rules for designated settlement funds provided in IRC § 468B apply in California. For both Personal Income and Bank and Corporation Tax purposes, the provisions of IRC § 468B(b) imposing a tax on a designated settlement fund are modified to provide that a tax will be imposed on the gross income of the fund at the corporate tax rate equal to that in effect for the taxable year under Rev & TC § 23501. The income tax imposed on gross income of the fund is in lieu of any

---

(21) § 17551; 24690.
(22) § 17081; 24275.

(23) IRC § 468A; § 17551; 24690.

other tax imposed by the Bank and Corporation Tax law or the Personal Income Tax law upon or measured by that income.[24]

Mitigation of effect of renegotiation of government contracts—repealed. For tax or income years starting on or after 1–1–91, California has adopted the federal repeal by OBRA '90 of the provisions of IRC §§ 1481–1482, relating to the mitigation of the effect of renegotiation of government contracts.[25]

SALES AND EXCHANGES

¶ 361   Sale or Exchange of Property—Gain or Loss

California law conforms to federal IRC § 1001(c). Gain or loss from a sale or exchange of property is recognized for tax purposes. The gain reportable on a sale is the excess of the net cash or fair market value of other property received for the property sold over the cost or other basis of the property sold.[26] In order to determine the extent to which a gain or a loss on a sale is included in the computation of taxable income in a given year, it is necessary to consider features of the sale in the light of various factors. Before the tax results of the sale or exchange are determined, the following factors must be considered:

    (a) Amount realized;
    (b) Basis of the property sold;
    (c) Any adjustments to the basis;
    (d) When is the gain or loss recognized;
    (e) Is it a capital gain or an ordinary gain.

Partial Exclusion of Gains on California Small Business Stock. Noncorporate investors may exclude 50% of the gain realized on the sale of qualifying California small business stock. To qualify the stock must have been issued after 8–9–93, and before 1–1–99. The stock must have been held by the taxpayer for five years. There is a lifetime limit on the amount that the taxpayer may exclude as gain with respect to qualifying stock issued by the same issuer. The limit is $10 million ($5 million for married individuals filing separately), or 10 times the taxpayer's original basis in the stock of the issuing corporation. To determine the limit for any one individual in later years, gain previously excluded on a joint return will be allocated equally between the spouses for purposes of measuring the limitation.

The eligible stock must be that of a 'C' corporation that is not a DISC or former DISC, a regulated investment company, a real estate investment trust, or a real estate mortgage investment conduit. Rules are provided to avoid abuses by issuers who purchased any of its stock from the taxpayer or a related party within the four years beginning two years before the issue date of the qualifying stock, or if the issuer within two years beginning one year before the issue date redeems more than 5% (by value) of its stock.

---

(24) § 24693.
(25) § 18351; 25201–25208.

(26) § 18031; 24901.

The issuer must be doing business in California and at all times on or after 7–1–93 and before the issuance of stock must have assets of $50 million or less when measured as a controlled group under modified federal rules, and must have at least 80% of the total dollar value of its payroll attributable to employment located within California.

Detailed rules are provided that the issuer must be actively involved in a qualified trade or business for substantially all of the taxpayers holding period. A qualified trade or business does not include a business in the fields of health, law, accounting, engineering, architecture, actuarial science, performing arts, consulting, financial or brokerage services, banking, insurance, financing, leasing, investing, athletics, farming or the raising and harvesting of trees, oil or gas extraction, or hotels, motels, and restaurants.

Nonrecognition of gain may be achieved through a partnership, S corporation, regulated investment company, or common trust fund if the entity held the qualifying stock for more than five years, and if the taxpayer sharing in the gain held the interest in the pass-through entity at the time the qualifying stock was acquired and at all times thereafter. Special rules are provided for estates and trusts.

The small business tax attribute will carryover to a taxpayer acquiring qualified stock by: (1) a gift or inheritance but the acquiring taxpayer must carryover both the transferor's basis and the transferor's holding period; and (2) by a partnership distribution of qualifying stock but only to the extent of the partnership interest held by the partner at the date the qualifying interest was acquired by the partnership. If nonqualifying stock is received by a taxpayer in a nontaxable exchange for qualified stock, the acquired stock is treated as qualified but only for the then accrued gain. One-half of the excluded gain is treated as a preference item for alternative minimum tax purposes.

It is the intent of the Legislature that in construing the provisions of the California small business stock, that the regulations issued by the Secretary of the Treasury for IRC § 1202(k) will apply, to the extent that those regulations do not conflict with the provisions of the California law, or regulations issued by the Franchise Tax Board.

Issuers are required to submit reports to the FTB and shareholders if requested, and penalties are imposed for failure to file required reports.[27]

Straddles are explained at ¶ 366.

Amount realized. The excess of the amount realized over the adjusted basis of the property is gain while the reverse is true for a loss. The amount realized includes the seller's personal obligations assumed by the buyer and also any other encumbrances outstanding against the property that the buyer assumes or satisfies. The amount realized in a taxable exchange of

---

(**27**) § 18152.5, as added by Stats. 1994, c. 1243, § 32.

property is the fair market value of the property received and any money received, reduced by any cost incurred in effecting the sale such as commissions, legal fees, advertising, etc. If property is subject to nonrecourse debt, fair market value must be not less than this amount.

Adjusted basis.   As indicated above, the amount realized is compared with the adjusted basis of the property in order to determine the gain or loss. The basis of property is its cost. However, if the property was acquired in a taxable exchange for other property, the property acquired has a basis of the fair market value of the property given up. If a group of assets is acquired, the basis of each asset is determined by apportioning the basis of the property given up to the assets received in relation to their relative fair market value. The adjusted basis is arrived at by increasing the original basis for all items or expenditures which are properly capitalized, such as improvements, purchase commissions, legal costs for defending or perfecting titles and recording fees. The original basis is reduced for any items that are considered to be a return of capital such as depreciation, depletion, recognized losses on involuntary conversions and deductible casualty losses.

IMPORTANT

In the purchase of a piece of property consisting of land and buildings, it is important to have a segregation of the cost between the two for depreciation purposes. IRS auditors will look for an apportionment on the values as determined by the local property tax assessor's office. However, an appraisal at the time of purchase by competent realtors or qualified property appraisal firms in the area in which the property is located will give a more valid separation of the cost between land and buildings. In fact, the county assessor in Los Angeles county, and probably other California counties, will issue a letter, upon request, to state that the figures used by the county based on proposition 13 valuation freeze are for the purposes of administration of property tax laws and should not be considered to represent the true market values of the land and building.

Bases of specific property are explained at ¶ 362.

Subtractions from basis.   California has adopted the federal IRC § 1016(a) rules which provide that the cost or other basis must be reduced by any deductions for depreciation and depletion to the extent allowed (but not less than the amount allowable). This reduction of basis must be made even if the taxpayer fails to claim any depreciation or depletion as a deduction in the year sustained if the deduction was "allowable".[28] California law also provides that in addition to adjustments to basis provided by IRC § 1016(a), proper adjustment shall also be made for amounts allowed as deductions for deferred expenses under former Rev & TC § 17689(b) and § 17689.5, relating to certain exploration expenditures, that resulted in reduction of taxes, but not less than amounts allowed or allowable under those sections for taxable

---

(28) § 18031; 24916.

¶ 361

year and prior years. Proper adjustments to basis must also be made for amounts deducted for depreciation by enterprise zone business, and expensed by qualified business in a program area or a Los Angeles Revitalization Zone.[29] No adjustments to basis shall be made for abandonment fees paid with respect to property on which an open space easement is terminated under Govt. Cd §§ 51061 or 51093, tax recoupment fees paid under Govt. Cd § 51142, or sales or use tax paid or incurred by taxpayer in acquiring machinery and parts subject to tax credit under Rev & TC § 17052.13.[30]

Additions to basis, at taxpayer's election, are at ¶ 362.

Recognition of gain or loss. Under federal IRC § 1001(c), when property is sold or exchanged the gain or loss is generally recognized. However, with respect to like kind exchanges, involuntary conversions, sales of residences (see ¶ 261), and so on, the gain or loss may not be recognized. In some cases there may be a partial recognition of the gain or loss. For instance, in a nontaxable exchange where there would ordinarily be nonrecognition of gain or loss, if boot is given or received in exchange, the gain or loss would be recognized to the extent of the boot. California, with exceptions noted below, follows federal rules on recognition of gain or loss.[31]

Deferred like-kind exchanges. IRC § 1031(a)(3) imposes a 45-day deadline on identifying substitute like-kind property, and a 180-day deadline on receipt of exchange property. Any property received or identified after the deadline isn't like-kind property. In California this rule applies to transfers affected by the federal rule after 10–1–85. If property to be received in exchange treated by taxpayer as part of like-kind exchange is identified in binding contract in effect on 10–1–85, and at all times thereafter until transfer, 1–1–89 will be substituted for 1–1–87 in provisions governing transfers on or before 10–1–85, and 1–1–91 for 1–1–89 in provisions governing deficiency.[32] In case of nonsimultaneous like-kind exchanges not covered under IRC § 1031(a)(3), the FTB has determined that it will follow the IRS position.[33]

Involuntary conversions. This type of exchange happens when your property is condemned and taken over by civil authorities, destroyed by fire or other casualty, or stolen, and taxpayer receives reimbursement from the government, an insurance policy, etc. Losses from involuntary conversions are treated as follows:

(1) Property used in the trade or business or for investment—a deductible loss.

(2) Personal (nonbusiness) property—not allowable as a deductible loss except as to items in (3).

(3) Personal property lost through fire or theft—a deductible loss in the individual income tax return.

(4) For corporations, the loss would be deductible in any case.[34]

---

(29) § 18036; 24916.
(30) § 18036(b)(1)–(2); 24916.2.
(31) § 18031; 24901(c).

(32) § 18043; 24941.
(33) FTB 1–30–86.
(34) IRC § 165; 1231.

Gains from involuntary conversions. Gains from involuntary conversions are not recognized if the property is converted into a property similar to or related in service or use to the property given up. If the taxpayer receives money or other property and elects not to recognize the gain, he may postpone paying tax on the gain by investing the proceeds in replacement property or in purchasing control (80%) of a corporation owning replacement property. If the entire net proceeds received are not reinvested, the gain is recognized to that extent. The purchase or replacement must be within a period which begins on the date of destruction, condemnation or other loss, or the date of the start of the threat of condemnation, whichever is earlier, and ends two years after the close of the first taxable year in which any of the gain from the involuntary conversion was realized.[35]

1993 NOTE   *Special rules for principal residences damaged by Presidentially declared disasters.* The federal Revenue Reconciliation Act of 1993 adopted an exclusion from income for insurance reimbursements of losses arising from a disaster as determined by the President of the United States. Insurance reimbursements for personal property which were not scheduled for insurance purposes may be excluded from income; insurance proceeds received for contents and residence will be treated as a payment for a single loss; and, the replacement period was extended from two years to four years. Federal law, in IRC 1061(h), applies for tax years ending on or after 9–1–91. California has adopted IRC § 1061(h) using the same effective dates as set forth in federal law. Refund claims for 1991 and 1992 may be appropriate.[36]

Note: California modifies federal rule. IRC § 1033(g)(3) relating to election to treat advertising displays as real property denies election if taxpayer has elected to expense asset on federal return. California will allow election under these circumstances.[37]

Illustrative case.   An individual received $360,000 in payment for about five acres of land from the state in a condemnation proceeding. After his death, the executors invested the proceeds in a parcel of land with a large commercial building on it. The Board of Equalization decided that the original land had been held for investment, and that the new land, even though with a building on it, was "like-kind" property. In addition, it was decided that the co-executors were acting on behalf of the deceased taxpayer for purposes of Section 18083. *Appeal of Estate of Howard W. Chase and Estate of Gladys C. Chase, SBE 6–22–76.*

Note: California does not conform to the provisions of (1) IRC § 1040 on transfer of certain farm real property; and (2) IRC § 1061 relating to nonrecognition of gain for certain vessels in transactions involving the Maritime Administration. California has conformed to IRC § 1042 relating to sales of stock to stock ownership plans, and eligible worker-owned cooperatives for taxable years starting on or after 1–1–90 and before 1–1–95. California has adopted the IRC § 1041 rule on nonrecognition of gain or loss on transfers between spouses, or to a former spouse if incident to divorce. No gain is recognized on the

---

(35) IRC § 1033(a).   **(37)** § 18037.
(36) § 18037(b)(1).

specified sales of assisted housing developments to tenant associations, nonprofit and profit-motivated organizations, individuals, or public agencies to maintain housing affordable to persons or families of low-income or very low income for a period of 30 years from the date of the sale or the remaining term of existing federal assistance. The state has also enacted additional provisions expanding nonrecognition of gain to other qualified projects.[38]

Capital gain or ordinary gain.   Capital gain is realized when a capital asset is sold or exchanged and the amount realized exceeds the cost or other basis of the asset. Generally, any gain from the sale or other disposition of property that does not qualify as a "capital asset" is treated as ordinary gain. However, a sale or exchange of qualifying business property—even those normally not considered as capital assets—may be either capital gain or ordinary gain, due to the netting effect of IRC § 1231.

IMPORTANT   For income years starting on or after 1–1–88, under the Bank and Corporation Tax Law, the tax treatment of capital gains and losses will be determined in accordance with IRC §§ 1201–1291. *Modifications.* IRC § 1201, relating to the alternative tax on corporations does not apply in California. IRC § 1211 is adopted. Capital losses can only be deducted to the extent of capital gains. A 5 year carryover is allowed. IRC § 1212, is modified by California as follows: IRC § 1212(a)(1)(A), relating to capital loss carrybacks does not apply; IRC § 1212(a)(3), relating to special rules on carrybacks does not apply; IRC § 1212(b) and 1212(c), relating to taxpayers other than corporations, does not apply. Also not applicable in California are the provisions of IRC §§ 1291–1297, relating to certain passive foreign investment companies.[39] For income years starting on or after 1–1–90, IRC § 1248, relating to gain from certain sales or exchanges of stock in certain foreign corporations, does not apply in California.[40]

Capital asset defined.   The definition in IRC § 1221, adopted by California, is stated in a negative manner. In other words, everything is a capital asset that the taxpayer owns except:

(1) Property held for sale in a trade or business, and material which will become part of the merchandise sold, such as inventories;

(2) Accounts and notes receivable acquired in the trade or business;

(3) Depreciable business property;

(4) Copyrights, literary, musical or artistic compositions, a letter or memoranda held by the taxpayer who either created it or acquired it from the person who created it in circumstances when the holder is entitled to use the basis of the one who created it;

(5) United States government publications.[1]

Limitation on capital losses-carryover.   For taxable years starting on or after 1–1–88, California Personal Income Tax Law adopts IRC § 1211, relating to limitation on capital losses. The Bank and Corporation Tax Law

---

(38) § 18031; 18040; 18041; 18041.5; 24955.   (40) § 24990.7.
(39) § 24990; 24990.5; 24995.   (1) § 18151.

adopts IRC § 1211(a) that provides that losses from the sales or exchange of capital assets are allowed only to the extent of gains from such sales or exchanges. This provision takes the place of Rev & TC § 24902 requiring the state to recognize the entire amount of gain or loss on corporation's sale of property. In the case of taxpayers other than corporations, losses from sales or exchanges are allowed only to the extent of the gains from such sales or exchanges, plus, if such losses exceed such gains, the lower of (1) $3,000 ($1,500 in case of a married individual filing separately), or (2) the excess of such losses over such gains. The California Personal Income Tax Law has also adopted IRC § 1212 on capital loss carryovers. The Bank and Corporation Tax law adopts IRC § 1212(1)(B) that allows a capital loss carryover to each of the five taxable years succeeding the loss year. This rule applies to income years starting on or after 1–1–90. Carrybacks are barred by California's conformity statute provisions.[2]

Built-in gains or losses—threshold.   California adopts IRC § 382, relating to the use of built-in gains or losses when a corporation changes ownership. A corporation that is acquired by another corporation is treated as having no net unrealized gain or loss only if the amount of gain or loss is not greater than $10 million or 15% of the fair market value of its assets, whichever is less. California also adopts another federal change that repealed a special provision relating to employee stock ownership plans. The repealed provision did not take into account certain employer securities in determining whether an ownership change had occurred, or whether the limit on the use of losses and credits preceding the change of ownership went into effect with respect to net operating loss rules. This repeal applies, for both California and federal purposes, to acquisitions of employer securities after 7–12–89.[3]

Special rules on capital gain or loss treatment.   Special rules on capital gain or loss treatment under both federal and California laws apply to:

(1) bonds or other evidences of indebtedness;
(2) short sales;
(3) options;
(4) patents;
(5) dealer's securities;
(6) real property subdivided for sale;
(7) emergency facilities;
(8) sales or exchanges between spouses, or between individuals and controlled corporations;
(9) amounts received for cancellation of lease or distributor's agreement;
(10) stock in firm operating under Small Business Investment Act; and
(11) transfer of franchise, trademark or trade name if transferor retains any significant power, right, or continuing interest.

---

(2) IRC § 1211–1212; § 17024.5; 24907; 24990; 24990.5; 24,995.

(3) § 24592.

Under IRC § 1253(c), amounts received or accrued by a transferor on account of a transfer, sale or other disposition of a franchise, trademark or trade name that are contingent on productivity, use or disposition of the franchise, trademark or trade name transferred must be treated as amounts received or accrued from the sale or other disposition of property that is not a capital asset. California has also adopted federal rules relating to contingent serial payments, payments in discharge of principal sum, and other payments made by transferee. For both California and federal purposes, these rules apply to transfers occurring after 10–1–89, unless the transfer is made under a binding written contract in effect 10–2–89 and at all times thereafter until the transfer takes place.

Holding periods.   California has adopted the 1986 TRA change that includes the entire amount of capital gains in gross income. In addition, California has adopted the $3,000 federal loss limit.

Table of holding periods.   The table reproduced below shows how the holding period was determined before 1987 for specified kinds of transfers.

HOLDING PERIODS

	Type of Transfer	**Holding Period of Assets**
1.	Tax-free exchange	Includes holding period of assets given up in the exchange
2.	Stock acquired through exercise of option	Begins on date the right to acquire was exercised
3.	Assets transferred to corporation	Includes holding period of transferor
4.	Assets received from decedent	Automatically in excess of one year (6 mos. if acquired after 6–22–84 and before 1–1–88) for federal purposes (IRC § 1223(11)) and for one to five years for California purposes (Rev & TC § 17024.5; 18162.5)
5.	Community assets held by surviving spouse	Begins on date acquired by community [LR 251, 10–30–59]
6.	Assets received as a gift	Includes period held by transferor
7.	Assets transferred to partnership	Includes period held by partner
8.	Assets transferred to a partner out of the partnership	Includes holding period of the partnership
9.	Replacement property in an involuntary conversion	Includes holding period of property given up
10.	Replacement residence when gain on sale was deferred	Includes holding period of principal residence sold
11.	Assets received in a transfer in trust	Includes holding period of transferor
12.	Stock dividend received	Includes holding period of stock which created dividend

Type of Transfer	Holding Period of Assets
13. Stock acquired in spin-off or split-off	Includes holding period of stock which gave rise to receipt of new stock
14. Stock acquired in "wash sale" transaction	If loss disallowed, the holding period of new stock includes that of stock sold
15. Restricted stock	Includes only the period beginning when the rights in the stock are transferable or not subject to substantial risk of forfeiture, whichever occurs first
16. Land and unharvested crops	Holding period of land [LR 257, 8–21–64]
17. Nontaxable partition of community property for surviving spouse	Date community acquired property [LR 275, 11–2–64]

¶ 362   **Sales or Exchanges—Basis**

Basis rules of general application in IRC §§ 1012—1021 are explained below. With exceptions noted, California laws conform to federal.[4]

This paragraph explains the basis of specific items of property for purposes of determining gain or loss. An explanation of basis and adjusted basis in general, is found at ¶ 361. Addition to basis for carrying charge—at taxpayer's election—is at ¶ 363.

Sale of stock. When shares of stock are sold or exchanged by a taxpayer who purchased or acquired lots of stock in separate transactions at different dates or at different prices, the basis of shares later sold is generally: (1) the cost of shares specifically identified; or (2) the earliest of the shares purchased (the "first-in-first-out" basis). Federal Regulations say that an adequate identification is made if it is shown that certificates representing shares of stock purchased on a certain date or for a certain price were delivered to the transferee. When stock is left in the custody of a broker or other agent, an adequate identification is made if at the time of the sale or transfer, the taxpayer specifies to the broker the particular stock shares to be sold, and within a reasonable period of time the broker confirms in writing that these are the shares which were sold or exchanged.[5]

Inventories. Under IRC § 1013, the basis of inventories is generally the value included in the last inventory for tax purposes, or if purchased since the last inventory, the purchase price. (See the section on inventories for specific information.)[6]

---

(4) § 18031; 24911–24919.
(5) Fed Reg 1.1012(c)(1)–(3).

(6) § 18031; 24913.

Accounts receivable. For an accrual basis taxpayer, if accounts receivable are sold or exchanged, the basis is the amount included in income. For a cash method taxpayer, the basis of receivables would be zero, unless they had been previously purchased.

Property acquired by gift. For property acquired by gift after 12–31–20, the basis for both federal IRC § 1015 and California purposes is the same as it was in the hands of the donor or the last person by whom it was not acquired by gift, except that if that basis is greater than the fair market value of the property at the date of the gift, then for purposes of determining loss the basis is the fair market value.[7]

> *Note:* The basis will be increased (but not above the fair market value at the date of gift) by the *federal* gift tax paid.[8] California has adopted IRC § 1015(d)(6) special rule for gifts made after 12–31–76 that limits amount of basis increase to portion of gift tax attributable to gift's net appreciation in value.[9]

Additional estate tax. California adopts IRC § 1016(c) that permits an increase in basis when an asset was initially valued at an amount less than its fair market value at decedent's death because it was used in certain family farm or closely held businesses, but was later assessed additional estate tax to essentially equal tax that would have been due if special use valuation had not been elected for federal estate tax purposes.[10]

Transfer in trust. Under IRC § 1015, when property is transferred to a trust, the basis in the hands of the trust is the grantor's basis, increased by the gain or decreased by any loss, recognized to the grantor on the transfer.[7]

Property acquired from a decedent. *Carryover basis.* California had adopted the "carryover" provisions of the Internal Revenue Code, and when they were repealed by the Congress retroactively in 1980, California conformed. As part of the repeal of IRC § 1023, Congress permitted an election for decedents' estates to retroactively elect either the "stepped-up" basis provisions of IRC § 1014, or the "carryover basis" under IRC § 1023 for persons dying between January 1, 1977 and November 6, 1978. California went along with the election by permitting the federal election to apply for California purposes unless notified to the contrary.

Current law. The basis of property acquired from a decedent is the fair market value at date of decedent's death for both federal and California purposes. Also, the estate tax return can be prepared using the date of death values or as an alternate, the values at a date six months later.[11]

Property acquired from a decedent includes the following:

(1) Property acquired by bequest, devise or inheritance, or by decedent's estate from decedent.[12]

---

(7) § 18031; 24914.

(8) § 18031; 24915.

(9) IRC § 1015(d).

(10) IRC § 1016(c); § 18036(c).

(11) IRC § 1014(a)(1)–(3); 2032; § 18031.

(12) IRC § 1014(b)(1).

(2) Property transferred by the decedent during his lifetime in trust to pay the income for life to the decedent or under his direction with the decedent retaining control.[13]

(3) Property passing without full and adequate consideration under a power of appointment exercised by the decedent by will.[14]

(4) Surviving spouse's one-half of the community property, if at least one-half of the community property was included in the California Inheritance tax base.[15]

(5) In case of decedents dying after 8–26–37, property acquired by bequest, devise or inheritance, or by decedent's estate from decedent, if it consists of stock or securities of a foreign corporation that, with respect to taxable year next preceding date of decedent's death was, under law applicable to that year, a foreign personal holding company. The basis is the fair market value at the date of death, or the basis in the hands of the decedent, whichever is lower.[16]

(6) In case of decedents dying after 12–31–50 and before 1–1–54, property that represents survivor's interest in joint and survivor's annuity, if value of any part was required to be included in determining value of decedent's gross estate under IRC § 811.[17]

(7) In case of decedents dying after 12–31–53, property acquired from decedent by reason of death, form of ownership, or other conditions, if by reason thereof property is required to be included in determining value of decedent's gross estate under IRC, Subtitle B, Ch. 11, or IRC of 1939. If property is acquired before death of decedent, basis will be determined using fair market value at date of death, or alternative valuation, reduced by amount allowed taxpayer in computing taxable income under current or prior IRC for deductions for depreciation, amortization, and depletion before decedent's death. Such basis applies to property starting on death of decedent, but doesn't apply to IRC § 72 annuities, property subject to (5) above, if acquired by bequest, and property described in any other paragraph of IRC § 1014(b).[18]

(8) Property includible in gross estate under IRC § 2044, relating to property for which marital deduction was previously allowed. Basis rules under (7) above apply.[19]

LR 423, 11–9–82 states that property acquired, transferred or passing under (1)–(3) above takes as basis the fair market value on the date of the decedent's death.

California adopts the federal rules in IRC § 1014(b)(6)–(7). Before 1987, state had its own rules for determining the basis of the surviving spouse's share of community property. California also did not adopt the federal rule in IRC § 1014(b)(5) that applied to stock of a foreign personal holding company. It did follow the federal rule in IRC § 1014(b)(9) for property acquired from a decedent by reason of death, form of ownership, or other conditions.

TAX TIP   For decedents dying after 1981, the stepped-up basis rules will not apply if (1) appreciated property is acquired by the decedent within one year of death by gift made after 8–13–81 and (2) the property passes from the

---

(13) IRC § 1014(b)(2)–(3).
(14) IRC § 1014(b)(4).
(15) IRC § 1014(b)(6).
(16) IRC § 1014(b)(5).

(17) IRC § 1014(b)(8).
(18) IRC § 1014(b)(9).
(19) IRC § 1014(b)(10).

decedent to the donor of the gift, or to donor's spouse. California has adopted this federal rule.[20]

Basis of community property. The basis of community property in the hands of a decedent's spouse and other beneficiaries depends in part on the date of death for California tax purposes. IRC § 1014(b)(6), adopted by California, states that the surviving spouse's one-half of community property is considered to be property acquired from a decedent so that it takes the fair market value (FMV) at the date of death (or the alternate valuation date of six months later).

Before 1987, the California rule in former Rev & TC § 18033(b)(1) stated that in case of decedents dying on or after 1–1–76, property that represents the surviving spouse's one-half share of the community property held by decedent and the surviving spouse under the community property laws of any state, territory or possession of U.S., or any foreign country, would be considered to have been acquired from or to have passed from the decedent, if the decedent's one-half of the whole of the community interest was transferred, within the meaning of Chapter 3 of the former California Inheritance Tax Law, to someone other than the surviving spouse.

For decedents dying on or after 6–8–82, after the repeal of the California Inheritance Tax, this rule could not be satisfied. The basis of the surviving spouse's share of community property is cost. Before the 6–8–82 repeal and prior to 1987, the surviving spouse's share got a stepped-up basis if decedent's share of the community property was acquired by a person other than the surviving spouse. If it passed to the surviving spouse, the surviving spouse got a stepped-up basis on the decedent's share, but used cost as basis for his or her own share of community property.

Quasi-community property. In general, property acquired while domiciled outside of California which would have been community property if domiciled in California is quasi-community property. For decedents dying after 4–7–53 and before 6–8–82, if quasi-community property was acquired in a noncommunity property jurisdiction, the surviving spouse's interest got stepped-up basis. The property was considered as acquired by inheritance. For 6–8–82 and later, the inheritance requirement could not be met. The basis is cost. In the case of decedent's dying before 6–8–82, if quasi-community property was acquired in another community property jurisdiction, the basis was cost if the decedent's share was transferred to the surviving spouse; if not so transferred, the surviving spouse's share got a stepped-up basis. For decedents dying 6–8–82 and later, the basis of the surviving spouse's share is cost.

Joint tenancy property. Federal rule applies. Property receives stepped-up basis if it must be included in decedent's estate for federal tax purposes.

---

(20) IRC § 1014(e); § 18031.

Basis of Property
Decedent and Surviving Spouse

CALIFORNIA FORM
1039

Type of Ownership By Decedent	Date of Death	Beneficiary of Decedent's Share	Basis of Property Decedent's Share	Surviving Spouse's Share
Separate Property.		Beneficiary	FMV	N/A
Community Property.	Prior to 4/8/53.	Spouse	FMV	Cost
	After 4/7/53	Husband—Any portion of wife's share.	FMV	Cost
	After 4/7/53— Prior to 9/15/61.	Wife—Any portion of husband's share.	FMV	FMV
	After 9/14/61. (See exception)	Wife—Any portion of husband's share.	FMV	Cost
	After 6/7/82— Prior to 1/1/87	Other than spouse	FMV	Cost
	After 12/31/86	Spouse or anyone other than spouse	FMV	FMV
Exception where husband dies between the following dates.	After 9/14/61— Prior to 9/17/65.	Wife—Life estate or power of appointment.	FMV	FMV
	After 4/7/53— Prior to 6/8/82.	Other than spouse	FMV	FMV
Property was originally separate property of either spouse and was converted to community property by agreement after 9/16/65.	After 9/16/65— Prior to 1/1/76.	Spouse	FMV	FMV
Quasi-community property acquired in a non-community property jurisdiction.	After 4/7/53.	Spouse	FMV	FMV
Quasi-community property acquired in another community property jurisdiction.	After 12/31/75.	Spouse	FMV	Cost
Quasi-community property acquired in any jurisdiction.	After 4/7/53— Prior to 1/1/76.	Spouse	FMV	FMV
Joint Tenancy with Spouse.				
a. Source of funds, not important	Prior to 1/1/55.	Spouse	Cost	Cost
b. Source of funds, not important unless c. below.	After 12/31/54— Prior to 9/7/55.	Spouse	FMV	Cost
c. Source of funds, separate property of spouses.	After 12/31/54— Prior to 1/1/81.	Spouse	Adj. FMV	Cost
d. Source of funds, originally community property of spouses.	After 9/6/55— Prior to 1/1/76.	Spouse	Cost	Cost
	After 12/31/75— Prior to 1/1/81.	Spouse	FMV	Cost
Exception where husband dies between the following dates.	After 9/6/55— Prior to 9/15/61.	Wife	FMV	Cost
e. Source of funds, quasi-community property of spouses.	After 9/14/61— Prior to 6/8/82.	Spouse	FMV	Cost
f. Source of funds, separate or community property of spouses.	After 12/31/80— Prior to 6/8/82.	Spouse	Cost	Cost
g. Source of funds, not important	After 6/7/82— Prior to 1/1/85.	Spouse	Cost	Cost
h. Source of funds, not important.	After 12/31/84.	Spouse	FMV	Cost
Decedents dying after 12/31/76 and prior to 11/7/78.				

¶ 362

Involuntary conversions. California law conforms to federal. The basis of property acquired as a replacement for property given up in an involuntary conversion is the same as that of the old property, if no gain was recognized on the exchange. When a gain is recognized because the proceeds exceed the cost of the replacement, the basis of the replacement property is the cost less the amount of gain not recognized. If a loss is recognized on the exchange, as when the basis of the property involuntarily converted is greater than the proceeds, the basis of the new property is merely the cost. If more than one property is acquired as a replacement, the basis is allocated to the respective properties in relation to their fair market values (their costs).[21]

Stock dividends. Distributions by corporations in the form of additional shares of their stock are generally nontaxable unless the shareholder has the option to take cash in lieu of the shares. The shareholder allocates the basis of the original shares to include the newly acquired shares for the purposes of later gain or loss on sales. Small amounts of cash in lieu of fractional shares are taxable in the year received and are not added to the basis. California conforms to federal.[22]

"Wash sales." California conforms to federal. The basis of stock purchased to replace stock sold in a wash sale transaction is the cost of the new stock plus the amount of the loss on the sale of the old stock which was not deductible. The change extending the treatment to short sales has been adopted by California as is the change that expands the rule to include contracts or options to buy or sell.[23]

Stock rights. California conforms to IRC § 307 which provides that the basis of rights which are nontaxable at issue is an allocated portion of the basis of the stock to which the rights pertain. If, however, the rights have a fair market value of less than 15% of the fair market value of the old stock, the basis of the rights is zero, although the shareholder can elect to apportion the basis between the stock and the rights. If the rights have a fair market value in excess of 15%, that is the basis because the same value is recognized for tax purposes in the year of receipt.[22]

Lessee improvements. California conforms to IRC § 1019 which provides that to the extent that the value of improvements to leased property by the lessee is not taxable to the lessor because of the exclusion provided in IRC § 109 (Rev & TC § 24309), the basis to the lessor will not be adjusted.[24]

Tax-free exchanges. For income and taxable years starting on or after 1–1–90, California has repealed former Rev & TC § 24941, relating to exchanges of property held for productive use or investment, and adopted IRC § 1031. California has picked the 1989 Revenue Reconciliation Act provisions on property received in an exchange between related persons, and

---

(21) IRC § 1033(b); § 18031; 24947.
(22) IRC § 307; § 17321; 24467; 24473.

(23) IRC § 1091(d); § 18031.
(24) § 18031; 24919.

¶ 362

the disqualification from IRC § 1031 rules for exchanges of foreign real property and real property located within the U.S. If property received in an exchange between related persons is disposed of before a date that is two years after the last transfer in the exchange, gain or loss unrecognized in the original exchange must be recognized as of the date of disposition, unless property is disposed of after the death of one of the parties to the exchange, or the disposition is an involuntary or compulsory conversion of the property, or neither the original exchange or the later disposition is tax motivated.[25]

California has also adopted IRC § 1035, relating to tax-free exchanges of life, endowment insurance, or annuity contracts, and IRC § 1036, relating to stock exchanged for stock of the same corporation, and repealed Rev & TC § 24950 and Rev & TC § 24951 that were in effect before 1990.[26]

Discharge of indebtedness.   California adopts IRC § 1017. Under this federal section, if an amount is excluded from gross income because of discharge of indebtedness under IRC § 108(a), and under IRC § 108(b)(2)(D) or § 108(b)(5), any portion of such amount is to be applied to reduce basis, such portion must be applied in reduction of basis of any property held by taxpayer at the start of the taxable year following the year in which such discharge occurs. Amount of reduction to be applied, and particular properties bases of which are to be reduced must be determined under the regulations of the Franchise Tax Board. A reduction in basis is not treated as a disposition.[27]

Bond redemption.   When U.S. bonds are applied in payment of estate tax at par value and valued at par for California inheritance tax purposes, the basis for computing gain or loss on redemption is par value.[28]

Sale and leaseback transactions.   California did not follow the federal treatment of arrangements qualifying as "safe harbor" leases under former IRC § 168(f)(8) (repealed by TRA 86). The state was guided by the provisions of Rev Proc 75–21, 1975–1 CB 715; Rev Proc 75–28; 1975–1 CB 752; Rev Proc 76–30, 1976–2 CB 647, and Revenue Ruling 55–540, 1955–2 CB 39 in determining whether certain transactions purporting to be leases were, in fact, leases for State tax purposes. If a transaction didn't qualify as a sale and leaseback, the sale and lease elements of the transaction were disregarded. Amounts received under such transaction would reduce the basis of the property in the hands of the so-called seller/lessee. The amounts paid by so-called buyer/lessor were viewed as purchase of federal tax benefits and were disregarded for California tax purposes. If a transaction purporting to be a standard lease failed to satisfy the above tests, the finance lease transaction would continue to be treated as conditional sales contract.[29]

Abandonment and tax recoupment fees.   No adjustments to basis may be made for abandonment fees paid with respect to property on which open-

---

(25) § 17024.5; 18041; 18043; 24941.

(26) § 17024.5; 18031; 24950; 24951.

(27) § 17024.5; 24918.

(28) LR 294, 4–23–65.

(29) § 17024.5(b)(16); LR 419, 12–3–81.

space easement is terminated under Govt. Cd § 51061; § 51093; or for tax recoupment fees under Govt. Cd § 51142.[30]

¶ 363   Addition to Basis for Carrying Charges

California law follows federal. Under IRC § 266, a taxpayer may elect to treat taxes or other carrying charges, such as interest, as capital charges rather than as an expense of the taxable year.[31] The items to which this election apply are:

(1) *Unimproved and unproductive real property.* Annual taxes, interest on a mortgage and other carrying charges.

(2) *Real property, whether improved or unimproved and whether productive or unproductive.* (a) Interest on a loan, (b) taxes of the owner of such real property measured by compensation paid to his employee, (c) taxes of such owner imposed on the purchase of materials or on the storage, use or other consumption of materials and (d) other necessary expenditures paid or incurred for the development of the real property or for the construction of an improvement or an additional improvement to such real property up to the time the development or construction work has been completed.

(3) *Personal property.* (a) Taxes of an employer measured by compensation for services rendered in transporting machinery or other fixed assets to the plant or installing them therein, (b) interest on a loan to purchase such property or to pay for transporting or installing the same, and (c) taxes of the owner imposed on the purchase of such property or on the storage, use or other consumption of such property, paid or incurred up to the date of installation or the date when such property is first put into use by the taxpayer, whichever date is later.

(4) *Any other taxes and carrying charges* with respect to property otherwise deductible which, in the opinion of the Commissioner or the Franchise Tax Board, are under sound accounting principles chargeable to capital account.

The election in (1) above is effective only for the year for which it is made and, therefore, must be renewed each year. The election in (2) is effective until the development or construction work is completed. The election in (3) is effective until the property is installed or first put to use, whichever date is later. Federal Reg 1.266–1(c) indicates that the election under (4) is effective and determined by the Commissioner.

Taxes enumerated in the elections above are social security taxes paid to construction employees and sales taxes on the purchases of machinery or construction materials.

TAX TIP   Here again, it may be advantageous to make an election to capitalize for federal purposes and deduct the same item for California purposes.

EXAMPLE 1   For two taxable years, Able pays annual taxes and interest on a mortgage on a piece of real property. During the first year, the property is vacant and unproductive, but throughout the second year Able operates a parking lot on the property. Able may

---

(30) § 18036(b); 24916.2.   **(31)** IRC § 266; Fed Reg 1.266–1(c); § 17201.

capitalize the taxes and mortgage interest paid in the first year, but not the taxes and mortgage interest paid in the second year.

EXAMPLE 2   Baker began the erection of an office building for himself. Baker, in connection with the erection of the building, paid $6,000 social security taxes which he elected to capitalize. Baker must continue to capitalize the social security taxes paid in connection with the erection of the building until its completion.

EXAMPLE 3   Baker also began the construction of a hotel. He pays $3,000 social security taxes in connection with the erection of the hotel. His election to capitalize the social security taxes on the office building started earlier in the year does not bind him to capitalize the social security taxes in erecting the hotel; he may deduct the $3,000 social security taxes on the hotel.

EXAMPLE 4   Michael began erecting a building which will take three years to complete. Michael, in the year the building erection was started, began to pay social security taxes and interest on the loan in connection with the building project. Michael has the election to capitalize the social security taxes even though he deducts the interest charges.

EXAMPLE 5   Charles purchases machinery for use in his factory. He pays social security taxes on the labor for transportation and installation of the machinery, as well as interest on a loan to obtain funds to pay for the machinery and for transportation and installation costs. Charles may capitalize either the social security taxes or both, up to the date on installation, or until the machinery is first put to use by him, whichever is the later.

¶ 364   Installment Sales

California has adopted the federal treatment of installment sales. The 1991, 1990, 1989 and 1987 changes are noted below.[32]

1991 change.   California has modified Rev & TC § 17560(e)(1) to provide that, in the case of any installment obligation to which IRC § 453A applies, and that is outstanding at the close of the tax year, instead of the provisions of IRC § 453A(c)(1), the tax imposed by Rev & TC § 17041 or 17048 (was the net tax defined by Rev & TC § 17039) for the tax year must be increased by the amount of interest determined in the manner provided by IRC § 453A(c)(2).

1990 changes.   The repeal of IRC § 453(c) by 1987 OBRA, § 10202(a), relating to the repeal of the proportionate disallowance of the installment method, applies to dispositions made in taxable or income years starting on or after 1–1–90. In case of any installment obligation IRC § 453(l)(2)(B), relating to timeshares and residential lots applies instead of IRC § 453(l)(3)(A) relating to payment of interest on timeshares and residential lots, the tax imposed under Rev & TC § 17041 and Rev & TC § 17048 for any taxable year for which payment is received on that obligation will be increased by the amount of interest determined under IRC § 453(l)(3)(B), relating to computation of interest. OBRA 1987, § 10202 and 10204 are modified to apply, respectively to dispositions in or costs incurred in taxable or income years starting on or after 1–1–90. Any adjustments required by IRC § 481, relating to adjustments required by changes in methods of accounting, must be included in gross income at 50% in the first taxable for

---

(32) § 17024.5; 17551; 17560(b)–(d); 24667–24669.

income year starting on or after 1–1–90, and 50% in the second taxable year starting on or after 1–1–90. In the case of any installment obligation to which IRC § 453A applies and that is outstanding at the close of the income or taxable year, instead of IRC § 453A(c)(1), the net tax, as defined by Rev & TC § 17039 must be increased by the amount of interest determined under IRC § 453A(c)(2). IRC § 453A(c)(3)(B), relating to maximum tax rate used to calculate deferred tax liability is modified to refer to Rev & TC § 17041 rate.

1989 changes. For purposes of applying IRC § 453C, if taxpayer does not elect, as provided by Rev & TC § 17560(a), to make IRC § 453C inapplicable, the provisions of 1986 TRA, §§ 811(c)(2), 811(c)(4), 811(c)(6), and 811(c)(7), as modified by 1988 TAMRA § 1008(f), will apply. 1986 TRA, § 812, relating to the disallowance of the use of the installment method for certain obligations, as modified by TAMRA, § 1008(g), will apply to taxable years starting on or after 1–1–87. The amendments to IRC §§ 453, 453A, and 453C made by 1987 OBRA, § 10202, relating to installment sales, shall not apply. 1988 TAMRA amendments to IRC §§ 453, 453A, and 453C, relating to installment sales will not apply. California adopts IRC § 453B(h), relating to S corporation liquidating distributions.

1987 changes. For taxable or income years starting on or after 1–1–88, installment sales shall be treated in accordance with IRC §§ 453, 453A, 453B and 453C, as enacted on 1–1–87, except as otherwise provided by California law. Any references in IRC to sections that have not been incorporated into either Bank and Corporation or Personal Income Tax Law by reference shall be deemed to refer to the corresponding section of these state laws. In the case of a taxpayer who made sales under a revolving credit plan and was on the installment method under former Rev & TC §§ 24667 or 24668 for the taxpayer's last income or taxable year starting before 1–1–88, the provisions governing IRC conformity in both California income tax laws will be treated as a change in the method of accounting for the taxpayer's first income or taxable year starting after 12–31–87. All of the following shall apply: (1) the change shall be treated as initiated by the taxpayer; (2) the change shall be treated as having been made with the consent of the Franchise Tax Board; and (3) the period for taking into account adjustments by reason of the change shall not exceed four years.

Under the California Personal Income Tax Law, a taxpayer could elect not to have the provisions of IRC § 453C, relating to certain indebtedness treated as payment on installment obligations, apply. TRA 1986, §§ 811(c)(2), 811(c)(4), 811(c)(6) and 811(c)(7) would apply if taxpayer does not make this election.[33]

Federal rules for reporting income from installment sales. On an installment sale, the gross profit is reported over the period in which the payments are received.

---

(33) § 17560(b)(i).

Income reportable.   Income reportable from an installment sale in any year is that proportion of the payments received in the year which the total gross profit on the sale bears to the "total contract price."

Total contract price.   Total contract price and not the selling price is the amount used to determine the part of each installment payment which is to be included in income. The total contract price is generally the total amount to be paid to the seller; that is, cash, notes and any other property such as new mortgage notes, but it does not include like kind property. If there is a mortgage on the property prior to the sale, the mortgage is part of the contract price only to the extent that it exceeds the seller's cost or other basis of the property. This is true whether or not the mortgage is assumed by the purchaser or the property is taken subject to the mortgage.

Any other obligations against the property which are to be discharged by the purchaser, are also to be included in the total contract price.

Sales to related parties.   Two special rules apply to installment sales between related persons. If you sell depreciable asset to a related person, you can't use the installment method. All the gain must be reported in the year of sale. Also, a special rule applies to a sale and resale involving related parties. The rules prevent related taxpayers from using the installment sales rules to avoid current tax on an asset's appreciation. A resale by a related purchaser will trigger recognition of gain by the initial seller. Gain will be recognized, based on the initial seller's gross profit ratio, to the extent the amount realized on the resale exceeds actual payments made under the installment sale. In calculating the gain, all payments received on the installment sale before the end of the tax year are taken into account, even if received after the second sale. Subsequent payments received by the initial seller will be recovered tax free until they equal the amount realized on the resale. For marketable securities, the rule applies without time limit to resales made before the installment obligation is fully paid. For other property, the rule only applies to resales within two years after the initial sale. The two-year period is suspended for any period that the installment buyer's risk of loss is substantially diminished by such things as holding a put or option or a short sale.

The rule does not apply to: (1) a nonliquidating installment sale of stock to the issuing corporation; (2) an involuntary conversion if the initial sale occurred before the threat or imminence of conversion; (3) a second disposition after the death of the installment seller or buyer; or (4) any transaction that does not have a tax-avoidance purpose.

If you sell certain depreciable property to certain related persons, you may not report the sale using the installment method. Instead, all payments to be received are considered to be received in the year of sale. Depreciable property for this rule is any property that can be depreciated by the person or entity to whom you transfer it. Payments to be received include the total amount of all payments that are not contingent and the fair market value of

¶ 364

any payment that is contingent as to amount. For any payments that are contingent as to amount but for which the fair market value is not reasonably ascertainable, the basis is recovered ratably and the purchaser may not increase the basis of any property acquired in the sale by any amount before the time the seller includes the amount in income.

Like kind exchanges. A taxpayer is entitled to use the installment method for gains on tax-free exchanges which include a taxable amount of boot. Under the installment sales provisions, like kind property is not treated as a payment when it is received with an installment obligation. If the exchange qualifies under the like kind exchange rules in IRC § 1031, the total contract price is reduced by the amount of like kind property exchange. Exchange of common stock for bonds paying 5½% interest and maturing as to 5% of principal amount in 22 years, and balance in 23 years was held reportable on installment method.[34]

Revolving credit sales. For dispositions made in taxable or income years starting 1–1–88 and later, dealers in personal property that dispose of personal property under a revolving credit plan cannot use the installment method. Payments are treated as received entirely in the year of sale. The same rule will apply to a dealer's installment obligations arising out of a sale of (1) stock or securities traded on an established securities market; and (2) to the extent provided in the regulations, property other than stock or securities of a kind regularly traded on an established market under regulations. The Franchise Tax Board can disallow the installment method in whole or in part for transactions in which these rules could be avoided by use of related parties or other intermediaries.[35]

Repossession of personalty sold by dealer. Under federal Regulation 1.453–1(d), a dealer in personal property using the installment method who is forced to repossess personal property has a current gain or loss equal to the difference between the fair market value of the repossessed property and the unpaid amount of outstanding obligations, less the amount which would be income if the notes were paid in full. The repossessed merchandise is included in the dealer's inventory at the fair market value.

If the dealer is not able to recover the property then he is entitled to a bad debt deduction. This deduction is based on the proportion of the defaulted payments which represents the cost of the goods sold and is an allowable deduction in the year of default.

A dealer in personal property is also allowed to use the reserve for bad debts method, if he so chooses.

Repossession of real estate. Under IRC § 1038, when a seller is forced to repossess real property sold by him, a limited amount of gain may be recognized, but no loss would be involved because of the repossession. The gain on the repossession is limited to the smaller of: (1) gain on the original

---

(34) LR 344, 10–5–70.   (35) § 17551; 17560; 24667.

sale reduced by income reported previously and by costs of repossession; (2) the amount of money and the fair market value of other property (other than buyer obligations) received prior to such reacquisition.

The amount of gain should not exceed the amount by which the price at which the real property was sold exceeded its adjusted basis, *reduced* by the sum of: (a) the amount of the gain on the sale of such property returned as income in prior periods; and (b) the amount of money, and the fair market value of other property (other than obligations of the purchaser received on the sale of the property) paid or transferred by the seller in connection with the reacquisition of the property. The basis of the repossessed real property is the adjusted basis to the seller increased by any gain recognized on the repossession and any cost incurred by the seller in the repossession.

Gain or loss on disposition of installment notes. Under IRC § 453B, gain or loss is recognized when installment notes are sold or disposed of. The gain or loss is the difference between the basis of the notes and (1) the amount realized in the case of satisfaction at other than face value or a sale or exchange or (2) the fair market value of the obligation at the time of the disposition.

Proportionate disallowance rule—repealed. IRC § 453 was repealed by 1987 OBRA for dispositions in taxable years starting after 12–31–87. California has adopted this repeal for taxable or income years starting 1–1–90 and later. Under prior California law, for dispositions in taxable or income years starting 1–1–88 and before 1–1–90, IRC § 453C provided a method for allocating installment debt to applicable installment obligations. These obligations were those that arose from the disposition of: (1) personal property under the installment method by a person who regularly sold or otherwise disposed of personal property on the installment plan; (2) real property under the installment method that was held for sale to customers in the ordinary course of trade or business; and (3) real property under the installment method that was property used in the taxpayer's trade or business or property held for the production of rental income, but only if the sales price was over $150,000 (all sales and exchanges part of same transaction or series of related transactions were treated as one sale or exchange). In addition, property had to be held by the seller, or member of the same affiliated group. Taxpayer could elect not to apply IRC § 453C to sales of specified timeshare rights or ownerships, or residential lots. IRC § 453C did not apply to installment obligations arising from disposition of tangible personalty by manufacturer to dealer if: (1) dealer was obligated to pay on obligation only when dealer resold or rented; (2) manufacturer had right to repurchase at fixed or ascertainable price no later than 9-month period starting with date of sale; (3) disposition was in income year and preceding income year in which aggregate face amount of installment obligations was at least 50% of sales to dealers giving rise to those obligations.[36]

---

(36) IRC § 453C; § 17551; 17560; 24670.

Deferred payment sales. If the obligations given by a buyer to a seller are not considered to be worth their face value, the seller may elect not to use the installment method of reporting.

TAX TIP	Instead of the installment method, seller can use a deferred payment method. Then, in the year of sale, the notes or obligations received are reported as income to the extent of their fair market value. In later years as payments on the notes are received, gain is realized and reported to pick up for each payment the difference in the face amount of the note paid in that year and the fair market value of that payment. This method of reporting is set forth in federal Regulation 1.453–6.

Imputed interest. The tax treatment of interest on certain deferred payments will be determined in accordance with IRC § 483. Adjustment is required on the return for the year in which the obligation matures or is otherwise disposed.[37] When property is sold and the proceeds are payable in installments, part of the installments may be treated as interest. In all types of installment sales, part of the deferred payments is treated as interest if either no interest or a low interest rate is provided.

Unstated interest. If the interest rate is specified, but the amount is not stated as a percent, the unstated amount must be determined as follows: (1) determine the sum of the sales price payments (excluding any stated interest payments) deferred for more than six months; (2) find the present value of all payments including stated interest, deferred for more than six months, using a discount rate equal to to the applicable federal rate determined under IRC § 1274(d).

If the amount in (2) is less than the amount in (1) there is unstated interest. To determine the amount of unstated interest, find the present value of the payments in (2) using a discount rate equal to the applicable federal rate determined under IRC § 1274(d), and subtract this amount in (1). The difference is treated as interest. If no interest is stated in the sales agreement, it is only necessary to figure the amount of the unstated interest as explained above. This unstated or imputed interest is not part of the sales price and is ordinary income to the seller. However, it is not included in the buyer's basis of the property and he can deduct it as interest currently.

Note: The imputed interest provisions do not apply to banks and corporations filing California franchise or income tax returns.

No imputed interest if:

(1) Sales price is fixed at $3,000.00 or less;
(2) No payment is deferred by the contract for more than a year; or
(3) Patents are sold;
(4) Carrying charges paid by purchaser treated under IRC § 163(b) (installment purchases where interest charge not separately stated) as if they included interest;

(**37**) IRC § 483(d); Fed Reg 1.483–2(b); § 17551; 23051.5.

¶ **364**

(5) Liability depending in whole or in part on life expectancy of one or more individuals that constitutes annuity to which IRC § 72 applies.

(6) Payments due under a debt instrument to which OID rules apply.[37]

OBSERVATION   *Payment deferred over a year.* A taxpayer sold a piece of real property in 1970 with a down payment made in escrow, and the large balance to be paid in a lump sum the following year, without interest charged. The Board of Equalization upheld the Franchise Tax Board in applying Rev & TC § 17617, stating that it is clear and unambiguous, requiring an interest computation even though the transaction qualified only by a matter of days beyond the one year requirement (see (2) above) *Appeal of Seymour and Arlene Grubman, SBE 4–22–75.*

Intra-family transfers. In case of any sale or exchange of land between members of the same family the maximum imputed interest rate is 6% compounded semiannually. The rule doesn't apply to any sale between family members made during any taxable year to the extent the sales price for such sale, when added to the aggregate sales price for prior sales made between such individuals for the calendar year, exceeds $500,000. Sales and exchanges in which any party is a nonresident alien don't come under coverage of rule.[37]

Recognition of recapture income in year of disposition.   For banks and corporations in income years starting 1–1–88 and later, California has adopted the IRC § 453(i)(1) rule that provides that in case of any installment sale to which the installment method applies, any recapture income shall be recognized in the year of disposition, and any gain in excess of recapture income shall be taken into account under the installment method.

Under its Personal Income Tax Law, California adopts the IRC § 453(i) rules on recapture income. Any recapture income is taken into account in the year of installment sale. Gain in excess of the amount recaptured may be taken into account under the installment method. "Recapture income" is the aggregate amount that would be treated as ordinary income under IRC § 1245 or § 1250 for the tax year of sale if all payments to be received were received in the year of sale.[38]

Enterprise zones and economic development program areas.   Under the Personal Income Tax Law, the sale of property subject to special depreciation or expensing provisions in installments is subject to the installment method treatment.

¶ 365   **Related Party Transactions**

California Personal Income Tax Law adopts IRC § 267. The Bank and Corporation Tax Law conforms to the same federal section.[39]

Under IRC § 267, no deduction is allowed on losses on transactions between "related parties" from the sale or exchange of property. California

---

(38) IRC § 453(i); 17551.   **(39)** § 17024.5; 17201.

adopts IRC § 267(a) that provide that this rule does not apply to any loss of the distributing corporation, or the distributee, in complete liquidation. In case of trade or business expenses or interest, the payor no longer loses deduction if, as accrual-basis taxpayer, accrued interest and business expenses are not paid in the year of accrual or within 2½ months thereafter. The deduction can be taken only when a cash-basis recipient must include it in income, or at later date, if another IRC section requires.

"Related parties." Related parties include: (a) members of a family (see following), (b) an individual and a corporation in which his direct and indirect ownership exceeds 50%, and (c) two corporations which are members of the same controlled group. Controlled group of corporations means a controlled group as defined in IRC § 1563(a), using a "more than 50%" test, rather than the "at least 80%" test.[40]

Members of a family. Members of a family include one's brothers and sisters (both whole and half-blood), spouse, ancestors and lineal descendants. Stock owned by a corporation, partnership, estate or trust will be considered to be owned proportionately by the stockholders, partners, or beneficiaries. California Personal Income Tax law adopts IRC § 267. The Bank and Corporation Tax Law conforms to IRC § 267.[1]

Basis if loss disallowed. If a loss on the sale of property is not allowed between the related parties, the basis for gain or loss or for depreciation to the transferee is his cost. However, on a sale of the property by the transferee, the gain is reduced by the loss disallowed to the transferor.[1]

EXAMPLE H sells to Corporation W, for $500, corporate stock with an adjusted basis for the purpose of determining loss to him of $800. The loss of $300 is not allowed because they are related parties. W later sells the stock for $1,000. Although W's realized gain is $500 ($1,000 minus a basis of $500) its recognized gain is only $200, the excess of the realized gain over the loss of $300 not allowed to the transferor.

Special rules for pass-through entities and controlled groups. California has adopted IRC § 267(e)–(f), including federal rules that apply to S corporations.[2]

¶ 366 **Straddles**

Straddles are offsetting positions as to personal property. To prevent deferring income and converting ordinary income and short-term capital gain into long-term capital gain on straddle transactions, the following rules will apply: The deduction of losses on straddle positions involving property not on the mark-to-market system (below) is limited to the amount by which such losses exceed unrealized gains on any offsetting straddle positions.

Deferred losses carry over to the next year. They are subject to the application of the deferral rules in that year. The losses are recognized in the

---

(40) IRC § 267(d); § 17201; 24427.
(1) § 17201; 24427.

(2) IRC § 267(e)–(8); § 17201; 24227.

first tax year in which there is no unrealized appreciation in offsetting positions acquired before the disposition of the loss position.

The loss deferral rules do not apply to losses on positions and straddles that taxpayers have clearly identified as straddles on their records on the day they were acquired. However, gain and loss on these identified positions must be netted. The positions must all have been acquired on the same day and either all closed on the same day or none closed by the end of the tax year. Straddles composed entirely of futures contracts are not subject to the loss deferral rules but will be taxed under the mark-to-market system. California has adopted the provisions of IRC § 1092 on straddle loss limits.

California conforms to federal provisions that apply loss deferral rules on straddles to stock and stock options. Exceptions to the rule on loss deferral apply to: (1) direct positions in stock; (2) hedging transactions; (3) stock options not deep in money. Capital loss is allowed on qualified covered call options. Identified straddle exemptions have become available for straddles wholly made up of positions in IRC § 1256 contracts covered by mark-to-market rules.[3] These provisions regarding straddles apply for personal income tax purposes, not bank and corporation taxes. California has adopted federal straddle rules on year-end positions that extend the limitation on losses on straddle positions to include loss on disposition of stock, where stock loss is offset by an unrecognized gain on an option, unless the unrecognized gain is offset by a qualified covered call and the option is held for at least 30 days after the sale of the stock.[4]

Interest and carrying charges. Interest and carrying charges allocable to property or positions belonging to a straddle and which would otherwise be deductible must be capitalized. The capitalization rules do not apply to any identified hedging transaction or any position not part of a straddle. California has adopted IRC § 263(g) on interest and carrying charges allocable to straddles.[5]

Gain or loss from regulated commodities futures contracts. Gain or loss from regulated commodities futures contracts not closed out during the year must be reported on an annual basis under the mark-to-market system and is taxed as if 60% of the capital gains and losses on them were long-term and 40% were short-term. The "mark-to-market" and 60%—40% rules applies to all listed nonequity options and dealer equity options. Each futures contract is treated as if it were sold for fair market value on the last business day of the year. A regulated futures contract is one that: (a) requires delivery of personal property or an interest in personal property; (b) is marked-to-market under a daily cash flow system of the type used by U.S. futures exchanges to determine daily gain or loss; and (c) is traded on or subject to the rules of a domestic board of trade designated as a contract market by the

---

(3) IRC § 1092; § 18031.
(4) IRC § 1092; § 18031.

(5) § 17201.

Commodities Futures Trading Commission or any other board or exchange approved by the Franchise Tax Board.

A taxpayer who has straddles clearly identified by the close of business on the day of acquisition as mixed straddles, those made up of positions in regulated futures contracts as well as positions in interests in property which are not, can elect to treat all of the positions in the straddle on a mark-to-market basis or can exclude them all from these rules. If taxpayer elects to exclude them, all of the positions in the straddle will be subject to the loss deferral, wash sales and short sales rules. Once made, this election is permanent and can be revoked only with Franchise Tax Board consent. Taxpayers can elect the new rules governing the taxation of straddles for positions which they held after 12–31–81. The election must cover all positions held after that date. The mark-to-market rules do not apply to hedging transactions. However, this exemption for hedging transactions does not apply to transactions entered into by a syndicate. The above rules on regulated futures do not apply to corporations.

Foreign currency transactions. IRC § 988 applies ordinary income and loss characterization and residence-based sourcing rules to certain gains and losses on foreign currency transactions. An IRC § 988 transaction refers to one in which the amount that the taxpayer is entitled to receive or must pay is denominated in a nonfunctional currency or is determined by reference to the value of one or more nonfunctional currencies. A foreign currency gain (or loss) means gain (or loss) from a an IRC § 988 transaction to the extent it doesn't exceed gain (or loss) realized due to changes in exchange rates on or after the booking date and before the payment date. Among other things, an IRC § 988 transaction includes entering into or acquiring a forward contract, futures contract, option, or similar financial instrument if it isn't marked to market at the end of the tax year under IRC § 1256.[6]

General rule. IRC § 988 transaction treatment won't apply to any regulated futures contract or nonequity option that would be marked to market under IRC § 1256 if held on the last day of the tax year.

Electing out. A taxpayer can elect to treat regulated futures contracts and nonequity options as IRC § 988 transactions whether or not they are or would be marked to market under IRC § 1256 if held at year end. The election applies to contracts held at any time during the tax year for which the election is made or later tax year unless it is revoked with IRS consent. For any tax year, an election must be made by the first day of that tax year or, if later, by the first day during the tax year on which the taxpayer holds the contract or option. For a partnership, an election must be made separately by each partner. For an S corporation, an election must be made separately by each shareholder. The election can't be made by a partnership that has elected "qualified fund" status.

---

(6) IRC § 988; 1092; 1256; § 17201.

Qualified funds receive capital gain treatment on foreign exchange gains and losses from certain financial instruments that would be marked to market under IRC § 1256 if held on the last day of the tax year. For IRC § 1256 purposes, a contract includes any contract held by a qualified fund that is, except as provided in regulations, a bank forward contract, a foreign currency futures contract traded on a foreign exchange, or to the extent provided in regulations, any similar instrument. Gains and losses on contracts treated as IRC § 1256 contracts will be short-term capital gains and losses.

A partnership is a qualified fund if:

(1) It has at least 20 unrelated partners, with no one partner owning more than 20% of its capital or profits interest at all times during the tax year and during each preceding tax year to which an election applies. A look-through rule applies. The 20% limit doesn't apply to certain general partners and to tax-exempt partners.

(2) Its principal activity for the tax year and each preceding tax year is buying and selling options, futures, or forwards as to commodities.

(3) At least 90% of its gross income for the tax year and each preceding tax year is from interest, dividends, gain from the sale or disposition of capital assets held to produce interest or dividends, and income and gains from commodities, futures, forwards, and options as to commodities.

(4) No more than a de minimis amount of its gross income for the tax year and each preceding tax year was derived from buying and selling commodities.

(5) An election applies to the tax year. The election for a tax year must be made by the first day of the tax year or, if later, by the first day during the year in which the partnership holds an instrument. The election applies to the tax year for which it is made and all later tax years, unless revoked with IRS consent.

If an electing partnership that fails to qualify had a net loss for the tax year or any later year, the loss is characterized under the rules that would have applied if it continued to be a qualified fund.

Straddles. The Treasury's regulatory authority under IRC § 1092(b) concerning gain or loss on positions that are part of a straddle will include authority on the timing and character of gains and losses for straddles, in which at least one position is ordinary and at least one position is capital.

Booking date. The term "booking date" no longer includes the date on which the financial instrument position is entered into or acquired.

Payment date. The term "payment date" means the date on which payment is made or received.

Measurement of gain or loss. Under federal law, the gain or loss from a IRC § 988 transaction is a foreign currency gain or loss if the transaction is a disposition of nonfunctional currency or a forward contract, futures contract, option, or similar financial instrument as to a nonfunctional currency.

Recognition on delivery under a futures contract. Federal law provides that making or taking delivery on or after 6–11–87, as part of an IRC § 988 transaction that is a forward contract, futures contract, option, or similar financial instrument is a gain or loss recognition event. In that situation, the payment date is the delivery date.

IRC § 988 hedging transactions. Under the IRC, when all transactions are integrated and treated as a single IRC § 988 hedging transaction or otherwise treated consistently, that treatment applies for purposes of all provisions of subtitle A of the IRC.

Sourcing rules. Generally, foreign currency gain is sourced (and losses allocated) by reference to the taxpayer's residence or the taxpayer's qualified business unit on whose books the underlying asset or liability is properly reflected. An individual's residence is the country in which his or her tax home is located. For nonindividuals, the residence of a U.S. person is the United States and of a foreign person is its foreign country. Under the federal law, for purposes of the currency sourcing rules, the residence of a U.S. citizen or resident alien who doesn't have a tax home is the United States. Anyone other than a U.S. citizen or resident alien who doesn't have a tax home will be treated as a resident of a foreign country. To the extent provided in the regulations, the residence of a partnership is determined at the partner's level.

DEPRECIATION AND AMORTIZATION

¶ 370   Depreciation and Amortization

For both Bank and Corporation Tax Law and Personal Income Tax Law, California has adopted the federal treatment of certain term interests. Depreciation or amortization deductions are denied for any term interest for any period during which the remainder interest is held, directly or indirectly by a related person. The basis of property for which the deduction is disallowed must be reduced by the amount of the deduction disallowed; the remainder interest must be increased by that amount. Remainder interest is not increased if the term interest is held by an exempt organization, nonresident individual, or foreign corporation, and income from term interest is not effectively connected with conduct of trade or business in the U.S.

California also adopts federal law concerning depreciation of luxury automobiles, computers, cellular telephones and similar telecommunications equipment (see ¶ 396).

California for taxable years starting on or after 1–1–89, allows taxpayers to elect to use the 150% declining balance method for regular tax purposes. The recovery period is the longer period used under the alternative depreciation system.

Grapevines. For tax years beginning on or after 1–1–92, newly planted grapevines in California which replace grapevines in the same vineyard damaged by phylloxera infestation, are classified as "five-year property" rather than "ten-year property" used for federal purposes. To qualify for the

California life of five years, the taxpayer must obtain a written certification from an independent state-certified integrated pest management advisor, or a state agricultural commissioner or advisor, that specifies that the replanting was required as a direct result of phylloxera infestation. The class life under IRC § 168(g)(2) and (3), which sets forth lives to be used for the alternative depreciation system, will be 10 years.

Amortization of cost of acquiring a lease.   California adopts IRC § 178. In determining the amount of the deduction allowable to the lessee for exhaustion, wear and tear, obsolescence or amortization in respect to the cost of any lease acquisition, the term of the lease must be treated as including all renewal options, and any other period for which the parties reasonably expect lease to be renewed, if less than 75% of the cost is attributable to the period of the term of the lease remaining on the date of its acquisition. Determination of period of term of lease remaining does not take into account any period for which the lease may later be renewed, extended or continued pursuant to an option exercisable by the lessee.[7]

MACRS depreciation.   IRC § 168, relating to the Modified Accelerated Cost Recovery System applies to assets placed in service on or after 1–1–87, in taxable years starting on or after 1–1–87. In the case of assets placed in service before 1–1–87, in taxable years beginning after 1984, and before 1–1–87, IRC § 168 (old ACRS) applies only to residential rental property as provided by former Rev & TC § 17250.5, as amended by Stats. 1985, c. 1461.[8]

Bank and Corporation Tax Law only.   California has not conformed to the federal law, and continues to use the mid-range ADR provisions.[9]

Modifications of IRC § 168.   California modifies IRC § 168 as follows:

(1) For purposes of the Personal Income Tax Law, any reference to "tax imposed by this chapter" in IRC § 168 means the net tax as defined in Rev & TC § 17039;

(2) Deduction for amortization of pollution control facilities is determined under IRC § 169, but deduction is available only for facilities located in-state, and the "state certifying authority" in IRC § 169(d)(2) means the State Air Resources Board in the case of air pollution, or the State Water Resources Control Board in the case of water pollution (eff. 1–1–91, the special rule on cogeneration equipment amortization is repealed);

(3) For property used in a trade or business, or held for the production of income, there shall be allowed as a depreciation deduction a reasonable allowance for the cost of a solar energy system and allowable conservation measures over a 60-month period for taxable years starting before 1–1–87;

(4) No deduction other than depreciation will be allowed for expenditures for tertiary injectants, as provided by IRC § 193;

(5) IRC § 263(a) on capitalization and inclusion in inventory of costs of certain expenses does not apply to expenditures under Rev & TC § 17265 for property acquired that is used exclusively within a program area or the Los Angeles Revitalization Zone;

---

(7) IRC § 178; § 17201; 24373.
(8) IRC § 168; § 17024.5; 17250.

(9) § 24349—24356.2.

(6) Before 1989, amortization of motor carrier, freight forwarding, and bus operating authorities over a 60-month period is not allowed in California[10];

(7) Alternative depreciation is used for property leased to governments and other tax-exempt entities.

What can be depreciated. Depreciation is allowable only for business or investment property that has a limited, useful life of more than one year. The type of property includes buildings, machinery, equipment, and vehicles but excludes land.[11]

Inventories are not depreciable property. Intangible property (not eligible for ACRS or MACRS) can be amortized if its use in the trade or business or in the production of income is definitely limited in duration. Examples would be patents, copyrights and in some cases leaseholds. Various licenses, franchises, contracts, and so on may be amortized on a straight line basis if they have a limited useful life. A covenant not to compete when separately stated in the sales agreement is also depreciable to the extent it is in effect for a certain term of years. On the other hand, trade names, trademarks, good will and trade brands are not depreciable because of their indefinite life. Returnable containers may be depreciated if they are used in a trade or business and if they have a useful life in excess of one year. Farmers may claim depreciation on farm buildings (except a dwelling occupied by the owner), farm machinery, and other physical property. Livestock used for dairy purposes or for breeding for use on the farm, are subject to depreciation as long as they are not included in inventory. Trees which have a definite useful life may also be depreciated.[12]

Who can deduct depreciation. Depreciation can be taken only by the taxpayer who would sustain an economic loss, due to the decrease in property value, from depreciation. Improvements by the lessee are generally depreciable by the lessee, rather than the lessor. If the leasehold improvement's life is less than the term of the lease, the improvement is depreciated over its useful life. On the other hand, if the useful life is no longer than the lease, the lessee may depreciate the improvement's cost over the remaining life of the lease. If the initial lease term is shorter than three-fifths of the estimated life of the improvements, the renewal period is included in determining the period for writing off the cost of improvements, unless the tenant is able to establish it is unlikely the lease will be renewed at the close of the tax year.[13]

Note: For property placed in service after 1986 generally, if a lessee makes improvements to leased property, the cost of building erected on leased property must be recovered over the 27½ or 31½ year period, regardless of the lease term. The cost of other improvements to leased property is recovered using the applicable ACRS recovery period. When the lease is terminated, the lessee figures gain or loss by reference to the improvement's basis at that time.

---

(10) IRC § 168; § 17250; 17260; 24349; 24372.

(11) Fed Reg No. 1.167(a)–1–1.167(a)–2.

(12) Fed Reg No. 1.167(a)–2—1.167(a)–3; 1.167 (a)–6.

(13) Fed Reg No. 1.167(a)–4.

When does depreciation start. Depreciation starts when an asset is placed in service. If property acquired for personal use is converted to business or investment use, depreciation is allowable from the time of the conversion.[14]

Note: For property placed in service after 1986 generally, depreciation under both the MACRS and the alternative depreciation system will be computed using the averaging conventions. The recovery period begins on the date property is placed in service under the applicable convention. Generally, a half-year convention applies under which all property placed in service or disposed of during a tax year is treated as placed in service or disposed of at the year's midpoint. A mid-month convention applies for both residential rental property and nonresidential real property. Special rules apply if there's a short tax year or if substantial property is placed in service during the last 3 months of the year.

WARNING   The deduction for depreciation and amortization can be lost by owners and transferors of an interest in real property or mobilehomes that fail to provide information as to Social Security numbers, identification numbers (if not individuals), and identification of property interests to the FTB as required by Rev & TC § 18802.3, or who provide false, misleading or inaccurate information in return. The deduction will be denied from 60 days after the due date of the Rev & TC § 18802.3 return until the FTB determines there is compliance. If noncompliance does not cover the entire calendar year, the denial of the deductions is at the rate of one-twelfth for each full month of non-compliance.[15] A taxpayer deriving rental income from a substandard housing can lose the deduction.[16]

¶ 371   Amortization of Intangible Property

Effective 1–1–94 California has adopted federal law which allows for the amortization of intangible property including goodwill. The federal provisions are found in IRC § 197 which has been adopted by reference, unless otherwise provided.

If the taxpayer has elected for federal purposes to claim amortization retroactively to July 25, 1991, for property acquired before August 11, 1993, or has made the election as provided in § 13261(g)(3) of the Revenue Reconciliation Act of 1993 for binding contracts as described in the federal Act, a separate election for California purposes shall not be allowed, but the federal election shall be binding for California. If the taxpayer has not made the above elections for federal purposes then they will not be allowed for California purposes.

In any event, no deduction shall be allowed for amortization under Rev & TC § 17279 for years beginning prior to 1–1–94; in addition no inference is to be drawn with respect to the allowance or denial of any deduction for amortization in any taxable year beginning before 1–1–94.

---

(14) Fed Reg No. 1.167(a)–10.
(15) § 17299.9; 24448.

(16) § 17274; 24436.5.

In the case of an intangible that was acquired in a taxable year beginning before 1–1–94, the amount to be amortized shall not exceed the adjusted basis of that intangible as of the first day of the first taxable year beginning on or after January 1, 1994, and beginning with the first month of the first taxable year beginning on or after January 1, 1994, and ending 15 years after the month in which the intangible was acquired.

To the extent the Revenue Reconciliation Act of 1993 also amended the following code sections to implement the adoption of amortization of intangible assets, those amendments are also recognized for federal purposes: IRC §§ 167(c) and (f), 642, 1016, 1060, 1245, and 1253.[17]

¶ 381   **Basis for Depreciation**

Personal Income Tax Law only.   California adopts MACRS system for taxable years starting on or after 1–1–87. Under this system MACRS applies to assets placed in service on or after 1–1–87 in taxable years starting on or after 1–1–87. The basis for depreciation for such assets would not be adjusted for any prior years' depreciation deduction. For assets placed in service on or after 1–1–87, in taxable years starting before 1–1–87, taxpayer may elect to amortize the difference between state and federal depreciation over a 60-month period starting with the first taxable year that begins on or after 1–1–87.[18]

Bank and Corporation Tax Law only.   Under IRC § 167(g), annual depreciation allowances are figured on the cost or other basis of depreciable property. Allowances reduce the "adjusted basis" of the property.[19] This basis is generally the same as that used for determining gain or loss upon the sale or other disposition of the property. When property is held for personal use, such as a residence, and it is converted to business or income-producing property, the basis for depreciation is the lesser of the adjusted basis of the property in the hands of the taxpayer, or the fair market value on the date of the conversion. The basis of inherited property is generally the fair market value at the date of death or at the alternative valuation date, for federal purposes.

When a piece of improved real property is acquired for a lump sum, the price must be allocated between the land and the building in order to determine the basis of the building for purposes of depreciation. The allocation is generally made by determining the proportion that their values bear to the total value, which is consistent with recognized trade practice as long as the method used is reasonable.[20]

---

(17) §§ 17249; 17279; 17748; 18060; 18166; 18173; 24355; 24355.5; 24966.3; 24990.8 and 24990.9, as added by Stats. 1994, c. 861, § 1–7, 9, 10, 12–14.

(18) IRC § 168; § 17250.
(19) IRC § 167(b); § 24353.
(20) Fed Reg No. 1.167(a)–5; 1.167(s)–1.

VALUATION

A taxpayer purchased two parcels of California property, which included land, buildings and orange groves on one and a walnut grove on the other. The taxpayer valued the buildings by projecting the rental income potential over the remaining useful lives. The groves were valued at estimated quantities of fruit to be produced times wholesale market values. The Board concluded that the values assigned by the county property tax assessor, while they might not be correct as to the overall value of the properties, would be the best evidence of the relative values as between buildings, land, and fruit groves. *Appeal of John E. and Amet Z. Newland, SBE, 9–17–75.*

Salvage value—Bank and Corporation Tax Law only. The amount that can be realized when property is no longer useful to the taxpayer has to be considered in determining the amount of depreciation. The salvage value may be a mere junk value or scrap value or if the asset has a useful life in some other business it may be a value higher than a junk or scrap value. Salvage value is determined when the property is acquired and once it is determined it cannot be changed merely due to price fluctuations.

As an alternative to salvage value, a taxpayer may use net salvage value which is salvage value reduced by cost of removal.

Effect on basis. California follows federal law.[21] The basis for depreciation must be reduced for estimated salvage value in computing depreciation on the straight-line method or the sum of the years digits method. However, salvage value is not subtracted from the basis in figuring declining balance depreciation, but it must be accounted for when the assets are retired. In any of the depreciation methods, the asset cannot be depreciated below the salvage value, less the 10% reduction if it applies. The 10% reduction is applied to the salvage value of personal property, other than livestock, with at least a three year useful life. The reduction is up to 10% of the original cost or other basis of the property.

Leased property. For corporate purposes only, when property subject to depreciation is acquired subject to a lease, no portion of the adjusted basis of the property shall be allocated to the leasehold interest, and the entire adjusted basis shall be taken into account in determining the depreciation deduction, if any, with respect to the property subject to the lease.[22]

¶ 382 **Methods for Figuring Depreciation**

Under the MACRS system in effect in California under the Personal Income Tax Law for taxable years starting on or after 1–1–87, the depreciation

---

(21) IRC § 167(g); Fed Regs No. 1.167(a)–1(c); 1.167(b)–1; 1.167(b)–3; 1.167(f)–1; § 17201; 24352.5.

(22) § 24353, as added by Stats. 1994, c. 861, § 8.

deduction is determined by using the applicable depreciation method, the applicable recovery period and the applicable convention.[23]

Applicable method. The applicable method, except where 15-year and 20-year property is involved, or the straight-line method applies, is the 200% declining balance method, switching to straight line for the first year for which its use will yield a larger allowance. A 15-year and 20-year property use the 150% declining balance method. Straight line applies to nonresidential real property, residential rental property, and property with respect to which taxpayer elects straight-line. Salvage value is zero.

Applicable recovery period. The applicable recovery period is 3 years for 3-year property; 5 years for 5-year property; 7 years for 7-year property; 10 years for 10-year property; 15 years for 15-year property; 20 years for 20-year property; 27.5 years for residential rental property; and 31.5 years for nonresidential real property.

Applicable convention. The applicable convention is generally the half-year convention. It's the mid month convention for nonresidential real property, and residential rental property.

Asset classes—3-year property. This class includes property with a 4-year-or-less midpoint life under the ADR (Asset Depreciation Range) system, other than cars and light-duty trucks (they are shifted to the 5-year class). Under the ADR system, property with a midpoint life of 4 years or less includes: special handling devices for the manufacture of food and beverages; special tools and devices for the manufacture of rubber products; special tools for the manufacture of finished plastic products, fabricated metal products, or motor vehicles; and breeding hogs. Racehorses more than 2-years old when placed in service, and other horses more than 12-years old when placed in service, are included in the 3-year class.

5-year property. This class consists of property with an ADR mid-point of more than 4 years and less than 10 years. This includes assets such as computers, typewriters, copiers, duplicating equipment, heavy general purpose trucks, trailers, cargo containers and trailer-mounted containers. The law specifically includes the following items in the 5-year class: cars, light-duty trucks, computer-based telephone central office switching equipment (assigned an ADR midpoint of 9.5 years), semiconductor manufacturing equipment (assigned an ADR midpoint of 5 years), renewable energy and biomass properties that are small power plant production facilities, qualified technological equipment and equipment used with research and experimentation.

The 5-year class life also includes, for income years beginning on or after January 1, 1992, grapevines planted in California to replace grapevines in the same vineyard damaged as a direct result of phylloxera infestation. (See ¶ 370 for certification requirements.)

---

(23) IRC § 168(a)–(d); § 17024.5.

7-year property. This class includes (1) any property with an ADR midpoint of 10 years or more and less than 16 years, and (2) property with no ADR midpoint that is not assigned to another class. Included in this class: office furniture, fixtures and equipment (was in the 5-year class), railroad track (assigned a 10-year midpoint) and single-purpose agricultural and horticultural structures (assigned a 15-year midpoint).

10-year property. This class includes property with an ADR midpoint of 16 years or more and less than 20 years (e.g., assets used in petroleum refining, or in the manufacture of tobacco products and certain food products).

15-year property. This class consists of property with an ADR midpoint of 20 years or more and less than 25 years. Specifically included in this class are municipal sewage treatment plants, telephone distribution plants, and comparable equipment used by nontelephone companies for the two-way exchange of voice and data communications (assigned a 24-year ADR midpoint). "Comparable equipment" does not include cable television equipment used primarily for one-way communication.

20-year property. This class consists of property with an ADR midpoint of 25 years and more, other than IRC § 1250 real property with an ADR midpoint of 27.5 years and more. Municipal sewers, which are assigned to a 50-year midpoint, are in this class.

In the case of a short tax year, the MACRS deduction for property in the 3, 5, 7, 10, 15, and 20 year classes is computed as if the property had been in service for half the number of months in the short tax year.

Averaging conventions and depreciation percentages. The half-year convention applies to all property assigned to the 3, 5, 7, 10, 15 or 20-year classes. All property is treated as placed in service (or disposed of) in the middle of the year. Thus, a taxpayer gets a half-year of depreciation when he places an asset in service and a half-year depreciation when the property is disposed of or retired from service. Salvage value is ignored. The original ACRS system had statutory depreciation percentages. The modified system prescribes the depreciation methods we've listed and does not provide recovery tables.

California Bank and Corporation Tax Law only. California follows IRC § 167(b).[24] No election is required to adopt either the ordinary straight-line method or accelerated depreciation. The appropriate method is used in the first tax return in which the property is put into service.

Straight-line method. In computing depreciation under this method the cost or other basis of the property is reduced by the estimated salvage value, and the resulting amount is deducted, in equal amounts, each year over the period of its remaining estimated useful life. The straight-line method may

---

(24) 24349(b).

¶ 382

be used for any property, real or personal, with any useful life in excess of one year.[25]

Declining balance method. Under this method the depreciation is the greatest in the first year and gets smaller in each succeeding year. The depreciation basis is reduced each year by the amount of the depreciation deduction. Salvage value is not taken into account in determining the amount of the depreciation each year, but the asset cannot be depreciated below a reasonable salvage value. California follows federal law.[26]

For availability of method, see below.

Sum of the years-digits method. Sum of the years-digit method is an alternative to the declining balance method and may be used for the same property which qualifies for the latter method. The annual depreciation deduction is figured by applying a changing ratio to the taxpayer's cost of the property reduced for salvage value as required, unless the Class Life, ADR system is elected. The numerator of the fraction each year represents the number of remaining years of the property's estimated useful life and the denominator which is used each year is the sum of the numbers representing the years of life of the property.

EXAMPLE   An asset with a four-year life would have as the denominator, 10, which is computed by adding one, two, three, and four, the number of years of the useful life. The numerator for the first year would be four, representing the number of years of remaining life of the asset. Four tenths, or 40% would be the factor to apply to the adjusted basis to determine the depreciation to be taken in the first year. California follows federal law.[27]

See below for availability of this method.

Component depreciation. Under the federal ACRS and MACRS, component depreciation is out. As a result, the same recovery period and method must be used, generally, for each component. Under the component method of depreciation, componensts of a new building could be depreciated separately in instances where the separate costs of the components could be determined. If a cost of a used building could be allocated to the various components, based on values determined by independent appraisers, the component method of depreciation was also allowable for used buildings.

OBSERVATION   Despite the fact that federal ACRS outlaws component depreciation for eligible property, components added to buildings placed in service prior to 1981 do qualify as eligible recovery property. However, the deduction for such components must be computed over the same period and under the same method as that elected for the first such component placed in service after 1980. For purposes of computing the deduction for the first component placed in service after 1980, the method of computing the allowable deduction is determined as if it were a separate building.

(25) IRC § 167(b)(1); Fed Reg No. 1.167(b)(1).
(26) IRC § 167(b)(2); Fed Reg No. 1.167(b)-2;
1.167(c)-1; § 17201; 24349(h).

(27) IRC § 167(b)(3); Fed Reg No. 1.167(b)-3;
1.167(c)-1; § 17201; 24349(6).

¶ 382

Furthermore, this break applies whether or not the components are substantial improvements.[28]

Other methods of depreciation. Any other method of depreciation may be used to determine the annual allowance for property, similar to that for which the declining balance method may be used. These methods may be used only if the total allowances for the property at the end of each year do not exceed during the first two years of the asset's useful life the total allowances that would result if the declining balance method were used. California follows federal law.[29] Among the other methods in use are:

(1) *Unit of production method.* This method is determined by figuring the number of units a machine will produce and using that as the denominator of a fraction, for which the numerator is the number of units produced in the year;

(2) *Operating day method.* To use this method a useful life of the asset is determined to be an estimated number of days. Using that estimate as the denominator the depreciable basis is prorated on the number of days the equipment is used;

(3) *Income forecast method.* The Internal Revenue Service and the Franchise Tax Board have adopted the income forecast method to depreciate the cost of rented television film, tape shows and motion picture film. The ratio is determined by using the income of the film in the year as the numerator and the estimated income to be received over the film's useful life as a denominator. The fraction then is multiplied by the adjusted cost of the films that produced the income during the year. The same authorities have allowed adjustments to be made for substantial over-estimates or under-estimates during the life of the film.[30]

TAX TIP   *Pre-release advertising and promotional expenses* of a motion picture are deductible as current expenses. They need not be capitalized. *Appeal of Screen Plays II Corp., SBE 6–25–57.*

Pre-release advertising and promotional expenses of motion pictures may be deducted as an expense in a year when the producer becomes legally liable to pay them under creditor's deferral agreement. They need not be amortized. *Appeal of Filmcraft Trading Corp., SBE 2–17–59.*

Assets acquired during the year. In order to determine depreciation on an asset acquired during a year, the depreciation is figured in the normal manner for an entire 12-month period, then an allocation is made to the respective tax years according to the proportion of that year that falls within the respective tax years.[31]

Available methods. *Double declining balance method.* The double declining method (at 200% of the straight line method) is allowable only for personal property having a useful life of at least three years which is new at the time it is placed in the service. The 200% method can be used for real estate only if the real property is new residential housing with the limitation that the gross rents from the dwelling units are at least 80% of the total.

---

(28) IRC § 167(m); 168(8)(1)(A)–(B).
(29) Fed Reg 1.167(b)–4; § 17201; 24349(b).

(30) Fed Reg 1.167(b)–0; 1.167(b)–4.
(31) Fed Reg No. 1.167(a)–10.

Personal property with a useful life of three years, which is used at the time it is placed in the service, can use 150% declining balance method (that is, the annual depreciation applied to the declining balance can be 150% of the straight line annual rate).

The 150% declining balance method may be used by a taxpayer for any new real estate acquired. Also new real estate can be depreciated by any other consistent method which does not give a greater allowance in the first two-thirds of its useful life than 150%.

For used commercial and industrial real property, and used residential rental property with a useful life of less than 20 years at the time of acquisition, straight line method of depreciation must be used. For used residential rental property with a useful life of 20 years or more at time of acquisition, 125% declining balance method can be used. This method is not allowed for used commercial and industrial real property.[32]

Sum of the years-digits method. The sum of the year-digits method may be used for the same kind of property that qualifies for the declining balance method.[33]

Changes in depreciation method. For banks and corporations, California follows IRC § 167(e). A change from declining balance to straight line method can be made at any time without obtaining prior consent from the IRS or the Franchise Tax Board. In order to be effective the change must be applied to all the assets in a particular account. The change must be made in the original return for the tax year in which the change is to be effective. A statement should be attached to the return showing the date the asset was acquired, the basis, the amounts previously recovered through depreciation, the salvage value, the character of the property, the remaining useful life, and similar information.[34] Election to change from sum of the years-digits, on declining balance method to straight-line for IRC § 1250(c) property is not available after 1990.[35] The same applies to boilers and combusters.[36]

Any other change in the method of depreciation, is a change in an accounting method and generally requires approval by the Internal Revenue Service and the Franchise Tax Board. The taxpayer must apply within 180 days after the start of the tax year in which the change is to be effective. The application is to be made on Form 3115 (the form used for applying for an accounting method change). The information to be put into the form includes:

(1) Date the property was acquired;
(2) If the taxpayer was the first user of the property;
(3) Location of the property;
(4) Property's character or type;
(5) Property's cost or other basis and adjustments to it;

---

(32) Fed Reg No. 1.167(b)–4; 1.167(j)–2–1.167 (j)–3.
(33) Fed Reg No. 1.167(b)–3.

(34) Fed Reg No. 1.167(e)–1(b); § 17201; 24352.
(35) § 24352.1.
(36) § 24354.3; 24354.4.

¶ 382

(6) Depreciation claimed in prior tax years;

(7) Estimated salvage value;

(8) Estimated remaining useful life in the hands of the taxpayer.

Note: The Internal Revenue Service has issued Rev. Proc. 74–11 to set out certain conditions which should be met by a taxpayer in applying for a change. If these conditions are met, the Revenue Service's consent can be assumed. The Franchise Tax Board has announced that it will follow the same treatment to give effect to Rev. Proc. 74–11. California will follow federal Rev. Ruling 74–324 on change from 150% of declining balance method on used property without consent.

¶ 383   Accounting for Depreciable Property

Personal Income Tax Law only.   California has adopted MACRS. The state also picks up the federal midquarter convention rules (¶ 370). Under IRC § 168, depreciation deduction is determined by using the applicable depreciation method, the applicable recovery period, and the applicable convention. For nonresidential real property, and residential rental property, the applicable convention is the mid-month convention. For other kinds of recovery property, the applicable convention is the half-year convention. A special rule applies where substantial property is placed in service during the last three months of the taxable year. Under this rule, if the aggregate bases of the property to which IRC § 168 applies, and which are placed in service during last three months of year, exceed 40% of the aggregate bases of property to which IRC § 168 applies placed in service during the taxable year, the applicable convention for all property placed in service during such taxable year will be the mid-quarter convention. This rule does not apply to nonresidential real property or residential rental property.[37]

Half year convention treats all property placed in service during taxable year, or disposed of during such year, as placed in service, or disposed on the mid-point of such taxable year.

Mid-month convention treats all property placed in service during any month, or disposed of, as placed in service or disposed of during the mid-point of that month.

Mid-quarter convention treats all property placed in service, or disposed of in any quarter, as placed in service or disposed of on the mid-point of that quarter.

Bank and Corporation Tax Law only.   A taxpayer can account for depreciable property by treating each individual item as an account or by combining two or more assets into a single account.[38]

Item accounts.   The cost of each asset is maintained separately with the useful life, the salvage value and the depreciation rate determined on an individual basis. Any reasonable method may be selected for each item of property as long as it is applied consistently, until the asset is disposed of or the basis less the salvage value is completely recovered. A different method

---

(37) IRC § 168(a); (d); § 17024.5.   (38) Fed Reg 1.167(a)—7—1.167(a)–8.

of depreciation: i.e., the straight line method, accelerated depreciation, sum of the year's digits and so forth, may be selected for each separate item of property.

In computing depreciation the average useful life of all the assets in the item accounts may be used as the expected useful life, or each asset may have its depreciation computed on its own useful life.[39]

Multiple asset accounts. A group of assets, whether or not they have the same life, or different useful lives, may be combined in one account and a single rate of depreciation used for the entire account. There are generally three types of multiple assets accounts. *Group accounts* contain assets similar in kind with approximately the same average useful lives. *Composite accounts* include assets without regard to their character or their useful lives. *Classified accounts* consist of assets classified as to use without regard to their useful life. In most cases classified accounts are used, such as machinery and equipment, furniture and fixtures, transportation equipment, etc.

Any reasonable method of depreciation may be used for each account, but it must be applied to that account consistently. If a different method of depreciation is to be used on similar property acquired later, the new assets can be set up in a separate account. In the straight line method for a group account, the rate may be based on the maximum expected useful life of the longest lived asset in the account, or on the average expected useful life of the assets in the account.[39]

Averaging conventions. The depreciation for each year may be determined using one of the averaging conventions as follows: (1) All additions and retirements are assumed to occur uniformly throughout the year. The depreciation rate is applied to the average of the beginning and ending balances in the asset account for the year. (2) All additions and retirements during the first half of the year are assumed to be made on the first day of the year and all those during the second half of the year are made on the first day of the following year. In this case a full year's depreciation is taken on the additions in the first half of the year and retirements in the second half of the year. On the other hand, no depreciation is taken on additions in the second half of the year and on retirements in the first half. Any averaging convention chosen must be consistently followed, unless it substantially distorts the depreciation allowance.[40]

¶ 384   **Retirement of Assets**

Personal Income Tax only. California has adopted MACRS. Generally, in case of retirement of an asset, taxpayer gets a half-year of depreciation when an asset is retired. Mid-month convention applies in case of nonresidential real property, and residential rental property.[1]

---

(39) Fed Reg 1.167(a)–7.
(40) Fed Reg 1.167(a)–10(b).

(1) IRC § 168(d); § 17024.5.

Bank and Corporation Tax only. California conforms to depreciation rules in effect before adoption of ACRS and MACRS. Retirement of assets means that the assets are permanently withdrawn from use in a trade business or in the production of income. The retirement may be due to a sale or an exchange, an abandonment or by putting the asset in the supplies or scrap account.

In the case of a sale or an exchange the usual rules for the recognition of gain or loss would apply. In an abandonment the recognized loss is the difference between the adjusted basis of the asset when it is abandoned and its salvage value. Transfer of a depreciable asset to a supplier's scrap account would not require that any gain be recognized. The recognized loss is the excess of the adjusted basis at the time of the retirement over the greater of (a) the salvage value or (b) the fair market value at the time of the retirement.[2]

Multiple asset accounts—normal retirement. If the depreciation rate is based on the maximum expected life of the longest lived asset in the account, the loss recognized is computed by the excess of the adjusted basis at the time of the retirement over the greater of the salvage value or the fair market value at that time. If the rate is based on average life, loss is recognized since the use of this rate assumes that some assets will be retired before and others after the expiration of the average life. The full cost of the asset reduced by salvage is charged to the depreciation reserve.[3]

Item accounts—normal retirement. If the rate is based on the average useful life and the taxpayer has a large number of assets, no loss is recognized. If there are only a few assets, the loss is computed if the use of the average life does not substantially distort income. The loss would be the excess of the adjusted basis over the salvage value or the fair market value at the time of retirement, whichever is larger. A retirement is considered as a normal retirement unless the withdrawal is from a cause not contemplated at the time the depreciation rate was set.[3]

¶ 385 Expensing Qualified Property

Personal Income Tax Law only. California has adopted IRC § 179, with modifications. Under this federal rule, a taxpayer may elect to treat some or all of the cost of qualifying property placed in service during the year as currently deductible expense, instead of depreciating the property. The amount expensed can't exceed $10,000 a year, and the basis of an asset is reduced by the amount expensed. California has repealed former Rev & TC § 17252 provisions that allowed a deduction for additional first-year depreciation, and § 17260(a)(2) provision disallowing expenditures for certain depreciable business assets as provided by IRC § 179(c).[4]

---

(2) Fed Reg 1.167(a)–8(a).
(3) Fed Reg 1.167(a)–8(b)–(e).

(4) IRC § 179; § 17024.5.

WARNING	The *Revenue Reconciliation Act of 1993* increased the amount which may be expensed under IRC § 179 from $10,000 per year to $17,500 for tax years beginning on or after 1–1–93. California has not adopted this change so that for personal income tax purposes expense deductions are limited to $10,000. The Bank and Corporation Tax Law does not recognize expense deductions under IRC § 179.

¶ 385A Clean-Fuel Vehicles and Refueling Property

California has adopted IRC § 179A which provides a deduction for the cost of clean-fuel vehicles and certain refueling property. While the federal deduction is allowable for property placed in service until the year 2004, California has modified the provisions to limit the deduction to qualifying property placed in service after 6–30–93, and before 1–1–95, regardless of the taxable year. In addition, IRC § 179A(e)(5) provides that the amount of deduction will not include any amount taken into account in expensing property under IRC § 179, or Rev & TC §§ 17252.5, 17265, or 17266, which relate to Los Angeles Revitalization zones, program areas, or enterprise zones.[5]

¶ 386 Useful Life and Class Life Asset Depreciation Range System

Personal Income Tax Law only. For taxable years starting on or after 1–1–87, California adopts federal MACRS. The depreciation deduction under IRC § 168 is determined by using the applicable depreciation method, the applicable recovery period, and the applicable convention.[6]

WARNING	The *Revenue Reconciliation Act of 1993* extended the recovery period for depreciating nonresidential real property from 31.5 years to 39 years for property placed in service by the taxpayer generally on or after 5–13–93. California has not adopted this change so that for personal income tax purposes the recovery period for nonresidential real property continues to be 31.5 years [Rev & TC § 17250], and for corporate tax purposes the recovery period is 40–60 years [Rev & TC § 24349; Reg. 24354.1; and FTB form 3885].

Useful life of depreciable property—Bank and Corporation Tax Law only. The useful life is the period the asset is expected to be used in the service of the taxpayer. It must be determined for each asset separately. The useful life is determined from the taxpayer's experience with similar property in the trade or business, or if his experience is inadequate, the general experience of the industry. Among the factors considered in determining the useful life are:

(1) wear and tear and decay or decline from natural causes;
(2) the normal progress of the arts, economic changes, conventions and current developments affecting the property;
(3) climatic conditions;
(4) the taxpayer's policy on repairs, renewals and replacements.

---

(5) § 24356.5.   (6) IRC § 168; § 17024.5.

Salvage value is not a factor in determining the useful life of depreciable property. Once the useful life is determined it can be changed only if the change is significant and there is a clear and convincing basis for the redetermination.[7]

Class Life Asset Depreciation Range (CLADR) System. In 1962 the Treasury Department set up the guideline system which was an industry-wide approach to depreciation. The 1971 Revenue Act established the Class Life system including ADR (asset depreciation range). The Class Life ADR (CLADR) system enables taxpayers to choose from a range of depreciable lives that are not more than 20% shorter nor 20% longer than the guideline lives established. The Class Life ADR system is an elective method. The federal election is made on Form 4832 and filed with a return for the year the assets are placed in service.[8]

California adopted the CLADR effective for 1976 and later years. Between 1962 and 1976, California had permitted the use of the federal Guideline Lives.

> *Note:* In adopting the federal system, California did not include the 20% upper and lower range limits established by the 1971 Revenue Act. In order to select the CLADR System for California purposes, a timely election must be filed with the return for the year in which the asset is placed in service. Form FTB 3888 is used for this purpose, and the Franchise Tax Board will not permit a taxpayer to use Federal Form 4832 in lieu of FTB 3888.

An additional averaging convention is available to a taxpayer who adopts the Class Life system. The rule uses a half-year approach for multiple asset accounts and treats all property acquired during the year as having been acquired in mid-year.[9]

¶ 387 Low-income Rental Housing

Both the California Bank and Corporation and Personal Income Tax laws grant taxpayers a credit against tax equal to the applicable percentage of the qualified basis of each qualified low income building located in California. The state credit is based on the federal credit under IRC § 42, applicable to taxable years ending after 12–31–86, including 1988 TAMRA amendments, unless modified by state law, and to buildings placed in service. State credit modifies federal provisions on applicable percentages, special rules for first year of credit, compliance period, and recapture provisions. California credit will remain in effect as long as federal.[10] For further details on California's Personal Income Tax Law credit, see ¶ 156; Bank and Corporation Tax Law credit, see ¶ 1235.

---

(7) Fed Reg 1.167(a)–1(b).

(8) Fed Reg 1.167(a)–11.

(9) Fed Reg 1.167(a)–11(c)(2).

(10) IRC § 42; § 17058; 23610.5.

¶ 388   Demolition of Structures

California follows federal provisions that require such expenses or losses to be capitalized.[11] Under IRC § 280B, no deduction is allowed to the owner or lessee of any structure for demolition expense or loss sustained on the demolition. Amounts are capitalized.

¶ 390   Child Care Centers

California has adopted IRC § 419(c)(3)(C) which allows a 5 year amortization of facilities used for child care centers using the straight line method and no salvage value. To be subject to amortization, rather than ordinary depreciation, the facilities must be provided as part of an employer provided benefit plan.[12]

¶ 392   Business Start-up Expenses

California Personal Income Tax Law adopts IRC § 195, relating to business start-up expenses. California Bank and Corporation Tax Law specifies that any IRC § 195 reference to IRC §§ 163(a), 164, 165 and 174 relating to interest, taxes, losses, and research and experimental expenditures refers to California law sections covering those subjects.[13]

Such expenses may, at the election of taxpayer, be treated as deferred expenses and deducted ratably over a period of not less than 60 months starting with the month the business commences. The election must be made no later than the due date of the return for the taxable year the business begins, including extensions of such due date. The period selected can't be changed. Start-up expenses are amounts paid or incurred in creating or investigating the creation or acquisition of an active trade or business or any activity engaged in for profit before the active trade or business begins in anticipation of the activity becoming an active trade or business, which aren't currently deductible under IRC §§ 163(a), 164 and 174. Such creation expenses, if paid or incurred in connection with expansion of existing trade or business in same field, to be deductible, would have to be allowable as deduction for taxable year in which paid or incurred. Start-up expenditures also cover those pre-opening costs which, if paid or incurred in the operation of an existing active trade or business, would be allowable as a deduction for the year paid or incurred. Expenses for the production of income incurred prior to the business activity must also be capitalized. The question of when an active trade or business begins will be answered by IRS Regulations. If the taxpayer disposes completely of the trade or business before the end of the amortization period, any unamortized start-up expenses may be deducted under IRC § 165 (losses).[14]

Note: Election must be made before the filing deadline for year (including extensions) in which business begins.

---

(11) § 17201; 24442.
(12) § 17501; 24601.

(13) § 17201; 24414.
(14) IRC § 195.

¶ 393   **Residential Rental Property**

Bank and Corporation Tax law only. For income years starting on or after 1-1-91, California has repealed its provisions for residential rental property depreciation. Before 1991, the ACRS provisions in IRC § 168 could be used to determine what was reasonable depreciation allowance for eligible residential rental property. This was real property that: (1) was located in California; (2) construction on which was started on or after 1-1-85 and before 7-1-88; and (3) complied with 80% or more of gross rental income from dwelling units requirement of IRC § 167(j)(2)(B). Eligible residential rental property was deemed "18-year real property" for purposes of applying IRC § 168. Calculation of depreciation was governed by IRC § 168(b) provisions on assignment of period and percentages and use of mid-month convention. Also applicable was the election of 18, 35 or 45 year recovery period using the straight-line method, use of single percentage for property in any class, and exclusion of property from half-year convention. MACRS provisions also applied.[15]

¶ 394   **Enterprise Zones**

A taxpayer may elect to treat the cost of any recovery property that is IRC § 1245 property, as defined in IRC § 1245(a)(3), as an expense not chargeable to a capital account. This treatment applies to any taxable or income year in which the property is placed in service. IRC § 1245 property is tangible personal property, other than an air conditioning or heating unit, or other tangible property, not including a building and its structural components, if such property is integral part of manufacturing, production, or extraction, or furnishing of transportation, communications, electrical energy, gas, water or sewage disposal services. Also included are research facilities, bulk storage facilities for fungible commodities, elevators and escalators, agricultural or horticultural structures, qualified rehabilitated buildings to extent of qualified expenditures, qualified timber property, and petroleum storage facilities. Recovery property must be used exclusively in trade or business conducted in an enterprise zone. Any amounts deducted with respect to expensed property that ceases to be used in an enterprise zone within two years after being placed in service must be included in income for that year. These rules do not apply to any property for which the taxpayer may not make an election for the tax year under IRC § 179 because of the application of IRC § 179(d) (applications and special rules). They also do not apply to any property described in IRC § 168(f), relating to property to which IRC § 168 does not apply.[16] Sound recordings shall be treated as recovery property only if so elected under IRC § 48(s).[17]

Election. The election to use expense treatment must specify the items to which it applies, and the portion of the cost to be taken into account. It must be made on the return for the taxable year. The election can only be

---

(15) § 24349.5.
(16) § 17252.5; § 24356.2.

(17) § 17250.

¶ 393

revoked with consent of the Franchise Tax Board. It's not available to estates or trusts.[16]

Aggregate cost. The aggregate cost that can be taken into account for expense treatment can't exceed $5,000 for taxable year of designation of enterprise zone; $5,000 for first taxable year thereafter; $7,500 for second and third such taxable years; and $10,000 for each succeeding taxable year. In the case of a husband and wife filing separately, with respect to each return, the applicable amount is 50% of the amount otherwise allowed.[16]

Other limits. A taxpayer who elects expense treatment can't take additional first-year depreciation, under IRC § 179. Rev & TC § 17252.5 does not apply to any property for which the taxpayer may not make an election under IRC § 179(d).[18] The section also does not apply to any property described in IRC § 168(f), relating to property to which IRC § 168 does not apply.[19] Prescribed elections must be in effect for special outdoor advertising display treatment.[20]

¶ 395   Economic Development Program Areas

A taxpayer who conducts a qualified business in an economic development program area can elect to treat 40% of the cost of: (1) machinery and machinery parts used for fabricating, processing and assembling; and (2) manufacturing machinery and machinery parts used to produce renewable energy resources or air or water pollution control mechanisms as an expense that is not chargeable to a capital account. Cost so treated will be allowed as a deduction for the taxable or income year in which the machinery or parts are placed in service. The property must be used as an integral part of qualified business in a program area. Estates and trusts are not eligible to use this treatment.[21]

Aggregate cost. The aggregate cost that may be taken into account for any taxable or income year can't exceed $100,000 in the taxable or income year of designation, and $100,000 in the first taxable or income year thereafter; $75,000 in the second and third years; and $50,000 in each taxable or income years following those years.

Election. The election must be made on the return for the taxable or income year, and must specify the items of property to which the election applies and the percentage of the cost to be taken into account. The election can't be revoked without the consent of the Franchise Tax Board.

Limitations. A taxpayer who elects a 40% cost write-off for machinery and parts can't claim the deduction under IRC § 179, relating to the election to expense certain depreciable business assets, and must reduce the basis of the property by the amount of the Rev & TC § 17265 deduction. But the taxpayer may claim depreciation by any method allowed under Rev & TC

---

(18) 17252.5(d)(5); 24356.2(c)(4).
(19) 17252.5(d)(7); 24356.2(c)(7).

(20) § 18151; § 24949.2.
(21) § 17265; 24356.3.

§ 17250 or Rev & TC § 24349 starting with taxable or income year following taxable or income year property is placed in service. Rev & TC § 17265 does not apply to any property for which the taxpayer cannot make an election during any tax year because of the application of the provisions of IRC § 179(d) (definitions and special rules). Installment method does not apply to extent of amount allowed as deduction under 40% cost write-off rule. Proceeds of installment sale, to extent of such deduction, will be deemed received in year of disposition. "Purchase" does not include property acquired: (1) from certain related parties; (2) by one component member of an affiliated group from another component member; (3) with basis determined in whole or in part by reference to adjusted basis in hands of person from whom acquired (excluding basis determined by basis of other property held at any time by acquirer).[22]

Property ceasing to be qualified property. Any amounts expensed with respect to property that ceases to be qualified property at any time before the close of the second taxable year after the property is placed in service must be included in income for that year.[23]

¶ 395A **Los Angeles Revitalization Zone**

Depreciable property. Depreciable property as defined in IRC § 1245(a)(3) purchased exclusively for use in the Los Angeles Revitalization Zone may be expensed in the year of acquisition.[24] The expensing provisions do not apply to property purchased from a related party, and the provision will not apply to so much of the basis of the property as is determined by reference to the basis of other property held at any time by the person acquiring the property. To qualify, the property must be purchased on or after September 1, 1992, but prior to December 1, 1998. Recapture provisions apply if the property ceases to be used in a trade or business within the Los Angeles Revitalization zone prior to the close of the second taxable year after the property is placed in service. There is no limit on the amount eligible for deduction in the year of acquisition. This deduction does not apply to property listed in IRC § 168(f).

Lender's deduction. A bank or financial institution lending money to businesses in the Los Angeles Revitalization Zone is not subject to tax on interest earned on the loan.[25]

¶ 396 **Luxury Automobiles and Mixed-Use Property**

Personal Income Tax law only. California has adopted IRC § 280F. IRC § 280F listed property, if used less than 50% for business, must be written off under the alternative depreciation system of IRC § 168(g). IRC § 280F provides that employees cannot claim an expensing deduction for listed property, unless it passes the convenience of employer and condition-of-employment tests. It places depreciation limits for luxury autos and certain

---

(22) § 17260; 17265; 17552.5; 24356.3; 24667.
(23) § 17265(h); 24356.3.

(24) § 17266; 24356.4.
(25) § 17233; 24385.

property used for personal purposes for income or taxable years starting 1–1–87 or later.

Caps on auto depreciation: Under IRC § 168, passenger autos placed in service after 1986 are depreciated over five years using a half year convention and 200% declining balance depreciation with a built-in switch to straight line. However, IRC § 280F in effect overrides IRC § 168 and "caps" the annual depreciation deductions that otherwise may be claimed, forcing the taxpayer to recover the cost of a higher-priced auto over a longer-than-normal period. For purposes of IRC § 280F, expensing deductions under IRC § 179 are treated as depreciation deductions.

Due to legislative changes, and an automatic inflation adjustment that applies to autos placed in service after 1988, the IRC § 280F dollar caps for business autos depend on when they were placed in service. For autos placed in service after 1986, the dollar caps are as follows:

Year	Autos placed in service during 1987 and 1988	Autos placed in service during 1989 and 1990	Autos placed in service during 1991	Autos placed in service during 1992	Autos placed in service during 1993
1	$2,560	$2,660	$2,660	$2,760	$2,860
2	$4,100	$4,200	$4,300	$4,400	$4,600
3	$2,450	$2,550	$2,550	$2,650	$2,750
Later	$1,475	$1,475	$1,575	$1,575	$1,675

For relevant earlier years, the limits were as follows: placed in service after April 2, 1985 and before 1987; $3,200 first year, $4,800 remaining years; placed in service after 1984 and April 3, 1985, $4,100 first year, $6,200 remaining years. The dollar caps must be reduced if business/investment use is less than 100%.[26]

EXAMPLE   In 1993, Taxpayer A and B each buy a $15,000 auto. Taxpayer A uses his car 100% for business and may claim a $2,860 depreciation deduction. Taxpayer B uses her car 70% for business and 30% for personal driving. Taxpayer B's 1993 depreciation deduction is limited to $2,002 (70% of $2,860).

Bank and Corporation Tax law only. California adopts IRC § 280F, with the following modifications:

(1) terms "deduction" or "recovery deduction" relating to depreciation deduction under IRC § 168 mean amount allowable as deduction under Bank and Corporation Tax Law;

(2) "recovery period" relating to property under IRC § 168 means class life asset depreciation range allowable by California;

(3) IRC § 280F investment credit provisions don't apply in California; and

(4) California definitions of "deduction", "recovery deduction" and "recovery period" don't apply to enterprise zone property subject to expense treatment (see ¶ 394).[27]

---

(26) IRC § 280F(a)(3); 17024.5.   **(27)** § 24349.1.

¶ 401 **Depreciation Recapture**

When business property is sold or exchanged or involuntarily converted, three terms relating to such property may come into play: IRC § 1231 property, IRC § 1245 property, and IRC § 1250 property. The purpose is to separate the gain realized into portions representing ordinary income and capital gains. The definitions and the treatment to which the respective assets are subject are set out below.

IRC § 1231 property. The property included in the definition is:

(1) property used in the trade or business or held for the production of rents or royalties held for more than one year,

(2) property used in a trade or business and involuntarily converted and also held for more than one year,

(3) crops sold with land held for the same period,

(4) livestock,

(5) timber, domestic iron ore or coal where the owner sells it under a contract with a retained economic interest.[28]

The specific treatment afforded "1231 assets" is that the gains are totaled separately from the losses. If the total of the gains exceeds the total of the losses, each gain or loss during the year is treated as though it was attributable to the gain or loss on the sale of a capital asset. If the losses exceed the gains, each gain or loss is treated as an ordinary gain or loss.[29]

WARNING | Federal Form 4797 is used to compute the results of the sale or exchange of IRC § 1231 assets. California has provided Schedule D–1 for the purpose and will not accept Form 4797 instead.

Recapture of net ordinary losses under IRC § 1231(c) must be offset against IRC § 1231 gains. California follows federal provisions on recapture of net ordinary losses.

IRC § 1245 property. For this purpose only (ignoring how the property may be treated under local law) IRC § 1245 property includes:[29]

(1) Personal property (tangible and intangible);

(2) An elevator or escalator;

(3) Real property other than in (4) below which has its adjusted basis reduced for amortization deductions for: (a) pollution control facilities (b) on-the-job training, or (c) child care facilities.

(4) A special purpose structure (other than a building or its components) which has been used for certain business activities, a research facility or a storage facility in manufacturing, production or extraction, or furnishing transportation, communications, electrical energy, gas, water, or sewage disposal services.

IRC § 1245(a)(2)(C) provides that deductions under IRC §§ 179, 190, and 193, will be treated as if they were deductions allowable for amortization. California expands that provision to provide that accelerated deductions for the write off of property under Rev & TC § 24356.2 relating to enterprise zone businesses, § 24356.3 relating to program areas, and

---

(28) IRC § 1231(b).   (29) § 18151.

¶ 401

§ 24356.4 relating to Los Angeles Revitalization Zones, will also be treated as if the deduction was allowable as amortization.[30]

In the computation of gain on the sale of IRC § 1245 property ordinary income results to the extent of the recapture of depreciation taken since 1961. To put it another way, the amount by which the lesser of: (1) the recomputed bases; or (2) the amount realized on the sale or exchange or involuntary conversion exceeds the adjusted basis of the property is ordinary income. The "recomputed basis" is the adjusted basis to which is added all of the depreciation taken since 1961.

The rule applies to sales or exchanges taking place during tax years beginning after 1962, except for elevators and escalators for sales after 1963.[31]

Note: California follows provisions of IRC § 1245(a)(5)–(6) defining recovery property in relation to ACRS provisions of IRC § 168, and special rule for qualified lease property in relation to same section of federal code. IRC § 1245 definition includes depreciable railroad grading or tunnel bore placed in service on or after 1–1–87.[32]

IRC § 1250 property. This group of assets includes all real property subject to the allowance for depreciation and which is not depreciable personal property within the meaning above of IRC § 1245 property. It includes leased property to which the lessee has made improvements which are depreciable. IRC § 1250 rules do not apply if: (1) the depreciation taken is straight line on assets held for more than a year; or (2) a loss results on the sale or exchange; or (3) the property is low-income rental property held for 16⅔ years or more.

Note: In reading following paragraphs dealing with depreciation of IRC §§ 1250 (Rev & TC § 18212) property, be sure to note different effective dates for state and federal rules governing depreciation periods.

To determine the amount of the gain treated as ordinary income compute the amount realized from the sale or exchange over the adjusted basis, figure the additional depreciation for periods after 1975 (after 1976 for California) and multiply by the applicable percentage below. The additional depreciation is the excess of actual depreciation taken over straight line depreciation taken since 1963. For example, by the use of declining balance depreciation, sum of the years-digits or other rapid depreciation method. If the real property has been held less than a year, any depreciation would be treated as additional depreciation.

For nonresidential real property the applicable percentage is 100% property sold or exchanged after 1969 (after 1970 for California).

Recapture of soil and water conservation expenditures. Under IRC § 1252, if a taxpayer sells farmland held less than ten years, a part of the gain, if any, can be recaptured as ordinary income if he or she had previously deducted the expenses of soil and water conservation expenditures. If the

---

(30) § 24990.6.
(31) § 18151.

(32) IRC § 1245; § 17024.5; 18151.

land had been held less than five years, 100% of the conservation expenses will be recaptured (to the extent of the gain). If the farmland is sold within six years after it was acquired, the recapture percentage is 80%. The amount decreases by 20% for each additional year held.[33]

Note: This recapture of soil and water conservation expenditures applies only under the Personal Income Tax Law and does not apply to corporations.

Recapture of oil, gas, geothermal or other mineral property.   Under IRC § 1254, adopted by California, if oil, gas, geothermal or other mineral property is disposed of, the lesser of: (1) the aggregate amount of expenditures deducted by the taxpayer or any person under IRC §§ 263 (intangible drilling and development costs), 616 (mine or other natural deposit development expenditures), or 617 (mining exploration expenditures that would have been included in adjusted basis; but not if expensed and later included in income); and the deductions for depletion under IRC § 611, or (2) the excess of, in the case of a sale, exchange or involuntary conversion, the amount realized, or in the case of any other disposition, the fair market value of the property, over the adjusted basis of the property shall be treated as a gain which is ordinary income. Gain is recognized despite any other provision of the IRC or California laws.[34]

Recapture of players' contract amortization.   Under IRC § 1245(a)(4), adopted by California, if a sports franchise is sold after December 31, 1975, the amortization taken on players' contracts is subject to a recapture computation. The "recomputed basis" of such contracts is the adjusted basis increased by the greater of (1) the previously unrecaptured depreciation on the contracts acquired by the transferor when he or she received the franchise, or (2) the previously unrecaptured depreciation on contracts set up since his or her acquisition of the franchise.[34]

Residential rental property.   IRC § 1250(a) depreciation recapture provisions apply to residential rental property.[35]

Sale of stock in S corporation.   The provisions of IRC § 1254(b)(2) for application of special rules under regulations of the Secretary of Treasury, similar to IRC § 751 rules on unrealized receivables and inventory items of a partnership, in case of sale of stock of S corporation apply in California. These rules, applicable under both California law and IRC, affect treatment of portion of excess of amount realized over adjusted basis of stock attributable to expenditures allocable to oil, gas or geothermal property that have been deducted as intangible drilling and development costs.[36]

---

(33) IRC § 1252.
(34) § 18151.

(35) IRC § 1250(a).
(36) IRC § 1254(b)(2).

DEPLETION

¶ 402   Depletion

With the exception of certain modifications noted below, California has conformed to federal IRC provisions on depletion.[37] California has not adopted IRC § 29 credit for producing fuel from:

- nonconventional sources;
- IRC § 40 credit for small producers of ethanol;
- IRC § 43 credit for enhanced oil recovery;
- IRC § 56;
- IRC§ 59 special energy deduction provisions for the alternative minimum tax; and
- IRC § 613(d) rules on percentage depletion for geothermal deposits.[38]

Corporations commonly owned or controlled. When either: (1) the income from sources within California of two or more corporations commonly owned or controlled is determined in accordance with California rules on allocation and apportionment, or the provisions of the Multistate Tax Compact adopted by California, or (2) two or more corporations commonly owned or controlled derive income from sources solely within California, whose business activities are such that, if conducted within and without California, the in-state source income would be determined under those provisions for allocation or apportionment, or the provisions of the Multistate Tax Compact, these corporations must determine percentage completion as if they were one corporation. As to wholly intrastate corporations, if the total depletion limitations apply, then the amount of percentage depletion, as so adjusted and limited, must be prorated among them in the ratio to which the percentage depletion of each, before applying the limitations, bears to the total percentage depletion for all corporations, before applying the limitations.[39]

Geothermal deposit. Geothermal deposit, for California purposes, means a geothermal reservoir consisting of natural heat that is stored in rocks, or in an aqueous liquid or vapor, whether or not under pressure.[40]

An owner of an interest in an oil, gas, geothermal well, or standing timber may deduct depletion. The deduction is available to both an operating owner and an owner of an economic interest in the mineral or standing timber in place. Economic interest depends on whether you have the right to the income from the extraction and sale of the mineral or the cutting of the timber to repay you for your investment in the property. It is possible for more than one person to have an economic interest in a property. In order to deduct a depletion allowance in any year, it is necessary that the holder of the economic interest have income from the property. The income may be

---

(37) IRC   § 611–638;   § 17681–17684;
24831–24834.
(38) § 17682; 24832.

(39) § 24833.
(40) § 17684; 24834.

¶ 402

from a working or operating interest from royalties, overriding royalties, production payments, or net profit interest.[40]

The amounts paid for the privilege of deferring development are ordinary income to the lessor of the property and are not subject to a depletion allowance.[1] If the taxpayer sells the property or his entire economic interest in the property, the gain on the sale is a capital gain, but no depletion deduction against that gain is allowed.[2]

Production payments.   In many instances the owner of an economic interest in property sells a share of the future production to be taken from the proceeds when the production of the mineral occurs.

"Carved-out payments."   Carved-out payments are created when the owner of a property sells or carves out a portion of his future production. California law conforms to IRC § 636 that treats the transaction as a loan rather than a sale of an economic interest. The owner of the property (the seller) is required to report the entire income from the property subject to depletion as the production takes place.

"Retained payments."   Retained payments are created when the owner of a mineral interest sells the working interest, but keeps production payments for himself. Retained payments are treated as purchase money mortgage loans, rather than economic interest in the mineral property. The production payment is part of the sales proceeds entering into the seller's gain or loss. The income from the property used to satisfy the payment is taxable to the buyer and is subject to depletion. He can deduct operating costs.

Payments retained by lessors.   Payments retained by lessors on leases of mineral interests are treated by the lessee as a bonus payable in installments. The lessee capitalizes the payments and recovers them through depletion. The lessor treats the production payments as depletable income.[3]

Adjusted for depletion.   California has adopted IRC § 612 that provides that basis is the adjusted basis for determining gain on a sale. In figuring the adjusted basis, certain additions must be made to the cost of the property. In the case of oil and gas properties, the owner or operator has an election to either charge intangible drilling and development costs to the capital account, recovering them through depletion or depreciation, depending on the type of property it is, or deduct the costs as expenses.[4]

Election.   The election to expense the intangible drilling costs must be made on the return for the first tax year the costs are sustained. If a taxpayer does not deduct the costs in the first return, he is considered to have elected to capitalize them.[5]

---

(1) IRC § 61; 611; 612.
(2) IRC § 611; 612; 617.
(3) IRC § 636.

(4) Fed Reg 1.612–4(a).
(5) Fed Reg 1.612–4(d).

In most instances it is preferable to expense intangible drilling costs, except that:

- Intangible drilling costs reduce taxable income, which might limit depletion because of the 50% net income limitation, and
- Intangible drilling costs are a tax preference item for noncorporate taxpayers.

Recapture.   California follows federal law.[6] Intangible drilling and development costs are considered to be similar to IRC § 1245 property to be recaptured when the property is disposed of in a sale. The amounts deducted in prior periods are treated as ordinary income to the extent they exceed the amounts that would have been deducted, had the costs been capitalized.

Cost depletion.   The purpose of cost depletion is to write-off the adjusted basis of the property over the term of the production in a simple form of depletion. It is based on an estimate of a number of units (barrels of oil, tons of mineral, thousands of cubic feet of gas, etc.). To determine cost depletion, the adjusted basis is divided by the number of recoverable units to give the cost depletion per unit.

This amount is multiplied by the units extracted and sold during the year to determine the amount of depletion allowable for the year. The adjusted basis of the property is reduced each year by the depletion deducted in the return for that year, whether it be cost or percentage depletion. The remaining basis is used to compute the cost depletion for the following year.

At any time when it is discovered that the remaining units have been incorrectly estimated, the depletion allowance for that year and later years will be based on the revised estimates.[7]

Percentage depletion.   The most beneficial way of computing depletion from a tax standpoint is the use of the percentage method, which applies to all types of depletable property except standing timber. This method allows a taxpayer to deduct a flat percentage of gross income from the property. The percentage depletion amount may not exceed 50% of the taxable income from the property, computed without regard to the depletion allowance taken in that year. You would generally compute depletion both by the cost method and the percentage method and take whichever results in the greater deduction. The tax laws state that cost depletion must be used if it results in a greater deduction than percentage depletion.

As with cost depletion, the adjusted basis of the depletable property is reduced each year by the percentage depletion deducted, but it should be noted that percentage depletion would still be allowable even though the basis of the property has been reduced to zero by prior depletion deductions. Cost depletion, however, would not be available once the basis of the property has been reduced to zero.[8]

---

(6) IRC § 1254; § 18151; 18175.   (8) IRC § 613; § 17683; 24833.
(7) IRC § 611(a); 612; § 17024.5; 23051.5.

"Gross income from the property," for the purposes of Rev & TC § 17683 provisions governing percentage depletion, does not include any lease bonus, advance royalty, or other amount payable without regard to production from the property.[9]

Oil and gas wells. The percentage depletion method for oil and gas wells was eliminated for federal purposes for tax years ending after 1974, with the exception of certain production from domestic gas wells and for independent oil producers and royalty owners.

For taxable or income years starting on or after 1–1–87, California follows the federal percentages for minerals, other than oil, gas or geothermal wells.

Exemption for small producers and royalty owners. California has adopted the federal rules in IRC § 613(d) and 613A which provides an exemption for small producers and royalty owners. *Federal rules.* The "average daily production" for the tax year from domestic oil and gas wells is the basis for computing the exemption for producers and royalty owners from the elimination of the percentage depletion deduction. Average daily production is arrived at by dividing the aggregate by the number of days in the tax year. The amount of the taxpayer's average daily production to which depletion applies is called "depletable oil (or gas) quantity".[10] These rules were first adopted as of January 1, 1993.

Aggregating operating oil and gas interests. A taxpayer's operating mineral interests in oil and gas in a separate tract or parcel of land or lease are combined and treated as one property. It is also possible to combine some of the interests into one property and treat all the other interests in that same tract as separate property. When a new interest is found in the property, it is combined with the existing combination unless the taxpayer elects to treat it separately. The election is made when filing the return for the first tax year an expenditure is made by the taxpayer on the new property.[11]

Unitization and pools. When these are required under state law, the taxpayer's interest in the unit or the pool is considered one property. If the formation of the unit or pool is voluntary, it is also considered one property, but the interests have to be in the same deposit or, if in more than one, must be logical and either contiguous or in close proximity.[12]

Aggregation rules—mines. A taxpayer can elect to aggregate and treat as one property all of the interests in a mine or two or more mines within an operating unit. It is necessary that all the interests in the mine be included in any aggregation, and it does not matter whether the interests are in the same or contiguous tracts or if the taxpayer makes more than one aggregation in an operating unit. However, you can elect to break up a single interest or tract containing one deposit into two or more properties if there is a mine

---

(9) § 17683(f).

(10) IRC § 613(d); 613A; § 17682; 24832.

(11) Fed Reg 1.614–8.

(12) Fed Reg 1.614–3.

in each segment. The election to put this into effect must be made no later than the time for filing the returns for the first tax year in which a development or operation expenditures are made.[12]

Timber depletion.   The only method of depletion allowed for timber is the cost method. Percentage depletion is not applied to timber. The depletion of timber takes place at the time the timber is cut, but the depletion allowable in most cases cannot be computed until the quantity of cut timber is first accurately measured in the process of getting it ready for sale. In figuring depletion on timber, it is necessary to calculate the "depletion unit". The depletion unit is the cost or adjusted basis of the standing timber on hand at the beginning of the taxable year, divided by the total number of units of timber on hand in the account at the beginning of the year measured in thousands of board feet or cords, etc. To figure the depletion allowance, multiply the number of timber units cut by the depletion unit. To the extent that depletion is allowable in a tax year on timber which has not been sold during the year, the depletion so allowable shall be included as an item of cost in the closing inventory for the year.

Treatment as sale or exchange.   California has adopted IRC § 631 which includes a special provision for timber which allows a taxpayer to treat the cutting of timber as a sale or exchange, whether for sale or use in his own trade or business, if he owned the timber or held the contract right to cut the timber for more than one year. Gain or loss is recognized to the extent of the difference between the adjusted basis of the timber, for depletion purposes, and the fair market value of the timber on the first day of the taxable year in which the timber is cut.

The fair market value then becomes the taxpayer's cost for the timber for all tax purposes, including gain or loss on the subsequent sale of the timber. Gain or loss on the sale would then be considered to be ordinary income.[13]

Election.   To use this special method, the election must be made on the return for the taxable year in which the timber is cut.

Exploration expenditures—mines.   Exploration expenditures paid or incurred during the income year in order to ascertain the existence, location, extent or quality of any deposit of ore or other mineral (other than oil, gas or geothermal properties) before the development stage begins may be deducted currently, or you have the option to capitalize them.

If you make the election to deduct exploration expenditures incurred, none can be capitalized.

Recapture.   Also, if you elect the deduction, the amounts must be recaptured when the mine reaches the producing stage or is sold or other-

---

(13) § 17024.5; 23051.5.

wise disposed of. For federal tax purposes in domestic exploration, the recapture will be handled by:

(1) Decreasing the depletion deduction when the mine reaches the producing stage, or

(2) Including such deductions in income when the mine reaches the producing stage, or

(3) By treating as ordinary income part or all of the gain if the mine is disposed of.[14]

Development expenditure—mines. Under IRC § 616, followed by California, development expenditures of a mine or natural deposit (other than oil or gas well) which is known to contain commercially marketable quantities of the ore or mineral are deductible as follows: (1) They can be deducted in the year paid or incurred; or (2) taxpayer may elect, regardless of when such expenses paid or incurred, to defer them to be deducted ratably as the ore or mineral benefited by them is sold.

Any election is not binding on future years. During the period the mine ore deposit is in the development stage this election is limited to the development expenses in excess of the net receipts from production in the tax year. On the other hand, the amount of such expenditures not in excess of such receipts may be deducted in full. The election is made in the return filed by the due date (including any extensions).

California follows federal rules on treatment of deferred development expenses.[15] Deferred development expenses are included in computing the adjusted base of the mine or deposit when the mine is sold. The base so adjusted must be reduced by such deferred expenditures allowed as deductions to the extent that they reduce tax liability (but not less than the amount allowable for the tax year and prior years). These expenditures are not considered in figuring the adjusted basis of the mine or deposit for purposes of depletion.

BAD DEBTS

¶ 403   Bad Debts—General

California has adopted IRC § 165, relating to losses; IRC § 166, relating to bad debts; and IRC § 582, relating to bad debts, losses and gains with respect to securities held by financial institutions.[16]

Under IRC § 166, a bad debt deduction can be taken either as a reduction of gross income in determining adjusted gross income or as an itemized deduction, depending on the type of debt. In order that a bad debt qualifies for a deduction, there must be certain facts present.

(1) There must be a true creditor—debtor relationship between taxpayer and the creditor;

---

(14) IRC § 617; § 17024.5; 23051.5.   (16) § 17201; 24347; 24348.
(15) IRC § 616; § 17024.5; 23051.5.

(2) There must exist a legal obligation to pay a certain amount of money;

(3) All necessary steps must have been taken to collect the debt. This does not mean that legal action is required. It may be that the bankruptcy of the creditor or his disappearance or something similar would create a situation where it is not necessary to take any further steps;

(4) It must be established that the debt is uncollectible, and that it will remain that way;

(5) Deduction is available only in the year that the debt becomes worthless. In some situations it is possible to prove worthlessness before the actual maturity of the obligation;

(6) Amounts owing for payment of goods or services provided by taxpayer are not deductible as bad debt unless taxpayer had reported the amount as income.

ILLUSTRATIVE CASES

The taxpayer corporation received an interest-bearing promissory note secured by a second deed of trust on some real property in exchange for a loan of $20,000 to a shareholder. The shareholder declared bankruptcy in 1969, and the bankruptcy was discharged in 1970. The real property was sold at a foreclosure sale in 1970. The taxpayer received nothing from the sale. The Franchise Tax Board determined that the debt went bad in 1970, rather than 1969 because it had not been proven that the amount would not be collected even though the debtor filed bankruptcy in 1969. *Appeal of Valley View Sanitarium and Rest Home, Inc., SBE 9–27–78.*

A deduction on a 1964 personal income tax return was disallowed because the debt had become worthless in a prior year. The Board stated: "On identical facts, and under substantially similar statutory provisions, the United States Tax Court recently resolved this issue adversely to the appellant . . .. Appellant has not provided us with any evidence which would justify our reaching a different conclusion." *Appeal of Ruth Wertheim Smith, SBE 10–16–73.*

¶ 404　Nonbusiness Bad Debts

California law conforms to IRC § 166(d)(1)(B).[17] Generally there are two kinds of bad debts: nonbusiness bad debts and business bad debts. A debt may be either totally or partially worthless. However, a deduction cannot be taken for a partially worthless nonbusiness bad debt. Generally, any debt which you did not get as a result of operating your trade or business is considered to be a nonbusiness bad debt. Such debts are deducted only as short-term capital losses on Schedule D of the individual income tax return.

TAX TIP　Example 1:　John Walker, a real estate broker, made loans to some of his clients, for the purpose of arranging their purchases and to retain their business. Client A later when bankrupt and was unable to pay his

---

(17) § 17201.

obligation. The loan would be considered to be related to his business and would be considered a business bad debt.

Example 2: Dr. Smith, a practicing physician, loaned some money to a couple of his clients. If these loans become uncollectible, they would be deductible only as nonbusiness bad debts since the doctor was not in the business of loaning money and the loans to his clients did not have a close relationship to his medical profession.

Loans to relatives. A taxpayer may lend money to a relative or a friend and take a deduction for the bad debt when it becomes worthless. As long as, at the time the transaction was entered into, there was an intention to repay; i.e., if the transaction was considered to be an arm's-length deal, both parties acknowledging that a debtor—creditor relationship was present.[18]

¶ 405 Business Bad Debts

In order to be deductible as a business bad debt, the debt must be closely related to the activity of the business with a valid business reason for entering into the transaction. Business bad debts are treated like other business expenses and deducted in arriving at adjusted gross income. For a corporate taxpayer there is no distinction between business bad debts and nonbusiness bad debts.[19]

Worthless accounts or notes receivable generally arise from the sales to customers of goods or services. A cash basis taxpayer would not include payment for such goods or services until such time as he actually receives payment. Therefore, he is not entitled to take a bad debt deduction for any such receivables which he cannot collect.

A taxpayer using the accrual method would report the income from such goods and services in income in the year in which he receives the account or note receivable. If he is unable to collect on the account or the note he has a valid bad debt.[20]

¶ 406 Guarantees

A taxpayer who guarantees the payment of another person or corporation's debt, and then has to pay it off, is entitled to a bad debt deduction. It does not matter whether the arrangement in which he participated was that of a guarantor, an endorsor, or an indemnitor. The only bad debt deduction allowable to a guarantor is one which is either entered into for profit, or related to the taxpayer's trade, business or employment. In other words, in order to show that you entered into it for a profit, you must be able to show that you were entitled to receive something in return. The distinction made is as follows: (1) A worthless debt will qualify as a business bad debt if it can be established that the dominant motive for guaranteeing the debt was proximately related to the guarantor's trade or business; (2) The worthless

(18) Fed Reg 1.166–5; § 17024.5(c).
(19) Fed Reg 1.166–1; 1.166–5; § 17024.5(c).

(20) Fed Reg 1.166–1(e); § 17024.5(c).

debt would be considered to be a nonbusiness bad debt if it is established that the guarantee was entered into for profit, but not as part of the guarantor's trade or business.[21]

Legal duty to pay.   In addition to the above, it should be noted that for a payment on a guarantee to be deductible, there has to be an enforceable legal duty upon the taxpayer to make the payment (except that legal action need not have been brought against the taxpayer) and the agreement was entered into before the obligation became worthless (or partially worthless in the case of an agreement entered into in the course of the taxpayer's trade or business).[22]

Subrogation rights.   When the agreement provides for a right-of-subrogation or other similar right against the issuer, the taxpayer is not entitled to deduct his payment as a worthless debt until the taxable year in which the right-of-subrogation or other similar right becomes totally worthless (or partially worthless in the case of an agreement which arose in the course of a taxpayer's trade or business).[23]

EXAMPLE   John Jones is the president and sole stockholder of ABC Corporation. The Corporation applied for a large loan at the local bank. The bank required that Mr. Jones guarantee payment. When ABC Corporation defaulted on the loan they called on Mr. Jones to make full payment to the bank. In order for Mr. Jones to prove that his guarantee payment was a business bad debt deduction, he would have to show that his purpose in guaranteeing the loan was his concern for his salary income. If his main purpose in guaranteeing the loan was to protect his investment in the stock of ABC Corporation then he has a nonbusiness bad debt deduction upon payment of the guarantee.

¶ 407   **Method of Deducting Bad Debts**

Bad debts are deducted in one of two ways:

Specific charge-off method.   Allows a deduction of all bad debts that became worthless during the taxable year;

Reserve method.   Under the California Bank and Corporation Tax Law, for income years starting 1–1–88 and later, this method is allowed only to banks, savings and loan associations, and financial corporations. The use of this method was repealed for taxable years beginning on or after 1–1–87.

Specific charge-off method.   Under this method, a deduction is allowed for bad debts that become partially or totally worthless during the tax year. However, deduction of partially worthless bad debts is limited to the amount actually charged off on taxpayer's books of account during the tax year. It is not necessary that a charge off and a deduction be made each year for partially worthless debts. The charge off can be postponed until a later year, when more of the debt has become worthless or, finally, when it is entirely worthless.[24]

---

(21) Fed Reg 1.166–9(a)–(c); § 17024.5(c).
(22) Fed Reg 1.166–9(d); § 17024.5(c).

(23) Fed Reg 1.166–9(a); § 17024.5(c).
(24) Fed Reg 1.166–3, § 17024.5(c).

TAX TIP   Although it is not necessary to write off on your books of account a totally worthless bad debt in order to get the deduction, it seems to be good business practice to do so. If you claim a debt as totally worthless in your tax return and a revenue agent rules that the debt is only partially worthless, you will not be allowed any deduction unless you have charged off that amount on your books.

Installment sales. A taxpayer who deals in personal property and uses the installment method of reporting the income from such sales may use the specific charge-off method for both partially and totally worthless bad debts. However, the deduction as a bad debt on the installment sale item cannot be more than the cost to the dealer of that item less the amount the dealer has received in payment on the sale.[25]

Reserve method. Using this method the taxpayer does not deduct bad debts directly from gross income. Instead, each year the taxpayer deducts as an addition to a reserve for bad debts, the amount calculated to cover expected bad debts in the future. When specific bad debts then become totally or partially worthless, they are deducted from the reserve. The addition to the reserve for that year, then, would be the amount required to build the reserve back up to the expected required level at the end of the year.

To determine the amount that is reasonable to have in the reserve at the end of a taxable year, it is necessary to consider the following facts:

- Type of business;
- General status of the economy in the area;
- Total amount of receivables at the end of the year;
- Net bad losses for the year;
- Amount in the reserve already.[26]

Collection history used. The Internal Revenue Service and the Franchise Tax Board field auditors generally take the position that the reasonable addition to a reserve depends primarily on the collection history of the particular business itself.

They will generally ask for information relating to the accounts receivable balances at the end of the five prior years, the bad debts loss and the recoveries in each of those years and then compute a reasonable addition to the reserve based on that information.

TAX TIP   Schedule F of the Federal corporation income tax return (Form 1120) and the California bank and corporation franchise tax return (Form 100) if filled in would provide that information on receivables, losses and recoveries to the taxing authorities.

Bad debt reserves for dealers' guaranteed obligations. For taxable years starting on or after 1–1–87, the California Personal Income Tax Law has

---

(25) § 17551; 24667–24669.   (26) Fed Reg 1.166.1(b); 1.166–4; § 17024.5(c).

adopted the 1986 TRA repeal of IRC § 166 provisions on dealer's bad debt reserve.[27]

Change from reserve method to specific charge-off method. Taxpayer must include in gross income in the year of the change the credit balance in the reserve for bad debts at the beginning of the tax year of the change. Again, it is required that Form 3115 be filed with the Commissioner of Internal Revenue and the Franchise Tax Board within 180 days after the beginning of the taxable year in which it is desired to make the change.

Going out of business. If you change your method of accounting for bad debts under Rev Proc 80–51 or Rev Proc 82–19 and go out of business during the one, three or up to 10-year period during which the adjustment is being made, the portion of the initial reserve which has not yet been deducted can be excluded from your income. A copy of Form 3115 should be attached to your tax return for the year in which you go out of business.[28]

¶ 408   Banks and Trust Companies—Bad Debt Reserve

The California rules for determining the bad debt reserve of qualifying banks, mutual savings banks, co-operative banks, building and loan associations and other savings institutions are substantially different from the federal rules. Only the California rules are discussed below.

A reasonable addition to the reserve for bad debts of any bank or savings and loan association for the income year may not exceed the amount necessary to increase the reserve at the close of the income year to the greater of:

(1) The amount which is determined by multiplying loans outstanding at the close of the income year by the ratio of (a) The total bad debts sustained during the income year and the five preceding years adjusted for recoveries of bad debts for such period to (b) The sum of loans outstanding at the close of such six income years. At the option of the taxpayer in lieu of the ratio obtained by this formula the ratio may be computed by using an average of annual averages for the six-year period.

(2) The amount which is determined by multiplying loans outstanding at the close of the income year by the ratio of (a) total bad debts sustained during the income year and the two preceding years, adjusted for the recoveries of bad debts for such period, to (b) the sum of loans outstanding at the close of such three income years; at the option of the taxpayer. Instead of this ratio, the ratio may be computed by using an average of annual averages for the three-year period.

(3) For income years beginning before January 1, 1989 the amount of the bad debt reserve determined as of December 31, 1976, provided that for income years beginning after December 31, 1984 the addition shall not exceed the amount necessary to increase the reserve to the amount that is five times the amount of the maximum reserve determined under paragraph (1).[29]

For income years starting 1–1–85 and later, if the taxpayer is able to establish that additions to reserve provided for by the rules in (1)—(3) above

(27) § 17201; 24348(b).   **(29)** Reg 24348(b)(3).
(28) Fed Reg 1.166–1(b)(3); 1.446–1(2)(3).

are insufficient to absorb anticipated losses, it may claim an addition to reserve in amount necessary to absorb such losses. In no event may amount of reserve exceed the lesser of the amount of the reserve required by or reported to bank and savings and loan association regulatory agencies and reflected in taxpayer's published financial statements, or 1% of amounts outstanding at close of income year. Taxpayer may establish inadequacy of addition to reserve by a review of creditworthiness of: (a) its largest loans not to represent less than 10% of its total loan portfolio, on an individual basis; (b) random selection of a reasonable percentage, not to be less than 5% of a particular class or classes of loans, such class to represent at least 50% of its remaining loan portfolio; and (c) the historic loan loss experience of the remaining loans determined under method in (1) above without consideration of specific loans or classes of loans for which review was made under (a) and (b). In no event may loss charged to reserve for any loan be greater than that charged or reported to regulatory agencies, or reported in financial statements.[30]

> *Note:* A newly organized bank or savings and loan association which does not have the required six years of loss experience may use the loss ratio which determines the allowable addition to the reserve by using the average of any combination it may select of its own loss experience or the industry-wide experience for each year of the six-year period. In the case of a savings and loan association the average loan loss experience of savings and loan associations located in the state for the income year may be deemed as the industry-wide loan loss experience.[31]

In computing the amount of loans outstanding at the end of the current year or any of the preceding five years, the bank or savings and loan association is required to exclude government insured loans to the extent that they are insured or guaranteed from the computation. Also if the bank or savings and loan association has control over the withdrawal of deposits in the lending bank or savings and loan association, loans secured by those deposits also are to be eliminated in computing the outstanding loans. Unearned interest or discount on outstanding loans of a bank or savings and loan association shall also be eliminated in computing the outstanding loans.[32] After statutory termination of deductions for special reserve for bad debts allowed on loans for low and moderate income housing,[33] existing reserve may be continued on loans remaining outstanding, subject to limitation of 10% maximum.[34] Savings and loan association can't retroactively increase amount of bad debt deduction, after date for filing return has expired, to amount greater than addition it made to bad debt reserve on its books for that year. To do so would require adjustment to self-determination addition entered on books. It would not reflect experiential loss on books.[35]

---

(30) Reg 24348(b)(3)(B)–(D).
(31) Reg 24348(b)(3)(b)(E)–(F).
(32) Reg 24348(b)(3)(G).

(33) § 24348(c).
(34) LR 351, 2–21–73.
(35) LR 417, 3–19–81.

¶ 409   **Recovery of Bad Debts**

California has adopted IRC § 111 which provides that a taxpayer who deducts a bad debt and later collects all or part of it must include the amount recovered in gross income on the tax return for the year of recovery. However, if the amount of the bad debt deduction in the prior year did not actually decrease the income subject to tax in that year, it is possible to exclude all or a portion of the recovered amount from gross income. IRC §§ 111(b) and IRC § 111(c), relating to treatment of credits and credit carryovers are applicable to credits allowed under both the Bank and Corporation Tax Law and the Personal Income Tax Law.[36]

INVENTORIES

¶ 411   **Inventories**

Inventories—at the beginning and end of each taxable year—are required when the production, purchase, or sale of merchandise is an income-producing factor. The use of inventories is necessary to assign the correct amount of income to each year of the trade or business.

Goods and items included in inventory. The inventory should include all finished or partly finished goods and, in the case of raw materials and supplies, only those which have been acquired for sale or which will physically become a part of the merchandise intended for sale. Containers such as kegs, bottles, and cases, whether returnable or not, are included in inventory if title to such items passes to the purchaser of the product. Finished goods should be included in the inventory until title of such goods is transferred to the buyer. Therefore, the seller should include in his inventory goods under contract for sale but not yet segregated and applied to the contract and goods out on consignment. Purchaser should include in inventory merchandise purchased (including containers), title to which has passed to him even though the goods may be in transit, or for other reasons have not been reduced to physical possession.

With the exception of farmers who are not required to use inventories, § 471 IRC the California Personal Income Tax Law, and the California Bank and Corporation Tax Law each state that the use of inventories is mandatory when in the opinion of the Commissioner of Internal Revenue or the Franchise Tax Board, it is necessary in order to clearly determine the income of the taxpayer.[37]

Uniform capitalization rules relating to inventory. California has adopted IRC § 263A and 460.[38] IRC § 263A provides uniform rules to determine which costs and expenditures must be capitalized.

---

(36) § 17131; 24310.
(37) § 17551; 24701.

(38) IRC § 263A; 460; 17551; 23051.5; 24422.5.

Items affected.   The following items must be capitalized and built into cost of goods sold.

- Costs incident to purchasing inventory (for example, wages or salaries of employees responsible for purchasing);
- Repackaging, assembly, and other costs incurred in processing goods while in the taxpayer's possession;
- Storage costs (e.g., rent or depreciation, insurance premiums, and taxes attributable to a warehouse and wages of warehouse personnel);
- A portion of general and administrative costs allocable to these functions;
- A portion of pension and profit-sharing costs; and
- Certain interest costs, including imputed interest.

The uniform capitalization rules only affect inventories valued at cost. The rules won't affect inventories valued at market by a taxpayer using the lower of cost or market method, or by a dealer in securities using the market method. But the rules will apply to inventories valued at cost by a taxpayer using the lower of cost or market method.

Items not covered.   The capitalization rules will not apply to the following:

(1) any portion of the cost constituting research and experimental expenditures, deductible mining development costs or intangible drilling costs,

(2) property produced in a farming business where the preproductive period is less than two years or consists of livestock held for slaughter,

(3) personal property acquired for resale if the taxpayer's average gross receipts are $10 million or less for the three prior tax years,

(4) to the growing of timber and certain ornamental trees (that is, those evergreen trees which are more than 6 years old when severed from roots and sold for ornamental purposes),

(5) any property produced by the taxpayer for use by the taxpayer other than in a trade or business or activity engaged in for profit, and

(6) property produced under a long-term contract.

Contributions to pensions.   For purposes of both the personal income tax and the corporation franchise and income taxes, California has adopted the IRC § 263A rules relating to the amortization of past service pension costs for income or taxable years starting on or after 1–1–90. Under these rules, an allocable portion of all otherwise deductible pension costs, whether for current or past services, must be included in the basis of property produced or held for resale. Before 1990, only current service pension costs had to be capitalized.

Special rules for interest.   California adopts IRC § 263A(f) which provides special rules concerning interest allocated to property produced by a taxpayer. Under these rules, interest on a debt must be capitalized if the debt is allocable to the production of:

- real and personal property having an IRC § 168 class life of 20 years or more produced for use or sale in the taxpayer's business; and
- the property has an estimated production period exceeding two years; or
- the property has an estimated production period exceeding one year and a production cost (excluding interest) of over $1 million.

¶ 411

The production period for real property starts when physical activity is first performed. For other property, it starts when cumulative production expenses equal or exceed 5% of the total estimated production expenses allocable to the property. The production period ends when the property is ready for service or sale.

In determining interest that must be capitalized for a property-producing asset, the general interest allocation methods apply to the asset's full cost. If it is not used only to produce a single property, the asset's total interest cost is allocated among the various properties produced. Any interest specifically traceable to such an asset must first be allocated to the produced property. Interest on the taxpayer's other debt is then allocated to the extent required under the avoided cost method. To avoid double counting, any interest allocated to property under this rule is not again allocated to property under the general interest allocation rule.

Aggregation rules similar to those for determining whether a business's annual gross receipts do not exceed $5 million for purposes of the small business exception to the accrual method requirement are applied to determine whether the $10 million threshold (under the above exception number three) is exceeded.

The 1986 TRA authorizes the Internal Revenue Service to provide a simplified method for applying uniform capitalization rules to property that is acquired for resale which can be separately used for each trade or business of the taxpayer. Taxpayers who do not elect to use the simplified method are required to use the same uniform capitalization rules that are applicable to manufacturers and their election may not be changed without the IRS's permission. In general, four categories of indirect costs will be allocable to inventory under this simplified method:

(1) off-site storage and warehousing costs (including, but not limited to, rent or depreciation attributable to a warehouse, property taxes, insurance premiums, security costs, and other costs directly identifiable with the storage facility);

(2) purchasing costs such as buyer's wages or salaries;

(3) handling, processing, assembly, repackaging, and similar costs, including labor costs attributable to unloading goods (but not including labor costs attributable to loading of goods for final shipment to customers, or labor at a retail facility); and

(4) the portion of general and administrative costs allocable to these functions.

Exempt property.   California has adopted IRC § 263A(c) which exempts the following property from the uniform capitalization rules:

● property for personal use, research and experimental costs deductible under IRC § 174;

● certain development and other costs of oil and gas wells and mineral property deductible under IRC § 263(c), 616(a), or 617(a);

● property produced under a long-term contract;

● growing of timber and certain ornamental plants.

¶ 411

The following costs are also exempt from the uniform capitalization rules:

- oil or gas well or mineral propert cost subject to amortization under IRC § 263(c), 263(i), 291(b)(2), 616, and 617;
- costs, other than circulation expenditures, subject to 10-year amortization under IRC § 59(e).

Special rules for farmers and ranchers. The uniform capitalization rules, including those requiring capitalization of interest, will generally apply to all crops and livestock (other than animals held for slaughter) having a preproductive period of more than two years. For this purpose, the preproductive period of plants is deemed to begin when the plant or seed is first planted or acquired by the taxpayer, and to end when the plant becomes productive or is sold. The preproductive period of animals begins at the time of acquisition, breeding or embryo implantation, and ends when the animal is ready to perform its intended function. The preproduction period of a plant grown in commercial quantities in the United States is to be based on the nationwide weighted average preproduction period for such plant. The IRS is authorized to issue regulations that permit a taxpayer to use reasonable inventory valuation methods to compute the amounts that have to be capitalized in the case of plants and animals.

Exception—Farming corporations. Farming partnerships with corporate partners and tax shelters who are required to use the accrual accounting method must capitalize preproduction costs without regard to whether the productive period is more than two years. Consistent with the general capitalization rules, such taxpayers are required to capitalize taxes and, to the extent the preproductive period exceeds two years, interest incurred prior to production.

Replacement of damaged crops. A special rule allows a taxpayer to deduct the cost of replacing crops that are lost or damaged because of freezing, disease, drought, pests or other casualty and were intended for human consumption so long as the replacement plants bear the same type of crop as was destroyed or damaged. The land on which the replanting takes place does not have to be the same land on which the lost or destroyed plants were located, and the replanting can take place on any parcel of land of the same acreage located anywhere in the United States. This exception applies to costs incurred by persons other than the taxpayer who incurred the loss, as long as the taxpayer (1) retains a more than 50% equity interest in the underlying property, (2) the person claiming the deduction materially participates in the planting or property maintenance during the four-tax-year period beginning with the loss year. The "other person" must hold an equity interest in the property.

Requirement (2), above, has been amended by allowing the deduction to material participant in the farm, other than the 50% or more equity owner, without regard to when the costs were incurred, or whether the other person's material participation occurs within the four-tax-year period following the loss. It further amends the 50% equity ownership interest by providing that ownership must be in the edible plants at all times during the tax year in which costs were incurred to replant the damaged crops. A similar amendment for less-than-50% owners who are material participants was made—material participation in replanting the edible crops is necessary. It should be noted, however, that the amended language requires the 50%-or-more equity owner to have the required interest at all times during the tax year in which the replanting costs were incurred or paid. The less-than-50% owner who is a material participant is required to own his interest and materially participate only during part of the tax year in which replanting costs were paid or incurred.

Election to deduct preproductive period expense. An exception to the rules requiring capitalization of productive period expenses for certain farmers is allowed. Under this exception, a farmer (including producers of livestock, nursery stock, Christmas and other ornamental trees and agricultural crops), may elect to deduct currently all preproductive cost of plants and animals that may be deducted under prior laws. If the election is made, any gain on disposition of the product is recaptured (generally treated as IRC § 1245 depreciation) and taxed as ordinary income to the extent of expensed deductions that otherwise would have been capitalized. Also, they are required to use the alternative cost recovery system (under IRC § 168(g)(2)) for all farm assets used predominately in farming and placed in service in any tax years covered by the election. The election can not be made by:

(1) tax shelters as defined in IRC § 6161(b)(2)(C)(ii);
(2) taxpayers required to use the accrual method; under Section 447;
(3) farming syndicates (as defined in IRC § 464(c)); and
(4) producers of pistachio nuts.

The election also does not apply to the cost of planting, cultivating, maintaining, or developing any citrus or almond grove, incurred before the end of the fourth tax year after the trees are planted. If a grove is planted over more than one tax year, the part of the grove planted in each tax year is treated as a separate grove for determining the year of planting. Partnerships and S corporations make the election at the partner or shareholder level. The election must be made in the first tax year that begins after 1986 during which the taxpayer is a farmer. Election can be revoked only with IRS consent.

Excluded from the UNICAP rules is the production of animals in a farming business, unless the farm is required to use the accrual method. 1989 Revenue Reconciliation Act makes it clear that the election to revoke the alternative depreciation system can only be made by farmers engaged in a farming business involving production of animals having a preproductive period of more than two years. Expenses having a preproductive period of less than two years are not covered by UNICAP. Taxpayers, other than those required to use the accrual method of accounting, may elect to deduct currently the cost of planting, cultivation, or development of pistachio trees. California adopts this rule relating to pistachio farmers for taxable income years on or after 1–1–88.

Free-lance authors, photographers and artists. California has adopted IRC § 263(h) which provides that qualified creative expenses of a writer, photographer, or artist, may be deducted currently. To qualify for the exemption, expenses must be incurred by an *individual* in the trade or business of being a writer, photographer, or artist. Further, this writer, photographer, or artist must be either self-employed or must own, either directly or with his family, substantially all of the stock of a personal service corporation. In this case, a personal service corporation is one whose principal activity is the performance of personal services that are substantially performed by employee-owners. Writers qualifying for the exemption include those whose personal efforts create a literary manuscript, musical composition, lyrics, or dance score. Photographers qualifying are individuals who through their personal efforts create a photograph, or photographic negative or transparency. Artists are qualified if they create through their personal efforts pictures, paintings, sculpture, etchings, drawings, cartoons, graphic designs, or original print editions. The exemption also applies to corporations owned by the writer, artist, photographer or family member. The principal activity of the corporation must be the performance of personal services directly related to the activities of the writer, artist or photographer. The exemption applies only to the expenses directly related to the writer's, artist's or photographer's activities.

Accounting for inventories involves two separate determinations to identify the quantity and the dollar value of the inventory. These are:

- *Inventory identification.* The method by which the quantity of goods on hand at the date of the inventory is identified, and
- *Valuation of inventory.* The method by which a cost or value is assigned to the various components of the inventory.

Inventory identification methods include the following:

- *Specific identification method* identifies items in an inventory with their cost by matching the goods with their invoices to find the cost of each item;
- *First in, first out (FIFO) method.* The items purchased or produced first are the first items sold, consumed or otherwise disposed of. The items in inventory at the end of the year are valued as the items most recently purchased or produced.
- *Last in, first out (LIFO) method.* By the use of this method a taxpayer assumes that the items of inventory which were purchased last are the ones which were sold and removed from inventory. The items included in the ending inventory are considered to be those from the opening inventory, plus any acquired items during the year still on hand using the LIFO reverse order of disposition. California conform to federal. The FTB may permit use of suitable published governmental indexes.[39]

---

(39) IRC § 472(b); § 17551; 24701.

EXAMPLE   For the taxable year you have an opening inventory of 2,000 units which cost $1.75 each. During the year you purchase 300 units @ $2.25 and 400 units @ $3.25, with an ending inventory of 900 units on December 31st.

Cost of goods sold using FIFO:

Opening inventory: 2,000 units @ $1.75		$3,500.00
Purchases:		
300 @ 2.25	675.00	
400 @ 3.25	1,300.00	1,975.00
Inventory available		$5,475.00
Closing inventory:		
400 @ 3.25	1,300.00	
300 @ 2.25	675.00	
200 @ 1.75	350.00	2,325.00
Cost of goods sold—FIFO		$3,150.00

Cost of goods sold using LIFO:

Inventory available (see above)	5,475.00
Closing inventory:	
900 @ 1.75	1,575.00
Cost of goods sold—LIFO	$3,900.00

FIFO and LIFO compared. The FIFO and the LIFO method will produce different results in income. As a result of the trend of price levels of the goods included in the inventories, when prices are rising, LIFO will produce a higher cost of goods sold and a smaller ending inventory. Under FIFO, the cost of goods sold will be lower and the closing inventory will be higher. On the contrary, during a period of time when prices are falling the LIFO method will produce a smaller cost of goods sold and a higher closing inventory. Under FIFO, during a time of falling prices, the cost of goods sold would be higher and the ending inventory would be lower.

During a period when prices are on the rise, a LIFO method results in relatively low closing inventory values. If the quantity of goods on hand in the inventory stays reasonably constant, the method is favorable to taxpayers, but if the taxpayer's source of supply of inventory should suddenly dry up, it would cause trouble for the taxpayer. The taxpayer would be forced to sell virtually his entire inventory and there would be a substantial profit because he would be selling inventory items which are on his books at a low value.

How to elect LIFO. A taxpayer may adopt a LIFO inventory method only with approval from the Internal Revenue Service. Application on Form 970 must be filed with the income tax return for the taxable year in which the method is first used. Once adopted, the method is binding for all future years, unless the Internal Revenue Service permits or requires the use of a different method. If the LIFO inventory method is used, the inventory must be taken at cost regardless of market value. In other words, the lower of cost or market method is not available for that part of the taxpayer's inventory valued under LIFO.[40] California follows Rev Proc 72–24 and Rev Proc 69–11 on discontinuance of LIFO inventory method.

> *Note: For California purposes* the regulations provide that the taxpayer must file an election to adopt the LIFO inventory method with return for year preceding year in which LIFO method will first be used. Copy of federal Form 970 may be submitted.[1]

> *California has adopted* IRC § 472(d) provision that any change in inventory value resulting from use of cost in beginning inventory for first year of LIFO method must be taken into account ratably in each of the three taxable years starting with the year of change.

California has adopted LIFO conformity rule that was extended to related corporations by the 1984 federal Tax Reform Act. Under this rule, a taxpayer can use LIFO method of inventory accounting only if it is also used for reporting to shareholders, partners, other proprietors, beneficiaries or for credit purposes. Conformity rules also apply to financially related corporations as if they were a single person. A group of financially related corporations means:

> (1) Any affiliated group of corporations as defined in IRC § 1504 (without regard to the exceptions in IRC § 1504(b)). However, for purposes of the IRC § 1504(a) percentage test, a 50% ownership test will take the place of the 80% ownership test; (2) Any other group of corporations which issue consolidated financial statements or reports to shareholders or others. The new law overrules *Insilco Corp. (1980)* 73 TC 589. However, several elections are provided that protect taxpayers who relied on *Insilco.*[2]

Costing under LIFO. The substantial federal provisions relating to LIFO inventories include the "dollar value method" of pricing in determining the increases in the quantity of the inventory items. The use of retail price method in connection with LIFO and the establishment of pools, such as the natural business unit pool, or the raw material content pool, which are prescribed in federal Regulations 1.472–4 to 1.472–8 have all been adopted verbatim for California purposes and are set forth in the corporation franchise and income tax regulations.[3]

Simplified dollar value LIFO inventories. California has adopted the provisions of IRC § 474. Under this federal section, an eligible small business is redefined as a business that has an average annual gross receipts of $5 million for the three preceding taxable years. The method of inventory pricing is changed from a single inventory pool to a "simplified method" in which separate inventory pools are maintained by major categories as provided in the indices published by the Bureau of Labor Statistics. Election to use the new method does not require consent of IRS. Taxpayers who made election

---

(40) Fed Reg 1.472–2—1.4721–3.
(1) Reg 24702–24706(c).
(2) IRC § 472(g) 17551; 24701.

(3) § 17551; 24701; Fed Regs 1.472–4—1.472–8; Reg 24702–24706(a)—24702–24706(g).

under the law in effect before 1986 TRA may continue under the provisions of that law for as long as their election remains in effect.[4]

Valuation of inventories. An inventory must conform to two tests:

- It must conform as nearly as possible to the best accounting practice in the trade or business, and
- It must clearly reflect income. Therefore, inventory rules cannot be uniform but must give effect to trade customs, which vary with the different types of businesses. The inventory practice of the taxpayer should be consistent from year to year and greater weight is given by the tax authorities to consistency, than to any particular method of valuing an inventory.[5]

Two most common methods used for valuing inventories are:

- Cost, or
- Cost or market, whichever is lower.[6]

The opening and closing inventories for a taxpayer must be valued by the same method.

Unsalable goods. Any goods in an inventory, which are unsalable at normal prices or unusable in the normal way because of damage, imperfections, shop wear, changes in the style, odd or broken lots, or similar causes, are to be valued at bona fide selling prices, less direct cost of disposition.

Raw materials or goods in process. Raw materials or goods in process held for use or consumption should be valued on a reasonable basis, taking into consideration the usability and the condition of the goods, but in no case should the value be less than the scrap value.[7]

Book inventories. If a taxpayer maintains book inventories on a sound accounting basis in which the respective inventory accounts are charged with the actual cost of goods purchased or produced and credited with the value of the goods used, transferred or sold, and calculated on the basis of the actual cost of the goods acquired during the taxable year (including the inventory at the beginning of the year), the net value shown by such inventory accounts will be used in the determination of the cost of goods on hand.[7]

WARNING Some of the methods used in taking or valuing inventories that are not acceptable are listed in the federal and California regulations and include the following: (1) Deducting from the inventory a reserve for price changes or an estimated depreciation in the value of the inventory; (2) Taking work in process or other parts of the inventory at a nominal price, or at less than its proper value; (3) Omitting a portion of the goods on hand; (4) Using a constant price or nominal value for so-called normal quantity of materials or goods in stock; (5) Segregating indirect production costs into fixed and variable production cost classification and allocating only the variable cost to the cost of goods produced, while treating fixed costs as period costs which are currently deductible

---

(4) § 17551; 24708; 59,223.　　　　　　　(6) Fed Reg 1.471–2(c).
(5) Fed Reg 1.471–2(a)–(b).　　　　　　　(7) Fed Reg 1.471–2(d).

("direct cost" method); (6) Treating all or most of the indirect production costs (either fixed or variable) as period costs which are currently deductible. This method is generally referred to as the "prime cost" method. Calif. reg. on inventory valuation is substantially same as federal.[8]

Inventories at cost. Cost means:

(a) The inventory price of goods on hand at the beginning of the taxable year;

(b) The invoice price, less trade or other discounts (except strictly cash discounts approximating a fair interest rate) for merchandise purchased during the taxable year. Transportation, or other necessary charges incurred in getting possession of the goods should be added to the net invoice price.

(c) For goods produced by the taxpayer, during the year the cost of raw materials and supplies entering into, or consumed in connection with the product, and direct labor expenditures and indirect production costs necessary for the production of the particular article, are included.[9]

Specialized businesses—valuation methods. The federal and California regulations state that in an industry in which the usual rules for the computation of cost of production are inapplicable, cost may be approximated on the basis which would be reasonable and in conformity with the established trade practice in the particular industry. The industries cited are: (1) farmers and raisers of livestock; (2) miners and manufacturers who, by a single process, or uniform series of processes, obtain a product of two or more kinds, sizes or grades, the unit cost of which is substantially alike and (3) retail merchants who use what is known as the "retail method" in determining the approximate cost.[10]

Manufacturers. Manufacturers are required to take into account, in order to clearly reflect income and to conform as nearly as possible to the best accounting practices, the "full absorption" method of inventory costing. Under this method the production costs must be allocated to the goods produced during the year, whether sold or included in the inventory at the end of the year. Thus, you are required to include as inventoriable cost all direct production costs and, as indicated below, all indirect production costs.[11]

Costs classified as "direct production costs" are those costs which are incident to and necessary in production or in manufacturing operations or processes, and which are components of the cost of either direct material or direct labor. The elements of direct labor cost include basic compensation, overtime pay, vacation and holiday pay, sick-leave pay and similar payments.[12]

The term "indirect production costs" includes both fixed and variable types of costs. Fixed indirect production costs are those costs which do not

---

(8) Fed Reg 1.471–2(d); Reg 24701(b).
(9) Fed Reg 1.471–3(a)–(c); Reg 24701(c).
(10) Fed Reg 1.471–3(d); Reg 24701(c).

(11) Fed Reg 1.471–11(a).
(12) Fed Reg 1.471–11(b)(1)–(2).

vary significantly with changes in the amount of goods produced at any level of production capacity, such as rents, property taxes on buildings and machinery, and so on. Variable indirect production costs are those costs which do vary significantly with a change in the amount of the goods produced. This classification would include indirect materials, janitorial supplies, utilities, repair expenses, etc.[13]

Some indirect costs, at the taxpayer's election, may be excluded from the computation of inventory costs and deducted currently. These would include marketing expenses, advertising expenses, selling and other distribution expenses, research and experimental expenses, etc. The third category listed in the regulations are those which may be included in or excluded from costs according to the way in which the taxpayer treats them in his financial statements.[14]

Note: The above information is pertinent to California taxpayers because the Franchise Tax Board has announced that it will follow the federal pronouncements in T.D. 7285. The Board also announced that it will follow Rev Proc 80–5 and Rev Proc 80–60 on inventory valuations. As a result of the *Thor Power Tool Co.* case dealing with markdowns of excess inventory amounts, the Internal Revenue Service has required substantial changes in the accounting for inventories.

Farmers. As indicated above, farmers may use the cash method of reporting income and deductions and, therefore, not be concerned with inventories. However, an accrual basis farmer, using inventories, may elect to value his inventory costs under one of the following methods: cost, the lower of cost or market, or farm price.

The "farm price method" provides for costing inventories at market price, less cost of disposition. When it is used, it must be applied to the entire inventory, unless the farmer elects to value his livestock inventory under the "unit-livestock-price method."

The "unit-livestock-price method" provides for a valuation of classes of animals raised, so as to include in the inventory such animals at a standard unit price within a class. The unit cost for each classification is determined by giving effect to the age and the kind of animals included within each class, in order to reflect a normal cost incurred in producing the animals.

It is necessary to get permission from the IRS or the California Franchise Tax Board to change from one method to another, except that a farmer who has used as a basis of his inventories the cost or cost or market methods, whichever is lower, may adopt the unit-livestock-price method without formal application.[15]

Retailers. Under the "retail method" the total of the retail selling prices of the goods on hand at the end of each year, in each department, or for each class of goods, is reduced to approximate cost by deducting an amount which bears the same ratio to such total as: (1) the total of the retail selling

---

(13) Fed Reg 1.471–11(b)(3).
(14) Fed Reg 1.471–11(c).

(15) Fed Reg 1.471–6; Reg 24701(f).

prices of the goods included in the opening inventory, plus the retail selling prices of the goods purchased during the year, with proper adjustments for all mark-ups and mark-downs, less (2) the cost of the goods included in the opening inventory, plus the cost of the goods purchased during the year, bears to (1).

The result should represent as accurately as possible, the amounts added to the cost price of the goods to cover selling and other expenses of doing business and for the margin of profit.

Mark-downs. Mark-downs which are not based on an actual reduction of retail sales prices (such as mark-downs based on depreciation and obsolescence), are not to be recognized in determining the retail selling prices of the goods on hand at the end of the taxable year.[16]

Change in method of valuing inventories. A new trade or business can adopt any method of valuing inventories. Any change from that method is an accounting change requiring approval from the tax authorities. See ¶ 352 explaining the mechanics of requesting accounting method changes.

---

(16) Fed Reg 1.471–8; Reg 2470(h).

TAXATION OF PARTNERSHIPS AND PARTNERS

¶ 421 **What is a Partnership**

Generally speaking, a partnership is an entity in which two or more persons join together to carry on a trade or business in which each contributes money, property, labor or special skills and each expects to share in the profits and losses from the business activity. A partnership includes a syndicate, group, pool, joint venture or other unincorporated organization through which any business, financial operation or venture is carried on and which is *not* a corporation, a trust or an estate.[1] It also includes foreign organized limited liability companies (LLCs) which are treated as partnerships for tax purposes by the Internal Revenue Service.[2]

Unincorporated organization. California has adopted IRC § 761(a).[3] Under IRC § 761(a) and Fed Reg 1.761–2, an unincorporated organization may be—by an election of all its members—excluded from the provisions affecting partnerships. The election applies only to those organizations which were formed for investment purposes only, or for the joint production, extraction or use of property. The election applies only if the group as such does not actively conduct a business for selling services or the property produced or extracted, and the members must be able to determine their income without computing partnership taxable income for the group.

If the management of the organization is centralized in one or more persons, and if the death of a partner does not interrupt the organization, there is a possibility that the taxing authorities would treat the organization as an association taxable as a corporation and not as a partnership.[4] IRC § 7701(a)(3) defines "corporation" to include an association.

IRC § 7704, adopted by California, provides for the treatment of publicly traded partnerships as corporations.[5]

Limited partnerships. Every limited partnership doing business in California, and required to file a return under the Rev & TC § 17932 partnership return provisions must pay California a tax for the privilege of doing business in California in an amount equal to the minimum tax amount specified in Rev & TC § 23153 for the current taxable year. For 1990 and later, this minimum tax is $800. The tax is due and payable with the return under the provisions of Rev & TC § 18432. "Limited partnership" means any partnership formed by two or more persons under the laws of California or any other jurisdiction, and having one or more general partners and one or more limited partners. Definitions of "taxable year" and "income year" will be applied to these partnerships.

Limited partnerships who file, or have on file, a certificate of limited partnership with the Secretary of State pursuant to § 15621 of the Corporations Code, must also pay the minimum tax discussed above, whether or not

---

(1) § 17008.
(2) FTB Notice 92–5, 8–21–92.
(3) § 17851.

(4) § 23038; Reg 23038(a)(2).
(5) § 17008.5.

the limited partnership is doing business in California, or is required to file a return with the state. The minimum tax on limited partnerships who become liable solely because of the filing with the Secretary of State is first due in 1994 for filing on or after 1–1–93. The tax would be due when the return for the year beginning on or after 1–1–93 is due.

The status of limited partnerships depends on the characteristics they have under the state law where they are created. Generally, limited partnerships in states whose laws are patterned after the Uniform Limited Partnership Act, usually are taxed as partnerships. If the death or retirement of a general partner dissolves the organization, it is considered to be a partnership.[6]

Family partnerships. To reduce taxes, the income of the principal wage earner of a family may be distributed among the members of his family by the creation of a partnership. California has adopted IRC provisions. Fed Regs are also applicable.[7]

WARNING   If, on the facts, the partners really intend to carry on the business and share the profits and losses, there is a valid partnership. The recognition of the partnership for income tax purposes by the taxing authorities is independent of its validity under the local state law.

A family member who actually owns an interest in a partnership in which capital is a material income-producing factor is considered to be a partner whether he bought his interest or received it as a gift. Capital is a material factor if a substantial part of business gross income is due to the use of capital as, for example, when inventories or investment in plant, machinery or equipment are required and are substantial. The family member will not be considered as actually owning the capital interest if the gift or sale of the interest to him was mere sham, or if the transferor retains so many incidents of ownership that he would continue to be recognized as actual owner.[8]

If capital is not a material income-producing factor (if the business income, for example, is primarily fees, commissions or other pay for personal services), the main guides to determine if a family member is a real partner are whether he shares in the management or control of the business, performs vital services or invests his own capital.[9]

IMPORTANT   If a family member received a valid gift of a partnership interest, the member would be taxed on the member's distributive share of such income, if the validity of the partnership is recognized, subject to two conditions: (1) the shares of partnership income must take into consideration an allowance for a reasonable compensation for services rendered to the partnership by the donor, and (2) the income allocated to the

---

(6) § 17851; 23041; 23042; 23081.
(7) IRC § 704(e); Fed Reg 1.704–1; § 170424.5; 17851.

(8) Fed Regs 1.704–1.
(9) Fed Reg 1.704–1(e)(iv).

family member donee cannot be proportionally greater than the share of the donor, attributable to his capital.[10]

¶ 422   Taxation of Partnerships

California has adopted federal IRC provisions. IRS regulations also apply in California.[10] Under IRC § 701 and Fed Reg 1.701–1, partnership profits and other items of income and gains are not taxed to the partnership but are, in effect, distributed to the individual partners and taxed to them.

California has adopted IRC § 702. IRS regulations also apply in California.[11] Under IRC § 702 and Fed Reg 1.702–1 in any case in which items of income or deductions would be limited on the individual partner's returns when added to the individual partner's other similar items of income or deductions, they are not used in the computation of the overall partnership profits, but are apportioned separately to the individual partners.

OBSERVATION   Most elections required in the law and regulations, which affect the computation of income, are made by the partnership rather than the individual partners. These include, among others, the election of the method of accounting, method of computing depreciation, amortization of any organization fees, etc. This regulation applies in California.[12]

Taxable year of partnership.   California has adopted IRC § 706. Fed Reg 1.706–1 also applies.[13] All partnerships are required to conform their tax years to that of the owners. A partnership must have the same tax year as that of its majority interest partners, unless it establishes, to the Treasury's satisfaction, a good business reason for having a different tax year. If the majority owners don't have the same tax year, the partnership must adopt the same tax year as its principal partners. If the principal partners don't have the same tax year, and no majority of partners have the same tax year, the partnership must adopt a calendar year as its tax year. Except as otherwise provided in regulations to be issued, required changes in partners' tax years are to be taken into account in determining a partnership's tax year. When the taxing authorities are satisfied there is a business purpose for having a different tax year, that year will be permitted provided deferral is three months or less. So a partnership that can establish a good business purpose can have a September 30, October 31, or November 30 year-end, even if all the partners are calendar year taxpayers. But taxpayers will not receive an automatic three-month deferral. A business purpose must exist, and wanting to defer the tax is not considered a business purpose. Taxpayers that have already obtained the taxing authorities' permission for a different year-end don't have to request permission again because of the law change.[13]

---

(10) Fed Regs 1.704–1(e)(ii).
(11) § 17024.5(c); 17851.
(12) Fed Regs 1.703.1; § 17024.5(c).

(13) IRC § 706; Fed Reg 1706–1; § 17024.5(c); 17851.

A partnership doesn't have to adopt the tax year of its majority interest partners unless partners having the same tax year have owned a majority interest in partnership profits and capital for the partnership's preceding three tax years. Tax years beginning before the new law's effective date are taken into account for determining whether the three-year test has been met. A partnership may not have a tax year other than its majority interest tax year. If it does not have a majority interest tax year, it may not have a tax year other than its principal partners' tax year, except as noted below. If it does not have a majority interest tax year and all of its principal partners do not have the same tax year (or it has no principal partners), the partnership must use the calendar year, unless another period is prescribed in regulations or elected under IRC § 444, which is effective for tax years beginning after 12–31–86. (California treatment of IRC § 444 is discussed below.) A partnership's majority interest tax year is the tax year (if any) that, on the testing day (that is, generally, the first day of its tax year), constituted the tax year of one or more partners having (on that day) a more-than-50% aggregate interest in its profits and capital. The IRC may provide that an alternate, representative period be used as the testing day, rather than the first day of the tax year, if that period is more representative of the partnership's ownership. A partnership required to change its tax year to its majority interest tax year is not required to change to another tax year for either of the two tax years following the year of change.[13]

Election of tax year other than required tax year. California adopts IRC § 444. IRC § 444(c), relating to effect of the election (required payments) does not apply in California. Generally, a partnership may elect to have a tax year other than the required tax year. Under IRC § 444(b)(1) an election may be made only if the deferral period of the tax year elected is not longer than three months. The "deferral period" with respect to any tax year of the partnership means the month between the beginning of such year and the close of the first required tax year ending in such year. Any election made under IRC § 444(a) remains in effect until the partnership changes its tax year. Any change to a required tax year may be made without consent of the taxing authorities. If the election is terminated, the partnership may not make another election. No election may be made with respect to a partnership that is part of a tiered structure other than a tiered structure comprising one or more partnerships all of which have the same tax year.[14]

A partnership that received permission to use a fiscal year-end under the provisions of Rev Proc 74–33, 1974–2 CB 489 (other than a year-end that resulted in a deferral of three months or less) can continue to use such taxable year. A partnership may adopt, retain, or change to a tax year established by IRS if the use of such tax year meets the requirements of the 25% test as described in Rev Proc 83–25, 1983–1, CB 689 (25% or more of gross receipts for the 12-month period in question are recognized in the last

---

(14) IRC § 444(a); (b); (d); § 17551; 17555.

two months of the period and the requirement has been met for the specified three consecutive 12-month periods).[13]

Annual returns of partnerships.   IRC § 6031 and Fed Reg 1.6031–1 provide that every partnership doing business in, or having income from sources within the United States, is required to file an annual information return (Form 1065).[15] California law requires that every partnership doing business in California, or in receipt of income from California is required to file a partnership return of income on Form 565. If one or more of the partners are California residents and an election is required to be made by the partnership affecting the computation of income, a return must be filed with California even though the partnership carries on no business in California or derives no income from sources within the state. Copies must be furnished partners or persons holding an interest in the partnership as nominee for another person at any time during the taxable year. A person holding an interest as nominee for another person must: (1) furnish the partnership, in manner set by the FTB, the name and address of that other person, and any other information the FTB requires; and (2) furnish information required by the FTB from partnership to that other person. The provisions of IRC § 6031(d), relating to the separate statement of items of unrelated taxable business income apply in California.[16] The FTB can provide for the filing of the group return by the partnership on behalf of electing nonresident partners or nonresident shareholders of S corporation doing business in or deriving income from California. S corp. or partnership makes return and payment as agent of electing nonresident partners and shareholders. Partnership or S corp. can deduct any amounts otherwise deductible by partner or shareholder under deferred compensation provisions, if partner or shareholder certifies to no earned income from any other sources.[17] Board can require resident partner to produce partnership records or other information on nonresident partnership.[18]

When return due.   The partnership return must be filed on or before the 15th day of the 4th month following the close of the fiscal year.[19]

OBSERVATION   IRC § 6698 provides for a penalty for failure to file a complete partnership return. The penalty is $50 per month (or fraction of a month) for each partner, up to a maximum of five months. California imposes a penalty of $10 a month multiplied by the number of partners.[20] For federal purposes, the partnership must apply for an extension of time if it is unable to file the tax return on or before the original due date. California law has a similar provision.[21]

WARNING   Rev & TC § 18633 which provides for the filing of partnership returns requires that the taxpayer identification numbers be included with the

---

(15) IRC § 6031; Fed Reg 1.6031–1.   (19) § 18566.
(16) § 18633.   (20) § 19172.
(17) § 18535.   (21) § 18567.
(18) LR404, 9–9–77.

¶ 422

return for each partner. If taxpayer identification numbers are not shown, the Franchise Tax Board could reject the return as being incomplete and assess late filing penalties computed based on the total number of partners in the partnership, not just the partners for which no tax identification number was shown. It is therefore important that correct taxpayer identification numbers be obtained for every partner.

¶ 423   Taxation of Partners

Under IRC § 702 and California Rev & TC §§ 17024.5; 17851, 17852, and 17858,[22] the individual partners must take into account on their personal income tax returns their distributive share (whether or not distributed) of certain partnership items:

- Gains and losses from sales or exchange of capital assets.
- Gains and losses from sales or exchange of property used in the trade or business.
- Gains and losses from involuntary conversions.
- Charitable contributions.
- Dividends.
- Taxes paid or accrued to foreign countries, or to possessions of the United States.
- Depletion.
- Political contributions credit.
- Other items of income, gains, losses and deductions.

Other items that have a special connotation to the individual partners, such as investment interest, net investment income, items of tax preference, property qualified for investment credit, excess intangible drilling costs tax credits, additional depreciation, payments to retirement plans, and similar items, are set forth on the K–1 of the federal Form 1065 and pages 2 and 3 of the California Form 565, to provide information necessary in the preparation of the individual partners' returns.

Apportionment of income or loss among partners. California has adopted IRC § 704(a)–(b). Federal regulations apply in California.[23] Under IRC § 704(a)–(b) and Fed Reg 1.704–1, the partnership agreement should provide information regarding the apportionment of income or loss among the partners. If the partners agree, specific items may be allocated among them in a ratio different from the ratio for sharing income or loss generally.

> *Note:* If the partnership agreement does not provide for the partner's share of income, gain, or loss, and the allocation under the partnership agreement does not provide for an allocation, or if the allocation under the agreement lacks "substantial economic effect", the allocation will be made in the ratio of the respective partners' interests in the partnership.

California has conformed to federal treatment of partners' shares of any items of income, gain, loss deduction or credit. If partners' interests change during year, interest, taxes and payments for services or use of

---

(**22**) IRC § 702; § 17024.5; 17851; 17852; 17858.   (**23**) § 17024.5(c); 17851.

property, that are accounted for under cash method, must be apportioned over each day in period during year to which they relate. The items are then allocated among the partners in proportion to their partnership interests at the close of each day to which they are assigned. For purpose of the allocations, an item relating to prior years is assigned entirely to the first day of taxable year, and an item relating to later years is assigned entirely to the last day of year. California rule applies to taxable years starting in 1985 and later.[24]

California has adopted the federal rules governing distributions of contributed property by a partnership. In the case of a distribution of contributed property, to other than the contributing partner within 5 years of the contribution, the contributing partner is treated as recognizing gain or loss equal to the difference between the contributing partner's basis and the fair market value at the time of distribution.[25]

¶ 424   Contributions to Partnership

California adopts IRC § 721[26] which provides that no gain or loss is recognized to the partnership or to any of the partners who contribute property to the partnership in exchange for a partnership interest, whether the contribution is made to an existing partnership or to a new partnership.

Basis to the contributing partner. The basis to the contributing partner of an interest in the partnership under IRC § 722, adopted by California, is the amount of the money transferred and the adjusted basis in the hands of the partner of the property transferred, increased by the amount (if any) of the gain recognized at such time.[26]

Services contributed. A partner may acquire an interest in a partnership as compensation in whole or in part for services rendered or to be rendered. The net value of this interest is taxable to him as ordinary income when he performs the services or, if they are for past services, he reports the income when he receives the interest. In a situation where one partner contributes cash or other property and the second partner contributes only services this is a problem. If one partner contributes cash or other property to the partnership and the second partner contributes only services, the first partner may surrender his right to a portion of the assets he contributes in exchange for services rendered by the second partner.

OBSERVATION   Fed Reg 1.723–1, also applicable in California, states that the partner who renders the services would receive ordinary income based on the fair market value of the interest in the property or cash that he receives. The income is realized by the partner at the time he renders the services or at

---

(**24**) IRC § 706(d).   (**26**) § 17851.
(**25**) IRC § 704(c).

the time the cash or other property right is transferred to him, whichever is later.[27]

Basis to the partnership. The basis to the partnership of property transferred by the partner under IRC § 723 is the adjusted basis in the hands of the partner at the time of the transfer, plus any gain recognized at that time. California has adopted IRC § 723.[27]

Holding period to the partnership. The holding period to the partnership for the property includes the holding period of the contributing partner. Fed Reg 1.723–1 applies in California.[27]

Note: Gain will be recognized if the property contributed in exchange for an interest in the partnership is transferred to a partnership that would be an investment company if it had been incorporated. The purpose of this provision in the IRC § 721(b) is to tax the gains realized by investors who transfer appreciated stock or securities or other property to an exchange fund operated as a partnership. However, a loss realized on the contribution to the partnership would not be recognized.

Character of gain or loss. California has adopted IRC § 724.[28] The character of the partnership's gain or loss on its disposition of contributed unrealized receivables, inventory and capital loss assets in the hands of the contributing partner will, under some circumstances, be the same as if the contributing partner has disposed of it.

The partnership's gain or loss on contributed unrealized receivables will be ordinary always. It will also have ordinary gain or loss on a taxable disposition of contributed inventory within 5 years of the contribution. (If it's disposed of more than 5 years after the contribution, the character of the gain or loss is determined at the partnership level.) And, on the disposition of a contributed capital asset within 5 years of receipt, any loss recognized by the partnership will be capital to the extent of the partner's unrealized loss potential.

If the partnership transfers the contributed property to a transferee who takes a substituted basis, the contributed property remains tainted in the transferee's hands. What's more, any property (other than C corporation stock received in a tax-free incorporation) received by the partnership in which it takes a substituted basis is also tainted. Rules similar to the foregoing also apply to a series of nonrecognition transfers.

Note: Inventory, for these purposes, doesn't include property that misses being a IRC § 1231 asset simply because it didn't meet the IRC § 1231 holding period requirements.

¶ 425 Basis of Partner's Interest

California adopts IRC § 722.[29] The basis of a partner's interest in a partnership equals the money and the adjusted basis of any property he contributes. If the transfer of property to the partnership results in taxable income to the partner, that income is an addition to the basis of the interest. An increase in

---

(27) Fed Reg 1.723–1; § 17024.5(c); 17581.   **(29)** IRC § 722; 17851.
(28) IRC § 724; 735(c).

the individual partner's liabilities because of his assumption of the partnership liabilities would be treated the same as a contribution of money to the partnership.

Mortgaged property contributed. Fed Reg 1.722–1 applies in California.[30] On the other hand, if the partner contributes property which is subject to a liability, or if the partner's liabilities are assumed by the other members of the partnership, the basis of his interest is reduced by the portion assumed by the others. It should be noted that if the contributing partner transferred property with a mortgage in excess of the contributing partner's basis, the excess would reduce the basis of the partnership interest in the hands of the contributing partner.

In addition, the excess of the mortgage assumed over the basis of the property would be treated as a capital gain to the partner from the sale or exchange of a partnership interest.

Increases in the original basis. California has adopted IRC § 705, and Fed Reg 1.705–1 applies in California.[31] Under IRC § 705 and Fed Reg 1.705–1, any further contribution to the partnership by a partner would increase the basis of the partnership interest in his hands. In addition, each year a partner's basis must be increased by his distributive share of:

(1) Taxable income;
(2) Capital gains and other income items, separately allocated to the partners;
(3) Partnership income exempt from taxation; and
(4) Excess of the deduction for depletion over the basis of the depletable property.

Reductions of partner's basis. A partner's basis in the partnership interest is reduced (but not below zero) by cash distributions made to him, his basis for other partnership property distributed to him, and by his distributive share of:

(1) Partnership losses (including capital losses);
(2) Partnership expenditure not deductible in figuring taxable income;
(3) The depletion deduction for oil and gas wells.

Partnership losses. California has adopted IRC § 704(d). Fed Reg 1.704–1(d)(1) also applies in California.[32] If distributions of money or property are made in a taxable year in which the partnership has a loss, the distributions must be taken into account before computing the amount of the partnership loss allowed to the partner as a deduction.

Partner's share of partnership liabilities. Fed Reg 1.704–(1)(b) applies in California.[33] A partner's share in the partnership's liabilities is determined in the same ratio as that set forth in the partnership agreement for

---

(30) Fed Reg 1.722–1; § 17024.5(c); 17581.
(31) IRC § 705 § 17024.5; 17851.
(32) IRC § 704(d); Fed Reg 1.704–1(d)(1); § 17024.5; 17851.

(33) Fed Reg 1.704–1(b); § 17024.5(c); 17581.

sharing losses. A limited partner's share of partnership liability cannot be greater than the difference between his actual contribution to the partnership and the total contribution which the partner would be obligated to make under the agreement. However, if the partnership were to acquire a piece of property with a mortgage for which the partnership and the individual partners did not assume nor have any liability, the liability would be shared in the same ratio as the profit sharing ratio of the partnership (including all partners, even the limited partners).

Limited partners. A limited partner is one whose personal liability for partnership debts is limited to the amount of money or other property that the partner has contributed to the partnership.

Alternative rule. California has adopted IRC § 705(b), and Fed Reg 1.705–1(b) applies in the state.[31] Under federal IRC § 705(b) and Fed Reg No. 1.705–1(b), the partner's adjusted basis for his partnership interest may be determined by reference to his proportionate share of the adjusted basis of the property of the partnership which would be distributed at the conclusion of the partnership. This rule may be used to determine the adjusted basis if: (1) The circumstances are such that you cannot practicably apply the general basis rules; or (2) where, from a consideration of all the facts, it is, in the opinion of the Commissioner or the Franchise Tax Board, reasonable to conclude that the result produced will not vary substantially from the result under the general basis rule.

Change of tax year—four-year spread. A partner's adjusted basis in its partnership interest is determined as if all of the income to be taken into account over the four-year-spread period were included in gross income in the first year. Accordingly, current distribution of an amount equal to a partner's income in the short tax year will not result in capital gain, unless the distribution would have resulted in capital gain had there been no four-year spread. If any partnership interest is disposed of before the last tax year in the spread period, any income related to the disposed interest that must be recognized under the spread is included in gross income in the same tax year that the disposal occurred. The IRS is not required to permit taxpayers an automatic change of a tax year.[31]

¶ 426   **Partnership Taxable Income**

Under IRC § 703(a), the taxable income of a partnership is computed in the same manner as that for an individual. There is no deduction for personal exemptions or the items set forth above (¶ 423), which are transferred to the individual partners for inclusion on their individual tax returns. The net operating loss under IRC § 172 can't be deducted by the partnership.

California has adopted IRC § 703 with the following exceptions:

(1) treatment of net operating losses is as provided by Rev & TC § 17276 for taxpayers other than those operating a business in enterprise zones and program areas, and as provided by Rev & TC §§ 17276.1 and 17276.2 for taxpayers operating businesses in enterprise zones and program areas;

(2) personal exemptions are granted in form of credits, not deductions;

(3) credit for political contributions are taken by individual partners, not the partnership (credit was repealed 1–1–92); and

(4) credit for taxes paid to another state is taken by partners, not the partnership.[34]

Deduction for business expenses. Fed Reg 1.703–1 applies in California.[35] A partnership is entitled to deduct all of the ordinary and necessary business expenses, paid or incurred, and the following will be considered in connection with some of them.

Organization and syndication expenses. The amounts paid to organize a partnership or promote the sale of an interest in a partnership are capital expenditures and are, therefore, not deductible. IRC § 195 is adopted by California and provides that the partnership can amortize the organization's expenses over a period of 60 or more months beginning with the month in which the partnership begins business. The balance sheet of the partnership return would show the unamortized balance of the organization's costs and all syndication expenditures (which are not amortizable).[36]

Salaries and wages. Fed Reg 1.703–1 applies in California.[37] Salaries and wages paid to employees are deductible in arriving at the distributable income of the partnership, including contributions to simplified employee plans (SEPs).

Guaranteed payments. California follows IRC § 707(c).[38] Payments or credits to a partner for services or for the use of capital are deductible by the partnership if the payments or credits are determined without regard to partnership income, except those which should be capitalized. The partner would report the payment on his return for the taxable year with which, or within which, ends the partnership year in which the partnership deducted the payments under its method of accounting. In case of nonresident partner, guaranteed payments are gross income from sources within California in the same manner as if those payments were a distributive share of that partnership.[38] A Franchise Tax Board release of 8–20–90 explains the withholding of tax from distributions to domestic (non-foreign) nonresident partners.[39]

Interest. Fed Regs 1.702–1; 1.703–1; and 1.707–1 apply in California.[40] Investment interest expense is not deductible by the partnership and should not be included on the partnership return. Interest expense for this purpose includes the interest on funds borrowed after December 16, 1969, to purchase or carry property held for investment. It is put on Schedule K of the tax return and treated by the individual partners on their separate income tax returns.

---

(34) § 17851–17853.
(35) Fed Reg 1.703–1; § 17024.5(c); 17851.
(36) § 17201.
(37) Fed Reg 1.703–1; § 17024.5(c).

(38) IRC § 707(c); § 17851; § 17854.
(39) FTB 8–20–90.
(40) Fed Reg 1.702–1; 1.703–1; 1.707–1; § 17024.5; 17851.

Interest paid by a partnership to a partner. Interest paid by a partnership to a partner as a result of a transaction in which the partner acts as other than a partner is deductible and included in interest expense on the tax return.

Taxes. Taxes paid or incurred on business property for carrying on a trade or business are deductible. Such taxes include federal import duties and federal excise and stamp taxes, but only if they were paid or incurred in carrying on the trade or business of the partnership.[40]

Bad debts. A partnership may deduct business bad debts, when they become wholly or partially worthless.[35]

Amortization. The partnership elects the deduction for amortization of certain expenditures:

    (1) Research and experimental expenses;
    (2) Mine or natural deposit development expenses.[35]

Depletion. The partnership may take a deduction for depletion only with respect to timber. Depletion deductions for oil and gas properties are included on Schedule K and go on the individual partners' returns.[1]

Retirement plans, profit sharing. Contributions made by the partnership for its employees under a qualified pension, profit sharing, annuity, bond purchase plan or bona fide employee pension plan and under any other deferred compensation plan are deductible. Payments for partners to these plans (except SEPs) are handled on the individual partner's returns.

IRA contributions. If the partnership contributes to an IRA for employees, the amount of the contribution for each employee is considered to be compensation. Contributions to an IRA for a partner are included on Schedule K and transferred to the partner's personal returns. The partnership's contribution to employee benefit programs for employees, which are not part of the retirement plans, are deductible by the partnership. Such plans include contributions for insurance, health and welfare programs.[1]

Other deductions. Any other deductions considered to be ordinary and necessary expenses of the partnership business would be included on the partnership return, except those cited as requiring a separate computation to be reported on Schedule K and transferred to each partner.[1]

¶ 427   Partnership Capital Gains and Losses

California adopts the IRC §§ 702 and 703 provisions on capital gains and losses. Fed Regs 1.702–1 and 1.703–1 apply.[2] Under IRC §§ 702 and 703, long-term and short-term capital gains and losses are disregarded in figuring partnership taxable income. They are, however, reported on the capital gain and loss schedule of the partnership return. Net recognized gains or losses from the short-term transactions and from the long-term transactions

---

(1) Fed Reg 1.702–1; 1.703–1   (2) § 17024.5(c); 17851.

are figured separately and 100% of each is shown on the capital gain and loss schedule.

OBSERVATION	Each partner picks up his share of these gains and losses whether distributed to him or not. Short-term or long-term treatment depends on the partnership's holding period, not the length of time a partner held his partnership interest.[1]

Depreciable business property (IRC § 1231 assets). Gains and losses from the sale, exchange or involuntary conversion of Section 1231 assets are excluded in calculating partnership income subject to tax. Each partner segregates his distributive share of such gains and losses and sets them off against his individual gains and losses of the same type.[2]

¶ 428   Partner's Distributive Share

California adopts the IRC § 704 provisions on distributive share determination. Fed Regs apply in California.[3] Under IRC § 704 and Fed Reg 1.704–1, each partner's distributive share of partnership income or loss is reported on his individual income tax return even though the partnership does not distribute any money to him. Generally, as indicated above, a partner's distributive share of any item or kind of income, gain, loss, deduction or credit is determined by the partnership agreement. If the partnership agreement does not provide for the partner's distributive share of income, gain, etc., or the allocation to a partner under the agreement does not have substantial economic effects, a partner's distributive share will be determined by the partner's interest in the partnership.

Distributions by the partnership are generally not taxable to the partners unless the distributions are treated as a liquidation or sale or exchange of all or part of their capital interest since the partners must include in their income their share of the partnership income whether distributed or not.

Limitation on losses. Each partner's distributive share of the partnership loss for the tax year and depletion on oil and gas properties of the partnership will be allowed only to the extent of the adjusted basis (without taking into consideration losses of the current year) of the partner's interest in the partnership at the end of the year of the loss.

In case of a limitation year, any excess of the loss over the basis will be allowed as a deduction in the succeeding year or years to the extent that the partner's adjusted basis for the partnership interest at the end of the succeeding year is greater than zero. California adopts IRC § 704(d). Fed Regs apply in Calif.[4]

EXAMPLE	At the end of partnership tax year (same as tax year of partners) partnership CD has a loss of $20,000. Partner C's distributive share of this loss is $10,000. The adjusted basis of his interest in the partnership (not taking into account his distributive share

---

(3) IRC § 704; Fed Reg 1.704–1; § 17024.5(c); 17851.

(4) IRC § 704(d); Fed Reg 1.704–1(d); § 17024.5(c); 17851.

of the loss) is $6,000. Therefore, $4,000 of the loss is not allowed. At the end of the partnership tax year, the partnership has no taxable income or loss, but owes $8,000 to a bank for money borrowed. Since C's share of this liability is $4,000, the basis of his partnership interest is increased from 0 to $4,000. C is allowed to use the $4,000 loss.

Liabilities assumed by partner. California adopts IRC § 752. Fed Reg 1.752–1 applies in California.[5] Under IRC § 752 and Fed Reg 1.752–1, an increase in a partner's share of the liabilities of the partnership is treated as a contribution of money to the partnership. This addition would serve to allow a partner, because of his higher basis, to use a larger partnership loss in his personal return. The same thing is true if the partner assumes on his own a share of the partnership debts. The liabilities assumable by the partner or by the partnership include not only notes and mortgages payable on partnership property, but other partnership obligations for payment of trade accounts, accrued expenses, notes payable, etc.

| WARNING | *At-risk loss limits.* IRC § 465 and Rev & TC § 17551 limit a taxpayer's loss to the amount that he has "at-risk" and could lose from the particular activity.[6] |

A partner is considered at-risk to the extent of the amount of cash and the adjusted basis of property contributed to the activity, the income retained by the partnership and the amounts borrowed by the partnership for use in the activity. He is not considered to be at-risk for amounts borrowed by a partner or the partnership unless he is personally liable for the repayment, or the amounts borrowed are secured by property other than that used in the activity.

¶ 428a Withholding on Distributions to Partners

California requires that partnerships withhold income taxes from any distributions of income to partners who are not residents of California if the distribution includes income derived from sources within California. The place of residence of the partner (that is, within the United States, or outside the U.S.), and the type of income being distributed (that is, sales proceeds from real property in California, etc.), determines the percentage of the distribution which is required to be withheld. These rules are explained more fully in ¶ 341, Chapter 6.

¶ 429 Partner's Dealings With Partnership

California adopts IRC § 707. Fed Reg 1.707–1 applies in California.[7] Under IRC § 707 and Fed Reg 1.707–1, if a partner engages in a transaction with the business of the partnership other than in his capacity as a partner, he would not be treated as a member of the partnership for that transaction.

---

(5) § 17024.5; 17851.
(6) IRC § 465; § 17551.

(7) IRC § 707; Fed Reg 1.707–1; § 17024.5; 17851.

¶ 429

Loss on sale or exchange.   On the sale or exchange of property, directly or indirectly between a person and a partnership, a loss would not be allowed if that person has an interest in the capital or the profits of the partnership of more than 50%. On the sale or exchange of property between two partnerships in which the same persons own more than a 50% interest of the capital or profits, the loss deduction will not be allowed.

Gain on sale or exchange.   Gain on the sale or exchange of property, directly or indirectly between a person and a partnership or between two partnerships, if more than 50% of the capital or profits interest is owned directly or indirectly by the same person or persons, would result in ordinary income treatment provided the property is other than a capital asset. Property other than a capital asset includes trade accounts receivable, inventory, stock and trade and depreciable or real property used in the trade or business.

Termination of a partnership.   California has adopted IRC § 708(a)[8] which provides that the existence of a partnership would be terminated only if (1) no part of any business, financial operation or venture of the partnership continues to be carried on by any of the partners in a partnership, or (2) there is a sale, within a 12-month period of an interest of 50% or more in the total capital and profits of the partnership. A sale to another partner would be included. However, a disposition of a partnership interest by gift, bequest or inheritance, or the liquidation of an interest is not considered to be a sale for this purpose.

The death of a partner in a two-man partnership does not terminate the partnership if the estate or other successor in interest continues to share in the profits or losses of the partnership.

Merger, consolidation or split-up.   California has adopted IRC § 708(b)[8] which provides that when two or more partnerships merge or consolidate into one, the resulting partnership is considered to be a continuation of the merging partnership the members of which own an interest of more than 50% of the capital and profits of the resulting partnership.

If a partnership divides into two or more partnerships, any resulting partnership or partnerships shall be a continuation of the prior partnership if its members had an interest of more than 50% in the capital and profits of the prior partnership.

California follows federal law that permits treatment of partner's transfer of money or other property to partnership as a sale if there's a related direct or indirect transfer of money (or other property) by the partnership to the transferor partner or to another partner and the setup is properly characterized as a sale. California also follows federal law that treats a partner's performance of services for, or transfer of property to, a partnership and its related direct or indirect allocation of income or gain to

---

(8) § 17851.

him, as a transaction between a partnership and a person not acting as a partner or as a transaction involving guaranteed payments if that's how the deal really stacks up. The related allocation is treated as a partnership payment to a nonpartner.[9]

¶ 430   **Sale or Exchange of Partner's Interest**

California adopts IRC § 741. Fed Reg 1.741–1 applies in California.[10] Under IRC § 741 and Fed Reg 1.741–1, when a partner sells or exchanges his interest in a partnership to one of the other partners or to a nonpartner, he realizes a capital gain or loss on the proceeds.

WARNING   There is no effect on the partnership itself; that is, no gain or loss is recognized to the partnership and the basis of its assets and the holding period are not affected. The selling partner must take into account the earnings of the partnership up to the date of the sale. He would report this as partnership income on his tax return and add the amount to the basis of his interest in the partnership. He withdraws his share of the partnership earnings and the withdrawal would serve to reduce his basis in the partnership interest.[11]

Whether the sale of the partnership interest is a short-term or a long-term capital gain or loss would depend on the holding period of the partnership interest by the partner.

Receivables or appreciated inventory.   California adopts IRC § 751. Fed Reg 1.751–1 applies in the state.[12] If the partnership has any unrealized receivables or substantially appreciated inventory at the time of the sale, the partner selling his interest must allocate the sales proceeds in part to the unrealized receivables and the appreciated inventories, and with respect to the gain on these items report as ordinary income, rather than capital gain.

WARNING   A partner who sells or exchanges all or part of his interest in the partnership, which has any unrealized receivables or substantially appreciated inventory, is required to file a statement with his income tax return for the year of the sale or exchange. The statement must set forth the following information: (1) the date of the sale or exchange; (2) the amount of the selling partner's adjusted basis for his partnership interest; (3) the portion of that basis assigned to the unrealized receivables and appreciated inventory assets; and (4) the amount of any money or the fair market value of any property received or to be received for the

---

(9) IRC § 707(a)(2)(b); § 17851.
(10) IRC § 741; Fed Regs 1.741–1; 17024.5(c); 17851.

(11) Fed Reg 1.741–1.
(12) IRC § 751; Fed Reg 1.751–1; § 17024.5(c).

interest in the partnership and the portion of those receipts attributable to the unrealized receivables and appreciated inventory assets.[13]

> *Note: California has not adopted* the provisions of IRC § 751(d)(2)(C) relating to appreciated inventory items subject to tax as gain on foreign investment company stock under IRC § 1246.[14]

"Unrealized receivables" means rights to income which have not been included in gross income under the method of accounting employed by the partnership, such as cash basis taxpayers. The term would not ordinarily apply to an accrual basis partnership which would include the income from the receivable in income at the time of the sale. The term means any rights (contractual or otherwise) to payment for goods delivered or to be delivered, or services rendered or to be rendered. The term unrealized receivables also includes "potential IRC § 1245 income" and "potential IRC § 1250 income". IRC §§ 1245 and 1250 property in this instance would be property on which the gain would be ordinary income.[15]

> *Note: California has not adopted* provisions of IRC § 751(c) that define term "unrealized receivables" to include (1) stock in certain foreign corporations described in IRC § 1248; and (2) oil, gas or geothermal property described in IRC § 1254.[16] IRC § 751(e) relating to limitation of tax on gains from sales or exchanges of stock in certain foreign corporations under IRC § 1248 does not apply in California.[17]

To prevent tax-wise corporations from using the partnership format to convert ordinary income (via recapture) into long-term capital gain (on sale of partnership interests), the federal law treats any sale or distribution of an interest in a partnership holding recognition (generally, inventory depreciable) property as an event triggering recognition income. The amount of such income equals what would have been recognized had the corporation sold the property (and for this purpose, FMV can't be less than the principal amount of any nonrecourse liability). Note that the selective use of loss properties won't reduce the amount of recognition income. The federal law also clarifies that the recognition income realized at the *corporate* level can be used to increase the basis of the partnership's recognition property under the IRC § 754 special election.

Transferring appreciated inventory and unrealized receivables into a second partnership basket won't divorce the ordinary income assets from the first partnership interest that's being sold. Each partnership shall be treated as owning its proportionate share of any other partnership's property in which it's a partner. And similar tax rules apply to tiered trust arrangements designed to convert ordinary income into capital gain.[18]

---

(13) Fed Regs 1.751–1(a)(3).
(14) § 17586.
(15) Fed Reg 1.751–1.

(16) § 17585.
(17) § 17587.
(18) IRC § 751; § 17851.

¶ 431   Retiring Partner's Interest

California adopts IRC § 736. Fed Reg 1.736–1 applies in California.[19] Under IRC § 736 and Fed Reg 1.736–1, a retirement from a partnership as compared to a sale happens when a partner withdraws from the partnership and his entire partnership interest is purchased by the partnership itself, rather than from the partner or other persons. When payments are made by the partnership to a retiring partner or to his estate or other successor in interest, the payments must be allocated between payments for his interest in the partnership property and his interest in unrealized receivables or appreciated inventory assets as described above.

Distribution vs. salary.

Distributions. The payments to the partner are treated as if they were distributions of the partnership. The money received reduces the retiring partner's basis for his interest in the partnership. If the basis is all used up, the payments in excess are capital gains. If some of the basis still remains after all payments have been applied against it, the remainder is capital loss. The following payments are not considered as made for an interest in partnership property and are not subject to the above rules:

(1) Payments for the partner's interest in unrealized receivables in excess of their partnership basis;

(2) Payments for the partner's share of partnership goodwill in excess of its partnership basis.

Payments, other than these, that are made in liquidation of a retiring or a deceased partner's entire partnership interest, are considered as either a distributive share of partnership income or a guaranteed payment. If the payments are based on partnership income, they are treated as distributive shares of partnership income and accordingly, are taxable to the recipient as though he continued to be a partner and they are excluded from the income of the remaining partners.

Precontribution gain rules apply. California has adopted IRC § 737 which provides that precontribution gains will be recognized to a partner receiving a distribution of property if there was a gain on that same property at the time it was contributed to the partnership by the partner receiving the distribution. This federal rule applies to distributions on or after 6–25–92. California's rule applies to distributions in taxable years beginning on or after 1–1–93.[20]

Salary. If the payments made are determined without regard to partnership income and they are not of the type treated above, they are considered as guaranteed payments (salary) made to one not a partner.

For all payments received, the recipient must segregate the portion of each payment which is in exchange for the partner's interest in partnership

---

(19) § 17024.5; 17851.   (20) § 17870.

property from the portion treated as a distributive share or guaranteed payments.

Fixed payments. If the amount to be received is fixed and is to be received over a fixed number of years, a certain portion of each year's total payments is treated as in exchange for partnership property. This portion is the total value of the retiring or deceased partnership interest in the partnership property, divided by the number of years over which the payments are to be made. The rest of the annual payment is treated as other payments.

Variable amounts. If the retiring partner receives payments that vary in amount, they are treated as payments in exchange for the interest in partnership property to the extent of the value of that interest and then as payments as either a distributive share of partnership income or a guaranteed payment.

¶ 432   **Gain or Loss on Distribution**

California has adopted IRC § 731. Fed Reg 1.731–1 applies in California.[21] Under IRC § 731 and Fed Reg 1.731–1, the income of a partnership is taxable to the partners whether or not the income is distributed to the partners. If the income is distributed when it is earned, the partners' basis of their interests cannot be changed because the partners' basis is increased by the fact of a partnership profit and decreased by the distribution of that profit to the partner.

On the other hand, any undistributed income will increase the basis of the partnership interest. If money is distributed to the partner in excess of the partnership's basis for his interest, the partner will realize a gain as though he had sold or exchanged his partnership interest.

IMPORTANT   Distributions of property can be made to the partners without the recognition of gain, but when the total amount of money distributed exceeds the partner's basis of his partnership interest, then he has taxable income.

Loss recognized. Loss is recognized only in instances where the distributions end the partner's interest in the partnership. The amount of the loss to the partner is the excess of the basis of the partner's interest over the sum of any money distributed and the basis to him of any unrealized receivables or inventory items.

Partnership realizes no gain or loss. A partnership realizes no gain or loss from a current distribution of property or a liquidation distribution.

¶ 433   **Special Basis to Transferee in Distributions**

California adopts the IRC § 732(d) provisions on special basis.[22] Under IRC § 732(d), a transferee partner who receives partnership property (other than

---

(21) § 17851.   (22) IRC § 732(d); § 17851.

money) in a distribution within two years after he acquired his partnership interest by transfer, may elect to adjust the basis of the distributed partnership assets. The election would serve to increase his basis for his partnership property to the adjusted basis of all partnership property. However, if the partnership had made such an election, this special election is not necessary.

| *TAX TIP* | To elect this method, the transferee partner must submit with his tax return, for the taxable year in which the distribution is made, a schedule showing: (1) a statement that he elects to adjust the basis of the property received under IRC § 732(d); (2) the computation of the special basis adjustment for the property distributed and its allocation to the different properties. |

Partner acquiring interest by transfer. A partner acquiring interest by a transfer when the partnership election to adjust the basis is not in effect, must determine his basis under this method, whether or not the distribution is made within two years of the transfer, if (1) the fair market value of all partnership property (except money) exceeds 110% of its adjusted basis to the partnership at the time he acquires his interest and (2) an allocation of basis under the regular method on a liquidation of his interest immediately after his transfer would have resulted in a shift of basis from property not subject to an allowance for depreciation, depletion, or amortization to property subject to such an allowance and (3) a special basis adjustment under IRC § 743(b), adopted by California, would change the basis to the transferee partner of the property actually distributed.

Distribution of depreciables or depletables. Federal Reg 1.732–1(d) applies in California.[23] If the property received in the distribution includes any property subject to depreciation, depletion or amortization, the election must be made in the year of the distribution. If it does not include any such assets, the election can be made at any time, but no later than the first taxable year in which the basis of any of the distributed property is pertinent in determining a partner's income tax.

Unrealized receivables and appreciated inventory. California adopts IRC § 751.[24] Fed Reg 1.751–1 applies. When a partnership distributes unrealized receivables or substantially appreciated inventory items in exchange for any part of a partner's interest in other partnership property (including money) or transfers partnership property (including money) other than unrealized receivables or substantially appreciated inventory items in exchange for any part of a partner's interest in the partnership's unrealized receivables or substantially appreciated inventory items, the distribution will be treated as a sale or exchange of property.

---

(23) Fed Reg 1.732–1(d); § 17024.5(c).
(24) IRC § 751; Fed Reg § 1.751–1; § 17024.5(c); 17581.

The partner is considered as having received the property in a current distribution and immediately thereafter having sold or exchanged it. In such case, the above rules apply in determining the partner's basis of the property which he is treated as having sold to or exchanged with the partnership (as constituted after the distribution).

However, the rules do not apply in determining the basis of that part of the property actually distributed to the partner, which is treated as received by him in a sale or exchange under IRC § 751 and Fed Reg 1.751–1.

¶ 434   Optional Adjustment to Basis of Partnership Assets

Liquidations. Under IRC § 734 and Fed Reg 1.734–1, adopted by California, when assets are distributed in liquidation to a partner, the basis in the hands of the distributee partner, may be less than the basis of the assets in the hands of the partnership. The partnership is not entitled to take a loss on the distribution, but it may elect to adjust the basis of its remaining assets to account for the unused basis.[25]

OBSERVATION   The partnership can elect to adjust the basis of its property on: (1) a distribution of partnership property as indicated and (2) a transfer of an interest in the partnership.

If the election is made, the partnership must adjust the basis for all distributions of property and all transfers of interest in the partnership during the tax year the election was made and for all later years. Such adjustments are not only for the purpose of determining gain or loss on a sale of partnership property, but also used for the purposes of computing depreciation, depletion and distributions of partnership property to the partners.

Note: Special adjustment on distributions. This adjustment allows the remaining partners to reflect their actual basis in the undistributed partnership property that is, in effect, purchased by them from the distributing partner. If the election is made the partnership's adjusted basis of its undistributed property is increased by: (1) a gain recognized to the distributee partner or (2) the excess of the distributed property's basis to the partnership immediately before the distribution over its basis to the distributee.

Transferee with special basis. If the distribution is to a transferee partner who has a special basis adjustment under IRC § 732(d), also adopted by California, special adjustment of the transferee partner must be taken into account in computing the partnership basis adjustment.

Rules are set forth in IRC § 755 and Fed Reg 1.755–1 for the allocation of any increase or decrease in basis among the various partnership assets. California follows federal.[26] These rules are discussed below.

Optional adjustment of basis on change in membership. A partnership interest may be transferred through the medium of a sale or an exchange or because of the death of a partner. Ordinarily, such a transfer would have no

---

(25) IRC § 734; Fed Reg 1.734–1; § 17024.5(c); 17851.   (26) § 17851.

effect on the basis of partnership assets. However, if there is a change in values because of current market conditions, the partnership may elect to adjust the basis of partnership assets to reflect the difference between the transferee's basis for his partnership interest and his proportionate share of the adjusted basis of all partnership property. The adjustment would be *mandatory* if a prior election, under IRC § 754 is in effect. The adjustment applies only to the transferee partners and does not change the basis of partnership assets as to the other partners.

OBSERVATION   The election will: (1) increase the adjusted basis of partnership property by the excess of the transferee's basis for his partnership interest over his share of the adjusted basis to the partnership of all partnership property; or (2) decrease the adjusted basis of partnership property by the excess of the transferee partner's share of the adjusted basis of all partnership property over his basis for his partnership interest.

The result is that, for purposes of depreciation, depletion, gain or loss and later distribution, the transferee partner will have a special basis for those partnership properties which are adjusted by this election. This special basis is his share of the common partnership basis (i.e., the adjusted basis of such property to the partnership without regard to any special basis adjustment of any transferee) plus or minus his special basis adjustments.

Partner's share of the adjusted basis. A partner's share of the adjusted basis of partnership property is equal to the sum of his interest as a partner in partnership capital and surplus, plus his share of partnership liabilities.

California has adopted IRC § 743(b) that requires partners to allocate gain, loss, depreciation and depletion as to property contributed by a partner by a method that takes into account the difference between the partnership's basis in the contributed property and the property's fair market value at the time of the contribution.[27]

Making the election. In order to make the election, the partnership shall include a written statement filed with a partnership return for the year during which the distribution or transfer occurs. The return must be filed not later than the due date of the return, including extensions thereof.

The statement must set forth the name and address of the partnership making the election, a declaration that the partnership elects under IRC § 754 to apply the provisions of IRC §§ 734(b) or 743(b).

Revocation of the election. If the partnership decides to revoke the election, it may do so with the approval of the District Director, or the California Franchise Tax Board. The application shall be filed not later than 30 days after the close of the taxable year for which the revocation is intended to take effect and it must be signed by any one of the partners. The Regulations cite reasons considered sufficient to approve the revocation such

---

(27) IRC § 734(b); § 17851.

as, a change in the nature of the partnership business, a substantial increase in the assets of the partnership, a change in the character of the partnership assets or an increased frequency of retirements or shifts of partnership interests so that an increased administrative burden would result to the partnership from the election. No application for revocation of an election would be approved when the purpose of the revocation was primarily to avoid stepping down the basis of partnership assets, upon a transfer or a distribution.

Rules for allocation of basis. The basis adjustment must be made to the kind of property involved in the distribution or transfer, as the case may be. The partnership property is divided into two classes:

(1) Capital assets or IRC § 1231 assets, and
(2) Any other property of the partnership.

If the adjustment is for a distribution of capital assets or IRC § 1231 assets, or for the transfer of a partnership interest in assets of this kind, the adjustment must be made only to capital assets or IRC § 1231 assets. If the adjustment is for a distribution of or transfer of a partnership interest in property other than capital assets or IRC § 1231 assets, the adjustment must be made to the basis of that kind of property.

Then the portion of the increase or decrease allocated to each class must be further allocated to the basis of the properties within the class in a manner which will reduce the difference between the fair market value and the adjusted basis of partnership properties.

Increase in basis. If there is an increase in basis to be allocated to partnership assets, such increase must be allocated only to those assets whose values exceed their basis and in proportion to the difference between the value and the basis of each.

No increase shall be made to the basis of any asset with an adjusted basis in excess of its fair market value.

Decrease in basis. If there is a decrease in basis to be allocated to partnership assets, the decrease must be allocated to assets whose basis exceeds their value and in proportion to the difference between the basis and the value of each.

No decrease shall be made to the basis of any asset with a fair market value which equals or exceeds its adjusted basis.

Goodwill. If good will exists and is reflected in the value of the property distributed, the price at which the partnership interest is sold or the basis of the partnership interest acquired from a decedent, some of the basis adjustment must be allocated to the goodwill.

No partnership property. If the adjustment cannot be made because the partnership owns no property of the character to be adjusted, then the adjustment must be made when the partnership acquires property of that character. If a decrease in the basis of partnership assets is required and cannot be made because the amount of the decrease exceeds the basis to the partnership of property of the required character, the basis must be reduced to zero and the balance of the decrease and basis must be applied when the partnership acquires the right kind of property at a later date.[28]

Applicable asset acquisition. California has adopted IRC § 1060 relating to special allocation rules for this kind of acquisition. These changes cover (1) binding agreements in writing as to allocation of consideration, and fair market value of any of the assets; (2) information required in case of transfers by 10% owners; and (3) penalties for failure to file a return under IRC § 1060. IRC § 1060 requires both the buyer and the seller in an "applicable asset acquisition" to allocate the purchase price using the residual method of allocation described in Fed Regs under IRC § 338 (see Temp Reg § 1.338(b)–2T). An applicable asset acquisition under IRC § 1060 is any transfer of assets constituting a business in which the transferee's basis is determined wholly by reference to the purchase price paid for the assets. IRC § 1060 covers both direct and indirect transfers of a business including a sale of a business by a partnership or a sale of a partnership interest in which the basis of the purchasing partner's proportionate share of partnership assets is adjusted to reflect the purchase price. Under the residual method of allocation, the purchase price of assets is first reduced by cash and cash-type assets. The balance is then first allocated, in proportion to their fair market values, to marketable security type assets (such as stock and securities) up to their fair market value, and then to all other assets except those in the nature of goodwill and going concern value up to their FMV; and finally to goodwill and going concern value.

IRC § 1060 applies to a partnership distribution or transfer of an interest in a partnership, where the partnership elects to adjust its basis under IRC § 755, but only for purposes of determining goodwill or going concern value. If IRC § 755 applies, then the distribution or transfer is treated as an applicable asset acquisition for purposes of the information reporting requirements of IRC § 1060(b).

¶ 435 **Estate or Other Successor as Partner**

California has adopted IRC § 708, and Fed Reg 1.708–1 apply in the state.[29] Under IRC § 708 and Fed Reg 1.708–1, when a partner dies, the partnership is not necessarily terminated. The estate itself or a beneficiary in interest may continue as a partner, if it is possible under local law, by an agreement with the other partners.

¶ 436 **Partnership Income of Nonresidents**

Nonresidents of California are taxable on taxable income from sources within this state computed as if they were residents multiplied by a ratio of California source adjusted gross income to total adjusted gross income from

---

(28) IRC § 755; Fed Reg 1.755–1.   (29) IRC § 708; § 17024.5(c); 17851.

all sources. Sourcing rules determine California source income. A Franchise Tax Board release of 8–25–90 explains the withholding of tax from distributions to domestic (non-foreign) nonresident partners.[30]

Income from California sources. The gross income of a nonresident, who is a member of a partnership includes that partner's distributive share of the taxable income of a partnership pool or syndicate to the extent that the income is derived from California sources. Also, amounts received from a partnership by a nonresident partner as payment for services or for use of capital constitute gross income of a nonresident.[31]

Allocation and apportionment. If the business, trade, or profession carried on by the partnership within this state is an integral part of a unitary business carried on both within and without California, or if the part within the state is so connected with the part without the state that the taxable income from the part within the state cannot be accurately determined independently of the part without the state, the gross income from the entire business, trade or profession must be reported.[32] The amount of this total income which has its source in California is to be determined in accordance with the provisions of the Uniform Division of Income for Tax Purposes Act, as set forth in Rev & TC §§ 25120—25139.[33]

CAUTION	Effective for income years beginning on or after 1–1–93, California revised the apportionment formula for multistate businesses, except those that derive over 50% of their gross receipts from agricultural or extractive business activities. Taxpayers affected must apportion their income to California using a fraction the numerator of which consists of the property factor plus the payroll factor plus *twice* the sales factor, and the denominator of which is four. Previously, the sales, payroll, and property factors had equal weights, and the denominator was three. The regulations have not been amended to reflect this change.[34]
	For years beginning on or after 1–1–94, the savings and loan industry has been added to the list of businesses which continue to use the three factor apportionment formula with sales equally weighted with property and payroll. If the FTB adopts the Proposed Multistate Tax Commission Formula for the Uniform Apportionment of Net Income from Financial Institutions, or its substantial equivalent, than banking and financial businesses will also be subject to the three factor formula.[34]

The first step in determining the California income of the partnership is to separate "business income" from "nonbusiness income". For definitions see Rev & Tax C § 25120 and the regulations thereunder.[35]

---

(30) FTB 8–25–90.

(31) Reg 17951–1(b); 17951–4(d); FTB 89–713, 9–5–89.

(32) Reg 17951–4(c).

(33) § 25120–25139.

(34) § 25128, as amended by Stats. 1994, c.861, § 15.

(35) § 25120; Reg § 25120.

The partnership's business income from California will generally be determined by the three-factor formula of property, payroll and sales.[36]

For specific information and examples of the computation of the factors in the apportionment formula applied to partnerships, refer to California Reg 25137–1.[37]

The California Franchise Tax Board has developed a method of apportioning the income from long-term contracts applicable to corporations but also used by partnerships which apportion their income within and without California.[38]

Capital gain or loss from selling a partnership interest is allocable to California in the ratio of the original cost of partnership property in the state to the original cost of partnership tangible property everywhere, determined at the time of the sale. In the event that more than 50% of the value of the partnership's assets consist of intangibles, gain or loss from the sale of the partnership interest is allocated to California in accordance with the sales factor of the partnership for its first full tax period immediately preceding the tax period of the partnership during which the partnership interest was sold.[39]

Professional partnerships—apportionment. If the nonresident is engaged in the practice of a profession, within the meaning set forth below, the apportionment formula developed by the California Franchise Tax Board has some special features.[40]

The payroll factor of the income apportionment formula will include 60% of the net income of a sole proprietorship or 60% of the distributive share of partnership income of each partner rendering professional personal services to the partnership. For this purpose, the net income of a proprietorship and a partner's distributive share of partnership income will be considered to consist only of income properly classifiable as business income.

However, if a partner does not render professional services to the partnership, no part of such partner's distributive share of partnership income shall be taken into account in the payroll factor. The amount deemed to be compensation paid shall be included in the denominator of the payroll factor and in the California numerator of the payroll factor if the principal location of such partner is in California.[1]

"Profession" defined. The regulations indicate that a profession for this purpose includes the practice of law, accounting, medicine or the performance of personal services in scientific and engineering discipline and the practice of any other profession in which capital is not a material income-producing factor and in which more than 80% of business gross income for the taxable year is from personal services actually rendered by the members

(36) § 25128; Reg 25128–25136.
(37) Reg § 25137–1.
(38) Reg 25137–2.

(39) § 25125(c)–(d).
(40) Reg 17951–4(e).
(1) Reg 17951–4(f).

¶ 436

of the partnership.[2] The regulations state that "other profession" includes any occupation or vocation in which a professed knowledge of some department of science or learning gained by a prolonged course of specialized instruction and study is used by practical application to the affairs of others, either in advising, guiding or teaching them or serving their interests or welfare in the practice of an art or science founded on it.[3]

Professional practice. For purposes of determining whether more than 80% of the partnership gross income is derived from personal services actually rendered by a member of the partnership, the gross income from the professional practice will be deemed derived from personal services rendered if: (1) Such income is personal service income as distinguished from income attributable to the sale of property or to the use of capital and (2) Such income represents fees or charges for professional services personally rendered or professional fees or charges for services which are attributable to the professional activities of the individual partners.[4]

Income of nonresidents through California investment partnerships. A nonresident of the State of California who's only contact with the state is through a broker, dealer, investment adviser, investment partnership, corporate fiduciary managing an investment account for a beneficiary of a qualifying estate or trust, or who is a unit holder in a regulated investment company, located in California does not realize California source income from interest, dividends, or gains and losses from qualifying investment securities. An investment partnership is one which has at least 90% of the partnership's cost of its total assets in qualifying investment securities, deposits at banks or other financial institutions, and office space and equipment reasonably necessary to carry on its activities, and no less than 90% of its gross income from interest, dividends, and gains from the sale or exchange of qualifying investment securities.

Qualifying investment securities include: common stock, including preferred shares or debt securities convertible into common stock, and preferred stock; bonds, debentures, and other debt securities; foreign and domestic currency deposits or equivalents and securities convertible into foreign securities; mortgage-or asset-backed securities secured by federal, state, or local governmental agencies; repurchase agreements and loan participations; foreign currency exchange contracts and forward and futures contracts on foreign currencies; stock and bond index securities and futures contracts, options on any of the forementioned investments, and regulated futures contracts. Qualifying investment securities does not include an interest in a partnership unless that partnership is itself an investment partnership.[4]

---

(2) Reg 17951–4(g).
(3) Reg 17951–4(h).

(4) § 17955.

DECEDENT'S FINAL RETURN TAXING ESTATE AND TRUST INCOME

DECEDENT'S FINAL RETURN

¶ 451   Decedent's Final Return

It is necessary to file an income tax return for a decedent for the period from the beginning of the taxable year in which he died to the date of death under the following circumstances: (1) If his income meets the gross income requirements for filing personal income tax returns; (2) If he had earnings from self-employment of $400 or more; (3) If a refund of taxes would be due. If an individual is unable to make a return, the return must be made by the fiduciary.[1]

When to file return.   The taxable year of the decedent ends on the date on which he dies. The final return of the decedent is due on the same date it would have been due if he had lived. So if the decedent is on a calendar year basis, his final return is due by April 15th of the year following that in which he died.

Joint return.   A joint return may be filed with the surviving spouse. In most circumstances the executor of the estate and the surviving spouse will jointly see that the return is prepared and filed. If, however, the court has not appointed a fiduciary by the due date of the income tax return, the surviving spouse may file the joint return.

If the fiduciary, when appointed later, does not agree to the filing of a joint return for the year of death, he may reject the filing of the joint return by the surviving spouse by filing a separate return for the year.

However, a joint return may not be filed if the surviving spouse marries before the close of the taxable year. A joint return cannot be filed by the surviving spouse if the tax year has been shortened by a change of accounting period.

If the return shows an overpayment of taxes, see ¶ 336 of this Handbook in regard to the filing of federal Form 1310.

If a joint return is filed, the return covers the income and deductions of the decedent from the beginning of the taxable year to the date of his death and the income and deductions of the surviving spouse for the full year.[2]

¶ 452   Estimated Taxes

The estate of a taxpayer is not required to make estimated tax payments for any taxable year ending before the date two years following the date of the decedent's death. This exception applies to the estate of the decedent or a trust all of which is considered owned by the decedent and to which the residue of the decedent's estate will pass. Federal and California law are the same.

---

(1) § 18503; 18505; Reg 18405(a).   (2) § 17551; 18505; 18506.

¶ 453   Income Reported on Final Return

If the decedent had been reporting for tax purposes on a cash basis, the final return would cover only income actually or constructively received up to the date of death and deductions only to the extent that they were paid during the period. The representative of the decedent preparing the final return has several unique elections that apply only with respect to a decedent's final return. For instance, an election is available to report accrued, but previously unreported, interest income on U.S. Government Series E bonds in the final return of the decedent, or not accrue the income so that the estate or beneficiaries report the interest income when received. An election is also available for medical expenses to be deducted in the final return of the decedent if paid within one year of the date of death (see ¶ 454).

If the taxpayer used the accrual method of accounting, the return would show the income accrued up to the time of death, except that income accruable only because of the taxpayer's death would not be included.

Income in respect of a decedent. California has adopted IRC § 691, with the exception of the provisions for (1) foreign tax credit; (2) capital gains; (3) special rule for generation-skipping transfers; and (4) § 691(c) deduction for estate tax paid.[3] Under IRC § 691 and Fed Reg 1.691(c)(1)–(2) and 1.691(d)(1), any amount of income which the decedent had earned or became entitled to, but which was not included in his final return because of the method of accounting he employed, is called "income in respect of a decedent." Such items are included in the federal estate tax return filed for the decedent's estate. At the same time, the person who collects such income, usually the estate, must include that income in the estate fiduciary income tax return in the year in which it is received. The amount would be offset by any itemized deduction available to the estate (there is no standard deduction available), and by an income tax deduction for any estate tax payable because of the gross income.

Sale of property. If a decedent completed the sale of his property and delivered the property before his death, but hadn't received payment, the right of the estate to collect the proceeds is an item of income in respect of the decedent. In such a case, the gain based on decedent's cost is taxable to the estate, or if it is realized in the final tax year of the estate, the gain may be taxed to the remainderman.

Successive decedents. The law treats as income in respect of a decedent income of a prior decedent, if the subsequent decedent acquired the item through the death of the prior decedent or through a bequest, devise or inheritance from him.

Transfer of right to receive income. Special rules apply if the right to receive income in respect of a decedent is transferred by the estate or person entitled to receive it. Either the fair market value of such right or the amount

(3) § 17024.5; 17731.

¶ 453

received for it, whichever is greater, is reported as income by the transferor. Such a transfer includes a satisfaction of an installment obligation at other than face value. However, transfers to the decedent's successors as a result of his death aren't taxed under this rule.

Installment obligations.   A special rule applies to installment obligations that the decedent would have reported under IRC § 453 had he lived. These are treated as income to his successor to the extent that the face value of the obligation exceeds its basis in the hands of the decedent. The law treats a satisfaction of such an obligation for other than face value as a taxable transfer by the successor of a right to receive income, to the extent that the greater of the amount received or the fair market value of the obligation at the time of the transfer exceeds the decedent's basis as adjusted for any payments received between the death and the transfer. If an installment obligation is transferred to the obligor, due to the decedent's death, or cancelled by the executor, then the decedent's estate will be liable for any previously unreported gain. A transfer that occurs at the death of the holder of the obligation is considered made by his estate. If the holder is a person other than the decedent, such as a trust, then the transfer is considered made by that person immediately after the decedent's death. If the decedent and the obligor were related, then the fair market value of the obligation can't be less than the face amount. Cancellation includes an installment obligation that becomes unenforceable.

Deductions.   Deductions denied to the decedent on his final return are allowed to his successor for obligations outstanding against property of the decedent that the successor receives. Business and nonbusiness expenses of the decedent, and deductions for interest and taxes, ordinarily can be deducted by the estate, if it pays them or is liable for them. If it isn't liable for their payment, and they're paid by an heir or other beneficiary who got the property subject to them, that person gets the deduction. A deduction for depletion also can be taken, but it is allowed to the person who gets the income to which the depletion relates, whether or not that person gets the property from which the income is derived.

Decedent-partner.   California has adopted IRC § 706, Fed Reg 1.706–1.[4] California has also adopted the IRC § 706(d)(2) rules dealing with proration of certain cash basis items over the period to which they are attributable. Under these rules, if the decedent is a partner in a partnership, his last return would include only his share of the partnership taxable income if the partnership taxable year ends within or with the decedent's final taxable year. In other words, if a partner dies and the partnership taxable year does not end within the period from the beginning of the decedent's last taxable year to the date of his death, the distributive share of the partnership income would not be included in his final return. In these cir-

---

(4) IRC § 706; Fed Reg 1.706–1; § 17851.

cumstances, the income would generally be reported on the estate income tax return for the period following.

Payments on an installment obligation. Payments on an installment obligation which had been incurred by the decedent prior to his death are considered to be items of income in respect of a decedent. Therefore, the estate or beneficiary, on receiving a payment on the installment obligation, would compute the taxable portion of the payment in the same manner and using the same gross profit computation as the decedent had been using even if the face amount of the installment obligation had been discounted on the federal estate tax return.[5]

¶ 454 Deductions on Final Return

California follows IRC § 461 and federal regulations.[6] Under IRC § 461 and Fed Reg No. 1.461–1(b), if the decedent was on a cash basis, only those expenses which were paid for as of the date of his death would be considered to be deductions on his final return. On the other hand, if he had used the accrual basis, the items which had accrued before his death would be deductible in the final return.

An exception to the above statement is that medical expenses, incurred for the care of the decedent and paid out of his estate within one year after his death, are considered to have been paid by the decedent at the time incurred. If, however, the expenses are also deductible for federal estate tax purposes, the deduction may not be claimed in the decedent's final return, unless the fiduciary files a statement that the deduction has not been claimed for estate tax purposes and a waiver of the right to claim the deduction for the estate tax return.

TAXING ESTATE AND TRUST INCOME

¶ 455 Estates and Trusts

Trusts and estates of decedents are considered to be taxable entities. They are required to report their entire taxable income, including income to the estate from community property.[7] They are allowed deduction for all business expenses and other expenses such as taxes and interest, and legal and accounting fees. In addition, these entities are allowed a deduction for the income included in gross income which is currently distributable to the beneficiaries, or is properly paid or credited to them. The taxability of trust depends on residence of fiduciaries and beneficiaries.[8]

The income distributed to the beneficiaries is taxable to them and retains the same tax status in their hands. That is, capital gains would have the same status as short or long term, state and municipal income would retain its same tax-exempt character, etc. Estates have the opportunity to

---

(5) § 17551.

(6) IRC § 461.

(7) LR 282, 4–23–65.

(8) § 17731; 17742–17745; LR 238, 10–27–59.

elect a same opportunity as any other taxpayer to elect the appropriate fiscal year and to adopt a method of accounting, either cash or accrual as the case may be.[9] A nonresident beneficiary is taxable on income distributed only to the extent it is derived from California sources.[10] Dividends, interest, and capital gains on the sale of securities are taxable to such beneficiary only if the securities giving rise to income were used in connection with trade or business in this state.[11] California beneficiaries of Hawaiian trust are liable for tax on their entire share of the trust income, distributed or distributable, if the Hawaiian trust fails to pay its California tax liability.[12]

Divorce or separation. For purposes of computing taxable income of an estate or trust and taxable income of spouse to whom IRC § 682(a) applies, that spouse will be considered as the beneficiary for the purposes of the rules governing the taxation of estates, trusts and beneficiaries.[13]

Simple trusts. California adopts IRC § 642 and 651, and applies Fed Regs No. 1.642(b)(1); 1.651(a)–1; 1.651(a)–4; and 1.652(a)–1.[14] Under these federal rules, a simple trust is one which, by the terms of the trust agreement, is required to distribute all of its income currently, except perhaps capital gains, and has no charitable beneficiaries. Because it is required to distribute all of its current income, with the possible exception of capital gains, and because it takes a deduction for the income distributed, the simple trust generally has no taxable income and no tax to pay, unless it retains capital gains subject to tax. However, for federal purposes it does have an exemption of $300. California allows an exemption credit of $1 instead of the federal exemption. The $1 credit against the tax imposed by Rev & TC § 17041 must be reduced by the interest added to the tax under Rev & TC § 17560(d)(1) and § 17560(e)(1), relating to dealer dispositions under IRC § 453, and special rules for nondealers under IRC § 453A.

Complex trust. A complex trust is any trust that is not a simple trust. In other words, it is a trust that may accumulate income or distribute corpus, but it may have charitable beneficiaries and may make accumulation distributions.[15]

¶ 456 Tax Rates

For California purposes, estates and trusts must pay tax according to a rate schedule (¶ 87). They cannot use the tax tables.[15]

¶ 457 Fiduciary Returns

Generally, a fiduciary acts for the estate or trust. The fiduciary is the term applied to a trustee, an executor, a personal representative, an administrator or any others acting in a trust relationship.[16]

---

(9) § 17731; 17745.
(10) § 17734.
(11) LR 291, 4–23–65.
(12) LR 371, 1–22–74.

(13) § 17737.
(14) § 17731—17733.
(15) § 17048; 17731; 17733.
(16) Fed Reg 301.6901–301, 6905–1.

When filing is required.   The fiduciary must file a federal Form 1041 for a domestic estate that has: (a) gross income for the tax year of $600 or more, or (b) any beneficiary who is a nonresident alien.[17]

The fiduciary must file Form 1041 for a trust that has: (a) any taxable income for the tax year; or (b) gross income of $600 or more regardless of the taxable income; or (c) any beneficiary who is a nonresident alien.[17]

For California purposes, the fiduciary must file a Form 541 for every estate with a taxable income of over $1,000 or with a gross income in excess of $8,000, or an alternative minimum tax liability, regardless of the amount of net income.[18]

For California purposes, the fiduciary must file a trust return, Form 541, for any trust that has a taxable income of over $100 or a gross income in excess of $8,000, or an alternative minimum tax liability, regardless of the amount of net income.[19]

Minors and incompetents.   A fiduciary who is in charge of the income of a minor or incompetent person must file the appropriate personal income tax return and pay the tax due on that return if the individual met the filing requirements, rather than filing a trust return.[20]

> *Note:* In California it is required that a certified copy of the will or trust instrument be filed with the first fiduciary return if the gross income of the estate or trust is over $5,000. If the trust instrument is amended in any way after the original copy has been filed, a copy of the amendment must be filed with the Franchise Tax Board.[21]

The federal regulations provide that the fiduciary must file a copy of the will or trust instrument with the Internal Revenue Service only if the Service requests it.[17]

¶ 458   **Payment of Tax**

Taxable year of trusts for both federal and California purposes must be a calendar year. Tax-exempt trusts under IRC § 501(a) and wholly charitable trusts under IRC § 4947(a)(1) may use a fiscal year. The entire amount of the tax shown on the federal trust return must be paid with the return. These rules apply to all trusts existing or created.[22]

Both new and existing trusts must pay estimated tax, but an estate need not pay estimated tax for its tax years ending within two years from the decedent's date of death. Generally the estimated tax for estates and trusts is calculated the same as for individuals, except that the periods for analyzing income are different. The cut-off dates for determining income to be annualized for estimated tax purposes of estates and trusts reporting on a calendar year are: 2/28, 4/31, 7/31, and 11/30. Federal and California law are the same.[23]

---

(17) Fed Reg 1.6012–3.
(18) § 18505(a)(4); (6).
(19) § 18505(a)(5); (6).
(20) § 18505(a)(1)—(3).

(21) Reg 18405–1(d).
(22) IRC § 645; § 17024.5; 17731.
(23) IRC § 6654(l).

For federal purposes, every executor, administrator, assignee or other person who pays any debt, or portion of debt, owing by the person or estate for which he acts without first satisfying the debts to the United States is personally liable for such payments to the United States. Excepted are the debts which have priority, such as administration expenses, funeral expenses, widow's allowance, etc. In the case of any other claims against the estate or trust for which the fiduciary acts, the fiduciary is liable if it pays them in whole or in part, or makes any distribution of the assets before satisfaction or payment of taxes, interest and penalties, except penalties due from the decedent. Liability extends to the full extent of payments or distributions made. Items that constitute a claim under the Personal Income Tax Law, or that are a lien or charge against the estate or trust, can also be collected from the fiduciary as a personal liability under this rule.[24]

Multiple trusts will be treated as one trust under IRC § 643(e), adopted by California, if they have substantially the same grantors and beneficiaries and principal purpose is tax avoidance.[25]

¶ 459   Capital Gains and Losses

Under IRC § 641 and Fed Regs No. 1.641(a)–1; 1.641(b)–1, gain on the sale or exchange of a capital asset by an estate or trust must be included in its gross income. For taxable years starting on or after 1–1–87, both California and federal include the entire amount of capital gains in gross income. Federal repealed the 60% capital gains, and California conformed by repealing its recognition percentages.[26]

The portion of the gain paid or credited or required to be distributed during the year to the beneficiary is deductible by the fiduciary and taxable to the beneficiary to the extent of the distributable net income. The capital loss is deductible only by the estate or trust and not by the beneficiary, except for the year of termination.[27]

If a fiduciary transfers a capital asset to a beneficiary to satisfy a cash legacy, it is treated as a sale or an exchange. Gain or loss is recognized equal to the difference between the fair market value of the property and its adjusted basis. The recipient is treated as a purchaser and takes as his basis for the property its fair market value at the date of distribution.[28]

Election to recognize gain. Under IRC § 643(d)(3), and California law, an estate or trust that distributes property other than cash, and which distribution is not in satisfaction of a pecuniary legacy, may elect to recognize gain or loss in same manner as if the property had been sold to the distributee at its fair market value. The amount taken into account under IRC § 661(a)(2) for any other amounts properly paid, credited or required to be distributed for the taxable year, and the amount taken into account under

---

(24) Fed Reg 301.6901–1; 301.6901–3.
(25) § 17731.
(26) § 17024.5(b); 17731.

(27) Fed Reg 1.643(a)–3.
(28) Fed Reg 1.661(a)–2.

IRC § 662(a)(2) for inclusion in gross income of beneficiary of other amounts distributed shall be the fair market value of the property.[29]

Gain recognized on a nonliquidating distribution of a trust interest by a corporation. Gain recognized on a nonliquidating distribution of a trust interest is computed without considering a loss from property which was contributed to the trust for the principal purpose of recognizing the loss on the distribution to offset gain otherwise taxable. California adopts IRC § 311(b)(3) for tax years starting on or after 1–1–89.[26]

Transfers between spouses incident to divorce in trust do not cause any recognition of gain or loss, except when spouse to whom property is transferred is a nonresident alien. The same rule applies to former spouses. California adopts IRC § 1041(d) for taxable years starting on or after 1–1–89.[26]

Basis of property to estate or trust. Under IRC § 1015(b) and Fed Regs 1.1015–2, the basis of the property to the trust, when the transfer is for a valuable consideration, is the grantor's basis increased by gain or decreased by loss recognized to the grantor on the transfer. California has adopted this rule.[30] For determining gain on the sale of an asset, California has adopted IRC § 1015(d)(6) that provides that the basis of property acquired by gifts after 1976 is the adjusted basis of the property in the hands of the donor increased by the gift tax attributable to the appreciation to the date of the gift.[31]

The basis of property acquired from a decedent is the fair market value on the date of the decedent's death, or on the alternate valuation date.[32]

¶ 461   Deductions—Generally

Specific items are explained below. See also ¶ 462.

Contributions. Under IRC § 642 and Fed Reg No. 1.642(c)–1, adopted by California, an estate or a complex trust can deduct any part of its gross income which, under the terms of the will or trust deed, is paid for charitable purposes. There is no limitation on the amount that can be deducted by a trust or an estate.[33]

IMPORTANT   There is a special provision in IRC § 642(c), adopted by California, to treat a current contribution as being paid during the prior taxable year. The election to take this course must be made no later than the due date (including extensions) of the income tax return for the year after the year for which the election is made.

The adjustment for deductions of amounts paid or permanently set aside for a charitable purposes found in IRC § 642(c)(4), which relates to

---

(29) IRC § 643(d)(3); 661(a)(2); 662(a)(2); § 17024.5; 17731.
(30) § 18031.

(31) § 17731; 18034.
(32) Fed Reg 1.1014–1–1.1014–2.
(33) § 17731.

excluded gains on federal qualified small business stock as described in IRC § 1202, is modified for California purposes by substituting the exclusion for California qualifying small business stock as described in Rev & TC § 18152.5.[33a]

Proration of deduction.   The charitable contribution must be from the gross income of the trust or the estate. If the organization has both taxable and tax-exempt income, the deduction is allowed only for contributions considered as coming from gross income in the return. Unless the governing instrument makes a different allocation, the contribution considered as coming from gross income bears the same proportion to the total contribution as the total gross income on the return bears to the total income including tax-exempt income. This federal reg. applies in California.

Qualified residence interest.   Interest paid or accrued by a trust or an estate on a debt secured by a qualified residence of a beneficiary is qualified residence interest.[33]

IRC § 469 passive loss rules.   California has adopted the IRC § 469 passive loss rules. Under these rules, when an estate or trust distributes its entire interest in a passive activity to a beneficiary, the basis of the interest immediately before the distribution is increased by the amount of any passive losses attributable to the distributed interest, and such losses shall not be allowable as a deduction for any taxable year. Committee reports indicate that gain or loss to the trust or estate and the basis in the hands of the beneficiary will then be determined under the usual rules applicable under the IRC.[33]

Depreciation.   California has adopted IRC § 167(d) which provides for the depreciation of life tenants and beneficiaries of trusts and estates. The federal rule provides that the depreciation of property held by a life tenant is computed as if the life tenant were the absolute owner; the depreciation is not apportioned with the remainderman. The deduction for depreciation of trust property is divided between the income beneficiaries and the trust as directed by the trust instrument. If the trust instrument does not indicate a method, the deductions are apportioned on the basis of the trust income allocable to each. In the case of an estate, the allowable deduction is apportioned between the estate and the heirs, legatees or devisees, according to the income of the estate allocable to each.[34]

If a reserve for depreciation is maintained, the depreciation deduction is allocated first to the trust to the extent that income is set aside for the reserve. The balance is apportioned between the trust and beneficiaries in accordance with the amount of trust income (over and above the reserve amount) allocation to each. Federal and California law are the same.[35]

(33a) § 17736.
(34) Fed Reg 1.642(e)–1; § 17201.

(35) Fed. Reg 1.167(h)–1(b).

Depletion. The treatment of depletion of property held in trust is the same as that of depreciation; namely, the deduction is apportioned between the income beneficiaries and the trust in accordance with the provisions of the instrument creating the trust or in the absence of such provisions, on the basis of the trust income allocable to each. In the case of an estate, the deduction under this section is apportioned between the estate and the heirs, legatees and devisees on the basis of the income of the estate allocable to each.[36]

Amortization. The benefit of deductions for amortization provided by IRC § 169 is allowed to estates and trusts in the same manner as for an individual. The allowable deduction must be apportioned between the income beneficiaries and the fiduciary as provided by regulations. In the absence of a specific California regulations, federal regulation prevails.[37]

Miscellaneous itemized deductions—2% floor. Estates and trusts may deduct miscellaneous itemized expenses only to the extent they exceed 2% of adjusted gross income (AGI). Estate or trust's AGI is computed the same way as an individual's, except that administration expenses incurred only because the property is held by a trust or estate are deducted in arriving at AGI. The distribution deduction allowed under IRC §§ 651 or 661, and the personal exemption allowed under IRC § 642(b) are also deducted in arriving at AGI. Also, deductions allowed to an estate or trust for IRC § 642(c) items paid or set aside for a charitable purpose, are not subject to the 2% floor.[38]

Other expenses. The estate or the trust can deduct the normal business and investment expenses subject to the same 2% reduction based on adjusted gross income which applies to individual itemized deductions. It can also deduct ordinary and necessary fiduciary's fees and litigation expenses relating administration and these expenses are not subject to the 2% floor on itemized deductions. Expenses attributable to the production and collection of tax-exempt income are not deductible. Interest on estate taxes can be deducted by an estate if the payments qualify as an administration expenses.

¶ 462   Deductions for Distributions to Beneficiaries

Simple trusts take a deduction for income required to be distributed currently, whether or not it was in fact distributed. If the amount exceeds distributable net income for the tax year, the deduction is limited to distributable net income computed without regard to items excluded from the trust's gross income.[39]

An estate or a complex trust can deduct the sum of: (1) trust income required to be distributed currently and (2) any other amounts paid, credited or required to be distributed for the tax year.

---

(36) Fed Reg 1.011–1–1.011–5; 1.642(2)–1.

(37) IRC § 169; § 17024.5; 17731.

(38) IRC § 67; § 17024.5.

(39) § 17731.

Note: The deduction cannot exceed lesser of distributable net income or accounting income available for distribution, and no deductions are allowed for amounts not included in the gross income of the estate. The amount deductible is treated as being composed of the same proportion of each class of items entering into the computation of distributable net income, as the total of each class bears to the total distributable net income, unless the governing instrument or the estate law makes a different allocation.

Excess deductions on termination.   When an estate or a trust has a capital loss carry-over or estate or trust deductions in the last taxable year in excess of the gross income for that year, then the carry-over or the excess deductions shall be allowed as a deduction to the beneficiaries succeeding to the property of the estate or trust subject to the 2% of gross income reduction of itemized deductions of individuals on Form 1040.[40]

Certain payments of tax treated as paid by beneficiary.   California has adopted federal rules that clarify that the election to distribute excess estimated tax to the beneficiaries need not be made on the tax return for the trust's preceding year. It can be made by the 65th day after the close of the tax year in a manner to be set by regulations. In addition, where the tax year is reasonably expected to be the last year of an estate, any reference in IRC § 643(g) to a trust is treated as including a reference to an estate, and the fiduciary of the estate is treated as the trustee.[1]

Distributable net income.   "Distributable net income" determines the amount of the deduction available to a trust or estate for distributions to the beneficiaries during the taxable year. In addition, the distributable net income determines the amount that the fiduciary reports as his or her share of estate or trust income. The distributable net income of the estate or trust is composed of the same items of gross income and deductions as those of the estate or trust, with certain modifications:

(1) Deduction for distribution to beneficiaries is not included;

(2) *Personal exemption* deduction is not included;

(3) *Gains from the sale or exchange of capital assets* are excluded to the extent they are allocated to corpus and not paid, credited or required to be distributed to any beneficiary during the year, or paid or permanently set aside for charities;

(4) *Losses from the sale or exchange of capital assets* are excluded, except to the extent that they are taken into account in determining the amount of gains which are paid, credited or required to be distributed to the beneficiary during the year;

(5) *Tax-exempt interest* is included, but reduced to the extent of expenses attributable to such income;

(6) *Extraordinary dividends* or taxable stock dividends allocated to corpus by the fiduciary are excluded, but only in the case of simple trusts.

In calculating the distributable net income, the exclusion of gain provided for qualifying California small business stock as described in Rev & TC § 18152.5, will not be taken into account.[1a]

---

(40) Fed Reg 1.642(h)–2.   **(1a)** § 17750.
(1) IRC § 643(g); § 17731.

Special 65-day rule. IRC § 663(b), adopted by California, allows a complex trust to consider any amount properly paid or credited within the first 65 days of any taxable year as having been paid or credited on the last day of the preceding taxable year, but only if the fiduciary of the trust makes an election on Form 1041 to have the section apply.[2]

Throw-back rules. The "throwback" rules have been put into the IRC § 665–667, adopted by California, except for provisions on foreign trusts, nonresident aliens, and the alternative minimum tax, to avoid accumulations of trust income by a complex trust over a period of years and to have distributions made to the beneficiaries in their low income tax years. Without the throwback rules, the year the income is distributed the beneficiary is taxable only to the extent of the distributable net income of the trust which is paid in the taxable year, and the excess distribution in the form of the accumulation distribution would be tax-free. The effect of the throw-back is to carryback to preceding years any distributions in excess of distributable net income for the year of the distribution and tax them to the beneficiaries in the same manner as if the income had been distributed in the year the income was accumulated by the trust.[3]

Accumulation distribution. To determine the accumulation distribution, follow these steps: (1) Take the total distribution for the tax year of the trust, reduced by the amount of income required to be distributed currently (including any amount that may be paid out of income or corpus to the extent that it was paid out of trust income for the year); (2) Subtract from (1) the distributable net income, reduced (but not below zero) by the income required to be distributed currently. The difference between (1) and (2) is the accumulation distribution for the tax year. The accumulation distribution is the total distribution for the tax year minus the distributable net income, both amounts reduced by the income required to be distributed currently.[4]

Undistributed net income. A trust has "undistributed net income" in any year in which the distributable net income is in excess of the amount of income actually distributed. To determine undistributed net income, find the distributable net income of the trust and subtract from it the amount of income required to be distributed currently, including any amount paid out of income or corpus to the extent it was paid out of trust income for the year, and subtract any other amounts paid, credited, or required to be distributed, plus the income tax on the undistributed portion of the trust's distributable net income. Ordinarily, this would be the tax paid by the trust, except in instances when the trust has capital gains not included in distributable net income. Any income accumulated by a trust before a beneficiary is born or while he or she is less than 21 years old would not be considered as part of an accumulation for this purpose, so that distributions of that accumulation would not be subject to the throw-back rules.[5]

---

(2) Fed Reg 1.663(b)–1–1.663(b)–2 § 17731.
(3) Fed Reg 1.665(a)–1A–1.667–1.

(4) Fed Reg 1.665(b)–1A.
(5) Fed Reg 1.665(a)–1A.

¶ 462

IMPORTANT	*Operation of the throw-back rules.* California follows federal law. When a trust makes an accumulation distribution for any tax year, the distribution is "thrown-back" to the earliest year after 1968 in which the trust had distributable net income in excess of the amounts actually distributed, or in excess of the undistributed net income for that year. The amount of the accumulation being thrown back to that year is considered to have been distributed on the last day of that year, but only to the extent of the undistributed net income of that year. The excess of the accumulation is then thrown-back to the next succeeding year which had undistributed net income and so on through the succeeding tax years until the accumulation distribution is all taken care of.

¶ 463   Tax Paid by Beneficiaries on Excess Distribution

California has adopted IRC § 667. Under this federal rule, the beneficiary is required to pay an additional tax for the current year (in which the accumulation distribution is actually paid or credited to him) on the amount considered to have been distributed to him by the trust in any of the throwback years. He is taxed on the accumulation distribution thrown-back to a particular year, and also an amount equal to the tax paid by the trust on the accumulation distribution so thrown-back. California has not adopted the federal rules on foreign trusts.[6]

TAX TIP	The tax computed on the beneficiary for the current year thus would be the sum of: (1) The partial tax on the beneficiary's taxable income for the current year and (2) The partial tax on the accumulation distribution. The partial tax is computed on a three year average basis as follows:

First the beneficiary takes his taxable income for the five years immediately preceding the distribution year and disregards the lowest and highest years. A loss year in any of the five years is considered to be zero. The accumulation distribution and the taxes considered to have been paid on the distribution is averaged over the number of years during which it was earned by the trust and this average amount is included in the beneficiary's taxable income for each of the three base period years.

The average increase in the beneficiary's tax for the three year base period is then computed by adding the tax increases for each of the three years and dividing the result by three.

The partial tax on the accumulation distribution is computed by multiplying the average increase in taxes by the number of throw-back years and by subtracting the amount of the taxes paid by the trust which are deemed to be an additional distribution. It should be noted that if the amount of taxes deem distributed is more than the partial tax computed on the accumulation distribution, the excess cannot be used to offset the beneficiary's tax liability arising from other sources.

---

(6) IRC § 667; § 17024.5(b); 17771.

SPECIAL RULES

¶ 471   Foreign Trusts

Under federal law, beneficiaries receiving distributions from foreign trusts are generally subject to the throw-back provisions discussed above. Foreign trusts are not allowed an exclusion from the throw-back rule for accumulation distributions covering years before the beneficiary reached 21. California has no similar provisions. The state's IRC conformity statute bars adoption of the IRC provisions on foreign trusts.[7]

¶ 472   Pooled Income Fund

California has adopted IRC § 642(c), except for the rules on (1) foreign trusts and (2) personal exemptions.[8] Under IRC § 642(c), a pooled income fund is a trust maintained by a charity to which a person transfers property retaining an income interest in the property for his life alone or for the life of one or more named living beneficiaries. The charity is given an irrevocable remainder interest in the property. The donor does not have a gain or loss from the contribution to the pooled income fund, unless he receives property in exchange from the fund or is relieved of a liability by the transfer.

The income payable by the fund to each beneficiary is determined by the rate of return of the fund. Such income must be distributed currently or within 65 days following the close of the taxable year and such income is, of course, taxable to the beneficiary.

The donor or his estate is entitled to receive a charitable contribution for the present value of the charitable remainder interest contributed to the charity. This value is computed in accordance with the Regulations and is essentially the present fair market value of the assets transferred, minus the present value of the life income interest retained.

¶ 473   Grantor Trusts

IRC §§ 671–679 cover treatment of grantor trusts. California has adopted those sections except for provisions on foreign trusts.[9] IRC § 672(f), relating to the special rule where the grantor to a nonforeign trust is a foreign person and the trust has a beneficiary who is a U.S. person, applies in California. In a grantor trust, the grantor or other persons who have substantial control over the trust property or income will be taxed on the trust income rather than the trust or the beneficiaries. If the grantor is taxed on the trust income, he is allowed the deductions and credits related to that income.

Family trusts. In Rev Rul 75–257, the IRS ruled that it will tax so-called "family estate" trusts as grantor trusts. Family estate trusts are arrangements that have been devised whereby an individual transfers his

---

(7) Fed Reg 1.665(c)–1A.
(8) IRC § 642(c); § 17024.5(b); 17731.

(9) IRC § 671–679; § 17024.5(b); 17731.

personal residence, business properties and the right to receive income in exchange for units of beneficial interests, which are essentially the right to enjoy the property. The California Franchise Tax Board follows this Revenue Ruling.

Reversionary interest. California follows federal rules which generally provides that income from 10-year and other grantor trusts is taxed to the grantor, not the beneficiary, if the property put into the trust will revert to the grantor or the grantor's spouse. It is immaterial how long the trust lasts.

Power to control beneficial enjoyment. The grantor is taxed on trust income if he retains the power to control the beneficial enjoyment of the corpus or the income of the trust. Any reference to the grantor includes a reference to the grantor's spouse.

Retention of administrative power. The grantor is taxed on the trust income, if he retains administrative powers which give him the right to financial benefits which would otherwise not be available. Some of these are the power to deal for less than adequate and full consideration, power to borrow without adequate interest or security, power to vote or direct the vote, voting of stock or other securities of a corporation in which the holdings of the grantor in the trust are significant from the viewpoint of voting control and others. IRC § 675 treats the grantor as the trust's owner if loans are made to the grantor's spouse.

Power to revoke trust. The grantor is treated as the owner of any portion of a trust where at any time the power to revest in the grantor title to such portion is exercisable by the grantor or a non-adverse party, or both. This rule does not apply to a power the exercise of which can only affect the beneficial enjoyment of income for a period starting after the occurrence of an event such that the grantor would not be considered as owner under IRC § 673 (beneficial enjoyment) if the power were a reversionary interest. The grantor may be treated as owner after the occurrence of that event unless the power is relinquished.

¶ 474 Charitable Remainder Trust

California has adopted IRC § 170(f)(2)(A).[10] Under this federal provision, no deduction is allowed for the transfer of a charitable remainder to a trust unless the trust is a charitable remainder annuity trust, a charitable remainder unitrust, or a pooled income fund. A charitable remainder annuity trust is one that pays only a specific sum to at least one non-charitable income beneficiary for his life or a term of not more than 20 years and transfers the remainder interest to (or for the use of) a charity. The income pay-out must be made at least once a year and cannot be less than 5% of the value of the property when it was placed in trust.[11]

---

(10) § 17731.   (11) IRC § 664(d)(1).

Charitable remainder unitrust. Charitable remainder unitrust is a trust from which a fixed percentage (which is not less than 5%) of the net fair market value of its assets, valued annually, is to be paid at least once annually to one or more persons for a term of not more than 20 years or for the life or lives of such individual or individuals.[12]

Character of distributable net income. The character of distributable net income does not pass through to the income beneficiary on a pro-rata basis. Income reportable by the beneficiary is deemed distributed as follows:

- First, from current or accumulated net taxable income,
- Then, from current or accumulated net short term capital gains,
- Then, from current or accumulated net long term capital gains,
- Last, from tax-exempt income.

California and federal law are the same. The federal reporting for split-interests is on form 5227, and unless all income is required to be distributed, form 1041-A. California reporting is on form 541–B and, unless all income is required to be distributed, form 541–A.

When taxed as complex trust. California has adopted IRC definitions and rule on unrelated business income.[13] These charitable remainder trusts are exempt from taxation unless they have unrelated business income, in which case they are taxed the same as a complex trust.

---

(12) IRC § 664(d)(2).   **(13)** IRC § 664(c); § 17731.

CHAPTER **10**

EXEMPT AND UNRELATED BUSINESS INCOME

¶ 951   **Who's Exempt—Application for Exemption**

Federal exemption.   The Internal Revenue Code exempts from income tax those organizations which are generally described as nonprofit organizations. These organizations may be in the form of an association, a trust, or a corporation. However, they are exempt only if they apply for and are granted an exemption as one of the organizations described in IRC § 501 or as an employee plan qualified under IRC § 401(a).

California exemption.   For California purposes the exemption for nonprofit organizations is included in the Bank and Corporation Tax Law under Chapter IV beginning with Rev & TC § 23701.[1] There is no provision for exempt organizations in the California Personal Income Tax Law. However, associations and trusts which would ordinarily be covered under the Personal Income Tax Law would be subject to the exempt provisions of the Bank and Corporation Tax Law.

Even though an organization may apply for and receive exemption from income tax for federal and California purposes, it may be necessary that it file an income tax return and pay tax in case it has "unrelated business income." This type of income is primarily from the operation of a business enterprise which is not related to the purpose of the organization for which it obtains its exempt status.

TAX TIP   The application for exemption from federal tax is made on Form 1023, Form 1024, Form 1028 or Form 1120–H, depending on the section of the IRC under which the exemption is claimed. The California exemption form is FTB 3500. It is to be filed by all organizations (except political organizations qualified under Section 23701r)[2] which claim an exemption from tax.

State filing needed.   If an organization is exempt from federal income tax, it does not become exempt from California franchise or income tax unless it files for and receives California exempt status. On the other hand, an organization which is granted an exemption from California tax must apply separately for an exemption from federal tax unless the organization is covered under a federal group ruling.

Political organizations.   A political organization that is incorporating should contact the Franchise Tax Board and obtain a certificate of exemption to avoid payment of the minimum franchise tax.

Unincorporated associations.   Unincorporated associations which are members of a group may be granted exemption on a group basis. The procedure is for the parent organization to file an application for exemption on its own and receive a letter of approval. Then the parent organization may file a separate application for a group exemption to cover all unincorporated organizations. This application should include a cover letter naming the

---

(1) § 23701.   (2) § 23701r.

¶ 951

subordinate associations which are affiliated with the parent and subject to the general supervision and control of the parent organization. Other items which are required are a sample copy of the uniform charter and affirmation that the subordinates are operating in accordance with the stated purposes and a statement that the subordinates have furnished a written authorization to the parent to be included in the group exemption application.

TAX TIP	If the organization requesting exempt status is being incorporated in California, the procedure is to mail five copies of the proposed articles of incorporation with fees to the Secretary of State, with a signed copy of the Exemption Application Form (FTB 3500) together with a copy of the proposed articles, a copy of the proposed bylaws and other supporting documents and a separate check to the Franchise Tax Board in the amount of $25.

Homeowners associations. IRC § 528 and Rev & TC § 23701(t) cover the exemption of homeowners associations. These organizations, which provide for the management, maintenance and care of *residential* real property are exempt if 60% or more of their gross income is from membership dues and assessments, and 90% or more of their expenses are for the acquisition, construction, management, maintenance, and care of association property. An association which has net income from sources other than membership fees is taxable on the net income from such activities less a $100 exclusion. Homeowners association includes a condominium management association, a residential real estate management association, and a cooperative housing corporation (defined in Rev & TC § 23701t(e)). Federal law, but not California, provides that an association has an annual election to have the homeowners association rules apply for the taxable year.[3]

Procedure for granting exemption. The Secretary of State will review the articles and approve the application for incorporation or notify the nonprofit organization if they have to be corrected. The exemption application, with a copy of the articles of incorporation and the bylaws and the supporting statements will be sent to the Franchise Tax Board department handling exempt organizations by the Secretary of State.

If the Franchise Tax Board approves the exempt status of the organization, it notifies the Secretary of State so that the corporation can then be approved as an exempt organization not subject to the franchise tax.

If the organization wants to complete the incorporation procedure first, it would accomplish that by filing the articles of incorporation for approval with the Secretary of State with a prepayment of the minimum franchise tax. After the corporation has been declared to be a California corporation by the Secretary of State, the corporation may then file the Exemption Application with the attachments to the Franchise Tax Board. If the exemption is approved by the Franchise Tax Board, it will normally be effective on the

(3) IRC § 528; § 23701t.

date of incorporation and the initial franchise tax will be refunded to the corporation; normally within four months.

Foreign corporations. If the organization being qualified is a foreign corporation, it must file with the exemption application a certificate of good standing from the public officer of the state having custody of the original articles of incorporation. If it qualified as an exempt organization in its state of legal residence, it must also file with the California Secretary of State a certificate to that effect. A copy of the application for exemption from California and the articles of incorporation and a copy of the federal determination letter should be included with the application.

TAX TIP   Because the Franchise Tax Board reviews the federal exemption application forms and revises the California Form FTB 3500 to conform to the federal application, it is generally advisable for an organization which is newly formed to obtain copies of each form and develop the information for both applications at the same time.

If the organization is a newly formed corporation, the federal exemption application will not normally be accepted until the articles of incorporation have been endorsed by the Secretary of State of California. In the case of an unincorporated association or a trust, it is advisable to file an application with the IRS first and furnish a copy of the federal determination letter with the state application.

If the Exempt Organization Bureau finds a flaw in the application or the articles of incorporation so that the corporation cannot be approved as an exempt organization, it will notify the organization's representatives.

WARNING   There are two basic reasons for denying an exemption from tax to an applicant: (1) Failure to furnish the information requested in the review of an application for exemption, and (2) The applicant does not meet the requirements of the law.

In either case the applicant will receive a letter from the Exempt Organization Bureau advising it of the reason for the denial. Generally, the information in the application can be verified, or the articles of incorporation amended, so that the organization will receive exemption approval. However, if the organization does not provide the necessary information or cannot change the articles of incorporation to conform to the requirements, the exemption is denied. There is no provision in the law for a protest or an appeal from a denial of the exemption by the Franchise Tax Board.

Note: In addition to the above requirements for applying for exemption, charitable organizations in California must register with the Registrar of Charitable Trusts, a part of the Attorney General's Office, and file annual reports with the Registrar.

¶ 952   **Chart of Exempt Organizations**

The chart that follows lists the various types of organizations that qualify for exemption. It also shows the Internal Revenue Code Section and the comparable Bank and Corporation Tax Law Section. The chart also indicates whether or not the contributions to the organization would be deductible as a charitable contribution on the tax return of the donor.

Code Sections		Type of Organization	Nature of Activities	Charitable Contribution Deductions Allowed?*
Calif.	**Federal**			
23701h	501(c)(2)	Title holding corporation for exempt organization	Holding title to property of an exempt organization	No
23701d	501(c)(3)	Religious, educational, charitable, scientific, literary, testing for public safety, etc.	The organization title is descriptive of the activities	Yes
23701f	501(c)(4)	Civic leagues, social welfare organizations, and local organizations of employees	Promotion of community welfare, charitable, educational, or recreational	No
23701a	501(c)(5)	Labor, agricultural and horticultural organizations	Educational and instructive, to improve work conditions and products	No
23701e	501(c)(6)	Business leagues, chambers of commerce, real estate boards	Improvement of business conditions, promotion of field of a business or area	No
23701g	501(c)(7)	Social and recreational clubs	Pleasure, recreational and social activities	No
23701b	501(c)(8)	Fraternal beneficiary societies	Lodge providing for payment of life, sickness, accident or other benefits to members	
23701i	501(c)(9)	Voluntary employees' beneficiary associations	Providing for payment of life, sickness, accident or other benefits to members	No

Code Sections		Type of Organization	Nature of Activities	Charitable Contribution Deductions Allowed?*
Calif.	**Federal**			
23701*l*	501(c)(10)	Domestic fraternal societies and associations	Lodge devoting its net earnings to charitable, fraternal and other specific purposes. No life, sickness, or accident benefits to members	
23701j	501(c)(11)	Teachers retirement fund associations	Teachers associations for payment of retirement benefits	No
23701c	501(c)(13)	Cemetery companies	Burials and incidental activities	Yes
None	501(c)(14)	State chartered credit unions, mutual reserve funds	Loans to members	No
None	501(c)(15)	Mutual insurance companies or associations	Providing insurance to members substantially at cost	No
24404	501(c)(16)	Cooperative organizations	Financing crop operations and marketing and purchasing	No
23701n	501(c)(17)	Supplemental unemployment retirement trusts	Provides for payment of supplemental unemployment compensation benefits	No
23701s	501(c)(18)	Employee funded pension trust	Payment of benefits under a pension plan funded by employees	No
23701w	501(c)(19)	Post or organization of war veterans	Organization title is descriptive of activities	Yes
23701q	501(c)(20)	Group legal services plan organizations	Legal services provided exclusively to employees	No
None	501(c)(21)	Black lung benefit trusts	Funded by coal mine operators to satisfy their liability for consequences of black lung diseases	Yes

Code Sections		Type of Organization	Nature of Activities	Charitable Contribution Deductions Allowed?*
Calif.	**Federal**			
23701k	501(d)	Religious and apostolic societies	Regular business activities. Communal religious activity	No
23704	501(e)	Cooperative hospital service organizations	Performs cooperative services for hospitals	Yes
None	501(f)	Cooperative service organizations of operating educational organizations	Performs collective investment services for educational organizations	Yes
23701r	527	Political organizations	Formed to support or defeat a candidate	No
23701t	528	Nonprofit home owners associations (incl. condominium & residential realty management, co-ops)	Provide acquisition, construction, management and protection of residential association property	No
23701x	501(c)(25)	Title holding companies	Acquiring real property, holding title to and collecting income	No
23701v	None	Mobilehome park tenant organization	Purchasing mobilehome park to convert it to condominium, stock cooperative or other resident interests.	No

[Footnote to Exempt Organization Chart]

   * In addition, a deduction for payments should also be considered as an ordinary or necessary business expense if paid by a business organization.

¶ 953   **Prohibited Activities**

Exempt organizations must operate within the framework of their articles of incorporation and by-laws and their Exemption Application information. However, those organizations that engage in specified types of prohibited activities may be subject to loss of exemption or other penalties.

WARRING   Organizations should regularly check their activities to be sure that they don't engage in prohibited transactions.

Problems for exempt organizations. Included among problems faced by exempt organizations are the following:

● *Prohibited transactions.* California law[4] lists transactions which are prohibited by certain organizations exempt under Rev & TC § 23701d[5] and Rev & TC § 23701n[6] except (a) religious organizations, or (b) educational organizations which normally maintain a regular faculty and an enrolled body of students and (c) organizations which normally receive a substantial part of support from the general public and government sources. For federal purposes the prohibited transaction sections apply to private foundations and supplemental unemployment benefit plans, qualified employee pension, profit-sharing or stock bonus plans and certain other employee pension plans. California has adopted the federal approach and now looks to only those organizations under Rev & TC § 23701n[6] to see if prohibited transactions exist. If so, the exempt status is removed from the organization for the taxable year following the year in which the organization is notified that the prohibited transaction occurred.

● *Organizations accumulating income.* An organization must have specific plans for the use of the capital to avoid the accumulation of an unreasonable amount. If an unreasonable accumulation of income exists without specific plans or if it is determined by the Franchise Tax Board that the accumulated earnings are not being invested wisely, the exempt status of the organization may be removed. This is particularly true of organizations holding title to property and exempt under Rev & TC § 23701h because such organizations are normally not allowed to accumulate income at all, except for current needs.[7]

● *Lobbying expenditures.* IRC § 501(c)3 and Rev & TC § 23701d[5] include in the provisions for an exemption for public charities the phrase that "no substantial part of the activities of which is carrying on propaganda or otherwise attempting to influence legislation". To avoid losing the exempt status because of excessive lobbying, public charities, except churches and affiliated group members, can elect to be subject to a tax equal to 25% of their excess lobbying expenditures for the tax year. "Excess lobbying expenditures" are defined as the greater of: (1) the excess of lobbying expenditures over the lobbying nontaxable amount, or (2) the excess of grass roots expenditures over 25% of the lobbying nontaxable amount.

Grass roots and lobbying expenditures are both attempts to influence legislation, but grass roots doesn't include communication with a government official or employee. "Lobbying nontaxable amount" is a certain percentage of the lobbying expenditures. California has adopted the same procedures and limitations on lobbying activities by public charities as the IRC § 501(h).[8]

At the same time, California adopted Rev & TC § 23740[9] to apply to lobbying expenditures for public charities. This section is the same as IRC § 4911 with the exception that it does not provide for a 25% tax on the excess lobbying expenditures for the tax year.

● *Participation in political campaign.* This activity will disqualify a Rev & TC § 23701d charitable organization. It cannot later qualify as a civic organization under Rev & TC § 23701f.[9a]

---

(4) § 23736.1.
(5) § 23701d.
(6) § 23701n.
(7) § 23737.

(8) § 23704.5.
(9) § 23740.
(9a) § 23704.6.

¶ 953

● *Benefiting members or officers.* An organization described in Rev & TC § 23701a through § 23701s[10], will lose its exemption if it permits its net earnings to inure in whole or in part to the benefit of a member, officer, director, employee, or creator of an exempt organization. Inurement of income for this purpose includes the use of the income, the services or property of an exempt organization in such a manner as to benefit a person having a personal or private interest in the organization.

Analysis of operation.   The current operations of an exempt organization have to be consistent with the primary purpose for which it was organized, and, in accordance with the premise on which it applied for and received its exempt status. Merely using the earnings from a function to further the exempt purpose is not enough if the function itself does not further the purpose for which the exemption is granted.

Educational purposes.   Educational purposes include providing care of children away from home, if (1) substantially all the care provided is to enable individuals to be gainfully employed; and (2) services provided by the organization are available to the general public.[11]

Nondiscrimination.   Voluntary employee's beneficiary associations and qualified group legal service plans must satisfy the nondiscrimination requirements of IRC § 505(b).[12]

Exempt title-holding companies.   These organizations must meet the requirements of IRC § 501(c)(25).[13]

Employee-funded pension plans.   To qualify, plans must meet elective-deferral requirements of IRC § 401(a)(30).[14]

¶ 954   Unrelated Business Income

Every organization exempt under Rev & TC § 17631[15] (described under IRC § 401a) or Rev & TC § 23701a through § 23701v[16] is taxable on its unrelated trade or business income, except a corporation formed to carry out a function of the state which is carrying out that function and is controlled by the State of California. An unrelated trade or business includes any type of activity carried on to produce income. It does not make a difference whether or not the activity is profitable—the trade or business could still be "unrelated." The organization's need for the income, or how it uses the profits has no bearing on whether it is unrelated business income.

Note: Income-producing activities always create the problem of whether or not there is unrelated business income. These activities should be checked in advance to make sure that they are within the same limits, if the organization wants to avoid unrelated business income tax. Get an official ruling in advance if necessary.

In the usual sense, if the business is not substantially related to the exercise or performance by the organization of the charitable, educational or

---

(10) § 23701a–23701s.
(11) § 23704.4.
(12) § 23705.
(13) § 23701u.

(14) § 23701s.
(15) § 17631.
(16) § 23701a–23701v.

other purpose constituting the basis for its exemption, it is an unrelated business.

California conforms to IRC § 513.[17] This federal provision states that the term "unrelated trade or business" does not include any trade or business (1) if substantially all the work in carrying on the trade or business is performed for the organization without compensation, or (2) which is carried on primarily for the convenience of its members, students, patients, officers, or employees, or (3) which is selling merchandise which has been received by the organization as gifts or contributions. Conduct of bingo games is also excluded. But the term, "trade or business" does include any activity which is carried on for the purpose of income from the sale of goods or the performance of services.

What's not taxable. Generally, unrelated trade or business income does not include: (1) qualified public entertainment activity, such as fairs and expositions conducted by exempt charitable, social, welfare or agricultural organizations or (2) qualified conventions or trade shows conducted by exempt unions or trade associations.

TAX TIP   In determining whether the income of an exempt organization from a trade or business is subject to unrelated business income tax, you have to determine: (1) whether it is income from business which is regularly carried on or is income from a sporadic activity, and (2) whether the business is unrelated. The business is substantially related only if the activity (not the proceeds from it) contributes importantly to the accomplishment of the exempt purpose of the organization.

Exclusions.   California conforms to IRC § 512.[18] Conformity includes rules on unrelated income of an exempt partner. Unrelated business income does not include:

(1) *Dividends, interest and annuities* and all deductions directly connected with such income,

(2) *All royalties* (including overriding royalties) whether measured by production or by gross or taxable income from the property and all deductions directly connected with royalty income,

(3) *All rents from real property* (including elevators and escalators) and all rents from personal property leased with such real property, if the personal property rents are an incidental amount of the total rents received.

(4) *All gains or losses* from the sale, exchange or other disposition of capital assets. These exclusions do not apply if the income is unrelated, debt financed income. The exclusion of dividends, interest, royalties, and rents, also does not apply if they are received from controlled organizations.

Note: The exclusions above refer only to the classification of such income with respect to the term "unrelated business income." This kind of income may be taxable to certain kinds of exempt organizations (other than those under Rev & TC § 23701d) as investment income.

---

(17) § 23051.1.   (18) § 23051.5; 23732.

Deductions from gross income. Deductions from gross income to arrive at taxable income from an unrelated business are those directly connected with the carrying on of the business, except that any deductions directly connected with the items that are excluded from income in the paragraph above are not deducted. Also the deduction for charitable contributions cannot exceed 5% of the unrelated business taxable income figured without the charitable contribution deduction.

The organization also has a special deduction of $1,000, except in the case of a diocese, province of a religious order, or a convention or association of churches. Each parish, church or local unit is entitled to a specific deduction of the lower of $1,000 or the gross income derived from any unrelated trade or business regularly carried on by the local unit.

Social clubs. Social clubs generally exclude exempt function income. Such clubs must pay tax on investment income they receive, but do not pay tax on dues, fees and similar charges paid by members for club services and facilities. Also, they do not pay tax on investment income set aside for religious, charitable, or educational purposes. A special rule applies to social clubs and other membership organizations to prevent those that are exempt from giving up their exempt status and escaping the tax on their business and investment income by using this income to serve the members at less than cost and then deducting the book loss.

Nonexempt membership organizations. California conforms to IRC § 277.[19] Nonexempt membership organizations can deduct the expenses incurred in supplying services, facilities, and goods to their members only to the extent of the income received from their members, including income from institutes and trade shows for the education of the members.

Unrelated debt-financed income is subject to the unrelated business tax for both federal and California purposes. The income to an exempt organization from debt-financed property, which is not related to the exempt function, is unrelated business income taxable in the same proportion that the average acquisition indebtedness bears to the property's adjusted basis. Acquisition debt does not include debt incurred by educational organizations, and affiliated support organizations to acquire or improve any real property. Same applies to any trust qualified under IRC § 401.[20] California adopts IRC § 514(c)(9), relating to computation of unrelated business taxable income of a disqualified shareholder (other than educational institution, its affiliated support organizations, or qualified pension trust) of a title-holding company.

Debt-financed property. Debt-financed property is defined as any property held to produce rental income that has an acquisition indebtedness at any time during the tax year or during the 12 months prior to its sale or

---

(19) IRC § 277; § 23051.5.

(20) IRC § 514; § 23051.5.

other disposition, unless its use is substantially related to the organization's exempt purpose.

The term acquisition indebtedness is defined as indebtedness incurred in acquiring or improving the property or indebtedness that would not have been incurred but for the acquisition or improving of the property.

Excluded from the definition of "debt-financed property:"

(1) Property to the extent that its income is subject to tax as income from the carrying on of an unrelated trade or business;

(2) Property to the extent that its income is derived from research activities; and

(3) Property to the extent its use is in the business where substantially all of the work of carrying on the business is performed without compensation or carrying on the business is primarily for the convenience of members, students, or patients, or the business consists of selling merchandise substantially all of which has been received as contributions.

Property subject to mortgage. Income from rentals of real property acquired by gift isn't taxable for period of 10 years after gift because the mortgage is not treated as acquisition indebtedness for that period.[20]

California adopts IRC § 514 that requires tax-exempt organizations in partnership with taxable entities to treat income from debt-financed real property as unrelated taxable income unless partnership allocations are either qualified allocations or permissible disproportionate allocations.

IMPORTANT   All income from unrelated trade or businesses has to be reported on the California return. If it is derived from sources within or without California an apportionment of income is required. For trusts which have unrelated trade or business from sources without California, the trust must report that proportion of such income as the number of resident trustees bears to the total number of trustees. Also, where a part or all of the unrelated trade or business income is taxed by more than one state, California or the other state may allow a tax credit for that portion of the income which is subject to double taxation in accordance with the credit for income taxes paid in Chapter 12 of the Personal Income Tax Law.

Tax credits. Unrelated business tax is subject to tax credits listed in the instructions to Form 109, Exempt Organization Business Income Tax Return.[21]

Details on these tax credits are found in Chapter 1 of this Handbook.

What tax rates apply. Corporations, associations, and business trusts are taxable on unrelated business income at the corporation tax rates. Trusts are subject to individual tax rates imposed under the personal income tax.[22]

---

(21) FTB Form 109 Instructions.   **(22)** § 17041(e); 17651; § 23731.

¶ 955   Private Foundations

The term "private foundation" means a domestic or foreign organization defined in IRC §§ 501(c)(3) and 509 and Rev & TC § 23701(d).[23] These generally are exempt organizations organized exclusively for religious, charitable or educational purposes, other than:

(1) Organization described in IRC § 170(b) qualifying for the maximum of 50% charitable deduction for federal purposes;

(2) Organization which normally receives more than ⅓ of its support in each taxable year from gifts, grants, gross receipts from admissions and sales of merchandise from the general public or from governmental units;

(3) Organization organized and operated exclusively for the benefit of one of the organizations described in (1) or (2) above; or

(4) Organization organized and operated exclusively for the testing for public safety.

California requirements.   Rev & TC § 23708(e)[24] provides that private foundations are required to include in their governing instruments certain provisions as follows:

(1) It must distribute its income for any taxable year so that it will not be subject to the penalty tax provided in IRC § 4942;

(2) Organizations cannot engage in any direct or indirect "self-dealing," such as the sale or exchange or leasing of property between them and a disqualified person; lending money or other extension of credit to a disqualified person; furnishing of goods and services or facilities or payment of compensation for expenses to a disqualified person at less than the fair value; or any other activity which would subject them to the tax for self-dealing under IRC § 4941;

(3) Have excess business holdings in the form of stock in a business enterprise so that the organization would be subject to tax on excess business holdings in accordance with IRC § 4943;

(4) Invest in such manner as to jeopardize the carrying out of its exempt purposes so that it would be subject to the tax on such investments under IRC § 4944.

California law, however, does *not* impose taxes on private foundations for the prohibited dealings, similar to the federal provisions.

Termination of private foundations.   California law provides that a private foundation may be terminated by action from the Attorney General of the state or by court ruling as set forth in IRC § 507. Also, the status of any organization as a private foundation may be terminated for California purposes if the organization distributes all of its net assets to one or more of the organizations which qualify for exemption under the 50% maximum deduction category as charitable organizations.[25]

Private operating foundation.   An operating foundation for federal purposes is one that spends substantially all of its adjusted net income or minimum investment return directly for the active conduct of its exempt

---

(23) § 23701d.
(24) § 23708(e).

(25) § 23707.

activities. In addition, it must meet certain other tests with respect to charitable activities and minimum investments.

Note: However, California law doesn't have provisions for private operating foundations.

¶ 960 **Annual Information Reports and Other Returns**

Form 199. All exempt organizations and some nonexempt charitable trusts must file the annual information return (Form 199) and pay a $10 filing fee. A copy of federal Form 990, Return of Organization Exempt from Income Tax must be attached to Form 199. Included in the requirement are charitable remainder trusts which are private foundations and must file Form 199 rather than a trust return. An organization exempt under Rev & TC § 23701v, should attach federal Form 1120, Corporation Tax Return, or 1120H, Return for Homeowners' Associations, instead of federal Form 990. An organization not required to file federal Form 990, need not file Form 199. Churches or religious orders and organizations with gross receipts normally less than $25,000 are not required to file Form 199. Private foundations must file Form 199, even if gross receipts are less than $25,000.[26]

● *Homeowners' associations* exempt under Rev & TC § 23701t, including condominium management associations, residential real estate management associations, and cooperative housing corporations must attach federal Form 1120 or 1120H to Form 199. If federal form 1120H is filed, also attach complete balance sheet and detailed financial statement reflecting income from all sources and all expenditures. Gross receipts are those from all sources before deductions.[26]

● *Exempt organization business income tax return, Form 109.* Exempt Organization Business Income Tax Return, Form 109, must be filed by the following:

(1) An exempt organization when the gross income derived from unrelated business is $1000 or more. Form 109 must be filed in addition to Form 199. *Exceptions to filing Form 109:* Political organizations (exempt under Rev & TC § 23701r), homeowners' associations (exempt under Rev & TC § 23701t) and organizations controlled by the state or other governmental municipalities.

(2) Stock bonus, pension or profit sharing trusts (exempt under Rev & TC § 17631) with unrelated business income of $1000 or more. There is no requirement to file Form 199.

Form 100. Corporation Franchise or Income Tax Return, Form 100 (or Form 100S for S corporations), must be filed by the following:[26]

(1) Political organizations (exempt under Rev & TC § 23701r) with taxable income in excess of $100. There is no requirement to file Form 199.

(2) Some mutual and cooperative organizations that are exempt under federal law but not exempt under California law.

(3) Homeowners' associations (exempt under Rev & TC § 23701t) with gross taxable income in excess of $100. Form 100 must be filed whether or not Form 199 is required to be filed. Homeowners' associations gross taxable income is defined as all income received during the taxable year other than amounts received from membership fees, dues or assessments.

---

(26) Forms 100, 109, and 199 instructions; § 23701; 23701k; 23701r; 23701t; 23771–23772.

Form 565. Form 565, Partnership Return of Income, must be filed by all religious or apostolic organizations described in Rev & TC § 23701k.[26]

Federal Form 1099 series and 596. Federal Form 1099 series, Information Return and Form 596, Annual Summary and Transmittal of Information Returns, must be filed to report payments of compensation (not subject to income tax withholding), dividends, interest, rents, royalties, annuities, pensions, etc. Every organization engaged in a trade or business (which includes for this purpose all exempt functions) is required to file.[26]

Organization statement. All corporations and exempt organizations incorporated or qualified in California are required to file an organization statement with the Office of the Secretary of State annually. Contact the Office of the Secretary of State at P.O. Box 944230. Sacramento, CA 94244–0230, or telephone (916) 445–2020.[26]

Nonexempt charitable trust. A nonexempt charitable trust described in IRC § 4947(a)(1), which is treated as a private foundation, is required to file Form 199 (not Form 541) and to comply with the reporting requirements of a private foundation. Other charitable remainder trusts and split interest trusts file Form 541.

Filing deadline. The forms must be filed on or before the 15th day of the 5th month, with the Franchise Tax Board. If the forms cannot be filed by the due date, the exempt organization has an additional seven months to file without need of filing a written request for extension.

Fees. All organizations are required to file Form 199 and, with the exceptions below, must pay a $10 filing fee. The fee is $25 if it is not paid on or before the due date (including extensions). Organizations exempt under Rev & TC § 23701d that don't have to pay a filing fee are the following:

(1) An exclusively religious organization;
(2) An exclusively educational organization which normally maintains a regular faculty and curriculum and student body;
(3) An exclusively charitable organization primarily supported by contributions from the general public or by the United States or any political subdivision;
(4) An organization operated, supervised or controlled by, or in connection with, an exclusively religious organization.

Large organizations with a central parent, state or district office and with numerous branches or local units may qualify to file a group return. In order to file on a group basis, written approval must be obtained from the Franchise Tax Board.

Farmers' cooperative associations. Cooperative marketing and purchasing organizations are exempt from tax for federal purposes under IRC § 521(a). This primarily means that their activities in connection with the cooperative for members are not subject to tax. However, any other income the cooperative derives from investments, capital gains on the sale of properties, and so on, is taxable at federal corporation rates. California does not provide for an exemption for farmers' cooperatives but, instead, provides that such associations organized and operating on a cooperative or mutual basis are entitled to deduct from income all income resulting from or arising out of business activities for or with their members carried on by them or their agents, or when done on a nonprofit basis, for or with nonmembers. In effect, the business income from activities for or with members is passed down to the members without tax at the cooperative level, and the members themselves are taxable on this income.[27]

Reports to Attorney General.   Reporting requirements are explained at ¶ 962.

¶ 961   Revocation of Exemption

The Franchise Tax Board may remove an organization's status as an exempt corporation for one or more of the following reasons:

(1) *Donations no longer deductible.*   The Internal Revenue Service has determined that donations are no longer deductible (the Internal Revenue Bulletin reports this information in the monthly issue of the bulletin);

(2) *Failure to report or register.*   The Attorney General's office has notified the Franchise Tax Board that the organization has failed to file reports or register with the Registrar of Charitable Trusts, or has determined that the organization is not operating in accordance with its exempt purposes;

(3) *Inactivity.*   The Franchise Tax Board received information that the organization is inactive or has ceased its existence;

(4) *Nonexempt activities.*   A field audit by the Franchise Tax Board shows that the corporation is not operating in accordance with its exempt purposes. If the Franchise Tax Board exempt section determines that the exempt status should be revoked, it issues Form FTB 2523M, Notice of Revocation, with a copy sent to the Registry of Charitable Trusts if the organization is subject to the Registrar's supervision.[28]

(5) *Failure to file statements or returns.*   An unincorporating organization fails to file its annual statements or returns.

(6) *Failure to complete incorporation procedures.*   An incorporating organization fails to complete its incorporation procedures within a specified period of time after being granted exemption, usually 60 days.

(7) *Failure to fulfill condition of exempt status.*   The organization is granted a conditional exempt status (for example, that it also obtain a federal exempt status) but fails to fulfill the condition.

IMPORTANT   The organization may re-establish its exempt status with the State of California by filing with the Franchise Tax Board: (a) a new application for exemption (Form FTB 3500) and payment of the $25 filing fee; (b) any information, returns, statements, notifications or amounts due, which were not previously submitted or paid and which caused the revocation and; (c) if the organization had its exemption revoked because it engaged in activities other than those permitted, it must submit satisfactory proof that it has corrected its nonexempt activities and that it will oper-

---

(27) § 24404.   (28) § 23777; Reg. 23777.

ate in an exempt manner in the future and pay the tax for any periods the organization was not qualified for exemption.[29]

Suspension of corporation. The corporation itself may be suspended for failure to file the required forms or pay the annual filing fees. Refer to the chapter on suspension and revivor of corporations for information as to how to obtain a revivor to put the corporation back in good standing.

Exempt purpose vs. unrelated business. The distinction between operating an unrelated business and operating a business for an exempt purpose, related to the organization's exempt function, is not clear and has led to numerous Revenue Rulings and court cases over the years. Generally, the business operated by an exempt organization must not be out of proportion with the exempt needs or it must be incidental or insubstantial when compared to the overall activities of the organization. The mere fact that the operation of an unrelated trade or business is used to earn funds for charitable or social welfare purposes does not qualify the organization for exemption from tax.

EXAMPLE The grey areas of what are unrelated business activities and nonexempt activities (for which organization could lose tax-exempt status) are shown by examples below.

(1) *Labor, agricultural, or horticultural organizations.* The operation of a bar, restaurant or similar activities or marketing livestock, putting on rodeos, or auction sales of animals;

(2) *Fraternal, beneficiary societies.* Operating a bar or restaurant open to the public, or food catering in a commercial manner;

(3) *Cemetery companies.* Operation of a mortuary or operation of a perpetual care fund;

(4) *Religious, charitable, educational, etc., organizations.* Income from sales of advertising space in publications;

(5) *Hospitals.* Operation of a pharmacy with sales to nonpatients; operation of a nurses' employment register;

(6) *Business leagues, chambers of commerce.* Multiple listing services by real estate boards, income from sale of advertising space in publications, operating a credit information service as a primary activity and operating trade shows on a commercial basis;

(7) *Civic leagues, local associations of employees, veterans' organizations.* Operation of bar or restaurant facilities available to the general public, operating a catering service and operating professional or semi-professional sports activities;

(8) *Social and recreational clubs.* Operating club facilities available to the general public.[30]

¶ 962 Supervision by Attorney General

In addition to the requirements that an exempt organization in California file an application and receive exempt status from the Franchise Tax Board and file annual reports with the FTB and submit to an examination of records or information by the Franchise Tax Board auditors, other state

---

(29) § 23778; Reg 23778.

(30) IRC § 512; 513; 514; 23731; 23733; 23734; 23735; 23736; 23736.1.

agencies also perform similar functions with respect to exempt organizations. The Office of the Attorney General of California through its Registry of Charitable Trusts is one of these. According to the general instructions for filing reports with that office "the Attorney General is responsible under California Law to protect the public interest in assets held for charitable purposes (purposes benefiting the public interest). This responsibility is carried out in part by requiring organizations and trusts, holding such assets to register and file periodic reports."

Registration application. At the inception of this law, the Attorney General's office provided Form CT–1 to be used by exempt organizations to register. At the present time, however, the organizations required to register and file periodic reports may submit a copy of the application for exemption which is filed with the Franchise Tax Board (FTB 3500) instead of filing Form CT–1.

Periodic reports. Form CT–2 is required annually of every corporation, association, or trustee holding assets for "charitable purposes," *except:*

(1) a government agency;
(2) a religious corporation sole;
(3) a cemetery corporation;
(4) a charitable corporation organized and operated primarily as a religious organization, educational institution or a hospital; and
(5) corporate trustees which are subject to the jurisdiction of the Superintendent of Banks of the State of California or to the Comptroller of Currency of the United States.

The type of organizations required to report are those generally exempt under IRC §§ 501(c)(3) or 501(c)(4) and Rev & TC § 23701(d) or § 23701(f). A nonexempt charitable trust, described in IRC § 4947(a)(1), which also meets the definition of a private foundation under IRC § 509(a) must comply with the reporting requirements of a private foundation by filing Form CT–2.

Filing exemption. Certain small organizations are excused from filing a periodic report for a maximum of ten years under the following conditions:

(1) a periodic report (CT–2) for the first year was filed;
(2) gross revenue for the current year is $25,000 or less;
(3) total assets at all times during the year were $25,000 or less;
(4) the purposes of the organization have not been amended or modified;
(5) there were no substantial sales of assets;
(6) there were no self-dealing transactions or loans to a director or trustee;

or

(7) the organization has not become inactive or dissolved.

Note: Private foundations are required by federal law to file a copy of Form 990 PF and 4720 with the Attorney General's office, even though the Foundation Trustee may be exempt from filing Form CT–2.

OBSERVATION   Form CT–2 will also partially meet the filing requirements of the Internal Revenue Service and the Franchise Tax Board. For example, private foundations may submit Form CT–2 in place of Form 990 AR, Annual

Report of Private Foundations. In addition, the Franchise Tax Board will accept the substitution of a completed copy of Form CT–2 for all of the information required on Form 199, except page 1.

When to file. The CT–2 Report must be filed on or before the 15th day of the 5th month following the close of the accounting period with the Registry of Charitable Trusts, P.O. Box 903447, Sacramento, CA 94203–4470.

Group report. A group report may be filed on Form CT–2 by a parent, central, state, district or like organization for two or more local units.

¶ 963 **California Nonprofit Corporation Law**

This law was enacted with an effective date of January 1, 1980. It has many sections which are significant for tax and accounting purposes. The provisions will be under the supervision of the Attorney General's office.[31]

Classifications for exempt corporations. The law puts exempt corporations into three different classifications:

(1) *Public benefit corporations.* This category includes charitable, scientific, literary, educational, and other organizations exempt from tax under Rev & TC § 23701d[32] except those classified under (2) below; this category also includes Rev & TC § 23701f organizations as well as Rev & TC § 23701h organizations that hold title to property for Rev & TC § 23701d and Rev & TC § 23701f corporations.

(2) *Religious corporations.* Those formed "primarily or exclusively for religious purposes";

(3) *Mutual benefit corporations.* The phrase is designed to include those organizations formed to benefit their members (fraternal organizations and the like); or which benefit those engaging in a particular type of business or activity. Rev & TC § 23701h and Rev & TC § 23701m organizations are not required to incorporate under the Nonprofit Mutual Benefit Corporation Law since the law specifically prohibits distribution of income and/or property except in dissolution. By their very nature, title holding companies and diversified management companies regularly make distributions to their members.

Each classification has some significant provisions of the law applicable to it in addition to the general rules.

Public benefit corporation requirements. Of special significance to Public Benefit Corporations are the following requirements:

(1) *Board of directors.* Not more than 49% of the Board of Directors can be "interested persons." An interested person is any person who is currently being compensated by the organization for services rendered by any relative of such persons;

(2) *Records.* Not only does the organization have to keep accounting records of financial transactions but the Code provides that it must keep written minutes of the proceedings of its members, boards and Committees, and a complete record of the members including their names and addresses.

(3) *Private foundations.* The Code provides that a private foundation has to distribute its income for each taxable year so that it is not subject to the corporation tax imposed by IRC § 4942 for failure to distribute income. In addition,

---

(31) Corp Cd § 5000–9600.　　　　　　　　(32) § 23701d.

private foundations may not engage in any act of self-dealing, retain excess business holdings or make prohibited investments. In other words, the Code does not provide for penalty taxes to a private foundation for engaging in these acts. It flatly prohibits such acts;

(4) *Annual report.*   Section 6321[31] of this California Nonprofit Corporation Code states that an annual report is required to be sent to the membership not later than 120 days after the close of the organization's year end. This Report is to include a statement of all the assets and liabilities as well as a recitation of the principal changes in the assets and liabilities and the trust funds, in addition, a complete listing of revenue and receipts and income and disbursements.

The report also is to disclose any transactions involving more than $50,000 between the organization and related parties such as an officer or director.

Note: The Code provides that the periodic report to the Attorney General (Form CT–2) can be used to submit this Annual Report to the membership, provided it contains all of the necessary information. However, it should be noted that the annual report to the members must be transmitted to them no later than 120 days after the close of the organization's year end, which is six weeks before the normal filing date for the CT–2.

Inspection of records.   The law allows the directors of the organization to inspect all records and membership lists and also gives members the right to review the same type of information.

Penalties and prohibitions.   Corporation Code § 6812[31] provides fines of $1,000 or penalty of up to one year in jail or both for directors and officers who file false reports or fail to make book entries or post required notices. There are also penalties up to one year in jail for directors or officers who are involved in fraudulent acquisition of corporate property or presenting false or fraudulent documents to public officials.

Memberships in public benefit corporations cannot be sold or exchanged or transferred through inheritance.

Religious corporations.   The provisions of the law involving religious organizations are similar to those set forth above for public benefit organizations, except that more reliance is placed on the articles and by-laws of the religious organizations. In addition, the Attorney General's office is not provided with the same supervisory powers for religious organizations as for public benefit organizations.[33]

Mutual benefit corporations.   Members of a mutual benefit corporation may have a proprietary interest in the organization's assets. Therefore, the Code permits memberships to be sold if the articles or by-laws of the corporations permit it.

There are provisions in the code for the merger, dissolution or sale of the assets of the organization requiring the Attorney General's office to be notified prior to undertaking any of these steps.[31]

---

(33) Corp Cd Annotated § 9110–9690.

CORPORATIONS TAXABLE

¶ 991   Federal-California Code Comparison Table

Listed in the table below are federal Internal Revenue Code (IRC) section numbers with the subjects that they cover, the California Bank and Corporation Tax Law and Administrative Tax Law section numbers and the paragraph numbers in this handbook where they are explained or to which they relate. "N" means none.

Federal IRC No.	Subject	Calif. Law No.	Handbook ¶ No.
11	Tax imposed	23151	1211
15	Effect of changes	24251	1057
30	Credit for qualified electric vehicles	23603	1240
41	Increasing research activities	23609	1237
42	Low income housing credit	23610.5	1239
51–52	Amount of targeted jobs credit	23621	1236
55–59	Alternative minimum tax	23400; 23455–23457; 23459	1223
61	Gross income defined	24271; 24323; 24308; 24314; 24315	402; 1079
63	Taxable income defined	24341	1067
64	Ordinary income defined	23049.1	1079
65	Ordinary loss defined	23049.2	1079
72	Annuities; insurance proceeds	24272.2; 24302	1097; 1115
77	Commodity credit loans	24273	1085
78	Dividends received from certain foreign corporations	N	1145
83	Property transferred in connection with performance of services	24379	1145
88	Certain amounts with respect to nuclear decommissioning costs	24275	1080
90	Illegal federal irrigation subsidies	24276	1080
101	Certain death benefits	24302; 24305	1115
108	Income from discharge of indebtedness	24307	1091
109	Improvements by lessee on lessor's property	24309	1086
111	Recovery of tax benefit items	24310;	1092
118	Contributions to capital	24324; 24325	1079
126	Certain cost-sharing payments	24308.5	1102
133	Interest income; loans & ESOPs	24306	1082
136	Energy conservation subsidies by local utilities	24326	1101
162	Trade or business expenses	24343; 24343.2; 24343.5	1145

Federal IRC No.	Subject	Calif. Law No.	Handbook ¶ No.
163	Interest	24344; 24344.5; 23384; 23385	1146
164	Taxes	24345–6	1147; 1148
165	Losses	24347–47.5	1157
166	Bad debts	24347	403
167	Depreciation	24349–24355	370; 387; 388; 391
168	Accelerated cost recovery system	24349	393; 394
169	Amortization of pollution control facilities	24372.3	306; 388
170	Charitable, etc., contributions and gifts	24357–24359	1149
171	Amortizable bond premium	24360–24363	1159
172	Net operating loss deduction	24416; 24416.1; 24416.2; 24416.3	1145; 1151
173	Circulation expenditures	24364	1151
174	Research and experimental expenditures	24365	1150
175	Soil and water conservation expenditures	24369	1161
176	Payments with respect to employees of certain foreign corporations	N	1145
178	Amortization of cost of acquiring a lease	24373	370; 381; 382
179	Expensing certain depreciable assets	24356.8; 24356.2–24356.4; 24356	385
179A	Clean-fuel vehicles and refueling property	24356.5	385A
180	Expenditures by farmers for fertilizer, etc.	24377	1160
190	Architectural barrier removal	24383	1145
192	Contributions to black lung benefit trust	N	1145
193	Tertiary injectants	N	1145
194	Amortization of reforestation expenditures	24372.5	305
194A	Contributions to employer liability trusts	N	1145
195	Business start-up expenses	24414	392
197	Amortization of goodwill and other intangibles	24355.5	371
216	Deductions for cooperative housing tenant-stockholder	24382	370; 1146; 1147
241	Allowance of special deductions	24401	1012–1013; 1081; 1155–1156
243	Dividends received by corporations	24402	1081
244	Dividends received on preferred stock	24402	1081
245	Dividends from foreign corporations	24402	1081
246	Rules applying to deductions for dividends received	24402	1081

¶ 991

Federal IRC No.	Subject	Calif. Law No.	Handbook ¶ No.
246A	Deduction reduced where portfolio debt financed	24402	1081
247	Dividends paid on public utilities preferred stock	24402	1081
248	Organizational expenditures	24407–09	1155
249	Limitation on deduction of bond premium on repurchase	24439	1146
261	General rule for disallowance of deductions	24421	321
263	Capital expenditures	24422–23	402
263A	Capitalization and inclusion in inventory costs of certain expenses	24422.3	411
264	Certain amounts paid in connection with insurance contracts	24424	1145
265	Expenses and interest relating to tax-exempt income	24425	291; 325
266	Carrying charges	24426	363
267	Losses, expenses, and interest with respect to transactions between related taxpayers	24427	364; 1115; 1166
268	Sale of land with unharvested crop	N	292; 1145
269	Acquisitions made to evade or avoid income tax	24431	1303
269A	Personal service corporations formed to avoid taxes	N	354
269B	Stapled entities	N	1079
271	Debts owed by political parties, etc.	24434	403; 1157
272	Disposal of coal or domestic iron ore	N	1145
274	Disallowance of certain entertainment etc., expenses	24443	292; 293; 1145
275	Certain taxes	24345	1147
277	Deductions incurred by certain membership organizations in transactions with members	24437	954
279	Interest on indebtedness incurred by corporation to acquire stock or assets of another corporation	24438	1146
280B	Demolition of certain historic structures	24442	388
280C	Expenses for which credits are allowed	24440	1146
280E	Expenditures in connection with illegal sales of drugs	24436	1145
280F	Limitation on investment tax credit and depreciation for luxury automobiles; limitation where certain property used for personal purposes	24349.1	396
280H	Personal service corporations; amounts paid to employee owners	24442.5	353

Federal IRC No.	Subject	Calif. Law No.	Handbook ¶ No.
291	Special rules relating to corporate preference items	24449	1223
301–385	Distributions of property	24451–24452	1115; 1116
302	Distributions in redemption of stock	24453	1117; 1118
303	Distributions in redemption of stock to pay death taxes	24451	1124
304	Redemption through use of related corporations	24451	1118; 1119
305	Distributions of stock and stock rights	24451	1120
306	Dispositions of certain stock	24456	1118; 1123; 362
307	Basis of stock and stock rights acquired in distributions	24451	362
311	Taxability of corporation on distribution	24451	1115
312	Effect on earnings and profits	24451	1115
316	Dividend defined	24451	1115; 1153
317	Other definitions	24451	1115
318	Constructive ownership of stock	24451	1118
331	Gain or loss to shareholders in corporate liquidations	24451	1125
332	Complete liquidations of subsidiaries	24451	1131
334	Basis of property received in liquidations	24451	1126
336	Gain or loss recognized on property distributed in complete liquidation	24451	1127
337	Nonrecognition for property distributed to parent	24461	1131
338	Stock purchases treated as asset acquisitions	24451	1133
341	Collapsible corporations	24451	1029
346	Definition and special rule; partial liquidation	24451	1125
351	Transfer to corporation controlled by transferor	24451	1103
354	Exchanges of stock and securities in certain reorganizations	24451	1104
355	Distribution of stock and securities of a controlled corporation	24451	1104
356	Receipt of additional consideration	24451	1104
357	Assumption of liability	24451	1104
358	Basis to distributees	24451	1104
361	Nonrecognition of gain or loss to corporations	24451	1103; 1104
362	Basis to corporations	24451	1103; 1104
367	Foreign corporations	24451	1103
368	Definitions relating to corporate reorganizations	24451	1017; 1104
381	Carryovers in certain corporate acquisitions	23253; 24471	1017; 1134

Federal IRC No.	Subject	Calif. Law No.	Handbook ¶ No.
382	Limitations on net operating loss carryforwards and certain built-in losses	24451	1017; 1134
383	Special limitations; excess carryovers of credits	24481	1017; 1134
384	Preacquisition losses to offset built-in gains	24451	1017
385	Treatment of certain interests in corporations as stock or indebtedness	24451	1017; 1104
401	Qualified pension, profit-sharing and stock bonus plans	23701p	952; 953
401–424	Pension, profit-sharing, stock bonus plans	24601	1079
404	Deduction for contributions of an employer to an employees' trust or annuity plan and compensation under a deferred-payment plan	24611	1145
404A	Foreign deferred compensation plan	24601	1145
406	Employees of foreign affiliates covered by § 3121(l) agreements	24601	1145
407	Certain employees of domestic subsidiaries engaged in business outside the United States	24601	1145
413	Collectively bargained plans, etc.	24612	1145
419	Treatment of funded welfare benefit plans	24601	1145
419A	Qualified asset account; limitation on additions to account	24601	1145
421	General rules; stock options	24601	309
422	Incentive stock options	N	309
423	Employee stock purchase plan	N	309
424	Definitions and special rules	N	309
441	Period for computation of taxable income	24631; 24632; 24633.5	351
442	Change of annual accounting period	24633	351
443	Returns for a period of less than 12 months	23113; 24634; 24636	351
444	Election of taxable year other than required year	24637	351
446	General rule for methods of accounting	24651	352
447	Method of accounting for corporations engaged in farming	24652	352
448	Limitation on use of cash method of accounting	24654	352
451	General rule for taxable year of inclusion	24661	353
453	Installment method	24667	364; 407
453A	Special rules for nondealers	24667	364; 407
453B	Gain or loss on disposition of installment obligations	24667	364; 407
454	Obligations issued at discount	24674	353
455	Prepaid subscription income	24676	353

Federal IRC No.	Subject	Calif. Law No.	Handbook ¶ No.
456	Prepaid dues income of certain membership organizations	N	353
457	Deferred compensation plans of state and local governments and tax-exempt organizations	N	353
458	Magazines, paperbacks, and records returned after the close of the taxable year	24676.5	353
460	Special rules for long-term contracts	24673.2	353
461	General rule for taxable year of deduction	24681	354
464	Limitations on deductions in case of farming syndicates	24682	354
465	Deductions limited to amount at risk	24691	354
467	Certain payments for use of property or services	24688	354
468	Special rules for mining and solid waste reclamation and closing costs	24689	354
468A	Special rules for nuclear decommissioning costs	24690	345
468B	Special rules for designated settlement funds	24693	354
469	Passive activity losses and credits limited	24692	325; 354
471	General rule for inventories	24701	411
472	Last-in, first-out inventories	24701	411
473	Qualified liquidations of LIFO inventories	N	411
474	Simplified dollar-value LIFO method for certain small businesses	24708	411
481	Adjustments required by changes in method of accounting	24721	352; 411
482	Allocation of income and deductions among taxpayers	24725	354
483	Interest on certain deferred payments	24726	1149
501	Exemption from tax on corporations, certain trusts, etc.	23701; 23701a–x; 23704; 23706	951; 952; 953; 954; 955
502	Feeder organizations	23702	952
503	Requirements for exemption	23736–36.4	953
504	Status after organization ceases to qualify for exemption under Sec. 501(c)(3) because of substantial lobbying	23704.6	953
505	Additional requirements for organizations described in paragraph (9), (17), or (20) of Section 501(c)	23705	953
507	Termination of private foundation status	23707	955
508	Special rules with respect to section 501(c)(3) organizations	23708	955
509	Private foundation defined	23709	955

Federal IRC No.	Subject	Calif. Law No.	Handbook ¶ No.
511	Imposition of tax on unrelated business income of charitable etc., organizations	23731	954
512	Unrelated business taxable income	23732	954
513	Unrelated trade or business	23710; 23734	954
514	Unrelated debt-financed income	23735	954
527	Political organizations	23701r	951; 952; 960; 1273
528	Certain homeowners associations	23701t	952; 960; 1299
541–547	Imposition of personal holding company tax	23051.5(b)(3)	1028
551–558	Foreign personal holding companies	23051.5(b)(4)	1028
561–565	Deduction for dividend paid	24402	1153
581	Definition of bank	23039	1006
582	Bad debts, losses, and gains with respect to securities held by financial institutions	24347(c)	408
584	Common trust funds	N	110
585	Reserves for losses on loans of banks	24348	408
591	Deduction for dividends paid on deposits	24370; 24403	1146
593	Reserve for losses on loans	N	408
595	Foreclosure on property securing loans	24348.5	403; 408
596	Limitation on dividends received deduction	N	408; 1081
611	Allowance of deduction for depletion	24831	402
611–638	Deductions	24831	402
612	Basis for cost depletion	24831	402
613	Percentage depletion	24831	402
613A	Limitations on percentage depletion in case of oil and gas wells	24831	402
614	Definition of property	24831	402
616	Development expenditures	24831	402
617	Deduction and recapture of certain mining exploration expenditures	24831	401–402
631	Timber, coal, iron ore; gain or loss	24831	402
636	Mineral production payments	24831	402
641–692	Estates, trusts, beneficiaries, and decedents	24271	451; 455; 471
701	Partners subject to tax	23081	423
701–761	Partners and partnerships	24271	421–436
851–855	Regulated investment company	24870–24871	1032
856–860	Real estate investment trust	24870–24872	353; 1031
860A–860G	Real estate mortgage investment conduits	24870–74	1038
861–865	Income from sources within the U.S.	25110; 24272.3	1165; 1170 1184
883	Exclusions from gross income	24320	1090
988	Foreign currency transactions	24905	1082

Federal IRC No.	Subject	Calif. Law No.	Handbook ¶ No.
991–999	Domestic International Sales Corporations	23051.5(b)(1)	1026
1001	Determination of amount of and recognition of gain or loss	24901–24902; 24955	361
1011	Adjusted basis for determining gain or loss	24911	361
1012	Basis of property—cost	24912	361
1013	Basis of property included in inventory	24913	362
1015	Basis of property acquired by gifts and transfers in trust	24914–15	362
1016	Adjustments to basis	24916–17	362
1017	Discharge of indebtedness	24918	362
1019	Property on which lessee has made improvements	24919	362
1031	Exchange of property held for productive use or investment	24941	362
1032	Exchange of stock for property	24942	362
1033	Involuntary conversions	24943–24949; 24949.1–24949.3	361; 1310
1034	Rollover of gain on sale of principal residence	N	362
1035	Certain exchanges of insurance policies	24950	362
1036	Stock for stock of same corporation	24951	362
1038	Certain reacquisitions of real property	24952	362
1040	Transfer of certain farm; etc., real property	N	361
1041	Transfers of property between spouses incident to divorce	N	361
1042	Sales of stock to employee stock ownership plans or certain cooperatives	24954	309; 361
1051	Property acquired during affiliation	24961	362
1052	Basis established by the Revenue Act of 1932 or 1934 or by the Internal Revenue Code of 1939	24962	362
1053	Property acquired before March 1, 1913	24963	362
1054	Certain stock of Federal National Mortgage Association	24965	362
1055	Redeemable ground rents	N	362
1056	Basis limitation for player contracts transferred in connection with the sale of a franchise	24989	362
1059	Corporate shareholder's basis in stock reduced by nontaxed portion of extraordinary dividends	24966	362
1059A	Limitation on taxpayer's basis or inventory cost; property imported from related persons	24966.1	362
1060	Special allocation rules for certain asset acquisitions	24966.2–24966.3	362
1071	Gain from sale or exchange to effectuate policies of F.C.C.	24971	1104

Federal IRC No.	Subject	Calif. Law No.	Handbook ¶ No.
1081	Nonrecognition of gain or loss on exchanges or distributions in obedience to orders of S.E.C.	24981	1104
1082	Basis for determining gain or loss	24988	362
1091	Loss from wash sales of stock or securities	24998	362
1092	Straddles	24998	366
1201	Alternative tax for corporations; capital gains and losses	24990.5	361
1211	Limitation on capital losses	24990	361
1212	Limitation on capital loss carrybacks and carryovers	24990.5(b)	361
1221–1245	Character of gain or loss; how determined	24990–24990.8	361
1271–1288	Original issue discount; stripped bonds	24990–94	361; 1082
1291–1297	Certain foreign investment companies	24995	361
1361–1379	S corporations	23800–10	1025
1381–83	Cooperatives	24404–24406.5	1087; 1012; 1154
1385	Amounts includable in patron's gross income	24273.5	952; 1012; 1013; 1154
1441	Withholding of tax on nonresident aliens	N	1278
1442	Withholding of tax on foreign corporations	N	1278
1445	Withholding of tax on dispositions of US real property interests	18662	1278
1501	Privilege to file consolidated returns	23362; 23364a	1003
1502	Regulations	23363; 25106.5	1003
1503	Computation and payment of tax	23364	1003
1504	Definitions	23361	1003; 1271
3402	Income tax collected at source	18667	5021–5023
4911	Lobbying expenditures	23740	953
6011	General requirements for returns	19524	1269
6012	Persons required to make returns	23771; 186801; 18606	960; 1269
6031	Partnership returns	23810	960; 1269
6033	Exempt organization returns	23772	960
6036	Notice of qualifications of executor or receiver	19089	1305
6037	S Corporation returns	18601	1269
6038	Information for foreign corporations	25111	1321
6038A	Information; certain foreign-owned corporations	19141.5; 25111	1321
6038B	Notice of certain transfers to foreign persons	19141.5	1321
6039C	Foreign persons; direct investments in U.S. property	N	1321
6041	Information at source	25111	960
6041A	Payments of remuneration for services and direct sales	18638	346

Federal IRC No.	Subject	Calif. Law No.	Handbook ¶ No.
6045	Brokers' returns	18642	346
6048	Returns of foreign trusts	23051.5(b)(6)	457
6050H	Mortgage interest received in trade or business	18645	346
6050I	Cash received in trade or business	18645	346
6050J	Foreclosure; abandonment of security	18645	346
6050L	Dispositions of donated property	18645	346
6050N	Payments of royalties	18645	346
6065	Verification of returns	18606; 18621	1269
6072	Time for filing returns	18601	1274
6081	Extension of time for filing	18604	1269; 1275
6091	Place for filing returns	18621	1274
6102	Computations on returns	18623	1055
6103	Confidentiality of returns	19543–49; 19551–19562	1323
6104	Publicity of information from exempt organizations and trusts	19565	960; 1323
6111	Tax shelter registrants	18547	346
6151	Time for paying tax on return	19001–19006	1293
6155–6167	Payment on notice and demand	N	1293
6159	Agreements to pay tax liability in installments	N	1293
6211	Definition of deficiency	19043; 23043	1303
6212	Notice of deficiency	19031–36; 19049–50	1303
6213	Petition to Tax Court	19041–44; 19046–48; 19051; 19332–34	1303; 6602
6301	Collection authority	19377–78	1325
6321	Lien for taxes	19221	1325
6331	Levy to collect tax	19231; 19262	1303
6335–38	Sale of seized property	N	1303
6342	Application of proceeds of levy	N	1303
6402	Authority to make refunds and credits	19301; 19314; 19354	1310
6404	Abatements	19104; 19431	1308
6501	Limitations on assessment and collection	19057–58; 19065–67; 19087	335; 1310
6502	Collection after assessment	19371	1310
6511	Limitations on credits and refunds	19306; 19308–09; 19311–13	1310
6521	Mitigation of effect of period of limitation	N	1310
6532	Limitation periods; suits	19384–85; 19388–89	1303
6601	Interest on underpayment, etc.	19101–03; 19105–19106 19108; 19111;	1309

Federal IRC No.	Subject	Calif. Law No.	Handbook ¶ No.
		19112–15	
6602	Suit to recover interest on erroneous refund	19411	1309
6611	Interest on overpayments	19340–41; 19349; 19351	1310
6621	Determination of rate of interest	19521(a)	1309
6651	Additions—failure to file return and pay tax	19131–32.5	1321; 3158
6652	Failure to file return	19133.5	1321
6653	Failure to pay tax	N	1321; 3158
6655	Failure to pay estimated tax	19004; 19010; 19023–27; 19142; 19144–45; 19147–51	1254; 1255
6657	Bad checks	19134	1321
6658	Coordination with Title II	19161	1255
6662	Accuracy-related penalty	19164	1321
6663	Fraud penalty	19164	1321
6664	Definitions; special rules	19164	1321
6665	Applicable rules	19164	1321
6694	Understatement by tax preparer	19166	1321
6700	Promoting abusive tax shelter	19177	1321
6701	Aiding understatement	19178	1321
6702	Frivolous returns	19179	1321
6706	Original issue discount information requirements	19181	1082
6721	Failure to file correct information return	19183	1321
6722	Failure to furnish correct payee statements	19183	1321
6861	Jeopardy assessments	19081;19086	1307
6863	Stay of collection—jeopardy assessments	19083–85	1307
6871	Claims in receivership proceedings	19088; 19090	1305; 1310
6872	Suspension of period of assessment	19089	1310
6873	Unpaid claims	19091	1310
6901	Transferred assets	19071–74	1307
7121	Closing agreements	19441	1308
7202	Willful failure to collect or pay tax	19708–09	1321
7203	Willful failure to file return	19701; 19705	1321
7206	Fraud and false statements	19706	1321
7213	Unauthorized disclosures	19542	1321
7405	Suit to recover erroneous refund	19411	1309
7408	Action to enjoin promoters of abusive tax shelters	19715	1321
7421	Prohibition of suits to enjoin collection	19381	333
7422	Action for refunds	19382; 19387	1311
7430	Awarding of costs and certain fees	N	338
7701	Definitions	23031–34; 23037–38; 23041; 23043.5;	354; 361; 362; 953; 1115; 1145

Federal IRC No.	Subject	Calif. Law No.	Handbook ¶ No.
		23045.1–6.; 23046–49	
7702	Life insurance contract defined	23045(a)	1088
7702A	Modified endowment contract defined	23045(b)	1088
7704	Publicly traded partnerships	23038.5	1039

¶ 995   **California-Federal Code Comparison Table**

Listed in the table below are the California Bank and Corporation Tax Law and Administrative Tax Law section numbers, the comparable federal Internal Revenue Code (IRC) section numbers and the paragraph number in this handbook where they are explained or to which they relate. "N" means none.

Calif. Law No.	Federal IRC No.	Handbook ¶ No.	Calif. Law No.	Federal IRC No.	Handbook ¶ No.
18602	N	1282	19025	6655(d)	1254
18604	6081	1269; 1275	19026	6655	1254
18605	N	1275	19027	6655	1255
18606	6012(b)	1269	19032	6212	1303
18606	6065	1269	19033	6212	1303
18621	6065	1269	19034	6212	1303
18621	6091	1269	19036	6212	1303
18621.5	N	1269	19041	6213	6602
18622	N	1277; 1281	19042	6213	6602
18623	6102	1055	19043	6211	1303
18634	N	1184–A	19044	6213	1303
18638	6041A	346	19045	N	1303
18642	6045	1269; 1274	19046	6213	6602
18645	6050I	341	19047	6213	6602
18649	1275	346; 960	19048	6213	6602
18662	1445	1278	19049	6212	6602
18667	3402	341	19050	6212	1303
18670	N	341	19051	6213	1303
18671	N	341	19053	N	1303
18674	N	341	19057	6501	1310
18675	6414	341	19058	6501(e)	1310
18676	N	341	19059	N	1310
19001	6151	1293	19060	N	1310
19002	6513	1278	19061	1033(a)(2)(D)	1310
19004	N	1293	19064	7609	1310
19004	6655	1254	19065	6501(c)	1310
19005	6151	1293	19066	6501(b)	1269
19010	6655	1254	19067	6501(c)	335; 1310
19011	N	1293	19071	6901	1307
19021	N	1007; 1211; 1212	19072	6901	1307
			19073	6901	1307
19022	N	1212; 1293	19074	6901	1307
19023	6655(g)	1254	19081	6861	1307
19024	6655(g)	1254			

Calif. Law No.	Federal IRC No.	Handbook ¶ No.	Calif. Law No.	Federal IRC No.	Handbook ¶ No.
19082	6862	1307	19231	6331	1325
19083	6863	1307	19232	N	1325
19084	6863	1304	19233	N	1325
19085	6863	1304	19234	N	1325
19086	6861	1304	19235	N	1325
19087	6501(c)	1310	19251–19254	N	1325
19087	6501(c)	1310	19262	6331	1325
19088	6871	1305	19263	N	1325
19089	6036	1305	19301	6402	1310
19089	6872	1310	19302	N	1310
19090	6871	1310	19306	6511(a)	1310
19091	6873	1310	19308–19309	6511(c)	1310
19101	6601(a)	1309	19311	6511	1310
19102	6601(b)	1309	19312	6511(d)	1310
19104	6404	1309	19314	6402	1310
19106	6601(e)	1309	19321–19324	N	1310; 1311
19108	6601	1309	19325	N	1310
19111	6601(e)	1309	19331	N	1310; 1311
19113	6601(f)	1308	19332–19334	6213	6602
19114	6601(g)	1309	19335	N	1310; 1311
19131	6651	1321	19340	6611(b)	1310
19131	6651	1321	19341	6611(c)	1310
19132	6651	1321	19342–19348	N	1310; 1311
19133	6652	1321	19349	6611	1310; 1311
19134	6657	1321	19350	N	1310; 1311
19135	N	1321	19351	6611(b)	1310
19141	N	1321	19363	6402	1310
19141.5	6038A; 6038B; 6038C	1321	19371	6502	1325
19141.6	N	1177B	19372–19373	N	1325
19142	6655(a)	1254	19374–19376	N	1325
19144	6655(b)	1254	19377–19378	6301	1325
19145	6655	1254	19381	7421	1311
19147	6655	1254	19382	7422	1311
19148	6655	1254	19384–19385	6532	1311
19149	6655	1254	19387	7422	1311
19150	6655	1255	19388–19389	6532	1311
19151	6655	1254	19390	N	1311
19161	6658	1255	19391	6612	1311
19164	6662	1321	19392	N	1311
19164	6663	1321	19411	6602	1311
19164	6664	1321	19411	7405	1311
19164	6665	1321	19412–19413	N	1311
19166	6694	1321	19431	6404	1308
19177	6700	1321	19441	7121	1308
19178	6701	1321	19442	N	1308
19179	6702	1321	19501	7621(a)	1325
19180	6703	1321	19503	7805	1325
19181	6706	1321	19504	7602	1325
19183	6721	341	19521(a)	6621	1309
19201	N	1325	19521(b)	6622	1309
19202	N	1325	19524	6011	1325
19221	6321	1325	19525	7623	1325
			19530	N	1325

Calif. Law No.	Federal IRC No.	Handbook ¶ No.	Calif. Law No.	Federal IRC No.	Handbook ¶ No.
19542	7213	1325	23151	11	1003; 1067; 1211
19543–19544	6103(b)	1325	23151.1	N	1003; 1004; 1015
19545	6103(h)	1325			
19546	6103(f)	1325	23151.2	N	1041
19547	6103(h)	1325	23153	N	1211
19549	6103(b)	1325	23154	N	1006
19551	6103(d)	1325	23155	N	1003; 1004; 1115
19552	7213	1325			
19562	6103	1325	23181	N	1003; 1006; 1067; 1212
19563	6108	1325			
19565	6104	1325	23182	N	1003
19701	7203	1321	23183	N	1003; 1006
19704	N	1321	23183.1	N	1003; 1006
19705	7203	1321	23183.2	N	1041
19706	7206	1321	23184	N	1006
19707–19708	7202	1321	23185	N	1006
19715	7408	1321	23186	N	1212
19717	N	338	23186.1	N	1212
19719	N	1321	23186.2	N	1212
19801–19802	N	1325	23186.5	N	1212
21001–21022	7811	1324	23201	N	1003; 1015
23036	26	1233	23202–23204	N	1003; 1015
23038	7701(a)(3)	421	23221–23224	N	1103
23038.5	7704	1039	23224.5	N	1003; 1016
23039	581	1006	23225–23226	N	1103
23040	N	1003; 1165; 1170	23251	368	1003; 1017; 1104
23043.5	7701(g)	354; 361	23253	381	1003; 1017
23044	N	1165	23281–23282	N	1003; 1042
23045	7702	362	23301	N	1003; 1042
23045.1	7701(a)(42)	361	23301.5	N	1042
23045.2	7701(a)(43)	361	23301.6	N	1042
23045.3	7701(a)(44)	361	23302	N	1042
23045.4	7701(a)(45)	361	23303	N	1042
23045.5	7701(a)(19)	408; 1004	23304.1	N	1042
23045.6	7701(a)(20)	1115	23304.5	N	1042
23046	7701(a)(46)	952; 953; 1145	23305	N	1042
23047	7701(e)	354	23305a–23305e	N	1042
23048	7701(i)	1003; 1004	23305.1	N	1042
23049	7701(h)	353	23305.2	N	1042
23049.1	64	1079	23305.5	N	1042
23049.2	65	1079	23331	N	1041
23051.5	7806	1079; 1082	23332	N	1211
23051.7	N	1233	23332.5	N	1041
23058	N	1057	23333	N	1041
23081	701	421	23334	N	1003; 1041
23091–23096	N	1040	23335	N	1041
23101	N	1003; 1170	23361	1504	1003; 1271
23101.5	N	1005	23362	1501	1003
23102	N	1003; 1030	23363	1502	1003
23113	443	351			

Calif. Law No.	Federal IRC No.	Handbook ¶ No.	Calif. Law No.	Federal IRC No.	Handbook ¶ No.
23364	1503	1003	23701x	501(c)(25)	952
23364a	1501	1003	23702	502	952
23400–59	55–59	1223–1224	23703	N	961
23501	N	1004	23704	501(e)	952
23503	N	1006	23704.4	501(e)	953
23504	N	1004	23704.5	501(h)	953
23561	N	1041	23704.6	504	953
23571	N	1042	23705	505	953
23572	N	1042	23706	501(c)(1)	953
23601.4	N	1235	23707	507	953
23601.5	48	1235	23708	508	955
23603	30	1240	23709	509	955
23605	161	1233	23710	513	955
23609	41	1237	23731	511	954
23610.4	N	1239	23732	512	954
23610.5	42	1239	23734	513	954
23612	N	1244	23735	514	954
23612.6	N	1244	23736	503(a)	954
23617	N	1246	23736.1	503(b)	953
23617.5	N	1246	23736.2	503(a)(1)	953
23621	51–52	1236	23736.3	503(a)(2)	953
23622	N	1244	23736.4	503(c)	953
23623	N	1236	23737	N	953
23623.5	N	1236	23740	4911	953
23624	N	1251	23741	N	953
23625	N	1236	23771	6012	954; 960
23666	N	1252A	23772	6033	960
23701	501(a)–(b)	951; 960	23774	N	954
23701a	501(c)(5);	952; 954	23775	N	1042
23701b	501(c)(8)	952; 954	23776	N	1042
23701c	501(c)(13)	952; 954	23777	N	961
23701d	501(c)(3); 501(j)	1149; 952;	23778	N	961
		953; 954;	23800–11	1361–1379	145; 266;
		955; 960;			1025
		963	24251	15	1057
23701e	501(c)(6)	952; 954	24271	61; 641–692;	
23701f	501(c)(4)	952; 954		701–761	1079
23701g	501(c)(7)	952; 954	24272	103; 141–150	1082
23701h	501(c)(2)	952; 954	24272.2	72	1097
23701i	501(c)(9)	952; 954	24272.3	865(b)	1184
23701j	501(c)(11)	952; 954	24273	77	1085
23701k	501(d)	952; 954	24273.5	1385	1012; 1087;
23701l	501(c)(10)	952; 954			1154
23701n	501(c)(17)	952; 953;	24275	88	1080
		954	24276	90	1080
23701p	401	952; 953	24301	101–136	1079
23701q	501(c)(20)	957; 953	24302	101	1115
23701r	527	951; 952;	24305	101(f)	1115
		960; 1273	24306	133	1098
23701s	501(c)(18)	952; 953	24307	108	1091
23701t	528	952; 960	24308	61	1095
23701v	501(c)	952	24309	109	1086
23701w	501(c)(19)	952	24310	111	1092

Calif. Law No.	Federal IRC No.	Handbook ¶ No.	Calif. Law No.	Federal IRC No.	Handbook ¶ No.
24314	61	1082	24365	174	1150
24315	61	1096	24368.1	167(e)	370
24320	883	1090	24369	175	1161
24321	881–882	1090	24370	591	1146
24322	597	1098	24371.5	188	390
24323	61	1099	24372.3	169	306
24324	118	1100	24372.5	194	305(d)
24325	118	1079	24373	178	370; 381; 382
24341	63	1067			
24343	162(a)	1145	24377	180	1161
24343.5	162(a)	1145	24379	83	1145
24344	163	1146	24382	216A	370; 1146; 1147
24344.5	163	1146			
24345	164; 275	1147	24383	190	1145
24346	164	1148	24384–24385	163	1146
24347	165; 166; 582	1157	24401	241	952; 1012–1013 1081; 1155 1156
24347.5	165	1157			
24348	585	403; 408			
24348.5	595	403; 408	24402	243–247; 561–565	1081
24349	167; 168	370, 391	24403	591	1146
24349.1	280F	396	24404	1381–1382	402; 952; 1012; 1087; 1154
24350	167(c)	382			
24351	167(d)				
24352	167(e)	382	24405	1381	1013; 1154
24352.5	167(f)	382	24406	1381	1013; 1154
24353	167(c)	381	24406.5	1381	1154
24354	167(d)	382	24407	248(a)	1155
24354.1	167(j)	382	24408	248(b)	1155
24355	167(f)	371	24409	248(c)	1155
24355.5	197	371	24410	243–247	1081; 1156
24356	179	385	24411	243–247	1081
24356.2–			24414	195	392
24356.5	179–179A	394	24415	161	1145
24356.8	179	395	24416	172	1145
24357	170(a)	1149	24416.1	172	1145
24357.1	170(e)	1149	24416.2	172	1145
24357.2	170(f)(3)	1149	24416.3	172	1145
24357.3	170(f)(4)	1149	24421	261	321
24357.4	170(f)(5)	1149	24422	263	402
24357.5	170(f)(1)	1149	24422.3	263A	411
24357.6	170(f)(6)	1149	24423	263	402
24357.7	170(h)	1149	24424	264	1145
24357.8	170(e)	1149	24425	265	291; 325
24357.10	170(l)	1149	24426	266	363
24358	170(b)	1149	24427	267	364; 1115
24359	170(c)	1149	24431	269	1303
24359.1	170(e)	1149	24434	271	325
24360	171(a)	1159	24436	280E	1145
24361	171(b)	1159	24436.1	280E	1145
24362	171(c)	1159	24436.5	161	370; 387; 391; 1146; 1147
24363	171(d)	1159			
24363.5	171(e)	1159			
24364	173	1151			

Calif. Law No.	Federal IRC No.	Handbook ¶ No.	Calif. Law No.	Federal IRC No.	Handbook ¶ No.
24437	277	954	24685	463	354
24438	279	1146	24688	467	354
24439	249	1146	24689	468	354
24440(a)–(b)	280C(b)–(c)	1146	24690	468A	354
24441	161	1147	24691	465	354
24442	280B	388	24692	469	354
24442.5	280H	353	24693	468B	354
24443	274	292	24701(a)–(b)	471; 472	411
24447	161	1145	24708	474	411
24448	161	1146; 1147	24721	481	352
24449	291	1223–224	24725	482	354
24451	301–385	104; 331; 361; 362; 1017; 1102-1104; 1115-1153	24726	483	364; 365
			24831–33	611–638	401; 402
			24870–74	851–860F	1038
			24901	1001	361
			24902	1001	361
24452	301	1115; 1116	24905	988	361; 1082
24453	302	1117; 1118	24911	1011	361
24461	337	1125–1183	24912	1012	361
24471	381	1017	24913	1013	362
24481	383	1017	24914	1015	362
24601	401–424; 421; 404A; 406; 407; 419; 419A	1145	24915	1015	362
			24916	1016	362
			24916.2	1016	362
24611	404	1145	24917	1016	362
24612	413	1145	24918	1017	362
24631	441	351	24919	1019	362
24632	441	351	24941	1031	362
24633	442	1054	24942	1032	362
24633.5	441	351	24943	1033(a)(1)	361
24634	443	351	24944	1033(a)(2)(A); (a)(2)(B)	361
24636	443	351			
24637	444	351	24945	1033(a)(2)(C)	361; 1310
24651	446	352	24946	1033(a)(2)(D)	361
24652	447	352	24947	1033(b)	361
24654	448	352	24948	1033(c)	361
24661	451	353	24949	1033(d)	361
24667	453; 453A; 453B;	364; 407	24949.1	1033(e)	361
			24949.2	1033(g)	361
24668.1	453	364	24949.3	1033(f)	361
24672	N	1127	24950	1035	362
24673	460	353	24951	1036	362
24673.2	460	353	24952	1038	362
24674	454	353	24954	1042	361
24675	N	353	24955	1001	301
24676	455	353	24961	1051	362
24676.5	458	353	24962	1052	362
24677	N	353	24963	1053	362
24678	N	353	24964	1011	362
24679	N	353	24965	1054	362
24681	461	354	24966	1059A	362
24682	464	354	24966.1	1059A	362
			24966.2	1060	362

Calif. Law No.	Federal IRC No.	Handbook ¶ No.	Calif. Law No.	Federal IRC No.	Handbook ¶ No.
24966.3	1060	371	25122	N	436; 182
24971	1071	1104	25123	N	436; 1178; 1184; 182
24981	1081	1104			
24988	1082	362	25124	N	436; 1178; 1184; 182
24989	1056	362			
24990–24995	1201–1297	353; 361; 371; 1093	25125	N	436; 1178; 1184; 182
24990.8	1245	371	25126	N	436; 1178; 1184; 182
24990.9	1253	371			
24995	1291–1297	361; 1093	25127	N	436; 1178; 1184; 182
24998	1091; 1092	362			
25101	N	1165; 1169	25128	N	436; 1180; 182
25101.1	N	1165; 1169			
25101.15	N	1169	25129	N	436; 1182; 182
25101.3	N	1187			
25102	N	1165; 1169; 1271	25130	N	436; 1182; 182
25103	N	1165	25131	N	436; 1182; 182
25104	N	1166; 1169			
25105	N	1166	25132	N	436; 1183; 182
25106	N	1179; 1186			
25106.5	1502	1162; 1184–A	25133	N	436; 1183; 182
25107	N	1165	25134	N	436; 182
25108	N	1165; 1169; 1170	25135	N	436; 1184; 182
25110	861–865; 951–964	1162; 1184–A	25136	N	436; 1184; 182
25111.1	N	1184–A	25137	N	436; 1184; 1187; 182
25114–15	N	1162; 1184–A	25138	N	436; 182
25120	N	436; 1162; 1165; 1178; 182	25139	N	436; 1162; 182
			25140	N	1178
25121	N	436; 182	25141	N	1187

¶ 1001 General

This chapter explains the taxes imposed on corporate income by the Bank and Corporation Tax Law. This law levies both the Bank and Corporation Franchise Tax and the Corporation Income Tax. The franchise tax is basically imposed on all corporations and financial corporations doing business in the state and on banks located in the state. The Corporation Income Tax principally affects: (1) foreign corporations engaged in carrying on business exclusively in interstate or foreign commerce between California and other states or foreign countries; (2) holding companies incorporated or having their principal place of business in California; and (3) inactive business corporations that derive income from California sources.[1]

---

(1) Franchise Tax Board, August 12, 1937.

WARNING - FEDERAL CONFORMITY, IF ANY, REMAINS AS OF JANUARY 1, 1993

Generally California has not confirmed its Bank and Corporation Tax Law (commencing with Rev & TC § 23001) with the Internal Revenue Code. Thus there are numerous difference in the determination of taxable income between that reported for federal and California purposes. These differences primarily arise in the areas of deductions.

California has however, conformed limited provisions of the Bank and Corporation law to the IRC by adopting, by reference, selected IRC provisions as of January 1 of each year. Although few in number, the conformed provisions were usually updated to January 1 of each year so that where appropriate California law mirrored the federal code.

As in the past, the Legislature passed legislation for 1994 to conform to selected provisions of the IRC as of 1-1-94, only to have that legislation (AB 2370) vetoed by the Governor. Accordingly when California law makes reference to specific provisions of the Internal Revenue Code, it is to those provisions as reflected in the IRC at 1-1-93, unless specific provisions of the Internal Revenue Code were adopted through the passage of other tax legislation. Provisions conforming at 1-1-94 are limited in number.

Care should therefore be exercised in treating California law as conforming to federal law. Some provisions will conform at 1-1-94 because individual tax bills may have resulted in limited conformity. In general however, those provisions enacted for federal purposes through the *Revenue Reconciliation Act of 1993,* and other federal tax legislation for 1993 as well, have not been adopted for California purposes.

¶ 1002   **History of Tax**

The bank and corporation tax became effective March 1, 1929. It was supplemented by the corporation income tax in 1937. Both these taxes were codified into the Bank and Corporation Tax Law with numerous changes, effective July 1, 1951. (L 1949, c. 557).

¶ 1003   **Franchise Tax on Corporations**

The Bank and Corporation Tax Law, under Chapter 2, imposes a franchise tax on all corporations incorporated in California or qualified by the office of the Secretary of State to do business in California.[2] California also collects an income tax from corporations deriving income from sources in-state.

Franchise tax is assessed against all corporations doing business in the state whether or not they are qualified. The law defines "doing business" as "actively engaging in any transaction for the purpose of financial or pecuniary gain or profit". A corporation organized in another state or a foreign country must engage in intrastate business to be subject to the franchise tax.

---

(2) § 23101-23405.

The regulations cite as examples foreign corporations which make complete sales by making deliveries from stocks of goods located in California by reason of orders taken by employees in California. These corporations are engaged in doing business in California and subject to the franchise tax, in spite of the fact that they might have no office or regular place of business in the state.[3]

Privilege year and base year. The concept of the franchise tax law is that the tax is a payment for a franchise for the privilege of doing business in California, measured by the income of the corporation from California sources in the prior year.

EXAMPLE
Income earned in calendar year 1993 is used to measure the tax payable for the privilege of doing business in California in 1994. When the corporation is incorporated or when it qualifies or begins doing business in the state, the tax for its first income year is the minimum tax $800. The income for the first year serves as the measure of the tax for the second taxable year. In a similar manner, the income of each succeeding year serves as the measure of the tax for the next following year.

OBSERVATION
In addition to the franchise tax, the California law imposes an income tax on all general corporations which derive income from sources within California even if they are not "doing business" in the state. Income derived from or attributable to sources within this state includes income from tangible or intangible property located or having a situs in this state and income from any activities carried on in this state, regardless of whether carried on in intrastate, interstate or foreign commerce.[4]

Note: In most cases, a corporation would not be subject to both the franchise tax and the income tax provisions. However, a corporation may be qualified to do business in California and, so, subject to the minimum franchise tax and also subject to the income tax because it would be deriving income from California sources; but it would not be doing business (intrastate) in California. In that circumstance, the minimum franchise tax would be allowed as an offset against the income tax paid on its income.

¶ 1004 Corporation Income Tax

In addition to providing for an income tax on those out-of-state corporations which are deriving income from sources within California, but which are not doing intrastate business, Chapter 3[5] of the Bank and Corporation Tax Law provides for an income tax for other "corporations" which are not doing business in California. The term "corporations" is not limited to incorporated bodies; it also includes associations, Massachusetts trusts and business trusts.

For this purpose, the term "association" includes any organization created for the transaction of designated affairs or the attainment of some object which, like a corporation, continues notwithstanding that its members or participants change, and the affairs of which, like corporate affairs,

---

(3) Reg 23040(b); 23101.
(4) § 23040.

(5) § 23501–23572.

are conducted by a single individual, a committee, a board, or some other group acting in a representative capacity.

An organization may be formed by an agreement, a declaration of trust, a statute or otherwise. Other labels used are a voluntary association, a joint stock association or company, a business trust, a Massachusetts trust, a common law trust, an investment trust, or a partnership or association.[6]

Differences between corporation income and franchise taxes. There are few differences between the taxability of a corporation subject to the franchise tax and one which is taxable under the corporation income tax (Chapter 3) provisions. The return used in either case is Form 100 and the tax rate is the same for both.

The franchise tax is on a prepaid basis; i.e., the income of one year is used to measure the tax for the privilege of doing business in the following year. Therefore, the income year precedes the taxable year of the corporation by one year. For income tax purposes, the income year and the taxable year coincide.

If a corporation doing business in California and subject to the franchise tax provisions ceases to operate in California, but does not dissolve or withdraw from the state and continues to derive income from California sources, it becomes subject to the income tax.

For the year in which this happens, Rev & TC § 23504 provides that the tax for the year in which the change occurred will be assessed under Chapter 2 (franchise tax). Rev & TC § 23151.1 which was added to the law because of the change in treatment of commencing corporations effective in 1972, says that a corporation ceasing to do business in California will pay a tax for that year measured by its income for the preceding year plus the income earned during the current year. The substance of both sections is that the corporation files a Form 100 for the entire year and reports the income earned for the entire year.

¶ 1005   Foreign Corporations

Generally speaking, whether an out-of-state corporation is subject to the franchise tax because it is doing intrastate business or, on the other hand, subject to the corporation income tax because it is doing business strictly in interstate commerce, will be determined by the following facts:

If the corporation has both employees working in the state and has an inventory or other real or tangible personal property located in the state, the corporation is doing business within the state of California. If it has employees, but not property, or property used in a business activity but no employees, the corporation is deriving income from California sources and would be subject to the corporation income tax.[7]

---

(6) Reg 23038(a); 23038(b).

(7) Reg 23040(b); 23101.

If a corporation is created in California, but remains inactive, or is a foreign corporation which qualifies to do business in California, and remains inactive, the corporation is subject to the minimum tax of $800 each year.[8]

For the year in which a corporation commences to do business in California it is also subject to the minimum tax for that year. For that year also, it should be filing estimated tax payments, based on its income for that year. The income for the year in which the corporation commences to do business, regardless of whether it is less than the 12-month period, is used as the measure of the tax for the following year. From then on the income of each year is used to measure the tax for the subsequent year as indicated previously.[9]

When corporation not "doing business" and not taxable. If a foreign corporation has limited activity in California it may not be subject to tax. It may not be doing business in California subject to the corporation franchise tax, nor deriving income from sources within the state subject to the corporation income tax. The determination would be made by the Franchise Tax Board after the submission of the required information by the corporation. A corporation may petition the Board to make the determination; it would remain in force for 5 years as long as the criteria below are met or indefinitely for corporations meeting them on or before 1–1–78 and continuing to do so. The three types of activities excluded under these provisions would be as follows:

(1) The purchase of personal property or services solely for the use of the corporation or its affiliates outside of the state would be subject to this exclusion, if the corporation does not have more than 100 employees in California at any one time, exclusive of employees temporarily present in California and employees in this state for educational purposes. The activities of the employees who are in the state must be limited to solicitation, negotiation, liaison, monitoring, auditing and inspecting of the property or services acquired, or providing technical advice with respect to the company's requirements. If the out-of-state corporation applying for the exclusion is engaged in a unitary business, the limitation of 100 employees applies to all corporations who are members of the unitary group.

(2) The maximum number of employees in California at any one time is increased to 200 if the personal property or services purchased by the corporation or its affiliate are used for the construction or modification of a physical plant or facility located outside California.[10] The presence of employees in this state only for the purpose of attending a public or private school, college or university or other educational training program, including those at industrial facilities, would also be within the exclusion. The number of employees in California for educational purposes are not counted for the above limits of 100 or 200 employees.

CAUTION

New for 1993. There is also a filing requirement placed on corporations who are doing business in California with those who have obtained a ruling under Rev & TC § 23101.5. Each taxpayer that sells property or services to the corporation with more than 100 employees in California

---

(8) § 23153; Reg 23151.   (10) § 23101.5.
(9) § 23221; 25563.

must annually file a statement with the Franchise Tax Board identifying the number of its employees within this state directly attributable to the construction or modification of a physical plant or facility located outside California.[11]

Initial application for exclusion under these provisions should be submitted to the Franchise Tax Board as soon as the corporation contemplates having employees within this state. The information to be reported under (1) and (2) above is set forth in Regulation 23101.5.[12]

In addition to the usual information with respect to the corporation's name and address, date of application, filing period, and so on, it is necessary that the corporation furnish the names and addresses of the businesses or individuals from whom the corporation expects to purchase personal property or services, and the names and addresses of the employees of the corporation who will be present within the state.

A further provision of the regulation is that the corporations must annually confirm within two months and fifteen days after the close of their fiscal year, that the facts relevant to the granting of that exclusion remain unchanged, or must state and explain the changes which have occurred.

Corporations shipping goods in-state. Foreign corporations which ship goods to customers in California from points outside of the state, in accordance with orders taken by employees in California, and which do not maintain stocks of goods nor engage in other activities here, are engaged in conducting business between California and the other states or countries exclusively in interstate or foreign commerce and are, therefore, not subject to the franchise tax. A portion of the income of such corporations, however, is attributable to activities in this state and is subject to the income tax, regardless of where the orders are approved or the billing is handled. Therefore, these corporations are required to file returns under the income tax provisions of the law.

IMPORTANT   It should be noted, however, that if the only activity of a corporation in California is solicitation by employees of orders for goods to be shipped to customers in California from points outside of the state, the corporation may not be subject to California income or franchise tax because of Federal Public Law 86–272, which is explained below.

In the same way, foreign corporations which send goods to California dealers or brokers on consignment or maintain stocks of goods here from which deliveries are made to fill orders taken by independent salesmen or brokers are subject to income tax since a portion of their income is attributable to investments represented by the property located in California.

(11) § 23101.5.

(12) 23101.5; Reg 23101.5.

Federal protection—Public Law 86–272. This federal law prohibits any state from imposing an income tax on income derived within the state from interstate commerce if the only business activity within the state consists of the solicitation of orders of tangible property by or on behalf of the corporation by its employees or representatives. If these orders are sent outside the state for approval or rejection, and when approved filled by shipment or delivery from a point outside the state of California, they would be subject to the provisions of Public Law 86–272. In addition, if the corporation, rather than having its sales solicited by employees, has the sales of tangible personal property solicited for it by an independent contractor (even though he maintains an office in this state), the sales do not cause the corporation to be subject to the state's tax jurisdiction.

An independent contractor is defined as a commission broker or other independent contractor who is engaged in selling or soliciting orders for the sale of tangible personal property for more than one principal and who holds himself out as such in the regular course of his business activities.

U.S. Supreme Court's interpretation of protected activity. A state's right to tax the net income of businesses who solicit sales within their state was limited by Congress when it passed Public Law 86–272 which set a minimum threshold of activity which would be protected. The protected activity has now been defined to include activities that are "entirely ancillary to requests for purchases - those that serve no independent business function apart from their connection to the soliciting of orders." A standard has also been established for *de minimis* activities which do not eliminate protection under P.L. 86–272 and these are defined as "nontrivial additional connections"(*Wisconsin Dept. of Revenue v William J. Wrigley, Jr., Co.,* (1992) 112 S Ct 2447; 120 LE2d 174). The Court then listed protected and non protected activities as:

(1) Automobile provided to salesmen
(2) Stock of free samples provided to salesmen
(3) Recruitment, training and evaluation of salesmen (but not in an owned or leased facility)
(4) Sales-related meetings in hotel and personal residences
(5) Advertising (print, radio and television) where directed from outside the state)
(6) The occasional use by salesmen of their homes for meetings and the use of a portion of one's home as one's office did not constitute the maintenance of an office by the taxpayer.

Nonprotected activities as defined by the *Wrigley* Court include:

(1) Maintenance of an office even if used exclusively for solicitation of sales (solicitation of sales is a protected activity under P.L. 86–272)
(2) Repair or servicing of company's products
(3) Replacement of products by salesmen
(4) Advance deliveries of product by salesmen for consideration
(5) Storage of product either with salesman or at a storage facility to facilitate (3) and (4) above
(6) Maintenance of a warehouse or inventory (other than free samples)

Note: Prior to the *Wrigley* decision California had taken the position that the following activities are not protected by the federal law and so would expose a corporation to taxation: maintenance of office or place of business, warehouse, inventory, repair shop, parts department, purchasing office, employment office, partnership or rental of real or tangible personal property. FTB Form 1050 also lists as activities that would lose immunity collection of delinquent accounts, credit investigation, installation and supervision of installation, conducting training courses or lectures, providing engineering functions, handling customer complaints, approving orders, repossession of company products, securing of deposits on sales, picking up or replacement of damaged or returned merchandise, hiring, training and supervising of personnel, providing shipping information and coordinating deliveries, maintaining sample or display room for more than two weeks of year, carrying samples for sale, exchange, or distribution in any manner for consideration or other value, owning, leasing or maintaining a meeting place for directors and officers or employees, telephone answering service, mobile stores, consigning tangible personal property, and conducting any activity in addition to immune activities that is not an integral part of order solicitation.

Other taxable activities. Other activities resulting in the loss of immunity from tax, depending on the circumstances, would include approval of credit, collection of accounts, repairing merchandise, handling complaints, supervision of personnel, installation of products, conducting training courses or lectures, etc. Form FTB 1050 lists the following permissible activities considered incidental to solicitation: advertising campaigns incidental to missionary activities, carrying samples for display, owning and furnishing autos for salesmen, passing on to home office inquiries and complaints, incidental and minor advertising, missionary sales activities, checking customer inventories, maintaining sample or display room for two weeks or less during year, and soliciting of sales by in-the-state resident employee of the taxpayer, if that employee maintains no in-the-state sales office or place of business, in-home or otherwise.[13]

¶ 1006   Banks and Financial Corporations

Banks located within the state are liable for franchise tax on net income.[14] Financial corporations doing business within the state are also liable for franchise tax.[15] Banks doing business in California and other corporations which are considered to be in substantial competition with national banks are subject to a higher franchise tax rate than other taxpayers under the California Bank and Corporation Tax Law.

In addition, financial corporations (not including banks) have received a tax credit called the financial offset against the franchise tax for other taxes they paid, such as personal property taxes.

Special tax rate. The reason for the special tax rate for banks and financial corporations stems from restrictions imposed by the federal government on the right of the states to tax national banks. National banks receive their charters from the federal government and perform certain

---

(13) Form FTB 1050, Rev 12–88.   (15) § 23183.1.
(14) § 23181.

functions for the government. Therefore, the Federal Congress, under the United States Government Code, has established methods of taxation which the states may use to assess the national banks.

California adopts method number (4) authorized by the Congress amending § 5219 of the Revised Statutes of the United States, Title 12, § 548, United States Code. Method number (4) allows a state to levy a tax according to or measured by the net income of the banks including income from tax-exempt federal securities.[16]

The provisions of the United States Code also state that the method chosen for taxing the banks has to be in lieu of all other taxes and licenses (state, county and municipal), except taxes on real property.

Another reason is that the tax against national banks cannot be discriminatory. Therefore, California taxes all state banks and all other financial organizations which are in "substantial competition" with national banks at the same rate. If the banks and financial corporations were to be assessed at the same tax rate as other corporations, there would be substantial discrimination in favor of the financial institutions in viewing their total tax picture because they do not pay the local taxes as other corporations do.

In order to correct this situation, California law provides that the banks and financial corporations are subject to a higher rate than general taxpayers, called the "Bank or Financial Rate." This surtax element is determined by computing the percentage of personal property taxes and business license taxes paid by general corporations to their net income and adjusting the basic general franchise tax rate to account for this additional tax to be assessed against banks and financial corporations.

The banks challenged the validity of the position taken by California in taxing them at a higher rate. The California Supreme Court ruled that the bank rate is not a violation of the federal restrictions on the taxation of national banks *(Security First National Bank v. the Franchise Tax Board, (1961) 55 Cal 2d 407)*.

In lieu tax—offset. The tax imposed on banks is in lieu of all other taxes and licenses, except taxes on their real property. However, financial corporations in substantial competition with national banks did not have the same immunity for income years starting before 1-1-81. Therefore, since they were subject to local taxes and licenses, they were allowed to offset such local taxes against their franchise tax.

On the other hand, for income years ending in 1980 and later, banks and financial corporations were no longer shielded by the "in lieu" provision from paying California sales and use tax and local utility users tax.[17]

Financial corporation defined. A landmark case in determining whether a corporation is a financial corporation or not is *Crown Financial Corpora-*

---

(16) § 23181.   (17) § 23182; 23184.5.

tion v. McColgan, (1943) 23 Cal 2d 280. It defined a financial corporation as one which deals in monied capital as distinguished from other commodities and is in substantial competition with national banks. Generally, monied capital is money employed in such a way as to bring it into substantial competition with the business of national banks. Such competition exists when loans are made of the same type as those made by national banks in the same general business area. This would be true even though the financial organization's requirements as to collateral, credit, etc., are not the same as the bank's. In other words, it doesn't necessarily follow that the bank and the financial corporation are soliciting the same customers. Also, a financial corporation is said to be in competition with a bank if one of its activities is in competition. It does not necessarily have to engage in all the functions of a national bank.

¶ 1007   State Chartered Credit Unions

A credit union, even though its membership is limited to members of an organization or a business, is in substantial competition with national banks and is classified as a financial corporation for tax purposes. This is true even though credit unions are allowed a deduction for all the income resulting from or arising out of business activities with their members. Income from outside investments in bonds, saving deposits, etc., is not considered to be income for or with members and is not deductible. Therefore, this type of income for a state chartered credit union would be taxable, offset by any direct expenses applicable to the income. In addition, indirect expenses apportioned to this investment income can be 1% of the gross taxable income, but not less than $100. For income years starting after 12–31–89, credit unions are not subject to minimum tax.

¶ 1008   Federal Chartered Credit Unions

Federal chartered credit unions are not taxable under the Bank and Corporation Tax Law, according to provisions of the United States Code.

¶ 1009   Small Business Investment Companies

The Franchise Tax Board takes the position that small business investment companies operating under the Small Business Investment Act of 1958 are not subject to tax as financial corporations. This is based on the conclusion that although they do deal in money as distinguished from other commodities, they are not in substantial competition with national banks.

¶ 1010   Federal Savings and Loan Associations

They are subject to tax, the same as state chartered savings and loan associations, at the financial rate.

¶ 1011   Credit Card Companies

The Diners Club was determined to be primarily engaged in the operation of an all-purpose credit card plan for its membership. It was said to be engaged on a large scale form of financing which brought it into substantial competition with national banks. It was, therefore, considered to be a financial corporation *(Appeal of Diners Club, Inc. SBE 9–1–67)*.

¶ 1012 **Farmers' Cooperatives**

Included in the group are cooperatives formed for purposes of marketing agricultural products or purchasing seed, fertilizers, packing supplies, etc., and also cooperatives that perform services such as dehydrating, providing farm labor camps, etc. Cooperatives are entitled to deduct all income from business done with members.[18] Advances to members by cooperatives, against crops to be delivered in future periods, are constructively received as income by such members. Co-ops can deduct advances when crops are delivered.[19] For deductions, see ¶ 1154.

¶ 1013 **Other Cooperatives**

Rev & TC § 24405[20] allows a deduction to other cooperatives dealing in intangibles such as credit unions, federal production credit associations, and so on, cooperative water companies, certified grocers and cooperative retail supermarkets selling agricultural products, for income resulting from or arising out of business activities for or with their members, including reciprocal transactions with member credit unions, in arriving at net income subject to tax.

Income derived from nonmembers on a profit basis is taxable. Income such as interest on government obligations, interest from savings and loan associations, rental income from nonmembers, etc. would be included in the measure of the tax. For deductions, see ¶ 1154.

Rev & TC § 24406 allows a special deduction for cooperative corporations dealing in tangible personal property except water, agricultural products, and food sold at wholesale.[21] For deductions, see ¶ 1154.

¶ 1014 **Corporations Commencing to Do Business**

A California corporation is considered to be doing business when it first engages in an activity other than incorporating. This takes place usually after the first meeting of the Board of Directors; because the corporate powers are vested in the Board of Directors under the Corporation Code, it is unusual for a corporation to be doing business at an earlier date. If pre-incorporation activities are ratified at the first board meeting, however, and the activities would normally constitute doing business, the corporation will be considered to have commenced doing business from the date of incorporation, but not prior to that date. If a corporation starts to do business in California and the period is less than one-half month before the end of its calendar or fiscal year, the corporation is subject to tax if it begins to do business or has any income from California sources during that short period.

---

(18) § 24404.
(19) LR 297, 4–23–65.

(20) § 24405.
(21) § 24406.

If, on the other hand, it can file affidavits (if requested) to the effect that it conducted no business in California and had no California income during the short period, it would not be required to file a return or pay a minimum tax.[22] Legal Ruling 310 indicates that the above is true if the articles of incorporation are filed with or the qualification by the Secretary of State takes place on the following dates:

(1) 28-Day month—15th of the month or later;
(2) 29-Day month—15th of the month or later;
(3) 30-Day month—16th of the month or later;
(4) 31-Day month—17th of the month or later.

TAX TIP

Rev & TC § 23221 provides that a minimum tax of $800 will be paid to the Secretary of State at the time articles of incorporation are filed, or a foreign corporation registers with the Secretary of State and qualifies to do business in California. Care should be exercised to assure that the payment of estimated tax for the following privilege year is not missed. Assuming a calendar year taxpayer, the estimated tax, which is in addition to the tax paid at time of incorporation or qualification is as follows:

Income Year Begins	# Of Installments	Installments Due On 15th Day Of	Percentage Of Taxes Due With Each Installment
1/1 to 1/16	4	Apr., June, Sept., Dec.	25%
1/17 to 3/16	3	June, Sept., Dec.	33%
3/17 to 6/15	2	Sept., Dec.	50%
6/16 to 9/15	1	Dec.	100%
9/16 to 12/31	None		

Penalties are assessed for failure to make timely estimates even in the initial year in which the corporation does business.

¶ 1015 Corporations Discontinuing Business

Because the corporation franchise tax is a prepaid tax—that is, the tax for the privilege of doing business in a given year is measured by the income of the preceding year—special provisions are necessary when a corporation ceases to do business during a given year.

The tax for the last year in which the corporation does business in California is measured by the income of the entire prior year, plus the income for the year of discontinuation from the beginning of the year up until the date it ceases to operate. Each year, however, stands on its own; i.e., the

---

(22) Reg 23222.

tax for each year is reported in a separate return and computed separately (the loss for one year cannot offset the income of the other year). If the corporation remains in existence as a California corporation, or if a foreign corporation continues to be qualified in California and does not withdraw, it is subject to the minimum franchise tax for all subsequent years until dissolution or withdrawal.[23] Starting 1–1–92, if all of the following conditions are satisfied, a minimum franchise tax will not be imposed with respect to the taxable year in which a tax clearance certificate is issued by the Franchise Tax Board. These conditions are: (1) the taxpayer does not do business in California at any time during the taxable year; (2) the taxpayer files a certificate of dissolution with the Secretary of State prior to the beginning of that taxable year, in accordance with Corporations Code § 1905. Before 1–1–92, if all of the following conditions existed, the minimum tax would not be imposed for the taxable year of cessation, dissolution or withdrawal if: (1) the taxpayer did not do business in the state at any time during the taxable year; (2) the taxpayer, pursuant to Rev & TC § 23334, filed a request for tax clearance at least 30 days before the beginning of the taxable year; (3) the taxpayer, pursuant to Rev & TC § 23334, satisfied all requirements pertaining to the issuance of the tax clearance certificate at least 30 days before the beginning of that taxable year; and (4) the taxpayer filed a certificate of dissolution or withdrawal with the Secretary of State, under Rev & TC § 23331, by the expiration date of the certificate of tax clearance issued by the Franchise Tax Board.[24]

Starting 1–1–92, filing a certificate of dissolution as provided in Corporations Code § 1905(c) is required before the Franchise Tax Board will issue its clearance certificate under Rev & TC § 23334. The expiration date of the tax clearance will be deemed renewed by the Franchise Tax Board, if the taxpayer submits either of the following documents to the Franchise Tax Board showing receipt of documents by the Secretary of State no later than the expiration date of the certificate of tax clearance: (1) a copy of the acknowledgement of receipt of documents issued by the Secretary of State under Rev & TC § 23331(c); or (2) a copy of the receipt of certified mailing from the U.S. Postal Service and a completed declaration of mailing, on a form and in a manner set by the Board, executed under penalty or perjury. These rules do not apply to corporations which are subject only to the corporation income tax since there is no prepayment for the right to do business in the following year.

¶ 1016   **Change of Tax Status**

If a corporation which has been subject to the provisions of Chapter 3 (income tax) of the law commences to do business in California so that it will have to pay a franchise tax on a prepaid basis rather than an income tax, it will pay an income tax under Chapter 3 for the entire year in which the change occurs. The following year the corporation will be subject to the

---

(23) § 23151.1; 23181; 23183.   (24) § 23332; 23334.

minimum tax. The return filed to report the income earned in the year following the year of changeover will determine the franchise tax for the following year.[25]

EXAMPLE   Corporation B derives income from California in 1988 and files a return on March 15, 1989 to report the income tax. On July 1, 1989, Corporation B sends employees into California and opens an office in the state to the extent it is doing business in California and subject to the franchise tax provisions. For calendar year 1989 it files its return by March 15, 1990 and pays the balance of the tax (over the estimates paid) on all of the 1989 income. For calendar year 1990 it pays only the minimum tax of $800. On March 15, 1991 the franchise tax return filed will report the income earned in 1990 and the tax on that income will be for the taxable year 1991.

¶ 1017   Corporate Reorganizations

Federal-state comparison. California has adopted IRC § 368 and therefore has identical definitions of corporate reorganizations.[26] These provisions are used to determine which transfers of property between corporations result in tax-free exchanges which would affect not only the corporations involved, but in some cases, their shareholders as well.

California follows the IRC § 368 definition of reorganization in handling commencing and dissolving corporations' reporting of income.[27] California has adopted the IRC § 381–384 carryover rules, subject to the following modifications: (1) IRC § 381(c), relating to items of the distributor or transferor corporation, is modified to provide that instead of paragraph (24), relating to credit under IRC § 38, and paragraph (25), relating to the credit under IRC § 53, the acquiring corporation must take into account, to the extent proper to carry out IRC § 381(c) purposes, the items required to be taken into account for purposes of each credit allowable under the Bank and Corporation Tax Law with respect to the distributor or transferor corporation; (2) IRC § 383, relating to special limitations on certain excess credits is modified to apply to the credits allowed under Bank and Corporation Tax Law, Ch 3.5, and the minimum tax credit allowable under Rev & TC § 23453.[28] If a short period year is required by use of IRC § 381(b), transferor's short tax year is computed using Rev & TC § 23151.1 for general corporations, and Rev & TC § 23181 for banks and financial corporations.[29]

Treatment of certain interests in corporations as stock or indebtedness. California conforms its law to the 1989 Revenue Reconciliation Act version of IRC § 385 that gives the Treasury authority to prescribe regulations necessary to determine whether an interest in a corporation is to be treated as stock or indebtedness, or as part stock or part indebtedness.[30]

---

(25) § 23224.5.
(26) § 23051.5.
(27) § 23251.

(28) § 24471; 24481.
(29) § 23151.1; 23181; 23253.
(30) IRC § 385; § 24580.

SPECIAL ENTITIES

¶ 1025   **S corporations**

The tax treatment of S corporations and their shareholders will be determined in accordance with Internal Revenue Code, Subtitle A, Chapter 1, Subchapter S, except that S corporations pay 2.5% tax, and do not pay the alternative minimum tax.[1] For income years ending on or after January 1, 1994, the tax rate is 1.5%.[2] (See Table of Ratios at ¶ 16 & 17.)

Application of IRC § 1374 (built-in gains) and § 1375 (passive investment income) for income years starting in 1988 and 1989. A corporation electing S corporation treatment was deemed to have made the election on the same date as that of its federal election under IRC § 1362(a).[3]

Election. An election under IRC § 1362(a), that is first effective for income years starting on or after 1-1-90, is an election to which Rev & TC § 23051.5(g), relating to elections, applies. It will be deemed to have been made on the same date as the federal election, unless the corporation files a California election to be treated as a "C" corporation. However, Franchise Tax Board Form 3560, S Corporation Election or Termination/Revocation must be filed with the Franchise Tax Board on or before the due date for the federal S Corporation Election. Form FTB 3560 is filed to:

(1) Report a federal S corporation election,

(2) Elect California C corporation status by a federal S corporation,

(3) Elect California S corporation status, by federal S corporation that had previously elected California C corporation status,

(4) Report a federal termination of S corporation status by a California S Corporation, and

(5) Elect termination of California S corporation status by revocation, without terminating the federal S corporation election.

To elect a C corporation treatment for California only, Form 3560 must be filed before the 16th day of the third month of the income year if the revocation is effective for the first day of that income year, at any time during its first year if the year is for only two months or less, or within two and one-half months after qualifying to do business in California. As with the federal election, a California S corporation election made after the 15th day of the third month but before the end of the income year is treated as having been made for the subsequent year.

For purposes of this election, a newly formed corporation's income year starts when it has shareholders, acquires assets or begins doing business, whichever occurs first.

In the event a corporation which is not doing business in California becomes subject to the Bank and Corporation Tax Law by qualifying to do business after filing a federal election to be treated as an "S" corporation, it is deemed to have made an election to be treated as an "S" corporation for the income year during which the corporation qualifies to do business in Califor-

---

(1) IRC § 1361–1379; § 23800.   (3) § 23801(a)(3).
(2) § 23802(b)(1).

nia unless it files a California election to be treated as a "C" corporation for that income year. This California election must be made in the form and manner set by the Franchise Tax Board no later than: (1) for an income year starting in 1990, two and one-half months after qualifying to do business in California; (2) for an income year starting on or after 1–1–91, the last date allowed for filing a federal S election under IRC § 1362(a) for that income year.

A corporation that is not qualified to do business in California, but which is treated as an "S" corporation for federal purposes, will be treated as an "S" corporation for purposes of California law. Its shareholders will be treated as shareholders of an "S" corporation. If a corporation, not qualified to do business in California and treated as an "S" corporation for federal purposes, elected to be treated as a "C" corporation before the 1989 amendments to Rev & TC § 23801 (eff. 10–2–89), that election will be revoked for income years starting on or after 1–1–90. It will be treated as an "S" Corporation, and its shareholders as "S" corporation shareholders.[4]

"Qualified to do business in California" or "qualifying to do business in California" means incorporating or obtaining a certificate of qualification to do business pursuant to the Corporations Code.[4]

A timely election to be treated as a "C" corporation will be treated as a revocation and IRC § 1362(g), relating to election after termination shall apply. An untimely election to be treated as a "C" corporation shall be null and void and shall not be applied to either the current or a later income year.[5]

IMPORTANT	Caution for those wishing to elect S corporation status for federal purposes only. There is a lack of consistency between Rev & TC § 23801(a)(4)(F) which provides that an election for a federal S corporation to retain its C corporation status for California purposes must be filed before the 16th day of the third month of the income year if the revocation is effective for the first day of that income year. If the election is not timely filed, Rev & TC § 23801(a)(4)(F) provides that the election will not be effective for the current year or any subsequent year. The instructions for Form 3560 would seem to allow an election made after the 15th day of the third month of the income year to be effective for the first day of the next income year. Care should be exercised to meet the timely filing requirements of the Code, and not rely on the instructions for the form.

Nonresident shareholders—trust with nonresident fiduciary. Each nonresident shareholder of an S corporation, or fiduciary must file with the S corporation return a statement of consent by that shareholder or fiduciary to be subject to the jurisdiction of California to tax the shareholder's pro rata share of income attributable to California sources. The S corporation must

---

(4) § 23801.   (5) § 23801(a)(4).

include in its return for each income year a list of the shareholders in the form and manner set by the Franchise Tax Board. Failure to meet these requirements will be grounds for retroactive revocation of California S corporation election.[6]

Combined report—inclusion—application of unitary combination methods to properly reflect income or loss of group including one or more S corporations. As a general rule, a corporation making a valid election to be treated as an S corporation will not be included in a combined report under Ch 17 of the Rev & TC, Art 1, starting with Rev & TC § 25101.

Exception to general rule. In cases where the FTB determines that the reported income or loss of a group of commonly owned or controlled corporations (under Rev & TC § 25105), that includes one or more corporations electing S corporation status, does not reflect clearly the income or loss of a member of that group, or represents an evasion of tax by one or more members of the group, and the FTB determines that the comparable uncontrolled price method set by IRC § 482 regulations cannot practically be applied, the FTB may, instead of other methods set by those IRC § 482 regulations, apply methods of unitary combination, under Ch 17, to properly reflect income or loss of group members. The application of this rule will not affect the S corporation's election.[7]

Short year—C corporation. Rev & TC Ch 13, starting with Rev & TC § 24631 will apply instead of IRC § 1362(e)(5).[8]

Termination of federal election. The termination of a federal election under IRC § 1362(d), that is not inadvertent pursuant to IRC § 1362(f), will, at the same time, terminate on S corporation election for purposes of the Personal Income Tax Law and the Bank and Corporation Tax Law. A federal termination by revocation is effective for purposes of California law and must be reported to the Franchise Tax Board using FTB Form 3560 no later than the last date allowed for filing the federal termination under IRC § 1362(d). A corporation may terminate by revocation its California S corporation election without revoking its federal election by filing a timely revocation on FTB Form 3560.[9]

Failure to elect C status or terminate by revocation. The result of such a failure will be the treatment of the corporation as an S corporation.[10]

Determination of taxable income. IRC § 1363(a) does not apply. California law governs.[11]

Rate of tax. The tax on S corporation under Rev & TC § 23151 (franchise) or Rev & TC § 23501 (corporation income) is 2.5% for years ending before 1-1-94; for years ending on or after 1-1-94, the tax rate is

---

(6) § 23801(b).

(7) § 23801(c)–(d).

(8) § 23801(e).

(9) § 23801(f).

(10) § 23801(g).

(11) § 23802(a).

1.5%.[12] In case of a financial corporation that is qualified as an S corporation, the rate is increased by the statutory equivalent (Rev & TC §§ 23183–23184) of personal property and business license taxes.[13]

Alternative minimum tax. An S corporation is not subject to the alternative minimum tax imposed by Rev & TC § 23400.[14]

Minimum tax. An S corporation is subject to the minimum tax under Rev & TC § 23151 or 23153.[15]

Net operating loss deductions. Net operating loss deductions will be allowed an S corporation under Rev & TC § 24416 or § 24416.1 only with respect to periods in which the corporation had in effect a valid election to be treated as an S corporation. IRC § 1371(b) denying carryovers between "C years" and "S years," applies, except as provided above. These rules do not affect the amount of any item of income or loss computed under IRC § 1366, relating to pass-thru items to shareholders.[16]

Limits on loss carryovers. Losses passed through to shareholders of an S corporation, to the extent otherwise allowable without application of Rev & TC § 17276(b), must be fully included in a shareholder's net operating loss. Rev & TC § 17276(b) must then be applied to the entire net operations.[16]

Deduction for built-in gains and passive investment income. For purposes of computing tax on an S corporation, a deduction from income is allowed for built-in gains and passive investment income for which a tax has been imposed under IRC §§ 1374 and 1375.[17]

Deduction for amortization and depreciation. S corporations must compute these deductions in accordance with the California Personal Income Tax Law. This permits use of MACRS depreciation by S corporations.[18]

Amounts at risk. IRC § 465, relating to limitation of deductions to amounts at risk applies to S corporations.[18]

Passive activity losses and credits. The passive activity losses and credit limits under IRC § 469 will apply to S corporations. For purposes of the tax imposed under Rev & TC §§ 23151 or 23501, as modified by Rev & TC § 23802, material participation must be determined in accordance with IRC § 469(h), relating to closely held C corporations and personal service corporations. For purposes of applying these IRC § 469 limits, the "adjusted gross income" of the S corporation shall be equal to its net income as determined under Rev & TC § 24341 with modifications required by Rev & TC § 23802(f), except that no deduction shall be allowed for contributions allowed by Rev & TC § 24357.[18] For income years starting on or after 1–1–88, the tax on passive investment income attributable to California sources, determined in

---

(12) § 23802(b)(1).
(13) § 23802(b)(1)–(2).
(14) § 23802(b)(3).
(15) § 23802(c).

(16) § 23802(d).
(17) § 23802(e).
(18) § 23802(f).

accordance with IRC § 1375, applies, but the tax will not be imposed on an S corporation that has no excess net passive income for federal purposes. The rate of tax is equal to the Rev & TC § 23151 rate, instead of IRC § 11(b). In case of an S corporation that is also a financial corporation, a rate adjustment will be made for personal property and business license tax equivalent. The tax will not be reduced for any financial corporation offset. The tax will not be reduced by any credits allowed under the Bank and Corporation Tax Law. "Subchapter C earnings and profits" under IRC §§ 1362(d)(3) and 1375 means those attributable to California sources. Consent dividend deduction is allowed in determining electing S corporation's Subchapter C earnings and profits at the close of the income year.[19]

Built-in gains attributable to California sources. Tax is imposed on built-in gains, determined in accordance with IRC § 1374, subject to the following modifications. The rate of tax is that specified in Rev & TC § 23151, not IRC § 11(b). An adjustment to the rate is made in the case of S corporations that are also financial corporations. The financial corporation offset does not apply. The tax is not reduced by any credits allowed under the Bank and Corporation Tax Law. IRC § 1374(b)(4), relating to coordination with IRC § 1201(a) (alternative tax for corporations) does not apply.[20]

Recapture of LIFO amount in case of elections by S corporations. The provisions of IRC § 1363(d) apply. IRC § 1363(d)(2)(C) is modified by California to refer to Rev & TC § 25901a provisions governing the rate of interest (adjusted annual rate established pursuant to Rev & TC § 19269 from due date if no extension had been granted until tax is paid). Under IRC § 1363(d), if an S corporation was a C corporation for the last taxable year before the first taxable year for which the IRC § 1362(a) election was effective, and the corporation inventoried goods under the LIFO method for that last taxable year, the LIFO recapture amount must be included in gross income of the corporation for that last taxable year, and appropriate adjustments must be made to the basis of inventory to take into account the amount included in gross income. The additional tax is payable in four equal installments. The first installment must be paid by the due date for the return of the tax imposed for the last taxable year the corporation was a C corporation; the 3 succeeding installments must be paid by the due date of the corporation's return for the three succeeding taxable years, IRC § 6601, relating to interest for the period of extension does not apply in California Rev & TC § 25901a governing the rate of interest applies.[21]

Exclusion for gains on California small business stock. An S corporation for California tax purposes may not exclude 50% of the gain on California qualifying small business stock as provided in Rev & TC § 18152.5. The gain may be eligible for special treatment at the shareholder level if the S corporation held the qualifying stock for more than 5 years, and

---

(19) § 23811.   **(21)** § 23802(g).
(20) § 23809.

if the shareholder sharing in the gain held the interest in the pass-through entity at the time the qualifying stock was acquired and at all times thereafter.[22]

Nonresident shareholders of S corporation—group return. If an S corporation has nonresident shareholders, these shareholders may elect to apply Rev & TC § 18408.5 relating to group return for nonresident shareholders of partnership.[23] The federal law on this matter was not followed by California.

Other provisions. Other California provisions apply to reduction, carryforward of credits; adjustments to basis of stock; partnership rules; distributions.[24]

¶ 1026   Domestic International Sales Corporations (DISCs)

The California Revenue and Taxation Code does not have provisions similar to the federal provisions covering DISCs. A DISC is a domestic corporation, whose income is primarily (95%) from export sales and rentals. Half of the DISC's income is taxed to the shareholders; and the tax on the other half is deferred until distributed, or when a shareholder sells his stock, or when the corporation no longer qualifies as a DISC. For California purposes, a DISC will be treated the same as any other corporation, taxable on its income currently. It would appear that in almost all cases the DISC would be involved in a unitary business with its affiliated corporations and would file on a combined report basis.

Note: Under federal 1984 TRA, Foreign Sales Corporations (FSC's) have replaced DISC's, effective generally for transactions after 12–31–84. California has not conformed to this federal change.

¶ 1027   Professional Corporations

The Franchise Tax Board has announced that there is no difference in the California tax treatment of shareholders, officers or directors of professional corporations and those of other corporations. No special taxes are imposed on professional corporations.

¶ 1028   Personal Holding Companies

IRC §§ 541—547 provide a 50% penalty tax for corporations found to be personal holding companies. These are corporations holding substantial amounts in investment portfolios to receive dividend and interest income which is not passed through to high-bracket stockholders. California with a personal income tax rate at the top reasonably close to the corporate rate has not seen fit to adopt similar provisions. See ¶ 1030 for the exemption from tax for holding companies, whether of the personal type or not.

---

(22) § 23802(f)(4).   **(24)** § 23803–23807.
(23) § 23810.

¶ 1029 Collapsible Corporations

For income years starting on or after 1–1–91, California has adopted IRC § 341 relating to collapsible corporations. Before 1991, California's Bank and Corporation Law had no provisions that applied IRC § 341 to banks and corporations. For income years starting on or after 1–1–91, California has also adopted IRC § 64, relating to the definition of ordinary income, and IRC § 65, relating to the definition of ordinary loss. Before 1991, the state had no distinction between capital gains and losses and ordinary income and losses for banks and corporations. In 1984, the state adopted the provisions for ordinary income and loss, and collapsible corporations as part of the Personal Income Tax Law. IRC § 341 provides that the sale or exchange of the stock of, or a distribution in partial or complete liquidation treated as in part or in full payment of the exchange of the stock of, a "collapsible corporation" results in ordinary income. A collapsible corporation for this purpose is a corporation formed or availed of to manufacture, construct or purchase certain property to be distributed to the stockholders before the property realizes substantial income to the corporation.[25]

¶ 1030 Holding Companies

Any corporation holding stocks or bonds of any other corporations and not trading in stocks or bonds or other securities held and engaging in no activities other than the receipt and disbursement of dividends from the stocks or interest from the bonds is not considered to be a corporation doing business in the state for purposes of filing a franchise tax return. However, the dividends and interest the holding company receives would be taxable under the income tax provisions.[26]

¶ 1031 Real Estate Investment Trusts (REITs)

Real estate investment trusts (REITs) will be treated by California in accordance with the provisions of IRC §§ 856—860, with the modifications by California set forth below.[27]

California modifications. IRC § 857(b)(1), relating to the imposition of tax on real estate investment trusts, shall not apply. Every real estate investment trust is subject to corporation franchise tax or corporation income tax, except that its net income as defined in Rev & TC § 24341, shall be equal to its real estate investment trust income. "Real estate investment trust income" means real estate investment company taxable income, as defined in IRC § 857(b) subject to these modifications:

(1) instead of IRC § 857(b)(2)(A), relating to special deduction for corporations, no deduction shall be allowed under Rev & TC § 24402, relating to dividends received;
(2) IRC § 857(b)(2)(D), relating to an exclusion for an amount equal to net income from foreclosure property does not apply in California;

---

(25) § 17024.5; 17074; 17075; 23049.1; 23049.2; 24451.

(26) § 23102.
(27) § 24872.

(3) IRC § 857(b)(2)(E), relating to deduction for an amount equal to the tax imposed in case of failure to meet 95% and 75% of income requirements, shall not apply in California; and

(4) IRC § 857(b)(2)(F), relating to exclusion for an amount equal to any net income derived from prohibited transactions, shall not apply.[27]

Income from foreclosure property.   IRC § 857(b)(4)(A), relating to imposition of tax on income from foreclosure property, does not apply in California. IRC § 857(b)(5), relating to imposition of tax for failure to meet 95% and 75% requirements does not apply. IRC § 857(b)(6)(A), relating to imposition of tax on income from prohibited transactions, does not apply in California.[27]

Alternative tax in case of capital gains.   IRC § 857(b)(3), relating to this tax does not apply in California.[27]

The income earned by REITS must be passive, rather than from the active conduct of a business in the real estate field. If a REIT distributes at least 95% of its taxable income to the investors, it is taxable only on the earnings retained. For California, the REIT would file a corporation income tax return.

Any distributions made by the REIT within 90 days following the final decision in the Tax Court or other court, or after the signing of a closing agreement setting forth a tax liability is a "deficiency dividend" and is allowable as a deduction against current income.[28]

Beneficiaries of real estate investment trusts must be taxed in accordance with IRC §§ 857—858.[29] All distributions are taxable to the recipients in the year received.

¶ 1032   Regulated Investment Companies

IRC § 852(b)(5) allows a regulated investment company (RIC) that invests in tax-exempt state and local bonds to pass through the interest on such bonds to be tax exempt in the hands of the shareholders if at least 50% of its assets is invested in tax-exempt bonds at the close of each quarter, and if at least 90% of its net tax exempt interest is paid during the taxable year of the fund or within 45 days thereafter. These dividends must be identified by written notice to the shareholders within the same period.

California allows a "management company" a similar pass-through of "exempt interest dividends." The company may pay such a dividend if 50% of the value of its assets, or series, consists of obligations interest on which is exempt from tax under U.S. or California constitution or California laws and the amount of dividend does not exceed the interest on obligations received by the company. The pass-through to be tax-free to the recipients applies to exempt interest received from California or local government bonds and on obligations of the U.S. that pay interest excludable from income under the Constitution or laws of the U.S. There is no 90% requirement in the Califor-

---

(28) IRC § 860; § 23051.5.   (29) § 17740.

nia law, however. A management company means a corporation, business trust or other organization that meets the requirements of Rev & TC § 24412 of the Bank and Corporation Tax Law, relating to deductions (see below).[30]

For deduction purposes, IRC §§ 851—855 and § 860 (deficiency dividends) apply, except that:

(1) IRC § 852(b)(i) on imposition of tax does not apply;

(2) every regulated investment company is subject to either franchise or income taxes; its net income is equal to its investment company income;

(3) investment company income means investment company taxable income as defined by IRC § 852(b)(2), as follows: (a) IRC § 852(b)(2)(A), relating to exclusion for net capital gain, shall not apply; (b) instead of IRC § 852(b)(2)(C), relating to special deductions for corporations, no deduction shall be allowed under Rev & TC § 24402; (c) the deduction for dividends paid, under IRC § 852(b)(2)(d), is modified to allow capital gain dividends and exempt interest, to extent included in gross income under Bank and Corporation Tax Law, to be included in the computation of the deduction;

(4) IRC § 852(b)(3)(A), relating to capital gains shall not apply;

(5) IRC § 852(b)(5)(B), relating to treatment of exempt interest dividends by shareholders, does not apply; and (6) IRC § 854, relating to limitations applicable to dividends received from a regulated investment company, is modified to refer to Rev & TC § 24402, instead of IRC § 243.[31]

California follows IRC § 852(b)(9), that requires a mutual fund to include dividends in income no later than the date the dividend was declared by the issuing corporation, or the date on which the mutual fund acquired the share.[32] The same conformity also applies to IRC § 852(f) that denies an increase in basis for load charges on the purchase of stock in a mutual fund where those shares are sold or exchanged within 90 days, if the shareholder subsequently acquires shares in the mutual fund pursuant to a reinvestment right.[33]

¶ 1037   Exempt Organizations

The Bank and Corporation Tax Law specifically exempts from tax various nonprofit organizations and entities.[34] However, these organizations are taxable on their unrelated business taxable income.[35] Exempt organizations are fully explained in Section VI of this Handbook.

¶ 1038   Real Estate Mortgage Investment Conduit

The taxation of a real estate mortgage investment conduit (REMIC) and the holders of regular or residual interest in that entity will be determined in accordance federal law, except that IRC § 860F, relating to the 100% tax on prohibited transactions does not apply in California.[36]

---

(30) § 17145.
(31) § 24871.
(32) IRC § 852(b)(9).
(33) IRC § 852(f).

(34) § 23701–23710.
(35) § 23731–35.
(36) § 17940; 24870; 24873.

What is a REMIC. A REMIC is a special tax vehicle for entities which issue multiple classes of investor interest backed by a fixed pool of mortgages.

Qualification. There are complex rules covering qualification as a REMIC. For REMIC status, the entity must be a calendar year taxpayer that elects REMIC status for the tax year, and if applicable, for all prior tax years.[37]

Asset test. Substantially all assets at the close of the fourth month ending after the "startup day" and each quarter ending thereafter, must consist of qualified mortgages and permitted investments.[37]

Investors' interests. All interests in the REMIC must be either regular interests or residual interests.

Regular interests are those with terms that are fixed on the "startup day" and which unconditionally entitle the holder to receive a specified principal amount and provide that interest payments (or similar payments) are payable based on a fixed rate.[38]

Residual interests. Residual interests are any REMIC interests which are not regular interests and which are designated as a residual interest by the REMIC. There can only be one class of residual interest, and distributions (if any) must be made pro rata to all holders.[39]

Taxation of interests. *Regular interests.* Holders of regular interests are taxed as if they held a debt instrument and must report REMIC income on the accrual basis.[38]

Residual interests. At the end of each calendar quarter, the holder of a residual interest has ordinary income or loss equal to his or her daily portion of the REMIC's taxable income or loss. Distributions up to the holder's adjusted basis are taxed as ordinary income and excess distributions are treated as gain from the sale or exchange of the interest.[39]

Taxation of the REMIC. A REMIC is subject to the minimum tax imposed under Rev & TC § 23153.[40] The income of the REMIC generally is taken into account by holders of regular and residual interests (above).

¶ 1039 **Publicly Traded Partnerships**

For income and taxable years starting on or after 1–1–90, California has adopted IRC § 7704. Under this federal rule, a publicly traded partnership is treated as a corporation, as a general rule. An exception for partnerships with passive-type income is provided under IRC § 7704(c). A "publicly traded partnership" is a partnership (1) whose interests are traded on an established securities market, or (2) whose interests are readily tradable on a secondary market, or the substantial equivalent thereof. The effect of becom-

---

(37) IRC § 860D.
(38) IRC § 860B.

(39) IRC § 860C.
(40) § 23153.

ing a corporation is that the partnership, as of the first day it has that status, will be treated as transferring all of its assets, subject to liabilities, to a newly formed corporation in exchange for the stock of the corporation, and distributing such stock to its partners in liquidation of their interests in the partnership. The exception for partnerships with passive-type income does not apply to certain partnerships that could qualify as a regulated investment company.[1]

¶ 1040   Limited Liability Companies

The organization of a Limited Liability Company (LLC) under California law is permitted effective September 30, 1994. An LLC is a legal entity created under state law. State law does not create a separate tax code for LLCs.[2]

Classification for tax purposes. An LLC will be classified under existing federal tax law which is generally mirrored in California's Revenue & Taxation Code. An LLC may be classified as: (1) a partnership; or (2) as an association taxable as a corporation. The criteria for this determination is found in U.S. Treas. Reg. § 301.7702–2(a)(1). To be treated as a partnership, the LLC may not have any more than two of the following characteristics: (1) limited liability; (2) centralized management; (3) continuity of life; and (4) free transferability of interest. Numerous revenue rulings and private letter rulings have been issued under federal law with respect to each of these characteristics in the context of classifying an LLC. The treasury regulations for the classification of an entity also include two additional criteria: (1) there being associates; and (2) an objective to carry on a business and divide gains. Since these last two characteristics are found in all business entities, the characteristics of associates and the objective to carry on a business and divide gains, are ignored in determining the classification of an LLC. The regulations treat an unincorporated association, such as an LLC, as an association taxable as a corporation if it has more corporate than non-corporate characteristics. Since, by definition, an LLC will almost always possess limited liability, an LLC must lack two of the remaining three criteria to avoid classification as a corporation.

Once an LLC has been classified under federal law as a partnership, or as an association taxable as a corporation, state law will follow the federal classification. California code provides that a "partnership" will include an LLC except where the context or specific provisions of California's Rev & TC otherwise require (Rev & TC § 28.5).

Member reporting. If an LLC is classified as a partnership for California purposes, a person with a membership or economic interest will take into account amounts required to be recognized under Chapter 10 (commencing with § 17851) of the Rev & TC as applied to individuals (Rev & TC § 17087.6).

---

(1) IRC § 7704. § 17008.5; 23038.5.   (2) Added by Stats. 1994, c. 1200.

The Code specifically authorizes the Franchise Tax Board to set forth the forms, conditions, and instructions, to provide for the filing of a group return for electing nonresident persons with a membership or economic interest in an LLC that is classified as a partnership for California purposes (Rev & TC § 18535).

Returns. The return of an LLC is required to be filed within three months and 15 days after the close of its taxable or income year (Rev & TC § 18633.5).

Each nonresident partner who is a member of a California LLC, must agree to file a return with the State of California, to make timely payment of all taxes imposed on the member, and if an agreement by a member has not been filed by the LLC with its return, then the LLC must agree to pay income taxes on behalf of each nonresident member computed at the highest marginal individual income tax rate then in effect.

The agreement with respect to nonresident members must be filed at the time the annual return is filed for the first taxable period of the LLC, or at the time the return is required and for which there is a nonresident member on whose behalf such agreement has not previously been filed (Rev & TC § 18633.5).

If an LLC is to be treated as a partnership, then any distributions to nonresident members are subject to withholding as is the case with partnerships (Rev & TC § 19002).

LLCs classified as corporations. Every LLC that is classified as a corporation for California tax purposes is required to file a tax return under Part 10.2 (commencing with Rev & TC § 18401) and pay the applicable taxes imposed by Part 11 (commencing with Rev & TC § 23001) which is commonly referred to as the Bank & Corporation Tax Law (Rev & TC § 18633.5). An LLC classified as a corporation is treated as any other corporate entity.

If an LLC is treated as a corporation, then it must abide by Rev & TC § 23211 relating to the payment of estimated taxes, including the minimum tax.

Credits. An LLC treats credits provided in California law in the same way as a credit is treated by a partnership (ie., passed through to its members) or a corporation, depending upon whether the LLC is classified as a partnership or an association taxable as a corporation.

Fees. A new Chapter 1.6, commencing with Rev & TC § 23091, is added to Part 11 of Division 2 of the Rev & TC which specifies the tax and fees for LLCs classified as partnerships. The tax and fees assessed shall be due on the 15th day of the fourth month following the end of the tax year. Estimated tax requirements are set forth in the Code for LLCs with respect to the tax imposed upon an LLC under Rev & TC § 23092.

The fees imposed on an LLC for a tax year beginning on or before December 31, 1995, and thereafter, are as follows:

| | Fee — Tax Year Beginning | |
Total Income	Before 12/31/95	After 1/1/96
$250,000–$499,999	$ 500	$ 500
$500,000–$999,999	1,000	1,500
$1,000,000–$5,000,000	2,000	3,000
$5,000,000 or more	4,000	4,500

The total income for purposes of calculating the above fee is income from all sources (Rev & TC § 23092). The above fees are in addition to the minimum tax under Rev & TC § 23153. The tax imposed upon an LLC is not deductible under California law (Rev & TC § 17220).

The above fees are for LLCs classified as a partnership for California tax purposes (Rev & TC § 18633.5).

Forms. An LLC which is treated as a partnership will file a return on a new form to be issued by the Franchise Tax Board, Form FTB 598.

Property tax change in ownership. The Rev & TC also provides that the determination as to whether a change in ownership of an LLC has occurred for property tax purposes, will be treated under Rev & TC § 64 in the same fashion as whether there has been a change in ownership which would require the reappraisal of real property if owned by a corporation or partnership. An LLC will be treated in a similar fashion if there is a change in more than 50% of the total ownership interest of the entity, as has previously been the case with respect to transfers of partnership or corporate interests where the entity holds real property (Rev & TC § 64).

Foreign LLCS. For California purposes, the legal determination of the tax classification of a foreign organized limited liability company doing business in California, or deriving income from California sources, will be made consistent with the determination of the IRS. Accordingly, if a foreign organized LLC is treated as a partnership by the IRS for federal tax purposes, the same partnership treatment will be given to the LLC by California.[3]

---

(3) FTB Notice 92–5, 8–21–92.

DISSOLVING, WITHDRAWING AND SUSPENDED CORPORATIONS

¶ 1041   **Corporate Dissolutions and Withdrawals**

If a California corporation wishes to dissolve its charter or if a foreign corporation intends to withdraw from the state, the procedure is to file papers with the California Secretary of State. Routinely, the organization files with the Secretary of State a "Notice of Intention to Wind-Up and Dissolve." Following that, it files a final certificate of winding up and dissolution with the Secretary of State's office. Eff. 1–1–92, Corporations Code § 1905 sets conditions of filing the certificate. The effective date of the dissolution is the date on which the Secretary of State files (stamps) the certified copy of the certificate of dissolution or the certificate of winding up and dissolution. For foreign corporations the procedure is to file a Certificate of Withdrawal and it would be effective on the date on which the Secretary of State's office files that certificate.[1] The Secretary of State must, through an information program and by forms and instructions provided to taxpayers, recommend that all documents required to be filed be sent, if mailed, by certified mail with return receipt requested. The Secretary must also notify taxpayers that receipt of the documents by the Secretary will be acknowledged within 21 days of receipt. On or before 21 days of receipt, the Secretary must provide the taxpayer with acknowledgement of the receipt of documents. See ¶ 1015 for special tax computation for corporation going out of business.

Tax clearance certificate.   The Secretary of State will not permit the dissolution or withdrawal of a corporation until it receives a tax clearance certificate from the Franchise Tax Board indicating that all taxes have been paid or provided for.[2]

TAX TIP   A tax clearance certificate is obtained by filing an Assumption of Tax Liability/Request for Tax Clearance (California from FTB 3555). When dissolving a California domestic stock corporation the Request is filed with the Secretary of State, 1230 J Street, Sacramento, CA 95814–2984. If you are dissolving a California domestic nonprofit corporation, surrendering a foreign corporation, or merging corporations, mail the completed form to: Franchise Tax Board, ATTN: Tax Clearance Unit, P.O. Box 1468, Sacramento, CA 95812–1468. The envelope should be clearly marked "Rush-Tax Clearance." The Franchise Tax Board is required within 30 days after receiving a request for a tax clearance to either issue the certificate or notify the person requesting the certificate of the conditions which must be met before the certificate will be issued. As a prerequisite, the taxpayer must have filed all the tax returns due and paid all the liability of record.

The Sacramento office, upon receipt of a tax clearance request, will review the returns and make sure that all taxes have been paid and that there are no questions requiring answers before the tax clearance certificate is issued. In many cases, it may be necessary that that office send

---

(1) § 23331; 23332; 23334; Corps Cd § 1905.   (2) § 23332; 23334; 23561. Corps Cd § 1905.

the return to one of the field offices so that various questions may be answered or that the returns for one or more years may be audited.

Returns marked as final returns. Commencing with returns filed on or after 1–1–93, if the taxpayer files a return marked "final return" and has not previously filed an Application for the Tax Clearance, the Franchise Tax Board will treat the return as a request for tax clearance. The taxpayer will then be provided with the forms and instructions, and other information and documents that are required to be filed with the Secretary of State, or the Franchise Tax Board, to complete the withdrawal or dissolution process.

Other methods. If the taxpayer wishes to get a tax clearance prior to the completion of the audit in the settlement of any issues involved, it can be done by one of the following methods: (1) assumption of liability; (2) surety bonds; (3) cash deposit bonds.

Assumption of liability forms. Assumption of liability forms may be filed by one or more individuals, provided they are residents of California, who can furnish proof of satisfactory financial responsibility. Generally, the individuals are stockholders or otherwise have a financial interest in the dissolution or withdrawal of the taxpayer. Proof of financial responsibility by the signers may be made by reference to balance sheets, financial statements, returns filed under the personal income tax law or other data. The Franchise Tax Board will determine whether or not one or more individual assumptions of liability are required depending on the financial responsibility of the individuals involved.

It is not necessary that the individual assumers constitute a majority ownership of the stock of the corporation. The FTB permits, if there is more than one assumer, that all sign one assumption, or a separate assumption may be filed by each individual. It is also possible to get an assumption of liability form filed by a corporation which is subject to the California franchise tax and has adequate resources within the state. Also, a corporate transferee in a reorganization who acquires the assets of the dissolving corporation and continues the business may file an assumption of liability.

TAX TIP

If it is not practical to get a corporate assumption of liability signed immediately because of the problems involving transfer of assets and reorganization, a cash bond may be deposited with the department until a valid assumption by a new corporation can be executed and submitted. This bond may be in the form of a certified check, payable to the Franchise Tax Board, and will be returned on receipt of the valid assumption.

Surety bond. The individuals or corporations desiring the tax clearance certificate may file a surety bond, generally in an amount equal to twice the estimated tax with interest, computed for a 12-month period.

¶ 1041

Cash deposit bond. If the corporation submits a cash bond, the Franchise Tax Board holds that bond as security. It is not applied to the taxpayer's account and will not draw interest during the period it is held by the Franchise Tax Board.

¶ 1042   **Corporate Suspension and Revivor**

If a corporation files a return, but fails to pay the tax shown on the return, or receives a notice and demand from the Franchise Tax Board for tax penalty or interest due, and fails to pay that tax, it may be subject to "suspension" for the failure to pay.[3]

Procedure for suspension.   Forfeiture and suspension of a taxpayer's rights and privileges under Rev & TC §§ 23301, 23301.5, and 23775 will occur and become effective only as expressly provided in Rev & TC § 23302. The notice requirements of Rev & TC § 21020 shall apply to forfeiture under Rev & TC § 23301, 23301.5 or 23775. The mechanics of the suspension is for the Franchise Tax Board to notify the Secretary of State that the corporation is subject to suspension and the Secretary of State then includes the corporation on the list of suspended corporations.[4]

Effect of suspension.   Except for the purpose of filing an application for exempt status or amending the articles of incorporation as necessary either to perfect that application or to set forth a new name, all of the corporation's powers, rights and privileges are suspended in these circumstances. During this period of suspension the corporation is not entitled to retain its own name, it does not have the right to defend itself in court, it also does not have the right to file a protest or an appeal with the Franchise Tax Board or the Board of Equalization with respect to the matters causing the suspension.[5] A domestic taxpayer is not entitled to sell, transfer or exchange real property in California during the period of forfeiture or suspension.[4] Rev & TC §§ 23301, 23301.5, and 23775 apply to a foreign taxpayer only if the taxpayer is qualified to do business in California. A taxpayer required under the Corporations Code to qualify to do business is not deemed qualified for the purpose of the Art 7 provisions on suspension and revivor unless the taxpayer has in fact qualified with the Secretary of State.[6]

Voidability of contract during period of suspension or forfeiture.   California has adopted Rev & TC §§ 23304.1 and 23304.5 relating to the voidability of contracts. Under Rev & TC § 23304.1, every contract made in California by a taxpayer during the period of suspension or forfeiture is voidable at the instance of any party to the contract other than the taxpayer. If a foreign taxpayer that is not qualified to do business, or has no corporate account number from the Franchise Tax Board fails to file a tax return, any contract made by that foreign corporation is voidable by another party. The applicable period for purposes of this rule is that starting on 1–1–91, or the

---

(3) § 23301.   (5) § 23301.5.
(4) § 23302.   (6) § 23301.6.

first day of the income year for which the taxpayer has failed to file a return or pay taxes, whichever is later, and ending on later of the date taxpayer qualified in California, or obtained corporate account number.[7]

CAUTION	*Criminal penalties.* In addition to the voidability of the corporation's contracts during the period of suspension or forfeiture, Rev. & TC provides a criminal penalty with a fine of not less than $250 or more than $1,000, and/or imprisonment of up to one year, for attempting to exercise the posers, rights, or privileges of a suspended corporation, or who transacts intrastate business in California on behalf or a foreign bank or corporation whose rights, powers, and privileges have been forfeited.

If a taxpayer fails to file a tax return, or pay tax, or file a statement or return required under Rev & TC §§ 23707 or 23774 within 60 days of receiving a demand from the FTB, any contract made during period starting at the end of the 60-day demand period, and ending on the date relief is granted under Rev & TC § 23305.1, or the date the taxpayer qualifies to do business, whichever is earlier, shall be voidable by any other party to the contract. This rule applies only if taxpayer has a corporate account number from the FTB, but has not qualified to do business under Corps Cd § 2105.[5] If a taxpayer has not complied with the 60-day demand, the taxpayer's name, corporate account number, date of demand, date of first day after the end of the 60-day demand period, and the fact taxpayer did not pay the tax or other amount, or file a statement or a return shall be a matter of public record.[7]

The exercise of the right to declare a contract voidable can be made only in a lawsuit brought by either party to the contract. The rights of the parties are not affected by Rev & TC § 23304.1 (see above), except to the extent determined by the court. Taxpayer must be allowed a reasonable opportunity to cure voidability. If the court finds a contract voidable, it must order it rescinded, but taxpayer must receive full restitution of benefits, before this can take place. Special rules apply to contracts entered into before and after effective date.[8]

During the period of suspension the corporation is not subject to the minimum tax, but if it carries on any business activities at a profit, or receives any income during the period, it is subject to the tax on that income.[9]

How to lift suspension or forfeiture. In order for a corporation to have the suspension lifted, the corporation, any officer, or any other person who has interest in the relief from the suspension or forfeiture must file an application for a Certificate of Revivor with the Franchise Tax Board. The application has to be accompanied by the filing of all the required tax returns and the payment of all taxes, additions to tax, penalties and any other amounts which caused its suspension, plus a minimum tax for the period of revivor and an affidavit to the effect that it conducted no business activities

---

(7) § 23304.1. (9) § 23303.
(8) § 23304.5.

during the period of suspension, or as an alternative, completed tax returns and made payment of the tax for such periods.[10] Clearance of name through the Secretary of State is also required before the issuance of the certificate of revivor.[11] A revivor may be effected by the FTB without full payment of taxes, if it determines that the revivor will improve the prospects for collection of the full amount due.[12] The FTB, when issuing a revivor, must notify the Secretary of State of the name of the taxpayer and its corporate number.[13] A taxpayer can apply for relief from voidability of contract. The period of relief must be specified and all taxes, penalties and interest must be paid. The Franchise Tax Board may assess a penalty of $100 per day for each day of the period for which relief from voidability is granted, not to exceed a total penalty equal to that amount of the tax that would otherwise be imposed, and the penalty will be no less than the minimum tax for the year. For exempt organizations the penalty will be no more than the tax otherwise imposed on unrelated business income.[14] The revivor or relief from voidability may be had if taxpayer provides the FTB with an assumption of liability, or bond, deposit, or other security.[15]

> *Note:* The tax computation for the year the suspended corporation is put back into good standing is determined in a manner similar to that for a commencing corporation. Rev & TC § 23282 provides that if the taxpayer was doing business in the year preceding the year in which the revivor took place, the tax for the year of revivor will be computed on the basis of the net income of that preceding income year. If that is not the situation, then the taxpayer resuming business in the year of revivor will pay a tax computed on the basis of the net income for the year in which the corporation ceased doing business, unless such income had already been subjected to tax. And in addition, the taxpayer in either case must pay an additional minimum tax. If the corporation had been suspended for nonpayment of the minimum tax (in other words, had never commenced doing business in California) its tax for the year of revivor would be the minimum tax.[16]

Confirmation of good standing. The Franchise Tax Board may provide letters of good standing, verifying a corporation's status for doing business in California. A fee will be charged by the Franchise Tax Board for responding to such requests.

---

(10) § 23305.
(11) § 23305a.
(12) § 23305b.
(13) § 23305c.

(14) § 23305.1, as amended by Stats. 1994, c. 357, § 3.
(15) § 23305.2.
(16) § 23282.

TAX ACCOUNTING AND TAX PERIODS

¶ 1053 General

For the rules on accounting methods, consult Section III of this handbook dealing with tax concepts that apply to corporations and individuals. This chapter deals with accounting period, rounding figures on returns, accounting period for new corporations, and tax period affected by changes in the law.

¶ 1054 Rounding Figures on Returns

The corporation may round off cents to the nearest whole dollar on the tax return and associated schedules.[1]

¶ 1055 Accounting Period

The established accounting period can be changed only with permission of the Franchise Tax Board. Conformity with federal is required. If the taxpayer does not have an established accounting period or does not keep books, the return must be filed on a calendar year basis.[2]

¶ 1056 New Corporations—Accounting Period

A new California corporation or a newly qualified foreign corporation is required to notify the Franchise Tax Board of its accounting period as soon as possible. The accounting period adopted should be identical with the period used for filing the federal corporation income tax returns. The first income period cannot end more than 12 months after the date of incorporation or qualification in California. If the first period is ½ month or less, it may be disregarded as far as filing a return is concerned provided the corporation was not doing business and receives no income from sources within California during this short period.[3]

¶ 1057 Tax Period Affected by Changes in Law

Except as otherwise provided by any law, the provisions of any act which affect the imposition or computation of taxes, penalties, or the allowance of credits against the tax must be applied to income years starting on or after January 1 of the year in which the act becomes law. Provisions which change Rev & TC §§ 25561 to 25563, inclusive, relating to payments of estimated tax or Rev & TC §§ 25951–25954.5, also relating to underpayment of estimated tax, must be applied to income years starting on or after January 1 of the year immediately following the year in which the act becomes law. The advance payment of taxes by use of estimates is not a tax, and the charge for underpayment of estimated tax is an "addition to tax," not a "penalty," so the changes in law relating thereto take affect on January 1, of the year following the year the act becomes law, unless otherwise provided in the statute.[4]

The tax on any taxpayer for a period beginning in one calendar year and ending in the following calendar year, when the law applicable to the

---

(1) § 25406.
(2) § 24631; § 24632; 24633.

(3) Form FTB 1060.
(4) § 23058.

computation of taxes for the second year is different from that of the first calendar year, must be computed for the entire period using the law and rates for the first calendar year, and then making the same computation using the law and rates for the second calendar year. The tax will be the sum of two amounts, each determined by the ratio of the portion of the total period falling within each year to the entire period.[5]

---

(5) § 24251.

BASIS OF TAX—GROSS INCOME

¶ 1067   **Basis of Tax**

Taxes on corporations and banks are levied or measured on the basis of net income.[1] Net income is gross income less allowable deductions.[2]

IRC conformity.   The term "Internal Revenue Code of 1954" or "Internal Revenue Code of 1986" for purposes of the Bank and Corporation Tax Law means USC Title 26, including all amendments thereto, as enacted on 1–1–92 for income years starting on or after 1–1–92, and on or before 12–31–93, as enacted on 1–1–93 for income years starting on or after 1–1–93.[3]

¶ 1079   **Gross Income Defined**

The traditional definition of "gross income", set forth in regulations under IRC § 61 and followed by the California Bank and Corporation Tax Law,[4] is that gross income means all income from whatever source derived unless excluded by law. Gross income includes income realized in any form, whether in money, property, or services. Income may be realized, therefore, in the form of services, accommodations, stock or other property as well as cash. For purposes of the Bank and Corporation Tax Law, a distributive share of partnership gross income will be determined under Rev & TC § 17001. Income from an interest in an estate or trust will be determined under Rev & TC § 17001.

IRC Section 61 (Rev & TC § 24271 for California) lists the more common items of gross income for purposes of illustration. Gross income, however, is not limited to the items so enumerated.

Contributions to capital of a corporation.   Prior to 1–1–92, California had no counterpart to IRC § 118 which provides that the gross income of a corporation does not include any contribution to the capital of the corporation. Effective 1–1–92, California enacted Rev. & TC § 24325 which provides that IRC § 118 will be followed by California so that it is clear that contributions to the capital of a corporation will not be treated as taxable income. Previously California had informally followed the federal treatment of IRC § 118.

IMPORTANT   The Bank and Corporation Tax Law contains provisions similar to the Personal Income Tax Law with respect to application of federal regulations, elections, filing applications and seeking consent.[5]

Investment income from investment partnerships.   Income derived from or attributable to sources within California shall not include the distributive share of interest, dividends, and gains from the sale or exchange of qualifying investment securities derived by a bank or corporation that is a

---

(1) § 23151; 23181; 23501.   (4) Fed Reg 1.61–1; § 24271.
(2) § 24341.   (5) § 23051.5(c)–(e).
(3) § 23051.5.

partner in a partnership that qualifies as an investment partnership under Rev & TC § 17955.

An investment partnership is one which has at least 90% of the partnership's cost of its total assets in qualifying investment securities, deposits at banks or other financial institutions, and office space and equipment reasonably necessary to carry on its activities, and no less than 90% of its gross income from interest, dividends, and gains from the sale or exchange of qualifying investment securities.

Qualifying investment securities include: common stock, including preferred shares or debt securities convertible into common stock, and preferred stock; bonds, debentures, and other debt securities; foreign and domestic currency deposits or equivalents and securities convertible into foreign securities; mortgage- or asset-backed securities secured by federal, state, or local governmental agencies; repurchase agreements and loan participations; foreign currency exchange contracts and forward and futures contracts on foreign currencies; stock and bond index securities and futures contracts, options on any of the fore-mentioned investments, and regulated futures contracts. Qualifying investment securities does not include an interest in a partnership unless that partnership is itself an investment partnership.[6]

WARNING   A corporation will not be exempt from tax as receiving only investment income from California if the bank or corporation participates in the management of the investment activities of the investment partnership, or that is engaged in a unitary business with another bank, corporation, or partnership that participates in the management of the investment activities of the partnership or has income derived from or attributable to sources within California other than the investment income described above.

Ordinary income and ordinary loss. California has adopted the provisions of IRC § 64, relating to the definition of ordinary income, and IRC § 65, relating to the definition of ordinary loss.[7]

¶ 1080   **Gross Income From Business**

In a manufacturing, merchandising or mining business, "gross income" means the total sales less the cost of goods sold, plus any income from investments and from incidental or outside operations or sources. Gross income is determined, without subtraction of depletion allowances based on a percentage of income, and without subtraction of selling expenses, losses, or other items not ordinarily used in computing cost of goods sold. The cost of goods sold should be determined in accordance with the method of accounting consistently used by the taxpayer.[8] Fed Reg 1.61–3 is highly persuasive in the interpretation of conforming California law.

(6) § 23040.1.
(7) § 23049.1; 23049.2.

(8) § 24271(a)(2).

For a California corporation operating entirely within the state, gross income means all types of income, except the income specifically excluded as outlined below. For a corporation operating within and without California in a unitary business, the income is apportioned in accordance with the formula and the rules for the determination of whether or not nonbusiness income is taxed are set forth below. For a corporation having nonbusiness income from sources in other states because of an investment of property there which is not associated with a unitary business, the income may be excluded from California taxation on a separate accounting basis.

Federal-state comparison. The starting point for reporting income on the corporation franchise tax return Form 100 is federal taxable income before net operating loss and special deductions (Federal Form 1120). Thus total federal income and deductions are reported on the state return. This amount, however, must be adjusted for state tax purposes to account for differences between the federal and state income and deductions. These adjustments are made on page 1 of Form 100.

¶ 1081 **Dividends**

"Dividend" means any distribution of profits made by a corporation to its shareholders out of: (a) earnings and profits accumulated after February 28, 1913; or (b) earnings and profits of the income year.[9]

A dividend is taxable to the shareholder when made subject to his demand. The date of payment rather than the date of declaration determines the time of taxability. An accrual basis stockholder will not include the dividend in income until it is made subject to his demand.[10]

The dividend may be paid in cash or other property. For an analysis of the treatment of dividends includable in gross income in the form of property, refer to chapter on dividends and other corporate distributions.

Dividend-received deduction. For federal purposes, (IRC § 243—246), a special deduction from gross income is available for dividends received from a domestic corporation which is subject to the income tax. The deduction is 70% of the dividends received, with certain dividends qualifying for a 100% exclusion.

Note: For income years starting on or after 1–1–90, California provides for deduction of a portion of the dividends received during the year declared from income which has been included in the measure of the taxes imposed by the franchise tax, the corporation income tax, and the alternative minimum tax. In case of a dividend received from a more than 50% owned corporation, the deductible percentage is 100%. If received from a 20% owned corporation, 80%. In the case of a dividend received from a less than 20% owned corporation, 70%. Before 1990, a 100% deduction was allowed by California if the income of the corporation paying the dividend was included in the measure of the taxes imposed by the franchise and corporation income taxes.[11]

---

(9) § 24495.
(10) Reg 24451.

(11) § 24402.

For more information on the computation, see the chapter on corporation deductions.

A dividend received from an insurance company, which has been paid out of gross premiums, subject to the tax imposed by part 7 (commencing with Rev & TC 12001), is deductible. The insurance company dividend must have been received by a California commercially domiciled corporation owning 80% or more of each class of stock of the insurance company to qualify for the deduction.[12]

If the insurance company subsidiary paying the dividend has gross income from sources within and without California, the deduction is a percentage of the dividend paid, computed by using a three-factor formula made up of gross receipts, payroll and property.

Water's edge election.   Taxpayers making the water's edge election under Rev & TC § 25110 can exclude 75% of qualifying dividends: (1) equal to the greatest amount of dividends received by the water's-edge group in any income year in the base period (12-month income year ending before 1–1–87 and two preceding 12-month income years); or (2) if the greatest foreign payroll factor for any base period year is the same as or less than the foreign payroll factor in any income year. A 100% exclusion applies if the greatest foreign payroll factor for any income year in the base period exceeds the foreign payroll factor for the income year. Dividends from construction projects with locations not subject to taxpayer's control may also qualify for the 100% exclusion. "Qualifying dividends" means those received by the water's-edge group from corporations regardless of the place incorporated if: (1) the average of property, payroll, and sales factors within the U.S. for the payor corporation is less than 20%; and (2) more than 50% of the total combined voting power of all classes of stock entitled to vote is owned indirectly by the water's-edge group. Foreign payroll factor for any income year is a fraction the numerator of which is the total amount paid outside the U.S. during the income year for compensation, and the denominator is total compensation paid everywhere by the water's-edge group and corporations that would have been combined with the group had not the water's edge election been made.[13]

Dividends received from foreign subsidiaries.   A state may not discriminate in its taxation of dividends from non-U.S. subsidiaries as compared with the taxation of dividends from its U.S. subsidiaries. The U.S. Supreme Court held that such discrimination violates the Foreign Commerce Clause of the U.S. Constitution (*Kraft General Foods, Inc. v. Iowa Department of Revenue and Finance* (1992) 112 S Ct 2365, 120 L Ed 2d 59).

¶ 1082   **Interest**

As a general rule, interest received by or credited to the corporation constitutes gross income, and is fully taxable. Interest income to a corporation

---

(12) § 24410.   (13) § 24411.

includes interest on banks or savings and loan deposits, coupon bonds, open accounts, promissory notes, mortgages, a corporate bond or debenture, the interest portion of a condemnation award, and interest on refunds of state or federal taxes.[14] Fed Reg applies in interpretation of conforming California law, in the absence of California regulation.[15]

<table>
<tr><td>

IMPORTANT

</td><td>

Franchise tax. Interest received from federal, state, municipal or other bonds is includable in the gross income of corporations taxable under the franchise tax (Chapter 2). Since the tax under Chapter 2 is a privilege tax for the right to exercise the corporate franchise, it is not a tax on the income received but merely uses such income of the year as the measure of the tax for the privilege of exercising the corporate franchise during the following year.[16]

Income tax. Interest on bonds and other obligations of the United States, the District of Columbia, and the territories of the United States, is exempt from taxation by the various states under the U.S. Constitution and the laws of the United States. Therefore, such interest is exempt from taxation for a corporation filing the corporation income tax return (Chapter 3). In the same manner, interest on bonds of the State of California, or its political subdivisions, is exempt from state taxation under the California Constitution and is likewise excluded on the corporation income tax return. The bank and Corporation Tax Law has not included an amendment to the California Personal Income Tax Law Rev & TC § 17133 that provides that the determination of whether a bond is issued by the state or local government must be made without regard to (1) the source of payment of the bond, or security for bond, public or private; and (2) whether or not public improvements are financed.

</td></tr>
</table>

Note: Gains and profits from the sale or other disposition of bonds and obligations of the United States or California municipalities are taxable to the same extent as gains and profits from the sale or exchange of other property on the corporation income and franchise tax returns.[17]

Original issue discounts.   When notes, bonds, or other certificates of indebtedness are issued by a corporation at a discount and are later redeemed by the debtor at the face amount, the original issue discount is considered interest and taxable to the receiving corporation.[14]

Treatment of bonds or other debt instruments.   For income years starting on or after 1–1–87, the tax treatment of bonds and other instruments of debt will be determined in accordance with IRC Subtitle A, Ch 1, Subch P, Part V, except as modified by California law. These IRC provisions are found in IRC §§ 1271—1288.[18]

---

(14) § 24271.   **(17)** § 24314.

(15) Fed Reg 1.61–7(a).   **(18)** IRC § 1271–1288; § 24990–24994.

(16) § 24272.

Modifications to IRC §§ 1271—1288. IRC § 1275(a)(3), relating to the definition of tax-exempt obligation does not apply in California. The term "tax-exempt obligation" means obligations the interest on which is exempt from tax under the Bank and Corporation Tax Law. A copy of the information return furnished under IRC § 1275(c)(2) must be furnished to the Franchise Tax Board by any issuer subject to tax by California, in the time and manner required by FTB. The treatment of loans with below-market interest rates will be determined in accordance with IRC § 7872. PL 101–179 of the Support for East European Democracy (SEED) Act of 1989, IRC § 307 does not apply for the purposes of the Bank and Corporation Tax Law. IRC § 1272, relating to current inclusion in income of original issue discount is modified as follows: (1) for income years starting on or after 1–1–87, and before the income year in which the debt obligation matures or is sold, exchanged or otherwise disposed, the amount included in gross income shall be the same as that included on the federal return; (2) the difference between the amount included in gross income on the federal return and the amount included in gross income under the Bank and Corporation Tax Law, with respect to obligations issued after 12–31–84, for income years starting before 1–1–87, shall be included in gross income in the income year in which the debt obligation matures or is sold, exchanged, or otherwise disposed. A taxpayer may elect, in the form and manner set by the Franchise Tax Board, to recognize the above difference ratably in each of the first four income years starting on or after 1–1–87, rather than at the time the debt obligation matures, is sold, exchanged, or otherwise disposed of, or to apply the provisions of IRC § 1272, relating to current inclusion in income of original issue discount, to obligations issued on or after the first day of the taxpayer's income years starting on or after 1–1–87.

Foreign currency transactions. California adopts IRC § 988 treatment of gain or loss on foreign currency transactions as ordinary income or loss, or as interest income or expense.[19] California does not adopt IRC § 988(a)(3) with respect to source of income.[20]

Passive foreign investment companies. California does not adopt Part VI of Subchapter P of Chapter 1 of Subtitle A of the Internal Revenue Code, relating to the treatment of certain foreign investment companies.[21]

¶ 1083 **State Government Contracts**

The profit from a contract with a state or a political subdivision of the state is to be included in gross income. If warrants are issued by a city, town, or other political subdivision and are accepted by the contractor in payment of public work done, the fair market value of the warrants is taxable. Then, in converting the warrants into cash, if the contractor does not receive and cannot recover the full value of the warrants, it can deduct any loss sustained from its gross income for the year in which the warrants were converted. Like-

---

(19) § 24905.
(20) § 24905.

(21) § 24995.

wise, if it realizes more than the value of the warrants, it must include the excess in its gross income for the year in which the conversion takes place. There is no difference between federal and California provisions on such contracts.[22] Fed Reg applies to the interpretation of conforming California law.[23]

¶ 1084   **Gross Income From Farming Corporations**

Cash accounting method. A farming corporation using the cash receipts and disbursements method of accounting should include in its gross income for the income year:

(1) Cash and the value of merchandise or other property received during the year from the sale of livestock and produce which it has raised;

(2) Profits from the sale of any livestock or other items which were purchased;

(3) All amounts received from breeding fees, from rents of teams, machinery or land, and other incidental farm income;

(4) Any subsidy or conservation payments which must be considered as income;

(5) Patronage dividends and other noncash allocations received from cooperatives unless the corporation has elected to exclude the amounts from gross income;

(6) Gross income from all other sources. Fed Regs 1.61–4(a) and 1.61–5 are highly persuasive in the interpretation of conforming California Law.[24]

Accrual method of accounting. This type of farming corporation must use inventories to determine gross income. The items of gross income included are as follows:

(1) Sale price of all livestock and other products held for sale and sold during the year;

(2) Inventory value of livestock and products on hand and not sold at the end of the year;

(3) All miscellaneous items of income such as breeding fees, fees from the rent of teams and machinery or land or other incidental farm income;

(4) Any subsidy or conservation payments which must be considered as income;

(5) Patronage dividends and other non-cash allocations received from cooperatives, if the corporation has not made the election to exclude the non-cash allocations from gross income;

(6) Gross income from all other sources.

From the total of the items (1) through (6), the corporation deducts the inventory value of livestock and products on hand and not sold at the beginning of the year and the cost of any livestock or products purchased during the year. Fed Regs apply to interpretation of conforming California law.[25]

---

(22) § 24271.

(23) Fed Reg 1.61–3(b).

(24) § 24271.

(25) § 24271; Fed Regs 1.61–4(a); 1.61–5.

¶ 1085 **Commodity Credit Loans**

Any amounts received by a corporation as loans from the Commodity Credit Corporation can be considered to be income in the year received at the election of the taxpayer. The same treatment, once elected, must be used for all subsequent income years, unless with the approval of the Franchise Tax Board it is changed to a different method as authorized.[26]

¶ 1086 **Rents and Royalties**

For both state and federal purposes, gross income includes rentals received or accrued for the use of real or personal property.[27] Under Fed Reg 1.61–8(a), that applies to conforming state law, royalties may be received from books, stories, plays, copyrights, trademarks, formulas, patents, or from minerals, oil or timber. Gross income includes advance rentals which have to be included in income in the year received regardless of the period covered or the method of accounting used by the taxpayer.[28]

Lease cancellation. Under Fed Reg 1.61–8(b), amount received by a lessor from a lessee for cancelling a lease is considered gross income for the year in which it is received, because it is essentially a substitute for rental payments. Fed Regs are highly persuasive in the interpretation of conforming state law.[29]

Lessee's improvements. As a general rule, if a lessee places improvements on real property which, in effect, constitute in whole or in part a substitute for rent, the improvements are considered rental income to the lessor. However, if there is no agreement between the lessor and the lessee that such amounts are to be considered as rent, then the increase in the value of such property attributable to buildings erected or other improvements made by the lessee received by the lessor on the termination of the lease is not to be included (or exempt) in gross income. Fed Reg 1.61–8(i) applies to the interpretation of conforming state law.[30]

¶ 1087 **Patronage Dividends**

If a taxpayer receiving non-cash patronage allocations elects to exclude these items from gross income until redeemed or realized, then only the amount realized when redeemed is required to be included in gross income. If the allocation bears interest, the interest is also not includible in gross income until the allocations are redeemed or realized, unless the interest has been paid in cash at a prior date. If the corporation includes the allocations in its gross income for the first taxable year beginning after 12–31–56, in which it receives any amount of non-cash patronage allocations, it has, in effect, made the election to include the face amount of such allocations in gross income for that year and all subsequent years. On the other hand, if it receives non-cash patronage allocations in any income year beginning after

---

(26) § 24273.
(27) § 24271.
(28) Fed Reg 1.61–8(a).

(29) Fed Reg 1.61–8(b).
(30) § 24309; Fed Reg 1.61–8(i).

12–31–56, and omits including the amount in gross income, the corporation is deemed to have elected to exclude such allocations from gross income for that year and subsequent years. The amount of the patronage allocations which are excluded should be disclosed in the return or by a written statement filed with the return.

The election may be made regardless of the taxpayer's method of accounting. Once an election has been made, it may be changed only with the consent of the Franchise Tax Board by application for permission to change, filed within 90 days after the beginning of the income year to be covered by the return.

If the taxpayer elects to exclude non-cash patronage allocations from gross income until they are redeemed or realized, the statutory period for the assessment of any deficiency attributable to the amounts excluded will not expire before the expiration of four years from the date the corporation notifies the Franchise Tax Board that the deferred allocations have been redeemed or realized.

"Non-cash patronage allocations" for this purpose means amounts allocated by the cooperative on the basis of the business done with or for a patron other than cash or merchandise, which is evidenced by any document which discloses the dollar amount of such allocations in the form of capital stock, revolving fund certificates of indebtedness, retain certificates or letters of advice.[31]

¶ 1088   **Life Insurance Proceeds**

Amounts received under life insurance endowment or annuity contracts—either during the term or at the maturity or upon surrender of the contract (other than amounts paid by reason of the death of the insured)—equal to the amount of premiums paid, are excluded from income. If the life insurance contract was acquired for a valuable consideration, the actual value of the consideration and the amount of the premiums subsequently paid are to be excluded from gross income. If, however, the contract was acquired in a nontaxable exchange so that the basis carries over from the transferor, the proceeds are not taxable. This is also true in the case of a transfer to a corporation in which the insured is a shareholder or officer.[32] Interest element in periodic payments made by the insurer, after the death of the insured, is taxable income. California adopts the IRC § 7702 definition of "life insurance contract," and the IRC § 7702A provisions, relating to modified endowment contracts.[33] This includes the expanded IRC § 7702A definition of a modified endowment contract to include "last-to-die" or "last survivor" life insurance contracts. Before 1985, California specifically adopted provisions of IRC § 101(f) on exclusion of proceeds of flexible premium contracts. Proceeds of flexible premium contracts were excluded from gross income only if, under such contract, (1) sum of premiums paid did not

---

(31) § 24273.5; Reg 24273.5.   (33) § 23045; 24305.
(32) § 24302.

at any time exceed guideline premium limitation; and (2) any amount payable by reason of death of insured, determined without regard to any qualified additional benefit, was not at any time less than applicable percentage value of contract's cash value. In addition, by terms of contract, cash value could not at any time exceed net single premium with respect to amount payable by reason of death of insured.

¶ 1090   Income of Certain Foreign Aircraft and Ships

The income from the operation of aircraft or ships by a corporation organized under the laws of a foreign country is excluded from California and federal gross income and is therefore exempt from tax.

The exemption applies if:

(1) The aircraft are registered or the ships are documented under the laws of the foreign country;

(2) The foreign country gives an equivalent exemption to corporations organized in the U.S., by treaty or agreement with the U.S.; and

(3) The exemption for U.S. aircraft and ships operating in the foreign country applies also to taxes assessed at the local level.[34]

¶ 1091   Income From Discharge of Indebtedness

California adopts the provisions of IRC § 108. The state modifies its adoption as follows:

(1) IRC § 108(b)(2)(B), relating to the general business credit is modified by substituting "this part" (Bank and Corporation Tax Law) for "Section 38 (relating to the general business tax credit);"

(2) IRC § 108(b)(2)(E), relating to foreign tax credit carryovers does not apply; where more than one credit is allowable under California law, the credit must be reduced on a pro rata basis;

(3) IRC § 108(b)(3)(B), relating to credit carryover reduction is modified by substituting 11.1¢ for 33⅓¢;

(4) IRC § 108(g)(3)(B), relating to adjusted tax attributes is modified by substituting $9 for $3.[35]

Before 1991, California conformed to the provisions of IRC § 108, relating to income from discharge of indebtedness, but IRC § 108(b)(2)(B) and (E) relating to tax attributes for the general business credit and foreign tax credit carryovers did not apply in California.[35]

Under IRC § 108, gross income does not include any amount that would be includible in gross income by reason of total or partial discharge of taxpayer's indebtedness, if discharge occurs in a Title 11 case, when the taxpayer is insolvent, or the indebtedness discharged is qualified farm indebtedness. Insolvency and farm exclusions do not apply to discharge occurring in Title 11 case. Such exclusion is limited to amount of insolvency. The amount excluded under either a Title 11 case, or insolvency must be applied to reduce the debtor's tax attributes. The order of reduction is: (1) net

---

(34) § 24320–24321.   (35) IRC § 108; § 23051.5; 24307.

operating loss; (2) capital loss carryovers. Reductions are on a dollar-for-dollar base. Taxpayer can elect to apply any part of the reduction first against depreciable property not to exceed aggregate adjusted bases of depreciable property held by taxpayer as of start of tax year following taxable year of discharge. These exclusion rules apply at partner level, and in case of S corporations, at corporate level. In Title 11 proceedings, reductions, in cases of individuals, must be made by the estate. California also conforms to the following general rules for discharge, including discharges not in Title 11 cases or insolvency:

(1) insolvency exception;
(2) income not realized to extent of lost deductions;
(3) adjustments for unamortized premium or discount;
(4) acquisition of debt by related person;
(5) purchase money debt reduction treated as price reduction;
(6) indebtedness contributed to capital;
(7) recapture of gain on later sale of stock;
(8) stock for debt exception;
(9) REIT qualifications;
(10) indebtedness satisfied by corporation's stock.

California has also picked up the federal provision on student loans, and the 1986 TRA and 1988 TAMRA changes on the discharge of qualified farm indebtedness of solvent farmers.

¶ 1092 Recovery of Bad Debts

California adopts IRC § 111, relating to recovery of tax benefit items. IRC §§ 111(b) and 111(c), relating to credits and the treatment of credit carryovers apply to credits under the Bank and Corporation Tax Law. Before 1991, California conformed to IRC §§ 111(a)–(b)(1)(2) and 111(c); IRC §§ 111(b)(3) and 111(d) did not apply in California.[36]

Credits. If an amount is recovered in a taxable year because of a price adjustment, etc., and a credit was based on that amount in a prior taxable year, the recipient's tax will be increased by the amount of the credit attributable to the recovered amount to the extent the credit reduced the amount of tax. And, an increase in a carryover which has not expired before the beginning of the taxable year in which the recovery or adjustment takes place will be treated as reducing the tax.

IMPORTANT   The amount of the exclusion for federal and California purposes will probably not be the same, because the tax benefit for federal purposes might depend on the relationship of net operating loss carry-backs and carry-overs or capital loss carry-overs, which are not applicable for Cali-

---

(36) § 24310.

fornia purposes, and numerous other differences between California and federal gross income and deductions.[36]

> *Note:* Prior to 1-1-92, California had no counterpart to IRC § 118 which provides that the gross income of a corporation does not include any contribution to the capital of the corporation. Effective 1-1-92, California adopted Rev & TC § 24325 which provides that IRC § 118 will be followed by California for contributions to capital after that date. The Franchise Tax Board had previously issued LR 362 to state that gratuitously forgiving a debt of a subsidiary corporation by the parent was a nontaxable contribution to the capital of the subsidiary.[37]

¶ 1093 Capital Losses

California adopts IRC § 1211. Under IRC § 1211(a) capital losses are netted against capital gains. If the capital losses are in excess of capital gain, no deduction is allowable. The corporation is allowed to carry back and over the unused capital loss.[38]

Corporate capital losses are allowed only as offsets against capital gains income. California also adopts IRC § 1212 that allows capital losses that exceed capital gains income to be carried forward five years. The state modifies this adoption of IRC § 1212, by providing that IRC § 1212(a)(1)(A) relating to capital loss carrybacks does not apply and that IRC § 1212(a)(3), relating to special rules on carrybacks does not apply. IRC § 1212(b)—1212(c), relating to taxpayers other than corporations also do not apply. Before 1990, IRC § 1211 and IRC § 1212 did not apply in California.[39]

¶ 1094 Securities Acquisition Loan

For income years starting on or after 1-1-90 and before 1-1-95, California has adopted IRC § 133, relating to interest on certain loans used to acquire employer securities. Under that federal section, gross income does not include 50% of the interest received by:

> (1) a bank;
> (2) an insurance company covered by IRC §§ 801–846;
> (3) a corporation actively engaged in the business of loaning money, or
> (4) a regulated investment company, as defined in IRC § 851, with respect to a securities acquisition loan.[40]

TAMRA changes eliminated the requirement that the commitment period on the loans could not exceed seven years. Federal law provides that only interest accrued during the seven-year period starting on the date of the loan can qualify for the 50% exclusion. Except in the case of immediate allocation loans and back-to-back loans, the term of the loan can exceed seven years, and 50% of the interest accrued on the original loan is excludible for the loan's entire term. The excludible period for a loan used to refinance the original loan is limited to the term of the original loan, or seven years, whichever is greater. IRC § 133 exclusion for interest earned on loans

---

(37) IRC § 118; § 24325.
(38) IRC § 1211(a).

(39) § 24990.5.
(40) § 24306.

to employee stock ownership plans will be denied unless the plan owns more than 50% of each class of stock, or more than 50% of the total value of all outstanding stock of the corporation.[40]

¶ 1095   Boundary Waters Canoe Act Payments

Qualified resort operators and commercial outfitters can exclude from gross income equity grants paid by the U.S. Forest Service as a result of restricting motorized traffic in the Boundary Waters Canoe Area. California does not follow federal provisions on pre-1985 payments or refund claims.[1]

¶ 1096   Empty Beverage Containers

Gross income does not include any amount received for empty beverage containers by a consumer from a recycling center or location as the recycling value.[2]

¶ 1097   Annuity Contracts Not Held By Natural Persons

California conforms to the IRC § 72(u) treatment of annuity contracts not held by natural persons. Under this federal provision, if any annuity contract is held by a person who is not a natural person, that contract will not be treated as an annuity contract, and the income on the contract for any taxable year of the policyholder is treated as ordinary income received or accrued during that year. Income on the contract is the excess of (1) the sum of the net surrender value as of the close of the taxable year plus all prior year distributions received during the taxable year, reduced by (2) the sum of the amount of net premiums under the contract for the taxable and prior years, and amounts includible in gross income for prior taxable years. Fair market value may be substituted for net surrender value to prevent avoidance. The above rules do not apply to annuity contracts that are:

(1) acquired by estate of decedent on account of decedent's death;
(2) held under IRC §§ 401(a) and 403(a) plans, an IRC § 403(b) program, and an individual retirement plan;
(3) qualified funding assets of IRC § 130 personal liability injury assignments;
(4) purchased by an employer on termination of IRC §§ 401(a) or 403(a) plan, and held by employer until employee's separation; or
(5) immediate annuities.[3]

¶ 1098   Domestic Building and Loan Association

Gross income of a domestic building and loan association, as defined in IRC § 7701(a)(19), does not include any amount of money or other property received from the Federal Savings and Loan Insurance Corporation pursuant to the National Housing Act, § 406(f)(1) USC, § 1729(f), regardless of whether any note or other instrument is issued in exchange therefor. No reduction in basis of assets of a domestic building and loan association will

---

(1) § 24308.
(2) § 24315.

(3) IRC § 72(u); 24272.2.

be made on account of money or other property received. Rev & TC § 24425, relating to amounts allocable to class or classes of income not included in measure of tax, shall not deny any deductions by reason of deductions being allocable to amounts excluded from gross income under this rule. This exclusion rule will not apply to any amounts received after 12–31–88, in income years ending after that date, unless payments are made by the FSLIC pursuant to an acquisition or merger that occurred on or before 12–31–88.[4]

¶ 1099 **Local Water Agency Rebates**

Any amount received as a rebate from a local water agency or supplier for any expenses paid or incurred for the purchase or installation of each water conservation water closet that meets the performance standards of the American National Standards Institute Standard A112.192, and uses no more than six gallons per flush will be treated as a refund or price adjustment of amounts payable to that water agency or supplier.[5]

¶ 1100 **Contribution to the Capital of the Taxpayer**

California conforms to IRC § 118(b) that provides that contributions to the capital of a taxpayer does not include any contribution in aid of construction or any other contribution as a customer or potential customer.[6]

¶ 1101 **Energy Subsidies Paid By Public Utilities**

California has adopted IRC § 136 which provides an exclusion from taxable income for energy subsidies paid by a public utilities to its customers for the purchase or installation of any energy conservation devise. The California exclusion is available only for amounts received on or after January 1, 1993, and before January 1, 1995, without regard to income year. The exclusion applies only to amounts received with respect to a dwelling unit.[7]

¶ 1102 **Cost-Share Payments Received By Forest Landowners**

For years beginning on or after 1–1–94, gross income does not include cost-share payments received by forest landowners from the Department of Forestry and Fire Protection pursuant to the California Forest Improvement Act, or from the United States Department of Agriculture, Forest Service, under the Forest Stewardship Program and the Stewardship Incentives Program, pursuant to the Cooperative Forestry Assistance Act. Such excluded amounts shall not be considered in determining the basis of property acquired or improved, or in computing any allowable deduction to which the taxpayer is entitled.[8]

---

(4) § 24322.
(5) § 24323.
(6) § 23051.5.

(7) § 24326.
(8) § 24308.5, as added by Stats. 1994, c. 22, § 3.

CORPORATE ORGANIZATIONS AND REORGANIZATIONS

¶ 1103   **Corporate Organization**

California adopts federal IRC provisions. California has adopted the provisions of Subchapter C of Chapter 1 of Subtitle A of the Internal Revenue Code, relating to corporate distributions and adjustments (IRC §§ 301—385), subject to certain modifications on 20% corporate shareholders, termination of interests, source of gain, recognition of gain or loss in liquidation, items of distributor or transferor corporation, and excess credit limits.[1]

CAUTION   While many of the corporate organizations and reorganizations are identified as "tax-free" due to various provisions in both the Internal Revenue Code, and the California Bank and Corportion Tax Law, the transaction may still attract either sales or use tax, or a reappraisal of property for property tax purposes. The tax advisor must consider all taxes prior to informing a client that the transaction is free of tax, because most taxpayers consider their tax advisor to advise them of "taxes," not just income or franchise tax.

Transfer of property to controlled corporation. No gain or loss is recognized in the transfer of property to a corporation by one or more "persons," solely in exchange for stock in the corporation, if immediately after the exchange the persons are in control of the corporation. The phrase, "one or more persons" includes individuals, trusts, estates, partnerships, associations, companies or corporations. For purposes of IRC § 351, stock issued for (1) services; (2) indebtedness of the transferee corporation not evidenced by security; or (3) interest on the indebtedness of the transferee corporation that accrued on or after the start of the transferor's holding period for debt can't be considered as issued in return for property. IRC § 351 doesn't apply to the transfer of a property of debtor under a plan while the debtor is under the jurisdiction of a court in a Title 11 or similar case under IRC § 368 to the extent the stock received in exchange is used to satisfy the indebtedness of such debtor.[2] With respect to transfers on or after 6–21–88, if property is transferred to a controlled corporation in an exchange with respect to which gain or loss is not recognized in whole or part to the transferor under IRC § 351, and the exchange is not in pursuance to a plan of reorganization, IRC § 311 (taxability of corporation on distribution) shall apply to any transfer in exchange by the controlled corporation, as if the transfer were a distribution to which IRC §§ 301–307 (effects on recipients) applied.[3]

To be in control. To be in control the person or persons must own at least 80% of the stock entitled to vote and at least 80% of the total number of shares of all other classes of stock of the corporation.

When property is transferred to a corporation by two or more persons in exchange for stock or securities, as indicated above, there is no requirement

---

(1) §§ 24451–24481.
(2) IRC § 351; 368; § 24451.

(3) IRC § 301–307; 351; § 24451; 24452; 24453; 24456.

that the stock received by each be substantially in proportion to his or her interest in the property immediately prior to the transfer to the corporation. If the stock received is in disproportion to the interest of the person receiving the stock, the transaction may be subject to investigation as to whether or not gifts between the parties might be involved.

In addition to transfers at the time of the formation of the corporation, the above provisions apply for transfers made to existing corporations as well, as long as the 80% control test is satisfied.[4]

"Boot." If, in addition to stock or securities, the transferor stockholder receives other property or money (or "boot"), gain is recognized but not a loss. The gain is recognized to the extent not in excess of the cash and the fair market value of the other property received.

Assumption of liability. Assumption of liability is treated as money received if the purpose was not a bona fide business purpose or tax avoidance. If the liabilities assumed plus the liabilities to which property is subject exceed the total adjusted basis of the property transferred, the excess is a gain from the sale or exchange of property that is a capital or noncapital asset. This rule doesn't apply to an exchange pursuant to a plan of reorganization under Title 11 or a similar case where no former shareholder of the transferor corporation receives any consideration for stock.[5]

Basis on transfer to controlled corporation. In the situation above, when one or more persons transfer property to a corporation in exchange for stock of the corporation, the basis to these persons of the stock acquired is the same as the basis of the property which they transferred. If, for any reason, gain is recognized, the basis would be increased to the extent of that gain. The basis of the property acquired by the corporation, is the same as it was in the hands of the stockholders, increased in the amount of any gain recognized to the stockholders on the transfer.

Taxable transfers. When a stockholder transfers property to a corporation in exchange for its stock in a situation where it is a taxable event to the stockholder because he does not have 80% control, the basis of the property to the corporation receiving it is the fair market value of the stock issued in the exchange, determined as of the date of the exchange. If the corporation's stock does not have a market value at the time of the exchange, it would be considered that its value was the same as the fair market value of the property transferred. To the transferring shareholder, the basis of the stock he receives would be the fair market value of the property given up, adjusted for the gain or loss on the transfer.

If property other than money is transferred to a corporation as contribution to capital by a non-stockholder, the basis of the property in the hands of the corporation would be zero. If money is transferred to a corporation as a contribution to capital by a non-shareholder, the basis of any property

---

(4) IRC § 368(c).

(5) IRC § 356(c).

acquired with the money during the 12-month period from the date of the contribution is to be reduced by the amount of the contribution. If the money received is not applied to the purchase of enough property during the year, the excess is to be used to reduce the basis of any other property held by the corporation.[6]

Sale to controlled corporation.   If a person owning at least 80% of the outstanding stock of a corporation sells depreciable property to the corporation, the gain is treated as ordinary income under IRC § 1239. The 80% ownership test follows the constructive ownership rules of IRC § 318 without regard to the 50% limit. The section also applies to sales or exchanges between two commonly controlled corporations.

Note: The Bank and Corporation Tax Law does not have provisions similar to IRC § 1239.

¶ 1104   Corporate Reorganizations

IRC § 368,[7] adopted by California deals with problems involving the exclusion of gain or loss on transfers in reorganizations between corporations, and the basis of stock or property acquired by the parties to the reorganizations. These provisions are discussed below. Rev & TC § 23251 provides that the term "reorganization" for purposes of determining which corporation files the franchise tax returns and reports the income earned during periods in which reorganizations occur, subsidiaries are formed, dissolved, etc., has the same meaning as the term is defined in IRC § 368.[8]

Essential elements.   Essentially, a reorganization is a change in the corporate structure or ownership; it occurs when one corporation, either a newly formed corporation or one in existence, acquires stock or property belonging to one or more other corporations or the stockholders in exchange for stock. If the Code requirements are met, the exchange is "tax free" and the gain or loss on the exchange is postponed until the stock, securities or property received in the exchange are disposed of. The reorganization definitions also include situations in which there is a change in the form of the corporate existence without the actual exchange of property.

Note: Definitions pertinent to reorganizations:

Party to a reorganization. This term includes a corporation resulting from a reorganization and both corporations in a transaction qualifying as a reorganization where one corporation acquires stock or properties of another corporation. An acquiring corporation remains a party to a reorganization, even if it transfers all or part of the stock or assets it acquired to a controlled subsidiary.[7]

Control. The term control means the ownership of stock having at least 80% of the total combined voting power of all classes of stock entitled to vote, and at least 80% of the total number of shares of all other classes of stock of the corporation.[8]

Plan of reorganization. Fed Reg 1.368–2(g) indicates that the term "plan of reorganization" refers to a consummated transaction specifically defined as a reorganization

---

(6) IRC § 362(c); § 24451.
(7) IRC 368, § 24451.

(8) § 17024.5; 23051.5; 23251.

under IRC § 368(a). It is not used in broadening the definition of reorganization but is to be taken to limit the non-recognition of gain or loss to the exchanges or distributions which are directly a part of the transaction specifically described as a reorganization in IRC § 368(a). The transaction, or series of transactions, embraced in the plan must not only come within specific language of IRC § 368(a), but readjustments involved in exchanges or distributions effected in consummation of plan must be undertaken for reasons germane to the continuance of business of a corporation party to the reorganization. This federal Reg provision is highly persuasive in the interpretation of conforming state law.

Transfers to foreign corporations. California has conformed to the changes in IRC § 367(a) that except from the general rule that transfers by a U.S. person to a foreign corporation will not be considered to be transfers to a corporation in determining the extent of gain recognized on (1) transfers of stock or securities of a foreign corporation that is party to an exchange or reorganization; and (2) transfers of certain property used in the active conduct of a trade or business. California also conforms to the rule that transfers of interest in a partnership to a foreign corporation in an exchange will be considered as a transfer of the U.S. person's pro rata share of the assets of the partnership. California also adopts the IRC § 367(d) rules on transfers of intangible property and the 1986 TRA provisions on IRC § 332 liquidations and IRC § 355 distributions.[9]

Requirements for tax-free reorganization. The reorganization must be in accordance with a plan adopted in advance by the participating corporations and the various exchanges of stock, securities or properties must take place in accordance with the plan. Other requirements include the following:

(1) *Valid business purpose.* Saving in taxes can be a contributing factor in adopting a reorganization plan, but the reorganization must serve a valid business purpose in addition.

(2) *Continuity of business enterprise.* The regulations state that a reorganization requires "a continuity of business enterprise under modified corporate form." Changes in the form or manner of conducting a business enterprise would satisfy the continuity-of-business-enterprise requirements, but if a substantial segment of a business were discontinued and the assets involved in that segment disposed of, it would appear to be a liquidation rather than a reorganization.

(3) *Continuity of ownership interest.* The regulations state that a continuity of interest on the part of those persons who, directly or indirectly, were the owners of the enterprise prior to the reorganization is required. The regulations state that there is not a reorganization if the holders of the stock and securities of the old corporation are merely the holders of short-term notes in the new corporation. An exception to the continuity of interest requirement is the "D" type of reorganization described below.

(4) *Same business classification.* The activity pursued after the reorganization must be under the same classification (manufacturing, retailing, etc.) as that pursued before the reorganization.

Property. The term "property" includes money except when the phrase, "property other than money" is used. It also includes securities and

----

(9) IRC § 367; § 24451.

stock other than the stock in the corporation making the distribution (or the rights to acquire such stock).

Securities. The term security means an instrument representing an unconditional obligation of the distributing corporation (other than an open account indebtedness) to pay a certain sum of money.

Not reorganizations. A transfer of assets and liabilities to a corporation which has been granted an exemption from tax under the Bank and Corporation Tax Law or for federal purposes cannot be a reorganization. A transfer of assets and liabilities to a foreign corporation which is not qualified to do business in California would also not qualify as a reorganization.

Nontaxable reorganizations described in the law[10] are as follows:

Statutory merger or consolidation. A statutory merger or consolidation is effective when made under local law, including the laws of the United States or a state or territory or the District of Columbia.

The corporation acquiring the assets may transfer some or all of them to a controlled subsidiary. A controlled corporation can use its parent's stock to acquire substantially all the properties of another corporation which merges into the subsidiary, as long as the exchange would have been a Type A reorganization if the merger had been with the parent and none of the subsidiary stock is used in the transaction.

Any money or property received will be "boot" and taxed accordingly, but boot would not prevent the reorganization from qualifying as an A-type reorganization.

Note: "Merger" is different from "consolidation." If Corporation A merges with Corporation B, and Corporation B is the continuing corporation, it is called a merger. If Corporation A merges with Corporation B to form a new corporation, C, it is called a consolidation. If a parent Corporation A merges into a subsidiary corporation, with the subsidiary corporation then continuing, it is called a down-stream merger.

Stock for stock. The acquisition by one corporation of stock of another corporation is a reorganization if the acquiring corporation transfers only its own voting stock or the voting stock of a corporation that controls it, and the acquiring corporation has control of the other corporation immediately after the acquisition (80%). It does not make any difference what percentage of the voting stock of the acquiring corporation or its parent is given in the exchange.

The effect of the transaction is that the acquiring corporation obtains a new 80%-controlled subsidiary in exchange for a portion of its stock or the stock of its parent corporation. Following the acquisition, the acquiring corporation can continue the operations of its new subsidiary or liquidate it. If the acquired corporation is liquidated under the plan of reorganization, any distribution to its creditors is treated as pursuant to that plan. A Type B

---

(10) IRC § 368; § 24551.

reorganization followed by the liquidation of the acquired subsidiary accomplishes the same result as a statutory merger or A-type reorganization.

The transaction would not be disqualified as a Type B reorganization if all or part of the stock acquired is transferred to a corporation controlled by the acquiring corporation.

It is possible for an acquiring corporation to purchase stock of the to-be-acquired corporation for cash prior to adopting the plan of reorganization. As long as the acquiring corporation at the end of the plan has 80% control, the reorganization is still non-taxable.

Stock for assets. In this type of reorganization, the acquiring corporation, in exchange solely for all or part of its voting stock (or in exchange solely for all or part of its parent's voting stock) acquires "substantially all" the properties of another corporation.

An exchange is still considered to be solely for voting stock if the acquiring corporation assumes liabilities of the other corporation or acquires its properties subject to a liability. As in a B reorganization, the acquiring corporation may transfer a small amount of cash to round off fractional shares without disqualifying the reorganization.

Note: The phrase "substantially all" of the properties is subject to interpretation, depending on the facts and circumstances. The Internal Revenue Service considers "substantially all" to be at least 90% of the fair market value of the net assets and at least 70% of the fair market value of the gross assets of the transferor corporation. The Franchise Tax Board follow these guidelines.

As stated above, the acquisition of property must be made solely in exchange for the acquiring corporation or its parent's voting stock in order to qualify as a Type C reorganization. The law states, however, that if the acquiring corporation receives at least 80% of the value of all of the property of the transferor corporation in exchange solely for the voting stock, other properties of the transferor corporation may be acquired for money or other consideration without destroying the nontaxable nature of the transaction.

The reorganization will not be disqualified because the acquiring corporation transfers some or all of the assets to its controlled subsidiary.

If the transaction qualifies as an acquisition of assets for stock (a C type reorganization) and also a transfer to a controlled corporation (a D type reorganization), the reorganization is treated as a type D reorganization.[11]

This type of reorganization will not meet requirements for nontaxability unless the acquired corporation distributes the stock, securities and other properties it receives, as well as its other properties, in pursuance of the plan of reorganization.

Transfer of assets to another corporation for controlling stock. The D reorganization requirements are that a corporation transfers all or a part of

---

(11) IRC § 368(b); § 24451.

its assets to another corporation and immediately after the transfer the transferor or one or more of its shareholders are in control of the corporation to which the assets are transferred. An additional necessary step in this type of reorganization is that the stock and securities of the transferee corporation have to be distributed to the shareholders of the transferor corporation in accordance with the plan of reorganization.

If the transferor corporation transfers all of its assets to an existing corporation in exchange for at least 80% of the voting stock, it is in effect a merger, particularly if the transferor corporation then liquidates. If, however, the transferor corporation transfers only part of its assets to a new corporation and then distributes the stock in the new corporation it received to its shareholders, the effect is that the shareholders of the transferor corporation as a result of the reorganization, now own the controlling interest in two corporations.

"Control" in non-divisive D reorganization means 50% of the total combined voting power of all classes of voting stock, or at least 50% of the total value of shares of all classes of stock in the corporation. California adopted changes made in IRC § 368(c) by 1984 federal Tax Reform Act. 80% requirement now applies only to divisive D reorganizations (see below). Both federal and California law apply to transfers made pursuant to plans adopted after 7–18–84.[12]

Recapitalization. This form of reorganization is ordinarily a change in the capital structure. Essentially, it is a readjustment of a corporation's stocks or bonds as to the amount, the income, or the priority. It might be a situation where a corporation pays off holders of its bonds by issuing new preferred stock or calls in outstanding preferred stock in exchange for common stock or other similar types of changes in the capital structure.

Change in identity, form, etc. This type of reorganization includes changes in form rather than substance. In other words, a corporation originally chartered in one state reincorporates in a different state, or it might be merely a filing to change the official name of the corporation. Definition is limited to change in identity, form, or place of organization of one operating corporation. The merger of a subsidiary corporation into its parent has been classified as an F reorganization, including the merger of separate corporations into one corporation. The advantage of having a reorganization classified as an F reorganization instead of, for example, an A or a B reorganization, is that for federal purposes there is more flexibility in carrying back net operating losses against pre-reorganization income. Rev Rul 75–561 provides requirements which, when met, will indicate that the combination of two or more corporations qualifies as an F reorganization.

Insolvency type reorganizations. California's treatment conforms to federal. Transfers of assets in Bankruptcy Act cases (Title 11, US Code),

---

(12) IRC § 368(c); § 24451.

receiverships, foreclosures and similar cases under federal and state law may qualify as reorganizations. To qualify, there must be a transfer pursuant to a court-approved reorganization plan of substantially all the assets of the debtor corporation to an acquiring corporation. Stock or securities of the acquiring corporation must be distributed in a transaction that qualifies under the provisions for nonrecognition of gain or loss on exchanges of stock and securities between corporate parties to the reorganization, and distribution of stock and securities of a controlled corporation. Owners of the debtor corporation must maintain substantial proprietary interest in the reorganized business. For acquisitions before 1–1–89, and income years starting before 1–1–89, in the case of a financial institution to which IRC § 593, relating to reserve for losses on loans, applies, the term "Title 11 or similar case" means only a case in which the Federal Home Loan Bank Board, Federal Savings and Loan Insurance Corporation, or equivalent state authority, if neither of those federal organizations has authority, which will be treated as a court in such case, certifies that a transaction otherwise meeting the requirements of Rev & TC § 24562(a)(7), relating to a qualifying transfer by a corporation of part or all of its assets to another corporation in a Title 11 case, in which the transferor corporation is a financial institution to which IRC § 593 applies, will not be disqualified as a reorganization if no stock or securities of the corporation to which the assets are transferred are received or distributed. This certification will be made only if the following conditions are met: (1) Rev & TC § 24531(b)(1)(A)—(B) requirements on substantial transfer of all assets, and distribution of stock, securities and other properties are met; (2) substantially all the liabilities of the transferor immediately before the transfer become liabilities of transferee after the transfer; (3) grounds set forth in Title 12, IRC § 1464(d)(6)(a)(i)—(iii) exist with respect to transferor or will exist in near future in absence of action by the appropriate authorities listed above.[13]

Recognition of gain or loss. The stockholders and security holders in a party to a reorganization can make exchanges without gain or loss recognition, if the exchange is solely for stock or securities in the same corporation or in another corporation which is a party to the reorganization. This rule doesn't apply to the extent that any stock, securities or other property received is attributable to interest that accrued on securities on or after the start of the holder's holding period.

> Note: No gain or loss is recognized to a corporation which exchanges property solely for stock or securities in another party to the same reorganization. If it receives anything else it is taxable as "boot," unless it redistributes the boot to the corporate shareholders as part of the reorganization plan.

When boot is received in the reorganization, together with stock and securities which can be received without recognition of gain or loss, gain is recognized to the extent of the boot but no loss is allowed. A corporation

---

(13) IRC § 368(d); § 24451.

¶ 1104

receiving boot does not have to recognize gain if the boot is distributed pursuant to the plan of reorganization to the shareholders.

The giver of boot recognizes gain or loss on his transfer to the extent of the difference between its adjusted basis and the fair market value at the time of the exchange.

Holders of securities who transfer them in a reorganization and receive securities greater in principal amount than the securities given up receive boot to the extent of the fair market value of the securities received in excess of the securities given up. If no securities are surrendered, the fair market value of the principal amount of the securities received is treated as boot.

If a stockholder in a nontaxable reorganization receives boot which is taxable, it may be treated as a dividend. The stockholder recognizes as a dividend the proportionate share of the earnings and profits accumulated after 2–28–13 as a dividend, and the remainder of the recognized gain is a gain from the exchange of this property.[14]

Basis to stockholder.   The basis of stock or securities received in a non-taxable exchange in a reorganization by a distributee stockholder is the same as the basis of the stock or securities exchanged decreased by (1) the money received, (2) the fair market value of any other property, and, (3) any loss that was recognized. The basis of the stock or securities is increased by any gain recognized on the exchange and the amount that was treated as a dividend. Also, the basis of any other property received is its fair market value on the date of exchange.

When a distributee receives several kinds of stock or securities, the basis must be allocated among the properties received in proportion to their relative fair market values.[15]

EXAMPLE 1   A, an individual, owns stock in Corporation X with an adjusted basis of $1,000. In a transaction qualifying under Rev & TC §§ 17435 to 17439, inclusive, (so far as the sections relate to Rev & TC § 17432) he exchanged this stock for 20 shares of stock of Corporation Y worth $1,200 and securities of Corporation Y worth $400. A realizes a gain of $600 of which $400 is recognized. The adjusted basis in A's hands of each share of the stock of Corporation Y is $50 determined by allocating the basis of the stock of Corporation X ratably to the stock of Corporation Y received in the exchange. The securities of Corporation Y have a basis in A's hands of $400.

EXAMPLE 2   B, an individual, owns a security in the principal amount of $10,000 with a basis of $5,000. In a transaction to which Rev & TC § 17432 is applicable, he exchanges this security for four securities in the principal amount of $750 each, worth $800 each, four securities in the principal amount of $750 each, worth $600 each, class A common stock worth $1,000, and Class B common stock worth $400. B realizes a gain of $2,000, none of which is recognized. The basis of his original security, $5,000, will be allocated 32/70ths to the four securities worth $800, 24/70ths to the four securities

---

(14) IRC § 354; 356; § 24451.   (15) IRC § 358; § 17321; 24451.

worth $600, 10/70ths to the class A common stock and 4/70ths to the class B common stock.

Basis to corporations. The basis of property acquired by a corporation in a tax-free reorganization is the same as the transferor's basis increased by any gain recognized to the transferor on the transfer.

TAX TIP

If the property acquired is stock or securities by a party to the reorganization, the basis of the stock or securities is the same as the basis of the property exchanged, decreased by (1) the fair market value of any other property received, (2) the amount of money received, (3) the amount of loss which was recognized and increased by (1) the amount which was treated as a dividend, and (2) the amount of the gain which was recognized on the exchange.

If the corporation exchanges its stock or securities (or its parent's stock or securities) as all or part of the consideration for the transfer and acquires stock or securities, they retain the basis they had in the hands of the transferor.[16]

Liabilities assumed. The assumption of liabilities of the transferor by the transferee or taking property subject to the transferor's liability is not treated as giving money or other property and does not ordinarily prevent the exchange from being tax free unless the purpose was to avoid taxes or the assumption had no valid business purpose. However, the assumption of liability decreases the transferor's basis for property received in the exchange.

In D-type reorganization, if the liabilities assumed (including liabilities against the property) exceed the adjusted basis of the property transferred, the excess is considered either a capital or ordinary gain, as the case may be.[17]

Records and information must be filed.

Corporations. The plan of reorganization has to be adopted by each of the parties to the reorganization, and the adoption must be shown on the official records of the corporations involved. Each corporation party to the reorganization should file with its return for the taxable year within which the reorganization takes place a statement of the following information:

(1) Copy of the plan of reorganization with a statement executed under the penalties of perjury showing in full the purposes of the plan and in detail all transactions incident to the plan.

(2) Complete statement of the cost or other basis of all property including stock and securities transferred as part of the plan.

(3) A statement of the amount of stock or securities and other property or money received from the exchange including a statement or any distributions made of these assets. Fair market value of the stock or securities or other property on the date of the exchange is to be included.

---

(16) IRC § 362; § 24451.   (17) IRC § 357; § 24451.

(4) A statement of the amount of any liabilities assumed in the exchange or the amount of any liabilities to which any of the properties acquired is subject [Fed Reg 1.368–3.]

Individuals. Every individual who receives stock or securities and other property or money in a tax-free exchange is to include in his tax return for the year in which the exchange takes place, a complete statement of the facts pertinent to the non-recognition of gain or loss, including:

(1) A statement of the cost or other basis of the stock or securities transferred, and

(2) A statement of the amount of stock or securities and other property or money received in the exchange including any liabilities involved. The amount of each kind of stock or securities or other property received is to be listed, showing the fair market value of each item at the date of the exchange. [Federal Reg 1.368–3.]

Divisive reorganizations. These reorganizations divide one corporation into two or more corporations, with the shares of each in the hands of the original shareholders of the one corporation.

OBSERVATION
In a *"split-up,"* a corporation is split up into two or more separate corporations. The stock of the new corporations is distributed to the shareholders of the old corporation, who surrender the stock of the old corporation. *In "split-off,"* a corporation transfers part of its assets to a new corporation in exchange for the stock of the new corporation. It then immediately distributes that stock to its shareholders who surrender part of their stock in the original corporation. A split-off may occur through a distribution by a parent of an existing subsidiary company stock to the shareholders who also surrender part of their stock in the parent corporation. *In a "spin-off,"* the transaction is the same as a split-off except that the shares of the new controlled corporation or of the existing controlled subsidiary are distributed to the shareholders, but they do not surrender any of their original stock.

Gain or loss recognition. A shareholder or security holder who receives only stock or securities of a controlled corporation has no recognized gain or loss if:

(1) The stock or securities received from the distributing corporation is stock or securities of a corporation that the distributing corporation controls immediately before the distribution;

(2) Each corporation is engaged in a trade or business that has been actively conducted for at least five years. An exception is made in the case of a parent if it is solely a holding company;

(3) The distributing corporation distributes all of the stock or securities in the controlled corporation held by it immediately before the distribution, or an amount of stock in the controlled corporation which constitutes control; and

(4) The reorganization is not principally a device to distribute earnings or profits of the distributing corporation or the controlled corporation.

Control.   Control means the ownership of stock with at least 80% of the total voting power, and at least 80% of the total number of shares of all other classes of stock of the corporation.

As long as the above requirements are met, the transaction is a tax-free reorganization and gain or loss is not recognized even if:

(1) The distribution is or is not pro rata to all of the shareholders of the distributing corporation.

(2) The shareholder does or does not surrender stock in the distributing corporation.

(3) The distribution is or is not pursuant to a plan of reorganization.

Only the principal amount of the securities surrendered for the securities received in the controlled corporation can be tax free. If securities in any greater amount are received, the fair market value of the excess is treated as boot. If no securities are surrendered, the fair market value of the securities received is treated as boot. Nonrecognition of gain or loss doesn't apply to extent any stock, securities or other property received is attributable to interest that has accrued on securities after start of holder's holding period.

The stock of a controlled corporation acquired by the distributing corporation in any transaction which occurs within five years of the distribution of the stock, and in which gain or loss was recognized, won't be treated as stock of a controlled corporation, but as other property.[18]

Active business.   Immediately after the distribution, the distributing corporation and the controlled corporation (or corporations) must be engaged in a trade or business that has been actively conducted for at least five years at the date of the distribution. If, however, immediately before the distribution the distributing corporation was a holding company and immediately after the distribution the controlled corporations are engaged in a trade or business that had been actively conducted for at least five years at the date of the distribution, the reorganization is nontaxable.

Each corporation has to be engaged in a separate trade or business immediately after the trade or distribution, but the distributing corporation can meet this requirement by dividing a single business formerly operated by it and then transferring part of it to the controlled corporation.[18] California has adopted IRC § 355(b)(2)(D) relating to the definition of active trade or business that requires that control of the corporation conducting an active trade or business at time of acquisition was not acquired by any distributee corporation directly, or through one or more corporations, whether the distributing corporation or otherwise, within the five-year period ending on the date of distribution, and was not acquired by the distributing corporation directly or through one or more corporations during that period, or was so acquired by any such corporation within the period, but only, in each case, by reason of a transaction in which gain or loss was not recognized in whole or in part, or only by reason of such transactions combined with acquisitions

---

(18) IRC § 355; § 24451.

before the start of such period. Distributee corporations that are members of a controlled group, under IRC § 368, will be treated as one distributee corporation.[19]

Bases in divisive reorganizations:

(1) When no stock is surrendered but stock of a controlled corporation is received (spin-off) the basis of the old and the new stock is found by allocating the basis of the original stock.

(2) When stock is surrendered in exchange for stock of a controlled corporation, the general basis rules apply; that is, the basis of the stock or securities received is the same as the basis of the stock or securities given up. If the stockholder receives more than one class of stock of the controlled corporation, the basis must be allocated among the classes of stock he now holds.

Transfers ordered by government agencies. When agencies or bureaus of the government require corporations to distribute or exchange a portion of their holdings, gain or loss on the transaction is generally not recognized. Basis of the property is adjusted accordingly. These situations include the following:

(1) *Securities and Exchange Commissions.* California conforms to IRC § 1081. Exchanges and distributions ordered by the Securities and Exchange Commission in accordance with the authority contained in the Public Utilities Holding Company Act of 1935 are nontaxable. Stock or securities received by a taxpayer in this type of exchange will have a basis the same as that of the stock or securities surrendered by the taxpayer.[20]

(2) *Federal Communications Commission.* Sales or exchanges of radio broadcasting properties (including stock of a corporation) certified by the Federal Communications Commission to bring about a change in policy may be treated as an involuntary conversion. Any gain which would be recognized within the application of the involuntary conversion rules may be deferred if the taxpayer elects to reduce the basis of its depreciable property.[21]

(3) *Railroad reorganizations.* No gain or loss is recognized to a shareholder on an exchange of stock or securities in a reorganization plan approved by the Interstate Commerce Commission for a railroad corporation.[22]

---

(19) IRC § 355; 368; § 24451.
(20) § 18031; 23051.5.

(21) § 18031; 24971.
(22) IRC § 354; § 24451.

DIVIDENDS AND OTHER CORPORATE DISTRIBUTIONS

¶ 1115 **Dividends Out of Earnings and Profits**

A dividend means any distribution of property made by a corporation to its shareholders out of earnings and profits accumulated after 2–28–13, or out of earnings and profits of the income year. The computation of the latter amount is as of the close of the income year without reducing the earnings and profits by any distribution made during the year.

IRC § 316, applicable in California, states that every distribution is made out of earnings and profits to the extent possible and from the most recently accumulated earnings and profits. In other words, if a dividend is distributed in a given year in excess of the earnings and profits of that year, the earnings and profits of the immediately preceding year are computed to determine the effect of the dividend on the distributees and if the dividend is in excess of those earnings and profits you next look to the income year immediately preceding that year.[1]

If the distribution is made from any other source, it is a tax-free distribution which will reduce the adjusted basis of the stock in the hands of the stockholders.

Earnings and profits. Determination is made by deducting from gross receipts the expenses of producing the profits. Therefore, in figuring earnings and profits you can deduct not only the costs deductible for tax purposes but also other items. Also in figuring gross income, types of income which are not ordinarily considered in a tax return are to be included in the computation.[2]

Items excluded from taxable income but includable in earnings and profits:

(a) Interest on state and municipal obligations.
(b) The proceeds of life insurance exempt from income under IRC § 101(a) and Rev & TC 24302.
(c) Compensation for injuries or sickness exempt under IRC § 104(a) and California Rev & TC 17131.
(d) Gain or losses realized from the sale or other disposition of property are used in computing earnings and profits only to the extent that the gain or loss is recognized in figuring taxable income. IRC § 312(f), adopted by California,[2] provides for the exclusion. The nonrecognition type of transactions included would be like-kind exchanges, replacements of voluntarily converted property, IRC § 351 transfers to a controlled corporation and reorganization transfers.

Items deducted in computing taxable income but not deductible in computing earnings and profits:

● Depletion must be based on cost even though depletion was used in computing taxable income.
● Dividends received must be included in full without regard to the 70% federal deduction or the California computed deduction.
● Depreciation in excess of straight-line depreciation is excluded.[3]

---

(1) IRC § 316; § 24451.
(2) IRC § 312; § 24451.

(3) IRC § 312(k); § 24451.

● Federal net operating loss deduction also cannot be used to reduce earnings and profits.

● Expenses nondeductible in computing taxable income but deducted in computing earnings and profits.

● Federal income taxes.

● Expenses and interests incurred in earning tax-exempt income.

● Charitable contributions not deducted in computing taxable income because of the 5% limitation.

● Premiums on term life insurance.

● Losses, expenses and interest not deductible under IRC Section 267.[4]

Excess distributions.   Distributions by corporations in excess of earnings and profits are not taxable dividends.

TAX TIP   If more than one dividend is paid during the year, the taxable and nontaxable amounts of each dividend are allocated as follows: (1) Allocate the earnings and profits of the tax year to each individual dividend. The proportion of each dividend which the total of the earnings and profits of the year bears to the total dividends paid during the year is regarded as out of the earnings and profits of that year. (2) Allocate the earnings and profits accumulated since 2–28–13, in sequence to the part of each individual dividend not regarded as out of earnings and profits of the tax year.

When a distribution exceeds the earnings and profits available for distribution, the excess reduces the shareholder's stock basis. After the excess has reduced the basis to zero, any additional excess is treated as gain from the sale or exchange of property unless it is a tax-exempt distribution.[5] Earnings and profits of a corporation shall not include income from discharge of indebtedness to extent of amount applied to reduce basis under IRC § 1017. If interest of any shareholder is terminated or extinguished in Title 11 or similar case, and there is deficit in earnings and profits, such deficit shall be reduced by amount equal to paid-in capital attributable to interest of such shareholder.[6]

California law conforms to IRC § 312(h) governing allocations of earnings and profits between acquiring and acquired corporations in Type C and Type D reorganizations.[7]

Adjustments to earnings to more properly reflect economic gain or loss. California has conformed to the IRC § 301(e) special rule for distributions received by 20% corporate shareholders (California applies Rev & TC § 24402 dividend deduction instead of IRC §§ 243—245), and the IRC § 312(n) adjustments for:

(1) construction period carrying charges;

(2) intangible drilling costs and mineral exploration and development costs;

(3) LIFO inventory adjustments;

(4) installment sales;

---

(4) § 24427.

(5) IRC § 301; § 24451.

(6) IRC § 312(l); § 24451.

(7) IRC § 312(h); § 24451.

(5) long-term contracts, and
(6) capital gain redemptions.[8]

It does not apply amortization provisions for circulation and organizational expenditures.

Effect of depreciation on earnings and profits. California conforms to IRC § 312(k). For purposes of determining earnings and profits of any corporation for any taxable year starting 7–1–72 and later, the allowance for depreciation and amortization will be deemed the amount that would be allowable for such year if the straight line method of depreciation had been used for each taxable year starting after that date. Adjustment to earnings and profits for depreciation may be determined under a method authorities find results in reasonable allowance under IRC § 167(a) that is not declining balance, sum-of-the-years digits method, or any other method allowable solely by reason of application of IRC § 167(b)(4) or § 167(j)(1)(c).[9]

Extraordinary dividend—reduction of basis. California conforms to IRC § 1059. If any corporation receives an extraordinary dividend with respect to any share of stock, and the corporation has not held such stock for more than two years before the dividend announcement date, the basis of that stock must be reduced, but not below zero, by the nontaxed portion of such dividends. In addition to any gain recognized under IRC income tax provisions, an amount equal to the aggregate nontaxed portions of any extraordinary dividends with respect to such stock that did not reduce the basis of the stock by reason of the below zero limitation will be treated as a gain from the sale or exchange of the stock for any taxable year in which the disposition of the stock occurs. Extraordinary dividend is any dividend with respect to a share of stock if the amount of the dividend equals or exceeds threshold percentage of taxpayer's adjusted basis in such share. Threshold percentage means 5% of taxpayer's adjusted basis in case of stock preferred as to dividends, and 10% in case of any other stock. The aggregation rules of IRC § 1059(c)(3) apply. The same applies to the special reduction rules of IRC § 1059(d), and distribution rules of IRC § 1059(e). California limits the taxable portion of the dividend to the amount described in Rev & TC § 24402 (included in measure of tax of declaring corporation). California adopted IRC § 1059(f) and IRC § 1059(g) relating to treatment of dividends on preferred stock.[10]

¶ 1116   Noncash Distributions

In addition to cash, corporations make distributions of other properties, some of which are:

(1) Distribution of property other than money.
(2) Distribution of obligations of the issuing corporation.
(3) Distribution of the issuing corporation's stock or rights to purchase its stock.

---

(8) IRC § 301(f); 312(n); § 24451; 24452.
(9) IRC § 312(k); § 24451.

(10) § 23051.5; 24966.

(4) Distributions in connection with corporate reorganizations.

(5) Distributions in redemption of stock including partial liquidations and complete liquidations (the amount of the distribution is the fair market value of the property on the date distributed). The amount of the distribution is reduced (but not below zero) by the amount of any liability of the corporation assumed by the shareholder in connection with the distribution and the amount of any liability to which the property received by the shareholder is subject immediately before and after the distribution.[11]

How to compute distribution and basis.   When a corporation receives distributions in property, the amount of the distribution and the basis of the property in the hands of the corporate distributee is the lesser of: (1) the fair market value of the property on the date of distribution; or (2) the adjusted basis of the property in the hands of the distributing corporation immediately before the distributions increased by any gain recognized to the distributing corporation through the distribution of inventories, property subject to a liability in excess of basis, appreciated property or recapture income.[11]

> *Note:* California follows the IRC § 311(b)(1) provisions relating to appreciated property that recognize a gain to the distributing corporation in amount equal to excess of fair market value of property distributed over its adjusted basis, as if property distributed had been sold at time of distribution.[12]

When liabilities assumed.   The amount of the distribution is reduced (but not below zero) by any liability of the distributing corporation assumed by the corporation shareholder in connection with the distribution and any liability to which the property is subject immediately before and after the distribution. In computing the basis of the property received, the deduction for liabilities is not included.

Property distributions other than money.   If property (other than money and other than the obligations of the distributing corporation) is distributed in kind to a corporate stockholder and the fair market value of the property is greater than the adjusted basis in the hands of the distributing corporation, the fair market value of the property is taken into account to reduce the basis of the property in the hands of the acquiring corporation.

Property distributed is money.   The amount of the distribution is the amount of the money received.

Stock or rights.   If the property distributed consists of the obligations of the distributing corporation, or stock of the distributing corporation, or rights to acquire such stock treated as property, the amount of the distribution is an amount equal to the fair market value of the obligations, the stock or the stock rights.

EXAMPLE   On January 1, 1993, Corporation M owned all of the stock of Corporation X with an adjusted basis of $2,000. During 1993 M received distributions from Corporation X totaling $30,000, consisting of $10,000 in cash and listed securities having a basis in the hands of Corporation X and a fair market value on the date distributed of

---

(11) IRC § 301; § 24451.   (12) IRC § 311(b)(1); § 24451.

$20,000. Corporation X's income year is the calendar year. As of December 31, 1992, Corporation X had earnings and profits accumulated after February 28, 1913 in the amount of $26,000, and it had no earnings and profits and no deficit in 1988. Of the $30,000 received by Corporation M, $26,000 will be treated as an ordinary dividend; the remaining $4,000 will be applied against the adjusted basis of its stock; the $2,000 in excess of the adjusted basis of the stock will either be treated as gain from the sale or exchange of property (under IRC § 301(b)(3)(A), or if, out of increase in value accrued before March 1, 1913, will, under IRC § 301(c)(3)(B), be exempt from tax). If Corporation M subsequently sells its stock in Corporation X, the basis for determining gain on the sale will be zero.

Extraordinary dividends. Reduction of stock basis is covered at ¶ 1115.

¶ 1117   **Redemption of Stock as Dividend**

A redemption of stock is considered to be a sale of the stock to the shareholders who receive capital gains treatment if the redemption satisfies any of the four conditions below. Otherwise the redemption is treated as a dividend and the basis of the remaining stock is adjusted. These rules do not apply to distributions in liquidation, except as stated under (4) below.

Stock redemption treated as sale.   One of the following conditions must be met:

(1) *Redemption is not essentially equivalent to a dividend.* A distribution in pro rata redemption of a part of a corporation's stock is ordinarily treated as a dividend if the corporation has only one class of stock outstanding. The redemption of all of one class of stock (exception IRC § 306 stock) is considered a dividend if all classes of stock outstanding at the time of the redemption are held in the same proportion.

(2) *Redemption is substantially disproportionate and the shareholder owns less than 50% of the total voting power after the redemption.* The definition of "substantially disproportionate" is that the percentage of the stockholder's ownership of the voting stock (and common stock whether voting or non-voting) after the redemption is less than 80% of the percentage owned by the stockholder before the redemption. An option to acquire stock is to be included in applying the 80% test. If the redemption is one of a series in total redemption, the total redemption must also meet the 80% test.

(3) *There is a complete redemption of all the stock* of the corporation owned by the shareholder.

(4) *Distribution in redemption of stock held by stockholder who is not a corporation that is in partial liquidation* of distributing corporation. Distribution will be treated as in partial liquidation of a corporation if (a) the distribution is not essentially equivalent to a dividend, determined at the corporate level rather than shareholder level; and (b) the distribution is pursuant to a plan and occurs within the taxable year the plan is adopted or within the succeeding taxable year.[13]

Note: California law follows IRC § 302(b)(4)-outlined in (4) above, and IRC § 302(e) that specifies when a distribution is treated as in partial liquidation. "What is a partial liquidation?" One setup that qualifies is a distribution, whether or not pro rata, because of the distributing corporation's ceasing to conduct, or consists of the assets of, a qualified trade or business where, immediately after the distribution, it's actively engaged in the

(13) IRC § 302; § 24451.

conduct of a qualified trade or business. What's a "qualified trade or business?" It's any trade or business that was actively conducted throughout the 5-year period ending on the date of the redemption, and wasn't acquired by the distributing corporation within that period in a taxable transaction.

California conforms to IRC § 317. The stock is treated as redeemed by a corporation if the corporation acquires its stock from a shareholder whether the stock is cancelled, retired or held as treasury stock.[14]

¶ 1118   **Constructive Ownership of Stock**

The ownership rules below apply to (1) the redemption of stock,[15] (2) the redemption of stock by a related corporation (California conforms to IRC § 304),[16] (3) the preferred stock bail-out,[17] etc.

Member of the family. An individual is considered as owning the stock owned directly or indirectly by or for his spouse, his children, grandchildren and parents.

Partnership and estates. Stock owned directly or indirectly by or for a partnership or estate is treated as owned proportionately by its partners or beneficiaries. Stock owned directly or indirectly by or for a partner or a beneficiary is treated as owned by the partnership or the estate.

Trusts. Stock owned directly or indirectly by or for a trust is considered as being owned by its beneficiaries in proportion to their actuarial interests in the trust. Stock owned directly or indirectly by or for a beneficiary of a trust is considered as being owned by the trust, unless such beneficiary's interest is a remote contingent interest. Stock owned directly or indirectly by or for any portion of a trust of which a person is considered owner under IRC §§ 671–678, relating to grantors and others treated as substantial owners, shall be considered owned by such person. Stock owned directly or indirectly by or for a person considered owner of any portion of trust under IRC §§ 671—678 shall be considered owned by trust.

Corporations. If any person actually or constructively owns 50% or more in value of a corporation's stock he is considered as owning any stock the corporation owns in the proportion that the value of his stock bears to the value of all the corporation's stock. If 50% or more in value of stock in corporation is owned directly or indirectly by or for any person, corporation shall be considered as owning the stock owned, directly or indirectly by or for such person.

Options. California conforms to IRC § 318 which provides that if a person has an option to acquire a stock, the stock is considered as owned by him.[18]

---

(14) IRC § 317; § 24451.
(15) IRC § 302; § 24451.
(16) IRC § 304; § 24451.

(17) IRC § 306; § 24451.
(18) IRC § 318; § 24451.

OBSERVATION   California conforms to IRC § 267 relative to transactions between related taxpayers.[19]

If there is a complete redemption of all the stock of a corporation owned by the shareholder, the rules for constructive ownership between members of a family do not apply if the distributee has no interest in the corporation and he does not acquire an interest within 10 years from the date of redemption. If he does acquire an interest in the corporation, the redemption will be taxed as a dividend in the redemption year. The rules on constructive ownership between members of a family will apply if the acquisition or disposition had as a principal purpose the avoidance of income or franchise tax.[20]

¶ 1119   **Stock Redemption Through Use of a Related Corporation**

California has conformed to IRC § 304 governing stock redemption through use of related corporations. IRC § 304(a) rule on acquisition by a related corporation not a subsidiary has been adopted.[21] In applying IRC § 304(b)(4), relating to certain intergroup transactions, the term "affiliated group" means a controlled group within the meaning of Rev & TC § 24564, relating to the 80% control rule. For income years starting on or after 1–1–90, IRC § 304, relating to nonrecognition of gain for distributions to corporations owning 80% or more of the stock of the distributing corporation, apply in California.

If one or more persons control two corporations and sell the stock of one to the other (a brother-sister transaction), the transaction is a distribution in redemption of the *purchasing* corporation's stock. And if a shareholder sells stock of one corporation to another corporation and the issuing corporation controls the purchasing corporation (a parent-subsidiary transaction), the transaction is a redemption of the issuing corporation stock. To determine the amount of the dividend the transaction is treated as though the "issuing" corporation (purchasing corporation in parent-subsidiary transactions) distributed the property to the purchasing corporation (issuing corporation in brother-sister transaction) which then redeemed its own stock from its shareholders. This rule was intended to provide dividend treatment for property received by shareholders to the extent of the aggregate E&P of both corporations.

Problem. The provision's application was unclear, because the amount treated as a distribution to corporate shareholders was limited to the distributing corporation's basis in the property, but was not so limited for noncorporate shareholders.

Clarification. The law provides that the amount of the dividend is determined by the purchasing corporation's E&P. If the dividend amount is less, the distribution does not affect the "issuing" corporation. If it is greater,

---

(19) § 24427.
(20) IRC § 302(c).

(21) IRC § 304; § 24451.

¶ 1119

the excess is treated as distributed by the "issuing" corporation to the extent of its E&P. The rules as to the characterization of a distribution as a dividend apply both to brother-sister and parent-subsidiary transactions.

Nonrecognition. IRC § 304 provides that a stock for property swap between one 50% controlled corporation and another is treated as a stock redemption and may be treated as a dividend. The provisions governing transfers to 80% controlled corporations (IRC § 351) did not apply to the extent of the nonstock consideration distributed, but did apply to exchanges governed by the corporate reorganization provisions.

Clarification. The law provides that the nonrecognition provisions governing transfers to 80% controlled corporations don't apply to exchanges between controlled corporations treated as redemptions. Therefore, where the reorganization provisions apply, the rules of IRC § 304(a) providing for stock redemption treatment would not apply.

Assumption of indebtedness. Redemption treatment does not apply where the property received was indebtedness on transferred stock, if incurred by the shareholder to acquire it.

Restriction. The law restricts this exclusion to cases where the indebtedness was incurred to purchase stock from a person whose stock ownership is not attributable to the person transferring the stock to the acquiring corporation. Ownership of an option is not considered attribution for this purpose.

Applicability. Redemption treatment is not applicable, even if the acquisition indebtedness was assumed in a transaction to which the nonrecognition rules would not apply (i.e., the transferors owned less than 80% of the acquiring corporation).

Extended application. The law provides that, where shareholders receive property consisting of the assumption of acquisition indebtedness in a corporation of which they have between 50% and 80% control, the transaction is subject to redemption and possible dividend treatment.

Bank holding companies. Stock redemption treatment did not apply to certain minority shareholders receiving securities in an exchange where bank stock was transferred to a newly formed holding company, so long as those receiving property in the exchange did not control the bank holding company.

Clarification. When a bank holding company assumes indebtedness in an acquisition, it will not be treated as property received by the shareholders controlling the bank holding company for purposes of applying the above exclusion. Therefore, the minority shareholders will not be subject to dividend treatment when they receive securities.

Constructive ownership. Generally, a 50% threshold applies under the constructive ownership rules, but not in applying the redemption rules to exchanges of stock for property of commonly controlled corporations. This could be interpreted to preclude the election of IRC § 338 treatment by the purchasing corporation.

De minimis rule. To determine whether control exists under IRC § 304, constructive ownership will not apply to and from a corporation and a shareholder owning less than 5% in value of the corporation's stock. Where a shareholder owns at least 5% but less than 50% in value of the corporation's stock, attribution of ownership from the shareholder to the corporation is limited to a percentage of the value of the corporation's outstanding stock owned by the shareholder.

Disposition of preferred stock. Shareholders who transfer stock from one controlled corporation to another may receive preferred stock in a non-recognition transaction instead of cash or other property. If cash had been received and would have been treated as a dividend, subsequent disposition of the preferred stock *may* result in ordinary income to the shareholders.

Problem. If the preferred stock is disposed of in a redemption, it is treated as a distribution by the acquiring corporation to determine if ordinary income results from such redemption. But the distribution may not constitute a dividend under this test if the acquiring corporation has little or no E&P.

Clarification. The law applies the dividend equivalence test to a hypothetical cash distribution at the time of redemption or other disposition *and* at the time of receipt. This allows the E&P of both corporations to be counted in determining if the stock's redemption is a dividend.

¶ 1120 **Stock Dividends Generally**

A dividend payable in stock is taxable if any shareholder can elect to take money or other property. If a distribution (or a series of distributions) is disproportionate then it is taxable. A distribution is disproportionate if some shareholders can get cash or other properties, and the others have an increase in their proportionate interests of stock, (including convertible debentures and stock rights).

If a distribution (or a series of distributions) has the effect of a distribution of preferred stock to some common shareholders and of common stock to other common shareholders, it is a taxable dividend.

A distribution with respect to preferred stock is taxable, except an increase in a conversion ratio solely to reflect a stock dividend or stock split.

If the distribution is of convertible preferred stock, unless it is established to the satisfaction of the Franchise Tax Board that its distribution will not have the effect of a disproportionate distribution, it will be taxed.

The provisions respecting the disproportionate distributions of preferred stock apply. Administrative authorities must use principles of IRC § 1272(a) and § 1273(a)(3).[22]

¶ 1121 Taxable Stock Dividends

A taxable stock dividend is treated as a property distribution. The amount distributed is the fair market value of the stock on the distribution date (except for regulated investment company distributions where the stockholder has an election). The basis of the new stock is its fair market value at the date of receipt. The basis of the old stock remains the same. The holding period of the new stock begins on the date the stock dividend is received.

¶ 1122 Nontaxable Stock Dividends

Stock dividends have no effect on the taxpayer's income in the year received unless the stock is sold or exchanged. When the dividend stock or the original stock is sold, the original basis must be allocated between the shares. Stock splits are treated the same as nontaxable stock dividends that are identical to the stock held. When the nontaxable stock dividend is of the same class (for example, common on common) the basis of each share is the cost of the old shares divided by the total number of old and new shares on hand. If stock dividends are paid on stock purchased at different times for different prices, the basis is computed by allocating to each lot of stock purchased a proportionate amount of the dividend attributable to it. When a nontaxable stock dividend is of a different class or preference (for example, preferred on common), your new bases are found by allocating the basis of your old stock to your old and new stock in proportion to the relative market values on the distribution date. When a nontaxable stock dividend is received the holding period for the new shares starts on the same date as the holding period of the old shares.

¶ 1123 IRC § 306 Stock

California adopts the IRC § 306, relating to preferred stock bailouts with the exception of IRC § 306(f) sourcing rules.[23] These sections were put into the Internal Revenue Code to circumvent a corporation that, by issuing preferred stock as a stock dividend to its shareholders, having the shareholders sell the stock at a capital gain, and having the corporation redeem the stock from the purchaser, attempts to avoid the reporting of dividend income.

Redemption. When the so-called "§ 306 Stock" is redeemed by the corporation, the amount realized is generally treated as a distribution of property, which may be a dividend, a return of capital or a capital gain. The amount taxed is a dividend as measured by the earnings at the time of the redemption.

---

(22) IRC § 305; § 24451.   (23) IRC § 306; § 24451; 24456.

Sale. When the stock is sold by the shareholder, ordinary income is realized to the extent that any part of the value of the stock sold would have been a dividend if paid in cash. The value used for this purpose is the value on the date of distribution. The sales proceeds are not treated as dividends so they do not reduce the corporate earnings and profits. Any excess of the amount received over the sum of the amount treated as ordinary income plus the adjusted basis of the stock disposed of is treated as gain from the sale of a capital or noncapital asset as the case may be. No loss would be recognized.

When not applicable. The rules for the treatment of the amounts realized from IRC § 306 stock do not apply when:

(1) The sale or redemption is of common stock that was issued to common stockholders as a nontaxable dividend.

(2) A stockholder's interest in the corporation's stock is completely terminated.

(3) The redemption is in complete or partial liquidation of the corporation.

(4) The stockholder is able to prove that the principal purpose of the sale or redemption is not tax avoidance.

(5) The transaction is one in which gain or loss is not recognized.[24]

Note: California adopts the IRC § 306(b) provision that redemption of IRC § 306 (Rev & TC § 24464) stock will not be treated as dividend if IRC § 302(b) rules relating to redemptions terminating shareholder's interest, or in partial liquidation of corporation apply. Anti-bailout rules also apply to stock other than common stock received by shareholder in IRC § 351 exchange (transfer to corporation controlled by transferor). Stock received in exchange is § 306 stock, if, had money been distributed instead, any part of distribution would have been dividend under IRC § 304.[25] California conforms to IRC § 306(c). Constructive ownership rules of IRC § 304(c)(3)(B) and § 318 apply.

¶ 1124 Redemption of Stock to Pay Death Taxes

California has adopted the IRC § 303 rules. A distribution in redemption of stock for this purpose is treated as a sale of the stock, receiving capital gain or loss treatment if all of the following conditions are satisfied:

(1) The value of the stock is included in determining the decedent's gross estate.

(2) The stock is redeemed after the decedent's death and within three years and 90 days after the filing of the decedent's estate tax return, or if a petition for the redetermination of a deficiency of the estate tax was timely filed within 60 days after the Tax Court decision becomes final.

(3) If an election has been made under IRC § 6166 where estate consists largely of stock in closely held corporation, and extended time of up to 15 years under that section expires later than time under (2) above, time limit under IRC § 6166 for payment in installments applies.[26]

California has not adopted the rules for generation-skipping transfers in IRC § 303(d).[27]

---

(24) IRC § 306(a)–306(e).
(25) IRC § 306(b)–306(c); § 24451.

(26) IRC § 303; § 24451.
(27) § 17024.5.

Also, the redemption proceeds cannot exceed the sum of the federal and state death taxes including interest, plus funeral and administration expenses allowable as deductions to the estate.

¶ 1125   Complete Liquidation of Corporation

California has adopted IRC §§ 331—338, relating to corporate liquidations. The federal rules relating to effective dates for recognition of gain or loss on distribution will generally apply. In the usual situation, whether a dividend is paid in cash or in property the stockholder continues to hold the stock of the corporation and pays income tax on his distributions. The same thing is true in the situation where there is a partial redemption of the stock in exchange for cash or property except that, in that instance, the problems as outlined above consist of whether or not the redemption is equivalent to a dividend or a return of capital.

TAX TIP	If for any reason it is decided to terminate the existence of the corporation entirely, the stockholder may receive a tax advantage. If the corporation has accumulated earnings and profits (which if paid out without a liquidation would be considered to be a distribution of profits and taxable as a dividend), their distribution would be part of the capital gain on the liquidation. The corporation after paying off its creditors would transfer all of the remaining cash and assets to the stockholders in exchange for their stock. The transaction, of course, would be considered to be a sale for income tax purposes, and the entire gain, if any, would be subject to capital gains treatment.[28]
OBSERVATION	California conforms to IRC § 346 that a distribution will be treated as in complete liquidation of a corporation if it is one of a series of distributions in redemption of all the stock of a corporation pursuant to a plan. Under federal rules, followed by the Franchise Tax Board, must make such regulations to ensure that provisions of TEFRA §§ 222(a)—(b), which repealed the special tax treatment of partial liquidations, may not be circumvented through the use of federal provisions.[29]

¶ 1126   Basis of Property Received in Liquidation

California conforms to IRC § 334(a). Unless the liquidation requires a special tax treatment (explained at ¶ 1129), the property received by the individual stockholder in the liquidation would take as its basis the fair market value at the time of the distribution.[30]

¶ 1127   Gain Realized on Liquidation

California conforms to and has adopted IRC § 336.

Under IRC § 336, gain or loss must be recognized to a liquidating corporation on the distribution of property in complete liquidation as if such

---

(**28**) IRC § 331; 24451.
(**29**) IRC § 346; § 24451.

(**30**) IRC § 334(a); § 24451.

property were sold to the distributee at its fair market value. If any property distributed in the liquidation is subject to a liability, or the shareholder assumes a liability of the liquidating corporation in connection with the distribution, for purposes of the general rule above, the fair market value of such property shall be treated as not less than the amount of such liability. See IRC § 361(c)(4) for rule that IRC §§ 336—338 do not apply to distributions in pursuance of plan of reorganization.[31]

No loss is recognized to a liquidating corporation on the distribution of any property to a related person, within IRC § 267, if such distribution is not pro rata, or such property is disqualified property (any property acquired by liquidating corporation to which IRC § 351 applied, or as contribution to capital during 5-year period ending on date of distribution).[32]

California has also adopted the special rules for certain property acquired in carryover basis transactions and liquidations to which IRC § 332 (complete liquidation of subsidiaries) applies.[33]

If a corporation owns stock in another corporation meeting 80% voting and value test of IRC § 1504(a)(2), and it sells, exchanges or distributes all of that stock, it may elect to treat such sale, distribution, etc, as a disposition of all the assets of the other corporation. No gain or loss will be recognized.[34] California conforms to federal treatment.

Installment sale income.   Gain not previously recognized on installment sales will also be recognized in the final return of the taxpayer. Abatement of the final year's tax as provided in Rev & TC § 23331 to 23333 shall not be allowed for any income recognized in that year from installment sales except with respect to those installment sales made in the year the taxpayer is no longer subject to California tax, or the immediate proceeding year. Previously unrecognized installment sale income will not be accelerated if the taxpayer ceases to be subject to tax because it is a party to a reorganization as described in IRC § 368(a), as defined in IRC § 368(c), or is transferred to a cemetery corporation as defined in § 23701c.[35]

¶ 1131   **Complete Liquidation of Subsidiary**

California conforms to IRC § 332 relating to complete liquidations of subsidiaries.[36]

If a parent corporation liquidates a subsidiary, no gain or loss is recognized by the parent on the receipt of property including money in the liquidation.

The distribution is considered to be in complete liquidation only if the corporation receiving the property is the owner of at least 80% of the voting stock and 80% of all other stock and the complete cancellation or redemption

---

(31) IRC § 336(a)–(c); § 24451.
(32) IRC § 336(d)(1); § 24451.
(33) IRC § 336(d)(2)–(3); § 24451.
(34) IRC § 336(e); § 24451.

(35) § 24672, as amended by Stats. 1994, c. 1243, § 67.
(36) IRC § 332; § 24451.

of the shares and the transfer of the property occurs within one taxable year. As an alternative it is possible for the liquidation to qualify for nonrecognition if the distribution is one of a series of distributions in complete cancellation or redemption of all of the stock in accordance with a plan of liquidation to be completed within three years from the end of the taxable year in which the first distribution is made.

If the transfer of the property to the parent doesn't occur within the taxable year, the Franchise Tax Board can require the posting of a bond, the waiving of the statute of limitations on assessment or both, if it considers it necessary to insure that all taxes will be collected if the transfer of the property is not completed within the 3-year period.

Nonrecognition for property distributed to parent in complete liquidation of subsidiary.   No gain or loss will be recognized to the liquidating corporation on the distribution to the 80-percent distributee of any property in a complete liquidation to which IRC § 332 applies. This IRC § 337 rule applies for both federal and California purposes.[37]

If a corporation is liquidated in an IRC § 332 liquidation, and on date of adoption of plan, the corporation was indebted to the 80-percent distributee, for the purposes of IRC §§ 336 and 337, and conforming California law, any transfer of property to the distributee in satisfaction of such indebtedness will be treated as a distribution in liquidation to the distributee.[37]

The above rules do not apply to a tax-exempt 80% distributee, other than an IRC § 521 cooperative. The exception applies where property is used in an unrelated business.[37]

¶ 1132   Filing Notices of Dissolution or Liquidation

The Internal Revenue Service requires that Form 966 be filed with the District Director of Internal Revenue within 30 days after the adoption of any resolution or plan for dissolution or liquidation of the corporation. The form contains information as to the terms of the plan.

TAX TIP	The California Franchise Tax Board does not have a similar printed form, but requires that a copy of Form 966 be filed with the Franchise Tax Board at the same time as the form is filed with the District Director.

¶ 1133   Sale of Corporation

California has conformed to IRC § 338, relating to certain stock purchases treated as asset acquisitions.[38] California conforms to the antiavoidance rule of IRC § 338(e)(3).

IRC § 338 rules, below, permit a corporation that buys a controlling stock interest in a target corporation to elect to treat the transaction as a purchase of the corporation's assets for tax purposes. To set up a purchase of

---

(37) IRC § 337; § 24451.   (38) IRC § 338; § 24451.

stock to get assets, the acquiring corporation must: (1) make a qualifying purchase (see below) of the stock of the acquired (target) corporation, and (2) not later than the 15th day of the ninth month following the month of the acquisition date, elect to treat the target corporation as if it sold all its assets at fair market value in a single transaction, and as a new corporation that purchased all of those assets as of the start of the day after the acquisition date. A qualifying purchase is a purchase of stock meeting the requirements of IRC § 1504(a)(2) applicable in determining whether that corporation qualifies as a member of an affiliated group, during a 12-month acquisition period.

Once an election is made, the target corporation's assets are treated as sold to and bought by it for an amount equal to the acquiring corporation's grossed-up basis in its recently purchased stock (stock purchased during the acquisition period) and the basis of any other stock held by the acquiring corporation in the target corporation that is not recently purchased stock. The target corporation *doesn't have to be liquidated.*

The target corporation's tax year as the selling corporation ends on the date of acquisition and it becomes a "new" corporation and a member of the affiliated group, including the acquiring corporation, on the next day.

No gain or loss is recognized by the target corporation as a result of an election by the acquiring corporation. However, the election will trigger any depreciation or investment credit recapture by the target corporation and will terminate its tax attributes, such as net operating loss carryovers. Normally, recapture items will be associated with the final return of the target corporation as the selling corporation for the tax year ending on the date of acquisition. However, if for some reason, recapture income is included in the income of the "new" corporation that is included in the consolidated return filed with the acquiring corporation, it must be separately accounted for and may not be absorbed by losses or deductions of other members of the group.

"Purchase" defined.   Stock is not purchased if it is acquired as follows:

- in a carryover basis transaction;
- from a decedent;
- in an exchange to which IRC §§ 351, 354, 355 or 356 apply;
- in a transaction described in the regulations in which the transferor does not recognize the entire amount of the gain or loss; or
- from a person such as a family member, partnership, estate or trust whose stock is attributed (options don't count) to the acquiring corporation under IRC § 318(a).

Stock acquired from a related corporation (including stock acquired in a carryover basis transaction following a qualified stock purchase and election with respect to the transferor) will satisfy the purchase requirement if at least 50% in value of the related corporation's stock was purchased. A purchasing corporation is not treated as having purchased stock in a third corporation which it constructively owns as a result of purchasing the stock in another (the second) corporation. Instead, if a qualified stock purchase and election are made with respect to the second corporation, the deemed purchase of the third corporation's stock will, if it satisfies the 80% ownership requirement, be treated as a qualified stock purchase permitting an election by the second corporation, or deeming an election to be made under the consistency requirements.

EXAMPLE   XYZ Corp. acquires 80% of the stock of Target Corp. which owns 80% of ABC Corp. stock. XYZ Corp. can't elect to treat ABC Corp. as a target because it is treated as owning only 64% (80% of 80%) of its stock. However, when the IRC § 338 election is made, Target Corp. is treated as having sold all of its assets, and as a new corporation which purchased the assets, including 80% of the stock of ABC Corp. Target Corp. can elect to have its deemed purchase of ABC Corp.'s stock treated as an asset acquisition. It may be required to do so under the consistency rules.

Consistency.   Consistency throughout a so-called "consistency period" is mandatory in the purchase-of-stock-to-get-assets area where the acquiring corporation makes qualified stock purchases of two or more corporations that belong to the same affiliated group. For this purpose, the consistency period is the one-year period preceding the target corporation's acquisition period, plus the period of acquisition, and the one-year period following the acquisition date. Some of the ground rules are as follows:

● Purchases by a member of the purchasing corporation's affiliated group, unless the regulations say otherwise, are treated as purchases by the purchasing corporation. In applying the consistency rules, you aggregate the purchases of members of an affiliated group to see if the 80% purchase requirement is met.

● A combination of a direct asset acquisition and a qualified stock purchase by a member of the purchasing corporation's affiliated group is, unless the regulations say otherwise, treated as made by the purchasing corporation.

● A direct purchase of assets within this period by the purchasing corporation from the target corporation or a target affiliate (except, for example, in the ordinary course of business) will result in the acquisition of the target corporation being treated as an asset purchase. A corporation is a target affiliate of a target corporation if each was, at any time during the portion of the consistency period ending on the acquisition date of the target corporation, a member of an affiliated group, within the meaning of IRC § 1504(a), that had the same common parent. This definition also applies in determining whether a purchase is made by a member of the same affiliated group as the purchasing corporation. The term "target affiliate" doesn't include foreign corporations, DISCs, FSCs, and possessions corporations.

● An acquisition of assets from a target affiliate during the consistency period applicable to the target corporation will result in the qualified stock purchase of the target corporation being treated as a purchase of assets.

● If during a consistency period, there are only qualified stock purchases of the target corporation and one or more target affiliates by the purchasing corporation, an election for the first purchase will apply to the later purchases, and a failure to make the election for the first purchase will knock out any election for the later purchases.

● The IRS has been granted broad authority to treat stock acquisitions, that have been deliberately timed to avoid the consistency rules, as qualified stock purchases. The IRS is also authorized to issue regulations to make sure that the consistency of treatment of stock and asset purchases, with respect to a target corporation and its target affiliates, aren't sidestepped through the creative use of other Code provisions or regulations, including the consolidated return regulations.

¶ 1134   **Carryovers to Successor Corporation**

California has adopted IRC §§ 381–384, relating to carryovers, with the following modifications: (1) IRC § 381(c) relating to items of the distributor or transferor corporation is modified to provide that, instead of paragraph (24), relating to the credit under IRC § 38 (general business credit), and paragraph (25), relating to the credit under IRC § 53 (prior year minimum tax liability), the acquiring corporation must take into account, to the extent proper to carry out the purposes of IRC § 381, the items required to be taken into account for the purposes of each credit allowable under the California Bank and Corporation Tax Law with respect to the distributor or transferor corporation; (2) IRC § 383, relating to special limitations on certain excess credits, etc. is modified to apply to credits allowable under the Bank and Corporation Tax Law, Ch 3.5, and the minimum tax credit under Rev & TC § 23453.[39]

---

(39) IRC § 381–384; § 24451; 24471; 24481.

DEDUCTIONS

¶ 1145   Ordinary and Necessary Business Expenses

An expense to be deductible for tax purposes must be ordinary and necessary and paid or incurred in the taxpayer's accounting period as an expense of a trade or business regularly carried on, or for the production of income, or the maintenance and preservation of property held for the production of income. Every expenditure would fit within the classic definition of an expense above. The principal problem is the determination of the accounting period in which to take the benefit of the deduction. The more common deductions are salaries and wages, rent, repairs, bad debts, interest, taxes, charitable contributions, casualty losses, medical malpractice indemnity payments, repairing and remodeling handicapped facilities, depreciation, advertising, contributions to employee benefit plans, and pensions.[1]

State-federal provisions compared. California conforms to IRC § 162 that specifies the following as being ordinary and necessary expenses:

(1) A reasonable allowance for salaries or other pay for personal services;

(2) The amounts expended for meals and lodging and travel expenses, other than amounts which are lavish or extravagant under the circumstances, while away from home in the pursuit of a trade or business; and

(3) Rentals or other payments required to be made as a condition to the continued use of property in which the taxpayer does not have an equity.

References in IRC § 162 to IRC § 170, relating to charitable contributions and gifts, are modified by California to refer to Rev & TC §§ 24357–24359.1.[2]

Illegal activities. No deductions are allowed against income from illegal activities, illegal bribes, kickbacks or other illegal payments made directly or indirectly to an official or employee of any government. Any payment to an official or an employee of a foreign government which would be an unlawful payment under U.S. laws is also not deductible.[3]

Net operating losses. For tax years beginning on or after 1–1–93, California has adopted the provisions of IRC § 172 relating to net operating loss carryovers, except as provided in Rev & TC §§ 24416.1 and 24416.2 (see below). IRC § 172(b)(2) is generally modified for California purposes to provide that only 50% of the entire amount of the net operating loss for any taxable year is eligible for carryover to any later taxable year. In addition, the carryover must be adjusted to eliminate the net operating loss carryover of a corporation which has a water's edge election under Rev & TC § 25110 to the extent that the net operating loss carryover was determined by taking into account the income and factors of an affiliated bank or corporation in a combined report whose income and apportionment factors would not have been taken into account if a water's edge election had been in effect for the income year in which the loss was incurred. No carrybacks are allowed.

---

(1) § 24343; 24415.   (3) § 24436; 24436.1.
(2) § 24343.

For the 1991 and 1992 tax years the deduction for net operating loss carryovers was suspended. For tax years beginning in 1993 the deduction for NOLs has been reinstated. With exceptions discussed below, the carryover period is generally five tax years.

EXTENDED NOL PERIOD

Because of the prior suspension of the NOL deduction, the carryover period for NOL's arising in tax years beginning in 1991 is seven years, and for those arising in tax years beginning in 1992, the carryover period is six years.

Year NOL Generated	Last Year Allowed
1986 or prior	Expired
1987	1994
1988	1995
1989	1996
1990	1997
1991	1997
1992	1997
1993	1998

New and small-businesses are allowed 100% deduction of their NOLs, and new businesses have an extended carryover period. For tax years beginning on or after 1–1–94, a new business, or a qualifying small-business, are allowed to deduct 100% of their NOL carryovers. A new business is one organized and first commencing business in California on or after 1–1–94. For new businesses, the extended carryover provision are limited to losses incurred in the first three years of operations. A new business may carryover its loss for its first tax year for 8 years; its second tax year for 7 years; and its third tax year for 6 years.

A small-business is one which has total receipts of less than $1 million.

Special rules are provided for those situations where the taxpayer conducts more than one business so that only the new business, or qualifying small business, losses are treated in a preferential manner. In addition Rev & TC § 24416(g) addresses those situations where a taxpayer acquires a portion of the assets of an existing trade or business.[4]

Taxpayers in bankruptcy. Taxpayers who are under the jurisdiction of a federal court under Title 11, any time prior to 1–1–94, or who are in receipt of assets acquired in a tax-free reorganization under IRC § 368(a)(1)(G) may carry over their net operating loss for years beginning on or after 1–1–87, and before 1–1–94, for 10 tax years. The extended carryover period does not apply to any loss incurred in an income year after the income year in which

---

(4) § 24416, as amended by Stats. 1994, c. 949, § 4.

the business is no longer subject to jurisdiction of the court in a Title 11 proceeding.[4]

NOL's arising in program areas, economic development zones, and Los Angeles Revitalization zones. Qualified taxpayers, as defined in Rev & TC § 24416.2, may elect to take the IRC § 172 net operating loss deduction, as modified by Rev & TC § 24416.1, with the following exceptions: (a) Rev & TC § 24416(a), relating to years in which allowable losses are sustained, will not apply; (b) Rev & TC § 24416(b), relating to 50% reduction of losses will not be applicable; (c) IRC § 172(b)(1) shall not apply; to the extent applicable, losses attributable to entities with losses described in IRC § 172(b)(1)(J) will be applied in accordance with IRC § 172(b)(1)(A) and (B); (d) corporations subject to Rev & TC §§ 25101 or 25101.15 make the computations required by Rev & TC § 25108; (e) election to compute net operating loss under Rev & TC § 24416.1 must be made in a statement attached to the original return, timely filed and is irrevocable. Qualified taxpayers are taxpayers engaged in conduct of business in an enterprise zone, a program area, the Los Angeles Revitalization zone, and a local Agency Military Base Recovery area. For these taxpayers, a two-factor formula of payroll and property will apply. Special rules apply for determining the net operating loss deduction and the income of the subsequent year against with the net operation loss can be applied.[5]

Cruise ship. Corporations can take a deduction for expenses of employees attending a convention, seminar, or other meeting held aboard a cruise ship, if specified conditions are met. California conforms to IRC § 274, including the rules on conventions in certain Caribbean countries and the rules on the disallowance of entertainment, gift or travel expenses.[6]

Meals—entertainment—gifts. Deductions are allowed for gifts of up to $25 per year directly or indirectly to an individual, and entertainment given as compensation for services or a prize to individuals not employees. To be allowed as a deduction, entertainment expenses must be directly related to the active conduct of a trade or business.[6]

General rule. The general rule is that the amount allowable as a deduction for any expense for food and beverages, or entertainment, amusement or recreation cannot exceed 80% (50% for tax years beginning after 12–31–93) of such expenses. California adopts IRC § 274(a)(1); 274(e); and § 274(n) (pre-1994 travel expenses).

Exceptions. The exceptions to the general rule are:

(1) expenses treated as compensation,
(2) reimbursed expenses,
(3) recreational expenses for employees,
(4) items available to the public,
(5) entertainment sold to customers,

---

(5) § 24416.2, as amended by Stats. 1994, c. 922, § 11.

(6) IRC § 274; § 23051.5; 24443.

(6) expenses includible in income of persons who are not employees,

(7) food and beverages for employees furnished on the business premises of the taxpayer,

(8) expenses directly related to a business meeting of employees, stockholders, directors, or agents, and

(9) expenses directly relating to a meeting of a business league defined in IRC § 501(c)(6) and exempt from tax under IRC § 501(a).[7]

Property transferred in connection with performance of services. California adopts IRC § 83. In case of a transfer of property to which IRC § 83 applies, or the cancellation of a restriction described in IRC 83(d), a deduction is allowed to the bank or corporation for whom the services were performed in connection with which the property was transferred. The amount of the deduction is equal to amount included in subsection (a), (b) or (d)(2) of IRC § 83 in the gross income of the person who performed those services. It will be allowed for the income year of the bank or corporation in which or with which ends the taxable year in which the amount is included in the gross income of the person who performed the services. Where property is substantially vested on transfer, the deduction shall be allowed to the corporation or bank in accordance with its method of accounting.[8]

Ridesharing. A deduction is allowed an employer as an ordinary business expense paid or incurred during the income year in carrying on any trade or business for expenses involved in:

(1) subsidizing employees commuting in van pools;

(2) subsidizing employees commuting in private commuter buses and buspools;

(3) subsidizing monthly transit passes for employees, or their dependents; but no deduction is allowed for transit passes issued for use of elementary and secondary school students;

(4) subsidizing employees commuting in subscription taxipools;

(5) subsidizing employees commuting in car pools.

An employer who offers free parking to employees, or offers cash equivalent to employees not requiring parking, or makes payments to employees under a qualified parking cash-out program is also allowed the deduction. Other activities of an employer qualifying for an expense deduction are: (1) providing free or preferential parking to carpools, vanpools, or any other vehicle used in ridesharing arrangement, (2) making facility improvements to encourage employees to participate in ridesharing arrangements, use bicycles, or walk; (3) providing company commuter van or bus service to employees and other commuters; and (4) providing employees transportation services required as part of employer's business activities to extent that transportation would be provided by employees without reimbursement in absence of employer-sponsored ridesharing incentive program. Capital costs of this service are not deductible.[9] "Employer" means either (1) a taxpayer for whom services are performed by employees, except entities not subject to the

---

(7) IRC § 501(c).

(8) IRC § 83; § 23051.5; 24379.

(9) § 24343.5.

Bank and Corporation Tax Law; or (2) a taxpayer that is a private or public educational institution that enrolls students at higher than secondary level.

Transfer of franchise, trademark and trade name. California adopts IRC § 1253 that allow transferees an IRC § 162(a) deduction for trade or business expenses for contingent serial and principal sum payments up to $100,000, and capitalization and recovery of other payments over a 25-year period.[10]

Premiums on life insurance covering officer or employee. California adopts IRC § 264. No deduction is allowed for: (1) premiums paid on any life insurance policy covering the life of any officer or employee or any person financially interested in any trade or business carried on by the taxpayer, when the taxpayer is directly or indirectly a beneficiary under such policy; (2) any amount paid or accrued on indebtedness incurred or continued to purchase or carry a single premium life insurance, endowment or annuity contract; (3) except as provided by specified restrictions in Rev & TC § 24424(c), any amount paid or accrued on indebtedness incurred or continued to purchase a life insurance, endowment or annuity contract, other than a single premium, or a contract so treated pursuant to a plan of purchase that contemplates systematic direct or indirect borrowing of part or all the increases in cash value; (4) any interest paid or accrued on any indebtedness with respect to one or more insurance policies owned by the taxpayer covering the life of any individual who is an officer or employee of the company, or financially interested in any trade or business of the taxpayer, if the aggregate amount of debt on the policies exceeds $50,000.[11]

New buildings—permanent improvements. No deduction is allowed for any amount paid out for new buildings or permanent improvements or betterments made to increase the value of any property.

Exceptions. The following are deductible:

(1) expenditures for development of mines or deposits deductible under IRC § 616;

(2) soil or water conservation expenditures deductible under Rev & TC § 24369;

(3) expenditures for farmers for fertilizer, etc. deductible under Rev & TC § 24377;

(4) research and experimental expenditures deductible under Rev & TC § 24365;

(5) expenditures for which a deduction is allowed under Rev & TC § 24356.2 (recovery property; enterprise zone);

(6) expenditures for which a deduction is allowed under Rev & TC § 24356.3 (machinery and parts used to fabricate and produce renewable energy resources or water pollution control mechanisms);

(7) expenditures for the removal of architectural and transportation barriers to the handicapped and elderly which the taxpayer elects to deduct under Rev & TC § 24383; and

(8) expenditures on certain property in a Los Angeles Revitalization Zone under Rev & TC § 24356.4.

---

(10) § 23051.5.   (11) § 24424.

No deduction is allowed for any amount expended in restoring property or making good the exhaustion thereof for which an allowance is or has been made.[12]

Loss of deduction. An entity or individual that fails to file information returns or give statements to payees of remuneration for personal services, or give an annual statement to employees of compensation paid, or furnish a statement with respect to services will not be allowed a deduction for the amounts paid as remuneration for personal services. Reasonable cause does not excuse failure.[13]

Substantiation is required. Substantiation is required under both federal IRC § 274(d) and California law to get a deduction or credit for travel expenses, items generally considered entertainment, recreation or amusement and facilities used in connection therewith, gift expenses, and with respect to any listed property as defined in IRC § 280F. This rule is not applicable to nonpersonal use vehicles.[6]

¶ 1146 **Interest**

All interest paid or accrued during the income year on a corporation's indebtedness is deductible in accordance with IRC § 163 allowable amounts except as indicated below.[14]

Related parties. The deduction for interest paid to related parties is limited in IRC § 163(j)(4), generally applicable interest paid or accrued in taxable years beginning after 7–10–89.

Combined groups. California treats all members included in a combined report as one taxpayer for purposes of determining the application of IRC § 163.[15]

Multistate taxpayers. Rev & TC § 24344(b)[16] provides for determining the amount of interest deductible in the case of a corporation which has income derived from sources both within and without California.

This provision is in the law so that interest which is incurred to obtain or maintain investments which produce income which is not taxable by California will not be allowed as a deduction.

Three-way split. The interest expense paid or accrued during the year (less nonbusiness interest expense which is allocated separately) is split into three portions. *The first portion* of interest expense will equal the unitary business interest (interest included in formula apportionment). *The second portion* of the interest expense is the amount to equal the dividends and nonbusiness interest income excluded from the apportionment formula. *The*

---

(12) § 24422.
(13) § 24447.
(14) § 24244(a).

(15) § 24344.
(16) § 24344(b).

third portion of the interest expense would be the amount applied to the balance of the unitary income.[17]

Rev & TC § 24344(b) allows an interest deduction for corporations to the extent the corporation had dividend or nonbusiness interest income which was not included in the measure of the tax. The exclusion from formula apportionment and the separate allocation of interest expense apply to both foreign and domestic corporations.

EXAMPLE

For a California domiciled corporation apportioning 60% of its unitary business to California, if it has $1000 of dividend income and $1000 of interest expense, the practical effect is that the $1000 of dividend income would be apportioned 100% to California and the interest expense would be 100% deductible, rather than 60% if it was included in the formula.

In calculating this interest offset, dividends (under Rev & TC § 24402) declared from income included in measure of tax imposed by the franchise or corporation income tax are excluded from dividends not subject to apportionment by formula; the exclusion will also apply to dividends subject to the deduction provided in Rev & TC § 24411 to the extent of that deduction. Notwithstanding the provision on dividends subject to special treatment under Rev & TC § 24411, interest expense incurred for the purpose of foreign investments, may be offset against dividends deductible under Rev & TC § 24411.[18]

California adopts the same effective date for limiting the deduction for certain interest paid to related persons as set forth in IRC § 163(j).

Installment sales with carrying charges. IRC § 163, adopted by California,[19] provides that when personal property or educational services are purchased on a contract payable in installments in which carrying charges are provided but no interest rate is specified, the taxpayer can consider that a portion of the monthly payment is to be considered to be interest computed using a 6% factor.

Investment indebtedness interest. IRC § 163(d) limits the deduction of "investment indebtedness interest." Both the California Bank and Corporation Tax Law and the Personal Income Tax Law have adopted this provision.[20]

Amortizable bond discounts. A deduction determined in accordance with IRC § 163(e) is allowed to the issuer of an original discount bond. The portion of the original issue discount allowable as a deduction is equal to the aggregate daily portions of the original issue discount for the days during the taxable year. Before the year of sale, exchange, maturity or other disposal, the deductible amount is same as on the federal return.

Acquisition indebtedness. No deduction is allowed for interest paid on corporate acquisition debt insofar as it exceeds $5 million, reduced by the

---

(17) LR 379, 4–1–75.
(18) § 24344(b)–(c).

(19) § 17201; 24344(a).
(20) § 17024.5; 24344.

amount of interest paid during the year on obligations that are not corporate acquisition debt, to provide consideration for the acquisition of stock or assets of another corporation.[21]

Federal tax deficiencies. Interest on such deficiencies is subject to statutory limits on deduction. It's like interest on borrowed money.[22]

Bonus interest accrued by savings and loan association. This can be deducted in the year credited on the certificate issued, even though the holder of the certificate will be paid interest in a later year on holding the certificate for the period not yet ended.[23]

Real property construction period interest and taxes. California has conformed to federal law.[24]

Enterprise zones and program areas. Net interest received in payment of debt of a qualified business located in a program area or a trade or business located in an enterprise zone is deductible by the recipient taxpayer provided it has no equity or ownership interest in the debtor, and the indebtedness is incurred solely in connection with the activity in the enterprise zone or program area.[25]

Loss of deduction. Owners and transferors of real property who have either (1) failed to give information that includes the federal identification number, identification of the property interest, and any other pertinent information; or (2) who have given false, misleading or incorrect information will be denied a deduction for interest that relates to that property.[26] Taxpayers deriving income from rental of substandard housing can lose the deduction.[27]

¶ 1147 **Taxes**

The principal difference between the federal and California treatment of the deduction for taxes is that California does not allow a deduction for any taxes on or according to or measured by income or profits, imposed by the United States, foreign country, or any state, territory or other political subdivision. This includes the California franchise tax itself.[28]

Deductible taxes. Deductible taxes or licenses include ad valorem property taxes, (see also ¶ 1148), automobile registration fees, city license fees, import or custom duties paid to federal customs officers, liquor or alcoholic beverage license fees, and other business, privilege or excise taxes paid to the United States or to a state.

Not deductible. So-called taxes, which are more properly assessments paid for local benefits such as street, sidewalk or other like improvements, easement abandonment and tax recoupment fees, are not allowable deduc-

---

(21) § 24438; LR 374, 7–2–74.
(22) LR 059, 12–5–58.
(23) LR 337, 3–5–70.
(24) § 17024.5.

(25) § 24384.
(26) § 24448.
(27) § 24436.5.
(28) § 24345(a).

tions from California gross income. A tax is considered assessed against local benefits when the property subject to the tax is limited to the property benefited. No deduction is allowed for federal stamp taxes, but the fact that any such tax is not deductible as a tax does not prevent its deduction as an ordinary and necessary expense paid or incurred during the year by the corporation in the conduct of a trade or business. Federal and California law are the same.

State and local general sales or use taxes. A deduction is allowed for state and local sales or use taxes that are paid or accrued within the income year in carrying on a trade or business, or an activity described in IRC § 212, relating to expenses for the production of income. However, any sales or use tax, except where credit is claimed under Rev & TC § 23612 (machinery in enterprise zones or program areas), Rev & TC § 23612.6 (machinery in a Los Angeles Revitalization Zone), and Rev & TC § 23645 (qualifying property in a Local Agency Military Base Recovery Area), that is paid or accrued in connection with an acquisition or disposition of property, must be treated as part of the cost of the property, or, in the case of disposition, as a reduction in the amount realized on the disposition.[29]

TAX TIP   The principal controversy arises in regard to taxes paid to other states and to foreign countries. If the tax imposed is on, or according to, or measured by income or profits, it is *not* deductible. The State Board of Equalization has consistently maintained that the question of whether a foreign tax is on, or according to, or measured by income has to be decided on the basis of the concept of income. The State Board of Equalization, in its decisions, takes the position that if the foreign tax is on net income, taxable income or even gross income, it would not be deductible for California purposes. If, however, the tax is on gross receipts, it would be an allowable deduction.

Foreign taxes on royalties. A deduction was disallowed for Japan's withholding taxes on receipts paid to a resident from domestic source income, such as royalties, dividends and motion picture rentals.[30] Taxes paid to a foreign country by a motion picture distributor and treated as distribution expenses, under the usual form of agreement between the distributor and producer, are taxes solely on the distributor, and a distribution expense to the producer. Distributor can't deduct them.[31]

---

(29) § 24345(e).   (31) LR 352, 2–21–73.
(30) LR 336, 3–5–70.

TABLE OF DEDUCTIBLE TAXES

This table is adapted from the corporation audit manual that lists state taxes paid by corporations and whether they are deductible or not. The distinction is that taxes on, according to, or measured by income are not deductible. The taxes listed below which are deductible are principally taxes based on capital stock or outstanding shares, rather than on earned income.

State	Fran	Inc.	Basis
AL	Ded		C. Stock
		Non-D	Net Inc.
AK	Nominal Flat Fee (Ded)	Non-D	Net Inc.
AZ	None	Non-D	Net Inc.
AR	Ded		C. Stock
		Non-D	Net Inc.
CO	None	Non-D	Net Inc.
CT	Non-D	None	Du. Basis
	Ded		C. Stock
DE	Ded		C. Stock
		Non-D	Net Inc.
DC		Non-D	Net Inc.
	Ded		C. Stock
FL	None	Non-D	Net Inc.
GA	Ded		Net Worth
		Non-D	Net Inc.
HI	None	Non-D	Net Inc.
ID	None	Non-D	Net Inc.
IL	Ded		St. Capital
		Non-D	Net Inc.
IN	None	Non-D	Net Inc.
IA	None	Non-D	Net Inc.
KS	Ded		C. Stock
		Non-D	Net Inc.
KY	Ded		C. Stock
		Non-D	Net Inc.
LA	Ded		C. Stock
		Non-D	Net Inc.
ME	None		
		Non-D	Net Inc.

State	Fran	Inc.	Basis
MD	Ded		An. Rpt.
		Non-D	Net Inc.
MA	Non-D		Du. Basis Net Income and Property
		Non-D	Net Inc.
MI	Nominal Flat Fee (Ded)	Non-D	Taxable Inc.
MN	Non-D		Net Inc.
		Non-D	Net Inc.
MS	Ded		Capital
		Non-D	Net Inc.
MO	Ded		Out. Shares
		Non-D	Net Inc.
MT	Non-D	None	Net Inc.
NE	Non-D	Non-D	Net Inc.
NV	None	None	
NH	Ded		C. Stock
		Non-D	Bus Profits
NJ	None		None
NM	Nominal Flat Fee (Ded)	Non-D	Net Inc.
		Non-D	Net Inc.
NY	Non-D	Non-D	Net Inc.
NC	Ded		C. Stock
		Non-D	Net Inc.
ND	None	Non-D	Net Inc.
OH	Ded	None	Cap. Stock
OK	Ded		Invest. Cap.
		Non-D	Net Inc.
OR	None		
		Non-D	Net Inc.
PA	Ded		C. Stock
		Non-D	Net Inc.
RI	Ded		C. Stock

¶ 1147

State	Fran	Inc.	Basis	State	Fran	Inc.	Basis
		Non-D	Net Inc.	VA	Ded		C. Stock
SC	Ded		C. Stock	WA	Nominal Flat Fee (Ded)	Non-D None	Net Inc. None
		Non-D	Net Inc.				
SD	None	Non-D	Net Inc.	W.VA	Ded		C. Stock
TN	Ded		C. Stock			Non-D	Net Inc.
		Non-D	Net Inc.	WI	None	Non-D	Net Inc.
TX	Ded Non-D	None	St. Capital Du. Basis	WY	Ded	None	Val. of Ass.
UT	Non-D	Non-D	Net Inc.				
VT	None	Non-D	Net Inc.				

Cooperative taxes. A deduction for cooperative taxes is allowed tenant stockholders in a cooperative housing corporation. Amounts allowable are determined by IRC § 216, adopted by California.[32]

Loss of deduction. Taxpayer who owns real property and has either (1) failed to give information that includes its federal identification number, identification of its property interest, and any other pertinent information; or (2) has given false, misleading or incorrect information will be denied deduction for taxes that relate to that property.[33] Renters of substandard housing can lose deduction.[34]

¶ 1148 Real Property Tax Deduction Divided Between Buyer and Seller

The portion of real property taxes allocated to the part of the property tax year preceding the sale is considered as imposed on the seller and is deductible by him. The portion allocable to the part of the property tax year beginning on the date of the sale is considered as imposed on the buyer and is deductible by him. This rule applies whether or not the seller and the buyer apportioned the tax between them.[35]

The purchaser does not take into account in totalling his cost of real property any amount paid to the seller as reimbursement for real property taxes which are treated under Rev & TC § 24346 as imposed on the purchaser. This is true, whether or not the contract of sale calls for the purchaser to reimburse the seller for such real estate taxes paid or to be paid by the seller. In California, real property sales are generally handled through escrow companies which routinely prorate the taxes between the buyer and the seller, so that the buyer does not pay any of the real property taxes assigned to the seller. However, if the purchaser does pay or assumes a liability for real estate taxes which are treated under Rev & TC § 24346 as imposed on the seller, these taxes are considered to be part of the cost of the property. It does not make any difference whether or not the contract of sale

---

(32) § 24382.
(33) § 24448.
(34) § 24436.5.
(35) § 24346.

specifies that the sale price has been reduced by real estate taxes allocable to the seller under Rev & TC § 24346.

EXAMPLE 1   Assume that the contract price on the sale of a parcel of real estate is $50,000 and that real property taxes on the property in the amount of $1,000 for the property tax year in which the sale occurred had been previously paid by the seller. Assume further that $750 of the taxes are treated under Rev & TC § 24346 as imposed on the purchaser and that the purchaser reimburses the seller for the $750, in addition to paying the $50,000 contract price. The amount realized by the seller is $50,000 and $50,000 is also the purchaser's cost. If, in this example, the purchaser made no payment other than the contract price of $50,000, the amount realized by the seller would be $49,250 since the sale price would be deemed to include the $750 paid to the seller for real property taxes imposed on the purchaser. Similarly, $49,250 would be the purchaser's cost.

EXAMPLE 2   Assume that the purchaser in the example above paid all of the real property taxes. Assume further that $250 of the taxes are treated under Rev & TC § 24346 as imposed on the seller. The amount realized by the seller is $50,250. Similarly, $50,250 is the purchaser's cost, regardless of the income year in which the purchaser makes actual payment of the taxes.

¶ 1149 Charitable Contributions

A corporation can deduct charitable contributions for the use of:

● *Governments.* The United States, the District of Columbia, possessions of the United States or any state or political subdivision if the contribution is made for exclusively public purposes;

● *Nonprofit organizations.* A corporation trust, community chest, fund or foundation created or organized in the United States or in any possession of the United States or under the law of the United States, the District of Columbia and organized and operated exclusively for religious, charitable, scientific, literary or educational purposes or to foster national or international amateur sports competition or for the prevention of cruelty to children or animals, no part of the net earnings of which enures to the benefit of any private shareholder or individual and which is not disqualified for tax exemption under Rev & TC § 23701(d)[36] for attempting to influence legislation and which does not participate in any political campaign;

● *Veterans' organizations.* A post or organization of war veterans or an auxiliary unit or society of such organization, organized in the United States or any of its possessions and none of the net earnings of which enures to the benefit of any shareholder or individual;

● *Cemetery company.* A cemetary company operated solely for burial purposes and not permitted to engage in any business, not necessarily part of that purpose, provided the company is operated on a nonprofit basis and no part of the net earnings enures to the benefit of any private shareholder or individual.[37]

Travel expenses. No deduction will be allowed for travel expenses, including amounts expended for meals or lodging, while away from home, whether directly or by reimbursement, unless there is no significant element of personal pleasure, recreation, or vacation in that travel.[38]

---

(36) § 23701d.   (38) § 24357(d).
(37) § 24357; 24359.

Educational organization—stadium tickets—80% limitation. If a taxpayer pays an amount to or for the benefit of an educational organization, described in IRC § 170(b)(1)(A)(ii) that is an institution of higher education as defined in IRC § 3304(f), and the amount would be allowable as a deduction under Rev & TC § 24357.10 but for the fact that the taxpayer receives, directly or indirectly, as a result of paying the amount, the right to purchase tickets for seating at an athletic event in an athletic stadium of the institution, 80% of the amount paid will be treated as a charitable contribution. If any portion of a payment is for the purchase of tickets, that portion and the remaining portion, if any, of the payment shall be treated as separate amounts.

Limit.   The charitable contribution deduction is limited to 5% of the corporation's net income (for federal purposes, the limitation is 10%). The deduction is computed without regard to any of the following: (1) Rev & TC § 23802(e), relating to a deduction for built-in gains and passive investment income; (2) Rev & TC §§ 24357 to 24359, inclusive, relating to deduction for contributions; (3) Article 2, starting with Rev & TC § 24401, of Ch 7 (except Rev & TC §§ 24407 to 24409, inclusive, relating to organizational expenses).[39] For California corporation tax purposes, there is no carryover of unused deduction.

Rev & TC § 24357.1[40] includes the provision that any charitable contribution of property is limited to the corporation's basis in the property (i.e., property's fair market value is to be reduced by the amount of the gain, which would have been realized if the property contributed had been sold by the corporation at its fair market value as of the time of the contribution).

Qualified research contribution.   Under IRC § 170(e)(4), a corporation contributing scientific property (held as inventory) to a college or university for research activities can get a deduction equal to the basis in the property plus ½ of unrealized appreciation but not more than twice the property's basis. The California deduction is limited to the greater of (1) the taxpayer's basis in the property, or (2) the fair market value of the property reduced by one-half the unrecognized gain in excess of twice the basis of the property.

California only excludes from the term "corporation" a service organization as defined in IRC § 414(m)(3). Federal law excludes both personal holding companies and small business corporations as well. California has no requirement that property must be constructed by taxpayer.[1] Further, California deduction applies only to gifts to colleges or universities located in California.

California extends the deduction coverage to scientific property used for instructional purposes. A taxpayer donating the instructional purpose property must receive from the donee a written statement that the property is a state-of-the-art equipment or apparatus and will be used as part of the

---

(39) § 24358.
(40) § 24357.1.

(1) § 24357.8; 24359.1.

instructional program. Reports to Franchise Tax Board are required. Also contributions, whether for research, experimentation or training or for instructional purposes, must be made on or after 7–1–83 and on or before 12–31–93. This deduction will not be disallowed on the basis that the contribution is made for the primary or incidental purpose of benefitting the donor by encouraging institutions to train students to use a computer, scientific equipment or apparatus, thereby enlarging the market for potential purchasers, or developing and maintaining a public image.[1]

Explanation at ¶ 326 covers rules on gifts of less than total interest in property.[2]

TAX TIP	*Charitable contribution computation for corporation apportioning income.*

Schedule R–6 is provided in Schedule R of the corporate tax return to limit the charitable contributions deduction to 5% of the California income which has been computed by formula apportionment plus or minus the allocation of nonbusiness income or loss to California. It is a complicated schedule and the results of using it can be stated as follows:

(1)   If the corporation has contributions less than the 5% limitation, use of the schedule will not change the amount of the deduction computed using the apportionment formula.

(2)   If the corporation has contributions up to or in excess of the 5% limitation, but has no nonbusiness income or loss, use of the schedule will not change the amount of the deduction.

(3)   If the corporation has contributions up to or in excess of the 5% limitation, and has nonbusiness income or loss allocated to California or other states, the result of the use of Schedule R–6 is to assign some of the charitable contribution to the nonbusiness income or loss, and increase or decrease the formula amount of the charitable contribution deduction in accordance with the increase or decrease in total California income.

If the return combines the income of two or more corporations engaged in a unitary business, the computation is made on a combined basis.

Essentially, what the schedule does is to apply the ratio of the total income before allocation and apportionment and before contributions deductions to the total income after allocation and apportionment and before the contributions deduction.[3]

¶ 1150   Research and Experimental Expenditures

California has adopted IRC § 174 relating to research and experimental expenditures. California modifies this adoption with respect to IRC § 174(b) by providing that Rev & TC § 24916(a), relating to items chargeable to capital will apply instead of IRC § 1016(a)(1). It also modifies IRC § 174(c) to

---

(2) § 24357.2; 24357.7.   (3) Form 100, Schedule R–6.

provide that Rev & TC §§ 24349 to 24356 will apply instead of IRC § 167, relating to depreciation of land and other property.

Under IRC § 174, as adopted by California, a taxpayer may treat research or experimental expenses which are paid or incurred during the taxable year in connection with trade or business as expenses that are not chargeable to capital account. The expenditures so treated are allowed as a deduction. The method of treatment may be adopted with the consent of the administrative authorities. It will apply to all of the above-described expenditures. A change to a different method in whole, or in part may be approved by those authorities.

Under IRC § 174(b), as adopted by California, a taxpayer can treat expenses incurred in trade or business as deferred expenses, if they have not been taken as deductions under IRC § 174(a), and are chargeable to a capital account, but not chargeable to property subject to depreciation under Rev & TC §§ 24349–24356, or IRC § 611. Such expenses are allowed as a deduction ratably over not less than a 60-month period, as selected by the taxpayer. In adjusting the basis of the property, Rev & TC § 24916(a) applies instead of IRC § 1016(a)(1). The election must be made by the time for filing the return, and must be adhered to unless the taxing authorities permit a change in the method or period. It does not apply to any years prior to the year of election. These rules for treatment of research or experimental expenditures do not apply to expenses for acquisition or improvement of land, or property subject to depletion, depreciation or exploration expenditures. Deductible or amortizable expenditures must be reasonable.

Expenses for which credits are allowable.   California adopts IRC § 280C(b), relating to the credit for qualified clinical testing expenses for certain drugs, and the provisions of IRC § 280C(c), relating to the credit for increasing research activities. These sections provide that no deduction will be allowed for amounts recognized as a credit.[4]

¶ 1151   **Circulation Expenditures**

Any expenditures by a corporation used to establish, maintain or increase the circulation of a newspaper, magazine or other periodical are deductible. However, expenditures for the purchase of land or depreciable property or for the acquisition of circulation through the purchase of any part of the business of another publisher of a newspaper, magazine or other periodical are not deductible. The taxpayer can elect to capitalize the total amount of the expenditures by attaching a statement to the return for the first income year to which the election is applicable. Once the election is made, all circulation expenditures in later years must be charged to the capital account and amortized unless the Franchise Tax Board, on application made to it in writing, permits a revocation of the election for any subsequent year.[5]

---

(4) § 24440.   (5) § 24364.

¶ 1153   **Dividends**

A corporation for federal income tax purposes is allowed a special deduction from gross income for dividends received from a domestic corporation subject to the federal income tax. The deduction is 70% of the dividends received. Affiliated corporations that do not file consolidated federal tax returns are allowed a 100% dividend received deduction for qualifying dividends from members of the affiliated group. Also, 100% of the dividends received from a small business investment company operating under the Small Business Investment Act of 1958 is deductible for federal purposes.[6]

California treatment.   A corporation receiving dividends can deduct a portion of the dividends received during the income year declared from income which has been included in the measure of taxes imposed upon the corporation declaring the dividends under the Bank and Corporation Franchise Tax, the Alternative Minimum Tax, and the Corporation Income Tax.

The portion of the dividends that may be deducted is: (1) in the case of any dividend received from a more than 50% owned corporation, 100%; (2) in the case of any dividend received from a 20% owned corporation, 80%; (3) in the case of any dividend received from a bank or corporation that is less than 20% owned, 70%. A "more than 50% owned corporation" means any bank or corporation if more than 50% of the stock of that bank or corporation, by vote and by value, is owned by the taxpayer. IRC § 1504(a)(4) stock shall not be taken into account. A similar definition is provided for a 20% owned corporation.

In order for the deduction to be available to the payee, the payor corporation must have had income from sources in California which require the filing of a California tax return.[7]

¶ 1154   **Special Deductions—Cooperative Organizations**

Corporations formed and operating on a cooperative basis are allowed special deductions under the Bank and Corporation Tax Law.[8]

Farmers' cooperative associations.   These associations consist of farmers, fruit growers and similar associations organized and operated on a cooperative or mutual basis for the purpose of marketing their products or for the purchase of supplies and equipment to be used in the farming and merchandising operations. In addition, other cooperatives would be included in this group if they perform services such as dehydrating, furnishing farm labor camps and similar services.[9]

This group of cooperatives is entitled to a deduction for "all income resulting from or arising out of business activities for or with their members, carried on by them or their agents or when done on a nonprofit basis for or

---

(6) IRC §§ 243–246.

(7) § 24402.

(8) §§ 24404–24406.5.

(9) § 24404.

with non-members." The amounts allocated to members include cash, merchandise, capital stock, revolving fund certificates, certificates of indebtedness, retain certificates, letters of advice or written instruments which in some other manner disclose to each member the dollar amount allocated to him. These allocations may be made after the close of the income year and on or before the 15th day of the 9th month following the close of the year (the due date of the return). It should be noted that non-member income, on a profit basis, is also not taxable to the cooperative if it is allocated to the members within the same 8½-month period.

Direct expenses are deductible from income to arrive at net income. In addition, indirect or overhead expenses would be allowed in the amount of $100 or 1% of gross taxable income, whichever is greater. The Franchise Tax Board has affirmed the practice of allowing deductions to farmers' cooperative associations based on allocation rather than source of income.[10] Farmers' cooperatives, described in Rev & TC § 24404, may deduct amounts allocated to members that are attributable to nonmember sales or transactions. The net income from transactions with members isn't taxable even if not allocated within eight months and 15 days after the close of the income year. The net income from transactions with nonmembers is taxable if not allocated within that period. The total amount of nonmember income should be included in determining the taxable portion after allowing reasonable expenses.[11] The payment of additional federal tax liability from current income would increase the taxable income reportable. A payment from equity capital wouldn't have any franchise tax consequences. The creation of reserve from equity capital for federal income tax wouldn't result in tax. Unallocated amounts from both co-op and nonco-op sources are taxable whether or not deposited in reserves.[12]

Other cooperatives. Rev & TC § 24405 gives a special deduction to cooperative corporations which do not sell tangible personal property, but instead deal in intangibles. Included would be credit unions, federal production credit associations and those dealing in water (cooperative water companies). Also included would be cooperatives which sell food products at wholesale or agricultural products. Under this section, income derived from nonmembers on a profit basis is taxable, as well as income from interest on investments, rental income from nonmembers, and so on. Direct expenses, such as depreciation on property used to earn income from nonmembers on a profit basis, are allowable as deductions in computing net income. Indirect expenses of $100 or 1% of gross taxable income, whichever is greater, are allowable as a deduction. Losses from member and nonmember operations on a nonprofit basis are not to be used to offset taxable income.[13]

Rev & TC § 24406 includes cooperatives whose income is derived from the sale of tangible personal property other than water, agricultural prod-

---

(10) LR 389, 8–25–76.
(11) LR 418, 5–12–81.

(12) LR 390, 8–25–76.
(13) § 24405.

ucts or food sold at wholesale. The deduction allowed this group of cooperatives is only the patronage refunds paid or accrued which are made: (a) in accordance with a pre-existing obligation created by the association's by-laws or other written instrument; (b) from earnings attributable to business done by the association with the patrons to whom the patronage refunds are made; and (c) allocated ratably according to the patronage with notification to the patrons on or before the due date for filing the franchise tax return (including any extension of time).[14]

For income years starting on or after 1–1–89, qualified gas producers' cooperative associations are entitled to a patronage refund deduction. These associations must certify their eligibility to the Franchise Tax Board. The deduction is for refunds paid to patrons of association out of earnings attributable to business done with the patrons. Refunds must be allocated according to patronage in accordance with preexisting obligation, association by-laws, or some other written instrument. Notice of allocation made must be given patrons before the return filing deadline for the year in which it occurred.[15]

¶ 1155   Organization Expenditures

The provisions in IRC § 248(a) and the California Bank and Corporation Tax Law on the amortization of organizational expenditures are the same. In addition, the regulations are substantially similar. They provide that a bank or corporation may elect to treat organizational expenditures as deferred expenses, amortizable on a straight line basis over a period of not less than 60 months, beginning with the month in which it began business.[16] For business start-up expenses, see ¶ 392.

Organization expenditures. The term includes any expenditure that:

   (a) Is incident to the creation of the bank or corporation;
   (b) Is chargeable to a capital account; and
   (c) Is of a character of which if expended, incident to the creation of a bank or corporation having a limited life, would be amortizable over such life.[17]

Examples of organizational expenditures. Legal services incident to the organization of the bank or corporation such as drafting the corporate charter, by-laws, minutes of organizational meetings, terms of original stock certificates and the like, necessary accounting services, expenses of temporary directors and of organizational meetings of directors or stockholders and fees paid to the state of incorporation.

Not qualifying. Any expenditures in connection with the issuing of, or selling shares of stock or in connection with the transfer of assets to the bank or corporation are not considered as organizational expenditures.

Election. This must be made in a statement attached to the taxpayer's return for the income year in which it begins business and should include the

---

(14) § 24406.
(15) § 24406.5.

(16) § 24407.
(17) § 24408.

description and the amount of the expenditures involved, the date they were incurred, the month in which the taxpayer began business and the number of months over which the expenditures are to be ratably deducted.[18]

¶ 1156   Dividends Received From Insurance Companies

Rev & TC § 24410 states that dividends received by a corporation domiciled in California from an insurance company subject to the California gross premiums tax at the time of the payment of the dividend, and at least 80% of each class of whose stock is owned by the corporation receiving the dividend are subject to a special deductible dividend computation.

If the payor insurance company has gross income from sources either within or without the state, the deduction is limited to that portion of the dividends received which correspond to the average percentage determined by applying an allocation formula consisting of the following three factors: (1) a gross receipts factor; (2) a payroll factor; (3) a property factor.

The second and third factors are determined under the provisions of the Uniform Division of Income for Tax Purposes Act (except that the property factor will include all intangible investment property allocated to the commercial domicile of the insurance company).[19]

¶ 1157   Losses

Any loss sustained during the income year and not made good by insurance or some other form of compensation is allowed as a deduction, with some limitations. The loss has to be evidenced by closed and completed transactions, fixed by identifiable events and actually sustained during the income year. The amount of the loss allowable as a deduction is limited to the adjusted basis for determining the loss from the sale or other disposition of the property involved. The loss is allowed as a deduction for California purposes only for the income year in which the loss is sustained. This means that the loss occurs when it is evidenced by closed and completed transactions and fixed by identifiable events occurring during the income year.[20] For federal purposes, but not California, disaster losses occurring between the close of the taxable year and the original due date of the return may be deducted in the prior taxable year.

If a casualty or other event occurs which results in a loss and in that year there exists a claim for reimbursement with respect to which there is reasonable prospect of recovery, the corporation cannot take a deduction for the year. The appropriate adjustment is to be made for the year in which the recovery is received or the corporation determines that it will not be received.[21]

---

(18) § 24409.
(19) § 24410.

(20) § 24347(a); Reg 24347–1(a)–(c).
(21) Reg 24347–1(d).

If any security becomes worthless during the income year, the loss is to be treated as a loss from the sale or exchange of the security on the last day of the taxable year.[22]

Theft losses are treated as sustained during income year taxpayer discovers the loss.[23]

For qualified disaster losses as listed below, a California deduction is allowed under IRC § 165(i) permitting the loss to be taken against the previous year's income, instead of the deduction under Rev & TC § 24347. Excess loss can be carried forward to five income years following the income year it is claimed. It must be carried to the earliest year. Excess loss remaining after the five-year period can be carried forward to each of the next 10 years to the extent of 50% of the loss. The governor must proclaim the affected county or counties to be in a state of disaster. Any corporation subject to the allocation provisions of Rev & TC § 25101 or 25101.15 that has disaster losses subject to Rev & TC § 24347.5 must determine excess loss to be carried to other years under Rev & TC § 25108 provisions relating to net operating losses. Loss taken under Rev & TC § 24347.5 can't be taken into account in computing net operating loss deduction under Rev & TC § 24416 or § 24416.1.[24]

OBSERVATION   *IMPORTANT LISTING OF DISASTER AREAS.* Disaster areas for years prior to 1991 are listed in Rev & TC § 24347. For years after 1990:

(1) the Oakland/Berkeley fire losses of 1991 or any other related casualty,

(2) earthquake, aftershock, or any other related casualty during April, 1992 in the County of Humboldt,

(3) losses as a result of riots, arson, or any other related casualty occurring in April or May, 1992,

(4) the Fountain Fire occurring in the County of Shasta or any other related casualty,

(5) earthquakes occurring in the County of San Bernardino in June, and July of 1992 and any other related casualty,

(6) fires in the Counties of Calaveras and Trinity that occurred in August, 1992, or other related casualty[25], and

(7) any loss sustained as a result of a fire in the County of Los Angeles, Orange, Riverside San Bernardino, San Diego, or Ventura, during October or November, 1993, or any other related casualty,

(8) any loss sustained as a result of the earthquake, aftershocks, or any other related casualty that occurred in the Counties of Los Angeles, Orange, and Ventura on or after January 17, 1994, and

---

(22) § 24347(d).
(23) § 24347(c).
(24) § 24347.5.

(25) § 24347.5; 24347.6; 24347.7; 24347.8; 24347.9.

(9) any loss sustained as a result of a fire that occurred in the County of San Luis Obispo during August, 1994, and any other related casualty.[26]

¶ 1158   Capital Losses

California modifies IRC § 1212 by providing that the provisions of IRC § 1212(a)(1)(A), relating to capital loss carrybacks do not apply. Also, the special rules of IRC § 1212(a)(3), relating to special rules on carrybacks will not apply. IRC §§ 1212(b) and 1212(c), relating to taxpayers other than a corporation, shall not apply.[27] A corporation under the federal provisions[28] may carry a capital loss not used during the current year back to each of the three taxable years preceding the loss year and any excess loss may be carried forward for five years following the loss year. California adopts only the carry forward rule.

¶ 1159   Amortization of Bond Premium

Bond premium is amortizable by the owner of the bond as follows:

(a) Amortization of bond premium is mandatory for fully tax-exempt bonds (the interest of which is excludable from gross income);

(b) Amortization of bond premium is optional at the election of the taxpayer for fully taxable bonds.[29]

In the case of a fully tax-exempt bond, the amortizable bond premium for the income year is simply an adjustment to the basis of the bond. However, in the case of a fully taxable bond, the amortizable bond premium is both an adjustment to the basis of the bond and a deduction in computing net income. The bond premium is the excess of the amount of the basis (for determining loss on the sale or exchange under Rev & TC § 24911) of the bond over the amount payable at maturity or at an earlier call date, if applicable.[30]

IRC § 171(b)(1)(B) provides that the amortization period may be determined by an earlier call date instead of the maturity date of the bond which is ordinarily used if it results in a smaller amortizable bond premium deduction. California has the same provision.

California conforms to IRC § 171(b)(3) relating to the method of determining the amortizable bond premium. Except as provided in the regulations, the determinations required under IRC § 171(a)–(b) must be made on the basis of taxpayer's yield to maturity, determined by (1) using the taxpayer's basis for purposes of determining loss on the sale or exchange of the obligation, and (2) compounding at the close of each accrual period, as defined in IRC § 1272(a)(5). If the amount payable on an earlier call date is used under the compounding provisions in determining the amortizable bond premium to the period before the earlier call date, that bond must be

---

(26) § 24347.5, as amended by Stats. 1994, c. 1245, § 5.
(27) § 24990.5(a)–(b).

(28) IRC § 1212.
(29) § 24362; 24363.
(30) § 24360.

treated as maturing on that date for the amount so payable, and then reissued on that date for the amount so payable.[31]

California adopts the IRC § 171(e) treatment as offset to interest payments. In the case of any taxable bond (1) the amount of any bond premium shall be allocated among interest payments on the bond under rules similar to Rev & TC § 24361(c); (2) instead of any deduction under Rev & TC § 24360, the amount of any premium so allocated to any interest payment shall be applied against, and operate to reduce the amount of the interest payment. Taxable bond is any bond the interest on which is not excludable from gross income.[32]

¶ 1160 **Soil and Water Conservation Expenditures**

Farmers can deduct in the tax year paid or incurred expenditures for soil and water conservation and the prevention of the erosion of land used in farming. California conforms to IRC § 175. Soil and water conservation expenses are limited to those consistent with a conservation plan, if any, approved by the Soil Conservation Service of the Department of Agriculture or, in absence of a plan, a plan of a comparable state conservation agency. Expenditures in connection with draining or filling of wetlands, or preparing land for installation or operation of a center pivot irrigation system are not eligible for the IRC § 175 deduction.[33]

Deductible. Deductible items include expenditures for the treatment, moving or cultivation of earth including leveling, conditioning, grading, terracing, contour furrowing and restoration of soil fertility, eradication of brush, planting of wind breaks and construction control and protection of diversion channels, draining ditches, irrigation ditches, earth and dams and the like.

Not deductible. Not deductible are taxpayer's expenditures to buy, construct, install or improve structures, appliances and facilities subject to depreciation.

Gross income limits. IRC § 175 has a limitation of 25% of the gross income from farming. Any excess expenditures incurred over the limitation may be carried over and deducted in a subsequent year (subject to the same 25% limitation for that year).

Land used for farming. The term "land used for farming" means land used by the taxpayer or his tenant for the production of crops, fruits or other agricultural products or for the sustenance of livestock.

Fertilizer and lime. Rev & TC § 24377 allows a corporate taxpayer to deduct, rather than capitalize, the amount paid or incurred during the income year for the purchase of fertilizer, lime, ground limestone, marl or other materials to enrich, neutralize or condition land used in farming. The

---

(31) § 24361(c).
(32) § 24363.5.

(33) § 23051.5; 24369.

election must be made within the time prescribed by law (including extensions) for filing the return for the year by claiming a deduction on the taxpayer's return.[34]

Land clearing expenses. The Bank and Corporation Tax Law did not conform to IRC § 182 that allowed expensing of land clearing expenses in tax years before 1986. Such expenses must be capitalized as part of basis of land.

---

(34) § 24377.

ALLOCATION AND APPORTIONMENT OF INCOME

¶ 1161   Introduction

This chapter explains the concept of unitary businesses and combined reporting of income. Also discussed are the methods of allocating nonbusiness income and apportioning business income by a formula of property, payroll, and sales. Special formulas are also discussed.

APPLICABLE LAWS

¶ 1162   Basic Law for Allocation and Apportionment

The Uniform Division of Income for Tax Purposes Act was originally drafted in 1957 by the National Conference of Commissioners on Uniform State Laws. In 1959, the United States Supreme Court issued its opinion in the case of *Northwestern States Portland Cement Company v. Minnesota,*[1] which discussed the rights of the states to assess a tax against an out-of-state corporation. As a result, Congress felt the need to establish rules on the rights of states to assess taxes on the income of corporations involved in interstate commerce. Public Law 86–272 defined the rights of a state to assess a tax against an out-of-state corporation which is engaged in selling personal property within the limits of the state. The UDITPA Act was adopted by the California Legislature in 1966.[2]

The provisions of the Act applied first for corporations filing California returns for income years beginning January 1, 1967, and later.

> *Note:* California did not adopt the definition of financial organization and public utility which are in the UDITPA Act. Also, UDITPA excludes financial organizations and public utilities from the provisions of the Act. The California version does not follow this exclusion; therefore, financial organizations and public utilities are taxed with other taxpayers under the California version of UDITPA. In addition, California has modified UDITPA with respect to the taxation of dividends and nonbusiness income.

OBSERVATION   Always rely on the California Revenue and Taxation Code (Bank and Corporation Tax Law) rather than the provisions of UDIPTA.

¶ 1163   Federal Law Protecting Interstate Businesses

Public Law 86–272. Public Law 86–272 was enacted by Congress in 1959 to place restrictions on the states in the taxing of businesses engaged in activities in interstate commerce. The principal provisions of P.L. 86–272 are as follows:

No state, or political subdivision thereof, shall have power to impose, for any taxable year . . . a net income tax on the income derived within such state by any person from interstate commerce *if the only business activities* within such state by or on behalf of such person during such taxable year are either, or both, of the following:

(1) 358 US 450.   (2) § 25120–25139.

¶ 1163

(1) The solicitation of orders by such person, or his representative, in such state for sales of tangible personal property, which sales are sent outside the state for approval or rejection, and if approved, are filled by shipment or delivery from a point outside the state, and

(2) the solicitation of orders by such person, or his representative, in such state in the name of or for the benefit of a prospective customer of such person, if orders by such customer to such person to enable such customer to fill orders resulting from such solicitation are orders described in paragraph (1).

U.S. Supreme Court's interpretation of protected activity. The protected activity under P.L. 86–272 has now been defined to include activities that are "entirely ancillary to requests for purchases - those that serve no independent business function apart from their connection to the soliciting of orders." A standard has also been established for *de minimis* activities which do not eliminate protection under P.L. 86–272 and these are defined as "nontrivial additional connections" *Wisconsin Dept. of Revenue v William J. Wrigley, Jr., Co. (1992) 112 S Ct 2447, 120 LE2d 174.* The Court then listed protected and nonprotected activities as:

(1) Automobile provided to salesmen

(2) Stock of free samples provided to salesmen

(3) Recruitment, training and evaluation of salesmen (but not in an owned or leased facility)

(4) Sales-related meetings in hotel and personal residences

(5) Advertising (print, radio and television) where directed from outside the state

(6) The occasional use by salesmen of their homes for meetings and the use of a portion of one's home as one's office did not constitute the maintenance of an office by the taxpayer.

Nonprotected activities as defined by the *Wrigley* Court include:

(1) Maintenance of an office even if used exclusively for solicitation of sales (solicitation of sales is a protected activity under P.L. 86–272)

(2) Repair or servicing of company's products

(3) Replacement of products by salesmen

(4) Advance deliveries of product by salesmen for consideration

(5) Storage of product either with salesman or at a storage facility to facilitate (3) and (4) above

(6) Maintenance of a warehouse or inventory (other than free samples).

Board's interpretation. The Franchise Tax Board has issued FTB 1050 "Application and Interpretation of Public Law 86–272" as a guide for out-of-state corporations making sales of tangible personal property within California. The brochure points out that the activity in California by an out-of-state corporation in order to be immune to taxation by California must be limited to solicitation and activities related to it.

WARNING   If there is any activity that exceeds solicitation, immunity is lost.

To be exempt from California's tax on net income, an out-of-state corporation must have its sales approved outside of California (except for independent contractors), and the deliveries must be made from inventories located outside of California. In other words, if a salesperson for an out-of-state corporation comes into California, sales of tangible personal property may be solicited and samples may be carried for display, advertising campaigns may be conducted, and missionary sales activity can take place. If the salesperson handles repairs, collection of delinquent accounts, credit investigations or installation of merchandise, the corporation would lose its immunity. If an out-of-state corporation maintains a sample or display room or sales office in California on a permanent basis it would be subject to California tax. If it maintains inventories in California, or a repair shop, or parts department, a purchasing office, employment office, warehouse, or similar activities, it would not be immune from California tax. If the sales in California are solicited by independent contractors, the company would not be taxable by California regardless of where the sale is approved and whether or not the independent contractor maintains his own sales office.

The interpretation by the Franchise Tax Board of P.L. 86–272 is important to the state in order to decide the taxability of out-of-state corporations having activities in California.

IMPORTANT   The California interpretation should also be used by taxpayers as well as by the Franchise Tax Board in determining whether or not the activity of the taxpayer in another state means that the taxpayer is taxable in that state under California's standards. This is important because in the sales factor of the apportionment formula, for example, UDITPA permits assigning sales filled from California inventories to any state where the taxpayer is subject to tax, as defined in PL 86–272.

Taxable in another state. A taxpayer is "taxable in another state" if (a) in that state it is subject to a net income tax, a franchise tax measured by net income, a franchise tax for the privilege of doing business, or a corporate stock tax, or (b) that state has jurisdiction to subject the taxpayer to a net income tax regardless of whether in fact it does or does not.

WARNING   If the taxpayer in filing a California return assigns sales in the sales factor to another state, it should be prepared to furnish evidence to the Franchise Tax Board that its activities in the other state qualify for an income tax to be assessed by the other state. Obviously, the best evidence is a copy of the tax return filed in the other state. In the absence of that, the Franchise Tax Board may require an affidavit from the taxpayer attesting to the existence of business activities in the other state which would make the taxpayer subject to the income or franchise tax in the other state.

The definition of "state" includes any state of the United States, the District of Columbia, Puerto Rico, territories and possessions of the United States, and any foreign country. Foreign countries and possessions of the United States are treated as other states to determine whether or not they have jurisdiction to tax a corporation on the basis of the activities in that country. If the activity in the other country were the same as that activity which would permit California to assess an income tax against a corporation, the foreign country would have jurisdiction to tax even though it did not have similar income tax laws, and even if there was a treaty between the foreign country and the United States. See SBE decision in *Appeal of Dresser Industries* (¶ 1184).

¶ 1164 **Multistate Tax Compact**

In addition to adopting UDITPA, California became a member of the Multistate Tax Compact.[3] This is an organization promoted by the Council of State Governments to assist in obtaining uniformity among the various states as far as taxation of interstate businesses is concerned. The apportionment rules set forth in UDITPA have been adopted by the Multistate Tax Compact. As provided in Article VIII, Paragraph 2 of the Compact, a major activity of the Multistate Tax Commission is a joint audit program which consists of performing audits of major corporate businesses on behalf of member states. The average number of states participating in each audit is around ten. Prime emphasis is placed on net income tax audits and sales and use tax audits; but the Commission also performs gross receipts tax audits and franchise tax audits for some states.

The Commission has audit offices in New York, Chicago and Houston, the centers of most of its auditing activity, although it has performed many audits elsewhere. The Commission claims that an audit for, say, ten states eliminates much of the duplicative effort which would take place if each of the ten states were to send one or more auditors across the country to perform a separate audit. The Commission also points out that, in many cases, a joint audit helps the states to take a more uniform approach to the determination of a taxpayer's tax liability than is the case where separate audits are performed by the various states. The validity of the Multistate Tax Compact was challenged and upheld by the United States Supreme Court in the matter of *U.S. Steel et al v. Multistate Tax Commission, et al. (1978) 434 US 452, 98 S Ct 799.*

Audits. Article VIII, Paragraph 2, of the Multistate Tax Compact states, "Any party, state, or subdivision thereof desiring to make or participate in an audit of any accounts, books and papers, records or other documents, may request the Commission to perform the audit on its behalf. The Commission may enter into agreements with party states or their subdivisions for assistance in performance of the audit. The Commission shall make charges to be paid by the state or local government, or governments for which it performs a service for any audits performed by it in order to reimburse itself for the actual costs incurred in making the audit." The information obtained by an audit under these rules is confidential and available only for tax purposes to the party states or their subdivisions or the United States.

---

(3) § 38001.

The Multistate Tax Commission can also act to pick and maintain an arbitration panel to resolve disputes arising between the states and taxpayers involving the Uniform Division of Income for Tax Purposes Act. The three-member arbitration panel is composed of one person chosen by the taxpayer, one by the state agency or agencies involved, and one member of the Multistate Tax Commission's panel.

The Compact has adopted as its apportionment formula the provisions of the Uniform Division of Income for Tax Purposes Act, including the definitions of business income, nonbusiness income and the provisions regarding the composition of the property, payroll and sales factors of the apportionment formula. The Compact is designed to assist a proper apportionment of income and franchise taxes between the various states. It has provisions for the equitable administration of sales and use taxes, gross receipts taxes and capital stock taxes.

¶ 1164A   **Income Through California Investment Partnerships**

California source income does not include income arising through a partnership which qualifies as an investment partnership in California as defined in Rev & TC § 17955. This exclusion applies whether or not the partnership has a usual place of business in California, if the income from the partnership is the bank's or corporation's only income derived from or attributable to sources within California. Such income includes income from interest, dividends, or gains and losses from qualifying investment securities. An investment partnership is one which has at least 90% of the partnership's cost of its total assets in qualifying investment securities, deposits at banks or other financial institutions, and office space and equipment reasonably necessary to carry on its activities, and no less than 90% of its gross income from interest, dividends, and gains from the sale or exchange of qualifying investment securities.

Qualifying investment securities include: common stock, including preferred shares or debt securities convertible into common stock, and preferred stock; bonds, debentures, and other debt securities; foreign and domestic currency deposits or equivalents and securities convertible into foreign securities; mortgage- or asset-backed securities secured by federal, state, or local governmental agencies; repurchase agreements and loan participations; foreign currency exchange contracts and forward and futures contracts on foreign currencies; stock and bond index securities and futures contracts, options on any of the forementioned investments, and regulated futures contracts. Qualifying investment securities does not include an interest in a partnership unless that partnership is itself an investment partnership.[4]

---

(4) § 23040.1.

UNITARY BUSINESSES

¶ 1165   **General Concept**

Basic California law.   The basic sections on which the Bank and Corporation Tax Law depends for the apportionment of income and the application of the unitary business concept are the following:

- Rev & TC § 25101[5] provides that when the income of the taxpayer is derived from or attributable to sources both within and without the state the tax must be measured by the net income derived from or attributable to sources within this state.
- Rev & TC § 23040[6] provides that income derived from or attributable to sources within this state includes income from tangible or intangible property located or having a situs in this state and income from any activity carried on in this state regardless of whether it is carried on in intrastate, interstate, or foreign commerce.
- Rev & TC § 25102[7] is authority for the rule that in the case of two or more "persons" owned or controlled, directly or indirectly, by the same interests, the Franchise Tax Board may permit or require the filing of a combined report and such other information as it deems necessary. It is authorized to impose the tax due under this part as though the combined entire net income was that of one person, or to distribute a portion or allocate the gross income or deductions between or among such persons if it determines such consolidation, distribution, apportionment or allocation is necessary in order to reflect the proper income of any such persons.

"Person" is defined in the California codes as including corporation, partnerships and other types of associations and ventures formed to carry out certain transactions. In application, the FTB does not require that partnerships owned by the same individuals as the corporation operating within and without California be combined with the corporation in a unitary return.

Major court decisions.   The first landmark case for California was that of *Butler Brothers v. McColgan ((1941) 17 C2d 664, 111 P2d 334).* In this case the three factor apportionment formula used by California was approved by the United States Supreme Court. The case involved a corporation which operated department stores in many states including California with the principal purchasing activities in the other state and primary sales activity in California. The taxpayer used a separate accounting method for its California operations and showed a net loss in California although the corporation as a whole had a profit on its Federal tax return. The Supreme Court said that the formula method should be used and applied to the combined income of the corporation. The Court stressed in particular the fact that because the company operated a number of department stores it was able to purchase in larger quantities and therefore obtain more favorable costs for merchandise than it would have been able to do had it only been operating the California store. The Court answered the separate accounting

---

(5) § 25101.   (7) § 25102.
(6) § 23040.

question by saying that the taxpayer would be entitled to use it to determine its California income depending on the nature of the business within and without the State. If the business within the State is so truly separate and distinct from its business without the State that an accurate segregation of income could be clearly and accurately made, the separate accounting method could be used.

TAX TIP	The California Supreme Court in an earlier decision in the *Butler Brothers* matter, stated that a business "is unitary if there is unity of ownership, unity of operation (as evidenced by central purchasing, advertising, accounting and management divisions), and unity of use in its centralized executive force and general system of operation."

These three unities have been cited by the California State Board of Equalization in innumerable decisions involving the unitary business question since the *Butler Brothers* case.

Edison California Stores case. Five years later another important decision involving California unitary business taxation occurred. This was the decision in *Edison California Stores v. McColgan ((1947) 30 C2d 472, 183 P2d 16)*. The California corporation was one of fifteen corporations whose parent corporation had its headquarters in St. Louis, Missouri. All the subsidiaries operated retail shoe stores, each in a different state. The parent company purchased shoes for all the subsidiaries, and provided close supervision in management services. The case was decided by the California Supreme Court following action of the Franchise Tax Commissioner in combining the income of all the corporations in apportioning the income within and without California by use of the standard three factor formula. The Court said the principles governing the allocation of income of a unitary business were the same whether the business was conducted by one corporation with divisions or by one corporation with several subsidiaries.

IMPORTANT	The *Edison California Stores* case is the authority for another distinctive test of the unitary business which the Board of Equalization has enumerated in many decisions since the *Edison Stores* case. The test is whether the operation of the portion of the business done within California is dependent upon or contributes to the operation of the business done without the State.

Superior Oil and Honolulu Oil cases. The third major case for California in applying the unitary approach (actually there were two cases combined for decision) was that of *Superior Oil Co. v. Franchise Tax Board ((1963) 60 C2d 406, 34 Cal Rptr 545)* and *Honolulu Oil Co. v. Franchise Tax Board ((1963) 60 C2d 417, 34 Cal Rptr 552, 386 P2d 40)*. Up until this time the principal single business factor which served to establish that a unitary business was present was whether or not one of the branches or the subsidiary of the parent company was selling a product manufactured by the parent. In other words, if there was a flow of inventory within or without

¶ 1165

California in any appreciable amount, it was almost prima facie evidence that a unitary business existed. If this transfer of product was present the Board was satisfied that a unitary business existed even though other factors might not be of particular consequence.

Note: The *Superior Oil and Honolulu Oil* cases were decided by the California Supreme Court, which determined that a unitary business was present in each case even though there was no intercompany flow of goods.

The companies were producing oil companies which sold their well production, oil or gas, at the wells and did not refine or market their product.

Among the unitary factors listed were:

(1) Strong management and central supervision—the heads of the company exercised strong administrative control and made policy decisions even covering comparatively minor problems.

(2) Centralized purchasing—the central purchasing office purchased pipelines, drilling equipment, and even office equipment such as typewriters. Any expenditure over $1,000 had to be approved at the top executive level.

(3) The training of technical personnel was carried out on a coordinated basis throughout the company.

(4) Departments handled land acquisition and exploration activities on a companywide basis.

(5) Research and development and testing laboratories in California were used by all divisions.

In addition, assets outside of California were used as security to finance projects in California and sources from outside the State provided funds used to finance projects within California.

The Court stated, "The evidence here revealed that such essential factors as land acquisition, exploration, technology, testing, availability of equipment and personnel, financing and many others are definitely interstate in character. It must also be considered that each producing well in a particular state is the end product of interstate activities which may involve many other unproductive wells in many other states."

Following the *Superior Oil and Honolulu Oil* cases the Franchise Tax Board took the approach that if affiliated corporations were engaged in similar businesses with a certain amount of centralization of the management function, the businesses would probably be unitary. In other words, the customary attributes of a unitary business would be present for the companies engaged in similar businesses without the flow of goods or inventory between the companies.

Chase Brass's Copper Co. case.   The next important case in the chronicle of the unitary business concept was *Chase Brass and Copper Co. v. Franchise Tax Board (1970) 7 CA3d 99; mod 10 C3d 496, 86 Cal Rptr 350.* Chase Brass and Copper Co., a subsidiary of Kennecott Copper Corporation, was manufacturer of brass, bronze and copper in rods, sheets, wire and tubes. The manufacturing was done entirely outside of California. The copper used in the manufacture was bought from Kennecott Sales, also a subsidiary of Kennecott Copper Corporation. The sales by Chase Brass inside of California were made by a subsidiary called Kennecott Sales Corporation. The Court decided that the parent corporation Kennecott Copper Corporation and the subsidiaries, Chase Brass and Copper, Kennecott Sales and Kennecott Wire and Cable were unitary. There was strong emphasis placed on the fact that there existed a strong central management and executive force which made all the major policy decisions. Another substantial factor was the purchase of copper from the parent by Chase Brass and the fact that Chase Brass had its sales made by another corporation in the affiliated group. Unitary factors in the case were common purchasing, common insurance programs, common retirement plans, tax and legal services and use of the trade name "Kennecott." Two other subsidiaries of Kennecott Copper Corporation called Braden Copper Company and Bare Creek Mining Company were held to be not part of the unitary group.

Whereas before the Franchise Tax Board had asserted that a unitary business was present when affiliated corporations were engaged in similar businesses and had a central management making day to day decisions, it began applying the unitary approach to a wider group of corporations following the *Chase Brass Copper* decision. The audit policy of the FTB became one of combining a group of corporations which had a strong centralized management making major policy decisions even if they were engaged in widely divergent types of business. Other unitary factors were also considered important and were usually found to be present in some degree such as central purchasing, loans between affiliates, and so forth. The regulations under Rev & TC § 25120[8] discussing whether there are two or more businesses or a single business bring out the importance of centralized management.

This regulation provides that two or more businesses may be unitary "when the central executive officers are normally involved in the operation of the various divisions." However, this is only one of several factors to be considered. Three recent cases before the State Board of Equalization which addressed centralized management and which concluded that the businesses were not unitary because there was not strong centralized management include: *Appeal of the Hearst Corp*, (SBE, 6–18–92); *Appeal of Dart Container Corp of California, SBE, 7–30–92;* and *Appeal of Lakeside Village Apartments, Inc., SBE, 7–30–92.*

Mole-Richardson Co. The recent case of *Mole-Richardson Co. v. Franchise Tax Board, Calif. Ct Appl 2nd District (1990) 220 CA3d 889* used the presence of a strong centralized management to find that diverse businesses were unitary. The taxpayer corporation claimed it was unitary. It was engaged in the design, rental, manufacture and sale of lighting equipment for motion picture and TV studios. It also ran farm and ranch operations in both California and Colorado. A separate company owned real property in

---

(8) § 25120; Reg 25120.

both states. A subsidiary of the taxpayer rented motion picture lighting equipment. All of the stock in both companies was owned by members of the same family or family trusts. The taxpayer was headquartered in California, and managed by one of the family members who made all the business decisions from that office. All financial and accounting operations of the diverse companies were carried on in California. One attorney was employed as counsel for all of the business operations. The Court found that both the three-unities—ownership, operation and use—and dependency and contribution tests were met.

IMPORTANT	In recent years the Franchise Tax Board has again changed its emphasis and no longer asserts that a unitary business is present when the corporations are involved in dissimilar businesses even though there is a strong central management accompanied by the usual factors of intercompany financing, insurance programs, etc. The auditors review the entire list of factors, which are generally considered to be factors of unitary business and apply the unitary business treatment only when their review indicates that it is appropriate.

¶ 1166   Auditors' Factors for Finding Unitary Business

The staff and the field auditors of the Franchise Board believe that a number of factors are significant in deciding whether a unitary business is present between two or more corporations or between out-of-state and instate branches of the same company. These are explained below.

> *Note:* Field auditors have a list of questions that they give to the officials of the taxpayer under examination, the answers to which will assist the auditors in finding the extent to which the factors listed below are present and whether or not in the particular case they are significant.

There is no formula that auditors use to determine whether or not on the basis of the factors listed a unitary business is present. That is, they wouldn't go down the list of the factors and say that because a majority of them are present it is a unitary business, or if less than a majority applies in a particular case the business is not unitary. On the other hand, it might be that one or two of the factors are of such importance in a particular business that it would indicate that that business should be treated as a unitary business even though most or all of the other factors are either absent or insignificant.

Intercompany sales.   For the many years that the FTB used the unitary business concept prior to the *Superior Oil and Honolulu Oil* cases in 1963, the fact that there was any degree of intercompany sales between the entities was highly significant in establishing the fact of a unitary business. Although the *Superior Oil* cases gave authority to the point that you could have a unitary business without appreciable intercompany sales or purchases, it is still a very important element in the determination of the presence of the unitary operation. Some of the cases which have pointed out the importance of intercompany sales or purchases since the *Superior Oil* case are:

  (1) *Appeal of White Motor Corporation,* SBE 12–15–66.
  (2) *Appeal of Joyce, Inc.,* SBE 11–23–66.
  (3) *Appeal of Cutter Laboratories,* SBE 11–17–64.
  (4) *Appeal of Hunt Foods and Industries, Inc.,* SBE 4–5–65.

Centralized management. FTB auditors always review this in the case of affiliated corporations, not only where there are centralized executive officers who perform management functions for the corporation involved, but they also note whether or not the boards of directors of the separate corporations include the same people.

The information should be important only if these officers are involved in making major corporation policies which affect the overall operations of the entire business as a group. The importance of centralized management was brought out in the *Superior and Honolulu Oil* cases mentioned in the discussion above. Other cases which stressed management as a strong factor include the *Appeal of Hunt Foods and Industries Inc., supra, Appeal of Cutter Laboratories, supra,* and the *Appeal of Servomation Corp., SBE 7–7–67.*

Centralized purchasing. This is always mentioned as a strong unitary factor because in many cases the economic advantages can be mathematically computed. The fact that a group of corporations combining their purchases (for example, into carload lots) would be able to get volume or quantity discounts which were not available if they purchased individually is a factor. Not only may discounts be available, but it is also stressed in cases that centralized purchasing leads to the advantages of better delivery schedules, better credit terms and prompt attention to adjustments and complaints. The *Butler Brothers* case, both in the California and the United States Supreme Court decisions, discussed the presence of central purchasing as a strong element in determining that a unitary business was present. On the other hand, several Board of Equalization opinions have expressed the view that centralized purchasing is not necessary in determining that the unitary business exists, that it is merely one of the important factors. These include the *Appeal of W.J. Bush and Co. Inc.* SBE 6–6–57; *Appeal of Beatrice Foods, Co., SBE 11–19–58.*

Financing. The fact that one corporation in need of capital is able to borrow from one of the other corporations in the group is considered to be a strong unitary factor. In addition, the fact that the group of corporations together are able in some cases to present a stronger balance sheet might enable the parent corporation or the group to use the balance sheet information to point out that there is substantial backing in the form of net worth of the group which would make it easier to obtain a larger volume of borrowing. The cases citing the joint financing include the *Appeal of Monsanto Co., SBE 11–6–70; Williams Furnace Co., SBE 8–7–69;* and the *Appeal of White Motor Corporation, supra.*

¶ 1166

Centralized advertising. The use of a centralized advertising department can be beneficial to the group of companies as a whole from the standpoint that it would be theoretically possible to effect economies in the advertising budget or obtain more advertising coverage by doing it on a combined basis. The field auditors' questions include whether or not a corporation advertises in a national magazine or trade journal for that particular industry. If so, whether or not the advertising includes the names, addresses, telephone numbers of the affiliated corporations. The importance of centralized advertising was mentioned in the *Appeal of Maryland Cup Corp., SBE 3-23-70;* and the *Appeal of Joseph Magnin Co., Inc., SBE 10-10-65.*

Information and "knowhow" transfer. The field auditor may wish to examine correspondence for a representative period during the examination to see if he can find instances where one division or one corporation transferred particular information or "knowhow" to another division which would result in benefits to the latter. For example, the files of a sales manager might indicate some sales tips which if transferred to another division would be helpful; or the engineering staff may have come up with a process or a time-saving short cut which would give benefit to other engineering facilities in the group. Ordinarily this would not be a particularly significant unitary factor but in a given set of circumstances it could be the most important element of all.

Research or laboratory facility. This is another instance where it would appear on the surface at least that economies could be effected if the parent organization established a research or laboratory facility which would serve all of the divisions or all of the members of the affiliated group. It is one of the factors that is always looked for by the field auditors and its presence is ordinarily mentioned in the Board of Equalization decisions.

Pension and employee benefit plans. The use of common pension plans and employee benefit plans by all members of an affiliated group or all the divisions of a corporation is quite common. While it is evident that by combining these plans there are certain economic or administrative advantages, the fact of the existence of such plans or their absence would not seem to be significant in determining whether or not a unitary business is present. It is one of the factors, however, which the field auditors will investigate.

Common legal counsel and independent auditors. The Board of Equalization decisions which have pointed out the existence of a single legal staff serving the needs of all the entities indicate that certain economies might be effected from their use. Be that as it may, it might be a fact that a legal staff serving the needs of all members of a particular business might more effectively perform its functions because of their knowledge of the history of the company and the activities of the various locations and their relationships. On the other hand, it could be argued that an attorney in the corporate headquarters in New York had little knowledge of real estate, or patent, or tax laws in California.

The cases which have indicated that the affiliated corporations use the same outside auditors point out the possible economies and possibly lower fees which would result from such use. This argument largely ignores the impracticality of having different public accounting firms issuing opinions on various portions of the business.

Common insurance plans. The use of the same insurance company to provide fire, public liability, workman's compensation, employee disability or health and welfare plans for all the units in the business, makes sense from a business standpoint because of the possibility of somewhat lower costs and the probability of better service through concentrating these plans in one insurance company rather than separate insurance companies for the various individual entities in the group. This is another factor which is present in almost all multiple entity businesses and its presence would therefore not seem particularly impressive as far as being an indication that the businesses are unitary.

Physical sharing of facilities. The sharing of a physical facility such as a warehouse used by two divisions to store inventory in a particular state would seem to be indicative of a unitary operation through the combining of the costs of the plant itself and the payroll of the employees involved. If an argument could be made that separate accounting rather than apportionment by formula is appropriate, this is one factor which could lend itself to separate accounting treatment because the costs for each division or each entity using the facility could be apportioned using ordinary cost accounting techniques.

Union bargaining. The fact that a particular corporation with plants or facilities in California and other states employs workers who belong to the same nationwide union and therefore union bargaining sessions are handled on a joint basis is considered to be a unitary element. It isn't a fact that has received any significant amount of discussion in the Board of Equalization appeals covering unitary business problems, however.

Trade names and trade marks. The use of an established trade name or trade mark by subsidiaries of a parent which developed it could be a very important unitary factor. A corporation formed in California to sell a product which is well known nationally, which was developed by its parent, would have immediate acceptance in California. A hotel constructed in California by an eastern corporation with a large number of hotels with fine reputations would also benefit from the name association. These would be unitary factors which could be important. The sharing of patents and trademarks was discussed in the *Appeal of Anchor-Hocking Glass Corp., SBE 8-7-67*.

Patents and processes. If one corporation develops an important patent or process and permits another corporation to use that patent or process to its economic advantage, certainly that would be an argument that a unitary business exists. The Board's staff would make that argument even though the corporation using the other's patent would pay appropriate royalties or compensation for its use. *Anchor-Hocking Glass Corp.* discusses the sharing of patents.

Transfer of personnel.   If a corporation hires an individual, trains him in the particular skills involved in the corporation's business, that person becomes an asset to the corporation at the completion of his training and months or years of experience. When the person is transferred to another division or another entity operating in the unitary business group, the training by one and the utilization of the resulting experience are considered to be unitary factors.

The factors listed above include all which are of principal significance in determining whether or not a unitary business exists. Certainly there are many other factors which could be considered to be important. And, different weight may be given to a factor, or factors, based on the facts and circumstances of each case as perceived by the auditor from the Franchise Tax Board.

¶ 1166A   Ownership or Control—Section 25104[9]

The authority in the law for requiring the filing of a combined report between affiliated corporations uses the phrase "a corporation owning or controlling either directly or indirectly another corporation or other corporations." For years beginning prior to 1–1–95, Rev & TC § 25105[10] states that direct or indirect ownership or control of more than 50% of the voting stock of the taxpayer constitutes ownership or control for this purpose.[11]

For income years beginning on or after 1–1–95 the Legislature has defined control more precisely. However, the new definition of control does not apply to Rev & TC § 25102 which addresses a combined return of two or more persons owned or controlled directly or indirectly by the same interests.

The newly expanded definition of "commonly controlled group" applies to corporations required to apportion its income as provided in Rev & TC § 25101 or 25101.15. A "commonly controlled group" means any:

(1) parent corporation and any one or more corporations or chains of corporations connected through stock ownership, or constructive ownership, with the parent, but only if: (A) the parent owns stock possessing more than 50% of the voting power of at least one corporation, and, if applicable; (B) stock representing more than 50% of the voting power of each of the corporations, except the parent, is owned by the parent, one or more corporations which are more than 50% owned by a corporation which is more than 50% owned by the parent, or one or more other corporations that are listed below,

---

(9) § 25104.
(10) § 25105.

(11) LR 410, 411, 1–16–79.

(2) two or more corporations, if stock representing more than 50% of the voting power of the corporations is owned, or constructively owned, by the same person,

(3) two or more corporations that constitute 'stapled entities' as specifically defined, or

(4) two or more corporations, all of whose stock representing more than 50% of the voting power of the corporations is owned, without regard to the constructive ownership rules, by or for the benefit of, members of the same family. For this purpose members of the same family are limited to an individual, his or her spouse, parents, brother or sisters, grandparents, children and grandchildren, and the respective spouses.

If because of the above rules a corporation is treated as a member of more than one commonly controlled group of corporations, the corporation shall elect to be treated as a member of only one commonly controlled group and that elections shall remain in effect unless revoked with the approval of the Franchise Tax Board.

Rules are provided for the attribution of stock ownership and these include, but are not limited to,

(1) an individual constructively owns stock that is owned by his or her spouse, children of that individual or the individual's spouse who have not attained the age of 21,

(2) stock owned by an estate or trust for which the individual is an executor, trustee, or grantor, to the extent that the estate or trust is for the benefit of that individual's spouse or children,

(3) stock owned through a corporation, directly or indirectly, which are more than 50% owned, or

(4) stock owned through a partnership, in proportion to the partner's capital interest, including limited partnerships in certain specified cases.

The Franchise Tax Board is authorized to prescribe any regulations necessary to carry out the purposes of describing relationships which result in a 'controlled group of corporation'.[12]

Even though there are minority shareholders, their interest in the income or the factors of the allocation formula are not considered in a combined report. In other words, the income and the apportionment factors are included 100% if the corporation itself through ownership or control is included in the unitary group.

The Board of Equalization took up the problem of ownership or control in the *Appeal of Signal Oil and Gas Company, SBE 7–14–70.* In that case Signal Oil and Gas Company formed a subsidiary and retained 50% ownership of the voting stock. The other 50% ownership was held by a German national. At the same time, Signal Oil entered into a contract with the other stockholder which provided that Signal Oil would have operational control in the new subsidiary with another of its subsidiaries. The Board of Equaliza-

---

(12) § 25105, as amended by Stats. 1994, c. 1243, § 68.

tion decided that 50% ownership plus the indirect control was sufficient to include that subsidiary in that combined report filed by Signal Oil and Gas.

In the *Appeal of Revere Copper and Brass, SBE 7–26–77,* the Board of Equalization did not permit a 50% owned company to be included in a combined report. The company was a producer of aluminum and 50% capitalized by two competitors in the aluminum industry. The two competing companies had exactly equal rights to control the operation and management of the subsidiary. Neither had controlling ownership. The Board distinguished the *Signal Oil and Gas Company* case by stating that in Revere Brass and Copper there was no indication of management control by either party.

In the *Appeal of Shaffer Rentals, Inc., SBE 7–14–70,* the Board of Equalization held that there was the required ownership or control in a different set of circumstances. In *Shaffer,* part of the stock of two closely held family corporations was owned by various relatives while the remainder of the stock was held in trust for the benefit of those relatives. No single individual or trust owned a majority interest in either corporation. However, the combined legal and beneficial interests of three relatives represented substantially all the stock of both corporations. In quoting the appeal of *Revere Copper and Brass,* the Board said, "Thus, in view of the parallel stock ownership interests in both corporations and the lack of any adverse or outside interests in either corporation, we concluded that the ownership requirement was satisfied and the two corporations should be combined pursuant to Rev & TC § 25101." (But see *Appeal of Douglas Furniture, Inc., SBE 1–31–84,* below, overruling *Shaffer Rentals.)*

Related taxpayers. California has adopted IRC § 267 rules relating to transactions between related taxpayers. Before 1985 California Rev & TC §§ 24428–24429 set the rules for constructive ownership of stock. The decision in the *Appeal of Shaffer Rentals, Inc.* followed the rule set forth in Rev & TC § 24429.[13]

Shaffer Rentals, Inc. overruled by SBE. In the *Appeal of Douglas Furniture, Inc., SBE 1–31–84,* the SBE overruled its determination in *Shaffer Rentals, Inc.* It held that unity of ownership of a California corporation and an Illinois corporation did not exist because no one individual or entity owned more than 50% of the voting stock of each corporation sought to be included in the unitary group. The ownership requirement was not satisfied even though the aggregate interests of family members constituted 100% ownership in each of the companies. Lacking unity of ownership the two companies would not be considered engaged in a single unitary business, even though all the other requirements for such a finding were met. Taxpayers could not compel the Franchise Tax Board to accept the filing of a combined report. This ruling was followed by the SBE in another case decided on the same date, that involved a manufacturing corporation, and a

---

(13) IRC § 267; § 24427.

sales corporation in which no single entity or individual owned more than 50% of the voting stock of each corporation, although more than 50% of each corporation was owned by a single family. (*Taylor Topper, Inc., SBE 1–31–84.*) The ruling in *Douglas Furniture, Inc.* was also followed in *B.K.I. Management Co., Inc., SBE 4–5–84,* where all ten companies in the group were owned by the same five individuals, all in the same proportions, with one shareholder owning 50% of each corporation, and the other four owning 12.5%. Since no single entity or owner owned more than 50% of each corporation, the SBE ruled they were not unitary.

Majority ownership held by a family rather than a single individual. In the case of *Rain Bird Sprinkler Mfg. Co. v. Franchise Tax Board (1991) 229 CA3d 784, 280 Cal Rptr 362,* the California Court of Appeal, 4th District held that majority ownership of corporations could be held by a family rather than a single individual or entity to satisfy the unity of ownership test of the three unities rule for finding the existence of a unitary business. In the situation presented, a family business had passed from its founder. The mother and children held virtually all the stock of each corporation in the unitary group. All the companies operated on a consensus basis, maintaining strict ownership and control within the family. Written stock purchase agreements for each corporation prohibited the transfer of stock by a shareholder to any other than the corporation or a shareholder. The court observed that nothing in Rev & TC § 25105 specified the degree of ownership necessary to meet the unity of ownership test. The language "direct or indirect" suggests that there can be attribution of ownership between related stockholders in satisfying the test.

Indirect ownership. In the case of *Hugo Neu-Proler International Sales Corp. v. FTB (1987) 195 CA3d 326, 240 Cal Rptr 635,* the Court held that a DISC that was 100% owned by a partnership of two corporations, each holding 50% interest in the partnership, was indirectly owned by the partners, and part of a unitary business consisting of the partners, the partnership, and the DISC.

Spouses, partnerships and trusts. The Franchise Tax Board in a 2–3–87 release has interpreted the controlling ownership test where these parties are involved.[14]

¶ 1167 **Court Rulings on Nonunitary Businesses**

Although the Franchise Tax Board wins an impressive number of cases which are appealed to the Board of Equalization, occasionally the taxpayers' arguments are found by the board to be persuasive. The Franchise Tax Board's Legal Ruling 274[15] asserted that the gain on selling all of the stock of a wholly owned subsidiary was to be allocated to the parent company's headquarters office even though the subsidiary had been part of a multicorporate unitary business and included in a combined report. The distinc-

---

(14) FTB 2–3–87.   (15) LR 274, 11–2–64.

tion made was that the parent company was selling the stock of the subsidiary and not the assets.

General Dynamics Corporation sold one million shares of the stock of Airlift International, Inc. General Dynamics itself is a large, diversified corporation engaging in unitary business operations in many locations. It has a commercial domicile in New York City. In its California unitary tax return it assigned the gain on the sale of the stock to its New York domicile. The Franchise Tax Board decided that the gain was business income apportionable to California by formula. Stock had been acquired by General Dynamics several years previously in partial satisfaction of the purchase price on aircraft sold. The State Board of Equalization held for the Franchise Tax Board in stating under the Uniform Division of Income for Tax Purposes Act and the regulations following it, the income from intangibles would now be business income subject to the apportionment by formula. *Appeal of General Dynamics Corp., SBE 1–17–75.*

The Pacific Telephone Company, in order to reduce the size of its operation, transferred all of its unitary business assets in three northwestern states to a newly formed corporation in exchange for stock, notes and the assumption of liabilities. Shortly after the transaction took place, Pacific offered the stock it received for sale. The Franchise Tax Board, in examining specific tax returns, asserted that the gain was nonbusiness income assignable to Pacific's state of commercial domicile, California. The State Board of Equalization decided that the sale of the stock was a part of the unitary business involving a reorganization, and should be apportioned according to formula. *Appeal of Pacific Telephone Company, SBE 5–4–78.*

OBSERVATION   The Franchise Tax Board in a later case tried to tax the gain on a sale of the stock of a subsidiary on the premise that it was nonbusiness income. The Times Mirror Company acquired the Sun Company in order to further the regular business operations of the unitary group of businesses which was headed by the Times Mirror Company. During the time it was owned by the Times Mirror, the Sun Company was managed as an integral part of the regular business operations of Times Mirror. The facts were stipulated between the parties. The court relied on the regulations under UDITPA and held that the income was business income apportionable by formula rather than nonbusiness income allocable to the commercial domicile in California. *Times Mirror Co. v. Franchise Tax Board (1980) 102 CA3d 872.*

Other major nonunitary decisions.   Lear Siegler had acquired several new businesses, which it incorporated as divisions, and became a "conglomerate" in effect. The businesses included in its nationwide activity were the manufacture and sale of furniture for children in California, commercial heaters and industrial and military communication equipment in California, radio and television in New York, and high fidelity equipment in New Jersey. Each of the divisions, primarily because they were separate and distinct types of businesses, operated with its own executive staff and maintained separate marketing, purchasing and engineering departments, and also, handled the accounting for its own division with no interchange of employees between the divisions. There were pension and profit sharing plans but the participation between the divisions was optional. Over all the divisions was a corporate services division providing financing and other overhead services. The expenses of operating the corporate services division were prorated to the various operating divisions.

The Franchise Tax Board argued that there was a dependency between divisions in the area of policy making by executives, administrative control, accounting personnel, budgeting, profit-sharing plan and exchange of technical knowhow. The Board of Equalization decided that the various divisions were *not* unitary for the following reasons:

(1) Each of the divisions had its own management team to carry out its business policies.

(2) The purchasing, accounting and other business activities were not centralized.

(3) There was no transfer of inventory or materials between divisions in any appreciable quantities, or there was no common sales force or marketing operations.

(4) The general pattern of interdependence seemed to be lacking.

Appeal of Lear Siegler, Inc., SBE 4–24–67.

TAX TIP   In an early case the State Board of Equalization found that a unitary business is not created merely by intercompany financing in the absence of a common business activity, or unity of operation or of use as set forth in *Edison California Stores, Inc. v. McColgan (1941) 30 Cal 2d 472; 183 P2d 334; affd. 315 US 501, 86 L Ed 991 (1942) (Appeal of Allied Properties, SBE, 3/17/64).* More recently the State Board of Equalization reached the same result that intercompany financing alone was insufficient to create a unitary business *(Appeal of Berry Enterprises, Inc., SBE 3/4/86).*

A second appeal where the SBE found a business to be not unitary was the appeal of Servomation Corp. Servomation was a nationwide supplier of vending machines in industrial plants through various subsidiaries. Many of the subsidiaries obtained a substantial part of their merchandise and supplies from a central purchasing facility. The members of the Board of Directors and the officers of the various companies were in some cases the same individuals. The coordination of the efforts of the various subsidiaries was handled through regional committees with the same individuals as members. In addition, the company provided a nationwide management training program. Servomation had one subsidiary which was involved in food preparation for sporting events, served hot at the time of preparation rather than through vending machines. The taxpayer presented evidence to show that the food preparation subsidiary operated in a manner dissimilar from that of the other subsidiaries and was practically autonomous from a management standpoint. The Board of Equalization held that all of the companies were unitary with the exception of this one manual food preparation company. *Appeal of Servomation, Inc., SBE 7–7–67.*

The *Appeal of Jaresa Farms, SBE 12–15–66,* is an interesting case because of the wording in it rather than because of the result. The taxpayer operated a farm in California, a farm outside of California and it also had a service station, motel, cafe and curio shops located in other states. The Board of Equalization said that the taxpayer did not have a unitary business in spite of the fact that the same officers headed all the operations. The Board indicated that merely because all of the operations were financed through the personal guarantee of the president and chief stockholder that there was not the required dependency affecting the operations of the various types of business included in the group. The interesting wording is that the Board stated that the fact of common officers and central financing is present in every closely held corporation and inferred that these then were not important unitary factors.

In the *Appeal of H & R Block, Inc., SBE 6–6–68,* the Board of Equalization decided that the California corporation was not unitary with the national organization of this well-known tax preparation firm. For the years involved in the appeal, the Board found that the links between the taxpayer and the national organization other than stock ownership were (1) the use of the name, H & R Block, (2) the taxpayers were in similar businesses and (3) the California corporation purchased a small amount of supplies and equipment from the headquarters office. The control of each operation was sufficiently separate, based on the facts then before the State Board of Equalization, so that separate accounting was appropriate.

¶ 1168   **Combining Foreign Subsidiaries**

The Franchise Tax Board takes the position that all corporations or divisions involved in a unitary business are to be included in a combined report regardless of their location, including foreign corporations. The first time a question was raised as to whether or not the income of foreign subsidiaries of a taxpayer could be included in a combined report of a parent was in the appeal of the American Can Company in 1958. The case involved a United States taxpayer with California activities and a subsidiary in Canada. The Board of Equalization decided that the unitary business concept would be applied to foreign branches of United States companies, or, in this case, to incorporated wholly controlled businesses, even those in foreign countries.

There are several difficulties involved in combining foreign corporations or foreign branches of U.S. companies. These were recited by the taxpayer in the appeal. In the first place, in dealing with foreign countries you have the problem of the blockage of foreign funds. If the funds are blocked or there are currency restrictions, it would make it difficult to pay the taxes on the income derived from including the foreign operation in a unitary return. Another argument raised by the taxpayer was that there was a treaty between the United States and Canada and California could not apply a tax on income earned in the foreign country because it was not included in the treaty provision. The Board held that the tax convention and protocol between the United States and Canada was not applicable to the individual state of the United States by its very terms, and it was not intended to apply to them. *Appeal of the American Can Co., SBE 11–19–58.*

Other cases in which the SBE upheld the Franchise Tax Board in combining foreign subsidiaries or branches were the *Appeal of 20th Century Fox Film Corporation, SBE 7–7–62;* the *Appeal of William Wrigley Company, SBE 12–15–66;* and the *Appeal of White Motor Corp., SBE 12–15–66.*

The Franchise Tax Board now applies the unitary concept equally to businesses operated entirely within the United States and a United States business with operations in foreign countries or a business headquartered in a foreign country which has operations within the United States. The FTB has issued Reg § 25137–6 for the preparation of combined reports which include foreign country operations.[16]

In addition to the problem of blocked foreign funds and conversion of foreign income to comparable United States dollar values, there are other problems in combining foreign entities. One of these is the unavailability of accounting information. The FTB's auditors, if they receive financial statements or tax returns prepared in foreign countries have difficulties with respect to language problems, reading balance sheets and financial operating statements. There is always a problem due to different methods of accounting for depreciation, values of properties, etc. In other cases, the information may be based on tax laws of the foreign country which could be quite different from the domestic tax laws, and without detailed information it might be difficult to make the information in the foreign tax return comparable to that in the domestic tax returns.

U.S. Supreme decisions. Recent U.S. Supreme Court cases have stressed that the linchpin of apportionability is the unitary business principle. *Mobil Corp. v. Commr. of Taxes of Vt. (1980) 445 US 425* upheld a Vermont corporate income tax, calculated by apportionment formula, on foreign source dividend income received by a parent from its subsidiaries. The Franchise Tax Board in a recent notice dated 10–31–89 stated that the *Mobil* test of contributions to income resulting from functional integration, centralization of management, and economies of scale would be the primary standard it would rely on in analyzing whether a unitary business exists. *Exxon Corp. v. Wis. Dept. Rev. (1980) 447 US 207* applied this concept to subject the total corporate income of a multistate oil company to a state apportionment formula. In both cases the activities of the foreign subsidiaries were related to the business done by the parent company in the taxing state. Such was not the case in *F.W. Woolworth v. New Mexico Tax & Rev. Dept. (1982) 102 SCt 3108* where the parent exercised no actual control over

---

(16) Reg 25137–6.

the business of the subsidiaries, or in *ASARCO, Inc. v. Idaho State Tax Comm. (1982) 102 SCt 3103* where the business activities of the subsidiaries had nothing to do with those of the corporate parent in the state. The Court said intangible income could not be considered part of unitary business by reason of the fact that the intangible property was acquired, managed or disposed of for purposes relating to or contributing to the taxpayer's business.

The ruling by the U.S. Supreme Court in the case of *Container Corp. of America v. Franchise Tax Board (1983) 103 SCt 2933*[17] involved a paperboard manufacturer that did business in California and elsewhere, and had subsidiaries overseas that were incorporated in the countries in which they operated. In upholding the decision of the California Court of Appeal, 1st District that the parent and its foreign subsidiaries were engaged in a unitary business, the U.S. Supreme Court found that the lower court's decision was based on a large number of factors that included: (1) filling personnel needs that could not be met locally; (2) substantial role of parent in loaning funds to subsidiaries and guaranteeing loans provided by others; (3) considerable interplay between parent and subsidiaries in area of corporate expansion; (4) technical assistance provided by parent; and (5) supervisory role played by parent's officers in providing general guidance to the subsidiaries. All these factors, taken in combination showed that state court's decision was within limits of permissible judgment. The Court did however limit its decision to corporate groups with the parent company in the United States. The Court recognized that there may be different issues where the parent company of a combined group was located outside the United States. Thus the U.S. Supreme Court has not yet ruled on the inclusion of a non U.S. parent company in a combined group where California has established jurisdiction based on a subsidiary operating in California.

The California Court in *F.W. Woolworth Co. v. Franchise Tax Board, (1984) 160 C3d 1154* cited the U.S. Supreme Court decisions in *ASARCO, Woolworth* and *Container* cases in finding that the parent company was not engaged in a unitary business with its Canadian subsidiary. There was no integration or unitary operation between the companies. The Canadian sub operated a discrete enterprise.

Groups which include foreign parent companies, subsidiaries, and/or other affiliates. On 6–20–94 the U.S. Supreme Court ruled in *Barclays Bank PLC v. Franchise Tax Board of California; Colgate-Palmolive Co. v. Franchise Tax Board of California,* U.S. Sup. Ct. Dkt. Nos. 92–1384 and 92–1839, that the worldwide combined reporting for unitary business groups was valid. The Court ruled that California's worldwide combined reporting (WWCR), as applied to a worldwide unitary business group with a foreign-based parent, didn't violate the Commerce Clause or the Due Process Clause of the U.S. Constitution. In the companion case of *Colgate Palmolive Co.,* The

---

(17) FTB 89–713, 10–31–89.

Court also reaffirmed its prior holding in *Container Corp. of America v. FTB (463 US 159)* that the WWCR method was constitutional as applied to worldwide unitary business groups with a U.S. Based parent. So ended the controversy as to the inclusion of foreign operations (either that of a parent, subsidiary, or other affiliated entity) in a combined report of a unitary business for California reporting, and the determination of California tax.

This does not, *per se,* mean that all groups which include foreign operations are required to file a combined report. Rather the nationality of a business will not be a determining factor; rather, the decision as to whether the foreign activities fall within a unitary business will be decided on the same factors as if all members of the group are domestic U.S. business activities. See the discussion of unitary business activities at ¶¶ 1165–1169.

¶ 1169   Combining Solely California Unitary Operations

The filing of combined reports for companies operating only within California is permitted by Rev & TC 25101.15[18] which states that if the income of two or more taxpayers is derived solely from sources within this state and their business activities are such that if conducted within and without this state a combined report would be required to determine their business income derived from sources within this state, then such taxpayers shall be allowed to determine their business income in accordance with Rev & TC 25101.[19]

The burden of proof is on the taxpayer or taxpayers to prove that the business operations within California which they want to combine are operating a unitary business. It is not sufficient that the corporation or corporations be owned or controlled by the same interests or that they have incidental overall common management and some financing. They have to be able to show that there are factors which prove that the earning of income by one entity depends on or contributes to the earning of income by the other entity or entities in California.

TAX TIP   Two California corporations can offset the profits of one by the losses of the other if they can establish the fact of a unitary business.

COMBINED REPORTING—AFFILIATED CORPORATIONS

¶ 1170   Description of "Combined Report"

The California combined report is different in several respects from a federal consolidated income tax return. In the first place, the law states that the Franchise Tax Board may permit or require the filing of a combined report. It does so only in cases where the corporations can show or have shown that they are engaged in a unitary business. There is no election to be made by the corporations to file a combined report as there is in filing a federal consoli-

---

(18) § 25101.15.   (19) § 25101.

dated tax return. The federal consolidated return requires a parent owning each subsidiary included in the return to directly or indirectly own each to the extent of 80%. For California combined reports, it is only necessary that the ownership be in excess of 50%. California combined reports may be filed by "brother-sister" corporations engaged in a unitary business while "brother-sister" corporations are not entitled to file federal consolidated tax returns. The federal consolidated return provisions apply only to domestic corporations, while foreign corporations are included in unitary combined reports.

The federal consolidated income tax returns ignore the separate status of the individual corporations, while the combined report maintains the separate identity of the corporations included in the group.

The provisions of the law require that every corporation taxable in California file its own return and pay the tax. This has been true over the years even though the corporations get together in filing a combined report. The procedures for filing the combined report include a method of apportioning the income to the various localities in which it is earned.

Note: Once the California portion of the income is determined by the apportionment formula, the income would then be apportioned to each of the separate corporations in the combined report, which are taxable in California. The corporation would pick up that income and add to it the gain or loss of nonbusiness income in California and report the total amount as its taxable income in its franchise tax return.

As indicated in the paragraphs above, the separate identity of the corporations is retained and each was required to file its own California return.

EXAMPLE This example derived from L.R. 234[20] apportions the California income to each corporation which has California numerators.

Unitary income	$1,000,000	$2,000,000	$3,000,000	$6,000,000
Apportionment percentage	20%	15%	–0–	35%
Apportioned income	1,200,000	900,000	–0–	2,100,000

Apportionment Formula

		Total Property	**California Property**	**%**
Corporation	A	$ 2,000,000	$2,000,000	20%
"	B	3,000,000	1,500,000	15%
"	C	5,000,000	–0–	
Combined		$10,000,000	$3,500,000	35%
		Total Payroll	*California Payroll*	*%*
Corporation	A	$ 1,000,000	$1,000,000	20%
"	B	1,500,000	750,000	15%
"	C	2,500,000	–0–	0

(20) LR 234, 10–27–59.

¶ 1170

Combined		$ 5,000,000	$1,750,000	35%
		Total Sales	*California Sales*	*%*
Corporation	A	$ 4,000,000	$4,000,000	20%
"	B	6,000,000	3,000,000	15%
"	C	10,000,000	–0–	0
Combined		$20,000,000	$7,000,000	35%

Property	35%
Payroll	35%
Sales (doubled)	70%
Total Percent	140%
Average percent (÷4)	35%

	Corporation A	Corporation B
Property	20%	15%
Payroll	20	15
Sales	40	30
Total	80%	60%
Average (÷4)	20%	15%

The percentages for each corporation are arrived at by using their California numerators over the totals of the denominators everywhere.

You will note in the example above, that the income of Corporation C is included in the combined report because it is engaged in a unitary business. However, none of the unitary business income is apportioned to corporation C because it is not taxable in California i.e., it does not have either property or payroll active in the State of California. It could be that corporation C has activities in California in the form of salesmen soliciting the sale of tangible personal property without maintaining an office here, or sales made by independent contractors with no inventory located in the state. If that is true, then the provisions of PL 86–272 might apply to C's California activity and it would not be taxable in California even though it might have some apportionment factors in California (payroll, for example, or sales).

Application of corporation income tax.   California imposes two taxes: The franchise tax is imposed under Chapter Two. The income tax is imposed under Chapter Three of the Bank and Corporation Tax Law. The franchise tax is imposed on corporations and banks organized in California and on foreign corporations and banks doing business in California. The tax is for the privilege of doing business (exercising the franchise) in California.

The California income tax started in 1937 and applies to those corporations engaged in interstate commerce as well as those corporations which are not doing business in California, but which are deriving income from California sources. In other words, the distinction between a corporation subject to the franchise tax (Chapter Two) and the corporation income tax (Chapter Three) is whether or not the corporation is "doing business" in the state. Rev

& TC § 23101[21] defines "doing business" as "actively engaging in any transaction for the purpose of financial or pecuniary gain or profit." A foreign corporation would have to engage in intrastate business in California to be subject to the franchise tax. Regulation 23101[22] states that a foreign corporation which maintains a stock of goods in the state and makes deliveries in the state according to orders taken by employees in the state is "doing business" and its entire income from sources within the state is subject to tax under Chapter Two. If the foreign corporation has property and payroll in California, it is subject to franchise tax under Chapter Two. Regulation 23040(b)[23] points out that if foreign corporations make sales in the state through employees, but do not maintain stocks of goods nor engage in other activities here, they are not subject to the franchise tax; however, they would be subject to the corporation income tax.

> *Note:* The regulation also indicates that foreign corporations which maintain inventories here to fill orders taken by independent dealers or brokers are also subject to the income tax rather than the franchise tax. In other words, if a foreign corporation has inventory located here but no employees, or employees in the state making sales but no inventories located here, the corporation would be subject to the corporation income tax provisions if there is no immunity because of the limited extent of the activity as described in P.L. 86–272.

Whether the corporation is taxable under corporation income tax or corporation franchise tax is immaterial in the filing of a combined report as long as it is part of the unitary business group. As indicated above, the California income resulting from the apportionment formula is assigned to each corporation which is taxable in California and that income is separately taxed to the corporation.

¶ 1171   **Two or More Formulas**

It may well be that a corporation or the several corporations in a unitary group may be engaged in different types of businesses so that they are not all unitary with each other. In that case, each business would have a separate three-factor apportionment formula applied to the total unitary income from that particular business in order to find out the extent of that business in California. The resulting California income of each of the unitary businesses would then be apportioned to each of the corporations taxable by California in each unitary group. All of the corporations would then add up their share of the California income from each of the unitary businesses of which it is a part and pay a tax on the combined income. Along the same line, a corporation may be engaged in a unitary business within and without California entirely on its own and also be engaged in another unitary operation with an affiliated corporation in an entirely unrelated business. In that instance, the first corporation would separate its business income into two categories, one attributable to each of the unitary businesses (and a third category if it has nonbusiness income). All of the direct expenses allocable to each of the

---

(21) § 23101.
(22) Reg 23101.

(23) Reg 23040(b).

businesses, and all of the indirect expenses apportioned to each of the businesses in accordance with ordinary accounting procedures would be assigned to each of the businesses. Each different corporation would pick up in its California return, if any, its share of the unitary income and any nonbusiness income or losses assigned to California.

It might be that one of the unitary businesses or the nonbusiness activity of the corporation would have a loss for the taxable year. This loss would serve to offset the income generated by the other unitary activity or nonbusiness activity. Losses in a unitary business are apportioned the same way as incomes so that the California loss from a unitary business and the California portion of the income or loss from a separate business or from a portion of another unitary business are totalled in the tax return schedules.

¶ 1172 **Contents of Combined Report**

The Franchise Tax Board requires the following information to be included in a combined return:

(1) A combined profit and loss statement in columnar form showing the usual income and expense items for Federal tax purposes for each corporation included in the unitary group.

(2) Combined beginning and ending balance sheets in columnar form for each corporation.

(3) Combined reconciliation of income in columnar form showing for each corporation the income as adjusted for federal tax purposes in accordance with the profit and loss statement discussed in (1), above.

(4) Combined property factor in columnar form showing for each corporation the composition of the numerator and denominator for each class of assets as shown in Schedule R–1 with a column showing the amounts of intercompany rents eliminated for both the numerator and denominator.

(5) Combined payroll factor in columnar form showing the numerator and denominator for each corporation.

(6) Combined sales factor in columnar form showing for each corporation the composition of the numerator and denominator for each class of sales as shown in Schedule R–1, with a column showing the amounts of all intercompany gross receipts eliminated from both the numerator and denominator.

(7) Supplemental schedules for each corporation showing:

(a) Taxes on, or measured by, income.

(b) California franchise or income taxes.

(c) Interest on government securities excluded.

(d) Sales or exchanges of capital assets including loss carryovers with an explanation of the business or nonbusiness nature of assets sold.

(e) Other adjustments as required by Form 100 for state tax purposes.

(8) Schedules of each corporation's nonunitary income items and expenses applicable to each item of income.

With this data, it is possible to compute the combined unitary income, the combined apportionment formula, the nonunitary income and expenses of each corporation, and the taxable income for the entire group. Computation verifications can also be made for allowable interest expense, contributions, and intercompany eliminations and for each of the apportionment factors.[24] Franchise Tax Board may adopt regulations to ensure correct reporting, determination, collection, assessment, computation, or adjustment of tax liability under either the provisions of Rev & TC § 25101 governing the combined report, or the provisions of Rev & TC § 25110 governing the water's-edge election.[25]

In addition, Schedule R of the return requires separate schedules to show the net income or loss of the rental of nonbusiness property, the computation of the interest offset, the deductible contributions adjustment, and the profit or loss of the sale of nonbusiness assets. These schedules can be submitted in columnar form if the number of corporations in the unitary group makes that a practical necessity.

Net operating loss deduction allowed by Rev & TC § 24416 must be deducted from the sum of the corporation's net income or loss apportioned to California and its income or loss allocable to California as nonbusiness income.[26]

¶ 1173   Common Accounting Period

A combined report for a group of related corporations should be filed on the basis of the same accounting period for all members of the group. If the group consists of a parent and subsidiaries, the probability is that they will all be on the same accounting year. Common business practice or reporting requirements for financial or other purposes will ordinarily necessitate their being on a common accounting year (unless for a specific purpose, an affiliate has a different year end such as a DISC corporation). If there are corporations in the group which are on a different year from that of the parent, for purposes of a combined report they would have their income and expenses reported by converting to the parent's year end. If there is no common parent corporation, the income of the related corporations should be determined generally on the basis of the income of the corporation required to file a California return and expected to have on a recurring basis the largest amount of income includable in the measure of the California tax.

If it is necessary to convert one or more corporations to the common accounting period of the parent, or otherwise, the taxpayer can use the actual figures taken from the books of account for that member of the group for each of the months in the common accounting period.

As an alternative, the income can be determined on the basis of the number of months falling within the income year.

EXAMPLE   If a parent corporation is on a calendar year and the subsidiary included in the unitary report is on a March 31 year end, the subsidiary would include nine months of its income for one taxable year, and three months of its income of the prior taxable year in the common calendar year of the parent. If this is done, it would also be

---

(24) UDITPA Manual, September 1984, 1100.   (26) § 24416; 25108.
(25) § 25101; 25106.5; 25110.

necessary to apportion the factors of the apportionment formula in the same nine-twelfths and three-twelfths fashion.

TAX TIP	A single unitary group may be in existence for only a portion of a year so that losses of a subsidiary in the last quarter of a tax year may be used to offset the income of the parent corporation even though the two were not unitary for the entire 12-month period. While this is not a common situation, and it may be very difficult to prove that a unitary group existed for only part of a year, under the facts of the case the State Board of Equalization held that the unitary group existed based on the "transactional test" in California Rev & TC § 25120(d) (*Appeal of The Signal Companies, Inc., SBE, 1–24–90*).

Once the California income of the combined group has been determined and apportioned to each of the companies using the common year and the apportionment factors for the common year, a separate computation has to be made for the subsidiary corporation which converted its year end. Its share of the California unitary income is allocated back to its respective year ends on the basis of the same nine-twelfths and three-twelfths type of computation. This is a cumbersome procedure because the subsidiary converting to the parent's year end will always have a short period hanging over to be applied to the return for the subsequent year. Franchise Tax Board Form FTB 1061 contains instructions for corporations having different accounting periods and gives examples of the required computation.[27]

TAX TIP	The Franchise Tax Board may allow a taxpayer to report the income of affiliates in the combined report of the parent company based on the affiliate's year ending within the tax year of the parent company. For instance, if the parent reported on a calendar year basis, it could, but only with prior approval, include the income of the subsidiary which reported on a 11–31–91 year end in the 1991 calendar year of the parent. The Franchise Tax Board, as a condition for granting this approval, would require the taxpayer to agree that the omitted income for the period December 1 to December 31, be picked up in a final return if the group was liquidating, or withdrawing from California so that none of the income would escape tax.

¶ 1174 Treatment of Partnerships

The Franchise Tax Board may not require, or permit the filing of a combined report by a corporation or corporations and a partnership which are engaged in a unitary business, even though the partnership and the corporations meet the requirements of ownership and control, and have sufficient unitary factors. Since corporations are addressed in Part 11 of the Revenue and Taxation Code in which the authority for combined reporting is found in Rev & TC §§ 25101 and 25102, and since partnerships fall within Part 10 of the Revenue and Taxation Code with individuals, there is considerable question

---

(27) FTB 1061.

that the Franchise Tax Board could require the combination of a partnership with a corporation even if they chose to try. The FTB may require, or permit a corporation that is a partner in a joint venture or partnership engaged in a unitary business with the corporate partner to include in the apportionment formula the corporate partner's share of the property, payroll and sales factors of the partnership. This treatment is based on the theory that the corporate partner has an undivided ownership in each asset, liability, income, deduction, or credit of the partnership, to the extent of its ownership interest.

EXAMPLE   Corporation A is a 40% partner in Partnership B, both reporting on a calendar year basis. For calendar year, partnership has taxable income of $100,000 all derived from its unitary business with Corporation A. In accordance with the usual tax procedures, Corporation A includes in its franchise tax return its $40,000 share of the partnership income. Because it is considered to be business income from the unitary operation, it would be included in the income subject to apportionment by formula. In addition, 40% of the property of Partnership B would be included in the property factor of the apportionment formula and 40% of the payroll and sales factors.

TAX TIP   This gives an advantage to a California corporation engaged in a unitary business with a partnership in which it is a partner. Instead of reporting its entire share of the partnership income as nonbusiness income assignable to California, it would not only include that income subject to apportionment within and without California, but it would also have a lower California percentage because of the out-of-state factors of the partnership. For further information, see special formula-partnerships at ¶ 1187.

Gain or loss on sale of partnership interest by corporate partner is apportionable business income.[28]

¶ 1175   Affiliated Corporations

Although each corporation subject to tax under the Bank and Corporation Franchise Tax Law is required to file a separate return and pay the tax shown on that return, the Franchise Tax Board, through an administrative decision, has agreed that one tax return may be filed by members of an affiliated group engaged in a unitary business activity. The election is made on Schedule R–7 to Form 100. The election should be filed for the first year in which a group elects to substitute the filing of separate returns by filing the one return. Changes in the composition of the unitary group would be explained in Schedule R–7. Schedule R–7 includes a list of all the corporations in the group, with notations to be made for any additional corporations acquired during the year or any dispositions during the year. Each member corporation which is incorporated or doing business in California is required to pay at least a minimum franchise tax, even though the corporations elect to file a single return.

---

(28) LR 415, 4–15–80.

WARNING	The Franchise Tax Board does not allow corporations which have different accounting periods to be included in a single return. A group of corporations, some of whose members are on a different accounting period will be required to conform to the method of filing for different accounting periods discussed above.

Corporations will also not be allowed to file a single return if one or more of the reporting corporations uses more than one apportionment formula in the determination of its California taxable income.

EXAMPLE	If Corporation A is engaged in a unitary business with Corporation B and a separate unitary business with Corporation C a single return may not be filed by A, B and C. A must file a separate return reporting its apportioned total share of income from separate businesses of A–B and A–C. Corporation B files a separate return, reporting the apportioned share of income from business A–B. Corporation C files a separate return reporting its apportioned share of income from business A–C.

Note: This election (as made on form FTB 4523–A) is not an election to file on a unitary basis—that filing is based on the facts and circumstances of each case. The election is merely an administrative matter; the election to file a single return for the group, rather than multiple returns—one for each member of the group.

Corporations that become a member of a unitary group after the beginning of the income year, or cease to be a member of the unitary group during the income year, are required to file separate returns.

EXAMPLE	If calendar year Corporation A sells all of its stock interest in unitary subsidiary Corporation B during the year, B must file a separate return for the entire year. B's income for the first months of the year is determined by combined report procedure with Company A and for its last months of the year it is determined by separate accounting.

UDITPA provides that if a corporation which is already doing business is acquired and becomes a member of the affiliated group filing a combined report, that corporation does not join in the filing of a combined report until such time as its activities become unitary with the other corporations engaged in the unitary business. The income earned by that corporation in the taxable or income year in which it is acquired prior to the date of acquisition has to be separately computed, as well as the income earned by that corporation from the date of acquisition until it becomes engaged in the unitary business. Note that this treatment is different from that of the corporation standing alone. If it becomes subject to UDITPA during its income year, the income apportionable to California is determined on the basis of apportionment from the beginning of the year, not from the date on which it becomes subject to the apportionment provision. The UDITPA manual points to an example of a corporation which has been doing business in California for many years and making sales to Oregon customers through its salesmen located there. At a given point during the year, the taxpayer, by establishing an inventory in Oregon and opening a sales office there, loses its prior immunity under PL 86–272. According to UDITPA and the example, the taxpayer is covered by the Uniform Act for the entire year. All sales to

¶ 1175

Oregon during the year are considered out-of-state sales for purposes of the allocation formula.[29]

A group of corporations electing to file on a single return basis is required to designate a key filing corporation. This corporation will be responsible for payment of all taxes and estimated taxes. The Franchise Tax Board will look to the key corporation for any later adjustments or audits of the single return file.

TAX TIP   In filing on a single return basis, the estimated taxes must be taken care of in order to prevent the imposition of filing penalties. The total amount paid as estimated tax is the total estimated group liability for the income year. The first installment, which is due three and a half months after the beginning of the income year, must include at least a minimum tax for each of the corporations in the group. The application of the provisions for exceptions to the penalty for estimated taxes will be made on a combined basis. If the corporations file separate returns in the preceding year, the "tax shown on the return" for purposes of the prior year exception will be an aggregate of the prior year tax liability of all the corporations in the electing group. Using the annualizing provisions for exception from estimated tax penalty, the income for each installment period will be determined on the basis of the final apportionment percentage used in computing the tax shown on the return for the year.

The election to file a single return will continue each year until terminated in writing by either the taxpayer or the Franchise Tax Board. Whenever a change is made in the corporations within the group, it is necessary that the corporate group file a new form FTB 4523A with the FTB.

¶ 1176   Expense Apportionment

Executive salaries, utility bills, rent, other expenses of operation of the headquarters office, are examples of indirect expenses which are ordinarily not directly attributable to any division or business activity of a corporate taxpayer. These expenses are apportioned to the separate business activities of the corporation by using methods in accordance with acceptable accounting principles. For example, gross receipts or square footage of floor space can be used for a certain type of expense. It is not required that all expenses be apportioned by the use of the same method.

Along the same line, it is possible to use a combination of separate accounting and apportionment by formula to determine the income from California sources. For example, a corporation operating hotels in California and retail operations within and without the state would use separate accounting for the hotel operations and apportionment by formula for the unitary retail stores in California. The taxpayer would pay a tax on its net income from operation of the hotels, its apportioned California income from

---

(29) UDITPA Manual September 1984, 0500.

the operation of the retail stores, plus any gain or minus any loss from nonbusiness income allocable to California.

¶ 1177   Intercompany Eliminations

Through the mechanics of preparing consolidated statements of income and deductions of members of the affiliated group, intercompany transactions, by and large, are automatically eliminated. In other words, a subsidiary paying rent for premises owned by the parent would have a rental expense deduction in the consolidated income statement offset by an equal amount of rental income in the same statement by the parent corporation. Intercompany sales would be eliminated in the same way because the sales shown in one corporation's income in the consolidated statement would be offset by purchases in the consolidated statements for another member of the group. Problems would arise only if the members of the group used different accounting methods or periods to report their income and deductions. If that were the case, then an adjustment would have to be made through intercompany eliminations. The principal item which would not be eliminated in combining the income and expense statements of an affiliated group of companies would be the intercompany profit in the beginning and ending inventories of a company purchasing from other members of the group. Adjustment is required to make this change in the income statements.

¶ 1177A   Information Returns

For income years beginning on or after 1–1–94, specifically identified taxpayers apportioning income pursuant to Rev & TC § 25101 must file information returns with the Franchise Tax Board. The taxpayers from whom information returns are required are those with total assets exceeding $200 million, or such higher amounts as may be subsequently established by regulation. The $200 million is calculated for all affiliated banks or corporations which are defined as those where more than 50% of the voting stock of one is directly or indirectly owned or controlled by the other, or if more than 50% of the voting stock of both is directly or indirectly owned or controlled by the same interest. The information return shall be filed once every three years unless there is a substantial change in the taxpayer's business activities, in which case it shall be filed for the year in which the change occurs. The information return is due within six months after the due date (including extensions) of the bank's or corporation's California return.

The information return must identify the corporate parent and those affiliates of which more than 20% of the voting stock is directly or indirectly owned or controlled by the parent. The information return must identify the percentage of ownership and the type of corporation (foreign organized, U.S. organized, foreign sales corporation, or other relevant descriptions. Willful failure to substantially comply with the filing requirements subjects the taxpayer to penalties described in Rev & TC § 19141.6(d) which are described below in the explanation of records to be maintained.

The information return filing requirements do not apply to any bank or corporation for any year that its payroll, property, and sales within the U.S. are less than $500,000.[30]

¶ 1177B   Records To Be Retained

A detailed listing of records to be retained for those corporations apportioning income pursuant to Rev & TC § 25101 are found in Rev & TC § 19141.6. Failure to maintain the records, including the information returns required pursuant to Rev & TC § 18634 of selected taxpayers, will result in a penalty of $10,000 for each income year with respect to which the failure occurred. If the failure continues for more than 90 days after the day on which the Franchise Tax Board mails a notice of the failure, an additional penalty will be assessed for each 30-day period during which the failure continues after the expiration of the 90-day period. The additional penalty imposed will not exceed a maximum of $50,000 if the failure to maintain or the failure to cause another to maintain the records is not willful.[31]

ALLOCATION OF NONBUSINESS INCOME

¶ 1178   Business vs. Nonbusiness Income

Step-by-step allocation procedure.   The first step in assigning income from a multistate operation is to determine the items of income which are not part of business income and which are specifically assigned to a particular state. The next step is to determine through an apportionment formula the amount of the business income to be assigned to each state in which the unitary business income is earned. The third step would be to combine the nonbusiness income attributable to a given state with that state's share of the operating or business income apportioned to it, giving as a result the total income subject to taxation in that state.

TAX TIP   *Nonbusiness income.*   The determination of the nonbusiness income involves three operations as well: (a) the designation of the amount and types of nonbusiness income, (b) to pick out the state to which that type of income is to be assigned, and (c) to identify the expenses directly or indirectly assignable to that nonbusiness income.

State tax officials and commentators in the field of state and local taxation make a distinction between the terms allocation and apportionment. Allocation generally means the assignment of specific items of income (nonbusiness or non-operating income) to a particular state and apportionment means the distribution of interstate business income to the various states by means of a formula.

---

(30) § 18634.   (31) § 19141.6.

Rev & TC § 25120[32] defines "business income" as income arising from transactions and activity in the regular course of the taxpayer's trade or business and includes income from tangible and intangible property if the acquisition, management and disposition of the property constitutes integral parts of the taxpayer's regular trade or business operations. The term "nonbusiness income" is defined in subparagraph (d) of that same section as all income other than business income. Gain or loss on sale of interest in partnership, whose activities are unitary with corporate partner, is apportionable business income.[33]

Regulation 25120(a)[34] observes that "the classification of income by the labels occasionally used such as manufacturing income, compensation for service, sales income, interest, dividends, rents, royalties, gains, operating income, nonoperating income, etc. is of no aid in determining whether income is business or nonbusiness income. Income of any type or class and from any source is business income if it arises from transactions and activity occurring in the regular course of a trade or business. Accordingly, the critical element in determining whether income is 'business income' or 'nonbusiness income' is the identification of the transactions and activity which are the elements of a particular trade or business. In general, all transactions and activities of the taxpayer which are dependent upon or contribute to the operations of the taxpayer's economic enterprise as a whole constitute the taxpayer's trade or business and will be transactions and activity arising in the regular course of and will constitute integral parts of a trade or business."

Principal types of nonbusiness income.   The principal types of nonbusiness income are as follows:

(1) Dividends
(2) Interest
(3) Income from rental property
(4) Gains from capital assets
(5) Royalties
(6) Partnership income

Rev & TC § 25123[35] in defining nonbusiness income states that rents and royalties from real or tangible personal property, capital gains, interests, dividends, or patent or copyright royalties to the extent that they constitute nonbusiness income shall be allocated as provided in Rev & TC § 25124 through 25127.[36]

Illustrative cases.   "Business income" as used by UDITPA was patterned after prior decisions of the State Board of Equalization defining "unitary income" under prior California law (*Appeal of General Dynamics Corp, SBE, 6–3–75*). Under that prior law, income from tangible or intangible property was considered to be unitary income subject to formula

---

(32) § 25120.
(33) LR 415, 4–15–80.
(34) Reg § 25120(a).

(35) § 25123.
(36) §§ 25124–25127.

apportionment if the acquisition, management, and disposition of the property constituted integral parts of the taxpayer's unitary business operations (*Appeal of National Cylinder Gas Co., SBE, 2–5–57*).

The disposition of property which is part of a unitary business is business income even though the disposition of the property is because of an extraordinary circumstance, or a sale which is not in the ordinary course of business (*Appeal of American President Lines, Ltd, SBE, 1–5–61*). The loss on the sale and liquidation of a California division, including a loss on goodwill related thereto, was business income subject to formula apportionment. It was of no consequence that goodwill had not been depreciated or otherwise charged against unitary income. The court also rejected the taxpayer's argument that it was not in the business of selling operating divisions and therefore the sale of this division, although admittedly part of its unitary operations, was not in the regular course of its business (*Appeal of Borden, Inc., SBE, 2–3–77*).

Intangible property has a business situs in California when the asset becomes identified with the economic activity in California (*Holly Sugar Corp v Johnson (1941) 18 Cal 2d 218; 115 P2d 8*).

Interest income earned on conditional sales contracts arising from the sale of merchandise in the ordinary course of business is income of a unitary business which is subject to formula apportionment, rather than income which is fully allocable to the commercial domicile of the taxpayer (*Appeal of Marcus Lesoine, Inc., SBE, 7–7–42*). As part of the income earned from a unitary business the Franchise Tax Board must include interest earned on accounts receivable which taxpayer received in the ordinary course of business. This income was not income earned on an intangible asset which was to be assigned to the commercial domicile of the corporation earning such income (*Appeal of M. Seller Company, SBE, 8–22–46*).

Sale of a subsidiary which is not operational with the parent results in nonbusiness income allocable to the commercial domicile of the parent company (*Allied-Signal, Inc. as Successor in Interest to Bendix Corp. v. New Jersey (1992) 112 S Ct 2251, 119 LE2d 533*). However, where a corporation sold five subsidiaries, the facts of the case allowed the gains or losses from the sale of three of the subsidiaries to be treated as business income subject to formula apportionment. The gain or loss on the sale of the other two subsidiaries were treated as nonbusiness since the two were not functionally integrated with the taxpayer's unitary business even though the original intent of the taxpayer in acquiring the two subsidiaries was to expand its unitary business (*Appeal of Occidental Petroleum Corporation, SBE, 3–3–82*).

The sale of a business unit, including physical assets, good will, and patent rights, which was located outside the state of California, created business income subject to apportionment since the out-of-state business was part of the unitary business being conducted in California. The fact that the plant had been shut down for three days prior to the sale did not cause the out-of-state activity to be separated from the unitary business (*Appeal of W.J. Voit Rubber Corp., SBE, 5–12–64*). The same result (treatment of gain or loss on the sale or disposition of assets upon the closing of a plant was business income subject to formula apportionment) where the plant had been idle for nine months, but had been part of the unitary business prior thereto (*Appeal of Steiner American Corporation, SBE, 8–7–67*).

¶ 1179   **Allocation of Nonbusiness Income**

The income from tangible nonbusiness assets and the gain or loss on disposition of the assets are allocated to the situs of the property. In addition, the income from intangible property and the gain or loss on the disposition of such property are also allocated to the situs of the property if the property has acquired a "business situs" there. Gains and losses and income earned by intangible property are generally allocated to the taxpayer's commercial or business domicile.

Commercial domicile.   Regulation 23040(a)[37] states that a corporation will be considered as having a commercial domicile in California if its principal office or place of business is located in this state or if its business is managed or controlled from within this state.

In the field of taxation there are two types of corporate domicile—legal and commercial. The legal domicile of a corporation is the state of incorporation. The business domicile is not as easily located and some of the considerations involved in making a determination of the location of the business domicile are listed below. In some cases the legal domicile of the corporation would not be entitled to any tax from income of the taxpaying corporation because the corporation may have no office in the state and may not engage in activities there. Commercial domicile on the other hand is the center of the corporate activity and the principal site which has an influence on the ability of the corporation to earn income.

Principal cases.   The principal California cases involving the determination of commercial domicile are *Southern Pacific Co. v. McColgan (1945) 68 CA2d 48; 156 P2d 81* and *Pacific Western Oil Corp. v. Franchise Tax Board, (1955) 136 CA2d 794, appeal dismissed* 352 US 805. In *Southern Pacific Company,* the Court decided that the commercial domicile of the corporation was in California rather than in New York City where the directors were. The Court said, "The true test must be to consider all the facts relating to the particular corporation and all the facts relating to the intangibles in question, and to determine from those facts which state among all the states involved gives the greatest protection and benefit to the corporation. Which state among all the states involved, from a factual and realistic standpoint, is the domicile of the corporation? That is partially a question of fact and partially a question of law."

---

(37) Reg. 23040(a).

IMPORTANT   Among the facts that the courts have considered in determining whether the principal office of a place of business of a corporation is located in a particular state or if its business is managed or controlled from within that state are:

History of the corporation. This would indicate where the principal activities of the corporation have been conducted and whether or not in the most recent years there is a trend which points to one location or the other as being the most active involving the affairs of the corporation.

Board of Directors meetings. The place where the Board of Directors meetings are held is always significant.

Location of stockholders meetings. The place where these meetings are held is of less importance than other factors unless it's a closely held corporation, in which case it could be important.

Location of the officers. The officers will be located at the principal business headquarters. If, because of the nature of the business, the officers are spread out into various divisions, a comparison of the number of officers, their duties, their compensation, etc. may indicate where the real headquarters of the corporation are.

Location of the executive. Location of the executive or operating committees.

Location of the books. Location of the books of account and other corporate records.

Location of banks. Location of banks in which the corporation has its principal account, the transfer agent handling the corporation's securities, and the insurance brokers and other financial correspondence.

Location of the legal staff. Location of legal staff and office of the independent accountants.

Dividends. Nonbusiness dividends have been taxed in a number of ways. They have been taxed by the state of legal domicile even though the payor corporation is doing business in other states. They have been taxed as California does by the state of commercial domicile, but cases have held also that the state in which the payor of the dividends is located may claim such dividends for tax purposes.

In the *Southern Pacific Company* case, the Court held that dividends received on stock were not from business done within the meaning of the Bank and Corporation Franchise Tax Act, and therefore, were taxable at the commercial domicile of the receiving corporation. The Franchise Tax Board and the Board of Equalization have followed that treatment for many years.

Regulation 25120(c)(4)[38] says that dividend income is business income where the stock with respect to which the dividends are received arises out of or was acquired in the regular course of taxpayer's trade or business operations or where the purpose for acquiring and holding the stock is related to or incidental to such trade or business operations. Most other dividends are nonbusiness income. Example is cited in which a taxpayer operating in a multistate chain of stock brokerage houses receives dividends on stock it owns for the purpose of making a market in that stock. The dividend income in that case would be business income. In another example, the taxpayer and several unrelated corporations own all of the stock of a corporation whose business operations consist solely of acquiring and processing materials for delivery to corporate owners. The taxpayer acquired the stock in order to obtain a source of supply of materials used in its manufacturing business. The dividends are business income. Reg 25120(c)(4) also gives examples involving (1) multistate construction business holding stock and securities for bonding purposes; (2) dividends from stock in a marketing agency; and (3) stocks and interest-bearing securities whose acquisition and holding is unrelated to taxpayer's manufacturing business.

Interesting example. The taxpayer is engaged in a multistate manufacturing and wholesale business. In connection with that business the taxpayer maintains special accounts to cover such items as workman's compensation claims, etc. A portion of the moneys in those accounts is invested in interest-bearing bonds and the remainder is invested in various common stocks listed on the national stock exchanges. Both the interest and any dividends would be business income.

The interesting point here is that because the interest and dividends are considered to be business income in the example, they would be subject to apportionment by formula rather than by allocation to a specific state.

Key law section. The law states that in any case in which the tax of a unitary group is determined by a combined report, the dividends paid by one corporation to another corporation in the unitary group will be eliminated from the income of the recipient and not be taken into account as long as the dividends are paid out of income which has been included in the unitary business.[39]

Under Rev & TC § 24402, a portion of the dividends received during the income year that has been included in the measure of taxes imposed under Ch 2 (franchise tax), Ch 2.5 (alternative minimum tax), and Ch 3 (corporation income tax) is deductible. In the case of any dividend received from a more than 50% owned corporation, 100%; in the case of any dividend from a 20% owned corporation, 80%; in the case of any dividend received from a less than 20% owned corporation, 70% of the dividends are deductible. For further details, see ¶ 1153.

---

(38) Reg § 25120(c)(4).　　　　　　　　　　　　**(39)** § 25106.

Interest.   California Reg 25120(c)(3)[40] states that interest income is business income where the intangible with respect to which the interest was received arises out of or was created in the regular course of the taxpayer's trade or business operations, or where the purpose for acquiring and holding the intangible is related to or incidental to such trade or business operations. Types of interest that would be considered to be business income would be service charges, interest or time price differentials, and similar amounts received with respect to installment sales and revolving charge accounts. Similarly, interest on federal and California tax refunds would be business income.

An example in the regulations points out that a corporation engaged in a multistate manufacturing and wholesaling business maintains special accounts to cover such items as workman's compensation claims, rain and storm damage, machinery replacement, etc. The moneys in those accounts were invested and earned interest. At the same time, the corporation temporarily invested funds which were intended for the payment for federal, state and local obligations. The interest income would be considered to be business income.

Another example given is a corporation that had working capital and extra cash totaling $200,000 invested in short-term interest-bearing securities. The interest income in that case was also decided to be business income. The final example, cites a corporation that sold all the stock it owned in a subsidiary for $20,000,000. The funds were placed in a separate interest-bearing account pending a decision by management as to how the funds were to be utilized. The interest income in this case was said to be nonbusiness income.

In summary, income from the corporation's investment of working capital on a long-term basis would be considered to be nonbusiness income, while interest from short-term investment of temporarily unused working capital would be business income.

Income from interest-bearing securities held by a Delaware corporation as a reserve against uninsured losses and for tax obligations was specifically allocable to California since the corporation had its principal place of business and a commercial domicile in the state. *Fibreboard Paper Products Corp. v. Franchise Tax Board (1968) 268 CA2d 363.*

Patent and copyright royalties.   Nonbusiness royalties are allocable to California if (1) the patent or copyright is used by the payor company in California, or (2) if the patent or copyright is used in another state in which the taxpayer is not taxable, and the taxpayer's commercial domicile is in California. For this purpose, a patent is considered to be used in a state if it is employed in the production, fabrication, manufacturing or other processing in the state, or to the extent that a patented product is produced in the state.

---

(40) Reg § 25120(c)(3).

A copyright is used in a state to the extent that the printing or other publication originates in the state. In any case in which the receipts from the royalties do not permit an allocation to the states in which the patent or copyright is used, or if the accounting procedures do not indicate the states in which the patents or copyrights are used, it is deemed that the use takes place in the state of the taxpayer's domicile.[1] Also, Reg 25120(c)(5),[2] states that patent and copyright royalties are business income where the patent or copyright with respect to which the royalties were received arises out of or was created in the regular course of the taxpayer's trade or business operations or where the purpose for acquiring and holding the patent or copyright is related to or incidental to such trade or business operations.

Royalties from the sale and lease of patents which were acquired, managed and protected in the regular course of a unitary business are includable in the unitary income even though the patents were not regularly sold or leased by the taxpayer and the products covered by the particular patents were not manufactured by the taxpayer. *Appeal of Velsicol Chemical Corp., SBE 10-5-65.*

Nonbusiness rents and royalties from real property.   Generally, rents from real property located in California are allocable to California. Rents or royalties from the use of tangible personal properties are allocable to California if the property is used in California or if the property is used in another state and the taxpayer is not taxable in that state or organized under the laws of that state. If the personal property is used in California and other states in the same year, the extent of utilization in California is determined by multiplying the rents or royalties by a fraction, the numerator of which is the number of days in which the property was physically located in California and the denominator is the number of days in which the property was located everywhere in the year, both considering only the days in which the property was actually in use. If the location of the property during the rental or royalty period can't be ascertained by the taxpayer, it is considered to be used in the state in which the property was located at the time the rental or royalty payor obtained possession of it.[1]

The above considers only rents and royalties from nonbusiness property. Rents from real and tangible personal property are business income if the property was used in the taxpayer's trade or business, or is incidental thereto, and, therefore, is includable in the property factor of the apportionment formula. Reg 25120(c)(1) gives an example in which the taxpayer operates a multistate car rental business. The income from the car rentals is business income. In another example, the taxpayer was engaged in heavy construction business using equipment such as cranes, tractors, and earth-moving vehicles. When the particular pieces of equipment were not needed on any particular project, the taxpayer made short-term leases of it. The rental income would be considered to be business income. In another exam-

---

(1) UDITPA Manual September 1984, 0612.   (2) Reg § 25120(c)(5).

ple, a taxpayer operated a multistate chain of men's clothing stores. It purchased a five-story office building for use in connection with its trade or business. It used the street floor as one of its retail stores and the second and third floors for general and corporate headquarters. The remaining two floors were leased to others. The rental of the remaining two floors is incidental to the operation of the trade or business, and, therefore, would be considered to be business income. Another example, the taxpayer operated a multistate chain of men's clothing stores and bought a twenty-story office building. It used the street floor and the second floor for its business purposes and leased the remaining eighteen floors to others. In this case, the rental of the eighteen floors was considered to be nonbusiness income.

Capital gains and losses.   Nonbusiness gains and losses from the sales of real property located in California are allocable to California. Gains and losses from the sales of nonbusiness tangible personal property are allocable to California if the property had a situs in California at the time of the sale, or, if it had acquired status in another state, but was not taxable there, and the taxpayer's domicile is in California.[3]

Gain or loss from the sale or the exchange of real or tangible or intangible personal property is business income if the property, while it was owned by the taxpayer, was used in the taxpayer's trade or business.

OBSERVATION   If the property had been used for producing nonbusiness income, or the property had been used in the business activities of the corporation and then removed from that activity and rented out, or otherwise used in a nonbusiness activity so that its value was removed from the property factor, the gain or loss would be nonbusiness income.

EXAMPLE   The taxpayer operates a multistate chain of grocery stores. It owned an office building which it occupied as its corporate headquarters. Because of inadequate space, the taxpayer acquired a new and larger building elsewhere for its corporate headquarters. The old building was rented to an unrelated investment company under a five-year lease. On the expiration of the lease, the taxpayer sold the building at a gain. The gain on the sale is nonbusiness income and the rental income received over the lease period is nonbusiness income.[4]

Intangibles—partnerships.   Except in cases of a partnership interest, gains and losses from the sale of intangible personal property are allocable to California if the corporate taxpayer's commercial domicile is in California. Gain or loss from the sale of a partnership interest is allocable to this state in the ratio of the original cost of the partnership tangible property in California to the original cost of the partnership tangible property everywhere determined at the time of sale. In the event that more than 50% of the value of the partnership's assets consist of intangibles, the gain or loss from the sale of the partnership is allocated to California in accordance with the sales factor of the partnership for its first full tax period immediately preceding

---

(3) UDITPA Manual September 1984, 0614.   (4) Reg 25120(c)(2).

the tax period of the partnership during which the partnership interest was sold.[5]

Gain or loss on subsidiary's stock.   Whether the gain or loss by a parent corporation on the sale of the stock or the liquidation of a subsidiary is business or nonbusiness income (see the discussion at ¶ 1167) an interesting point is raised if the subsidiary had operated a unitary business with the parent corporation and/or other corporations in the affiliated group. Federal Reg 1.1016–6 states that the basis of the subsidiary stock must be adjusted for the subsidiary's losses for the years it was included in a consolidated return. Former California Reg 24916(e) had adopted similar wording and Legal Ruling 186 to the same effect had been issued by the FTB. On the strength of the *Safeway Stores* decision *(SBE 3–2–62)* the Legal Ruling was withdrawn by L.R. 394, dated 12–17–76.[6] The corporate parent has the benefit of having offset the subsidiary's losses in the combined return without having to reduce the basis of the subsidiary stock on the sale or liquidation.

BUSINESS INCOME APPORTIONMENT FORMULA

¶ 1180   Introduction

Effective for income years beginning on or after 1–1–93, generally all business income must be apportioned to California by multiplying the income by a fraction, the numerator of which is the property factor plus the payroll factor plus twice the sales factor and the denominator of which is four.[7] These factors are explained in this section.

Apportionment Formula

$$
\text{Business Income} \times \frac{\dfrac{\text{Calif. Property}}{\text{All Property}} + \dfrac{\text{Calif. Payroll}}{\text{All Payroll}} + 2 \times \left(\dfrac{\text{Calif. Sales}}{\text{All Sales}} \right)}{4} = \text{Apportioned Income}
$$

For years beginning on or after 1–1–93 the double weighting of the sales factor does not apply when the business drives more than 50% of its gross receipts from an extractive or agricultural business.

For years beginning on or after 1–1–94, extractive industries and the savings and loan industry have been added to the list of business which

---

(5) § 25125(c)–(d).
(6) LR394, 12–17–76.

(7) § 25128 as amended by Stats. 1994, c. 861, § 15.

continue to use the three factor apportionment formula with sales equally weighted with property and payroll. If the FTB adopts the Proposed Multistate Tax Commission Formula for the Uniform Apportionment of Net Income from Financial Institutions, or its substantial equivalent, than banking and financial businesses will also be subject to the three factor formula.[7]

¶ 1182   **Property Factor in Apportionment Formula**

The property factor includes all real and tangible personal property owned or rented and used during the income year to produce business income. The numerator of the property factor is the average value of all property owned or rented, real and tangible personal property, located in California, and the denominator is the total of all such property owned or rented by the taxpayer, wherever located.[8]

Property owned by the taxpayer is valued at its original cost without any deduction for such items as depreciation, depletion, etc.

The phrase "original cost" of property owned by the taxpayer is deemed to be the basis of the property for federal income tax purposes (prior to any federal adjustments) at the time of acquisition by the taxpayer, adjusted for any capital additions, and partial disposition thereof, by reason of sale, exchange or abandonment, etc. Capitalized intangible drilling and development costs shall be included in the property factor, whether or not they have been expensed for either federal or state tax purposes. If the original cost is not available, a taxpayer is entitled to use the fair market value of the property at the date of acquisition. In a tax-free reorganization, the transferor's basis is carried over to the transferee and is then considered to be the transferee's "original cost."[9]

In order for property to be considered, it has to be either used in the unitary business or available for use, or capable of being used to produce income. If the property is used to produce nonbusiness income, it should be kept out of the property factor. Property which is available for use, but not actually being used would include, for example, a manufacturing plant which is temporarily idle, but could be used currently if circumstances required that it be opened up. Other examples include timber tracts for lumber companies, oil leases for oil companies, and mineral leases. Once property is used in the regular course of trade or business, it remains in the property factor until it is removed permanently from possible unitary business use. Identifiable events which would remove it from the property factor would be its conversion to nonbusiness use, its sale or the lapse of an extended period of time (normally five years) during which the property is held for sale. Property used in the unitary business and also used in the production of nonbusiness income should be included in the property factor only to the extent of the use of the property in the unitary business.[10]

---

(8) Reg 25129.
(9) Reg 25130.

(10) Reg 25129(b).

Generally, the "average yearly value" to be used in the property factor is determined by averaging the values at the beginning of the year and those at the end of the year. In some cases the monthly averages might be required if the Franchise Tax Board feels that they should be used to properly reflect the average value for the income year. This would be true if substantial fluctuations in the values of the property take place in the income year, or in instances where the property is acquired or disposed of after the beginning of the income year.[11]

Property or plants being constructed during the year are excluded from the property factor until the property is actually placed in use in the business. However, inventories of work in progress are included in the property factor.[9]

TAX TIP	From a tax planning standpoint, it is important to classify all property as business or nonunitary business property. If a substantial item of property is to be sold and its location is in California, it should be part of the unitary group if a gain is to be realized, so the gain can be apportioned. If California property would be salable at a loss, it might be converted to rental use, so that the ultimate loss on the sale is 100% California rather than apportioned.

Inventory. Inventory is included in the property factor with a cost computed by using the same valuation method as that used for federal income tax purposes.[12]

In transit. Property owned by a corporation in transit between locations is to be considered at the destination in computing the numerators of the fraction. Property in transit between a buyer and seller also is included in the property factor according to the location of the destinations.[13]

Leasehold improvements. Leasehold improvements are considered to be owned by the taxpayer regardless of whether the taxpayer is entitled to remove the improvements at the end of the lease or they revert to the lessor.[14]

Mobile property. The value of mobile or movable property, such as construction equipment, trucks or leased electronic equipment, which is located within or without the state during the year is determined for purposes of the numerator of the factor on the basis of the total time within California during the year. An automobile assigned to a traveling employee is to be included in the property factor in the numerator of the state in which the employee's compensation is apportioned in the payroll factor, or in numerator of state in which automobile is licensed.[15]

---

(11) Reg 25131.
(12) Reg 25130(a)(2).
(13) Reg 25129(d)(2).

(14) Reg 25130(b)(5).
(15) Reg 25129(d).

Offshore wells. The value of offshore oil wells should be included in the property factor. Wells located outside the state boundary are to be included in the denominator but not the numerator, while the property within the state boundary of California is to be included in both the numerator and the denominator.[16]

Outerspace property. Satellites used in the communication industry are included in the denominator of the property factor. The numerator is based on the ratio of earth stations served.[17]

Partnership property. A partnership's real and tangible personal property owned or rented and used in the unitary business is included in the property factor to the extent of the taxpayer-partner's interest in the partnership.[18]

Property rented. Property rented by the taxpayer is valued at eight times the net annual rate. The "net annual rent rate" for any item of rented property is the annual rental paid by the taxpayer for such property, less the total of annual sub-rental rates paid by subtenants of the corporation. Any amount paid as additional rent in the form of a percentage of sales, taxes or interest, insurance or repairs, are considered to be paid as rent and are capitalized in the property factor.[19] Annual rent does not include (1) incidental day-to-day expenses such as hotel or motel accommodations, daily rental of automobiles, etc., and (2) royalties based on extraction of natural resources, whether represented by delivery or purchase. For this purpose, a royalty includes any consideration, conveyed or credited to a holder of an interest in property which constitutes a sharing of current or future production of natural resources from such property, irrespective of the method of payment, or how such consideration may be characterized, whether as royalty, advance royalty, rental or otherwise.[20]

Rent paid in advance, which is not an allowable deduction in the year of payment is not to be included in the property factor. If the first and last month's rent of a five-year lease were paid during the first month, the last month's rent would not be capitalized and in the factor until the fifth year.[21] The "net annual rental rate" is the amount paid as rental for the property for a 12-month period. If property is rented for less than a 12-month period, the rent paid for the actual period of rental will be considered to be the annual rental rate for the year.[22]

If a taxpayer is involved in a government contract and uses government facilities for no rent or for a very nominal rent, a reasonable rental rate should be determined for property factor purposes.[23]

---

(16) UDITPA Manual September 1984, 0720.

(17) UDITPA Manual September 1984, 0722.

(18) UDITPA Manual September 1984, 0723.

(19) Reg 25130(b)(1).

(20) Reg 25130(b)(4).

(21) UDITPA Manual September 1984, 0752.

(22) Reg 25130(b)(2).

(23) UDITPA Manual September 1984, 0756.

In determining the annual rental rate, the aggregate of the annual sub-rental rates paid by subtenants of the corporation are deducted unless the sub-rents are business income.[24]

Replacement property. If property is acquired as result of involuntary conversion or exchange, original federal cost is carried over to replacement property. Adjustments are made for later capital additions and partial disposition. Unrecognized gain and depreciation previously deducted (federal adjustments) are disregarded.[25]

Property not owned by the taxpayer may be included in the property factor. The property factor generally only includes inventory, depreciable assets, and land owned or rented by the taxpayer and used in a unitary business. However where the taxpayer uses property, such as buildings owned by the federal government, free of charge in its unitary business, the value of such property should be included in the property factor since the property is used to produce unitary income subject to tax (*McDonnell Douglas Corp. v Franchise Tax Board, 69 Cal 2d 506; 72 Cal Rptr 465; 446 P2d 313*).

¶ 1183   **Payroll Factor in Apportionment Formula**

Compensation paid—salaries, wages, commissions, and any other form of payment—is included in the payroll factor of the apportionment formula. Compensation also includes the value of property and services provided by the corporation to employees, such as room and board, housing, rent, and similar benefits whenever these payments are considered to be taxable income to the employee under the provisions of the Internal Revenue Code, and the California Personal Income Tax law.[26]

> *Note:* It is only compensation paid to employees that is included in the payroll factor. Any amount paid to agents, brokers and other independent contractors is excluded. The California Employment Development Department, which administers the unemployment insurance provisions of the Revenue and Taxation Code, is continually making determinations in the employee versus independent contractor issue in California, and their decisions are routinely followed by the Franchise Tax Board in questions arising as to whether a payment made to an individual should be included as part of the payroll in the determination of the payroll factor.

The amount to be included in the factor depends on the method of accounting used by the paying corporation. The accrual basis employer would include all compensation properly accrued for the benefit of employees in the payroll factor. However, an accrual basis taxpayer can elect to include its payroll in the payroll factor by the use of the cash method to conform to the taxpayer's method of reporting the compensation for unemployment compensation purposes.[27]

---

(24) § 25129–25131; Reg 25130(b)(1).

(25) LR 409, 9–8–77.

(26) § 25132–25133; Reg 25132(a)(3).

(27) UDITPA Manual September 1984, 0820.

Any compensation paid to an employee for services rendered in connection with producing nonbusiness income should be excluded from the payroll factor.[28]

Who's an employee.   A person is considered an employee when the corporation for which he performs the services has the right to control and direct the individual, not only as to the result to be accomplished, but also as to the manner of accomplishing that result, including setting forth general working conditions, time in which to perform the job, etc. In other words, the right of the "employer" to direct and control the performance of the services, rather than the actual exercise of the right, is the critical factor in determining whether or not an employment relationship exists.[29]

Note: Facts indicating that the corporation receiving the benefit of the individual services exercises the amount of control to qualify the individual as an employee: (1) Wage payments on a periodic basis, (2) establishing the hours for beginning and ending the daily work, (3) requirement that full time and best efforts be devoted to work, (4) furnishing of work space, (5) requirement of detailed and regular reports be provided, (6) prevention of the other individual's engaging in other work at the same time, (7) restriction on right of worker to employ assistants.[29]

The denominator of the payroll factor includes all compensation paid to employees wherever they are located. Accordingly, if compensation is paid to employees whose services are performed entirely in a state where the corporate payor is immune from taxation under PL 86–272, the compensation is nevertheless included in the denominator of the payroll factor.[30]

The numerator of the payroll factor is the total amount of compensation paid to employees in California.

Assigning pay.   UDITPA follows the Uniform Unemployment Compensation Act in using four criteria for determining an employee's compensation to be assigned to a particular state:

(1) The place where services are performed;
(2) The base of operations of the employee;
(3) The location from which the services are directed or controlled;
(4) The state of residence of the employee.[31]

Compensation is assigned to California if the employee's services are performed entirely within the state or if individual services are performed both without and within the state, but the services performed without the state are incidental to the services within the state. For this purpose the word "incidental" means any service which is temporary or transitory in nature or which is rendered in connection with an isolated transaction.

If the employee's services are performed within and without California they are assigned to a state depending on the factual situation.

---

(28) Reg 25132(a)(2).
(29) UDITPA Manual September 1984, 0830.

(30) Reg 25132(b)(1).
(31) UDITPA Manual September 1984, 0890.

The term "base of operation" is the place of more or less permanent nature from which the employee starts his work and to which he customarily returns in order to receive instructions from the employer or communications from his customers or other persons or to replenish his stock or other materials, to repair equipment, or to perform any other functions necessary to the exercise of his trade or profession.[32]

TAX TIP   The tests are applied consecutively, so that if an employee's services are performed entirely within California, or if his services outside the state are incidental or transitory, as indicated above, the first test is applicable, and the remaining tests are ignored. If the employee's services cannot be localized in any particular state, the second test, base of operations, would be used. If the employee's base of operations is not in any state in which some part of his services are performed, then the third test would become the one to be used.

¶ 1184   **Sales Factor in Apportionment Formula**

General. For income years beginning on or after 1–1–93, the sales factor is generally given double weighting in the apportionment formula.

The numerator is the total "sales" of the taxpayer in the state during the income year. The denominator is the total sales of the taxpayer everywhere during the year.[33] The definition of sales includes all gross receipts of the taxpayer not allocated under Rev & TC §§ 25123 through 25127 (these are the sections which define nonbusiness income).[34]

Double weighting of the sales factor. The sales factor is double weighted. This means that the result of dividing the numerator by the denominator of the sales factor is multiplied by 2 in determining the apportionment formula.

The double weighting of the sales factor applies to business income subject to apportionment other than that from an agricultural business activity, or an extractive business activity.

An agricultural business activity means an activity relating to any stock, dairy, poultry, fruit, furbearing animal, or truck farm, plantation, ranch, nursery, or range. It includes the cultivating of soil or raising or harvesting of any agricultural or horticultural commodity, including, but not limited to, the raising, shearing, feeding, caring for, training, or management of animals on a farm as well as the handling, drying, packing, grading, or storing on a farm of any agricultural or horticultural commodity in its unmanufactured state, but only if the owner, tenant, or operator of the farm regularly produces more than one-half of the commodity so treated.

An extractive business activity means activities relating to the production, refining, or processing of ore, natural gas, or mineral ore.[35]

---

(32) Reg 25133.
(33) § 25134.

(34) § 25120(d); 25123–25127.
(35) § 25128.

How sales are assigned.   Rev & TC § 25135 sets forth the rules to determine when a sale of tangible personal property is to be assigned to California:

> (1) A sale of tangible personal property (including unprocessed timber) is in California if it is delivered or shipped to a purchaser in this state and the corporation is taxable in this state.
>
> (2) A sale of tangible personal property (including unprocessed timber) is in this state if the property is shipped from an office, store, warehouse, factory or other storage location in California and the corporation is not taxable in the state of the purchaser.[36]

Unprocessed timber is softwood, including any log, cant, or similar form of timber, cut from an area in this state, and which is delivered or shipped to a purchaser outside the United States. The rules for unprocessed timber remain in effect only for years beginning prior to December 1, 2000.[37] The California treatment mirrors § 13239(c) of the *Revenue Reconciliation Act of 1993* (PL 103–66).[38]

What's included in sales.   *Manufacturers.*   For a corporation manufacturing and selling or purchasing and reselling goods or products, gross receipts from such sales (less returns and allowances) include, in addition to the purchase price, such items as interest income, service charges, carrying charges or time-price differential charges incidental to such sales. Federal and state excise taxes are included if such taxes are passed on to the purchaser.

Contractors.   In cost-plus-fixed-fee contracts, such as the operation of a government owned plant for a fee, "sales" includes the entire reimbursed cost plus the fee.

Services.   In the case of a taxpayer engaged in providing services, such as the operation of an advertising agency, research and development activities, or the performance of equipment service contracts, "sales" includes the gross receipts from performing these services, including fees, commissions and similar items. In the case of a corporation engaged in renting real or tangible property as part of the unitary business, the term "sales" includes the gross receipts of the rental, lease or licensing the use of the property.

Intangibles.   If the corporation's trade or business includes the sale, assignment or licensing of intangible personal property, such as patents or copyrights, sales would include the gross receipts from this business.

Income from the sale of equipment.   Income from the sale of equipment used in the corporate business would be included in the sales factor. For example, a truck express company owning a fleet of trucks would include the revenues from the sale of some of their trucks under a replacement program.[39]

---

(36) § 25135.

(37) § 25135, as amended by Stats. 1994, c. 1296, § 5.

(38) § 24272.3, as added by Stats. 1994, c. 1296, § 4.

(39) Reg 25134(a)(1).

Special exclusions.   The regulations under Rev & TC §§ 25134(a)(2) and 25137[40] (the law section providing for other apportionment methods) indicate that gross receipts from unusual circumstances should be disregarded in computing the sales factor, so that the formula will operate fairly to apportion to California the correct amount of income. One of the circumstances is where substantial amounts of gross receipts come about from an incidental or occasional sale of fixed assets which have been used in regular business operations of the corporation. An example would be gross receipts from the sale of a factory or plant, which would be excluded because of the distortion it would give to the formula. A second circumstance pointed out in the regulations is where minor amounts of gross receipts arising from incidental or occasional transactions can be excluded from the sales factor unless keeping the items out of the formula would materially affect the amount of income apportioned to California. The examples would be a gross receipt from the sale of fixed assets used in the unitary business of a minor nature such as office furniture, business automobiles, and so on.

Sales of tangible personalty.   Gross receipts from the sales of tangible personal property, other than sales to the United States government, are in California if the property is delivered or shipped to a purchaser within California, regardless of the F.O.B. point or other conditions of sale; or if the property is shipped from an office, store, warehouse, factory or other place of storage within the state and the taxpayer is not taxable in the state of the purchaser.[1] Advertising receipts must be included in numerator of sales factor in a ratio of instate-to-total sales of magazines and periodicals.[2]

IMPORTANT   If, for example, a California corporation sends employees into another state to make sales of personal property and has no other activity within that state, and ships the merchandise to fill the orders into the other state from a location outside the other state, the corporation would not be taxable in the other state because of the provisions of PL 86–272. The sales are not assignable to the other state but are "thrown back" to California or the state in which the inventory from which the order was filled is located.

In *Appeal of Dresser Industries, Inc. SBE 6–29–82*, the California State Board of Equalization considered whether, in computing the sales factor of the apportionment formula, taxpayer properly applied the throwback rule to various sales of products manufactured in California and sold and shipped to customers in foreign countries. It decided that the provisions of PL 86–272 did not apply to foreign commerce. Congress limited the application of that law to interstate commerce Reg 25122 states that jurisdiction to tax is not present when the state is prohibited by PL 86–272 from imposing net income tax. No prohibition applies when the income sought to be taxed is derived from foreign commerce.

---

(40) Reg §§ 25134(a)(2); 25137.   (2) LR 367, 12–14–73.
(1) Reg 25135.

In the *Appeal of Finnigan Corporation, 88–SBE–022, 8–25–88,* the State Board of Equalization specifically ruled that the word "taxpayer" as used in Rev & TC § 25135(b)(2) means "all of the corporations within the unitary group." Therefore, the SBE held that when sales were shipped from California to another state by a member of a group conducting a unitary business in California, the throwback rule does not apply if *any* of the corporations within the unitary group is taxable in the other state. In the *Appeal of Finnigan Corporation.* Opn. on Pet. for Rehg., 88–SBE–022A, January 24, 1990, the SBE expressly overruled the apportionment rule announced in the *Appeal of Joyce, Inc., SBE 11–23–66* (but see CAUTION below), that the income attributable to the California activities of a corporation exempt from taxation by this state because of Public Law 86–272 had to be separately computed by application of the apportionment method and then excluded from the measure of the franchise tax. In practice, the *Joyce* rule was accomplished by excluding from the numerator of the apportionment formula, but not the denominator, the California factors of corporations within the unitary group that were not themselves taxable by this state. Under *Finnigan,* this restriction no longer applies.

Accordingly, the Franchise Tax Board's administrative practice with respect to multi-entity apportionment formula rules previously governed by *Joyce* has now changed as follows: (1) Sales of goods shipped from California to other states are to be assigned to this state under the throwback rule only when none of the corporations within the unitary group is taxable within the destination state. (2) The California property, payroll and sales of each corporation within a unitary group will be taken into account in the apportionment of business income to this state, including amounts attributable to entities exempt from taxation in this state because of Public Law 86–272. The total business income thus apportioned to California will be assigned to the individual corporations taxable by this state by use of the "revised method" currently authorized by Legal Ruling 234.[3]

CAUTION	A Los Angeles superior court, in a Minute Order, has endorsed *Joyce, Inc.* and rejected *Finnigan Corp.* The court said that the *Finnigan Corp.* approach to apportioning the income of certain unitary groups is contrary to P.L. 86–272. *Brown Group Retail, Inc. Minute Order, Calif. Super. Ct., Cty. of Los Angeles, No. C714010, 10–8–93.*

Note that the taxability or immunity of a corporation under PL 86–272 is discussed in ¶ 1163. In addition, Circular FTB 1050 issued by the Franchise Tax Board may be consulted.

Sales to U.S. Government. Gross receipts from the sales of tangible personal property to the government are considered to be in California if the property is shipped from an office, factory, warehouse or store in California. In other words, under UDITPA, sales to the U.S. government of personal

---

(3) FTB Notice 90–3, 6–8–90.

property are treated in a different manner from other sales. They are assigned to the state from which the product was shipped. The sales to the United States government to which this applies are those sales for which the U.S. government makes direct payment to the seller under the terms of the contract. Therefore, sales made by a subcontractor to the prime contractor are not considered to be sales to the United States government for this purpose.[4]

Sales other than sales of tangible personal property. Rev & TC § 25136 provides for the assignment of sales of other than tangible personal property in the numerator of the sales factor of the apportionment formula. These sales are assigned to California if the "income-producing activity" which gave rise to the sale is performed wholly within California. At the same time, gross receipts are included in the California numerator if the income-producing activity is performed within and without California but the greater proportion of the income-producing activity is performed in California based on "costs of performance."[5]

Income-producing activity. The term "income-producing activity" applies to each separate item of income and means the transactions and activity directly engaged in by the corporation in the regular course of its trade or business for the purpose of obtaining gains or profit. Examples given in the regulations include the following:

(1) The rendering of personal services by employees or the use of tangible and intangible property by the taxpayer in performing a service;
(2) The sale, rental, leasing, licensing or other use of real property;
(3) The rental, leasing, licensing or other use of tangible personal property;
(4) The sale, licensing or other use of intangible personal property.[6]

Costs of performance. The term "costs of performance" means the direct costs determined in a manner consistent with generally accepted accounting principles and also in accordance with the accepted conditions or practices in the trade or business of the taxpayer.[7]

Item (1) above. In the application of item (1) above, the gross receipts from the rendering of personal services by employees or the utilization of tangible or intangible property by the taxpayer in performing the services are in California to the extent the services are performed in the state. If these services relate to a single item of income and are performed partly within or without California but the greater amount is performed in the state based on costs of performance, the service revenue would be assigned to California. The usual situation is that when services are performed partly within and partly without California, the services performed in each state will constitute a separate income activity, so that a portion of the total revenue would be assigned to each of these locations. The gross receipts for this purpose would be measured by the ratio which the time spent in per-

---

(4) Reg 25135(b).
(5) § 25136; Reg 25136.

(6) Reg 25136(b).
(7) Reg 25136(c).

forming the services in California bear to the total time spent in performing such services everywhere.

Item (2) above.   Regarding item (2) above, the sale, rental, leasing, licensing or other use of real property is assigned to the state in which the property is located.

Item (3) above.   Gross receipts from the rental, leasing, licensing or other use of tangible personal property are assigned to the state in which the property is located during the period of the rental. For property which is moved from one state to another, each location is considered to be a separate income-producing activity. Consequently, the gross receipts attributable to California in this activity are to be measured by the ratio which the time the property was physically present or used in California bears to the total time or use of the property everywhere during the year.

Item (4) above.   Assigning the income from intangible personal property as pointed out in item (4) above to California depends on whether the income-producing activity can be readily identified. For example, on deferred payments on sales of tangible personal property, the interest, carrying charges or time price differential charges are included with the gross receipts of the sale and would be assigned in accordance with the sale of the personal property. If the business income from intangible property cannot readily be attributed to any particular income-producing activity, it would be excluded from the numerator of the sales factor and also from the denominator. This would include dividends received on stock, royalties on patents or copyrights, interest received on bonds, debentures or government securities, all resulting from the mere holding of the intangible personal property and which would be excluded from both the numerator and the denominator of the apportionment formula.[8]

"Delivered" and "shipped" defined.   Legal Ruling 348 issued in 1973 defines the term "delivered" as being the place at which the purchaser takes possession and control of the property and "shipped" means the transportation of the property (including delivery) to the purchaser.

Mail order sales.   Mail-order sales sent to a state in which the taxpayer is not taxable, when shipped from an inventory in California, are "thrown back" to California and are included in the numerator of the sales factor.[9]

¶ 1184A   **Water's-Edge Election**

The law affecting water's-edge elections for income years beginning on or after 1–1–94, have been significantly changed by the California Legislature in Stats 1993, c. 881, SB 671, signed by Governor Wilson on 10–6–93. The changes made by the Legislature include:

---

(8) Reg 25136(d); 25137(c).   (9) Reg 25135(a)(6).

- Elimination of the water's-edge spreadsheet filing requirement and instead requires an information return for all apportioning corporations whose assets exceed $200 million with or without the water's-edge election.
- Repeal of the election fee.
- Rescinded all existing water's-edge elections. New elections must be filed by corporations desiring to continue a water's-edge election.
- Extended the term of the water's edge election from 5 to 7 years.
- Eliminated several conditions under which taxpayers could terminate a water's-edge election prior to the end of the 7-year period.
- Eliminated provisions that allow the Franchise Tax Board to disregard the water's-edge election for specified reasons.

Changes in the statute have been integrated into the explanations which follow.

WATCH ALERT

The Franchise Tax Board has issued extensive proposed regulations for the apportionment of income of unitary businesses (Rev & TC § 19141.6), and records and responsibilities of those making a water's-edge election (Rev & TC § 25111.1). These proposed regulations have been subject to a Hearing, but have not yet been implemented. Care should be exercised to comply with the regulations interpreting these sections of the Rev & TC once the regulations have been issued.

Pre-1994 elections.   For income years starting on or after 1–1–88, a bank or corporation engaged in a unitary business with one or more other banks or corporations may elect to determine its taxable income by means of a water's-edge combined report.

For years beginning prior to 1994, if a bank or corporation makes such an election, it must pay a fee of .03% of its property and payroll assigned to California for an income year of 12 full months ending during the calendar year 1986 and its sales assigned to California for the current income year. The election fee will be offset by additional investments in California. The reduction will be permanent, but there is a minimum fee of .01%. On the other hand, no election fee is imposed on a bank or corporation that shows a loss on a worldwide combined report basis. The election is for an initial period of five years, but the taxpayer can terminate the election before the end of the five-year period, if it meets any of the conditions specified in Rev & TC § 25111(b), or the Franchise Tax Board may disregard an election when any of the conditions specified in Rev & TC § 25111(c) are met (see details below).[10]

Recission of pre-1994 elections.   For years beginning on or after 1–1–94, the existing water's-edge contracts under law in effect for years beginning prior to 1–1–94 are no longer in effect. Those contracts are rescinded for any periods remaining on the contracts commencing on the first day of the taxpayer's income year that begins on or after 1–1–94. Any

---

(10) § 25110; 25111; 25115.

fiscal year taxpayer whose contract is in effect as of 12–31–93, will continue to be bound by that contract until the close of its income year after 1–1–94, and before 12–31–94.[11]

| *CAUTION* | Taxpayers must make new elections for years beginning on or after 1–1–94, if they wish to continue a water's-edge election under the new rules. |

Income and apportionment factors of affiliated entities.   A bank or corporation that elects to determine its California net income pursuant to a water's-edge election must take into account the income and apportionment factors of the following affiliated entities:

(1) Banks and corporations that are eligible to be included in a federal consolidated return, other than corporations making an election under IRC § 936;

(2) Domestic international sales corporations and foreign sales corporations;

(3) Any corporation whose property, payroll, and sales factors average 20% or more within the United States;

(4) Banks and corporations not included in (1) that are incorporated in the United States (excluding corporations making election pursuant to IRC Sections 931 to 936), more than 50% of whose stock is controlled directly or indirectly by the same interests;

(5) A bank or corporation not described in any of these categories, but only to the extent of its income derived from or attributable to sources within the United States determined from its books of account and its apportionment factors assignable to a location in the United States; and

(6) Export trade corporations.

(7) An affiliated bank or corporation which is a controlled foreign corporation as defined in IRC § 957, if all or part of the income of that affiliate is included in U.S. income under IRC § 952 (Subpart F income). Special apportionment factors apply for apportioning subpart F income.[12]

The income and apportionment factors of the above-enumerated banks and corporations shall be taken into account only if the income and factors would have been taken into account under Rev & TC § 25101, had Rev & TC § 25110 not been enacted. The income and factors of a bank or corporation that is not described in Rev & TC § 25110(a)(1) through (4) and (6) above and that is an electing taxpayer under Rev & TC § 25110(a) shall be taken into account in determining income only to the extent set forth in Rev & TC § 25110(a)(5). The income and apportionment factors of a controlled foreign corporation will be taken into account to the extent that it has Subpart F income. An electing bank will take into account only that income from sources in the United States and apportionment factors assignable to a location in the United States.[10]

An affiliated bank or corporation means a bank or corporation that is related to a bank or corporation required to file under the Bank or Corporation Tax Law, because either (1) it owns directly or indirectly more than 50% of the voting stock of the bank or corporation required to file under that law;

---

(11) § 25111.1.   (12) § 25110(a)(7).

or (2) more than 50% of its voting stock is owned directly or indirectly by a bank or corporation required to file under that law; or (3) more than 50% of voting stock of both it and the bank or corporation required to file under this part is owned or controlled directly or indirectly by any bank or person, as defined in IRC Sec 7701(a)(1).[10]

Consent to depositions—acceptance of subpoena. To be eligible to make an election, a bank or corporation must file along with its tax return a consent to the taking of depositions from key domestic corporate individuals and to the acceptance of subpoenas duces tecum requiring reasonable production of documents to the Franchise Tax Board as required by statute, the State Board of Equalization, or the courts. The consent will remain in effect as long as the election is in effect. It will be limited to information necessary to review or to adjust income or deductions under IRC §§ 482, 861, Subpart F, and similar provisions of the Code. It would also be limited to information necessary to conduct an investigation with respect to any unitary business in which the electing bank or corporation may be involved.[10]

Agreement on treatment of dividends as business income. An electing bank or corporation must also agree that dividends received by any bank or corporation included in the water's-edge combined report group will be deemed to be business income and apportionable to California provided that: more than 50% of the voting stock of the dividend payor is owned directly or indirectly by members of the unitary group and is engaged in the same general line of business as the unitary group; or that the dividend payor supplies 15% or more of the needs of the unitary business, purchases 15% or more of the output of the unitary business, sells 15% or more of its output, or obtains 15% or more of its raw materials or input from the unitary business.[10]

How election is made. A water's-edge election is made by contract with the Franchise Tax Board in the original return for a year and is effective only if every taxpayer that is a member of the water's-edge group and that is subject to tax under the Bank and Corporation Tax Law makes the election. A single taxpayer that is engaged in more than one business activity subject to allocation and apportionment under UDITPA (starting with Rev & TC § 25120) may make a separate election for each business. An affiliated bank or corporation that is a member of the water's-edge group or is a nonelecting taxpayer which is subsequently proved to be a member of the water's-edge group pursuant to Franchise Tax Board audit determination, as evidenced by a notice of deficiency proposed to be assessed or a notice of tax change, and later becomes subject to tax under the Bank and Corporation Tax Law will be deemed to have elected. No water's-edge election can be made for an income year beginning prior to 1–1–88. The form and manner of the election will be prescribed by the Board.[10]

Duration of election—change—conditions. For income years beginning after 1993, the term of the contract is seven years, and the contract continues to be renewed annually for a seven-year period unless a notice of nonrenewal is given to the Franchise Tax Board. If a notice of nonrenewal is given, the water's-edge contract remains in effect for the remaining period of the contract (generally six years).

For income years beginning prior to 1994, each contract could be for an initial term of five years, except as provided in the termination provisions of Rev & TC § 25111(b), or disregard of election by the Franchise Tax Board the provisions of former Rev & TC § 25111(c). Each contract needed to provide that on the anniversary date of the contract, or any other annual date specified by the contract, a year was added automatically to the initial term unless a notice of nonrenewal was given. Each contract was conditioned by an agreement to pay the repealed water's-edge fee.

Termination of water's-edge election. For income years beginning after 1993, a water's-edge election can only be terminated if (1) the taxpayer is acquired directly or indirectly by a nonelecting entity that alone or together with those affiliates included in its combined report is larger than the taxpayer as measured by equity capital, or (2) with the permission of the Franchise Tax Board, the election is terminated.

For income years beginning prior to 1994, a water's-edge election was terminated by a taxpayer before the end of the five-year period, if any of the following occurred: (1) the taxpayer was acquired directly or indirectly by a nonelecting entity that alone or together with those affiliates included in its combined report was larger than the taxpayer as measured by equity capital; (2) the taxpayer ceased to be affiliated with any bank or corporation whose income and apportionment factors the taxpayer was required to take into account in determining its income, but for the election, and the taxpayer was not a bank or corporation doing business within and without the U.S.; (3) with the permission of the Franchise Tax Board, the election was terminated; (4) pursuant to an FTB determination, as evidenced by a notice of deficiency or tax change, a substantial modification was made to the composition of the water's-edge group as filed. The election was terminated only with respect to income years starting on or after January 1 of the year the audit determination was made. No amounts paid under former Rev & TC § 25115 for the years the election was in effect was allowed to be refunded.

Disregard of election by the FTB. For only those years beginning prior to 1994, the Franchise Tax Board could disregard the water's-edge election by the affiliated group if certain conditions described below exist. For tax years beginning after 12–31–93, all of the provisions allowing the Franchise Tax Board to disregard the water's-edge election have been repealed. For income years beginning prior to 1–1–94, the FTB could disregard the election when: (1) bank or corporation willfully failed to comply substantially with former Rev & TC § 25401(d) requiring the filing of domestic disclosure spreadsheets and any federal law requiring those spreadsheets; or (2) after reasonable adjustment of transfer prices, royalty rates, allocation of common expenses, and similar adjustments, return filed failed to prevent a willful evasion of taxes; or (3) an otherwise qualified taxpayer willfully failed to (a) retain and make available upon request the documents and information, including IRS or qualified state questionnaires that were necessary to audit issues involving attribution of income to U.S. or foreign jurisdictions under IRC §§ 482, 863, 902, 904 and Subpart F, Part III, Subchapter N, or similar sections; (b) identify, on request, principal officers and employees who had substantial knowledge, and access to, documents and records that discussed pricing policies, profit centers, cost centers, and methods of allocating income and expense among them; (c) retain and make available upon request all documents and correspondence ordinarily available to taxpayer included in the water's-edge election that were submitted to or obtained from the IRS, foreign countries, or their territories or possessions, and competent authority relating to rulings, requests, settlement resolutions, and competing claims involving jurisdictional assignment and sourcing of income that affected assignment of income to the U.S.; (d) prepare and make available, on request, for each bank or corporation included in the domestic disclosure spreadsheet in which taxpayer was included, a list of each state and foreign country in which taxpayer had payroll, property, or sales (determined by destination); (e) retain and make available, on request, forms filed with IRS under IRC §§ 6038, 6038A, 6038B, 6038C and 6041; (f) prepare and make available to each 50% voting stock owned or controlled corporation the information included in IRC §§ 6038, 6038A, 6038B, 6038C and 6041 forms; (g) retain and make available all state tax return forms filed by water's-edge group members; (h) comply with reasonable requests for information to determine or verify net income, apportionment factors or geographic source income pursuant to the IRC. Information had to be retained for the period of time that the tax liability could be subject to adjustment, including all periods additional income could be assessed, or appeals or lawsuits were pending in California and federal courts. Ninety days' written notice of the intent to disregard was required to be given by the FTB. A superior court review of the FTB decision was available.

Evasion of tax—reflection of income. The Franchise Tax Board has authority to impose conditions, and make regulations to prevent the avoidance of tax, and clearly reflect income for the period the election was, or was purported to be, in effect.[13]

Nonrenewal of contract. Taxpayer must serve a written notice upon the FTB in advance of the renewal date of a contract. If notice is not served at least 90 days before the annual renewal date, the contract will be renewed. If the taxpayer serves notice of intent not to renew, the existing contract will remain in effect for the balance of the period remaining since the original execution, or last renewal.[11]

---

(13) § 25106.5.

Penalties.   Penalties may be imposed for failure to supply required information. Failure to comply with a document request may result in a court bar against the introduction of any documentation covered by that request in a civil proceeding in which treatment of the item is in issue.[14]

Other procedural provisions.   These cover: start of time period and reasonable cause; formal document request; proceedings to quash; jurisdiction of courts; documentation; extension; toll of statute of limitations.[14]

Information returns.   For income years beginning on or after 1–1–94, specifically identified taxpayers making a water's-edge election pursuant to Rev & TC § 25110 must file information returns with the Franchise Tax Board. The taxpayers from whom information returns are required are those with total assets exceeding $200 million, or such higher amounts as may be subsequently established by regulation. The $200 million is calculated for all affiliated banks or corporations which are defined as those where more than 50% of the voting stock of one is directly or indirectly owned or controlled by the other, or if more than 50% of the voting stock of both is directly or indirectly owned or controlled by the same interest. The information return shall be filed once every three years unless there is a substantial change in the taxpayer's business activities, in which case it shall be filed for the year in which the change occurs. The information return is due within six months after the due date (including extensions) of the bank's or corporation's California return.

The information return must identify the corporate parent and those affiliates of which more than 20% of the voting stock is directly or indirectly owned or controlled by the parent. The information return must identify the percentage of ownership and the type of corporation (foreign organized, U.S. organized, foreign sales corporation, or other relevant descriptions). Willful failure to substantially comply with the filing requirements subjects the taxpayer to penalties described in Rev & TC § 19141.6(c)(1) which are described below in the explanation of records to be maintained.

The information return filing requirements do not apply to any bank or corporation for any year that it's payroll, property, and sales within the U.S. are less than $500,000.[15]

Records to be retained.   A detailed listing of records to be retained for those corporations making a water's-edge election pursuant to Rev & TC § 19141.6. Failure to maintain the records, including the information returns required pursuant to Rev & TC § 18634 of selected taxpayers, will result in a penalty of $10,000 for each income year with respect to which the failure occurred. If the failure continues for more than 90 days after the day on which the Franchise Tax Board mails a notice of the failure, an additional penalty will be assessed for each 30-day period

---

(14) § 25112.
(15) § 18634, as amended by Stats. 1994, c. 756,
§ 6.

during which the failure continues after the expiration of the 90-day period. The additional penalty imposed will not exceed a maximum of $50,000 if the failure to maintain or the failure to cause another to maintain the records is not willful.[16]

Examination of returns. If the examination of returns reveals a potential noncompliance, a detailed examination must be made, unless the taxpayer is being examined by the IRS for the same year. In the case of two or more controlled organizations, trades, or businesses, the FTB may distribute, apportion, or allocate gross income, deductions, credits, or allowances between or among these organizations, etc., if necessary to prevent tax evasion or more clearly reflect income. The FTB must generally follow rules, regs, and procedures of IRS in making audits under IRC § 482. Federal rules are not subject to review by California Office of Administrative Law. Rebuttable presumptions apply to IRS adjustments on audit, or audit resulting in no IRS adjustments.[17]

Annual fee. There is no annual fee for years beginning in 1994. For years beginning prior to 1994, the election contract was conditioned upon an agreement to pay an annual fee to the FTB. The amount of the fee was equal to thirty-thousandths of 1% (.03%) of the sum of the electing bank or corporation's property and payroll assigned to California for an income year of 12 full months ending during the calendar year 1986 and its sales assigned to California for the current income year. A single corporation that was engaged in more than one business for which it was making separate elections determined the amount for each business for which it was electing to determine its income. A bank's or corporation's property, payroll, and sales in California was determined under UDITPA. Property included only property defined in Rev & TC §§ 25129–25131. Sales didn't include gross receipts from the sale of real property and improvements thereto, or the sale of the stock of a subsidiary unless that activity occurred as a regular part of the taxpayer's business.[11]

CAUTION   Stats. 1993, c. 881 repealed the water's-edge election fee effective for calendar years beginning on or after 1994 or fiscal years beginning in 1994. The Legislative Counsel has issued an informal opinion that the fee must still be paid for elections in effect through calendar year 1993 or fiscal years beginning in 1993.

Reduction in fee base for investment in new plants in-state; hiring of new employees. Under the law in effect for income years beginning prior to 1-1-94, the sum of the property, payroll, and sales in California was reduced by the cumulative amount expended after 1-1-87 for investment in new plants or facilities in California and by the amount expended for new employees. A new plant or facility was new construction as defined in Rev & TC § 70 constructed by or for the taxpayer, or new tangible personal prop-

---

(16) § 19141.6.   (17) § 25114.

erty, the original use of which commenced with the taxpayer in California, but may not be a replacement for an existing plant or facility. New tangible personal property meant the current year's acquisition of personal property classified as machinery and equipment for industry, profession, or trade, tools, molds, dies and jigs, and computers and related equipment, as reported to the county assessor, or the State Board of Equalization. A plant or facility was deemed a replacement if the electing bank or corporation or an affiliated bank or corporation closed, took out of service, sold, or leased to an unrelated party (in either the three immediately preceding or the three immediately succeeding years from the time the new plant or facility was operational), a plant or facility with a cost basis equal to 25% or more of the cost basis of the new plant or facility.

The amount expended for new employees in California was equal to the product of the number of new employees and the average wages paid for each work year for the income year in question. The number of new California employees was determined by comparing the total number of work years in California for the income year to the greater of (1) the average of the total number of work years for the income years ending in 1985, 1986, and 1987, or (2) the total number of work years for the income year ending in 1987. A work year, in the case of hourly-paid employees, was 2,000 paid hours and, in the case of salaried employees, a total of 12 paid months. Apparently, the transfer of employees from an affiliated corporation or the reduction in the number of an affiliated corporation's employees did not affect the computation of the election fee.

For years prior to 1–1–94, the election fee could not be less than ten-thousandths of 1% (.01%) of the sum of the electing bank's or corporation's property, payroll, and sales in California for the income year. No statutory changes in the amount of the election fee could be made for the period a contract was in effect without the consent of the electing bank or corporation. Any statutory change would be applicable for any renewal year beginning five years after the statutory change. The election fee was collected in the same manner and subject to the same interest and penalty provisions as taxes.

If a taxpayer was reorganized into two or more separate entities, the 1986 property and payroll factors for the new entities were determined by the ratio of the current property and payroll factors, excluding intangible property, for each new entity subject to tax in California to the total of all entities subject to tax in California for the year in which those entities were created. This ratio was applied to the 1986 property and payroll and each entity was allocated a portion of the 1986 payments and payroll based on this ratio. Notwithstanding Rev & TC § 24345 (taxes or licenses paid or accrued), the amount imposed by Rev & TC § 25115 was allowed as a deduction in computing taxes.

Final appellate determination of unconstitutionality. In the event of a final appellate level determination by a California or a federal court that the application of the worldwide combined report method, or the requirement that amounts be paid under former Rev & TC § 25115 is unconstitutional, for income years starting on or after 1–1–88, such amounts shall, to the extent ordered by the court, or as otherwise provided in applicable law and regulations as of 1–1–88, be refunded with interest, as provided in Rev & TC § 19340, from funds in the California Unitary Fund, or from the General Fund, if there are insufficient funds in the Unitary Fund.[11]

Domestic disclosure spreadsheet. The requirement to file a domestic disclosure spreadsheet is repealed effective for years beginning in 1994. For years beginning prior to 1994, any taxpayer making the water's-edge election had to file with the Franchise Tax Board within six months after it filed its California return a domestic disclosure spreadsheet, if it and its related banks' or corporations' payroll, property, or sales in foreign countries exceeded $10 million, or it and its related banks' or corporations' total assets exceeded $250 million. The spreadsheet had to be filed every three years, unless there was a substantial change in the taxpayer's business activities, in which case it had to be filed in the year that the change occurred. The spreadsheet provided for full disclosure as to the income reported in each state, the state tax liability, and the method used for apportioning or allocating income to the states, and any other information required by regulation necessary to determine the amount of taxes due each state and to identify the corporate parent and affiliates of which more than 20% of the voting stock was directly or indirectly owned or controlled by the parent. The FTB had to review the spreadsheet for completeness. Incompleteness incurred penalties. The spreadsheet rule didn't apply to any corporation or bank, if property, payroll and sales were each less than $500,000 in any year. Although domestic disclosure spreadsheets are not required for years beginning after 1993, much of the information is still required to be retained by the taxpayer under Rev & TC § 19141.6. See discussion of records to be retained, above.

Exclusion of qualifying dividends. Taxpayers who make water's-edge election under Rev & TC § 25110 will be allowed to exclude 100% of qualifying dividends if the taxpayer's foreign payroll factor for any income year in the base period exceeds the foreign payroll factor for the income year. The base period is the 12-month income year ending before 1–1–87, and the two immediately preceding 12-month income years. A 75% exclusion of qualified dividends can be taken if the greatest foreign payroll factor for any year in the base period is the same as or less than the foreign payroll factor for the income year.[18]

"Qualifying dividends" means those received by the water's-edge group from corporations regardless of the place incorporated if both following conditions are met: (1) the average of property, payroll and sales factors in the U.S. for the corporation is less than 20%; and (2) more than 50% of the total

---

(18) § 24411.

combined power of all classes of stock entitled to vote is owned directly or indirectly by the water's-edge group.

"Foreign payroll factor" for an income year is a fraction whose numerator is the total amount paid outside the United States during income year for compensation by the water's-edge group and corporations that would have been combined with the water's-edge group had the election pursuant to Rev & TC § 25110 not been made, and whose denominator is the total compensation paid everywhere by the water's-edge group and corporations that would have been combined with the water's-edge group had the election pursuant to Rev & TC § 25110 not been made, during the income year. The amount and location of compensation will be determined under Rev & TC § 25133 and regulations thereunder.

"Water's-edge group" consists of banks or corporations whose income and apportionment factors are taken into account pursuant to Rev & TC § 25110.

The 100% exclusion is determined as follows: (1) foreign payroll factor is subtracted from the greatest foreign payroll factor for any year in the base period; (2) amount so determined is divided by the greatest foreign payroll factor for any year in the base period; (3) the percentage obtained is multiplied by total qualifying foreign dividends. This amount is the amount of the fully excluded dividends. It can't exceed the amount of the qualifying dividends in excess of the base dividends determined in Rev & TC § 24411(b). Base dividends are qualifying dividends equal to greatest amount of qualifying dividends as described in Rev & TC § 24411(a) received by the water's-edge group in any one of income years constituting base period. If fully excluded dividend amount is less than the amount of qualified dividends in excess of base dividends, the difference is added to the base dividends. The 100% exclusion also applies to qualifying dividends derived from construction projects, the locations of which are not subject to the taxpayer's control.

The 75% exclusion is determined as follows: (1) the greatest foreign payroll factor for any year in the base period is subtracted from the foreign payroll factor in the income year; (2) the amount determined is divided by the foreign payroll factor for the income year; (3) the percentage is multiplied by the total qualifying foreign dividends; (4) subtract this amount from the excess of the qualifying dividends over the base dividends; (5) the balance is the partially excluded qualifying dividends. 75% of qualifying dividends equal to greatest amount of dividends received in any one of base period income years may be excluded in the alternative.

¶ 1185 **Computation of Interest Offset**

The interest expense deductible by corporations using the apportionment formula, will be an amount equal to the interest income subject to the apportionment formula plus the amount by which the balance of interest expense exceeds interest and dividend income not subject to apportionment by formula. Interest expense not included in the preceding sentence is to be applied as a direct offset against interest and dividends not subject to apportionment by formula. For further information, refer to section on corporate deductions (¶ 1146).

¶ 1186   Intercompany Dividends

In any case where an affiliated group of corporations is engaged in filing a combined return and one of the corporations pays a dividend out of its share of the unitary income to its parent corporation which is also a member of the unitary group, the dividends will be eliminated from the income of the recipient.[19]

SPECIAL APPORTIONMENT FORMULAS

¶ 1187   Special Formulas Allowed—Petition to Change Formula

Rev & TC § 25137 provides that a taxpayer may petition for, or the Franchise Tax Board may require, deviation from the ordinary three-factor formula in any case in which that formula does not fairly represent the extent of the taxpayer's business in California. Changes offered are the following:

(a) Separate accounting;
(b) The exclusion of one or more of the factors;
(c) The inclusion of one or more additional factors; or
(d) The employment of any other method to "effectuate an equitable allocation and apportionment of the taxpayer's income."

The Franchise Tax Board has issued rules regarding special apportionment formulas. Usually the special formulas are established only after discussions with representatives of the particular industry involved.[20]

Banks and financial corporations.   Property, payroll and sales factor of apportionment formula for banks and financial corporations must be computed under Rev & TC §§ 25128—25137 and applicable regulations.

Special rules apply to property factor: Special rules apply to the following items in the property factor: (1) Owned intangible personalty; (2) Goodwill; and (3) Coin and currency.

Owned intangible personalty includes:

(1) loans;
(2) participating bank's portion of participation loan;
(3) loans solicited by travelling loan officers;
(4) bank credit card and travel and entertainment credit card receivables;
(5) investment of bank in securities, income from which constitutes business income;
(6) securities used to maintain reserves against deposits;
(7) securities owned by bank but held by state treasurer or other public official;

---

(19) § 25106.   (20) § 25137.

(8) investments by financial corporation in securities yielding business income; and

(9) leases of tangible personalty.

Special rules applicable to sales factor: The special rules cover:

(1) receipts from lease or rental of tangible personalty;

(2) receipts from intangible personalty, including interest from loans, participation loans and loans solicited by travelling loan officers;

(3) interest or service charges from credit cards and cardholder fees;

(4) merchant discount income;

(5) fiduciary services;

(6) investment in securities yielding business income;

(7) receipts from securities used to maintain reserves against deposits;

(8) receipts from securities held by state treasurer or other public official, or pledged to secure public trust funds;

(9) fees for issuance of travelers checks or money orders by bank, financial corporation or independent agent; and

(10) receipts from investments of financial corporation.[21]

For income years starting on or after 1–1–89, Reg 25137–10 gives the rules for combining a general corporation (predominant activity other than financial) and a financial corporation in a unitary report. Before 1989, LR 370 gave the rules. FTB Notice 89–610, eff 9–22–89 gave notice of the proposed withdrawal of LR 370, and modified the rules for the inclusion of intangibles in the property and receipts factors.[22]

Where financial corporation is dominant member of unitary group, Reg 25137–4[21] is applied in determining factors of banks and financial corporations included in combined report. UDITPA is used for general corporations.[22]

International banking facility. Facility maintained by a bank within California is considered doing business outside of the state. Intangible personal property and sales reflected on segregated books and records recognized by the Federal Reserve System as attributable to the facility must be so attributed in determining the property, payroll and sales factors of the bank.[23]

Partnerships. When a corporation has an interest in a partnership and that partnership's activities and the corporation's activities constitute a unitary business under established standards, the corporation's share of the partnership's income is to be combined with the taxpayer's unitary business income and apportioned on the basis of the formula.[24]

Construction contractors. Construction contractors engaged in a unitary business are required to make a special computation for their unitary business during the years in which they have long-term construction contracts. The contractors using the percentage of completion method for long-

---

(21) Reg 25137–4.
(22) Reg 25137–10; LR 370; FTB 89–610, 9–22–89.

(23) § 25107.
(24) Reg 25137–1.

term contracts include in income each year of the contract the amount by which the gross contract price which corresponds to the percentage of the entire contract which has been completed during the year exceeds expenditures made during the year on the contract, taking into account the materials and supplies on hand at the beginning and the end of each income year. Under the completed contract method, the taxpayer reports the entire income from the contract in the year in which the contract is completed and accepted, and deducts the expenditures incurred on the contract. All receipts and expenditures on contracts using the completed contract method, whether completed or not at the end of each income year, are excluded from business income each year and included in income in the final year of the contract. Business income from other sources, for example, short-term contracts and rents, would be apportioned by the regular three-factor formula of property, payroll and sales for each of the years of the contract prior to the termination year.

TAX TIP

A general contractor operating both in and outside California, and reporting its income on the completed-contract method of accounting, must use the special apportionment formula designed by the Franchise Tax Board for apportioning income to California. The burden is on the taxpayer to show that the formula apportionment method used by the state is unfair and the lack of fairness is not demonstrated by merely showing that a different formula would generate different results (*Appeal of Robert E. McKee, Inc., SBE, 12–13–83*).

If the construction contractor using the percentage of completion method has income from within and without California on the contract, he follows the ordinary rules for apportionment of income in determining the property factor percentage and the payroll factor percentage.

Sales factor computation. For the sales or revenue factor the following computation is made:

(a) Gross receipts are assigned to California if (1) the project is located in California; or (2) if the contract is performed both within and without California, the percentage of the contract performed in California is based on the ratio which the costs in California bear to the total costs of the contract.

(b) The sales factor would include only that portion of the total contract price which was completed during the income year, figured by using the percentage amount completed.

Reporting revenue from a completed contract within and without the state. In reporting the revenue from a completed contract, which takes place both within and without California, the following method is used:

(a) The income or loss from the contract is determined.

(b) The income or loss from the contract is apportioned to California as follows:

(1) A fraction is determined for each year the contract is in progress. The numerator of the fraction is the amount of the construction costs paid or

accrued each year of the contract, and the denominator of the fraction is the total of all such construction costs for the project.

(2) Each percentage determined in (1) is multiplied by the apportionment formula percentage for that year as determined under the ordinary apportionment rules.

(3) The products determined at (2) for each year the contract was in progress are totalled.

(4) The total percentage determined in (3) is applied to the total income or loss on the particular contract. The result is the amount of business income from the contract derived from sources within California.[25]

Motion picture and television producers and television network broadcasts. Reg 25137–8 applies to motion picture and television film producers, producers of TV commercials, and TV networks. It also applies to independent TV stations to extent they are members of a chain of commonly owned stations all of which operate as network affiliates or all of which are unaffiliated with network but which operate collectively in purchasing properties for telecast or in marketing air time or which operate as a producer.

The property, payroll and sales factor of the apportionment formula will be computed according to Rev & TC §§ 25128 through 25137, and regs, under those sections, except as provided in Reg 25137–8.

Property factor. Property factor rules cover: (1) net annual rental rate; (2) lump-sum rental payments; and (3) value of films, video cassettes, and discs.

Payroll factor. Payroll factor rules cover compensation paid, including talent salaries, residual and profit participation payments, and payments for services of actor or director loaned or provided by another corporation.

Sales factor. Sales factor rules cover receipts from films to theater, TV, or TV network, and sales and rentals of video cassettes and discs. Instate-outstate attribution rules will apply.

Bus and truck companies. Transportation companies operating within and without California use the standard three-factor formula with the following adjustments:

(1) *Property factor.* Nonmovable property such as warehouses, offices, repair shops, etc., are apportioned under the ordinary rules of the formula. If the corporation is providing buses, a percentage is computed using the ratio of California revenue miles to the total revenue miles and this percentage is applied to the original cost of the equipment. If rented buses are used, the same percentage is applied to the capitalized annual rent on the buses. If the company provides trucking services rather than buses, the ratio of ton-miles (or actual miles) for each piece of equipment is used instead of revenue miles.

(2) *Payroll factor.* The denominator is the total compensation paid to all employees wherever located. For the numerator, a computation is made for the bus and truck drivers and the helpers operating interstate equipment, using the same ratios as explained above for the property factor.

---

(25) Reg 25137–2.

(3) *Sales factor.* The denominator includes gross revenue from all sources. For the California numerator for revenues received from intrastate and interstate hauling, the same percentages computed under the property factor are used to compute the California portion of the income from buses or trucks, as the case may be.[26]

Airlines. With the exception of movable property and flight personnel, airline corporations follow the usual apportionment rules. Rev & TC 25101.3 sets up a special apportionment formula relating to the aircraft of an air carrier, or foreign air carrier, or the operator of an air taxi. The numerator of the property factor for aircraft is based on the ratio that the air and ground time for the aircraft is in California, to the total air and ground time everywhere. This portion of the computation is weighted at 75%. The ratio of total arrivals and departures of aircraft in California to the total arrivals and departures of the aircraft everywhere is weighted at 25%. The Franchise Tax Board has determined that "air time," which is determined in minutes, means the time from the California border to the airport or vice versa. For this purpose, the California border as it applies to the California coast is the three-mile limit. Ground time includes the time for loading, unloading, minor repairs and so on, but not including time in storage. Use of taxpayer's owned or rented aircraft in exchange program with another carrier isn't rental or subrental. Such aircraft must be accounted for in property factor. Rotables, parts and other expendables, including parts for use in contract overhaul work must be valued at cost. Statistics to be used in computing time and arrivals and departures factors shall be the taxpayer's annual statistics or those for a representative period for the taxpayer's income year should be used if available. Otherwise the statistics for the representative period should be used. These periods are periods designated by the State Board of Equalization for the current property tax assessment year and the immediately preceding or succeeding property tax assessment year. The FTB can designate alternate periods to fairly reflect the taxpayer's activities in-state.[27]

Payroll factor. The payroll factor for flight crews in California is determined by the ratio that the air and ground time in California bears to the total air and ground time everywhere.

Sales factor. For the revenue factor, the denominator is the total business revenue of all sources. The numerator for California is the revenue for hauling passengers, freight, mail or baggage, determined by the ratio of the air time of the aircraft in California to the total everywhere, weighted at 80%, and the ratio of arrivals and departures in California to total arrivals and departures, weighted at 20%. Air time and arrivals and departures by type of aircraft shall be used in computing revenue attributable to state derived from hauling passengers, freight, mail and excess baggage. If records of actual revenue by type of aircraft aren't maintained, the total revenue shall be divided into passenger and freight and allocated to aircraft

---

(26) UDITPA Manual September 1984, 1010. (27) § 25101.3; Reg 25137-7.

type on ratio of revenue passenger miles and revenue freight ton-miles. Taxpayer's annual statistics should be used in computing time and arrival and departures, or statistics for the representative period.[27]

Personal service companies.   Included in this category are advertising agencies, architectural firms, engineering firms, insurance agencies, consulting agencies and management companies. The property factor, if any, for a service organization is determined in accordance with the usual rules. The payroll factor is assigned to the state in which the services are rendered, computed in accordance with the rules for unemployment insurance reporting. Sales factor for service companies is the only factor which presents any major variation from the usual apportionment rules. The denominator of the sales factor is business receipts from all sources. The numerator assigns receipts to California if the services are performed in California, and if the services are performed partly within and partly without California, the receipts attributable to California are determined by the ratio of the time spent in performing the services in California to the total time spent in performing services everywhere.[28]

Stockbrokers.   The rule established by the Franchise Tax Board for stockbrokers operating a unitary business is different from the usual formula only in the sales factor. The denominator of the sales factor would be the total receipts of the business except receipts from the sale of stocks and bonds. The numerator of the factor is determined as follows: (a) Commissions from buying and selling. (1) Stocks—60% to the originating office and 40% to the selling office. (2) Bonds—50% to the originating office and 50% to the selling office. (b) Dividends—To the extent dividends constitute business income, they are assigned to the state of domicile of the corporation. (c) Other gross receipts are apportioned in accordance with the ordinary rules.[28]

Professional sports.   The Franchise Tax Board has repealed the formulas for professional baseball, football, basketball, and ice hockey clubs, which were applied uniformly to those teams based in California and those based in other states that visit California.

A special three-factor apportionment formula applies to professional athletic teams that are members of professional leagues and located in California and other states and foreign countries. If the team's operation is based in California (state under which it derives its territorial rights under the rules of the league of which it is member), (1) the average value of all its property, wherever located, owned or rented and used during income year will be deemed to have been owned, rented and used in-state during the income year; (2) the total compensation paid everywhere will be deemed paid in-state; and (3) the total sales everywhere will be deemed made in-state. Similar apportionment rules apply to a team with operation based out-of-state—its property, payroll and sales will be deemed owned, paid or made in-state in which it has its base of operations. For purposes of the minimum tax,

---

(28) UDITPA Manual September 1984, 1010.

an entity that operates as a professional athletic team will be treated as a corporation. Any corporation owning part of entity can satisfy its minimum tax liability by paying that tax, if not otherwise doing business in-state.[29]

Commercial fishing. The Franchise Tax Board adopted Reg 25137–5 for the apportionment of income from commercial fishing. The regulation follows the ordinary apportionment formula rule with the exception of the value of a ship and ship's equipment in the property factor, and ship's personnel and fishermen in the payroll factor, and the receipts in the revenue factor. In each of the three factors, the California ratio for the numerator is determined by the ratio of the number of port days during which the ship was within California to the total number of port days of the ship everywhere during the income year.[30]

Installment sales. Legal Ruling 413 provides that installment sale gains will be apportioned to California using the factors for the year of sale. Collections in installment sales in subsequent years are not included in the income subject to apportionment in that year, but are reported separately using the original apportionment percentage from the year in which the property was sold.[31]

Combined reports including foreign country income. The translation method for determining income is the profit and loss method. This method excludes unrealized exchange rate gain or loss resulting from a restatement of the assets and liabilities, while taking into account exchange gains or losses attributable to income transactions.

Determining income. For purposes of determining income:

(1) Profit and loss statement must be prepared for each foreign branch in currency in which books of account are regularly maintained.

(2) Adjustments must be made to conform to generally accepted accounting principles accepted in the U.S., except as modified by regulation.

(3) Adjustments must be made to conform to Rev & TC, Part 11, Div 2 accounting standards.

(4) Profit and loss statement of each branch or corporation, U.S. or foreign, must be translated into currency used by the parent to maintain books.

(5) Business and nonbusiness income under California law must be identified and segregated.

(6) Nonbusiness income must be allocated to specific state under UDITPA provisions of Rev & TC §§ 25124–25127.

(7) Business income must be included in combined report.

(8) Income from California sources must be expressed in dollars, and taxes computed.

Alternate method. If the FTB allows, a unitary business with operations in a foreign country may determine income on the basis of a consolidated profit and loss statement prepared for related corporations of which a unitary business is a member prepared for filing with the SEC. If not

---

(29) § 25141.
(30) § 25137–5.

(31) LR 413.

required to file with the SEC, a consolidated report prepared for shareholders may be used.

Exchange rates. Translations must be made at the following exchange rates: (1) Depreciation, depletion, or amortization must be translated at the appropriate exchange rate for the transaction period in which the historical cost of underlying asset was incurred. (2) All other items must be translated at either the year-end exchange rate or the simple average exchange rate for the period. Repatriated income takes the rate at the date of repatriation. The currency of the parent is used for all factors, unless the FTB sets the dollar or other currency at a fairer rate.

Computation of factors—property factor. Property factor is computed as follows: (1) Fixed assets—use original cost and exchange rate at the date of acquisition. (2) Rented property is capitalized at eight times the annual rental rate—use simple average of beginning and end-of-year rate. (3) Inventories—use original cost and rate as of the date of acquisition. (4) Financial corporation—financial assets are translated at year-end rate, and defined as assets reflecting fixed amount of currency. Securities held or expected to be held for less than six months must be translated at year-end rates. If held longer, at the appropriate exchange rate for the translation period in which the historical cost of the asset is determined.

Payroll and receipts factors. Translation must be made at simple average of beginning and end-of-year exchange rates unless there is substantial fluctuation. If there is such fluctuation, the appropriate exchange rate shall be either (1) the simple average of the month-end rates, or (2) the weighted average taking into account the volume of transactions for the calendar months ending with or within that period.[32]

Franchisors. Trade or business that includes granting of license by franchisor of trademark, trade name or service mark to market or use a product or service under such mark or name according to methods prescribed by franchisor computes property, payroll and sales factors of apportionment formula under Rev & TC §§ 25128–25137.

Exceptions—payroll factor. In determining the numerator, compensation paid to traveling employees regularly providing administrative or advisory services at the franchisee's place of business must be determined on the basis of the ratio of time spent in performing such services in-state to the total time spent in performing such services everywhere.

Sales factor. In determining the numerator the following receipts must be attributed to the state in which the franchisee's place of business is located, provided taxpayer is taxable in such state: (a) fees received from the franchisee for national or regional advertising placed by the franchisor; (b) fees received for site investigation, selection and acquisition of place of business of the franchisee or potential franchisee. If the taxpayer isn't taxable in

---

(32) Reg 25137–6.

the state of business location, receipts must be attributed to the state in which the principal office of the taxpayer's employee or employees performing the services is located, except that if the services are performed by an independent contractor, receipts shall be attributed to the state of the taxpayer's commercial domicile; (c) fees for administrative or advisory services. Fees or royalties received for the use of a trademark, trade name, etc. or the right to market product or service must be attributed to the state in which the franchisee's place of business is located, if the taxpayer is taxable there; otherwise to the taxpayer's commercial domicile.[33]

Other special group industry formulas have been provided for[34] railroads[35], pipeline companies, freight forwarding companies and offshore drilling companies.[36]

SEPARATE ACCOUNTING

¶ 1188   When Applicable

The statute says that if the allocation and apportionment provisions don't represent the extent of the taxpayer's business activity in California, the taxpayer can petition or the Franchise Tax Board may require use of separate accounting.[37] See special apportionment formulas ¶ 1187.

ALTERNATIVE MINIMUM TAX—PREFERENCE ITEMS

¶ 1189   Apportionment Formula

The alternative minimum tax on items of preference income applicable to corporations is discussed at ¶ 1223.

California adopts IRC § 57, relating to items of tax preference, with the following modifications: IRC § 57(a)(5), relating to tax-exempt interest does not apply. IRC § 57(a)(6)(A) is modified to refer to amounts allowed as a deduction by Rev & TC § 24357, rather than IRC § 170 (future interest in tangible property contributed). The last sentence of IRC § 57(a)(6)(B) relating to tangible personal property shall not apply. IRC Sec 57(a)(7), relating to accelerated depreciation or amortization on certain real property placed in service before 1–1–87, is modified to read: With respect to each property as described in IRC § 1250, as of 4–1–70, the amount by which the deduction allowable for the income year for depreciation or amortization exceeds depreciation deduction that would have been allowable for the income year had taxpayer depreciated property under the straight-line method of each income year of its useful life, without regard to Rev & TC §§ 24354.2 or

---

(33) Reg 25137–3.
(34) Reg § 25137.
(35) Reg 25137–9.

(36) LR 366, 12–14–73; LR 396, 8–9–76; UDITPA Manual September 1984, 1010.
(37) § 25137.

24381, for which taxpayer held the property.[38] California also adopts IRC § 55(b)(2), relating to the definition of alternative taxable income but modifies the federal rules to provide that for corporations whose net income is determined under the allocation and apportionment provisions of Ch 17, starting with Rev & TC § 25101, alternative minimum taxable income shall be allocated in the same manner as net income is allocated and apportioned for purposes of the regular tax.[39]

---

(38) § 23457.   **(39)** § 23455(b).

TAX RATES, TAX CREDITS

2002 Section VII/BANK AND CORPORATION INCOME TAXES

TAX RATES

¶ 1211   Corporation Tax Rate

The rate of tax is 9.3%[1].

Minimum tax. Every corporation doing business in California, except financial corporations, must pay annually to the state a minimum tax, if the minimum tax specified in Rev & TC § 23153 is greater than the tax according to or measured by its net income computed at the applicable rate.[2] For income years starting after 12–31–89, the minimum tax is $800.[3] A domestic bank or corporation that files a certificate of dissolution in the office of the Secretary of State pursuant to § 1905 of the Corporations Code, and does not thereafter do business, is not subject to the minimum franchise tax for income years beginning on or after the date of filing.[4]

Beginning 1–1–94, for nonprofit cooperative associations organized on or after that date, an exemption from the minimum franchise tax is provided for five consecutive income years commencing with the first income year that a certificate is prepared by the county board of supervisors certifying that: (1) the association is in an economically distressed area; (2) at least 90% of the association's members are, or have been, within the previous 12 months unemployed or dependent on public social services for their income; and (3) the request for the certificate is made during the association's first income year. The requirements for exemption are more specifically set out in Food and Agricultural Code § 54042.[5]

¶ 1212   Bank and Financial Tax Rate

For income years ending in 1988, and before December 31, 1995, the rate of tax on banks and financial corporations shall be the lesser of 11.7% or a percentage equal to the sum of (1) the rate of tax specified in Rev & TC § 23151, relating to the general tax on corporations, and (2) the in-lieu rate, as defined by Rev & TC § 23186(c) or Rev & TC § 23186(e).

1994 rate. For taxpayers filing on a calendar year basis, the rate for 1994 is 11.470% (11.107% for 1993). The 1994 rate consists of the 9.3% general tax rate and the in lieu rate, computed at 2.170%, for income years ending in 1994. For fiscal year taxpayers, the rate must be prorated to reflect the in lieu rate change.

In-lieu rate for income years ending after 1991 and before 12–1–95. For income years ending after 1991 and before December 1, 1995, the in-lieu rate is defined as a fraction which is multiplied by an adjustment factor equal to 0.51535.

---

(1) § 23151(d).
(2) § 23151(a).
(3) § 23153(d).

(4) § 23153(e).
(5) § 23153, as added by Stats. 1994, c. 427, § 2.

The numerator of the fraction is the total amount required to be paid to the political subdivisions of California as personal property taxes and business license, decreased by the product of the franchise tax rate and the total amount required to be paid to the political subdivisions of California as personal property taxes and business license taxes. Personal property taxes required to be paid shall be the statewide locally assessed personal property taxes reported by the State Board of Equalization for the state's fiscal year ending in the calendar year before the beginning of the bank tax rate year. Business license taxes required to be paid shall be the statewide locally assessed business license taxes reported by the Controller's office for the state's fiscal year ending in two calendar years prior to the beginning of the bank tax rate year.

The denominator is the total amount of net income derived from or attributable to sources in California by every corporation taxable under the franchise tax, other than public utilities, as defined in the Public Utilities Act, for income years ending in three calendar years prior to the beginning of the bank tax rate year, determined pursuant to information compiled from tax returns filed with the Franchise Tax Board, increased by the total amount required to be paid to the political subdivisions of California as personal property taxes and business license taxes.[6]

The in-lieu rate, so calculated, shall never be less than 1.3%.

The bank tax rate year is the calendar year in which taxpayer's income year ends.

Rate— income years ending on or after 12–31–95. For income years ending on or after 12–31–95, the rate shall be the rate of tax specified in Rev & TC § 23151, plus 2%.[7]

WARNING   Taxpayers who decline or refuse to furnish information to the Franchise Tax Board with respect to personal property and business license taxes, or net income required to determine rate will lose deductions for those taxes, and be subject to $5,000 penalty.[8]

Minimum tax. For income years beginning after 12–31–89, the minimum tax is $800.[3]

¶ 1214   Water's Edge Election Fee

For income years starting 1–1–88 and later, qualified taxpayers whose income subject to tax is derived from or attributable to sources both within and without California may elect to determine their income derived from or attributable to sources within California according to the Bank and Corporation Tax Law, as modified by the water's edge election provisions.

---

(6) § 23186(e).

(7) § 23186(f).

(8) § 23186(h).

For years beginning prior to 1–1–94, the election was made by contract with the Franchise Tax Board that must provide for payment of an annual amount to the FTB equal to thirty-thousandths of 1% (.03%) of the sum of qualified taxpayers' property, payroll and sales in-state, subject to adjustments that: (1) use property and payroll factors for an income year of 12 full months ending during calendar year 1986, and sales assigned to the state for the current income year; a single corporation engaged in more than one business for which it is making separate elections must determine the fee for each of these businesses; and (2) reduce the sum of property, payroll and sales by the cumulative amount expended since 1–1–87 in new plants or facilities in-state, and the amount expended for new employees in-state. In no event may the annual amount be less than ten-thousandths of 1% (.01%) of the sum of taxpayer's property, payroll and sales in-state for current year.[9]

CAUTION   Stats. 1993, c. 881 repealed the water's-edge election fee effective for calendar years beginning on or after 1994 or fiscal years beginning in 1994. The Legislative Counsel has issued an informal opinion that the fee must still be paid for elections in effect through calendar year 1993 or fiscal years beginning in 1993.

¶ 1223   Alternative Minimum Tax Rate

California has adopted the federal alternative minimum tax imposed by IRC §§ 55—59, subject to certain state modifications.[10] California's conformity provisions are similar to those in ¶ 135 of this handbook that explains the tax as it applies under the Personal Income Tax Law, but there are special provisions for corporations that file a combined report, and for commencing, dissolving and withdrawing corporations, and those that cease doing business during the year.

In computing the alternative minimum tax, adjustments are made based on adjusted current earnings as set forth in IRC § 56(g). Such adjusted current earnings for California purposes determined on a separate entity basis, even though the corporate entity may be included in a combined report.[11]

Federal-state conformity.   California adopts IRC § 55(b)(1), modified as follows: (1) With respect to corporations subject to the franchise tax under Ch 2, other than financial corporations, according to or measured by net income, for the privilege of doing business in California, the rate is 7% of the amount of alternative minimum taxable income for the taxable year as exceeds the exemption amount. (2) With respect to corporations subject to corporation income tax under Ch 3, the rate is 7% of alternative minimum taxable income as exceeds the exemption amount. (3) With respect to corporations subject to tax on unrelated business income from in-state sources, the rate is 7% of alternative minimum taxable income for the taxable year

---

(9) § 25101; 25110; 25111; 25115.
(10) § 23400; 23453–23459.

(11) § 23456, as added by Stats. 1994, c. 948, § 5.

that exceeds the exemption amount.[12] The minimum tax credit determined in accordance with IRC § 53, as modified by California, is allowed against the regular tax, as defined by Rev & TC § 23455(c). The amount determined under IRC § 53(c)(1) is the regular tax, as defined by Rev & TC § 23455(c), reduced by the sum of the credits allowable under the Bank and Corporation Tax Law, other than that portion of any credit that reduces the tax below the minimum tax as provided in Rev & TC § 23036(d)(1).[13]

Credits which reduce the minimum tax. Only the following credits are allowed to reduce the tax below the tentative minimum tax, and then only after allowance of the minimum tax credit allowed by Rev & TC § 23453: (1) the credits allowed by Rev & TC §§ 23601, 23601.4, and 23601.5 relating to solar energy; (2) the credit allowed by Rev & TC § 23609.5 relating to clinical testing; (3) the credit allowed by Rev & TC § 23610.5 relating to low-income housing; (4) the credit allowed by Rev & TC § 23612 relating to the sales and use tax credit; (5) the credit allowed by Rev & TC § 23612.6 relating to the Los Angeles Revitalization Zone sales tax credit; (6) the credit allowed by Rev & TC § 23622 relating to the enterprise zone hiring credit; (7) the credit allowed by Rev & TC § 23625 relating to the Los Angeles Revitalization Zone hiring credit; (8) the credit allowed by Rev & TC § 23623 relating to the program area hiring credit; and (9) the credit allowed by Rev & TC § 23649 relating to qualified property.[14]

California has not adopted the change on the calculation of the AMT by mutual life insurance companies. California only applies the gross premiums, not the income tax to these companies.

Tax benefit rule. California conforms to IRC § 111 on recovery of tax benefit items, except that IRC § 111(b)(3) (investment tax credit and foreign tax credit) and IRC § 111(d) (special rules for accumulated earnings tax and personal holding company tax) do not apply in California.[15]

¶ 1224   **Banks and Financial Corporations—Alternative Minimum Tax Rates**

California adopts IRC § 55(b)(1) with respect to rates for banks and financial corporations, with the following modifications: (1) With respect to banks taxable under Rev & TC § 23181, the rate is 7% of alternative minimum taxable income that exceeds the exemption amount, and at the rate determined under Rev & TC § 23186, less the rate determined set by Rev & TC § 23151, upon the basis of net income for the taxable year. (2) With respect to financial corporations, the rate is 7% of so much of the alternative minimum taxable income as exceeds the exemption amount, and at the rate set by Rev & TC § 23186, less the Rev & TC § 23151 rate, on the basis of net income for the taxable year. The Rev & TC § 23184 offset shall be applied to the tentative minimum tax in same manner and to same extent as offset is applied to tax imposed by Rev & TC § 23101.

---

(12) § 23455(a).

(13) § 23453.

(14) § 23036 as amended by Stats. 1993, c. 881.

(15) § 24310.

TAX CREDITS

¶ 1233 Tax Credits—General

Specific credits against tax are allowed. These are explained below. The table of tax credits for individuals and corporations is at ¶ 158. The order of credits is specified. Credit carryovers to which taxpayer was entitled under pre-1987 law are allowed by Rev & TC § 23051.7.[16]

If two or more taxpayers share in costs that would be eligible for a tax credit, each taxpayer may take the tax credit in proportion to its respective share of costs paid or incurred.[17]

¶ 1235 Commercial Solar Energy System Credit

For income years starting on or after 1–1–90 and before 1–1–94, a credit is allowed against the tax, as defined in Rev & TC § 23036, in an amount equal to 10% of the cost of a solar energy system, installed on premises used for commercial purposes, which are located in California, and are owned by the taxpayer during the income year. If taxpayers lease a solar energy system, the tax credit shall only apply to the principal recovery portion of the lease payments, for the term of the lease, not to exceed 10 years, that are made during the income year, and to amounts expended on the purchased portion of the solar energy system, including installation charges, during the income year.[18]

The commercial solar electric system credit is claimed on FTB Form 3805L.

System with generating capacity in excess of 30 megawatts. The credit may not be claimed for any solar energy system with a generating capacity in excess of 30 megawatts for any income year or portion thereof for which the Internal Revenue Code does not allow at least a 10% tax credit for those solar energy systems with a generating capacity in excess of 30 megawatts that is equivalent in scope to the credit available under the Internal Revenue Code for the 1989 calendar year.

When claimed. The solar energy tax credit must be claimed on the state income tax return for the income year in which the solar energy system was installed. A taxpayer who claimed the solar energy tax credit in the state income tax return for the income year in which the solar energy system was installed may claim the credit in subsequent years for additions to the system or additional systems.

Cost reduced by grant of public entity. For purposes of computing the credit, the cost of any solar energy system eligible for the credit is reduced by any grant provided by a public entity for that system.

---

(16) § 23036; 23051.7.
(17) § 23036(g).

(18) § 23601.5.

Basis reduced by credit and grant of utility or public agency. The basis of any system for which a credit is allowed is reduced by the amount of the credit and the amount of any grant provided by a utility or public agency for the solar energy system. The basis adjustment is made for the income year for which the credit is allowed.

More than one owner. If there is more than one owner of a premises on which a solar energy system is installed, each owner shall be eligible to receive the solar energy tax credit in proportion to its ownership interests in the premises.

Partnership. Solar energy credit may be divided between the partners pursuant to written partnership agreement.

Carryovers. When the credit allowed under this section exceeds the "net tax" for the income year, that portion of the credit which exceeds the "net tax" may be carried over to the "net tax" in succeeding income years, until the credit is used.

No credit—expenditures claimed as credit for energy conservation measures. No tax credit may be claimed for any expenditures which have been otherwise claimed as a tax credit for the current or any prior income year as energy conservation measures under this part.

Lessees of solar energy system. Taxpayers who lease a solar energy system installed on premises in California receive a tax credit, if the lessee can confirm, if necessary, by a written document signed by the lessor that: (1) the lessor irrevocably elects not to claim a state tax credit for the solar energy system; and (2) if the system is installed in a locality served by a municipal solar utility, that the lessor holds a valid permit from the municipal solar utility. Leasing requirements may be established by the State Energy Resources Conservation and Development Commission as part of the solar energy system eligibility criteria.

Guidelines and criteria. The State Energy Resources Conservation and Development Commission shall, after one or more public hearings, establish limits on eligible costs of solar energy systems in terms of dollars per kilowatt and guidelines and criteria for solar energy systems which shall be eligible for the credit. These guidelines and criteria may include, but are not limited to, minimum requirements for safety, market readiness, reliability, and durability of solar energy systems. Any solar energy system with generating capacity in excess of 100 kilowatts is eligible for the credit only if the owner of the solar energy system first obtains a finding from the commission that the system is eligible for the credit under established guidelines and criteria. Any system certified by the commission under Public Resources Code, Div 15, Ch 6 (starting with § 25500) is deemed eligible for the credit. The Franchise Tax Board shall prescribe such regulations as may be necessary to carry out the purposes of the credit provisions.

¶ 1235

Taxpayer's identification number. The Commission may obtain a claimant's taxpayer identification number through its tax credit application or certification process for purposes of identifying a qualifying taxpayer to the Franchise Tax Board. This number must be used exclusively for state tax administrative purposes.

Construction—associated expenditures by the end of the income year. Notwithstanding Rev & TC § 23601.5(a), relating to the credit amount, and Rev & TC § 23601.5(b)(1), relating income year of claim, a taxpayer who, on or before the end of the income year, has commenced construction, or made expenditures, associated with the installation of a solar energy system, shall be eligible in that income year for the tax credit to the extent of the cost paid or incurred during that income year for construction or expenditures for which a credit is otherwise allowable, if the installation is completed by the end of the sixth month of the taxpayer's next income year.

System that continues to qualify under former Rev & TC § 23601. Systems that continue to qualify under former Rev & TC § 23601 by meeting the eligibility requirements of former Rev & TC § 23601(j) is not covered by the credit discussed above. The carryover rules of Rev & TC § 23601.4(g) will apply to such a system.

Sunset date. The sunset date of the solar energy system credit is 12–1–94. Unused credits may continue to be carried forward until exhausted.

¶ 1236   **Jobs Tax Credit**

A credit is allowed in an amount equal to 10% of the amount of wages paid to each employee who is certified as meeting the requirements of Unemployment Insurance Code § 328.[19]

The jobs tax credit is claimed on FTB Form 3524.

To qualify an employer for the credit, each employee must have, by the day of starting work (1) received a certification from the Employment Development Department, or (2) have requested in writing a certification from that Department. If by the start of work, the employee has received from the Department a written preliminary determination that he or she is a member of a targeted group, the requirement of (1) or (2) above will apply by the fifth day on which the employee starts work.

The credit does not apply to wages over $3,000 paid by the taxpayer to any one individual. The aggregate credit can't exceed $600 with respect to each qualified employee.

The credit also does not apply to wages paid to an individual who (1) is a dependent, as described in IRC § 152(a)(1)–(8), of an individual who owns directly or indirectly, more than 50% in value of taxpayer's outstanding

---

(19) § 23621.

stock, determined by application of IRC § 267(c); or (2) is a dependent described in IRC § 152(a)(9) of the individual described in (1).

The credit does not apply to wages paid to an individual, if, before the hiring date, that individual had been employed at any time he or she was not certified by the Department to meet the requirements of Unempl Ins Cd § 328.

If certification has been revoked because false information was provided the Department under Unempl Ins Cd § 328(c), the credit will not apply to wages paid after the date on which the notice of revocation is received.

The credit is in addition to any deduction allowed taxpayer, and will be applied to wages paid each qualifying employee during the 24-month period starting on the date the employee commences work.

Taxpayer may elect to have Rev & TC § 24330 not apply for any income year. The election may be made or revoked at any time before the end of a 4-year period starting on the last day for filing the return for that income year, determined without regard to extensions. The election must be made in the manner set by the Franchise Tax Board.

In case of a successor employer referred to in IRC § 3306(b)(1), the determination of the amount of credit with respect to wages paid by the successor will be made in the same manner as if the wages were paid by the predecessor employer.

No credit will be determined with respect to remuneration paid by employer to employee for services performed for another person unless the amount the employer can reasonably expect to receive for those services from that other person exceeds the remuneration paid to the employee.

IRC § 51(c)(3), relating to payments for services during labor disputes, is not included in the meaning of the term "wages."

The credit expires 12–31–93.

Economic development area. A qualified business in an economic development program area that hires a qualified employee can take a credit against net tax for each qualified employee who has been unemployed for at least six months before being employed equal to: (1) 50% for qualified wages in the first year of employment; (2) 40% for qualified wages in the second year of employment; (3) 30% for qualified wages in the third year of employment; (4) 20% for qualified wages in the fourth year of employment; and (5) 10% for qualified wages in the fifth year of employment. The credit for each qualified employee who has been unemployed for at least three months, but less than six months, shall be (1) 25% of qualified wages for the first year of employment; (2) 40% of qualified wages for the second year; (3) 30% of qualified wages for the third year; and (4) 20% of qualified wages for the fourth year; and (5) 10% of qualified wages for the fifth year.[20]

Unused credits may be carried over to succeeding income years, but must be applied first to the earliest income years possible.

The credit can't exceed the amount of tax that would be imposed on the income attributed to the business activities of the taxpayer within the program area as if such attributed income represented all of the net income subject to tax. The attributed income must be determined under the UDITPA rules using a two-factor factor formula apportionment formula.

Qualified wages. "Qualified wages" means that portion of wages not in excess of 150% of the minimum wage paid or incurred by the qualified business during the income year to the qualified employee.

Qualified business. "Qualified business" means any corporation or other entity subject to the Bank and Corporation Tax Law certified by a city, county, or county and city and by the Department of Economic and Business Development that, during the designation of the program area, is engaged in the active conduct of trade or business within the program area and meets the percentage requirements (30%) as to: (1) employees resident in a high density unemployment area; (2) setting up community service programs approved by the local government and community advisory council; (3) engaging in a joint venture with business owned by a resident or residents of the high density unemployment area. The percentage requirements with respect to the employment of residents of a high-density unemployment area are applicable only to those employees hired within 12 months immediately preceding the date the business seeks certification from the Department of Commerce and not to the entire workforce of the business. For purposes of Rev & TC § 23623 only, a business will be qualified if the Department of Commerce certifies that it meets the requirements of Govt Cd § 7082.

Qualified employee. "Qualified employee" means an employee who has been an unemployed resident of a high density unemployment area before being employed by a qualified business. The participation by a prospective employee in a state or federally funded job training or work demonstration program shall not constitute employment, or effect the eligibility of an otherwise qualified employee. Qualified employee includes an otherwise qualified employee who is employed by a qualified business in the 90 days before its certification by Department of Commerce as a qualified business for purpose of becoming eligible for that certification.

The credit must be reduced by the amount allowed for the jobs tax credit under Rev & TC § 23621. It must also be reduced by the IRC § 51 credit relating to payments for services during labor disputes. No deduction is allowed under Rev & TC § 24343 for the portion of wages or salaries paid or incurred for the income year on which the credit allowable is based.

---

(20) § 23623.

Recapture of credit. Termination of employment within a specified period will result in an increase in the employer's tax by the amount for the income year in question and all prior years attributable to qualified wages. The employment relationship between the taxpayer and an employee will not be treated as terminated by reason of a mere change in the form of conducting the trade or business, if the employee continues to be employed in that trade or business, and the taxpayer retained a substantial interest in that trade or business. Any increase in the employer's tax shall not be treated as a tax imposed by the Bank and Corporation Tax Law for the purpose of determining the amount of any credit allowable.

Limit on credit. The amount of credit cannot exceed the amount of tax that would be imposed on income attributed to the business activities of the taxpayer in the program area, as if that attributed income represented all of the income of taxpayer subject to tax determined in accordance with the provisions for allocation and apportionment under Art. 2, Ch. 17, starting with Rev & TC § 25120. A two-factor formula of payroll and property will apply to determine income within the program area.

¶ 1236B   **Enterprise Zone Hiring Credit**

For income year starting on or after the designation of an area as an enterprise zone, a credit against tax will be allowed an employer for 50% of qualified wages for the first year of employment; 40% of qualified wages for the second year of employment; 30% of qualified wages for the third year of employment; 20% of qualified wages for the fourth year of employment; and 10% of qualified wages for the fifth year of employment.[21]

Qualified wages. "Qualified wages" means wages paid or incurred by an employer during the income year to qualified disadvantaged individuals. The term "qualified wages" means that portion of hourly wages that does not exceed 150% of minimum wage. "Qualified years one through five wages" means, with respect to any individual, qualified wages received during 60-month period starting on day the individual commences employment in enterprise zone. "Minimum wage" means the wage established by the Industrial Welfare Commission as provided for in Chapter 1, commencing with Section 1711, of Part 4 of Div. 2 of the Labor Code. Qualified wage does not include amounts paid or incurred after the enterprise zone designation is terminated.

Qualified employee. "Qualified employee" means an individual at least 90% of whose services during the income year are directly related to the conduct of taxpayer's trade or business located in an enterprise zone, and who performs at least 50% of the services for the taxpayer in the enterprise zone. "Qualified disadvantaged individual" means an individual who is (1) a qualified employee; (2) hired by the employer after the designation of the

---

(21) § 23622, as amended by Stats. 1994, c. 755,
§ 4

area as an enterprise zone; and (3) is any of the following: (a) an individual who is eligible for services under the federal Job Training Partnership Act (29 USC 1501 et seq.); (b) is eligible for voluntary or mandatory registration under the Greater Avenues for Independence Act of 1985 (Welfare & Institutions Cd., Div. 9, Pt. 3, Ch. 2, Art. 3.2); and (c) any individual who is eligible under the federal Targeted Jobs Tax Credit program, as long as that program is in effect. The employer must obtain and have available for the FTB certification that the employee qualifies as set forth in (3) above.[21]

Recapture of credit. The termination of employment within a specified period will result in the increase in the employer's tax by the amount of the credit for the income year in question, and all prior income years attributable to qualified wages.

Reduction of credit. The jobs tax credit allowed under Rev & TC § 23621 will reduce the credit allowed for wages paid in an enterprise zone. The target jobs credit allowed under IRC § 51 will also reduce this credit. No deduction will be allowed under Rev & TC § 24343 for such wages or salaries.

Controlled group of corporations. All employees of all corporations that are members of the same controlled group of corporations will be treated as employed by a single employer. In any such case, the credit, if any, allowable to each member will be determined by reference to its proportionate share of the qualified wages giving rise to the credit. The term "controlled group of corporations" has the meaning given by IRC § 1563(a)(1), except that "more than 50 percent" must be substituted for "at least 80 percent" each place it appears in IRC § 1563(a)(1), and the determination of the share of qualified wages will be made without regard to IRC § 1563(a)(4) and (e)(3)(C). If an employer acquires a major portion of a trade or business of another employer ("predecessor") or the major portion of a separate unit of a trade or business of a predecessor, then, in applying Rev & TC § 23622, other than employment termination rules, for any calendar year ending after that acquisition, the employment relationship between an employee and an employer shall not be treated as terminated if the employee continues to be employed in that trade or business.

In case of financial organizations covered by IRC § 593 (domestic building and loan association, mutual savings bank, and cooperative banks), and regulated investment companies and real estate investment trusts, the rules on treatment of controlled group of corporations and the definition of an enterprise zone will apply.

Carryover—limits. Unused credits may be carried over. The credit can't exceed the tax on income attributable to the enterprise zone, determined under UDITPA rules. A two factor formula of payroll and property applies.[21]

¶ 1236C   **Los Angeles Revitalization Zone—Hiring and Sales Tax Credits**

A "Los Angeles Revitalization Zone" has been established in Los Angeles County and within cities that suffered from civil disturbances in April and May, 1992. Local jurisdictions are responsible for identifying and mapping the business areas damaged during the civil disturbances. These designated zones must be approved by the Department of Commerce by January 1, 1993.[22]

Hiring credits—construction workers. For each tax year beginning on or after 1–1–93, and before 1–1–98 a hiring credit will be allowed to employers who hire construction workers who are residents of a "supportive residential area" equal to the sum of:

(1) For the period between May 1, 1992, and June 30, 1993, 100% of the wages not exceeding $6.38 per hour earned during that period by employees who were hired during that period, and

(2) For the next six month period, 75% of the wages not exceeding $6.38 per hour earned during that period by employees hired during that period, and

(3) For the next four years, 50% of the wages not exceeding $6.38 per hour earned during that period by employees hired during that period.

The credit is recaptured in the event of early termination in the same manner as credit is recaptured for the Economic Development Area credits (see ¶ 1236) except that termination as a result of a contractual agreement will not result in recapture.

No deduction is allowed for wages for which a credit is claimed. The amount of credit in any taxable year can not exceed the amount of tax that would be imposed on income attributed to the business conducted in the "Los Angeles Revitalization Zone". Special rules are included for the determination of income earned in the Revitalization Zone. Carryovers are allowed for the excess credit.

A "business zone" is a defined area within which businesses can take advantage of the tax benefits granted for the Los Angeles Revitalization Zone. A "supportive residential area" is an area where employees must reside in order for employers to receive job-related tax incentives.

The hiring credit must be reduced by other credits available including the Jobs Tax Credit (Rev & TC § 23621), the Enterprise Zone Employer's Credit (Rev & TC § 23622), and the Economic Development Area Employer's Credit (Rev & TC § 23623), and the Enterprise and Program Area Credit (Rev & TC § 23623.5).

Hiring credits—employees other than construction workers. For each tax year beginning on or after 1–1–92, and before 1–1–98, a hiring credit will be allowed to employers who hire qualified disadvantaged individuals on or after 5–1–92. The credit against the "net tax" (as defined by Rev & TC 23036) is equal to the sum of the following: (1) 50% of qualified wages in the first

---

(22) §§ 23612.6; 23623.5; 23625.

year of employment; (2) 40% of qualified wages in the second year of employment; (3) 30% of qualified wages in the third year of employment; (4) 20% of qualified wages in the fourth year of employment; and (5) 10% of qualified wages in the fifth year of employment. The period for measuring the credit commences with the first day the individual commences employment within the Los Angeles Revitalization Zone.

Qualified wages means the wages, not in excess of 150% of the hourly minimum wage, paid or incurred by the employer during the taxable year to qualified disadvantaged individuals.

A qualified disadvantaged individual is one who is a resident in the Los Angeles Revitalization Zone who performs services for the taxable year which are at least 90% directly related to the conduct of the taxpayer's trade or business located in the Zone, and who performs at least 50% of the services in the Zone. Special rules apply to multiple businesses under common control which have not been incorporated.

The credit is recaptured if an employee's employment is terminated by the taxpayer at any time during the first 270 days of that employment, or before the close of the 270th calendar day after the day in which the employee completes 90 days of employment with the taxpayer. Recapture does not apply if the termination of employment is voluntarily, the employee becomes disabled, the termination is due to misconduct, there is a substantial reduction in the trade or business of the employer, the employee is replaced by other qualified employees so as to create a net increase in both the number of employees and the hours of employment, there is a mere change in the form of conduction the trade or business and the employee continues to be employed, or if an employer acquired the major portion of a trade of business of another employer, or the major portion of a separate unit of a trade or business of a predecessor, and the employee continues to be employed in that trade or business.

The hiring credit shall be reduced by the credit allowed under Rev & TC §§ 23621 (jobs tax credit), 23622 (enterprise zone employers' credit), 23623 (employer's credit for wages paid to qualified employees), 23625 (credit for wages paid to a construction employee in the Los Angeles Revitalization Zone discussed above), and for the credit allowed under IRC § 51 (targeted jobs credit). The deduction for wages paid such qualified employees will be reduced by the amount of the credit.

The credit may be carried over to subsequent years for a maximum of 15 years.

The credit can only offset the amount of tax that would be imposed on income attributed to business activities within the Zone as if it represented all of the taxpayer's income. Attribution of income will be made under

UDITPA apportionment rules using a two factor formula based only on property and payroll.[23]

Sales tax credit. A sales tax credit may be claimed by a person or entity engaged in a trade or business within the Los Angeles Revitalization Zone for (1) constructions materials to repair or replace the taxpayer's building and fixtures, and (2) machinery and equipment used exclusively in the zone. The credit is equal to the sales or use tax paid or incurred for the purchase of qualified property. No depreciation shall be allowed on the amount claimed as a credit. Recapture of the credit is required if the property is no longer used by the taxpayer in the Los Angeles Revitalization Zone at the end of the second taxable year after the property is placed in service.

The amount of sales tax credit which can be claimed in any one year is limited to the tax on the income earned in the Los Angeles Revitalization Zone. Special rules are provided for determining the amount of tax which can be reduced by the credit. Carryovers are available for the excess credit. In the event that the designated zones are later amended, the incentive programs identified below (eg., hiring credits for construction workers and others, and the sales tax credit) become inoperative for the next following tax year. Prior credits are not lost retroactively, and any unused credits for periods prior to the amendment of the designated zone may continue to be carried forward.[24]

¶ 1236D   Local Agency Military Base Recovery Area—Incentives

The California Trade and Commerce Agency is authorized to specify certain geographical areas as Local Agency Military Base Recovery Areas (LAMBRA). For taxable years beginning on or after January 1, 1995, and before January 1, 2003, a taxpayer engaged in a trade or business within a LAMBRA is entitled to certain incentives including a sales tax credit, a hiring credit, an accelerated deduction for the cost of specified property acquired by purchase for exclusive use in the LAMBRA, and special treatment of net operating loss carryovers.

To be eligible for the incentives the taxpayer must be doing business in the LAMBRA, and generate at least one additional new full time job in the state, and in the LAMBRA, within the first two taxable years of doing business in the LAMBRA. Specific methods for calculating if a new job has been created are provided.

If there are similar incentives available to the taxpayer under more than one part of the Revenue and Taxation Code, then the taxpayer may elect the section under which the incentive will be claimed.

The amount of credits which may be used in any one year, including carryovers, is limited to the amount of tax that would be imposed on the

---

(23) § 23623.5.
(24) § 23612.6(f), 23625(g), & 23623.5(g), as amended by Stats. 1994, c. 756, § 9, 10, & 11.

income attributable to business activities within the LAMBRA. The income of a taxpayer operating within and outside a LAMBRA is apportioned based on the property and payroll factors, divided by 2. Credits may be carried forward if not fully utilized in the year the credit is earned by the taxpayer.[25]

Sales tax credits. A credit against the taxpayer's income tax equal to the amount of sales or use tax paid in connection with the purchase of qualified property is allowed. Qualified property may not exceed $20 million cumulative cost of qualifying property. Qualified property must be used exclusively in a LAMBRA, and is defined as: (1) high technology equipment; (2) aircraft maintenance equipment; (3) aircraft components; and (4) any property that is IRC § 1245 property as defined in IRC § 1245(a)(3). To be eligible for the credit, the property must be manufactured in California unless qualified property of a comparable quality and price is not available for timely purchase and delivery from a California manufacturer.

The sales tax credit is recaptured if the property is disposed of, or moved outside the LAMBRA, before the close of second tax year following the date the property is placed in service. The credit previously claimed will be recaptured on the return for the second taxable year after the property was placed in service.[25]

Hiring credits. A credit will be allowed for hiring a disadvantaged individual, or a qualified displaced employee, during a taxable year equal to the sum of the following:

(1) 50% of qualified wages in the first year of employment;
(2) 40% of qualified wages in the second year of employment;
(3) 30% of qualified wages in the third year of employment;
(4) 20% of qualified wages in the fourth year of employment;
(5) 10% of qualified wages in the fifth year of employment.

Qualified wages means the amount paid to qualified disadvantaged individuals, or qualified displaced individuals. These are individuals who work at least 90% of the time in activities directly related to the taxpayer's business in a LAMBRA, and who spend at least 50% of their time actually in the LAMBRA. The wages for which a credit is claimed can not exceed that portion of a wage paid to an individual which exceeds 150% of the minimum wage, and cannot exceed $2 million during years one through five. The credit is also limited to those wages paid to employees hired after the designation of the area as a LAMBRA.

A qualified disadvantaged employee is one: (1) who has been determined eligible for service under the federal Job Training Partnership Act; (2) any voluntary or mandatory registrant under the California's Greater Avenues for Independence Act of 1985; or (3) any individual who has been certified eligible by the Employment Development Department under the federal Targeted Jobs Tax Credit Program. A qualified displaced employee

---

(25) § 23645; 23646, 24356.8, & 24416.2.

means an individual who was a civilian or military employee of a base or former base that has been displaced as a result of a federal base closure act.

Provisions are made for recapture of the credit if an employee is terminated within 270 days of employment; whether or not consecutive, or within 270 calendar days after the day in which that employee completes 90 days of employment. Special rules are provided for termination because of disability, mergers and divestitures, misconduct, or substantial reduction in operations of the taxpayer. The tax upon recapture will be added to the tax otherwise due by the taxpayer for the year in which the termination occurred.

All employees of trades or business that are under common control shall be treated as employed by a single employer, and each business shall be entitled to the credit based on their proportionate share of qualifying wages.

The amount of credit will be reduced by credits claimed under Rev & TC § 23621 (California Jobs Tax Credit), and by the credit allowed under IRC § 51 (federal Targeted Jobs Tax Credit).[25]

Deduction for qualifying property acquisitions. Taxpayers may elect to deduct the cost of qualifying property purchased for exclusive use in a trade or business conducted within a LAMBRA in the year of acquisition. The election will be made on the taxpayer's return and may not be revoked except with the consent of the Franchise Tax Board. No form is specified for the election, and as with property claimed as a deduction under IRC § 179, the election is made by the decision, as reflected in the computation of tax, to deduct the qualifying property. Qualifying property means property as defined in IRC § 1245(a)(3) used exclusively in a trade or business conducted within a LAMBRA. A purchase does not include: (1) property acquired from a person whose relationship to the person acquiring the property would result in the disallowance of losses under IRC §§ 267 or 707(b), but with modification of the federal attribution rules under IRC § 267(c)(4); (2) where the basis of the property in the hands of the acquiring person is determined by reference to the adjusted basis of the property in the hands of the person from whom it was acquired; or (3) where the basis is determined under IRC § 1014 relating to property acquired from a decedent.

Eligible property excludes that property for which no election can be made under IRC § 179 because of the rules set forth in IRC § 179(d).

The deduction shall not exceed the following amounts for the taxable year of the designation of a LAMBRA and each taxable year thereafter:

Taxable year of designation, and the first year thereafter	$5,000 per year
Second and Third taxable year following designation of a LAMBRA	7,500 per year
Each taxable year thereafter	10,000 per year

Recapture of the deduction is provided if the property ceases to be used in the trade or business within a LAMBRA at any time before the close of the second taxable year after it has been placed in service.

Any taxpayer who elects to deduct property under this provision will not be entitled to claim a deduction for the same property under IRC § 179.[25]

Special treatment of net operating losses.   Rather than the normal 5 year period for carryover of net operating losses, the net operating loss incurred in a LAMBRA may be carried over for 15 years. The net operating loss carryover shall be a deduction only with respect to income attributed to the business activities of the taxpayer in the LAMBRA by applying the two factor formula based on payroll and property as described above.[25]

¶ 1237   Research Expenditures Credit

A credit against tax is allowed for amounts paid or incurred for research in accordance with IRC § 41, as modified by California.[26]

The research credit is claimed on FTB form 3523. The research credit for start-up companies is claimed on FTB form 3505.

California modifications.   The applicable percentage is 8% (20% federal) of excess of qualified research expenses for an income year over the base period research expenses, and 12% (20% federal) of the basic research payments. The terms "qualified research" and "basic research" include only research conducted in California. In computing gross receipts for IRC § 41(c)(5), only gross receipts from the sale of property held for sale in the ordinary course of business, which is delivered or shipped to a purchaser within California will be included.[27]

Basic research.   California modified the federal definition in IRC § 41(e)(7)(A) by providing that basic research includes any basic or applied research including scientific inquiry or original investigation for advancement of scientific or engineering knowledge or the improved effectiveness of commercial products, except the term does not include any of following: (1) basic research conducted outside California; (2) basic research in social sciences, arts or humanities; (3) basic research for purpose of improving a commercial product if the improvements relate to style, taste, cosmetic, or seasonal design factors; (4) any expenditure paid or incurred to ascertain existence, location, extent or quality of any deposit of ore or other mineral, including oil or gas. Under federal law, basic research means any original investigation for the advancement of scientific knowledge not having a specific commercial objective, except that it does not include basic research conducted outside the United States, and basic research in the social sciences, arts or humanities.

Carryovers.   In the case where the credit exceeds the net tax for the income year, that portion of the credit which exceeds the net tax may be

---

(26) § 23609.   (27) § 23609.

carried over to the net tax in succeeding income years. IRC § 41(h) does not apply for California purposes. Thus the Research Expenditures Credit if permanent for California purposes, unless the Legislature takes specific action to terminate the credit.[28]

¶ 1238   **Clinical Testing Expenses Credit**

For income years starting on or after 1–1–87 a credit against net tax is allowed for 15% of qualified clinical testing expenses paid or incurred by a taxpayer for clinical testing conducted in California. This credit is repealed effective 12–1–93. Carryovers of excess credit to succeeding income years are permitted.

California adopts IRC § 28, except for the modifications for applicable percentage, carryovers, conduct of testing and termination. The applicable percentage for federal purposes is 50% of qualified clinical testing expenses. The federal credit is limited to testing within the U.S., unless the testing is conducted outside the U.S. because there is insufficient testing population in the U.S., and the testing is conducted by a U.S. person or any other person not related to the taxpayer to whom designation under Federal Food, Drug and Cosmetic Act § 526 applies.

California adopts the IRC § 28(b) definitions of qualified clinical testing expenses and clinical testing; IRC § 28(c) rules on coordination with credit for increasing research expenditures; IRC § 28(d) on rare disease or condition, and election by taxpayer.[29]

The credit was claimed on FTB form 3528.

¶ 1239   **Low-income Housing Credit**

A California low-income housing credit is allowed in an amount determined by IRC § 42 as it was in effect on January 1, 1992, subject to certain California modifications outlined below. Originally the federal and California credits were to expire on June 30, 1992. The federal *Revenue Reconciliation Act of 1993* however reinstated the federal credit retroactively to July 1, 1992. As Rev & TC § 23610.5(r)(2) provided that the California credit would remain in effect during the same periods that the federal credit was operative, California automatically reinstated the low-income housing credit retroactively to July 1, 1992. The low-income housing credit is one of those credits that may reduce tax below the tentative minimum tax.[30]

The California credit is claimed on Form 3521, which must be attached to the return together with a Certificate of Final Award of California Low-Income Housing Tax Credits (Form 3521A) issued by the Mortgage Bond and Tax Credit Allocation Committee.

Note: Due to the retroactive reinstatement of the California low-income housing credit, refund claims may be appropriate for the 1992 tax year.

---

(28) § 23609(f), as amended by Stats. 1994, c. 1243, § 63.5.

(29) § 23609.5.
(30) § 23610.5.

California Tax Credit Allocation Committee authorizations. California requires that credit allocated to a housing sponsor be authorized by this committee based on the project's need for the credit for economic feasibility. It is the intent of the Legislature that the amount of the state low-income housing tax credit allocated to a project shall not exceed an amount in addition to the federal credit that is necessary for the financial feasibility of the project and its viability throughout the extended use period.

The low-income housing project must be located in California, and must satisfy either of the following requirements: (1) the housing sponsor of the project must have been allocated a credit for federal income tax purposes by the Committee under IRC § 42; or (2) the project must qualify for credit under IRC § 42(h)(4)(B), providing for a special rule where 70% or more of the building is financed with exempt bonds subject to a volume cap. The Committee can't require fees for the credit under California law in addition to the fees required for a credit application under IRC § 42. The Committee must certify to the housing sponsor the amount of the State tax credit to which a taxpayer is entitled for each credit period. In the case of a partnership or S corporation, the housing sponsor must provide a copy of the California Tax Credit Allocation Committee certification to the taxpayer who must attach it to the return.

Special rule applies to any government assisted building, and any building purchased by a qualified nonprofit organization that agrees to satisfy the requirements of IRC § 42(g) for the useful life of the building. All elections made by the taxpayer pursuant to IRC § 42 apply to California. No credit shall be allocated to buildings located in a difficult development area or a qualified census tract, as defined in IRC § 42, for which the eligible basis of a new building or the rehabilitation expenditure of an existing building is 130 percent of that amount pursuant to IRC § 42(d)(5)(C), unless the committee reduces the amount of federal credit, with approval of the applicant, so that the combined federal and state amount does not exceed total credits allowed by § 17058 and IRC § 42(b), computed without regard to IRC § 42(d)(5)(C).

Transfer of credit. For years beginning on or after January 1, 1993, banks or corporations eligible for the low-income housing credit may elect to transfer that credit to an affiliated bank or corporation. An affiliated bank or corporation is defined as in § 25110 substituting "100%" for "50%" as used in § 25110. This election is irrevocable for the income year once it has been made. It may be changed for any subsequent year if the assignment is expressly shown on the returns of the affiliated banks or corporations.[31]

Applicable percentage. California modifies IRC § 42(b) to provide (1) in case of qualified income housing placed in service by the housing sponsor during 1987, applicable percentage means 9% for the first three years, and 3% for the fourth year for new buildings, whether or not the building is

---

(31) § 23610(r).

federally subsidized, and for existing buildings (federal is 9% for new buildings not federally subsidized, or 4% for new building federally subsidized, and existing buildings); (2) in case of any qualified low-income building placed in service by the housing sponsor after 1989 that is a new building not federally subsidized, applicable percentage means either (a) for each of the first three years, the highest percentage set under IRC § 42(b)(2) for the month placed in service, instead of the 9% and 4% federal percentages set in IRC § 42(b)(1)(A), or (b) for the fourth year the difference between 30% and the sum of the applicable percentages for the first three years. In the case of a qualified low-income building that receives an allocation after 1989, and that is a new building that is federally subsidized, or an existing building that is at risk of conversion, applicable percentage means: (1) for the first three years, the percentage set by the Secretary of the Treasury for new buildings federally subsidized for the taxable years; (2) for the fourth year, the difference between 13% and the sum of the applicable percentages for the first three years. "At risk of conversion" is defined by Rev & TC § 23610.5(c)(4).

Qualified low-income housing project. California modifies IRC § 42(c)(2) by adding the following requirements: (1) the taxpayer must be entitled to receive a cash distribution from the operations of the project, after funding required reserves, which, at the election of the taxpayer, is equal to (a) an amount not to exceed 8% of the lesser of the owner equity which shall include the amount of capital contributions actually paid to the housing sponsor, and shall not include any amounts until they are paid on an investor note, or 20% of the adjusted basis of the building as of the close of the first taxable year of the credit period; or (b) the amount of the cash flow from those units in the building that are not low-income units (for purposes of computing cash flow, operating costs are allocated using "floor space fraction)." Any amount allowed to be distributed under (a) that is not available for distribution during the first five years of the compliance period may be accumulated and distributed at any time during the first 15 years of the compliance period, but not thereafter. The limitation on return shall apply in the aggregate to the partners if the housing sponsor is a partnership and in the aggregate to the shareholders if the housing sponsor is an S corporation. (2) The housing sponsor must apply any cash available for distribution in excess of the above amount to reduce rent on rent-restricted units, or increase number of rent-restricted units subject to IRC § 42(g)(1) tests.

Credit period. California uses a 4-year period instead of the federal 10-year period. California does not apply the special federal rule under IRC § 42(f)(2) for the first taxable year of the period. California modified IRC § 42(f)(3) rule on the increase in qualified basis after the first year of the credit period. If, as of close of any taxable year after the first year of the credit period, the qualified basis of any building exceeds the qualified basis of that building as of the close of the first year of the credit period, the housing sponsor to the extent of its tax credit allocation shall be eligible for a credit on the excess in an amount equal to applicable percentage determined pursuant to Rev & TC § 23610.5(c) for the four-year period beginning with the later of the income years in which the increase in qualified basis occurs.

Rent restriction and income. California adopts definition in IRC § 42(g)(1) providing that taxpayer can elect either the 20–50 or 40–60 test for rent restriction and income. California also adopts the definition of rent-restricted units in IRC § 42(g)(2); the rules on the date for meeting requirements on restriction and income in IRC § 42(g)(3); the rules on the determination of low-income qualification in IRC § 42(g)(4); and election after compliance period in IRC § 42(g)(5).

Limitation on aggregate credit allowable on projects located in-state. California adopts IRC 42(h) with the following modifications: (1) instead of applying IRC § 42(h)(2) (allocated credit application), the total amount for the four-year credit period of the housing credit dollars allocated in a calendar year to any building shall reduce the aggregate housing credit dollar amount of the California Tax Credit Allocation Committee for the calendar year in which the allocation is made; (2) IRC § 42(h)(3)–(5) (6)(E)(i)(II), (6)(F), (6)(G), (6)(I), (7) and (8), relating to credit dollar amount, special rules and definitions do not apply in California. The aggregate housing credit dollar amount that may be allocated annually by the California Tax Credit Allocation Committee is an amount equal to the sum of the following: (1) $35 million; (2) the unused housing credit ceiling, if any for the preceding calendar years; (3) the amount of the housing credit ceiling returned in the calendar year. The amount in (3) equals the housing credit dollar amount preciously allocated that does not become a qualified low-income project within the period required by Rev & TC § 23610.5, or to any project with respect to which an allocation is canceled by mutual consent of the Committee and the allocation recipient.

The definitions and special rules of IRC § 42(i) are adopted, but the state uses a 30-yr. compliance period instead of the federal 18-year period.

Recapture of credit. California does not follow IRC § 42(j). It provides that a regulatory agreement be entered into between the Committee and the taxpayer as to the enforcement of the state provisions on low income housing credit. The agreement may be subordinated, when necessary, to any lien or encumbrance of banks or financial institutions. The regulatory agreement entered into pursuant to Health & Safety Cd § 50199.14(f) shall apply, subject to specified conditions.

Carryovers. Carryovers of excess credits are provided.

Election to accelerate credit not applicable in California. California has not adopted the provisions of PL 101–508, § 11407(c), relating to the election to accelerate the credit.

Duration of credit.   California credit will remain in effect for as long as the IRC § 42 low-income housing credit remains in effect.[32]

¶ 1240   **Low-emission Vehicle Credit**

For income years starting on or after 1–1–91 and before 1–1–96, a credit is allowed against the net tax equal to 55% of the costs, including installation, but excluding interest charges, of a device designed to and installed to convert a motor vehicle, that is intended to be used on the public roads and highways of the state, to a low-emission motor vehicle. The credit also applies to 15% of the purchase price of a nonrecreational motor vehicle that is low-emission and is intended to be used on private roads, private school campuses, or commercial or industrial worksites in California.[33] The credit can be claimed in the income year that the device is installed. The credit cannot exceed $1,000 per automobile, motorcycle, or two person passenger vehicle, or $3,500 for a vehicle whose weight is in excess of 5,750 lbs. A credit will also be allowed for the cost differential of a new motor vehicle which is equipped from the factory to operate as a low-emission vehicle and is certified by the state Air Resources Board to be a low-emission motor vehicle. Differential cost is determined by the California Energy Commission.

To qualify for the credit, all vehicles must be registered in the state. The taxpayer or a partnership must make the application to the California Energy Commission which must certify that: (1) the device or vehicle qualifies for the credit under Rev & TC § 17052.11; and (2) a credit allocation is available. The application for credit allocation and certification must contain all information required by the Energy Commission. Taxpayers must notify the Commission that a device or vehicle has actually been purchased. A copy of the Commission certificate must be retained. The Franchise Tax Board can require taxpayers to make the certification available. A partnership must disclose on its return the partner's social security number or identification number, and the name of each partner receiving the credit allocation, and the amount of the allocation. Guidelines and criteria are to be established by the California Energy Commission.

The credit can be carried over to subsequent years if it exceeds the net tax in the year the credit is earned.

The differential costs for which credit may be claimed must be reduced by those costs for which a federal credit is allowed under IRC § 30 for qualified electric vehicles.[34]

The low-emission vehicles credit is claimed on FTB form 3554.

¶ 1244   **Sales or Use Tax Paid on Purchase of Qualified Property**

A qualified business in an economic development area and a bank or corporation engaged in a business in a designated enterprise zone can take a credit

---

(32) § 23610.5, as amended by Stats. 1994, c. 1164, § 40.

(33) § 23603.

(34) § 23603.

for sales tax paid in connection with the purchase of qualified property. "Qualified property" means machinery and machinery parts used for: (1) fabricating, processing, assembling and manufacturing; and (2) machinery and machinery parts used for the production of renewable energy resources, or air and water pollution control mechanisms up to value of $20 million. Excess credit may be carried over to succeeding income years until used. It must be applied first to the earliest years possible.

A taxpayer who elects to take the credit can't increase the basis of the property as otherwise required by IRC § 164(a) for sales tax paid or incurred in connection with the purchase of qualified property.

The amount of the credit can't exceed in any year the amount of tax that would be imposed on the income attributed to the business activities of the taxpayer within the program area, or enterprise zone. Attributed income will be determined under UDITPA rules. A two-factor formula of payroll and property applies for determining income earned in the program area or enterprise zone.

If taxpayer has purchased property on which use tax has been paid or incurred, the credit will be allowed only if qualified property of comparable quality or price is not timely available for purchase in-state.[35]

The credit for sales or use tax paid on equipment purchases used in an enterprise zone is claimed on FTB form 3805Z. The Franchise Tax Board also publishes a separate booklet detailing the deductions and credits that businesses may qualify for if they are operating in an enterprise zone or program area.

¶ 1245   **Employer's Child Care Credit**

Start-up expenses—child care program—construction of facility.   For taxable years starting on or after 1–1–88 and before 1–1–98 a credit is allowed for 30% of either or both of (1) the start-up expenses of establishing a child care program, or constructing a child care facility in California for the benefit of the employees of the taxpayer; and (2) the cost paid by a taxpayer for contributions to the California child care information and referral services for the employees of the taxpayer. This credit is extended for years beginning on or after 1–1–93 for expenses incurred by the taxpayer for the start-up expenses of establishing a child care program or constructing a child care facility in California, to be used primarily by the children of employees of tenants leasing commercial or office space in a building owned by the taxpayer. The amount of credits allowed cannot exceed $50,000 for any taxable year.[36]

If a child care facility is established by two or more taxpayers, the credit will be allowed if it is to be used primarily by the children of each of the taxpayers.

---

(35) § 23612.
(36) § 23617, as amended by Stats. 1994, c. 748,
§ 4.

"Start-up expenses" include, but are not limited to, feasibility studies, site preparation, and construction, renovation, or acquisition of facilities to establish on-site or near-site centers by one or more employers.

The credit to employers incurring start-up expenses of establishing a child care program, or constructing a child care facility, is claimed on FTB Form 3501.

If two or more taxpayers share in the costs eligible for the credit, each taxpayer will receive a tax credit with respect to its respective share of the costs.

Credits that are unused can be carried over beyond the 12–1–95 repeal date until exhausted.

If credit carryovers from preceding years plus the credit allowed for the current year exceed an aggregate of $50,000, the credit allowed to reduce the net tax is limited to $50,000. The amount in excess may be carried over and applied against net tax in later years. The carryover amount when added to the credit allowed for the current year cannot exceed $50,000.

No deduction will be allowed for that portion of the expenses paid in an income year that is equal to the amount of the credit allowed attributable to these start-up expenses.

Depreciation can be taken instead of the credit under Rev & TC § 24371.5.

The basis of the facility must be reduced by the amount of credit taken.

¶ 1246   **Dependent Care Plan for Employees**

For income years starting before 1–1–95, a credit against tax is allowed for 50% of the cost paid or incurred for contributions to a qualified care plan made on behalf of any dependent of the taxpayer's California employee under the age of 15. The amount of the credit cannot exceed $600 per qualified dependent.[37]

The credit to employers incurring expenses for a dependent care plan for employees is claimed on FTB Form 3501.

"Qualified care plan" includes, but is not limited to, onsite service, center-based service dependent care center, and in-home or home-provider care, provided the facility is located in California, and operated under the authority of a license when the state law requires it.

"Dependent care center" includes a specialized center with respect to short-term illnesses of employee's dependents.

In the case where child care received is of less than 42-week duration, the employer may claim a prorated portion of the allowable credit. The ratio used is the number of weeks of care received divided by 42 weeks.

---

(37) § 23617.5 as amended by Stats. 1994, c. 748,
§ 5.

If an employer makes contributions to a qualified care plan and also collects fees from parents to support a child care facility owned and operated by the employer, no credit is allowed to extent the sum of contributions and fees exceeds the total cost of providing care.

The credit is not available to the employer if the care provided on behalf of an employee is provided by an individual who qualified as a dependent of that employee or spouse under Rev & TC § 17054(d)(1) (exemption allowable for employee), or is within Rev & TC § 17056, a son, stepson, daughter, or stepdaughter of that employee under the age of 19 at the close of taxable year.

Contributions to the plan can't discriminate in favor of officers, owners, or highly compensated employees or their dependents.

The Child Care Credit is reduced for years commencing on or after January 1, 1995, and before January 1, 1998 to 30% of eligible costs, and the credit can not exceed $360 per qualified dependent. In addition, the qualified dependent must be under 12 years of age.

Excess credits may be carried over until exhausted.[38]

¶ 1248   Ridesharing

Purchase of company shuttle and commuter buses or vans, or motor-pool vehicles.   For taxable years before 1–1–96, an employer with 200 or more employees will be allowed a credit for 20% of the cost paid or incurred for the purchase of company shuttle buses, commuter buses or vans, motor pool vehicles provided as part of an employer-sponsored ridesharing incentive program for employees conducted principally in California. An employer with less than 200 employees will be allowed a credit of 30% of the cost.

The credit must be claimed in the state income tax return for the taxable year that the vehicles are purchased and placed in service. The credit is claimed on FTB Form 3518.

The basis of any ridesharing vehicle purchased must be reduced by the amount of the credit. The adjustment is made in the year for which the credit is allowed.

In the event of disposal of the vehicle, or nonuse within three years of acquisition, the portion of the credit that represents the pro-rata share of that remaining three-year period is added to the employer's tax liability in year of disposition or nonuse. The basis of the vehicle must be increased by the amount added to the employer's tax liability.[39]

Cost of leasing or contracting for vehicles.   An employer with 200 or more employees, will be allowed a credit of 20% of the cost paid or incurred. The credit is based on the total payments to the lessor or vehicle provider

---

(**38**) § 23617.5, as amended by Stats. 1994, c. 748, § 6.

(**39**) § 23605.

during the life of the lease or contract. The lessor or vehicle provider is not eligible for the credit. An employer with less than 200 employees will be allowed credit of 30% of the cost.

The credit will be claimed in the state income tax return for the taxable year in which the vehicles are first placed in service under the lease or contract. If first leased or contracted prior to the 1989 taxable year, the credit may be claimed on the 1989 return based on total payments to the lessor or vehicle provider in that year, and the total payments to be made during the remaining life of the contract.

In case of disposal or nonuse, the portion of the credit representing the pro rata share of the remaining life of the lease or contract will be added to the employer's tax liability in the year of disposition or nonuse.[39]

Subsidized transit passes. A credit will be allowed for the cost paid or incurred by employers for providing subsidized public transit passes to employees: (1) 40% of cost if employers provide no free or subsidized parking; (2) 20% of cost if the employers provide subsidized parking; (3) 10% of cost if employers provide free parking.[39]

Carryovers. Excess credits may be carried over until exhausted, even beyond the 12–1–96 repeal date of the credit.

Credit in lieu of deduction. The credit is in lieu of any other deduction to which the employer might be entitled under the Personal Income Tax Law.

When vehicle credits do not apply. The credit will not be allowed for the cost of the purchase, lease or contract of vehicles that would otherwise be required as part of the employer's business activities in the absence of the ridesharing program.

¶ 1250   **Recycling equipment**

For income years starting on or after January 1, 1989, and before January 1, 1994, a credit against net tax will be allowed in an amount equal to 40% of the cost of qualified property purchased and placed in service on or after January 1, 1989, and before January 1, 1994.[40] The credit for qualified purchases of recycling equipment is claimed on FTB form 3527.

Qualified property. Machinery or equipment located in California which has not been certified and is used by the taxpayer exclusively to manufacture finished products composed of at least 50% secondary waste material with at least 10% composed of postconsumer waste generated from within California. Qualified property may include manufacturing equipment that utilizes 100% secondary waste including at least 80% postconsumer waste where all of that material is contained within a finished product regardless of the finished product's percent postconsumer content. It

---

(40) § 23612.5.

can include deinking equipment used to produce fine quality paper and equipment used to reclaim plastic used as raw material or in the fabrication or manufacture of finished products, equipment utilized in the production of compost, equipment that processes used plastic milk bottles into flakes, equipment that processes resin pellets from the flakes, and equipment that manufactures toys from the pellets.

How claimed. Taxpayers can claim the credit as follows: 20% of the cost in the year the recycling equipment is placed in service as limited (see below); 15% of the cost, as limited, in the income year immediately succeeding the income year placed in service; 5% of the cost, as limited, in the following income year. The amount of credit cannot exceed $625,000 for each facility over the 5-year tax credit period.

Basis reduced by credit. The basis of any qualified property, for which the credit is allowed must be reduced by the amount of the credit; the adjustment is made in the year the credit is allowed.

Conditions of credit. The credit shall only be allowed if: (1) the total adjusted basis of all qualified property owned on the last day of the income year exceeds the largest total adjusted basis of all qualified property owned at any one time during the base year; (2) the total capacity of qualified property to use recycled materials on the last day of the income year exceeds the largest total capacity of qualified property at any one time during the base year. In case of replacement, eligible costs shall be proportional to the increase in capacity.

California Integrated Waste Management Board. The board must certify the purchase and use by the taxpayer, and provide an annual listing to the Franchise Tax Board of qualified taxpayers who were issued a certification. It must also provide taxpayer with a copy of the certification for taxpayer's records.

Taxpayer's duties. Taxpayer must provide the California Integrated Waste Management Board with documents to verify the purchase of qualified property, and that the machinery or equipment meets recycling requirements. Taxpayer must also retain the Board certificate in its records.

Carryover of credit. Excess credit may be carried over to succeeding years until exhausted. Carryover also applies beyond the law's 12–1–94 repeal date.

Disposal of qualified property. Any amount otherwise allowable as credit for the year of disposition or nonuse will not be allowed.

Two or more taxpayers. Each taxpayer sharing in the expenses is eligible to receive credit in proportion to its respective share of the expenses paid or incurred. In case of a partnership, the tax credit may be divided between the partners pursuant to the written partnership agreement.

¶ 1250

Report to legislature. The FTB's report to the legislature is due 3–1–94. The report must show the number of taxpayers claiming the credit, the total dollar amount allocated, and the equipment for which credit was used. It must also determine the extent that the tax expenditure increased recycling activities in the state.

¶ 1251 **Prison inmate labor**

A credit against tax is allowed equal to 10% of the amount of wages paid or incurred to each prisoner who is employed in a joint venture program established pursuant to Penal Code, Part 3, Title 1, Art 1.5 through agreement with the Director of Corrections. The Department of Corrections must forward annually to the Franchise Tax Board a list of all employers certified by the Department as active participants in the joint venture program. The list must include the participant's federal employer identification number.[1] The credit for prison inmate labor is claim on FTB Form 3507.

¶ 1252 **Investment Tax Credit For Manufacturing Equipment**

For acquisitions of qualified property on or after January 1, 1994, qualified taxpayers will be entitled to a 6% credit against the "net tax" as defined in Rev & TC § 23036, of the amount paid or incurred on or after January 1, 1994, for qualified property that is placed in service in California.

Time for taking credit for the 1994 year. For qualified cost paid or incurred on or after January 1, 1994, and prior to the first taxable year of a qualified taxpayer beginning on or after January 1, 1995, the credit shall be claimed for the first taxable year beginning on or after January 1, 1995.

Special transition rules apply for those contracts in existence on or before January 1, 1994, but for which costs are incurred after December 31, 1993. Contract costs for qualified property which qualify for the credit shall be the amount determined by the ratio of cost actually paid before January 1, 1994, and total contract cost actually paid. For this purpose, a cost paid shall include contractual deposits and option payments. For any contract that is entered into on or after January 1, 1994, that is a replacement contract to a contract that was binding prior to January 1, 1994, shall be treated as a binding contract in existence prior to January 1, 1994. An option contract in existence prior to January 1, 1994, shall be treated as a binding contract for purposes of determining the credit. Special rules apply when the option holder will forfeit an amount less than 10% of the fixed option price in the event that option is not exercised. Contracts shall be considered binding even if they are subject to conditions.

Qualifying persons. Qualifying persons entitled to the credit for acquisitions of qualifying property are those who are engaged in those lines of business described in Codes 2,000 to 3,999 inclusive of the Standard Industrial Classification Manual published by the U.S. Office of Management and

---

(1) § 23624.

Budget, 1987 edition (these are generally referred to as SIC Codes). Generally, Codes 2,000 to 3,999 include all manufacturing businesses but exclude agriculture, communication, construction, forestry, fishing, mining, real estate, retail trade, services, transportation, utilities and wholesale trade.

Manufacturing is defined in the Code and generally means converting or conditioning property by changing the form, composition, quality, or character of the property for ultimate sale at retail or use in the manufacturing of a product to be ultimately sold at retail. It includes any improvements to tangible personal property that result in a greater service life or greater functionality than that of the original property. Fabricating means to make, build, create, produce, or assemble components or property to work in a new or different manner.

Qualified property. Qualified property means for all of the following:

(1) Tangible personal property purchase for use primarily (defined as 50% or more) in any stage of the manufacturing, processing, refining, fabricating, or recycling of property, beginning at the point any raw materials are received by the qualified person and are introduced into the process and ending at the point at which the manufacturing, processing, refining, fabricating, or recycling has altered the property to its completed form.

(2) Tangible personal property purchased for use primarily (defined as 50% or more) in research and development.

(3) Tangible personal property purchased to be used primarily (defined as 50% or more) to maintain, repair, measure, or test any property which is otherwise qualified property.

(4) For pollution control that meets or exceeds standard established by any local or regional governmental agency within the state.

(5) Recycling equipment.

The value of any capitalized labor cost that is directly allocable to the construction or modification of property which is otherwise qualifying property, is included in the cost subject credit.

In the case of any qualified taxpayer engaged in manufacturing activities described in SIC Codes 357 or 367, or for those activities related to biotech processes described in SIC Code 8731, or those activities related to biopharmaceutical establishments only that are described in SIC Codes 2830 to 2836 inclusive, "qualified property" also include special purpose buildings that are constructed or modified for use by a qualified taxpayer primarily in a manufacturing, processing, refining, or fabricating process, or as research of storage facility primarily used in connection with a manufacturing process. Such costs for special purpose buildings include capitalized labor costs. Special rules are included limiting the definition of "special purpose building and foundation". If the entire building does not qualify as a "special purpose building" a taxpayer may establish that a portion of the building, and foundation, qualify. Biopharmaceutical activities are specifically defined.

Qualified properties specifically excludes furniture, facilities used for warehousing purposes after completion of the manufacturing process, inventory, equipment used in the extraction process, equipment used to store finished products that have completed the manufacturing process, tangible personal property that is used in administration, general management, or marketing, and any vehicle for which credit is claimed as a low-emission vehicle under Rev & TC §§ 17052.11, or 23603. Qualifying property includes property that is acquired by or subject to a lease by a qualified taxpayer subject to special rules set forth in Rev & TC § 23649(f).

Recapture. If the qualified property is removed from the state of California in the same taxable year as the property is first placed in service, no credit shall be allowed. If qualified property for which a credit was allowed is thereafter removed from the state of California, or disposed of to an unrelated party, or used for any purpose not qualifying for the credit within one year from the date the qualified property is first placed in service in California, the amount of the credit allowed will be recaptured by adding that credit to the net tax of the qualified taxpayer for the taxable year in which the qualified property is disposed of, removed, or put to ineligible use.

Carryover of unused credit. The credit in excess of the amount allowed in any one year can be carried over for seven years. A "small business" can carry the credit over for an additional two years for a total of nine years. A "small business" is one which either has less than $50 million in gross receipts, less than $50 million in net assets, or a total credit of less than $1 million in the year for which the credit is allowed.

Coordination with sales tax exemption. No credit shall be allowed for any qualified property for which an exemption from sales and use taxes was allowed and claimed as provided in Rev & TC § 6377.[2]

¶ 1252A   **Salmon And Steelhead Trout Habitat Credit**

Beginning January 1, 1995, taxpayers will be entitled to a credit of 10% of the qualified costs paid or incurred by the taxpayer or partnership for salmon and steelhead trout habitat restoration and improvement projects. The credit is allowed for the taxable year in which the expense for the habitat restoration or improvement project is paid or incurred. The California Department of Fish and Game must certify that the requirements as set forth in the Code have been met. These conditions include: (1) that the project meets the objective of the Salmon, Steelhead Trout, and Anadromous Fisheries Program Act of California, (2) the project provides employment to persons previously employed in the commercial fishing or forest products industry within a county with a rate of unemployment that is higher than the mean annual unemployment rate as specified in the Code, (3) the work to be undertaken in not otherwise required to be carried out pursuant to the Public Resources Code of the state of California, and (4) the project does not involve certain activities as listed in Rev & TC § 23666(b)(4). Carryover

---

(2) § 23649 as amended by Stats. 1994, c. 751, § 3.

provisions are provided. The credit will remain in effect until December 1, 2000.[3]

(3) § 23666, as added by Stats. 1994, c. 1296, § 3.

RETURNS AND PAYMENTS

ESTIMATED TAX

¶ 1253   **Estimated Tax Requirements**

An estimate is required from each bank and corporation incorporated in California or qualified to do business in the state or doing business in the state, whether active or inactive, or having income from sources within California, unless expressly exempted by the provisions of the Bank and Corporation Tax Law. The estimate form should be filed even though the bank or corporation may have a credit resulting from an overpayment for a prior year.

Federal rule.   For federal purposes it is not necessary to file a form with the Internal Revenue Service. The estimate is made by making a deposit with the Federal Reserve Bank or other bank with which the corporation carries on banking functions.

Note: For California, however, Form 100–ES is to be filed and the tax paid by sending it and the payment to the Franchise Tax Board in Sacramento, CA 95857.

¶ 1254   **Paying Estimated Tax**

The payment made to the Secretary of State at the time of incorporation or qualification is a payment for the privilege of doing business during the corporation's first income year. This payment cannot be claimed as an estimated tax payment or credit against tax.

If the amount of the estimated tax does not exceed the minimum tax specified in Rev & TC § 23153, the entire amount of the minimum tax is payable as an estimate on or before the 15th day of the 4th month of the corporation's income year. If the amount of the estimated tax exceeds the minimum tax specified in Rev & TC § 23153, the estimated tax is payable in four installments. These installments are due and payable on the 15th day of the fourth, sixth, ninth and twelfth months of the year.[1]

If, however, the filing requirements for making payments of the estimated tax are not applicable until after the first day of the fourth month, the payments should be spread over the remaining quarters. The new estimate spreads difference in the tax over the remaining quarters.[2]

Underpayment or late payment.

An underpayment or a late payment   of an installment of estimated tax may result in additional charges for the period from the due date of each installment until paid, or until the due date for filing the tax return, whichever is earlier. An underpayment of any installment is defined as the amount required to have been paid if the estimated tax were equal to 95% of the tax shown on the return, or if no return is filed, 95% of the tax for such year over

---

(1) § 19023; 19025.   (2) § 19025(b); 19026.

the amount actually paid on or before its due date.[3] "Tax shown on return" refers to the final return filed on or before the due date of the original return.[4] The term means the tax after the correction of mathematical errors, not the tax shown on the amended return filed after the due date, or the tax as finally determined.[4] The computation of the penalty for failure to pay an estimated tax of a minimum tax must be treated as if the tax were payable in installments the same as the payment of estimated tax for a larger amount. Payment of estimated tax due after the due date doesn't bar penalties associated with the due dates of earlier installments.[4]

No addition to tax. There is no charge for underpayment of estimated tax if the amount paid on or before the due date equals or exceeds the amount required to have been paid, on or before the due date if the estimated tax were the lesser of the *exceptions listed below.*

Note: Rev & TC § 19147 relating to not imposing an addition to tax for underpayment of any installment, is almost word for word with IRC § 6655(d), so that the rulings issued by the Internal Revenue Service would be applicable for California.

The exceptions are:

(a) The tax shown on the return for the preceding income year, if a return was filed and covered a period of 12 months and showed a tax liability.

(b) An amount equal to the tax computed at the rates applicable to the taxable year but computed on a basis of the facts shown on the return for and the law applicable to the prior taxable year;

(c) An amount equal to 95% of the tax for the taxable year computed by placing on an annualized basis the income of: (1) the first three months for the installment due in the fourth month; (2) the first three or five months for the installment due in the sixth month; (3) the first six or eight months for the installment due in the ninth month; and (4) the first nine or eleven months for the installment due in the 12th month of the income year.[5] Corporations subject to the tax on unrelated business taxable income under Rev & TC § 23731 substitute two months for three months, four months for five months, seven months for eight months, and eleven months for twelve months.[5]

(d) An amount equal to 95% of the tax for the taxable year is withheld pursuant to Rev & TC § 18662; or, 95% or more of the net income for the income year consists of items from which an amount was withheld pursuant to Rev & TC § 18662 and at the time the first installment of estimated tax is due, the amounts credited from such withholding, together with estimated tax payments, equaled at least the minimum franchise tax due at the first installment date.[5]

Large corporations. Banks or corporations with taxable income of $1 million or more during any of three preceding income years during the testing period, computed without regard to the deductions allowed by Rev & TC §§ 24416 and 24416.1 (net operating loss), must pay estimated tax equal to 95% of the tax shown on the return for the income year, or, if no return was filed 95%, of the tax for that year.

---

(3) § 19142; 19144.

(4) LR326, 2–28–68; LR383, 4–1–75; LR384, 4–1–75.

(5) § 19147.

WARNING   Effective for income years beginning on or after 1–1–93 California has abandoned the safe harbor estimated tax payment rules which applied only to *large worldwide corporations*. All large corporations, including those previously identified as "large worldwide corporations" will have met the 95% pay in requirement set forth above.

The reduction in the first required installment based, under Rev & TC § 19147(a)(1)(A), on the tax shown on the return for the preceding year must be recaptured by increasing the amount of the next installment by the amount of the reduction. "Taxable income," as used in Rev & TC § 19147, means "net income," as defined by Rev & TC § 24341, or "alternative minimum taxable income," as defined by Rev & TC § 23455. "Testing period" means the three years means the three income years immediately preceding the income year involved.

WARNING   The exception from underpayment penalty if estimated tax payments equal or exceed tax liability for preceding year is limited by the above percentage factors for large corporations.

Corporations with seasonally recurring income. The addition to tax with respect to any underpayment of any installment shall not be imposed if the total amount of all payments of estimated tax made on or before the last date prescribed for payment of that installment equals or exceeds 95% of the amount determined by: (1) taking net income for all months during the income year preceding the filing month; (2) dividing that amount by the base period percentage for all months during the income year preceding the filing month; (3) determining the tax on the amount computed under (2) above; and (4) multiplying the tax computed under (3) above by the base period percentage for the filing months and all months during the income year preceding the filing month.[6] "Base period percentage" for any period of months shall be the average percent that net income for corresponding months in each of three preceding income years bears to net income for three preceding years.[7]

Note: The rules above only apply if the base period percentage for any six consecutive months of the income year equals or exceeds 70%. The FTB can provide by regulations for the determination of the base period percentage in case of reorganizations, new corporations and other similar circumstances.

Note: Use Form 100ES to compute seasonal income pattern and amount of installment.

Estimated tax due on minimum tax imposed by Rev & TC § 23153. If only the minimum franchise tax is required to be paid under Rev & TC § 19025, then the addition to tax with respect to underpayment of any installment must be calculated only on basis of amount of minimum tax. The rule does not apply to large corporation as defined in Rev & TC § 19147(b).[8]

---

(6) § 19148(b).   (8) § 19149.
(7) § 19148(c)(1).

Exempt organizations. Notwithstanding Rev & TC § 19142 and the provisions of Rev & TC §§ 19131—19149, the addition to tax with respect to underpayment of any installment will not be imposed on an exempt corporation whose exemption is retroactively revoked, unless the corporation has notice that the estimated tax should have been paid. The denial of the organization's exemption application or revocation of its exemption by the IRS normally satisfies the notice requirement.[9]

For banks and financial corporations the term "estimated tax" means the amount determined using the rate published by the Franchise Tax Board, less the financial offsets, if any, but not less than the minimum tax. In case of increase or decrease in rate imposed by Rev & TC § 23151, bank or financial corporation must increase or decrease rate determined by Franchise Tax Board for preceding year by same amount as change in rate imposed under Rev & TC § 23151 determined in accordance with Rev & TC § 24251 (computation of tax when law changed).[10]

The penalty is computed on the amount of the underpayment at adjusted rate established under Rev & TC § 19521, from the due date of each installment to the due date of the return (excluding extension of time), or to the date on which the underpayment was paid, whichever is earlier. As in the federal estimated tax penalty computation, the taxpayer can use a different exception for each installment if it qualifies.[11]

¶ 1255 **Estimated Tax Payment for Short Period**

A corporation whose accounting period is less than 12 months should apportion its estimated tax over the number of installments that come due within its period as follows:

Calendar Year Taxpayer (Fiscal year taxpayers— adjust dates accordingly) If income year begins:	Number of Installments	Due Dates of Installments— On or before the 15th day of	Percentage of Estimated Tax Payable Each Installment*
Jan. 1 through Jan. 16	4	April-June-September-December	25 percent
Jan. 17 through Mar. 16	3	June-September-December	33⅓ percent
Mar. 17 through June 15	2	September-December	50 percent
June 16 through Sept. 15	1	December	100 percent
Sept. 16 through Dec. 31	None	————	————

* Amount of first installment cannot be less than the minimum tax.

(9) § 19151.
(10) § 19024.

(11) § 19142; 19147; 19148.

RETURNS

¶ 1269   **Filing Annual Returns**

The law specifies the annual dates when the return must be filed (Form 100). This applies to returns filed by banks and corporations as well as returns filed by farmers' cooperative associations.[12] The principal officer of the taxpayer must sign the return. The return must be verified.[13] For returns by receivers and trustees in Title 11 case, see ¶ 1272. The Rev & TC § 18642 provisions relating to the reporting of real estate transactions apply for purposes of the Bank and Corporation Tax Law.[14] The return must be filed and statements furnished to the person whose name is required to be set forth on the return for certain payments of remuneration for services under IRC § 6041A. No return need be filed if a statement with respect to services must be furnished under Unemployment Insurance Code, Division 6, relating to withholding taxes on wages. No return is required with respect to direct sales pursuant to IRC § 6041A(b).[15]

Electronic imaging technology.   The Franchise Tax Board will set forms, declarations, statements or other documents to be used when filing returns in the medium of electronic imaging technology. Any of these filing documents filed in a traditional medium and captured using electronic imaging technology will be deemed a valid original document on reproduction to paper by the FTB.[16]

Any form which is filed electronically is not complete, and therefore not filed, until an electronic filing declaration is signed by the taxpayer. The FTB is to prescribe instructions for the declaration to be retained by the taxpayer or the tax preparer. Such declaration must be made available to the FTB upon request.[16]

Magnetic media.   Forms may also be on magnetic media as well as electronic imaging technology.[17]

For time and place to file, see ¶ 1274.

WARNING   Official United States Post Office postmarks will be considered primary evidence of the date of filing of income tax documents and/or payments. Postage meter dates will not be considered as proof of filing for the dates shown.

Automatic extension.   Form FTB 3504 (application for automatic maximum extension of time for filing a return) is to be used for requesting an extension of time. The application is for an automatic seven-month extension requiring no statement of the reason for the delay. If it is filed on or before the due date for filing a return, and if the total additional tax due is paid with

---

(12) § 18601.   (15) § 18638.
(13) § 18621.   (16) § 18621.5.
(14) § 18642.   (17) § 18621.

the application, the acceptance of the extension by the Franchise Tax Board is automatic. No extension beyond the seven months from the original due date for filing the return may be granted.[18] See also ¶ 1275.

Paperless extension. The FTB will allow an automatic seven-month extension without the need to file a written request for bank and corporation returns required to be filed on or after 3–15–93. The paperless extension applies to all taxpayers in good standing filing FTB Form 100, including REITs, RICs, and REMICs, S corporations filing Form 100S, water's-edge corporations filing Form 100-FEE, and exempt organizations filing Forms 109 and 199. The extension period for fiscal and calendar year taxpayers is the original due date plus seven months. The extension is conditioned on the filing of a return within the automatic extension period. The extension of time to file doesn't extend the time to pay tax.[19]

¶ 1270 Combined Reports

When two or more corporations are engaged in a unitary business, the members of the entire unitary group must compute the measure of the tax on the combined income of all members of the group. This is called the "combined report" approach. The purpose of the combined report is to (1) determine the California income of those members of the unitary group doing business in-state; and (2) adjust intercompany transactions or transactions between corporations and stockholders, and prevent avoidance of taxes by the shifting of income and deductions between members of group.[20] Every corporation doing business in California, whether it is a California corporation or a qualified foreign corporation, is generally required to file a California Franchise Tax Return on Form 100. However, under the combined report approach, one return may be filed by one of the corporations in the affiliated group to report the combined income of all the members. If a unitary business includes both general corporations and financial corporations, the corporations should be included in the combined report.[21] If the dominant member in the combination is a general corporation, other than a financial corporation, Rev & TC § 25128 governs the allocation and apportionment of income.[22] If the dominant member in the combination is a financial corporation, Reg 25137–4 should be used to determine the factors of the financial corporations involved.[23]

CAUTION   Effective for income years beginning on or after 1–1–93, Stats. 1993, c. 946, revised the apportionment formula for multistate businesses, except those that derive over 50% of their gross receipts from agricultural business activity. Taypayers affected must now apportion their income to California using a fraction the numerator of which consists of the property factor plus the payroll plus *twice* the sales factor, and the denominator of which is four. Previously, the sales, payroll, and property

---

(**18**) § 18604.
(**19**) § 25402; FTB Notice 92–11, 10–23–92.
(**20**) LR 241, 10–28–59; FTB 1061.

(**21**) LR 370, 1–11–74.
(**22**) § 25128; Reg 25137–10.
(**23**) § 25137; Reg 25137(j).

factors had equal weights, and the denominator was three. The regulations have not been amended to reflect this change.

A California corporate insurer engaged in a unitary business must be excluded from the combined report. The state Constitution exempts these corporations from franchise and income taxes.[24] Three subsidiaries engaged in a unitary business with an exempt insurance company parent must be included in the combined report, but the parent must be excluded.[25] The same rule was applied to three subsidiaries engaged in a unitary business when the parent company wasn't engaged in such business.[25] For further information, see ¶ 1170–1177.

¶ 1271   **Consolidated Returns**

There is no blanket provision in the Bank and Corporation Franchise Tax Law where affiliated corporations may elect to file a consolidated return. Section 25102[26] of the law states that "the Franchise Tax Board may permit or require the filing of a combined report and such other information as it deems necessary and is authorized to impose the tax due under this part, etc."

The lone exception to the rule is that an affiliated group of railroad corporations may file a consolidated return, whether or not it is engaged in a unitary business. Affiliated group means one or more corporations connected through stock ownership with a common parent corporation, whereby there is 80% control and each of the corporations, except the common parent corporation, is either a corporation whose principal business is that of a common carrier by railroad or a corporation whose assets consist principally of stock in railroad corporations.[27]

¶ 1272   **Returns by Receivers**

Receivers, trustees in bankruptcies, trustees in dissolution, and assignees operating the properties or business of a corporation must make the returns and pay the taxes on behalf of the corporation. Whether they are engaged in carrying on the business for which the corporation was organized or only in marshalling, selling, and disposing of its assets for the purposes of liquidation they will be deemed to be operating the trade or business and the corporation would be subject to the franchise tax.[28] If receivers and trustees in a case under Title 11, or assignees are operating the property or business of a bank or corporation, they must make returns for such bank or corporation in same manner and form as such bank or corporation.[29]

---

(24) LR 385, 4–1–75.

(25) LR 411, 1–16–79.

(26) § 25102.

(27) § 23361–23364.

(28) § 23038; 23039.

(29) § 18606.

Federal trustee or receiver. A federal trustee or receiver who is liquidating a bankrupt and nonoperating corporation must file return and pay minimum franchise tax.[30]

¶ 1273 Political Organization

A political organization exempt under Rev & TC § 23701r must file the corporation return Form 100 and report its "political taxable income" in excess of $100. Political taxable income means all amounts received during the taxable year other than:

(1) Contributions of money or other property;
(2) Membership dues, fees, or assessments;
(3) Proceeds from political fund-raising or entertainment events or proceeds from the sale of political campaign material which are not received in the ordinary course of any trade or business. Political organizations are not required to file Form 199. The income tax is computed without regard as to whether the political organization is a corporation, unincorporated association, trust, or fiduciary.[31]

¶ 1274 Time and Place to File

The annual bank or corporation franchise tax or corporation income tax return is to be filed within two months and fifteen days after the close of the accounting period. Returns of farmers' cooperative associations must be filed by the 15th day of the 9th month following the close of the income year. The returns should be addressed to the Franchise Tax Board, Sacramento, California 95857.[32]

Official United States Post Office postmarks are considered to be primary evidence of the date of the filing of corporate returns, extensions of time and payments. Postage meter dates are not considered as proof of filing for the date shown.

WARNING	If mail is received by the Franchise Tax Board which does not bear a postmark assigned by the United States Post Office, the question of whether or not the return was filed on time will be determined by the date of receipt and other appropriate evidence.

If the due date for filing a return, an extension of time or an estimated tax falls on a Saturday, Sunday or legal holiday, the documents can be filed on the next business day following.

With the exception of corporations filing tax returns as part of a unitary business group, other corporations which dissolve or withdraw from the state are to file the tax return within two months and fifteen days after the close of the month in which the dissolution or withdrawal takes place.

California has adopted IRC § 381(b) that provides that the taxable year of the distributor or transferor corporation in a reorganization ends on the date of distribution or transfer.[33]

---

(30) LR 407, 9–16–77.
(31) § 23701r.
(32) § 18601.
(33) § 23253.

¶ **1274**

CAUTION   Except for cooperative associations, for income years beginning on or after January 1, 1995, if a short period return is required by Rev & TC § 24634, then the return is due when the federal return is due which includes the net income of the taxpayer for the short period. If no federal return is required to be filed for the period that includes the short period California return, then the California return is due on the fifteenth day of the third month following the close of the short period.[34]

¶ 1275   Extension of Time Request

California has an automatic extension of time request to be filed by corporations requesting an extension of time for filing franchise or income tax returns, exempt organization business income tax returns (Form 109) and exempt organization annual information returns (Form 199).[35]

The total unpaid expected tax for the income year has to be paid with the application and filed prior to the due date of the return. If these conditions are met the extension is automatic for the seven-month period. No reason for the necessity of filing the return after the original due date is required to be included with the application. See also ¶ 1269.

Members of a combined group.   For members of a combined group who have made an election to file a single return, only the member electing to file the return has to apply for an extension. If the election to file the single return is not on file with the Franchise Tax Board, each separate member of the combined group has to apply for the extension of time to file.

Mechanics for filing.   The mechanics for filing are the same as that for filing Federal Form 7004; that is, that an original signed California application on FTB Form 3504 may be submitted, and the second copy retained to be attached to the return when filed. No reply will be received from the Franchise Tax Board unless the application is denied.

¶ 1276   New Corporation Requirement

If the first accounting period of a newly incorporated or newly qualified corporation is one-half month or less, it may be disregarded as far as filing a corporate tax return for the period, if the corporation was not doing business in and received no income from sources in California. For a portion of a month to be disregarded under this rule, the corporation's articles of incorporation or qualification would have to be filed in the case of: (a) a 28-day month: on the 15th day or after; (b) a 29-day month: on the 16th day or after; (c) a 30-day month: on the 16th day or after; (d) a 31-day month: on the 17th day or after.[36]

---

(34) § 18601, as amended by Stats. 1994, c. 35, § 1.   **(36)** FTB 1060.
(35) § 18604.

¶ 1277 **Amended Returns**

Form 100X is used to file an amended corporation franchise or income tax return for any period. Form 100X can be filed at any time after the original return is filed.

It is also used as a claim for refund. If used for this purpose, it can be filed within four years from the original due date, the approved extended due date of the return or within one year from the date the tax was paid, whichever is later. If an amended return is filed for federal purposes, it is required by California law that an amended return showing the changes be filed with the Franchise Tax Board within 90 days of the federal filing. Form 100X requests information as to whether or not the federal amended return was filed, and whether or not the corporation had been approached in regard to a Federal examination of the amended return.[37]

¶ 1278 **Out-of-State Corporate Tax Return Filers**

The Franchise Tax Board has always had problems with corporations located outside of California which send employees, inventory or other property into California, and, therefore, become subject to either the corporation income or franchise tax filing requirements. The Board has, in the past, adopted various procedures for reviewing records of the Employment Development Department (to determine employees of out-of-state corporations located in California), county property tax assessment rolls (to determine inventories in public warehouses owned by out-of-state corporations) and consulted financial and entertainment newspapers and publications to determine information about foreign corporations and their activities within California.

Note: Rev & TC § 18662[38] permits the Franchise Tax Board to require any bank, corporation or person having control of income subject to withholding payable to a corporation which does not have a permanent place of business in California, to withhold from such income and transmit to the Franchise Tax Board the amount of tax specified. Even if the corporation has a permanent place of business in California, the Franchise Tax Board may require withholding of tax from the income of the corporation by filing a notice with the person having control or custody of the income, if it considers it necessary. Notice from Board will require payment at such time as it may designate. In case of depositary institution, amounts must be transmitted to Board not less than 10 business days after receipt of notice. To be effective, such notice must state amount due and be delivered or mailed to branch or office where credit or property is held, unless another branch or office is designated.[39]

The types of income referred to in the law are interest, dividends, rent, prizes and winnings, premiums, annuities, emoluments, partnership income and gains, compensation for services, including bonuses and other fixed or determinable annual or periodic gains or profits and income. In addition, withholding is required for services of performers furnished in the amuse-

---

(37) § 18622.
(38) § 18662.

(39) § 18670.

ment, artistic or recording fields who fulfill engagements carried on in California, and payments of prizes, premiums, awards winnings, and so on, to corporations participating in or entering horses, dogs, etc., in races or other contests in California. This includes payments to corporations for performances by dance bands, orchestras, circuses or for payments of services of actors, singers, performers, entertainers, wrestlers, boxers, and other similar types of amusement or sporting activity in California, when payment for such performances is made to a corporation rather than directly to the performer.[40]

A corporation for purposes of this section has a permanent place of business in California if it is organized and existing under the laws of this state, or if it is a foreign corporation qualified to transact intrastate business. A corporation which has not qualified to transact intrastate business will be considered as having a permanent place of business in California only if it maintains a permanent office in this state which is permanently staffed by its employees.[1]

When withholding not required. Withholding pursuant to Reg 26131–2 is not required unless and until income payments with respect to each payee by same payor either exceed $1,500 during calendar year, or payor is directed to withhold by Franchise Tax Board.[2]

Computation of tax withheld. The amount to be withheld will be computed by applying a rate of 7%, or such lesser rate as authorized in writing by the FTB.[2]

Documentation of overwithholding. The FTB may consider documentation that the 7% rate results in overwithholding, and waive withholding requirements in whole or in part, or authorize the use of a lower rate. Compliance bond, deposit or other security may be required. Notices of waiver or lower rate by the FTB must be in writing and mailed to the payor.[2]

Disposition of California real property interest—IRC § 1445. In the case of any disposition of a California real property interest by a corporation, the transferee must withhold an amount equal at least to 3⅓% of the sales price of the real property conveyed, if the corporation immediately after the transfer of title to the California real property has no permanent place of business in California. For this purpose, a corporation has no permanent place of business in California if all of the following apply: (1) it is not organized or existing under the laws of California; and (2) it does not qualify with the office of the Secretary of State to do business in California; and (3) it does not maintain and staff a permanent office in California. Withholding will not be required if the sales price does not exceed $100,000. The transferee cannot be required to withhold unless a written notice of the above requirements is given to the real estate escrow person. Withholding is not

---

(40) Reg 26131–2.   **(2)** Reg 26131–2.
(1) Reg 26131–1.

required if the transferor is bank acting as a trustee other than a trustee of the deed of trust. The transferee need not withhold if it is a bank and corporation beneficiary under a mortgage, or beneficiary under the deed of trust, and the California property is acquired in a judicial or nonjudicial foreclosure, or by deed in lieu thereof. The Franchise Tax Board may authorize a reduced rate of withholding, or no withholding.[3] For failure to withhold, the penalty is $500, or 10% of the amount required to be withheld, if greater. Other provisions deal with liability of real estate escrow person, and required written notice to the transferee.[3]

Information with respect to certain foreign-owned corporations. California adopts IRC § 6038A. Under this federal IRC section, if at any time during a taxable year, a corporation is a domestic corporation or a foreign corporation engaged in trade or business within the U.S., and is 25% owned at any time during the taxable year by one foreign person, that corporation must furnish, at such time and manner set by the tax authorities by regulation, certain required information, and maintain appropriate records to determine the correct treatment of transactions with related parties. The required information includes:

(1) name, principal place of business, nature of business, and country or countries in which organized or resident, of each person that is a related party to the reporting corporation, and had any transaction with the reporting corporation during the taxable year;

(2) the manner of relationship between the reporting corporation and the person;

(3) transactions between the reporting corporation and the person; and

(4) such information as tax authorities require to carry out IRC § 453C, relating to certain indebtedness treated as payment on installment obligations.

Foreign person is any person not a U.S. person, as defined in IRC § 7701(a)(30) (term includes corporations, partnerships and trusts). A related party is any 25% foreign shareholder of the reporting corporation, a related person within meaning of IRC § 267(b) or IRC § 707(b)(1) or § 482. IRC § 318, relating to constructive ownership of stock applies with certain exceptions. For penalties and enforcement, see ¶ 1321.[4]

WARNING   California has adopted regulations which require the filing of federal form 5472, Information Return of a 25% Foreign-Owned U.S. Corporation or a Foreign Corporation Engaged in a U.S. Trade or Business, with the California return if it is required to be attached to the federal return. California has also adopted the federal penalty provisions which provide a fine of $10,000 for failure to file the form 5472 when it is due. The

---

(3) § 18662(e).   (4) § 19141.5.

penalty also applies for failure to maintain records as required by Federal Reg. 1.6038A–3 which has been adopted by California by reference.

Cash received in trade or business.   The Franchise Tax Board must require a copy of the federal information to be filed, if a federal information return was required under IRC § 6050I.[5]

Return of tax withheld at source.   If notice to withhold has been issued for a particular engagement, the tax withheld must be remitted by the 20th day of the month following the month of the close of the engagement. The original copy of the notice to withhold will serve as a return of the tax withheld (Form 592) as well as a statement of the tax withheld at source. The remittance must be sent to the FTB office that issued the notice to withhold. If a notice to withhold is not issued, the return of tax withheld is due by the 20th day of the month following the month in which the total amount withheld and not remitted during the calendar year exceeds $2,500. Amounts withheld and not previously remitted because the total did not exceed $2,500 must be submitted by 1–31 following the close of the calendar year. Both Form 592 (return) and Form 591 (statement) must be remitted to the FTB whenever a notice to withhold is not issued.[6]

¶ 1279   Home Owners' Association

A home owners' association exempt under Rev & TC § 23701(t) must file corporation return Form 100 if it received "Home Owners' Association taxable income" in excess of $100. This is in addition to the filing of an annual information return or statement on Form 199.

"Home Owners' Association taxable income" means the excess over $100, of gross income for the taxable year over deductions allowed that are directly connected with the production of such gross income, other than the amounts received from membership fees, dues, or assessments. The income tax is computed with no minimum tax required.[7]

¶ 1280   Special Form to Secretary of State

Section 3301 of the California Corporation Code requires that every domestic corporation file Form S/0200 with the California Secretary of State at the following times:

(1) Domestic corporations other than non-profit:
    (a) Within 90 days after filing articles of incorporation;
    (b) Thereafter annually, between April 1 and June 30;
    (c) Each time the corporation changes its principal office address.
(2) Domestic nonprofit corporations:
    (a) Within 90 days after filing articles of incorporation;
    (b) Each time there is a change in corporate officers. If there is no change in officers, a filing is required every five years.

---

(5) § 18645.
(6) Reg 26131–5.

(7) § 23701(t).

The form is to be filed with the Secretary of State, P.O. Box 2830, Sacramento, CA 95809, accompanied by a fee of $5 (nonprofit corporations are exempt from filing the fee). If the corporation fails to file the form, even after demand by the Secretary of State, the corporation may be deemed in default and have its corporate powers, rights and privileges suspended by the Secretary of State.

¶ 1281   **Reporting Federal Changes**

In any case in which an audit by the Internal Revenue Service results in an increase in federal taxable income or tax liability, the corporation is required to submit a copy of the changes to the Franchise Tax Board within 6 months after the "final determination" of such change. The same is true if a contract or subcontract with the United States is renegotiated resulting in a change in income or deductions. Also, any corporation filing an amended return with the Internal Revenue Service is required to file an amended return with the Franchise Tax Board within 6 months.[8]

When the changes are reported, or the amended return filed, the Franchise Tax Board has a period of 2 years within which to issue a Notice of Proposed Assessment on the increases in the taxable income resulting from the changes. The 2 year period commences on the date the notification or amended return is filed with the Board and may extend beyond the normal statute of limitations period.

If the corporation reports the change, but fails to do so timely within the 6-month period, the statute of limitations is extended for a period of four years from the date the notice is finally received or the amended return is filed with the Board.[9]

WARNING   If the taxpayer fails to report a federal change in income or correction to the Franchise Tax Board, the Franchise Tax Board may issue a notice of proposed deficiency assessment resulting from the adjustment *at any time* after the change, correction, or amended return is reported to or filed with the federal government. Failure to make the required report to the Franchise Tax Board results in the suspensions of the statute of limitations for additional California taxes which are do with respect to the item being changed.

Note: Both the Bank and Corporation Tax Law and the Internal Revenue Code include reciprocal provisions permitting an exchange of information. As a result of these provisions the FTB receives copies of the revenue agent's finding directly from the Internal Revenue Service. Notices of Proposed Assessment are issued directly from these reports may be issued without waiting for the corporation to submit a copy as required.

It should be emphasized that the extension of the statute of limitations for reporting the federal changes 6 months, or not reporting the federal changes within that period, applies to only the additions to taxable income

(8) § 18622.   (9) § 25673–25674.

resulting from the change. The statute is not extended for other potential adjustments nor claims for refund.

IMPORTANT   The "final determination" is the last level to which the federal matter is referred. For example, if the case is settled by a Tax Court decision, that is the final decision for this purpose.

The FTB will issue its assessment notices based on the revenue agent's report even if the corporation is filing an appeal. Taxpayer has 60 days after the notice is mailed to file a written protest. Use FTB 3532 (reproduced at ¶ 6602) for automatic protest of federal deficiencies. FTB 3531 (reproduced at same paragraph) is also acceptable to the FTB in most circumstances.

¶ 1282 Effect of Paying Wrong Tax

If taxes, penalty, or interest have been assessed or paid as a franchise tax and it is determined that the corporation should have been filing and/or paying tax as a corporation income tax instead, the Franchise Tax Board will consider that the taxes, etc. have been filed under the appropriate Chapter without the necessity of refiling returns or making other payments.[10]

PAYMENTS

¶ 1293 Payment Due Date

For general corporations, the entire amount of the tax liability unpaid as shown on the return when filed is due by the due date for filing the tax return.[11] Payment may be made by check payable in U.S. funds, if not paid by the bank on which drawn, taxpayer remains liable for all taxes, interest and penalties, as if the check had never been given in payment. Remittances can also be made by a credit account number and authorization. Remittances may also be drawn on account with a financial institution.[12] All payments required under the Bank and Corporation Tax Law must be remitted by electronic funds transfer, if (1) the estimated tax payment averages $50,000 or more per payment in any tax year starting on or after 1–1–93, or $20,000 or more per payment in any income year starting on or after 1–1–95; (2) the total tax liability for any income year starting on or after 1–1–93 was in excess of $200,000, or $80,000 or more in any income year starting on or after 1–1–95. The penalty for failure to remit payments by electronic transfer when required is 10% of the amount paid by other means, unless proof is made that the failure was for reasonable cause and not wilfull neglect. Taxpayers not required to remit by electronic transfer may apply to the Franchise Tax Board for permission to do so. The conditions for a Franchise Tax Board waiver of the requirement for remission by electronic funds transfer are specified. Payment is deemed complete on the date the funds transfer

---

(10) § 19059—19060.
(11) § 19001.

(12) § 19005, as amended by Stats. 1994, c. 271, § 1.

is initiated, if settlement to the state's demand account is by the next banking day; otherwise payment is deemed to occur on the date of settlement.[13]

---

(13) § 19011.

ASSESSMENT, COLLECTION, REFUND

¶ 1303   **Deficiency Assessment**

If after the Franchise Tax Board examines returns it finds that the tax is less than that disclosed by its examination, it will mail a notice of the additional tax proposed to be assessed.[1] Any interest, penalty or addition to tax may be collected in the same manner as if it were a deficiency.[2] Taxpayer may file a protest against the additional tax within 60 days after the mailing of the notice.[3] If no protest is filed, the proposed assessment is final after the end of the above 60 days.[4]

Hearing and appeal.   If a protest is filed and a hearing is requested, the Franchise Tax Board will reconsider the assessment and grant the taxpayer an oral hearing. The FTB's action on the protest is final after 30 days from the date of the notice to taxpayer unless an appeal is filed with the State Board of Equalization at Sacramento. The SBE will hear and determine the appeal and it becomes final after 30 days from its determination unless within that time a rehearing petition is filed, in which case its determination becomes final after 30 days from the time the SBE issues its opinion.[5]

TAX TIP   The Franchise Tax Board will grant a hearing only if it is requested in the original protest. If no hearing is requested the FTB will act on the written record. It is always wise to request a hearing. If it is later decided that a hearing is not desirable, or not needed, it can be waived.

¶ 1304   **Jeopardy Assessment**

If the Franchise Tax Board decides that the assessment or collection of a tax or a deficiency for any year will be jeopardized by a delay, it can issue a notice to the taxpayer or its transferee with a demand for immediate payment of the tax or deficiency declared to be in jeopardy, including interest and penalties. The FTB may also declare the income year of a taxpayer immediately terminated and make an assessment on the basis of the income for the period up to the date of the termination. This procedure is used in a case where no return is filed and the FTB has an indication that the corporation was active in California during the period.[6]

A jeopardy assessment is immediately due and payable and the FTB can proceed with collection procedures at once. Collection may be stayed if the taxpayer (1) files a bond, (2) posts other securities, or (3) files with the Franchise Tax Board acceptable evidence that the collection of tax is not in jeopardy.[7]

A written statement of the information upon which the Franchise Tax Board relied in issuing the notice and demand for payment, or the notice and demand for return and payment under Rev & TC § 19082 must be mailed or

---

(1) § 19032; 19033.
(2) § 19036.
(3) § 19041.
(4) § 19042.

(5) § 19044; 19045; 19046.
(6) § 19081; 19082.
(7) § 19083.

issued to taxpayer within five days after the date of the issuance or mailing of the notice and demand under Rev & TC § 19082.[8]

Within 30 days after the date on which the taxpayer is furnished with the written statement of information, or within 30 days after the last day of the 5-day period for furnishing the statement, the taxpayer may petition the Franchise Tax Board to review whether its finding under Rev & TC § 19081 is reasonable. The petition must specify grounds. Filing of the petition does not stay collection. It can only be stayed by a Rev & TC § 25761a procedure (filing bond or other security). The petition will also be considered a protest against the additional tax under Rev & TC § 19041. If the petition is not made within the 30-day period, the finding of the Franchise Tax Board will be final.[8]

After the petition for review is filed, the Franchise Tax Board must determine whether or not its issuance of the notice and demand is reasonable. In making this determination, it must grant taxpayer, or representative an oral hearing, if so requested. The burden of proof on the issue of the existence of jeopardy as to collection or assessment rests on the Franchise Tax Board. A determination by the FTB must be made within 90 days of filing of the petition for review, unless the taxpayer requests additional time in writing. The determination must consider all relevant factors, including the likelihood of jeopardy of collection, assets of the taxpayer, and the amount of the assessment as it relates to the existence of jeopardy status. The burden of proof is on the taxpayer, as to the amount of the assessment for purposes of determining jeopardy status.[8]

Appeals to State Board of Equalization. An appeal to the State Board of Equalization can be made within 60 days after the earlier of (1) the day the FTB notifies the taxpayer of the determination on reasonableness of issuance of the notice and demand; or (2) one day after the 90-day time period for the FTB to make its determination on the taxpayer's petition for review. If appeal is not made within these periods, the FTB determination is final. Filing of appeal does not stay collection.[8]

Superior Court action. The State Board of Equalization decision on reasonableness of the notice and demand may be the subject of action brought by either party.[8]

¶ 1305   **Bankruptcy and Receivership**

The receiver or the trustee in a case under Title 11, U.S. Code proceeding, the debtor in possession or other person in control of assets in any bankruptcy proceeding by order of the Court must give notice of his appointment or qualification as such to the Franchise Tax Board. In the same manner, a receiver in a receivership proceeding or an assignee for the benefit of creditors or other like fiduciary is required to give notice in writing to the FTB.[9]

---

(8) § 19084.   (9) § 19089.

Rev & TC § 19088[10] permits the Franchise Tax Board to make an immediate assessment of any deficiency it determines to be due and to file the appropriate claim with the Court having jurisdiction.[11] The unpaid portion of claim allowed in the receivership proceeding must be paid on notice and demand by the Franchise Tax Board after the termination of such proceeding, and may be collected like delinquent taxes at any time within 6 years after the termination.[12]

¶ 1306   Consent Letter

If the Franchise Tax Board in making adjustments to tax returns filed by the corporation finds that for one or more years there is an additional tax to pay, and for other years an overpayment of tax, it will issue a standard form letter summarizing the amounts involved and asking the corporation's permission to offset the overpayments against the deficiency. If the corporation does not agree with the proposed adjustments, it should still file a protest whether or not it would agree to the offsetting of the overpayments to the deficiencies if the notices become final.

¶ 1307   Transferee Liability

The Franchise Tax Board may assess additional taxes against the transferee of a corporation if it has reason to believe it cannot collect from the corporation itself. In order to establish that a transferee liability exists, it must be shown that (a) the transferor transferred assets of value to the transferee, (b) that this transfer left the transferor insolvent, (c) the transferor was liable for the assessment in question, (d) the transfer was made after the liability had accrued.[13]

The statute of limitations for assessment of a liability against a transferee is one year after the expiration of the statute of limitations for assessment against the corporation.[14]

¶ 1308   Closing Agreements

The Franchise Tax Board or a member of its staff designated to do so, may enter into an agreement with a corporation to settle any matter pertaining to the taxes under the Bank and Corporations Tax Law. The agreement must be approved by the Franchise Tax Board. The agreement is then final and conclusive unless either fraud or misrepresentation of a material fact is disclosed. The case cannot be reopened for the matters agreed on by any officer, employee or agent of the state; in any court action, the agreement cannot be set aside, modified or disregarded.[15]

---

(10) § 19088.
(11) § 19090.
(12) § 19091.
(13) § 19073.

(14) § 19074.
(15) § 19441, as amended by Stats. 1994, c. 726, § 38.

¶ 1308-A **Settlement Authority**

The Franchise Tax Board may settle civil tax disputes. The executive officer or chief counsel of the Franchise Tax Board must first submit the proposed recommendations to the Attorney General who is, within 30 days of receiving the recommendation, to advise the executive officer or chief counsel of the Franchise Tax Board of the Attorney General's conclusions as to whether the recommendation is reasonable from an overall perspective. Once submitted to the Franchise Tax Board, following the receipt of the Attorney General's findings, the Franchise Tax Board has 45 days to accept or disapprove the recommendation for settlement. If there is no action within 45 days of submission, the recommendation is treated as approved. All settlements pursuant to Rev & TC § 19442 are final and nonappealable.[16]

Whenever a reduction of tax in excess of $500 is approved pursuant to the settlement authority granted to the Franchise Tax Board, a public record will be created to show the name of the taxpayer, the amount originally involved, the amount of the settlement, a summary of the reasons why the settlement is in the best interests of the State of California, and the Attorney General's conclusions that the recommendation of settlement was reasonable from an overall perspective.

A settlement of any civil tax matter in dispute involving a reduction of tax or penalties which does not exceed $5,000, may be approved by the executive officer and chief counsel of the Franchise Tax Board without referral to the Attorney General's office.[17]

¶ 1309 **Interest on Assessment and Refunds**

Any tax or any portion of the tax not paid on or before the due date is assessed interest on the unpaid amount at the adjusted rate established under Rev & TC § 19521[18] from the date prescribed for its payment until paid. Legislation provides that the rate will be determined in accordance with IRC § 6621, except that the overpayment rate specified in IRC § 6621(a)(1) shall be modified for California purposes to be equal to the underpayment rate determined under IRC § 6621(a)(2). Determination of the interest rate is made on a semiannual basis, rather than quarterly, as under the federal law.[18] The adjusted rate applies to extensions of time for payment from the date payment would have been due, if there had been no extension, until paid.[19] It also applies to deficiencies from the date prescribed for payment of the tax, or, if tax is paid in installments, from the date prescribed for first installment, until the date tax is paid. If any portion of the deficiency is paid before the date it is assessed, interest accrues on that portion until the date it is paid. If the Franchise Tax Board makes an erroneous payment to the taxpayer, that amount may be assessed and collected pursuant to Rev & TC § 19051, relating to mathematical errors, but

---

(16) § 19442.
(17) § 19442, as amended by Stats. 1994, c. 138, § 3.

(18) § 19521.
(19) § 19102.

interest at the rate set under Rev & TC § 19521 on that amount does not accrue until 30 days from the date the FTB mails a written notice demanding repayment. The Franchise Tax Board may abate the assessment of all or any part of an interest assessment for any period if (1) any deficiency is attributable in whole or in part to any error or delay by an officer or employee of the FTB acting in his or her official capacity in performing a ministerial act; or (2) to the extent any payment of additional tax under Rev & TC § 19034 is attributable to that officer being dilatory in performing a ministerial act. Error or delay will be taken into account only if no significant aspect of that error or delay can be attributed to the taxpayer involved. The Franchise Tax Board must have contacted taxpayer in writing with respect to that deficiency or payment. The FTB must abate all interest on any erroneous refund for which recovery action is provided under Rev & TC § 19411 until the date a demand is made for repayment, unless the taxpayer, or a related party, has caused that erroneous refund, or it exceeds $50,000.[20] The same adjusted annual rate applies to interest in respect of any assessable penalty as follows: (1) in the case of a penalty, additional amount, or addition to tax, that, when assessed, is payable on notice and demand, other than a penalty for failure to file on time, the penalty for underpayment of tax, or the accuracy-related penalty, from the date of notice and demand to the date of payment; (2) in the case of a penalty, additional amount, or addition to tax, if initially assessed as deficiency, other than failure to file on time, the penalty for underpayment of tax, or the accuracy-related penalty, from date of notice of proposed assessment to date of payment; (3) with respect to a penalty or addition to tax for failure to file on time, the accuracy-related penalty, or underpayment, for the period starting on the date the return is required to be filed, including extensions and ending on the date of the payment of the addition to tax. Interest will not be imposed if payment is made within ten days of the notice.[21] The same rate also applies to overpayments credited or refunded and erroneous refunds and credits.[22]

Large corporate underpayments. Eff 1–1–92, the interest rate charged on underpayments in excess of $100,000 will be the short-term federal rate plus 5 percentage points. This amount of interest applies to the amount determined to be an underpayment, regardless of the amount of the tax assessed. This rate does not apply to self-assessed interest charges using a method of accounting or reporting that defers payment of tax. Before 1992, the rate was the short-term federal rate plus 3 percentage points.[23]

¶ 1310 **Time Limits for Tax Deficiencies and Refunds**

The Franchise Tax Board must mail any notice of additional tax to the taxpayer within four years after the return was filed. In a case under Title 11 of the United States Code, the running of the period must be suspended for any time during which the Franchise Tax Bd. is prohibited by reason of such

---

(20) § 19104.
(21) §§ 19106; 19111.

(22) §§ 19340; 19391; 19411.
(23) §§ 23051.5; 19521; 19104.

case from mailing the notice of the additional tax proposed to be assessed and 60 days thereafter.[24] The FTB may ask the taxpayer to sign a waiver of the statute of limitations (FTB 3570) for a limited period of time, generally to the normal expiration date of the following year's return. Acceptance of the waiver by the taxpayer by signing the form will, in addition to extending the statute of limitations for the issuance of the notices of additional tax, also extend the statute within which a claim for refund may be filed.[25] Receipt of a written document signed by the taxpayer showing the additional amount due within the 60-day period ending on the day that the time for assessment would expire extends that time to 60 days after the receipt.[26]

IMPORTANT   If the corporation signs a federal waiver, the period for mailing California notices of proposed deficiency or filing claims for refund will be the normal four-year statute of limitations or six months after the date of expiration of the date of the federal waiver, whichever period expires the later.[27]

If the taxpayer omits from gross income an amount properly includable which is in excess of 25% of the amount of gross income shown on the return, the statute is open for six years, rather than four years. The omitted gross income does not include any amount of gross income disclosed in the return, or in the statement attached to the return in the manner which would inform the Franchise Tax Board of the nature and the amount of the income. For purposes of this provision, the term "gross income" in the case of a trade or business carried on by the corporation means the total of the amounts received or accrued from the sales of goods or services, if such amounts are required to be shown on the return before the cost of these sales or services is deducted.[28]

STATUTE OF LIMITATIONS—CORPORATIONS

Situation	Tax Deficiency	Claim for Refund
Normal, not including false or fraudulent returns	4 years from the date the return was filed or 4 years after the due date including extensions, whichever is later.[29]	4 years from the due date (not including extensions) or 1 year from date of overpayment, whichever is later.[30]
California waiver of the statute in effect	The period of the waiver.[31]	The period of the waiver or 1 year from date of payment, whichever is later.
Omission of 25% of gross income	6 years from due date of the date return was filed, whichever is later.[28]	Not applicable.

(24) § 19065; 19057.
(25) § 19066; 19308.
(26) § 19057(c).
(27) § 19065.

(28) § 19057(d).
(29) § 19065.
(30) § 19306.
(31) § 19067.

¶ 1310

Situation	Tax Deficiency	Claim for Refund
Federal waiver in effect	6 months after the expiration of federal waiver.[29]	6 months from expiration of federal waiver, or 1 year from date of payment, whichever is later.[32]
Federal change reported by taxpayer, (or amended return filed), within 6 months	2 years after notification by taxpayer or amended return filed with Franchise Tax Board (applies to federal adjustments but not general changes in audit).[33]	Two years from notice or amended return or ordinary waiver period, whichever is later.[34]
Federal change reported by taxpayer, or amended California return filed, but after 6-month period for timely reporting had expired	4 years from the final determination by the Internal Revenue Service or from date amended return filed. (applies only to federal changes).[35]	Not applicable
Federal changes not reported and no amended return filed	At any time; statute of limitation suspended[33]	Not applicable
Bad debt, worthless security, or erroneous inclusion of recoveries	Not applicable	7 years after due date.[36]
Election regarding gain on involuntary conversion	4 years after notification by taxpayer of replacement or intention not to replace.[37]	Not applicable
Renegotiation reported within 6 months (or amended return filed)	2 years after notification by taxpayer or amended California return filed.[38]	4 years from due date or 2 years after date excess profits returned.
Renegotiation changes reported or amended return filed, but after 6-month period for timely reporting had expired.	4 years after final determination or amended return filed.[38]	4 years from due date or 2 years after date excess profits returned.
Patronage dividends (noncash dividends elected to be excluded)	4 years after taxpayer notifies the Franchise Tax Board of gain realized from noncash dividends.[39]	Not applicable

(32) § 19308.
(33) § 19059.
(34) § 19311.
(35) § 19060.

(36) § 19312.
(37) § 19061; 24945.
(38) § 19060(b).
(39) § 24273.5.

Situation	Tax Deficiency	Claim for Refund
Title II, USC case	Running of statute suspended for up to 2 years based on notification date.[40]	Not applicable
Fraud, or no return filed	No statute	Not applicable
Original transferee	1 year beyond the normal statute of limitations.[1]	Not applicable
Transferee of a transferee	Within 1 year after the expiration of the statute for the preceding transferee.[2]	Not applicable

If the Franchise Tax Board makes changes in returns which have been filed and the computation of income for any year results in an overpayment for one year and a deficiency for another year, the overpayment will be credited against the deficiency if the statutes of limitations for both years are open, and the balance will be charged or credited, as the case may be. Interest then is assessed or allowed only on the net amount of the change.

¶ 1311 **Claims for Refund**

As in personal income tax cases, if the Franchise Tax Board decides that there has been overpayment of tax, penalty or interest by a taxpayer, the amount of the overpayment maybe credited against any amount then due from the corporation and the balance refunded. Every claim for refund must be in writing, be signed by taxpayer or representative of taxpayer, and state specific grounds. A claim filed for or on behalf of a class of taxpayers must meet these requirements, and be accompanied by a written authorization from each taxpayer sought to be included in the class.[3]

How to file. If the corporation wants to initiate a claim for a refund, it will file with the Franchise Tax Board one of the following:

(1) *Form 100X.* Amended corporation franchise or income tax return. This form may be used to file a claim for refund for any year.

(2) *Ordinary letter.* The FTB will accept a letter from the taxpayer as a claim for refund if it states the reason for the claim with enough information so the FTB can process the letter as a claim for refund.

(3) *Payment of tax after filing a protest.* If a taxpayer pays the tax which he has protested before the Franchise Tax Board has acted upon his protest or if the taxpayer has filed an appeal with the State Board of Equalization and the taxpayer pays the tax before the SBE has handled the appeal, the Franchise Tax Board treats the protest or the appeal as a claim for refund.[4]

Failure to mail notice of action on refund claim. If the Franchise Tax Board fails to mail a notice of action on any refund claim within 6 months after the claim is filed, taxpayer may, prior to the mailing the notice of

---

(40) § 19089(b).
(1) § 19074(a).
(2) § 19074(b).

(3) § 19322.
(4) § 19335.

action, consider the claim disallowed, and appeal to the SBE, or bring a refund action. See US Code, Title 11, § 505(a)(2) for substitution of 120-day for 6-month period in Title 11 case.[5]

Payments credited.   If an overpayment of tax is credited against the estimated tax for the succeeding income year, and no claim for credit or refund will be allowed for the income year in which the overpayment arises.

Refunds over $50,000.   Refunds in excess of $50,000 must be approved by the State Board of Control unless the refund arises from (1) the payment of estimated tax, (2) a rate redetermination relating to banks or other financial corporations, or (3) a settlement made by the FTB under the compromise authority provided in Rev & TC § 19442.[6]

¶ 1321   Penalties Imposed

The Bank and Corporation Tax Law imposes the following penalties:

Failure to file return.   Any corporation which fails to file a return on or before the due date (including extensions of time) is assessed a penalty of 5% of the tax for each month or fraction elapsing between the due date of the return and the date filed, with a maximum of 25% of the tax. If any failure to file any return is fraudulent, 15% will be substituted for 5%, and 75% for 25%. This penalty is assessed on the net amount of the tax due on the return. In other words, the amount of tax shown on the return is reduced by the amount of any part of the tax paid on or before the due date of the payment of tax and by any credit against tax that can be claimed on the return. The Franchise Tax Board has the authority to waive the penalty if it can be shown by the taxpayer that the failure to file is due to reasonable cause and not due to willful neglect. Generally speaking, the Franchise Tax Board will accept the same reasons for failure to file that have been acceptable for federal purposes in various court cases.[7]

WARNING   *Filing enforcement fee.* The Franchise Tax Board may impose a filing enforcement fee of $119 if a taxpayer required to file a return required under Part 11 of the Revenue & TC (relating to corporations) fails or refuses to make and file a tax return within 25 days after a formal legal demand to file the return is mailed by the Franchise Tax Board. For fees to be charged during the 1994 calendar year, the amount can be modified to reflect actual costs of filing enforcement as set in the annual Budget Act. The filing enforcement fee is in addition to the failure to file penalty. The amount assessed as a filing enforcement fee will not bear interest.[8] The fee for the 1994–95 fiscal year of the state is $119 for a bank of corporation.

Accuracy-related penalty—general.   For income years starting 1–1–90 and later, California imposes an accuracy-related penalty in accordance with

---

(5) § 19331; 19385; 19388; 19389.
(6) § 19302.

(7) § 19131.
(8) § 19254.

IRC § 6662. It also imposes a fraud penalty in accordance with the provisions of IRC § 6663. The definitions and special rules in IRC § 6664 will apply in California. Applicable provisions of IRC § 6665 will also apply in the state.

Accuracy-related penalty, under IRC § 6662, is 20% of the amount of underpayment of tax, if any portion of the underpayment is attributable to one or more of the following:

(1) negligence or disregard of rules or regulations;
(2) any substantial understatement of income tax;
(3) any substantial valuation overstatement;
(4) any substantial overstatement of pension liabilities.

This rule does not apply to IRC § 6663, relating to the fraud penalty. For the definition of negligence, IRC § 6662(c) applies.[9]

Accuracy-related penalty—substantial understatement of income tax. Under IRC § 6662(d), there is a substantial understatement of income tax for any taxable year if the amount of the understatement for the taxable year exceeds the greater of 10% of the tax required to be shown on the return, or $5,000. In the case of corporations, other than S corporations, or personal holding company, as defined in IRC § 542, substitute $10,000 for $5,000. The term "understatement" means the excess of the amount of the tax required to be shown for the taxable year on the return, over the amount of the tax imposed that is shown on the return, reduced by any IRC § 6211(b)(2) rebate. A reduction of the understatement can be made due to the position of the taxpayer on a disputed item. The abusive tax shelter penalty does not apply if this penalty is assessed.[9]

Accuracy-related penalty—substantial valuation misstatement under Chapter 1. Under IRC § 6662(e), there is a substantial valuation misstatement under Ch. 1 if the value of any property, or the adjusted basis of any property, claimed on any return of tax imposed by that chapter is 200% or more of the amount determined to be the correct amount of such valuation or adjusted basis. California has adopted the federal provisions relating to valuation misstatements on transactions between persons described in IRC § 482, and the net IRC § 482 transfer price adjustments. For purposes of the 400% gross misstatement penalty, substitute 400% for 200%. No penalty applies unless the portion of the underpayment for the taxable year attributable to the substantial valuation misstatement exceeds $5,000 or $10,000 in the case of a corporation other than an S corporation or personal holding company.[9]

Accuracy-related penalty—substantial overstatement of pension liabilities. California adopts IRC § 6662(f). A penalty will apply if the actuarial determination of liabilities taken into account in computing the deduction under IRC § 404(a)(1) or § 404(a)(2) is 200% or more of the amount determined to be correct. For purposes of the 400% gross misstatement penalty,

---

(9) § 19164.

substitute 400% for 200%. No penalty applies unless the underpayment for the taxable year attributable to the substantial overstatement of these liabilities exceeds $1,000.[9]

Accuracy-related penalty—definitions and special rules.   California adopts IRC § 6664, relating to the definition of underpayment, charitable deduction property, qualified appraiser, qualified appraisal, and the special rules on reasonable cause exception and valuation overstatements.[9]

Fraud penalty.   California imposes a fraud penalty as determined by IRC § 6663. Under this federal rule, if any part of any underpayment of tax required to be shown on a return is due to fraud, an amount equal to 75% of the portion of the underpayment attributable to fraud must be added to the tax. If the tax authorities establish that any portion of an underpayment is attributable to fraud, the entire underpayment must be treated as so attributable, except with respect to any portion of the underpayment that the taxpayer establishes, by a preponderance of the evidence, is not so attributable.[10]

Penalty for failure to file corporate organization statement.   If a corporate taxpayer fails to file with the California Secretary of State the annual statement (Form S/0200), the Franchise Tax Board may assess a penalty of $250. The penalty for failure to file the nonprofit corporation report is $50.[11]

Failure to pay tax by the due date.   In case of failure to pay either (1) the amount of tax shown on the return by the due date, without regard to any extension; or (2) any amount in respect of any tax required to be shown on the return that is not so shown, including excess tax assessed due to mathematical error, within 10 days of the date of the notice and demand, unless it is shown that the failure is due to reasonable cause and not willful neglect, a penalty is imposed of (1) 5% of the total tax unpaid; and (2) an amount computed at the rate of ½% per month of the remaining tax for each additional month or fraction during which that tax is greater than zero, not to exceed 25% in the aggregate. No interest shall accrue on the "remaining tax" part of the penalty. "Total tax unpaid" means the amount of tax shown on the return, reduced by the amount of tax paid by the due date, and any credit that may be claimed on the return. "Remaining tax" means the total tax unpaid reduced by the amount of payment. If the amount of tax required to be shown on the return is less than the amount shown, the penalty provisions will be applied by substituting lower amount. Penalty is not assessed if for the same taxable year, the penalties for failure to file, or failure to file after demand are equal to or greater than this penalty for failure to pay the tax.[12]

---

(10) § 19164.
(11) § 19141.

(12) § 19132.

WAIVER OF LATE PAYMENT PENALTIES

Late payment and late filing penalties will be waived for qualified taxpayers who as a result of the Northridge earthquake in January 1994, suffered a (1) significant property loss, (2) a loss of employment due to property damage suffered by his or her employer, or (3) a significant loss of business income from a business located in the Northridge earthquake area. The late payment will be waived only if the tax is paid by an individual, partnership, or fiduciary within 6 months of the original due date of the return, or by a corporation within 7 months from the original due date of the return. The return must be filed timely, including extensions, for the waiver of the late payment penalty to apply.[13]

WARNING

Collection costs. The Franchise Tax Board is empowered to add a fee when any person or bank taxable under Part 11 of the Revenue & TC (relating to corporations) fails to respond to a notice to the person for payment of tax, penalty, addition to tax, interest, or other liability imposed and delinquent. This fee can be imposed only after a notice has been mailed to the person for payment that advises the taxpayer that continued failure to pay the amount due may result in collection action, including the imposition of a collection cost recovery fee. For fees to be charged after 1–1–94, the amount can be modified to reflect actual costs of collection as set forth in the annual Budget Act. The assessment of collection costs is in addition to failure to pay penalty. The amount assessed as a collection fee will not bear interest.[14] The fee for the 1994–95 fiscal year of the state is $183 for banks of corporations.

Substantial understatement by tax preparer—aiding and abetting. Substantial understatement by a tax preparer incurs a $100 penalty if due to negligence or intentional disregard of rules and regulations; $500 if due to willful understatement of liability. California follows IRC § 6694.[15] Aiding and abetting understatements is subject to a $10,000 penalty, if the return, document, affidavit, or claim relates to the tax liability of a corporation; otherwise the penalty is $1,000. Only one penalty per person per period is imposed. California follows IRC § 6701.[16] Aiding and abetting can be enjoined.[17]

Abusive tax shelters. The promotion of abusive tax shelters incurs a penalty of the greater of $1,000 or 10% of gross income derived or to be derived by the promoter. California follows IRC § 6700.[18] Abusive tax shelter promotion may be enjoined.[17]

---

(13) § 19132.5, as added by Stats. 1994, c. 735, § 2.

(14) § 19254.

(15) § 19166.

(16) § 19178.

(17) § 19715.

(18) § 19177.

Filing frivolous returns.   California adopts IRC § 6702 imposing a $500 penalty for filing a frivolous return. A taxpayer must pay the entire penalty before bringing a suit for relief from the penalty.[19]

The basis of the penalty is the correct net tax due on the proper filing date.[20]

Effect of extension.   An underpayment of tax existing at the regular due date isn't excused because an extension is granted.[21]

Single penalty rule.   If a taxpayer could be assessed a penalty for failure to file a return on time and a penalty for failure to pay the tax shown on that return on time, the only penalty which will be assessed will be the larger of the two. The same thing is true for failure to pay a tax on a deficiency with an assessment for a penalty for failure to file information or a return on notice and demand or a deficiency due to negligence or a deficiency due to fraud. In other words, either the penalty for failure to pay or the failure to furnish the information will be assessed, whichever is the larger.[22]

Title 11, USC case pending.   No addition to tax shall be made under Rev & TC § 19132 or 19142 for failure to pay tax on time with respect to a period case was pending under Title 11 of US Code (1) if the tax was incurred by the estate and failure occurred pursuant to an order of the court finding probable insufficiency of funds of the estate to pay administrative expenses; or (2) if such tax was incurred by the debtor before the earlier of the relief, or, in an involuntary case, the appointment of a trustee, and the petition was filed before the due date, including extensions, for filing the return, or the date for making the addition to tax occurs on or after the day on which the petition was filed. This rule does not apply to liability for addition to tax arising from failure to pay or deposit tax withheld and required to be paid to California.[23]

Information with respect to certain foreign-owned corporations.   California has also adopted the IRC §§ 6038A, 6038B, and 6038C rules relating to information reporting and record maintenance to all foreign corporations doing business in the U.S. The penalty imposed for failure to furnish information or maintain records is $10,000 for each tax year for which the failure occurs. The penalty can be increased if the failure continues after notification for more than 90 days after tax authorities mail the notice of failure. The increase is $10,000 for each 30-day period after the 90-day period above that the failure continues. Information required to be filed with the FTB must be a copy of the information filed with the IRS. The information required is specified in IRC § 6038A(b). Definitions of terms are in IRC § 6038A(c). Enforcement of requests for certain records is in IRC § 6038A(e). See ¶ 1278 for details of reporting requirement.[24]

---

(19) § 19179.
(20) LR 381, 4–1–75.
(21) LR 392, 10–30–76.

(22) § 19132.
(23) § 19161.
(24) §§ 19141.5; 19135.

Whenever any foreign corporation that fails to qualify to do business in California, or whose powers, rights and privileges have been forfeited, or any domestic corporation has been suspended, does business in California and fails to make and file a return, the Franchise Tax Board must impose a penalty of $2,000 per income year, unless the failure is due to reasonable cause, and not willful neglect. This penalty is in addition to any other penalty. This penalty will be imposed if return is not filed within 60 days after the FTB's notice and demand.[24]

Bad checks. The provisions of IRC § 6657, relating to bad checks will apply in California. Under this federal IRC section, a penalty of 2% of the amount of the check is payable on notice and demand of the administrative authorities by the person tendering the check. The penalty is $15, or the amount of the check, whichever is less, if the check is less than $750. The penalty does not apply if tender was made in good faith and with reasonable cause to believe it would be paid.[25] California has modified the federal rules to include credit card remittance's and electronic funds transfers that are not paid when presented to the financial institution upon which they are drawn.[26]

Cash received in trade or business. The penalty for failure to file the information return required by Rev & TC § 18645, relating to cash received in trade or business will be determined according to IRC § 6721. Under that IRC section, a $50 penalty is imposed for each return not filed before the due date, and for failure to include all required information. The total amount imposed cannot exceed $250,000. The penalty is reduced where correction is made within 30 days of the due date, or by August 1 of due date calendar year.[27]

Criminal penalties. In addition to above, Rev & TC §§ 19705—19715 provide severe fines, and in some cases jail sentences for criminal and willful violations of the laws with respect to filing false returns, failing to file returns, failing to collect and pay withheld taxes, supplying false information, etc.[28]

WARNING   These criminal penalties can also be applied to those who willfully aid, assist, counsel, or offers advise which results in the filing of a false return, claim, document, etc.

Original issue discount reporting requirements of Rev & TC § 18649. The penalty for failure to meet these requirements is determined by the provisions of IRC § 6706. Under that federal section, the penalty for failure to show information on debt instruments is $50 per instrument, unless reasonable cause and not wilful neglect is shown. The penalty for failure to

---

(25) § 19134.
(26) § 19134.

(27) § 18645.
(28) § 19705—19515.

furnish information to authorities is 1% of aggregate price of the issue, not to exceed $50,000 for such issue. Reasonable cause will excuse.[29]

Waiver—reliance on board opinion.   The Franchise Tax Board is required to waive interest, additions to tax, and penalties if it determines that the following conditions are satisfied: (1) taxpayer or its representative requested in writing an opinion as to the tax consequences of particular acts or activities contemplated, setting forth all the pertinent facts; (2) based on the facts presented and the applicable law, the FTB issued a written opinion as to the tax consequences that was reasonably relied on when the activities were started and the action taken; (3) the tax consequences were not later changed by a change in statutory law, case law, federal interpretation on which the FTB's opinion was based, or the material facts or circumstances relating to taxpayer. Taxpayer seeking relief must file the required documents, including the request and opinion. Misrepresentation or omission of one or more material facts makes this rule inapplicable. Waiver extends only to penalties and interest attributable to actions taken after receipt of the opinion.[30]

¶ 1322   Accumulated Earnings Tax

IRC §§ 531—537 provide for a tax to be imposed on a corporation formed or availed of for the purpose of avoiding the income tax to its principal individual shareholders by accumulating rather than distributing its earnings and profits. That is, an accumulation beyond the reasonable needs of the business. The Federal tax is imposed on the income of the current year with some adjustments less the dividends paid and the accumulated earnings credit. California has not adopted the provisions for this type of penalty tax.

¶ 1323   Disclosure of Information

Provisions cover

    (1) misdemeanor to divulge business income or business affairs of taxpayer;
    (2) availability of exemption application to public inspection;
    (3) disclosure of standards or data used to select returns for audit;
    (4) disclosure under judicial order;
    (5) furnishing information to government officials, including tax authorities of other states;
    (6) restrictions on disclosure; and
    (7) certain disclosures allowed.[31]

Exchange agreement with Mexico.   Effective 1–1–94, California tax authorities are authorized to exchange tax information with Mexican taxing authorities, if a reciprocal agreement between the two agencies exists, Mexican authorities will receive information from California only on Mexican nationals. California will receive information only on California residents.[32]

---

(29) § 19180.
(30) § 21012.

(31) §§ 19542—19565.
(32) § 19551.

¶ 1324   **Taxpayers' Bill of Rights**

Rev & TC §§ 21001–21022 governing assessment, audit, and collection of corporation income taxes by the Franchise Tax Board provide for the protection of the privacy of taxpayers and the protection of their property rights. The FTB must establish the position of Taxpayers' Rights Advocate to coordinate resolution of taxpayer complaints and problems. The FTB must also develop a taxpayer education and information program. Annually, it must systematically identify areas of taxpayer noncompliance. When explaining procedures and remedies to taxpayers, the FTB must use simple nontechnical language. Performance of officers and employees in contact with taxpayers must be evaluated by FTB. A plan must be developed to reduce the time required to resolve refund claims, protests, and appeals. Other provisions cover waiver of interest, protest hearing procedure, reimbursement for reasonable fees and expenses, restriction on surveillance, release of levy, exemptions from levy, reimbursement of bank charges after erroneous levy, filing and recording of liens, notice of suspension, penalties for reckless disregard of FTB procedures, and extension of time for filing.[33]

¶ 1325   **Other Collection Remedies**

The Franchise Tax Board can issue a warrant for the collection of any tax or the enforcement of any lien. Taxes may also be collected by seizure and sale. Collection suits may be brought to collect delinquent taxes. The FTB can use debt collection services outside the state. It can also enter into agreements with one or more persons for the collection of delinquent accounts.[34]

Miscellaneous provisions deal with cumulative remedies, priorities of tax claims and judgment for tax. Also covered are powers and duties of the FTB, examinations of books, papers and testimony, subpoenas, preservation of reports or returns, filing on magnetic media, and reward programs.[35]

¶ 1326   **Voluntary Disclosure Program for Business Entities**

Effective August 26, 1994, the State of California has adopted a voluntary disclosure program which allows business entities, other than those organized under the laws of the state of California, or those which have qualified to do business in California, to enter into negotiations with the Franchise Tax Board for the waiver of taxes, additions to tax, fees, or penalties with respect to each taxable or income year ending prior to six years from the signing date of the voluntary disclosure agreement. For the first six years prior to the signing of the voluntary disclosure agreement, the Franchise Tax Board could waive certain specified penalties.

The FTB is to provide guidelines and establish procedures for business entities to apply for voluntary disclosure agreements. They are to accept

---

(33) § 21001–21022.
(34) § 19221;   19231—19235;   19262—19263;
19371—19378.

(35) § 19251—19253; 19201; 19501—19531.

applications on an anonymous basis. In determining if a voluntary disclosure agreement is to be accepted, the FTB is to consider:

(1) the nature and magnitude of the business entity's previous presence and activity in California and the circumstances by which the nexus of the business entity as established,

(2) the extent to which the weight of the factual circumstances demonstrates that a prudent business person exercising reasonable care would conclude that the previous activities and presence in California were or were not immune from taxation by California by reason of Public Law 86–272, or otherwise,

(3) reliance on the advice of a person in a fiduciary position or other competent advise that the business entity's activities were immune from taxation by California,

(4) lack of evidence of a willful disregard or neglect of the tax laws of California,

(5) demonstration of good faith on the part of the business entity, and

(6) the benefits accruing to California by entering into a voluntary disclosure agreement.

The voluntary disclosure agreement is to be acted upon with 120 days of receipt.

If a voluntary disclosure agreement is accepted, then the FTB shall waive its authority to assess or propose to assess taxes, additions to tax, fees, or penalties with respect to each taxable or income year ending prior to six years from the signing date of the voluntary disclosure agreement. In addition with respect to each of the six taxable or income years ending immediately preceding the signing date of the voluntary disclosure agreement, the FTB may exercise its discretion to waive any or all of the following penalties: failure to file, failure to pay, any penalty for underpayment of estimated tax, failure to maintain records, and any penalty related to contract viodability.

Businesses will be eligible for a voluntary disclosure agreement if they meet all of the following criteria:

(1) they are a bank, or corporation, and

(2) the business entity, including any predecessors to the business entity, had never filed a return with the FTB, and

(3) the business entity, including any predecessors to the business entity, had never been subject to an inquiry by the FTB with respect to any tax liability on its income, and

(4) the business entity voluntarily comes forward prior to any unilateral contact from the FTB, and makes application in the form and manner proscribed by the FTB, and

(5) makes a full and accurate statement of its activities in California for the six immediately preceding taxable or income years.

A business is ineligible to qualify if it is organized and existing under the laws of the state of California, is otherwise qualified or registered with the California Secretary of State's office, or maintains and staffs a permanent facility in California other then the storing of materials, goods, or products in a public warehouse in California.

¶ 1326

Rev & TC § 19194 sets forth the circumstances which will make a voluntary disclosure agreement null and void.[36]

---

(36) § 19191 & 19192, as added by Stats. 1994, c. 367, § 2.

CHAPTER **23**

VALUATION, ASSESSMENT, PROPOSITION 13

¶ 3001   **Introduction**

The laws governing the imposition of property taxes in California are part of the California Revenue and Taxation Code. Amendments to the law are made by the California legislature. Nevertheless, except for certain intercounty and utility property, the property taxes are not administered, assessed or collected by a state agency, but rather by local tax authorities. The California State Board of Equalization, in addition to acting in its position of equalizing property taxes between various districts or counties of the state (Rev & TC § 1815 et seq.) plays a minor role in assessing taxes. The SBE annually assesses canals, ditches, pipelines and aqueducts lying within two or more counties, and property owned or used by regulated railway, telegraph or telephone companies, car companies operating on railways and companies transmitting or selling gas or electricity.[1]

Political subdivisions which assess and collect property taxes in California are the various counties, and certain cities which have not agreed to have the county perform the assessment and collection functions. Unlike the situation in many other states, in California the County Assessor of each county performs the assessment function for the county, the cities within the county and the special school, irrigation and other districts within the limits of the county.[2]

¶ 3002   **Administering the Tax**

The County Assessor has primary responsibility for valuing and assessing all taxable property in the county.[3]

The County Board of Supervisors is responsible for ensuring that the values of property throughout the county are assessed equitably. The county board is authorized to sit as an appeal body to hear protests as to valuation. Counties can set up Assessment Appeals Boards to equalize the values of property on the local assessment rolls by adjusting individual assessments.[4]

The Auditor-Controller receives the assessment roll from the Assessor and extends the taxes on it.[5]

The Tax Collector prepares and distributes tax bills.[6]

Mandatory audits by the assessor. When trade fixtures and business tangible personal property owned by a taxpayer engaged in a profession, trade or business has a full value of $300,000 or more, the assessor is required to audit the books and records at least once every four years.[7]

¶ 3003   **Who Is Taxable**

All real property is assessed to the owner. Assessment is done in the same manner whether it is owned by individuals or business corporations. The

---

(1) Const Art XIII, § 19.
(2) § 128.
(3) § 128; 601.
(4) § 1601–1630.

(5) § 1646.
(6) § 2601; 2610.5; 5; 2611; 2611.5.
(7) § 469.

land and the improvements to the land are separately assessed. Cultivated and uncultivated lands of the same quality and similarly situated are assessed at the same value. For more details, see *Assessments* ¶ 3008.

Possessory interest.   This is an interest in real property which exists as a result of possession, exclusive use or right to possession or exclusive use of land and/or improvements unaccompanied by the ownership of a fee simple or life estate in the property.[8] Rev & TC § 107[9] defines possessory interests as follows: (a) possession of, claim to or right to the possession of land or improvements, except when coupled with ownership of the land or improvements in the same person; (b) taxable improvements on tax-exempt land. Possessory interests are not ordinarily assessed separately from the fee interest. An exception occurs when the owner of the fee interest is a nontaxable government entity. When valuing possessory interests in real property created by the right to place wires, conduits, and appurtenances along or across public streets, rights-of-way, or public easements contained in a cable television franchise or license, the assessor must value these possessory interests consistent with the full value requirements of Rev & TC § 401. Methods of valuation include, but are not limited to, the comparable sales method, the income method, or the cost method. The preferred method of valuation is the capitalization of annual rent, using the appropriate rate.[10]

¶ 3004   **Property Taxable**

Generally.   Property includes all matters and things, real, personal and mixed, capable of private ownership.[11] All property in the state, not exempt under U.S. or state laws, is taxable.[12] Realty and tangible personalty are taxed except when exemptions apply.[13] Intangible personalty isn't taxed (see below). "Interest" in any property includes any legal or equitable interest.[14]

For examples of exempt intangibles and taxable tangible personalty existing in the same property, see the discussion of copyrights, computer programs, and records below.

Timber and race horses.   Timber and race horses are specially taxed (see ¶ 3012).

Imported property.   Imported personal property from outside the United States was subject to property tax by a state even though the property was being sorted by size and type at the warehouse of the wholesale distributor. After the items were sorted they were to be shipped to dealers in a number of other states. The court held that the protection afforded under the Import-Export Clause of the U.S. Constitution did not protect the goods from a nondiscriminatory property tax since they were no longer in import transit (*Michelin Tire Corp. v. Wages et al. (1976) 423 US 276*).

---

(8) Reg 21.
(9) § 107.
(10) § 107.7.
(11) § 103.

(12) § 201.
(13) Art XIII, § 1.
(14) § 115.

A property tax exemption for goods manufactured outside the United States and brought into California for storage and reshipment to customers outside California discriminated against similar goods manufactured in California and stored in California pending shipment out-of-state. The state exemption for foreign goods was found to be in violation of the Commerce Clause of the U.S. Constitution and was therefore invalid (*Zee Toys, Inc. v. County of Los Angeles; Sears, Roebuck & Co. v. County of Los Angeles, (1978) 85 Cal 3d 763; 149 Cal Rptr 750*)

Real property. "Real property" is defined as including the possession of, claim to, ownership of or right to possession of land, and included are all mines, minerals, quarries and improvements. Improvements include buildings, structures, fixtures and fences, fruit, nut-bearing or ornamental trees and vines, which are not of natural growth and not exempted (except date palms under eight years of age are not included).[15]

IMPORTANT

Fixtures. A fixture is an item of tangible property, the nature of which was originally personalty, but which is classified as realty for property tax purposes because it is physically or constructively annexed to realty with the intent that it remain annexed indefinitely. The manner of annexation, the adaptability of the item to the purpose for which the realty is used, and the intent with which the annexation is made are important elements in deciding whether the item has become a fixture or remains personal property. Proper classification as a fixture or as personal property, results from a determination made by applying these criteria to the facts in each case. Reg 122.5[16] explains physical annexation, constructive annexation, and intent, and gives examples. Reg 124[17] includes a list of items which have been classified as either land or improvements.

Tangible personal property. All property that may be seen, weighed, measured, felt, touched, or is in any other way perceptible to the senses—except land and improvements—is tangible personal property.[18]

Property which is movable within and without the county is assessed as follows:

● *Aircraft.* Aircraft of United States registry operated by certificated air carriers and flown in intrastate, interstate or foreign commerce, is assessed by the county assessors where the aircraft normally touch down, based on an allocation formula. The formula is composed of two factors: (1) ground and flight time, and (2) aircraft arrival and departures. The factor of ground and flight time is weighted at 75% and the factor of arrivals and departures from airports is weighted at 25% to obtain the allocation ratio to be applied to the full cash value of the aircraft.[19] Specific information is set forth in Reg 202.[20]

● *Vessels.* Vessels are ordinarily assessed by the county where they are habitually moored. If a vessel is documented in a county different from the resi-

---

(15) § 104; 105.
(16) Reg 122.5.
(17) Reg 124.

(18) § 106; Reg 123.
(19) § 1150–1152.
(20) Reg 202.

dence of the owner, the owner gives written notice to the assessor that the vessel is moored in a different county so that it will not be taxed by both assessors. Ferry boats connecting points in more than one county are assessed in equal proportion by the counties they connect. Wharves, storehouses and stationary property connected with the ferry boat are assessed by the county in which that property is located. Vessels other than ferry boats regularly engaged in transporting passengers or cargo between two or more ports and vessels concerning which notice of habitual place of mooring has not been given are assessed only in the county where documented. Vessels which are not required to be documented are assessed in the county where they are habitually moored.[21]

● *Movable property.* Property which is intended to be and is moved from time to time from one location to another has a situs (or tax location; i.e., place where it is assessed) for tax purposes determined as follows: (1) it has a situs where it is located on the lien date if it has been in the county for more than six of the 12 months immediately preceding the lien date, and if it is to remain in that county for any substantial period during the following 12 months; (2) property which has been in the county for less than six of the 12 prior months which is committed to use in the county for an indeterminate time or for more than six months, has a situs in the county; and (3) property which does not have a situs or location on the lien date as indicated above has a situs at the location where it is normally returned between uses.[22]

● *Leased property.* Property leased or rented on a daily, weekly or short-term basis has a situs or tax location at the place where the lessor normally keeps the property. Property leased for an extended but unspecified period or for a lease of more than six months, has a situs on the basis of the lessee's use.[23]

Intangible personal property. This category of property is *exempt* from taxation and includes money, notes, debentures, shares of capital stock, solvent credits, bonds, deeds of trust, mortgages and any interest in similar property.[24] The taxable status of copyrights, business records and computer programs are explained below.

Copyright. Copyright is not subject to tax. In a leading case, *Michael Todd Co. v. Los Angeles (1962) 57 C 2d 684, 21 Cal Rptr 604* the court concluded that a film negative was taxable as personal property, based on the production costs of the film. The Court indicated that the value of the copyright itself was not being taxed. The full value of motion pictures, including negatives and prints, for purposes of assessing property tax is limited to the value of the tangible materials upon which the motion pictures are recorded.[25] It does not include the value of or any value based on any intangible rights such as a copyright or the right to reproduce.

TAX TIP   The State Board of Equalization has held that the intangible attributes (technology) may be considered by assessors in valuing real and tangible personal property for property tax purposes (*Mike Todd Co. v. County of Los Angeles, 57 Cal 2d 684; 21 Cal Rptr 604*). The assessors use of a capitalized flow of value method of appraisal has been upheld for cable television companies (*Cox Cable San Diego, Inc. v. County of San Diego*

---

(21) § 1136–1141.   (24) § 212.
(22) Reg 205.   (25) § 988.
(23) Reg 204(a).

(1986) 229 Cal Rptr 839; Stanislaus County v. Assessment Appeals Board (1992, unpublished)) and for companies with possessory interests (*Hertz Corporation v. County of San Diego, November, 1992, unpublished).*

Business records. The cash value of business records for property taxation is the cash value only of the tangible material in which the records are recorded, maintained or stored. The following items are not included in the definition of business records: (1) books, (2) old newspapers on microfilm, (3) computer programs and storage media, otherwise taxable, (4) records which are held for sale in the ordinary course of business.[26]

Computer programs. Computer programs other than "basic operational programs" are exempt from taxation, although the storage media for computer programs are taxable. The storage media include such things as punch cards, tapes, discs or drums on which the computer programs are stored. Computer program is defined in Rev & TC § 995[27] as a set of written instructions, magnetic imprints, required documentation or other process designed to enable the user to communicate with or operate a computer or other machinery. Tax applies to "basic operational program" or "control program" (the terms are interchangeable) which is defined as a program which controls the operation of a computer by managing the allocation of all system resources including the central processing unit, main storage, input/output devices and processing programs. The law[28] defines terms and excludes selected programs from the category of taxable basic operational systems, including programs for payroll, inventory control and production control.

Motor vehicles. Automobiles, trucks and other items of motor equipment are assessed fees. These fees consist of a registration fee under the Motor Vehicle Code, and a license fee under the Revenue and Taxation Code. The license fee is in lieu of property tax on vehicles subject to registration—whether or not registered.[29]

Mobile homes and manufactured homes. Mobile homes and manufactured homes on permanent foundations are taxed as real property. Mobile homes and manufactured homes first sold new after 7–1–80, and mobile homes and manufactured homes that were, at the request of the owner following notification of the Department of Housing and Community Development and the assessor, made subject to personal property taxation are subject to personal property taxation under Rev & TC §§ 5800–5842. All other mobile homes and manufactured homes are subject to motor vehicle license fee.[30]

---

(26) § 997.
(27) § 995.
(28) § 995.2.

(29) § 10758.
(30) §§ 5800–5842; 10758.

¶ 3004A   **Rebate of Tax On Economic Revitalization Manufacturing Property**

The governing body of a local agency will have the authority for fiscal years 1994–1995 and thereafter, to rebate all or a portion of the personal property tax on economic revitalization manufacturing property [ERMP]. The rebate shall continue for the first five years after the property was placed in service.

Qualifying ERMP. Qualifying ERMP is tangible personal property which meets the following requirements: (1) the property is directly involved in the manufacturing process in California, and is not in a preliminary or subsequent activity, or one incidental to manufacturing, and (2) use of the property will lead to the creation of at least 10 new full-time manufacturing jobs or positions at salary levels of at least $10 per hour (or $20,000 per year), and those jobs will continue in existence for a continuous five-year period.

Manufacturing process. Manufacturing means the activity of converting or conditioning property by changing the form, composition, quality, or character of the property for ultimate sale at retail or use in the manufacturing of a product to be ultimately sold at retail.

Creating new jobs. The 10 new jobs must be created in California. Detailed rules are provided for measuring the number of new jobs. It is not clear in the legislation if the 10 new jobs must be created in the year the property is placed in service. Only property acquired on or after 1–1–94, shall be eligible for rebate.

Recapture of rebate. The rebate will be recaptured if at any time within five years after granting a rebate the recipient taxpayer no longer uses the manufacturing property in a manufacturing process as described above, or the required increase in jobs has not occurred.[31]

¶ 3005   **Exempt Property**

The California Constitution[32] lists the following property as being exempt from property taxation:

(a) Property owned by the state of California.
(b) Property owned by a local government.
(c) Bonds issued by the state or a local government in the state.
(d) Property used for libraries and museums that are free and open to the public, and property that is used exclusively for public schools, community colleges, state colleges and state universities.
(e) Buildings, land, equipment, and securities used exclusively for educational purposes by a non-profit institution of higher education.
(f) Buildings, land on which they are situated, and equipment used exclusively for religious worship.
(g) Cemetery property.
(h) Growing crops.
(i) Fruit and nut trees under the age of four years and grapevines under the age of three years.
(j) Immature forest trees.

---

(31) § 5108.   (32) Calif. Constitution, Article XIII, § 3.

¶ **3005**

(k) Homeowners exemption. $7,000 of the full value of the principal residence of the owner is exempt. The exemption does not apply if the owner received an exemption as a veteran or disabled or blind veteran. The exemption includes a multiple dwelling unit if the owner occupies one of the units as his principal residence, and also applies to a condominium or cooperative apartment occupied by the owner.

(l) Vessels of more than 50 tons engaged in the transportation of freight or passengers.

(m) Household furnishings and personal effects not used in connection with a trade or business.

(n) Any debt secured by land.

(o) Property in the amount of $4,000 owned by a veteran, his widow, his parents, if he is deceased. The exemption is not available to an individual who owns more than $5,000 in property value or a married person, who, together with his spouse, owns property valued at $10,000 or more.

For the 1994–95 and 1995–96 property tax fiscal years, $40,000 of the full value of the property which is owned by, and is the principal place of residence of, a veteran or the unmarried surviving spouse of a veteran, in the case of a veteran who was blind in both eyes or had lost the use of two or more limbs, is exempt from tax. The exempt amount is increased to $100,000 of full value in the case of a veteran who was totally disabled. The deceased veteran which results in the eligibility of the surviving spouse would have had to qualify in all respects for the exemption under the laws effective on 1–1–77, except that the veteran died prior to 1–1–77, or died of a service connected disease. The $40,000 exempt amount is raised to $60,000, and the $100,000 is increased to $150,000 if the household income (as defined in Rev & TC § 20504) of the unmarried surviving spouse does not exceed that amount set forth in Rev & TC § 20585, which is currently $24,000.

For subsequent fiscal years, the exemption is limited to $40,000 and $100,000 as described above without the increased exemption amount based on income.[33]

TAX TIP

Homeowner exemption—1991 fire storms and 1992 civil disturbance. The homeowners exemption can normally be claimed only if the homeowner occupies the property as their primary residence on March 1 of each year, and the property is not rented, vacant, or under construction. The homeowners exemption will not be denied however, if the property is temporarily damaged, destroyed, or is being reconstructed as a result of fires occurring between October 20, and November 1, 1992 in a disaster area as declared by the Governor, or as a result of fire occurring during a civil disturbance in California in April or May, 1992, which was declared a disaster by the Governor. To qualify under these special rules, the

---

(33) § 205.5.

property must not have changed ownership since the commencement of the fire or civil disturbance.[34]

Filing claims for exemption. In some cases it is necessary for the property owner listed in the above exemption categories to annually file a claim for exemption. Forms for the filing are provided by the Assessor's office and are required as follows:

- Aircraft of historical significance exemption (Rev & TC § 220.5), April 1;
- Artistic works on public display (Rev & TC § 217(b)), file by March 15;
- Cemetery exemption (Rev & TC § 256.5), March 15;
- Church exemption (Rev & TC § 256), and religious exemption (§ 257), March 31;
- College exemption (Rev & TC § 258), March 15;
- Disabled veteran's exemption (Rev & TC § 277), April 15;
- Homeowner's exemption (Rev & TC § 253.5), April 15;
- Property on exhibit (Rev & TC § 259), March 15;
- Vessels (documented) (Rev & TC § 254), April 1;
- Veteran's exemption (Rev & TC § 252), April 15;
- Veteran's organization exemption (Rev & TC § 254.5), March 15;
- Welfare exemption (Rev & TC § 254.5), March 15.[35]

An applicant granted the welfare exemption, and owning any property exempted under Rev & TC § 231 (property owned by a nonprofit organization and leased to government) need not reapply for exemption in any later year in which there has been no transfer of, or change in title to exempted property, and the property is used exclusively by a government entity for its use and benefit.[36]

CAUTION   Partial exemptions.

Failure to file the exemption application by the date specified above may not be fatal. Alternative late filing dates for some of the exemptions are available which, if the criteria for receiving the exemption are met, results in a partial allowance of the applicable exemption. The practitioner should refer to the statutes for the particular exemption to determine if alternative filing dates are available.[37]

National and state banks. In addition, Article XIII, Section 27[38] of the California Constitution provides that national and state banks will pay property taxes only on their real property.

Statutory exemptions. Other types of property exempt from taxation under various sections of the Revenue and Taxation Code are as follows:

Aircraft. Any aircraft which is in California on the lien date solely for the purpose of being repaired, overhauled or modified is exempt from property taxation, unless it is normally based in California or operated intrastate

---

(34) §§ 218; 218.1.
(35) § 251; 255.
(36) § 254.5.

(37) § 270–286.
(38) Calif Const Art XIII, § 27.

or interstate in and into California.[39] So is aircraft of historical significance made available for public display. The exemption extends only to the individual owner who does not hold the aircraft primarily for purposes of sale and does not use the aircraft for commercial purposes or general transportation.[40] Aircraft made available for display in a publicly owned aerospace museum, or museum operated by qualified nonprofit corporation regularly open to the public are also exempt. The aircraft must have been restored or maintained, whether or not certified, or have been donated to the museum in perpetuity.[1]

Cargo containers. Cargo containers principally used for the transportation of cargo by vessels in ocean commerce are exempt from property tax.[2] The exemption does not apply to a cargo-carrying vehicle subject to the registration provisions of the California Vehicle Code. Description of the "container" is included in the code.

Hand tools used owned by an employee as a condition of employment. Up to $20,000 of the assessed value of hand-held implements and equipment, including hand-held power tools, necessary for the ordinary and regular performance of the employee's work, are exempt from tax. The tools must be owned by the employee such that the employee will continue to own the tools following the termination of employment.[3]

Nonprofit educational TV and FM broadcasting. All personal property owned or leased by such an organization and used exclusively in the production of programs as a noncommercial educational broadcast is exempt from taxation.[4]

Noncommercial vessels. A vessel with a market value of $400 or less is to be free from taxation if it is used or held for noncommercial purposes. The exemption does not apply to lifeboats or other vessels used in conjunction with operation of larger vessels.[5]

Property used exclusively for the preservation of plants or animals. Property which is used exclusively for the preservation of native plants or animals, biotic communities, geological or geographical formations of scientific or educational interest, or open-space lands used solely for recreation and for the enjoyment of scenic beauty, which is open to the general public, and is owned and operated by a scientific or charitable entity, may be exempt from property tax if the requirements of Rev & TC § 214.02 are met.

Welfare (religious, hospital, scientific, charitable, educational) exemption. An exemption from property taxes is available for property used exclusively for religious, hospital or charitable purposes and owned or held in trust by corporations or other entities, that (i) are organized and operating

---

(39) § 220.
(40) § 220.5.
(1) § 217.1.
(2) § 232.

(3) § 241, as added by Stats. 1994, c. 527, § 1.
(4) § 215.5.
(5) § 228.

for those purposes (occasional fund-raising activities will not disqualify), (ii) are non-profit, and, (iii) no part of whose net earnings inures to the benefit of any private shareholder or individual. Included is property used exclusively for these purposes if it is in the course of construction, including the land on which the facilities are located.[6]

Among the types of property specifically exempt under the welfare exemption is property used exclusively for nursery school purposes owned and operated by religious, hospital or charitable funds, property used exclusively for a noncommercial educational FM broadcast station, or educational television station, owned and operated by religious, hospital, scientific or charitable funds. The list also includes property used exclusively for housing and related facilities for elderly or handicapped families and financed by the federal government and owned and operated by religious, hospital, scientific or charitable funds, foundations, corporations, or by a qualifying veterans' organization. Low-income rental housing and emergency or temporary shelters and related facilities for homeless persons are exempt. Property leased for a term of 35 years or more, or any transfer of property leased with remaining term of 35 years or more, used solely and exclusively for rental housing and related facilities for persons of low income, is exempt if leased and operated by religious, charitable, or scientific funds, foundations, organizations, or by a qualifying veterans' organization. A determination of exemption under IRC § 501(c)(3) must have been received. Operation in accordance with exempt purpose is required. Exemption under the welfare exemption provisions also includes schools of "less than collegiate grades." Such schools provide teaching for students who are exempted from attendance at a public, full-time elementary or secondary day school under sections of the Educational Code and which are operated exclusively by religious, hospital, or charitable funds or organizations.[6]

A golf course used by students and faculty for physical education courses, intercollegiate and intramural college competition, and by alumni and the public for recreational and social purposes qualified for exemption from property tax as part of the educational property associated with the university. Its use by alumni and the public did not disqualify the property from its primary commitment to legitimate educational purposes (*Board of Trustees of The Leland Stanford Junior University v. County of Santa Clara, 86 Cal App 3d 79; 150 Cal Rptr 109*).

Exemptions are also provided in the Revenue and Taxation Code for real property of veterans organizations used for charitable purposes and all of their personal property; housing and related facilities for employees of religious, charitable, scientific, or hospital organizations; property of volunteer fire departments; property of the civil air patrol; disabled veterans; property open to the public and preserved in its natural state, etc. aircraft made available for display in aerospace museum, artistic works on public

---

(6) § 214.

display, property owned by nonprofit corporation and leased to government, property owned by nonprofit entity solely owned by transit development board, property used or possessed by nonprofit corporation in conduct of agricultural fair, property owned by nonprofit entity, devoted to public purposes, in which chartered city of over 750,000 population has sole ownership interest, property used for museum purposes, and certain possessory interests and fee interests in the City of Palm Springs devoted to conventions and related purposes.[7]

The derivation of unrelated business taxable income by an organization entitled to welfare exemption will result in a proportionate reduction of the value of the property subject to exemption.[7]

Inventories.   Business inventories are exempt. Business inventories include goods intended for sale or lease, and raw materials and work in process in respect to such goods. Inventory also includes goods held by contract and not yet incorporated into realty. Animals and crops held for sale or lease are included. Inventory also includes business machinery and equipment held for sale in ordinary course of business[8], but does not include office furniture and equipment which is not held for sale in the ordinary course of business.

Tangible personal property held for lease is included as inventory and is exempt from tax. Tangible personal property actually leased on the lien date is subject to tax, as is any property held by the lessor for lease but with the intent of the lessor to use the property prior to or subsequent to the lease.[8]

Bookstore property of schools and colleges.   This property will be subject to property tax in the ratio of the store's unrelated business taxable income to its gross income as applied to the bookstore's property.[9]

Qualified computer equipment.   All the computer equipment of the San Diego Supercomputer Center located on the campus of the University of California, San Diego, is exempt, including supercomputer and other equipment related to the system.[10]

¶ 3006   **Returns—Reports**

Property statement.   The State Board of Equalization provides a form for business to file with the county assessors setting forth the information on the value of business personal property it owns. The form is designated as a Business Property Affidavit. Many of the California counties, however, have their own form of property statement, including supplemental schedules. The property statement has the usual declaration that it is prepared and signed under penalty of perjury. It is to be filed with the assessor generally between the lien date, March 1 and the last Friday in May, though the

---

(7) § 201.1; 201.2; 201.3; 201.4; 205.5; 213.6; 213.7; 214.02; 214.05; 214.14; 215; 215.1; 217; 217.1; 231; 236.

(8) § 129; 219.
(9) § 202–203.
(10) § 226.

Assessor may require a date earlier than the last Friday in May (but not earlier than April 1 each year).

A signed property statement must be filed with the county assessor by each person owning taxable personal property with an aggregate cost of $30,000 or more for the initial assessment year, and by other owners of personal or real property, if requested by the assessor. For years subsequent to the initial assessment year, a signed property statement is not required unless the aggregate cost of the property exceeds $100,000, or the property statement is requested by the assessor. The statement should show all of the taxable property owned, claimed, possessed, controlled or managed by the person filing it and required to be reported on the form. The property statement should show a description of the property in the detail required, including the cost if it is known or can be determined from available records.[11]

Penalty for late filing. If a person is required to file the property statement by the due date, or if, after written request by the assessor, a person fails to file an annual property statement within the time specified, a penalty of 10% of the assessed value of the unreported taxable tangible personal property of the person is assessed. The penalty can be abated if the person establishes to the satisfaction of the county Board of Equalization or the Assessment Appeals Board that the failure to file the statement was due to reasonable cause and not due to willful neglect.[12]

¶ 3007   **Valuation**

Property is valued (and assessed) as of its lien date according to its full cash value.[13] However, the full cash value of realty (and personalty by virtue of Cal. Const. Art XIII, § 2) is equivalent to its fair market value as of the 1975 lien date or as of the date it's purchased or newly built after the 1975 lien date (2% inflation factor may be added annually). See "Proposition 13" at ¶ 3020 for a fuller explanation.

Commercial fishing, or research vessels. Documented vessels are assessed at 4% of their full cash value if the vessel is used: (1) for the taking and possession of fish and other living resource of the sea for commercial purposes; (2) as an oceanographic research vessel for instruction or research studies; or, (3) to carry or transport seven or more people for hire for commercial passenger fishing purposes and holds a current certificate of inspection issued by the U.S. Coast Guard for this purpose (more than 85% of the total operating time as logged in the immediate preceding assessment year must meet the specifically described activities for the commercial passenger fishing use to qualify).[14]

Historical structures. The owner of a qualified historical property may contract with a city, and/or county which has created a historical zone, to

---

(11) § 441 as amended by Stats. 1993, c. 173;442.
(12) § 463.

(13) § 110.1; 401; 401.3.
(14) § 227, as amended by Stats. 1994, c. 940, § 2.

restrict the use of property for a minimum of 10 years. Detailed rules are provided for qualification, termination or nonrenewal of contracts. Valuation methods are provided for the valuation for single family dwellings which are owner-occupied, rental properties, and other restricted historical property.

Qualified historical property includes qualified historical improvements and land on which the improvements are situated as specified in the historical property contract. If the property contract does not specify the land to be included, only that area of reasonable size that is used as a site for the historical improvements is included.[15]

Replacement grapevines. The initial base year value for qualifying replacement grapevines that are planted to replace grapevines less than 15 years of age that were removed solely as a result of phylloxera infestation, as certified in writing by the county agricultural commissioner, is the base year value of the removed vines factored to the lien date of the first taxable year of the replacement vines.[16]

Restricted property. In valuing property the assessor is to consider the effect of any enforceable restrictions to which the land may be subjected. These restrictions include:

(1) zoning;

(2) recorded contracts with governmental agencies;

(3) permit restrictions from the California Coastal Commission and the regional coastal commissions, the San Francisco Bay conservation and Development Commission, and the Tahoe Regional Planning Agency;

(4) development controls;

(5) environmental constraints;

(6) hazardous waste land use pursuant to Health and Safety Cd § 25240; and

(7) recorded conservation, trail, or scenic easements as described in Civil Cd § 815.1. Special valuation rules apply and there are detailed provisions regarding presumptions as to future use.

Special rules also apply to agricultural preserve property which includes property subject to: (1) a scenic restriction entered into prior to 1–1–75; (2) an open-space easement; or (3) a wildlife habitat contract.[17]

¶ 3008   **Assessment**

Assessment dates. All taxable property in California is assessed to the owner as of the lien date or the assessment date, March 1 of each year. The taxes assessed as of that date apply to the fiscal year of the taxing authorities, commencing on July 1 following the March 1 date and ending on June 30 of the subsequent year. Two assessment rolls are prepared by the taxing authorities as follows:

(1) *Secured roll.* The property included on the secured roll is all real property and all taxable personal property in the same location.

---

(15) §§ 439—439.4.
(16) § 53.

(17) § 402.1; 421—422.

(2) *Unsecured roll.* The law states that the unsecured roll includes the remainder of the assessable property which is not included on the secured roll. Essentially, this means tangible personalty that is not assessed to the owner of the realty on which it is located, and, at the discretion of county board of supervisors, possessory interests in land.[18]

Assessment percentage. All property within a county on the lien date of March 1 each year is assessed at full valuation.[19] The rate of tax applied to this assessed value varies from county and district to district, depending on the various budgets involved. Certain "enforceable restriction" (open-space) land may be assessed at less than 100% of full cash value.[20]

Who's assessed the tax. If the owner of the property and the holder in possession of the property on the lien date are not the same persons, the following is an explanation of who is assessed the tax:

Grantor and grantee. In California, the grantor and grantee put their deeds and consideration into an escrow which provides for apportionment of the tax due in the taxable year in which the property is sold, the buyer paying his pro rata share of the year's taxes from the date of sale to the end of the year.[21]

Landlord and tenant. Leased lands are assessed to the lessor or the landlord. Possessory interest is assessed to the lessee if the lessor is exempt. The lessee of personal property owned by a bank or financial institution is conclusively presumed to be owner of that property.[22] Property subject to a contract designated as a lease that qualifies for exemption as a free library or museum, or as exclusively used by an institution of higher education under Cal. Const. Article XIII, § 3(d)–(e) will be regarded as owned by the lessee, if the lessee has the option to acquire it at end of lease term for $1, or any other nominal consideration.[23]

Life tenant and remainderman. The owner of a life estate in real property must pay taxes and other annual interest charges on the property.[24]

Partners. The assessments are made in the firm name and each partner is liable for the whole tax assessed against the partnership.[25]

Executors and administrators. Undistributed or unpartitioned property of deceased persons is assessed to the heirs or executors or administrators, and the payment of taxes made by one binds all parties in interest for their equal proportions.[26]

Receivers. Property in litigation and in possession of the County Treasurer, Court, County Clerk or receiver, is taxable to the officer in possession and taxes are paid under the direction of the Court.[27]

---

(18) § 107.

(19) § 401.

(20) § 421–430.5.

(21) Civ Cd § 1113–1114.

(22) § 235.

(23) § 442.

(24) Civ Cd § 840.

(25) § 405.

(26) Probate Cd § 1024; § 612; 982.

(27) § 983.

Separate assessments. When improvements are owned by a person other than the owner of the real property on which the improvements are located, either the owner of the improvements or the owner of the real property can apply for separate assessments. Once the application is made and the county records separate assessments, they will continue until the disposition of the property or a request for a discontinuance of the separate assessments.[28] Separate assessment can also be obtained for the pro rata portion of a mobile home park that changes ownership under Rev & TC § 62.1.[29] The assessor may separately assess individual units shown on the condominium plan of a proposed condominium project, provided required documents are recorded, unless the record owner of the real property records with the condominium plan a request that the property be assessed as an entire parcel.[30]

Escape assessments. When an item of property escapes assessment in a given year, the assessor will make an "escape assessment" when it is discovered. The value of the property on the lien date for the year in which the property escapes assessment is used and the tax rate applied is the tax rate for that year. Escape assessments are subject to interest at the rate of three-fourth of one per cent a month from the date the taxes would have become delinquent if they had been timely assessed, to the date the additional assessment is added to the assessment rolls, and a penalty of 10% with the usual waiver for reasonable cause. If the assessee didn't cause the escaped assessment, no penalty attaches. Escape assessments are also used when there has been an under-assessment or faulty assessment by the assessor or faulty reporting by the owner.[31] If a county board of supervisors has adopted the necessary resolution, escape assessments can be prorated between previous owners and purchasers.[32]

Supplemental assessments. Whenever a change in ownership occurs or a new construction resulting from actual new physical construction on site is completed, the assessor must appraise the property changing ownership or the new construction at its full cash value on the date the change in ownership occurs or the new construction is completed. The value so determined is the new base year value of the property. If the change in ownership occurs on or after March 1 and on or before May 31, the first supplemental assessment to be placed on the roll will be the difference between the new base year value and the taxable value on the current roll. The second supplemental assessment in case of change in ownership of a full interest in real property is the difference between the new base year value and the taxable value to be placed on the roll being prepared. If the change in ownership is of only the partial interest in real property, the second supplemental assessment is the difference between the sum of the new base year value of the portion transferred plus the taxable value on the roll being prepared of the remainder of

---

(28) § 2188.2.
(29) § 2188.10.
(30) § 2188.6.

(31) § 110.1; 531.
(32) § 531.2(c).

the property, and the taxable value on the roll being prepared of the whole property. For new construction, the second supplemental assessment shall be the value change due to the new construction. If the change in ownership occurs or the new construction is finished on or after June 1 but before following March 1, the supplemental assessment will be the difference between the new base year value and the taxable value on the current roll. The removal of structure and fixtures must be taken into account in valuing property for supplemental assessment purposes. Other provisions of this law cover: (1) additions to roll for new real property construction; (2) when assessment is not treated as escape assessment; (3) report on fixtures; (4) application of inflation rate; (5) treatment of exemptions; (6) notice to assessee of new base year value and procedure for filing exemption claim; (7) application of tax rate; (8) refunds; (9) collection.[33]

WARNING	*Statute of limitations on supplemental assessments.* A supplemental assessment will have no force or effect, unless it is placed on the supplemental roll on or before the fourth July 1 following the July 1 of the assessment year in which the event giving rise to the supplemental assessment occurred. This period shall be extended for an additional two years if the penalty for concealment (Rev & TC § 502) or fraud (Rev & TC § 503) is imposed by Rev. & TC § 504. A further extension of an additional two years is added if the change in ownership or control is not reported, and the required report of a change in ownership is not filed.[34]

Disaster relief. Any taxpayer who files a claim for reassessment of eligible property under Rev & TC § 170 which provides for a reassessment of property damaged or destroyed by misfortune or calamity, or whose property is so reassessed, may apply for a deferral of the next installment of property taxes due on the regular secured roll which immediately follows the disaster which resulted in substantial disaster. If a timely claim for deferral is filed, the payment is deferred without penalty or interest until the assessor has reassessed the property and a corrected bill prepared pursuant to Rev & TC § 170. There are penalties if the claim for deferral is not made in good faith. The deferral also does not apply to property taxes paid through impound accounts.[35]

¶ 3010   Rate of Tax

The County Board of Supervisors, in addition to administering the county ordinances, also acts as the administrator of the property tax provisions. The county board establishes its budget for the fiscal year and receives from the assessor the county tax rolls which show the extent of the taxable property within the county. With this information the Board of Supervisors in each county sets up a tax rate which covers all of the county assessments as well

---

(33) § 75–75.80.   (35) § 194.1.
(34) § 75.11.

as the assessments which the county is handling for the cities and the special tax districts within the county.

Maximum rate. The maximum rate is 1% of full cash value, but may be increased to pay interest and redemption charges on any indebtedness approved by the voters before 7–1–78, or any bonded debt for the acquisition or improvement of real property approved by two-thirds of votes cast by voters on or after 7–1–78.[36]

Tax areas. Because of varying boundaries of cities, schools, and special districts, taxpayers who want to check the computation shown on the tax bill must know the tax rate for their particular "tax rate area" within a city—or for their "tax rate area" outside a city.[37]

Unsecured roll. An important difference between the secured and unsecured roll is that the property tax rate on the unsecured roll is the same as the rate on the secured roll due for November 1st of the prior year.[38]

¶ 3011   Payment and Collection

Payment dates. The entire amount of tax on personal property which is secured by real property and one-half of the real property tax is due on November 1 each year and is delinquent if unpaid at 5:00 p.m. on December 10. If December 10 falls on a Saturday, Sunday or holiday, the taxes are due on the next business day. The second half of the tax on real property is due February 1, and is delinquent if unpaid on April 10 of the following year. The tax on unsecured property is due on March 1, which is the lien date, or when the local tax collector demands payment. Generally speaking, the tax on property on the unsecured roll is due on July 31 and is delinquent after August 31 at 5:00 p.m. or the close of business, whichever is later.[39] Tax collectors are authorized to accept credit cards for payment of fees, charges, or taxes due to the agency. The agency could impose a fee on the persons using a credit card for payment of fees, charges, and taxes generally, or in payment of property taxes.

Tax bills. Secured tax bills are normally mailed by the Tax Collector by Nov. 1st of each year. It's the owner's responsibility to pay tax whether a tax bill is received or not.[40]

Electronic funds transfers. On or after 7–1–93, unless otherwise delayed by the State Controller, taxpayers with aggregate payments of $100,000 or more for the two most recent installments of property tax on the secured roll may be required by the Tax Assessor for the city or county to make subsequent payments by electronic funds transfer.[1]

Penalties for delinquencies. If the tax is not paid by the delinquency date, the penalties on tax on the secured rolls is 10%; for unpaid taxes on the

---

(36) Art XIII A, § 1 and 2.
(37) § 443.
(38) Art XIII, § 12.

(39) § 2605; 2606; 2617; 2618; 2901; 2922.
(40) § 2610.5.
(1) § 2503.2.

unsecured rolls, 10% plus 1½% a month starting the first day of the 3rd month after the 10% penalty attaches. Actual costs of collection of taxes on the unsecured roll incurred up to time delinquency is paid can be charged by collector. The Tax Collector or auditor can cancel the penalty with the approval of the Board of Supervisors if they find that the delinquency in payment of the tax is due to reasonable cause and circumstances beyond the assessee's control and occurred notwithstanding exercise of ordinary care and in the absence of willful neglect, provided payment is made within 90 days of the first delinquency date or 30 days of the second delinquency date. The penalty can also be waived if there was an inadvertent error in the amount of the payment by the assessee, provided the payment is made within 10 days after the notice of shortage is mailed by the Tax Collector.[2] The law also provides procedures for seizure and sale of delinquent property to effect tax collections.[3]

> *Note:* No penalties or interest with respect to delinquent installments of property taxes for the 1992–1993 fiscal year shall be imposed or collected against a property owner who suffered economic hardship as a result of the civil unrest that occurred in Los Angeles in April and May, 1992. The treasurer or tax collector is precluded from taking any collection action until on or after 1–1–94. Claims for relief may be filed if any interest or penalties have been paid.[4]

Penalties for willful evasion, or fraud. Rev. & TC § 503 and 504 provide penalties equal to 25%, and or 75% of the escape assessment, where there has been a willful evasion of tax, or a fraudulent action resulting from the escape assessment, respectively. These penalties apply for an escape assessment due to the underassessment of tangible personal property.[5]

In-lieu taxes. Until 1–1–95, the county assessor of a county with a population exceeding 8 million who determines that corrections of property tax assessments or applications of base year-year value limitations or transfers cannot be accomplished before delinquency of currently due amounts may notify the county auditor-controller and collector. The collector must accept in-lieu amounts and make adjustments to property tax records reflecting correction or application of base-year value limits or transfers, and notify the assessee that in-lieu amounts will be accepted, and the amount and time of payment.[6]

¶ 3012   Specially Taxed Property

Timber yield tax. The tax is imposed on owners of timber maintained for eventual harvest for forest product purposes, including Christmas trees, but not including nursery stock. The tax is at the rate of 6% of the immediate harvest value of that timber. The "immediate harvest value" means the amount that each species of timber would sell for on the stump at a voluntary sale made in the ordinary course of business for purposes of immediate

---

(2) § 2617; 2618; 2922; 4985.2.
(3) § 2903; 2951; 2937; 2958.
(4) § 171.

(5) § 504, as amended by Stats. 1994, c. 544, § 2.
(6) § 4833.

harvest. The immediate harvest value of Christmas trees is the sale price of the Christmas trees in quantities of 100 trees or more in the market area nearest to the place where the trees are cut. The immediate harvest value is determined as of the scaling date, which means the date when the quantity of timber harvested by species is first definitely determined.

In December of each year, after public hearings, the county board will adjust the timber yield tax rate to the nearest 1/10 of 1%, in the same proportion that the average rate of general property taxation in the current tax year differs from the average rate of general property taxation in the preceding tax year.[7]

Tax on race horses. An annual tax is imposed on the owners of race horses in California counties for the privilege of breeding, training, caring for and racing such horses. The fee is in lieu of any property taxes. A table showing the scale of taxes imposed on the owner for race horses domiciled in the county is provided[8]. The rates vary depending on whether the animal is 12 years old or younger in one category and 13 years and older in the other category. Different rates apply for stallions depending on the amount of stud fees and for brood mares and active race horses depending on the previous calendar year's earnings. Special breeding and racing requirements apply to Arabian horses. The tax is determined as of January 1 for the calendar year imposed. It's due and payable immediately to the tax collector of the county in which the racehorse is domiciled. The tax is delinquent at 5 p.m. on February 15. The State Board of Equalization administers the tax.[9]

¶ 3015   Senior Citizens' Tax Relief

Property tax assistance. Taxpayers, 62 years of age and older, with limited income are entitled to a certain amount of property tax relief. Claimants for such relief have to be 62 years of age or older on the last day of the year, or blind or disabled as defined in the Welfare and Institutions Code, and either the owner-occupant of a residential dwelling, or the renter of a residence on or before the last day of the year. The relief provisions also apply to the owner-occupant of a mobile home subject to property tax.

The benefit provided is an elimination of a portion of the property taxes on the first $34,000 of assessed valuation of the property. The percentage applied to the $34,000 begins at 96% for $3,300 of total household income and decreases in steps depending on the recipient's "household income." Household income for this purpose means the adjusted gross income for income tax purposes plus (1) public assistance and relief, (2) gross amount of pensions and annuities, (3) social security payments except Medicare, (4) railroad retirement benefits, (5) unemployment insurance payments, (6) veterans benefits, (7) interest received from any source, (8) gifts and inheritances in excess of $300, and similar income items. The percentage reduces

---

(7) § 38115; 38202.
(8) § 5722.

(9) § 5701–5783.

to 4% on an income not in excess of $13,200. For example, if an individual's income is $3,300, he is entitled to relief from property tax to the extent of 96% of the first $34,000 of assessed valuation of the property. If the income is $3,520 the relief is based on 94% of the first $34,000 of assessed valuation, and continues in similar steps. If his household income is $13,200, the person gets a reduction in assessed valuation of 4% of $34,000.

Renters who qualify are entitled to relief based on a similar table applied to $250. In other words, a renter with no more than $3,300 of household income would be able to obtain relief to the extent of 96% of $250.

Whether the individual recipient is a homeowner or a renter, the procedure for obtaining the relief is the same. The relief does not operate automatically as a reduction of the property tax bill itself, rather, it is necessary that the recipient file a claim with the Franchise Tax Board after May 15 of the fiscal year for which the assistance is claimed, but on or before August 31 of the succeeding fiscal year.[10]

Property tax postponement. Taxpayers, 62 years of age and older or blind or disabled, may defer property taxes on their principal residence if they meet certain conditions. The taxes which they do not pay when they enter the program become a lien on the property, and become due and payable when the claimant sells the property or dies or otherwise ceases to occupy the property as his residence. If the claimant dies and leaves a spouse occupying the residence, the tax would be due and payable only when the spouse ceases to occupy the property, dies or sells the property or becomes delinquent in the payment of property taxes. To qualify, taxpayers must have gross household income of less than $24,000 ($34,000 if taxpayers filed and qualified in 1983), must have at least a 20% equity in the home and the home must be their principal residence (a condominium or mobile home would be included).

The California State Controller's office prepares the forms that must be filed with that office after May 15 of the calendar year in which the fiscal year for which postponement is claimed begins and by December 10 of such fiscal year.[11]

The Legislature can provide for a manner in which a disabled person could postpone the payment of property tax on a dwelling owned and occupied as a principal residence. (Proposition 33.) All property tax postponement acts now apply to the blind and disabled.

¶ 3018   **Proposition 13**

In 1978, the people of California adopted a change in the property tax system in California by approving Proposition 13 which added Cal. Const. Art. XIII–A.[12] Because of the innumerable problems caused by the varying interpretations of the basic wording of Proposition 13, the Legislature has been

---

(10) § 20501–20504.
(11) § 20581–20646.

(12) Cal. Const. Art XIII–A.

active since 1978 passing bills to clarify some of the confusing language and interpretations. It has added Part 0.5 to the Revenue and Taxation Code implementing Article XIIIA. These provisions cover (1) base year values; (2) change in ownership; (3) new construction; (4) supplemental assessments; (5) assessment appeals; and (6) taxpayer reporting. Valuation provisions and taxpayer reporting are discussed below. For assessment appeals, see ¶ 6604 in Section XIII, Protests and Appeals. For supplemental assessments, see ¶ 3008.

Although Proposition 13 concerns itself with real property, the impact of the valuation system change (converting from current value method to an acquisition value system) and the rate limitation (1% of value plus additional amount to pay off pre-7-1-78 indebtedness, or any bonded indebtedness for the acquisition or improvement of real property approved on or after 7-1-78 by two-thirds of votes cast by voters voting on the proposition) apply also to tangible personal property. This is so because Cal. Const. Art. XIII, § 2 provides that the "tax per dollar of full value shall not be higher on personal property than on real property in the same taxing jurisdiction."[13]

Proposition 13's full text (Article XIII-A), as originally approved by the voters, is as follows:

ARTICLE XIII A (Proposition 13)

SECTION 1   (a)   The maximum amount of any ad valorem tax on real property shall not exceed one percent (1%) of the full cash value of such property. The one percent (1%) tax to be collected by the counties and apportioned according to law to the districts within the counties.

(b)   The limitation provided for in subdivision (a) shall not apply to ad valorem taxes or special assessments to pay the interest and redemption charges on any indebtedness approved by the voters prior to the time this section becomes effective.

SECTION 2   (a)   The full cash value means the county assessor's valuation of real property shown on the 1975-1976 tax bill under "full cash value" or, thereafter, the appraised value of real property when purchased, newly constructed, or a change in ownership has occurred after the 1975 Assessment. All real property not already assessed up to the 1975-1976 full cash value may be assessed to reflect the valuation.

(b)   The full cash value base may reflect from year to year the inflationary rate not to exceed 2% for any given year or reduction as shown in the consumer price index or comparable data for the area under taxing jurisdiction, or may be reduced to reflect substantial damage, destruction, or other factors causing a decline in value.

SECTION 3   From and after the effective date of this article, any changes in State taxes enacted for the purpose of increasing revenues collected pursuant thereto whether by increased rates or changes in methods of computation must be

---

(13) Art. XIII, § 2.

imposed by an Act passed by not less than two-thirds of all members elected to each of the two houses of the Legislature, except that no new ad valorem taxes on real property, or sales or transaction taxes on the sales of real property may be imposed.

SECTION 4   Cities, Counties and special districts, by a two-thirds vote of the qualified electors of such district, may impose special taxes on such district, except ad valorem taxes on real property or a transaction tax or sales tax on the sale of real property within such City, County or special district.

Principal areas requiring clarification include the meaning of "base year value," "change of ownership" and the effects of new construction. A brief summary of the important aspects of Proposition 13 is set forth below. Specific information is set forth in Division I, Part 0.5, Chapters 1 through 5.5 of the California Revenue and Taxation Code, which includes Section 50 to Section 93.[14]

Definitions.   The more important definitions relating to Proposition 13 are as follows:

Base year values.   Essentially the base year value in any year is the fair market value or full cash value on the lien date in 1975. It is compounded annually since 1975 by an inflation factor. For property acquired or having a change in ownership since 1975, the base year value is the amount which the assessor places on the tax rolls at the lien date following the date of acquisition or change. Provisions for the transfer of the base year value to comparable replacement property in the event of disaster loss apply if the replacement property is acquired or newly constructed within three years.[15] The Legislature has set conditions under which persons over 55, and severely disabled persons regardless of age, could transfer the base year value of property entitled to a homeowner's exemption to any replacement dwelling of equal or lesser value within the same county, purchased or newly constructed as principal residence within two years after the sale of the original property.[16]

On 11–8–88, California voters at the general election approved an amendment to the California Constitution that permits the transfer of the base year value to replacement dwellings in different counties, if the county of the replacement dwelling adopts an ordinance participating in the program. Substantially damaged or destroyed property retains its base year value.[17] Eff. 1–1–90 and through 12–31–98, the specific applicable date of the ordinance authorizing the intercounty transfer of base year value may be a date earlier than the date the county adopts the ordinance.[18]

On 11–2–93, California voters also approved a constitutional amendment that would allow a property owner to transfer the current assessed value of his original property to a replacement property in another county,

---

(14) § 50–93.
(15) § 69.
(16) § 69.5.

(17) Calif Const Art XIII A, § 2(a); § 69; 69.5.
(18) § 69.3.

but only if the county in which the property is located has agreed to participate, by adopting a special valuation program ordinance. This applies to comparable replacement property acquired on or after 10–20–91, under the following conditions: (1) the Governor must have declared that a disaster occurred; (2) the disaster must have reduced the market value of the property by more than one-half; and (3) the replacement property must be comparable to the damaged property and acquired or constructed within three years of the damage to the original property.[19]

Change of ownership as a basis for the timing of the reappraisal of real property under Cal Const Art § XIII(A)(2) is not invalidated because in practice, the ownership of a personal residence changes more frequently than does the ownership of business real property. In addition the fact that the owners of personal residences with equal current fair values may pay different property taxes based on the value at the date of acquisition is not prohibited. The Equal Protection Clause of the 14th Amendment of the U.S. Constitution is not violated (*Stephanie Nordlinger v. Lynch, Los Angeles County Tax Assessor, and Los Angeles County (1992) 112 S Ct 2326*.

Full cash value. Full cash value or fair market value is the amount of cash or its equivalent which property would bring if exposed to sale in the open market under conditions in which neither buyer nor seller could take advantage of the exigencies of the other, and both with knowledge of all of the uses and purposes to which the property is adapted and for which it is capable of being used and of the enforceable restrictions upon those uses and purposes.[20] For the purposes of determining "full cash value" or "fair market value" of real property, other than possessory interests, being appraised upon a purchase, "full cash value" or "fair market value" are the purchase price paid in the transaction unless it is established by a preponderance of the evidence that the real property would not have transferred for that purchase price in an open market transaction. Purchase price shall be rebuttably presumed to be the "full cash value" or "fair market value" if the terms of the transaction were negotiated at arm's length between a knowledgeable transferor and transferee if neither could take advantage of the exigencies of the other.

Full cash value of real property. Full cash value within the meaning of § 2(a) of Article XIII–A means the fair market value as determined in the above paragraph for either (1) the 1975 lien date, or (2) for property which is purchased, is newly constructed or changes ownership after the 1975 lien date: (a) the date on which a purchase or change of ownership occurs; or (b) the date on which new construction is completed, and if uncompleted, on the lien date. Value thus determined is called the base year value for the property.[21]

---

(19) Proposition 171; § 69.
(20) § 110.

(21) § 110.1.

Taxable value of real property. For each lien date, the taxable value of real property is the lesser of (1) a base year value compounded annually since the base year by an inflation factor which is the percentage change in the cost of living, provided that any percentage increase does not exceed 2% of the prior year's value or (2) its full cash value on the lien date, taking into account any reduction in value due to damage, destruction, depreciation, obsolescence or other factors causing a decline in value.[22]

Purchase. A purchase is defined as a change in ownership (defined below) for consideration.[23]

Newly constructed property. Rev & TC 70(a) defines new construction as any addition to real property whether land or improvements (including fixtures) and any alteration of land or of any improvement including fixtures which constitutes a major rehabilitation or which converts the property to a different use. Any rehabilitation, renovation or modernization which converts an improvement or fixture to the substantial equivalent of a new improvement or fixture is a *major rehabilitation* of such improvement or fixture.[24]

"New construction" does not include the timely reconstruction of property damaged or destroyed by a disaster to a level equivalent to the original property. Only that portion which exceeds substantially equivalent reconstruction is considered to have a new base year value and a reappraisal.[24]

New construction and newly constructed does not mean the portion of reconstruction or improvement to structure, constructed of unreinforced masonry bearing wall construction necessary to comply with a local ordinance. The exclusion remains in effect for the first 15 years following the reconstruction or improvement, unless the property is purchased or changes ownership. In the sixteenth year following the reconstruction or improvement the assessor must place the property on the roll at current full cash value.[25]

Also, "newly constructed" excludes construction or addition of any active solar energy system which exists on the lien dates for the 1991–1992 to 1993–1994 fiscal years. For purposes of supplemental assessment, Rev & TC § 73 applies only to qualifying construction completed on or after 1-1-91.[26]

Fire sprinkler, fire detection, or other fire extinguishing systems are excluded from term "new construction".[27]

The construction, modification or installation of any portion or structural component of a single or multiple family dwelling that is eligible for the homeowner's exemption will not be included in the meaning of "new construction", if the construction, installation or modification is for the purpose

---

(22) § 51.
(23) § 67.
(24) § 70.

(25) Art XIII A, § 2(a); § 70.
(26) § 73.
(27) Art XIII A, § 2c; § 74; 74.3.

¶ **3018**

of making the dwelling more accessible to a severely disabled person. This includes home additions that duplicate existing facilities and which are for disabled persons.[27]

The term "newly constructed" does not include the portion of reconstruction of or installation in a building of seismic rehabilitation improvements, or earthquake hazard mitigation technologies.[28]

WARNING	New construction to make a personal residence more accessible to the severely and permanently disabled will be eligible for exemption only if (1) a statement signed by a licensed physician or surgeon, certifies that the person is severely and permanently disabled, and identifies specific disability-related requirements necessitating accessibility improvements or features, and (2) there is a statement that identifies the construction, installation, or modification that was in fact necessary to make the structure more accessible. The assessor may charge a fee to reimburse the assessor for the costs of procession and administering the required statements.[29]

Change of ownership. A change in ownership means a transfer of a present interest in real property including the beneficial use thereof, the value of which is substantially equal to the value of the fee interest.[30]

As indicated above, the county assessor is entitled to change the base year value following any year in which there has been a change in ownership, or a purchase of the property, or new construction on the property. The circumstances which raise the question of whether or not a reappraisal of the property value is called for are set forth below.[31]

Leases. Leasehold interest in taxable real property for a term of 35 years or more (including renewal option) is considered to be a change of ownership. Therefore, the creation or termination of a 35-year lease will cause a reappraisal, as well as any transfer of a lease with the remaining term, including options, of 35 years or more. When a lease has less than 35 years to run, its transfer does not cause a reappraisal. The transfer of a lessor's interest subject to a lease with a remaining term of less than 35 years is a change of ownership; but a transfer of a lessor's interest in a lease with a remaining term of more than 35 years *is not* a change of ownership.[32]

Joint tenancies. When a joint tenancy is created or when additional joint tenants are added, there is no reappraisal as long as the transferor is one of the joint tenants. The same thing is true when there is a transfer of a joint tenancy interest. Other transfers of joint tenancy interests may or may not cause a reappraisal. For specific information refer to Rev & TC §§ 62(f), 65(a), or Rev & TC § 65(b).[33]

---

(28) § 74.5.   (31) § 61–66.
(29) § 74.3.   (32) § 61–62.
(30) § 60.   (33) § 62; 65.

Interspousal transfers. Transfers between spouses do not constitute changes in ownership, including transfers which are caused by the death of a spouse or transfers in connection with a property settlement or decree of dissolution of a marriage or legal separation. Voters have incorporated similar provisions in Proposition 13.[34]

Intrafamily transfers. Intrafamily transfers of eligible dwelling units from parent(s) or legal guardian(s) to minor child or children or between or among minor siblings as a result of a court order or judicial decree due to the death of a parent or parents are not considered changes in ownership. To be eligible, the dwelling unit must be the principal place of residence of the minor child or children before the transfer and remain so afterward. The terms "purchased" and "change in ownership" do not include purchase or transfer between parents and children of (1) the principal residence of the transferor; and (2) the first $1 million of full cash value of all other real property. The exclusion includes voluntary transfers and those resulting from court decree.[35]

WARNING	To be eligible for the exemptions from reappraisal of a property transferred between parents and child a claim for exemption must be timely filed. In the case of a qualifying transfer on or before 9–30–90, the claim must be filed within three years following the date of transfer; in the case of a qualifying transfer after 9–30–90 the claim must be filed prior to the transfer of ownership of the property to a third party or within three years following the qualifying transfer, whichever is earlier. If a claim is not otherwise filed timely, a claim for exemption will be considered timely if it is filed within six months after the date the assessor mails a notice of supplemental or escape assessment, as a result of the purchase or transfer of real property for which the claim is made. If the qualifying transfer between parent and child is a result of the death of the parent or child (that is the transfer may go either way), the date of death is considered the date of the qualifying transfer.[36]

Trusts. A change of ownership is not considered present when property is transferred by the grantor to a trust (i) if the transferor or his spouse is one of the present beneficiaries, or (ii) if the trust is revocable, or (iii) if the trust is a Clifford trust for not more than 12 years. However, a change of ownership does occur when the grantor dies or is removed as the current beneficiary or where the trust becomes irrevocable.[35]

Tenancies in common. The creation, transfer or termination of any joint tenancy interest is considered a change in ownership requiring a reappraisal of the value of the property. However, a transfer between the co-owners which results in a change in the method of holding title to the real

---

(**34**) Const Art XIIIA, § 2(g).

(**35**) Const Art XIIIA, § 2(h); § 62; § 63.1.

(**36**) § 63.1.

property without changing the proportional interest of the co-owners is not a change in ownership.[32]

Mineral rights. The creation, renewal, sublease, assignment or other transfer of the right to produce or extract oil, gas or other minerals in paying quantities is a change in ownership, regardless of the period during which right may be exercised.[37]

Water conservation equipment for agricultural use. The installation of water conservation equipment for agricultural use is not new construction. Water conservation equipment is defined to include any device, system, pipeline, mechanism, or improvement that is installed to replace or improve an existing system which will result in the reduction of water usage as specifically defined.[38]

Possessory interests. The creation, renewal, sublease, or assignment of a taxable possessory interest in tax-exempt real property for any term is considered a change in ownership. Renewal does not include the granting of an option to renew an existing agreement pursuant to which the term of possession of the existing agreement would, upon exercise of the option, be lengthened, whether the option is granted in the original agreement or later.[37]

Corporations. A transfer of real property interest between a corporation and a shareholder is not a change in ownership unless the proportional interests of the holders are changed by the transfer. However, a sale of over 50% of the stock of the corporation creates a change of ownership. Any reorganization of farm institutions pursuant to the federal Farm Credit Act of 1971 (P.L. 92–181), as amended, is not a change of ownership.[39]

Partnerships and limited liability companies. A transfer of real property interest between a partnership and a partner, or a limited company and a member, is not a change of ownership if the interest of the owner is proportionally the same after the transfer. A sale or exchange of partnership interest or interests amounting to over 50% is a change in ownership.[39]

Involuntary conversion. Change in ownership does not include the acquisition of real property as replacement for a comparable property if the person acquiring it has been displaced from that property in-state by eminent domain proceedings, acquisition by public entity, or governmental action resulting in judgment of inverse condemnation. The rule applies to proceedings, acquisitions or judgments after 3–1–75, and affects only those assessments that occur after 6–8–82. Comparable property means property similar in utility, size, and function, or conforming to regulations defined by the Legislature governing relocation of persons displaced by governmental actions.[40]

---

(37) § 61.
(38) § 73.5.

(39) § 62; 64.
(40) Art XIII A, § 2(d); § 68.

Correction or reformation of deeds. No change of ownership occurs if such transfer is made to express the true intentions of the parties, provided the original relationship between the grantor and grantee is not changed.[35]

Transfer by will, devise, or inheritance to disabled children or wards. Change in ownership does not include any transfer of an eligible dwelling unit, whether by will, devise, or inheritance from a parent or parents to a child or children, or from a guardian or guardians to a ward or wards, if such transferees have been disabled for at least five years preceding the transfer, and have adjusted gross income, that, when combined with adjusted gross income of the spouse, or spouses, parent or parents, and child or children does not exceed $20,000 in the year of the transfer. Eligible dwelling means a dwelling unit that was the principal place of residence of the transferees for at least five years preceding the transfer, and remains so after the transfer.[35]

Mobilehome park transfers. Change of ownership does not include, for the 1985 through 1999 calendar years, any transfer of a mobilehome park to a nonprofit corporation, stock cooperative corporation, limited equity stock co-operative or other entity formed by the tenants of the park to purchase the park. Transfers of rental spaces in the park to individual tenants are also excluded, if 51% of the spaces are bought by tenants who are renters prior to the purchase; if, after such transfer, the park has not been converted to condominium, stock cooperative ownership, or limited equity cooperative ownership, any transfer, on or after 1–1–89, of shares of voting stock, or other ownership or membership interests, in the entity that acquired the park is a change of ownership of the pro rata portion of the real property of the park unless the transfer is for the purpose of converting the park to condominium, stock cooperative ownership, or limited equity ownership, or is excluded from change of ownership by Rev & TC §§ 62, 63 or 63.1.[1] Change of ownership shall not include any transfer on or after 1–1–89, of a mobilehome park to a nonprofit corporation, stock cooperative corporation, or other entity, including a government entity, if, within 18 months after the transfer, the mobilehome park is transferred by that corporation or other entity, including a governmental entity, to a nonprofit corporation, stock cooperative corporation, or other entity formed by the tenants of the mobilehome park in a transaction that is excluded by Rev & TC § 62.1(a), or at least 51% of the mobilehome park rental spaces are transferred to the individual tenants of those spaces in a transaction that is excluded by Rev & TC § 62.2(b) from change of ownership.[2]

Undivided interests. Only a unit or lot within a co-op, community apartment project, condominium, planned unit development, shopping center, industrial park or similar residential or commercial or industrial land subdivision complex that is bought or changes ownership will be reappraised.[3]

---

(1) § 62.1.
(2) § 62.2.

(3) § 65.1.

Employee benefit plans. Change in ownership does not include: (1) the creation, vesting, transfer or termination of a participant's or beneficiary's interest in an employee benefits plan; (2) any contribution of real property to such plan; and (3) any acquisition by the plan of employer corporation stock through which the plan obtains the direct or indirect control of the company.[4]

Report of change in ownership. The new property owner (transferee) acquiring an interest in real property or a mobile home subject to local property taxation, is required to file a change-in-ownership statement with the County Recorder or Assessor. Administrators and executors must file with recorder or assessor of county where decedent owned property at time of death. The change-in-ownership statement has to be filed at the time of the recording of the transfer, or if it is not recorded, then within 45 days of the date of the change in ownership. If the transfer occurs as a result of the death of the owner, than the personal representative (or trustee if the property is held in trust) shall file a change of ownership statement with the County Assessor or County Clerk of the county in which the property is located within 150 days of the date of death, or if the decedent's Estate is subject to probate, at the time the inventory and appraisement of the decedent's property is filed with the County Clerk.[5] Changes in control or ownership of corporation, partnership or other legal entity must be reported to the Property Taxes Department of the State Board of Equalization, P.O. Box 1799, Sacramento, California 95808.[6] A preliminary change of ownership report may be filed with the recorder along with any document effecting change in ownership.[7] Secrecy rules apply.[8]

The failure to file the required statement within 45 days after receipt of a written request by the Assessor, causes a penalty of $100 or 10% of the current year's taxes on the real property or mobile home, not to exceed $2,500, whichever is greater. A 10% penalty applies to corporations, partnerships or other legal entities in the event of change of control or ownership. The penalty also applies to the successor in interest to a decedent's property. The penalty may be waived if the assessee proves to the Board of Supervisors that the failure to file the statement was due to reasonable cause and not to willful neglect.[9]

Statute of limitations. In the absence of negligence or fraud, property may be added to the assessment roll anytime within four years after July 1 of the assessment year in which the property escaped taxation or was underassessed. The period is extended to six years if a penalty under Rev & TC § 504, for willful negligence or fraud, is added to the assessment.

If property has escaped taxation, or has been underassessed following a change in ownership, then the statute of limitations shall not commence

---

(4) § 66.
(5) § 480, as amended by Stats. 1994, c. 1222, § 13.3.
(6) § 480; 480.2.

(7) § 480.3; 480.4.
(8) § 408; 408.2; 481.
(9) § 482–482.2.

until July 1 of the assessment year in which the change in ownership statement, is filed with respect to the event giving rise to the escape assessment or underassessment.[10]

Tax limits. A 1986 statutory initiative added Art 3.7, §§ 53720–53730 to the California Government Code. This law defines special taxes and general taxes. It requires two-thirds approval of voters of any local government or district before a special tax can be imposed. A general tax must be approved by a majority of voters. Any tax imposed by localities on or after 8–1–85 and before 11–5–86 can continue to be imposed if approved by a majority of voters voting in an election held within two years of 11–5–86. If authority for tax is not given by voters, or sought by the locality, the tax can't be imposed after 11–15–88. A penalty of dollar-for-dollar reduction of allocated tax revenues is set for noncompliance or action in excess of taxing authority. Any citizen or taxpayer can bring action to invalidate a tax that violates the above rules.[11] A 1988 legislation authorized (1) public library special taxes, effective 9–26–88; and (2) hospital district special taxes, effective 1–1–89.[12]

¶ 3019 Property Taxpayers' Bill Of Rights

In an attempt to achieve better understanding and communication between taxpayers' and tax administrators with respect to the property tax system, a Property Taxpayers' Bill of Rights has been enacted (Rev & TC § 5900—5910). The intent is to disseminate information on property assessments and collection of tax, promote uniform practices among the various jurisdictions for property tax appraisal and assessment, and to establish a Property Taxpayers' Advocate position within the State Board of Equalization. The advocate is to assist in the prompt resolution of board, assessor, and taxpayer inquiries, and taxpayer complaints and problems. The advocate is to be designated by, and report directly to, the executive office to the State Board of Equalization, and is to report at least annually on the adequacy of existing procedures, or the need for additional or revised procedures to enhance taxpayer understanding. Educational and information programs on property tax assessments are to be established. Materials in nontechnical language are to be prepared explaining the taxation of property in California, property tax exemptions, supplemental assessments, escape assessments, assessment procedures, the obligations, responsibilities, and rights of both taxpayers and the tax authorities.

A program for county assessors to respond to a taxpayer's written request for a written ruling as to the property tax consequences of an actual or planned particular transactions, or as to the property tax liability of a specific property, is to be established. If a taxpayer relies on such a ruling addressed to him or her and fails to timely report information or pay amounts of tax, the taxpayer shall be relieved of any penalties, or interest

---

(10) § 532, as amended by Stats. 1994, c. 544, § 4.
(11) Govt. Cd. § 53720–53730.

(12) Govt.   Cd.   § 53717–53717.b;
53730.01–53730.02.

assessed or accrued, with respect to the property taxes not paid. The taxes will not be relieved or abated.[13]

---

(13) § 5900—5910.

ESTATE AND OTHER TRANSFER TAXES

¶ 3101 Introduction

On 6–8–82, the California electorate approved the repeal of the state inheritance and gift tax and added a new section to the Revenue and Taxation Code banning the state from imposing any inheritance or gift tax. The new law provides for a "pick-up" estate tax equal to the federal credit for state death taxes. The tax was effective as of the date of its passage, and applies to the estates of persons dying "on or after such date." The California Court of Appeals held that the "pick-up" tax applied to estates of persons dying at any time on 6–8–82, the date of its passage, and not only after the closing of the polls at 8:00 p.m. on that date. Accordingly, the inheritance tax was repealed as of the start of 6–8–82. [Estate of Jessie Cirone, 153 CA3d 199, 200 Cal Rptr 511.]

The pick-up estate tax is provided for in Part 8 of Division 2 of the Revenue and Taxation Code. It is imposed to allow California to obtain the maximum amount of tax without increasing the estate's total California and federal estate tax liability.

For estates of resident decedents, all of a decedent's real and personal property sited in California and all of a decedent's intangible property wherever situated is subject to the pick-up tax. For a U.S.-resident decedent who wasn't a California resident, the pick-up tax is apportioned to California based on the value of the decedent's real and personal property sited in California as compared to the total of such value everywhere.

Who administers the taxes. Estate and other death transfer taxes are administered by the State Controller who has offices in Sacramento, San Francisco, and Los Angeles. Death and gift tax liabilities incurred before 6–9–82, are determined and enforced under the law in effect at the time of the transfer.

¶ 3105 Definition of Estate or Property

The California estate tax equals the portion of the maximum allowable federal credit for state death taxes attributable to the decedent's estate or property located in California. Rev & TC § 13402 defines estate or property as the real or personal property or property interest of a decedent or transferor, and also includes:

● *Intangibles of resident decedents.* All intangible personal property of a resident decedent within or without California or subject to its jurisdiction;

● *Intangibles of nonresidents of U.S.* All intangible personal property in California belonging to a deceased nonresident of the United States, including all stock of a California corporation, or a corporation that has its principal place of business or does the major part of its business in California, but not including savings accounts and bank deposits except deposits held and used in connection with a California business (see *Estate of Herbert N. Banerjee, Deceased* (1978) 21 C3d 527; 580 P2d 657, 147 Cal Rptr 157).

Definition of resident decedent. A resident decedent is a decedent who was domiciled in California at the time of death.[1] A nonresident decedent is a decedent who was domiciled outside of California at the time of death.[2] The statute doesn't define domicile. California recognizes that a decedent could have had only one domicile at the time of death. *(Cory v. White* (1982) 102 S Ct 2325, No. 80–1556.)

California has adopted the Uniform Act on Interstate Compromise of Death Taxes. Under the Act, when the Controller claims that a decedent was domiciled in California at the time of death and the taxing authorities of another state or states make a like claim, the Controller may enter into a compromise agreement with the other authorities and the executor of the estate. The agreement will conclusively fix the amount of death taxes owed to California.[3] Also, if the personal representative of an estate claims that the decedent wasn't a resident decedent, the Controller and personal representative can compromise the estate tax liability.[4]

California has also adopted the Uniform Act on Interstate Arbitration of Death Taxes.[5] The Act provides for the submission of a dispute over a decedent's domicile to a board of arbitrators on written agreement of the Controller, the executor, and the taxing authorities of the other state or states making the claim that decedent was domiciled in their state. The board's determination of domicile is final for the purpose of imposing and collecting death taxes.

¶ 3106   Calculation of Estate Tax—Rate

California imposes a California estate tax whenever a federal estate tax is payable to the U.S. and the estate includes property located in California. The tax equals the portion of the maximum allowable federal credit for state death taxes under IRC § 2011 attributable to property located in California.

The maximum allowable credit for state death taxes under IRC § 2011 is called the "federal credit."[6] To determine the federal credit, you must first calculate the value of the "gross estate." The gross estate's value is the fair market value of all interests in the property of a citizen or resident of the U.S. at the date of his death, or on the alternate valuation date. Within three months of the date of appointment, the estate's personal representative must submit to the clerk of the probate court an inventory and appraisement of the fair market value of the assets of the decedent's estate.[7] The estate representative is responsible to appraise, under oath, all cash, currency, bank accounts, life and accident insurance policies, as well as retirement plans, payable upon death in a lump-sum amount.[8] All other assets are valued by a court-appointed probate referee, whose commission is paid by

(1) § 13407.
(2) § 13408.
(3) § 13810.
(4) § 13801.

(5) § 13820.
(6) § 13411.
(7) Probate Cd § 600.
(8) Probate Cd § 605(a)(1)

the estate.[9] The court may waive the appointment of a probate referee for good cause, such as economic hardship.[10] Any person who wants to object to an appraisement must file a written objection with the court at any time before the decree of final distribution of the estate, and must notify all interested parties, including the probate referee, of the hearing. [11] Once the gross estate is so determined, the "taxable estate" is calculated by subtracting from the gross estate all deductions allowed under IRC §§ 2053—2057. The adjusted taxable estate is the taxable estate less $60,000. After you have determined the adjusted taxable estate, use the following table to determine the federal credit.

---

(9) Probate Cd § 609.
(10) Probate Cd § 605(a)(2).

(11) Probate Cd § 608.5.

If the adjusted taxable estate is:	The federal credit is:
Not over $90,000	8/10ths of 1% of the amount by which the adjusted taxable estate exceeds $40,000.
Over $90,000 but not over $140,000	$400 plus 1.6% of the excess over $90,000.
Over $140,000 but not over $240,000	$1,200 plus 2.4% of the excess over $140,000.
Over $240,000 but not over $440,000	$3,600 plus 3.2% of the excess over $240,000.
Over $440,000 but not over $640,000	$10,000 plus 4% of the excess over $440,000.
Over $640,000 but not over $840,000	$18,000 plus 4.8% of the excess over $640,000.
Over $840,000 but not over $1,040,000	$27,600 plus 5.6% of the excess over $840,000.
Over $1,040,000 but not over $1,540,000	$38,800 plus 6.4% of the excess over $1,040,000.
Over $1,540,000 but not over $2,040,000	$70,800 plus 7.2% of the excess over $1,540,000.
Over $2,040,000 but not over $2,540,000	$106,800 plus 8% of the excess over $2,040,000.
Over $2,540,000 but not over $3,040,000	$146,800 plus 8.8% of the excess over $2,540,000.
Over $3,040,000 but not over $3,540,000	$190,800 plus 9.6% of the excess over $3,040,000.
Over $3,540,000 but not over $4,040,000	$238,800 plus 10.4% of the excess over $3,540,000.
Over $4,040,000 but not over $5,040,000	$290,800 plus 11.2% of the excess over $4,040,000.
Over $5,040,000 but not over $6,040,000	$402,800 plus 12% of the excess over $5,040,000.
Over $6,040,000 but not over $7,040,000	$522,800 plus 12.8% of the excess over $6,040,000.
Over $7,040,000 but not over $8,040,000	$650,800 plus 13.6% of the excess over $7,040,000.
Over $8,040,000 but not over $9,040,000	$786,800 plus 14.4% of the excess over $8,040,000.
Over $9,040,000 but not over $10,040,000	$930,800 plus 15.2% of the excess over $9,040,000.
Over $10,040,000	$1,082,800 plus 16% of the excess over $10,040,000.

In administering an estate, the personal representative must construe wills, trusts, and other written instruments in compliance with the provisions of the Internal Revenue Code.[12] With regard to marital deduction gifts and charitable gifts, the estate representative is prohibited from taking any action that might impair or limit these federal deductions. [13] If the governing instrument provides that a fiduciary may satisfy a pecuniary gift wholly or partly by distribution of property other than money, the property must be

---

(12) § 21500–21503.   **(13)** § 21522(b); § 21541.

valued as of the date of distribution.[14] Unless the instrument provides otherwise, the gift is to be satisfied by an amount of property with an aggregate value on the distribution date not less than the amount of the pecuniary bequest.[14] The representative may also value assets as of a date other than distribution, if the instrument grants that authority.

Note: In preparing wills, trusts, and other instruments, attorneys should consider granting to fiduciaries both the authority to satisfy pecuniary bequests with property other than money, as well as the authority to value this property as of a date other than the date of distribution. The express provision of that authority will provide the fiduciary with great flexibility in the administration of the estate, which could result in significant income tax savings.

Apportionment of tax for estate with out-of-state property. If a decedent leaves some property having a situs in California, and some property having a situs in another state or states, the California estate tax is a portion of the federal credit. To find the California estate tax, multiply the federal credit by the percentage that the gross value of property having a California situs bears to the value of the gross estate.[15] The value of property for the purpose of apportioning the federal credit is the value of the property as determined for federal estate tax purposes.

¶ 3107 Filing of Return

The personal representative of an estate subject to California estate tax must file a California estate tax return and a true copy of the federal estate tax return with the Controller. The returns are due on or before the due date of the federal estate tax return, which is nine months after a decedent's death. [16]

Note: If the estate receives an extension of time for filing the federal return, the due date for the California return will also be extended to that date. The personal representative must file a copy of the federal extension with the Controller.[17]

A penalty is imposed for late filing of the return without reasonable cause. The penalty is 5% of the tax due for each month, or portion thereof, that the return is late, but the total penalty can't exceed 25% of the tax due.[18]

Reporting federal changes. A copy of an amended federal estate tax return must be filed with the Controller.[19] The personal representative must give the Controller notice of the final determination of the federal estate tax due within 60 days after the determination.[20]

¶ 3108 Payment of Tax

The personal representative is individually liable for taxes, penalties, and interest to the extent of any payments or distributions from the estate before satisfaction of the estate's tax liability.[21] Except in cases where the governing

---

(14) § 21120.
(15) § 13303.
(16) § 13501.
(17) § 13502.

(18) § 13510.
(19) § 13503.
(20) § 13504.
(21) § 13530; § 19625.

instrument or federal law provides otherwise, the personal representative is directed to equitably prorate the estate tax among "persons interested in the estate," before distribution of estate assets.[22] A "person interested in the estate" is any person, including a personal representative, who is entitled to receive or who has received any property from a decedent, whether at the decedent's death or during his lifetime.[23] The prorated amount of estate tax due is determined by multiplying a fraction, the numerator of which is the value of the estate received by each person interested in the estate and the denominator of which is the value of the estate received by all persons interested in the estate, by the total estate tax due. [24] The personal representative is charged with the duty to recover the tax from persons who received property outside of the representative's control, or if recovery is impossible, to prorate this portion of the tax among the remaining interested persons. Unpaid taxes, interest, and penalties become a perfected and enforceable state tax lien. The lien expires 10 years after the deficiency determination is issued if no notice of the lien was recorded or filed within that 10-year period.[25]

The tax must be paid within nine months after the decedent's death [26] or interest will be charged from that date until it is paid. [27] There is no provision for installment payment of tax.

Delinquent tax bond.   If the tax isn't paid on time, the Controller may require the personal representative to execute a bond for twice the amount of tax due, plus interest from the time the tax became delinquent.[28] The Controller can have the personal representative's letters revoked if the personal representative doesn't file the bond within 20 days after being ordered to do so.[29]

Collection of tax.   *Deficiencies.* The Controller has four years from the date the return is filed to determine a deficiency.[30] However, if a false or fraudulent return was filed, or if no return was filed, the deficiency may be determined at any time. [31] The Controller also has three years to set aside or amend a determination in an erroneous amount.[32] The Controller must give notice of deficiency determined and penalty, if any, to the person filing the return, or the person liable for the tax if no return is filed. [33] If an erroneous deficiency determination is claimed, the person liable for the tax has three years from the deficiency determination to bring action in the appropriate superior court to have the tax modified in whole or in part.[34] The current rate of interest on deficiencies is 12% simple interest.

---

(22) § 20110; § 20116.

(23) § 20100.

(24) § 20111.

(25) § 13610.

(26) § 13532.

(27) § 13550.

(28) § 13555.

(29) § 13557.

(30) § 13516.

(31) § 13517.

(32) § 13518.

(33) § 13519.

(34) § 13520.

Refunds. If the Controller determines that an overpayment was made, the payor will be entitled to a refund of the amount overpaid.[35] Application for refund must be made within one year after final determination of the federal estate tax.[36] The interest rate on refunds will be determined annually, but it won't exceed 7%. Interest will accrue from the later of the date the tax would have been delinquent, if not paid, or the date it was actually paid, until a date no less than 30 days before the Controller issues his refund warrant to the Treasurer.[37] The rate of interest on refunds for 1993 is 6%; for 1992, it was 6.5%.

Collection methods. California can institute a civil suit against any person liable for the tax or any property subject to the lien to enforce its claim for the tax due. [38] The superior court having jurisdiction over the probate estate has jurisdiction to decide tax questions.[39] For nonprobate estates, the superior court of the county of decedent's residence at the date of his death has jurisdiction.[40] If a nonresident decedent leaves property in more than one county, the first superior court to invoke jurisdiction obtains jurisdiction over all property situated in California.[1] The provisions of the California Code of Civil Procedure are followed except when the Estate Tax law provides otherwise. [2]

The Controller can collect by issuing a warrant for collection of tax, or by having a writ of execution issued to enforce a judgment that tax is due. [3] The Controller can use any or all of these methods to collect the tax.[4]

Time limits for collection. The Controller must begin collection proceedings within 10 years after a delinquency determination is issued.[5]

¶ 3109   Generation-Skipping Transfer Tax

Sections 16700 to 16950 of the California Inheritance Tax law provide for a "generation-skipping transfer tax." This California tax is another pick-up tax equal to the amount allowable as a credit under the Generation-Skipping Transfer Tax provisions of the Internal Revenue Code of 1986, as amended.

When tax applies. Section 16702 states that the tax applies where the original transferor is a resident of California at the date of the original transfer, or where the property transferred is real or personal property located in California.

The tax applies to all generation-skipping transfers[6] and is due when there is a taxable distribution or a taxable termination. [7] The person liable for payment of the federal generation-skipping tax is also liable for the state

---

(35) § 13560; 13562.
(36) § 13561.
(37) § 13563.
(38) § 13601.
(39) § 14000.
(40) § 14001.
(1) § 14002.

(2) § 14010.
(3) § 13615–13622.
(4) § 13684.
(5) § 13680.
(6) § 16710.
(7) § 16751.

tax.[8] The tax due is sent to the Controller, payable to the State Treasurer, [9] and becomes delinquent on the day after the last day that the generation-skipping transfer tax return is permitted to be filed. [10]

The California tax will be reduced if any of the property transferred is real property in another state or personal property having a business situs in another state that requires the payment of a tax for which credit is received against the federal generation-skipping transfer tax. The California tax is to be reduced by an amount bearing the same ratio to the total state tax credit allowable for federal generation-skipping transfer tax purposes as the value of such property taxable in the other state bears to the value of the gross generation-skipping transfer for federal generation-skipping transfer tax purposes.[6]

Time for filing. The time for filing the California return to report a generation-skipping transfer is the same as the last day prescribed for filing the federal return. A copy of the federal return must be attached to the California return.[11] If the federal authorities increase or decrease the amount of the federal generation-skipping tax, an amended return is to be filed with the California State Controller showing the changes made in the original return and the amount of increase or decrease in the federal generation-skipping transfer tax. [12]

Collection of tax. The state may enforce its claim for the generation-skipping transfer tax by civil action in any court of competent jurisdiction.[13] The delinquent tax bears interest from the date it becomes due until the date it is paid.[14] The generation-skipping transfer tax is a perfected lien on the property transferred from the time the transfer is made for a period ending on the earlier of 10 years after a deficiency determination is issued or the tax is paid.[15] The Controller may have a writ of execution issued to enforce a judgment to collect the delinquent tax. [16] It may be executed against any property of the person liable for its payment or any property subject to the tax lien. [17]

Refunds. Overpaid generation-skipping transfer taxes are refundable to the taxpayer, but not after the later of the four-year period beginning on the last day a return is due or one year after the date of overpayment unless a claim for overpayment refund is filed by the taxpayer before the end of the period or the Controller refunds the overpayment before the period expires.[18] Suits for refund in the superior court having jurisdiction are allowed within specific time limits.[19] If the overpayment was not caused by taxpayer error or results from a judgment, interest will be allowed to the taxpayer.[20]

---

(8) § 16750.
(9) § 16753.
(10) § 16752.
(11) § 16720.
(12) § 16722.
(13) § 16800.
(14) § 16760.

(15) § 16810.
(16) § 16820.
(17) § 16821.
(18) § 16850; 16851.
(19) § 16860.
(20) § 16870; 16871.

¶ 3109

¶ 3110   Gift Tax

There is no California tax on transfers of property by gift.

RETAILERS, GROSS RECEIPTS, USE TAX

¶ 4001   **General—Scope**

California imposes either a sales or a use tax on the transfers of tangible personal property. Almost all of the transactions in tangible personal property are covered by the sales tax sections of the California Revenue and Taxation Code, with the balance of transactions covered by the use tax provisions. The two taxes are complementary taxes, and a transaction would be subject to one or the other but not both.

The sales and use tax provisions are administered by the California State Board of Equalization. The SBE issues what are now called "Sales and Use Tax Regulations" which are part of the California Administrative Code.[1]

The sales and use tax rates are generally as follows:

State 6.00%

Local county rate 1.25%

Transactions and transportation taxes,
if adopted in a local level .... .25% to 1.75%

Thus the combined minimum rate throughout the state is 7.25%. Individual counties or cities may have a rate as high as 9.0%. At the general election on 11–2–93, the voters approved a permanent extension of the 0.5% portion of the state tax rate that was scheduled to expire 12–31–93.

¶ 4002   **Nature and Purpose of Tax**

The sales tax is a tax on retailers for the privilege of selling tangible personal property at retail in California. The tax is assessed as a percentage of the gross receipts of the retailer from the sale of the tangible personal property in California.[2]

While the sales tax is imposed on the California retailer, the retailer may by written or oral contract be reimbursed for the tax by the purchaser. The California Civil Code provides for the addition for sales tax reimbursement to the sales price. (*Pacific Coast Engineering Co. v. SBE (1952) 111 CA2d 31, 244 P2d 21; Livingstone Rock & Gravel Co., Inc. v. DeSalvo (1955) 136 CA2d 156, 288 P2d 317; Clary v. Basalt Rock Co. (1950) 99 CA2d 458, 222 P2d 24; Op Atty Gen No. 52–178, 12/16/52;* Cal CC § 1656.1.)[3]

(a) Whether a retailer may add sales tax reimbursement to the sales price of the tangible personal property sold at retail to a purchaser depends solely upon the terms of the agreement of sale. It shall be presumed that the parties agreed to the addition of sales tax reimbursement to the sales price of tangible personal property sold at retail to a purchaser if: (1) the agreement of sale expressly provides such addition of sales tax reimbursement; (2) sales tax reimbursement is shown on the sales check or other proof of sale; or (3) the retailer posts in his premises in a location visible to the purchasers or includes on a price tag or in an advertisement or other printed material directed to purchasers, a notice to the

---

(1) Regs 1500–1704.   (3) CC § 1656.1.
(2) § 6051.

¶ 4001

effect that reimbursement for sales tax will be added to the sale price of all items or certain items, whichever is applicable.

(b) It shall be presumed that the property the gross receipts from the sale of which is subject to the sales tax is sold at a price which includes tax reimbursement if the retailer posts in his premises or includes on a price tag or an advertisement (whichever is applicable) one of the following notices: (1) "All prices of taxable items include sales tax reimbursement computed to the nearest mill"; (2) "the price of this item includes sales tax reimbursement computed to the nearest mill."

The provisions of the Civil Code Section have been explained and amplified by Regulation 1700.[4] The regulation states that every retailer who adds to the sales price of property sold at retail an amount from a consumer in reimbursement of sales tax on gross receipts must compute the amount of the sales tax by reference to schedules prepared by the Board of Equalization. As an alternative, the retailer may compute the sales tax on each item to the nearest mill, but if he does he must post a sign to that effect.

¶ 4003 **Important Definitions**

The following definitions are important to know in working with California sales and use tax problems:

Sale. "Sale" means any transfer of title or possession, exchange or barter, conditional or otherwise, in any manner, or by any means whatsoever, of tangible personal property for a consideration. "Transfer of possession" includes only transactions found by the SBE to be in lieu of a transfer of title, exchange or barter.[5]

An assumption of liabilities is "consideration" even where the transferring party remains liable on the indebtedness based on Cal Corp Code § 15015 (*Newco Leasing Inc. v. SBE* (1983) 143 Cal App 3d 126, 191 Cal Rptr 588).

Work on consumers' materials. "Sale" also includes the producing, fabricating, processing, printing or imprinting of tangible personal property for a consideration for consumers who furnish either directly or indirectly the materials used in such producing, fabricating, etc.[6]

Lease—exceptions. "Sale" also includes any lease of tangible personal property in any manner or by any means whatsoever for a consideration *except* a lease of: (1) motion picture, including television films and tapes; (2) linen supplies and similar articles when an essential part of the lease agreement is the furnishing of the recurring service of laundering or cleaning the articles; (3) household furnishings with a lease of the living quarters in which they are to be used; (4) mobile transportation equipment for use in transportation of persons or property; (5) tangible personal property leased in substantially the same form as acquired by the lessor or leased in substantially the same form as acquired by a transferor as to which the lessor or the

---

(4) Reg 1700.
(5) § 6006(a).
(6) § 6006(b).

transferor has paid the sales tax reimbursement or as to which the lessor or transferor has paid use tax measured by the purchase price of the property.[7] Video cassettes, videotapes and videodiscs are not covered by the exceptions for leases of motion pictures, including TV films and tapes under (1), or tangible personalty leased in substantially the same form as acquired under (5), if the lease is for private use and gives lessee no right to license, broadcast, exhibit, or reproduce.[8]

Any person who receives no more than 20% of total gross receipts from the alteration of garments during the preceding calendar year is a consumer and not a retailer with respect to the property used or furnished in altering new or used clothing. To get the exemption, the person must be licensed by the state to pick up and deliver cleaning, or provide spotting or pressing services on the premises, but not garment cleaning, or operate garment cleaning or dyeing plant on the premises; and 75% or more of total gross receipts must be charges for garment cleaning or dyeing.[9]

Lease defined. Lease includes rental, hire and license. "Lease" does not include the use of casual personal property for a period of less than one day for a charge of less than $20 when the privilege to use the property is restricted to the use on the premises or at a business location of the grantor of the privilege. Where a contract designated as a lease binds the lessee for a fixed term, and the lessee is to obtain title at the end of the term upon completion of the required payment or has the option at that time to purchase the property for a nominal amount, the contract shall be regarded as a sale under a security agreement from its inception and not as a lease. In case of such contract designated as a lease with any state or local government body, agency or instrumentality thereof, lessee will be treated as bound for a fixed term even though the lessee has the right to terminate the contract if sufficient funds are not appropriated to pay amounts due under contract.[10]

Seller. Seller includes every person engaged in the business of selling tangible personal property of a kind, the gross receipts from the retail sale of which are required to be included in the measure of the sales tax. Such tangible personal property includes all tangible personal property of a kind the gross receipts from a retail sale of which is, or would be, required to be included in the measure of sales tax, if sold at retail, whether or not the tangible personalty is ever sold at retail, or suitable for sale at retail.[11]

¶ 4004 Who's a Retailer?

Retailer includes:

(a) Every seller who makes any retail sale or sales of tangible personal property and every person engaged in the business of making retail sales at auction of tangible personalty owned by the person or others.

---

(7) § 6006(g)(1)–(5).
(8) § 6006(g)(7).
(9) § 6018.6.

(10) § 6006.4.
(11) § 6014.

(b) Every person engaged in the business of making sales for storage, use or other consumption or in the business of making sales at an auction of tangible personalty owned by the person or others for storage, use or consumption.

(c) Any person conducting a race meeting under the provisions of Chapter 4 of Division 8 of the Business and Professional Code with respect to horses which are claimed during such meeting.[12]

(d) Notwithstanding (b) above, a newspaper carrier is not a retailer. The retailer is the publisher or distributor for whom the carrier delivers the newspapers. The publisher or distributor is responsible for the tax measured by the price charged to the customer by the carrier.[13]

Person deemed retailer. In addition to the general definitions of retailer listed above, Rev & TC § 6275 adds specific types of retailers, as follows: (a) every person making any retail sale of a mobile home or commercial coach required to be registered under the Health and Safety Code, or a vehicle required to be registered under the Vehicle Code or subject to identification under that code or vessel or aircraft, is a retailer, or, (b) every person licensed or certificated under the Vehicle Code or Health and Safety Code as a dealer is the retailer of a mobile home, commercial coach or vehicle required to be registered or subject to identification under such codes when a retail sale of the vehicle is made through him and such person provides to the Department of Motor Vehicles or Department of Housing & Community Development, a notice of transfer on the vehicle pursuant to Health and Safety Cd § 18080.5, or Vehicle Cd § 5901 or § 38200. For purposes of this subdivision, "sale" does not include a lease.[14]

Mail order sellers from outside California. California's attempt to require out-of-state seller's to collect California's use tax and pay it over to the state based on the seller's substantial and recurring solicitations of sales and acceptance of credit cards issued by California financial institution, was struck down as overreaching in *Direct Marketing Association, Inc. etc. v. William M. Bennett, etc., et al.*, (ED Cal, Docket No. CIV S–88–1067, 7/12/91). The court held that *National Bellas Hess, Inc. v. Department of Revenue of the State of Illinois* (1967) 386 US 754 controlled. California's former Rev & TC § 6203(f) was held to be invalid.[15]

Person making more than two retail sales. Every individual, firm, co-partnership, joint venture, trust, business trust, syndicate, association or corporation, making more than two retail sales of tangible personal property during any 12-month period, including sales made as assignee for benefit of creditors, or receiver or trustee in bankruptcy, is considered a retailer. The purpose of this rule is to include in the definition those persons who engage in enough sales transactions to be considered to be retailers when they would not ordinarily hold themselves out to be in that category. Such a person would not be considered to be a retailer until he had made the third sale during a 12-month period. In that situation, each of the first two sales would also be subject to sales tax even though at the time he made the sales he did

---

(12) § 6015.
(13) § 6015(c).

(14) § 6275.
(15) § 6367; Reg 1595.

not know such would be the case. If the person did not include in the first two transactions a provision for contingency that sales tax might later be assessed, that person should try to postpone the third sale until after the twelve-month period from the first sale has passed.[16]

Occasional sale rule—activities requiring seller's permit.   The tax applies to all retail sales of tangible personal property held or used by the seller in the course of an activity or activities for which a seller's permit or permits is required or would be required if the activity or activities were conducted in California. Generally, a person who makes three or more sales for substantial amounts in a period of 12 months is required to hold a seller's permit. A person who makes a substantial number of sales for relatively small amounts is also required to hold a seller's permit. The tax does not apply to a sale of property not held or used in the course of such activities which requires a seller's permit, unless the sale is one of a series of sales sufficient in number, scope and character, to constitute an activity for which the seller is required to hold a seller's permit or would be required to hold a seller's permit if the activity were conducted in California.[16] For an expanded explanation of "occasional sale," see ¶ 4017.

¶ 4004A   Engaged in Business

Retailers "engaged in business" in California are subject to California's taxing jurisdiction. This is frequently referred to as 'nexus'. Nexus in California is created when the California activities of the retailer include any of the following:

(1) maintaining, occupying, or using, permanently or temporarily, directly, or indirectly, or through a subsidiary, or agent, on office, place of distribution, sales or sample room or place, warehouse or storage place, or other place of business.

(2) having any representative, agent, salesperson, canvasser, independent contractor, or solicitor operating in this state under the authority of the retailer or its subsidiary for the purpose of selling, delivering, installing, assembling, or the taking of orders for any tangible personal property,

(3) deriving rentals from a lease of tangible personal property in California,

(4) soliciting orders for tangible personal property by means of a telecommunication or television shopping system which utilizes toll free numbers which is intended by the retailer to be broadcast by cable television or other means of broadcasting, to consumers in California,

(5) contracting with a broadcaster or publisher located in California to solicit orders for tangible personal property by means of advertising primarily to consumers located in California,

(6) soliciting orders for tangible personal property by mail if the solicitations are substantial and recurring and if the retailer benefits from any banking, financing, debt collections, telecommunication, or marketing activities occurring in California, or benefits from the location in California of authorized installation, servicing, or repair facilities,

---

(16) § 6019.

(7) any retailer owned or controlled by the same interests which owns or controls any retailer engaged in business in the same or a similar line of business in California,

(8) any retailer having a franchise or licensee operating under its trade name if the franchise or licensee is required to collect sales or use tax, and

(9) solicits orders for tangible personal property by means of advertising which is transmitted or distributed over a cable television system in California.

A retailer doing business in California as set forth in (4) - (9) above, but is not conducting activities as set forth in (1) - (3) above, is a retailer engaged in business in California for purposes of use tax collections only.

Effective 1–1–95, a retailer is not engaged in business in California if its only activities are the taking of orders from customers in California through a computer telecommunications network located in California which is not directly or indirectly owned by the retailer, when the orders result from the electronic display of products on the same network. This exclusion applies only to a computer telecommunications network that consists substantially of on-line communications services other than the displaying or taking of orders for products. This exclusion sunsets on 12–31–99.[17]

Voluntarily disclosure. If a retailer voluntarily comes forward and discloses that it is engaged in business in California, the statute of limitations, notwithstanding Rev & TC § 6487, during which a deficiency determination may be mailed to a qualifying retailer is limited to three years after the last day of the calendar month following the quarterly period for which the tax is proposed to be assessed, rather than the eight year period when no return has been filed. A qualifying retailer is one who meets all or the following conditions:

(1) is located outside California and has not previously registered with the State Board of Equalization,

(2) the retailer is engaged in business in California as defined in Rev & TC § 6203,

(3) the retailer voluntarily registers with the board,

(4) the retailer has not been previously contacted by the State Board of Equalization or its agents regarding doing business in the State of California, and

(5) the State Board of Equalization determines that the retailer's failure to file a return or failure to report or pay the tax or amount due was due to reasonable cause and was not a result of negligence or intentional disregard of the law, or because of fraud, or an intent to evade tax.[18]

¶ 4005   What Are Gross Receipts?

"Gross receipts" means the total amount of the sale or lease or rental price as the case may be of the retail sale of retailers valued in money whether received in money or otherwise without any deductions on account of any of the following:

(1) The cost of the property sold.

---

(17) § 6203, as amended by Stats. 1994, c. 851, § 2.   **(18)** § 6487.05, as added by Stats. 1994, c. 903, § 5.

(2) The cost of the materials used, labor or service cost, interest paid, losses or any other expense.

(3) The cost of transportation of the property.

(4) The amount of any tax imposed by the United States on producers and importers of gasoline.

(5) Total amount of the sale, lease or the rental price includes all of the following:

(a) Any services that are a part of the sale;

(b) All receipts, cash, credits and property of any kind;

(c) Any amount for which credit is allowed by the seller to the purchaser.[19]

Exclusions. In computing gross receipts the retailer can exclude: (1) cash discounts allowed and taken on sales; (2) the sales price of property returned by customers when that amount is refunded either in cash or credit; (3) the price received for labor or services used in installing or applying the property sold if separately stated; and (4) the amount of any taxes imposed by the United States (except manufacturers' or importers' excise tax, other than the amount of manufacturers' or importers' excise tax imposed by IRC § 4091 for which the purchaser certifies entitlement to either a direct refund or credit against federal income tax for excise tax paid), California, or local tax authorities measured by a stated percentage of sales price or gross receipts; (5) separate stated charges for transportation from place of shipment directly to the consumer; (6) motor vehicle, mobile home or commercial coach fees and taxes of California measured by a percentage of the sales price of the motor vehicle; (7) the charges for transporting landfill from an excavation site to a site specified by the purchaser if, either the charge is separately stated and does not exceed a reasonable charge, or the entire consideration consists of payment for transportation.[19]

Consumer cooperatives' "gross receipts" from the sale of property don't include the value of initial or periodical membership fees, labor performed in place of, or as part of monthly membership fees. The cost of property sold is not excluded from "gross receipts."[20]

Technology. The State Board of Equalization has held that the value of technology transferred on computer tape and discs is not subject to sales tax. The sales tax applies only to the value of the computer tape itself, including the cost of copying the information onto the tapes and discs (*Appeal of Intel Inc.*, SBE, 3/92, unpublished).

Bad debts. A retailer is allowed to recover sales tax which has been paid on tangible personal property items sold on a credit basis in which the retailer suffered a bad debt. A bad debt deduction may be claimed on a current sales tax return if the original sale was made after 9–30–57, and the sales tax or use tax was actually paid to California. Regulation 1642 states that the measure of the reduction of the tax is represented by the accounts

---

(19) § 6012.   (20) § 6012.1.

which have been found to be worthless and charged off for income tax purposes or, if the retailer is not required to file income tax returns, charged-off in accordance with generally accepted accounting principles. If the retailer repossesses an item of personal property, a bad debt deduction is allowed to the extent that the retailer sustains a net loss of gross receipts on which tax has been paid.[21]

TAX TIP   The State Board of Equalization will only allow a bad debt to be recognized for sales tax purposes in the same year it is written off for income tax reporting.

Tax paid property resold. A retailer who has paid sales tax to a vendor on tangible personal property which was intended for self use, and instead of using it sells it in a retail sale, is entitled to take a deduction on the sales tax return for the tax paid under the heading, "Cost of tax-paid purchases resold prior to use." The deduction must be taken on the retailer's return in which the sale of property is included. If the deduction is not taken in the proper quarter, a claim for refund must be filed.[22]

¶ 4006 Service Enterprises

The performance of services that are not subject to sales tax is sometimes difficult to separate from the sale of tangible personal property which is subject to sales tax. According to Regulation 1501, the basic distinction that must be made in deciding whether a transaction involved a sale of tangible personal property or the transfer of personal property incidental to the performance of a service, is distinguishing the "true object" of the contract; that is, the real object sought by the buyer—whether it is the service per se, or the property produced by the service. If the true object of the contract is the service the transaction is not subject to tax even though some tangible personal property is transferred.

TAX TIP   Research and development contracts may result in prototypes which have been prepared to demonstrate that the technology being developed actually works. It has been the practice of the State Board of Equalization to tax the transfer of prototypes by valuing them at the actual costs of material and labor content of the prototype itself, plus a factor for overhead and profit. The technology is not included in the value subject to tax.

¶ 4007 Exemption Certificates

The gross receipts from all sales of tangible personal property delivered in California by a retailer in California are subject to sales tax unless purchased for resale by the buyer. The gross receipts are presumed to be taxable unless the seller can prove that the purchase was for resale. The best evidence that the sale of tangible personal property was for resale by the

---

(21) § 6055; 6203.5; Reg 1642.   (22) Reg 1701.

purchaser is for the seller to get a resale certificate from the purchaser showing that the item was for resale in the ordinary course of the purchaser's business.

Resale certificates.   A "Resale Certificate" is given by a purchaser of tangible personal property to the California retailer to claim exemption from the sales tax because the purchaser will sell the purchased property in the ordinary course of the purchaser's business. Regulation 1668 specifies the information that must be included in the resale certificate and also provides a specimen form. If the seller accepts the resale certificate in good faith and has no reason to believe that the person offering the certificate is other than a retail dealer, the seller is relieved of any liability for sales tax on the transaction.

Conversion to taxable use.   If a retailer acquires property from a vendor, and gives a resale certificate instead of paying sales tax, and then consumes the property for self-use, the retailer is required to pay use tax on the property by including it in its sales and use tax return under the category of "purchase price of tangible personal property purchased without California sales or use tax, and used for some purpose other than resale."[23]

Demonstration and display.   A purchaser of tangible property who gives a resale certificate to the seller and does not pay sales tax at the time of purchase and later uses the property solely for purposes of demonstration or display during the period in which it is held for sale in the regular course of business, is not required to pay tax attributable to such use. However, if the property is used for any other purpose, such as making deliveries, personal use by employees, etc., the purchaser is required to include in the measure of

latter case, in addition to recording the sales tax on the rental receipts, the dealer is required to include in gross receipts the retail sale of the demonstration property following its rental to the salesman. Regulation 1669.5 sets forth the rule for the demonstration, display and use of motor vehicles by automobile dealers and their salesmen. It states that automobile dealers who provide vehicles to schools, colleges and veterans institutions for driver training or other educational purposes are exempt from paying use tax on such use.

Catering truck operators.   The State Board of Equalization may require any sellers to operators of catering trucks, operated out of their facility, who resell property in regular course of business, to verify validity of operators' permits. The SBE may also require the listing of the purchasing operators, identifying information on operator, and notice of operator's fail-

---

(23) § 6421.

ure to provide evidence of a valid permit. Sellers without valid permits, or those whose permits have been revoked, must report and pay tax as if the sale was one at retail.[24]

Use of fuel in manner not qualifying for income tax credit or refund. A purchaser is liable for sales or use tax measured by the amount of federal excise tax paid to the extent the seller has not remitted sales or use tax measured by that amount.[25]

Direct sales permits. The State Board of Equalization is authorized to adopt rules and regulations that provide for issuance of direct sales permits.[26]

¶ 4008   **Exempt Tangible Personalty**

Tangible personal property not included in the measure of the sales tax includes:

Food and beverages. The tax does not apply to sales of food products for human consumption. From 7–15–91 through 11–30–92, candy, confectionery, nonmedicated chewing gum, snack foods, and noncarbonated and noneffervescent bottled water sold in individual containers of ½ gallon or more were taxable. Beginning 12–1–92, the exemption for these food products were reinstated. The tax does not apply to sales of purified water through vending machines and retail outlets or local supply lines, if dispensed into the customer's own container. It also does not apply to sales of water in bulk quantities of 50 gallons or more to an individual for use in a residence not serviced by lines, mains, or pipes. Reg 1602 outlines the tax treatment of foods. The furnishing, preparing or serving of food, meals or drinks for a consideration is taxable unless the items prepared are used by patients and inmates of hospitals, alcoholism or drug abuse recovery facility, child care centers, aged persons centers, etc. There is also an exclusion for: (1) meals and food products served to low-income elderly people at or below cost by nonprofit organizations; (2) the sale of hot prepared foods by caterers to air carriers engaged in interstate or foreign commerce; and (3) meal or food products furnished to and consumed by senior citizens living in a condominium, who own equal shares in common kitchen facility, provided meals and food products are served to them on a regular basis. Food products, but not prepared hot meals, sold for consumption at national and state parks, monuments, marinas, campgrounds, and recreational vehicle parks are exempt.

Any organization listed below is the consumer of, and will not be considered a retailer with respect to food products, nonalcoholic beverages or other tangible personal property made or produced by its members, provided its sales are made on an intermittent basis, and the organization's profits from

---

(24) § 6074.   **(26)** § 7051.1.
(25) § 6423.

those sales are used exclusively in furtherance of the organization's purposes.

● Any nonprofit organization that: (a) qualifies for tax-exempt status under IRC § 501(c); (b) whose primary purpose is to provide a supervised program of competitive sports for youth, or to promote citizenship in youth; and (c) the organization does not discriminate on the basis of race, sex, nationality, or religion.

● Any youth group sponsored by or affiliated with a qualified educational institution, as defined, including, but not limited to any student activity club, athletic group, or musical group. The term qualified educational institution includes public schools for kindergarten through grades 1 to 12, and college undergraduate programs operated by state or local government, any nonprofit private educational institution, providing education for kindergarten, grades 1 to 12 and college undergraduate programs that meet the requirements of the State Board of Education, and any local laws in effect 1–1–90; discrimination is barred.

● Little League, Bobby Sox, Boy Scouts, Cub Scouts, Girl Scouts, Campfire, Inc., YMCA, YWCA, Future Farmers of America, Future Homemakers of America, and 4–H Clubs. Exemption also extends to Distributive Education Clubs of America, Future Business Leaders of America, Vocational Industrial Clubs of America, Collegiate Young Farmers, Boys' Clubs and Girls' Clubs, Special Olympics, Inc., American Youth Soccer Organization, California Youth Soccer Association, North, California Youth Soccer Association, South, and Pop Warner Football.

Meals served by care facilities. Effective 1–1–95, gross receipts subject to sales tax excludes receipts from the sale of meals and food products for human consumption furnished or served to and consumed by residents or patients of: (1) a health facility defined in Health and Safety Code § 1250; (2) a community care facility as defined in Health and Safety Code § 1502; (3) a residential care facility for the elderly as defined in Health and Safety Code § 1569.2; (4) a house or institution supplying board and room for a flat monthly rate and serving as a principal residence exclusively for persons 62 years of age or older, or any housing that primarily serves older persons and is financed by state or federal programs; (5) an alcoholism recovery facility as defined in Health and Safety Code § 11834.11; or (6) a drug abuse recovery or treatment facility as defined in Health and Safety Code § 11834.11. In all cases the facilities qualify for exemption only if they meet certain licensing requirements as specified in the code.[27]

Vending Machines In case of food products, for 1990 and later, 33% of retailer's gross receipts will be subject to tax, when sold through vending machines. For 1989, the percentage was 55%; for 1988, 77%. For purposes of this Rev & TC § 6359.2 partial exemption, food products include hot coffee, hot tea, and hot chocolate when sold through a vending machine for a separate price, but do not include other hot prepared food products. Any vending machine operator is the consumer, not the retailer of food products sold at retail for 25¢ or less through a vending machine.[28]

---

(27) § 6363.6, as amended by Stats. 1994, c. 702, § 1.
(28) § 6006(d); 6359–6359.1; 6359.2; 6359.4;

6359.45; 6359.5; 6361; 6363.6; 6366.4; 6374; 6376.5; Reg 1602.

Carbon dioxide packing. Effective 1–1–95, gross receipts subject to sales tax does not include receipts from the sale of carbon dioxide used in packing and shipping fruits or vegetables for human consumption when those fruits or vegetables are not sold to the ultimate consumer in the package which contains the carbon dioxide, and any nonreturnable materials containing the carbon dioxide atmosphere.[29]

Works of art. Commercial artists are retailers of commercial art work sold to advertising agencies. Works of art are exempt when they are purchased by (1) the state or a political subdivision, (2) any nonprofit organization operating a museum for such governmental entity, (3) any nonprofit organization qualified for exemption under Section 23701d for a museum open to the public and (4) purchased for donation and actually donated to the government entity or nonprofit organization. The exemption applies only for art purchased to become a permanent part of the museum collection, that of a nonprofit organization meeting tests regarding loans of its collection, and local government entities buying or commissioning art for public display. Items having value as museum pieces, and used exclusively for display purposes that are purchased by specified nonprofit museums to replace property destroyed by fire, flood, earthquake or other calamity are exempt provided museum meets conditions as to time, space and the segments of population to which it is open without charge to public. The exemption also includes the purchase of property used exclusively for display within the San Diego Aero-Space Museum, and the California Museum of Science and Industry, and sprung instant structures used as temporary exhibit housing at these two museums.[30]

Newspapers and periodicals. The sale of newspapers, periodicals, and other publications is generally taxable. However, newspapers or periodicals distributed without charge, and regularly issued at average intervals not exceeding three months, are exempt. Also exempt are periodicals issued at average intervals not exceeding three months that are sold by subscription and delivered by mail or common carrier. Tangible personal property that became ingredients or components of a free newspaper or periodical or a subscription periodical are also exempt.

For purposes of the free periodical and subscription periodical exemptions, a "periodical" means a publication that appears at stated intervals of at least four times, but not more than 60 times, a year. Each issue of the periodical must contain news or information of general interest to the public, or to some particular organization or group of persons. Each issue must bear a relationship to prior or later issues and there must be some connection between the different issues of the series. The term does not include printed sales messages, shopping guides, or other publications, of which the advertising portion is over 90% of the printed area of the entire issue in more than

---

(29) § 6359.8, as added by Stats. 1994, c. 624, § 1.   **(30)** § 6365; 6366.3; 6366.4; 6403; Reg 1540(c).

½ of the issues during any 12-month period.[31] Newspapers for which a pre-paid subscription was made before 7–15–91 are also exempt.[32] Newspapers published or purchased by an organization qualifying for tax-exempt status under IRC § 501(c)(3), and newspapers distributed by a nonprofit organization similarly exempt. In both of these cases, the distribution must be to members of the organization in consideration of payment of the organization's membership fee. Qualifying IRC § 501(c)(3) organizations can make distributions of the publication to contributors. To qualify for the exemption, the IRC § 501(c)(3) organization cannot receive revenue from, or accept any commercial advertising to be included in the exempt publication. In the case of nonprofit organizations, the cost of printing the newspaper or periodical must be less than 10% of the membership fee for the period of distribution.[33]

> *Note:* The exemption for tangible personal property sold to become an ingredient or component part of any newspaper, etc., was repealed effective 7–15–91 and reinstated for sales on or after 11–1–92.[34]

Poultry litter.   Wood shavings, sawdust, rice hulls, or other products that are used as litter in poultry and egg production and are ultimately resold as, or incorporated into, fertilizer, is exempt from sales and use tax effective 1–1–94.[35]

Qualified organizations receive partial exemption.   Sales of organizations which are exempt from tax pursuant to IRC § 501(c)(3) which has as its primary purpose the providing of services to individuals with developmental disabilities, and which does not discriminate on the basis of race, sex, nationality, or religion, qualify for an exemption from tax if the: (1) property sold is of a handcrafted nature and is designed, created, or made by individuals with developmental disabilities who are members of, or receive service from, the organization; (2) the price of each item sold does not exceed $10; (3) the organization's profits from those sales are used exclusively in furtherance of the purposes of the organization; and (4) the organization's sales are made on an irregular or intermittent basis. The exclusion applies to transactions on or after 1–1–94.[36]

Intangible rights.   The amount charged for intangible personal property transferred with tangible personal property in any technology transfer agreement, under which certain rights are assigned or licensed, is not subject to sales or use tax if the agreement separately states a reasonable price for the intangible personal property or if the tangible personal property or like tangible personal property has been previously sold, leased, or offered for sale or lease at a separate price as specified. If there is no comparable price of the tangible personal property and if the price of the intangible personal property is not stated, then other valuation rules apply. The exclusion applies to transactions on or 1–1–94.[37]

---

(31) § 6362.7; Reg 1590.
(32) § 6362.3.
(33) § 6362.7; 6362.8.
(34) § 6362.7.

(35) § 6358.2, as amended by Stats. 1994, c. 1&6, § 199.
(36) § 6361.1.
(37) § 6011(c)(10) and 6012(c)(10).

TAX TIP	The exclusion from sales of amounts received from the transfer of intangible rights set forth in Rev & TC §§ 6011 and 6012, was declared by the Legislature to be a clarification of existing law. Accordingly, claims for refund of tax previously paid should be considered if the statute of limitations has not already expired.

Mailing lists. Mailing lists sold or rented for one-time use are exempt from sales or use tax effective 1–1–94. A mailing list means a written or printed list of names and addresses that is intended for circulating material by mail. It may be in the form of a manuscript list, directory, Cheshire tax, Dick tape, gummed labels, index cards, or other similar means of communication including magnetic tape or similar device used to produce written or printed names and addresses by electronic or mechanical means.[38]

Medical identification tags. Medical identification tags are exempt from tax. For years prior to 1994 the exemption applied to medical alert tags. The change in description of the tags is not meant to change the incidence of tax.[39]

Catalogs, circulars, letters, brochures and pamphlets. Catalogs, circulars, letters, brochures, and pamphlets consisting substantially of printed sales messages and services printed to special order of purchaser are exempt from sales and use taxes, if mailed or delivered by seller, its agent or a mailing house, acting as agent for the purchaser, through the U.S. Postal Service or by common carrier to any other person at no cost to the person who becomes the owner of these messages.[40]

Medicines. Medicines prescribed by physicians for the treatment of human beings are exempt. This includes sutures, insulin and insulin syringes furnished by registered pharmacists and drug infusion devices, and other items of personal property which are implanted in the body for specific purposes. Medical oxygen delivery systems purchased by individual patients are also exempt. It does not include nonprescription drugs or medicines, or articles in the nature of splints, bandages and so on, without prescription. Exemption also extends to receipts from transactions involving hemodialysis products; gross receipts from sale, storage or use of wheelchairs, crutches, canes, quad canes, white canes (for the blind) and walkers when sold to individual for personal use on order of physician, orthopedic shoes and supportive devices, and items and materials used to modify vehicle for physically handicapped persons, including portion of vehicle modified. Licensed hearing aid dispenser is consumer, not retailer of hearing aids dispensed. Licensed veterinarian is consumer, not retailer, of drugs and medicines furnished in performance of professional services. Food stamp coupons are exempt.[1]

---

(38) § 6379.8.   (40) § 6379.5.
(39) § 6371.   (1) § 6369–6369.5; 6373.

The exemption for medicine, effective 1–1–95, would also include medicines furnished without charge by a pharmaceutical manufacturer or distributor to a licensed physician, surgeon, dentist, podiatrist, health facility, or to an institution of higher education for instruction and research. The exemption includes the related packaging, materials, elements, and ingredients of such medicine. The exemption is limited to medicines that can be dispensed only for the treatment of a human being and pursuant to prescriptions issued by persons authorized to prescribe medicines.[2]

Charitable organizations qualifying for welfare exemption. Tangible personal property made, prepared, assembled or manufactured by such organizations is exempt from both sales and use tax, if the organizations are engaged in and make donations, as well as sales, pursuant to relief efforts.[3]

Auction items sold to fund shelter for homeless individuals and families. Effective 1–1–95, gross receipts subject to sales tax do not include the proceeds of the sale of tangible personal property sold at an auction conducted by, or affiliated with, a nonprofit organization to obtain revenue for the funding of a shelter for homeless individuals and families. This exemption can apply only to one auction by a qualified organization during any 12-month period.[4]

Nonprofit zoological societies. There is exempt from sales or use tax transfers of an endangered or threatened animal or plant species, as defined, between nonprofit zoological societies or between a member of the American Zoo and Aquarium Association and a nonprofit zoological society. Any retailer, other than a nonprofit zoological society, that stores, uses, or otherwise consumes in California an endangered or threatened animal or plant species acquired through a trade or exchange with a nonprofit zoological society shall be liable for use tax.[5]

Ships and marine supplies. Exempt from tax are the receipts from the sales of vessels of more than one thousand tons burden, by the builders.[6]

Used floating homes. Used floating homes subject to local property taxation are exempt from payment of use tax on resale or transfer.[7]

Gas, electricity, water. Gas, electricity and water are exempt.[8]

Transfer between family members or to a revocable trust. Transfers of mobilehomes or commercial coaches required to be registered annually under the Health and Safety Code, vehicles required to be registered or identified under the Vehicle Code, vessels and aircraft are exempt from sales/use tax when the person selling the property is either the parent, grandparent, child, grandchild, or spouse, or the brother or sister if the sale

---

(2) § 6369, as amended by Stats. 1994, c. 857, § 2.

(3) § 6375.

(4) § 6363.2, as added by Stats. 1994, c. 855, § 1.

(5) § 6010.50, 6202.5 & 6366.5, as added/amended by Stats. 1994, c. 771, § 1–3.

(6) § 6356.

(7) § 6379.

(8) § 6353; 6359.6.

between that brother or sister is between two minors related by blood or adoption, of the purchaser, and the person selling is not engaged in the business of selling that type of property for which the exemption is claimed. This exemption also applies to sales or transfers to a revocable trust if: (1) the seller has unrestricted power to revoke the trust; (2) upon revocation the property will revert wholly to the seller; (3) the sale does not result in any change in the beneficial ownership of the property; and (4) the only consideration for the sale is the assumption by the trust of an existing loan for which the tangible personal property being transferred is the sole collateral for the assumed loan.[9]

Monetized bullion. Bulk sales that are substantially equivalent to transactions in securities or commodities through national securities or commodities exchanges are exempt; also storage, use or consumption of monetized bullion so sold. Nonmonetized gold or silver bullion, or numismatic coins are exempt. California gold medallions are exempt. Bulk sales are defined as transactional with a value of $1,000 or more. For years after 1994, the $1,000 value is to be adjusted annually for inflation.[10]

Rail freight cars. Rail freight cars are exempt.[11]

Watercraft. Watercraft used in interstate or foreign commerce for transportation, in deep sea commercial fishing operations, and, functionally 80% or more of time in transporting property or persons for hire to vessels or offshore drilling platforms outside territorial waters of state. A rebuttable presumption that a person is not regularly engaged in such operations applies if gross receipts are less than $20,000.[12] The sale or use of diesel fuel used to operate such watercraft is taxable.

Low-emission motor vehicles. The incremental cost (difference between estimated cost or sale of low-emission motor vehicle, and cost of comparable gasoline or diesel fueled vehicle) is exempt from sales or use tax; also net receipts from sale or use of any retrofit device converting conventional into low-emission vehicle. The exemption expires 1–1–95.[13]

New motor vehicle sold to resident of foreign country. The sale or use of any new motor vehicle is exempt if sold to a purchaser who is a resident of a foreign country who arranges for the purchase through an authorized dealer in a foreign country before arriving in U.S. In-transit permit under Vehicle Cd § 6700.1 must be secured, and before its expiration, the retailer must ship or drive the motor vehicle to a point outside the U.S. by means of its facilities, or by delivery to a carrier, customs broker, or by delivery to carrier, customs broker, or forwarding agent for shipment to that point.[14]

Tangible personal property brought or shipped into California by purchaser. The first $400 of tangible personal property purchased in a foreign

---

(9) § 6285.
(10) § 6354; 6355; Reg. 1599.
(11) § 6358.5.

(12) § 6368; 6368.1.
(13) § 6356.5.
(14) § 6366.2.

country by an individual from a retailer and personally hand carried into California by the purchaser within any 30-day period is exempt from use tax.[15]

Aircraft. Aircraft sold to common carriers, foreign governments, aircraft leased to common carriers and foreign governments.[16]

Containers. Exempted from sales tax are the gross receipts from the sale of and the storage, use or other consumption in California of:

(a) *Nonreturnable containers* when sold without the contents to persons who place the contents in the container and sell the contents together with the container.

(b) *Containers when sold with the contents* if the sale price of the contents is not required to be included in the sales tax.

(c) *Returnable containers* when sold with the contents in connection with the retail sale of the contents or when resold for refilling.[17]

Fuel. The gross receipts from the distribution of, and storage, use or consumption of motor vehicle fuel used to propel aircraft, except jet fuel, if distributions are subject to the motor vehicle fuel tax are exempt.[18] Fuel sold to air common carriers for immediate consumption or shipment in the conduct of their business as air common carriers, on an international flight is exempt. An international flight is one whose final destination is outside the United States. Prior to 1–1–93, the exemption only applied if the first destination of the flight was outside the United States.

Until 7–15–91, an exemption applied to fuel and petroleum products sold to certain common carriers where the fuel and petroleum products were to be immediately shipped outside the state for use and consumption by the common carrier after the first out-of-state destination. For sales on or after 1–1–92 to water common carriers, the exemption was reinstated.[19]

Dry ice or ice. Dry ice or ice used or employed in packing and shipping or transporting food products for human consumption is exempt when the food products are shipped or transported in intrastate, interstate, or foreign commerce by common carriers, contract carriers, or proprietary carriers.[20]

Carriers. Sales of tangible personal property to common carriers are exempt when the property is shipped by the seller via the purchasing carrier under a bill of lading to the out-of-state point, and is actually transported to that point for use by the carrier in the conduct of its business. Also exempt are gross receipts from the sale of tangible personalty, other than aircraft fuel and petroleum products, purchased by a foreign air carrier, and transported to a foreign destination for use in its business as a common carrier by air of persons and property. The seller has reasonable time to request the foreign air carrier to submit a certificate that the property will be trans-

---

(15) § 6405.
(16) § 6366; 6366.1.
(17) § 6364.

(18) § 6357.
(19) § 6357.5; 6385.
(20) § 6359.7.

ported and used in the manner required to qualify for the exemption.[21] New or used trailers or semitrailers are exempt from use tax if in-state storage, use or consumption involves moving them or operating them while laden under a one-trip permit.[22]

U.S. agencies—American Red Cross. Sales of tangible personalty to the U.S., its agencies or instrumentalities, and the American Red Cross are exempt from sales tax.[23]

¶ 4008a   **Sales Tax Exemption For Manufacturing Equipment**

Beginning on or after 1–1–94, and continuing until at least tax years beginning on or before 1–1–2001, property purchased by qualified taxpayers will be partially exempt from sales or use tax if the property is placed in service in California and meets detailed requirements as to use. Beginning 1–1–95, the exemption applies to 5% of the state tax; from 1–1–94 through 12–31–94, the exemption applied to the full 6% state tax.[24]

Qualified property.   Qualified property means all of the following:

(1) Tangible personal property purchased for use primarily (defined as 50% or more) in any stage of the manufacturing, processing, refining, fabricating, or recycling of property, beginning at the point any raw materials are received by the qualified person and are introduced into the process and ending at the point at which the manufacturing, processing, refining, fabricating, or recycling has altered property to its completed form, including packaging, if required.

(2) Tangible personal property purchased for use primarily (defined as 50% or more) in research and development.

(3) Tangible personal property purchased to be used primarily (defined as 50% or more) to maintain, repair, measure, or test any property described in (1) or (2).

(4) Tangible personal property purchased for use by a contractor either as an agent of a qualified person or for the contractor's own account and subsequent resale to a qualified person for use in the performance of a construction contract for the qualified person who will use the tangible personal property as an integral part of the manufacturing, processing, refining, fabricating, or recycling process, or as a research or storage facility for use in connection with the manufacturing process.

Qualifying property does not include any tangible personal property that is used primarily in administration, general management, or marketing. Tangible personal property as specifically defined in Rev & TC § 6377(b)(9) includes, but is not limited to:

(1) Machinery and equipment, including component parts and contrivances such as belts, shafts, moving parts, and operating structures.

(2) All equipment or devices used or required to operate, control, regulate, or maintain the machinery, including, without limitation, computers, data processing equipment, and computer software, together with all repair and replacement parts with a useful life of one or more years, whether purchased separately or in

---

(21) § 6385.   (23) § 6381.
(22) § 6410.   (24) § 6377.

conjunction with a complete machine and regardless of whether the machine or component parts are assembled by the taxpayer or another party.

(3) Property used in pollution control that meets or exceeds standards established by California, or any local or regional governmental agency within California.

(4) Special purpose buildings and foundations used as an integral part of the manufacturing, processing, refining, or fabricating process, or that constitute a research or storage facility used during the manufacturing process. Buildings used solely for warehousing purposes after completion of the manufacturing process are not included.

(5) Fuels used or consumed in the manufacturing process.

(6) Property used in recycling.[25]

Qualifying persons. Qualifying persons must be engaged in a new trade or business. A person shall not be considered in a new trade or business if they have purchased or otherwise acquired all or any portion of the assets of an existing trade or business, irrespective of the form of entity, that is doing business in California if the aggregate fair market value of the total assets of the trade or business being conducted by the acquiring person, or related person. For this purpose the measurement date shall be the last day of the month following the quarterly period in which the person first uses any of the acquired assets in his or her business activity. Special rules apply to property acquired which is defined in IRC § 1221(1), inventory. In addition, if a person is engaged in one or more trades or businesses in California within 36 months prior to the acquisition, and thereafter commences an additional trade or business, the new trade or business will be considered as a new business only if it is classified under a different division of the SIC Manual published by the U.S. Office of Management and Budget, 1987 edition, than are any of the person's, or any related person's, current or prior trade or business activities in California.

In any case where a person is engaged in a trade or business wholly outside the state of California, and that person first commences doing business in California after 12–31–93, other than by purchase or other acquisition described above, the trade or business activity in California will be treated as a new business.

If there is merely a change in legal form under which a trade or business is being conducted, the change in form shall be disregarded and the determination of whether the trade or business activity is a new business shall be made by treating the person as having purchased or otherwise acquired all or any portion of the assets in an existing trade or business as described above.

A related person shall mean any person that is related under IRC §§ 267 or 318. To 'acquire' includes any gift, inheritance, transfer incident to a divorce, or any other transfer, whether or not for consideration.

---

(25) § 6377, as amended by Stats. 1994, c. 751, § 1.

A qualifying person will not include any person who has conducted business activates in a new trade or business for three or more years.[25]

Qualifying persons entitled to the credit for acquisitions of qualifying property are those who are engaged in those lines of business described in Codes 2000 to 3999, inclusive, of the Standard Industrial Classification Manual published by the U.S. Office of Management and Budget, 1987 edition (these are generally referred to as SIC codes). Generally, codes 2000 to 3999 include all manufacturing businesses, but exclude agriculture, communication, construction, forestry, fishing, mining, real estate, retail trade, services, transportation, utilities, and wholesale trade.

Manufacturing means converting or conditioning property by changing the form, composition, quality, or character of the property for ultimate sale at retail or use in the manufacturing of a product to be ultimately sold at retail. It includes any improvements to tangible personal property that result in a greater service life or greater functionality than that of the original property. Fabricating means to make, build, create, produce, or assemble components or property to work in a new or different manner.[25]

Investment tax credit.   No credit shall be allowed for any qualified property for which an investment tax credit has been claimed pursuant to Rev & TC §§ 17053.49 or 23649.[25]

In the event the person acquiring the qualified property paid the retailer reimbursement for sales tax at the time of acquisition, or self-assessed use tax, a claim may be filed with the SBE for refund of 6% tax paid. The claim may be filed by the person who paid the tax reimbursement to the retailer, it does not have to be filed by the retailer. When making the Claim the owner of the property must irrevocably waive the equivalent amount of credit allowed as an investment tax credit for manufacturing property under Rev & TC §§ 17053.49, or 23649. To claim the refund, the person filing the claim must include proof of payment of tax to the retailer with a copy of an invoice or purchase contract that shows when the purchase occurred, a description of the property purchased, the price paid for the property and the amount of tax paid with the purchase.[26]

Recapture.   The sales/use tax will be assessed against the purchaser if qualified property is disposed of, or removed from California, within one year of the date of purchase.[25]

Exemption certificate required.   No exemption from sales/use tax will be recognized unless the buyer delivers to the seller an exemption certificated, completed in accordance with any instructions or regulations as proscribed by the board, and the retailer subsequently furnishes the board with a copy of the exemption certificate. The certificate must specifically state that the purchase is an exempt transaction under Rev & TC § 6377, and state the amount of the purchase price exempt from tax.[25]

---

(26) § 6902.2, as added by Stats. 1994, c. 547, § 1.

Local taxes apply. The exemption from tax does not apply to any county, city, or district tax levied pursuant to, or in accordance with the Bradley-Burns Uniform Local Sales and Use Tax Law, or the Transactions and Use Tax Law.[25]

¶ 4008b   Sales Tax Exemption Vandenberg Space Center

Beginning on or after 1–1–94, and continuing until at least tax years beginning on or before 12–31–2003, tangible personal property with spaceflight capability are exempt from sales/use tax. The space flight must originate at Vandenberg Air Force Base. Material not *intended* to be launched into space is taxable. Fuel which is not adaptable for use in ordinary motor vehicles, but is produced, sold, and used exclusively for space flight is exempt.[27]

¶ 4009   Some Effects of Tax on Business

The following paragraphs illustrate some applications of the tax to businesses shown:

Manufacturers. Manufacturers purchase tangible personal property to be used in their manufacturing process. If the tangible personal property is incorporated into the manufactured article to be sold, its purchase is not taxable. For example, any raw material becoming an ingredient or component part of the manufactured article does not require that sales tax be paid when the manufacturer purchases it. However, sales tax does apply to the sale of tangible personal property to a manufacturer who purchases it for the purpose of use in the manufacturing, production or processing, but not for the purpose of physically incorporating it in the manufactured article sold. Examples of the latter are machinery, tools, furniture, office equipment, chemicals used as catalysts, etc.[28] However, effective 1–1–94, specified manufacturing equipment purchased by qualified taxpayers are partially exempt (see ¶ 4008a).

In some cases, the manufacturer acquires tangible personal property for use in the manufacture of finished goods for a customer and transfers the property to the customer at the completion of the contract. This would be true of dies, patterns, jigs, toolings, etc., which may be used in producing the finished products and then delivered to the customer with the finished goods inventory. The SBE has ruled that in these cases, a single tax applies at the time of the purchase of the property by the manufacturer and not at the time of the transfer to the customer.[29]

Construction contractors. Reg 1521 sets forth the application of sales and use tax to construction contractors on portions of their contracts for construction and sale of improvements to real property including items of tangible personal property. Construction contractors are considered to be the consumers of materials such as asphalt, electrical wiring, lumber, paint

---

(27) § 6380.
(28) Reg 1525.

(29) § 6007–6009.1.

¶ 4008b

and linoleum which become integral parts of the completed real property (without exemption for U.S. contracts). Also included are supplies and tools which are used in the performance of the construction contract, such as, oxygen, acetylene, hand tools, lumber and similar items which are substantially consumed in the construction. On the other hand, fixtures and machinery and equipment, which do not lose their identity as accessories when installed, are taxable under sale for resale rules. Included would be air conditioning units, prefabricated cabinets and counters, and machinery and equipment items such as drill presses, electric generators, lathes and machine tools. Under specified circumstances, a construction contractor may contract to sell materials and also install the materials sold. For further information, see Reg 1521, which lists many other taxable and nontaxable items. Gross receipts from the sale of factory-built housing, and sales price of such housing, sold, stored or otherwise consumed in-state are 40% of sales price of factory-built housing to consumer.[30] A similar exemption applies to factory-built school buildings.

Generally a construction contractor must actually install the tangible personal property used in the construction project to qualify as the consumer of the materials and pay tax on the purchase price thereof, rather than the installed value.[31] The court rejected this argument by the State Board of Equalization where the taxpayer was responsible for the engineering services in the design of the materials, purchased and modified the materials, was responsible for the installation, supervised the unloading at the job site, and supervised, tested, and corrected the installation work done by others. All of the employees of the general contractor who installed the materials were working under the supervision of the taxpayer. Under these circumstances the taxpayer was the consumer of the materials and paid tax only on the purchase price thereof (*Western Concrete Structures, Inc. v. SBE (1977) 66 Cal App 3d 543; 136 Cal Rptr 93*).

Repairmen. Any charges for labor or services used in installing or applying personal property sold are excluded from sales tax. If the retail value of parts and materials furnished in connection with the repair work is more than 10% of the total charge, or if the repairman makes a separate charge for these materials, the repairman is the retailer and tax applies to the fair retail selling price of the property. If the retail value of the property is more than 10% of the total charge, the repairman must segregate on the invoices to the customers the fair retail selling price of the parts and materials from the charges for labor or repair installation or other services performed. If the price of tangible personal property is not separately stated, the entire gross receipts are taxable. If the retail value of the parts and materials is 10% or less of the total charge, and if no separate charge is made for such property, the repairman is the consumer of the property and tax applies to the sale of the property to him.[32]

---

(30) § 6012.7; Reg 1521.4.
(31) 1521(a)(1)(B)(2).

(32) Reg 1546.

Motion pictures. The terms "sale" and "purchase" do not include the performance of any qualified production services in connection with the production of all or any part of any qualified motion picture. Persons performing those qualified production services are consumers of paintings, models, and art work used by those filming special effects, titles, or credits, and of film, tape, or other embodiment on which sound, visual images, or computer-generated graphics are created or recorded. "Sale" or "purchase" also do not include any transfer of all or any part of a qualified motion picture, or any interest therein, or any rights relating thereto when either: (1) any transfer is made before the date the picture is broadcast or exhibited to a general audience or (2) the transfer is made to any person, or persons holding, either directly or indirectly, or by affiliation, any exploitation rights obtained before the date that the picture is exhibited to general audience. These rules do not apply to: (1) any sale or purchase of raw film or videotape stock; (2) any sale or purchase of release prints or tapes for exhibition or broadcast; and (3) any rentals or leases of videocassettes, videotapes, or videodiscs for private use, as described in Rev & TC § 6006(g)(7) and § 6010(e)(7).[33] See also Reg 1529.

Recording industry. Reg 1527 has been issued in the same manner to explain the extent to which activities in the recording industry are taxable, and which are not.[34]

Automatic data processing. Reg 1502 gives extensive information as to which transfers of property or information to the customer are taxable and which are not. Included in the transfers subject to tax are: (1) the transfers of tangible personal property on which information has been recorded or incorporated; (2) charges for producing, fabricating, processing or printing consumer-furnished tangible personal property (cards, tapes, etc.); and (3) transfers of tangible personal property which has been produced, fabricated or printed to the special order of the customer. On the other hand, charges for processing customer-furnished information (sales data, payroll data, etc.) are generally not subject to tax. For information as to specific personal property items or services, please refer to the regulations.[35] "Sale" and "purchase" do not include the design, development, writing, translation, fabrication, lease, or transfer for consideration of title or possession of custom computer program (other than basic operational program), either in the form of written procedures, or storage media or any required documentation or manuals designed to facilitate use of such program.[36]

U.S. Government contracts. Under Rev & TC § 6381, consumable supplies included as overhead in contracts with the United States government are exempt from sales tax. The supplies had been used by the contractor after title had passed to the U.S. government. The passage of title was determined by the court in *Lockheed Aircraft Corporation, 81 Cal App. 3d*

---

(33) § 6010.6; Reg 1529.
(34) Reg 1527.

(35) Reg 1502.
(36) § 995.2; 6010.9.

¶ 4009

257. The tax paid and charged to the U.S. government had to be refunded. Reg 1618 providing for the collection of sales tax was arbitrary, and beyond the rulemaking authority of the State Board of Equalization. *(Aerospace Corporation v. SBE 218 CA3d 1300; 267 Cal Rptr 685).*

Goods in interstate commerce. Interstate commerce does not enjoy free immunity from taxation. A sales tax which is a percentage of gross receipts levied for the "privilege of engaging or continuing in business or doing business" in a state which is not discriminatory against interstate commerce, is not constitutionally prohibited under the Commerce Clause of the U.S. Constitution. The taxpayer transported goods into a state and shortly thereafter (usually within 48 hours) the goods were delivered to dealers for sale. The court noted that there were many decisions where a state tax imposed upon companies which operated exclusively in interstate business had been sustained if the tax met the test of being related to local activities, was fairly apportioned, and where the tax was for benefits and protection by a state for which it was receiving fair compensation *(Complete Auto Trans, Inc v. Brady 430 US 274)).*

¶ 4010 Leasing or Renting Personalty

Rentals or leases of tangible personal property are considered as sales, with certain exemptions listed (see ¶ 4003). Ordinarily, the lessee pays a use tax based on the fair rental value of the property. If the lessor has not paid the sales tax when the property is acquired, and the property is rented in substantially the same form as it was when acquired, an election may be made to pay a sales tax on the purchase price rather than on the basis of rental receipts. The election is made in the tax return for the period in which the property is first leased. If, however, the sales tax was paid at the time of purchase, it is considered that an irrevocable election has been made not to pay tax measured by rental receipts. The lessor cannot change this election by reporting tax on rental receipts and claiming a tax-paid purchase resold deduction. The measure of tax on the lease is the lease or rental payments provided in the agreement between the lessor and the lessee.[37] If the agreement provides that the lessee is to pay the county property tax on the personal property, then that tax would be included as a rental payment for purposes of the sales tax computation. Special rules applicable to leases of mobile transportation equipment are set in Reg 1661.[38]

Sale and leaseback transactions. Transactions structured as sales and leasebacks will be treated as financing transactions if (1) the "lease" transaction would be regarded as a sale at inception under Reg 1660(a)(2); (2) the purchaser lessor does not claim any deduction, credit or exemption with respect to the property for federal or state income tax purposes; and (3) the amount which would be attributable to interest, had the transaction been structured originally as a financing agreement, is not usurious under Cali-

---

(37) Reg 1660. (38) Reg 1661.

fornia law. Transactions treated as financing transactions are not subject to sales or use tax.[38]

Transactions structured as sales or leasebacks will also be treated as financing transactions if all the following requirements are met: (1) initial purchase price of the property has been paid by the seller-lessee to the equipment vendor; (2) seller-lessee assigns to the purchaser-lessor all of its right, title and interest in the purchase order and invoice with the equipment vendor; (3) the purchaser-lessor pays the balance of the original purchase obligation to the equipment vendor on behalf of the seller-lessee; (4) the purchaser-lessor does not claim any deduction, credit or exemption with respect to the property for federal or state income tax purposes; (5) the amount which would be attributable to interest had the transaction been structured originally as a financing agreement is not usurious under California law; and (6) seller-lessee has an option to purchase the property at the end of the lease term, and the option price is fair market value or less.[38]

In the case of an acquisition sale and leaseback, the terms "sale" and "purchase" do not include any transfer of title to, nor any lease of tangible personal property. An acquisition sale and leaseback is a sale by a person and a leaseback to that person of tangible personal property, if both of the following conditions are satisfied: (1) that person has paid sales tax reimbursement or use tax with respect to that person's purchase of the property; and (2) the acquisition sale and leaseback is consummated within 90 days of that person's first functional use of the property. "Sale" and "purchase" include transfer of title to the lessee upon termination. These rules apply to arrangements executed on or after 1–1–91 and before 1–1–95.[39]

Mass transportation vehicles.   "Sale" and "purchase" do not include any transfer of a qualified mass commuting vehicle pursuant to a safe harbor lease arrangement described in IRC § 168(f)(8), or pursuant to a sale-leaseback or lease-leaseback arrangement that includes a safe harbor lease arrangement.[40] The California Department of Transportation is the consumer of and not the retailer with respect to passenger transportation vehicles, including but not limited to rail passenger cars, locomotives, other rail vehicles, bus and van fleets, and ferryboats that it sells to and leases back from any person under Govt Cd §§ 14060–14066.[1] The sales-use tax does not apply to passenger transportation vehicles sold or leased to the Department of Transportation by any person who received title to property from that department under Govt Cd §§ 14060–14066.[2]

¶ 4011   The Use Tax

The California use tax is imposed in the storage, use or other consumption in California of tangible personal property purchased from any retailer for the purpose of storage, use or other consumption in California measured by a

---

(39) § 6010.65.
(40) § 6010.11.

(1) § 6018.8.
(2) § 6368.7.

percentage of the sale price of the property. The use tax supplements the sales tax by providing a means for collecting tax on personal property sold outside of California and brought into California for storage, use or consumption in the state.[3] The property in California is exempt from use tax if the gross receipts from the sale of the property were included in the measure of the sales tax.[4] Terms, storage, use and consumption as defined in the Code take the ordinary meaning of the word.

Collection by out of state sellers (nexus). The maintenance of two offices in California with two employees to solicit advertising sales was sufficient activity to require taxpayer to collect use tax on sales of mail order items shipped to California residents from out-of-state (the taxpayer had argued that the California business activity—advertising sales—was unrelated to the mail order business or distributing maps, books, and similar items) *(National Geographic Society v. SBE 430 US 551).*

In its most recent decision addressing multistate jurisdiction, the U.S. Supreme Court held that a state may not compel a seller to collect and remit the state's sales or use tax if the seller has no physical presence in the state. The U.S. Supreme Court found that unless there was physical presence, North Dakota's requirement for collection of tax violated the Commerce Clause of the U.S. Constitution *(Quill Corp v. North Dakota (1992) 112 S Ct 1904, 119 LE2d 91).* This finding is important because the prior U.S. Supreme Court's decision in *National Bellas Hess, Inc. v. Illinois Department of Revenue (1967) 386 U.S. 753,* which held that the activities of an out-of-state mail order seller of selling to residents in a state and delivering the items sold by common carrier or mail, and the occasional mailing of catalogs and advertising circulars were insufficient activities to allow a state to require collection of the use tax by the seller, was based on the Due Process Clause. The Court in overruling that portion of *National Bellas Hess, Inc.* which said that Due Process required physical presence in a state and in finding that it was the Commerce Clause which applied, was inviting Congress to enact legislation if it so desired permitting the states to impose collection responsibilities. The Congress can change laws which are impacted by the Commerce Clause more easily than it can change the limits under the Due Process Clause. However, until there is a change in federal law, the physical presence test is the one to be applied.

Purchased for use in California. In order for a use tax to be imposed, the property purchased has to be purchased for the purpose of storage, use or consumption in California. It is presumed that property sold for delivery in California is sold for storage, use or other consumption in California, and personal property brought into California by the purchaser is also presumed to have been purchased from a retailer for storage, use or other consumption in California.[5] The first $400 of tangible personalty bought in a foreign

---

(3) § 6201.
(4) § 6401.

(5) § 6246–6248.

country and hand carried into California is exempt (See "Exempt tangible personalty" at ¶ 4008).

If the first use of the property after purchase is in California, then there seems to be little doubt that the purchase of the property is subject to use tax. If, however, the purchaser made use of the property after purchase in another state for a period of time before bringing the property to California, there is a question as to whether or not the property was purchased for the purpose of storage, use or consumption in California. The only definitive period of time specified in the law is set out in Rev & TC 6248, which indicates that there is a rebuttable presumption that any motor vehicle purchased outside of California, which is brought into California within 90 days from the date of its purchase, was acquired for storage, use or other consumption in California.

Donated property. Property donated by a retailer to any organization described in IRC § 170(b)(1)(A) (namely, charitable, educational, religious, medical care or research organizations, colleges, etc.) and located in California is exempt from the use tax.[6]

Credit for out-of-state taxes. Out-of-state sales or use tax paid is credited ratably against California state and state-administered local use taxes. Out-of-state taxes aren't allowed as credits (against California taxes measured by periodic payments under lease) when the outstate taxes were measured by periodic payments under a lease for a period before the property's consumption in California.[7]

¶ 4012 State and Local Tax Rates

The total state sales tax rate is 6%.[8] The city and county tax rate, also known as the Bradley-Burns Uniform Local Sales and Use Tax, discussed below, is 1¼%. For those counties and cities that do not impose a transit or other special district tax, the total tax rate is 7.25%. There are 38 counties that fall into this category. The Sonoma County Rate is 7.5%. The counties of Del Norte, Fresno, Imperial, Inyo, Madera, Orange, Riverside, Sacramento, San Benito, San Bernardino, San Joaquin, and Santa Barbara impose a single ½% district tax and have a total tax rate of 7.75%. But a 7.85% rate is imposed in the Fresno Metropolitan Projects Authority and its sphere of influence. In the City of Calexico in Imperial County, the rate is 8.25%. The counties of Alameda, Contra Costa, Los Angeles, San Mateo, Santa Clara and Santa Cruz that impose two district taxes have a total tax rate of 8.25%. The San Francisco County rate is 8.5%.[9]

TAX ROLLBACK--REFUND OF INVALID TAXES

Beginning 4–1–94, and continuing until further notice, the effective sales-use tax rate in San Diego County is reduced to 7%. The 0.75% tax rollback, in conjunction with a tax credit program for retailers, is

---

(6) § 6403.
(7) § 6406.

(8) § 6051; 6051.2; 6051.3; 6051.4; 6051.5.
(9) § 6051; 6201; 7202; 7261.

designed to refund revenues to the public previously collected under the invalid San Diego Regional Justice Facility Tax.

Under a similar program, the tax in Monterey County was rolled back to 6.5% beginning 10–1–94. The rollback is intended to refund revenues collected under the invalid Monterey County Public Repair and improvement Authority Tax.

Bradley-Burns Uniform Local Sales and Use Tax Law. Counties are authorized to impose a 1¼% tax. Cities within a county can impose a 1% sales-use tax. The city tax displaces the county tax. Redevelopment agencies within a city can also impose a 1% sales-use tax. Reg 1802 sets forth the provisions for determining where a sale takes place for purposes of the Bradley-Burns local sales and use taxes. For a retailer having more than one place of business in California that participates in a sale, the regulation states that the sale occurs where the principal negotiations are carried on. Other information on specific types of sales can be obtained from the regulation.[10] Releases by the State Board of Equalization cover analysis of transactions and use tax law; district taxes as applied to leases; and questions and answers relating to transactions in districts.[10] Counties are authorized to impose .25% to 1.75% sales and use tax as a transaction or transportation tax.[11] Stanislaus County is authorized to add an additional transactions and use tax at a rate of .25% for a period not in excess of five years, subject to voter approval.[12] In addition, the Legislature authorized the cities of Lakeport and Clearlake to add a transactions and use tax at a rate not specified but also subject to voter approval.[13]

TAX TIP

Two-thirds vote required for passage. A sales and use tax (transactions tax) imposed by the San Diego County Regional Justice Facility Financing Agency was invalid because it was not approved by two-thirds of the voters from the district in which the tax was to be imposed. The tax was a "special tax" imposed by a "special district" and therefore within the scope of Cal Const Art § XIII(A)(4) even though the agency levying the tax had no authority to tax real property *(Richard J. Rider et al. v. County of San Diego et al. 1 CA4th 1, 2 Cal Rptr 490)*. The Court distinguished its finding in *Los Angeles County Transportation Comm. v. Richmond. (1982) 31 CA3d 197, 643 P2d 941.* The *Richmond* Court found that a "special district" could levy a "special tax" with only the majority approval of the voters when the district did not have authority to levy a property tax. However in *Richmond* the special district was

---

(10) Reg 1802.
(11) Pub Util Cd § 131000–131108.
(12) § 7262.7, as added by Stats. 1994, c. 244, § 1.

(13) § 7286.40 & 7286.45, as added by Stats. 1994, c. 1240, § 1&2.

created prior to the passage of Cal Const Art § XIII, and therefore could not have been limited as envisioned by Cal Const Art § XIII(A)(4).

Timeshare estates.   Local occupancy tax on timeshare estates is barred. Cities or counties can collect transient occupancy tax from timeshare projects in existence as of 5–1–85, that were then subject to such tax imposed by an ordinance duly enacted before that date.[14]

State park campsites.   State park campsites are not subject to any city, city and county, county, or district tax for the privilege of occupying such sites.[15]

Smog impact fee.   In addition to any fees required to be paid under the Sales-Use Tax Law, and the Vehicle Code at the time of the registration of a motor vehicle, a person who applies for registration of a 1975 or later model year gasoline-powered motor vehicle, subject to the requirements of Veh Cd § 4000.2, must pay to the Department of Motor Vehicles a motor vehicle smog impact fee of $300 for any motor vehicle that, before the date of the application, was last registered outside of California, unless the vehicle has been certified under the Health & Safety Code § 43100. Registration of motor vehicles barred from entering California is not authorized. Vehicles not bearing an emission control label will be presumed not certified, unless the manufacturer proves otherwise. The smog impact fee does not apply to a commercial vehicle with unladen weight in excess of 6,000 lbs. It also does not apply to a vehicle, owned by a person, who, pursuant to military orders or following discharge or release from active duty in the armed forces of the U.S., enters California to establish or reestablish residence or accept gainful employment, if the vehicle was acquired by the owner in a foreign jurisdiction where those military orders required the owner's presence. Both civil and criminal penalties are set for violations.[16]

¶ 4012A   Refunds of Unconstitutional Taxes

Existing provisions of the California Constitution require that a special tax imposed by a county, city, or special district must be approved by two-thirds of the qualified voters of that entity, and prohibit any special tax so imposed from including an ad valorem property tax or a tax on the sale of real property. Effective 10–6–93, procedures have not been established for the refund of tax collected where the enabling legislation was subsequently determined to be invalid by a court.[17]

Credit allowed.   Retailers located in jurisdictions where taxes have already been erroneously collected will be allowed a credit against the sales or use tax otherwise due equal to .75% after receiving notice from the State Board of Equalization that the credit is to be allowed. No application for the benefits of this section are required; the period during which the credits are

---

(14) § 7280.
(15) § 7282.

(16) § 6261–6263.
(17) § 7275–7279.6.

to be allowed is to be determined by the SBE who is to notify retailers of their eligibility for claiming the credit. The credit shall be allowed during that period proscribed by the SBE until it is estimated that all of the taxes erroneously collected, less allowable expense reimbursements to the county for administration, have been credited. The retailer is required to reduce taxes reimbursed from purchasers by the amount of credit being claimed by the retailer. The credit, and reduced collection of tax, apply only in those jurisdictions where a tax was unconstitutionally collected as determined in a final, nonappealable decision of a court of competent jurisdiction and where the revenue derived from that unconstitutional tax are paid to the SBE and held in an impound account.[18]

Refund claims. Pending refund claims which were filed timely before the enactment of the refund procedures set forth in Chapter 4, Part 1.6 of Division 2 of the Revenue & TC (commencing with Rev & TC § 7275) which have not been paid by the SBE with respect to unconstitutionally collected tax are to be paid. The refund procedures herein described became effective 10–6–93.

For claims arising after the effective date of these refund procedures, individual purchasers who have reimbursed a retailer for the payment of the unconstitutional tax may file a claim for refund with the SBE if: (1) the claim is in writing and accompanied with proof of payment such as a copy of an invoice, bill of sale, or purchase contract that indicates the date and place where the purchase occurred, a description of the property purchased, the price paid for the property, and the amount of transactions and use tax collected with respect to the purchase; (2) if the tax is a use tax the claimant will also report the period during which the tax was remitted; and (3) the claim for refund made with respect to a single purchase or aggregate purchases is $5,000 or more of tax to be refunded.[18]

Time limit for filing claim. The claim by the party reimbursing the tax to the retailer in the case of a sales tax, or the taxpayer in the case of the use tax, must file the claim within one year of the first day of the first calendar quarter commencing after the effective date of enactment of Rev & TC § 7277, or after the date upon which the court decision becomes final and nonappealable, whichever occurs later. If that one-year period does not end on the last day of a calendar quarter, it shall end on the last day of the preceding calendar quarter or on the last day of the calendar quarter which is nearest to the date of the one-year period ends.[19]

WARNING   Claims for refunds of taxes previously paid and which have been declared unconstitutional may be appropriate. Taxes which have previously been declared unconstitutional by the California Supreme Court include: (1) the San Diego County Regional Justice Facilities district tax

---

(18) § 7276.   (19) § 6451–6459.

- suspended 2–14–92, and (2) the Monterey County Public Repair and Improvement Authority tax suspended 10–1–92.

¶ 4013   Filing of Returns

Every retailer and every other person liable for sales tax is required to file returns on a quarterly basis on or before the last day of the calendar month following the end of the quarter. An extension of time for filing the reports may be granted for not over one month for reasonable cause.[19]

An extension of time for filing a return for a period of more than one month may be granted if: (1) a budget for the state has not been adopted by July 1, and (2) the person requesting the extension is a creditor of the state who has not been paid because of the state's failure to timely adopt a budget. The extension shall expire no later than the last day of the month in which the budget is adopted or one month from the due date of the return, whichever come later.[20]

Preparers required to sign return.   If a sales and use tax return is prepared by a paid preparer, the preparer shall enter their name, social security number, and business name and address in the space provided on the return. Failure to provide the specified information will result in a $50 penalty for each failure to provide the requested information.[21]

¶ 4014   Payment

Due date.   Taxes are due and payable to the state quarterly on or before the last day of the month succeeding the quarterly period—unless prepayment is required.[22]

Electronic fund transfers.   Effective 1–1–93, an electronic funds transfer for payment of tax is required of any person whose estimated tax liability averages $50,000 or more per month. Persons whose estimated tax liability is less than $50,000, and those who collect use tax on a voluntary basis, may voluntarily remit by electronic funds transfer, if the State Board of Equalization approves. These rules apply to regular payments and prepayments. Penalties are set for failure to file returns, and pay tax through an electronic funds transfer if required.

Effective 1–1–95, payment by use of electronic funds transfer is required for payment of tax by any person whose estimated tax liability averages $20,000 or more per month.[23]

Extension of time to pay tax.   An extension of time for paying the sales or use tax may be granted for not over one month for reasonable cause. An extension of time to pay the tax for a period of more than one month may be granted if: (1) a budget for the state has not been adopted by July 1, and (2) the person requesting the extension is a creditor of the state who has not

---

(20) § 6459.
(21) § 6452.

(22) § 6451.
(23) § 6479.3–6479.5.

been paid because of the state's failure to timely adopt a budget. In the latter case the extension shall expire no later than the last day of the month in which the budget is adopted or one month from the due date of the return, whichever comes later. In all cases interest is due on the deferred payment of tax, except when the taxpayer is a creditor of the state which has not yet adopted its budget. In that case no interest will be due on that portion of the payment equivalent to the amount due to the person from the state on the due date of the payment.[20]

Prepayment. On written notification by the SBE, any person whose estimated measure of tax liability averages $17,000 ($50,000, if required certification to Legislature and SBE is made by the Attorney General) or more per month, without regard to measure of tax in any one month, make the following prepayments: (1) in the first, third and fourth calendar quarters, prepay not less than 90% of state and local tax liability for each of the first two monthly periods of each quarterly period; and (2) in the second calendar quarter, prepay a first prepayment of 95% of the amount of state and local tax liability for the first monthly period of each quarterly period, and a second prepayment of either (a) 95% of the amount of such liability for the second monthly period of the quarterly period plus 95% of such liability for the first 15 days of the third monthly period of the quarterly period, or (b) 95% of the amount of state and local tax liability for the second monthly period plus 50% of 95% of liability for the second monthly period.[24] Figures for the corresponding quarter of the preceding year may be used if the business or its predecessor operated during the full quarter.

To find the current prepayment for the first, third and fourth calendar quarters, multiply one-third of the tax base reported on the return(s) for that quarter by the state and local tax rate in effect for the month of prepayment. Prepayment requirements for the second calendar quarter may be satisfied by the first prepayment of an amount equal to one-third of the measure of tax liability reported, and the second prepayment of an amount equal to one-half of the measure of the tax liability reported on the return(s) filed for that quarterly period of the preceding year, multiplied by the state and local tax rate in effect for the month of prepayment.[25] Report and prepayment must be made: (1) in the first, third and fourth calendar quarters by the 24th day next following the end of each of the first two monthly periods of the quarter; and (2) in the second calendar quarter (a) the first prepayment must be made by the 24th day next following the end of the first monthly period of each quarterly period; and (b) the second prepayment must be made by the 23rd day of the third monthly period for the second monthly period and the first 15 days of the third monthly period of each quarterly period.[26]

Any person required to make a prepayment in accordance with the above who fails to make the payment on or before the last day of the monthly

---

(24) § 6471.
(25) § 6471(b).

(26) § 6472.

period following the quarterly period in which the prepayment became due and who files a timely return and payment for the quarterly period in which the prepayment became due must pay a penalty of 6% of 95% of the tax liability for each of the monthly periods during that quarterly period for which the required prepayment was not made. If the failure to make the prepayment was due to negligence or intentional disregard of the rules, the penalty is 10% instead of 6%.[27]

Effective 1–1–94, any person who is relieved of the penalties for failure to timely prepay sales-use taxes must pay interest at the modified adjusted rate per month or fraction from the date the prepayment was due until the date of actual payment.[28]

Distributors and brokers of motor vehicle fuel (does not include aviation fuel) are not required to make additional prepayment under prepayment rules explained above if more than 75% of their gross receipts are from retail sale of motor vehicle fuel. Instead, they must collect prepayment of sales tax from their distributees. Every April 1, the State Board of Equalization will establish the rate per gallon to be prepaid based on 80% of the combined state and local tax rate on arithmetic average selling price, excluding sales tax, as determined by the State Energy Resources Commission, of all grades of gasoline through self-service stations. The SBE's rate determination must be made by November 1. A notification of the new rate must be given by January 1. The rate may be readjusted. Report and payment of prepayment amounts must be made in the period the fuel is distributed. A 25% penalty, plus interest at the modified adjusted rate per month, applies from the due date to the date of payment, if prepayment is not made on time.[29]

Effective 1–1–92, after written notice from the State Board of Equalization, importers and producers must collect prepayment of retail sales tax from the person to whom the fuel is first sold in California. Jobbers, defined as anyone other than a producer or importer, must also collect the retail sales tax from the person to whom the fuel is sold. The term "jobber" does not include anyone dealing in fuel only as the operator of a service station. "Fuel" is defined in Rev & TC § 8604; it includes aircraft jet fuel, but not liquefied petroleum gas, compressed natural gas, liquid natural gas, and methanol and ethanol containing not more than 15% gasoline and diesel fuels. The rate of prepayment is equal to the prepayment rate in Rev & TC § 6480.1(f) (prepayment rate for sales tax on motor vehicle distributions), less 1½¢ per gallon. The SBE must notify every producer, jobber, importer and retailer of the rate by January 1. The rate may be readjusted by the SBE. Sales or exchanges of fuel between persons exempt under Rev & TC § 7401(a)(3) (fuel distributed and distributor) are exempt from prepayment.[30]

---

(27) § 6476–6479.
(28) § 6592.5.

(29) § 6471.4; 6480–6480.8.
(30) §§ 6480.10–6480.23.

¶ 4015   Assessment

If the State Board of Equalization isn't satisfied with a return or the amount of tax required to be paid, it may levy additional (deficiency) assessment for one or more periods.[31]

Statute of limitations. The SBE is required to issue its notice of deficiency determination within three years after the last day of the calendar month following the period for which the amount is proposed to be determined or within three years after the return is filed, whichever period expires the later. The period for which the amount is proposed may be a calendar quarter for those filing quarterly, or for a one-year period for those which file annual returns. If no return is filed, the notice of determination is to be mailed within eight years after the end of the calendar month following the quarterly period for which the amount is proposed to be determined.[32]

Interest and penalties. The SBE must assess a penalty of 10% of the amount of any deficiency determination for negligence or intentional disregard of the law. A penalty of 25% of the deficiency determination is applicable in the case of fraud.[33] The modified adjusted rate per annum that applies at simple interest to underpayments is the adjusted rate plus 3 percentage points. The rate is determined semi-annually. Effective 1–1–93 the adjusted rate is determined by reference to the rate established under IRC § 6621 for both over and underpayments of tax. Thus, interest on deficiencies will be 3 percentage points higher than the interest to be paid on refunds. In addition, the interest rate determined under IRC § 6621 for January 1 of a given year will be used by the State Board of Equalization for the subsequent July 1 to December 31 period, and the interest rate determined under IRC § 6621 for July 1 will be the interest rate applied by the State Board of Equalization for the following January 1 to June 30.

Interest may be relieved if the failure to make a timely return or payment was due to a disaster, and occurred notwithstanding the exercise of ordinary care and the absence of will neglect. Any person seeking to be relieved of the interest should file a statement with the board under penalty of perjury setting forth the facts of the disaster.[34]

Denial of interest on refunds. The State Board of Equalization may refuse interest if it determines that the overpayment occurred intentionally or as a result of carelessness.[35]

Innocent spouse relief from taxes, penalties, and interest. If the application for the seller's permit was made in the names of both spouses and there is an underpayment of tax resulting from the failure to file a return, or by the omission of an amount properly includable as subject to tax, or by the claim for erroneous deduction or credits, and the understatement of tax liability is

---

(31) § 6481.
(32) § 6487.
(33) § 6484–6485.

(34) § 6593.
(35) § 6591.5; 6596.

attributable to one spouse, then the other spouse will be relieved of tax, penalties, and interest if: (1) the innocent spouse establishes that they did not know of, and had no reason to know of, that understatement; and (2) taking into account whether or not the innocent spouse significantly benefited directly or indirectly from the understatement, it is determined that it is inequitable to hold the other spouse liable for the deficiency. This determination will be made without consideration of community property laws. The question as to whether the tax was attributable to one spouse may be determined by whether a spouse rendered substantial service as a retailer of taxable items. If neither spouse rendered substantial services as a retailer, then the attribution of applicable items of understatement shall be treated as community property. An erroneous deduction or credit will be attributable to the spouse who caused that deduction or credit to be entered on the return.[36]

Jeopardy assessments.   If the SBE decides that collection of the tax will be jeopardized by a delay, it may make a jeopardy determination which causes the tax to be immediately due and payable. The taxpayer has 10 days after the notice of the determination is issued to pay the jeopardy assessment or petition for a redetermination. If he takes no action, the jeopardy assessment becomes final.[37]

Taxpayers' bill of rights.   The purpose of the taxpayers' bill of rights law is to ensure that the rights, privacy, and property of California taxpayers are adequately protected during the process of the assessment and collection of taxes. The State Board of Equalization administers the law. The SBE is required to establish the position of the Taxpayers' Rights Advocate, who is responsible for facilitating resolution of taxpayers' complaints and problems. The SBE must also develop and implement a taxpayer education and information program. It must annually perform a systematic identification of areas of recurrent taxpayer noncompliance. Brief but comprehensive statements in simple language must be issued explaining procedures, remedies, and rights and obligations of the SBE and taxpayers. The SBE can set goals and evaluate performance with respect to productivity and efficient use of time. Evaluation of officers' and employees' performances with respect to taxpayers must be made. The SBE must develop a plan to reduce the time required to resolve petitions for redetermination and claims for refund. Protest hearings before the SBE must be held at a reasonable time at a convenient SBE office. Surveillance for nontax administration purposes is barred. Settlement of tax matters involving disputed liability of $5,000 or less may be made by an executive officer. Taxpayers may file claim for reimbursement of bank charges in event of erroneous levy, or notice to withhold. Preliminary notice must be given of filing or recording of liens. Taxpayer may bring action for damages if an officer or employee recklessly

---

(36) § 6456.   (37) § 6536–6539.

disregards SBE-published procedures. Actual and direct monetary damages sustained and reasonable litigation costs can be recovered.[38]

¶ 4015a Successor and/or Predecessor Liability

Purchase of business. A purchaser of a business may be held liable for the predecessor's sales or use tax liability and has the affirmative duty to withhold tax from the proceeds which might be due to the predecessor unless: (1) the purchaser obtains a receipt from the board showing that the tax has been paid; or (2) a certificate from the board is received stating that no tax is due. Failure to comply exposes the purchaser to liability for tax equal to the amount paid for the business.[39]

Sale or withdrawal from business. If a permitholder fails to surrender a seller's permit upon transfer of a business, then the permitholder becomes liable for any tax, interest, and penalty incurred by the transferee if the permitholder has actual or constructive knowledge that the transferee is using the permit in any manner. The predecessor's liability is limited to the quarter in which the business was transferred, and the subsequent three quarters. The limit on liability will not apply is 80% of more of the real or ultimate ownership of the business transferred is held by the predecessor.[40]

Withdrawal from partnership. An individual who was a general partner on the board's records and withdraws from the partnership causing a change in ownership, and failed to notify the board, may be liable under a notice of determination for the tax that becomes due during the three years after the last day of the calendar month following the quarterly period in which the change in ownership occurred. The notice of determination must be mailed within four years after the last day of the calendar month following the quarterly period in which the change of ownership occurred. The limit on the period of assessment will not apply if the partner retains an ownership interest in a corporation that is a successor to the partnership, or in cases of fraud or intent to evade tax.[1]

¶ 4016 Audits, Adjustments, Appeals

Information regarding sales and use tax audits and appeals procedures is included in the chapter "Protests and Appeals" under Section XIII.

¶ 4016a Settlement Authority

The State Board of Equalization has been granted the authority to settle civil tax disputes. The executive director or chief counsel of the State Board of Equalization must first submit the proposed recommendations to the Attorney General who is, within 45 days of receiving the recommendation, to advise the executive director or chief counsel of the State Board of Equalization of the Attorney General's conclusions as to whether the recommendation is reasonable from an overall perspective. Once submitted

---

(38) § 7080–7099.
(39) § 6811.

(40) § 6071.1.
(1) § 6487.2.

to the State Board of Equalization, following the receipt of the Attorney General's findings, the State Board of Equalization will have 45 days to accept or disapprove the recommendation for settlement. If there has been no action within 45 days of submission, the recommendation shall be deemed approved. All such settlements will be final and nonappealable.[2]

Whenever a reduction of tax in excess of $500 is approved pursuant to the settlement authority granted to the State Board of Equalization, a public record will be created to show the name of the taxpayer, the amount originally involved, the amount of the settlement, a summary of the reasons why the settlement is in the best interests of the State of California, and the Attorney General's conclusions that the recommendation of settlement was reasonable from an overall perspective.[3]

¶ 4017 Occasional Sales

There are two types of occasional sales:

● A sale of property not held or used by a seller in the course of activities for which he is required to hold a Seller's Permit, provided the sale is not one of a series of sales sufficient to constitute an activity for which he is required to hold a Seller's Permit.

● A transfer of all or substantially all the property held or used by a person in the course of an activity for which a sales permit is required when after the transfer the ownership of the property is substantially similar to that which existed before.[3]

Transfers of tangible personal property which meet either of the two tests are not subject to sales tax. As stated above, (¶ 4004) a person who makes three or more sales for substantial amounts in a period of 12 months is required to hold a seller's permit and this occasional sale exception would therefore not apply.

Separate businesses. To illustrate the first kind of occasional sale, a person may own a hardware store in one location and a real estate brokerage business at another location, with no relationship between the two activities. A sale of the furniture used in the brokerage business would not be a sale of property held or used in an activity requiring the holding of a seller's permit. A sale of the tangible personal property used in the hardware business would be a sale of property held or used in an activity requiring the seller's permit.

The second type of occasional sale mentioned above happens when a company which holds a retail seller's permit transfers all or substantially all of its property to another entity and the ownership of the property remains substantially unchanged. "Substantially all the property" means 80% or more of all the tangible personal property including that located outside of California. The real or ultimate ownership is "substantially similar" to that which existed before a transfer if 80% or more of that ownership is unchanged after transfer.[4]

---

(2) § 7093.5.   (4) Reg 1595.
(3) § 6006.5.

Statutory merger. Sales tax does not apply to the transfer of tangible personal property of a corporation to a surviving corporation or a new corporation due to a statutory merger applying under sections of the California Corporation Code or similar laws of other states, if only stock is received in the exchange.[1]

New corporation or partnership. Sales tax does not apply to a transfer of tangible personal property to a new corporation or partnership in exchange solely for the first issue of the stock of the corporation or a partnership interest. If, however, the transferor receives consideration such as cash, notes or an assumption of indebtedness, the sales tax does apply and the transfer does not qualify for exemption. Sales tax would be measured by the amount and the consideration attributable to the tangible personal property transferred.[4]

A transfer of tangible personal property to a newly formed partnership in return for cash, notes, and the assumption of indebtedness, was subject to sales tax. Such a transfer is exempt as provided in Reg 1595 only if the transfer of tangible personal property is solely for an interest in the partnership. The fact that the partners remained jointly and severally liable for the debts assumed by the partnership was of no consequence since the partnership became the primary obligor for the indebtedness *(Industrial Asphalt, Inc. et al. v. SBE 5 CA4th 1237, 7 Cal Rptr 2d 444)*. An assumption of liabilities is "consideration" even where the transferring party remains liable on the indebtedness based on Cal Corp Code § 15015 *(Newco Leasing Inc. v. SBE (1983) 143 Cal App 3d 126, 191 Cal Rptr 588)*.

Distributions and dissolution. A transfer of assets by a corporation or partnership to the stockholders or the partners in accordance with the dissolution of a corporation or partnership is not a taxable sale as long as holders or partners receive assets in proportion to their ownership interest. If only a portion of the business is transferred, however, sales tax may apply. If a partial liquidation is complete and in reality is a liquidation of one portion of a business, transfer may qualify under the occasional sale rule. The Sales Tax Counsel has ruled that a distribution in complete liquidation or a distribution of the assets used in a segment of business is nontaxable distribution if the partners receive title to property as tenants in common in the same ratio as their interest in the partnership. Where there is a single withdrawal of a single asset by one partner, this amounts to a taxable sale.[5]

Specific types of reorganization. The following are the types of reorganization which are nontaxable for federal income and California income or franchise tax purposes, and their sales tax consequences:

Statutory merger or consolidation. As discussed above this qualifies as an occasional sale under the second occasional sale rule.

---

(5) § 6367.

Stock-for-stock exchange. The transfer of intangible personal property (stock) is not subject to sales tax even if the acquiring corporation liquidated its newly acquired subsidiary. Transfer of tangible personal property in the liquidation would not be a taxable event because of the occasional sale exclusion.

Acquisition by one corporation for all or part of its stock, or the stock of its parent company of substantially all the properties (assets) of another corporation. This is not a transaction exempt under the occasional sales rules and therefore a sales tax applies on the transfer of all the tangible personal property based on their fair market value.

Transfer of assets by a corporation to another corporation if immediately after the transfer the transferor corporation or its stockholders are in control of the corporation to which the assets were transferred. The sales tax is not applicable even if followed by a subsequent transfer of the acquired stock to the stockholders of the transferor. A transfer of all or a part of the assets of a corporation to a new corporation in exchange solely for the stock ownership of the new corporation is exempt from sales tax under the occasional sale rule, even if less than 80 percent of the total assets are transferred, as long as the exchange is for the initial issuance of stock of the new corporation.

Vehicles, mobilehomes, commercial coaches, vessels and aircraft. The transfer of such items would not be exempt under the first occasional sale rule. Therefore sales tax could apply to the transfer of vehicles, vessels and aircraft even if the seller is not required to hold a seller's permit and the other items of personal property transferred are exempt from tax. Generally speaking, in this circumstance, the tax would be a use tax imposed on and payable by the transferee.[6] If vehicles, mobilehomes, commercial coaches, vessels and aircraft are included in a transfer of all or substantially all the property held or used in the course of the business activities of the person selling the property and the real or ultimate ownership of the property is substantially similar to that which existed before the transfer, the transfer is exempt from sales tax.[4]

Producers of hay. The sale of property by a producer of hay, other than hay, is exempt if the sale is not one of series of sales sufficient in scope, or character to constitute an activity for which the producer would be required to hold a seller's permit, if the producer were not also selling hay.[7]

¶ 4018   **Sale of Property Shipped Out of California**

When a retailer in California delivers personal property to a purchaser or his representative in California, sales tax applies whether or not the purchaser

---

(6) § 6271–6277; 6367.   (7) § 6006.5(c).

¶ 4018

then ships the property out of California for his use in another state.[8] However, the sale for resale exemption may apply.

Sales tax does not apply when the property is shipped to a point outside of California under a contract of sale by transportation facilities of the retailer or by delivery by the retailer to a common carrier, customs broker or forwarding agent, whether hired by the purchaser or not for shipment out of California.[9]

Also the sales tax does not apply when property is sold by a California retailer for shipment to a foreign country by the facilities of the retailer, or forwarded by the retailer to a carrier, forwarding agent, export packer or ship, airplane or other conveyance furnished by the purchaser for shipment to the foreign location.[10]

---

(8) § 6007.
(9) § 6396; Reg 1620.

(10) § 6387; Reg 1620.

UNEMPLOYMENT—DISABILITY INSURANCE, WITHHOLDING OF PERSONAL INCOME TAX

EMPLOYMENT TAXES—GENERAL

¶ 5001   Administration

The California Employment Development Department administers the provisions of the California Unemployment Insurance Code regarding employment taxes. California unemployment insurance is funded by payroll taxes paid by California employers. The State Disability Insurance program is provided by amounts withheld from employees and collected by employers and transferred to the department. In addition to these two programs, the Employment Development Department administers the withholding provisions of the personal income tax law and provides an employment service throughout California.

¶ 5002   Employers

An employer is any person or organization making a payment of wages or fees to individuals for services performed as an employee. The Code distinguishes between three types of employers as follows:

●*Employment in general.* An employer is considered to be an employing unit if it has during the current year or had within the preceding calendar year one or more employees and paid wages for employment in excess of $100 during any calendar quarter.

● *Government entities.* Included in the term is the State of California, any instrumentality of the state, and any political subdivision of the state, various public authorities and agencies. Government entities are liable for unemployment insurance coverage for employees and in some cases, for disability insurance.

● *Employment for household service.* An employing unit becomes liable as a household employer by employing individuals to perform domestic service in a private home, local college club or local chapter of a college fraternity or sorority and paying wages in cash of $1,000 or more ($750 for disability purposes) for this type of service during any calendar quarter in the current year or the preceding year. Both cash and noncash payments are included in wages for this purpose.

Employer identification number.   Every employer subject to the California Income Tax withholding provisions and/or the California Unemployment Insurance Code, is assigned an 8-digit number separated as follows: 000–0000–0. This number is called the employer's "account number."

Strike force on the underground economy - enhanced penalties The Legislature has authorized a Strike Force on the Underground Economy. As part of that legislation, enhanced penalties for failure of an employing unit to register, or file a return or report within the time provided by law, have been added.

Failure by an employer to register as required by Unemployment Insurance Code (UI Cd § 1086), due to intentional disregard or intent to evade the law or regulations, will result in a penalty of $100 per nonreported employee which will be added to an assessment for failing to make a return.[1]

---

(1) § 1126.1, as added by Stats. 1994, c. 1117, § 6.

In addition to the penalties provided in the UI Cd §§ 1126 and 1127, an additional penalty of 50% of the amount of contributions assessed will be added when the employing unit has failed to file a return or report timely due to fraud or an intent to evade the law or regulations. In the event the employing unit has, in addition, failed to file the required Information Returns under UI Cd § 13030 (wage statements), or Rev & TC §§ 18637 or 18638, an additional penalty of 50% will be added to the assessment so that the total penalty will be 100%.[2]

¶ 5003 Definition of Employee

"Employee" means any officer of a corporation and any individual who under the usual common law rules applicable in determining the employer-employee relationship has the status of an employee. Section 621 of the California Unemployment Insurance Code also provides that the term "employee" includes agent drivers, commissioned drivers, traveling or city salespersons and home workers, who under common law rules could be considered to be independent contractors.

¶ 5004 California Employment

In order for the employment of an individual to be considered as California employment, the services must be performed within the state of California. However, there are exceptions to this rule.

¶ 5005 Multistate Employment

A uniform set of tests has been adopted by all states to provide a method of determining which state is the state where the employee's services are reported, even though he or she may perform part of the services in several states.

The four tests are as follows:

- Whether services are localized and if so, where.
- Whether there is a single base of operations and if so, where it is.
- Whether there is a central point from which services are directed or controlled and if so, where it is.
- Where the employee resides.

The four tests are applied individually beginning with the first test. In other words, if an employee is assigned to a state by the application of the first test, there is no necessity to look to the application of the three remaining tests.

Service in California. The service is considered to be localized in California if the service is performed entirely within California or the service is performed both within and without California, but the service performed out of the state is incidental to the service within the state; for example, service

---

(2) § 1128, as added by Stats. 1994, c. 1117, § 7.

out-of-state is temporary or transitory in nature or consists of isolated transactions.

If the employee performs services entirely outside of California his or her salary would generally be excluded from coverage. However, if the services are not covered under the laws of any other state, California considers that they are under California law if the services are performed within the United States or Canada and are directed or controlled by the employer located in California. If the services of a citizen are performed outside of the United States there are rules which will cause the employment to be reported to California, such as the fact that the employer has its principal place of business in California. See § 610 of the California Unemployment Insurance Code.

¶ 5006 Wages

Wages includes any remuneration payable to an employee for personal services performed, such as salary and wages, commissions and bonuses, and the reasonably estimated cash value of payment in kind (such as meals and lodging). Tips are included in wages if an accounting is furnished to the employer. Wages also include payment of an employee's Social Security taxes, state disability insurance, and sick pay (except payments received under a workers' compensation law).

Excluded from the term wages are: (1) payments to the employee as a reimbursement for travel expenses, and (2) payments made by an employer to a survivor or estate of a former employee after the calendar year of death.

Meals and lodging. It should be noted that meals and lodging furnished an employee are wages for purposes of California unemployment and disability insurance. Meals are not subject to state and federal income tax withholding if they are furnished on the employer's premises for the employer's convenience and lodging is not subject to withholding if furnished on the employer's premises for its convenience and as a condition of employment.

¶ 5007 Excluded Employment

The services of some employees are excluded from coverage under the Unemployment Insurance Code and can be covered only if the employer files an application for elective coverage. There are also various categories of employees who are excluded from both unemployment and disability insurance provisions such as persons who work for nonprofit religious organizations and orders, elected officials, members of the California National Guard, individuals hired by the state on a temporary basis in case of fire, storm, flood or other emergencies, students providing services under certain categories, etc. A person performing services as a real estate, mineral, oil and gas, or cemetery broker or as a real estate, cemetery, or direct-sales salesperson who is licensed or engaged in the trade or business of primarily in-person demonstration and sales presentation of consumer products in the home or to any buyer on a buy-sell, deposit-commission or any similar basis for non-retail resale is excluded if remuneration is directly related to sales or other output, and a written contract provides that the person will not be treated as an employee for state tax purposes.

¶ 5008 **Reporting Wages**

New wage reporting rules for 1995. Employer reporting of wages and employer taxes have substantially changed for the calendar year 1995. An employer may elect out of the new rules for 1995 only, by filing an exemption request on form DE3086, before January 15, 1995, if because of computer reprogramming, or other reasons a hardship would be created for application of the new employer responsibilities.

For 1995 a Quarterly Contribution Return (form DE 3 DP) will not longer be required. A new Quarterly Wage Report (DE 6) will be used by employers to report personal income tax withholdings for employees, and the form will list the name, quarterly wage, social security number, and the amount of personal income tax withheld for each employee. All tax payments, including unemployment insurance, employment training tax, disability insurance, and personal income tax, will be made with a new tax deposit coupon (DE 88), and the deposits will be reconciled only once a year with an Annual Reconciliation Return (DE 7). An Annual Reconciliation of California Personal Income Tax Withheld will no longer be required on form DE 43.

CAUTION	The lack of a quarterly reconciliation for employer tax withholdings does not mean that tax payments are only required annually. Tax deposits are required at the same time as under the law in effect prior to 1995, although as described below, some of the thresholds for deposits have been changed. DEPOSIT TIME FRAMES REMAIN THE SAME.

The deposit threshold for inter quarter deposits has been raised from $75 of California personal income tax withheld, to $500 of California personal income tax withheld, for employers which have federal deposit requirements. For employees who have no federal deposit requirements, the threshold remains at $75 as in 1994. Copies of the Wage Statement (form W-2) will no longer have to be filed with the Franchise Tax Board.

In conformity with federal law, employers with more than 250 employees will have to submit their wage report on magnetic media. A separate exemption may be requested to be relieved of the magnetic media filing requirement - as with federal law.[3]

Unemployment insurance. The maximum taxable wage of an employee is $7,000 for a calendar year. The Department notifies the employers of their unemployment insurance contribution rate each year, during the first quarter of the year. This rate is applied to the total taxable wages up to

(3) Added by Stats. 1994, c. 1049.

the $7,000 limit per employee to compute the employer's unemployment insurance tax liability.

Disability insurance. The maximum amount of wages for each employee is four times the maximum weekly benefit for each calendar year, multiplied by 13, and divided by 55%. Employees pay a contribution rate equal to the rate for the immediately preceding calendar year as adjusted, depending on the balance in the disability fund and the fund adequacy percentage. For 1994 and 1995 the disability insurance taxable wage base is $31,767. The employer's tax rate for 1994 and 1995 is 1.3%. The maximum contribution per employee for 1994 and 1995 is $397.09. The disability insurance tax is assessed only on the employee.

Personal income taxes withheld. The total of the unemployment insurance contributions, the disability insurance contributions and personal income tax withheld is remitted to the department as payment voucher, DE 88.

If the worker is obligated for contributions required in any one month because the cash tips and gratuities exceed the wages of the worker under the control of the employer, the worker may furnish the employer, on or before the 10th day of the following month, or if the amounts are estimated, on or before the last day of the month following the calendar quarter, an amount equal to the excess to be paid over to the Disability Fund by the employer. If the amount is not paid by the employee to the employer, then the employee is required to pay the excess directly to the department within 30 days from the written statement furnished by the employer pursuant to UI Cd § 1088.6.

Each employer is required to furnish a written statement to an employee showing the excess of the worker disability insurance contributions required with respect to cash tips and gratuities, and the employer shall furnish a copy of that statement to the Employment Development Department. If the employer fails to furnish the statement as required by regulations, the employer shall be liable for the excess of the worker contributions.[4]

Tips. Tips are subject to unemployment and disability insurance contributions when the employee includes the amount of tips received in a written statement and furnishes that accounting to his or her employer. Withholding of personal income tax is required if an employee receives $20 or more in cash tips per month.

Payment in kind. Meals, lodging or any payment in kind received by an employee in addition to or instead of cash wages is taxable on the basis of a reasonably estimated cash value to an employee, as determined or approved by the Employment Development Department. The Department annually publishes regulations setting forth the reportable cash values that

---

(4) UI Cd 987.7 and 1088.6.

have been determined for meals and lodging for use during the calendar year.

¶ 5009 Filing Tax Returns

For 1995 a quarterly wage report (form DE-6) is required to be filed on or before the end of the month following the end of the calendar quarter. Payment of unemployment insurance, disability insurance and personal income tax withheld is required at the same time as the return is filed. In addition, employers that are not required to deposit state taxes according to the federal schedule must remit the total amount withheld during each month of a calendar quarter by the 15th day of the next month, if the amount withheld for any three months, or, cumulatively for two or more months is $350 or more. Remittances are made with Form DE 88. Any amount of disability insurance tax withheld during these periods must be paid at the same time the personal income taxes withheld are paid.

Employers who are required to deposit federal taxes must deposit state taxes within the same number of banking days that deposits of federal taxes are due (this includes the federal one-banking day rule), if the accumulated amount of state tax withheld for 1995 is more than $500. An employer may be allowed to submit amounts due from multiple locations if necessary in order for the employer to comply with these requirements.

Employers who are required to withhold and pay over amounts withheld for federal income tax purposes under IRC § 6302, and who have accumulated more that $500 of state income tax withheld during 1995, are required to pay over the state employer taxes and employee withholding on the same day that the federal tax deposits are due as provided in IRC § 6302.[5]

OBSERVATION If the Governor declares a state of emergency, the director may extend the time for filing returns and reports of wages required by UI Cd § 1088, and contributions required by UI Cd § 1110. The extension granted by the director will apply only to employers prevented by the conditions giving rise to the state of emergency from timely filing their returns and timely payment of taxes due.[6]

Electronic funds transfer. For calendar years beginning before 1–1–95, if, in the 12-month period ending June 30 of the prior year, the cumulative average payment for any deposit period is $50,000 or more ($20,000 or more, eff. 1–1–95), employers must remit the amounts owed California on the same day the federal payment is due under IRC § 6302. Payments must be made by electronic funds transfer for one calendar year beginning on January 1. The department notifies employers by October 31 of the prior year if they must pay electronically. Electronic funds transfers may be made by ACH Debit, ACH Credit, Fedwire, or other pre-approved meth-

---

(5) UI Code § 13021.   (6) UI Cd § 1111.5 and 13071.

ods. Employers not required to remit electronically may elect to do so. Elections are subject to the department's approval, and must be made by October 31. Elections are operative for one calendar year, beginning January 1.

A penalty of 10% of the tax required to be remitted by electronic funds transfer is assessed if the payment is made by a method other than by electronic funds transfer.

Compromise of amount due.   When an employer owes delinquent contributions, withholdings, penalty, or interest to the Employment Development Department, the director may enter into an agreement to accept partial payment in satisfaction of the full liability. The same provisions apply to officers who fail to make payments and are individually assessed tax under UI Cd § 1735.

The offer in compromise may be considered only for liabilities of inactive out-of-business taxpayers, and for those assessed tax under UI Cd § 1735, only if the individual assessed no longer has a controlling interest or association with the business that incurred the liability to which the offer in compromise applies. In addition the employer or assessed individual must: (1) not have access to current income which would allow payment of the accumulating interest and 6.7% of the liability on an annual basis; (2) not have reasonable prospects of acquiring increased income to liquidate the obligation on a reasonable basis; and (3) has insufficient assets, that if sold, would satisfy the liability. The amount offered in compromise must be more than the department could reasonably expect to collect through involuntary means during the four-year period beginning on the date on which a compromise agreement is tendered. The offer must be submitted by the taxpayer in writing and must be accompanied by a cashier's check, or money order equal to the amount of the offer. The payment can not be applied against the liability unless the offer is accepted. Only final nondisputed tax liabilities shall be considered for compromise. Liabilities arising as a result of fraud or actions that resulted in a conviction for violation of the Unemployment Insurance Code will not be compromised.

When the Employment Development Department believes that it is in the best interest of the state, the director may permit the agreed amount to be paid in installments under a payment agreement not to exceed five years in length.

If the amount of liability is reduced by $10,000, the negotiated amount must be approved by the Unemployment Insurance Appeals Board.

If the amount due is a joint and several liability of several parties, the acceptance of an offer from one of the parties will not relieve the other obligated parties from liability.[7]

---

(7) UI Cd § 1870—1875.

Nonresident independent contractors. Certain payments to nonresident independent contractors are subject to withholding and filing of tax returns (see ¶ 5022). Payers receiving a Notice to Withhold Tax at Source (Form 594) for a particular engagement must remit the amount withheld by the 20th day of the month following the close of the engagement. If no notice is issued, tax must be remitted by the 20th day of the month following the month in which the total amount withheld during the calendar year and not remitted exceeds $2,500. Any amount withheld but not previously remitted because the total did not exceed $2,500 must be submitted by Jan. 31 following the close of the calendar year. Payers must file Form 592, Return of Tax Withheld at Source and Copy A of Form 591, Statement of Tax Withheld at Source. A Notice to Withhold Tax at Source (Form 594) substitutes for Forms 559 and 592.

¶ 5010 Transfer of Ownership

If there is a change in the form of doing business during the year (for example, a sole ownership transfers its business to a partnership or incorporates), and one or more of the owners of the predecessor business continues as an owner of the transferee, the transaction is considered to be a change in the business form rather than a sale or a transfer of the business. In addition to continuity of ownership, it is also considered a change in the business form if there is continuity of control between the old and new businesses. Control may be shown by ownership, security, or lease arrangements of assets necessary to conduct the business. The new entity must file the employment reports as though there was one business in existence for the entire year. When a statutory merger or consolidation occurs the continuing corporation is required to file one return as though it and the corporation going out of existence constituted one entity.

If you acquire substantially all of the property used in a trade or business you may, by obtaining written approval from the Employment Development Department, assume responsibility for the filing of Form DE 43 and Forms W–2 of the predecessor, and continue as the employer, using the seller's reserve account.

¶ 5011 Experience Rating

The Department keeps separate records of the amounts paid into the unemployment insurance fund by each employer and the charges to the account in payment of benefits.

The California Unemployment Insurance Code includes provisions by which employers can qualify for basic contribution rates either lower or higher than the rate of 3.4%. This "experience rating" system has seven rate schedules, which apply depending on the ratio of the balance of the state's unemployment fund to total wages in covered employment on December 31 of the prior year.

If the fund balance on December 31 of any year is greater than 1.8% of the wages for the preceding 12-month period, Schedule AA will be in effect for the following calendar year; if the fund balance is not greater than 1.8% and greater than 1.6%, Schedule A will be in effect; if the fund balance is not greater than 1.6% and greater than 1.4%, Schedule B will be in effect; if the fund balance is not greater than 1.4% and greater than 1.2%, Schedule C will be in effect; if the fund balance is not greater than 1.2% and greater than 1%, Schedule D will be in effect; if the fund balance is not greater than 1% and greater than or equal to 0.8%, Schedule E will be in effect; if the fund balance is not greater than 0.8% and greater than or equal to 0.6%, Schedule F will be in effect. If the fund balance is less than 0.6%, employers will pay contributions at emergency solvency surcharge rates, which will be 1.15 times the Schedule F rates, rounded to the nearest one-tenth of 1%.

Employers whose reserve accounts have not been subject to benefit charges for at least 12 complete consecutive calendar quarters pay at the basic rate of 3.4%. New employers whose reserve accounts have been subject to benefit charges during the period of 12 complete consecutive calendar months ending on the June 30 computation date are eligible for experience rating.

When a new employer becomes subject to the provisions of the Code an "employer's reserve account" is set up. This is the basic factor of the experience rating system used to determine whether or not the employer qualifies for a reduced unemployment insurance contribution rate. The reserve account contains a record of the employer's contributions, the charges for unemployment benefits paid to former employees, the reserve balance (the difference between contributions and charges to the account) and the taxable wages paid during the most recent three years.

All of the contributions are actually put into one fund from which unemployment benefits are paid. Payments are not limited to the amount of the reserve account for the individual employer. If enough former employees are paid benefits out of the fund, the employer may end up with a negative reserve balance.

¶ 5012   **Computing the Rate**

The employer's basic contribution rate is computed by the ratio of its reserve balance at the computation date of June 30 to the average base payroll of the employer. The ratio is then checked against the applicable rate schedule and the employer's basic rate for the following calendar year is determined.

¶ 5013   **Employment Training Fund**

All employers, except those with a negative reserve account balance and employers of those providing domestic services and in-home supportive services, must pay an additional 0.1% each quarter. Contributions to the Employment Training Fund are used to provide training to the unemployed.

¶ 5015   **Reserve Account Transfer**

As indicated above, when a business changes hands the new owner may apply for a transfer of the reserve account of the previous ownership at any time within 90 days. If the transfer is granted the new owner acquires the reserve account of the former owner, and the former owner's contribution rate and experience term (which may make it possible to meet the 12-month requirement to qualify for a reduced rate at an earlier date). The successor also acquires charges accumulating during the current year based on unemployment insurance benefits paid to the predecessor's former employees and notices as to claim actions concerning former employees.

TAX TIP   If the predecessor had a reduced rate or a favorable reserve balance with not many benefit charges accumulating, the transfer could mean an immediate tax reduction and would be, therefore, advantageous. On the other hand, if the reserve balance is negative, the successor may acquire a rate higher than 3.4%. Also, if the facts indicate that there is likelihood of substantial benefit charges to be applied against the reserve, the possibility of gaining a reduced rate would be adversely affected.

The employer is officially notified during the first quarter of the calendar year of its unemployment insurance tax rate on form DE 2088. It includes instructions for filing protests if the employer is not satisfied with the rate. The form shows the previous reserve balance, employer contributions for the 12-month period, the benefit charges during the year, the new reserve balance with taxable base payroll, the ratio between the reserve balance and the average base payroll (only for employers who have qualifying experience) and the employer's basic contribution rate for the year. Also included is the Employment Training Fund tax rate, which is not part of the contribution rate. This tax is computed and shown as a separate tax on the quarterly contribution return, Form DE 3 DP. Negative reserve account employers, which are not subject to this tax, will have a 0.0% entry shown for an Employment Training Fund Tax rate.

The employer is notified of all charges made against its reserve account in the fiscal year ending the previous June 30. These notices are usually mailed during the last three months of the calendar year.

¶ 5016   **Basis for Charges**

The amount of unemployment insurance payable to a claimant is based on wages received during the previous one-year period known as the "base period." The benefits paid to a claimant are charged against the reserve account of the base-period employer. If there are two or more employers during the base period, the charges are prorated on the basis of the percentage of the total base-period wages each employer has paid. The account of a base-period employer is not charged with the benefits paid to a former employee whom the department has ruled quit that base-period employer without good cause or was discharged for misconduct connected with work.

¶ **5016**

The account is not charged for benefits paid to a student employed on a temporary basis during a school vacation period or benefits paid to a part time employee who received wages less than the weekly benefit amount.

An employer has a right to protest charges against its reserve account. To do this a written protest should be filed with the department within 60 days of the mailing of the notification form.

¶ 5017   **Payment of Benefits**

Unemployment insurance is payable to covered employees who are unemployed through no fault of their own, able to work, available for work and actively seeking employment, and who have met all the eligibility requirements of the law. The weekly benefit amount to be paid to an unemployed worker is based on the amount of wages paid in the highest quarter of his or her base period.

Maximum benefit. The maximum amount of state unemployment insurance payable during a benefit year is 26 times his or her weekly benefit amount or one-half of the total base-period earnings, whichever is the lesser.

To qualify. Claimants have to meet the following requirements to qualify for unemployment insurance benefits:

- Be unemployed and registered for work;
- Have received a minimum amount of wages during the base period;
- Be physically able to work;
- Be available for work (which means ready and willing immediately to accept suitable work);
- Be actively seeking work on their own behalf;
- Comply with the regulations regarding the filing of claims.

¶ 5019   **Employee Versus Independent Contractor**

One of the principal areas of dispute between employers and auditors of the Employment Development Department has to do with the status of workers as between employees and independent contractors. If an employer has treated one of the workers as an independent contractor and the department auditor determines that the worker should be classified as an employee, the department will issue an assessment against the employer for the amount of unpaid unemployment insurance and also the amount of disability insurance and personal income taxes that the auditor claims should have been withheld from the worker's wages and forwarded to the Employment Development Department.

If the employer does not agree with the finding of the auditor (that a worker is an employee rather than an independent contractor) it has the right of protest. Information regarding the filing of appeals is included in chapter 28 of the handbook entitled "Protests and Appeals."

If the employer accepts the finding of the auditor or files an appeal and loses after the matter has been reviewed and a decision made, the employer is entitled to reduce the amount of the deficiency by getting evidence from the worker that the worker included the amount of the payments he or she received from the employer in his or her California personal income tax return for the appropriate year.

The Employment Development Department states that the determination of the status of a worker as an employee or an independent contractor is to be made in accordance with the principles of common law based on a group of factors that have been developed in a series of court cases. Though the factors are looked at as a group, a certain amount of emphasis is generally placed on the extent to which the employer has the right to control the worker's manner, mode, methods and means of performing the details of the work. It is important to note that it is the right to control rather than the actual exercise of control which is important in the determination. Another important evidence of an employment relationship is the right of the employer to discharge the worker at will without cause, which would be indicative of the fact that the worker is an employee rather than an independent contractor. A written contract stating that a person is an independent contractor is not valid if there is actually an employer-employee relationship.

Federal Public Law 97–248 prohibits the IRS from reclassifying any individual as an employee prior to 1980, whom a taxpayer "reasonably" treated as an independent contractor. This was done in order that a congressional committee establish some rules to be used from then on for a determination of whether a worker was an employee or an independent contractor. The California Employment Development Department is proceeding with its own audit program and making its own determinations without regard to the federal moratorium or the prospective set of rules to be eventually issued by the federal government. Federal law excludes from the definition of "employee" licensed real estate agents and direct sellers where substantially all remuneration paid for their services is directly related to sales or other output and services are performed under a written contract that provides that they will not be treated as employees for federal tax purposes.

¶ 5020 **Disability Insurance**

The program is designed to protect workers against wage loss because of unemployment resulting from nonoccupational illness or injury. As indicated above, the contributions withheld from employees' wages by the employer are paid by the employer to the State Disability Fund or a private plan. Employers, self-employed persons, individuals in family employment, employee organizations of public school employers, and some government entities that are not covered under the state disability insurance plan can obtain coverage by voluntary elections. Employers must give new employees and employees who leave work on account of pregnancy or nonoccupational sickness or injury notice of their rights under the disability law.

To be eligible for disability insurance, a claimant must: (1) be unable to perform regular or customary work because of illness or injury; (2) have earned at least $300 in covered employment during a previous 1-year base period; (3) file a claim for benefits within 41 days; and (4) serve a 7-day waiting period (unless the person is confined in a hospital or nursing home; under a physician's orders, receives treatment in a hospital surgical unit or clinic which requires a stay of less than 24 hours and is disabled for at least 8 days or is unemployed and disabled for more than 14 days). Benefits are paid weekly on the basis of the amount of wages paid during the base period. Maximum benefits are 52 times the weekly benefit amount but not more than total base-period wages. Effective beginning 2–9–93, by order of the Director of the Employment Development Department, the minimum and maximum weekly benefit amounts are $50 and $226.

The employer who pays the employee's share of social security contributions and state disability insurance premiums is required to add these payments to the wages reported, by IRC § 3121(a)(6). Unemployment Insurance Cd § 935 is ineffective. Payments by an employer of FICA and SDI are wages subject to employment taxes for California purposes.

PERSONAL INCOME TAX WITHHOLDING

¶ 5021   What's Subject to Withholding

Wages subject to personal income tax withholding include all compensation paid to an employee for services performed for the employer, with certain exceptions listed below. Wages include, but are not limited to, salaries, fees, bonuses, dismissal pay, payment of an employee's Social Security tax or state disability insurance, commissions and payment in forms other than cash or checks. If wages are paid in any other form than cash or checks, they are measured by the fair market value of the goods, lodgings, meals or other consideration given. If one-half or more of the employee's time in the employ of a particular employing unit in a pay period is spent performing services subject to withholding, all amounts paid to the employee for services performed in that pay period are subject to withholding. On the other hand, if less than one-half of the employee's time is spent performing services subject to withholding, none of the amounts paid to the employee are subject to withholding. Reporting of tips is explained at ¶ 5008.

¶ 5021A   Employment Tax Amnesty

For three months beginning 4–1–95, employers who voluntarily reclassify independent contractors as employees will be granted waivers for unpaid interest, penalties, and interest owed on unpaid penalties imposed on or before December 31, 1993 pursuant to various sections of the Unemployment Insurance Code. This amnesty program is to bring employers into compliance with § 4304–7 of Title 22 of the California Code of Regulations, which addresses the classification of workers as independent contractors.

To qualify an employer must file an Application for Amnesty on forms to be proscribed by the Franchise Tax Board during the amnesty period, and must do the following: (1) files, with the Application for Amnesty, contribution returns reporting unreported wages and taxes for the quarter that ended June 30, 1993, and prior quarters, for which amnesty is be sought; and (2) pays the full amount due, exclusive of amounts waived pursuant to the amnesty program, or enters into an installment agreement in lieu of complete payment and meets the obligations of that agreement timely. No waiver of tax, penalties, or interest, shall be approved if the employing unit has outstanding delinquent quarters for which liabilities have not been established as of the date of the application for amnesty.[8]

¶ 5022   Exclusions From Withholding

California Personal Income Tax is not withheld from wages paid to:

● Members of the Armed Forces of the United States on active duty, who are stationed outside of California or claim domicile in another state (not including members of the National Guard or the Ready Reserve).

● A master, officer or other seafarer who serves on a vessel engaged in foreign coastwide, intercoastal, interstate or noncontiguous trade.

● Employees of interstate carriers by rail, motor vehicle, water or air to the extent that their compensation is exempted by Public Law 91–569.

● Workers on a fishing boat, paid on a share-of-the catch basis, if the crew of the boat is less than 10 persons.

Agreement to withhold. Withholding is not required from the categories listed below but the employees and their employers are permitted to enter into a voluntary agreement to withhold personal income taxes from compensation paid.

● Agricultural labor;
● Domestic service in a private home or a local college club or fraternity or sorority;
● Services to an employee for which cash wages less than $50 are paid;
● Newspaper carriers under 18 years of age;
● Newspaper and magazine vendors;
● Ministers of churches.

Supplemental employment compensation benefit plans. California employers who have supplemental employment compensation benefit plans must withhold personal income tax from all payments which are includable in the gross income of the employee except to the extent that the employee makes contributions to the plan.

Annuities or pensions. Pensions, annuities, and other forms of deferred income are wages and subject to state income tax withholding. However, individual payees may elect not to have income tax withheld. An election not to have federal taxes withheld applies for purposes of state

---

(8) § 1152, as amended by Stats. 1994, c. 999, § 2.

withholding, unless the payee elects, with the payer's consent, to have the state tax withheld.

Sick pay. Sick pay paid to employees under wage continuation plans for periods that the employees were absent from work because of personal injury or sickness are subject to withholding to the extent the payments are the result of contributions made by the employer which were not includable in the employee's gross income or paid by the employer. Benefits attributable to the employee's contributions are excludable without limit.

Nonresident employees. Wages paid to nonresident employees for services performed in California are subject to withholding. If the nonresident employee performs services both within and without California, only the wages for services performed within the state are subject to California income tax withholding, determined by the ratio of the number of working days in California to the total number of working days employed within and without the state.

Nonresident independent contractors. A payer who pays more than $1,500 to the same nonresident independent contractor during a calendar year for services rendered in the state must withhold 7% of the payment. Nonresident independent contractors include corporations not having a permanent place of business in the state, and nonresident individuals. Individual payees may file an original and one copy of a Certificate of Residency (Form 590) with payers who must submit the original to the Franchise Tax Board before making payment; no withholding is required. Payments subject to withholding include commissions paid to salesmen or agents for orders received or sales made in the state, fees for professional services, and payments to entertainers. No withholding is required if services are performed entirely outside the state, regardless of whether payment is made within the state, or if a nonresident performing services outside the state occasionally enters the state for purposes of reporting or receiving instructions.

¶ 5023 **Withholding Allowance Certificates**

California provides Form DE 4 for an employee to declare the number of withholding exemptions to which he or she is entitled; however, its use is optional and employers can use Federal Form W–4 instead. California will allow the employer to compute the withholding amounts using all of the additional exemption allowances shown on the Federal W–4.

Filing copy of W–4 with tax authorities. The IRS requires that employers who receive W–4s from employees which show more than 10 withholding exemptions, or complete exemption from withholding and wages usually exceed $200 per week, file a copy with the IRS for audit purposes. If copies of a certificate are reported with the IRS, employers need not submit copies to the State. A federal determination that a certificate is invalid will also apply for State purposes.

¶ 5024   Withholding Method

The amount of income tax to be withheld can be computed by using any one of two methods.

Wage bracket table method.   There are separate tax tables for single, married, or heads of household taxpayers and weekly, biweekly, semi-monthly, monthly, and daily or miscellaneous pay periods. Tables are based on progressive tax rates that automatically allow the California standard deduction and credits for personal and dependent exemptions. The wage bracket table method is essentially similar to the federal tax table method.

Exact calculation method.   It is somewhat similar to the percentage withholding method used for federal withholding purposes. To compute the amount of tax to be withheld, the first step is to subtract from gross wages an amount obtained from an "itemized deduction allowance table." The effect of the taxpayer's standard deduction is obtained by a reference to a "standard deduction table." This amount is subtracted from the balance obtained from the calculations made in the first step. The result is the taxpayer's taxable income. To obtain the amount of withholding, a "tax rate table" is used for the applicable payroll period as in the federal percentage method. The resulting California amount is subject to one more deduction derived from "the tax credit table." The final resulting figure is the amount of tax to be withheld for California purposes.

Supplemental wage payments.   If supplemental wages, such as bonuses, commissions, overtime pay, sales awards, back pay, etc., are paid at the same time as regular wages, the personal income tax to be withheld is computed by the employer on the total of the supplemental and the regular wages for the payroll pay period.

If the employer has not withheld personal income tax from the regular wages (as, for example, where an employee's withholding exemptions exceed wages) the regular and supplemental wages must be added together and the tax computed on the total amount.

If income tax has been withheld from the employee's regular wages, the withholding on the supplemental wages can be handled in one of two ways.

● The tax is computed on the combined regular and supplemental wages. The computed tax less the amount of tax withheld from the regular wages is the tax to be withheld from the supplemental wages.

● Withhold at a flat rate of 6% without allowing for any withholding exemptions claimed on the employee's withholding allowance certificate.

Return.   Return filing is explained at ¶ 5009.

FORMS

¶ 5025   **California Forms for Employment Taxes-1995**

	California Form Number	Federal Form Number
Quarterly contribution return and report of wages—Unemployment insurance, disability insurance, and personal income tax withheld	DE 3 DP	941
Deposit of state personal income tax withheld and disability insurance contributions	DE 88	FTD 501 or 511
Reconciliation of income tax withheld	DE 43	W-3
Combined federal and state wage and tax statement	Use federal form	W-2
Annuitant's wage and tax statement	Use federal form	W-2P
Employer registration	DE 1	SS-4
Employee's withholding allowance certificate	DE 4 or Use federal form	W-4
Withholding exemption certificate (when employees anticipate no tax liability)	DE 4 or Use federal form	W-4
Annuitant's request for income tax withholding	DE 4P or Use federal form	W-4P
Annual reconciliation return	DE7	
Quarterly wage report	DE6	
Request for state income tax withholding from sick pay	DE 4S or Use federal form	W-4S
Certificate of residency	590	
Statement of tax withheld at source	591	
Return of tax withheld at source	592	
Notice to withhold tax at source	594	

¶ 5025

Insurance Companies Doing Business in California

¶ 6000   **Overview**

Insurance companies doing business in California are generally not subject to the franchise or income tax on their net income. Rather, the tax is based on a percentage of their gross premiums, the underwriting profits of ocean marine insurers transacting business in the state, the net income of title insurance companies, and the retaliatory tax imposed on insurers of other states or countries where the other state or country discriminates against California insurers. The tax on insurers is "in lieu" of a franchise or income tax on net income as imposed on regular commercial corporations. The taxes are administered by the State Insurance Commissioner. The filing of returns, and the assessment and effect of the taxes, are prescribed in detail in the Insurance Code, and/or Revenue and Taxation Code, as are payment and prepayment dates, interest and penalties, and collection of delinquent accounts. Nonpayment of delinquent amounts may result in revocation of the insurer's certificate of authority. Cancellation is authorized of amounts improperly assessed, as is refund or credit of amounts improperly paid or collected. Suit may be brought on a claim for refund or credit.

The California rules for the taxation of insurance companies are found in Part 7, Chapter 1–7, of the California Revenue & Taxation Code, and for surplus line brokers the tax is prescribed in Part 2, Chapter 6, of the Insurance Code. California law does not conform to federal law set forth in IRC § 801–845.

¶ 6001   **Constitutional and Statutory Authority for Taxation of Insurance Companies**

The State Constitution provides for an annual tax on every insurer doing business in the state of California. It provides a separate tax on ocean marine insurance companies and for a retaliatory tax on insurers of a state or country that discriminates against California insurers.[1] A tax on domestic insurance company based on business done in California is a privilege tax. *Occidental Life Insurance Co. v. SBE, 139 CA2d 468, 293 P2d 870.* While the Code refers to insurance companies, Rev & TC § 12003(c) provides that "companies" for purposes of the taxation of insurance companies will include persons, partnerships, joint stock associations, companies and corporations.

The tax is an annual tax on the amount of gross premiums, less return premiums, received during the year on the business done in California. The business done from, or on which, a premium received is something other than the receipt of the premium itself and, as a consequence, the receipt of a premium outside the state of California, is not determinative that the business on which the premium was received was business done outside the state. *Occidental Life Insurance Co. v. SBE, 139 CA2d 468, 293 P2d 870.*

The Constitutional provision formerly Const Art XIII, § 14 4/5 relating to the taxation of insurance companies imposes a tax on "gross premiums"

---

(1) Cal Const. Art XIII, § 28.

from all insurance, whether life, fire, marine, or casualty, the only exceptions being title insurance, reinsurance, and ocean marine insurance.[2] *Allstate Insurance Co v State Board of Equalization, 169 CA2d 165, 336 P2d 961.* Title insurance, reinsurance, and ocean marine insurance are treated under separate provisions of the California Revenue & Taxation Code.

The California State Board of Equalization, the Insurance Commissioner, and the Controller may each prescribe, adopt, and enforce rules and regulations relating to the administration and enforcement of the tax code relating to insurance companies with respect to the constitutional or statutory responsibility which each of these agencies posses.[3] Each of the agencies may adopt rules and regulations either with or without retroactive effect.

TAX TIP	Insurance is a contract that furnishes protection to the insured against a risk of loss by distributing the actual losses of a few amongst a much larger group of insurers who are subject to the same risk of loss.

The purpose of the "in lieu" exemption granted to insurers and other enumerated businesses was to impose a tax obligation measured by given percentages of gross receipts—gross premiums in the case of insurance companies—revenue from which are allocated to California, rather than local, purposes. The gross premiums tax is not a tax on property, but a franchise or excise tax extracted for the privilege of doing insurance business in California. Thus the "in lieu" tax exemption granted insurers is tied to the gross premiums tax. The more burdensome gross premiums tax is imposed, but is offset by an exemption which insulated insurers and their property from all other taxes, except real property taxes, retaliatory taxes and vehicle registration fees and taxes.[4] The "in lieu" exemption also protects the insurer from any tax on income derived from other than the insurance business on investment income.[5] *Mutual Life Insurance Company of New York v City of Los Angeles, 50 C3d 402, 267 Cal Rptr 589, 787 P2d 996.* The effect of the decision in *Mutual Life Insurance Co. of New York* is to overrule FTB Legal Ruling 427, 2–11–87, and prior rulings of the Franchise Tax Board that insurance companies were taxable on income generated from activities not related to the insurance business.

The tax on reciprocal insurers is addressed in Chapter 3 of the Insurance Code.[6] In lieu of all other taxes, licenses or fees whatever, each exchange and its corporate attorney in fact is considered as a single unit and shall pay the same fees (tax) on its business as are paid by mutual insurers, except that each corporate attorney in fact of a reciprocal or interinsurance exchange will be subject to all taxes imposed upon other corporations doing business in California, other than taxes directly attributable to property used exclusively in, or on income derived from its principal business as corporate attorney in fact. In any event such corporate attorney in fact shall

---

(2) § 12203.
(3) § 13170.
(4) §§ 12102; 12204.

(5) Cal Const. Art. XIII, § 28.
(6) Ins Cd § 1530.

file an annual return and pay the minimum tax provided in Rev & TC § 23151 which is imposed upon regular commercial corporations. Ins. Code also defines the term "gross premiums" for purposes of the gross premiums tax[7] imposed on reciprocal or interinsurance exchanges.

The following insurance contracts are subject to the gross premiums tax:

(1) A check surety agreement under which the insured may require the purchase of checks that have been dishonored or refused by a surety (*Atty Gen Op No 49–96, 16 Ops Cal Atty Gen 172 (1950)*).

(2) A contract that provides for the cancellation of an outstanding obligation on the death of the insurer obligor (*Atty Gen Op No 52–118, 20 Ops Cal Atty Gen 29 (1952)*).

¶ 6002 Gross Premiums Tax

Insurers, unless otherwise excepted, pay a tax based, generally, on its gross premiums, less return premiums, received during the year on it business done in California.[8]

Tax rate. The tax rate is set each year by the State Board of Equalization.[9] Since 1990 the tax rate has been 2.35%. The Constitutional delegation of authority to the State Board of Equalization to establish the tax rate was challenged in the courts and upheld. *State Compensation Ins. Fund v. SBE*, 1993, Cal. Ct. of Appeal, 1st Dist, Div. 1, #A058211.

"Return premiums" are that portion of the gross premiums that are unearned and that insurers are lawfully bound to return. They do not extend to that portion of income in excess of the cost in insurance which mutual benefit companies and associations use to distribute as dividends among their life membership. *Northwestern Mutual Life Insurance Co v. Roberts, 177 C 540, 171 P 313*. Premiums generated from insurance contracts with exempt or qualified pension or profit sharing plans under IRC §§ 401(a), 403(b), 404, 408(b) and 501(a) are subject to tax at a rate of .5%.

Items included in gross premiums. The following amounts are to be included for determining gross premiums subject to tax:

(1) Amounts received by insurance companies under contracts which provide: (a) A reserve for the payment of claims, and (b) Operating costs including sales commissions *Allstate Insurance Co. v. SBE (1959) 169 CA2d 165, 336 P2d 961;*

(2) Amounts received from the sale of annuity contracts. *Equitable Life etc. Society v. Johnson (1942) 53 CA2d 49, 127 P2d 95;*

(3) Advance payments for the purchase of annuity contracts at a future date. These payments may be reported as gross premiums subject to tax either at the time they are received or at the time the annuity contract is purchased;[10]

(4) The interest earned on advanced payments (see 3 above). Funds that are received as an advance payment on annuities to be purchased may be reported under either of the methods described above and once an election has been made

---

(7) § 12221.
(8) Cal Const Art XIII, § 28(c); § 12221.

(9) Cal Const. Art XIII, § 28(d); Rev & TC § 12202.
(10) § 12222.

as to the accounting methods to be used by the insurance company, the election cannot be changed without the approval of the State Insurance Commissioner;

(5) Home protection contract revenue;[11]

(6) Amounts received under excess risk contracts from fiduciary of employee benefit plans. *General Motors Corp. v. SBE (9th Cir 1987), 815 F2d 1305;*

(7) Service fees collected by an insurer from a club with which it has contracted to provide insurance to the club members. *Interinsurance Exchange v. SBE (1984) 156 CA3d 606, 203 Cal Rptr 74;*

(8) Service fees on installment payments of premium *Allstate Insurance Co. v. SBE (1959) 169 CA2d 165, 336 P2d 961;* and

(9) Amounts paid as fees to a membership organization that qualify members to buy insurance. (*Atty Gen Op No CV 75–132, 58 Ops Cal Atty Gen 768 (1975)*).

Exclusions.   The following amounts have been determined to be excluded from the definition of gross premiums against which the tax is applied:

(1) The insurer may elect to treat advance payments received for the purchase of annuity which are returned to the subscriber before an annuity policy is purchased. If the election is made, these are considered return premiums;[12]

(2) Interest charged to policy holders that pay premiums by an installment note are not considered gross premiums subject to tax—the interest income is investment income. *Mercury Casualty Co. v. SBE (1983) 141 CA3d 43, 190 Cal Rptr 72;*

(3) Amounts received under reinsurance contracts;[13] and

(4) Dividends returned to an insurer because the premiums received by the insurance company was in excess of the amount required to provide insurance coverage and meet overhead expenses. The amount is excluded whether it is refunded in cash or applied to future premium payments. *California State Auto Assn Inter-Ins Bureau v. SBE (1974) 44 CA3d 13, 118 Cal Rptr 334.*

Illustrative Cases.   Sums retained by an insurance company as part of the wages owed to employees participating in a non-compulsory retirement plan are not premiums received by the company on its business done within this state, within the constitutional provisions imposing a tax on insurance companies. Though such a plan contains many features generally found in group annuity policies regularly sold by insurers, it cannot, in view of the total absence of a profit motive, be classified as an insurance business. *California-Western States Life Insurance Co. v. SBE, 151 C2d 559, 312 P2d 19.*

Insurance companies are not immune from sales tax paid to retailers who sell personal property to insurance companies. The legal incidence of the retail sales taxes is on the retailer and not the consumer, even though most often the real economic burden of the tax eventually falls on the consumer. Therefore neither Cal Const Art XIII § 28(f), nor Rev & TC § 12204, both of which provide that the gross premium receipts tax imposed on insurance companies shall be in lieu of all other taxes, prohibits the passing of the

---

(11) § 12221; Ins. Code § 12740.
(12) § 1222.

(13) § 12221.

sales tax onto insurance companies by retailers. *Occidental Life Insurance Co. v. SBE (1982) 135 CA3d 845, 185 Cal Rptr 779.*

Under a group medical insurance plan which required employers to assume the obligation to pay all employee claims for benefits up to a "trigger-point" amount, defined as the actuarially predicted, the monthly average level of aggregate employee claims, and require the insurer to pay all claims in excess of that amount, the entire cost of the plan, including not only the amount paid directly to the insurer as a premium for the coverage in excess of the trigger-point amount, but also the amount paid out of the employer's funds to satisfy the employee's claims, was taxable to the insurer as gross premiums. Under the plan, the employers did not function as independent insurers; as a matter of law, they functioned only as agents of the insurer for collection of premiums. Accordingly, the "trigger-point" was analogous to the "net premium" under a standard group policy, and the amount paid directly to the insurer for cost of administration and to compensate the insurer for assuming the risk that claims experienced might fluctuate above the expected level (or trigger-point) was analogous to the loading under a standard arrangement. Thus the gross premium which was subject to the gross premiums tax was composed of the sum of the actual pre-trigger-point claims payments and the amount paid directly to the insurer as premiums. *Metropolitan Life Insurance Co. v. SBE (1982) 32 C3d 649, 186 Cal Rptr 578, 652 P2d 426.*

A gross premiums tax was properly imposed on two foreign insurers who solicited business by mail from outside the state, where either or both the investigation and settlement of claims was performed in-state by the insurer's resident agents. The fact that agents were independent contractors was of little significance for purposes of determining whether the requirements of due process (nexus) were satisfied. What was significant was that the investigation in settlement of claims was an integral and crucial aspect of the business of insurance. Further, the investigation of 153 claims in a two-year period by one of the insurers and 331 claims by the other insurer could not be viewed as conduct so sporadic and peripheral to their insurance businesses that it amounted only to a slight presence in the state for purposes of taxation. To the contrary, the character and extent of the insurer's activities in the state were sufficient to form the "definite link" and "minimum connection" required to justify imposition of the tax. They also received the benefit of state laws through the protection afforded to their agents. *Illinois Commercial Mens Association v. SBE (1983) 34 C3d 839.*

With respect to the "gross premiums" tax on insurance companies, an insurance company doing business in California and writing only "casualty" insurance, was not subject to the tax for interest charged on installment notes executed by its insureds for the payment of premiums. The insurance company offered, as an alternative to paying the premiums in cash in advance, a method of payment whereby part of the premiums were paid in cash, and the balance by an installment note, which included both a "service" charge, that is, an amount calculated to cover the increased overhead to the company for handling the notes and collecting them, plus a sum equal to interest at the going rate on the principal of the notes. Although the "service" charges were subject to the "gross premiums" tax, the interest collected was no more than income from an investment, that is a loan to the insured, and thus was not subject to the gross premium tax. *Mercury Casualty Co. v. SBE (1983) 141 CA3d 43, 190 Cal Rptr 72.*

In determining the amounts that are to be included within the meaning of the term "gross premiums" for purposes of the gross premium tax imposed on insurers, the insurer is to be assessed a tax based on the total cost of the insurance coverage provided to the insured. *InterInsurance Exchange v. SBE (1984) 156 CA3d 606, 203 Cal Rptr 74.*

The gross premiums tax on insurance companies was intended to preclude the state or any of its subdivisions from extracting any other revenue from the specified corporation (except local taxes on real estate) and was granted in exchange for the payment of tax on gross rather than net premiums, and at an adjustable rate higher than would otherwise be applied. Be excepting real property taxes from the in lieu provision, however, the constitutional provision kept in place the traditional funding source for local governments, thereby accommodating the revenue needs of counties and municipalities. *Mutual Life Insurance Co. v. City of Los Angeles (1990) 50 C3d 402, 267 Cal Rptr 589, 787 P2d 996.*

Doing insurance business that is subject to the gross premiums tax confers upon the insurer a status that entitles it to broad exemption from paying state and local taxes of any kind except real property and motor vehicle taxes and fees.[14] Thus an insurance company was exempt from taxes imposed by a city on revenues derived from the rental of an office building and the operation of a parking lot owned by the company, and from a tax on the use of electric power in the building. There is no ambiguity in Cal Const Art XIII § 28, either patent or latent, allowing a court to look beyond the plain meaning of the words. Even if the Section did require interpretation, the result would be the same. The electorate, in creating exceptions to taxes on real property and motor vehicles, could have made a further exception for taxes incidental to the operation of a commercial real estate business, but did not. Further, considerations of policy support the exemption of investment income from taxation: to tax investment income would be to minimize the value of the investment and reduce the sums available for reserves, to the potential detriment of policy holders. (Disapproving, to the extent it holds to the contrary, *Massachusetts Mutual Life Insurance Co. v. City and County of San Francisco (1982) 129 CA3d 876, 181 Cal Rptr 370); Mutual Life Insurance Co. v. City of Los Angeles (1990) 50 C3d 402, 267 Cal Rptr 589, 787 P2d 996.)*

---

(14) Cal Const Art XIII, § 28(f).

A life insurance company that owned two office buildings for investment purposes was entitled to a refund of municipal taxes on the parking facilities in the building, which it paid under protest. *Mutual Life Insurance Co. v. City of Los Angeles (1988) 206 CA3d 943, 254 Cal Rptr 80.*

¶ 6002A   Low-Income Housing Credit

The California low-income housing credit for corporations is addressed at ¶ 1239.

The California low-income housing credit allowed to insurers differs from the California credit allowable under the Bank and Corporation Tax Law provisions in that the insurers may not assign the credit to affiliated organizations as can banks and other corporations under Rev & TC § 23610(r).[15]

¶ 6003   Title Insurers

Title insurers are taxed at the same tax rate as applied to the gross premiums tax of insurance companies in general. That amount is 2.35%. However, the tax rate is applied to the title insurer's income as specifically defined. Income subject to tax is defined as the income from business done in California except: (1) interest and dividends, (2) rents from real property, (3) profits from the sale or disposition of investments, and (4) income from investments.[16]

The taxable income of a title insurer equals the total of the following: (1) title insurance premiums received, (2) all income received on reinsurance assumed, without any deduction for reinsurance placed by it, (3) policy losses paid by underwritten title companies on behalf of the insurer, and (4) all other income, exclusive of income received from the insurer's trust department, and exclusive of income received from investments as described above.

If a title insurer also operates a trust department, it excludes from its income the income of the trust business and any income from the trust department's assets provided that the trust business is subject to tax under the California Bank and Corporation Tax Law.[17]

A title insurer may not divert premiums to a title company with which it has contracted to act as its agent and escape tax thereon. The premiums that the title companies are permitted to retain are included in "all income" of the title insurer from business done in California. *Title Insurance Co of Minnesota v. SBE (1991) 231 CA3d 626, 282 Cal Rptr 570.*

Dividends received by a title insurer from a company whose income is derived from the use of a title plant or title records is excluded from the title insurer's income. Premiums received by a title insurer are subject to tax even though they may pay others for the title search. Income derived directly or indirectly by a title insurer from the use of title plants and title records

---

(15) § 12206.

(16) Cal Const Art XIII, § 28(c); § 12231.

(17) § 12233.

whether owned by the title insurer or others is included in the basis of tax.[18] (*Atty Gen Op No NS 5510, 4 Ops Cal Atty Gen 62 (1944)*).

Since income from investments of a title insurance company are not subject to tax, any investments that include property owned by the insurer as a reserve to be used in the settlement or adjustments of claims is not subject to tax. Exempt investment income excludes any income earned directly or indirectly from the investment in title plants and title records.

The taxable income of a title insurance company is equal to:

(1) Title insurance premiums,

(2) Reinsurance premium income (no deduction is allowed for reinsurance ceded),

(3) Policy losses paid by title companies under-written by the insurer and paid on behalf of the insurer, and

(4) All other income other than the income received from the insurer's trust department and excluding income from investments.

¶ 6004   Surplus Line Brokers

There are special and unique arrangements for the taxation of brokers who transact business in insurance contracts with special risk or for those contracts which are not within the usual lines of authorized business.

A tax of 3% of the gross premiums is imposed by California on business done by surplus line brokers. The base for computing the tax is the gross premiums on business done by surplus line brokers during the preceding calendar year less 3% of return premiums paid by the broker in that year because of cancellations or reductions. There are carry forward provisions which allow deductions in subsequent years in the event that the return premiums paid by the surplus line broker exceed 3% of gross premiums. As an alternative to the carry forward provisions the broker may elect to receive and be paid a refund equal to the amount of taxes paid on the excess of return premiums over gross premiums received.[19]

For 1995 the tax on surplus line brokers is prepaid in monthly installments if the prior years annual tax was $5,000 or more.

The tax imposed on surplus line brokers is found in Ins Code §§ 1760–1780 rather than the Revenue & Tax Code.

Surplus line brokers are subject to a 10% penalty plus interest at the rate of 1% per month or fraction thereof for failure to make the required quarterly prepayments. Interest accrues from the date the required quarterly payment is due to the original due date for the return. The penalty is increased to 25% of the unpaid amount in the case of fraud by the insurer.[20]

---

(18) Cal Const Art XIII, § 28(c); § 12232.   **(20)** Ins Cd § 1775.4(f).
(19) Ins Cd § 1775.5.

¶ 6004A   **Nonadmitted Insurance Tax**

Insurers must be admitted to do business in California. Those who are not admitted will, subsequent to 12–31–93, not be able to avoid tax on premiums resulting from business done in California.

For gross premiums paid or to be paid on insurance contracts that take effect or are renewed on or after 1–1–94, a gross premium tax of 3%, less 3% of returned premiums that were previously subject to tax but returned by reason of cancellation or reduction of the premium, will be paid by every person who effects insurance governed by Chapter 6 of Part 2 of Division 1 of the Insurance Code dealing with surplus line brokers. Those subject to tax include any individual, bank, corporation, partnership, society, association, organization, joint stock company, estate, or trust, or a receiver, trustee, assignee, referee or any other person acting in a fiduciary capacity, whether appointed by a court or otherwise, or any combination thereof. The Nonadmitted Insurance Tax does not apply if the gross premium tax imposed by the Ins Cd § 1775.5 is due or has been paid, or for business reported by a surplus line broker as provided in Ins Cd § 1760.5. The tax is due whether there is a single transaction with one underwriter, or a group of underwriters, or whether there are one or more policies during the reporting quarter.

Returns are required to be filed with the Franchise Tax Board on or before the 1st day of the 3rd month following the close of the calendar quarter during which a taxable insurance contract took effect or was renewed. The tax, penalties, and interest imposed under this Nonadmitted Insurers Tax law will be administered by the Franchise Tax Board as though they are taxes imposed under Part 10 (commencing with Rev & TC § 17001) or Part 10.2 (commencing with Rev & TC § 18401) of the Revenue and Tax Code.

The Nonadmitted Insurers Tax has its own penalties for noncompliance. A penalty of 10% of the amount of the payment due is imposed for failure to pay timely, unless the failure was due to fraud for which the penalty is increased to 25%.

Refunds must be claimed within four years from the date of cancellation or reduction of premium (not four years from the date of overpayment of tax as generally is the case for refunds of overpayments of other taxes). Interest will be paid on refunds (Rev & TC § 13210).[21]

¶ 6005   **Exempt Insurers**

The following organizations are exempt from tax:

    (1) The California insurance guarantee association,[22]
    (2) Nonprofit cooperative marketing associations,[23]
    (3) Special line surplus line brokers[24]—but see the above discussion for a gross premiums tax as a licensing requirement,

---

(21) § 13201.
(22) Ins Cd § 1063.8.

(23) Ins Cd § 1280.5.
(24) Ins Cd § 1760.5.

(4) Fraternal benefit societies,[25]

(5) Nonprofit hospital service plans,[26]

(6) A nonprofit hospital corporation (see discussion below),

(7) Those insurance companies that do not have minimum connections within the state of California.

"Minimum connections" has been interpreted by the California Supreme Court to allow California to tax an insurance company that received premiums from California insured residents even though the company had no employees and owned no real property in California and conducted most of its business within California by mail from outside the state. The Court found that the company's use of third-party contractors within California to research claims data from doctors, police, claimants and other parties was such that California had jurisdiction to impose a tax. *Illinois Commercial Men's Association v. SBE (1983) 34 C3d 839, 196 Cal Rptr 198, appeal dismissed (1984) 466 US 933, 104 S Ct 1901, 80 L Ed 2d 452.*

To qualify for exempt status, a non-profit cooperative marketing association must be organized under Chapter 4 of Division 6 of the Agricultural Code.

A fraternal benefit society is exempt from all state, county, district, municipal, and school taxes other than taxes on real estate and office equipment.[27] A fraternal benefit society may be any incorporated nonprofit society, order, or supreme lodge that does not have capital stock, is conducted solely for the benefits of its members and their beneficiaries, is operated on a lodge system with ritualistic forms of work, and makes provisions for the payment of benefits.[28]

A non-profit hospital corporation organized under Insurance Code Chapter 11A is a charitable organization. Accordingly, it is not subject to tax. All of the funds of such hospital are exempt from any state, county, district, municipal or school taxes other than taxes on real estate and office equipment.[29]

¶ 6006   Tax on Ocean Marine Insurance

Every insurer transacting the business of ocean marine insurance in this state must annually pay a tax measured by the portion of the underwriting profit from ocean marine insurance written in the United States which the gross premiums of the insurer from ocean marine insurance written in this state bear to its gross premiums from ocean marine insurance written within the United States. The rate of tax is 5%.

"Ocean marine insurance" means insurance written within California upon hulls, freights, or disbursements, or upon goods, wares, merchandise, and all other personal property and interests therein, in the course of expor-

---

(25) Ins Cd § 10993.   **(28)** Ins Cd § 10990.

(26) Ins Cd § 11493.5.   **(29)** Ins Cd § 11493.5.

(27) Ins Cd § 10993.

tation from, importation into any country, or transportation coastwide, including transportation by land or water from point of origin to final destination in respect to, appertaining to, or in connection with, any and all risks or perils of navigation, transit or transportation, any portion of which exportation, importation, transportation, navigation, transit, or shipment is upon any ocean, or upon the property while being prepared for and while awaiting shipment, and during any delays, storage, transshipment or reshipment incident to or in connection with the shipment or transportation. "Ocean marine insurance" includes marine builders and war-risk insurance. "Ocean marine insurance" does not include insurance written upon a hull, which is not a documented vessel registered with the Transportation Department of the United States or anything carried in, attached to, or used in transportation or of any risk written in connection with any hull, unless the insurance is written upon a customary ocean marine form and such hull and the risks with respect thereto are covered for one who is in the business of (1) renting or chartering boats, (2) using boats for commercial purposes, or (3) building or rebuilding boats.[30]

"Underwriting profit" with respect to any one calendar year of an ocean marine insurer, means the amount arrived at by deducting losses and expenses from the net earned premiums of the calendar year on ocean marine insurance contracts written within the United States. In arriving at "underwriting profit," expenses incurred in any amount exceeding 40% of the gross premiums on ocean marine insurance contracts written during the current calendar year may not be deducted.[31]

The tax on an ocean marine insurer is generally computed on the average annual underwriting profit of the insurer from ocean marine insurance during the preceding three calendar years.[32]

The tax measured by an ocean marine insurer's underwriting profit is in lieu of all other state and local taxes except (1) taxes on real estate, (2) retaliatory taxes, (3) motor vehicle registration fees, other taxes or license fees imposed on vehicles or the operation of vehicles in California, and (4) any taxes incurred by the insurer as a result of writing other forms of insurance.

In determining the expenses incurred to be deducted from net earned premiums during the taxable year, expenses must be classified as "specific" and "general." Specific expenses are those which are identified with ocean marine insurance activities.[33] Specific expenses are deductible from net earned premiums. General expenses do not relate to any particular class of insurance[34] and are allocated to the ocean marine insurance business based on the ratio of net premiums of ocean marine insurance to the total net premiums of all classes of insurance written by the company.

---

(30) § 12002.
(31) § 12073.
(32) § 12103.

(33) § 12077.
(34) § 12088.

¶ 6007   **Retaliatory Tax on Foreign Insurers**

When the laws of any other state or foreign country impose on California insurers, their agents, or representatives, any taxes, licenses, or other fees, in the aggregate, and any fines, penalties, deposit requirements, or other material obligations, prohibitions, or restrictions, that are in excess of similar taxes and other extractions directly imposed on similar insurers, or their agents or representatives, of such other state or country, than the same taxes and other extractions so imposed by the other state or foreign country on California insurers, or their agents or representatives, are imposed on the insurers, or their agents or representatives, of such other state or country doing business or seeking to do business in California. Such retaliatory taxes are imposed so long as such laws of such other state or country continue to be enforced or so applied. The authority for the retaliatory tax is found in Const Art XIII § 28(f)(3) and the Ins Cd §§ 685, and 685.1. Personal income taxes and property taxes on real and personal property are not considered in determining whether a retaliatory tax should be levied.

If the retaliatory tax statute operates as to a particular foreign state, to impose a retaliatory tax on a few of the smaller insurance companies of that state doing business in California, while not imposing such a tax on larger insurance companies of that state doing business in California, there is no denial of equal protection of the law to a small insurer of that state compelled to pay the retaliatory tax where the foreign state discriminates only against smaller California insurers doing business there and taxes them more than California taxes a foreign state insurer doing a similar amount of business, whereas the California gross premium tax on a larger insurer from a foreign state exceeds the comparable foreign state tax on a California insurer doing a similar amount of business. *Franklin Life Insurance Co. v. SBE, 63 C2d 222, 45 Cal Rptr 869, 404 P2d 477.*

The "retaliatory" tax on foreign insurance companies has been held to be constitutional if the company's home state imposes a higher tax on foreign insurers than does California. By its enactment of the McCarran Act,[35] which provides that the business of insurance should be subject to the law of the several states which relate to the regulation or taxation of such business, Congress clearly put the full weight of its power behind existing and future state legislation to sustain it from any attack under the commerce clause to the extent that may be done with the force of that power behind it. *Western & Southern Life Insurance Co. v. SBE (1979) 99 C3d 410, 159 Cal Rptr 539.* The same case held that "the retaliatory" tax did not violate the equal protection clause of the 14th Amendment to the U.S. Constitution.

The tax imposed on workers' compensation carriers by the state of Arizona was not a special purpose obligation or assessment within the meaning of Cal Const Art XIII § 28(f)(3) or California Ins Cd § 685.1 (both containing virtually identical language with the effect that if a foreign state

---

(35) 15 USCS §§ 1011–1015.

¶ **6007**

charges a California insurance company a greater tax for doing business in that state than is levied by California on an insurance company doing business in California, then California will levy an additional tax upon insurers domiciled in that foreign state and doing business in California, except as to specified taxes and special purpose obligations or assessments). The Arizona tax was not a charge for benefits conferred upon the taxpayer (which is the distinction between assessments and taxes). Thus the State Board of Equalization properly imposed a retaliatory insurance tax upon an Arizona insurance company doing business in California, since the insurance company had to pay less tax in California for certain years than a hypothetical citizen of California would have had to pay for the privilege of doing business in Arizona. *American Alliance Insurance Co. v. SBE (1982) 134 CA3d 601, 184 Cal Rptr 674.*

It should be noted that the charges incurred by an insurance company with respect to the foreign state's taxes, licenses, or fees, are to be aggregated to determine if those fees imposed by the foreign state or country are more than those imposed in California. Even though isolated charges of a foreign jurisdiction may be higher than those in California, it is the aggregate of this foreign state or country charges that determine whether a retaliatory tax will be incurred. (*Atty Gen Op No 60–79, 35 Ops Cal Atty Gen 182 (1960)*). The Attorney General has also ruled that the license fees paid by insurance agents must be included when determining whether the retaliatory tax should be applied. (*Atty Gen Op No 84–402, 67 Ops Cal Atty Gen 341 (1984)*).

¶ 6008 **Returns, Assessment, and Payment of Tax**

The return filing requirements for the Nonadmitted Insurance Tax are explained at § 6004A.

Every insurer subject to tax or taxes imposed on insurers must file an insurance tax return annually with the Insurance Commissioner. The return must show such information pertaining to its insurance business in this state as will reflect the basis of its tax as prescribed by law, the computation of the amount of tax for the period covered by the return, the total amount of any tax prepayments, and such other information as the Commissioner may require. Separate returns must be filed with respect to insurance generally, life insurance (or life insurance and disability insurance), ocean marine insurance, and title insurance.

The return forms are available directly from the state Insurance Commissioner.

It is required that the return be signed by the insurer, or on behalf of the insurer by an officer, under oath and contain a written declaration that it is made under penalties of perjury. An out-of-state insurer's return may be signed by a manager residing in California. A foreign insurer's return may be signed and verified by the United States manager for the foreign insurer.[36]

The State Board of Equalization initially assess the tax in accordance with the data as reported by the insurer on its return.[37] The Board must promptly transmit notice of its initial assessment to the Insurance Commissioner and to the Controller, and if the initial assessment differs from the amount computed by the insurer, notice must also be given to the insurer.[38] As soon as practicable after the return is filed, the Insurance Commissioner must examine it, together with any information within the Commissioner's possession, or that may come into the Commissioner's possession, and determine the correct amount of tax.[39] If the Commissioner determines that the amount of tax disclosed by the return and assessed by the SBE is less than the amount of tax disclosed by the Commissioner's examination, the Commissioner must propose in writing to the SBE a deficiency assessment for the difference, setting forth the basis for the deficiency assessment and the details of the computation.[40] The SBE is required to make a deficiency assessment on the basis of the proposal as submitted.[1] The SBE must promptly notify the insurer of such deficiency assessment. The insurer must then petition for a redetermination of the deficiency assessment within 30 days after service upon the insurer of the notice of the deficiency.[2] The petition protesting the deficiency assessment must set forth the grounds for the insurer's objection and the correction sought. At the time the petition is filed with the SBE, a copy of the petition is also filed with the Insurance Commissioner. If no petition for reconsideration is filed, the additional assessment of tax becomes final at the end of the 30 day period.

Generally, each insurer subject to the imposition of a retaliatory tax must file annually with the Insurance Commissioner a retaliatory tax return self-assessing tax.[3] The returns are due, together with the payment of the tax, on April 1 of the year following the calendar year in which the insurer is doing business in California. Returns for ocean marine insurers are due on June 15. Insurers subject to the retaliatory tax must also file their returns by April 1 as do surplus line brokers. The Insurance Commissioner may extend the time for filing a tax return for a period up to 30 days.[4] Interest is charged on any delayed payment of tax during the period of extension.

A duplicate copy of the return is filed with the State Board of Equalization. The originals of the returns are filed with the State Insurance Commissioner.

Any tax on an insurer levied by the State Board of Equalization is a lien on all property and franchises of any kind and nature belonging to the insurer, and has the effect of a judgment against it.[5] Any such lien has the

---

(36) § 12303.
(37) § 12412.
(38) § 12413.
(39) § 12421.
(40) § 12422.

(1) § 12424.
(2) § 12428.
(3) § 12287.
(4) § 12306.
(5) § 12491.

effect of an execution duly levied against all property of the delinquent insurer,[6] and no judgment is satisfied or lien removed until either the taxes, penalties, and costs are paid or the insurer's property is sold for their payment.

Electronic funds transfers. Commencing with tax payments due on or after 1–1–94, insurers with tax payments in excess of $50,000 per year will make their tax payments by electronic funds transfers. A penalty of 10% is imposed on those required to transfer funds electronically who make tax payments by some other means. For tax payments due after 12–31–94, the threshold for payments by electronic funds transfers is reduced to include all insurers with tax payments in excess of $20,000 annually.

The requirement for payments by electronic transfer include payments due by those subject to retaliatory taxes (Ins Cd § 685), reciprocal insurers (Ins Cd § 1531), surplus line brokers (Ins Cd § 1776.8), all taxes, penalties, interest and other fees payable to the Insurance Commissioner (Ins Cd § 12976.5), and all taxes, penalties, interest and other fees payable to the Franchise Tax Board (Rev & TC § 12602).

Insurance Cd § 45 authorizes several alternative methods of electronic funds transfer including an automated clearinghouse debit, an automated clearinghouse credit, a Federal Reserve Wire Transfer (Fedwire), or an international funds transfer, at the option of the insurer. Payment of the amount due is not completed until the date of settlement occurs if settlement to the state's demand account does not occur on or before the banking day following the date of transfer.[7]

¶ 6009   Payment and Collection

Payment dates of taxes imposed on insurers are prescribed by the statute. Generally, payments are due in quarterly installments payable on April 1, June 15, September 15, and December 15 of the current tax year. Each prepayment is equal to ¼ of the annual insurance tax liability reported on the insurer's tax return for the preceding calendar year.[8] Surplus line brokers are also required to make installment payments of the tax due which for calender year 1995 are to be made monthly.[9]

While the retaliatory tax is due and payable by April 1, any additional retaliatory tax due on account of an ocean marine insurer is due and payable on June 15.

Amounts of taxes, interest, and penalties not remitted to the Insurance Commissioner with the original return of the insurer are payable to the Controller.[10]

---

(6) § 12493.
(7) Ins Cd §§ 45, 685, 1531, 1776.8, 12976.5; § 12602.
(8) §§ 12253; 12254.

(9) Ins. Code § 1775.3, as amended by Stats. 1994, c. 455, § 4.
(10) § 12601.

No prepayments may be required with respect to the tax on ocean marine insurance underwriting profit or the retaliatory tax.[11]

Penalties and interest are imposed for failure to pay taxes or deficiency assessments within the time required.[12]

At any time within a stated period after any amount of tax becomes due and payable, and at any time within a shorter prescribed period after any deficiency assessment of tax becomes due and payable, the Controller may bring action in the name of the state in a court of competent jurisdiction in any county or city and county in the state in which the Attorney General has an office to collect delinquent taxes, together with interest and penalties. The time periods for filing are set forth in the California Code of Civil Procedure.[13] In the action, certificate of the controller or the secretary of the State Board of Equalization, showing unpaid taxes against the insurer, is prima facie evidence of the assessment of the taxes, the delinquency, the amount of taxes, interest, and penalties due and unpaid, that the insurer is indebted to the state in that amount, and that there has been compliance with all the requirements of the law in relation to the assessment and levy of the taxes.[14] The payment of the amount of the judgment recovered must be made to the Controller.[15] The Controller is likewise authorized to sue and recover any refund or pardon thereof that is erroneously made and any credit or part thereof that is erroneously allowed.[16]

The penalty for failure to file or make timely payment may be waived by the State Board of Equalization if the insurer's failure to make the timely return or payment was due to reasonable cause and to circumstances beyond the insurer's control.[17] The law[18] also provides that if a person's failure to make a timely return or payment was due to disaster, and occurred not withstanding the exercise of ordinary care in the absence of willful neglect, the person may be relieved of interest payments.

Payment and collection of the Nonadmitted Insurance Tax is explained at ¶ 6004A.

¶ 6010   **Suspension of Rights of Delinquent Insurers**

Each year the Controller is required to transmit to the Insurance Commissioner between December 10th and December 15th, a statement showing the names of all insurers that have failed to pay the tax, penalties, or interest owed to the state of California, or any part thereof. The statement must show the amount of tax, interest, and penalties due from each insurer.[19] The Commissioner must then give a notice in writing to each delinquent insurer of the time and place for a hearing to show cause why a certificate of authority should not be revoked. The notice of hearing must be given at least 10

---

(11) § 12251.
(12) § 12631.
(13) § 12677.
(14) § 12681.
(15) § 12682.

(16) § 12691.
(17) § 12636.
(18) § 12637.
(19) § 12801.

days in advance of the scheduled hearing date. Upon completion of the hearing the certificate shall be revoked unless it is established that the tax, interest, and penalties, due from the insurer have been paid (Rev & TC § 12802). An insurer whose certificate is revoked may have it restored by the Commissioner during the period for which it is issued on payment of all taxes, interest, and penalties due, plus an additional fee of $500 to the Insurance Commissioner.[20]

Every person who attempts or purports to exercise any of the rights, privileges, or powers of a suspended domestic insurer or attempts to transact any intrastate business in this state on behalf of a forfeited foreign insurer is guilty of a misdemeanor.[21]

¶ 6011   Cancellations, Refunds and Credits

If an amount in excess of the tax due has been incorrectly assessed, the State Board of Equalization must set forth that fact in its records and, generally, then certify to the Controller the amount of assessment in excess of the amount legally assessed and the insurer against whom the assessment has been made and authorize the cancellation of the amount on the records of the controller. The State Board of Equalization must mail a notice to the insurer of any cancellation authorized.[22] If the Insurance Commissioner discovers an amount assessed by the State Board of Equalization that the Commissioner believes to have been illegally or improperly assessed, the Commissioner must notify the State Board of Equalization in writing of such fact, together with a statement of any information that may be in the possession of the Commissioner concerning the correctness of the assessment.[23]

If the State Board of Equalization determines that any tax, interest, or penalty has been paid more than once or has been erroneously or illegally collected or computed, it must set forth that fact in its records and, generally, certify to the State Controller the amount of taxes, interest, or penalties collected in excess of what was legally due, and from who they were collected or by whom paid. The Controller, on receipt of a certificate of credit or refund, must credit the excess on any amounts then due and payable from the insurer and refund the balance.[24] No credit or refund may be approved or allowed unless claim therefore is filled with the Insurance Commissioner within four years after the due date of the return, or within six months from the date the deficiency assessment becomes final, or within six months from the date of the overpayment, which ever expires the later.[25]

Failure to file a claim within that time period constitutes a waiver of any demand against the state on account of the overpayment.[26]

---

(20) § 12803.

(21) § 12832.

(22) § 12951, as amended by Stats. 1994, c. 726, § 33.

(23) § 12952.

(24) § 12977, as amended by Stats. 1994, c. 726, § 34.

(25) § 12978.

(26) § 12980.

Interest is allowed on the amount of any overpayment of the tax at a stated rate from the due date of the tax for the year for which the overpayment was made, but no refund or credit is made of any interest imposed on the claimant with respect to the amount being refunded or credited,[27] and if the State Board of Equalization determines that any overpayment has been made intentionally or made not incident to a bona fide and orderly discharge of a liability reasonably assumed by the insurer to be imposed by law, no interest will be allowed on the overpayment.[28]

Interest is also disallowed on overpayments refunded or credited within 90 days after the due date of the tax year for which the overpayment was made.[29]

Plaintiff, an insurance company that paid gross premium taxes to the State Board of Equalization under protest while it was litigating its tax liability for previous years, failed to exhaust its administrative remedies, and thus the trial court properly denied Plaintiff a refund of those taxes, where Plaintiff did not seek a refund for the later year until more than one year after the judgment favorable to the plaintiff became final in its litigation with the Board. The checks by which Plaintiff paid the taxes and which had "paid under protest" written on their backs did not meet the provisions of Rev & TC § 12979[30] (claim for refund must be in writing and state specific grounds upon which it is founded). The complaint in the present action could not be treated as a timely claim, since it was not filed within six months of the overpayment as required by Rev & TC § 12978. *Mercury Casualty Co v. SBE (1986) 179 CA3d 34, 224 Cal Rptr 781.*

¶ 6012   **Taxpayers Suit**

Unless a claim for refund or credit has been duly filed in accordance with Rev & TC § 12978 et seq. no refund or proceeding may be maintained in any court for the recovery of any amount alleged to have been erroneously or illegally assessed or collected.[31] Within 90 days after the mailing of a notice of action of the State Board of Equalization on a claim for refund or credit, the claimant may bring an action against the SBE on the grounds set forth in the claim in a court of competent jurisdiction in any county or city and county in the state in which the Attorney General has an office for the recovery of the whole or any part of the amount with respect to which the claim has been disallowed.[32] Rev & TC § 13104 provides that if the SBE fails to mail notice of its action on a claim for refund or credit within six months after a claim is filed with the SBE, the claimant may, prior to mailing of notice by the SBE of its action on the claim, consider the claim disallowed and bring action against the SBE based on the grounds set forth in the claim for the recovery of the whole or any part of the amount claimed as an overpayment.[33]

(**27**) § 12983.
(**28**) § 12984.
(**29**) § 12983.5.
(**30**) § 12979.

(**31**) § 13102.
(**32**) § 13103.
(**33**) § 13104.

CAUTION	The basis for the appeal before the Superior Court of the State of California against the denial of a claim for refund is limited solely to those issues set forth in the original claim. New issues will not be permitted after the claim is denied and action is brought before the Superior Court.

Failure to bring suit within the time specified constitutes a waiver of all demands against the state on account of the alleged overpayment.[34] If judgment is rendered for the plaintiff, the amount of the judgment must first be credited on any tax due and payable from the plaintiff, and the balance is then refunded.[35] Rev & TC § 13107 provides for interest on the judgment.[36] Judgment may not be rendered in favor of the plaintiff when the action is brought by or in the name of an assignee of the insurer paying the tax, interest or penalties or by any person other than the insurer that paid the tax, interest, or penalties.[37]

No injunction or writ of mandate or other legal or equitable process may issue in any suit, action, or proceeding in any court against the state or any state officer to prevent or enjoin the assessment or collection of any tax or any amount of tax required to be collected.[38]

In an action by the Insurance Commissioner for a refund of taxes paid under protest, application of the doctrine of equitable tolling did not relieve plaintiff of its failure to file a claim within six months of the overpayment as required by Rev & TC § 12978, where the latest possible date for the commencement of the period set forth in Rev & TC § 12978 would be the date of the final decision favorable to the plaintiff in its litigation with the State Board of Equalization regarding the same taxes for earlier years, and plaintiff did not bring the present action until one year after that date. *Mercury Casualty Co v. SBE (1986) 179 CA3d 34, 224 Cal Rptr 781.*

(**34**) § 13105.
(**35**) § 13106.
(**36**) § 13107.

(**37**) § 13108.
(**38**) § 13101.

MISCELLANEOUS TAXES AND FEES

MOTOR VEHICLE TAXES AND FEES

¶ 6500   **Motor Vehicle License Tax**

The provisions of the law governing motor vehicle taxes and fees are also included in the California Revenue and Taxation Code, Division 2, Part 5, including Rev & TC §§ 10701 to 11108.[1] The law is administered by the Department of Motor Vehicles. It requires that every vehicle (subject to registration under the Vehicle Code) using California highways pay a license fee each year.[2]

The Department assigns a "registration year" for each vehicle in the state, usually the twelve-month period beginning with the time it was first registered in California. The purpose is to have an equal renewal case-load each month during the year rather than have peak periods.[3]

The rate of license fee or tax is 2% of the market value of the vehicle as determined by the Department.[4] Effective 8–1–91, a 2.2% temporary surcharge is added to the 2% motor vehicle license fee. The surcharge must be added to the regular motor vehicle license fee for any initial or original registration of any motor vehicle never before registered in California for which the fees become due on or after 8–1–91, and before 8–1–92, and for any renewal of registration with an expiration date on or after 8–1–91 and before 8–1–92. The surcharge will cease to operate on the first day of the month following the month in which the Department of Motor Vehicles is notified by the Department of Finance of a final California Supreme Court decision, or California Court of Appeal determination on (1) the allocation of funds pursuant to Article XI, § 15 of the Constitution, and (2) the obligation of the state to reimburse counties for costs of providing medical services to the medically indigent adults under specified laws. Rev & TC §§ 10753 and 10753.2 require reclassification of vehicles upon their sales to consumers as used vehicles. Formerly, classification occurred only when the vehicle was first sold new to a consumer, or purchased or assembled by the person applying for original registration. A new schedule of annual depreciation applies, ranging from 100% to 15% of value by the 11th succeeding year; old schedule ranged from 85% to 5% for the tenth and each succeeding year. These changes are also subject to termination on the same terms as the surcharge.[5]

Note: In addition, if any vehicle is modified or added at a cost of $200 or more, the owner is required to notify the Department so that an adjustment in the price can be made (unless the modification was for a disabled person to enable him to use the vehicle, or for the installation of emission control systems).[6] The tax is in lieu of personal property taxes.[7]

---

(1) § 10701–11108.
(2) § 10751.
(3) § 10705.
(4) § 10752.

(5) § 10753; 10753.1; 10753.2; 10753.7; 10753.8.
(6) § 10753(b)–(e).
(7) § 10758.

Mobile homes, manufactured homes, truck campers and commercial coaches. The Department of Housing and Community Development administers the vehicle license fee imposed by Rev & TC § 10751 on mobile homes not subject to local property taxation under Part 13, Div 1 of Rev & TC §§ 5801–5842, manufactured homes, truck campers and commercial coaches. The fee is 2% of the market value of a mobile home or commercial coach. The market value is determined on the basis of original sales price.[8]

¶ 6501 **Motor Vehicle Registration and Weight Fees**

Every vehicle subject to registration must be registered with the Department of Motor Vehicles.[9] Effective 1–1–92, the vehicle registration fee under § 9250 of the Vehicle Code is increased to $27. The increased fee will apply to: (1) the initial registration, on or after 1–1–92, of a vehicle not previously registered in California; and (2) the renewal of registration of a vehicle for which the registration expires on or after 1–1–92, without regard to when the renewal application was mailed; and (3) the renewal of registration of a vehicle for which the registration expired on or before 12–31–91, but the registration fee is not paid until 1–1–92 or later. Before 1991, this registration fee was $22. It applied only to the: (1) initial registration, on or before 12–31–91, of a vehicle not registered in California; and to (2) the renewal of registration of a vehicle for which the registration fee expired on or before 12–31–91, and for which the registration fee had been paid by that 12–31–91 date.[10] Effective 1–1–93, an additional $1 registration fee may be imposed by a County Board of Supervisors to fund a program to deter the theft of vehicles.[11]

Publicly owned vehicles are subject to registration. Annual renewal is unnecessary. When vehicles are transferred to private ownership, plates are surrendered and the vehicle is reregistered.[12] In addition to the registration fee and any weight fee, a service fee of $10 must be paid for the registration in California of every vehicle purchased new out-of-state, or previously registered out-of-state. If the vehicle has been registered or operated in this state during the same registration year in which the registration application is made, the fee is $6.[13] Effective 1–1–94, the County of San Francisco may impose a vehicle license fee surcharge of $4 on vehicles registered or garaged in the County of San Francisco.[14] The South Coast Air Quality Management District also assesses a $1 fee for a clean fuels program.

Weight fees for commercial vehicles. Electric vehicles, $87 for unladen weight less than 6,000 lbs to $325, unladen weight 10,000 lbs or more. Vehicles not more than two axles, $8 for 3,000 lbs or less unladen weight to $560 for unladen weight 14,001 lbs and over. Three or more axles, $39 for unladen weight of 2,000–3,000 lbs to $924 for unladen weight 15,001 lbs or

---

(8) Health & Safety Cd § 18115–18115.5.
(9) Veh Cd § 290; 670; 4000.
(10) Veh Cd § 9250.
(11) Veh. Cd. § 9250.14.

(12) Veh Cd § 4155.
(13) Veh Cd § 9252.
(14) § 11151.

more. Effective 7–1–94, a further increase on commercial weight fees is scheduled.[15]

Mobile homes, manufactured homes, truck campers and commercial coaches. Mobile homes, manufactured homes, truck campers, and commercial coaches are subject to an annual registration fee of $11 for each transportable section.[16] Mobile and manufactured homes subject to local property taxation under Part 13[17] of Div 1 of the Revenue & Taxation Code, and not installed on a foundation system, are subject to registration only at the time of sale, resale, or transfer of title. Mobile and manufactured homes installed or to be installed on foundation systems are exempt from registration so long as they remain affixed to foundation system, or are removed from the foundation only for dismantling or reinstallation on another system.[18]

Administration. The Department of Motor Vehicles administers registration and weight fees.[19] The Department of Housing and Community Development administers registration and titling of mobile homes and commercial coaches.[20]

¶ 6502   Motor Carriers

The property carrier rate regulation percentage fee is ⅓ of 1% of gross operating revenue unless the Public Utilities Commission, with Department of Finance approval sets a lower rate. The flat fee is $15 quarterly.[21] Highway carriers license tax is 1/10 of 1% of gross operating revenue.[22] The fee is payable quarterly at the same time as the rate regulation percentage fee. Various other registration, initial filing, and permit processing fees are provided by statute.

FUEL TAXES

¶ 6503   Motor Vehicle Fuel License Tax

The tax is imposed on distributors of gasoline in California, based on the number of gallons sold during the month less the gallons exempt from tax.[23] The provisions of the Law (Part 2 of Division 2 of the Revenue and Taxation Code) are administered by the California State Board of Equalization.[24]

Rates. 1994, 18¢ per gallon; 1993, 17¢; 1992, 16¢; 1991, 15¢; and 1990, 14¢.[25] The aircraft jet fuel tax is 2¢ per gallon.[26]

---

(15) Veh Cd § 660; 661; 5000; 9400.

(16) Health & Safety Cd § 18114.

(17) § 5800–5842.

(18) Health & Safety Cd § 18075–18114.5.

(19) Veh Cd § 1650–1652.

(20) Health & Safety Cd § 18002.8; 18020; 18022; 18075–18114.5.

(21) Pub Util Cd § 5003.1.

(22) Pub Util Cd § 4304.

(23) § 7351; 7401; 7651.

(24) § 8251–8256.

(25) § 7351.

(26) § 7370–7380.

¶ 6504 **Use Fuel Tax**

The use fuel tax supplements the motor vehicle fuel license tax.[27] The tax is an excise tax on each gallon of fuel used. If federal fuel tax rate is reduced, the rate increases so that combined state and federal rate stays the same.[28]

Rates. 1994, 18¢ per gallon; 1993, 17¢; 1992, 16¢; 1991, 15¢; and 1990, 14¢.[28]

Other fuel rates. The rate for liquefied petroleum gas is 6¢ per gallon, unless a flat rate is paid.[29] The rate for natural gas is 6¢ per gallon in liquid form, and 7¢ per 100 cu ft of compressed natural gas, unless a flat rate is paid.[30] The rate on ethanol or methanol containing not more than 15% is one-half of the rate per gallon for motor vehicle fuel: 7½¢ for 1991; 8¢ for 1992; 8½¢ for 1993.[31]

Annual flat rate. The owner or operator of a vehicle propelled by a system using liquefied petroleum gas, liquid natural gas, or compressed natural gas may pay an annual flat rate according to the following schedule: (1) all passenger cars and other vehicles of unladen weight, 4,000 lbs or less, $36; 4,001–8,000 lbs, $72; 8,001–12,000 lbs, $120; 12,001 lbs or more, $168.[32]

Diesel Fuel Tax. Effective 7–1–95 California imposes a tax on the removal, entry, sale, and delivery of diesel fuel. Generally the tax must be collected by the vendor. The tax is imposed at a rate of 18 cents per gallon of diesel fuel subject to tax. Provisions are provided so that if the federal fuel tax is reduced below the rate of 15 cents per gallon, then the California diesel fuel tax is automatically increased so that the combined state and federal tax rate per gallon equals 33 cents. Exemptions are provided. The tax also applies to diesel fuel used by interstate truckers. Licenses are required for suppliers, exempt bus operators, vendors, highway vehicle operator and end sellers. Returns are required monthly.[33]

---

(27) § 8604.
(28) § 8651.
(29) § 8651.5.
(30) § 8651.6.

(31) § 8651.8.
(32) § 8651.7.
(33) § 60001, as added by Stats. 1994, c. 912.

ALCOHOL BEVERAGE FEES—TAXES

¶ 6506   **License Fees**[34]

Distilled spirits manufacturer	$276 per year plus $52 enforcement fee
Beer manufacturer	828 per year
Beer manufacturer (60,000 barrels or less a year)	100 per year
Wine grower or blender	$ 22 to $165 per year depending on gallons produced
Importers:	
Beer and wine	$ 56
Distilled spirits	276 per year plus $52
Wholesalers:	
Beer and wine	$ 56 per year
Distilled spirits	276 per year plus $52
Off-sale stores:	
Beer and wine	$ 24 per year ($100 initial fee)
General	350 per year plus $24 for enforcement ($6,000 initial fee)
On-sale licenses:	
Beer and wine	$168 per year
General	$360 to $580 depending on population of the city

¶ 6507   **Excise Tax**

Tax is imposed on sales of alcoholic beverages made in California. The provisions of the law are administered by the State Board of Equalization. Returns must be filed and the tax paid by the 15th of each month on sales made during the preceding month. An extension of time for one month may be granted for filing the return, but a charge of interest at the modified adjusted rate (adjusted rate plus 3%) is payable. If the monthly liability is under $100, the SBE is authorized to permit quarterly filing.[35]

Excise tax rates. Starting 7–15–91, the combined state excise tax and surtax rates are as follows: Beer, 20¢ a gallon; still wines, 14% or less alcohol, 20¢ per wine gallon; greater than 14% alcohol, 20¢ per wine gallon; sparkling hard cider, 20¢ per wine gallon; distilled spirits, proof strength or less, $3.30 per wine gallon; greater than proof strength, $6.60 per wine gallon. Floor tax was imposed, as of 2:01 a.m. on 7–15–91 to pick up the increases from the old rates.[36]

(**34**) Bus & Prof Cd § 23053.5; 23320; 23954.5.
(**35**) § 32201; 32251; 32251.5; 32253; 32451; 32456.

(**36**) § 32151; 32201.

PRIVATE RAILROAD CAR TAX

¶ 6510 General

The private railroad car tax is based on the value of private railroad cars operated in-state. The average number of each class of private railroad cars physically present in-state in the year immediately preceding the year the tax is imposed is multiplied by the full cash value for the car of each class. Value includes materials or supplies held, stored or used in-state by the owner, but not tools or equipment used to repair them. The rate of tax is the average rate of general property taxation in-state. Special taxes, and assessments on property subject to uniform statewide tax rate are excluded in fixing the rate. Report must be made to the State Board of Equalization by April 30. The SBE mails a notice of assessment, rate and amount of tax by October 15. Payment is due by December 10. Penalties and interest are imposed for failure to file and pay the tax.[37]

Rate. The rate for the 1993–94 assessment year is $1.056 per $100 of assessed value. For the 1992–93 assessment year, it was $1.054 per $100 of assessed value.

CIGARETTE TAX

¶ 6511 General

Effective 1-1-94, a tax of 37¢ per pack of 20 cigarettes is payable by the distributor on distributions.[38] The rate prior to 1-1-94 was 35¢ per pack of 20. Distribution includes in-state sale of untaxed cigarettes, placing cigarettes in vending machines, in-state use or consumption of cigarettes and distributing to retail stores for sales to consumers.[39]

A tax on tobacco products, other than cigarettes, is imposed at a rate, determined by the State Board of Equalization, that is equivalent to the cigarette tax. The rate is $.2303 for the period from 7-1-93 through 6-30-94.

REALTY TRANSFER TAX

¶ 6513 Local Taxes

Cities and counties can tax any deeds or conveyances that transfer and convey any interest in real estate within the taxing county or city. The consideration or value of interest or property conveyed, over and above any lien or encumbrance, must exceed $100. The county rate is 55¢ for each $500 or fraction. The city rate is half of the county rate. The city must be located in

---

(37) § 11201–11655.
(38) § 30101.

(39) § 30008.

a county imposing a similar tax. Credit is allowed against a county tax for amount paid to a city. Payment is made to the county recorder.[40]

OTHER FEES AND TAXES

¶ 6514   Business License Taxes

Statewide license taxes are imposed on a wide variety of professions and occupations. They are administered by many different state agencies and officials.

Local taxation.   Local taxation of businesses can be authorized by the Legislature.[1] A city charter may permit the city to make and enforce all ordinances and regulations subject only to limits set in the charter.[2] Incorporated cities may, for the purpose of regulation, and not otherwise, license any kind of business not prohibited by law.[3]

¶ 6515   Oil and Gas Production Charge

Operators of oil and gas wells, and owners of royalty or other interests in connection with such wells are subject to an annual oil and gas production charge.[4]

¶ 6516   Motor Oil Fees

Producers selling to retailers or dealers, retailers transporting oil in-state, and on any other sale, dealers pay maximum a 2¢ fee to the Department of Agriculture for each gallon of motor oil sold or purchased.[5]

¶ 6517   Toll Bridges, Ferries, Roads

The Department of Public Works must grant a franchise for their operation. The fee is $10–$100 a month as fixed in the franchise. Reports are due annually by March 15.[6]

¶ 6518   Electric Energy Surcharge

Persons consuming electric energy purchased from an electric utility, the US or agency are liable for an electric energy surcharge. Each electric utility must add the surcharge to the cost of electric energy sold to consumers. The Legislature may lower the rate. Each utility must make quarterly payments to the State Board of Equalization.[7]

¶ 6519   Telephone Users Surcharge

A surcharge is imposed on amounts paid by every person in-state for intrastate telephone communication services. The rate charged is determined by

(40) § 11901–11914.
(1) Calif Const Art XIII, § 24.
(2) Calif Const Art XI, § 5.
(3) Bus & Prof Cd § 16000.
(4) Pub Res Cd § 3000–3433.

(5) Bus & Prof Cd § 13430–13434.
(6) Streets & Highways Cd § 30800–30811.
(7) Pub Res Cd § 25801; Pub Util Cd § 443; § 40001; 40082.

the Department of General Services and cannot exceed ¾ of 1%. Service suppliers are liable for the tax and must collect it from service users.[8]

¶ 6520 **Hazardous Waste Tax**

Hazardous waste disposal fee. On-site disposers of hazardous waste, and every person that annually submits more than 500 lbs of hazardous wastes for off-site disposal must pay a fee directly to the State Board of Equalization for that disposal. The fee must also be paid by every person submitting hazardous waste in-state for transportation and disposal out-of-state. Each operator of a hazardous waste disposal facility must pay the fee for wastes disposed of at the facility unless the submitter of waste for disposal provides the operator with a properly completed manifest that includes the Hazardous Waste Tax Account number assigned by the State Board of Equalization.[9]

Disposers and operators of facilities must pay a specified percentage of the base rate. The percentage depends on the type of the hazardous waste involved. It applies to each ton or fraction of ton of hazardous waste disposed of on or applied to land.[10] The rate per ton, or fraction thereof, for the first 500 tons of hazardous waste by a producer is calculated at 25% of the base rate.[11]

Reports and payments. Disposers must file a return and pay the fee to the State Board of Equalization on a quarterly basis by the 15th day of the calendar month following the quarterly period for which it is due. The SBE may allow a combined return covering operations at more than one facility.[12] Disposers must register with the State Board of Equalization.

Facility fee. In addition to the hazardous waste disposal fee, each operator of a hazardous waste facility must pay a facility fee for each state fiscal year, or any portion thereof in which the facility is operated. The fee is based on the size and type of the facility.[13]

The State Board of Equalization administers and collects the fees. Any fee is considered a tax. Facility fees are due and payable in two installments, by November 1 and April 1, each year. Facility operators must register with the State Board of Equalization.[14]

Facilities with postclosure permits. For the first five years of the postclosure care period, the annual fee ranges from $7,500 a year for a small facility to $22,500 a year for a large facility. For the rest of the period of postclosure, the fees range from $4,000 for a small facility to $13,500 for a large facility. The fees are not indexed for inflation.[15]

Generator fees. The Department of Health Services must establish the generator fees for November 1 each year and submit a bill by December 1.

---

(8) § 41001–41131.
(9) Health & Safety Cd § 25117.12; 25174.
(10) Health & Safety Cd § 25174; 25174.1; 25174.2; 25174.6.
(11) Health & Safety Cd. § 25174.6.

(12) § 43101; 43151.
(13) Health & Safety Cd § 25205.1–25205.5.
(14) § 43001; 43008; 43101; 43152.6.
(15) Health & Safety Cd § 25205.5–25205.6.

The base rate is $3,110 for 1993 calendar year. The fee is indexed annually. The fee paid by each generator of hazardous waste is determined by the amount of hazardous waste generated during the state's fiscal year. Per ton, or fraction thereof, fees are assessed based on the following schedule:[16]

Tons Generated During Year	% Of Base Fee
5 but less than 25	5%
25 but less than 50	40%
50 but less than 250	base rate
250 but less than 500	5 × base rate
500 but less than 1000	10 × base rate
1000 but less than 2000	15 × base rate
2000 or more	20 × base rate

Fees for a local hazardous waste management program paid in a preceding year may be offset.[15]

Generator fees and hazardous waste reporting surcharges billed on December 1 by Department of Health Services must be paid by the following January 31. Generators must register with the State Board of Equalization which administers fees and collects them.[16]

Generator fees - medical waste. A separate schedule of fees is provided for generators of medical waste. The fee effective 1-1-94, for small quantity generators is $25 annually. This same fee applies to limited quantity hauling exemption.

Other fees are set as follows:

General acute care hospital with:

less than 100 beds	$600
100 to 199 beds	860
200 to 250 beds	1,100
more than 250 beds	1,400

Specialty clinic providing surgical,

dialysis, or rehabilitation services	350

Skilled nursing facility with:

less than 100 beds	275
100 to 199 beds	350

---

(16) Health & Safety Cd § 25205.6; 25205.9; Rev & Tax Cd § 43001; 43008; 43101; 43152.6; 43152.7.

more than 199 beds 400

Acute psychiatric hospital 200

Intermediate care facility 300

Primary care clinic 350

Licensed clinical laboratory 300

Health care service plan facility 350

Veterinary clinic or hospital 200

Generator medical office 200

An additional charge is imposed for large quantity generators of medical waste who shall pay an annual medical waste treatment facility inspection and permit fee of $300. An offsite medical waste treatment facility fee of .002¢ for each pound of medical waste, or $10,000, whichever is greater is also imposed. Application fees are also provided.[17]

Potentially responsible parties—fee. Potentially responsible parties are subject to fees for costs incurred in connection with the oversight of any action specified in the law that is taken by the potentially responsible party, or the Department of Toxic Substances Control's estimate of the size and complexity of a hazardous substance release site to establish a fee, or a preliminary endangerment assessment. Fees are credited against costs that the Department is entitled to recover.[18]

Annual verification fee. The Department of Toxic Substances Control may impose a fee for verification of compliance upon all generators, transporters, and facility operators according to the following schedule:

Number of employees	Fee
50 but less than 75 employees	$150
75 but less than 100 employees	175
100 but less than 250 employees	200
250 but less than 500 employees	225
500 or more employees	250

Solid waste disposal fee. Every operator of a solid waste landfill must have a solid waste facilities permit under the Solid Waste Disposal Site Hazardous Reduction Act of 1987. An annual fee must be paid to the State Board of Equalization on all solid waste disposed at each disposal site. The State Board of Equalization will establish the amount of the fee based on the amount, by weight or volumetric equivalent, handled at each disposal site.

---

(17) § 25079.3.   (18) Health & Safety Cd § 25340–25360.

The total receipts from fees collected each year must approximate $20 million. The State Board of Equalization may adjust the rate so the balance in the General Fund account for solid waste disposal on 7-1 does not exceed $100 million. The State Board of Equalization may exempt any operator of solid waste landfill that receives less than a monthly average of five tons of solid waste per operating day. Recycled materials and inert waste removed and not disposed must be used in statistics used to determine the fee. Registration with the State Board of Equalization is required for each solid waste landfill operator. The State Board of Equalization may require a reasonable security. Reports are due by 3-1 every year. The fee must be paid by 7-1. A one month extension may be granted by the State Board of Equalization. A 10% penalty is added to the fee if not paid by due date; the fee bears interest at the adjusted rate per month. The deficiency assessment time limit is 3 years; this does not apply if there is fraud, intent to evade, or failure to make a report. The limit is 8 years in case of failure to report. A petition for redetermination must be filed within 30 days of a deficiency determination.[19]

Solid waste landfill operators—quarterly fee. An additional fee is imposed based on all solid waste disposed of at each site. It is due 25 days after the end of the calendar quarter. For 7-1-91 and later, the fee will be set by the State Board of Equalization annually at a rate of not more than $1 per ton. Any operator receiving a less than monthly average of 5 tons may be exempted by the State Board of Equalization.[20]

Corporations' annual fee. Corporations that employ at least 50 people and use, generate, store or conduct activity related to hazardous materials must pay an annual fee based on the number of employees.[21]

Exempt. A local government agency transporting wastes from a household hazardous waste facility that receives the waste from small quantity commercial resources. Government agencies and their contractors when they investigate, remove, or remedy a release of hazardous waste caused by another person.

Post-closure permit. This permit is required when hazardous wastes remain after the closure of a facility.[22]

¶ 6521   **Propane Safety Inspection Surcharge**

Effective 7-1-95, a surcharge is imposed on the owner of mobilehome parks, or the distributions system of not more than 25 cents per month per mobilehome space for funding California's propane safety inspection and enforcement program. Reporting and payment will be no more frequent than on a quarterly basis.[23]

---

(19) Govt Cd § 66799–66799.55; Rev & Tax Cd § 45001–45984.
(20) Pub Res Cd § 46800–46811; 48000–48010.
(21) Health & Safety Cd § 25205.6; Rev & Tax Cd § 43152.9.
(22) Health & Safety Cd. § 25205.7.
(23) § 4200, as added by Stats. 1994, c. 388, § 2.

¶ 6522   **Petroleum Underground Storage Tank Fee**

Every owner of an underground storage tank who is required to obtain a permit to own and operate a tank under Health & Safety Code § 25284 must pay a storage fee of 6 mills ($0.006) for each gallon of petroleum placed in an underground storage tank. The fee is due and payable quarterly.[24]

Commencing 1–1–95 and additional fee of 1 mill ($0.001) per gallon of petroleum placed in underground storage will be imposed and this additional fee will increase to 2 mills ($0.002) effective 1–1–96, and 3 mills ($0.003) effective 1–1–96, for funding claims made under the Barry Keene Underground Tank Cleanup Trust fund Act of 1989.[25]

---

(24) § 25299.41, as amended by Stats. 1994.
(25) § 25299.43, as added by Stats. 1994, c. 1191, § 4.

FIELD AUDITS, APPEALS—BUSINESS, PROPERTY AND EMPLOYMENT TAXES

FIELD EXAMINATION INFORMATION—TAXES ON INCOME

¶ 6601   Procedure in Field Audits

The Franchise Tax Board maintains field audit offices in various cities in California and also two offices in New York City, one in Chicago, Illinois, and one in Houston, Texas. Field auditors in the California offices will examine personal income tax returns, partnership returns, estate and trust income tax returns and bank and corporation franchise and income tax returns. The field auditors located in Chicago and New York City will examine only bank and corporation franchise and income tax returns. These auditors concentrate their efforts almost exclusively on examination of the apportionment formula and establishing whether or not the activity in California is a unitary business with the activity carried on by the taxpayer and its affiliates in other locations. The field auditors will almost always either telephone ahead for an appointment to examine the books and records at a time convenient to the taxpayer, or send a written inquiry in the mail to arrange a time and place for the examination.

Under Rev & TC § 19504, the Franchise Tax Board, for the purpose of administering its duties, including determining the correctness of any return or making a return where none has been made, or determining or collecting the liability of any person with respect to any tax, has the power to require by demand that an entity of any kind including, but not limited to, employers, or financial institutions provide information or make available for examination or copying at a specified time and place, or both, any book, papers, or other data that may be relevant for that purpose. Any demand to a financial institution must comply with the California Right to Financial Privacy Act set forth in Govt Cd, Title 1, Div 7, Ch 20, starting with § 7460. Information that may be required includes, but is not limited to: (1) addresses and telephone numbers of persons designated by the Franchise Tax Board; and (2) information contained in federal Form W–2 (Wage and Tax Statement), federal Form W–4 (Employee's Withholding Allowance Certificate), or state Form DE–4 (Employee's Withholding Allowance Certificate). It may require the attendance of the taxpayer or any other person having knowledge of the facts and may take testimony and require material proof for its information and administer oaths, and it may also issue subpoenas or subpoenas duces tecum.[1]

The field auditor will conduct routine audits in sequence as received for examination. In some cases, the audit of selected returns will be accelerated. Some of the situations in which this happens are:

(1) cases in which the statute of limitations will expire in the near future;
(2) cases in which the collection of tax may be in jeopardy;
(3) tax clearance audits to permit corporations to dissolve;
(4) request for early estate audits;

---

(1) § 19504.

          (5) post-dissolution audits;

          (6) claim for refund audits;

          (7) audits where waivers have already been given to extend the statutory period; and

          (8) cases where an early audit may have been requested by the taxpayer or his representative.

The Franchise Tax Board will grant an early audit in such case if good cause is cited.

When the field auditor completes the examination, the adjustments must be explained to the taxpayer or the taxpayer's representative and, if possible, agreement must be reached that the proposed adjustments are correct. If there are substantial questions or problems, the field auditor will generally discuss them with a supervising auditor prior to discussing them with the taxpayer or representative.

IMPORTANT   It is the policy of the Franchise Tax Board to grant a taxpayer or the authorized representative an informal conference in the field office with the audit supervisor of the field auditor on any matter of dispute which the auditor thinks might possibly be settled without requiring the filing of a formal protest. In instances where the field examination discloses an adjustment which would affect a prior year or a subsequent year, the field auditor may request the other tax returns from the Franchise Tax Board's central office or inspect the taxpayer's retained copies of the return to determine whether the change in tax would be sufficient to warrant an adjustment of this other year.

The Franchise Tax Board receives copies of federal examination reports of changes made in personal income tax and also partnership returns, estate and trust returns, and bank and corporation income tax returns. Both the California Personal Income Tax Law and the Bank and Corporation Tax Law have provisions whereby the taxpayer is required to submit copies of the adjustments made by the Internal Revenue Service or copies of amended or changed returns filed with the Internal Revenue Service by the taxpayer within two years of the date of final determination of the federal liability.[2] If a revenue agent's report is available, the field auditor will ask that a copy be made available, and set up the additional tax liability from items in the federal report even though the taxpayer informs him that the revenue agent's adjustments have not been agreed to and are under protest or appeal. It is the policy of the Franchise Tax Board to issue the assessment in such cases and inform the taxpayer that he should file Form FTB 3532, Notice of Protest to protect the taxpayer's interests until the federal controversy is settled. The auditor will make these adjustments when the California and federal tax laws are substantially similar.

If the federal examination was concluded with an agreed tax, the field auditor will try to determine the basis of the federal settlement to determine

---

(2) § 18622.

whether or not a similar course of action is appropriate for California purposes. The Franchise Tax Board authorities have issued instructions to the field auditors that they are required to submit a completed audit report four months prior to the expiration of the statute of limitations for any of the years involved in the audit. Therefore, the field auditor may request that the taxpayer sign a waiver of the statute of limitations in order that the return may be processed normally.

> *Note:* If the field audit results in an overpayment, the auditor in discussing the proposed adjustments with the taxpayer or representative, will suggest that the taxpayer file a claim for refund within the statute of limitations to protect the taxpayer's rights. The field auditor is not required by the Franchise Tax Board to prepare the claims for refund.

> The Franchise Tax Board, under their reciprocity arrangement, will send copies of the results of the field examination to the Internal Revenue Service whenever the statute of limitations for the year concerned is open for federal purposes and when the federal Internal Revenue Code provides for a similar adjustment as that made on the California return.

> The Franchise Tax Board has adopted the practice of issuing a "no change" letter on all completed audit years that do not result in additional tax or overassessment. These letters are issued from the Sacramento office of the Franchise Tax Board and not by the field auditor. The "no change" letter will be sent directly to the taxpayer and if the taxpayer's representative wishes a copy, the field auditor will see that the representative receives one in the mail.

IMPORTANT   The policy of the Franchise Tax Board is not to reopen audited years unless there is a material change in fact or consideration of a significant issue not previously examined. An audited year is one where there has been a contact between the Franchise Tax Board and the taxpayer or the taxpayer's representative, either by letter or personal contact, concerning verification of an item or items in the returns. In some instances the Notice of Proposed Assessment or the abatement and refund papers will clearly state that the returns remain subject to audit. In such cases, the Franchise Tax Board will reopen the audited years if it is determined to be necessary. If an agreement has been reached between the taxpayer and the Franchise Tax Board covering the treatment of certain items, this treatment will be followed for prior years still open and for later years unless the auditor finds a material difference in facts in those other years.

In some cases, a substantial period of time can elapse after the proposed adjustments have been discussed with the taxpayer and before the Notices of Assessment are actually issued. Because interest continues to accrue on unpaid deficiencies, the field auditors should, at the close of the audit, explain to the taxpayer or the taxpayer's representative the approximate length of time (normally, two to four months) it will take before they receive the Notices of Proposed Assessment and give the taxpayer the opportunity to pay the proposed assessment at the close of the audit to stop the running of the interest.

¶ 6601

¶ 6602   **Appeals and Review Function**

If there is a deficiency after a field examination or a desk audit has been made, the Franchise Tax Board mails to the taxpayer a Notice of Proposed Assessment (NPA). This Notice includes a very short explanation of the adjustments and the computation of the deficiency. The taxpayer has 60 days after the mailing of the NPA to file a written protest against the proposed additional tax. The protest must be addressed to the Franchise Tax Board, Protest Section, P.O. Box 942867 Sacramento, Ca. 94267–5540. The protest should be in writing, should state that it is a protest and it must include the following information:

(1) the name and the address of the taxpayer;

(2) the identification number of the taxpayer (Social Security number or corporation number);

(3) each year which is being protested and the amount of tax for each year;

(4) the date and the number of the NPA;

(5) a brief statement as to the reason for the taxpayer's disagreement with the items which he is protesting;

(6) whether or not an oral hearing is requested;

(7) points and authorities to support his contention; and

(8) the signature of the taxpayer or his representative.

TAX TIP   A meeting with a hearing officer (oral hearing) will only be granted if it is requested in writing. The request should be made in the initial protest. The hearing can always be waived at a later time. However, if an oral hearing is not requested in the protest, or prior to the Notice of Action by the Franchise Tax Board, none will be granted and the protest will be decided based on the written record.

Two copies of specimen protest letters are reproduced on pages 2906—2907, one for the automatic protest for federal deficiencies (FTB 3532) and the other an acceptable protest, which may be adapted in most circumstances (FTB 3531). If this type of protest is used, because of its brevity and lack of adequate support of the taxpayer's position, the Appeals and Review officer (hearing officer) of the Franchise Tax Board may request in writing that the taxpayer or his representative submit additional arguments and points of authority to support his position before the hearing officer sets up the hearing itself.

TAX TIP   A protest may be filed by addressing a letter to the Protest Section of the Franchise Tax Board. The use of a special form is not necessary. It is only necessary that the Franchise Tax Board have written notice in a timely manner that the taxpayer does not agree with the assessment.

[Text continues on page 2908]

STATE OF CALIFORNIA
FRANCHISE TAX BOARD
P.O. BOX 942840
SACRAMENTO, CA 94240–0040

NOTICE OF PROTEST
Proposed deficiency results from
adjustments which correspond to
adjustments proposed in a Revenue
Agent's Report.

PLEASE TYPE OR PRINT PLAINLY

NAME OF TAXPAYER

PRESENT ADDRESS

CITY, TOWN OR POST OFFICE, STATE AND ZIP CODE

Taxpayer or representative to fill in applicable items

A. YOUR SOCIAL SECURITY NO.	SPOUSE'S NO., IF JOINT RETURN	B. CORP./EXEMPT ORG. NO.	C. FED. EMPLOYER I.D. NO.

FRANCHISE TAX BOARD'S NOTICE OF PROPOSED ASSESSMENT

Number _____   Year _____   Amount ($) _____

The proposed federal income tax deficiency has been protested and the above-numbered Notice(s) of Proposed Assessment is protested on the same grounds. Please defer further action until the federal income tax liability has been finally determined, at which time the documents submitted in explanation of the federal determination will be forwarded for consideration in connection with this protest.

If a joint return was filed, this protest should be signed by both husband and wife. If the taxpayer is a corporation, the protest should be signed with the corporate name, followed by the signature and title of the officer having authority to sign for the corporation.

Signed _____

Dated _____ 19_____   _____

NOTE: Protest must be filed within 60 days after the date of mailing the above Notice(s) of Proposed Assessment.

Form FTB 3532

FRANCHISE TAX BOARD
P.O. BOX 942840
SACRAMENTO, CA 94240-0040

Date _____, 19_____

PROTEST

NAME		DLN NO./CORP. NO.
ADDRESS		YEAR
CITY	STATE	ZIP CODE

Re: NPA No. _____

Account No./Corp. No. _____

Date of NPA _____

Amount $_____

Protest is hereby made against the above-mentioned proposed assessment for the following reasons:

Signed _____

Signed _____

Address _____

NOTE: Protest must be filed within 60 days after the date of mailing the above NPA. An oral hearing will be granted, if requested. If a joint return was filed, this protest should be signed by both husband and wife. If the taxpayer is a corporation, the protest should be signed with the corporate name, followed by the signature and title of the officer having authority to sign for the corporation.

(Attach letter-size sheet if space is not sufficient.)

FTB 3531 (REV 7–87)

Form FTB 3531

¶ 6602

Special apportionment formula. *Application under Rev & TC § 25137.* A special procedure for protest is available to any corporate taxpayer which feels that its activity in California is unique and that the standard three-factor apportionment does not fairly represent the extent of the taxpayer's business activity in the state. A petition may be filed under Rev & TC § 25137 for permission to apply a variation of the normal UDIPTA apportionment method (see Chapter 19).[3]

The taxpayer can file a "petition" under Rev & TC 25137 with the Franchise Tax Board setting forth its reasons for the use of a special apportionment formula. There is no prescribed form for the petition, but it should indicate the taxable years involved, a complete description of the corporate activity in and out of California and the special activity or function which would call for the unusual adaptation. The advantage of using this appeal procedure is that the petition may be filed at any time within the statutes of limitations—that is, even after the corporation has been turned down in an oral hearing by the Franchise Tax Board or on an appeal to the Board of Equalization.

The audit and legal staffs of the FTB's Sacramento office will ordinarily handle petitions under Rev & TC § 25137. However, Reg 25137(g) states that the Franchise Tax Board itself may hear and decide the petition. Such a hearing would be in open session at a regularly scheduled meeting of the FTB. The taxpayer would be required to waive the confidentiality provisions of Rev & TC § 19542.[3]

Handling of protests.   Protests are classified by the Protest Section of the Franchise Tax Board as "docketed" or "undocketed" protests. The undocketed protests are transferred to the audit field office which originated the audit and are assigned to a field auditor for handling. Protests are designated as undocketed if:

(1) their principal issues are the subject of a pending State Board of Equalization appeal for another taxpayer or a pending case in either federal or state courts;

(2) the matter is minor or routine and it appears that it can be settled satisfactorily;

(3) the taxpayer is in the process of being audited by the Internal Revenue Service; or

(4) it is possible that additional facts may be developed by the field office which will serve to settle the matter.

If the amount of tax at issue is substantial and the taxpayer and its representatives believe that their treatment of the issue should be upheld even if all of the undeveloped facts are brought out, it might be appropriate to request that the protest be docketed so that the hearing will take place with a hearing officer other than one in the field office of the auditor who initiated the proposed assessment of additional tax.

---

(3) § 25137; 26451; Reg. 25137(g).

On routine protests of NPAs, the hearing officers will hold hearings in the Sacramento office of the Franchise Tax Board or in San Francisco or Los Angeles. The present policy of the Franchise Tax Board is to have attorneys in the Appeals and Review office conduct the hearings in Sacramento while the hearings in San Francisco and Los Angeles are handled by senior field auditors whose training and experience qualify them to conduct the oral hearings, although they may have no legal training.

The Appeals and Review office has no policy for regularly scheduled hearings to be held in any other offices of the Franchise Tax Board. However, at times it may schedule a series of hearings in one of the other offices of the FTB, including Chicago and New York, if it can schedule enough hearings within a short period of time to make it worthwhile to send a hearing officer to that location.

Of course, if an oral hearing is not requested, the Appeals and Review officer assigned to the case in Sacramento will initiate correspondence to enable the taxpayer and/or his or her representative to submit answers to questions to determine whether or not the protest is valid.

TAX TIP	The oral hearing itself is an informal procedure. The Appeals and Review officer in most instances will have the field auditor who conducted the examination sit in on the conference with a copy of his audit work papers available. The purpose is to verify any factual information submitted by the taxpayer during the hearing.

When a decision has been made, the taxpayer will be notified by the issuance of a Notice of Action in the mail.

WARNING	The taxpayer may appeal to the State Board of Equalization within 30 days after the mailing of the Notice of Action. Two copies of the appeal and two copies of any supporting documents should be mailed to the SBE's offices in Sacramento, California. Upon receipt of the appeal, the SBE will mail one copy of the appeal and one copy of the supporting documents to the Franchise Tax Board.[4] If no such appeal is filed within the 30-day period, the deficiency becomes final and the tax is due and payable within 10 days after demand for payment is mailed to the taxpayer.

The advantages of filing an appeal with the State Board of Equalization rather than suing in California courts at this stage are:

(1) it is not necessary to pay the deficiency in order to file the appeal;
(2) the taxpayer would have the opportunity to present arguments and authorities to a different person or persons;
(3) if the Franchise Tax Board hearing was held by other than an attorney, the taxpayer will have an opportunity to present the appeal to attorneys;
(4) the procedure before the Board of Equalization is fairly informal and the rules on the introduction of evidence are less stringent than in the Superior Court;

---

(4) § 19044; 19045; 19046.

(5) even if the appeal with the State Board of Equalization is unsuccessful, the taxpayer still has an opportunity to pay the tax and proceed with filing a claim for refund, which are the first steps required to be completed prior to action before the Superior Court of California.

The appeal to the State Board of Equalization has no particular format but it must be in writing and should include the following:

(1) the name of the appellant taxpayer;
(2) the amount of tax for each year and the years involved;
(3) the number and the mailing date of the Franchise Tax Board's Notice of Action;
(4) a statement of the facts in the case;
(5) points and authorities to support the taxpayer's appeal.

The State Board of Equalization is composed of five members, four representing districts in the state and the fifth is the State Controller. There is no requirement that these officials be attorneys and, in fact, they may have little or no knowledge of the tax laws involved in the various appeals. However, the State Board of Equalization has a staff of attorneys who handle the research and advise the five members. The Franchise Tax Board is represented by attorneys from its legal staff and the taxpayer may be represented by an attorney or certified public accountant, or any person qualified to present the case on behalf of the taxpayer, or the case may be presented in person by the taxpayer without representation.

Memorandums.   After the filing of the appeal, the Franchise Tax Board will be allowed 30 days in which to file a memorandum in support of its position. The appellant will then be allowed 30 days thereafter in which to file a reply if he so desires. Two copies of the memorandum are to be filed with the State Board of Equalization which will pass one copy on to the other party. Reasonable extensions of time for filing of the memoranda may be granted upon written request to the State Board of Equalization. The Franchise Tax Board will be allowed to file a supplemental memorandum to deny allegations of fact in the reply of the appellant if it so desires. The supplemental memorandum should be filed by the Franchise Tax Board within 30 days of the filing of the reply unless, upon written request, an extension of time has been granted. The appellant and the Franchise Tax Board may file at any time during the proceedings a stipulation of the facts upon which they agree, the facts which are in dispute and the reasons for the dispute. The State Board of Equalization may require the parties to file such a stipulation.

Dismissal or settlement.   An appeal may be dismissed at any time at the written request of the appellant or upon the basis of a written stipulation between the appellant and the Franchise Tax Board. Prior to the issuance of a decision, the appellant and the Franchise Tax Board may enter into negotiations at any time for settlement of an appeal.

TAX TIP   Special settlement procedures are now in place under both the Bank and Corporation Tax Law and the Personal Income Tax Law for civil cases existing on January 1, 1994 where a settlement proposal is made to the Attorney General prior to June 30, 1994. This appears to be an excellent opportunity to resolve a case without a lengthy dispute. (See ¶ 1308a.) The settlement authority set forth in this special procedure is not limited to only cases where the disputed tax is $50,000 or less which is the general authority granted in Rev & TC 21015.[5]

Hearings. After all memoranda are filed, the appeal will be set for oral hearing unless a hearing has been waived. Oral hearings may be waived and the appeal submitted for decision on the basis of the memoranda, on the written request of either party and the agreement by the other party. The State Board of Equalization issues a written notice of the time and the place of the hearing, approximately 30 days in advance of the date. The hearing may be postponed for good cause at the written request of either party.

Generally, an appeal involving an appellant or representative living in the southern part of the state will ordinarily be held in the Pasadena office of the State Board of Equalization. Other appeals will ordinarily be held in Sacramento. The hearing is usually scheduled to last for not more than one hour, although additional time may be arranged in advance if it is estimated that it will be needed.

TAX TIP   The hearing ordinarily would proceed in the following manner: A member of the legal staff of the SBE summarizes the undisputed facts and the issues. The appellant will state its position and present its evidence. The Franchise Tax Board attorney will thereafter state its position and present its evidence. The appellant will then be given an opportunity to reply. The acting Chairman of the State Board of Equalization may call a party or any other person who is present to testify under oath or affirmation. Any member of the SBE or its legal staff may question the witnesses.

The rules of evidence are as follows: (a) oral evidence will be taken only on oath or affirmation; (b) each party may call and examine witnesses, introduce exhibits, cross-examine opposing witnesses on any matter relevant to the issues even though that matter was not covered in the direct examination, impeach any witness regardless of which party first called the witness to testify and rebut the evidence. Either party to the appeal or employee or agent may be called by the opposing party and examined as if under cross-examination; (c) Any relevant evidence, including affidavits and other forms of hearsay evidence, will be admitted if it is the sort of evidence on which responsible persons are accustomed to rely in the conduct of serious affairs.

The burden of proof will ordinarily be upon the appellant as to all issues of fact. In any proceeding involving the issue whether the appellant has been

_____

(5) § 21015.

guilty of fraud with intent to evade tax, the burden of proof as to that issue is upon the Franchise Tax Board.

Disclosure of contributions.   Prior to setting a hearing before the State Board of Equalization to adjudicate a contested tax, the taxpayer, the tax-payer's representative, and any one appearing on behalf of the taxpayer, or as a witness, will be asked to sign a statement that they have not made a contribution to a member of the State Board of Equalization during the prior 12 months which aggregates more than $250. The gathering of this information is authorized by Gov't Code § 15626. Failure of the appellant or participant to disclose such contributions is a criminal offense.[6]

IMPORTANT   It should be noted that the decision of the State Board of Equalization in an appeal brought before it is final as far as the Franchise Tax Board is concerned, but not insofar as the taxpayer is concerned. The Franchise Tax Board is not allowed to file an appeal from a State Board of Equalization determination against it. The taxpayer on the other hand may file action in Superior Court after a denial by the State Board of Equalization by paying the tax and filing a claim for refund. The situation is different, however, after the California Superior Court has rendered its decision. Either the Franchise Tax Board or the taxpayer may file an appeal from the decision of Superior Court to the California Appellate Court and/or the California Supreme Court.

All of the State Board of Equalization decisions in income or franchise tax cases are published and may be obtained from the library of the State Board of Equalization, in Sacramento. They are also reproduced by the various tax services. The law allows for a rehearing requested by either the taxpayer or the Franchise Tax Board within 30 days of the date of the decision of the State Board of Equalization. If no rehearing petition is filed, the SBE's decision becomes final within 30 days after its decision, or within 30 days after the SBE's decision on a rehearing if a petition for rehearing was filed.[7]

Handling of claims for refunds.   If the Franchise Tax Board denies a claim for refund, the taxpayer must file a complaint with the Superior Court prior to the later of: (1) four years after the date for filing of the return; (2) one year after the date the tax was paid; (3) 90 days after Notice of Action by the Franchise Tax Board on the claim for refund; or, (4) 90 days after a final Notice of Action by the State Board of Equalization on the appeal from the Franchise Tax Board's decision.[8] Two copies of the appeal and two copies of any supporting documents should be addressed and mailed to the State Board of Equalization. Upon receipt of the appeal, the SBE shall provide one copy of the appeal and one copy of any supporting documents to the Franchise Tax Board.[9] Similar rule applies to appeals from disallowance of

---

(6) Govt. Cd § 15626.
(7) § 19046—19048.

(8) § 19323—19324.
(9) § 19332—19334.

interest on refund.[10] If the taxpayer pays the tax and timely files a claim for refund with the Franchise Tax Board and it fails to act on the claim within six months after it is filed, the taxpayer is entitled to file the action with the Superior Court in the same manner as though the claim had been formally denied by the Board.[11]

The official forms for filing a claim for refund are Form 540X under the Personal Income Tax Law, and Form 100X under the Bank and Corporation Tax Law, although the claim may be in letter form. A complete statement of the basis for the refund should be included because Rev & TC § 19082 (personal income tax) and Rev & TC § 26102 (bank and corporation franchise and income tax) state that the suit for refund may be based only on the grounds set forth in the claim for refund.[12]

Any action against the Franchise Tax Board may be commenced and tried in any city or city and county in which the Attorney General maintains an office. A copy of the complaint and summons should be served on the Franchise Tax Board or its Executive Officer. The Attorney General or a counsel for the Franchise Tax Board may defend the action, although it is generally handled by the Attorney General's office.[13]

If a taxpayer files a protest to an assessment and then pays the amount of tax under protest, the case is treated as claim for refund from that point on by the Board's staff. This procedure does not affect the statutes of limitations or interfere with the taxpayer's rights of carrying on the protest, however.[14]

TAX TIP   *Special appeals procedures for nonresidents of California in disputes which involve a residency issue.* If the contested tax involves the issue of alleged California residency for a nonresident, it is not necessary that the tax be paid before an appeal is filed with the Superior Court of the State of California. Rev & TC § 19381 provides that the taxpayer can file for review by the Superior Court in Sacramento, San Francisco, or Los Angeles within 60 days of a final determination by the State Board of Equalization. The taxpayer must exhaust its administrative remedies before the Franchise Tax Board and the State Board of Equalization before commencement of the Superior Court action.

APPEALS AND REVIEW PROCESSES FOR BUSINESS TAXES

¶ 6603   The Field Audit Program

The program of the California State Board of Equalization is administered from the SBE's offices in various cities in California as well as Chicago and New York City. The business taxes handled by the field auditors include the California Sales and Use Tax, the Bradley Burns Uniform Local Sales and

---

(10) § 19342—19348.   (13) § 19387—19389.
(11) § 19385.   (14) § 19335.
(12) § 19382.

Use Tax, the Transactions and Use Tax, Motor Vehicle Fuel License Tax, the Use Fuel Tax, Cigarette Tax and the Alcoholic Beverage Tax.

During the course of the examination, the taxpayer or representative should keep in close contact with the field auditor and discuss questions and problems so that additional information can be presented to clarify an issue prior to the completion of the audit. After the audit is completed, the taxpayer is entitled to discuss the audit thoroughly with the auditor and if possible, convince the auditor that the proposals are erroneous.

IMPORTANT   However, if the taxpayer and the auditor are not able to agree on the adjustments proposed by the auditor, a meeting can be arranged with the auditor's Supervisor. At that meeting the taxpayer may discuss the reasons for disagreement and mutually agree on steps to be taken to resolve the disagreement. After the conference with the Supervisor, if you still do not agree, the audit report will be processed by the local office with the notation that it is an unagreed case. You will then receive a letter from the local office giving you the opportunity to appear before a local board representative for a discussion of your case before the Notice of Assessment is issued.

The letter will give you 10 days within which to make an appointment for an informal hearing. At that hearing you may present any matter which you think is pertinent to the adjustments made by the auditor. If the issues are not resolved at this hearing, the report will be sent to the Sacramento headquarters for processing. A Notice of Determination of the amount of underpaid tax will then be issued.

If your audit report has been marked that you do not agree with the results and you do not receive a notice of hearing from the local office, it is generally due to the fact that the statute of limitations will expire shortly, or that the matters at issue could not be resolved by the local office in any event. If such is the case, the local office would send you a letter informing you that the audit has been forwarded to the Sacramento headquarters. That office will then send, by mail, a Notice of Determination.

Petition for redetermination. Upon receipt of a Notice of Determination, you have 30 days from the date of mailing within which to file a petition for redetermination in all business tax cases except those pertaining to payment for cigarette tax, stamps and meter register settings. In the latter case, petitions for redetermination must be filed within 10 days from the date of mailing the notice of determination. The petitions must be in writing and filed with the State Board of Equalization, c/o The Petitions Unit, PO Box 1799, Sacramento, CA 95808.[15]

There is no prescribed form for the petition, but it should identify the protested items by taxable period and must contain a statement of the

(15) § 6561.

specific grounds or reasons why you believe the tax should not be assessed. If you want an oral hearing before the SBE, you should include that request as part of your petition for redetermination.

Hearing on petition. In some cases, when you have not asked for an oral hearing and in all cases when you have requested an oral hearing, the SBE's offices will notify you of the time and place where you may appear for a preliminary hearing and present your case to an SBE hearing officer. After this hearing, you will receive a written notice of the hearing officer's recommendations and if you do not agree, you may proceed with your oral hearing before the SBE.

At its discretion, the State Board of Equalization may continue the hearing to a later date or grant a rehearing on a Petition For Redetermination. However, the action granting the rehearing has to be taken before the time the determination becomes final.

When the hearing is concluded, the State may issue its order or decision or take the matter under consideration for a later decision. The final decision will be sent to the taxpayer in the form of a Notice For Redetermination of the tax or a Notice of Denial of the Petition or a Notice of Denial or Granting of a claim for refund. The State does not issue written opinions in business tax hearings.

Disclosure of contributions. Prior to setting a hearing before the State Board of Equalization to adjudicate a contested tax, the taxpayer, the taxpayer's representative, and any one appearing on behalf of the taxpayer, or as a witness, will be asked to sign a statement that they have not made a contribution to a member of the State Board of Equalization during the prior 12 months which aggregates more than $250. The gathering of this information is authorized by Gov Cd § 15626. Failure of the appellant or participant to disclose such contributions is a criminal offense.[16]

Payment of tax and claim for refund. Rather than protesting an unpaid assessment, you may pay the amount of tax involved and file a claim for refund. The claim for refund must be in writing and filed with the State Board of Equalization within six months from the date the determination became final or within three years (four years for insurance tax) from the due date of the return for the period for which the overpayment was made (or within three years from the due date of payment for cigarette tax, stamps or meter register settings) or within six months from the date of overpayment; whichever date expires the later. The claim must set forth all the grounds or reasons which you believe render the items not subject to tax.[17]

If the SBE makes no change in your assessment, then if you wish to pursue the matter, it is necessary that you go to a civil court. A complaint in the civil court must be filed within 90 days after the mailing of the Notice by

---

(16) Govt. Cd § 15626.   (17) § 6902; 6905.

the SBE that your claim has been denied.[18] If the SBE fails to act on your claim within six months after you file it, you may consider the claim to be disallowed and commence a suit for refund without prior notice by the SBE.[19] It is suggested that you be represented by legal counsel when your case is presented to the Superior Court, although taxpayers may represent themselves. You are limited in your court action to the grounds for refund which were presented to the SBE in your original claim.

PROPERTY TAX ASSESSMENT APPEALS

¶ 6604 **Appeals, Hearings**

Most of the protests and appeals of property tax assessments deal with the valuation of real property. Tangible personal property is reported to the county assessor by the taxpayer in the form of an affidavit each year and assigned a value on the basis of its original cost and number of years of service.[20] Since Proposition 13 has been in effect, the assessor is required to use the value of real property as of the lien date in 1975 for valuation purposes; unless the property has been sold, has had additions to, or subtractions made from it or had a change in value due to causes such as fire, earthquake or flood.[21]

IMPORTANT   If the property owner does not agree with the assessed valuation, an Application for Change in the assessed value must be filed between July 2 and September 15.[22]

The county provides the forms on which the application for change is to be made which will show, in addition to the name and address of the applicant and/or the applicant's agent, a description of the property which is the subject of the application, the taxpayer's opinion of the full value (market value) of the property on the lien date, the full value on which the assessment of the property was based and the facts relied on to support the claim that the Assessment Appeals Board should order a change in the assessed value or classification of the subject property.

List of property transfers.   In addition, the county clerk notifies the taxpayer that a list of property transfers within a county, which have occurred within the preceding two-year period, is open to inspection at the assessor's office to the applicant upon payment of a fee of $10. The clerk also is to notify the taxpayer that written findings of fact will be available on request and the taxpayer must so indicate on the form that the findings of fact are requested. In order to file such a protest, the taxpayer must determine the value used by the assessor for the property. The information should be available in the offices of the assessor during May, June or early July each

---

(18) § 6933.
(19) § 6934.
(20) § 441.

(21) Calif Const Art XIII A; § 50–73.
(22) § 1603.

¶ 6604

year. The law requires that the assessor inform the property owner by mail or by publication of any increase in the assessor's market value figure over the figure used in the prior year. Many counties will notify all property owners, even if there is no increase. These notices generally are mailed around July 1 each year, but if a notice is not received or would like to find out the assessed valuation prior to July 1, the county assessor should be able to provide the information upon request.[23]

TAX TIP	In any event, prior to filing the appeal, you should go to the assessor's office and: (1) Review the assessor's records and compare your property with others in the same area as to valuation, size, etc.; (2) obtain evidence of sales in the same neighborhood; and (3) find out from the assessor as much information as is possible about the estimate of market value.

The base year for assessments under Proposition 13 was 1975. If your property was on the assessment rolls in 1975 and a review by the assessor of your property was made in that year, then that base year value is the amount which must be used for calculation of the assessed valuation in each subsequent year. An inflation factor of 2% each year can be added by the assessor in computing the full value for subsequent years.[21] If the property tax bill is for an escaped assessment or an assessment made by the assessor outside the regular assessment period, applications for equalization on such assessments can be filed within 60 days after you are notified of the assessment.[24]

New owner of real property acquired after March 1 and before July 1 can file written applications for equalization no later than November 15, if the acquired property's full value has increased and the new owner did not receive a notice concerning the reassessment of the property.[25]

For property with a base year after 1975, an application may be filed during the regular equalization period for the year in which the assessment is placed on the assessment roll or in any of the three succeeding years.[26]

Property tax assessment appeals are heard by the county Board of Supervisors sitting as a "county board of equalization". In some counties, however, the Board of Supervisors has appointed an Assessment Appeals Board to handle these appeals. The hearing before the board is informal. It is not essential to have legal counsel, but it would be desirable in an instance where a taxpayer intends to go to court after an adverse decision, because the record made before the local board may be very important.[27]

Generally, the burden of proof is on the taxpayer to demonstrate that the assessor's fair market value estimate is too high, except in the case of owner-occupied single-family residences. In those cases, the assessor has the

---

(23) § 408.1; 619; 1603.
(24) § 1605.
(25) § 620.5.

(26) Reg 305.5.
(27) Const Art XIII, § 16; § 1620.

burden of establishing, by competent evidence, the value that he placed on the residence.

IMPORTANT	If the property has a 1975 base year in accordance with Proposition 13, the only issues to be resolved in a board hearing are: (1) whether the assessor performed a periodic appraisal in 1975 on the property and if not, (2) whether the correct "indicia and factors" were used to set the base year value. For properties with other than a 1975 base year, the evidence of the fair market value should be presented to support your application. The actual sales prices of comparable properties are the best evidence of fair market value and are the guidelines generally used by the assessors. Replacement costs, less accrued depreciation, and rental values are two other typical evidences of fair market value.[28]

The county board of supervisors can appoint one or more assessment hearing officers or contract with the Office of Administrative Procedure for the services of a hearing officer. These officers conduct hearings on any assessment protests and make recommendations to the county board of equalization or assessment appeals board regarding these protests. Applicant must be assessed and file application. For counties where the board of supervisors has not adopted Rev & TC § 1641.1 provisions on the request of the protesting party and assessor to accept the hearing officer's recommendation, the total assessed value of property cannot exceed $100,000, or the property under consideration must be a single-family dwelling, condominium or cooperative, or multiple-family dwelling of four units or less. Applicant must request a hearing before the hearing officer. Board may, by resolution, require assent of the assessor in cases where the total assessed value exceeds the figure set by resolution. This last rule does not apply to cases involving owner-occupied residential property. For property taxes levied in 1989–90 and later fiscal years, assessee of a mining or mineral property located in more than one county may request a hearing before a panel of one assessment hearing officer from each county. If property is located in an even number of counties, hearing officers must designate an additional officer; otherwise the Office of Administrative hearings may do so.

Exchanges of information. When the assessed valuation of the property involved is $100,000 or less, the applicant may file a written request for an exchange of information with the assessor. If the assessed value before the deduction of any exemption is greater than $100,000, either the taxpayer or the assessor's office may request such an exchange. The request should be filed with the clerk of the appeals board at any time prior to 20 days before the commencement of the hearing. The request should contain the basis of the requesting party's opinion of value and the following data:

(1) *Comparable sales data.* For each property sold, the information should include the date of the sale, the price paid, the terms of the sale and the zoning of the property;

---

(28) § 1636–1637; 1642.

(2) *Income data.* In instances where the value is to be supported with evidence based on an income study, the information must include the gross income, the expenses, the capitalization method and the rate or rates employed;

(3) *Cost data.* If the value is to be supported with evidence of replacement cost, there should be presented the date and type of construction and replacement cost of improvements to real property, the date of installation, replacement cost of machinery and equipment and any information regarding the functional or economic obsolescence or remaining life of the assets.[29]

If the party requesting the exchange has filed the above information on time, the other party has to mail a response at least 10 days prior to the date of the hearing and support his response with the same type of information required of the person who requested the exchange.[30]

If information has been exchanged in this manner, the parties are allowed to introduce evidence only on those same matters, unless the other party agrees to the introduction of other evidence. At the hearing each party may introduce new material relating to the information received from the other party.[31]

Hearings need not be conducted according to technical rules relating to evidence and witnesses. Any relevant evidence may be admitted if it is the sort of evidence on which responsible persons are accustomed to rely on in the conduct of serious affairs. The board may announce its decision at the end of the hearing, but may take the matter under submission and notify the taxpayer at a later date. The decision of the board is final, the board is not required to reconsider or rehear the application. There is also no right for the taxpayer to appeal to the State Board of Equalization.[32]

Refund action. If the appeal before the local board was considered to be a claim for refund, or if a separate claim was submitted to and denied by the Board of Supervisors, then a suit from the denial of the claim must be filed in a California Superior Court within six months of the effective date of the denial of the claim. The review by the Court is based only on the record of the hearing in the local equalization proceeding and the Court does not receive new evidence involving value.[33] Actions by state assessees are governed by special rules.[34]

DEPARTMENT OF EMPLOYMENT DEVELOPMENT

¶ 6605 **Administrative Procedure**

The Department of Employment Development has field offices throughout California with field auditors who review the employer's records to determine the correctness of the employer's filings for California Unemployment Tax, Disability Insurance, and Income Tax Withholding.

---

(29) Reg 305.1(a).
(30) Reg 305.1(b).
(31) Reg 305.1(c).

(32) Reg 313; 325; 326.
(33) § 5140–5143.
(34) § 5148.

At the completion of the field audit, the employer is given a Notice of Assessment by the Field Auditor and he has five days within which to request an office conference if he does not agree with the adjustments proposed. The conference will be held by the Field Auditor's Supervising Tax Auditor. After the conference, the referee will notify the taxpayer that he will either uphold or amend the notice of assessment issued by the Field Auditor. If the employer is not satisfied with the result and intends to carry on a further appeal, he has 30 days from the date of the original notice within which to petition for reassessment by the department. An additional 30 days for the filing of the petition will be granted for reasonable cause.

The petition for reassessment will be handled by a referee. He will review the assessment and, if the employer has requested it, grant a hearing unless the grounds stated in the petition are the same grounds on which a previous hearing had been held with the employer. The referee is required to give 20 days' notice of the time and place of the hearing. The referee is required to give a decision in the matter and notify the petitioner and the Director of the Department of Employment Development promptly as to his increase or decrease in the amount of the assessment and his reasons for his action.

Appeals.   Within 30 days after the mailing of the referee's decision, the employer or the Director of the Department may file an appeal to the California Unemployment Insurance Appeals Board. The 30-day period can be extended if good cause is determined.

The hearing is held before an administrative law judge. The burden of proof is on the employer or petitioner. Testimony is taken only on oath, or affirmation on penalty of perjury. Each party has the right to call and examine parties and witnesses, to introduce exhibits and to question opposing witnesses on any matter relevant, even though that matter was not covered in direct examination. Any relevant evidence is admitted if it is the sort of evidence in which responsible persons are accustomed to rely in the conduct of serious affairs.

The order and decision of the Appeals Board and the assessment become final 30 days after service on the employer of the notice of the order or decision.

Appeals to Appeals Board as a panel.   It is possible to file an appeal to the Appeals Board from a decision by the administrative law judge. In this instance, the Appeals Board means the Board as a whole or a panel of the Board. The appeal must be filed within 20 days after the date of mailing or personal service of a copy of the administrative law judge's decision. The Appeals Board considers only those issues raised by the Department of Employment Development in their notice of action. If the employer or the Department wishes to present new or additional evidence before the Appeals Board, an application to that effect must be filed with the Board within 10 days after the Board sends to the parties a notice that an appeal has been filed. Similarly, if the Department or the employer wants to present oral or written argument to the Appeals Board, that application must also be in writing and filed within the same 10-day period. Then, on the basis of the record of the previous hearing, before the administrative law judge and any oral or written arguments and new and additional evidence presented to the Appeals Board, a decision is made by the Board at its regular meeting or if made by a panel of the Board, it has to be adopted by a motion before the Board and a majority vote.

¶ 6605

TABLE OF CASES

———————————— All References are to PARAGRAPH [¶] Numbers ————————————

TABLE OF LEGAL RULINGS OF FRANCHISE TAX BOARD

Caution. The legal rulings listed below were issued by the state before California's 1983 adoption of federal Internal Revenue Code (IRC) on gross income and adjusted gross income. These rulings are not strictly binding as to the 1983 law changes. However, they may nevertheless be persuasive in appropriate situations.

——————————— All References are to PARAGRAPH [¶] Numbers ———————————

LR	Handbook ¶	LR	Handbook ¶	LR	Handbook ¶
58	183	336	324	384	1254
59	1146	337	1146	385	1270
97	255	338	215	386	336
98	174	340	182	389	1154
132	183	344	364	390	1154
178	255	345	182	392	1321
234	1170	348	1184	396	1187
238	455	351	408	399	201
241	1270	358	171	402	336
248	183	365	255	404	422
255	216	366	1187	407	1272
266	216	367	1184	408	150
274	1167	368	268	409	1182
282	455	370	1270	410	1166-A
291	455	371	324; 455	411	1270
294	362	372	341	412	253
297	1012	375	145	413	1187
300	110; 181	376	1153	415	1174; 1178
319	121	379	1146	417	408
323	325	380	150	418	1154
326	1254	381	1321	419	362
329	182	383	1254	425	215

TABLE OF IRS REVENUE RULINGS AND PROCEDURES

Listed below are federal revenue rulings (RevRul) and revenue procedures (RevProc) issued by the Treasury Department that have been approved by the California Franchise Tax Board for use in the determination of income and franchise taxes. Although the list is considered to be comprehensive, the fact that an IRS revenue ruling or revenue procedure is not listed does not indicate that the Franchise Tax Board has rejected it as inappropriate for California purposes.

_____ All References are to PARAGRAPH [¶] Numbers _____

RevRul	Handbook ¶	RevProc	Handbook ¶
55-540	362	64-16	352
57-461	323	67-10	352
68-295	323	69-11	411
72-191	255	70-27	352
73-529	292	71-21	353
74-22	254	72-24	411
74-23	254	72-51	351
74-324	382	74-11	382
75-257	473	75-20	346
75-561	1104	75-21	362
		75-28	362
		76-30	362
		80-51	352
		82-19	352
		82-32	352
		90-59	293

INDEX

——————— References are to Paragraph [¶] Numbers ———————

_____ References are to Paragraph [¶] Numbers _____

Foreign subsidiaries
. combined report . . 1168
Foreign taxes
. carryovers . . 258
. royalties, on . . 1147
Foreign trusts . . 471
Forest Assistance Act
. forest landowners exclusion from gross income . . 289; 1102
Forest landowners
. cost-share payments exclusion . . 289; 1102
Forest products
. property tax . . 3012
Forestry
. manufacturing equipment, investment tax credit for . . 142
Forgery of signature
. returns . . 338
Forms
. electronic imaging technology . . 1269
. employment taxes . . 5025
. federal (See Federal forms)
. state tax forms
. . 100 . . 407; 960; 1004; 1080; 1273; 1279
. . . Sch. F . . 407
. . . Sch. R . . 1172
. . . Sch. R-7 . . 1175
. . 100-ES . . 1253
. . 100X . . 1277; 1311
. . 109 . . 960; 1275
. . 199 . . 960; 1273; 1275; 1279
. . 540 . . 111; 165; 181
. . . Sch. D-1 . . 401
. . . Sch. S . . 145
. . 540A . . 111; 165; 336
. . 540NR . . 111; 145; 165; 181; 182
. . 540X . . 173; 336
. . 541 . . 457
. . 565 . . 423; 960
. . 591 . . 341
. . 592 . . 341; 1278
. . CT-2 . . 962; 963
. . DE-4 . . 6601
. . FTB 2523M . . 961
. . FTB 3500 . . 951; 961; 962
. . FTB 3502 . . 165
. . FTB 3504 . . 1269
. . FTB 3531 . . 6602
. . FTB 3532 . . 6601; 6602
. . FTB 3545 . . 336
. . FTB 3570 . . 1310
. . FTB 3888 . . 386
. . FTB 4523A . . 1175
. . S/0200 . . 1280
Foster care
. payment exclusion . . 287
Foster grandparent program . . 272
401(k) plans . . 276
Franchise
. engaged in business, as factor in determination of . . 4004A
. transfers . . 1145
Franchise tax
. application
. . commencing to do business . . 1014
. . first year of operations . . 1003
. base year . . 1003

Franchise tax—Cont'd
. corporations subject . . 1001; 1003
. distinguished from income tax . . 1004
. nonprofit cooperative association exemption . . 1211
. privilege year . . 1003
. tax rate computation . . 1003
Franchise Tax Board
. audit office locations . . 6601
. certificate tax paid . . 342
. field audit procedures . . 6601
. protests of deficiency notices . . 6602
. section 25137 appeals . . 6602
Franchisors
. special apportionment formula . . 1187
Fraternal beneficiary societies
. exempt organization . . 952
Fraudulent actions
. property tax . . 3011
Fraudulent return
. compromise of amount due . . 5009
. penalty . . 338; 1321
. statute of limitations . . 335
Free-lance authors
. inventories . . 411
Fringe benefits . . 282
Frivolous return
. penalty . . 338; 1321
Fruit
. carbon dioxide packing exemption . . 4008
Fruit trees
. property tax . . 3005
FSC (See Foreign sales corporations)
Fuel
. defined for sales tax . . 4014
. investment tax credit, qualified property . . 1252
. prepayment of sales tax . . 4014
. sales tax . . 4008
. sales-use taxes
. . exemption, partial . . 4008a
Fuel from nonconventional sources
. depletion allowance . . 402
Fuel taxes
. motor vehicle fuel license tax . . 6503
. use fuel tax . . 6504
Full absorption inventory method . . 411
Full cash value . . 3018

— G —

Gain or loss
. abandonment and tax recoupment fees . . 362
. acquisitions in liquidation . . 1126
. additional estate tax . . 362
. adjusted basis . . 361; 362
. adjustment for improvements by lessee . . 362
. allocation . . 1179
. amount realized . . 361
. basis (See Basis for gain or loss)
. capital asset . . 361
. collapsible corporation . . 1029
. computation
. . installment sales . . 364
. control defined . . 1104

Interest penalty—Cont'd
. innocent spouse . . 4015
. overpayments . . 337; 1309
. recovery by FTB . . 337; 1309
Interest statement
. penalty for failure to file . . 338
International banking facility
. special apportionment formula . . 1187
Interplay; 80% rule and other limits . . 292
Interspousal transfers . . 3018
Interstate and foreign commerce
. sales and use tax . . 4008
Interstate businesses
. federal law protecting . . 1163
. protected activities defined . . 1163
Intrafamily transfers . . 364; 3018
Inventories
. appreciated, partnerships . . 430
. basis; sale . . 362
. income, use in assigning . . 411
. interest, special rules for . . 411
. partnerships . . 430
. property tax . . 3005
Investment advisors
. investment partnerships, noresident income
      through . . 436
Investment interest
. passive activity losses . . 325
Investment partnerships
. income as California source income . .
      1164A
. noresident income through . . 436
Investment seminars . . 292
Investment tax credit
. manufacturing equipment . . 142; 1252;
      4008a
Involuntary conversions . . 361
. basis of new property . . 362
. change of ownership . . 3018
. defined . . 361; 362
. gains not recognized . . 362
IRC adoption
. personal income tax . . 106; 201
Irrigation subsidies . . 224
Item accounts . . 383; 384
Itemized deductions . . 321-328
. adoption expenses . . 323
. casualty losses . . 327
. charitable contribution . . 326
. disaster losses . . 327
. earthquake relief . . 327
. education expenses . . 328
. employee's expenses . . 328
. gambling losses . . 328
. gifts . . 326
. golden parachute . . 328
. health insurance for self-employed persons
      . . 321
. interest . . 325
. IRC section 68 . . 321
. job hunting expenses . . 328
. limitations, overall . . 321
. lobby groups . . 326
. losses on deposits in insolvent banks . . 327
. medical expenses . . 323
. miscellaneous deductions . . 328

Itemized deductions —Cont'd
. Olympic Training Fund . . 326
. political contributions . . 328
. production of income expenses . . 328
. state lottery . . 326
. taxes . . 324
. travel-expenses . . 326
Items of tax preference (See Alternative
      minimum tax)

— J —

Japanese ancestry
. income exclusion
. . reparations . . 285
Jeopardy assessment
. appeal to SBE . . 1304
. corporation taxes . . 1304
. hearing . . 333
. individual possession of cash in excess of
      § 10,000 . . 333
. personal income tax . . 333
. petition for reassessment . . 333
. sales and use tax . . 4015
. stay of collection procedures . . 333
. Superior Court action . . 1304
. termination of tax year . . 333
Jet fuel
. sales tax . . 4008
Job hunting expenses . . 328
Job Training Partnership Act, federal
. hiring credits, Local Agency Military Base
      Recovery Areas . . 1236D
Jobs tax credit
. corporations . . 1236
. personal income tax . . 149
Joint returns
. deceased spouse . . 121
. fiduciary changes . . 451
. divorce granted . . 121
. extension for filing . . 165
. husband and wife . . 121
. . change to, after filing separately . . 121
. innocent spouse . . 338
. nonresident spouse . . 121
. renter's credit . . 150
. requirements for filing . . 121
Joint stock companies
. nonadmitted insurers tax . . 6004A
Joint tenancy property
. basis . . 362
. change of ownership . . 3018
Joint venture
. partnership status . . 421
Joint venture programs
. prison inmate labor
. . credits against tax . . 164; 1251
Jury duty
. fees as compensation . . 202

— K —

Keogh plans
. premature distribution . . 136; 300
. prohibited transactions . . 136
. self-employed individuals . . 211; 300

Kickbacks
. government officials . . 224
Kiddie tax
. unearned income . . 115

— L —

L.A. riots
. exemption . . 3005
Labor organizations . . 952
LAMBRA (See Local Agency Military Base
    Recovery Areas)
Land
. farm . . 305
Landlord and tenant . . 3008
Lease
. defined . . 4003
. engaged in business, as factor in determina-
    tion of . . 4004A
Leased property
. amortization, cost . . 381; 382
. property tax . . 3004; 3018
. sales and use tax . . 4010
Legal services
. group plan organization . . 952
Legislators' expenses . . 115; 223
Lessee
. improvements to property . . 259
. . basis . . 362
Letters, sales tax on . . 4008
Leverage leases
. income taxes . . 362
Liability
. fiduciaries . . 457
. husband and wife
. . community income . . 201
. . separate returns . . 121
. transferee . . 339; 1307
License tax, vehicles . . 6500
Licenses
. deduction . . 324
. straight line amortization . . 370
Lien dates
. property tax . . 3011
Life insurance
. beneficiary, loan . . 253
. contracts
. . corporations . . 1088
. . personal income tax . . 253
. group term
. . employer's payments . . 202
. . exclusion . . 253
. interest . . 253
. lump sum option . . 253
. premiums covering officer or employer, de-
    ductions . . 1145
. proceeds
. . corporation tax . . 1088
. . exclusion, personal income tax . . 353
. . payments to beneficiary . . 353
Life tenant and remainderman . . 3008
LIFO method, inventories . . 411
Like-kind exchanges
. deferred . . 361
. installment method . . 364
Limitation of time
. deficiency assessment . . 335; 1310

Limitation of time—Cont'd
. refund claim . . 335; 1310
Limited liability companies
. corporations . . 1040
. partnerships . . 421; 1040
. recognition of . . 1040
Limited partnerships . . 421
Liquidation
. basis . . 1126
. complete . . 1125
. corporation . . 1125-1132
. filing notice of . . 1132
. gain . . 1127
. installment sale, gain not previously recog-
    nized . . 1127
. nonrecognition . . 1131
. partners interest . . 431
. subsidiary, complete . . 1131
Liquor taxes (See Alcoholic beverages)
Litigation costs . . 338
Livestock
. inventory method . . 411
Living expenses
. convenience of employer . . 263
. deduction . . 321; 328
. employee
. . meals and lodging provided . . 263
. . insurance payments . . 262
LLC (See Limited liability companies)
Loans (See also Bad debts)
. Commodity Credit Corp . . 219; 1085
. relatives . . 404
. student . . 265
Lobbying expenses
. deduction . . 292
Local Agency Military Base Recovery
    Areas
. deduction for qualifying property acquisi-
    tions . . 164a; 1236D
. hiring credits . . 164a; 1236D
. incentive, entitlement to . . 164a
. net operating losses . . 1236D
. . deduction . . 164a; 295-A
. sales tax credits . . 164a; 1236D
. specification of . . 1236D
Local taxes
. assessment . . 6514
. sales-use taxes manufacturing equipment
    exemption . . 4008a
Local water agency rebates . . 1099
Lodging
. convenience of employer . . 263
. ministers and clergy . . 257
. reporting . . 5008
. wages, status as . . 5006
Long-term contracts
. year of inclusion . . 353
Los Angeles Revitalization Zone
. construction workers, hiring credits . .
    1236C
. credits against tax . . 140
. deductions . . 395A
. depreciation . . 395A
. depreciation recapture . . 401
. disadvantaged individuals, hiring credits . .
    1236C
. hiring credits . . 161

New jobs
. Economic revitalization manufacturing property rebate . . 3004A
New law
. nonconformity, relief for unintentional . . 350
Newly constructed property . . 3018
Newspapers
. circulation expense deduction . . 1151
. retailer status of carrier . . 4004
. sales tax on . . 4008
Nexus
. creation of . . 4004A
Non-exempt plans . . 212
Nonadmitted insurers
. tax on . . 6004A
Nonbusiness bad debts . . 404
Nonbusiness income
. allocation . . 1178; 1179
Noncash distributions . . 1116
Nonconformity to new law
. unintentional, relief for . . 350
Nonproductive assets . . 296
Nonprofit organizations (See Exempt organizations)
Nonrecreational motor vehicle
. low-emission vehicle credit . . 1240
Nonresidents
. adjustments to gross income . . 182
. alimony . . 182
. alimony paid . . 301
. allocation of gross income . . 182
. alternative minimum tax . . 135
. beneficiary of estate or trust . . 182
. . certificate tax paid . . 342
. business, trade or profession . . 182
. change of status . . 183
. contracts, long-term . . 182
. credits against tax . . 182
. deductions . . 182
. defined . . 181
. estates or trusts . . 182
. gain or sale of residence . . 182
. income from sources in California . . 182
. independent contractors
. . returns . . 5009
. . withholding . . 5022
. installment sale gains . . 182
. intangible income . . 182
. investment partnerships . . 436
. military personnel . . 181
. moving expenses . . 183; 297
. net operating loss . . 181
. noncontributory pensions . . 183
. part-year . . 181
. partnership income . . 182; 436
. personal service income . . 182
. professional athletes . . 183
. professional income . . 182
. profits, gains . . 182
. real or tangible personal property . . 182
. returns
. . preparation . . 182
. royalties . . 183
. separate accounting . . 182
. shareholders of S corp . . 1025
. stock sales . . 183

Nonresidents—Cont'd
. tangibles . . 182
. trade or business . . 182
. unitary business . . 182
. withholding of tax . . 341
Nonstatutory stock options . . 309
Nonunitary businesses . . 1167
Northridge earthquake
. waiver of late filing penalties . . 1321
Not for profit activities
. adjustments to income . . 308
Notice
. bankruptcy
. . corporate . . 1305
. . personal . . 332
. corporation
. . notice filed with Secretary of State . . 1280
. dissolution or liquidation, corporate . . 1132
. employment tax, electronically remitted . . 5009
. fiduciary . . 343
. Franchise Tax Board, notice to
. . bankruptcy . . 332; 1305
. . executors . . 343
. . fiduciary . . 332; 343
. penalties
. . failure to deposit taxes after notice . . 338; 1321
. proposed assessment . . 6602
. protests of deficiency notices
. . Franchise Tax Board . . 6602
. sales-use tax determination . . 6603
. withholding, nonresident . . 341
Nuclear power plant decommissioning . . 354

— O —

Obligations, government . . 216
. corporation tax . . 1082
. debt, federal rules followed . . 106
. personal income tax . . 216
Occasional sale rule
. sales and use tax . . 4004; 4017
Office
. engaged in business, as factor in determination of . . 4004A
Office at home . . 302
Offsets . . 1006
Oil and gas wells
. aggregation of properties . . 402
. depletion limitations . . 402
. . small producers . . 402
. drilling expense, partner . . 423
. intangible drilling costs . . 402
. . recapture . . 401
. percentage depletion . . 402
. production charge . . 6515
. production payments . . 402
. tax shelters . . 354
Olympic Training Fund
. Itemized deductions . . 326
One-voice rule
. unitary business . . 1168
Open-space easements
. valuation, effect on . . 3007

Use fuel tax
. rates . . 6504
Use tax (See also Sales-use taxes)
. deduction . . 324; 1147
. explained . . 4011
. property purchased outside California . . 4011
Useful life, depreciation . . 386
Utility services . . 353
. manufacturing equipment, investment tax credit for . . 142

— V —

Vacating real property-payments
. exclusion from gross income . . 268
Vacation pay
. accrual of deduction . . 354
Valuation
. inventories . . 411
. property . . 3007
. restricted property . . 3007
Vandenberg Space Center
. sales-use taxes exemption . . 4008b
Vegetables
. carbon dioxide packing exemption . . 4008
Vehicle conversion credit . . 153; 1240
Vehicles
. carriers . . 6502
. license tax . . 6500
. registration and weight fees . . 6501
Vendors
. diesel fuel tax . . 2805
Vessels
. family members or revocable trust, transfers to . . 4008
. noncommercial . . 3005
. valuation of commercial or research . . 3007
Veteran's exemptions
. property tax . . 3005
Veterans' organizations
. charitable contributions . . 1149
Voluntary disclosure
. business entities negotiating waiver . . 1326
. engaging in business in California, retailer . . 4004A

— W —

Wages
. Department of Industrial Relations, collection of wages for . . 202
. employment taxes . . 5006
. enterprise zones . . 159
. gross income . . 202
. reporting . . 5008
Waivers
. income and franchise taxes . . 335; 338; 1310; 1321
. voluntary disclosure program for business entities negotiating waiver . . 1326
War veterans organizations . . 952

Warehousing
. engaged in business, as factor in determination of . . 4004A
Wash sales, basis . . 362
Water conservation
. expense . . 305
Water conservation water closet expenses
. gross income exclusions . . 286
Watercraft, sales tax . . 4008
Water's edge election . . 1081; 1162; 1184-A; 1214
Welfare benefit plans . . 311
Welfare exemption . . 3005
Welfare recipients
. disclosure of information . . 344
Wholesale trade
. manufacturing equipment, investment tax credit for . . 142
Wildlife habitat contracts
. valuation, effect on . . 3007
Wind energy systems . . 151
Windfall profits tax (repealed) . . 324
Wines
. excise tax . . 6507
. license fee . . 6506
Withdrawal of savings
. interest penalty . . 298
Withholding of tax (See also Employment taxes)
. allowance certificates . . 5023
. application . . 341; 5021-5024
. compromise . . 5009
. credit . . 157
. disposition, real property . . 1278
. exclusions . . 5022
. list of forms . . 5025
. methods . . 5024
. nonresidents . . 341
. out-of-state corporate tax . . 1278
. partner, distributions to . . 428a
. payment . . 5009
. personal income tax (See Personal income tax withholding)
. return of tax withheld . . 341; 5009
. supplemental wages defined for . . 341
Works of art
. sales tax . . 4008
Wrong tax paid . . 1282

— Y —

Year
. accounting period: (See Accounting period)
. base year and privilege year, corporation tax . . 1003; 1004
. deductions taken . . 354
. inclusion of gross income items . . 353

— Z —

Zoological societies
. sales tax on . . 4008